ATLANTIC STUDIES ON SOCIETY IN CHANGE

NO. 138

Editor-in-Chief, Ignác Romsics
Founder, Béla K. Király

MINORITY HUNGARIAN COMMUNITIES IN THE TWENTIETH CENTURY

edited by
Nándor Bárdi
Csilla Fedinec
László Szarka

Translated by Brian McLean
Copyedited by Matthew Suff
Typeset by Andrea T. Kulcsár

Social Science Monographs, Boulder, Colorado
Atlantic Research and Publications, Inc.
Highland Lakes, New Jersey

Distributed by Columbia University Press, New York
2011

EAST EUROPEAN MONOGRAPHS, NO DCCLXXIV

The publication of this volume was made possible by grants from
the Hungarian Academy of Sciences,
the National Cultural Fund,
the Hungarian Book Foundation,
the Hungarian Institute of International Affairs,
and the MOL Hungarian Oil and Gas Company.

Nemzeti Kulturális Alap

HUNGARIAN BOOK
FOUNDATION

Magyar Külügyi Intézet
Hungarian Institute of International Affairs

Table of Contents

Preface to the Series xi
Introduction 1

I. Changes of Sovereignty
and the New Nation States in the Danube Region
1918–1921

1. The Break-Up of Historical Hungary
   László Szarka 29
2. Hungary at the Peace Talks in Paris
   László Szarka 43
3. The Creation of Hungarian Minority Groups
   Romania (*Nándor Bárdi*) 52
   Czechoslovakia: Slovakia (*Attila Simon*) 58
   Czechoslovakia: Transcarpathia (*Csilla Fedinec*) 62
   The Serb-Croat-Slovene Kingdom (*Enikő A. Sajti*) 65
   Austria (*Gerhard Baumgartner*) 69

II. Between the Two World Wars
1921–1938

1. Nation States and Minorities in Central Europe
   László Szarka 81
2. International Minority Defense System: The League of Nations
   Ferenc Eiler 92
3. The Policies Towards Hungarian Communities
   Pursued by Hungary's Neighboring Countries
   Nándor Bárdi 102
4. Disputes, Plans and Proposals for Handling the Minority Question
   Nándor Bárdi 117
5. Territorial Revision and Minority Protection in Hungarian Politics
   Nándor Bárdi and *Ferenc Eiler* 128

6. Outcomes and Inconsistencies
   in Hungarian Policy on Territorial Revision
   László Szarka 142
7. Minority Hungarians and Central European Land Reforms
   Attila Simon and *Attila Kovács* 157
8. Minority Hungarian Societies
   Nándor Bárdi 164
9. Minority Hungarian Culture, Art, Science and Scholarship
   Tamás Gusztáv Filep 178
10. Case Studies
   Romania (*Nándor Bárdi*) 194
   Czechoslovakia: Slovakia (*Attila Simon*) 202
   Czechoslovakia: Transcarpathia (*Csilla Fedinec*) 207
   Yugoslavia (*Enikő A. Sajti*) 214
   Austria (*Gerhard Baumgartner*) 218

**III. The World War II Years
1939–1944**

1. Returnee Hungarians
   Tamás Gusztáv Filep 235
2. The Autonomy Question in Transcarpathia
   Csilla Fedinec 248
3. Case Studies
   Romania (*Béni L. Balogh* and *Nándor Bárdi*) 256
   Slovakia (*Árpád Popély*) 261
   The Banat (*Enikő A. Sajti*) 265
   The German Reich: Burgenland (*Gerhard Baumgartner*) . 269

**IV. From the End of World War II to the Communist Takeover
1944–1948**

1. Hungary and the Situation of the Hungarian Minorities in 1945
   László Szarka 279
2. The Losses of Hungarian Minorities
   Mihály Zoltán Nagy 287

3 Case Studies
  Romania (*Csaba Zoltán Novák*).....................295
  Czechoslovakia (*Árpád Popély*)...................299
  The Soviet Union (*Csilla Fedinec*).................304
  Yugoslavia (*Enikő A. Sajti*).......................306
  Austria (*Gerhard Baumgartner*).................311

**V. In the Eastern European Single-Party States
1948–1989**

1. The Models for Communist Minority Policy
  Stefano Bottoni and *Zoltán Novák*..................323
2. Hungary and the Hungarians Beyond Its Borders
  Nándor Bárdi.................................340
3. Demographic Features
  Patrik Tátrai.................................357
4. Collectivization and Rural Change
  Nándor Bárdi and *Márton László*..............366
5. The Education Question
  Csilla Fedinec.............................379
6. The Development of Cultural, Artistic and Scientific Institutions
  Tamás Gusztáv Filep.....................386
7. Case Studies
  Romania (*Stefano Bottoni* and *Csaba Zoltán Novák*)......397
  Czechoslovakia (*Árpád Popély*)...............403
  Yugoslavia (*Árpád Hornyák*).................408
  The Soviet Union (*Csilla Fedinec*)...............413
  Austria (*Gerhard Baumgartner*).................419

**VI. From the Change of Regime to the Recent Past
1989–2005**

1. Minority Rights in International Relations
  Balázs Vizi.................................435
2. Hungarian Minorities and the Change of System, 1989–1991
  László Szarka..........................441

3. The Policy of Budapest Governments
   towards Hungarian Communities Abroad
   Nándor Bárdi 456
4. Demographic Processes in Minority Hungarian Communities
   László Gyurgyík 468
5. The Education Issue
   Attila Papp Z. 480
6. The Position of the Hungarian Language
   Orsolya Nádor 493
7. Cultural and Scientific Activity
   Among Hungarian Minority Communities
   Nándor Bárdi, Csilla Fedinec and *Attila Papp Z.* 503
8. Case Studies
   Austria (*Gerhard Baumgartner*) 517
   Croatia (*János Vékás*) 521
   Romania (*Nándor Bárdi*) 525
   Serbia (*János Vékás*) 538
   Slovakia (*Judit Hamberger*) 545
   Slovenia (*János Vékás*) 552
   Ukraine (*Csilla Fedinec*) 556

**VII. Other Hungarian-Speaking Communities
In and Beyond Hungary's Neighboring Countries**

1. Hungarian-Speaking Jews in the Carpathian Basin
   Viktória Bányai 585
2. Hungarian-Speaking Jewish Communities Overseas
   Viktória Bányai 598
3. The Csángós of Moldavia
   Zoltán Ilyés 605
4. Hungarian-Speaking Gypsies in the Carpathian Basin
   Péter Szuhay 618
5. The Hungarian Diaspora Beyond the Carpathian Basin up to 1989
   Ilona Kovács 628

6. Some Social and Demographic Features
   of the Hungarian Diaspora in the West and Its Institutions
   Attila Papp Z. 642
7. The Contact Dialects of Hungarian
   Miklós Kontra 661
8. Population Movements in the Carpathian Basin
   Tamás Stark 680

Biographies of Key Personalities 697
The Authors 713
Bibliography 741
Historical Regions of Minority Hungarian Communities
   in the Carpathian Basin. 806
Maps (made by László Sebők) 809
Name Index 831
Place Index 840
Volumes Published in "Atlantic Studies on Society in Change". 851

Preface to the Series

The present volume is a component of a series that is intended to present a comprehensive survey of the history of East Central Europe.

The books in this series deal with peoples whose homelands lie between the Germans to the west, the Russians, Ukrainians and Belorussians to the east, the Baltic Sea to the north and the Mediterranean and Adriatic Seas to the south. They constitute a particular civilization, one that is at once an integral part of Europe, yet substantially different from the West. The area is characterized by a rich diversity of languages, religions and governments. The study of this complex area demands a multidisciplinary approach, and, accordingly, our contributors to the series represent several academic disciplines. They have been drawn from universities and other scholarly institutions in the United States and Western Europe, as well as East and East Central Europe.

The editor-in-chief is responsible for ensuring the comprehensiveness, cohesion, internal balance and scholarly quality of the series that he has launched. He cheerfully accepts these responsibilities and intends this work to be neither justification nor condemnation of the policies, attitudes and activities of any person involved. At the same time, because the contributors represent so many different disciplines, interpretations, and schools of thought, our policy in this, as in the past and future volumes, is to present their contributions without major modifications.

The authors of this volume are distinguished scholars in the field to which the theme of this book belongs to.

Special thanks are due to the Hungarian Academy of Sciences, the MOL Hungarian Oil and Gas Company, and the *Közéletre Nevelésért Alapítvány* [Training for Public Life Foundation], and the *Bethlen Gábor Alap* [Gábor Bethlen Fund] whose contribution to the production costs made this publication possible.

Budapest, March 15, 2011   Ignác Romsics
                                             Editor-in-Chief

INTRODUCTION

The Versailles peace process redrew the map of Europe after World War I, as new states emerged on the territories of the dismembered Austro-Hungarian Monarchy. Hungary, one of the successor states to finally gain full independence, was in a difficult position. Its historical borders within the Monarchy had embraced large non-Hungarian communities that obtained state-constituting rights under US President Wilson's idea of national self-determination, which became the organizing principle for post-war state construction. The peace conference, however, presented the new Hungarian state with borders beyond which lay wide areas with ethnically nearly homogeneous or majority Hungarian populations that became annexed to neighboring states. Consequently, the new states of Austria, Czechoslovakia, a much-expanded Romania and the Kingdom of the Serbs, Croats and Slovenes (later Yugoslavia) began their existence with sizable Hungarian minorities. This book traces the history of these minority communities from 1918 until the 2000s – including native Hungarian-speakers whose ethnic self-identification might have classified them as Jewish, Roma (previously known as "Gypsy") or Moldavian Catholic. Additionally, the volume includes accounts of Hungarian diasporas in Western Europe and overseas. The book is an edited and annotated translation of a work published in Hungarian in 2008 in conjunction with the Institute for Ethnic and National Minority Studies of the Hungarian Academy of Sciences.[1] The most significant changes for the English edition include the addition of more extensive annotations and the omission, for reasons of space, of the photographs, source documents, dictionary of terms, bibliography and statistical materials found in the original. Structurally, individual accounts of each country for each period in the Hungarian edition have been grouped together into chapters covering particular countries in the English edition. The volume is written for all those with an interest in the history of Central Europe and some basic knowledge of it.

In our effort to bring together the histories of Hungarian minorities outside Hungary in a comprehensive volume, we were mindful of the fact that these histories belong to multiple and contested national historiographies. Without questioning the relevance of country-specific research on Hungarian minorities, we believe that a regional comparative perspective can offer invaluable insights into the situation of these minority communities. The evolution of Hungarian communities in seven states in the region (Austria, Slovakia, Ukraine, Romania, Slovenia, Croatia and Serbia, in total numbering almost 2.5 million today) can be better understood if these separate histories are situated in the region's varying political and socio-historical conditions. Hungarian minorities have been for the most part citizens of their current country of residence, but they have still considered themselves linguistically and culturally as part of a shared Hungarian ethnic and cultural community. The territories in which they live form buffer zones in neighboring state- and nation-building processes.

The scope of the volume is to explore the histories of these minorities through a comparative lens, incorporating perspectives from a broad range of Hungarian historians. Half the contributors to this volume were born outside Hungary, and a majority of those still live in neighboring countries.

The emphasis in the book is on tracing the influence of historical events on minority communities in the various regions, examining them in a comparative framework. The chapters covering six main periods are intended to explore the impact of international changes, sketching the situation in each country and developing each theme in a comparative manner. Socio-economic history features in these chapters as a background to political events. Several chapters discuss the impact of successive waves of land reform and collectivization on the opportunities available to members of the minority community – including minority elites, peasants, and also workers and employees living in majority regions (sometimes far from their place of origin). These studies demonstrate how the history of Hungarian minority communities has been intertwined, from the beginning until today, with international changes, domestic and foreign policy developments in neighboring countries and the relative status of these minorities themselves in the countries in which they live.

These minorities share three important characteristics: (1) Hungarian minority communities were created forcibly by post-war political and territorial changes as late as the early twentieth century, rather than by earlier and more gradual processes of demographic change or migration – as is the case with other ethnic minorities in Europe or around the world. Hungarians in neighboring countries became minorities in their native lands against their will, within states formed after 1918. They formed themselves into national minority communities over the course of the last nine decades under significantly different conditions, striving to maintain their regional positions and purposefully organizing themselves as minority communities. (2) The Hungarian minority communities that exist in the Carpathian Basin today live in ethnically diverse regions (representing differing degrees of ethnic concentration) and in varying institutional structures of opportunity. Consequently, each regional Hungarian minority community can also be seen as a distinct "society" organized into social groups of differing composition, structured according to specific historical, economic and cultural attributes. (3) The history of relations between each Hungarian community and its neighboring nations is one of parallel nation-building. The minority groups severed in 1918 from the Hungarian nation-building process have continually been confronted with the nation-state efforts of majority nations in their "host states" – and have done so in a context of sometimes drastically shifting international power relations. Against this backdrop, ever since then, minority elites have framed their conceptions about the appropriate structures of minority social and communal life in terms of national cultural reproduction, striving to minimize the disadvantages of minority status and to increase the space available for community self-organization.

In mainstream Hungarian interpretations of Hungarian minority history, three distinct narratives have emerged as dominant. One is the *narrative of grievances*, which focuses on experiences of loss – including lost property and rights, continuous demographic decline and individual suffering. A complementary narrative, with various degrees of influence in different periods, concentrates on the absurdities of the means by which Hungarians ended up in minority status. This interpretation offers conspiracy theories about the illegitimate dismemberment of the state imposed on the Hungarian people by the 1920 Treaty of Trianon, which could be rectified only by a restoration of the pre-1918 status quo. During the interwar period and in the period of communist consolidation, a moderate segment of the Hungarian minority intelligentsia tried to sideline the narratives of grievances and injustice, and to introduce instead a more pragmatic approach, which addressed majority–minority inequalities, emphasized the notion of minority self-improvement, and called for political and public participation. In other words, this narrative advocated the need for minorities to make *efforts to influence the course of their history*. Dominant from the outset were the goals of self-organization, legal protection and mediation between national communities. This meant that hard-won, specific results in daily life gained more importance than the grand narratives about national grievances and symbolic victories. The editors of this volume consider this pragmatic approach to be the most realistic one, enabling people to move beyond the interpretations focusing on past grievances. This narrative treats the minority condition as an ongoing *process of permanent adaptation*. From this perspective, demographic decline, emigration, scattering, loss of language and loss of rights become issues that can mobilize the minority to organize itself and keep itself on the alert, while bilingualism and multilingualism, together with the various ties and identities, become lines of defense against majority domination, as well as a routine for adaptation to circumstances.

Underlying all of these interpretations is the view that, under the constraints of being in a non-dominant political and economic situation, Hungarian minority communities have become focused on a shared set of goals: to preserve and strengthen their linguistic and cultural heritage, to maintain control over their churches and their educational and cultural institutions, and to seek continual unhindered cooperation with other parts of a larger Hungarian national society. This self-assessment, along with the awareness that it is difficult to distinguish the minority from the majority when linguistic or cultural matters are not the issue, has driven the Hungarian minority intelligentsia to look beyond the problems of specific minority communities and to focus on the idea of a broader national community.

In the remainder of this introduction, we focus on three areas of issues that we think are important to explore if we want to gain a comparative understanding of the history of Hungarian minorities. First, we discuss the meanings of the names of regions inhabited by Hungarian minorities. Secondly, we place Hungarian minority communities into a typology of European minorities. Finally, we reflect upon the limitations of past research on this subject, which led us to the compilation of this volume.

A Framework of Key Spatial Concepts
Related to Hungarian Minorities

The names of the regions that are today inhabited by Hungarian minorities have undergone significant changes over the last ninety years.

Beyond the southern border of Hungary, the Kingdom of the Serbs, Croats and Slovenes was formed in 1918 and took the name Yugoslavia in 1929. The Yugoslav federation began to show signs of breaking up in 1991, when referendums in Slovenia, Croatia and Macedonia indicated a high level of popular support for independence, leading to declaration of such and recognition of the same, and this culminated in 1992, when Bosnia-Herzegovina also gained recognition as an independent state. In the same year, Serbia and Montenegro (Crna Gora) formed the Federal Republic of Yugoslavia: this lasted until 2003, when it became the State Union of Serbia and Montenegro. The two parts of this confederation became separate states in 2006. Regarding the region inhabited by Hungarian minorities, the term *Southern Region* (Délvidék in Hungarian) in Hungarian usage denotes the territories of the former Hungarian kingdom (Croatia not included) that were annexed to the

Yugoslav state after 1918: Prekmurje, Bačka, the Baranja triangle and the Banat. The term Vojvodina (Vajdaság in Hungarian) was originally associated with partially successful efforts to obtain Serb autonomy for this region within the Hungarian kingdom. This (earlier) territorial entity, Serb Vojvodina, existed as an administrative unit in Hungary from 1849 to 1860. After 1945, the region known as Srem (Srijem, Szerémség) was added to Bačka, the Baranja triangle and the Banat, to form the ostensibly Autonomous Province of Vojvodina.

The term *Transylvania* (Erdély – originally meaning "beyond the forest" just as the Latin name does – in Hungarian, Ardeal or later Transilvania – meaning the same – in Romanian, and Siebenbürgen – "seven castles" as there are seven cities, which were once fortified, in the region – in German) is applied today to all the territories of "historical Hungary" annexed to Romania after World War I, but the names originated in the Middle Ages. The pre-1920 and post-1920 territories of Transylvania differ, however, and are distinguished in contemporary scholarly discourse (both in Hungary and elsewhere) as "historical Transylvania" and "present-day Transylvania." The former took shape in the early centuries of the Hungarian state as an administrative unit under royal rule, stretching from the mountains on the eastern side of the Great Hungarian Plain to the west on one side to the northern, eastern and southern lines of the Carpathian Mountains on the other, covering an area of some 52,000 square kilometers. It became customary in the twelfth century for the king to appoint a chief (*vajda*) to govern Transylvania, with strong military and administrative powers, expressed also in a separate system of public law. The county system applied elsewhere in the Hungarian kingdom did not cover the whole of Transylvania, which also contained autonomous areas for the Székely (occasionally known in English as Szekler) and Saxon peoples (or nations in the medieval sense). Hungary split into three parts in the aftermath of the Battle of Mohács in 1526: the central part, with Buda as its administrative center, came under Ottoman rule, the west and north of the kingdom came under the rule of the Habsburgs, as titular kings of Hungary, and "historical

Transylvania" gained limited independence as the Principality of Transylvania, which was a vassal state of the Ottoman Empire. The three feudal estates of Transylvania (Hungarians, Saxons and Székelys) sent representatives to diets convened by the prince as head of state, who also commanded the army, minted currency and maintained wide diplomatic connections.

The prince also ruled over a varying number of adjacent Hungarian territories, depending on the relative strengths of Transylvania and the Habsburg dominions. These territories together were known as the *Partium*. The Principality of Transylvania annexed Máramaros, Bihar, Zaránd, Közép-Szolnok and Kraszna, Kővárvidék Counties under the 1571 Treaty of Speyer. The east of Arad County and Szörény County also joined the Partium later. In 1691, after the expulsion of the Turks, the Habsburg Emperor Leopold I assumed the title of prince of Transylvania. In 1768, the Empress Maria Theresa raised Transylvania to the rank of a grand principality within the Habsburg Empire, which was ruled in the monarch's name by a governor (*gubernator*). Transylvania remained a formally independent state, with its own diet, government and legal system, although in practice it became an increasingly backward eastern province. During the 1848–1849 Hungarian War of Independence from the Habsburgs, Transylvania's union with Hungary was declared by the Transylvanian Parliament amidst widespread unrest on May 29, 1848, but this union could not be fully implemented until the Austro-Hungarian Compromise (*Ausgleich*) of 1867 – due to the crushing of the War of Independence when Habsburg military rule was imposed on Hungary. A major defeat suffered by the Habsburgs in the Austro-Prussian War accelerated the Compromise. (Meanwhile, the Transylvanian Diet that was reconvened in Nagyszeben (today Sibiu) in 1863–1864 became the only one ever to declare the equality of Romanians, Hungarians and Saxons in Transylvania.)

The Austrian emperor, in his capacities as king of Hungary and grand prince of Transylvania, recognized in 1867 the act of union that had been adopted in 1848. This act reincorporated Transylvania into the Hungarian kingdom and reduced the term Transylvania to a regional geographical designation, as it had been in the Middle

Ages. The county system of governance was extended to Transylvania in 1876, when the separate "seats" of the Székelys and the Saxons were abolished. The once independent principality was superseded by fifteen counties of Királyhágóntúl (the region beyond the Királyhágó) (as these appeared in Hungarian public discourse). Less than half a century later, the 1920 Treaty of Trianon ceded 102,000 square kilometers of Hungary's territory to Romania, the majority of which consisted of "historical Transylvania" and the Partium (62,000 square kilometers). These territories ("historical Transylvania" and the Partium) were incorporated into "present-day Transylvania." The remainder of "present-day Transylvania" (40,000 square kilometers) consists of areas of Hungary adjacent to "historical Transylvania" made up of larger or smaller parts of what had been the counties of Máramaros, Szatmár, Ugocsa, Bihar, Arad, Csanád, Krassó-Szörény, Temes and Torontál. The enlarged Romanian state that incorporated "present-day Transylvania" thus expanded its frontiers from the ridge of the Carpathian Mountains to embrace a set of "trans-Carpathian" territories that soon became known in Romanian simply as Ardeal or Transilvania. This territory was later split by the Second Vienna Award in August 1940 into Northern Transylvania (which was reannexed to Hungary), and Southern Transylvania (which remained in Romania). The previous status quo was restored after World War II.

The region known as *Transcarpathia* (Kárpátalja in Hungarian) took shape as a political entity only in the twentieth century, under names that varied over time and between languages. The geographical extent of the territory also changed several times. Before 1918, most of it belonged to the Hungarian counties of Ung, Bereg, Ugocsa and Máramaros. With the addition of Zemplén (in the nineteenth century), the territory became known as *Északkeleti Felvidék* (North-East Upper Hungary). From December 25, 1918, to September 10, 1919, it was known as the *Ruszka-Krajna Autonomous Area*, but the continuing warfare prevented the establishment of exact boundaries for this territory.

After the fall of the Hungarian Soviet Republic (March 21 to August 6, 1919), this area of 12,617 square kilometers took the name of *Podkarpatská Rus* and became part of Czechoslovakia under the terms of the Treaty of Saint-Germain. The province became known unofficially among Hungarians as *Ruszinszkó* (by analogy with Szlovenszkó, which denoted the then-emerging Slovakia), but during the 1930s it became increasingly referred to as Subcarpathia, a term reflecting its geographical position as seen from Hungary. Although the geographical name of Subcarpathia had existed since the later part of the nineteenth century, it came to be employed in an administrative sense during the period of the Czechoslovak Republic. During the brief period of a federated Czecho-Slovakia (October 1938–March 1939), the region was designated on November 22, 1938, as an autonomous territory of 11,094 square kilometers, with the official name of *Carpathian Ukraine* (Karpats'ka Ukrai'na in Ukrainian, Kárpáti Ukrajna in Hungarian). This territory then became independent for a few hours on March 15, 1939. Occupied by Hungary, and thereafter remaining under Hungarian control, the region became a Hungarian administrative entity as the *Subcarpathian Governorship* (Regents'kyj komisariat Pidkarpats'koi' terytorii' in Ukrainian, Kárpátaljai Kormányzóság in Hungarian), with an area that varied between 11,500 and 12,171 square kilometers, due to territorial changes under the Second Vienna Award of 1940 and local-level administrative changes. The territory then came under Soviet control in October 1944 as *Transcarpathian Ukraine*, and became formally incorporated into the Soviet Union on January 22, 1946. On August 24, 1991, the region became the Transcarpathian *oblast* (county) of independent Ukraine, covering 12,800 square kilometers. The term Subcarpathia, banned in the Soviet period as reminiscent of Hungarian military rule and of Hungary's aspirations towards territorial revision, became unofficially acceptable again in Hungarian public discourse towards the end of the 1980s. Today the region is commonly known among Hungarians as Kárpátalja (Subcarpathia), but the official name is *Transcarpathia* (Zakarpattia) in Ukrainian.[2]

The term *Slovakia* first appeared in political discourse after 1918. After the trisection of medieval Hungary in 1526, mentioned earlier, the regions of the Habsburg-ruled kingdom further from Vienna (such as Szepes and Abaúj Counties) became known as

Upper Hungary and those closer to Vienna as Lower Hungary (such as Selmecbánya and Körmöcbánya Counties). The term *Felvidék* (Upper Hungary or Upland) began to be used in both a geographical and a historical sense, gradually replacing the sixteenth-century term *Felföld* (which was the mountainous counterpart of Alföld – the Plain, also known as the Great Hungarian Plain). In the nineteenth century, the term Felvidék covered not only the Tátra and Fátra Mountains, but also the hills of Zemplén, Bükk, Mátra, Cserhát and Börzsöny, which still belong to Hungary. The flat country of Csallóköz (Žitný ostrov), which is today commonly included in the Hungarian term Felvidék, was not included at the time. Under the Dual Monarchy of Austria-Hungary, Felvidék gained political meaning as the territory of the northern counties of Hungary either with a Slovak majority (Trencsén, Árva, Turóc, Liptó, Zólyom, Szepes and Sáros) or a sizable Slovak population (Pozsony, Nyitra, Hont, Bars, Nógrád, Gömör, Abaúj-Torna, Zemplén and Ung). The term projected the image of a region of Hungarian dominance and identity, as opposed to the term *Slovensko* (Szlovenszkó or Szlovákia in Hungarian), which Slovaks preferred as it suggested their own right to the area. A further change in the meaning of Felvidék ensued in Hungarian public discourse after 1920, as it became a politically slanted synonym for Slovakia as an administrative unit within Czechoslovakia. This interpretation of the term – according to which the name Felvidék covers the whole of Slovakia, with current state borders as its boundaries, rather than the geographical area of the original concept – survives to this day in Hungarian discourse, and is often employed in ways that Slovaks regard as manifestations of revanchist or Hungarianizing ambitions. Due to the ambiguities associated with the term Felvidék, the term *southern Slovakia* (Dél-Szlovákia) has become more commonly used in both Hungarian and Slovak references to the strip of Hungarian-inhabited territory along the country's border with Hungary.[3]

The parts of three western Hungarian counties (Moson, Sopron and Vas) that were annexed in 1918 to (almost 4,000 square kilometers) gained the name *Burgenland*, from the German word "Burg" found in the German name of those three county names (Wieselburg, Ödenburg and Eisenburg).

The Hungarians among Europe's Minorities

In an article published in 2003, Alesina *et al.* summarize the cultural (ethnic, linguistic and/or religious) divisions of the early 1990s in the countries of the world in the following table:[4]

States, majorities and minorities in the world (1990s)

	World	EU	Central Europe and CIS	N. and Central America	S. America and the Caribbean	Asia	Africa
No. of countries	190	28	27	19	34	38	44
Percentage of all countries	100	15	14	10	18	20	23
Number of groups	1,054	132	175	83	146	183	335
Percentage of all groups	-	13	16	8	14	17	32
Average percentage of majority	68	82	72	69	71	76	44
Average percentage of next largest group	16	9	15	19	18	14	19
Countries with an absolute majority nation	144	25	25	16	27	34	14
Countries with a majority nation of over 90%	44	17	2	4	7	13	1

According to censuses taken around the turn of the millennium, the 39 countries of geographical Europe, including European Russia but discounting the mini-states, contain 329 national or ethnic groups with an aggregate population of 86,674,000, or 11.45 percent of the total population.[5] The countries of Europe can be placed in four main groups in terms of national divisions, according to ethno-demographic composition.[6] A country can be classified as a nation state *stricto sensu*, which is to say a homogeneous nation state, if its indigenous ethnic minorities account for less than 10 percent of the population and there are no sub-state areas where a minority is in a regional majority. Of the 15 European countries that meet these criteria today – Albania, Austria, the Czech Republic, Denmark,

Germany, Greece, Hungary, Iceland, Ireland, Malta, Norway, Poland, Portugal, Slovenia and Sweden – only Ireland and Malta lack any sizable indigenous ethnic minority, but substantial bilingualism exists in both states, as well as a linguistic minority of Gaelic-speakers and of English-speakers respectively. All other European countries that qualify as nation states *stricto sensu* according to the criteria listed above include indigenous minorities, such as the Sorbs in Germany, the Samis in Sweden and Finland, and so on. In some of the countries on the list, the size of indigenous minorities fell in the twentieth century as a result of forced resettlement (in the Czech Republic, Greece, Poland and Hungary). In the second half of the twentieth century, sizable immigrant minorities appeared in many of these countries: their proportions of the total population in 2008 were 16.7 percent in Ireland, 15.3 percent in Austria, 13.9 percent in Sweden, 7.3 percent in Denmark, and 6.1 percent in Portugal.[7]

Finland, France, the Netherlands and Italy can be described as relatively or historically homogeneous nation states, as their indigenous minorities amount to less than 10 percent of the population. These states, however, cannot be classified together with the 15 countries listed above, as their minorities form a sub-state majority in some districts or provinces. This applies to the following: the Swedes of Finland along the west and south coasts and in the Åland Islands, the Germans of Alsace and Lorraine in France, the Bretons, Catalans, Corsicans and Flemings of France, and the West Frisians of the Netherlands. Furthermore, the last two countries have sizable immigrant groups, amounting to 10.9 percent of the Netherlands' population and 8.4 percent of France's.

States whose minorities amount to 10–25 percent of the population can be grouped as what may be termed "nationalities states" – that is, countries with prominent minorities. The United Kingdom, Luxembourg, Romania, Slovakia, Lithuania, Bulgaria and Croatia fall under this category. The Scots, Welsh and Northern Irish of the United Kingdom have undergone a revival of their cultural and political traditions (and have a high degree of autonomy, as well as being in majority status within their own regions, which are formally recognized as constituent nations, although the official nomenclature for them ranges from principality to province), while Luxembourg incorporates both a German and a French cultural heritage. Additionally, both of these countries include a high proportion of non-indigenous minorities (10.8 and 37.3 percent respectively). The other states listed in this group all contain one sizable minority – Hungarians in both Romania and Slovakia, Russians in Lithuania, Turks in Bulgaria and Serbs in Croatia – as well as several smaller ethnic groups. Among the countries in geographical Europe that are not likely to join the European Union in the near future, Russia, Belarus and Ukraine are distinct cases, with proportions of minority populations as high as 20 percent, 18.8 percent and 17.3 percent respectively. A similar situation may be seen in Moldova, where the Russian minority enjoys a better-than-average social position (in terms of urbanization, school achievement and employment structure), similar to the position of the Germans and Jews in the pre-war nation states of Central Europe.

The last group consists of countries in which the national majority represents less than 75 percent of the population, which may thus be termed "multinational states": Switzerland, Belgium, Spain, Cyprus, Bosnia-Herzegovina, Macedonia, Montenegro, Serbia, Estonia and Latvia. These are states that either operate on a federal principle, or have a dominant nation whose proportion of the population is less than 75 percent. Switzerland is a federation of three-plus-one language communities. Belgium includes differentiated Walloon and Flemish communities and a smaller community of German-speakers. Spain has granted autonomy to 17 communities since 1978, so that the Catalans, Basques, Galicians and others enjoy rights in addition to their overarching Spanish national affiliation. Cyprus contains two separate and ethnically homogeneous national communities, each of which has claimed rights as a separate political entity. Some of the ex-communist countries mentioned here have political and cultural traditions dating back several decades or even centuries, for instance the countries that resulted from the fragmentation of Yugoslavia (Bosnia-Herzegovina, Macedonia, Montenegro and Serbia). Others were products of the break-up of the Soviet Union (Estonia and Latvia) and consequently have large Russian minorities, the descendants of twentieth-century immigration. (Moldova too could be counted in this latter group.)

According to the censuses of the 1920s, Europe after World War I (discounting the European part of the Soviet Union) had 352 million inhabitants, of whom 308 lived in majority status. (The latter figure includes also groups that formed multinational federations together with other nations, such as Belgium's Flemings and Walloons, Czechoslovakia's Slovaks, Yugoslav Serbs, Croats and Slovenes, and German, French and Italian Swiss; a total population of 9.6 million.) Alongside the 38.4 million persons classified in the censuses as belonging to a national minority, there were 5.4 million in the miscellaneous category, so that 43.9 million Europeans, or 12.4 percent of the total, can be classified as belonging to a minority. The largest of these groups, according to the official census data, was that of the 9.6 percent of Germans who at the same time formed a majority nation in five countries (Germany, Austria, Switzerland, Luxembourg and Liechtenstein). Those living in minority status accounted for 11.6 percent of all Germans. Ukrainians represented the second-largest minority population, with 8 million people, of whom 26.8 percent lived in minority status outside the Soviet Union. (That is not to imply that Soviet Ukraine constituted a nation state within the Soviet Union.) The 2.7 million minority Hungarians amounted to 27.4 percent of the whole population of Hungarians. Next were the 1.4 million minority Bulgarians (comprising 24.4 percent of all Bulgarians). In terms of the proportion of a national group living as a minority, the Hungarians were second only to the Albanians, 50.7 percent of whom (651,000 persons) lived in minority status.[8] Thus, Hungarians currently feature as prominent minority groups in two states (Romania and Slovakia) and as smaller minorities in other states. The comparative place of Hungarian minorities on the broader European scale of majority–minority ethnic demography was even more prominent during the interwar period.

As stated earlier, 86,674,000 million Europeans lived as minorities in the early 2000s. The countries of greatest ethnic/ national diversity are Russia, Ukraine and Romania (with 43, 23 and 19 recognized groups respectively). Roma, Germans and Hungarians constitute the overall largest European minorities (living in minority status in 28, 22 and 8 countries respectively). Russians in Ukraine represent the overall largest minority (11 million), followed by Catalans in Spain (6.4 million), and Scots in the United Kingdom (4.8 million). The largest national/ethnic minorities in Central and Eastern Europe (CEE) are Romania's Hungarians and Roma. The CEE region's largest minority groups are Russians (12.8 percent), followed by Roma (8.5–10 million), Turks (6 million), Poles and Hungarians (each with 2.6–2.7 million).

The minority communities of Hungary and of Central Europe[9] can be classified according to five criteria: historical emergence, geographical location, characteristics of language use, legal status and group identity. The authors of this volume have taken those criteria into consideration, as below:[10]

1. Historically speaking, in order of their emergence, European minorities can be placed into four groups. *Indigenous* minorities are groups that have dwelt continuously in their present locations since the period preceding the creation of nation states. *Historical* minorities emerged in the Middle Ages through processes of special feudal rights, colonizations or migrations. *Involuntary* minorities were separated from their ethno-cultural kin living in another country by border changes based on externally imposed political decisions. *Recent* minorities, which is to say *immigrant* minorities, appeared mainly in the second half of the twentieth century through emigration for economic reasons to richer Western European countries. The majority of minorities in present-day Hungary are historical minorities, while the Hungarian minorities of neighboring countries are involuntary minorities.

Central European minorities emerged in four main periods: (1.1) Medieval colonization and migration processes resulted in the incorporation of the region's formerly sovereign kingdoms that could have formed into nation states during the nineteenth century into the multinational Habsburg, Tsarist and Ottoman Empires. Consequently, the historical roots of today's minority communities of Central Europe are found in the period between the thirteenth and the seventeenth century. (1.2) After the period of Ottoman occupation, waves of repopulation resettlement and migration significantly rearranged the region's ethnic demography. The multiple partitions of Poland also contributed to demographic developments that together produced an ethnic mosaic in the region. This was epitomized in such ethnically mixed areas as Bačka (with its mixed communities of Germans, South Slavs and Hungarians), the Banat (Germans, Hungarians, South Slavs and Romanians) and Dobrudja (Bulgarians, Romanians, Turks and Tatars). (1.3) Urbanization and industrialization in the nineteenth century triggered large-scale regional, international and inter-continental migrations and assimilation processes. Long-established inter-ethnic relations were dramatically altered by the homogenization projects of nation states. (1.4) A series of dramatic changes in state boundaries and political systems during the early decades of the twentieth century replaced multi-ethnic empires with smaller nation states that reduced many previously dominant ethnicities (German, Hungarian, Greek and Turkish groups) to minority position.

Another major factor in the formation of ethnic minorities was the stage that the nation-building process in question had reached by the time that the given minority splintered from a larger national community. Most Hungarian minority communities outside Hungary were already part of a robust nation-building project when they became annexed to neighboring countries after 1918. By contrast, ethnic minority groups that found themselves in places that were geographically remote from the larger part of their ethno-cultural kin at the beginnings of modern nation-building were in a different position: they were able to participate in the nation-building process only through a small intelligentsia. Examples are the Moldavian Catholics known as Csángós, and the various ethno-/linguistic minorities of present-day Hungary. So it is hard to compare the loyalty of the Slovaks, Germans or Rusyns of Hungary towards their wider nation to that of the Central European Hungarian minorities, which were integral parts of Hungarian statehood at their time of severance.

The twentieth-century history of the minorities of Central and Eastern Europe is marked by demographic decline, forced assimilation, ethnic annihilation and genocide, ethnic cleansing and the negative effects of forcible resettlement. The ethnic map of Central Europe has altered considerably since the beginning of the twentieth century: communities of Germans and Jews have vanished, while the proportion of minorities within present-day Hungary has shrunk, and the proportion of minority Hungarians in the neighboring countries has halved. Most of the minorities in Central Europe after World War I were *forced minorities*. Today they tend to be *residual minority communities*, while the Roma groups belong largely to the *underclass*. *Historical minorities* that still exist only in fragments include the Jews, the Germans, the Slovaks and the Rusyns.

2. A minority community's development and cohesion depends, apart from historical factors, also on its *geographical position* and settlement structure. The legacies of the original patterns of minority settlement and of the population movements of the twentieth century (migration, urbanization and involuntary resettlement) mean that most minorities today are scattered or were turned from a majority into a minority (10–50 percent of the local population) at the beginning of the last century. Being scattered means that communities can only maintain institutions for cultural reproduction with outside help, and the native language is confined to private life. In this process, linguistic islands have developed in villages (or parts of villages) and in urban minority communities. Ethnic blocs of Hungarians – such as Žitný ostrov in Slovakia, the Berehove district in Ukraine, the Székely Land and the Bihor County border zone in Romania, northern Bačka and the area along the Danube in Serbia – are exceptions. Thanks to the existence of these blocs, 75 percent of Hungarians in Slovakia, 61 percent of those in Transcarpathia, 56 percent of those in Transylvania, and 49 percent of those in Vojvodina live in settlements where Hungarians form a majority. All of these regions, except for the Székely Land, are border areas, which eases contacts with Hungary, but at the same time turns the minority question into a matter of state security (due to its being, for example, a possible source of irredentism) in the eyes of majorities in the neighboring states.

3.   Concerning majority–minority relations, the most significant change in *language use* during the twentieth century is that most members of minority groups have become bilingual, while members of majority nations have remained monolingual. A distinction can be drawn according to whether the minority language or the majority language has become dominant among minorities in their daily life. The native language has primacy among the Hungarians of Slovakia, Ukraine, Romania and Serbia, the Slovaks of Romania and Serbia, the Rusyns of Ukraine and Serbia, the Poles of the Czech Republic, the Lithuanians, Ukrainians and Belorussians of Poland, the Serbs of Croatia and Romania, the Albanians (and to a certain extent the Roma and Turks) of Macedonia, the Turks of Bulgaria, and the Russians of Transcarpathia. Among minorities in Hungary (including Slovenes, Germans, Slovaks and Czechs) and Hungarians in Slovenia and Croatia, the majority language dominates in daily contacts and increasingly also in the family.

The linguistically assimilated minorities can be divided into two sub-groups. One sub-group comprises people who maintain their native language through inter-generational communication and the teaching of the literary language in schools – as is the case of Hungarians in the Burgenland region of Austria, minority groups in Hungary that identify themselves as such in the national census and claim language instruction in their schools, and some Roma communities in the region. Another sub-group of assimilated minorities is made up of people who have lost the language but retain a cultural memory of it – such as minorities that once spoke Armenian, Yiddish or German.

4.   In some instances, minorities can also be given a partial categorization on the basis of *legal and political status*, which varies according to the regime under which they live. Some political systems grant group rights, cultural and/or language rights, others grant individual rights, and some political systems are designed to erode such rights through systematic discrimination. In terms of political recognition, the status of European minorities ranges from constitutional recognition and regional or local self-government through minorities who form their own political parties to minorities

with other organizations to represent their interests. The Hungarian minorities are communities having cultural and/or language group rights, and according to political recognition, all three categories include Hungarian minority groups. 5. Three types of minorities can be distinguished according to the strength of *ethnic identification*. Sociological studies conducted among the four largest Hungarian minority communities in neighboring countries have shown that they hold a Hungarian national identity, identifying themselves as members of the universal Hungarian nation as commonly understood. Similar adherence to a universal *national identity* (that is, involving such things as attachment to the broader national cultural community and to the kin-state) is exhibited by South Slav national minorities living in neighboring countries, and also by Poles in the Czech Republic and by Russian minorities living outside Russia. Minorities that formed several hundred years ago and show fluctuating signs of ethnic identity represent a second type. Ethnic identification (or at least awareness of ethnicity) is manifested in these cases as respect for one's native language, the fostering of local ethnic traditions, and a strong sense of *ethnic identity* based on awareness of one's origins. This type of ethnic awareness, however, differs from national identity in that group identity here is largely confined to the local minority community, and broader ethno-cultural ties are seen merely as extensions of local ties. This type of identification is found among most minorities in Hungary, and also among Bulgarian, Slovak, Czech and Slovene minorities in the region. An important auxiliary element, a complement to the identities of both ethnic and national groups, is regional or local identity: the awareness that they belong to the minorities of Central Europe. Another significant attribute of group identification among Hungarians in Slovakia, Ukraine, Romania and Serbia is their identification with specific regions (such as Žitný ostrov, the region along the River Bodrog, Transcarpathia, Satu Mare, Țara Călatei, the Székely Land, the Banat, Bačka or Baranja). Similarly strong *regional identifications* can be found among the Slovenes, Slovaks and Baranja Germans of Hungary. From the point of view of group identity, particularly important here is a third type of identification: dual identity. *Dual identification* is typical among historical minorities living in locations where the majority language has become dominant, and where there are efforts to integrate particularistic ethnic or national group awareness into a broader affiliation with the community of citizens living in the same country. Dual identities are built on a fragile balance that can be easily tipped by negative impulses. In this region, this type of identity leads most often to inter-generational assimilation, largely through mixed marriages. In the case of the Hungarian minorities, there is not the kind of "hybridization" that led to mass adoption of "Yugoslav" or "Soviet" identity, but of concurrent affiliation to the Hungarian community and the wider community of the home country.

Based on the typology outlined above, it is possible to place the minorities of Central Europe into three overlapping categories: (1) *national minorities*, with a strong awareness of a broader national identity, who exhibit an awareness of their belonging to a national community and consider it to be a decisive element of their national identity; (2) *ethnic minorities*, whose group identity has for a long time developed separately from their original larger ethno-cultural or national communities, with which their connection is now based mainly on origins and the language that they speak; (3) *regional minorities*, who have lost their language and ethnic identity, but preserve a sense of origin and local attributes that distinguish them from the majority nation.

A Short Overview of Previous Research

Research into the history of Hungarian minorities began with the materials prepared in 1919–1920 for the Versailles peace process.[11] These materials described the ethnic, communal and social relations in the territories likely to be claimed by Hungary's neighboring states. During the decades that followed the signing of the Trianon peace treaty, numerous accounts of Hungarian minority grievances appeared in Hungary. Educational and cultural grievances concerning Hungarians in several states were first aired in accounts by Gyula Kornis and Ferenc Olay.[12] The main outlet for related documents and analyses, however, was the journal *Magyar Kisebbség* (1922–1942), which was published in Romania (and had Romanian, French and German versions). On a European level, a report on the continent's national minorities prepared according to uniform criteria by Ewald Ammende appeared in 1931 at the suggestion of the Hungarian delegation to the League of Nations' minority congresses.[13] By the end of the 1930s, the history of Hungarian minority communities became documented in monographs that focused largely on grievances. This framework became gradually surpassed and replaced by a comparative approach in the post-World War II minority research conducted in Hungary during the period of peacemaking. This research agenda resulted in works such as András Rónai's *Közép-Európa atlasza* (Atlas of Central Europe) and a three-volume collection of studies and data edited by Elemér Radisics and entitled *Dunatáj* (The Danube Region).

Given the tight political control of the period, it became possible only in 1972–1973 for the Hungarian Academy of Sciences' Institute of Literature to initiate research into cultural contacts with neighboring countries, with Lajos Für, Csaba Kiss, Béla Pomogáts, Rudolf Joó and others taking part in this endeavor. However, neither the several thousand pages of material that emerged from this research on the situation of Hungarians beyond the country's borders nor a short summary of this material could be made public at that time. Only a decade and a half later did the journal *Medvetánc* produce a special issue of reports on the situation of the Hungarians in four neighboring countries. Early in the 1990s, monographs appeared about the folklore of Hungarians outside Hungary,[14] their ethnic geography[15] and their "living language."[16] Attempts were made to compensate for the absence of a comprehensive study of minority history with a textbook of Hungarian national studies, followed by the publication of a handbook.[17] Since the early 1990s, several journals of minority affairs have appeared: *Fórum Társadalomtudományi Szemle* in Slovakia, *Korunk, Magyar Kisebbség and Székelyföld* in Romania, and the journals *Pro Minoritate, Regio* and *Kisebbségkutatás* in Hungary.

Concerning institutional antecedents, the most important interwar institution was the Institute of Governance and Public Policy, founded in 1926, which gathered data and analyses in support of Hungary's ambitions for territorial revision. University seminars were also offered on minority law, most notably at the Minority Institute of the University of Pécs (1936–1949). After 1940, the Institute of Governance and Public Policy was divided into the Hungarian History Institute, the Transylvanian Scientific Institute (in Cluj) and the Pál Teleki Institute. The latter provided background expertise for the post-war peace preparations. These institutions were abolished in 1948, and for several decades the issue of minorities was shrouded in silence.

As an aspect of the "softening" of communism in Hungary towards the end of the 1980s, research on Hungarian minorities abroad became once again acceptable, and an Institute for Hungarian Studies was founded in Budapest (1985–1992) to carry out primary research that would document the situation of Hungarians beyond the country's borders. The successor of this institute was the László Teleki Foundation's Institute of Central European Studies (1992–2006), which published monographs, edited volumes of studies and documents, and began a systematic processing of source materials and the compilation of chronologies and bibliographies. Earlier work had relied largely on press reports, memoirs and historical studies, all treated within the framework of cultural history. A major goal of the research conducted at the Teleki Foundation was to complement that body of work with archival research and in-depth studies of political and economic institutions – in other words, to move beyond description and documentation to a scholarly examination of how minority communities "work". By the turn of the millennium, research on Hungarian minorities (mainly ethnographic, sociological and anthropological studies) intensified in institutions outside Hungary leading to new avenues of contact between researchers and institutions inside and outside Hungary. The most visible outcome of this process was the creation of internet databanks in Transylvania, Slovakia, Vojvodina and Hungary, which provided access to research tools, sources and publications.[18]

New research projects and workshops contributed to an increase in volume of publications on minority history (including numerous monographs and thematic volumes) and created higher scholarly expectations in the field. Building on the work accumulated in the study of Hungarian minority history, the studies launched since 1998 under the auspices of the Institute for Ethnic and National Minority Studies of the Hungarian Academy of Sciences have aimed at synthesizing the results of this body of research.

In parallel with the publication of the Hungarian-language original of our present volume, some methodologically outstanding works have appeared on the history and operation of the Hungarian minority communities. A monographic analysis of the everyday operation of Central European nationalism is given in the monograph of Rogers Brubaker and his colleagues at Cluj, and the research of everyday ethnicity is represented by the volume of essays edited by Margit Feischmidt.[19] The demographic conditions of Hungarians in Romania and the discourses reflecting on them are presented in a new way by Tamás Kiss.[20] On the history and institutional world of the American Hungarians, different aspects of a summary were prepared by Béla Várdy, Agnes Huszár Várdy, Károly Nagy and Attila Papp Z.[21] The research dealing with the Hungarian minority communities within the regional relationships of the Carpathian Basin has brought about a breakthrough in two respects. First, the 15-volume program on the region's social and economic geographical conditions, expounded according to uniform diagnostic criteria, edited by Gyula Horváth is nearing completion.[22] Furthermore, the first comprehensive book on the twentieth-century history of the region, edited by Csilla Fedinec and Mykola Vegesh, was published – and what is more, as the joint work of the historians of the two neighboring nations of Hungary and Ukraine – in both countries and in both languages.[23]

The historiography of the Hungarian minorities has been shaped to a great extent by an urge to record and document the numerous serious political, economic and social grievances that these communities have indubitably suffered, and the dominant historical narratives that have emerged in the course of the past nine decades reflect the centrality of those grievances and react to them. This volume shifts the focus from a discourse based on grievances, and focuses instead on strategies of survival and interest-promotion, as it was largely these that were largely responsible for shaping the evolution of minority communities during the twentieth century. The work concentrates on the history of relations among four interconnected fields: minority, majority, a Hungarian kin-state and international actors. Our intention is to contribute to the comparative history of societies and nationalisms in Central Europe. We hope that readers will find this book useful in understanding the place of Hungarian minority communities in that history.

The Editors

Notes

1 Nándor Bárdi, Csilla Fedinec and László Szarka, eds., *Kisebbségi magyar közösségek a 20. században* [Minority Hungarian Communities in the 20th Century] (Budapest, 2008).

2 Details: Csilla Fedinec's "Kárpátalja" entry in the Slovakian Hungarian Data Bank: http://www.foruminst.sk/index.php?p=lexikon&t=a&xp=& w=&MId=&Lev=&Ind=9&P=index.hu. Retrieved November 20, 2010.

3 The account draws on the "Felvidék" entry by József Liszka and Attila Simon in the Slovakian Hungarian Data Bank: http://www. foruminst.sk/index.php?p=lexikon&t=a&xp=&w=&MId=&Lev=& Ind=9&P=index.hu. Retrieved November 20, 2010.

4 A. Alesina *et al.*, "Fractionalization," *Journal of Economic Growth* (2003) 8: 155–194.

5 Thomas Benedikter, "Legal Instruments of Minority Protection in Europe," at http://www.gfbv.it/3dossier/eu-min/autonomy-eu.html. Retrieved November 20, 2010.

6 Iván Nagy, "Európa kisebbségei" [Europe's Minorities], *Magyar Kisebbség* (1929) 19: 710–719.

7 Source: "Stocks of Foreign-Born Population in OECD Countries," at http://www.oecd.org/dataoecd/7/40/45594799.xls. Retrieved November 20, 2010.

8 Nagy, "Európa kisebbségei," pp. 710–719.

9   Defined as the present territories of Poland, the Czech Republic, Slovakia, western Ukraine, Romania, Serbia, Croatia, Slovenia, Austria and Hungary.

10 Details: László Szarka, "A közép-európai kisebbségek tipológiai besorolhatósága" [Typology of Central European Minorities], *Kisebbségkutatás* (1999) 2: 168–175.

11 *A magyar béketárgyalások. Jelentés a magyar békeküldöttség működéséről Neuilly s/S.-ben 1920 január–március havában.* I–III/B kötet [Hungarian Peace Talks. Report on Work of the Hungarian Peace Delegation at Neuilly s/S in January–March 1920. Vols I–III/B] (Budapest, 1920–1921).

12 Gyula Kornis, *Az elszakított magyarság közoktatásügye* [The Education Issue for the Detached Hungarians] (Budapest, 1927); Ferenc Olay, *A magyar művelődés kálváriája az elszakított területeken 1918–1928* [The Suffering of Hungarian Education in the Detached Territories 1918–1928] (Budapest, 1930).

13 Ewald Ammende, ed., *Die Nationalitäten in den Staaten Europas* (Vienna/Leipzig, 1931).

14 Iván Balassa, *A határainkon túli magyarok néprajza* [Ethnography of Hungarians beyond the Borders] (Budapest, 1989).

15 Károly Kocsis and Eszter Hodosi Kocsis, *Hungarian Minorities in the Carpathian Basin. A Study in Ethnic Geography* (Toronto, 1995).

16 Miklós Kontra, ed., *Tanulmányok a határainkon túli kétnyelvűségről* [Studies of Bilingualism beyond Hungary's Borders] (Budapest, 1991).

17 J. Alföldy *et al.*, eds., *Haza a magasban. Magyar nemzetismeret* [Homeland on High. Hungarian National Knowledge], 2 vols. (Lakitelek, 2002); Zoltán Bihari, ed., *Magyarok a nagyvilágban. Kézikönyv a Kárpát-medencében, Magyarország határain kívül élő magyarságról* [Hungarians in the Wide World. Handbook on the Hungarians beyond Hungary's Borders in the Carpathian Basin] (Budapest, 2000).

18 www.adatbank.ro, www.foruminst.sk, www.dda.vmmi.org, and www.mtaki.hu respectively.

19 Rogers Brubaker, Margit Feischmidt, Jon Fox and Liana Grancea, *Nationalist Politics and Everyday Ethnicity in a Transylvanian Town* (Princeton, NJ, 2006); Margit Feischmidt, ed., *Etnicitás. Különbségteremtő társadalom* [Ethnicity. Society that Creates Differences] (Budapest, 2010).

20   Tamás Kiss, *Adminisztratív tekintet. Az erdélyi magyar demográfiai diskurzus összehasonlító elemzéséhez. Az erdélyi magyar népesség statisztikai konstrukciójáról* [Administrative Look. Comparative Analysis of the Transylvanian Hungarian Demographic Discourse. On the Statistical Construction of the Hungarian Population of Transylvania] (Kolozsvár, 2010).

21   Béla Várdy and Agnes Huszár Várdy, *Hungarian Americans in the Current of History* (New York, 2010); Károly Nagy, *Amerikai magyar szigetvilágban* [In the American Hungarian Archipelago] (Budapest, 2009); Attila Papp Z., ed., *Beszédből világ. Elemzések, adatok amerikai magyarokról* [A World from Speech. Analyses, Data on American Hungarians] (Budapest, 2008).

22   The book series *A Kárpát-medence régiói* [Regions of the Carpathian Basin] of the MTA Regionális Kutatások Központja [The Center for Regional Studies of the Hungarian Academy of Sciences] has been being published since 2003. The editor of the series is Gyula Horváth. Up to 2010, 12 volumes in the series have been published: Vol. 1. *Székelyföld* [The Székely Land] (2003); Vol. 2. *Dél-Szlovákia* [Southern Slovakia] (2004); Vol. 3. *Dél-Dunántúl* [Southern Transdanubia] (2006); Vol. 4. *Északnyugat-Erdély* [Northeastern Transylvania] (2006); Vol. 5. *Nyugat-Dunántúl* [Western Transdanubia] (2007); Vol. 6. *Közép-Magyarország* [Central Hungary] (2007); 7. *Vajdaság* [Vojvodina] (2007); 8. *Észak-Alföld* [The Northern Great Plain] (2008); 9. *Dél-Erdély és a Bánság* [Southern Transylvania and the Banat] (2009); 10. *Dél-Alföld* [The Southern Great Plain] (2009); 11. *Kárpátalja* [Transcarpathia] (2010); 12. *Közép-Dunántúl* [Central Transdanubia] (2010).

23   Csilla Fedinec and Mykola Vegesh, eds., *Kárpátalja 1919–2009: történelem, politika, kultúra* [Transcarpathia 1919–2009: History, Politics, Culture] (Budapest, 2010); M. Vegesh and Cs. Fedinec, eds., *Zakarpattja 1919–2009 rokiv: istorija, polityka, kul'tura* [Transcarpathia 1919–2009: History, Politics, Culture] (Uzhhorod, 2010).

I. CHANGES OF SOVEREIGNTY AND THE NEW NATION STATES IN THE DANUBE REGION 1918–1921

1. THE BREAK-UP OF HISTORICAL HUNGARY

László Szarka

By the fifth year of the Great War, the opposing Entente or Allied Powers (notably France, the United Kingdom, and from 1915–1916 Italy and Romania) and Central Powers (Germany, Austria-Hungary, Turkey and Bulgaria) were nearing the limits of their endurance. Austria-Hungary under its new monarch Charles[1] had been making diplomatic moves in the last year-and-a-half of the war to reach a separate peace with the Entente, but public revelations of this by France in April 1918 obliged Austria-Hungary to commit itself to the Central Powers more closely than ever for fear of German military occupation. Since the monarch lacked the power to break with Germany openly, the Allied Powers, especially France and the United Kingdom, began in the spring of 1918 to treat Austria-Hungary in the same hostile way as they did Germany, and the idea of breaking up the Austro-Hungarian Monarchy after the war was soon being mooted.

The only force inside pre-1918 Hungary to press for looser constitutional ties with Austria and rapprochement with the Entente was the opposition Independence and '48 Party headed by Mihály Károlyi. But this had no influence on foreign policy in the Monarchy before the end of the war. So the Western allies did not treat Hungary as a separate international factor in any sense. This was unfortunate, as the Hungarian government might have gained much from a separate national and state presence during the war years.

The Entente Powers had managed to win neutral Italy and Romania over to their side in 1915 and 1916 with the secret treaties of London and Bucharest. The latter, concluded on August 17, 1916, offered Romania the whole of Transylvania, and the ethnically mixed

29

regions of the Banat (Bánság) and the Partium, all other Hungarian territory east of the River Tisza, and Austrian-ruled Bukovina, in exchange for joining the Allies in the war and not making a separate peace. By early 1917, successful political and propaganda work and military organization had also turned the Czechoslovak and South Slav émigré communities in London and Paris into a significant international force able to influence the Western Allies' policy on the aims of the war.

Regular, fairly accurate intelligence on the existence of the secret treaties and the aims of the émigré Czechoslovak, Romanian and South Slav committees reached leading Monarchy politicians, including István Tisza, the Hungarian prime minister, but no clear steps to realign the Monarchy's international relations were taken. Tisza, for instance, had regularly rejected the idea of Transylvanian autonomy, for which the German High Command pressed as a way of forestalling Romania's entry into the war.

In the event, Romania's invasion of Transylvania in August 1916 was driven back with German assistance. Defeat was acknowledged by Romania in another Treaty of Bucharest concluded with the Central Powers on May 7, 1918, but it managed to retain much of its army. This allowed Romania in the final stage of the war to reenter on the Entente side and occupy the territories that it claimed. France and Britain also supported the ambitions of the Czechoslovak and Yugoslav political émigrés to form states, and recognized the Czechoslovak and South Slav committees abroad as *de facto* governments in the early autumn of 1918. The territorial claims that they made were treated as fact in the final stage of the war, which made possible the Czechoslovak, Romanian and Yugoslav military actions that took place after the armistice agreement, including those in the Slovak- and Rusyn-inhabited regions of Northern Hungary, the northern border areas of Croatia and Slovenia, and the Vojvodina (Vajdaság) region of Southern Hungary.[2]

In January 1918, the American President Woodrow Wilson was still only calling for autonomy for the nations of the Monarchy in his draft 14 points for a post-war settlement, but in June the American administration, in consultation with the French and the British, decided to support the efforts to found independent states being made by the émigré Czechoslovaks led by T. G. Masaryk and the Poles inspired by Ignacy Paderewski, along with the movement for South Slav unity headed by the Croat Ante Trumbić and Frano Supilo and the Serb Nikola Pašić, and the Greater Romanian movement led by Ion I. C. Brătianu. Washington accordingly issued a statement on June 28 supporting the independence efforts of all the ostensibly oppressed nations of the Monarchy.[3]

On October 17, 1918, István Tisza, who had been Hungarian prime minister in 1913–1917, told the Hungarian Parliament that the Central Powers had lost the war. The Hungarian National Council was set up a week later on October 23, and the break-up of the Monarchy became visible in a succession of national revolutions: the Czechs in Prague on October 28, the Austrians in Vienna and Slovaks in Turócszentmárton[4] on the 30th, and the Hungarians in Budapest on the 31st all broke with the Monarchy or the Hungarian Kingdom. In Budapest, Archduke Joseph appointed a new government headed by Mihály Károlyi on October 31; on the same afternoon, István Tisza was murdered by soldiers in his villa on Hermina út.

But the victorious powers wanted at all costs to conclude an armistice with the united Habsburg Monarchy, so that their demands could be imposed on the successor states. Such an armistice was signed by the Monarchy in Padua on November 3, 1918, and in Germany on November 11, after the serious defeats on the Balkan, Italian and Western fronts. Since that left Hungary without a separate armistice agreement, Prime Minister Mihály Károlyi headed a delegation to Belgrade on November 11, 1918, to find a substitute, and managed to agree with the French General Louis Franchet d'Espèrey on military conditions for ending the war. But only Hungary recognized the Belgrade Convention signed two days later as valid. This agreement, which would have given *de facto* recognition to the independent Hungarian People's Republic (proclaimed on November 16, 1918) was rejected by the Allied and Associated Powers and by Hungary's neighbors, leaving the country's international legal status still in question.[5]

There was no foreign military presence on the soil of historical Hungary at the end of World War I, but the collapse of the Balkan Front left an imminent danger of attack by Romanian, South Slav and Czechoslovak forces. The well-equipped Serbian army duly crossed the border at the beginning of November, the first units of Czechoslovakia[6] on November 8, and Romanian forces on November 13. The Austro-Hungarian army broke up and the Hungarian army that was being formed was unable to put up any resistance for some time. The Károlyi government was trying to disarm as quickly as possible the old multinational military units, which were coming under Anarchist and Bolshevik influence, and then build up the new army. This basically rational decision had catastrophic consequences, as it prevented the defensive capabilities of the country from developing in the Hungarian-inhabited areas.

Active propaganda and diplomatic activity took place during World War I. The central issue in East-Central Europe from the outset was concerned with the efforts at self-determination and establishment of independent states made by non-German, non-Hungarian nations in the Monarchy. The principle of national self-determination was also emphasized in November 1917 by Vladimir Ilyich Lenin, leader of the Russian Bolshevik Revolution. That and defeat in the war were what prompted him to recognize the rights of Finland and the Baltic states to self-determination and secession. US President Wilson also stressed national self-determination early in 1918 as the underlying principle for the post-war reorganization of Eastern and Central Europe. But implementation of the principle of national self-determination related closely to post-war power relations and to realization of the diplomatic and economic aims of the peace for the victorious powers and their allies.

The big problem with the principle of national self-determination was that the new states advanced exaggerated territorial claims incompatible with the historical legal and ethnic positions of the Hungarians and the Germans of pre-1918 Hungary. Czechoslovakia, for instance, successfully claimed Sudetenland, where three million Germans lived, and aspired not just to territories of the historical

Hungarian state where a majority of the population was Slovak, but to a zone running through Pest, Nógrád, Heves, Borsod and Zemplén Counties, with an estimated 1.2–1.6 million Hungarian inhabitants. Ultimately it obtained at the Paris peace talks only the part of the claimed zone lying north of the Danube–Ipoly line and the Rusyn Region of Transcarpathia, together with 800,000–850,000 Hungarian inhabitants.[7] Romania also put a curious interpretation on the principle of national self-determination. The Romanians formed a bare majority over the Hungarians and the German-speaking Saxons and Swabians in the claimed territories of Transylvania and Eastern Hungary, but the claim for the whole was formulated in the name of that fragile majority, so that it could unite with the Romanian Kingdom. The opposing Hungarian plans for federation and cantonization, on the other hand, were designed to defend the country's historical integrity.[8]

Between November 1918 and May 1919, the Czechoslovak, Romanian and Yugoslav armies occupied all the territory that their countries were to be awarded a year later under the Treaty of Trianon. The dwindling Hungarian state found itself in a very difficult diplomatic and military situation, under conditions of military isolation while facing the superior forces of its enemies and the detrimental territorial decisions of the peace conference. Indeed the Károlyi government had misjudged the potentials in the situation, the strength of post-war international pacifism, the peacetime objectives of the victorious powers, and the actual chances of saving the country's territorial integrity. Having demobilized the soldiers returning from the world war fronts, its attempts at rapid organization of a separate Hungarian army were unsuccessful. Nor could it push back or contain the organizing efforts of the Communist Party of Hungary or the extreme right-wing nationalists.[9]

The continual losses of territory prevented the promised parliamentary elections based on universal suffrage for men and women. A combination of the Entente notes, the ceaseless advances by neighboring countries, and the internal divisions meant that the government could not place on war alert forces great enough to represent serious resistance to annexation in areas with a majority Hungarian population.

The government of Mihály Károlyi and from January 19, 1919, of Dénes Berinkey entrusted a "ministry for national minorities" under Oszkár Jászi, minister without portfolio, with the task of drawing up agreements with the movements of other national communities. These were to protect the rights of Hungarian self-determination in regions dominated by such communities and to be shown to the peace conference as domestic pacts, as counters to the idea of founding new states, which the Great Powers supported. The apparatus behind Jászi, "charged with preparing for self-determination of non-Hungarian nations living in Hungary," followed Mihály Károlyi's policy of pacifism and banking on help from the Entente. It pressed for a negotiated peace and for order to be restored provisionally by the peace conference, with the aim of turning Hungary into an Swiss-type federal state, an idea that had long since been overtaken by events.[10]

Jászi and his staff drafted several ideas. One was to prepare for plebiscites to decide the future of the areas earmarked for detachment from Hungary. The first such preparations were made in the Slovak region of Upper Hungary, where signatures were collected for a petition printed in Hungarian, German and Slovak, supporting the country's territorial integrity. The other central element in the Jászi proposals was to initiate Swiss-style cantonization ("Helveticization") throughout the public administration. A surviving draft by Jászi's team envisaged ethnic Hungarian and non-Hungarian cantons having ethnographic cantons (such as for the Palóc)[11] and cantons embracing cities (Budapest, Debrecen, Kassa, and so on) and distinct geographical areas (for example Balaton). Related to this were plans for demarcating national groups by drawing ethnic boundaries around districts in Upper Hungary and Transcarpathia with a majority Slovak or Rusyn population.

Early in December 1918, the Hungarian government promised broad ethnic autonomy to a Slovak delegation led by Milan Hodža visiting Budapest as an official representative of the Czechoslovak government. On December 6, a short-term agreement was reached on a demarcation line to follow the linguistic boundary. Meanwhile Act X/1918 granted autonomy to Transcarpathia (officially called Rus'ka-Krajna).[12]

Jászi also looked to the Swiss model for an acceptable negotiating basis when he proposed having Romanian, Hungarian, German and mixed cantons in Transylvania, at Hungarian–Romanian talks held in Arad on November 13–14. But the idea was rejected by the Transylvanian Romanian National Council delegation headed by Iuliu Maniu. Furthermore, the Romanians made radical efforts to obstruct any movement inclining towards resistance or self-determination for the Hungarians of the Székely (Szekler) counties or Transylvania. Strong constraints were placed on the Hungarian National Council of Transylvania led by István Apáthy, which was tied closely to Jászi's ministry. Shortly after the Romanians occupied Kolozsvár, Apáthy was arrested and there were attempts to make the work of the Transylvanian Hungarian National Council and the Eastern Hungarian Chief Commission impossible. The Transylvanian Hungarian civilian and military high command was summarily abolished in January 1919.

Jászi's ministry also supported for a time the movements intending to found an independent Transylvanian republic: the Budapest group headed by Elek Benedek, Gyula Györffy, Benedek Jancsó and Vilmos Nagy, and the other Székely National Council headed by the Transylvanians Miklós Bánffy, István Bethlen, Lajos Lóczy, Pál Teleki and Gábor Ugron. After the failure of the Arad talks and the advance by the Romanians, the prime Transylvanian objective became to save the territories west and north of the Mureş (Maros) line. So the declaration adopted at the November 28 Grand Székely Assembly at Marosvásárhely aimed primarily at the integrity of the Hungarian state.

The organization in Temesvár headed by Ottó Roth that intended to proclaim an independent Banat People's Republic was broken up by the opposing Romanian and South Slav armies moving into the territory. The Romanian force did not respect the Belgrade Convention or the later Berthelot–Apáthy Transylvanian demarcation line (see below). It was held up at Csucsa for a couple of weeks only by resistance from Hungary's Transylvanian Division. The first small Romanian units crossed the Hungarian state border at Gyergyótölgyes on November 12. The government initially took incisive action against the Romanians, sending three armored trains into Transylvania. Károlyi appealed to President Wilson against the advance. But on December 2, 1918, one day before the Romanian Assembly at Gyulafehérvár declared Romanian unification, Franchet d'Espèrey consented, with Prime Minister Clemenceau's approval, to the Romanians' crossing the Mureş demarcation line drawn in the Belgrade Convention, which they did on December 18. The Hungarian military command hastened to reinforce its Transylvanian positions, notably Kolozsvár, but could not muster appreciable forces against the Romanians, who had orders to occupy the whole province.

When the Károlyi government saw that the Belgrade Convention had been ignored, it requested through Lieutenant Colonel Fernand Vix that the nine main Transylvanian cities be placed under French military occupation, in an effort to secure the ceasefire terms.

The Kolozsvár Assembly of the Transylvanian Hungarians took place on December 22, 1918, calling for "full equality, liberty and self-government for all nations here living... within a united and undismembered Hungary." But Kolozsvár was occupied on December 24, 1918, by the advancing Romanian army under General Constantin Neculcea, which had met no resistance. Three days later Neculcea declared a state of siege in the city, introduced internment, and placed a ban on public assembly. Six days after that, Apáthy and the French General Henri Mathias Berthelot, seconded to command the military forces of Allied Romania, reached agreement on a new demarcation line past Nagybánya, Kolozsvár, and Déva. After Berthelot's departure, the Romanian military administration disbanded the Eastern Hungarian Chief Commission – the Hungarian government's highest body of state in Transylvania –

and arrested Apáthy. Emil Grandpierre, who succeeded him as chief commissioner, was removed from office on January 28. The city's Romanian officials were appointed on the same day.[13]

By December 1918, several ministers in the Károlyi and the Berinkey governments, including Jászi and Minister of Agriculture Barna Buza, were calling for abandonment of the pacifist stance. The strategy of waiting out the decisions of the peace conference had failed, as the majority of the country's territory was occupied by neighboring armies by the end of 1918. Károlyi ultimately changed his position, having seen that the Czechoslovak, Romanian and South Slav armies were not waiting for the peace conference decisions before taking military action, that many conflicts were breaking out on Transylvanian and Upper Hungarian soil, and that an attitude inimical to Hungary would dominate the Paris peace conference when it opened on January 29. By that time there was no hope of Hungary regaining the occupied territories or of non-Hungarians in them exercising self-determination within a Hungarian framework.

The Hungarian regiments in the Székely counties and in the other regions of Transylvania refused to lay down their arms. They and other volunteers in the Romanian-occupied Székely counties then formed a 2,000-strong Székely Division, which along with the other Transylvanian Hungarian military units was under the command of Austro-Hungarian army Brigadier Károly Kratochwill, as military commander of Transylvania. The previous local and national guard units and the Székely Division may have together numbered 10,000–12,000 men by the end of 1918, and in January 1919, Kratochwill's Székely Division managed to hold up the Romanians at the Király-hágó, the pass on the main road between Kolozsvár and Nagyvárad, on the traditional border between Transylvania and Hungary. Fatally late in the day, Mihály Károlyi outlined an alternative policy in an address to the Székely Division at Szatmárnémeti on March 2.[14]

There were only local attempts at resistance by the Hungarians of Upper Hungary, such as those at Érsekújvár, Balassagyarmat, Kassa and Abara. Lacking a history of regional self-determination, they looked on passively at the rapid advance of the small but organized Czechoslovak military forces. In February 1919, a people's assembly at Jóka adopted a memorandum in the name of the people of the Csallóköz protesting against annexation of the district by Czechoslovakia. There was also resistance to annexation from the Germans of the region of Zips (Spiš, Szepesség), who planned an independent Zipser Republic (Szepesi Köztársaság). Such local pockets of resistance in areas of Hungary awarded to Czechoslovakia were easily dealt with by the Czechoslovak forces, drawn from the Czech and Slovak legions in Italy. On February 3, 1919, the minister plenipotentiary for Slovakia, Vavro Šrobár, moved from Zsolna to Pozsony), to set up there Slovakia's new seat of government, Bratislava.

Among the Hungarian peace notes can be found a protest by the Hungarians of the Banat (Bánság) and Bačka (Bácska) districts, claimed by the South Slavs, and one by the Hungarians of the Western Hungarian areas being claimed by Austria (Burgenland), dismissing such claims and demanding a plebiscite.[15]

The proclamation of the Hungarian Soviet Republic[16] on March 21, 1919, was followed by a coordinated attack by the Romanian and Czechoslovak armies. The Romanians entered Debrecen on April 23, and then met up with the Czechoslovaks at Csap. The forces mobilized by the Hungarian Soviet Republic were placed under new command and took up defensive positions against the Romanians along the River Tisza. Kratochwill, still in command of the Székely Division, issued orders on April 25, 1919, effectively disbanding the Division, citing antagonism from the Hungarian Red Army, but some units fought on as the Székely Brigade.

On May 20, a counter-attack to the north beat back the Czechoslovak units. Léva, Kassa, Selmecbánya, and Bártfa were recaptured between June 1 and 6. The Hungarian Soviet Republic lasted 133 days, during which Béla Kun in his capacity as commissar for foreign affairs proved willing, unlike Károlyi's government, to abandon territorial integrity when faced with the peace conference decisions.[17] It was conceded in notes to the Czechoslovak, Romanian and South Slav governments on April 30 that the three countries had admissible national and territorial claims, but Kun demanded in exchange an immediate end to hostilities and any interference in the internal affairs of the Hungarian Soviet Republic, freedom of transit, and protection for the remaining minority communities in the neighboring countries.[18] The constitution of the officially named Socialist Federal Soviet Republic of Hungary was adopted on June 23, 1919, by the National Assembly of Federal Soviets, which met only once. It designated the Soviet Republic as a federal state of the nations dwelling within it. But none of this could take effect in practice. On June 13, the Hungarian Soviet government was informed in the Clemenceau Note of the decision of the Paris Peace Conference on Hungary's borders and ordered the Hungarian army to withdraw inside them. On July 1, a Czechoslovak–Hungarian ceasefire was signed in Bratislava.[19] After the northern retreat, the Tisza front collapsed and the Hungarian Soviet Republic fell. The Romanian army marched into Budapest on August 4.

Notes

1   Charles I of Austria and IV of Hungary succeeded Francis Joseph I as emperor and king on November 21, 1916, and was crowned king in Budapest on December 30.

2   On the outcome of World War I for Central Europe: Béla K. Király, Peter Pastor and Ivan Sanders, eds., *Essays on World War I: Total War and Peacemaking, a Case Study on Trianon* (New York, 1982); Hugh Seton-Watson and Christopher Seton Watson, *The Making of a New Europe: R. W. Seton-Watson and the Last Years of Austria-Hungary* (Seattle, 1981); Mária Ormos, *From Padua to Trianon, 1918–1920* (New York, 1982). In Hungarian: Ernő Raffay, *Erdély 1918–1919-ben* [Transylvania in 1918–1919] (Budapest, 1987); Lajos Arday, *Térkép, csata után. Magyarország a brit külpolitikában (1918–1919)* [Map after Battle. Hungary in British Foreign Policy (1918–1919)] (Budapest, 1990); Enikő A. Sajti, *Impériumváltások, revízió, kisebbségek. Magyarok a Délvidéken 1918–1947* [Sovereignty Changes, Revision, Minorities. Hungarians in the Southern Region 1918–1947] (Budapest, 2004). On Hungarian–Romanian relations:

Cornel Grad and Viorel Ciubuta, eds., *1918: Sfarsit si inceput de epoca* [1918: The End and the Beginning of an Era] (Satu Mare/ Zalau, 1998); Ignác Romsics, *The Dismantling of Historic Hungary: the Peace Treaty of Trianon, 1920* (New York, 2002).

3   On the Central European policies of the United States and the Entente and national relations in Central Europe: Romsics, *The Dismantling of Historic Hungary*; Zsuzsa L. Nagy, "Peacemaking after World War I: The Western Democracies and the Hungarian Question," in Stephen Borsody, ed., *The Hungarians: a Divided Nation* (New Haven, CT, 1988), pp. 35–36; Géza Jeszenszky, "A dunai államszövetség eszméje Nagy-Britanniában és az Egyesült Államokban az I. világháború alatt" [The Danube Federation Idea in Britain and the United States in World War I], *Századok* 122 (1988) 4:648–663; Joseph P. O'Grady, *The Immigrants' Influence on Wilson's Peace Policies* (Lexington, KY, 1967); Eva Schmidt-Hartmann and Stanley B. Winters, eds., *Grossbritannien, die USA und die böhmischen Länder 1848–1938* (Munich, 1991); Peter Pastor, ed., *Revolutions and Interventions in Hungary and Its Neighbor States, 1918–1919* (Boulder, CO/Highland Lakes, NJ, 1988).

4   *Translator's note:* The intention with place names in this English edition is to use the official name and spelling at the time being discussed, except where there is an established English name (e. g. Belgrade). However, this has not been done for the relatively short periods of reoccupation by Hungary immediately before and during World War II. The place names and their equivalents in other languages are indexed at the end of the book.

5   Mária Ormos, "The Military Convention of Belgrade," in Béla K. Király and László Veszprémy, eds., *Trianon and East Central Europe* (Boulder, CO/Highland Lakes, NJ, 1995), pp. 55–91.

6   The independent Republic of Czechoslovakia or Czecho-Slovak State was declared by the National Council on October 28, 1918.

7   Dagmar Perman, *The Shaping of the Czechoslovak State* (Leyden, 1962); Géza Jeszenszky, *The British Role in Assigning Csallóköz (Žitný Ostrov, Grosse Schütt) to Czechoslovakia*, at http://www. hungarianhistory.com/lib/jeszenszky/jesz12.doc (last consulted March 2, 2009); Marián Hronský, *The Struggle for Slovakia and the Treaty of Trianon* (Bratislava, 2001); Yeshayahu Jelinek, "The Treaty of Trianon and Czechoslovakia: Reflections," in Király, Pastor and Sanders, eds., *Essays on World War I*, pp. 201–216.

8	Stephen Fischer-Galati, "Trianon and Romania," in Király, Pastor and Sanders, eds., *Essays on World War I*, pp. 185–200.

9	Peter Pastor, "Hungarian Territorial Losses during the Liberal-Democratic Revolution of 1918–1919," in Király, Pastor and Sanders, eds., *Essays on World War I*, pp. 165–184.

10	Pál Schönwald, A *magyarországi 1918–1919-es polgári demokratikus forradalom állam- és jogtörténeti kérdései* [Issues of Constitutional and Legal History in Hungary's Bourgeois Democratic Revolution of 1918–1919] (Budapest, 1969); László Szarka, "Keleti Svájc – illúzió vagy utópia? A Károlyi-kormány Nemzetiségi Minisztériumának működése" [Eastern Switzerland – Illusion or Utopia? The Operation of the Károlyi Government's Ministry of Nationalities], in Idem, *Duna-táji dilemmák. Nemzeti kisebbségek – kisebbségi politika a 20. századi Kelet-Közép-Európában* [Danubian Dilemmas. National Minorities and Minority Policy in 20th-Century East-Central Europe] (Budapest, 1998), pp. 113–125 and 281–284.

11	An ethnographic Hungarian group found in wide areas of northern Hungary and southern Slovakia, who speak a distinctive dialect.

12	See Chapter 3.

13	Raffay, *Erdély 1918–1919-ben*, pp. 76–110 and 168–199; Ioan Scurtu, "Integrarea provinciilor romanesti unite in 1918 in cadrul statului national roman" [Integration of the Romanian Provinces United in 1918 in the Romanian National State], in Grad and Ciubuta, eds., *Sfarsit si inceput de epoca*, pp. 47–71.

14	Konrád Salamon, *Nemzeti önpusztítás 1918–1920. Forradalom-proletárdiktatúra–ellenforradalom* [National Self-Destruction 1918–1920. Revolution – Proletarian Dictatorship – Counterrevolution] (Budapest, 2001), pp. 114–125.

15	Magda Ádám and Győző Cholnoky, eds., *Trianon. A magyar béreküldöttség tevékenysége 1920-ban. Válogatás A magyar béketárgyalások. Jelentés a magyar béreküldöttség működéséről Neuilly-sur-Seine-ben I–II. kötetéből.* (Térképmelléklet: III/B. kötet) [Trianon. The Activity of the Hungarian Peace Delegation in 1920. Selection from the Hungarian Peace Negotiations. From Vols. I–II of the Report on the Work of the Hungarian Peace Delegation in Neuilly-sur-Seine (Map Supplement, Vol. III/B)] (Budapest, [1921] 2001), pp. 289–296 and pp. 345–350; Katalin Soós, *Burgenland az európai politikában 1918–1921* [Burgenland in European Politics, 1918–1921] (Budapest, 1971), pp. 58–65.

16   *Translator's note:* The bourgeois democratic administration of Mihály Károlyi adopted the name Hungarian People's Republic (*Magyar Népköztársaság*) on November 16, 1918. This style persisted after the communist takeover of March 21, 1919, but gave way officially to the name Hungarian Soviet Republic (*Magyar Tanácsköztársaság*) when a new constitution was published by the Revolutionary Governing Council on April 2. The latter has sometimes been translated into English as the Hungarian Republic of Councils. After the communists seized power a second time in 1948–1949, the style Hungarian People's Republic was used again.

17   After the coup on March 21, 1919, Sándor Garbai became chairman of the new Revolutionary Governing Council, with Béla Kun as commissar for foreign and for military affairs, but in practice Kun was in full charge of the "proletarian dictatorship" until its collapse on August 1.

18   Mária Ormos, "The Hungarian Soviet Republic and Intervention by the Entente," in Király, Pastor and Sanders, eds., *Essays on World War I*, pp. 93–105.

19   The official name of the city was changed from Pozsony (Pressburg, Prešporok) to Bratislava in March 1919.

2. HUNGARY AT THE PEACE TALKS IN PARIS
László Szarka

There were preliminary discussions among the victorious Great Powers – the United States, France, the United Kingdom, Italy and Japan – before the Paris Peace Conference opened ceremoniously on January 18, 1919. The Conference was unparalleled in size – with delegates from over 30 countries, including Romania, Czechoslovakia, Poland and the South Slavs – and level of organization, but the defeated countries were excluded from it, although its prime aim was to devise peace treaties with them, above all with Germany. Delegates of defeated countries were only invited to Paris to be handed the completed draft of each treaty.

The basic principles of the settlement were decided by a Supreme War Council of the prime ministers and ministers of foreign affairs of the five Great Powers. They set the main political issues, reviewed commitments made in the war, and weighed proposals by the Conference's committees. Then they heard the demands of the affected neighboring countries. Finally they decided, on the recommendations of territorial and specialist committees (for ports, waterways and railways, for territorial questions, and so on), what the German, Austrian, Hungarian, Bulgarian and Turkish peace treaties would contain.

After each draft treaty had been handed over, the Supreme War Council listened to the delegation head of each defeated country, but the latter had no right to ask questions or negotiate with Supreme War Council members.

Hungary's status at the peace conference was especially complex, as the Great Powers had still not recognized Hungary officially since the break-up of the Austro-Hungarian Monarchy. Thus the Allied and Associated Powers did not accept, for instance, the Belgrade Military Convention of November 13, 1918, as an armistice or see it as a commitment. Moreover, the Peace Conference was intent on ending the Hungarian Soviet Republic, which had succeeded the Hungarian People's Republic on March 21, 1919. So Hungary was not invited to the Peace Conference until December 1919.[1]

The most important decisions for Hungary derived from the border demarcation work of the Czechoslovak and the Romanian–Yugoslav territorial committees, meeting between February 10 and mid-April 1919. Representatives of the Great Powers took part, but in cases of dispute, the delegation heads of the Allied and Associated powers concerned – Czechoslovakia, Romania and the South Slav state – were heard. The criteria in drawing the state borders of the new Hungary were these:

-   Commitments made in the Great War or the months leading up to the Peace Conference (such as the 1916 Bucharest Treaty, the armistice agreements, and the territorial decisions of the various demarcation agreements reached between November 1918 and June 1919).

-   The ethnic principle, although from the outset the Great Powers differed greatly in their interpretations of it. The principle for settling ethnic disputes was to decide in favor of Allied states.

-   The territorial claims of Allied countries, in which the utmost attention was paid to historical, geographical, economic and other criteria designed to support the demands expressed in the Czechoslovak, Romanian and South Slav peace notes. So in demarcating and justifying the territories of the Czechoslovak, Polish, South Slav and Romanian states, the arguments for the legitimacy of the territorial demands made in the beneficiary states' peace memoranda rested sometimes on historical grounds and sometimes on those of ethnicity or ethnography.

- The main aim of the Great Powers' efforts at peace-making was to avoid further military action and strive to withdraw and demobilize their forces as fast as possible. This meant working to boost local Allied countries, which could monitor Eastern Central Europe militarily, economically and politically, as an adequate counterweight to Germany and Russia.

- Strategic military criteria came to the fore in connection with military plans of Soviet Russia and the Hungarian Soviet Republic. The regional strategic and military purposes of the Great Powers were thought to be best served by so-called railway borders: along the River Ipoly, in Transcarpathia, and between Szatmárnémeti, Nagyvárad, Arad and Temesvár in Eastern Hungary. In each case these lines fell within the borders of Allied states, to reinforce their economic and military predominance.

- An attempt was also made to apply to the defeated countries the principle of economic viability, although this occurred in Hungary's case only with the coalmines of Salgótarján, Miskolc and the Mecsek Hills.

Demarcation of the new Hungarian state borders was completed by the territorial committees at the end of March and beginning of April 1919. The aim had been to prepare and conclude the peace treaties with Austria and with Hungary at the same time, but the declaration of the Hungarian Soviet Republic and the activity of the Hungarian Red Army intervened.[2] On June 13, 1919, a note from French Prime Minister Georges Clemenceau on behalf of the Supreme War Council informed Béla Kun, in his capacity as commissar for foreign affairs of the Hungarian Soviet Republic, of the Conference decisions on the new borders of Hungary. No substantive change in them ensued before the Treaty of Trianon was signed.

These borders meant that Hungary lost substantial amounts of territory with a majority of Hungarian inhabitants, to Czechoslovakia, Romania and the Serb-Croat-Slovene Kingdom: the Csallóköz and Mátyusföld, the land along the Garam, Gömör, Upper Bodrogköz, the Ung district, Bereg, Szatmár and Bihar, as well as Arad County, the Székely Land (Szeklerland) and Kalotaszeg, and the Banat (Bánság) and Bácska. This meant that larger or smaller Hungarian-speaking areas and village communities became minority regions or parts of them. Among the ceded cities with a majority Hungarian population were Érsekújvár, Komárom,

Rozsnyó, Kassa, Munkács, Ungvár, Szatmárnémeti, Nagyvárad, Kolozsvár, Arad, Marosvásárhely, Csíkszereda, Szabadka, Zenta, and several others.[3] The advent of the Hungarian Soviet Republic and the success and reception of its Red Army's northern campaign were a warning to the Great Powers at the Peace Conference that neglect of the principle of ethnic justice and equity was causing appreciable new tensions in the Danube basin. So the Supreme War Council tried to rein in the territorial ambitions of the Romanians, Czechoslovaks and South Slavs, and order their armies to withdraw behind their agreed state borders.

But the other main Allied objective in Hungary was to avert and eliminate the danger of Bolshevism. This led them to condone the occupation of Budapest by the Romanian army in August 1919. They sought through diplomats sent out by the Peace Conference to consolidate the situation in Hungary as fast as possible. But there was no chance of progress while the complexity of the domestic political and military situation in Hungary prevented either the Peidl or the Friedrich government from taking substantive decisions, and the Romanians followed up their occupation of Budapest by overrunning most of Transdanubia as well.

The British diplomat Sir George Clerk arrived in Budapest on October 23, 1919, as a special envoy of the Supreme War Council, with a mandate to consolidate the political situation and create stable conditions for the end to the Romanian occupation. He agreed on November 5 with local party leaders and the commander-in-chief of the National Army, Miklós Horthy, on the composition of a new government to include members of all parliamentary parties. He then won from the Romanian army's Budapest command a commitment to withdraw from the city before November 14.

Horthy entered Budapest on November 16 at the head of his army units and gave a well-remembered speech on Gellért tér in which he called Budapest a "guilty city" for the way in which it had helped the Commune to power. The "concentration" (coalition) government[4] formed by Károly Huszár on November 24 was recognized by the

Peace Conference on the following day, and, based on Clerk's report in Paris, was invited on December 1, 1919, to receive the draft treaty. The government appointed Count Albert Apponyi to head the peace delegation. While neighboring countries did all that they could to prevent the protests of Hungarians in the territories under their control from reaching the Peace Conference, the Hungarian peace delegation appended several such documents to its peace memorandum. The tensions prompted the Czechoslovak government to declare a lengthy state of emergency, which lasted a year and a half in Transcarpathia, and it did not wait for the Treaty of Trianon before holding general elections in April 1920. Meanwhile Hungarian civil servants and professionals were under pressure from Romania and the Serb-Croat-Slovene Kingdom to resign their jobs or even leave the country, requiring public employees, for instance, to take an oath of allegiance to the new state. In the event, several hundred thousand Hungarians who had been transferred to neighboring countries fled into the Trianon territory of Hungary during 1919 and 1920.[5]

The Apponyi delegation arrived in Paris on January 6, 1920, and was handed the peace conditions, which is to say the draft Hungarian peace treaty. Apponyi told the Supreme War Council on January 16 that Hungary was willing to submit to plebiscite all disputed territory. Citing Wilson's self-determination principle, he said "We demand a plebiscite for the parts of our country that you now wish to detach from us. I declare that we will submit to the results of this plebiscite whatever they may be."[6] Those running the Peace Conference paid no more heed to this demand than to other Hungarian observations on the draft, for instance on ecclesiastical, cultural and regional autonomy for minority Hungarian communities or assurance of broad rights to use their language.

After secret Hungarian–French negotiations in April–May 1920 had failed, the Hungarian peace treaty was initialed on June 4, 1920, at the Grand Trianon in the grounds of Versailles, by Ágoston Bernárd, minister of labor and public welfare, and Alfréd Drasche-Lázár, envoy extraordinary and minister plenipotentiary. The structure of the Treaty of Trianon followed that of the Austrian peace treaty signed in the Palace of Saint-Germain-en-Laye on September 10, 1919. It covered not only political and territorial matters, but rules, implementing measures and miscellaneous measures to do with war reparations, military commitments and restrictions, and international economic, commercial and transport links, as well as international minority protection measures, which were covered in relation to the victorious countries in the region in the form of a separate agreement.[7]

Hungary had no option but to sign the treaty, due to its succession of domestic crises in 1919, continuing political isolation, and consequent military and economic defenselessness. Yet for several reasons the treaty remained anathema to the Hungarian public between the wars, on whichever side of the Trianon frontier they lived. It was seen as a grave injustice to detach compact Hungarian-inhabited areas along the borders and cities with a majority Hungarian population, putting more than three million Hungarians in a minority situation. The historical Hungarian state was seen as a thing of great value, to which the foundation of the new, still multi-ethnic, states compared badly, as for a long time the Hungarian public would not even acknowledge the right of neighboring nations to self-determination. None of the rapidly changing state systems in Hungary in 1919 – people's republic, soviet republic, republic, kingdom – or any of the governments had managed to spur Hungarian society to defend itself or its country, even in areas with a Hungarian majority in an ethnic sense. That absence of national resistance, the desertion of hitherto loyal minorities (notably the Saxons), and defenselessness against merciless assimilation policies in neighboring states would lead to grave dilemmas and traumas in Hungarian society.

US President Woodrow Wilson took the initiative to establish on May 1, 1919, the Committee on New States and Minorities, which drafted the minority protection treaties with certain European Allied and Associated Powers – Czechoslovakia, Greece, Poland, Romania and the Serb–Croat–Slovene State – and the minority protection passages in the treaties with the two defeated successors to the

Habsburg Monarchy – Austria and Hungary – and with Bulgaria and Turkey. These laid the foundations for a minority protection system based on a guarantee system that allowed individual minorities to take complaints before the League of Nations. The minorities were granted, in the identical texts of the minority protection treaties and the minority protection chapters of the peace treaties, not only civil but linguistic, educational, cultural and religious rights. These general legal principles were accompanied by other provisions specific to each treaty. Article 10 of the Romanian Minority Protection Treaty, for instance, follows the others in stipulating that "Roumania will provide in the public education system in towns and districts in which a considerable proportion of Roumanian nationals of other than Roumanian speech are resident adequate facilities for ensuring that in the primary schools the instruction shall be given to the children of such Roumanian nationals through the medium of their own language," but adds a special provision in Article 11: "Roumania agrees to accord to the communities of the Saxons and Szeklers [*Székely*] in Transylvania local autonomy in regard to scholastic and religious matters, subject to the control of the Roumanian State."[8]

The Hungarian government's attitude was criticized on several occasions by representatives of the Hungarians now in a minority position. The Hungarians of Transylvania, Upper Hungary and the Southern Region saw it as a great error, indeed treachery, to have signed the treaty without reference to the minority communities concerned or consistent, unconditional representation of their position. The most harrowing document to reflect this view is a memorandum called "Cry for the Hungarian-ness of Transylvania, Bánság, Körösvidék and Máramaros" issued by Károly Kós, Árpád Paál and István Zágoni in Cluj in 1921. A similar warning came on June 2, 1920, in Parliament in Prague from the Czechoslovakian Hungarian members who had gained seats in the 1920 general elections, on whose behalf a joint statement of Hungarian parties was read by Lajos Körmendy-Ékes.[9] This insisted on the right of the Czechoslovakian Hungarians to self-determination, pointing out that nobody in the Hungarian peace delegation had received a mandate to sign on behalf of the Hungarians transferred to Czechoslovakia a peace treaty that denied the right of self-determination to the Hungarian communities of Slovensko and Rusinsko[10] (Slovakia and Ruthenia).

Notes

1   Works by Hungarians covering the talks with Hungary at the Versailles Peace Conference: Mária Ormos, *From Padua to Trianon, 1918–1920* (New York, 1982); József Galántai, *Trianon and the Protection of Minorities* (Boulder, CO/Highland Lakes, NJ, 1991); József Galántai, *A trianoni békekötés 1920. A párizsi meghívástól a ratifikálásig* [The Trianon Peace Settlement 1920. From the Paris Invitation to Ratification] (Budapest, 1990); György Litván, ed., *Trianon felé. A győztes nagyhatalmak tárgyalásai Magyarországról (Paul Mantoux tolmácstiszt feljegyzései)* [Towards Trianon. Negotiations of the Victorious Great Powers with Hungary – Notes by Interpreting Officer Paul Mantoux] (Budapest, 1998); Béla K. Király, Peter Pastor and Ivan Sanders, eds., *Essays on World War I: Total War and Peacemaking, a Case Study on Trianon* (New York, 1982); Béla K. Király and László Veszprémy, eds., *Trianon and East Central Europe* (Boulder, CO/Highland Lakes, NJ, 1995); Magda Ádám and Győző Cholnoky, eds., *Trianon. A magyar békeküldöttség tevékenysége 1920-ban. Válogatás* A magyar béketárgyalások. Jelentés a magyar békeküldöttség működéséről Neuilly-sur-Seine-ben I–II. *kötetéből.* (Térképmelléklet: III/B. kötet) [Trianon. The Activity of the Hungarian Peace Delegation in 1920. Selection from the Hungarian Peace Negotiations. From Vols. I–II of the Report on the Work of the Hungarian Peace Delegation in Neuilly-sur-Seine (Map Supplement, Vol. III/B)] (Budapest, [1921] 2001); Ignác Romsics, *The Dismantling of Historic Hungary: the Peace Treaty of Trianon, 1920* (New York, 2002); László Szarka, ed., *Hungary and the Hungarian Minorities. Trends in the Past and in Our Time* (Boulder, CO/Highland Lakes, NJ, 2004). From the international literature: Margaret Macmillan, *Paris 1919: Six Months That Changed the World* (New York, 2003); Marian Hronský, *The Struggle for Slovakia and the Treaty of Trianon* (Bratislava, 2001).

2　The Treaty of Saint-Germain-en-Laye was signed with Austria on September 10, 1919, and that of Trianon with Hungary on June 4, 1920. The Austro-Hungarian border was later amended by plebiscites in 1921 and 1923. See Section 2.10.

3　The frontiers were drawn at meetings of the Czechoslovak and Yugoslav–Romanian territorial committees, selected materials of which appear in Magda Ádám, György Litván and Mária Ormos, eds., *Documents diplomatiques français sur l'histoire du Bassin des Carpates 1918–1932. Vol. 1–2. Octobre 1918–août 1919, août 1919–juin 1920* (Budapest, 1993–1995).

4　The centers of resistance to the Hungarian Soviet Republic in the south of the country and in Vienna were both represented in the new government.

5　I. István Mócsy, "Partition of Hungary and the Origins of the Refugee Problem," in Király, Pastor and Sanders, eds., *Essays on World War I*, pp. 239–256.

6　Litván, ed., *Trianon felé*.

7　Galántai, *Trianon and the Protection of Minorities*, pp. 167–169; Galántai, *A trianoni békekötés 1920*, pp. 135–140.

8　Galántai, *Trianon and the Protection of Minorities*, pp. 165–166. Spelling taken from the original.

9　László Szarka, "Artificial Communities and an Unprotected Protective Power: the Trianon Peace Treaty and the Minorities," in Szarka, ed., *Hungary and the Hungarian Minorities*, pp. 14–35.

10　*Translator's note*. The terms referred to the actual or perceived Slovak and Rusyn-inhabited areas. These did not overlap perfectly with what became the Czechoslovak provinces of Slovakia and Ruthenia or Transcarpathia.

3. THE CREATION OF
HUNGARIAN MINORITY GROUPS

Romania (*Nándor Bárdi*)

The period under discussion here can be divided into two parts. One ran from the Aster Revolution to the signing of the Treaty of Trianon (October 31, 1918, to June 4, 1920). The other covered the subsequent period in the former areas of Eastern Hungary, when the Romanian state administration was acknowledged also by the Hungarian community, up until the formation of the National Hungarian Party[1] in Romania in December 1922.

On the minority question the Károlyi government (October 31, 1918, to January 8, 1919) supported Wilson's principle of self-determination, hoping to defend Hungary's territorial integrity by granting rights to self-determination to its national minorities. In the first half of November, events in Budapest and the influence of returning soldiers revolutionized the mining districts of Eastern Hungary and the urban working class and the peasantry, who were under local military government. But only sporadically did the military and social revolts that broke out assume a national character. The government turned for help in curbing these to the local authorities: the Hungarian and Romanian national councils that had begun to form at the end of October. Many rural administrative staff had fled and the influence of urban authorities was reduced. The Transylvanian Hungarian military force of some 4,000 was too small to keep order, which meant relying on national guard units that the national councils had organized. This new power system was riven by two conflicting sets of objectives. The radicalized Hungarian and Székely national councils thought in terms of the republican movement; the question of the country's integrity came to the fore only gradually. Not so with the parallel Romanian organizations, where national interests were foremost.[2]

On November 9, the Romanian National Council issued from Arad an ultimatum to the government calling for the transfer of 26 Romanian-inhabited counties in Eastern Hungary, based on Wilson's principle of self-determination and the need to preserve public order. Then negotiators in Arad headed by Minister of Nationalities Oszkár Jászi (November 13–14) offered, until the peace negotiations were over, rights to self-determination to areas with a Romanian majority on a kind of cantonal system. This the Romanian National Council representatives rejected as being too complex. A second proposal from Jászi was for the areas with a Romanian majority to be subject to the Romanian National Council, which would be represented in Parliament, while the local minorities (Saxons, Romanians and Hungarians in this case) would be under the protection of the 1868 Nationalities Act. This the Romanian side also rejected, demanding complete secession.[3]

On December 1 came the Romanian Assembly at Gyulafehérvár (Alba Iulia). During the preparations, some representatives of Transylvania's Romanian National Party (the initiators of the Romanian National Council) and the Social Democrats regarded the democratization of Romania as a precondition for the union, and were planning partial autonomy for Transylvania. However, only the democratic principles (universal franchise, freedom of the press and assembly, agrarian reform, extension of working-class rights, and broad minority rights) made it into the final draft. Later the Romanian King Ferdinand I assented only to Point I of the resolution, the act of union.[4] The 1,228 delegates of the Romanians of Hungary at Gyulafehérvár passed the resolution and proclaimed it to a crowd of a hundred thousand. They then elected a 200-member Grand National Council that appointed a 15-member Governing Council, headed by Iuliu Maniu, which was set up on December 7 in Nagyszeben (Sibiu) as a provisional government for the province.[5] The Hungarian government on December 8 named as high governing commissioner of Eastern Hungary István Apáthy, a Kolozsvár professor and head of the Transylvanian Hungarian National Council. His aspiring government office sought to control the civil unrest in the province.[6]

The rivalry of the two ethnically based regional centers of administration and power was decided by military events. The November 3 Padua ceasefire agreement had simply ordered the evacuation of areas occupied in the war without affecting Hungary's borders, except for the secession of Croatia. The armistice was made concrete in the Belgrade Military Convention of November 13. One of its terms required the Hungarian government to withdraw behind a demarcation line along the Upper Nagy-Szamos river as far as Marosvásárhely (Oşorhei/Tărgu Mureş), then along the River Maros to Szeged, but it allowed Hungarian administration to remain in the ceded territories. On the day that the treaty was signed, Romanian forces arrived at the passes over the Eastern Carpathians and went on to occupy Marosvásárhely on December 2, Beszterce (Bistriţa) on the 4th, Székelyudvarhely (Odorhei/Odorheiu Secuiesc) on the 6th, and Brassó (Braşov) on the 7th, and reached the demarcation line. The local Hungarian administration treated the Romanian units as Entente forces in control of the territory up until the peace negotiations, and there was no appreciable resistance. During the days after the Gyulafehérvár Assembly, the Romanian forces overstepped the demarcation line in some places. On December 12, General Henri Berthelot, in command of the Entente's Danube Army, arbitrarily allowed the Romanian forces to advance to a line running from Szatmárnémeti (Satu Mare) through Nagykároly (Carei) and Nagyvárad (Oradea) to Arad.[7]

The Károlyi government in Budapest put up no military resistance, partly out of faith in the Belgrade Convention and its acceptance as a partner by the Entente, but also because the soldiers returning from the war were causing huge social tensions and the government aimed to disarm these masses as quickly as possible. Nor did it have enough funds for setting up the new army. Of the new Hungarian republican defense force, only 3,000–4,000 Transylvanian local guards were available to face an advancing Romanian force of 20,000–40,000 men. So on December 24 Kolozsvár (Cluj) was ceded without a fight to the Romanian troops, who reached the Máramarossziget (Sighetu Marmaţiei)–Nagybánya

(Baia Mare)–Zilah (Zalău)–Csucsa (Ciucea) line before mid-January. The only opposing force consisted of the Székely Division recruited among refugees from occupied territories. By the end of January, experience had persuaded Károlyi in favor of armed defense of the country, but he still had no adequate military force available. But he could not accept the peace conference decision allowing the Romanians to advance to a line from Szatmárnémeti to Arad, fronted to the west by a neutral zone that was to embrace Debrecen, Békéscsaba and Szeged. Seeing that his policy of cooperating with the Entente had failed, Károlyi resigned. The only remaining chance of preserving the country's integrity lay in a foreign policy of alignment with Soviet Russia.[8]

In mid-November, the Hungarian and Székely national councils in Transylvania responded to the Romanian self-determination effort by coming out in support of government from Budapest or alternatively of Transylvanian self-rule. A plan for an independent Székely state was also mooted. A rally of 40,000 held in Kolozsvár on December 22 called for national equality before the law in a "united, unmutilated Hungary." There were attempts during the change of sovereignty to fill the power vacuum with autonomous local centers of authority: the Banat Republic, centered in Temesvár (Timişoara), the Székely Republic (Székelyudvarhely) and the Republic of Kalotaszeg (Bánffyhunyad/Huedin).[9]

The Romanian forces, having taken Nagyvárad on April 20, 1919, introduced press censorship, a curfew and corporal punishment, banned the operation of political and social organizations, and suspended freedom of assembly and movement everywhere. On January 15, 1919, a delegation headed by Judge Emil Grandpierre met in Nagyszeben with Iuliu Maniu, head of the Governing Council. The Hungarian position – until the final legal settlement emerged from the peace talks – was for public administration in Hungarian-inhabited areas of Transylvania to be Hungarian, in Romanian-inhabited areas Romanian, and in mixed areas mixed. Officials should not be required to take an oath, just give an undertaking, for which the delegation had brought the wording. The proposal was rejected by the Governing Council. Two days later, István Apáthy was arrested and his High Governing Commission for Eastern Hungary[10] wound up forthwith. Meanwhile, control of the railway and postal services was assumed by Romanian army units. In March, the courts in Kolozsvár were taken over, as were the University of Sciences and the National Theater in May. Public officials, lawyers and railway employees were made to swear allegiance to the Romanian king, but refused on the grounds that the peace talks had not been completed. This meant loss of the franchise, employment and pensions, and most of them fled to Hungary. In all, about 145,000 persons left Transylvania for Hungary in 1918–1920, mostly from the urban middle class and officialdom. Conditions worsened further as dwellings were requisitioned by the military authorities. In September 1919, Romanian became the language of instruction in state secondary schools.[11]

After the High Governing Commission was closed and its head was arrested, there continued to be an illegal Transylvanian Center[12] headed by Judge Emil Grandpierre, the lord lieutenant of Kolozsvár appointed by the Károlyi government. The Center kept in touch with politicians in Budapest and Szeged, organized passive resistance among officials, gave what financial support it could to institutions and officials, and, last but not least, gathered information for those in Budapest who were preparing for the peace talks and for local Hungarian leaders in Transylvania.[13]

Once the Treaty of Trianon had been signed on June 4, 1920, were made to seek ways of settling in within the Romanian state. The Hungarian postal and administrative officials and lawyers who were still in their posts swore their oaths of allegiance in the same month. The land reform began to be implemented in September. The undertakings necessary for alleviating its effects (appeals, matters to do with expropriations of estates) made it essential to institutionalize some kind of political interest protection. A group consisting of Grandpierre and the former heads of the Hungarian state administration, on the grounds of the minority protection treaty signed by Romania in December 1919, sought foreign help for remedying Hungarian grievances. By November 1920 they were thinking in terms of a legal body to represent the Hungarian community before the League of Nations, using the terms of the treaty, and the Hungarian Association emerged on January 9, 1921.[14] Meanwhile, another group appeared in Transylvanian public life in 1918–1919, a group of younger, socially sensitive radical bourgeois, advocating integration into the Romanian state and the democratic organization of the Hungarian community within it. They promised loyalty to Romania in return for democratization that would have granted national autonomy to the annexed Hungarian community. The decisive influences were architect Károly Kós and journalist Árpád Paál (a former deputy lieutenant of Székelyudvarhely who had sworn loyalty along with county officials to the Székely Republic and then spent a year and a half in prison).[15] Essentially these were the two groups that competed to represent the Hungarians of Romania in 1921–1922: the traditional Transylvanian Hungarian elite (including church leaders), trying to defend their positions, and the bourgeoisie and the intellectuals, who were setting the agenda of the press and were urging democratic self-organization and political, economic and social modernization.

It was essential to create a united body to represent Hungarian interests against the discriminatory policies that Romania was pursuing. In the spring of 1921, the Hungarian Church leaders (Roman Catholic, Reformed and Unitarian) swore allegiance, for they were the one remaining institutional umbrella over the Hungarian community, able to offer some political representation, mainly for grievances over the school system and land reform, but representation in Parliament became essential. This meant running in the elections as a political party. The Hungarian People's Party (Magyar Néppárt) was formed in the summer of 1921 by the "activists" among the Hungarian minority elite,[16] and in July, integration went further when the "passivists" united with the People's Party and joined the Hungarian Association, which was now headed by Baron Sámuel Jósika, the last speaker of the Hungarian Upper House (the House of Lords), and as such, formerly the highest-ranking public figure in Transylvania. The Association (as their self-governing organization) saw itself as the legal embodiment of the Hungarians of Romania. This claim prompted the government to fabricate reasons to suspend its operation in October 1921. For the general elections due in 1922, first the People's Party in January and then Grandpierre's Hungarian National Party (*Magyar Nemzeti Párt*) in February reorganized and agreed on common candidates. They were not helped by the fact that much of the Hungarian community had been left off the electoral rolls and most of the Hungarian candidates were not allowed to stand for various reasons. These and other electoral abuses – designed to ensure a majority for the Liberal Party in the constituent assembly – resulted in a House of Representatives and a Senate with only three Hungarian members each, whereas their proportion of the population would have warranted 25–30. When the operation of the Hungarian Association remained banned in the autumn of 1922, the leaders of the two parties agreed at the end of December to merge as the National Hungarian Party (*Országos Magyar Párt*), which essentially continued with the program of the Hungarian Association, this way preventing the Romanian political parties from forming organizations to represent the Hungarians.[17]

Czechoslovakia: Slovakia (*Attila Simon*)

The Czechoslovak state was proclaimed on October 28, 1918, but its borders were not settled for several months. Minister of Foreign Affairs Edvard Beneš intended to present the Paris Peace Conference with a *fait accompli*, and so Czech forces (without any warrant to do so) tried unsuccessfully in November 1918 to occupy the northern counties of Hungary, where the administration was falling apart. Only at the end of the month did the Entente draw a provisional demarcation line between the two countries, running along the Danube and Ipoly rivers, then under Rimaszombat (Rimavská Sobota) as far as the River Ung. The Hungarian government only learnt of this in the so-called Vix Note of December 23.

Czech legions ordered back from Italy began on December 31, 1918, to occupy the southern, Hungarian-inhabited areas of Upper Hungary (the future Slovakia) and gained control before mid-January. Local inhabitants saw the Czechoslovak rule as temporary and received the Czech soldiers peacefully, except in a few places near Érsekújvár (Nové Zámky) and in the Mátyusföld (Matúšov) villages of Deáki (Deakovce) and Pered, where local guard units opposed them.

There was resistance in the form of a rail strike in the occupied areas called in the early days of February by the Pozsony (Bratislava) Social Democrats, who also held a mass rally of Hungarian and German inhabitants of Pozsony on February 12, 1919, protesting against social grievances and the Czechoslovak occupation. The intervention by the authorities led to Czechoslovak soldiers firing on the peaceful demonstrators, causing eight fatalities and 14 injuries.

The Czechoslovak army went on to attack the Hungarian Soviet Republic, seeking to push Slovakia's borders still further south to a line along the ridge of the Mátra and Bükk hills, but without success. The Paris Peace Conference in June 1919 drew the final border along the December demarcation line, but with some alterations, to Hungary's detriment. Ethnic principles were ignored, meaning that 890,000 of the 2.9 million inhabitants of the new Slovakia appear to have been Hungarians if the 1910 census data are projected onto the new state borders. Most of the Hungarians lived in a homogeneous Hungarian-speaking zone along Slovakia's southern borders.[18]

In terms of its nature, Czechoslovakia's history from the foundation of the state up to the first parliamentary elections in the spring of 1920 can be called a period of Czechoslovak national dictatorship.[19] Legislative power was held by a provisional National Assembly in which the German and Hungarian inhabitants were unrepresented. This body adopted the basic laws that would remain in force until the autumn of 1938: the Constitution, the language act, land reform act, public administration act, and so on. The National Assembly granted full powers to govern Slovakia to a minister plenipotentiary, Vavro Šrobárt. There commenced a de-Hungarianization of Slovakian public life using a series of new laws and regulations and the means available to the military dictatorship that had been declared due to the presence of the Hungarian Soviet Republic. It meant that large numbers of Hungarian officials, teachers and other state employees were dismissed. Many others left rather than take an oath of allegiance to the new state. As a result, several thousand families (about 120,000 persons) who had lost their livelihood fled to Hungary. A process of rapid ethnic transformation began in the cities along the ethnic border. Suddenly several important centers such as Eperjes (Prešov), Nagyszombat (Trnava) and Nyitra (Nitra) became predominantly Slovak-speaking. Over the next couple of years, Hungarian monuments and statues disappeared as well. The statue of Maria Theresa in Pozsony was broken to pieces by Czech legionaries, as were the Millenary moments in Dévény (Devín) and Nyitra, the statue of an 1848 Hungarian soldier in Kassa (Košice) and statues of Lajos Kossuth in Rozsnyó (Rožňava), Losonc (Lučenec) and Érsekújvár.

The constitutional changes soon affected Slovakia's ethnic structure. The census of 1921 recorded 637,000 Hungarians, a fall of over 250,000 in the number in Slovakia since 1910, due to the many who had left the country and tens of thousands of bilingual city dwellers now more inclined to record themselves as Slovaks than as Hungarians.[20]

The Constitution adopted by the provisional Czechoslovak National Assembly on February 29, 1920, ended national dictatorship and created a basis for parliamentary democracy. The First Republic was a centralist state run from Prague, with an ideology of "Czechoslovakism," whereby the Czech and Slovak nations were one. So the official language of state was Czechoslovak, which did not exist in reality. Relations between the Czechs and the Slovaks remained unresolved throughout the period, as Czechoslovakism was widely rejected by Slovaks pressing for autonomy for Slovakia.

Czechoslovak legislation was relatively generous with minority rights, allowing minorities to found political and cultural organizations, and to use their language in official contacts if they accounted for over 20 percent of the population. But there were obstacles to applying this in practice, as the Czech officials who had replaced the Hungarians were unable to speak the local language.

Development of Hungarian political and cultural institutions in Slovakia was assisted by the new Constitution and the first parliamentary elections, but went slowly due to uncertainty over the borders and a want of distinct political traditions in Upper Hungary. Most Hungarians voted in the elections in April 1920 for parties that advocated self-determination for minorities. Two Hungarians entered the Prague Parliament on the list of the left-wing German–Hungarian Social Democratic Party and another six on those of the right-wing National Christian Socialist Party and the National Hungarian Smallholders', Agriculturalists' and Artisans' Party. The popularity of left-wing ideas also appears in the fact that a further two Hungarians won seats for the biggest Czechoslovak party, the Czechoslovak Social Democratic Movement.[21]

Opposition Hungarian members set out to exploit the scope of Czechoslovak parliamentarianism, speaking up in their native language for the right of the Hungarian minority to self-determination and the minority rights assured to them by international agreement and under the Czechoslovak Constitution. Lajos Körmendy-Ékes, presenting a joint declaration by the right-wing Hungarian parties in the Prague legislature on June 2, 1920, picked out well the cardinal policies to be pursued by the Hungarians of Czechoslovakia in the coming years: "It is our parliamentary duty to the Hungarian community over a million strong, forced into alien frames and under strong pressure there, and to our German brethren suffering a similar fate, to afford them at all times, by legal means but without compromise, devoted protection, until such time as all people realize and it be the truth In everyone's eyes that the Hungarians may well have been the sole combatants in the world war who sought to win without taking aught from others, striving simply for their existence and national honor on the grounds that a word given is sacred. Although we have now through others' crimes lost all, yet has our honor remained; precisely this is what obligates us to state clearly and decisively that we shall never in any wise abandon our right of self-determination, for that we reserve, that we demand."[22]

Czechoslovakia: Transcarpathia (*Csilla Fedinec*)

The government of Mihály Károlyi, in Act X/1918,[23] granted autonomy to the Rusyn (Ruthenian) people of the variously named northeast Felvidék (Upper Hungary), one of the most backward parts of the country. The name given to the territory in the act was Ruszka Krajna (Rus'ka Krajna, in English: Ruthenian Border Territory). In December 1918, a Ministry for Rus'ka Krajna was set up under Oreszt Szabó (Orest Sabov), and a Munkács-based governor, Avgusztin Stefán (Avgusthyn Shtefan), was appointed, but foreign armies advanced into the territory in January 1919 and the borders of Rus'ka Krajna receded before them.[24] The Upper Tisza district came under Romanian control, while Czechoslovak forces occupied the western part up to the River Ung, including the city of Ungvár (Ukrainian: Uzhhorod, Slovak: Užhorod). The foreign forces continued to advance under the Hungarian Soviet Republic (March 21–August 6), whose constitution[25] recognized a Rusyn autonomous area, but it existed for only 40 days in March and April before being overrun by Czechoslovak and Romanian military forces.[26] But the major influences on the destiny of Transcarpathia were not confined to the Hungarian government, which sought to retain possession of the Rusyn-inhabited areas and to prevent secessions or detachments from them.[27]

One such influence was the so-called Ukrainian line, which had the strongest influence in the Máramaros County. Its main aim was to annex Transcarpathia to Ukraine. From November 1918 to May 1919, a body called the Hutsul People's Council was based at Kőrösmező (Ukrainian: Jasyna, Slovak: Jasiňa) and declared a Hutsul Republic, but this was ended by the Romanian invasion.

The other main initiative came from the Rusyn-Ukrainian émigré community in North America. Several organizations were founded but the decisive influence on events was the American National Council of Ruthenians founded at Homestead, Florida, and chaired by Nicholas Chopey. The aims of the Council were formulated by Gregory Zhatkovych, a lawyer. It joined the Mid-European Democratic Union chaired by T. G. Masaryk, signed the Declaration of Common Aims of the Independent Mid-European Nations, and voted at Scranton, Pennsylvania, on November 12, 1918, for annexing the Rusyn-inhabited counties of historical Hungary (Szepes, Sáros, Zemplén, Abaúj, Gömör, Borsod, Ung, Bereg and Máramaros) to the new Republic of Czechoslovakia, provided that the latter gave autonomy to the majority population, the Rusyns. US President Woodrow Wilson was informed of the Scranton resolution as well.

Thereafter, the Rusyns who were invited to the Paris peace conference that opened on January 18, 1919, by Edvard Beneš and Karel Kramař, representing the Czechoslovak government, were not local figures sympathetic to Hungary or the Ukrainian line, but representatives of the émigré American National Council of Ruthenians, including Gregory Zhatkovych and Anton Beszkid (Anton Beskyd), president of the Rusyn Council of Eperjes (Slovak: Prešov), who was resident in Czechoslovakia by then. The Czechoslovak claims in Transcarpathia were endorsed by the Paris peace conference on March 12, 1919. On May 8, 1919, the Rusyn councils of Eperjes, Ungvár and Huszt (Ukrainian: Khust, Slovak: Chust) held a joint meeting in Ungvár (by then occupied by Czechoslovakia) to found the Central Russian (i.e. Rusyn) National Council, which declared "voluntary" annexation to Czechoslovakia. The Czechoslovak government took steps in August to introduce civil government alongside the military administration in force there since the beginning of the occupation.

That was the situation when the Treaty of Saint-Germain-en-Laye was signed by the Allied and Associated Powers and the new Republic of Austria on September 10, 1919.[28] To the Czechoslovak Republic was ceded Transcarpathia – the most of the counties of Ung, Bereg, Ugocsa and Máramaros, under the designation "Podkarpatská Rus" (Subcarpathian Russia) – with more than 600,000 inhabitants, of whom 370,000 described themselves in 1921 as Rusyn (or Russian or Ukrainian), 102,000 as Hungarian, 80,000 as Jewish, and smaller numbers as Romanian, Czech, Slovak, German and Gypsy.[29] Czechoslovakia committed itself under the treaty to running the territory as an autonomous self-governing unit. Until this commitment should be met, a provisional Rusyn Autonomous Directory was appointed under the chairmanship of

Gregory Zhatkovych, who moved to Užhorod with his family in the summer. The constitution of the Czechoslovak Republic adopted on February 29, 1920, confirmed that Transcarpathia was to receive wide autonomy.[30] On May 5, Zhatkovych was appointed as governor, again provisionally, until autonomy should be granted. One reason given for the provisional status was the fact that the Romanian army had yet to withdraw. That was also why the region was omitted from the first Czechoslovak elections to the National Assembly and the Senate, held in the spring of 1920. The Romanian withdrawal was completed at the end of August that year, but still no change was made in its status. Zhatkovych could make no progress in his talks with the government and resigned in disillusionment. After an official farewell to Užhorod on May 17, 1921, he moved back to the United States over the summer.[31]

Simultaneously with these Transcarpathian events, of importance primarily to the Rusyns, the Hungarian community was following its own route. It took a long time for it to sink in with the Hungarians that these new borders were permanent, not temporary. The first steps were to try to save Hungarian as a language of instruction in secondary schools – petitions were drawn up or efforts made to start private gymnasia in Munkács (Ukrainian: Mukacheve, Slovak: Mukačevo), Beregszász (Ukrainian: Berehove, Slovak: Berehovo) and above all Ungvár – and to establish political organizations. That early period marked the beginning of several Hungarian parties in Transcarpathia: the Hungarian Party of Law, the Autonomous Party of the Indigenous, the Christian Socialist Party and the Smallholders, Artisans and Agriculturalists' Party. The Hungarian branch of the Czechoslovak Communist Party also had a strong influence on the public initially.[32]

The Hungarian population of Transcarpathia experienced the change of state sovereignty and its results in a way specific to itself. It took a while before people realized what life under a new state entailed. People interpreted the events around them quite unrealistically until the peace treaties had been concluded. Officials and government employees in the early days refused to swear allegiance to the new Czechoslovak state. The Hungarian intelligentsia viewed uncomprehendingly the sudden political self-confidence of the Rusyns, who now had no desire to fall back on Hungarian politics and wanted to further their own interests. Only after the international treaties that decided the fate of the whole of Transcarpathia had been concluded did the Hungarians grasp their real situation, treating what had happened to them and their mother country as a drama, a tragedy. As a way of suffering the tragedy more easily, they sought a scapegoat for what had happened, and their choice fell on the Jews. Once it was realized that the borders could not be changed, their attention shifted: if there was to be a border between them and their mother country, let it be permeable, not sealed. The Hungarian community experienced for the first time what it was like to live as a minority. The Austro-Hungarian Monarchy had contained a great many national groups, and the peace agreements that ended the First World War typically acknowledged them by detaching them as new states, and by creating a new national minority, the Hungarians themselves.[33]

The Serb-Croat-Slovene Kingdom (*Enikő A. Sajti*)

The Zagreb National Council of the Serbs, Croats and Slovenes declared its secession from Austria-Hungary on October 29, 1918, and proclaimed the State of the Serbs, Croats and Slovenes. On November 24, it announced the unification of the South Slav lands, including Vajdaság (Vojvodina). Due to a dispute with Zagreb about unification procedure, the Novi Sad Grand National Assembly, on the advice of the Serbian National Council in Újvidék (Novi Sad), announced separately on November 25 that the Bánát (Banat), Bácska (Bačka) and Baranya (Baranja) were detached from Hungary and annexed to the Kingdom of Serbia. This assembly did not reflect the ethnic composition of Vajdaság: 750 of the 757 delegates were Slavs – 578 Serbs, 84 Bunjevci (Bunyevác), 62 Slovaks, 21 Rusyns, 3 Šokci and 2 Croats – with only 6 Germans and 1 Hungarian, but it passed a resolution proposed by Jaša Tomić, head of the Újvidék Council of Nationalities ensuring minority rights for non-Slav peoples.[34]

Formation of the Royal State of the Serbs, Croats and Slovenes was announced formally in Belgrade on December 1, 1918. This became the Serb-Croat-Slovene Kingdom with the adoption of the St. Vitus' Day Constitution of June 28, 1921 (*Vidovdanski ustav*).

On November 13, 1918, the Károlyi government signed the Belgrade Military Convention (in effect an armistice), which confirmed the Serb military occupation of the Southern Region, and obliged the Hungarian government to evacuate the areas of Transylvania and the Banat east of the Upper Szamos river and south of the River Maros, and also the lands south of the Szeged–Baja–Pécs–Varasd (Varaždin) railway. In addition, the city of Pécs, with part of Baranya (Baranja), and Baja with its environs came under Serbian military occupation. These were not evacuated as required under the Treaty of Trianon until August 24, 1920. The Convention did not apply to the Muravidék (Pomurje), but the Serbian army occupied it for a time. A Croatian unit took over the Muraköz (Međimurje) in December 1918. Only on February 20, 1919, could the Serbian military command take over the Banat from the Bánát National Council, which had envisaged a measure of autonomy under French supervision.[35]

The Belgrade Military Convention left the administration of Serbian-occupied areas to "local organizations": Hungary should have run them up to the signing of the peace treaty. However, the Grand National Council elected by the Grand National Assembly in Újvidék set up for administrative purposes a new regional Serbian body (people's government) called the People's Administration for the Banat, Bačka and Baranja,[36] headed by Joca Lalošević. This was abolished by a royal decree of March 11, 1919, that centralized and regulated the provisional administration of the new state. Thereafter the Southern Region territories annexed to the Kingdom of Serbs, Croats, and Slovenes were administered directly from Belgrade through the separate Bačka, Banat and Baranja Department of the Ministry of the Interior.

Up to the end of September 1919, successive Hungarian governments urged the Southern Region officials (and those of other detached territories) to resist openly. They were to take orders only from Budapest and refuse to take the oath of allegiance to the new state. The Friedrich and the Huszár governments changed this stance before the peace treaty was signed and began to accept "seeming integration," but there were serious conflicts between the Southern Region Hungarians and the new South Slav authorities.

The National Directorate, ignoring the terms of the Belgrade Convention, immediately started to dismiss Hungarian lord lieutenants, deputy-lieutenants, mayors and notaries in favor of mainly Serbian officials, often current, as being more reliable in their allegiance. Non-compliance by the old Hungarian judges and prosecutors led to some civil cases being brought before Serbian military courts. Censorship was imposed, and Hungarian-language theater performances and film shows were banned, as were assemblies of "unreliable elements," including family gatherings. A curfew was introduced, and officers of the Austro-Hungarian army were placed under police surveillance, while officials and teachers who refused to swear an oath of allegiance were dismissed from their posts and had their property confiscated. Nor were armed clashes between the Serb military and locals rare.

In March 1920, the Belgrade government ordered the conscription of young men in the Southern Region. There was a mass refusal to join on the part of the Germans and Hungarians of Bačka and the Banat, which sparked shooting incidents between the military and the local population. One such left 15 dead and 20 wounded in Torzsa (Torž) and another 10 dead and 20 wounded in Zombor (Sombor). The authorities took hostages in several places as a way to keep order. The Szabadka (Subotica) Rail Directorate sacked two thirds of the Hungarian railway staff in an attempt to crush a strike, during which the Szabadka police department was attacked and two men were killed.[37]

The borders of the South Slav state emerged from the peace treaties and frontier agreements of 1919–1920. Under Trianon, Hungary (excluding Croatia–Slavonia) lost 20,551 square kilometers with 1,509,295 inhabitants to the South Slav state (in Muravidék/

Prekmurje, the Baranya Triangle, part of the Banat, and Bácska/ Bačka), where 30.3 percent of the population had been Hungarian at the time of the 1910 census. According to the Yugoslav census of 1921, the area ceded by Hungary to the South Slav kingdom held 467,658 Hungarians, of which 378,107 dwelt in Vojvodina (the Banat, Bačka and Baranja). The "Southern Region" in Hungarian parlance and historical terminology means the areas (except Croatia) annexed to the Yugoslav state after 1918 (the Banat, Bačka, Baranya and Muravidék/Međimurje), while the term Vajdaság (Vojvodina) was linked with nineteenth-century autonomy efforts, partly successful, by Hungary's Serbian national minority. The Serbian Vojvodina existed from 1849 to 1860. After 1945, the Autonomous Province of Vojvodina included the Banat, Bačka and Baranya, and also Srem (Szerémség/Srijem).

A total of 44,903 Hungarians left the Serb-Croat-Slovene Kingdom between 1918 and 1924, as deportees, refugees, or optants.

Inroads into the Hungarian school system began right after the Serbian troops arrived, as teachers were dismissed in large numbers for refusing to take the oath. By 1920, the Serbian system of elementary and secondary state schools had spread over the Southern Region and the teacher training college in Subotica had been closed. The old system of communal, denominational and private schools, including Serbian ones, was almost completely eliminated by the nationalization.

Article 16 of the St. Vitus's Day Constitution provided for mother-tongue education in elementary schools for "citizens belonging to another race and speaking another language." Children were to be raised in a spirit of "state self-awareness and national unity," and so even a minimum of Hungarian national subjects was left out of the curriculum. In June 1920, Minister of Education Svetozar Pribičević issued a notorious "name-analysis" order that limited the right to mother-tongue education for Hungarians. The order, which remained in force under the new constitution, right up to 1938, gave access to mother-tongue instruction only to Hungarian children whose parents and grandparents bore surnames deemed by a committee to be Hungarian. This also meant that all those classed as ethnic Germans or as Jews were barred from enrolling their children in Hungarian-taught classes.

Nationalization of the economy began in the autumn of 1918 with the freezing of ostensibly foreign assets. Local Hungarian owners were obligated under an order, which has never been found, to elect "reliable Serbs" onto the boards of directors of their companies.

After some hesitation, Yugoslavia stated on December 5, 1919, in connection with the Austrian peace treaty, that it would endorse the international minority protection treaty. This committed the country to providing mother-tongue elementary education for the minorities in its territory (except for the Albanians and Macedonians) and requisite funding for that from the state budget. The treaty also contained option rights for Hungarians. Yugoslavia's Hungarians were not able to exercise their rights as citizens until the option right expired on July 26, 1922. They could not take part in the 1921 elections to the constituent assembly or found any business, political or cultural organizations.[38]

Austria (*Gerhard Baumgartner*)

The Allied Powers, after the proclamation of republics in Austria and Hungary, proposed at talks with them that western areas of the counties of Moson, Sopron and Vas be annexed to Austria. Yet these areas had not been included in the new Republic of Austria's territorial claims.[39]

These areas (the future Burgenland) were inhabited chiefly by Germans (75.1 percent), Croats (15.2 percent) and Hungarians (8.4 percent). Those whose native language was Hungarian were unevenly distributed over the annexed territory. Most lived in mixed communities or were scattered. There was mainly Hungarian habitation only in the Oberwart (Felsőőr) and western Neusiedl (Nezsider) districts. The 1920 census recorded 22,867 native-speaking Hungarian inhabitants in Burgenland. Only in the villages ceded from Vas County did the Hungarians exceed 10,000, but there they made up only 8 percent of the population. The highest proportion of Hungarians was in the ceded areas of Moson County: 14.3 percent. The ceded community with the highest proportion of Hungarians was Eisenstadt (Kismarton, 35.0 percent), the future provincial capital. The most important Hungarian communities were in Oberwart (Felsőőr) with 3,138 Hungarians, Unterwart (Alsóőr) with 1,230, and Eisenstadt with 1,020. There were altogether 53 communities with over 100 Hungarian inhabitants. A more significant picture emerges if the number of Hungarian-speakers, rather than native speakers, is taken. These were in an absolute majority in the Neusiedl and Oberpullendorf (Felsőpulya) districts and the towns of Eisenstadt and Rust (Ruszt), and their proportion in the whole of Burgenland was 35.1 percent (78,686 persons).

Most people (67.7 percent) were engaged in farming, the rest in industry (16.2 percent), commerce and credit (1.9 percent), mining and smelting (1.9 percent), public service (1.2 percent), armed forces (1.6 percent) and transport (1 percent), and 1.8 percent were self-employed. Only Neufeld an der Leitha (Lajtaújfalu) had a sizeable mine, employing 549, and a yarn factory, employing 603.[40]

The German-speaking inhabitants of Burgenland began to organize themselves in November 1918 with the foundation of the German People's Council for Western Hungary[41] in Mattersdorf (Nagymarton, after 1924 Mattersburg), to which 200 communities later became affiliated. A month later, Mattersdorf was again the center for a "Republic of Heanzenland," instigated on the initiative of the Austrian Social Democratic Party as a way of easing accession to Austria.[42] Participants in a German People's Day in Sopron in January 1919 called for territorial autonomy, which the Hungarian government legislated for ten days later. This brought into being a *Deutsches Gouvernement* for the German-inhabited parts of the country, allowing the Germans cultural autonomy.[43]

The 1919 peace treaty of Saint-Germain annexed Burgenland to Austria. Hungary was forced to acknowledge this in the 1920 Treaty of Trianon. In 1921, the Austrian government passed legislation making Burgenland a separate province, although it was not yet able to occupy the whole of it. The Hungarian Soviet Republic was replaced by one appointed by Miklós Horthy as regent, but there were legitimists who sought to place Charles IV back on the throne. One legitimist center was the Erdődy mansion at Rotenturm (Vörösvár). The legitimist units played a key part in resisting the Austrian forces that began to take over in 1921. The first clash took place between the Austrian police and Hungarian irregulars at the border village of Pinkafeld (Pinkafő). The irregulars managed to expel the Austrian forces from the whole of Burgenland during September. On October 4, the "Lajtabánság" (the Banat of Leitha) was proclaimed as an independent state at Oberwart.[44] Thereafter negotiations between the Austrian and Hungarian states began, leading to the Venice Memorandum of October 13, in which Hungary undertook to cease supporting the irregulars and Austria agreed to a plebiscite to decide the fate of Sopron and eight neighboring villages.

Austrian troops occupied Burgenland on November 26, 1921, and took over the public administration, but they withdrew from Sopron and district before the plebiscite, held on December 14–15, in which 72.8 percent of the votes were in Hungary's favor. The town and eight villages remained Hungarian.[45] Contributing to the result was the fact that the majority of the inhabitants of Sopron were Evangelical (Lutheran), whereas Austria was almost entirely Catholic. Thus the Hungarian-speaking citizens were joined in voting for Hungary by German-speakers known as the Ponzichter – mainly market gardeners and vineyard owners.[46] The Hungarian government awarded Sopron the honorary title of *Civitas fidelissima* (most faithful city).

No self-governing organizations ever emerged among the minority Hungarians in the territories ceded to Austria, only cultural associations in Hungarian communities, which had been functioning since the late nineteenth century – the Alsóőr Reading Circle since 1890 and the Reformed Youth Reading Circle since 1899, for instance. Apart from those, Hungarian cultural associations were found in Austria after 1918 only in Vienna and Graz. The oldest was the Hungarian Reading Circle of Vienna, founded in 1864, and the Graz Hungarian Cultural Association, founded in 1888.[47]

Notes

1 *Országos Magyar Párt.*

2 Zoltán Szász, "Az erdélyi román polgárság szerepéről 1918 őszén" [The Role of the Transylvanian Romanian Citizenry in the Autumn of 1918], *Századok* 106 (1972) 2: 304–335.

3 László Szarka, "A méltányos nemzeti elhatárolódás lehetősége 1918 végén. A Jászi-féle nemzetiségi minisztérium tevékenységéről" [The Chance of Equitable National Delimitation at the End of 1918. The Activity of Jászi's Ministry of Nationalities], *Regio* 1 (1990) 1: 49–65; Zsolt K. Lengyel, "'Keleti Svájc' és Erdély 1918/1919. A nagyromán állameszme magyar alternatíváinak történetéhez" ["Eastern Switzerland" and Transylvania 1918–1919. The History of Hungarian Alternatives to the Greater Romania Idea], *Regio* 3 (1992): 77–89.

4 Royal assent was given to the Act on Unification of Transylvania, the Banat, Crişana, Sătmar and Maramureş with the Old Regat of Romania (*Lege asupra Unirei Transilvaniei, Banatului, Crişanei, Sătmarului şi Maramureşului cu Vechiul Regat al României*) on December 11, 1918. It covered the province of Transylvania including about 60 percent of the Partium as then understood, the rest of the latter going to Czechoslovakia or remaining in Hungary. The term Partium today normally refers only to the parts ceded to Romania at that time.

5 *Marele Consiliu Naţional Român; Consiliul Dirigent.*

6 Zoltán Szász, "Revolutions and National Movements after the Collapse of the Monarchy (1918–1919)," in Béla Köpeczi, ed., *History of Transylvania* (Budapest, 1996), pp. 643–660.

7 Mária Ormos, *From Padua to Trianon, 1918–1920* (New York, 1982), pp. 114–135.

8 Ernő Raffay, *Erdély 1918–1919-ben* [Transylvania in 1918–1919] (Budapest, 1987), pp. 255–304.

9 Nándor Bárdi, "Impériumváltás Székelyudvarhelyen" [Sovereignty Change in Székelyudvarhely], *Aetas* (1993) 3: 76–120.

10 *Kelet-magyarországi Főkormánybiztosság.*

11 Ernő Raffay, *Erdély 1918–1919-ben*, pp. 195–254; Nándor Bárdi, "'Action Osten'. Die Unterstützung der ungarischen Institutionen in Rumänien durch das Mutterland Ungarn in den 1920er Jahren," *Ungarn-Jahrbuch* 23 (1997).

12 *Erdélyi Központ.*

13 Nándor Bárdi, "Action Osten."
14 *Magyar Szövetség.*
15 They authored the most important minority political program of the period. Károly Kós, Árpád Paál and István Zágoni, *Kiáltó szó. A magyarság útja. A politikai aktivitás rendszere* [Exclamatory Word. The Hungarians' Road. The System of Political Activity] (Budapest, [1921] 1988).
16 *Magyar Néppárt.*
17 Emil Grandpierre, "Az erdélyi magyarság politikai küzdelmei az egységes magyar párt megalakulásáig" [The Political Struggles of the Transylvanian Hungarians until the Founding of a United Hungarian Party], *Magyar Szemle* (1928) 10: 130–136; Imre Mikó, *Huszonkét év. Az erdélyi magyarság politikai története* [Twenty-Two Years. A Political History of Transylvanian Hungarians] (Budapest, 1941), pp. 9–38.
18 Gyula Popély, *Népfogyatkozás. A csehszlovákiai magyarság a népszámlálások tükrében 1918–1945* [Depopulation. Czechoslovakian Hungarians in the Light of the Censuses 1918–1945] (Budapest, 1991), p. 24.
19 The designation appears also in contemporary Czech analyses. Cf. Zděnek Kárnik, "Volby na jaře 1920. Československo na ceste od národně rovoluční diktatúry k parlamentní demokraci" [Elections in the Spring of 1920. Czechoslovakia on Its Way from the National Revolutionary Dictatorship to Parliamentary Democracy], in Jindřich Pecka, ed., *Acta contemporanea. K pětašestdesátinám Viléma Prečana* [Elections in the Spring of 1920. Czechoslovakia on Its Way from the National Revolution Dictatorship to Parliamentary Democracy] (Prague, 1998), pp. 95–131.
20 Another factor was the fact that the Czechoslovak census introduced Jewish as an ethnic option. Many Jews had classed themselves as Hungarian, not least on linguistic grounds.
21 The voting pattern among the Slovakian Hungarians is discussed in Béla Angyal, *Érdekvédelem és önszerveződés. Fejezetek a csehszlovákiai magyar pártpolitika történetéből 1918–1938* [Interest Protection and Self-Organization. Chapters from the History of Czechoslovakian Hungarian Party Politics 1918–1938] (Galánta/ Dunaszerdahely, 2002)
22 Digitální knihovna, NS RČS 1918–1920, Poslanecká sněmovna – stenoprotokoly, 3. schuze, 2. června 1920. http://www.psp.cz/ eknih/1920ns/ps/stenprot/003schuz/prilohy/priloh01.htm. Accessed

February 22, 2010. Also on the home page: "Příloha k těsnopisecké zprávě o 3. schůzi poslanecké sněmovny. Národního shromáždění republiky Československé v Praze ve středu dne 2. června 1920" [Notes to the Stenographic Report of the 3rd Meeting of the House of Commons. National Assembly of the Czechoslovak Republic in Prague on Wednesday, 2 June 1920], in *Národní shromáždění republiky Československé, 1920–1925* [National Assembly of the Czechoslovak Republic, 1920–1925], at http://www.psp.cz/eknih/1920ns/ps/stenprot/003schuz/prilohy/priloh01.htm. Accessed February 22, 2010.

23 *Magyar Törvénytár. 1918. évi törvénycikkek és néptörvények* [Hungarian Statute Book. Articles and People's Acts of 1918] (Budapest 1919), pp. 214–215.

24 V. Hudanych and V. Bodnar, "Rus'ka Krajna v 1918–1919 rokah" [Rus'ka Krajna in 1918–1919], in *Kul'tura ukrai'ns'kyh Karpat: tradycii' i suchasnist'. Materialy mizhnarodnoi' naukovoi' konferencii' (Uzhhorod, 1–4 veresnja 1993 roku)* [The Culture of Carpatho-Ukraine: Traditions and Modernity. Proceedings of the International Scientific Conference (Uzhhorod, 1–4 September, 1993)] (Uzhhorod, 1994), p. 275.

25 The constitution appears in *Tanácsköztársasági Törvénytár. V. 1919. június 10–30.* [The Statute Book of the Hungarian Soviet Republic. Vol. V. June 10–30, 1919] (Budapest, 1919), p. 21.

26 P. Smijan, *Zhovtneva revoljucija i Zakarpattia (1917–1919)* [The October Revolution and Transcarpathia 1917–1919] (Lviv, 1972); Ivan Granchak, ed., *Vstanovlennja radjans'koi' vlady na Zakarpatti u 1919 r.* [Soviet Power in Transcarpathia in 1919]; B. Spivak and M. Trojan, *Felejthetetlen 40 nap. Az 1919-es tanácshatalomért a Kárpátontúlon vívott harc történetéből* [Unforgettable 40 Days. From the History of the 1919 Struggle for Soviet Power in Transcarpathia] (Uzhhorod, 1969).

27 S. Vidnjans'kyj, "Problema samovyznachennja i rozv'jazannja pytannja pro derzhavnu prynalezhnist' Zakarpattia pislja pershoi' svitovoi' vijny" [Transcarpathia's Status in the Period after World War I], *Problemy Istorii'i' Ukrai'ny – fakty, sudzhennja, poshuky* (2007) 16: 104–115; M. Vegesh, *Gromads'ko-politychni vzajemovidnosyny Shidnoi' Galychyny i Zakarpattia v 1918–1919 rokah* [The Socio-Political Relations of Eastern Galicia and Transcarpathia in 1918–1919] (Uzhhorod, 1996); M. Boldyzhar, *Zakarpattia mizh dvoma*

svitovymy vijnamy. Materialy do istorii' suspil'no-politychnyh vidnosyn [Transcarpathia between the World Wars. Materials on the History of Socio-Political Relations] (Uzhhorod, 1993), p. 107; S. Klochurak, *Do voli: Spomyny* [Towards Freedom: Memoirs] (New York, 1978); "Ukra'ins'ki Karpaty" [Ukrainian Carpathians], Materialy mizhnarodnoi' konferencii' "Ukra'ins'ki Karpaty: etnos, istorija, kul'tura". Uzhhorod, 1991. VIII. 26.– IX. 1. [Proceedings of the International Conference "Ukrainian Carpathians: Ethnicity, History, Culture". Uzhhorod, August 26–September 1, 1991] (Uzhhorod, 1993); Vincent Shandor, *Carpatho-Ukraine in the Twentieth Century. A Political and Legal History* (Cambridge, MA, n. d.), pp. 3–34.

28   *From Trianon to the First Vienna Arbitral Award. The Hungarian Minority in the First Czechoslovak Republic 1918–1938* (Montreal, 1981), pp. 187–190.

29   *Československá statistika. Svazek 9. Sčítaní ludu v republice Československé ze dne 15. února 1921* [Czechoslovak Statistics. Vol. 9. Census in the Republic of Czechoslovakia of 15 February 1921] (Prague, 1924), pp. 41–42.

30   "A Csehszlovák Köztársaság Alkotmánylevele" [The Constitutional Document of the Czechoslovak Republic], in Csilla Fedinec, ed., *Iratok a kárpátaljai magyarság történetéhez 1918–1944. Törvények, rendeletek, kisebbségi programok, nyilatkozatok* [Documents on the History of the Transcarpathian Hungarians 1918–1944. Laws, Regulations, Minority Programs and Statements] (Dunaszerdahely, 2004), pp. 61–63.

31   G. Zhatkovich, *Otkrytoe-Exposé* [Open Exposé] (Homestead, FL, n. d.); *Ruszinszkói Magyar Hírlap*, March 18 and July 29, 1921

32   M. Tokar, *Polityčhni partii' Zakarpattia v umovah bagatopartijnosti (1919–1939)* [The Multi-Party System in Transcarpathia (1919–1939)] (Uzhhorod, 2006); Csilla Fedinec, "Magyar pártok Kárpátalján a két világháború között" [Hungarian Parties in Transcarpathia between the Two World Wars], *Fórum Társadalomtudományi Szemle* (2007) 1: 83–110.

33   Cs. Fedinec, "Perehid m. Uzhhorod pid vladu Chehoslovachchini (za materialamy miscevoi' ugors'komovnoi' presy 1918–1920)" [Change of State in Uzhhorod (Reflected in the Contemporary Local Press 1918–1920)], in *Naukovyj Visnyk Chernivec'kogo universitetu. No. 378–379. Istorija. Politychni nauky. Mizhnarodni vidnosyny. Zbirnyk naukovyh prac'* [Scientific Bulletin of Chernivtsi University.

Issue 378–379. History. Political Science. International Relations.
Scientific Papers] (Chernivtsi, 2008), pp. 114–119.

34 *Arhiv Vojvodine* (AV): Narodna uprava za Banat, Bačku i Baranju.
F.76.22/1918.

35 Magda Ádám, György Litván and Mária Ormos, eds., *Documents diplomatiques français sur l'histoire du Bassin des Carpates 1918–1932. Vol. 1. Octobre 1918–août 1919* (Budapest: 1993)

36 *Narodna uprava za Banat, Bačku, i Baranju.*

37 Magyar Országos Levéltár [The National Archives of Hungary] (MOL) K-26. A miniszterelnökség központilag iktatott és irattározott iratai 1867–1944 [Centrally Entered and Archived Documents of the Prime Minister's Office] 1920-XLI-994. Reprinted in Ignác Romsics *et al.*, eds., *Magyarok kisebbségben és szórványban. A Magyar Miniszterelnökség Nemzetiségi és Kisebbségi Osztályának válogatott iratai, 1919–1944* [Hungarians in a Minority and in Sporadic Settlements. Selected Papers of the Hungarian Prime Ministry's Department of Nationality and Minority Affairs 1919–1944] (Budapest, 1995), pp. 421-425.

38 Enikő A. Sajti, "Impériumváltás a Délvidéken" [Change of Sovereignty in the Southern Region], *Limes* (2005) 1: 7–19.

39 Nina Almond and Ralph Haswell Lutz, eds., *The Treaty of St. Germain. A Documentary History of Its Territorial and Political Causes, with a Survey of the Documents of the Supreme Council of the Paris Peace Conference* (Stanford, 1935); John D. Berlin, *Akten und Dokumente des Außenamtes [State Department] der USA zur Burgenland-Anschluss-Frage 1919–1920* (Eisenstadt, 1977); Gerald Schlag, *Die Kämpfe um das Burgenland 1921* (Vienna, 1970); Gerald Schlag *"Aus Trümmern geboren!" – Burgenland 1918–1921.* Wissenschaftliche Arbeiten aus dem Burgenland 106 (Eisenstadt, 2001).

40 *Die Bevölkerungsentwicklung im Burgenland zwischen 1923 und 1971* (Eisenstadt, n. d.); *A Magyar Szent Korona Országainak 1910. évi népszámlálása* [1910 Census of the Lands of the Hungarian Holy Crown] (Budapest, 1912); György Éger, *A burgenlandi magyarság rövid története* [Short History of the Burgenland Hungarians] (Budapest, 1991).

41 *Deutscher Volksrat für West-Ungarn.*

42 Cornelia Kurz, *Deutschsprachige Propaganda und Agitation während des Anschlußkampfes des Burgenlandes an Österreich 1918-1921* Ms. dissertation (Vienna, 1983); Irmtraut Lindeck-Pozza, "Zur

Vorgeschichte der Venediger Protokolle," in *50 Jahre Burgenland.* *Burgenländische Forschungen* (Eisenstadt, 1971) pp. 15–44.

43 Johannes Seedoch, "Deutschösterreichische Bemühungen um den Anschluss des Burgenlandes," *Burgenländische Forschungen* 7 (1984): 28; Gerald Schlag, "'Um Freiheit und Brot.' Die Arbeiterbewegung von ihren Anfängen im westungarischen Raum bis zur Verbannung in die Illegalität," in Walter Feymann, Gerald Schlag and Fred Sinowatz, eds., *Aufbruch an der Grenze. Die Arbeiterbewegung von ihren Anfängen im westungarischen Raum bis zum 100-Jahre Jubiläum der SPÖ* (Eisenstadt, 1989), pp. 9–94.

44 Gerald Schlag, "Zur Burgenlandfrage von St. Germain bis Venedig (10. September 1919–11. Oktober 1921)," *Burgenländische Heimatblätter* 24 (1970) 3: 97–125; Mária Ormos, *Civitas Fidelissima. Népszavazás Sopronban 1921* [Referendum in Sopron 1921] (Győr, 1990), pp. 111–131; László Fogarassy, "Paul Prónays Erinnerungen an das 'Lajta-Banat'," *Burgenländische Heimatblätter* 1 (1990).

45 August Ernst, *Geschichte des Burgenlandes* (Vienna, 1987), p. 197; Gerald Schlag, "Die Grenzziehung Österreich-Ungarn 1922/23," in Harald Prickler, ed., *Burgenland in seiner pannonischen Umwelt. Festgabe für August Ernst* (Eisenstadt, 1984), pp. 333–346.

46 Eugen Házi, *Unser Recht auf Ungarn* (Budapest, 1920); László Fogarassy, "Die Volksabstimmung in Ödenburg (Sopron) und die Festsetzung der österreichisch-ungarischen Grenze im Lichte der ungarischen Quellen und Literatur," *Südostforschungen. Internationale Zeitschrift für Geschichte, Kultur und Landeskunde Südosteuropas* (1976) 35: 150–182.

47 Gerhard Baumgartner, "Idevalósi vagyok – Einer, der hierher gehört. Zur Identität der ungarischsprachigen Bevölkerungsgruppe des Burgenlandes," in Gerhard Baumgartner, Eva Müllner and Rainer Münz, eds., *Lebensraum und Identität* (Eisenstadt, 1989), pp. 69–84; Ernö Deák, "Streiflichter aus der Geschichte der Wiener Ungarn in der Neuzeit," in *Aus dem Kulturleben der Wiener Ungarn. Exhibition catalogue* (Vienna, 1982), p. 9; Gerhard Baumgartner, "Ungarn in Wien," in *Wir. Zur Geschichte und Gegenwart der Zuwanderung nach Wien* (Vienna, 1999), pp. 125–130.

II. BETWEEN THE TWO WORLD WARS
1921–1938

1. NATION STATES AND MINORITIES
IN CENTRAL EUROPE
László Szarka

The radical post-war changes of sovereignty and state borders in Europe still left sizeable minorities. The majority of the continent's 62 million minority citizens dwelt in the 17 newly constituted states of non-Russian East-Central Europe and in Turkey, but there were 12 million in Western Europe and 11.5 million in the interwar territory of Russia as well.[1]

Only in six European locations was an attempt made to settle territorial disputes by plebiscite – four involving Germany (Schleswig-Holstein, southeastern Prussia, Upper Silesia and the Polish Corridor[2]) and two involving Austria (southern Carinthia, and the Sopron/Ödenburg district). Plebiscite plans in three other areas (Teschen/Cieszyn/Těšín, and parts of former Árva/Orava and Szepes/Spiš/Zips, disputed between Czechoslovakia and Poland, and the territories of Eupen–Malmedy, disputed between Belgium and Germany) were abandoned.

A plebiscite in the Austrian provinces of Tyrol and Salzburg in April and May 1921 showed 99 percent voter support for union with Germany, in contravention of the terms of the Treaty of Saint-Germain-en-Laye, which specifically forbade Austria's accession to Germany. The Austrian regime bowed to international pressure and quashed these initiatives. When the new borders of Hungary were being drawn, neighboring countries combined to protest against the solution by plebiscite urged by the Hungarian peace delegation under Albert Apponyi. Except in the Sopron/Ödenburg district, Hungary's Trianon borders were settled administratively even in places where local demands for a vote were insistent (Salgótarján and Prekmurje).[3]

In Western and Northern Europe, the borders agreed in the treaties ending World War I created four sizeable new ethnic minorities in the following cases: the annexation of the Germans of South Tyrol to Italy, the annexation of Alsace-Lorraine to France (a longstanding conflict involving dual identity), the cession of largely German-speaking Eupen and Sankt Vith to Belgium, and the incorporation of the Swedish-speaking Åland islanders into Finland. These recipient countries opposed the demands of the minority communities with their own, concerning defense or the territorial aspirations of neighboring parent countries. The Swedish and German minority regions now have settled legal status, but all except Åland were the source of numerous conflicts in the interwar period. In the final third of the twentieth century, exemplary and *well-functioning* forms of minority autonomy were devised for self-government in South Tyrol and German-speaking Belgium, but on the back of very unsteady interwar backgrounds. However, the cases of much larger historical ethnic groups in Western Europe – Basques and Catalans in Spain, Bretons and Corsicans in France, Frisians in the Netherlands, or speakers of Celtic languages in the United Kingdom – were left unmentioned in the treaties and uncovered by the international system for minority protection.[4]

Most countries in Western and Southern Europe – Britain, France, Spain and Italy – became nation states by seeing the commonwealth of citizens as the basic concept and framework of the "nation". Historical and regional minority communities would steadily lose their language, and with it their potential for forming a separate nation. A "political nation" in Western Europe, in raising its language to the status of a state language, would strive to impede the development of parallel national movements. Certain countries in Northern and Western countries afforded language-use rights to a chosen minority. Finland made both Finnish and Swedish official languages under the 1922 Constitution. Belgium in the 1930s counteracted the political and cultural supremacy of French by granting broad language-use rights to the Flemings. In Spain, on the other hand, the Catalans' rights of language use were curtailed in 1918.[5]

Far bigger conflicts took place after World War I in East-Central Europe and the Balkans, in both the victorious and the defeated successor states to the Habsburg Monarchy. To the east of Germany, which Versailles had deprived of several border regions and provinces with a German majority, there arose a plethora of separatist movements and local plebiscites. Just after the foundation of Czechoslovakia, representatives of the Sudeten Germans tried to set up provinces of German Bohemia (Deutschböhmen), German Moravia (Deutschsüdmähren) and Bohemian Forest Region (Böhmerwald) as units of German Austria, rejecting the idea that Sudetenland should belong to Czechoslovakia, although these initiatives were easily defeated by military force. Similar efforts were made in Silesia and several other Polish/German border areas.[6]

The populations of the buffer-zone states created by the Versailles peace system – Czechoslovakia, Estonia, Latvia, Lithuania, Poland and Yugoslavia, with the radically altered Germany, Austria, Hungary, Bulgaria and Romania – included about 80 million people (50 percent) whose citizenship changed. It was mainly in the ostensible nation states of Central and Eastern Europe that the minority issue assumed great importance through the enhanced political weight of old and new minority ethnic groups and the minority protection agreements attached to the peace treaties and the League of Nations guarantee system.[7]

The Versailles peace system rested on what proved an erroneous French geostrategic notion, the idea that France could only manage in conjunction with Eastern allies to contain the revisionist efforts of Germany, and the Soviet Russian efforts to expand into the Baltic, Poland's Ukrainian areas, Bessarabia and Bukovina. Germany managed with the 1925 Treaty of Locarno to break out of its diplomatic isolation, having accepted and guaranteed the Rhine border laid down in the Treaty of Versailles, in other words relinquishing its claims to Alsace-Lorraine and the German-speaking parts of Belgium. In return for the five-nation Rhine guarantee pact, France and Belgium ceased to occupy the Ruhr and Germany could rejoin the international community as a member of the League of Nations.[8]

The Versailles process left only three self-declared nations in East-Central and Southeastern Europe without separate constitutional status: the Rusyns, Bosnians and Macedonians. All other nations (along with the Austrians, Hungarians, Serbs, Romanians, Bulgarians, Finns, Albanians and Greeks, who had attained statehood in some form before 1918) were equipped with a nation state in some sense. The borders for the nations with historical statehood – the Czechs, Poles, Lithuanians and Croats – and those of the nominal "Soviet republics" and "autonomous areas" of the Soviet Union were drawn on the basis of ethnic regions. The Estonians and Letts gained independent statehood for the first time. Others, who had never had a "national" state – the Slovaks, Slovenes and Croats, and the Belorussians within the Soviet Union – were accommodated with nations that spoke a related language.

The most ethnically diverse of the new states in East-Central Europe and the Balkans were Czechoslovakia and Yugoslavia, although their constitutions spoke of composite "Czechoslovak" and "Serbo-Croat" nations that hardly featured in the declared affiliations of their inhabitants. Their pseudo-federal systems caused serious problems not only for the national minorities within their territories but for minority nations within them as well – the Slovaks and Rusyns, and the Croats, Slovenes, Macedonians and Bosnians.[9]

Both East-Central and Southeastern Europe contained large numbers of sizeable national minority groups old and new. The two most numerous were 4.4 million minority Ukrainians living mainly in Poland but to some extent in the Baltic states, and 8.9 million ethnic Germans living in 13 states. The two biggest minorities in a single state were Poland's Ukrainians and Czechoslovakia's Sudeten Germans, each numbering about 3 million.[10]

Even post-war Hungary still had sizeable minority communities, a fact that Czechoslovakia in particular cited in its minority-related diplomatic activity, both bilateral and through the Little Entente. For 10.4 percent of the population of post-Trianon Hungary had a native language other than Hungarian, the most numerous being the

Germans (551,000), followed by the Slovaks (132,000), the Croats (37,000), the Serbs (36,000) and the Romanians (24,000). The native language of the vast majority of the Jews in Hungary was Hungarian. They numbered over 470,000 in 1920. No official cognizance was taken of two non-Hungarian Gypsy languages.[11]

The number of ethnic Hungarians on the post-war territories of the new neighboring countries of Austria, Czechoslovakia, Romania and the Serb-Croat-Slovene Kingdom, now minority communities, had fallen significantly since the census of 1910. The assimilation processes of the pre-war period had given way to dissimilation. This was especially the case in the cities of Slovakia and Transcarpathia (Ruthenia). The proportion of Hungarians among the inhabitants of Bratislava and Košice, for instance, had sunk below 20 percent by 1930, with the result that that Hungarian language-use rights there had lapsed. Resettlement, flight and the opting process for citizenship had led to a sizeable loss of 426,000 between 1918 and 1924, or 13 percent of altogether 3.3 million minority Hungarians in Czechoslovakia, Romania, Yugoslavia and Austria. Another factor, however, was the fact that many in the previously assimilated Jewish communities of the northern and southern regions of pre-1918 Hungary and Transylvania dissimilated themselves by designating themselves as Jewish in an ethnic sense, not just a religious one.[12]

The nation states concerned sought to settle the status of these minorities by legal means. It might have sufficed in principle to strengthen the League of Nations' minority protection terms if these had been enshrined in domestic law, but the constitutions promulgated in 1920 in Czechoslovakia, Poland and Austria, in 1921 in Yugoslavia, and in 1923 in Romania defined each country as a unitary nation state. The Czechoslovak constitution endorsed and incorporated the minority protection treaties, exceeding them in terms of language rights, and the country concluded bilateral minority protection treaties with neighboring Austria and Poland. The Yugoslav St. Vitus' Day constitution of June 28, 1921, put a limiting interpretation on the minority protection treaties. The 1923

Romanian constitution (a version of the constitution of 1866) failed to consider the minorities, even though the population of expanded Romania was only 71.9 percent Romanian.

Inadequate regulation of minority rights in Romania left ample room for discriminatory and assimilatory practices in minority policy. The Hungarian, Ukrainian, Jewish, Bulgarian and Russian minorities made almost 50 submissions to the League of Nations minority protection panel in just ten years.[13] The Yugoslav and Austrian constitutions named the minorities and stated what their language and educational rights were, but Yugoslavia opposed from the outset the founding of minority parties and sought to curb native-language educational and cultural activity. National cultural and educational associations could not be formed. Yet Yugoslavist ideology proved even less successful than the Czechoslovakist one. The idea of South Slav national unity was rejected outright by the Croats, which left the Serb nation in the fatally weakened position of a minority.[14]

The nationalism of nineteenth-century Western Europe had led to serious ethnic conflicts, but also to strong, linguistically almost homogeneous, nation states. The patterns chosen by Eastern European nations were primarily those of Britain and France, not Switzerland or Belgium, although the latter were cited by Hungary and its neighbors even in the most critical situations in the nineteenth and twentieth centuries. The states that formed in 1918–1920 could only aspire to resemble either of these Western ideals. They declared themselves unitary nation states in their constitutions, yet remained multinational throughout the interwar period, with severe problems of regional development and differentials and of historical and national identity. Only on the rarest occasions did members of the minorities concerned – Hungarians, Germans or Slavs – accept the proffered option of assimilation into the majority.

It is usual to interpret the nation states and ethnic features of interwar Central, Eastern and Southeastern Europe in terms of a classic triad of relations between parent states ("kin states"), citizenship-awarding states, and minorities.[15] All nations had a state of their own, or at least formed part of the political nation of a nation state, and all without exception had national minorities within the borders of "their" states. So all peoples in East-Central and Southeastern Europe had ambitions relating to their parent state and their citizenship state: that is, national tasks and aims of a cultural and political nature. The majority nations of Western European nation states retained almost exclusive state power over their territories, despite language and assimilation battles in the nineteenth century. Most nations east of the Oder, Elbe and Leitha gained state means of nation-building and assimilation (state nationalism) only after Versailles.

This specifically Eastern European lag – discernible in the development of nationalism as well – gave rise to serious conflicts. Most of the national minorities within the new nation-state structure of the region, simultaneously subject to the triad system of relations and participants in it, faced a duality of state, cultural and political identities and loyalties. In striving to create the economic, political and cultural foundations of their own minority, to campaign for individual and communal rights, and to found and operate their institutions, they were the subject of scarcely compatible expectations from their wider national community and the state in which they dwelt.

What those running the nation states expected was a pattern of assimilation and integration, rapid acquisition of majority language and culture, acceptance of proffered cultural and political patterns, and unquestioning cooperation and loyalty, in most cases without gaining in exchange any state support for their own aspirations. Meanwhile, the parent country expected its interwar minorities to retain their national language and cultural identity, insulate themselves from the majority offer, and behave in a way that pointed back to an earlier status. So it was rare in most minorities to find cooperation with majority parties, as such "activism" would displease the parent country. The commonest minority stance was one of grievance, shown in documentary activity important for minority legal protection and community building, and providing some kind of momentum for mobilization.[16]

Of all the nation states of East-Central and Southern Europe, the one that went furthest in minority rights was Czechoslovakia, but not even Masaryk's First Republic could bring itself to implement Slovak and Rusyn autonomy or grant communal rights to 3.3 million Germans, almost 800,000 Hungarians, or the Polish minority in Czech Silesia. Czechoslovak democracy and "nationalism with a human face" did not produce in the twenty years available any substantive integration processes with the first two, or still less the second three, which contributed to the secession of the minorities during the months of grave international crisis in 1938–1939.[17]

The outcome of minority policy in Yugoslavia and Romania was more negative still. Despite efforts by some of the Transylvanian Romanian elite to alter the direction of Bucharest government policy towards the minorities, the successive short-lived governments, fearing demands for territorial revision from parent countries, thought it too risky to support minority community building and proceeded with a policy of assimilation instead. This is even truer of the South Slav state (the *Serbo-Croatian-Slovene Kingdom*), suffering from constant structural crisis and sheltering for a time behind a mask of royal dictatorship. The neighboring states that "inherited" the three populous Hungarian minorities tried to curb Hungary's revisionist aspirations with the consultative mechanisms of the Little Entente, while laming the minority political elite, reliant throughout the period on its close political and financial relations with Budapest.

Notes

1   A statistical review of Europe's minority populations at the time: Wilhelm Winkler, *Statistisches Handbuch der europäischen Nationalitäten* (Vienna, 1931). Situation reports by minorities themselves: Ewald Ammende, ed., *Die Nationalitäten in den Staaten Europas* (Vienna/Leipzig, 1931); minorities in states created since World War I: József Galántai, *Trianon and the Protection of Minorities* (Boulder, CO/Highland Lakes, NJ, 1991), pp. 13–20.

2   Like many disputed areas, this went under different names in different languages at different times: *Polnischer Korridor, Danziger*

Korridor, Pomorze, korytarz polski, korytarz gdański, województwo pomorskie, etc. Regardless of political implications, the commonest term in English was the Polish Corridor. Some inhabitants of the corridor identified themselves as Kashubians, who have sometimes been seen as an ethnic or linguistic entity distinct from the Poles.

3   On the Sopron/Ödenburg plebiscite, see Peter Haslinger, *Der ungarische Revisionismus und das Burgenland 1922–1932* (Frankfurt a. M./Bern/New York/Paris, 1994), Peter Haslinger, *Hundert Jahre Nachbarschaft. Die Beziehungen zwischen Österreich und Ungarn 1895–1994* (Frankfurt a. M./Bern/New York/Paris, 1996), and Mária Ormos, *Civitas Fidelissima* (Szekszárd, 1999).

4   Accounts of individual cases with historical background: Guy Héraud, *L'Europe des ethnies* (Paris, 1974); Hannum Hurst, *Autonomy, Sovereignty, and Self-Determination. The Accommodation of Conflicting Rights* (Philadelphia, PA, 1990). The failure to cover all European states was one of the main objections of states obliged to sign a minority protection treaty at the Paris peace conference: Harold Temperley, ed., *A History of the Peace Conference of Paris*, Vol. V (London, 1924), pp. 128–132. Effects on Hungarian minorities: László Szarka, "Artificial Communities and an Unprotected Protective Power: The Trianon Peace Treaty and the Minorities," in László Szarka, ed., *Hungary and the Hungarian Minorities (Trends in the Past and in Our Time)* (Boulder, CO/Highland Lakes, NJ, 2004), pp. 14–35; on the Jews, see Carole Fink, *Defending the Rights of Others: The Great Powers, the Jews, and International Minority Protection, 1878–1938* (Cambridge, 2004).

5   Heinz Kloss, *Grundfragen der Ethnopolitik im 20. Jahrhundert* (Vienna/Stuttgart, 1969), pp. 343–348.

6   Susanne Maurer-Horn, "Die Landesregierung für Deutschböhmen und das Selbstbestimmungsrecht 1918/19," *Bohemia* 38 (1997) 1: 37–55; Martin Zückert, "Zwischen Nationsidee und staatlicher Realität: Die tschechoslowakische Armee und ihre Nationalitätenpolitik 1918–1938" (Munich, 2006), pp. 30–31 and 141–142; Emil Brix, "Die 'Entösterreicherung' Böhmens Prozesse der Entfremdung von Tschechen, Deutschböhmen und Österreichern," *Österreichische Osthefte* 34 (1992) 1: 5–12.

7   On the installation and operation of the minority protection system, see Galántai, *Trianon*; on its operation in practice, see Ignác Romsics, *Nemzet, nemzetiség és állam Kelet-Közép- és Délkelet-Európában a*

19. és 20. században [Nation, Nationality and State in East-Central
and Southeastern Europe in the 19th and 20th Centuries] (Budapest,
1998), pp. 203–227.

8   Marshall M. Lee, "Gustav Stresemann und die deutsche
Völkerbundspolitik 1925–1930," in Wolfgang Michalka and Marshall
M. Lee, eds., *Gustav Stresemann* (Darmstadt, 1982), pp. 350–375.

9   On the conflict between the interwar concept of a "united
Czechoslovak political nation" and ethnic realities, see Martin
Schulze Wessel, *Loyalitäten in der Tschechoslowakischen Republik,
1918–1938: politische, nationale und kulturelle Zugehörigkeiten*
(Munich, 2004).

10   Raymond Pearson, *National Minorities in Eastern Europe 1848–
1945* (London, 1983), pp. 147–189; Romsics, *Nemzet, nemzetiség és
állam*, pp. 193–202.

11   János Vékás, "Spectra: National and Ethnic Minorities of Hungary
as Reflected by the Census," in Ágnes Tóth, ed., *National and Ethnic
Minorities in Hungary 1920–2001* (Boulder, CO/Highland Lakes,
NJ, 2005), pp. 19–23 and 90–156; Ágnes Tóth, "The Hungarian
State and the Nationalities," in *ibid.*, pp. 171–183; Loránt Tilkovszky,
Nemzetiségi politika Magyarországon a 20. században [National
Minority Policy in 20th-Century Hungary] (Debrecen, 1998), pp.
39–123.

12   István I. Mócsy, *The Effects of World War I. The Uprooted:
Hungarian Refugees and Their Impact on Hungary's Domestic
Politics* (Boulder, CO/Highland Lakes, NJ, 1983); Károly Kocsis
and Eszter Kocsis-Hodosi, *Ethnic Geography of the Hungarian
Minorities in the Carpathian Basin* (Budapest, 1998), pp. 15–37.

13   The constitutional situation is discussed in detail in the minority
situation reports: Ammende, *Die Nationalitäten*; comprehensive
analysis of the situations in Czechoslovakia and Romania: József
Gyönyör, *Államalkotó nemzetiségek* [State-Creator National
Communities] (Bratislava, 1989), pp. 7–192; coverage of the
complaints made to the League of Nations: Miklós Zeidler, "The
League of Nations and Hungarian Minority Petitions," in Ferenc
Eiler and Dagmar Hájková, eds., *Czech and Hungarian Minority
Policy in Central Europe 1918–1938* (Prague/Budapest, 2009), pp.
79–109.

14   Dejan Djokić, ed., *Yugoslavism. Histories of a Failed Idea 1918–1992*
(London, 2003).

15 Rogers Brubaker, *Nationalism Reframed: Nationhood and the National Question in the New Europe* (Cambridge, 1996), pp. 55–78.

16 This is detailed in two Central European minority journals, *Nation und Staat* (1927–1944) and *Magyar Kisebbség* (1922–1942), and the translations of them: *Glasul minorităţilor/Die Stimme der Minderheiten/La voix des minorités*. On cooperation among European minority movements, see Sabine Bamberger-Stemmann, *Der Europäische Nationalitätenkongreß 1925 bis 1938. Nationale Minderheiten zwischen Lobbyistentum und Großmachtinteressen* (Marburg, 2000).

17 The expression "nationalism with a human face" occurs in Roman Szporluk, *The Political Thought of Thomas G. Masaryk* (Boulder, CO, 1981).

2. INTERNATIONAL MINORITY DEFENSE SYSTEM: THE LEAGUE OF NATIONS

Ferenc Eiler

The League of Nations, which set to work soon after the Great War, on January 10, 1920, was intended mainly to monitor observance of the peace treaties, mediate in conflicts between states, and provide an international forum for cooperation among them. The victorious Great Powers saw it as essential to peace in Europe to ensure some form of international protection for the minorities of smaller states affected by the border changes. The almost identical minority protection treaties concluded with victorious countries and minority protection clauses in the peace treaties concluded with defeated countries were placed under League of Nations guarantee.[1]

The international stipulations for minority protection had taken more or less their final form at the Paris Peace Conference. Not so the League of Nations guarantee procedures, which were built up step by step in the 1920s.[2] The minority treaties already implied that the victors would not place the future procedures in the hands of the General Assembly of delegates of member countries, but with the Council, a narrower body operating under Great Power influence and composed largely of their political representatives. For it was stipulated that every Council member had a right to bring to the attention of the Council any infraction or any danger of infraction of any such obligations, and that any such member was to take action against the state concerned. Any difference that arose between a member of the Council and a state signatory to the minority treaty obligations counted as an international dispute, and at the member's request, it could be referred to the Permanent Court of International Justice in the Hague, whose decisions were final.

Under the established procedural system, minority organizations and even minority members had rights like those of Churches, governments and individual citizens to place complaints before the League of Nations. But such petitions counted as informal, and petitioners were not equal in rank at the proceedings to the state against which they complained. Indeed, before 1929 they were not even informed officially whether the League was dealing with their complaints or not.

The petitions arrived at the Secretariat of the League of Nations, where they were examined by its Minority Section to see if they met the formal and substantive criteria for submission. Complainants could only request protection from infractions for which international protection was stipulated in the treaty; they could not demand political secession of the minority from the state concerned. Nor could the reports emanate from anonymous or unauthenticated sources, and they had to abstain from violent language. Finally, they could not concern matters already investigated.

If the Section found the petition acceptable, the results of the investigation were conveyed to the state accused, which had two months in which to submit its observations in official form. After the response arrived, the Section put the case before the Council, which appointed a Committee of Three (later of Five in some cases) to examine the case, usually in continual consultation with the state accused. The committee could reach a decision in three different ways: it could place the matter on file, formulate a proposal for remedying the complaint, or initiate official proceedings. The last was relatively rare, as the Council and the states concerned tried to avoid investigations that would attract big publicity. Even if an investigation reached that stage, there was no guarantee that the complaints would be fully remedied. The Council might issue a final decision calling on the state to cease its breach of the law, but it might recommend a compromise solution, or it might dismiss the case.[3]

So at the center of the complaints procedure was the Council of the League of Nations and its Committee of Three, but the Secretariat's Minority Section, confined to administrative tasks and with no decision-making powers, yet managed to develop into the decisive factor in the process.[4] For the Secretariat was the only body within the League of Nations with staff at work in Geneva all the year round. Those in the Minority Section were well able to orient themselves in the diplomatic jungle of Geneva, and they gained great expertise, as they had to collect the arriving petitions and government responses, and all the information, legislation, proposed legislation and press accounts to do with the situation of the minorities. In addition, the Section was regularly visited by delegates of the reported governments and even by minority politicians. Furthermore, the Section head – strictly with the permission of and at the invitation of the government concerned – could visit the location and talk there with government representatives and on some occasions those of minorities as well.

The Section would present at the first meeting of the Committee of Three a summary of the petition and the reported government's response to it. This was often augmented with specific proposals on the matter. If the Committee of Three saw fit, it could hold with the government concerned confidential talks, which the chief of the Section would usually be charged with heading. Typical of the work of the Committee of Three and of the Section was mediation and secret discussions behind closed doors. In fact the aim was to reach compromises acceptable to the state concerned and to the Council of the League of Nations. They never set out to harass a state publicly and were well aware that implementing a League of Nations resolution depended in practice on states being willing to cooperate.

The guarantee clause in the minority treaties named as an important factor in the guarantee process the Permanent Court of International Justice in the Hague, as the highest resort of international law. The Council might refer a minority protection case to the Court for two purposes. It could call for a professional opinion – in which case the Court's decision counted only as a legal opinion and had no compulsory force – or it could request a final, enforceable judgment. In the event, the Court played only a marginal role in interwar minority protection, principally because the Council, essentially a political forum, also exercised a kind of judicial function in such cases, and as such, favored compromise solutions wherever possible, to avoid the publicity and serious political risk entailed in official proceedings.

Almost 500 petitions – about one half of those submitted between 1921 and 1938 – were judged after preliminary examination to be acceptable and fit for forwarding to the Council.[5]

Table 1. Distribution of acceptable petitions by states accused[6]

Poland	203	Bulgaria	2	Hungary	9
Germany	29	Greece	41	Estonia	1
Lithuania	3	Albania	12	Yugoslavia	35
Romania	78	Iraq	2	Austria	9
Turkey	12	Czechoslovakia	36	Latvia	1

Most petitions submitted to the Secretariat concerned the minority policy of smaller states that gained territory out of the Great War (Czechoslovakia, Poland, Romania, Yugoslavia, and so on), the complainants naturally being minorities of those countries.

Table 2. Distribution of acceptable petitions by complainants[7]

Germans in Poland	163	Ukrainians in Poland	25
Greeks in Albania	21	Hungarians in Yugoslavia	12
Hungarians in Romania	43	Poles in Germany	25
Germans in Czechoslovakia	15	Macedonians in Yugoslavia	11

The legal grounds for the complaints were very varied. Besides the petitions against general discrimination, the commonest claimed infringements were to do with education, land reform, labor law, freedom of worship, cultural and association activity, freedom of the press, confiscation of private property, citizenship, and use of the mother tongue.

The interwar system of international minority protection was often criticized from several sides. These criticisms were aimed alike at countries that had gained by the war and those that had lost by it, and at various international bodies and minority political, cultural and economic organizations.

The smaller countries on the winning side saw the imposed minority protection treaties as an infringement of sovereignty. Their objections were strengthened because the League of Nations proclaimed the equality of its member states, and yet only a few European countries were bound by the minority protection system. They demanded that it should be extended to all members. That did not succeed because the Great Powers (the United Kingdom, France and Italy) were not prepared to be bound in that way.

The defeated countries now with high numbers of compatriots abroad (Germany, Hungary and Bulgaria) and the minorities themselves were dissatisfied with the efficacy of the guarantee procedure. They saw the Secretariat and its Minority Section as biased and considered it to be unacceptable that these bodies should decide legal issues on political grounds. In terms of the minority protection treaties, they saw it as the biggest shortcoming of the system that it aimed at minimal average protection with a view to the sensibilities of the states, instead of moving towards providing the conditions for minority self-administration. They were undoubtedly right in concluding that the degree of protection accorded to different minorities was not uniform. While the prospect of territorial autonomy was mooted for Transcarpathia, with its population of 430,000, the far more numerous Székely and Saxon communities in Transylvania were only given a general promise of limited local autonomy in religious and educational affairs, and the 4.75 million Ukrainians of Poland were given no hope of any kind of self-administration.

A great number of problems arose when resolutions were not phrased precisely enough, leaving room for various interpretations. Statements, for instance, that the minority would receive adequate relief, or statements about districts where they lived in a significant proportion, or receiving a substantial and appropriate part of public wealth, in practice left the minorities at the mercy of the legislature and administration of the state concerned. There were similar consequences if the definitions of obligations were not categorical enough or no time limit was placed in the treaties for meeting them. Governments duly took advantage of this by indefinitely prolonging the process of putting the regulations into practice, or in most cases, simply sabotaging them.

Naturally there were several proposals for improving the guarantee procedure. One of the major demands was to create a status under international law for minorities submitting petitions, as a way of recognizing them as legal entities, which would have radically changed the legal complexion of the procedure. In that case the complainant could have featured in the proceedings as a party of equal rank with the reported state. But there was never any chance of acceptance for this, as it would have been at variance with the treaties and governments were not prepared even to consider it. Another idea for reform was to establish a permanent minority committee alongside the Council, with the task of reviewing the complaints with a professional competence that the *ad hoc* Committees of Three lacked.[8] The legal side of the guarantee procedure would also have been strengthened by the ideas for reinforcing the influence of the Permanent Court of International Justice.[9] But these proposals came to nothing, achieving only a little in the publicity field in 1929, after which the secretary-general gave statistics on the fate of petitions from the minorities in his general report, and member states might, with the consent of the state concerned, publish Committee of Three reports. Moreover, the Committees of Three (thenceforward sometimes Five) might meet more frequently.[10]

The minority protection treaties had many shortcomings, but neither the Great Power delegations nor the states concerned desired to offer the minorities more than the accepted terms stipulated. International minority protection between the world wars cannot be assessed in terms of a non-existent normative level of minority protection, desirable though it might be in principle. League of

Nations protection of minorities left open the possibility of positive domestic legislation, and despite its shortcomings, set a minimum for minority rights in some states of Central Europe. Well or badly, it policed through its guarantee procedure the respect for such rights, which was a leap forward compared with the minority protection of earlier times. The main obstacle to the League's regionally delimited international system of minority protection was its place within the international security system, unable to insulate itself from the prevalent divisions in broader politics. Any notion of minority protection remaining a purely legal matter was precluded by the antagonisms of interest groups pursuing disparate aims. From behind the debate there soon emerged the real endeavors of states: revision of the peace treaties in the case of those that had lost territory through the war, and the fastest possible assimilation of minorities into a nation state in those created or enlarged by the treaties. The fate of international minority protection was ultimately sealed when Hitler's Germany withdrew from the League of Nations in 1933, and Poland in September 1934 repudiated its obligations under the minority protection treaty and refused to cooperate with the international forum until minority protection should be made general. Although petitions continued to arrive at the Secretariat up to 1939, the system of minority protection had been dead for years when the Second World War broke out.

The foundation of the League of Nations and development of its system of minority protection was the political background to the establishment of another international organization that focused on the national minority question and the struggle for minority rights. The European Congress of Nationalities was founded near Geneva in 1925 with the tacit support of the Hungarian prime minister, István Bethlen, but with initial disapproval from the German Ministry of Foreign Affairs; its exclusive concern was to tackle minority problems that arose.[11] Having grown out of Baltic German initiative, it held an annual forum of consultation for the legitimate member organizations' official delegates, who represented the political and social elite of the minorities. In most years they conferred for two or three days in Geneva. During the rest of the year, the members of the Board (representing Ukrainian, Jewish, Hungarian, German, Catalan and some smaller Slav groups) normally met three times a year to prepare for the next conference and discuss legal and political matters that had arisen. The secretary-general and driving force, the Estonian German Ewald Ammende, headed until his death in 1936 a small Congress office in Vienna and kept in touch with minority leaders through correspondence and personal meetings.

Ammende had wanted to found a body that presented mainly theoretical work to the outside world. Building on the solidarity among minorities and international publicity, it was to position itself as an autonomous component in international politics and lobby effectively on behalf of member organizations, on the one hand presenting to states the need for cultural autonomy, and on the other urging the League of Nations to make its international system of minority protection more effective.

During the 14 years in which the European Congress of Nationalities existed, 49 European national minorities sent at least one delegate to one of the annual conferences. The frequency of participation was influenced by several factors, apart from interest from the minority political elite. The first filter was the degree of security felt at home by minority politicians, but the stance of the minority's parent state could also play a part. But the decisive factor was how long the groups could continue to accept the basic principles of the Congress or follow its political line. So in 1933, 14 minorities announced that they would withdraw permanently. The minorities in Germany and another four Polish minorities in solidarity with them withdrew after the third conference, sensing pan-German intentions in the background. The seven Jewish organizations that had hitherto taken a regular part left the Congress, as it was not prepared to publicly condemn the 1933 anti-Semitic atrocities in Germany, pointing out that the valid statutes of the Congress forbade direct criticism of states.

Up to 1933, the course and activity of the Congress was decided largely by the German, Hungarian and Jewish delegates. The withdrawal of the Jewish minorities and increased interest from the German Ministry of Foreign Affairs – including financial support – meant that the Congress came clearly and definitively under German influence. The Hungarian government also surreptitiously provided the organization with substantial sums for foreign policy reasons (bearing in mind its publicity value), and the minority Hungarians were extremely active in the Congress for the same reason.

The Congress never managed to persuade the League of Nations or the states concerned to radically alter their approach to minority protection. But its resolutions over 15 years covered and brought to international notice its position on all the important issues, most of which remain cogent today. The way in which it catalogued all the expectations of the national minorities, passing them through a legal filter, has certainly left a serious, if only theoretical, legacy, despite the efforts of the German and Hungarian governments to use the organization for their own ends.

Notes

1   For analysis of the treaties, see the following: Artúr Balogh, *A kisebbségek nemzetközi védelme* [The International Protection of Minorities] (Berlin, 1928); Zoltán Baranyai, *A kisebbségi jogok védelmének kézikönyve* [Handbook of Protection of Minority Rights] (Berlin, 1925); László Buza, *A kisebbségek jogi helyzete* [The Legal Position of Minorities] (Budapest, 1930); Erzsébet Sándor Szalayné, *A kisebbségvédelem nemzetközi jogi intézményrendszere a 20. században* [The International System of Legal Institutions for Minority Protection in the 20th Century] (Budapest, 2003), pp. 79–112; Erwin Viefhaus, *Die Minderheitenfrage und die Entstehung der Minderheitenschutzverträge auf der Pariser Friedenskonferenz 1919* (Würzburg, 1960); Ferenc Eiler, *A két világháború közötti nemzetközi kisebbségvédelem rendszere* [The System of International Minority Protection between the Two World Wars], *Pro Minoritate* (1987) 3–4: 69–76.

2   On the guarantee procedure, see the following: Heinrich Rauchberg, *Die Reform des Minderheitenschutzes* (Breslau, 1930), pp. 9–15 and 28–48; Christoph Gütermann, *Das Minderheitenschutzverfahren des Völkerbundes* (Berlin, 1979); Sebastian Bartsch, *Minderheitenschutz*

in der internationalen Politik (Opladen, 1995), pp. 99–181; Buza, *A kisebbségek jogi helyzete*, pp. 152–244; Szalayné, *A kisebbségvédelem nemzetközi jogi intézményrendszere a 20. században*, pp. 112–135.

3   The texts of six resolutions of the Council of the League of Nations on such procedures, passed between October 22, 1920, and June 13, 1929, appear in Appendix 5 of József Galántai, *Trianon and the Protection of Minorities* (Boulder, CO/Highland Lakes, NJ, 1991).

4   The structure and operation of the Secretariat is analyzed in detail in the following: Gütermann, *Das Minderheitenschutzverfahren des Völkerbundes*, pp. 273–287; Miklós Zeidler, "A Nemzetek Szövetsége és a magyar kisebbségi petíciók" [The League of Nations and Hungarian Minority Petitions], in Nándor Bárdi and Csilla Fedinec, eds., *Etnopolitika. A közösségi, magán- és nemzetközi érdekek viszonyrendszere Közép-Európában* [Ethno-politics. The Relation System in Communal, Private and International Interests in Central Europe] (Budapest, 2003), pp. 67–78.

5   Bartsch, *Minderheitenschutz in der internationalen Politik*, p. 104.

6   *Ibid.*, p. 105.

7   *Ibid.*

8   The Inter-Parliamentary Union and the League of Nations Association dealt for several years with the question of establishing a Permanent Committee, the former in 1922, 1923 and 1925, and the latter in 1922, 1923, 1928 and 1929. See Rauchberg, *Die Reform des Minderheitenschutzes*, p. 39.

9   Otto Junghann, *Das Minderheitenschutzverfahren vor dem Völkerbund* (Tübingen, 1934), pp. 56–59.

10   On the 1929 proposals and their results, see Martin Scheuermann, *Minderheitenschutz contra Konfliktverhütung? Die Minderheitenpolitik des Völkerbundes in den zwanziger Jahren* (Marburg, 2000), pp. 377–393.

11   On the activity of the European Congress of Nationalities, see the following: Rudolf Michaelsen, *Der Europäische Nationalitäten-Kongreß 1925–1928. Aufbau, Krise und Konsolidierung* (Frankfurt am Main, 1984); Sabine Bamberger-Stemmann, *Der Europäische Nationalitätenkongreß 1925 bis 1938. Nationale Minderheiten zwischen Lobbyistentum und Großmachtinteressen* (Marburg, 2000); Ferenc Eiler, *Kisebbségvédelem és revízió. Magyar törekvések az Európai Nemzetiségi Kongresszuson (1925–1939)* [Minority Protection and Revision. Hungarian Efforts at the European Congress of Nationalities (1925–1939)] (Budapest, 2007).

3. THE POLICIES TOWARDS HUNGARIAN COMMUNITIES PURSUED BY HUNGARY'S NEIGHBORING COUNTRIES

Nándor Bárdi

The situation of a national minority depends basically on three factors: the settlement structure and demographic, economic and social attributes of the ethnic group concerned, the policy of the host state towards its minorities, and the relations and ties of the minority group to its kin-state – the state or states in which it was in a majority. The section examines the second factor as it applied in Czechoslovakia, Romania and Yugoslavia. The national question also became decisive in Austria in the 1930s (especially because of the *Anschluss* in March 1938), but the minorities played no direct part in this. The Hungarians of Austria – bilingual, and forming a tiny proportion of the population – were not a domestic political issue.

The attitude towards the national minorities in the Entente countries was determined mainly by the change in international power relations and the ambitions of the three new states to build a uniform nation.

The minority protection treaties attached to the peace treaties that concluded the First World War were rejected initially by the Yugoslav and Romanian prime ministers. Then Nikola Pašić of Yugoslavia signed after certain concessions had been made, but Ion Brătianu of Romania preferred to resign, and the treaty was signed for Romania by another peace delegation member, Alexandru Vaida-Voevod of Transylvania. Hungary accepted the Trianon minority stipulations with resignation, as it was ethnically more homogeneous than its neighbors. Only about 10 percent of the population belonged to a national minority, and these lived scattered across the country. Furthermore, the terms allowed for the rights of Hungarian minorities abroad to be raised internationally. Although the minority protection treaties were ratified, not one country in the region codified the rights of its minorities. Instead they declared the equal rights of all citizens in their constitutions, and then enshrined the interests of the state in relation to the minorities through sectorial legislation. None of these countries, not even Hungary, met its obligations to the minorities to the full.[1]

One aim of the Little Entente that Czechoslovakia, Romania and the Serb-Croat-Slovene Kingdom formed in the 1920s was to make a military and political alliance against Hungary's ambitions for territorial revision, but they were also interested in regional economic cooperation. However, the latter called also for participation by Hungary, which saw the problems of the Hungarian minorities as a precondition for consolidating relations with these countries. Budapest also needed to assert its interests, but its geopolitical weight was too low to do so. For in terms of area and population, Hungary was only half the size of any of the three neighbors. All that Hungary could rely on were the Italian and German discontent with the European status quo and the chance to win over British public opinion.

By 1935, it was clear that the Little Entente countries could not base their defense against German and Italian threats on support from Britain or France. Since defense against any German or Italian attack would be precluded by Hungarian action, Yugoslavia and Czechoslovakia set out to normalize relations with Budapest. This was opposed by Romania, whose domestic political legitimacy rested on anti-revisionism and a Hungarian enemy, but as its two partners were ready to negotiate with Budapest even without Bucharest, the latter agreed to join after all. Hungary, however, was only interested in agreement with Yugoslavia and temporary settlements with Romania. For Czechoslovakia in 1935–1936 was the only place where Hungary, with Hitler's support, had some chance of territorial revision.[2]

In 1937, the Hungarian government attempted to reach a separate agreement with Yugoslavia. The essential aims were to settle the educational situation of the Hungarian minority, to ensure ethnically proportional local government representation, and to obtain land for landless Hungarian farm laborers out of the redistribution scheme. Initially the Yugoslav prime minister, Milan Stojadinović, seemed willing to tackle the minority problems and reach a separate agreement, but he rejected the advance from Budapest after the Italian–Yugoslav pact of March 25, 1937, fearing the reactions of the other members of the Little Entente.

Romania and Czechoslovakia, sensing that the alliance system was weakening, agreed with Yugoslavia at the Belgrade meeting of the Permanent Council of the Little Entente in April 1937 that before any of them concluded a bilateral agreement with Hungary, they were to consult the other two members and request their consent. They also agreed to recognize Hungary's equal right to arm (easing the Trianon military restrictions) if the Hungarian government concluded a treaty of non-aggression with them in return. There were talks on this in August 1937 at Sinaia in Romania, where László Bárdossy, the Hungarian ambassador in Bucharest, tried to tie this to a remedy for the minority problems, but the Romanians refused.[3]

Romania again sat down to negotiate at the request of the other two Little Entente members in Geneva in the autumn, but Hungarian Minister of Foreign Affairs Kálmán Kánya found his Romanian counterpart, Victor Antonescu, implacable. The upshot was that Yugoslavia and Czechoslovakia held Romania responsible for the breakdown of negotiations and announced that they would agree with Hungary nonetheless. On March 11, 1938, one day before German troops overran Austria, Bucharest indicated to Budapest a desire to resume the negotiations and the imminent appointment of a high commissioner for minorities to handle minority grievances. The talks with the Little Entente states then continued. But it had been clear since Hungarian Prime Minister Kálmán Darányi's visit to Berlin in November 1937 – when it emerged that Hungary would not give military support to Austria in the event of a German occupation and was in agreement with the idea of revising the borders of Czechoslovakia – that Budapest was in no hurry to agree with Prague. At the same time, the Czechoslovak position was the most flexible, as a start had been made on drafting new minority legislation. Hungary's armed forces were not strong enough to impose such revision, and it was not certain that Yugoslavia and Romania would remain neutral in such an eventuality. On August 21–22, 1938, the Little Entente states agreed in Bled to recognize Hungary's equal right to arm, and agreed to negotiate in the future about the situation of the minorities, and Budapest renounced the use of force to alter the frontiers. But only a month later, the Munich Agreement brought about a new situation in Central Europe.[4]

It is time to examine how the two key concepts of nation-building and the nation state operated in the minority policy of the neighboring countries, which also affected the loyalty of the local Hungarians to the new states.[5]

Two of the three were constitutional monarchies and the third, Czechoslovakia, a bourgeois democracy. But the real difference was the fact that the last had kept the Austro-Hungarian model of public administration, while the other two followed the pre-1918 administrative patterns of the small Balkan states. While the Monarchy had had regional and local governments and self-governing commonality of farmland and vineyards, the headsmen of the villages of the Romanian Old Kingdom, for instance, had been dependent on central government, and individuals were at the mercy of appointed local officials. The same applied to urban property, where the local authorities and councils in the Monarchy could manage the property for themselves. So the concept of decentralization of power was interpreted differently in the two political cultures. While the guarantee of this was seen in the Monarchy to lie in the decision-making powers of the elected communal and county organizations, the local and regional power in the two Balkan states was in the hands of officials appointed by the center. The three differed also in the Orthodox Churches' dominance in the areas that had lain outside the Austro-Hungarian Monarchy – pre-1918 Romania and Serbia – where they had not performed the social functions that the Churches in the Monarchy had (for instance in education).

Similarly, Romania and Serbia had no organized minority groups, or had assimilated them. They had not had to reckon before 1918 with such groups in their nation-building or state organization. At the same time the two countries had assumed the role of a kin- state for the Romanians of Transylvania and Serbs of the Southern Region, and were the potential ally for the Croatian and Slovenian national movements. A further difference: the regions acceding to Romania and Yugoslavia were much more developed than the core regions. In Czechoslovakia's case, the Sudeten German territories were at the same level of industrialization as the core Bohemian/Moravian regions, or a slightly higher one, but the territories annexed from Hungary were far less developed.

What the three had in common were significant national groups other than the country's dominant nation. The proportion of Czechs in Czechoslovakia was 50.5 percent, of Serbs in Yugoslavia 39.2 percent, and of Romanians in Romania 71.9 percent (in 1930–1931). So it was necessary to draw related nations into the nation-building process: the Slovaks (15.7 percent) in Czechoslovakia, and the Croats (23.4 percent) and Slovenes (8.1 percent) in Yugoslavia through the Yugoslavist program. The Slovenes had gained a system of institutions through their permanent provincial status under Austria, and the Croats of the Kingdom of Hungary, without an army or foreign policy of their own, could count on military protection against Italy from the Serbs. But 22.5 percent of the Czechoslovak population were ethnic Germans and 4.9 percent Hungarians, as were 4.1 and 7.9 percent respectively in Romania and 3.6 and 3.4 percent in Yugoslavia. The German minority posed a revisionist threat only to Prague. Those of the other two countries (not bordering Germany) followed the traditional German minority (*volksdeutsch*) policy of loyalty to the extant regime. But the Hungarian minorities represented a security concern for all three countries.[6]

Two strategies towards the Hungarians appeared in Romania, the land least divided in national terms. Iuliu Maniu, the leader of Transylvania's Romanians, thought in terms of integration through socio-economic reinforcement of the Romanians and introducing a modern system of institutions, rather than open discrimination. There would be equal civil rights, and as with Hungary's minority policy, the minority issue was to be limited to language usage, and minority education left to the Churches.[7]

The Liberal Party's aim in Bucharest, on the other hand, was to break the socio-economic strengths of the minorities by force. The discriminatory approach became dominant. The Transylvanian cities were Romanianized, as the only way to gain the economic positions rapidly. In party political rivalry, even the smallest concessions to the Hungarians were branded as un-national. Essential minority problems were not solved by the Minority State Secretariat (1931), the Minority High Commission (1938), or the Minority Statutes, which served propaganda purposes abroad.[8]

Yugoslavia adopted a clearly discriminatory policy, steered by relations with Hungary, rivalries among the regional parties in Vojvodina, and fear of a rapprochement with the Croats. In socio-economic terms, the Hungarians of Yugoslavia were not even of great regional weight.[9]

In Czechoslovakia the edge was taken off discriminatory measures by the region's most democratic, pluralist political system, with correctly held general and local elections, effective local government, and freedom of the press. In principle, greater stress was placed on winning the loyalty of the Hungarians. A big role here was played by President Masaryk, who sought to integrate the minorities by affording them equal civil rights and full linguistic and educational rights, initially proclaiming Czechoslovakia "the Switzerland of the East" for its minority policy. Certainly a third of the Hungarians there voted for the social democratic and communist parties, which were not organized on national lines, while in the 1930s, the governing Agrarian Party of Czechoslovakia gained 10–15 percent of the poll in Hungarian communities.[10]

None of the three states recognized the national minority autonomy urged by Hungarian minority parties in exchange for loyalty to the new state. The main minority policy measures of the three countries did not even secure the equality of individual rights offered instead of collective rights. Only the Czechoslovak constitution made mention of the minorities. This, apart from according equality of civil rights, stated that membership in a minority could not be an obstacle to official employment and that any language could be used in commerce and in public. Some stipulations were taken over from the minority protection treaty: the right to use the minority language in the courts, the right to found institutions, and the right to gain access to mother-tongue education supported by the state.[11] The 1923 Romanian constitution defined Romania as a "unitary and indivisible nation state." No concept of a national minority was recognized, only that of a religious minority. The 1921 constitution of the Serb-Croat-Slovene Kingdom likewise afforded only basic civil rights. The 1931 constitution of the royal dictatorship stated that no political party or association could have a racial or religious basis.[12]

The basic condition for equal rights under the new state was granting nationality in the sense of citizenship. The article of the minority protection treaty covering this would have granted nationality to all inhabitants of the new territories, but Czechoslovakia instead passed separate legislation (Act 236/1920) whereby citizenship went to those who had gained entitlement (domicile, payment of communal tax) by 1910. Later arrivals underwent a complicated process of application and examination. The problem was settled in part by Lex Dérer et Szent-Ivány (Act 152/1926), seen as one of the great achievements of the activist Hungarian policy.[13]

Romania also passed separate legislation on citizenship (Act 41/1924), requiring evidence of domicile on December 1, 1918, i. e. four years of residence and evidence of payment of local taxation, as communal registration had not been compulsory before 1918. But "racial Romanians" obtained citizenship with no difficulty through a different procedure. The seriousness of the problem becomes apparent from the fact that the nationality of almost 100,000 heads of family (300,000–400,000 people) was still unsettled in 1939.[14]

Yugoslavia likewise did not implement the citizenship article of its minority protection treaty. The option right included in it was used until July 26, 1922, to justify a ban on political and cultural activity by Hungarians, who did not have voting rights either.

Under the option stipulation, those resident in the new territories on January 1, 1910, could apply for citizenship or emigrate to Hungary. The deadline for this was extended to November 1930. Altogether 45,000 Hungarians migrated from the Southern Region in 1918–1924. Even in 1934, there were still over 21,000 option holders in Yugoslavia whose citizenship was unsettled. Furthermore, politically motivated expulsions were common, the most important wave (of 2,700 people) being expelled after the Marseille assassination of King Alexander I.[15]

One key aspect of minority rights was use of native language. The most generous provision was the Czechoslovak language law passed at the same time as the constitution (Act 122/1920). This named "Czechoslovak" as the republic's state and official language. So after an initial nation-building process in which the Slovak language was classed as a dialect of Czech, there were two state languages, as Slovak was used in Slovakia. Article 2 stated that in districts where the proportion of "non-Czechoslovaks" exceeded 20 percent, it was compulsory to allow use of a minority language in the courts, public administration and local government. Where the proportion of the minority reached two thirds, administration could be conducted using just the language of the minority. But the law did not prevent Slovakization, as it was enough to redraw the administrative districts or change the legal status of cities, or to produce situations where it was worthwhile for those with a dual allegiance to return themselves as Slovaks in the census. The main measure of this kind was the 1922 act on the status of cities, which left only four of Slovakia's 39 cities with full municipal rights – Bratislava, Košice, Užhorod and Mukačevo. The 1930 census put the proportion of Hungarians at less than 20 per cent in the first three, but 82 percent of Hungarians still lived in localities where their language rights remained.[16]

The constitution of Romania designated Romanian the official language of state. No separate language legislation was passed, the use of Romanian being governed by various regulations from 1921 onwards. The courts were obliged to use Romanian under Order No. 28.819/1921, and minority languages were forbidden in public administration under Order No. 19.654/1922. Internal regulations in public offices and in transportation ordering staff to communicate only in Romanian appeared continually in the second half of the 1920s. By the 1930s, adequate knowledge of Romanian was a prime condition for employment in the civil service and education, and members of the minorities were subjected to several language tests, causing over 10,000 Hungarian employees to be dismissed. Language use in local councils was governed not by the 1925 and 1929 acts on public administration but by local executive authorities, which forbade minority representatives to use their native language. A surtax was levied on businesses keeping their books or putting up signs in a non-Romanian language, and there was an extra charge for such telegrams. In the second half of the 1930s, the Romanian language was prescribed exclusively for business use. In 1937, Hungarian place names and geographical names were banned from the press.[17]

Of the three official languages of the Serb-Croat-Slovene Kingdom, Serbian was preferred in official forums. It was forbidden to speak Hungarian in public offices or local administration. There was official interference in language use in business and private affairs as well. Hungarian was confined to the first four grades of elementary school, the cumbersome cultural societies, Church activity, the Hungarian press, and private life. This was unchanged until the end of the 1930s.

The role of the state in social organization and local communities increased across Europe after the Great War. This administrative change had marked significance in the minority-inhabited areas of the new states of Central Europe. The change of sovereignty in all three countries discussed here entailed dissolving county, district and local representative bodies and chambers and appointing new personnel to run them.

In Czechoslovakia the administrative changes meant that the counties lost their regional political powers, while one third of the members of district, city, county and provincial assemblies were government appointees, which was usually enough, with the governing party representatives elected, to control them and the appointments that they made.[18]

Romanian laws on public administration would change every four or five years, which prevented the system from operating effectively. Transylvania had a regional Governing Council from the union until April 1920, which from a national point of view adapted the pre-1918 legal system to the new situation. Standardized public administration ensued in 1925, when new legislation significantly curtailed the powers of cities, and the names and seats of counties were altered to suit Romanian national interests. Altered borders meant that four counties (Mureş–Turda, Braşov, Bihor and Satu Mare) gained Romanian majorities. The group of those summoned to the representative bodies was reduced to state-appointed officials and representatives of the Romanian Churches. The most important change came in the 1929 act on public administration, whereby the communal, county and city councils elected in often rigged local government elections (in 1926 and 1930) could be dissolved by government decree and their powers vested in provisional committees. As a result, the sizeable local government assets in Transylvania came under the control of the Romanian state. Meanwhile, the judges and public officials were also changed, so that the Hungarians were underrepresented everywhere by the 1930s.[19]

The 1922 local administration system in Yugoslavia consisted of 33 provinces, with the majority of the Hungarians living in those of Bačka and Belgrade. There were elections to provincial and local assemblies in 1927. The Hungarian Party, under an agreement with the ruling Radical Party, gained six seats in both provincial assemblies, i. e. 10 percent representation. After the local elections in November, the local assemblies of Ada, Čantavir, Horgoš, Mol and Senta had Hungarian majorities, although they achieved little beyond airing grievances. Even that modicum of local representation was lost with the coming of the royal dictatorship in 1929.[20]

The key institutions for sustaining the Hungarian minority community belonged to the education system. Schools were a central issue in all regions. In Czechoslovakia and Romania, the Churches sought to fill the gap left by the previous state and village schools teaching in Hungarian. In Czechoslovakia, the body to decide and authorize the language of instruction was the schools bureau of the Slovakian Ministry Plenipotentiary. Church schools came to play the decisive role in Hungarian-language schooling in Slovakia. In 1922, 22.7 percent (29,000) of lower and upper elementary pupils of Hungarian ethnicity were not taught in their mother tongue. Nor were 33.3 percent (1,500) of such secondary students in 1926. For higher education, most Czechoslovakian Hungarians applied initially to German-language universities in Czechoslovakia or to universities in Hungary, but degrees from Hungary ceased to be recognized in 1928. By that time, the first students of Hungarian ethnicity were graduating from the Czechoslovakian gymnasia (academically oriented high schools), who were more inclined to enroll in Czech or Slovak colleges and universities. The 1922 schools act raised the period of compulsory schooling from six years to eight. (This did not happen in Hungary until after World War II.)[21]

The language measures in Romania extended beyond the state education system to impede the operation of non-Romanian Church schools. Church schools had hardly been a factor in pre-1918 Romania. Nationalizing Transylvanian schools was seen as a measure of national modernization. There the pre-war Romanian community had had its own denominational school system, while the Hungarians had relied on state schools teaching in Hungarian. With the change of sovereignty, the Romanian state closed more than two thirds of the lower and upper elementary schools teaching in Hungarian, and three quarters of such high schools and teacher-training institutions. The Greek Orthodox and Greek Catholic institutions teaching in Romanian (2,600 institutions) were nationalized. All 645 Hungarian kindergartens and 59 day-care centers were closed, as were peoples' schools for repeating the upper elementary course (3,500), and trade and industrial apprentice schools (almost 200). To compensate, 403 lower elementary schools (319 Reformed, 62 Catholic and 23 Unitarian) had been founded by 1923 by the Churches, as had 33 upper elementary schools, 7 trade schools and 5 teacher-training colleges.[22] This burst of Church-based self-organization prompted the Romanian Liberal Party to frame an assimilatory schooling policy by withdrawing state subsidies from Church schools, and through three pieces of legislation. Under the 1924 act on state elementary education a state permit was needed to found a school. State Hungarian-language elementary schools were to be formed in minority communities, even if a Church school existed. There would be kindergartens for minority communities, but teaching would be conducted in Romanian. Families deemed officially to be of Romanian origin would be obliged to enroll their children in Romanian-language schools. One special measure was to designate a "culture zone": Romanian elementary teachers taking posts in 20 counties with predominantly minority inhabitants were offered a 50 percent salary supplement, 10 hectares of land and a removal allowance. Despite protests from the minorities and the Churches on the international level, the private education act of 1925 demoted Church schools to the status of private schools and curtailed their right to issue certificates of entitlement to further education, tying it to a permit, which one third of denominational schools failed to obtain. The same act set Romanian as the language of instruction for five subjects, and as the exclusive language in schools run by religious orders; Jewish institutions were to teach only in Romanian or Hebrew. The third major measure was the 1925 act on the baccalaureate, whereby high school graduation was awarded not at the school attended, but before a board of teachers from other state schools, who could only be Romanians. Even subjects taught in Hungarian were to be examined in the state language. Thus 73 percent of Hungarian candidates failed their examinations in 1925.[73]

Yugoslavia imposed on the rest of the country the pre-1918 Serbian school system, in which the village schools and denominational schools important under the Monarchy for minority education found no place. There was no chance of setting up a system of Church schools. Apart from the dismantling of the Hungarian school system and dismissal of its teachers, the most damaging measure was to enroll children in schools based on analysis of their family names. Several regulations on schools were followed in December 1929 by an act on people's schools, introducing eight years of compulsory education. The sizeable number of communities with a minority population were instructed to set up separate sections for such pupils, but with a Serbian director in charge. Here the pupils were officially to be taught the lower four elementary grades in their native language. In 1929–1930, there were 528 classes taught in Hungarian in the Danube Banat, with 364 teachers, a third of whom were not ethnic Hungarians. The Hungarian community itself had no representatives with a say in how these institutions were run. The teaching staff were trained in the Belgrade teacher-training college. Two high school sections teaching in Hungarian remained at Senta and Subotica in the mid-1920s; only 14.5 percent of the Hungarian high school students were taught in Hungarian. About 500 Hungarians received college or university degrees in Belgrade, Zagreb or Subotica between the two world wars; the majority of them became clergy, lawyers or pharmacists. An attempt to fill the gap was made by the Hungarian Party, various left-wing movements and local cultural associations, providing literacy classes, adult education and educational lectures, taking advantage of an easier political atmosphere in the second half of the 1930s.[24]

Notes

1   József Galántai, "The Paris Peace Conference (1919–1920) on Protection of the Minorities," in Ferenc Glatz, ed., *Etudes Historiques Hongroises 1990. II. Ethnicity and Society in Hungary* (Budapest, 1990), pp. 303–320.

2   Magda Ádám, "The Little Entente and Issue of the Hungarian Minorities," in *ibid.*, pp. 321–338.

3   *Ibid.*, pp. 328–330.

4   *Ibid.*, pp. 331–335.

5   A contemporary summary with reports of the situation of Hungarian minorities appears in Ewald Ammende, ed., *Die Nationalitäten in den Staaten Europas* (Vienna/Leipzig, 1931). Ignác Romsics, *Nemzet, nemzetiség és állam Kelet-Közép- és Délkelet-Európában a 19. és 20. században* [Nation, Nationality and State in East-Central and Southeastern Europe in the 19th and 20th Centuries] (Budapest, 1998), pp. 193–232, surveys the whole field.

6   Lajos Pándi, ed., *Köztes-Európa 1763–1993. Térképgyűjtemény* [In-Between Europe 1763–1993. Map Collection] (Budapest, 1995), pp. 368, 394 and 406.
7   Iuliu Maniu, *Problema minorităţilor* [The Minorities Issue] (Bucharest, 1924), p. 21.
8   On regional standardization in Romania, see Irina Livezeanu, *Cultural Politics in Greater Romania: Regionalism, Nation Building, and Ethnic Struggle, 1918–1930* (Ithaca, NY, 2000), pp. 89–188. On the search for a Hungarian minority policy, see Franz S. Horváth, *Zwischen Ablehnung und Anpassung: politische Strategien der ungarischen Minderheitselite in Rumänien 1931–1940* (Munich, 2007). On the constitutional and nationality policy frameworks, see Lajos Nagy, *A kisebbségek alkotmányjogi helyzete Nagyromániában* [The Constitutional Position of Minorities in Greater Romania] (Kolozsvár, 1944), pp. 16–40.
9   Enikő A. Sajti, *Hungarians in the Voivodina 1918–1947* (Boulder, CO/Highland Lakes, NJ, 2003), pp. 164–171.
10 On the national and democratic nature of nationality policy in Masaryk's Czechoslovakia, see Tamás Gusztáv Filep, "Maléter István és a balítélete" [István Maléter and His Prejudice], in Idem, *A hagyomány felemelt tőre. Válogatott és új tanulmányok az 1918–1945 közötti [cseh]szlovákiai magyar kultúráról* [The Raised Sword of Tradition. Selected and New Studies on Czechoslovakian and Slovakian Hungarian Culture in 1918–1945] (Budapest, 2003), pp. 25–119. On election results of Hungarian parties in Czechoslovakia, see Béla Angyal, *Érdekvédelem és önszerveződés. Fejezetek a csehszlovákiai magyar pártpolitika történetéből 1918–1938* [Interest Protection and Self-Organization. Chapters from the History of Czechoslovakian Hungarian Party Politics 1918–1938] (Galánta/Dunaszerdahely, 2002).
11 For a view of the creation and content of the constitution, see József Gyönyör, *Közel a jog asztalához. A csehszlovák állam kezdeti nehézségei, területi gyarapodása, ideiglenes alkotmánya, alkotmánylevele és annak sorsa* [Near the Table of the Law. Czechoslovakia's Initial Difficulties, Territorial Expansion, Provisional Constitution, and Constitution and Destiny] (Bratislava, 1992). On minority and language-use sides of the constitution, see Gyula Popély, *Népfogyatkozás. A csehszlovákiai magyarság a népszámlálások tükrében 1918–1945* [Depopulation. Czechoslovakian

Hungarians in the Light of the Censuses 1918–1945] (Budapest, 1991), pp. 40–46.

12 Nagy, *A kisebbségek alkotmányjogi helyzete*, pp. 16–75; Sajti, *Hungarians in the Voivodina*, pp. 90–125.

13 Popély, *Népfogyatkozás*, pp. 106–107.

14 Nagy, *A kisebbségek alkotmányjogi helyzete*, pp. 76–84.

15 Sajti, *Hungarians in the Voivodina*, pp. 19–20; Enikő A. Sajti, *Impériumváltások, revízió, kisebbségek. Magyarok a Délvidéken 1918–1947* [Sovereignty Changes, Revision, Minorities. Hungarians in the Southern Region 1918–1947] (Budapest, 2004), pp. 25–27 and 85.

16 Popély, *Népfogyatkozás*, pp. 109–111.

17 Nagy, *A kisebbségek alkotmányjogi helyzete*, pp. 109–116; Sándor Bíró, *The Nationalities Problem in Transylvania 1867–1940* (Boulder, CO/Highland Lakes, NJ, 1992), pp. 443–459.

18 Tamás Gusztáv Filep, "Kormánypárton vagy ellenzékben. A pozsonyi magyar polgár és az 1925-ös választások" [In Government or Opposition. The Hungarian Citizens of Pozsony in the 1925 Elections], in Idem, *A humanista voksa. Írások a csehszlovákiai magyar kisebbség köréből 1918–1945* [The Humanist Voice. Writings from the Czechoslovakian Hungarian Minority] (Pozsony, 2007), pp. 26–55.

19 Zsombor Szász, *The Minorities in Roumanian Transylvania* (London, 1927), pp. 95–118; Nagy, *A kisebbségek alkotmányjogi helyzete*, pp. 176–196.

20 Sajti, *Hungarians in the Voivodina*, pp. 25–89.

21 The question is covered comprehensively in Popély, *Népfogyatkozás*.

22 For an overall view, see Bíró, *The Nationalities Problem*, pp. 507–618. A statistical review: Júlia Balogh, *Az erdélyi hatalomváltozás és a magyar közoktatás 1918–1928* [Change of Power in Transylvania and Hungarian Public Education 1918–1928] (Budapest, 1996), pp. 87–108.

23 Bíró, *The Nationalities Problem*, pp. 570–579 and 541–548; Endre Barabás, "A magyar iskolaügy helyzete Romániában" [The State of Hungarian Schooling in Romania], *Kisebbségi Körlevél* 7 (1943) 3: 271–287, and 7 (1943) 4: 351–368.

24 Sajti, *Hungarians in the Voivodina*, pp. 142–163.

4. DISPUTES, PLANS AND PROPOSALS
FOR HANDLING THE MINORITY QUESTION
Nándor Bárdi

Strategies that evolved in the twentieth century for handling ethno-cultural conflicts can be placed in two categories. One aims to eliminate ethno-cultural differences, the other to preserve communities exhibiting them. Under the first heading come genocide (exemplified by the Holocaust), deportation, population exchange (such as that between Slovaks and Hungarians), founding new states on grounds of national self-determination (for example, the disintegration of Yugoslavia), and integration by assimilation (as in the United States or Australia). Methods of handling ethnic conflict that belong to the other category include authoritarian control (for example, by the Serb minority in Kosovo or the white minority in South Africa), international control and adjudication (for example, the UN role in the Middle East or Cyprus), also public administration within ethnic borders, cantonization (Switzerland), federalism (Canada), territorial autonomy (Alto Adige), and personal and cultural autonomy (indigenous Swedes in Finland). The most advanced model for coexistence of ethnic groups and nations within one state is power-sharing, that allows each group to retain its collective identity and culture. The requirements are a constitutional right of veto, communal self-government, proportional representation, labor opportunities, budget share, and a grand coalition government in which the minority has a permanent place.[1]

About half the inhabitants of In-Between Europe[2] before World War I, some 50 million people, lived as a minority without their own nation state. After World War I, there were still 32 million living as a national minority. The Austro-Hungarian Monarchy was the one Great Power in pre-World War I Europe whose ruling nations formed only a plurality of the population (44.8 percent in 1910).

117

Under the Versailles system between the two world wars, the Serbs in Yugoslavia formed only 47.7 percent of the population (the "Serbo-Croats" 74.4 percent), and the Czechs in Czechoslovakia 49.8 percent (the "Czecho-Slovaks" 65.5 percent). Poland and Romania had dominant nations (forming 68.9 and 71.9 percent of the population respectively). Meanwhile 37.5 percent of Albanians, 27.6 percent of Hungarians, and 11.2 percent of Germans lived outside the borders of their nation state (or in the Germans' case, outside the three states of Germany, Austria and Switzerland). Taking the absolute figures of the 1930 censuses, the largest minority in In-Between Europe was that of the Germans (8.9 million in 12 countries), then the Jews (6.5 million in 11 countries), then the Ukrainians (4.4 million). There were 2.7 million Hungarians in five neighboring countries. Other nations with over a million members spread over several countries were the Poles, Byelorussians and Russians. The biggest minorities in a single country were the Ukrainians of Poland (4 million), the Germans of the Czech Lands (3.2 million), the Polish Jews (3 million), the Romanian Hungarians (1.4 million) and the Polish Germans (1 million).[3]

The architects of the post-World War I peace system, after the break-up of the three Central European empires, started from the principle of national self-determination in responding to the nation-building efforts of less numerous peoples by creating new states. The 1919 minority protection treaties and the foundation of the League of Nations brought into being the concepts of international minority protection and of national minorities, whereas the question of national groups had been handled as a domestic matter in the 1910s. The rules of minority protection devised at that time were built into the five minority protection treaties, the four peace treaties and the Covenant of the League of Nations. These can be classified in three groups: stipulations on citizenship and on equal rights, and guarantees of implementation. The several treaties also contained stipulations specific to local conditions. These went beyond the equality of citizens to cover elements of national autonomy and territorial autonomy. Concerning the Hungarian minority, Article 11 of Romania's minority protection treaty referred briefly to granting "the communities of the Saxons and Székelys in Transylvania local autonomy with regard to scholastic and religious matters," but these rights were not meant by the Romanian government for the community recognized as a self-standing legal entity, but for their existing religious and educational organizations. Articles 11–13 of the treaty with Czechoslovakia raised the prospect of territorial autonomy for the Rusyns, extending to linguistic, religious and local government affairs. The treaty promised a provincial assembly as a separate legislative authority and a governor appointed by the Czechoslovak president as a separate executive authority.[4] But these expectations were not met in political practice.[5] The minorities themselves were divided on the matter. A common minority view of the future was clarified at the meetings of the Congress of European Nationalities held between 1925 and 1939, where it seemed possible to treat the question as one of autonomy for national minorities. But that seemed too little for the minorities living in blocs of continuous territory in Poland, and too big a challenge for the minorities of Germany. When the Jews, divided over the question of cultural autonomy, quit the organization in 1933, the National Socialist leanings of the German minorities left the Hungarian minority representatives as the sole consistent advocates of autonomy in international minority politics.[6]

The nation-building elites of the new states were also divided both ethnically and regionally. The divisions were something that Hungarian diplomacy and the Hungarian minority parties aspired to exploit in the 1920s, to gain a base for minority and regional interests against central governments.

Attempts were made in Czechoslovakia to defend local interests via the Czech–Slovak antagonisms and ideologies (of indigenousness) found in Slovensko and Transcarpathia. The strongest political group in the former was the Slovak People's Party, which sought Slovak national autonomy and in 1927 joined the governing coalition in Prague. Thereby the so-called Slovak Ministry gave way to greater provincial autonomy, but constitutional settlement of the Czech–Slovak relationship and greater decentralization were not gained.

Nor was the Rusyn or Transcarpathian autonomy prescribed in the minority protection treaty, on the one hand because Prague feared that it might set a precedent for Sudeten German or Slovak devolution, and on the other because some of the Rusyns, in what was the poorest and most divided part of the new country, were oriented towards Hungary, which represented a threat to its integrity and the whole Little Entente system of military defense. (Transcarpathia provided a common Czechoslovak–Romanian border to set against possible Polish or Hungarian designs.)[7]

In Romania, relations between the Bucharest-based National Liberal Party and the National Peasant Party, rooted in Transylvania and Bessarabia, can be seen in terms of the decisive political and administrative position gained after 1918 by the Romanians in lands transferred from Hungary to Romania. So the Romanians of Transylvania had to struggle on two fronts. They sought on the one hand to change by state means the economic and social structure that had emerged historically in Transylvania, and on the other to defend and strengthen their own positions against colonizing efforts from the Regat.[8] The idea of recognizing any form of autonomy (internal self-determination) or the historical and social particularities of Transylvania was quashed by the constitution of 1923, with its aims of unification. Indeed, the 1925 and 1929 public administration acts placed question marks over the introduction of viable local government precisely because the cities of Transylvania were dominated by non-Romanian elements. If fair and democratic local government elections had been held, most Transylvanian cities and half of the counties would have come under the political control of minorities that opposed the unifying, nation-building endeavors of the Romanian state. So no interest was shown even by Romanian political forces in Transylvania in retaining local government autonomy. The process of institutionalizing the regional politics of the Transylvanian Romanians came to an end in 1926, when the Romanian National Party of Transylvania merged with the Peasant Party of Bessarabia, as Iuliu Maniu and his group needed a national program to put up against the National Liberal Party. Thus even the

National Peasant Party government of 1928–1932 failed to bring decentralization, let alone provincial or institutional autonomy.[9]

Politics in Yugoslavia were dominated by the antagonism between the Croats and the Serbs, mainly because the centralist efforts of the new state system founded by the Serbian nation, whose embourgeoisement was less developed, conflicted with the interests of the Croats and Slovenes, who had more advanced social and economic institutions. Lukács Peszkovics, head of the People's Circle in Subotica in the 1920s, tried to represent regional interests and the minority interests of the Germans and Hungarians, with a view to attaining "Vojvodina autonomy" (as a successor to the Vojvodina set up after 1848), but this was rejected even by the Hungarian Party in Yugoslavia, which was just forming. The Hungarian leaders in the Vojvodina were looking for concessions from Belgrade, and also rejected the advances of Iván Nagy's group, which was advocating an alliance with the Croatian national movements.[10]

Efforts at national autonomy, seen at the time as the best way to handle the issue, appeared among Hungarians abroad alongside trust in border revisions, as a view of the future that might be held openly. The political leaders of the minority Hungarians stated everywhere that in return for loyalty to the new state, they sought the right to institutions that they ran and controlled themselves.[11] Administrative autonomy for the minority was mooted in three contexts. (1) The Hungarian minority parties viewed themselves in terms of representing the minority as an (unrecognized) institution of self-government. This appeared as an item in the 1922 program of the National Hungarian Party in Romania and the United Hungarian Party in Czechoslovakia, although not in that of the National Hungary Party in Yugoslavia.[12] (2) These parties spoke out both for equality of rights and for retention of the pre-1918 local and communal self-government, especially autonomy of the Churches and the independence of Church schools in Transylvania. But there was central control of local government in all three countries. In Czechoslovakia, otherwise the most democratic of the three, the elected local government authorities could be dissolved by government-appointed bodies at the *župan* (county) level, or after 1927 the provincial level, and new elections held. In Romania, the central government manipulated the actual local government elections. Later the self-governing bodies in most Transylvanian counties and cities were replaced by extraordinary committees, which could dispose over city and county property almost without restriction. In Yugoslavia, the Hungarians found it hard even to register themselves as voters, and there were seldom any local elections. The whole public administration operated with officials appointed from above.[13] (3) The Hungarian minority parties devised specific proposals for handling the problems. This remained in Yugoslavia on their level of demanding equal civil and political rights.[14]

In Czechoslovakia, the Hungarian political forces in Trans-carpathia supported the Rusyn efforts to gain political autonomy throughout the period.[15] The efforts of the Hungarian parliamentary parties were directed either at enrolling the pro-Hungarian (or pro-Hungary) Christian Socialists in Slovakia, or at activism, or at setting up social institutions of their own. In the spring of 1938, after the two main Hungarian parties had merged, there was an official demand for a national quota system in offices and factories and for minority powers over schools and adult education institutions.[16] The background to this was a debate in Czechoslovakia initiated at the end of 1937 by Pál Szvatkó, which started from a proposal for three "cantons" with a Hungarian majority, which were to have special rights of language use and education.[17] In Romania, more than 50 Transylvanian Hungarian proposals were drawn up between the world wars to settle the Transylvanian question in some way.[18] These can be grouped in terms of their objectives: ideas for frontier changes; plans for independence for Transylvania or autonomy within Romania or Hungary; drafts of minority legislation; plans for national (Hungarian or Székely) autonomy. Those mooted in the period of the change of sovereignty, in 1918–1920, usually proposed decentralization and regionalization. Those that emerged in 1928–1931 were plans for minority legislation or public administrative reform influenced by the prospect of a minority act and unsuccessful plans for administrative decentralization. At the end of the 1930s, plans for cultural autonomy and maps of border changes were simultaneously drafted for the awaited negotiations on territorial revision.

In the debates in Romania in the 1920s, lack of a Romanian partner meant that ideas of Hungarian national autonomy gained ground over those of Transylvanian autonomy (political "Transylvanianism").[19] Again, opinion was divided, as there was only the minority protection treaty to cite under international law, and that referred only to communal autonomy for the Székelys. So potential cultural autonomy for the Székely Land would have split the Hungarian community, and the local government school system would have come up against the Székely Land's widespread system of Church education.[20] Iuliu Maniu as prime minister held out the prospect in 1929 of amending the minority act, and two drafts for that were prepared by the National Hungarian Party. One by Árpád Paál took cultural self-government for the Székely Land's Hungarians as its starting point, thinking in terms of an independent school system funded by self-taxation and of defending the area's communal wealth (ensuring a prior right of purchase for locals).[21] The other, by Elemér Jakabffy, envisaged cultural self-government organizations covering the whole territory of the country, brought about through voluntary enrollment into a special register.[22] National councils elected in that way were to control a system of minority educational and cultural institutions, which the state would support out of a proportion of the taxes paid by those featuring on the land registry. Romania's promised minority act did not even get so far as to formulate a proposal. When Romania and Yugoslavia reached an international agreement in 1933 on schools for the Serbs of the Banat, this prompted the National Hungarian Party, at its grand assembly in July 1933, to include in its program the question of autonomy for the Székelys, but that meant little under the political situation prevailing at the time. In the following year the National Hungarian Party unsuccessfully requested the Romanian parties to formulate a clear common stance of the majority regarding the minorities, such a standpoint was never clarified. Neither was the measure calling for an end to the discrimination against the Hungarian community implemented, which was part of the government's minority statute of 1938.[23]

The Little Entente countries were intent on building homogeneous nation states. The League of Nations and international public opinion started out from requiring individual civil rights and condemned only measures of forcible assimilation that infringed those. How the Hungarian minorities were treated was related directly to the measure of democratization in each country. The worst measures of assimilation and discrimination were suffered by the Hungarians of Yugoslavia.

The larger Hungarian state that resulted from the Vienna Awards of 1938 and 1940 broke with its earlier official ideology of calling for national autonomy and collective minority rights. Thereafter the national minority question was treated as one of language and public administration and the national minority act of 1868 was taken as a basis for handling it.[24]

Notes

1   John McGarry and Brendan O'Leary, "The Macro-Political Regulation of Ethnic Conflict," in Idem, eds., *The Politics of Ethnic Conflict Regulation. Case Studies of Protracted Ethnic Conflicts* (London/New York, 1993), pp. 1–40.

2   In-Between Europe is taken here to mean the region of small nations between Russia and Germany, from Finland to Greece.

3   Ignác Romsics, *Nemzet, nemzetiség és állam Kelet-Közép- és Délkelet-Európában a 19. és 20. században* [Nation, Nationality and State in East-Central and Southeastern Europe in the 19th and 20th Centuries] (Budapest, 1998), pp. 206–223; Lajos Pándi, ed., *Köztes-Európa 1763–1993. Térképgyűjtemény* [In-Between Europe 1763–1993. Map Collection] (Budapest, 1995), pp. 368, 394 and 406.

4   The minority treaties of each country are analyzed in tabular form in Miklós Zeidler, "A Nemzetek Szövetsége és a magyar kisebbségi petíciók" [League of Nations and the Hungarian Minority Parties], in Nándor Bárdi and Csilla Fedinec, eds., *Etnopolitika. A közösségi, magán- és nemzetközi érdekek viszonyrendszere Közép-Európában*

[Ethno-Politics. The System of Relations in Communal, Private and International Interests in Central Europe] (Budapest, 2003), pp. 64–65.

5 For a summary in Hungarian of the literature of the period, see András Rónai, "A nemzetiségi kérdés területi megoldásai" [Territorial Solutions to the Minority Question], *Magyar Szemle* 30 (1937) 11: 201–209, and Idem, "A nemzetiségi kérdés nem-területi megoldásai" [Non-Territorial Solutions to the Minority Question], *Magyar Szemle* 31 (1938) 8: 303–312.

6 Ferenc Eiler, *Kisebbségvédelem és revízió. Magyar törekvések az Európai Nemzetiségi Kongresszuson (1925–1939)* [Minority Protection and Revision. Hungarian Efforts at the European Congress of Nationalities, 1925–1939] (Budapest, 2007), pp. 117–123, 190–194 and 248–250; Árpád Hornyák, *Magyar–jugoszláv diplomáciai kapcsolatok 1918–1927* [Hungarian–Yugoslav Diplomatic Relations 1918–1927] (Novi Sad, 2004).

7 László Szarka, *A szlovákok története* [History of the Slovaks] (Budapest, 1993), pp. 159–173.

8 The *Vechiul Regat* (Old Kingdom) was a term current between the world wars for the territories of Wallachia, Moldavia and Northern Dobruja, which had become the Kingdom of Romania in 1881, as opposed to territories annexed later, such as Transylvania and Bessarabia.

9 Nándor Bárdi, "Die minderheitspolitischen Strategien der ungarischen Bevölkerung in Rumänien zwischen den beiden Weltkriegen," in *Südost-Forschungen 1999* (Munich, 1999), pp. 285–292.

10 Enikő A. Sajti, *Hungarians in the Voivodina 1918–1947* (Boulder, CO/Highland Lakes, NJ, 2003), p. 98 ff; János Csuka, A *délvidéki magyarság története 1918–1941* [History of Southern Region Hungarians 1918–1941] (Budapest, 1995), pp. 81–82; Dénes Sokcsevits, Imre Szilágyi and Károly Szilágyi, *Déli szomszédaink története* [History of Hungary's Southern Neighbors] (Budapest, 1994).

11 This was expressed most forcefully in Károly Kós, Árpád Paál and István Zágoni, *Kiáltó szó* [Exclamatory Word], Facsimile edition (Budapest, 1988 [Cluj, 1921]).

12 On the National Hungarian Party in Romania: Imre Mikó, *Huszonkét év* [22 Years] (Budapest, 1941), pp. 271–273. On the Czechoslovak program: László Szarka, "Autonómia elképzelések a kisebbségi magyar pártok két világháború közötti politikájában" [Ideas of

Autonomy in the Politics of the Minority Hungarian Parties between the World Wars], in Tibor Valuch, ed., *Hatalom és társadalom a XX. századi magyar történelemben* [Power and Society in 20th-Century Hungarian History] (Budapest, 1995), pp. 250–254; Gyula Popély, "A magyar pártok 1936. évi fúziója Csehszlovákiában" [The 1936 Merger of the Hungarian Parties in Czechoslovakia], *Regio* 1 (1990) 4: 92–111.

13   Sajti, *Hungarians in the Voivodina*, p. 48 ff; László Fritz, "A Iorga-kormány 'interimár-bizottságai' és a magyar nemzetkisebbség" [The "Interim Committees" of the Iorga Government and the Hungarian National Minority], *Magyar Kisebbség* 10 (1932) 3–4: 75–83.

14   The founding program of the Hungarian Party issued at Senta on September 17, 1922, is published in Csuka, A *délvidéki magyarság*, pp. 66–70.

15   Csilla Fedinec, "Kárpátaljai autonómia-koncepciók 1918–1944 között" [Transcarpathian Concepts of Autonomy 1918–1944], *Kisebbségkutatás* 10 (2001) 3: 450–469.

16   The demands of the United Hungarian Party were summarized by Andor Jaross in the Prague Parliament on April 5, 1938. Szarka, "Autonómia elképzelések," pp. 250–254.

17   Pál Szvatkó, "A svájci példa. A három magyar kanton" [The Swiss Example. The Three Hungarian Cantons], *Új Szellem* 1 (1937) 21: 9; Kálmán Berecz, "Megvalósítható-e a svájci példa?" [Can the Swiss Pattern Be Attained?], *Új Szellem* 2 (1938) 3: 3–5.

18   Nándor Bárdi, "Javaslatok, modellek az erdélyi kérdés kezelésére – A magyar elképzelések 1918–1940" [Proposals and Models for Handling the Transylvanian Issue – Hungarian Ideas 1918–1940], in Idem, ed., *Konfliktusok és kezelésük Közép-Európában* [Conflicts and Handling of Them in Central Europe] (Budapest, 2000), pp. 137–180.

19   For a survey at the time, see Emil Grandpierre, "Az erdélyi magyarság politikai küzdelmei az egységes magyar párt megalakulásáig" [The Political Struggles of the Transylvanian Hungarians until the Founding of a United Hungarian Party], *Magyar Szemle* 21 (1928) 10: 130–136. On the attempt at political Transylvanianism as a scheme of regionalism, see Zsolt K. Lengyel, *Auf der Suche nach dem Kompromiss. Ursprünge und Gestalten des frühen Transsilvanismus 1918–1928* (Munich, 1991).

20 Imre Mikó, "A székely közületi kulturális önkormányzat" [Székely Communal Cultural Self-Determination], *Magyar Kisebbség* 12 (1934) 13: 365–378, and 12 (1934) 15–16: 441–464.

21 Árpád Paál, "Törvény a székely közületek közművelődési önkormányzatáról, a Párizsban 1919. december 19-én kötött nemzetközi szerződés 11. cikke alapján" [Act on Educational Self-Determination for Székely Communes, Based on Article 11 of the International Treaty Concluded in Paris on December 19, 1919], *Magyar Kisebbség* (2004) 1–2: 424–465.

22 Elemér Jakabffy, "Tervezet a 'kisebbségi törvény' javaslatához" [Draft Proposal for a "Minority Law"], *Magyar Kisebbség* (2004) 1–2: 377–423.

23 On the minority rights contained in the statute, see Lajos Nagy, *A kisebbségek alkotmányjogi helyzete Nagyromániában* [Constitutional Position of Minorities in Greater Romania] (Kolozsvár, 1944), pp. 38–40 and 56–61.

24 Act XLIV/1868 on Equal Rights of National Communities was well summarized and defended comprehensibly at the time in Imre Mikó, *Nemzetiségi jog és nemzetiségi politika* [National Minority Law and National Minority Policy] (Kolozsvár, 1944), pp. 493–498. On the post-1940 change in policy stance by the elite of what had been the Hungarian minority in Romania, see Nándor Bárdi, "A múlt, mint tapasztalat. A kisebbségből többségbe került erdélyi magyar politika szemléletváltása 1940–1944 között" [The *Past* as *Experience*. Change of Political Outlook by the Transylvanian Hungarians on Turning from Minority to Majority, 1940–1944], *Limes* 19 (2006) 2: 43–70.

5. TERRITORIAL REVISION AND MINORITY PROTECTION IN HUNGARIAN POLITICS

Nándor Bárdi and *Ferenc Eiler*

Hungarian society and the Hungarian communities that came under other sovereignty were alike shocked by Trianon's economic, social and territorial terms. The stipulations were felt to be unfair in every detail. The clear rejection of them by the whole of society immediately placed territorial revision in the forefront of interwar Hungarian foreign policy.[1]

Such revision was a foreign policy objective and a way for the Horthy regime to gain social legitimacy. Apart from the cult of territorial revision, the determination to regain the lost territories was inherent in the system of expectations and arguments that ran through the whole system of power, and this aim was often given precedence over the social and economic problems confronting the country. So policy in pursuit of territorial revision needs to be treated separately from minority protection or nationhood policy, known today as policy towards the Hungarian community.

Since creating conditions for territorial revision was a permanent feature of Hungarian foreign policy between the world wars, the search for allies in this became a crucial diplomatic endeavor. Hungary had little room for diplomatic maneuver in the early post-war years, due to the demands of economic stabilization and the constraints placed on its sovereignty. France and Britain, despite their sporadic disputes and differences of interest, were committed to keeping things as they were. Italy deepened its relations with the neighboring countries (Czechoslovakia, Romania and Yugoslavia) that had formed the Little Entente expressly to contain Hungary. Germany was busy with economic reconstruction and stabilizing its domestic and foreign political position. Hungary unsuccessfully attempted to weaken the Little Entente through bilateral negotiations with its members. Seeking a relationship with Germany founded on the minority question failed as well. In this way Hungarian foreign policy in 1921–1927 took the form of an "achievement policy" designed to seek leverage in the new European order.[2]

Mussolini, on the other hand, sought to base his efforts as a Great Power on his policy and alliances in the Danube Basin, with the result that the Italian–Hungarian Treaty of Friendship of 1927 won the Hungarian prime minister István Bethlen an ally ready to give support to limited Hungarian revisionist intentions against Czechoslovakia. Thereafter the Italian connection played a prominent role in Hungarian diplomacy, even though the collaboration was far from serene and still less a unilateral commitment. This period saw the first, still general, reference made by Bethlen in a public speech to territorial demands by Hungary on the successor states. At about the same time, the British newspaper owner Lord Rothermere began an international press campaign calling for fairer borders for Hungary based on ethnic proportions.[3]

As early as 1927, Bethlen was also trying to extend Italian–Hungarian cooperation to Germany, thus giving it greater importance. This idea was rejected by the German minister of foreign affairs, Gustav Stresemann, as a potential danger to the steadily improving relations of Germany with the Western powers, which were in his country's fundamental interest. Nor did he want to strain relations with the other countries in the region by putting friendship with Hungary to the fore.

Even in the 1930s, Germany firmly refused to enshrine its cooperation with Hungary in a political treaty. The idea of German–Italian–Hungarian–Austrian cooperation returned to Hungary's agenda under Gyula Gömbös's premiership, only to be rejected by Germany again. For the two countries' economic and strategic interests in the region were at variance for a long time. Even in principle, Nazi Germany would only have been willing to support Hungary's efforts at territorial revision in relation to Czechoslovakia, and it bluntly turned down the suggestion that it try to bring the German minorities in the successor states to cooperate with the Hungarians on revision.[4]

While seeking allies, the Hungarian Ministry of Foreign Affairs tried several times to drive a wedge between the members of the Little Entente, whose efforts were directed mainly against Hungary. This was certainly a driving force behind the talks with Yugoslavia in 1926–1927, Romania in 1928, and all three Little Entente countries in 1937–1938.[5]

The theoretical possibility of redrawing Hungary's frontiers was raised seriously only once in the twenty years up to the Munich Agreement of September 29–30, 1938, during preparatory talks for the Four Power Pact of July 15, 1933. The plan drawn up by the British prime minister, Ramsay MacDonald, and Mussolini in March 1933 raised the questions of the Polish corridor and of restoring to Hungary the Hungarian-inhabited lands across its borders, but both points were omitted from the final pact.[6]

Hungarian views on territorial revision seemed united to outsiders. In practice the closest that they came to consensus was in stating that the frontier changes had to be peaceful, as the military forces of Hungary's neighbors were an order of magnitude stronger than Hungary's. But the specific revisionist goals were left vague. Only the Gömbös government went so far as to set concrete revisionist goals. This secret draft prepared for Mussolini's benefit weighed ethnic, economic and strategic criteria when abandoning the idea of territorial integrity in favor of sharing the disputed territories roughly half and half with the other states involved. Hungary's area would have grown from 93,073 to 195,000 square kilometers, but only 1.65 million of the minority Hungarians would have rejoined their parent country,[7] while the proportion of the non-Hungarian minorities in the total population would have risen from 10.4 to 37 percent. The model envisaged a peaceful transfer. In fact Gömbös himself did not believe that the frontiers could be altered by negotiation.[8]

The version of revision most stridently advocated (by social organizations) was to restore the integrity of pre-1918 "historical" Hungary, but to diplomatic minds, the idea of revision on ethnic grounds seemed the most attainable, even if this was drowned out in domestic politics by the cult of "No, nay, never!" among the general public. Experts were thinking mainly of annexing the Hungarian-inhabited areas just across the border. What was envisaged for Transylvania was a corridor through Cluj and Sălaj districts connecting the Hungarian settlements around Satu Mare and Salonta with the Székely Land. Plebiscites were proposed for ethnically mixed areas and for those where the majority community in the state concerned formed a minority.[9]

No comments on such plans came from representatives of Hungarian political parties beyond Hungary's borders, whose programs advocated schemes of national autonomy that cited motions passed at the unification rallies of 1918 and the stipulations of the minority protection treaties.[10]

The main arguments advanced in Hungarian revisionist propaganda can be grouped under four types. (1) First came the arguments resting on the geographical and economic integrity of the Carpathian Basin, backed by age-old historical processes (the highland/lowland relation and the function of Budapest) and the economic anomalies that arose after 1918.[11] (2) This covers the discourse on the historical virtues of Hungarian statehood and the cultural superiority of the Hungarian people.[12] (3) The starting point here was the geopolitical need to offset the power of Germany and Russia, which only strong and stable countries such as Poland and a Hungary that ruled the Carpathian Basin could do.[13] (4) It was argued that the new states had been unable since 1918 to handle the minority question, with the result that the situation had become less stable and the relations of the various national groups more inimical than they had been before 1918 under the Austro-Hungarian Monarchy.[14]

The propaganda for territorial revision was made by the Ministry of Foreign Affairs and by various social organizations. Several dozen societies pledged to struggle for the territorial integrity of Hungary had arisen in 1918. The most active was the Territory Protection League (TEVÉL), which sought to appeal to the patriotic feelings of Hungarians and win over the former minorities of pre-1918 Hungary. However, this was dissolved by the government under the stipulations of the Treaty of Trianon. Still, TEVÉL was one of the forerunners of the National Federation founded in 1920. This organization refused to recognize Trianon, so it was suitable only for domestic propaganda. In April 1920, the Hungarian Society for Foreign Affairs was founded by a group of foreign policy experts, intending to raise the awareness of the Hungarian public about foreign policy issues.[15] Scholarly research was specifically the aim of the Sociographic Institute, founded in 1924 to tackle social issues in Hungary, as it was of the Political Science Institute (*Államtudományi Intézet*) founded two years later and headed by Pál Teleki. The latter set out to gather social, economic and political data on the neighboring countries and their Hungarian minorities and to provide data based upon which decisions could be made.[16] The newspaper propaganda that strengthened with the campaign by Lord Rothermere gave rise in April 1927 to the Hungarian Revisionist League, as an association of more than 500 member organizations. It set up offices abroad (in London, Milan, Paris, Amsterdam, Berlin, Washington, Warsaw and Geneva) and by 1940 had published 270 books in various languages (English, Italian, French and German). In 1931, the League took over the publication of the foreign policy journal *Magyar Külpolitika*.[17]

The minority protection efforts of Budapest governments appeared openly both in revisionist politics and on international forums, in conjunction with support for the self-organization and political activities of the minority Hungarian communities. This policy towards the Hungarian community was represented at the time by Benedek Jancsó's idea: territorial integrity had been lost, but not cultural integrity, which was backed by the minority treaty and had to be sustained, along with the demographic, economic and cultural positions, so that use could be made of all this as a basis at new peace negotiations in the future.[18] For this reason, great emphasis was placed in Hungary's interwar support policy on denominational education and maintaining the means of minority publicity (via the press).

During the change of sovereignty (1918 to 1920–1922), Budapest advised the former elite of officials in Transylvania to take a politically passive stance, while in Czechoslovakia it supported restoration of the old party frameworks. (Uncertainty over citizenship and political rights remained in Serbia until 1922, when the opting period expired.) As it emerged that the alteration in international relations had to be accepted in the longer term and as emphasis shifted onto consolidation in Hungary (in 1923–1926), Budapest came to support the idea of integrating minority Hungarians into the politics of the successor states, through a framework of distinct Hungarian parties.[19] Beyond the organization of Hungarian political activity, Budapest encouraged cooperation with other ethnic groups in Hungarian-inhabited regions (Slovaks, Rusyns, Croats, Šokac, Bunjevac or Germans), as well as with local members of the majority group (the Romanians of Transylvania), on asserting regional interests against the nation-state center, and tried to support such programs (Transylvanianism, or the Slovensko idea and other ideologies of "indigenousness" in Slovakia and Transcarpathia). It was clear by the end of the 1920s that this was not working. Hungary could not supply sufficient political or economic resources to persuade non-Hungarian regional groups to turn against Prague, Belgrade or Bucharest.[20] Moreover, some of the non-Hungarian regional parties and some of the minority Hungarian parties joined the government, to pursue a policy of concluding pacts with the authorities of the day.[21] So Hungarian parties everywhere were on the defensive by the end of the 1920s, pursuing their grievances through appeals to the League of Nations that were backed by Budapest, while seeking at home to extricate the minority question from party politics by persuading the majority parties to introduce some kind of legal and political regulation. In the 1930s, a period of national drawing together, government policy in Budapest shifted towards internal organization and unification of Hungarian minority societies. The main goal became to maximize the institutional organization of each such society.[22] By the second half of the 1930s, preparations for territorial revision had become the focus, despite negotiations on the minority question with the Little Entente and with neighboring countries individually (Yugoslavia and Romania).

Budapest governments between the world wars saw the Hungarian political elites of neighboring countries as part of the Hungarian political class and their parties as pursuing Hungarian national goals. Although many Hungarian politicians in neighboring countries stayed loyal to the policy of Budapest, they were also seeking scope for political integration at home by the end of the 1920s. Later they trusted simultaneously in the prospect of revision and in gaining acceptance for their minority as a political entity (in Transylvania, the Southern Region, Transcarpathia or Slovakia) by building up their own social institutions.

The dominant strand in the overlapping, cross-supporting arguments of the Hungarian minority elites and of Budapest in its policy towards those communities was reference back to the minority protection treaties of 1919, with utilization in the second half of the 1930s of the League of Nations' minority complaints procedure. Emphasis went on the language-use problems in Vojvodina, the absence of the Székely cultural autonomy promised in Romania's minority protection treaty, and the failure of Prague to provide the oft-promised administrative autonomy for Transcarpathia.[23]

The second line of argument (especially in the 1920s) involved the post-unification conflicts between central government and the regions in the new nation states. Hungarian leaders of Romania sought to ally with advocates of "Transylvania for the Transylvanians" against the liberal economic and political elite of Bucharest. With Slovensko and Transcarpathia, they argued against intrusions of the Czech economy and administrative apparatus and in favor of the rights of "indigenousness" championed by the Slovak national movement. In Yugoslavia, Hungarian leaders sought to magnify regional conflicts between Vojvodina and Belgrade or between Zagreb and Belgrade to assert the interests of Hungary or the Hungarian minority.

The third group of arguments consisted of appeals to decisions made before 1918, at the time of the change of sovereignty, or made earlier to promote it. It included (1) calls to new national political elites over national demands made by movements gaining a majority after 1918, (2) comparisons of the current situation with stated political aims at the time of secession from the Monarchy, and (3) comparisons of the liberal minority policy of pre-1918 Hungary with current policy towards Hungarians in the successor states.[24]

The work of the Ministry of Foreign Affairs through the legations in Prague, Bucharest and Belgrade tied in with that of the Nationalities and Minority Department of the Prime Minister's Office, headed by Tibor Pataky from its foundation until 1944.[25] The latter did not deal with the Austrian or Western Hungarian communities, only those of Czechoslovakia, Yugoslavia and Romania, and non-Hungarian communities in Hungary. It performed the day-to-day operative tasks of maintaining relations and mediating in certain cases, and had advisory powers, preparing summaries on certain subjects or mediating between persons or social organizations and the prime minister or Ministry of Foreign Affairs. The latter had the task of bringing minority problems to the attention of Great Power governments and to contributing international propaganda. Hungarian missions in Central Europe began in the later 1920s to establish close ties with Hungarian minority leaders and to make regular reports on minority questions. Their mediating role covered policy and information, and under Bethlen's premiership they reported only to him. Later the Second Department of the Prime Minister's Office became the decisive factor. Apart from preparing the international ground for revision, the Ministry of Foreign Affairs pursued Hungary's interests through bilateral contacts with neighboring countries and international campaigns for minority rights, by preparing minority petitions to the League of Nations and managing them in Geneva, secret funding for the European Congress of Nationalities, and propaganda for minority rights.[26]

In the spring of 1920, István Bethlen and some confidants of his of Transylvanian origin – some of whom had taken part in the peace preparations before joining the Second Department – set up the Bocskay Association to give support to the "detached Eastern

Hungarian territories." This later changed its name to the Populist Literary Society. Since the relations between the government and such social organizations were unclear, a government meeting on August 12, 1921, endorsed Bethlen's proposal for a Center for the Association of Social Societies[27] (TESZK), headed by Pál Teleki, with Antal Papp as executive deputy. The government decision stated that only the prime minister could take action on questions concerning the Hungarians beyond the borders, having listened to the requisite minister on each specific question. The task of TESZK was to coordinate social activity in Hungary to protect and support the interests of Hungarians abroad. This meant in practice that during Bethlen's premiership TESZK dispensed the funding for Hungarian social institutions, through the Rákóczi Association in Czechoslovakia, the Society of St. Gellért in the Southern Region (including the parts of the Banat south of the River Mureş ceded to Romania), and the Populist Literary Society in other parts of Romania.[28]

The allocation for operating the system and forwarding the subsidies amounted to 0.178–0.443 percent of the annual central budget in 1921–1931, or 10–35 percent of the Ministry of Foreign Affairs' allocation. The associations were not funded equally. This depended not only on the number of Hungarians that they covered, but also on the projects to fund and the relative lobbying powers of their officers. The Rákóczi Association (the Association of Upland Societies[29] after 1924) mainly channeled subsidies for political purposes: operation of the Hungarian parties and infrastructural support for them. Only 10–12 percent of the total went on cultural and educational purposes, whereas the Populist Literary Society[30] and the Society of St. Gellért spent the bulk of their funds on Church (educational) and cultural matters.[31]

But the task of the associations went beyond channeling subsidies. They gathered information, published books, and up to the end of the 1920s, ran hostels for Hungarian students in higher education from abroad.

The operation of TESZK falls into three stages. The first (1921–1925) was one of coordinating the work of the associations abroad financially and through propaganda for revision. In the next (1925–1932) it simply organized assistance from Hungary through the associations, and with the end of the Bethlen era in 1931, its task of channeling subsidies ceased. The government replaced it in the 1930s with a new framework that operated through the diplomatic missions and consulates. Of the three social associations, only the Populist Literary Society retained a more important role, as it continued to run the university hostel and scholarship schemes.[30]

Notes

1   For comprehensive accounts of Hungarian foreign policy at the time, see Ignác Romsics, *Hungary in the Twentieth Century* (Budapest, 1999), pp. 191–204. A monographic treatment of the question of territorial revision: Miklós Zeidler, *Ideas on Territorial Revision in Hungary 1920–1945* (Boulder, CO/Wayne, NJ, 2007).

2   Pál Pritz, "Revíziós törekvések a magyar külpolitikában 1920–1935" [Revisionist Efforts in Hungarian Foreign Policy 1920–1935], in Miklós Zeidler, ed., *Trianon* (Budapest, 2008), pp. 810–817.

3   Rothermere's articles: "Hungary's Place in the Sun. Safety for Central-Europe," *Daily Mail,* June 21, 1927. In book form: Lord Rothermere (Harold Sidney Harmsworth), *My Campaign for Hungary* (London, 1939), pp. 60–68. See also Ignác Romsics, "Hungary's Place in the Sun. A British Newspaper Article and Its Hungarian Repercussions," in László Péter and Martin Rady, eds., *British–Hungarian Relations since 1848* (London, 2004), pp. 193–204.

4   Ignác Romsics, "Magyarország helye a német Dél-Kelet-Európa politikában 1919–1944" [Hungary's Place in Germany's Southeastern Europe Policy 1919–1944], *Valóság* 35 (1992) 10: 12–39.

5   Magda Ádám, "The Little Entente and Issue of the Hungarian Minorities," in Ferenc Glatz, ed., *Etudes Historiques Hongroises 1990. II. Ethnicity and Society in Hungary* (Budapest, 1990), pp. 321–338.

6   On the Anglo-Italian plan for "peaceful revision" and the reactions of the Danube countries to it, see Mária Ormos, *Franciaország és a*

keleti biztonság 1931–1936 [France and Eastern Security 1931–1936] (Budapest, 1969), pp. 190–203.

7 The effect of the 1920 Treaty of Trianon had been to reduce the area of Hungary from 325,111 sq. km to 92,963 sq. km. The population in the 1910 census was 20,886,487 million (including Croatia–Slavonia) and in the 1920 census 7,986,875 million.

8 Miklós Zeidler, "Apponyi Albert, a 'nemzet ügyvédje'" [Albert Apponyi, "the Nation's Attorney"], *Európai Utas* 12 (2001) 1: 56–58.

9 A fuller, more professional exposition appears in Ödön Kuncz, *A trianoni békeszerződés revíziójának szükségessége. Emlékirat Sir Robert Gowerhez* [The Need to Revise the Treaty of Trianon. Memorandum to Sir Robert Gower] (Budapest, 1934). In English: pp. 18–31.

10 László Szarka, "Autonómia elképzelések a kisebbségi magyar pártok két világháború közötti politikájában" [Ideas of Autonomy in Minority Hungarian Parties in Politics between the World Wars], in Tibor Valuch, ed., *Hatalom és társadalom a XX. századi magyar történelemben* [Power and Society in 20th-Century Hungarian History] (Budapest, 1995), pp. 250–254.

11 This all provided the basis for arguments used in the peace talks at the end of World War I: "A magyar békedelegáció II. jegyzékének összefoglaló kivonata (Neuilly 1920. január 14.)" [Summary of the 2nd Note of the Hungarian Peace Delegation, Neuilly, January 14, 1920], in Zeidler, ed., *Trianon*, pp. 110–120. A monograph justification: László Buday, *A megcsonkított Magyarország* [Severed Hungary] (Budapest, 1921). On the outlook and activity of the Political Science Institute that provided the basis for revisionist propaganda and preparations, see András Rónai, *Térképezett történelem* [Mapped History] (Budapest, 1989), pp. 107–192, and Idem, *Atlas of Central Europe* (Balatonfüred/Budapest, 1945).

12 This was advocated internationally mainly by Albert Apponyi: Zeidler, "Apponyi Albert"; "Address of the President of the Hungarian Peace Delegation, Count Apponyi, to the Supreme Council, Jan. 16, 1920," in Francis Deák, *Hungary at the Paris Peace Conference. The Diplomatic History of the Treaty of Trianon* (New York, 1972 [1942]), pp. 539–549. It also dominated in the examinations of the history of relations between Hungary and its minorities and neighbors, of which the highest-quality example was József Deér and László Gáldi, eds., *Magyarok és románok* [Hungarians and Romanians], 2 vols. (Budapest, 1943).

13 This defined the foreign policy ideas of István Bethlen and Pál Teleki.

14 For a comparative summary, see Andreas [András] Rónai, "Herrschaftswechsel in Siebenbürgen. Anhang Nationalitätenpolitik vor Trianon und nach Trianon," in József Deér, ed., *Siebenbürgen* (Budapest, 1941), pp. 243–249. A post-war comparative work compiled in preparation for the post-World War II treaty: Sándor Bíró, *The Nationalities Problem in Transylvania 1867–1940* (Boulder, CO/ Highland Lakes, NJ, 1992).

15 Miklós Zeidler, "A Magyar Külügyi Társaság és folyóirata: a *Külügyi Szemle* (1920–1944)" [The Hungarian Foreign Policy Society and Its Journal, *Külügyi Szemle* (1920–1944)], *Külügyi Szemle* 1 (2002) 1: 151–176.

16 Albin Márffy, "A Magyar Statisztikai Társaság Államtudományi Intézete" [The Political Science Institute of the Hungarian Statistical Society], in Károly Mártonffy, ed., *Közigazgatásunk nemzetközi kapcsolatai* [International Relations of Our Public Administration] (Budapest, 1941), pp. 586–591.

17 Miklós Zeidler, "A Magyar Revíziós Liga" [The Hungarian Revisionist League], *Századok* (1997) 2: 303–351.

18 Benedek Jancsó, "A magyar társadalom és az idegen uralom alá került magyar kisebbség sorsa" [Hungarian Society and the Fate of the Hungarian Minority under Alien Rule], *Magyar Szemle* 1 (1927) 1: 50–57.

19 Béla Angyal, *Érdekvédelem és önszerveződés. Fejezetek a csehszlovákiai magyar pártpolitika történetéből 1918–1938* [Interest Protection and Self-Organization. Chapters from the History of Czechoslovakian Hungarian Party Politics 1918–1938] (Galánta/ Dunaszerdahely, 2002), pp. 39–55, 75–89 and 102–111; Nándor Bárdi, "Az ismeretlen vízmosás és a régi országút. Stratégiai útkeresés a romániai Országos Magyar Pártban, 1923–1924" [Unknown Gully and Old Highway. Strategic Path-Seeking in Romania's National Hungarian Party, 1923–1924], in Nándor Bárdi and Csilla Fedinec, eds., *Etnopolitika. A közösségi, magán- és nemzetközi érdekek viszonyrendszere Közép-Európában* [Ethno-Politics. The System of Relations in Communal, Private and International Interests in Central Europe] (Budapest, 2003), pp. 153–195; in Hungarian–Yugoslav relations, neither capital attached much significance to the Vojvodina Hungarians in reaching diplomatic decisions: Árpád Hornyák,

Magyar–jugoszláv diplomáciai kapcsolatok 1918–1927 [Hungarian–Yugoslav Diplomatic Relations 1918–1927] (Újvidék, 2004).

20 For an account of the Transylvania experiment, see Zsolt K. Lengyel, *Auf der Suche nach dem Kompromiss. Ursprünge und Gestalten des frühen Transsilvanismus 1918–1928* (Munich, 1991).

21 The successor to the Transylvanian Romanian National Party that Iuliu Maniu led – the National Peasant Party – gave the country its prime minister in 1928–1930 and 1931–1932. Romania's National Hungarian Party concluded electoral pacts with Averescu's People's Party in 1923, with the Liberal Party in 1926, and again in the same year with the People's Party. At the center of the Slovak People's Party's program in 1925 was autonomy for "Slovensko", but it only managed to win provincial administration when it joined the government coalition in 1927. The Smallholders' Party in Czechoslovakia, headed by József Szent-Ivány, tried an activist policy in 1926 (aiming to join the government), but failed for domestic political reasons – a governing majority was obtained instead by allying with a Sudeten German party. In the Serb-Croat-Slovene Kingdom, members of the Hungarian Party could only gain seats in Parliament on governing party tickets.

22 Gyula Popély, "A kisebbségi magyar pártpolitika megújulása a harmincas évek első felében" [Renewal of Minority Hungarian Party Politics in the First Half of the 1930s], *Regio* 1 (1990) 3: 97–132; Idem, "A magyar pártok 1936. évi fúziója Csehszlovákiában" [The Merger of Hungarian Parties in Czechoslovakia in 1936], *Regio* 1 (1990) 4; Franz Sz. Horváth, *Zwischen Ablehnung und Anpassung: politische Strategien der ungarischen Minderheitselite in Rumänien 1931–1940* (Munich, 2007), pp. 101–184.

23 The regular forum for argument and documentation in 1922–1942 was the periodical *Magyar Kisebbség* (Hungarian Minority), which appeared also in other languages (*Glasul Minorității̦lor, Die Stimme der Minderheiten, La Voix des Minorités*). For an overview of League of Nations publications, see Miklós Zeidler, "A Nemzetek Szövetsége és a magyar kisebbségi petíciók" [The League of Nations and Hungarian Minority Petitions], in Bárdi and Fedinec, eds., *Etnopolitika*, pp. 59–85.

24 See Note 13.

25 Ignác Romsics *et al.*, eds., *Magyarok kisebbségben és szórványban. A Magyar Miniszterelnökség Nemzetiségi és Kisebbségi Osztályának*

válogatott iratai, 1919–1944 [Hungarians in a Minority and in Isolated Settlements. Selected Documents of the Hungarian Prime Ministry's Department of Nationality and Minority Affairs 1919–1944] (Budapest, 1995).

26 Zeidler, "A Nemzetek Szövetsége," pp. 59–83; Ferenc Eiler, *Kisebbségvédelem és revízió. Magyar törekvések az Európai Nemzetiségi Kongresszuson (1925–1939)* [Minority Protection and Revision. Hungarian Efforts at the European Congress of Nationalities (1925–1939)] (Budapest, 2007).

27 *Társadalmi Egyesületek Szövetségének Központja.*

28 For an overall view of the whole subsidy system, see Nándor Bárdi, "'Action Osten'. Die Unterstützung der ungarischen Institutionen in Rumänien durch das Mutterland Ungarn in den 1920er Jahren," in *Ungarn-Jahrbuch 1997* (Munich, 1998).

29 Béla Angyal, "A csehszlovákiai magyarság anyaországi támogatása a két világháború között [Subsidies from the Kin-state for Czechoslovakia's Hungarians between the World Wars], *Regio* 11 (2000) 3: 133–178.

29 *Felvidéki Egyesületek Szövetsége.*

30 *Népies Irodalmi Társaság.*

31 "Keleti Akció, a Népies Irodalmi Társaság iratai" [Eastern Action. Documents of the Populist Literary Society], 1930–1943, 12 vols., Magyar Országos Levéltár (MOL) P 1077.

6. OUTCOMES AND INCONSISTENCIES IN HUNGARIAN POLICY ON TERRITORIAL REVISION

László Szarka

The Treaty of Trianon imposed on Hungary on June 4, 1920, remained a factor in Hungarian public thinking through the twentieth century – as an act of injustice by the Great Powers, evidence of unbridled nationalist expansionism in Hungary's neighbors, an obstacle to sober consideration of the question, or populist demands for full return of the lost territory. All appreciable political and public forces in interwar Hungary saw some revision of the borders laid down in the treaty as inevitable and essential.

It was commonly held across the political spectrum (for instance by Albert Apponyi, Miklós Horthy, Gyula Gömbös and even Ferenc Szálasi) that the ultimate aim was "integral revision" – full territorial restitution. The commonest arguments for this cited the geographical unity of historical Hungary or reformulated and updated versions of traditions of a multi-ethnic historical state ascribed to its founder, St. Stephen of Hungary.[1] Some, mainly in the opposition and on the left wing, accepted in part the nation-state realities of the new Central Europe and sought only the return of areas with an ethnic Hungarian majority. Yet others (among them two prominent prime ministers, Pál Teleki and István Bethlen) cited diplomatic realities, the need for international support for Hungary's claims, and maintenance of independence as reasons for asserting the territorial claims in stages.[2]

One influential writer of the period, Dezső Szabó, took a position that altered from time to time. Another, László Németh, saw a lasting solution in idealized cooperation among the Danubian peoples, with gradual extension of minority rights and "spiritualization" of national borders. A similar view was taken by the émigré Oszkár Jászi, who echoed the sentiments of more sober figures in Hungarian

142

government, having discovered at first hand, as a member of the short-lived Hungarian National Council of 1918–1919, the risks of armed conflict inherent in a policy of territorial revision.[3]

Ultimately, the chances depended not on domestic political debate in Hungary, but on power relations in interwar Europe.[4] After Hitler came to power in 1933, there was increased antagonism between the Great Powers, divided between those for and those against preserving the Versailles status quo. The situation prompted Hungary to press for Great-Power support for its territorial objectives, where possible seeking peaceful, diplomatic means of attaining them, although this was only successful for the predominantly Hungarian-inhabited parts of Czechoslovakia, recovered in the autumn of 1938.[5]

Britain and France stood back from the problem, which meant that Hungary's plans to revise its borders could be furthered only by Germany and Italy. There was no thought in Berlin of accommodating Hungary's claims during the *Anschluss* of March 13, 1938, either in Burgenland or in Devín and Petržalka, two former Hungarian villages in Slovakia annexed at the same time. At the Kiel talks in August 1938, Hitler offered Hungary the whole of Slovakia if it would act as an initiator of the dismemberment of Czechoslovakia. This was rejected by Governor Miklós Horthy on the advice of Hungarian Minister of Foreign Affairs Kálmán Kánya and the Hungarian chief of staff. Hitler then went ahead with stepping up pressure on Czechoslovakia. Britain and France, anxious to resolve the crisis and avert world war, came to see detachment of minority-dominated areas of Czechoslovakia as the means to do it, which prepared the way for the Munich Agreement on September 29, 1938, after four-power negotiations to which Czechoslovakia was not invited.[6]

So Hungary's insistence on "integral revision" had to be abandoned (for Slovakia and then Transcarpathia) in favor of the ethnic principle and a bilateral deal presaged by an addendum to the Munich Agreement. Czechoslovakia lost the Sudeten German territories, and after an ultimatum from Warsaw, the mainly Polish settlements in Silesia and Orava County. On October 6, 1938, Slovakia's autonomy

was proclaimed at Žilina.[7] A few days later, an autonomous Transcarpathian government formed under András Bródy (Andrej Brody)
at Khust, and was recognized by Prague two days later.[8]

Referring to the Munich Agreement, Hungary sought a bilateral
agreement with Czechoslovakia as fast as possible, basing its ethnic
claims on the 1910 census returns. At talks held in Komárno on
October 9–13, 1938, the Hungarian government delegation was
headed by Teleki and Kánya and the Czechoslovak one by Jozef Tiso,
but these foundered on rival interpretations of the Hungarian and
Czechoslovak census returns, especially as they concerned the four
largest cities in the territory affected: Bratislava, Nitra, Košice and
Užhorod. At that point, Italian diplomacy, orchestrated by Mussolini
and Ciano, tended to favor Hungarian arguments, and the Third
Reich's diplomacy, under Hitler and Ribbentrop, Czechoslovakia's.
A decision was reached on November 2, 1938, by means of German–
Italian arbitration, as the First Vienna Award. This took the 1910
census returns as its starting point and awarded Hungary two of the
cities: Košice and Užhorod.[9]

The Hungarian politicians of Slovakia and Transcarpathia worked
to ensure a calm atmosphere for the bilateral and international
negotiations. They prepared a memorandum and also gave an oral
report to the British negotiator, Lord Runciman, as well as making
contact with Warsaw and Rome, but this won them no invitations to
the Komárno talks or the Vienna tribunal. On October 3 they formed
a Slovensko Hungarian National Council, and shortly afterwards a
Transcarpathian National Council as well. These two bodies broke
with the earlier autonomy policy and demanded that the borders
be changed. However, the views of the Hungarian minority played
practically no part in either negotiating process.[10]

The territory granted to Hungary by the First Vienna Award
was occupied in the first half of November 1938. After twenty
years of Czechoslovak rule, the "return" was greeted by most of
the population of former Upper Hungary with euphoria, as an act
of historical justice. The rulings of the German–Italian tribunal
were given specific form in several bilateral agreements, finalizing

the new frontier, exchanging certain settlements, dealing with the Czechoslovak settlers in the reannexed areas and their property, addressing the minority question, and settling matters such as trade, and postal and rail services. Britain and France endorsed the First Vienna Award, with some reservations, although they had played no part in arbitrating it.

Western assessments of the Czechoslovak question and of Hungarian border revision changed radically when Hitler invaded Czechoslovakia on March 14, 1939, thrust qualified independence on Slovakia, and *de facto* annexed the remainder of the country to the Reich as the Protectorate of Bohemia and Moravia. At the same time, Berlin concurred with a Hungarian invasion of the Transcarpathia of Avgusthyn Voloshyn, then known officially as "Podkarpatská Rus." The Hungarian forces defeated the *Sich* Guards of the Voloshyn government and advanced to the Polish frontier, also annexing 65 settlements along the eastern border of Slovakia.[11]

Administrative efforts ensued to integrate the reoccupied areas economically and culturally into the Hungarian state. Despite some success, this soon precipitated regional differences of interest. The Hungarians of the returned Upper Hungary had met in the minority period with the democracy prevalent in Czechoslovakia and did not feel that they were receiving clear support from Hungarian officialdom, notably in the case of the Hungarian reversal of the Czechoslovak land reform and in the parent country's stance in administrative political decision-making.[12]

The autonomous and then semi-independent Slovakia was dismayed by the First Vienna Award, as it had lost the city of Košice and three islands of largely Slovak settlement in Slovenský Meder/ Šurany, Nógrád and Gemer. The Slovak legislature began to apply the principle of reciprocity, placing obstacles to the operation of János Esterházy's Hungarian party and infringing Hungarian cultural and economic interests.[13]

Hungary's territorial demands on Romania in Transylvania were affected by three main factors: the international position of Romania, especially after the Molotov–Ribbentrop pact of August

23, 1939; the ethnic topology of the territories ceded to Romania after Trianon; and the places of both countries in Hitler's plans for a second world war. Furthermore, the Teleki government was keen to ensure at least tacit agreement from the Western powers for its moves to revise its frontiers, which it could not expect from either Britain or France in the case of Transylvania.[14]

The German–Soviet pact proved advantageous to Hungary over Transylvania in several respects. The German/Soviet occupation of Poland had made the Soviet Union an immediate neighbor, and both powers were prepared to support Hungary's demands in Transylvania. During the short pre-war period of Soviet–Hungarian rapprochement, the Soviet Union stated several times that it had no objections to Hungary's revisionist efforts there. Britain and the United States were prepared to accept limited border changes based on bilateral agreement. Germany, as it prepared for war on the Soviet Union, sought the soonest possible end to the Hungarian–Romanian dispute, by mutual agreement.

The next development was a four-day Soviet military campaign against Romania, launched on June 28, 1940. The Soviet Union occupied northern Bukovina and Bessarabia, thereby becoming the first power to overturn Romania's territorial settlement under the Versailles system. Budapest made strong use of the Bessarabian precedent, but sought to avoid any appearance of cooperating with the Soviet Union. As Hungary weighed up the risks of armed intervention in Romania, it was interrupted a second time by joint German–Italian arbitration. Pressure from Berlin induced the two countries to hold talks at Turnu Severin in mid-August. The formula of a German–Italian tribunal was revived after the Romanian government found Hungary's alternative territorial proposals unacceptable.

The Second Vienna Award of August 30, 1940, came out in favor of a Northern Transylvanian "ethnic corridor" to link Hungarian-majority areas and other areas with a relatively strong Hungarian ethnic presence in the Partium, Northern Transylvania and the Székely Land. The division of historical Transylvania caused grave concern and antagonism among the Hungarian and the Romanian public alike, especially the Hungarian Székelys (Szeklers). For a time public delight in Hungary at the return of Transylvanian cities with a mainly Hungarian population and of the Székely Land overrode the anxieties about new conflicts after the border change. But the Romanian public was deeply offended by this second almost immediate infringement of the country's sovereignty, involving territory seen as vital to Romanian national development and a transfer to Hungary of some 1.1 million ethnic Romanians. The subsequent riots led to the king's abdication and rapid installation of the totalitarian Antonescu regime.[15]

Based on agreements at Borşa and Debrecen between military delegations of the two governments, the Hungarian army occupied the land granted under the Second Vienna Award on September 5–15, 1940. There was a huge welcome for the arriving army from Hungarian society in Transylvania, after decades of indignities, persecution and grievances as a minority. Celebrations of the "return of Transylvania" were remembered by many for the rest of their lives, and the annexation greatly reinforced the Hungarian identity of the Hungarians in the reoccupied region. But the ensuing months of Hungarian military administration brought about many local conflicts. The bloodiest reprisals for attacks on the army took place in Sălaj County, at Treznea on September 9 and at Ip and Marca on September 13–14. Altogether 243 people lost their lives in these brutal reprisals.[16]

During September and October 1940, the two sides held so called liquidation talks to find mutually acceptable solutions for the Hungarian and Romanian inhabitants of divided Transylvania, but the initiative was swamped by the waves of refugees and deportees in both directions and by the related confiscations of property. From the outset the Antonescu regime with its totalitarian methods opposed any rapprochement with Hungary, thereby expressing its refusal to recognize the validity of the Second Vienna Award. This was underlined by a statement issued by the Romanian government on March 15, 1941.[17]

The Hungarian government sought to consolidate the conditions in Northern Transylvania and the Székely Land as rapidly as possible. Once civilian government had been introduced on November 26, 1940, attempts were made to address the grievances of the Hungarians. Major investments were made in education and culture, transport and infrastructure.[18]

The two Vienna Awards left the Hungarian government strongly indebted and committed to Hitler's Germany. It had already subscribed to the Anti-Comintern Pact in February 1939, and it joined the Tripartite Pact on November 20, 1940. Despite some promising diplomatic moves, neither Horthy nor the Teleki government was willing to cooperate with the Soviets, as such action would probably have led to rapid German occupation.[19]

After the German occupation of Poland, the one weak alternative to alliance with the Axis that remained was Hungarian–Yugoslav cooperation. Teleki had pressed deliberately for the so-called treaty of eternal friendship between the two countries, seeking thereby to preserve Hungary's neutrality and to encourage confidential relations with the Western Allies. The treaty signed in Belgrade on December 12, 1940, simply alluded to the unsettled political questions between the two countries (concerning territory and the minorities) and sought to postpone mutual agreement on them.

As the Germans and Italians spread ever more aggressively through East-Central and Southeastern Europe, the Balkans became a strategically important region, especially Western-oriented Yugoslavia. Two days after the latter's sudden accession to the Tripartite Agreement on March 25, 1941, there was a *coup d'état* in which the now pro-German Regent Paul was replaced by his young nephew King Peter II and a government headed by Dušan Simović. Hitler immediately began to prepare an invasion.

Hungary, indebted to Germany for the Vienna Awards, faced a grave dilemma. Joining in Germany's military aggression irrevocably lost it the goodwill of the Western Allies, and subsequently any chance of retaining the territorial gains that it had made. Yet to have rejected Germany's overture would have gone against the revisionist aims pursued through the period, by precluding the recovery even of territories with a majority of Hungarian inhabitants, still living in the ignominious state of a minority. The dilemma appeared in its most extreme form in the case of Yugoslavia, less than four months after the treaty of eternal friendship had been signed. Horthy, with an eye to the territorial claims that Hungary was still making against Yugoslavia, had assured Hitler on March 28 that there could be Hungarian–German military cooperation, in view of the "common lot" of the two countries.

Prime Minister Teleki tried to make Hungary's military participation in the invasion conditional on circumstances that might excuse his country breaching the treaty of eternal friendship. But participation meant abandoning two basic ideas behind Hungary's policy for territorial revision. None of the Western Allies was prepared to condone Hungary's attack on Yugoslavia, and they stated their opposition to Hungary's pursuing its territorial objectives by military means. As the German forces began to pass through Hungary on April 2 to launch the attack, it became clear that Hungary was now in a dependent position. It can be assumed from a suicide note, addressed to Horthy, that this moral problem, or some aspects of it, prompted Pál Teleki to take his own life on the night of April 3, 1941.[20]

Military action by Hungary, commencing on April 11, 1941, after the formation of the so-called Independent Croatian State, resulted within three days in the capture of Bačka, south Baranja and Međimurje. Southern Region Hungarians greeted the invaders as a liberating army freeing them from oppression as a minority, although there was disappointment that the Banat came under German military control and part of Međimurje went to Croatia under a bilateral agreement. In the event only 55 percent of the lands lost to the South Slav state under Trianon was regained – 11,475 square kilometers, with some 1,300,000 inhabitants, of whom 39 percent were Hungarians.[21]

The Hungarian army met with no appreciable resistance from the Serbs before Yugoslavia capitulated on April 17, but the number of Serb civilian victims rose steadily, due to a spate of charges brought in the occupied territories. Serious local incidents proliferated, due to false intelligence and poor knowledge of local conditions. The worst of these occurred at Sirig, a village of Serb settlers that belonged to Temerin, where locals were driven out to greet the Hungarian forces, who suddenly surrounded them and killed over 100 of them (470 according to one Serb report).

Cleansing operations began all over Bačka on April 18. During these, several tens of thousands of post-war Serb settlers (*dobrovoljac*), Jews, and others labeled unreliable were interned, and a still larger number of Serbs were deported to German-occupied Serbia, the Banat and Croatia.[22] To replace them the Hungarian government imported 3,279 northern Bukovina Székely families (about 13,200 people) into 14 settler villages in Bačka in May and June 1941, under an agreement with Romania signed on May 11, 1941, whereby the land-starved Székelys (descendants of eighteenth-century settlers in Bukovina) would evacuate the villages of Józseffalva, Istensegíts, Hadikfalva, Andrásfalva and Fogadjisten (now Vornicenii Mici, Țibeni, Dornești, Măneuți and Iacobești respectively).[23]

Alongside the cleansings and internments that continued throughout the year, costing many civilian lives, there appeared signs of Serb and communist partisan resistance. Acts of sabotage proliferated in October 1941. Martial law and summary trials were introduced by Lieutenant General Ferenc Szombathelyi, successor to Henrik Werth as chief of staff, but were approved only subsequently, on October 28, by the Hungarian government, and were aimed mainly at diversionary and partisan actions by the Serb communists.

The incidents in Čurug and Žabalj, which had slid into armed conflict, were followed on January 4, 1942, by a full-scale raid from the direction of the Šajkaš district of south Bačka, ordered by Szombathelyi and led by Lieutenant General Ferenc Feketehalmy-

Czeydner. The increasingly savage operations aimed at suspected Chetniks,[24] partisans and communists, as well as Serbs and Jews accused of assisting them, spread on January 15 to Stari Bečej and Srbobran and the city of Novi Sad. The three-day raid across Novi Sad became a pogrom in which innocent Jews of all ages were massacred by Hungarian forces. Those days in Bačka are estimated to have cost several thousand civilian lives. There was a temporary lull in the communist and partisan actions against the Hungarian regime, but they did more damage to Hungary's international reputation than any military act before them.[25]

The four border changes brought Hungary's area to 172,200 square kilometers at the end of 1941, and brought its population to 14.7 million. The Romanians, Rusyns, Serbs and Slovaks in the acquired territories made the country more multi-ethnic: the proportion of native Hungarian speakers in the population fell to 77.5 percent. So the result was equivocal in terms of an ethnically based policy of territorial revision.[26]

Notes

1   See, for example, Jenő Szűcs, *Nemzet és történelem. Tanulmányok* [Nation and History. Studies] (Budapest, 1984), p. 35.
2   Summarizing the revisionist ideology and strategy: Miklós Zeidler, *Ideas on Territorial Revision in Hungary 1920–1945* (Boulder, CO/Wayne, NJ/New York, 2007); Anikó Kovács-Bertrand, *Der ungarische Revisionismus nach dem Ersten Weltkrieg. Der publizistische Kampf gegen den Friedensvertrag von Trianon 1918–1931* (Munich, 1997). Trianon: Béla K. Király, Peter Pastor and Ivan Sanders, eds., *Essays on World War I: Total War and Peacemaking, a Case Study on Trianon* (New York, 1982); Miklós Zeidler, ed., *Trianon* (Budapest, 2008); Miroslav Michela, *Pod heslom integrity. Slovenská otázka v politike Maďarska 1918–1921* [Under the Slogan of Integrity. The Slovak Issue in Hungarian Policy 1918–1921] (Bratislava, 2009). For revisionist views of Hungarian politicians and public figures, see Ignác Romsics, ed., *Trianon és a magyar politikai gondolkodás, 1920–1953* [Trianon and Hungarian Political Thinking, 1920–1953] (Budapest, 1998); the following contributions are worth

listing: sections on Pál Teleki (by Balázs Ablonczy), pp. 12–30; István Bethlen (by Lóránt Péteri), pp. 31–50; Gyula Gömbös (by Miklós Zeidler), pp. 70–97; Ferenc Szálasi (by Krisztián Ungváry), pp. 117–133; Jászi Oszkár (by Gábor Richly and Balázs Ablonczy), pp. 134–155; László Németh (by Nándor Bárdi), pp. 175–192.

3   Jászi covers the most important issues, dilemmas of the revision in his English-language works. See for example Oscar Jászi, *Revolution and Counter-Revolution in Hungary* (London, 1924); Idem, *The Dissolution of the Habsburg Monarchy* (Chicago, 1929); Idem, "Neglected Aspects of the Danubian Drama," *The Slavonic and East European Review* 14 (July 1935) 40: 53–67.

4   The limited scope in Hungarian foreign policy: Pál Pritz, "Magyarország külpolitikája a formálódó Berlin–Róma tengely árnyékában," *Századok* (1981) 5: 921–954; Idem, "Entscheidungsprozesse in der ungarischen Aussenpolitik (1919–1944)," in Gábor Máthé, ed., *Theorie und Institutionsystem der Gewaltentrennung in Europa* (Budapest, 1993), pp. 173–191; Idem, "Hungarian Foreign Policy in the Interwar Period," *Hungarian Studies* 17 (2003) 1: 13–32; Magda Ádám, *The Little Entente and Europe (1920–1929)* (Budapest, 1993).

5   Hungary's claims against Czechoslovakia and actions in 1938: K. Jörg Hoensch, *Der ungarische Revisionismus und die Zerschlagung der Tschechoslowakei* (Tübingen, 1967), p. 323; Henry Delfiner, *Vienna Broadcasts to Slovakia, 1938–1939: a Case Study in Subversion* (Boulder, CO/New York, 1974); Edward Chaszar, *Decision in Vienna: the Czechoslovak–Hungarian Border Dispute of 1938* (Astor, FL, 1978); Nandor F. Dreisziger, *Hungary's Way to World War II* (Astor Park, FL, 1968); Eric Roman, "Munich and Hungary: an Overview of Hungarian Diplomacy during the Sudeten Crisis," *East European Quarterly* 8 (March 1974) 1: 71–97; Thomas L. Sakmyster, *Hungary, the Great Powers and the Danubian Crisis, 1936–1939* (Athens, 1980).

6   Magda Ádám, "The Munich Crisis and Hungary: the Fall of the Versailles Settlement in Central Europe," in Igor Lukes and Erik Goldstein, eds., *The Munich Crisis 1938, Prelude to World War II* (London, 1999), pp. 82–121; Gergely Sallai, *"A határ megindul..." A csehszlovákiai magyar kisebbség és Magyarország kapcsolatai az 1938–1939. évi államhatár-változások tükrében* ["The Frontier Moves Off..." Relations between the Czechoslovakian Hungarian

Minority and Hungary in the Light of the 1938–1939 Border Changes]
(Bratislava, 2009), pp. 81–112.

7   The question of Slovak autonomy: K. Jörg Hoensch, *Die Slowakei
und Hitlers Ostpolitik. Hlinkas Slowakische Volkspartei zwischen
Autonomie und Separation 1938/1939* (Cologne/Graz, 1965); James
Ramon Felak, *At the Price of the Republic: Hlinka's Slovak People's
Party, 1929–1938* (Pittsburgh, PA, 1995).

8   Paul R. Magocsi and Ivan Pop, *Encyclopedia of Rusyn History and
Culture* (Toronto, 2005); Christian Ganzer, *Die Karpato-Ukraine
1938/39: Spielball im internationalen Interessenkon☐ikt am Vorabend
des Zweiten Weltkrieges* (Hamburg, 2001); Albert S. Kotowski,
"Ukrainisches Piemont? Die Karpatenukraine am Vorabend des
Zweiten Weltkrieges," *Jahrbücher für Geschichte Osteuropas* 49
(2001) 1: 67–95; Mykola Vegesh, "Ukrajna belpolitikai helyzete,
1938–1939" [Ukraine's Domestic Situation, 1938–1939], in Csilla
Fedinec, ed., *Kárpátalja 1938–1941. Magyar és ukrán történeti
közelítés* [Transcarpathia 1938–1941. Hungarian and Ukrainian
Historical Rapprochement] (Budapest, 2004), pp. 21–36; Vasyl
Hudanych, "Mi volt a Kárpáti Szics?" [What Was the Carpathian
Sich?], in *ibid.*, pp. 37–52. The *Sich* was a separatist defense force.

9   László Szarka, "The Principle and Practice of Ethnic Revision in
Hungary's Foreign Policy in Connection with the First Vienna
Award," in Ferenc Eiler and Dagmar Hájková, eds., *Czech and
Hungarian Minority Policy in Central Europe 1918–1938* (Prague/
Budapest, 2009), pp. 135–153.

10   Comprehensive Slovakian Sourcebook on the Vienna Award, see
Ladislav Deák *Viedenská arbitráž. 2 november 1938.* [The Vienna
Award, November 2, 1938] Vol. I–III (Bratislava, 2002–2006); Gergely
Sallai, "Az első bécsi döntés diplomáciai és politikai előtörténete"
[Diplomatic and Political Antecedents to the First Vienna Award],
Századok (2000) 3: 597–631; Gyula Popély, "A müncheni döntéstől
a komáromi tárgyalások megszakadásáig" [From the Munich
Agreement to the Break-Up of the Komárno Talks], *Magyar Szemle*
7 (1993) 11: 1133–1151.

11   Ladislav Deák, *Malá vojna* [The Little War] (Bratislava, 1993); Paul
R. Magocsi, *The Rusyn-Ukrainians of Czechoslovakia: an Historical
Survey* (Vienna, 1983); Iryna Haponenko-Tóth, "Kárpáti Ukrajna
magyar megszállása (1938. november–1939. március)" [Hungarian
Occupation of Carpathian Ukraine, November 1938–March 1939],
in Fedinec, ed., *Kárpátalja 1938–1941*, pp. 71–86.

12   On the first Slovakian state: Mark W. A. Axworthy, *Axis Slovakia –*
     Hitler's Slavic Wedge, 1938–1945 (Bayside, NY, 2002). Hungary's
     image of Czechoslovakia's Hungarian elite: Tamás Gusztáv Filep,
     "Két előadás a visszatért magyarokról. Felföldi társadalomkutatók az
     1938 utáni magyarországi viszonyokról" [Two Lectures on Returned
     Hungarians. Upland Social Researchers on Conditions in Hungary
     after 1938], in Idem, *A humanista voksa. Írások a csehszlovákiai*
     magyar kisebbség történetének köréből 1918–1945 [Humanist Voice.
     Writings on the History of the Czechoslovakian Hungarian Minority
     1918–1945] (Pozsony, 2007), pp. 187–221. The "return" problem
     is treated in detail in László Bukovszky, "A visszacsatolt Felvidék
     (Dél-Felvidék) közigazgatási szervezete" [The Administrative
     Structure of the Reannexed Upland (The South Upland)], *Limes* 20
     (2007) 4: 53–64, Gábor Demeter and Zsolt Radics, "A Dél-Felvidék
     reintegrációjának gazdaság- és társadalomföldrajzi vonatkozásai"
     [Economic and Socio-Geographical Aspects of Reintegration in the
     South Upland], *ibid.*, pp. 65–82, István Gaucsík, "Bankstratégia
     a dél-felvidéki területeken (1938–1941)" [Bank Strategy in South
     Upland Territories (1938–1941)], *ibid.*, pp. 83–97, and Gyula Popély,
     "Az iskolai nemzetnevelés problémái az 1938 novemberében
     felszabadult felvidéki területeken" [Problems of School National
     Education in Upland Territories Liberated in November 1938], *ibid.*,
     pp. 133–140.

13   On Esterházy: Gabor Szent-Ivany, *Count Janos Esterhazy. The Life*
     and Works of the Great Son of the Hungarian Highland (Astor, FL,
     1989), at http://www.hungarian-history.hu/lib/esterh/esterh00.htm.
     A detailed picture: *A szlovákiai magyarság élete 1938–1942* [Life of
     the Slovakian Hungarians 1938–1942] (Budapest, 1948). The lessons
     and community strategies of the second minority period: János
     Esterházy, "A szlovákiai magyar család élete a második sorsforduló
     óta" [Life of the Slovakian Hungarian Family after the Second Turn
     of Events], in *ibid.*, pp. 7–20; Rezső Peéry, "Perem-magyarok"
     [Marginal Hungarians], in *ibid.*, pp. 21–34.

14   Pál Pritz, "La crise de guerre internationalle et la Hongrie (1938–
     1941)," *Guerres mondiales et conflits contemporains: revue d'historie*
     (September 2001): 67–82; Zeidler, *Ideas on Territorial Revision*, pp.
     255–279; András D. Bán, *Hungarian–British Diplomacy, 1938–1941.*
     The Attempt to Maintain Relations (London/Portland, OR, 2004).

15 Preparations: András Rónai, *Térképezett történelem* [Mapped History] (Budapest, 1989). Diplomatic and political ties: Béni L. Balogh, *A magyar–román kapcsolatok 1939–1940-ben és a második bécsi döntés* [Hungarian–Romanian Relations in 1939–1940 and the Second Vienna Award] (Csíkszereda, 2002).

16 Péter Illésfalvi, "'Édes Erdély itt vagyunk.' Az 1940-es erdélyi bevonulás során történt atrocitásokról" ["Dear Transylvania, Here We Are." The Atrocities during the 1940 Entry into Transylvania], *Pro Minoritate* 9 (2004) 1: 58–77.

17 Béni L. Balogh, "A magyar–román viszony és az erdélyi kérdés 1940–1944 között" [Hungarian–Romanian Relations and the Transylvania Question 1940–1944], in Gyöngy Kovács Kiss, ed., *Történelmünk a Kárpát–medencében 1926–1956–2006* [Our History in the Carpathian Basin 1926–1956–2006] (Kolozsvár, 2006), pp. 19–27.

18 For works on conditions in Northern Transylvania in 1940–1944, see the following: digital text base www.adatbank.ro; Zeidler, *Ideas on Territorial Revision*, pp. 279–286; Holly Case, *Between States: The Transylvanian Question and the European Idea during World War II* (Stanford, CA, 2009), pp. 67–198; the whole of *Limes* 19 (2006) 2 (a themed issue), especially the following: Csaba Gidó and László Márton, "Észak-Erdély és Magyarország 1940. évi gazdasági fejlettségének összehasonlítása" [Economic Development Comparison between Northern Transylvania and Hungary, 1940], *Limes* 19 (2006) 2: 19–42; Edit Csilléry, "Közalkalmazottak és köztisztviselők Észak-Erdélyben a második bécsi döntést követően" [Public Employees and Officials in Northern Transylvania after the Second Vienna Award], *ibid.*, pp. 73–92; András Tóth-Bartos, "Háromszék vármegye gazdaságának fejlesztésére tett próbálkozások 1940–1944 között" [Attempts to Develop the Economy of Trei Scaune County 1940–1944], *ibid.*, pp. 107–118; Nándor Bárdi, "A múlt, mint tapasztalat. A kisebbségből többségbe került erdélyi magyar politika szemléletváltása 1940–1944 között" [The Past as Experience. Change of Outlook in Transylvanian Hungarian Politics after the Minority/Majority Shift], *ibid.*, pp. 43–70.

19 Miklós Zeidler and Béni L. Balogh, "Az 'Erdély-kérdés' a magyar–szovjet külkapcsolatokban" [The "Transylvanian Question" in Hungarian–Soviet Relations], *2000* 14 (2002) 3: 41–67.

20   The background and farewell note appear in Zeidler, *Ideas on Territorial Revision*, pp. 273–279; also see Balázs Ablonczy, *Pál Teleki (1874–1941): The Life of a Controversial Hungarian Politician* (Boulder, CO, 2006) on Teleki. The note, to be delivered to Horthy if the suicide attempt succeeded, read as follows: "Your Serene Highness! We have become breakers of our word – out of cowardice – in defiance of the Treaty of Eternal Friendship. The nation feels this, and we have thrown away its honor. We have placed ourselves on the side of the scoundrels – for there is not a word of truth in the stories of atrocities – against either the Hungarians or the Germans! We shall become the despoilers of corpses, the most abominable of nations! I did not restrain you. I am guilty." Quoted in translation in Paul Lendvai, *The Hungarians: a Thousand Years of Victory in Defeat* (London, 2003), p. 408.

21   Enikő A. Sajti, *Hungarians in the Voivodina 1918–1947* (Boulder, CO/ Highland Lakes, NJ, 200), pp. 191–233; László Göncz, *Felszabadulás vagy megszállás? A Muramente 1941–1945* [Liberation or Occupation? Along the Mura 1941–1945] (Lendava, 2006).

22   Sajti, *Hungarians in the Voivodina*, pp. 234–249.

23   *Ibid.*, pp. 250–297; Enikő A. Sajti, *Székely telepítés és nemzetiségi politika a Bácskában* [Székely Settlement and Minority Policy in Bačka] (Budapest, 1987).

24   Originally a Serbian nationalist and royalist organization, the Chetniks turned after 1941 to supporting the Axis occupation against Tito's partisan forces.

25   Sajti, *Hungarians in the Voivodina*, pp. 342–402.

26   Detailed socioeconomic statistics appeared in the following: "A vissza-csatolt északi terület" [Reannexed Northern Territory], *Magyar Statisztikai Szemle* 6 (1938) 1–12: 1011–1158; "Az 1939. március közepén birtokba vett kárpátaljai terület" [Transcarpathian Territory Obtained in Mid-March 1939], *Magyar Statisztikai Szemle* 7 (1939) 8: 196–240; "A visszacsatolt keleti terület" [Reannexed Eastern Territory], *Magyar Statisztikai Szemle* 8 (1940) 8: 657–787; "A visszafoglalt délvidéki terület" [Reannexed Southern Region Territory], *Magyar Statisztikai Szemle* 9 (1941) 11: 767–821.

7. MINORITY HUNGARIANS
AND CENTRAL EUROPEAN LAND REFORMS
Attila Simon and *Attila Kovács*

The objective of the interwar Czechoslovak, Yugoslav and Romanian governments, sometimes tacitly, sometimes openly, was to establish nation states. One method employed was to weaken the economic power of the minorities and nationalize industry, agriculture and banking. For economic power brought political power, and a Hungarian minority shorn of its property became more vulnerable in political, cultural and educational terms as well. The main vehicle of the Czechoslovak, Yugoslav and Romanian nationalization process was land reform, to transfer land ownership to the nation that constituted the state.

Almost every country in Europe took up the question of reorganizing land ownership after the First World War. Land ownership in most of the still mainly agricultural countries of Central Europe was skewed, most of the farmland being owned by a few aristocratic landowners, while most villagers owned little or no land. The land reforms of the 1920s in Romania, Yugoslavia and Czechoslovakia showed great similarities: (1) Aside from their social and economic objectives, they were intended to weaken the politico-economic positions of the Hungarian minority. (2) They were accompanied by resettlement campaigns that brought Romanian, South Slav or Czechoslovak colonists into Hungarian-speaking areas.

Slovakia and Transcarpathia

Land reform was announced in Czechoslovakia in November 1918, just after the republic had been declared. Apart from its social and economic intentions, it had the open objective of transferring land from German and Hungarian to Czech and Slovak ownership. The Sequestration Act of April 1919 set upper limits on permissible land ownership of 150 ha for farmland and 250 ha for other land (forest, pasture, and so on). Land that exceeded those limits was seized by the State Land Office against compensation. The area of land seized in Slovakia and Transcarpathia was 740,000 ha, of which 113,000 ha could be claimed back by its original owners, while the rest was put up for sale to legitimate claimants under the Allocation Act of January 30, 1920. Although one objective of the land reform was to reinforce peasant farming, most of the best sequestered land was parceled into so-called residual estates of 100 ha for sale to those close to the government. This created a new, loyal stratum of middling landowners who were not German or Hungarian, but Czech or Slovak.

The land reform had a particularly strong effect in the southern Slovakian region inhabited by Hungarians. On the one hand that was where most of the large sequestered estates lay, but on the other more than 60 percent of the inhabitants were earning their living from agriculture. There were plenty of potential Hungarian claimants, and the number of landless agricultural workers and day laborers in agriculture was much greater among the Hungarians (42 percent) than the national average. Yet the partiality of the State Land Office meant that only 20 percent of the land redistributed in the Hungarian-majority districts of southern Slovakia and Transcarpathia went to local Hungarian people. The rest went to residual estate owners, settlers and other claimants, or passed into state ownership. That left large numbers of Hungarian estate workers and poor peasants without a livelihood and highly susceptible to communist agitation.[1]

The national objectives of the Czechoslovak land reform became clearer during the ensuing colonization campaign, for claimants under the Allocation Act could also apply for land outside their place of residence. Using this loophole, the State Land Office set out to attract tens of thousands of Czech and Slovak claimants to the southern, Hungarian-inhabited districts of Slovakia and

Transcarpathia, where they were granted holdings averaging 12 ha of farmland and received substantial subsidies to buy the holding and start farming it. The colonies were usually sited so as to break up the uniform Hungarian character of the district, place a buffer between the Hungarian-language area and a nearby city (such as Bratislava or Galanta), or extend the Slovak-language area southward to the border.

One type of colony consisted of villages founded to defend the border and populated with legionnaires from the Czechoslovak foreign legions that had fought in World War I. These legionnaires living right by the Hungarian border were still army reservists who could be mobilized at any time. They were also used to guard railway junctions. Major legionnaire settlements were sited at Buzitka (formerly Nógrád County), Gerňov (formerly Gömör–Kishont County) and Solomonovo by the River Tysa in Transcarpathia.

The Czechoslovak colonization program brought over 3,300 Czech, Moravian and Slovak families to 143 communities in southern Slovakia, and some 300 families to 16 colonies in Transcarpathia.[2] The colonists, mainly from the northern mountains, found it hard to adjust to strange natural and farming conditions, and many had financial troubles. Furthermore, it was hard to gain acceptance from local inhabitants, who had been overlooked in the reform, and as a result there were constant ethnic tensions.

When the Hungarian-inhabited areas of Slovakia and Transcarpathia were reannexed to Hungary under the First Vienna Award in the autumn of 1938, over 70 percent of the settlers came under Hungarian rule. Some 400 families left their colonies before the Hungarian army arrived, and double that number were deported by the Hungarian authorities. The remaining 1,200 or so colonists stayed put throughout the war.[3]

Romania

The unusual feature of the land reform in Romania was that separate arrangements were made for each part of the country (the Regat, Transylvania, Bessarabia and the Banat). The main reason was not simply the topographical differences, but the aims of nation-building policy as well.

The Land Ownership Act of July 30, 1921, that applied to the annexed territories of Eastern Hungary and Transylvania differed from the legislation in the Regat in not setting an upper limit to the total area of land to be sequestered, and it gave greater scope for expropriating the land of public institutions (schools and churches) than the legislation in other parts of the country. It also stipulated that land could be seized without compensation from those who had resided abroad other than on public business between December 1, 1918, and publication of the act. This affected thousands of Hungarians who had fled from Transylvania to Hungary for a longer or shorter period (even a few days) at the time of annexation.

As in Czechoslovakia, the act discriminated against the Hungarians of Romania in the way in which sequestered land was reallocated. According to official statistics issued on June 1, 1927, the land reform in Transylvania benefited 212,803 Romanians, 45,628 Hungarians, 15,934 Saxons and Swabians, and 6,314 members of other minority groups. The losses were especially great for the largely Hungarian Churches (the Catholics and Reformed), weakening their ability to contribute to Hungarian education and culture in Romania.

The land reform in Romania was also accompanied by colonization campaigns. These brought into being 111 settlements, mainly in Hungarian-inhabited areas of Transylvania, in which almost 5,000 Romanian families were settled on altogether 40,000 ha of land.

Application of the Land Ownership Act for Transylvania caused tensions between Romania and Hungary, as the Romanian state also seized the estates of those who had moved to Hungary and taken Hungarian citizenship, thereby contravening the terms of the Treaty of Trianon. It affected, for example, former Transylvanian aristocrats who were prominent in Hungarian politics, including Prime Minister Bethlen. The diplomatic debate finally ended with international agreements in the early 1930s.

Yugoslavia

The land reform in the Yugoslav state that came into being after World War I took place under very intricate conditions, mainly because of the great differences between the territories that were uniting.

The purpose of the Yugoslav agrarian reform was to apply the Serbian system of peasant smallholdings to other parts of the country. So there was support for land reform and for regulations and acts on colonization that would produce smallholdings. Land was granted only to the landless and to those with less than 10 cadastral *hold* (5.7 ha), the latter receiving one 1 *hold* per family member, for which they had to pay. Colonists, however, received up to 8.7 cadastral *hold* (5 ha), again having to pay, with the exception of the *dobrovoljac*, "men of goodwill" or volunteers who had fought for Yugoslav unity, who had the sum paid for them by the state. The upper limit before great estates had to be parceled out varied by region. In Slovenia, estates over 200 ha were confiscated, while in Vojvodina it was as much as 500 ha. The minorities were entirely excluded from the redistribution, which was especially unfortunate for the Hungarians in the northern areas, where the proportion of Hungarians with no land or less than 10 cadastral *hold* was highest. Yugoslavia alone of the successor states first rented out to the claimants the lands expropriated from the great estates. Only after the act concluding the land reform had been passed in June 1931 did the redistributed land pass into the ownership of the claimants.[4]

The colonization took place in parallel with the Yugoslav land reform, with settlers of Serb national origin in the main settling in areas inhabited by the minorities. The authorities used the settlers to spread Slav influence over the newly acquired territories, to assist in assimilating the non-Slav population, and in Macedonia's case, to forestall the spread of a Macedonian national identity and Serbianize the inhabitants. The settlements carried out in Yugoslavia between the world wars were aimed mainly at two regions: Kosovo and the northern territories. In both cases most colonists were sent to border communities, where they were supposed to constitute a Slav stratum unconditionally loyal to the Yugoslav state. These people were used by the authorities, especially in the 1920s, to keep the minorities under surveillance and intimidate them.[5]

The colonization campaign in Vojvodina was concentrated in the north, where the greatest number of great estates (mainly Hungarian- and German-owned) were found and there lived populous minority communities (Hungarians, Germans, Romanians, Rusyns, Slovaks, and so on). The colonists brought into the plains were mainly from mountainous areas of the country and were interested in stockbreeding. Their farming knowledge was woefully inadequate and they were also short of the tools for farming. At least 20,000 South Slav families with about 100,000 dependants were brought into the northern areas of Slovenia, Croatia and Vojvodina between the world wars, setting in motion changes in the ethnic complexion of those regions, compounded by strong emigration from the minorities excluded from the land reform.[6]

Notes

1   For more on land reform and colonization in southern Slovakia, see Attila Simon, *Telepesek és telepítések Dél-Szlovákiában a két világháború közötti időszakban (1918–1938)* [Settlers and Settlements in southern Slovakia in the Period between the Two World Wars (1918–1938)] (Somorja, 2008).

2   *Ibid.*

3   *Ibid.*

4   For more on interwar land reform in Yugoslavia, see Erić Milivoj, *Agrarna reforma u Jugoslaviji 1918–1941* [Agrarian Reform in Yugoslavia 1918–1941] (Sarajevo, 1958), and Attila Kovács,

Földreform és kolonizáció a Lendva-vidéken a két világháború között [Land Reform and Colonization in the Lendava District between the Two World Wars] (Lendva, 2004).

5   Enikő A. Sajti, *Kényszerpályán. Magyarok Jugoszláviában, 1918–1941* [Forced Path. Hungarians in Yugoslavia, 1918–1941] (Szeged, 1997), pp. 93–105.

6   Kovács, *Földreform és kolonizáció*, pp. 181–186; Enikő A. Sajti, *Hungarians in the Voivodina 1918–1947* (Boulder, CO/Highland Lakes, NJ, 2003), pp. 165–170.

8. MINORITY HUNGARIAN SOCIETIES
Nándor Bárdi

The positions held by the minority communities in society were decided in general by their historical and cultural heritage, the legal and political framework in which they lived, the institutional scope available to them, and the structural attributes of society. This section examines how social and economic conditions changed for the Hungarian communities that became minorities after 1918. Then there is the separate question of whether these ethno-cultural communities can be called "minority societies," although they certainly saw and proclaimed themselves as such.[1]

Around 1930, the number of Hungarians outside Hungary but within the Carpathian Basin was 2.6 million. There had been 3.3 million in 1910, and 3.24 million declared themselves so in 1941, after the reannexations. In all the countries of the region, the proportion of the community constituting the state nationality increased at the expense of the minorities. The proportion of self-described Hungarians in Hungary rose from 88.4 to 92.1 percent. In Czechoslovakia, the proportion of Slovaks and Czechs in the territory of today's Slovakia rose from 58 to 72 percent, while the proportion of Romanians in Transylvania rose from 54 to 58.2 percent. The population of Trianon Hungary in 1920 was 7.98 million, which had risen by 700,000 by 1930, and to 9.32 million in 1941, making a growth of 16.8 percent over the 1920–1941 period.[2]

Table 1. The number and proportion of those with Hungarian as a native language (1910) or with Hungarian as a national affiliation (1930 and 1941) in the areas annexed by successor states[3]

	1910		1930		1941	
Slovakia/ Czechoslovakia	881,326	30.2%	585,434	17.6%	761,434	21.5%
Trans- carpathia	185,433	30.6%	116,584	15.9%	233,840	27.3%
Transylvania	1,658,045	31.7%	1,480,712	25.8%	1,711,851	28.9%
Vojvodina	425,672	28.1%	376,176	23.2%	456,770	28.5%
Croatia	119,874	3.5%	66,040	1.7%	64,431	-
Prekmurje	20,737	23.0%	15,050	-	16,510	20.1%
Burgenland	26,225	9.0%	10,442	3.5%	2,076	-

The 1910–1930 decrease in the recorded Hungarian population was greatest numerically in Czechoslovakia (295,894) and proportionally in the new Austrian province of Burgenland (by about two thirds). The causes of the declines in the numbers of Hungarians fall into two groups: actual processes and manipulative census-taking techniques. About 350,000 people moved to Hungary from lost territories in 1918–1924 (197,000 from Transylvania, 107,000 from the former Upper Hungary, 45,000 from the southern counties).[4] Another reduction in the statistical size of the community came from the many Hungarians of unsettled citizenship: some 30,000 in Czechoslovakia and over 100,000 in Romania counted as foreigners.[5] A big contribution to the change in the national structure of the regions concerned was made by colonization. Some of these colonists filled places left by the Hungarian official class. The colonization connected with the land reform was designed to break up the blocs of Hungarian settlement along the borders with Hungary, for security and social reasons. A total of almost 120,000 Czech officials, workers and colonists moved into Transcarpathia and Slovensko.[6] In Romania, 34,000 families were moved into new villages in the Partium and the Banat,[7] and in 1930 Transylvania had 245,000 non-native inhabitants.[8] In the Southern Region, over 50,000 Slav colonists were moved into the 50-kilometer border zone during the Yugoslav land reform.[9] The post-1918 censuses in neighboring countries treated the Hungarian-speaking Jews as a separate national group and did not usually group them with the Hungarian-speakers. In Czechoslovakia, five sixths – 110,000 – of the Jews declaring themselves Hungarian-speakers in 1910 were treated separately in later censuses, as were 40 percent – 60,000 – of those in Transylvania.)[10] Similarly, Hungarian-speaking Greek Catholics were counted as Rusyns in Transcarpathia and as Romanians in Transylvania. Romania treated the Hungarian-speaking Gypsies and the Csángó (Ceangăi) in the same way.[11] So the Romanian census of 1930 under-recorded the number of native Hungarian speakers by about 100,000–120,000.[12]

In terms of ethnic spatial structure, the Hungarian presence shrank due to the factors just mentioned and also because many of the bourgeois in the smaller cities (Bratislava, Nitra, Levice, Komárno, Lučenec, Rimavská Sobota, Košice, Trebišov, Užhorod, Mukačevo and Berehovo) had a multiple identity (Hungarian/German/Jewish/Rusyn/Slovak) and were drawn towards Czechoslovakia, which meant the assimilation of about 100,000 people by 1930. (There were 786 localities in Czechoslovakia with a Hungarian majority in 1921, but only 46 in 1930.) A similar process took place in the Partium[13] (Satu Mare, Sighetu Marmației, Baia Mare, Carei and Oradea), except that there was substantial immigration of Romanians. In Yugoslavia, the land reform was used to replace the native farm laborers on the Hungarian-, Jewish-, or German-owned estates with immigrants from southern Serbia. The number of Vojvodina localities with a Serb majority rose from 203 in 1910 to 258 in 1930, while the number with a Hungarian majority fell from 134 to 90.

The area inhabited by Serbs increased in the Bačka Topola, Novi Sad and Veliki Bečkerek districts.[14] There the number of localities with a Hungarian majority fell from 139 to 59 in 1931. In Prekmurje the number fell from 33 to 15.[15]

The biggest changes of proportion in the urban population occurred among the multi-identity bourgeoisie of the northern cities. In 1910, 44 percent of the urban population of the future Slovakia were Hungarians, but this had fallen to 11 percent by 1930. The shifts over that period were from 40.5 to 16.1 percent in Pozsony/ Bratislava, 75.4 to 17.9 percent in Kassa/Košice, 80.3 to 17.7 percent in Ungvár/Užhorod, and 73.4 to 22.5 percent in Munkács/Mukačevo. In all except the last, this meant the loss of language rights by the Hungarians, who had to make up 20 percent of the inhabitants to qualify. The extent of the census manipulations in these cities and the expedient shift to the majority ethnic allegiance become clear in a post-1941 resurgence of the Hungarians, when the number of votes cast for the Hungarian parties exceeded the self-declared Hungarian population.[16]

Transylvania was far more rural than the Upland: 83 percent of the population in 1930 lived in villages, and a third of the city-dwellers were also involved in agriculture. In 1910, 59 percent of urban Transylvanians were Hungarian-speakers, 23.1 percent Romanian-speakers, and 16.2 percent German-speakers. By 1930 the proportion of Hungarians was down to 45 percent, partly through emigration to Hungary by some 50,000, mainly of the official class, and by a similar number to villages for reasons of livelihood. The second reason was that only 2 of the 10 localities raised to city rank had a Hungarian majority. The third was that some 120,000 city-dwellers counted in the 1930 census were not native to Transylvania. Although 32 of the 49 Transylvanian cities had a Hungarian majority in 1918, the figure was 27 in 1930. The number with a Romanian majority rose from 8 to 18 and those with a German majority fell from 9 to 4. (The cities to lose their Hungarian majorities were Deva, Alba Iulia, Lugoj, Beiuş, Făgăraş, Hunedoara and Ibaşfalău. By 1930, Timişoara had gained a Hungarian plurality due to a rapidly growing Hungarian working class.)[17]

By comparison with Hungary's 36.3 percent proportion of urban inhabitants in 1930 (including Budapest's 16.6 percentage points), the Hungarians of Transylvania and Slovakia were more urbanized and those of Transcarpathia and the Southern Region less so.

The employment structure of the interwar Hungarians in neighboring countries was less favorable than the average in Czechoslovakia and more favorable in Romania. In the Southern Region it was worse than that of the majority nations in the region.[18] In Czechoslovakia, 65.4 percent of active Hungarians worked in agriculture and forestry (which accounted for 57.4 percent of the region's total employment), but they were underrepresented in industry (16.9 percent) and commerce (6.30 percent), where the regional totals represented 18.8 and 10.1 percent respectively. The proportion of self-employed among the Hungarians and that among the Slovaks were almost the same (38.7 and 37.8 percent respectively) and the same applied to the working class (25.2 and 26.8 percent). Looking at the sectors more closely, it emerges that of the 374,000 working in agriculture, 53,000 (with 210,000 dependants) owned land and 110,000 did not. But most of those with land (about 38,000) had more than the 10 ha required to make a living. Of the 100,000 Hungarians working in industry, 10,000 were proprietors (in small-scale industry) and 86,000 were workers. There were 6,000 Hungarians in public employment, and about 10,000 were out of work. But unemployment was worse than the recorded figure, especially in the Transcarpathian timber industry.

The Hungarians, like the Germans and the Jews, were overrepresented in Transylvania's service sector. While 26.7 percent of the Transylvanian population were ethnically Hungarian in 1930, that applied to 40 percent of those working in industry (70–80 percent in small-scale industry), 39.9 percent in credit and commerce, 33 percent in mining, and 30 per cent in transport. The proportions in 1910 had been 52.5 percent in industry, 58.8 percent in commerce, 41.2 percent in mining, and 74.2 percent in transport.[19] So the continued overrepresentation was coupled with a sense of retreat in Hungarian society, compounded by the ground lost in the professions. The proportion of Hungarian lawyers fell from 73.1 percent in 1913 to 20.4 percent (542 persons) in 1935. The case was similar in health care, where only 27 of the 257 physicians in Cluj were Hungarian by 1930, while the proportions in 1935 were 24 out of 157 in Mureş County, 10 out of 34 in Odorhei County, and 5 out of 64 in Bihor County. Only 10.9 percent of the district doctors in Transylvania in 1936 were Hungarians. The proportion of Hungarians in public administration was down to 11.9 percent and among local notaries it was 2.4 percent.[20]

The territories ceded to Yugoslavia after World War I had been rural, agricultural areas dominated by large estates. Much of the small urban population had also lived by agriculture. Industry mainly meant small-scale industry and food processing, and the middle class meant the staff of state and county offices. Even in 1910, the Hungarian agricultural labor force showed the highest rate of landlessness (53.2 percent). The Hungarians accounted for 35.5 percent of the landowners in Vojvodina, 43.2 percent of the landless peasantry, and 48.9 percent of the farm servants. The indicators for the Germans, Serbs, Slovaks and Rusyns were all better in this regard.[21] The disadvantage was compounded by the fact that two thirds of the teachers moved to Hungary after the change of sovereignty.[22] In the absence of ethnic breakdowns of employment in the 1931 census returns, it is only possible to compare the ten Southern Region districts with a Hungarian majority with the aggregate figures for Bačka, the Banat and Baranja. (The 231,737 Hungarians in the ten districts, 53.4 percent of the population, accounted for 61 percent of the Hungarian population in Yugoslavia in 1931.) It emerges from the regional figures that the Hungarians in the districts with a Hungarian majority were underrepresented in all sectors except agriculture.[23]

The Hungarians formed 31.4 percent of Vojvodina's urban population in 1931 (and 29 percent of Hungarians lived in urban localities). That figure and contemporary accounts of Hungarians still poorer after the land reform seeking work elsewhere in Yugoslavia yield an estimated 18–20 percent of Hungarians (80,000–90,000) as working in industry (small-scale industry).[24] The closest to the 1930 position was the employment structure of the Hungarians in Transylvania. (Comparative figures for Hungary were 51.8 percent in agriculture, 23 percent in mining and industry, 5.4 percent in commerce and credit, and 3.9 percent in transport.)

As for educational achievement, illiteracy was a grave concern in Romania and Yugoslavia. In Slovakia, 88.6 percent of Hungarians over the age of five could read and write, as could 83.17 percent in Transcarpathia. Czechoslovakia introduced eight years of compulsory schooling in the 1920s, and illiteracy among the Hungarian community almost entirely disappeared. In Transylvania, half of the population could not read or write in 1910, 75 percent of the illiterates being Romanians (20 percent being Hungarians and 2 percent Germans). In 1930, 42.9 percent of the inhabitants of Greater Romania over seven were illiterate, but the proportion was only 32.6 percent in Transylvania, and it was lowest in Odorhei and Trei Scaune Counties (14.9 and 15.7 percent), and highest in the Romanian-dominated Maramureş and Someş Counties (61.2 and 51 percent).[25] The illiteracy rate in Yugoslavia was still 51.5 percent in the mid-1920s, but the proportion in Vojvodina was 23.3 percent, and as the social structure of the Hungarians there can be gauged as average or below average, it must have been 15–20 percent among them as well.[26] In Hungary before World War I, illiteracy among the agricultural population was about one third, but in Trianon Hungary it had halved by 1930, just as it had fallen in industry (to 5 percent).

The parts of the school system in the greatest danger were the secondary schools teaching in Hungarian. The number of state-run Hungarian-language gymnasia in Czechoslovakia and Yugoslavia was a source of dissatisfaction. There were only five Hungarian-language middle schools and a single women's teacher-training college in the whole Upland and Transcarpathia. There were 5,135 ethnic Hungarian middle school students in 1921–1922, but the number fell to 4,006 in 1929–1930, of whom only 2,838 were being taught in Hungarian. So the Hungarians accounted for 4.97 percent of the country's middle school students, which was slightly higher than their proportion of the population (4.78 percent).[27] Only two gymnasia teaching in Hungarian remained in the whole Vojvodina.[28] In Transylvania, teaching in minority languages was done mainly in Church schools, and the scope for this was narrowed by the state through the medium of the baccalaureate examinations. Most of the vocational training in all three countries was conducted in the majority language, which presented a serious obstacle to Hungarian students seeking upward employment mobility in industry.

In higher education, altogether about 500 Yugoslav Hungarians obtained a university degree during a twenty-year period, mainly in Zagreb, but also in Belgrade and Subotica, most of them qualifying as clergy, lawyers or pharmacists. In Romania, most Hungarian undergraduates attended university in Cluj, where their proportion rose from 5 percent at the beginning of the 1920s to 15–20 percent. Nationally, there were 1,434 Hungarian undergraduates in 1935–1936, of which 550 were studying law, the same number training to be teachers, and 160 doing medicine. The number of Hungarian college and university students in Czechoslovakia varied strongly: 1,200 in 1921–1922 and 779 in 1925–1926, but 1,127 in 1929–1930, when they represented 3.62 percent of the country's university students. In other words, the Hungarians were underrepresented in higher education.[29]

In terms of economic positions, the land reforms in all three countries meant that Hungarian individual, collective and Church estates lost land to claimants of other national groups. In other ways the role and development of the three regions differed, as did the consequent economic development of the Hungarian community. Žitný ostrov was a granary for Czechoslovakia, as was the Banat/Bačka for Yugoslavia, but they differed strongly in their land ownership structures. Žitný ostrov producers were able to modernize by changing products (from grain to truck farming to supply the capital and smaller cities), mechanizing, and forming cooperatives, but not so the Vojvodina Hungarians, as day laborers or owners of small or dwarf holdings. Transylvania was Romania's most developed region, and the Southern Transylvanian industrial centers (Arad, Timişoara, Sibiu and Braşov) grew rapidly. The worker supply was recruited mainly from the increasingly impoverished Hungarian artisans and surplus labor in the Székely Land. According to the statistical comparisons made after the reannexations, Žitný ostrov developed in parallel with neighboring Transdanubia, but eastern Slovakia, Transcarpathia and Transylvania had only reached the level of pre-war Hungary. Vojvodina had not even managed that.[30]

The Hungarian farmers of Yugoslavia were the most indebted stratum of all, in a country burdened by high interest rates. Serbian nation-building at the time was focused on nationalizing agricultural land and eliminating Hungarian financial institutions and credit cooperatives. By 1930, Hungary too had stopped subsidizing these, with the result that Southern Region Hungarian farmers were left without institutional financial back-up. Furthermore, the region had the highest taxes.[31]

Nation-building economic policy in Czechoslovakia was governed by the interests of heavy industry and the financial sector. Small-scale and local industry in the Upland and Transcarpathia failed against competition from large-scale Czech industry, while agricultural incomes were siphoned off by rapid rises in the prices of industrial and consumer goods.[32]

Rapid development of the timber, textile and chemical industries in Transylvania in the 1920s brought appreciable economic growth. The state imposed a unitary economic policy mainly at the expense of newly acquired territories and the minorities. The main features were the following: land reform (1920–1921); colonization in border areas (1921 and 1930); nationalization of natural resources to turn the oil and gas reserves into national capital; nationalization of corporations by tightening state permits and controls and banning the use of foreign bank credit; transport tariffs to discourage raw-material exports; location of new industry away from cities near the Hungarian border; a taxation policy whereby the tax yield in counties with a Hungarian majority rose to three times the national average.[33]

The demographic, social and economic positions of all the lost areas of Hungary deteriorated and fell behind Hungary itself. The biggest lags developed among the Hungarians in Vojvodina and Transcarpathia. In every region, the biggest losers of the political transformation, followed by the economic and social ones, were the urban middle and artisan classes.

Notes

1   Important inside social accounts and reconstructions were provided by the following: László Fritz and István Sulyok, eds., *Erdélyi Magyar Évkönyv* [Transylvanian Hungarian Yearbook] (Cluj, 1930); Sándor Kacsó, ed., *Erdélyi Magyar Évkönyv. A kisebbségi magyar polgár kézikönyve, 1938* [Transylvanian Hungarian Yearbook. The Minority Hungarian Citizen's Handbook, 1938] (Braşov, 1937); József Fazekas, ed., *Vagyunk és leszünk. A szlovenszkói magyarság társadalmi rajza 1918–1945* [We Are and Will Remain. The Sociography of the Hungarians of Slovensko 1918–1945] (Bratislava, 1993); the banned summer 1935 issue of *Kalangya* reprinted 60 years later: *Létünk* (1994) 4.

2   Károly Kocsis, "Society and Economy in the Carpathian Basin of the Present," in Béla Bulla and Tibor Mendöl, eds., A *Kárpát-medence földrajza / The Geography of the Carpathian Basin* (Budapest, 1999), pp. 359–364.

3   The author's calculations from census data. The 1910 census recorded only the native language.

4   Of the refugees arriving in Hungary in 1918–1924, 105,000 were active earners with 245,000 dependants, 57,000 having been in public employment and 86,000 teachers and university students. Emil Petrichevich Horváth, *Jelentés az Országos Menekültügyi Hivatal négy évi működéséről* [Report on the Four Years' Activity of the National Bureau for Refugee Affairs] (Budapest, 1924), p. 37.

5   Lajos Nagy, *A kisebbségek alkotmányjogi helyzete Nagyromániában* [The Constitutional Position of Minorities in Greater Romania] (Cluj, 1944), pp. 76–84; Gyula Popély, *Népfogyatkozás. A csehszlovákiai magyarság a népszámlálások tükrében 1918–1945* [Depopulation. Czechoslovakian Hungarians in the Light of the Censuses 1918–1945] (Budapest, 1991), pp. 106–107.

6   On the colonization, see the previous chapter of this book and Attila Simon, *Telepesek és telepes falvak Dél-Szlovákiában a két világháború között* [Colonists and Colony Villages in Southern Slovakia between the Two World Wars] (Šamorin, 2008).

7   Victor Jinga, *Migrațiunile demografice și problema colonizărilor în Romania* [The Question of Migration, Demography and Colonization in Romania] (Brasov, 1941).

8   Most arrived from other parts of pre-1918 Hungary. Altogether 68,000 came from outside the Carpathian Basin, from pre-1918 Romania. Árpád E. Varga, "Városodás, vándorlás, nemzetiség" [Urbanization, Migration, National Affiliation], in Idem, *Fejezetek a jelenkori Erdély népesedéstörténetéből* [Chapters from the History of Contemporary Transylvanian Demography] (Budapest, 1998), p. 200.

9   Attila Kovács, *Földreform és kolonizáció a Lendva-vidéken a két világháború között* [Land Reform and Colonization in the Lendava District between the Two World Wars] (Lendava, 2004); József Venczel, *Az erdélyi román földbirtokreform* [The Romanian Land Reform in Transylvania] (Kolozsvár, 1942).

10   Árpád E. Varga, "Népszámlálások a jelenkori Erdély területén" [Censuses in the Present-Day Area of Transylvania], in Idem, *Fejezetek*, pp. 34 and 54–57; Popély, *Népfogyatkozás*, pp. 106–107. On the search for identity by Jews among the minority Hungarian-speakers, see Éva Kovács, *Az asszimiláció ellentmondásai. A kassai zsidóság a két világháború között (1918–1938)* [Contradictions of Assimilation. Jews of Košice between the Two World Wars (1918–1938)] (Somorja/Dunaszerdahely, 2004); Attila Gidó, *Úton. Erdélyi zsidó társadalom és nemzetépítési kísérletek (1918–1940)* [On the Road. Transylvanian Jewish Society and Nation-Building Attempts (1918–1940)] (Miercurea-Ciuc, 2008).

11   The name refers usually to two groups of native Hungarians living in scattered rural areas in Moldavia and border Transylvania (Ghimeş). It has sometimes been applied to other groups of Hungarians beyond the main area of Hungarian settlement (e. g. Bukovina and Ţara Bârsei).

12   Varga, "Népszámlálások a jelenkori Erdély területén," in Idem, *Fejezetek*, p. 34.

13   The term refers here to the parts of the historical Partium annexed by Romania in 1918: the Crişana and the eastern Banat.

14 Veliki Bečkerek was renamed Petrovgrad in 1935 and Zrenjanin in 1946.

15 Károly Kocsis and Eszter Kocsis-Hodosi, *Ethnic Geography of the Hungarian Minorities in the Carpathian Basin* (Budapest, 1998), pp. 15–37, 54–64, 84–93, 111–120, 142–151, 168–179, 189–191 and 199–202.

16 Popély, *Népfogyatkozás*, pp. 111–113.

17 László Szarka, "A városi magyar népesség számának alakulása a Magyarországgal szomszédos országokban (1910–2000)" [Change in the Urban Hungarian Population in Neighboring Countries (1910–2000)], *Kisebbségkutatás* (2001) 4: 57–67; Varga, "Városodás, vándorlás, nemzetiség," in Idem, *Fejezetek*, pp. 180–217.

18 Detailed national studies: Béla Angyal, *Érdekvédelem és önszerveződés. Fejezetek a csehszlovákiai magyar pártpolitika történetéből 1918–1938* [Interest Protection and Self-Organization. Chapters from the History of Czechoslovakian Hungarian Party Politics 1918–1938] (Galánta/Dunaszerdahely, 2002); László Gyurgyík, "A (cseh)szlovákiai magyarság demográfiai valamint település- és társadalomszerkezetének alakulása 1918–1998" [Demographic, Settlement Structure and Social-Structural Development of the (Czecho)Slovakian Hungarian Community 1918–1998], in Tamás Gusztáv Filep and László Tóth, eds., *A (cseh) szlovákiai magyar művelődés története 1918–1998* [The History of (Czecho)Slovakian Hungarian Education 1918–1998] (Budapest, 1998), pp. 101–102; Pál Opra, *Erdély lakosságának foglalkozások szerinti megoszlása* [Transylvania's Population by Employment], ms., 1930, OSZK Kézirattár [Teleki László Alapítvány kézirattára 1518/95]; Béla Köpeczl, ed., *History of Transylvania* (Budapest, 1996), pp. 674–677; Lajos Arday, "A jugoszláviai magyarság demográfiai, gazdasági és társadalmi helyzete 1918 és 1944 között" [The Demographic, Economic and Social Situation of the Yugoslavian Hungarians in 1918–1944], in Idem, *Magyarok a Délvidéken, Jugoszláviában* [Hungarians in the Southern Region, Yugoslavia] (Budapest, 2002), pp. 121–173 and 137–139.

19 The employment structure among Transylvania's Hungarians, according to the 1930 census: 58 percent worked in agriculture (as did 67.7 percent among the employed population of Transylvania), 19.9 percent in mining and manufacturing (12.6 percent), 4 percent in commerce (3.6 percent), 3.8 percent in transport (2.5 percent) 13.4

percent in professional jobs (11.1 percent). Of those employed in manufacturing, 28.6 percent were in the textile industry, 21 percent in metallurgy, 17.3 percent in timber-related industry, and more than 10 percent each in food processing and consumer goods. See Opra, *Erdély lakosságának.*

20 Sándor Makkai, "Erdély társadalma" [Transylvanian Society], in József Deér, ed., *Erdély* [Transylvania] (Budapest, 1940), p. 257.

21 Arday, "A jugoszláviai magyarság," p. 138.

22 Enikő A. Sajti, "Az impériumváltás hatása a délvidéki magyarok társadalomszerkezetére" [The Effect of the Change of Sovereignty on the Social Structure of the Southern Region Hungarians], *Limes* (2002) 2: 41–50.

23 "At the end of the interwar period, the number of Vojvodina agricultural workers and their dependants reached 350,000, the vast majority of them Hungarians. The agricultural workers performed an average of 40–45 days of hired laboring, mainly at reaping and corn-snapping time. There were years such as 1934 when 20,000 families were left quite without work." Arday, "A jugoszláviai magyarság," p. 138.

24 *Ibid.*, p. 139. The estimated employment structure of the Yugoslavian Hungarians according to the 1931 census was as follows. Agriculture provided a livelihood for 74.5 percent of the employed in the ten districts with a Hungarian majority and for 69 percent of the working population in Bačka, the Banat and Baranja. For manufacturing and mining the proportions were 13.7 percent and 10 percent, for transport and commerce 5.2 percent and 6.6 percent, and for services and the self-employed 3.9 percent and 4.9 percent. *Ibid.*, pp. 170–171.

25 Alajos Kovács, "Erdély népesedési viszonyai" [Transylvania's Population Relations], in Deér, ed., *Erdély*, pp. 236–237.

26 László Gulyás, *Két régió – Felvidék és Vajdaság – sorsa. Az Osztrák-Magyar Monarchiától napjainkig* [Fate of Two Regions: the Upland and Vojvodina. From the Austro-Hungarian Monarchy to Today] (Pécs, 2005), p. 87.

27 Béla László, "Az iskolai művelődés a statisztikák tükrében" [School Education in the Light of Statistics], in Béla László, László A. Szabó and Károly Tóth, eds., *Magyarok Szlovákiában IV. köt. Oktatásügy* [Hungarians in Slovakia IV. Education] (Šamorin, 2006), pp. 59–63.

28 Enikő A. Sajti, *Impériumváltások, revízió, kisebbség. Magyarok a Délvidéken 1918–1947* [Sovereignty Changes, Revision, Minority.

Hungarians in the Southern Region 1918–1947] (Budapest, 2004), pp. 142–163.

29   Gyula Kornis, *Az elcsatolt területek magyar egyetemi ifjúsága* [Hungarian University Youth of the Detached Territories] (Budapest, 1937); László, "Az iskolai művelődés a statisztikák tükrében," pp. 59–63.

30   For a statistical survey of the territories reannexed by Hungary in 1938–1941, see Gidó, *Úton*, and László, "Az iskolai művelődés." A good account of the interwar conditions emerges from the statistical surveys made of the reannexed territories: "A visszacsatolt északi terület" [The Reannexed Northern Territory], *Magyar Statisztikai Szemle* (1938) 10: 929–933; "A visszacsatolt keleti terület" [The Reannexed Eastern Territory], *Magyar Statisztikai Szemle* (1940) 8–9: 657–733; "A visszafoglalt délvidéki terület" [The Reannexed Southern Region Territory], *Magyar Statisztikai Szemle* (1941) 11: 768–857.

31   Arday, "A jugoszláviai magyarság," pp. 127–130.

32   Lajos Jócsik, *Idegen igában. Húsz év cseh uralom alatt* [Under a Foreign Yoke. Twenty Years under Czech Rule] (Budapest, 1940), pp. 41–49 and 175–196.

33   A work from Romania putting forward the positive side of the transformation was Illés István Győri, ed., *Metamorphosis Transylvaniae. Országrészünk átalakulása 1918–1936* [Transformation of Our Part of the Country 1918–1936] (Cluj, 1937). For an analysis from Hungary, see András Rónai, "Erdély gazdasági élete Romániában" [Transylvania's Economic Activity in Romania], in Deér, ed., *Erdély*, pp. 239–254.

9. MINORITY HUNGARIAN CULTURE, ART, SCIENCE AND SCHOLARSHIP
Tamás Gusztáv Filep

The beginnings of minority life and of minority culture in the strict sense did not coincide.[1] This is not just because institutions were banned, communal forms paralyzed, and a state of emergency declared after the military occupations of 1918–1919. Before cultural activity could begin, there had to be awareness of the formation of political-cum-legal communities, separate by necessity, which had to assess for themselves their specific problems and find the responses to them. The position as a minority – there would later be an extensive theoretical literature on it – decided in practice the character and purpose of the arts and scholarship and invested them with social tasks. Members of the public who were prepared to speak out called on culture to interpret the "minority destiny," examine its attributes, and document its experiences. The most important demand by the fragmented society was for art to help them to survive and preserve their national identity, language and threatened values. Of course the values in question were mainly ones that reflected unmistakable features. The aims were attained where the attributes specific to the minority could be tied to universal criteria on a theoretical level. That was the basis for more or less effective Hungarian minority ideologies in the successor states, such Transylvanianism, or the local-color theory in the Southern Region.[2] Respect for regional values meant in principle denying provincialism. That was also the origin of the oft-heard theory in Upper Hungary that the urbane tradition of the region's rich ensured close contact with Western Europe.[3]

One constant attribute of minority intellectual life was its truncated, partial nature; its viable elements performed a kind of supplementary, gap-filling purpose. An especially large number of functions fell to literature (and its background areas).[4] It is typical to find permeability between forms of consciousness and expertise: journalism, literature and scholarship were often blurred together by the higher social functionality expected of them. Later it became generally accepted in Hungarian intellectual life that Hungarian literature and Hungarian culture were universal, but they were organized into separate centers because of the political disunity. The aim was for the parts to cooperate and build relations.[5] The early period brought an extraordinary expansion of the press, which became rich and varied, and was increasingly divided by political trends, areas of knowledge, occupations and religious denominations. The previous readerships of the small, localized papers multiplied, and new papers were founded with the aim of influencing public opinion. This role was retained by the press until the end of the period, although many papers died or dwindled in the meantime. On the other hand, a system of minority cultural institutions grew up to some extent.

The detached minorities, naturally, saw themselves as part of the global Hungarian community and its common spirit. However, when the intellectual barriers finally came down, the Czechoslovakian, Romanian and Yugoslavian Hungarian communities proved capable of supporting cultural life, if not their own culture. But the required edifice lacked foundations.

Many provincial cities at the turn of the century had been calling for culture to be decentralized,[6] for institutions to be shared between the capital and provincial centers. Furthermore, the period had seen many modern centers of culture begin to emerge – the most important being Nagyvárad, which had launched the generation of the poet Endre Ady – but the critical weight would not have been reached: the necessary figures would have been lacking, had many of the participants in the 1918 bourgeois revolution and the 1919 proletarian dictatorship not withdrawn into territories occupied by the successor states.[7] One of the period's most influential Hungarian editors in Czechoslovakia, Pál Szvatkó, referred to the first phase in Czechoslovakian Hungarian literature as one of struggle between the émigrés and the dilettanti,[8] a comment that could apply largely to Romania and Yugoslavia too. The difference is more that the frontlines were not equally sharp, and the modernizers did not have equal chances of integrating into the new environment. It depended on the structure and proportions of the minority political forces, on the effectiveness with which the advocates of a bourgeois democratic "people's republic" took part in establishing Hungarian party politics there. Nor did the generations raised in the minority situation identify completely with their modernist or conservative elders, aiming rather to build on and synthesize the various effects. In the literature[9] and borderline areas of all three emerging minority cultures, there was a conspicuous advance by avant-garde groups, associated partly with bourgeois radicalism[10] and partly with the labor movement,[11] against which more conservative circles could not bring appreciable forces to bear, although the latter had greater chances of reaching a mass public. The most important members of the groups whose ideas developed the népi schools of thought[12] tended up to the 1930s to cooperate with the bourgeois humanists, with regional groups still connected with the world trends, and to establish creative community with them. Then in the 1930s, younger members gained steadily more interest in "reality literature" based on knowledge of the people and "sociographical" or even sociological matters, which became the basis for a new concept of the collective.[13] The respect for value-based literature that seemingly consolidated during the decade was shaken by an increasing number of more or less scientifically conducted pieces of social research. The demand for culture shifted from literature towards social research.[14]

The development of literary and scholarly life was impeded by the inadequate system of institutions: there was a want of well-capitalized publishers, scientific establishments, or institutes of higher education, where scientific and scholarly thinking might develop and thrive. Higher education in Hungarian for the leading intelligentsia ceased, except in theology. Every field of culture and scholarship suffered from a shortage of state and municipal (city, village) subsidies. Books most often had to be published privately, in editions from periodicals and enterprising local printers (who soon failed), under the auspices of local literary societies, or with a covert subsidy from the Hungarian state.[15] The space that the supplements of the daily papers and the periodicals were prepared to give to scholarship and literature meant that they preferred methods appealing directly to the public, rather than scholarly immersion. But the focus on news also gave rewards: the newspapers took literature and literary journalism to a relatively wide readership. Some papers that played such a role, in some periods and some regions, included *Kassai Napló* (Košice), *Prágai Magyar Hírlap* (Prague), *Ellenzék* and *Keleti Újság* (Cluj), *Bácsmegyei Napló* (Subotica) and *Reggeli Újság* (Novi Sad). Apart from some fleeting periodicals, they were the sites where there began to appear regularly, alongside the literature and the journalism with a basis in social science, the scientific studies needed for informed discussion of minority social problems.[16] Many researchers were self-taught, or dealt with subjects that drew on local knowledge.[17] There were some experts in minority law, and one respected publication commanding attention throughout the language area: *Magyar Kisebbség* ("Hungarian Minority"), edited by Elemér Jakabffy and published in Lugoj.[18] Only in the second decade did sociological and psychological works begin to appear, mainly from researchers now socialized into the minority situation. That was when life's work of permanent value appeared: in Transylvania, for instance, from archivist Lajos Kelemen, philologist Attila T. Szabó, jurist Artúr Balogh and sociologist József Venczel;[19] in Czechoslovakia from historian Andor Sas[20] and educationalist and social psychologist Jenő Krammer.[21] Only in Transylvania was there a longstanding tradition of scholarship. Drawing on a background of Kolozsvár's Francis Joseph University of Sciences, the turn-of-the-century school of philosophy surrounding Károly Böhm, espousing the neo-Kantian theory of value, had several members who continued their careers in Hungary after World War I, but many others remained in Transylvania. The most important philosophers to have studied at Kolozsvár were the Reformed Bishop Sándor Makkai, also a theologian, prose writer and apologist for Endre Ady, and the Unitarian Bishop Béla Varga. The most interesting experiment was associated with the Kolozsvár/Cluj philosopher and theology professor Sándor Tavaszy, who sought to develop a new philosophy out of Kantian ethics, theory drawn from his experience of the minority way of life, and new recognitions of the existentialism that began with Kierkegaard. Tavaszy was among the first to bring to public attention in Hungary the ideas of the existentialist Martin Heidegger, one of the most influential thinkers of the twentieth century.[22] He played a similar pioneering role in introducing into the Hungarian-speaking world, through the Transylvanian Church, the main strand of new Protestant theology: the dialectic philosophy of Karl Barth.[23] The neo-scholastic theologian Cecil Bognár was among the Hungarian scholars in Czechoslovakia to contribute several important works.[24]

The importance of literature grew immeasurably, but the frames for this were only created to a limited extent, at a cost of great efforts.

Contemporaries stressed the importance not only of arranging book publication, but of setting up regular literary and cultural forums, having journals and literary workshops based on criteria of quality not ideology, and, where possible, collaboration between societies, periodicals and publishers. This had lasting results only once, in Transylvania, where in 1926 Baron János Kemény set up at his mansion in Brâncovenești the *Helikon* literary society, which from 1928 to 1944 published the *Erdélyi Helikon,* the period's leading literary paper, alongside an earlier publishing company, the Transylvanian Arts Guild.[25] The bourgeois democratic, liberal, conservative liberal and Transylvanian *népi* writers were still working together at that time.[26] Discounting some private initiatives, the Guild published most of the literary work that still has validity and become symbolic of the Transylvanian community in the period: the prose of Áron Tamási, Károly Kós, Miklós Bánffy and Benő Karácsony, the lyric poetry of Lajos Áprily and Sándor Reményik, exploring the symbols of standing one's ground, and the verse of Jenő Dsida, the poet of modern neo-Catholicism. Later the Guild co-published several series with Révai in Budapest, sometimes reaching six-figure sales in Hungary, although the sales were not always proportionate to literary worth, having more to do with adept promotion. Still, many were expecting a renascence of Hungarian literature to come out of Transylvania, in the light of major achievements around the turn of the 1920s and 1930s.[27] This coincided partly with a growing demand for literature dealing with communal and social problems. The radical left wing congregated around the Marxist periodical *Korunk*.[28] *Pásztortűz* overlapped strongly with *Erdélyi Helikon* in its authors and editors;[29] the latter was a more traditional journal of the middle class, taking on board the achievements of the influential Hungarian journal *Nyugat*, but without breaking off relations with the old conservative authors who had founded the Transylvanian Literary Society[30] and its paper the *Erdélyi Irodalmi Szemle*. An institution operating more traditionally was the Transylvanian Museum Society,[31] whose periodical the *Erdélyi Múzeum* was revived in the 1930s.[32] The generation growing up in the 1930s (some having split off from the *Helikon*) showed a strong will to influence public life and share knowledge of the common people in their journal *Erdélyi Fiatalok*, as did a still younger generation in theirs, *Hitel*.[33] The last three journals no longer found room for literature.

The landowning politician József Szent-Ivány attempted to form a united Hungarian literary front in Czechoslovakia, by inviting to Liptovský Ján in 1930, 1931 and 1932 a number of writers without reference to their world outlooks, but either the right or the left would stay away. The fragmentary program that came out of the gatherings, known as the Szentiván Curiae, was not applied, for want of funding and for lack of interest. The Kazinczy publishing company, formed after earlier efforts at unity, brought out a three-volume publication, only to have it confiscated, which took the company to the brink of failure, with the result that it only vegetated after that, failing even to support a periodical throughout the whole period.

The role of a central literary periodical was taken by M*agyar Írás* and at the end of the period by *Tátra*, under the auspices of the Czechoslovakian Hungarian Literary Association,[34] with which talented prose writers such as Mihály Tamás, István Darkó and Pál Neubauer were more closely or loosely associated, as was the poet

Dezső Vozári. The novelist and short story writer Piroska Szenes was more directly connected with forums in Hungary. Partly due to connections with the lively Czech intellectual scene, many outlooks opposed to the cult of minority survival also had advocates among Czechoslovakian Hungarians, but the most popular body of poetic work proved to be that of Dezső Győry, who managed to proclaim in publicist form the emotions of the first generation of Hungarians to grow up as a minority.[35] Neither the dogmatic Marxists (with the poet Imre Forbáth to the fore) nor the new generation's *Sarló* movement[36] managed to launch a periodical comparable to *Korunk* in Transylvania, but the neo-Catholic youth group succeeded in carrying their periodical *Új Élet* over into the new period. One feature of the situation was that the government and president launched what was intended to be a central organization, the Hungarian Scientific, Literary and Art Society (known colloquially as the Masaryk Academy), although it operated in practice only for a few years.[37]

Both Ernő Ligeti in Transylvania and Pál Szvatkó in Czechoslovakia set up papers that gathered together the value of the bourgeois, non-totalitarian world view and included contributions from writers, scholars and public figures: *Független Újság* and *Új Szellem* respectively.[38]

The work of building up a strong Hungarian cultural presence in Czechoslovakia was impeded by a small potential readership and absence of the kind of patrons found in Transylvania. In the Southern Region, almost everything was lacking, including local cultural traditions.[39] There it was for the longest time that newspaper columns, supplements and anthologies had to make up for the absence of literary journals. Not until 1928 was there a meeting of writers with a view to founding an overall body, and in the event, there was no continuation of the *Helikon* meeting at Bečej. Several short-lived literary reviews appeared (the poet Zoltán Csuka being the main organizer), but not until 1932 did the periodical *Kalangya*[40] appear, focused on the theory of local color. This was edited by Kornél Szenteleky and survived until 1944. Szenteleky, an exponent of three genres, was criticized by many for seeing local color not as a set of external, random constituents, but as the depiction of minority life. As an organizer of literary activity, he hardly got beyond the stage of calling together writers of varying talent. After Szenteleky's death in 1933, the task of running *Kalangya* passed to the prose writer Károly Szirmai, under whom it really became a periodical that mapped the reality for Hungarians in the Southern Region. *Kalangya* was also involved in some successful book publishing. Two other careers to mention are those of the prose writers János Herceg and Mihály Majtényi. In addition to *Kalangya*, there appeared a Marxist publication entitled *Híd*,[41] which was mainly devoted to disseminating factual knowledge, and so was not associated with any appreciable literary initiatives.[42]

Theater, closely related to literature,[43] was hampered by bans and systematic state control in Czechoslovakia and Romania, along with a lack of state or municipal subsidies, problems of recruitment, restriction of the theater season, and arbitrary limits on the number of venues. Some theaters were requisitioned by the state (for instance in Bratislava, Cluj and Košice). Concessions to run theaters often went to those thought to be sufficiently loyal. Here as in other areas of the arts, the politically motivated state controls led to a fall in standards. (In Transylvania, most theater companies dwindled or merged into weaker groups.) Impoverishment of the theater-going public encouraged artistically undemanding programs. The theater directors who stood out were in Transylvania Jenő Janovics in Cluj, and in the Upland Ödön Faragó. Janovics spiked his program of classical drama and opera with work by Romanian Hungarian playwrights, and even encouraged drama to spread in Transylvania by running competitions. By the end of the 1920s his company was providing seasons in Oradea and Timişoara as well. (Janovics was also a pioneer of Hungarian film production, making movies in Transylvania up to the end of the 1920s, in a studio established at the beginning of the century.)[44] Ödön Faragó's programs and artistic objectives were outstanding as well. He too strove to incorporate local dramatists. Eventually his budget became so overburdened by extra assignments that he was forced to hand matters over to Imre Kádár in 1934–1935 and leave for Hungary. Although he returned several times, he could never make the company pay. Both countries spawned voluntary societies to support drama. The Theater Patrons' Association was founded in Romania in 1922, the Slovakian Hungarian Theater Patrons' Association in 1925, and the Transcarpathian Rusyn Theater Patrons' Association in 1926.[45] Professional theater companies were banned in Yugoslavia in 1920. Not one professional performance of a Hungarian play was given in the period up to 1941. Nor were companies from Hungary, Romania or Czechoslovakia allowed to appear, and even amateur theater was banned in the sensitive border city of Subotica. Without professionals, the already depleted traditions became confined to nineteenth-century popular peasant plays and operettas. In other fields, efforts to save the arts were made by denominational, local, youth, and many other societies and groups, which sponsored performances and evenings that took more traditional forms, or followed the new ideological trends, but even so, often did good service among an audience deprived of more organized and expert cultural manifestations or indifferent to them. In many localities, the choral society or the farmers' union was the one basis for preserving cultural values. In Yugoslavia, for instance, the People's Circle in Subotica organized shows and literature courses throughout Vojvodina, in the absence of professional bodies to do so, and it was not until 1940–1941 that the Southern Region Hungarian Education Association was formed.[46] The main integrating, and to some extent representing, role in Czechoslovakia was played by the Hungarian Cultural Associations in Slovensko and Transcarpathia,[47] but by the end of the period some use was being made of the state-instituted district public education boards as well.[48]

Notes

1   A sharp picture of early events in Transylvania: Ernő Ligeti, *Súly alatt a pálma. Egy nemzedék szellemi élete. 22 esztendő kisebbségi sorsban* [Palm under a Weight. A Generation's Intellectual Life over 22 Years of Being a Minority] (Csíkszereda, [1941] 2004). On Czechoslovakian Hungarian intellectual movements, press and literature, see Pál Szvatkó, *A visszatért magyarok. A felvidéki magyarság húsz éve* [Returned Hungarians. Twenty Years of the Upland Hungarians] (Budapest, 1938), pp. 115–151, 179–182 and 192–196.

2   See Zsolt K. Lengyel, *Auf der Suche nach dem Kompromiss. Ursprünge und Gestalten des frühen Transsilvanismus 1918–1928* (Munich, 1991) (= *A kompromisszum keresése. Tanulmányok a 20. századi transzszilvanizmus korai történetéhez* [Csíkszereda, 2007]); Kornél Szenteleky, *Ugartörés* [Ground-Breaking], chosen by János Herceg (Novi Sad, 1963). An anti-regionalist view: Izidor Milkó, "Erdélyi Helikon és vajdasági irodalom" [Transylvanian *Helikon* and Vojvodina Literature], in Idem, *Harun al Rasid és egyéb írások* [Harun al Rashid and Other Writings] (Novi Sad, 1966), pp. 157–160.

3   Aladár Kuncz, "Erdély az én hazám. Csendes beszélgetés Áprily Lajossal" [Transylvania Is My Home. A Quiet Talk with Lajos Áprily], in *Tanulmányok, kritikák* [Studies, Reviews], compiled etc. by Béla Pomogáts (Bucharest, 1973), pp. 243–251. For and against: Jenő Krammer, "Európa és a csehszlovákiai magyarság" [Europe and the Czechoslovakian Hungarians], in István Borsody, ed., *Magyarok Csehszlovákiában* [Hungarians in Czechoslovakia] (II: 6) (Budapest, 1938), pp. 205–211. Also see Pál Szvatkó, "Indogermán magyarok" [Indo-German Hungarians], in Idem, ed., *A változás élménye. Válogatott írások* [Experience of Change. Selected Writings] (Pozsony, 1994), pp. 56–80.

4   Miklós Béládi, "Kisebbségi irodalom – nemzetiségi irodalom" [Minority/Ethnic Group Literature], in Idem, *Válaszutak. Tanulmányok* [Dilemmas. Studies] (Budapest, 1983), pp. 431–444.

5   See the "Schism Trial" papers: *Erdélyi Helikon* (1928) 1: 55–58 and 2: 146–150.

6   A concise account of pre-war cultural centralism: Marcell Benedek, "Az erdélyi magyar irodalom" [Transylvanian Hungarian Literature], *Századunk* (1926) 1: 52–54.

7   Lajos Turczel, "Egy különös írói csoport. Magyarországi emigráns
    írók és újságírók Csehszlovákiában" [Unusual Writers' Group.
    Hungarian Emigré Writers and Journalists in Czechoslovakia], in
    Idem, *Arcképek és emlékezések* [Portraits and Memories] (Bratislava,
    1997), pp. 164–195; Lajos Jordáky, "A Magyar Tanácsköztársaság
    emigránsainak szellemi tevékenysége Romániában" [Intellectual
    Activity in Romania of Emigrés of the Hungarian Soviet Republic], in
    Idem, *A szocialista irodalom útján* [On the Path of Socialist Literature]
    (Budapest, 1973), pp. 209–217; Ferenc Mák, "A baranyai köztársaság
    délvidéki menekültjei – Emigránsok a vajdasági közírásban 1920
    után" [Southern Region Refugees from the Baranya Republic –
    Emigrés in Vojvodina Journalism after 1920], *Aracs* (2008) 1: 27–35.
8   On the author, see Tamás Gusztáv Filep and László G. Kovács, "Egy
    európai polgár emlékezete..." [Memoir of a European Citizen...],
    in Szvatkó, ed., *A változás élménye*, pp. 7–26. Study cited: Szvatkó,
    "Szlovenszkói magyar irodalom" [Slovensko Hungarian Literature],
    in *ibid.*, pp. 138–148.
9   Lajos Kántor and Gusztáv Láng, *Romániai magyar irodalom 1944–
    1970* [Romanian Hungarian Literature 1944–1970] (Bukarest,
    1973), pp. 5–24.
10 On its presence in Transylvanian self-identity ideology, see
    Gusztáv Láng, "Egy önmeghatározás tanulságai. Jegyzetek a
    transzszilvanizmusról" [Lessons of a Self-Identification. Notes
    on Transylvanianism], in Idem, *Kivándorló irodalom. Kísérletek*
    [Emigrant Literature. Experiments] (Kolozsvár, 1998), pp. 5–26.
11 See for example Imre József Balázs, *Az avantgárd az erdélyi magyar
    irodalomban* [The Avant-Garde in Transylvanian Hungarian Literature]
    (Marosvásárhely, 2006).
12 The *népi* (sometimes translated misleadingly as "populist") writers
    and thinkers of the interwar period sought the sterling qualities of
    the Hungarian nation in rural, as opposed to urban, society, and
    made efforts to encapsulate these in lengthy, detailed, description of
    rural life ("sociography"), sometimes of great literary merit. Their
    lines of argument bore some resemblance to those of Tolstoy or the
    early *völkisch* movement in Germany. For a brief outline, see Lóránt
    Czigány, *A History of Hungarian Literature from the Earliest Times
    to the Mid-1970s*, Ch. XXII, at http://mek2.niif.hu/02000/02042/
    html/index.html. Last accessed: June 24, 2009. On the beginnings of
    this, see Ferenc Balázs, "Erdélyi magyar irodalom" [Transylvanian

Hungarian Literature], and "Székely mitológia" [Székely Mythology], in Idem, ed., *Versek – elbeszélések – tanulmányok tizenegy fiatal erdélyi irótól erdélyi művészek rajzaival* [Verses, Stories, Studies by 11 Young Transylvanian Writers, Drawings by Transylvanian Artists] (Cluj, 1923), pp. 7–20.

13 See the new edition of a scholarly work of his and accompanying study: Imre Mikó, ed., *Az erdélyi falu és a nemzetiségi kérdés* [The Transylvanian Village and the Minority Question] (Miercurea-Ciuc, 1998); Nándor Bárdi, "Egy magyar girondista Erdélyben" [A Hungarian Girondist in Transylvania], in *ibid.*, pp. 5–33; Pál Szvatkó, "Bata-cipős magyar ifjúság; új szellem Szlovenszkón" [Hungarian Youth in Bata Shoes. New Spirit in Slovensko], in Idem, ed., *A változás élménye*, pp. 117–125 and 196–205.

14 The divisions in the young elite in the 1930s appeared in socio-political movements and social scientific debates, not literary movements. See Sándor Balázs, *Szociológia és nemzeti önismeret (A Gusti-iskola és a romániai magyar szociográfia) Kritikai tanulmány* [Sociology and National Self-Awareness (The Gusti School and Romanian Hungarian Sociography). A Critical Study] (Bukarest, 1979).

15 István Monoki, compiler, *Magyar könyvtermelés Romániában (1919–1940). I. Könyvek és egyéb nyomtatványok* [Hungarian Book Production in Romania (1919–1940). I: Books and Other Printed Matter] (Kolozsvár, 1997).

16 Only one was the subject of a monograph: Lajos Gyüre, *Kassai Napló 1918–1929* [Kassa Diary 1918–1929] (Bratislava, 1986). The best newspaper history: Miklós Hornyik, "Az országföld őrzői" [Guardians of the Land], in Idem, *Határsértés. Válogatott és új írások 1965–2001* [Border Encroachment. Selected and New Writings 1965–2001] (Budapest, 2002), pp. 9–130.

17 József Liszka, *Magyar néprajzi kutatás Szlovákiában (1918–1938)* [Hungarian Ethnographic Research in Slovakia (1918–1938)] (Pozsony, 1990).

18 Sándor Balázs, *Lugosi üzenet* [Message from Lugoj] (Szatmárnémeti, 1995).

19 New editions: Artúr Balogh, *A kisebbségek nemzetközi védelme. A kisebbségi szerződések és a békeszerződések alapján* [International Protection of Minorities. Based on the Minority Treaties and Peace Treaties], 2nd rev. ed. (Csíkszereda, 1997); Idem, *Jogállam és*

kisebbség [Constitutional State and Minority] (Budapest/Kolozsvár, 1997); József Venczel, *Az önismeret útján. Tanulmányok az erdélyi társadalomkutatás köréből* [On the Road to Self-Awareness. Studies in Transylvanian Social Research] (Bukarest, 1980).

20   Antal Párkány, *Sas Andor helye a csehszlovákiai magyar kulturális életben* [The Place of Andor Sas in Czechoslovakian Hungarian Cultural Life] (Pozsony, 1975), with bibliography (pp. 158–170).

21   Tamás Gusztáv Filep, "A humanista voksa. Krammer Jenő szlovákiai pályaszakaszához" [Humanist Voice. The Slovak Period in Jenő Krammer's Career], in Idem, *A humanista voksa. Írások a csehszlovákiai magyar kisebbség történetének köréből 1918–1945* [Humanist Voice. Writings on the History of the Czechoslovakian Hungarian Minority 1918–1945] (Pozsony, 2007), pp. 65–120.

22   Sándor Tavaszy, *A lét és valóság. Az exisztenciálizmus filozófiájának alapproblémái* [Existence and Reality. Basic Problems of the Philosophy of Existentialism] (Cluj, 1933). Selected earlier work: Idem, *Válogatott filozófiai írások* [Selected Philosophical Writings] (Kolozsvár/Szeged, 1999).

23   On major members of the Cluj School: Tibor Hanák, *Az elfelejtett reneszánsz. A magyar filozófiai gondolkodás századunk első felében* [Forgotten Renaissance. Hungarian Philosophical Thinking in the First Half of This Century] (Budapest, 1993), pp. 131–152.

24   A more recent edition of work on him and by him: Erzsébet Hász, ed., *Bognár Cecil* [Cecil Bognár] (Budapest, 2002).

25   *Erdélyi Szépmíves Céh.*

26   See Ildikó Marosi, ed., *A Helikon és az Erdélyi Szépmíves Céh levelesládája (1924–1944)* [Helikon and the Letterbox of the Transylvanian Arts Guild (1924–1944)], 2 vols. (Bukarest, 1979). The latter were connected only loosely to the later political *népi* movement.

27   On problems of regionalism and the value system in Transylvanian literature at the time, see Mihály Babits, "Erdély" [Transylvania], in Idem, *Írók két háború közt* [Writers between the Two World Wars] (Budapest, 1941), pp. 155–163 and 261–266.

28   Zádor Tordai and Sándor Tóth, eds., *Szerkesztette Gaál Gábor 1929–1940* [Edited by Gábor Gaál 1929–1940] (Budapest, 1976) – fictitious 1976 issue of the journal *Korunk*; Lóránt Kabdebó, ed., *50 éves a Korunk. Az 1976. május 20–21-i emlékülés* [50 Years of *Korunk*. Memorial Session on May 20–21, 1976] (Budapest, 1977).

29 Mária Palotai, *Pásztortűz (1921–1944). Egy erdélyi irodalmi folyóirat története* [*Pásztortűz* (1921–1944). History of a Transylvanian Literary Periodical] (Budapest, 2008). Covering a later period of *Pásztortűz*, *Erdélyi Helikon* and *Hitel*, but also looking at antecedents: Júlia Vallasek, *Sajtótörténeti esszék. Négy folyóirat szerepe 1940–1944 között az észak-erdélyi kulturális életben* [Essays in Press History. The Role of Four Journals in the Cultural Life of Northern Transylvania in 1940–1944] (Kolozsvár, 2003).

30 *Erdélyi Irodalmi Társaság.*

31 *Erdélyi Múzeum Egyesület.*

32 György Lajos, ed., *Az Erdélyi Múzeum-Egyesület három-negyedszázados tudományos működése 1859–1934* [Three Quarters of a Century of Scholarly Work by the Transylvanian Museum Society 1859–1934] (Cluj, 1938).

33 Ferenc László and Péter Cseke, eds., *Erdélyi fiatalok. Dokumentumok, viták* [Transylvanian Young People. Documents, Debates] (Bukarest, 1986); Éva Záhony, ed., *Hitel. Kolozsvár 1935–1944* [*Hitel.* Kolozsvár 1935–1944] (Budapest, 1991).

34 *Csehszlovákiai Magyar Irodalmi Szövetség.*

35 Monographs on interwar Czechoslovakian Hungarian literature: Gábor [G.] Kemény, *Így tűnt el egy gondolat. A felvidéki magyar irodalom története 1918–1938* [How an Idea Disappeared. History of Upland Hungarian Literature 1918–1938] (Budapest, 1940); Zoltán Fónod, *Üzenet. A magyar irodalom története Cseh/Szlovákiában 1918–1945* [Message. The History of Hungarian Literature in Czechoslovakia 1918–1945] (Pozsony, 2002). On the broader context: Lajos Turczel, *Két kor mezsgyéjén (A magyar irodalom fejlődési feltételei és problémái Csehszlovákiában 1918 és 1938 között)* [Between Two Periods (Development Conditions and Problems of Hungarian Literature in Czechoslovakia 1918–1938)] (Pozsony, 1983).

36 "Sickle." Jenő Krammer, *A szlovenszkói magyar serdülők lelkivilága. Szociálpszichológiai tanulmány* [The Psychological World of Slovensko Hungarian Adolescents. Social Psychological Study] (Budapest, 1935); Sándor László, ed., *Ez volt a Sarló. Tanulmányok, emlékezések, dokumentumok* [That Was *Sarló*. Studies, Memoirs, Documents] (Budapest, 1978).

37 Its history: Gyula Popély, *A Csehszlovákiai Magyar Tudományos, Irodalmi és Művészeti Társaság* [Czechoslovakian Hungarian Scientific, Literary and Arts Society] (Pozsony, 1973).

38   Ligeti, *Súly alatt a pálma*, pp. 271–274; Ildikó Marosi, "A fedél-
      zetközi utas palackpostája" [Below-Decks Passenger's Message in
      a Bottle], in *ibid.*, pp. 307–314; G. Kovács, "Az Új Szellem avagy
      a csehszlovákiai magyar »egységfront« megteremtésének kísérlete"
      [The New Spirit, or an Attempt to Form a Czechoslovakian Hungarian
      "United Front"], *Kalligram* (1993) 3: 25–31.

39   See the relevant chapters of Imre Bori, *A jugoszláviai magyar
      irodalom története* [The History of Yugoslavian Hungarian
      Literature] (Novi Sad/Belgrade, 1998).

40   "Stook" [of corn]. Csaba Utasi, *Irodalmunk és a* Kalangya [Our
      Literature and *Kalangya*] (Novi Sad, 1984).

41   "Bridge."

42   An anthology of articles from it: János Kovács, ed., *Híd 1934–1941*
      [*Híd* ("Bridge") 1934–1941] (Novi Sad, 1964).

43   Tamás Bécsy, Tamás Gajdó and György Székely, eds., *Magyar
      színháztörténet III. 1920–1949* [Hungary Theater History III, 1920–
      1949] (Budapest, 2006); László Tóth, "A (cseh)szlovákiai magyar
      színjátszás nyolcvan éve 1918–1998" [Eighty Years of (Czecho)
      Slovakian Hungarian Theater 1918–1998], in Idem, *Köz – Művelődés –
      Történet. Három tanulmány* [Public – Education – History. Three
      Studies] (Budapest, 2000), pp. 95–153.

44   Lajos Jordáky, *Az erdélyi némafilmgyártás története (1903–1930)*
      [The History of Transylvanian Silent Film-Making (1903–1930)]
      (Bucharest, 1980).

45   *Színpártoló Egyesület*; *Szlovákiai Magyar Színpártoló Egyesület*;
      Podkarpatszka Ruszi Színpártoló Egyesület.

46   *Délvidéki Magyar Közművelődési Szövetség.* On Yugoslavian
      Hungarian public education in the period, see János Csuka, *A
      délvidéki magyarság története 1918–1941* [The History of Southern
      Region Hungarians 1918–1941] (Budapest, 1995), pp. 28–136, 232–
      244, 391–398, 411–413, 428–429, 479–481 and 494–499, and Gyula
      Krámer, "A Délvidéki Magyar Közművelődési Szövetség feladatai
      és munkája" [Tasks and Activity of the Southern Region Hungarian
      Public Education Association], in Zoltán Csuka, ed., *A visszatért
      Délvidék* [The Returned Southern Region] (Budapest, 1941), pp.
      43–46.

47   *Szlovenszkói Magyar Kultúregyesület* and *Podkarpatszka Ruszi
      Magyar Kultúregyesület.*

48   On this and overall educational chances for the Czechoslovakian
      Hungarian minority, see Imre Molnár, "A szlovenszkói magyar
      közművelődés meghatározó összetevői 1920–1945 között" [Decisive
      Factors in Slovensko Hungarian Education 1920–1945], in László
      Tóth and Tamás Gusztáv Filep, eds., *A (cseh)szlovákiai magyar
      művelődés története 1918–1998* [The History of (Czecho)Slovakian
      Hungarian Education 1918–1998], Vol. 2 (Budapest, 1998), pp. 179–
      233.

10. CASE STUDIES

Romania (*Nándor Bárdi*)

The policy of interwar Bucharest governments towards the Hungarians can be seen mainly in terms of a centrally directed homogenization process for the regions at various levels of development (Transylvania, Bukovina, Bessarabia) and of international relations between Romania and Hungary. The pattern for the Romanian model envisaged was a homogeneous nation state such as nineteenth-century France. Attainment of this was envisaged differently by the Romanian National Party in Transylvania and by the Bucharest politicians. The former sought individual integration of the minorities, or state reinforcement of the Romanian national (ethno-cultural) community, while the then dominant Liberal Party wished to continue the assimilatory, discriminatory national policy of the pre-war period, which had been successful for the Romanian nation in Dobruja and Moldavia.[1] The underlying question in the period was how the Romanians of Transylvania, having gained political power, could make headway against the dominant Germans, Jews and Hungarians in the economic, cultural and social fields.

The 1918–1921 period – of the Sibiu Governing Council and the first governments led by Alexandru Vaida-Voevod and by Alexandru Averescu – saw the transfer of the institutional system, removal of Hungarian officials, and implementation of a land reform that weakened the Hungarian landowners. The Governing Council's policy on the Hungarians, decisively influenced by the Transylvanian Romanian National Party, took as its starting point Hungary's minority policy before 1918: leaving education to the religious denominations, and obstructing minority self-organization. The succeeding Liberal government led by Ion I. C. Brătianu took the view that Hungarians should exercise their political rights

194

individually within the existing Romanian party structure. This was rejected by the Saxons, with their long traditions of minority politics, and by the rapidly organizing Hungarians, with their strong urban bourgeoisie.

During the rule of the Liberal Party in the 1922–1926 period, the means employed to erect a homogeneous, unified nation state were rooted in a discriminatory model determined by Ion and Vintilă Brătianu, which gained precedence over the integration techniques advocated by Iuliu Maniu. This discriminatory strategy contained two strands: on the one hand, it involved Hungarian industrial corporations and financial institutions being nationalized and smaller Hungarian banks and artisan industry suffering systematic economic discrimination, and on the other an education policy devised by Minister Constantin Angelescu that became institutionalized in the limitation of language rights and self-determination (the act on private education, the baccalaureate system, cultural zones, and so on).

The third period, between 1927 and 1931, brought relative peace and prosperity under the government by the National Peasant Party and Maniu. Policy on the Hungarians focused on individual rights such as the pensions of former public officials who had not taken the oath of allegiance to Romania. But antagonism towards minorities remained a feature of party political competition, meaning that little was achieved.

The 1931–1934 period was marked by economic crisis. The Hungarians received no government support of any kind, and lost their gains from the period of economic prosperity. New Romanian worker and clerical strata produced by the national school policy of the 1920s appeared and demanded jobs, further reducing the scope for Hungarians on the labor market.

What marked the 1934–1938 period were anti-revisionist movements. One reaction to the changed international situation was for Romanian governments to regard the Hungarians as hostages against Hungary's territorial ambitions. So the economic and language-rights positions of the Hungarian minority continued to narrow.

The likelihood of territorial revision increased in 1938–1940, prompting three defensive moves. Bucharest's Minority Statute was meant to show the world that the minority Hungarian question had been settled legally. At the same time, measures of labor, language and economic discrimination continued. Yet the period of royal dictatorship gave rise to a Hungarian branch of the National Front for Rebirth – the Hungarian People's Community[2] – which undertook effective work of building up society and organizing the community among the Hungarians.[3]

Romanian government policy on the Hungarian community took the form of legal and economic measures. There were five available sources of legitimacy for minority demands in interwar Romania. The only part of the Gyulafehérvár (Alba Iulia) Resolutions of December 1918 to be adopted as legislation was the union of Transylvania with Romania, and thus this did not count as a constitutional source. The Minority Protection Treaty of December 1919 was ratified, but as an international treaty it ranked lower than domestic legislation. The official Romanian policy was to claim that the autonomy obligations towards the Székelys and Saxons had been met through the system of Church institutions. Both the 1923 and the 1938 Constitution only recognized the concept of a religious minority, but not that of a national minority (on a racial or linguistic basis). The Minority Statute of 1938 set up a minority government commissionership to show the world that efforts were being made to handle the minority question, but gave it no decisive powers, while the Council of Ministers minutes that spelled out the minority rights did not count as a legal regulation.[4]

The discrimination that most affected Hungarians in their daily lives concerned citizenship. The 1924 Nationality Act prescribed domicile (four continuous years of residence and certified payment of local dues), not just place of residence, as the criterion for Romanian citizenship. So even in 1939 there were tens of thousands of Hungarians in Romania whose citizenship was unsettled. On the labor market in the 1930s, there were regulations stipulating that 80 percent of a firm's employees and 50 percent of its managers were to be of Romanian nationality (ethnicity), while use of the Romanian language became compulsory in the judiciary, commercial bookkeeping, the postal services, and city and county public offices. In the second half of the 1930s it became illegal for the Hungarian-language press to use Hungarian names for geographical features and places in Romania.[5]

The most important change in the economy was the land reform. Four separate land reform acts were introduced for the country's four big regions, of which the legislation for Transylvania was the most radical, although it had the least unequal ownership structure. The expropriation in Transylvania covered whole estates, whereas in the Regat it included only cultivable land. Also expropriated were the lands of those who had been abroad between December 1, 1918, and the summer of 1921, and the same applied to the lands of those who had opted for Hungarian citizenship. Altogether 3,192,508 *hold* (1,819,730 hectares) in Transylvania were redistributed, 24.9 percent to applicants for ownership and 65.6 percent for public pasture and forest to strengthen the position of local Romanians. The beneficiaries up to 1927 were 212,803 people of Romanian, 45,628 of Hungarian, 15,934 of German, and 6,314 of other ethnicity.

Also discriminatory was the expropriation of the estate of the Ciuc Border Guard (62,000 *hold* mainly of forest and other valuable pieces of real estate), while that of the Romanian-recruited Năsăud Border Guard of similar origin remained in communal ownership. The compensation was paid as an annuity bond after the 1913 price had been converted into lei, which meant that the estates were valued at next to nothing. The biggest institutional sufferers by the land reform were the Hungarian Churches, which were deprived of 84.5 percent of the 372,000 *hold* used for educational and other public purposes.[6]

There was economic discrimination also in the fiscal system. The amount of tax levied on Transylvania in the mid-1920s increased twice as fast as the national average increase, and the tax collection results in the Hungarian counties was far more effective than in the Romanian counties (96.8 percent in Ciuc County, 99.9 percent in Mureş-Turda, and 100.2 percent in Trei Scaune).[7]

Interest assertion specific to the Romanian Hungarians can be distinguished in party political and social policy strategy.[8] The former encompassed four kinds of political stance: a pact policy, formation of a minority bloc, separate political activity by Transylvanian Hungarians, and integration into the royal dictatorship. By social policy is meant internal construction of society and institutions. Romania's National Hungarian Party concluded three pacts with Romanian parties in 1923–1926, thus integrating itself into the Romanian political system and obtaining seats in the legislature. But much of the Hungarian community was not even on the electoral roll, and it was always the government supervising the elections that won them, through substantial ballot rigging, an agreement had to be reached with the party expected to govern in the future. The Liberal Party, however, denied the need for any separate minority party, while the National Party in Transylvania feared for its regional urban votes, which left Averescu's People's Party as the sole possible ally, as it needed Transylvanian votes. The secret Ciucea Pact with it in 1923 envisaged revision of the electoral rolls and settlement of minority grievances, not just parliamentary representation.[9]

The Liberal Party held negotiations on a pact with the National Hungarian Party before the local elections of 1926, to prevent the National Party from gaining exclusive positions. This was never signed, although local organizations cooperated, and the largely Liberal Party lists supported by the National Hungarian Party won 30 of the 49 cities in the province, while Hungarians were added to the electoral rolls and the National Hungarian Party became a nationally accepted political force. However, the king appointed Averescu to form a government, and parliamentary elections were called in May. This put the 1923 pact with the People's Party back on the agenda. István Ugron (having dissolved the pact a few weeks earlier in favor of one with the Liberal Party) stepped down as National Hungarian Party leader in favor of György Bethlen, who renewed the earlier pact almost unchanged and gained his party 14 seats in the Lower House and 12 in the Upper House. But the promised redress of the minority grievances came to nothing, as the

Romanian parties vied for two decades to accuse the government of the day of betraying the Romanian nation if it proposed changing the disadvantageous position of the Hungarians. In 1927, the Liberal Party returned to power, but offered the National Hungarian Party only seats in the Parliament in that summer's elections.[10]

Electoral law stated that a party had to poll 2 percent of the vote nationally or an absolute majority in one county to qualify for seats. This prompted the leaders of the German and Hungarian parties to form a joint minority bloc, for fear of electoral fraud (1927). The 15 seats obtained were divided 8:7 between them, although there were twice as many Hungarians as Germans in Romania. Such political arrangements worked well elsewhere in Europe, but not in Romania, owing to the size of the Hungarian minority, its regional weight, the kin-state's open aim of territorial revision, and the conflict between Hungarian/Jewish and Hungarian/German dual identity as opposed by separate Jewish and German parties.[11]

Another problem was the German minority insistence (ever since the Austro-Hungarian *Ausgleich* of 1867) on concluding a pact with the government parties of the day, and cooperation was offered also to Iuliu Maniu when he took power in November 1928. This would not work for the Hungarians, because the National Peasant Party (successor to the Romanian National Party in Transylvania) was threatening further land reform at Hungarian expense. So thereafter the National Hungarian Party stood alone in elections,[12] during a decade of separate political activity from 1928 to 1938. Apart from its parliamentary presence, the National Hungarian Party represented the Hungarian cause before local and ministerial bodies, transmitted the Hungarian standpoint to the Romanian public, and helped to run Hungarian social organizations. Furthermore, it worked internationally, for instance in the European Congress of Nationalities, where Elemér Jakabffy, Artúr Balogh and other National Hungarian Party politicians were active.[13] On 54 occasions it made complaints on behalf of the Romanian Hungarians to the League of Nations, with little success.[14] The minority policy of Maniu's National Peasant Party in 1928–1931, although representing a community that had itself been a minority up to 1918, was a big disappointment. As the international situation changed and the anti-Hungarian mood in Romania increased, in 1934 the National Hungarian Party recommended accepting the Romanian Parliament's inter-party agreement on the minority issue, but eventually this was rejected by the other parties. The main achievement in this period was to keep the Hungarian political community together and obstruct some of the anti-minority measures that were mooted.[15]

All political parties and associations were dissolved by royal decree on March 31, 1938. The National Front for Rebirth brought into being by the royal dictatorship managed to win over the entire organized Hungarian community after talks with the former leaders of the National Hungarian party, the Hungarian bishops, Miklós Bánffy (former Hungarian minister of foreign affairs (1921–1922) who had returned to Transylvania), and Pál Szász (president of the Transylvanian Hungarian Agricultural Association).[16] Under the January 1939 agreement, special departments were set up in Hungarian settlements and their trade associations admitted into corporatist national trade bodies. Bánffy was the man that the king appointed to head the comprehensive economic, social and cultural institution known as the Hungarian People's Community, which took over the tasks carried out hitherto by the National Hungarian Party and worked intensively in the social field. However, much of its work after the First Vienna Award shifted to offsetting or diluting the mounting anti-Hungarian campaigns and measures in the parts of Transylvania that remained under Romanian control.[17]

The most extensive system of institutions among the Romanian Hungarians consisted of the Churches and their school system. It was mentioned in Section 2.3 that teaching in Hungarian became largely confined to denominational schools unsupported by the state. These numbered, in 1930–1931, 483 maintained by the Reformed Church, 297 by the Catholics, 36 by the Unitarians, and 6 by the Evangelicals. In fact 57.6 percent of the Hungarian children for whom school was compulsory (76,255 pupils) attended a denominational school. The number of state schools teaching in Hungarian had fallen to 112 by 1934–1935. There were 23 Hungarian-language denominational middle schools (17 lyceums, 7 teachers' training colleges, 4 upper commercial schools, and 4 winter commercial schools) provided native-language teaching for 54 percent of Hungarian secondary students. Some 6–7 percent of those receiving university degrees were of Hungarian ethnicity. There was no separate Hungarian institution: university education was attempted in jointly run Church colleges set up in Cluj, providing separate Hungarian-language teaching in each major subject. The broadest Church organizations in society were the women's associations.[18]

The long-established Hungarian cultural associations in Transylvania confined themselves in this period mainly to preserving what they had accomplished in the past. The library and collections of the Transylvanian Museum Society[19] were used by the University of Cluj, but no rent was paid for that[20] and the Society was not recognized legally until 1926. The funds for the Hungarian Cultural Association of Transylvania[21] all but dried up after the transfer of power. Its statutes were not recognized until 1935 and its interwar activity was negligible. The Transylvanian-Hungarian Economic Association (*Erdélyi Magyar Gazdasági Egyesület*, EMGE), founded in 1844, had no village branches until Pál Szász took over as president in 1936. Thereafter it began widespread work of information and organization in support of small provincial farmers and managed to attract almost 40,000 members within a few years.[22] There was intensive organization of choral societies, with 150 of them affiliated to the Romanian Hungarian Singers' Association by 1930.[23]

Public opinion among the Hungarians of Transylvania was shaped by the political newspapers and periodicals and by a variety of "internal parliaments" (general assemblies of the National Hungarian Party, and meetings of the executives of the Roman Catholic Status[24] and the Transylvanian Reformed Church District). Some 25–30 Hungarian-language newspapers appeared in Romania between the world wars, of which the most influential were the *Keleti Újság, Ellenzék, Erdélyi Lapok* and *Brassói Lapok.* The periodical with the largest circulation was *Magyar Nép*. Other influential periodicals were the internationally recognized journal of the minorities *Magyar Kisebbség*, and the standard-bearer of conservative literature in Transylvania, *Pásztortűz*. Miklós Bánffy was instrumental in launching the most prestigious literary journal in the province: *Erdélyi Helikon*, which published the pick of the literary output in that period. The periodicals and movements of most importance in the field of social policy were *Erdélyi Fiatalok*, *Hitel* and *Korunk*.[25]

The Hungarian minority in interwar Romania strove to establish its own national minority institutions, to oppose the efforts to build a uniform Romanian nation state. In a situation where the state support for building the Hungarian nation had ceased, and against the intentions of both the Bucharest and the Budapest government, the Hungarians began to protect their positions by building up a separate regional and political community.

Czechoslovakia: Slovakia (*Attila Simon*)

It is important to note, when examining the policy, culture and public life of Slovakian Hungarians, that they had never had traditions of their own (unlike the Transylvanians): Kassa, Pozsony, Komárom, and so on had looked to Budapest for examples. It was some time after the change of sovereignty before the Slovakian Hungarians could build up a system of institutions from scratch and establish their own traditions, although the democracy prevalent in interwar Czechoslovakia assisted them in doing so in the 1920s.

The scope available to the Slovakian Hungarians was decided largely by Prague's minority policy, which was inconsistent, despite the country's democratic system and the broad rights that it ensured for its minorities. For instance, there was insistence throughout the period on building up the Czechoslovak nation state. Plans for German, Hungarian and even Slovak autonomy were rejected mainly due to fear of possible efforts by the Sudeten Germans to secede. On the other hand, Prague generally made broader concessions to the

Sudeten Germans than to the Hungarians, for reasons that included the greater numbers of the former, the greater flexibility of minority German policy (the role of the activist school), and the greater respect felt for Germany.

There were three main political strands among the Slovakian Hungarians. The strongest gave electoral backing to the right-wing opposition Hungarian parties, which trimmed their policies to Budapest's expectations. They insisted throughout on self-determination for the Hungarian minority, being prevented by Czechoslovak law from stating their real aim of peaceful revision of the borders. The deciding figures in the mainly Christian Socialist Party[26] were Jenő Lelley, then Géza Szüllő, while the Hungarian National Party,[27] popular mainly among Reformed Church members, was led by József Szent-Ivány. Despite several initial conflicts, the two parties managed steadily to consolidate their cooperation. By the 1930s, they had a joint parliamentary club, and they merged in 1936 as the United Hungarian Party,[28] whose national president was Andor Jaross and executive president János Esterházy.

Support for the Communist Party of Czechoslovakia, affiliated to the Third International, was much higher among the Slovakian Hungarians (20–25 percent) than it was among the majority Slovaks (12–14 percent). This was due partly to its attitude on the minority question and the influence of its social rhetoric on the Hungarian agricultural workers excluded from the land reform. Hungarians played important roles in the communist movement in Slovakia, notably Jenő (Eugen) Fried[29] in the national leadership and István Major in minority public life in Slovakia.

The third strand of Hungarian minority politics, Activism, was less successful. It mainly took the form of Hungarian sections within the two main Czechoslovak parties, the right-wing Agrarians and the Social Democrats. What it lacked was the strong economic motivation that made it popular among the Sudeten Germans. The groups headed by the Agrarian István Csomor and the Social Democrat Ignác Schulcz could hardly point to any autonomy within their parties or political results. Although the example of the Sudeten Germans seemed to justify Activist politics, it was vehemently opposed by Budapest: Slovakian Hungarian activists were often branded as traitors to their nation.

The authorities may have eliminated Hungarian-language teaching in the cities beyond the linguistic border, but it was profoundly important to the identity of Slovakian Hungarians that Hungarian-language elementary schooling largely remained in the districts where they predominated. Still, there was no Hungarian higher education in Czechoslovakia, while the Germans had their own universities in Prague and Brno.

The Hungarian-language press was extensive and varied. The total of more than 500 Hungarian papers of various kinds that appeared for longer or shorter periods in interwar Slovakia included plenty of political and popular dailies, cultural magazines, and even sports papers. The foremost daily was the *Prágai Magyar Hírlap*, a mouthpiece of the opposition, but the *Kassai Napló* in Košice and the moderate pro-government *Magyar Újság* of the 1930s were of a high standard as well.

Cultural life was as divided as politics, each institution being tied to some party or political trend. The main national body was the Hungarian Cultural Association in Slovensko,[30] closely associated with the opposition. This had broadly active branches in every region, maintaining drama and folklore groups, and holding lectures and celebrations. The main regional bodies were the Kazinczy Society (*Kazinczy Társaság*) in Košice, the Toldy Circle (*Toldy Kör*) in Bratislava, and the Jókai Cultural and Museum Society (*Jókai Közművelődési és Múzeum Egyesület*) in Komárno, but there were many reading circles, boys' brigades, Church groups, workers' academies and middle-class clubs that played a crucial local role. A donation from President Masaryk prompted the formation in 1931 of the Czechoslovakian Hungarian Scientific, Literary and Artistic Society[31] (known colloquially as the Masaryk Academy), to act as a kind of academy of sciences for the Hungarian community, but it foundered on the hostility of opposition Hungarians and fell into dilettantism.

Slovakian Hungarian youth was organized initially into the Scout movement and the Association of Czechoslovakian Hungarian Academics,[32] which encompassed university students, but ideological and political polarization had invaded by the end of the 1920s. The more left-wing *Sarló* (Sickle) movement in Slovakia was inspired by the rural researchers and folksong collectors, while the Prohászka Circles[33] were focal points for Catholic young people. But Slovakian Hungarians growing up after Trianon shared an acquaintance with Czech and Slovak culture, to which they were more open than their elders. They saw the solution to the minority question primarily in cooperation among the nations of the Carpathian Basin.

Sports in interwar Czechoslovakia were organized on a national basis as well, so that the Hungarians and other minorities had autonomous sports institutions, in the former case the Czechoslovakian Hungarian Physical Education Association.[34] This ran championships in association football, tennis, athletics, swimming, water polo and even ice hockey.

Despite the relative comprehensiveness of minority life, the Hungarian minority in Slovakia had numerous grievances, mainly to do with the efforts in Prague to build up a Czechoslovak nation state. The Hungarian parties criticized not only the 1920 Language Act, but also the failure of the authorities to observe its terms. The Hungarians lost by the reform of public administration, which replaced the traditional system of counties and restricted local self-government. Particularly detrimental was the conduct of the land reform, in which the Slovakian Hungarians were hardly included at all, while thousands of them were left jobless by the break-up of the great estates. Another recurrent complaint was over the expulsion of Slovakian Hungarians from state offices and public administration. The authorities treated all Hungarians as unreliable from the state's point of view, with the result that they were almost entirely eliminated from central and district state offices, and even from the post office and the railways, where they no longer made up even one percent of the workforce.[35] The lack of Czechoslovak generosity towards the minorities appeared also in the legislation that banned public use of Hungarian national symbols or public celebration of Hungarian national feasts. The authorities discerned irredentism in anyone who wore or hung out a flag in the Hungarian national colors, or sang the Hungarian national anthem. Prosecution would follow any infringement of these regulations.

Prague's attitude to the minorities changed in the second half of the 1930s, when the actions of Hitler brought radical changes in international relations and placed Czechoslovakia in direct danger. In the spring of 1938, in the shadow of the German/ Austrian *Anschluss*, Prime Minister Milan Hodža tried to rescue his fragmenting country by abandoning nation-state ideology and preparing a so-called Nationality Statute. This promised to eliminate national grievances, accord equal rights to the languages of the minorities, and grant them cultural and educational autonomy, but it was never introduced, due to the heightening antagonism between the government and the Sudeten Germans, who wished to join the German Reich. The imminent threat of world war was lessened by the four-power Munich Agreement between France, Britain, Germany and Italy concluded on September 29–30, 1938, but the areas of Czechoslovakia with a German-speaking majority were incorporated into Germany. The Hungarian minority initially hoped that the talks on the Statute would improve the situation in Czechoslovakia,[36] but the United Hungarian Party reacted to the changed conditions by issuing a statement on September 17 demanding rights of self-determination. The Hungarians in many Hungarian-inhabited areas held demonstrations after Munich, in the early days of October, calling for annexation to Hungary.[37] On October 7, Hungarian representatives and senators formed a Hungarian National Council[38] aimed at ensuring that the return to Hungary took place peacefully, without disorderliness. Although the Hungarian communists in Czechoslovakia had initially given support for the integrity of the country, Slovakian Hungarian politics became united after Munich, as they and the Activists fell in behind the Hungarian National Council and the aim of peaceful revision of the borders. Of course the choice made by the Slovakian

Hungarians facilitated in residual Slovakia, which had gained autonomy from Prague, the arrival of a regime headed by Jozef Tiso that was intolerant of all differences (Jews, Gypsies, Hungarians or Freemasons) and intent on imposing a Fascist model of state.

Czechoslovakia: Transcarpathia (*Csilla Fedinec*)

After the first Transcarpathian governor, Gregory Zhatkovych, resigned, his successors – Anton Beszkid (Anton Beskyd) (1923–1933) and then Konstantin Hrabar (1935–1938) – were still appointed by Prague. Fulfillment of the repeated promise that this was a temporary arrangement until autonomy continued to be postponed. Transcarpathia was needed mainly for strategic reasons of access to the other Little Entente countries (Romania and thereby Yugoslavia), it being in the Little Entente's interest to keep Hungary surrounded.

The governorship was the only difference in public administration between Transcarpathia and the rest of Czechoslovakia, after it had been declared a province of the republic in 1928. Elsewhere there was a uniform two-tier system of local and district offices, but in Transcarpathia there remained a governor's office, attached to the provincial governor (known colloquially as the national governor).[39] The head of the National Office was Antonín Rožypal from 1928 to 1937, after which the post was left vacant due to the "imminent introduction" of autonomy, and the regular tasks were carried out by the national vice-president, Jaroslav Meznik. Uzhhorod (Slovak: Užhorod; the center of the territory) and Mukachevo (Slovak: Mukačevo) retained the rank of incorporated cities, but Berehove (Slovak: Berehovo), the one Transcarpathian city to keep its Hungarian majority throughout the century, was demoted to a large civil parish. According to the 1930 census returns, the population of Transcarpathia exceeded 750,000, of whom almost 450,000 were Rusyns (Ukrainians or Russians), about 110,000 were Hungarians, and 91,000 were Jews. In their religious affiliation, about 50 percent were Greek Catholic, 15 percent Orthodox, 15 percent Jewish, 10 percent Reformed, and 10 percent Roman Catholic.[40]

The first practical move towards the promised autonomy came in 1937, with an act defining the powers of the governor.[41] The autonomy act followed on November 22, 1938,[42] but its form was affected by the war situation, with the public demanding autonomy on national lines, in other words demanding that Transcarpathia should be declared a Rusyn autonomous area.

The official explanations for postponing autonomy usually cited the territory's backwardness and poverty. An attempt to alleviate the poverty had been made at the turn of the century in a so-called Highland Economic Campaign headed by Ede Egan. Transcarpathia certainly was the most backward corner of pre-1918 Hungary and then of the whole East-Central European region. It remained so despite success in the Czechoslovak period in reducing illiteracy. The land reform, on the other hand, did not have the desired results. The stratum of officials consisted almost wholly of immigrant Czechs. "Czech settlements" were placed on the old great estates. Almost 70 percent of the population worked in agriculture and forestry, with hardly any small or large-scale industry (about 10 percent) or commerce (about 5 percent). There was a long tradition of winemaking and beekeeping. Flooding was a constant problem, especially in 1933.

The most obvious changes after Transcarpathia's annexation to Czechoslovakia were in infrastructure development and construction. Paved roads and bridges were built, and there were extensive water regulation works, along with several construction projects in cities. The Galagó district was added to Uzhhorod/Užhorod in Czech constructivist style. Hospitals went up in Mukacheve/Mukačevo, Berehove/Berehovo and Vynohradiv (Slovak: Sevľuš), and a gymnasium (high school) was built in Khust (Slovak: Chust). Solotvyno (Slovak: Slatinské Doly) underwent planned development.[43]

The Hungarian parties in interwar Transcarpathia got little further than defining themselves and establishing relations with each other. After 1927, there were no exclusively Transcarpathian parties, as they operated only as district organizations of national (Czechoslovak) parties up to the turn of events in 1938, when there was a ban, followed by conversion into the "Highlands." The two exclusively Transcarpathian parties in the 1920s were the Hungarian Party of Law (1920–1922, chaired by Endre Korláth, publishing the *Ruszinszkói Magyar Hírlap* and later the *Ungvári Közlöny*)[44] and the Autonomous Party of the Indigenous (1921–1927, chaired by Ákos Árky, publishing the *Ruszinszkói Magyar Hírlap*).[45] The other parties operated as *Transcarpathian* branches of so-called national parties, which sought to maintain vestiges of a separate political complexion, mainly for reasons of financing. These were the Christian Socialist Party (1920–1936, chaired by István Kerekes, publishing the *Kárpáti Napló*, later the *Határszéli Újság*), and the Smallholders', Artisans' and Agriculturalists' Party (1921–1926, after which it became the Hungarian National Party, chaired by Ferenc Egry, publishing the *Beregi Hírlap* and later the *Kárpáti Magyar Gazda*).[46] From 1920 to 1936, the Hungarian parties operating in Transcarpathia were grouped in the Hungarian Party Association chaired by Endre Korláth (publishing the *Ruszinszkói Magyar Hírlap*, later the *Kárpáti Magyar Hírlap*). This lost its function when the Christian Socialists and the Hungarian National Party merged as the United Hungarian Party in 1936. On March 15, 1940, the United Hungarian Party was declared to be dissolved, or rather subsumed into the Hungarian Party of Life (established by Pál Teleki in 1939 and in government in Hungary until March 1944).[47]

The Hungarian parties in Transcarpathia cooperated closely with the eponymous Hungarian parties in Slovakia, but as separate entities, not parts of a uniform national organization. The Hungarian parties made an electoral alliance with the German parties of Slovakia. The main figures in Hungarian politics included Endre Korláth, Ferenc Egry and Károly Hokky (Charles J. Hokky). The public role of Egry, a respected senator and a famous bell-founder, was enhanced, as many church bells had been melted down to make guns in the war, and he could use the social occasion of consecrating new ones to make speeches encouraging people to take heart. These Hungarian parties and the Rusyn ones pressing strongly for autonomy received regular financial support from official sources in Hungary.

An appreciable part was also played by the Communist Party of Czechoslovakia, which opposed autonomy but made strong social demands. It set up youth organizations and "red" trade unions, organized hunger strikes in the early 1930s, and began in the mid-1930s to campaign strongly against fascism. It came to the republic's defense during the crisis of 1938, as the only party to embrace all ethnic groups, and oriented itself towards the Soviet Union. Its Hungarian-language paper was the *Munkás Újság*.

Election results in the 1920s show that some 70 percent of voters in Transcarpathia supported the working-class parties (as opposed to about half nationally). The centralist parties had more support than those demanding autonomy, and this stayed largely unchanged. The Communists consistently polled more votes in Hungarian-inhabited districts than the Hungarian parties did.[48] However, irredentist movements gained strength during the depression at the turn of the 1920s and 1930s. Official Hungarian government support for Hungarian politics in Transcarpathia came through the Center for Alliance of Social Associations[49] or directly through the Prime Minister's Office or the Ministry of Foreign Affairs. Separate support went to the autonomist Rusyn parties, notably the Autonomous Agriculturalists' Association[50] headed by Iván Kurtyák (Ivan Kurtiak) and then András Bródy (Andrej Brody).[51] The united indigenous demands for autonomy were broken in 1938 by the idea of Hungarian national autonomy, whose main exponent was the Hungarian National Party, although the same politicians rejected all forms of autonomy after Hungary overran Transcarpathia in 1939. There were several Hungarian papers appearing in Transcarpathia during the Czechoslovak period, including the *Ruszinszkói Magyar Hírlap* (later *Kárpáti Magyar Hírlap*), *Határszéli Újság*, *Az Őslakó*, *Kárpátalja*, *Kárpáti Híradó*, *Kárpáti Magyar Gazda* and *Munkás Újság*, almost all with clear political affiliations.

Most Hungarians in Transcarpathia belonged to the Reformed Church, with some Roman and Greek Catholics,[52] the latter being organized into the Greek Catholic Diocese of Mukacheve/ Mukačevo. Under an agreement between the Czechoslovak government and the Vatican, that and the Diocese of Prešov were removed from the Province of Esztergom, to which they had belonged since September 1918, and temporarily placed directly under the Apostolic See, although the former was returned to Esztergom in the summer of 1939. In 1921, the twelve parishes of the former Diocese of Ung remaining in Transcarpathia expressed a wish to split off as a separate Diocese of Transcarpathia. On October 31, 1922, the formation of the Transcarpathian Reformed Diocese was declared, and it was recognized soon afterwards by the first legislative synod of the Combined Reformed Church of Slovakia and Transcarpathia. This was followed on December 16, 1925, by the first ordination of Reformed clergy to have taken place in Transcarpathia since the war. The diocese received official state recognition in 1932.

Authority over Roman Catholic parishes in this part of Czechoslovakia was exercised by the bishop of Satu Mare in Romania. A movement began in Transcarpathia in 1928 to have a separate Roman Catholic bishopric for the territory. In 1929 the Holy See concluded a concordat with Romania whereby the ordinary authority of Satu Mare over the Transcarpathian parts of the diocese ceased, and in 1930 it ended the authority of Satu Mare, passing it to a Transcarpathian Roman Catholic Apostolic Governorship.

The Czechoslovak Republic inherited in Transcarpathia elementary schools (with various languages of instruction), three gymnasia (in Užhorod, Mukačevo and Berehovo, teaching in Hungarian), a vocational middle school, and three teachers' training colleges (two in Užhorod and one in Mukačevo, teaching in Rusyn and Hungarian). These were under the authority of the schools department in Užhorod, although the governor had certain powers of appointment and administration. The elementary system was left largely unchanged. The civil schools were expanded but parallel classes teaching in Hungarian remained only in Užhorod and Mukačevo, and the time spent in such schools was reduced from four years to three in the 1930s, although an additional fourth year was made available in some places. The Hungarian classes were steadily run down in the Czechoslovak system's real gymnasia (the more practically oriented type of gymnasium, the other being the human gymnasium) in Užhorod and Mukačevo, until the Hungarian language of instruction remained only in one place: the parallel classes of the bilingual real gymnasium in Berehovo. In addition, a bilingual Rusyn–Czech gymnasium opened in Khust, as well as a Jewish gymnasium in Mukačevo and, in the 1930s, a Hebrew gymnasium in Užhorod. Many Hungarian teachers lost their positions and their citizenship after the change of sovereignty. The so-called Small Schools Act stated that pupils in educational institutions were not obliged to attend religious education. The Library Act, on the other hand, had a beneficial effect, ensuring good supplies of Hungarian books to village and city public libraries.[53]

Transcarpathia had no prominent regional literary traditions. This was the region where literary thinking veered furthest away from the development path of Hungarian literature as a whole, into regional frames. Despite attempts to raise the literary standard, the regional awareness behind them remained a literary standard as such. It is not possible to draw a sharp line between Transcarpathian and Slovakian Hungarian literature in the 1920s and 1930s, apart from pointing to the peripheral state of the former. Yet it is not possible to omit this from the history of Hungarian literature, as it was an indispensable part of Transcarpathian awareness. The foremost writers included Árpád Fülöp, Pál Ilku, Margit Prerau, Pál Rácz, László Sáfáry, Menyhért Simon and Mihály Tamás. But Transcarpathia accounted for only a tiny proportion of over 2,000 Hungarian-language books published in Czechoslovakia. The main source, with about 25 publications, was the Kálvin Press in Berehovo, which belonged to the Transcarpathian Reformed Church.[54]

In the arts, the general opinion today is that the self-organizing activities of the local Hungarians under the Czechoslovaks were directed from Košice and other Slovakian cities. But the social and cultural organizations of Transcarpathia resembled the parties in emphasizing their autonomy and objected to attempts to incorporate them or influence them from Slovakia. There was an independent dramatic society in the 1920s that was merged in the 1930s with that of East Slovakia, to constant protests in

Transcarpathia. An independent Transcarpathian Hungarian Drama Patronage Society[55] was formed in Mukačevo in 1926. This ran acting courses and published a drama periodical for long or short periods (the *Színházi Újság*, later *Ruszinszkói Színházi Élet*). The members of the Transcarpathian Hungarian theater company often appeared in Budapest as unemployed actors looking for parts. The amateur societies presented work by local playwrights that later appeared in print. Interestingly, the press reports of the time suggest that amateur theatricals were important social occasions, arousing more momentary interest than the professional performances did. The commercial survival of the theater companies depended on the fluctuating audiences. The breakthrough often came by appealing to the national sentiments of the audience or by suggesting that these might be waning. So consumption of Hungarian culture became a means of professing one's ethnicity.[56]

The most successful of the Transcarpathian Hungarian cultural groups was the Mosaic Cultural Society, which became the Transcarpathian Hungarian Cultural Society in the 1930s, then the Literature and Drama Society in Berehovo.[57] There were also several larger and smaller local societies organizing innumerable events, evenings, commemorations, readings, evening classes and other occasions, even ice-cream afternoons. The most prestigious event on the Hungarian calendar was the Hungarian National Ball in Berehovo. There was mass participation in the gymnastics and sports associations, which were prominent cultural events as well. The Athletics Club in Užhorod started a flower carnival and election of a rose queen in 1926, long before Debrecen did. It was a matter of pride for a community to support a singing circle, and there was a "national" (Transcarpathian) review of them. These were hosted by Sevľuš, Berehovo, Mukačevo and Užhorod in the 1930s, while a children's song contest was held in Vylok (Slovak: Ujlak) and Berehovo. Beauty queen contests were already being held in the 1930s. In 1935 the Three Borders Community organized a march of several thousand to the Rákóczi Memorial Column in Tiszabecs, which was revived in the 1990s by the Transcarpathian Hungarian Cultural Association, although it is now held at the restored Turul Statue in Vylok, which was destroyed in the 1920s. Young people were brought together in the Scout movement, the Transcarpathian Scout Federation founded in 1920 having Czech/Slovak, Rusyn/Ukrainian, Jewish and Hungarian sections. The latter was set up in 1923 by Ferenc Haba. There was another association for Transcarpathian students in higher education. There were freemasons' lodges in Užhorod and later (known as Pro Libertate) in Berehovo.[58]

One important arts event was the establishment in 1921 of the Artists' Club in Mukačevo (or Transcarpathian Painters' Club) under the painter Gyula Virágh. Then in 1931, József Boksay, Béla Erdélyi and the Czech painters Bedrich Oždian and Jaroslav Kaigl initiated the Podkarpatska Rus Artists' Association, of which Erdélyi remained president for many years. There were regular exhibitions in the province from 1921.[59] The big celebrations in 1922–1923 to mark the centenary of the birth of the Hungarian poet Sándor Petőfi initiated, according to Ferenc Sziklay, cultural secretary of the National Hungarian Party Association, "'minority' awareness and a sense of community among Slovakian and Transcarpathian Hungarians."[60] A reproduction of a full-length painting of Petőfi by Gyula Ijjász appeared in the Christmas 1922 supplement of the *Ruszinszkói Magyar Hírlap.* The works of Transcarpathian painters were exhibited in Paris in February 1938.

Yugoslavia (*Enikő A. Sajti*)

After the law on opting for citizenship expired, the Southern Region Hungarians became the last community in the successor states to enter formal politics. The Yugoslavian Hungarian Party[61] was founded at a congress in Senta on September 22, 1922, chaired by the physician Dr. György Sántha, who was elected president. The party never established branches in Baranja or Prekmurje, and the Catholic Hungarians of Novi Sad did not join either. In Prekmurje, there was a short-lived United Party of Prekmurje to represent local interests.[62]

The Hungarian Party worked strictly within the framework of the Vidovdan (St. Vitus' Day) Constitution of June 28, 1921, although it was subject to official harassment throughout the period. Its main policies were to ensure native-language education, free operation of cultural associations, lifting of electoral measures that discriminated against the Hungarians, freedom of business associations, alteration of the detrimental tax system in Vojvodina, reinstatement of dismissed Hungarian officials, and recognition of pension claims obtained in Hungary. Its activity was subsidized through St. Gellért's Society by the Hungarian government's Center for Alliance of Social Associations.[63] The president of St. Gellért's Society was the writer Ferenc Herczeg.

The party first put up its own candidates in the parliamentary elections of February 8, 1925, but failed to gain seats. However, in the provincial elections of 1927, won by the Radicals, the Hungarian Party gained six of the 60 seats in the Bačka *oblast* and a similar number in that of Belgrade, to which the Banat belonged. In the 1927 general elections, an alliance with the ruling Radicals ensured seats for Dr. Dénes Streliczky and Dr. Imre Várady in the Belgrade legislature. No aggregate figure for the seats gained in communal assemblies is available, but in Subotica, for instance, with the Hungarian population in majority, the party won only 14 out of 100 seats. In Senta it was 55 out of 80, but some communities (Mol, Čantavir, Horgoš and Ada) elected purely Hungarian assemblies.[64]

The scope for Hungarian political and cultural representation was severely curtailed by the royal dictatorship that ensued on January 6, 1929, when King Alexander dissolved the legislature, banned political parties and national and other cultural associations, introduced censorship, and dissolved the provincial and communal assemblies. Under the "imposed" constitution of September 3, 1931, an organization loyal to the regime was formed within the monopoly of the Yugoslav National Party in December, but this was boycotted by leaders and members of the dissolved Hungarian Party. In the second half of the decade, Hungarians studying in Zagreb started an anti-Belgrade radical movement within the Croatian Peasant

Party, proposing autonomy for Vojvodina (previously opposed by the leaders of the Hungarian Party) and a right-wing radical solution to the land question.

Yugoslavia's international position was being eroded by Germany's advances. On August 20, 1938, a pact between the rival Croatian and Serbian power centers was made, to shore up domestic political stability. Belgrade also began to take a more tolerant attitude to the Hungarians.

The Yugoslav government addressed several longstanding grievances among Yugoslavia's Hungarians in the months preceding the Hungarian–Yugoslavian Treaty of Eternal Friendship of December 12, 1940. After long hesitation, permission was given on January 30, 1940, to form the Yugoslavian Hungarian Public Education Association, of which Gyula Kramer became president. The first officially licensed Hungarian-language theater in Yugoslavia opened in the same year.[65]

Southern Region Hungarians belonged to three denominations: Roman Catholic, Evangelical and Reformed. There are no exact figures for their relative sizes, and diocesan boundaries in any case underwent big changes after 1918. Agreement on disputed issues was reached in 1922 between the Vatican and the Serb-Croat-Slovene Kingdom, covering the interim government of Southern Region Catholic dioceses and two new bishoprics in Subotica and Veliki Bečkerek. The Catholic priesthood was trained in seminaries in Croatia, which meant an acute shortage of Hungarian-speaking priests. The 1935 concordat between the Vatican and the Kingdom of Yugoslavia was not ratified after Orthodox protests. The Reformed Church at an inaugural synod in Sombor decided in favor of an independent Yugoslav province. Its clergy would be trained at Hungarian theological colleges in Cluj, and in Bratislava and Lučenec. The Evangelical Church retained its links with Hungary to the greatest extent. It received permission to hold a founding synod in 1926, but the Slovak parishes did not attend. Yugoslavia's Churches failed to play the kind of role in preserving language, culture and self-awareness that they did, for example, in Transylvania.

One factor destructive to the general economic situation in the Southern Region was the fact that the border broke contacts that had existed for centuries. The Yugoslav land reform promised a fair solution to the land question and abolition of the great estates, to make small-scale peasant farming general in Serbia and eliminate the remnants of serfdom. However, it served openly nationalist purposes. The Hungarians were excluded from the reform on the grounds that their citizenship was unclear (due to the opting law), and colonies of settlers (*dobrovoljac*) loyal to the Yugoslav state were established near the Hungarian border. Of the private land redistributed in the reform, 4.4 percent (110,684 hectares) had been in Hungarian hands. Hungarian optant landowners (61 persons) lost 71.2 percent (90,062 hectares) of their holdings and Hungarian landowners who had taken Yugoslav citizenship 38.6 percent (20,622 hectares). The 364 redistributed estates owned by the state, communities, the Churches and charitable foundations covered 247,565 hectares (36 percent of the land was in this type of ownership), while 61.5 percent of the estates belonging to Hungarians was redistributed. Of the redistributed land in Bačka, 42.55 percent was communally owned, 39.9 percent privately owned, and 8.3 percent in Church ownership.

The land reform granted land to 43,500 families, mainly Serbs and Montenegrins. Of these 6,175 families received holdings in Bačka (6,912 families according to other sources) and 235 did so in Baranja. Furthermore, 45 Slovene families from the sea coast were resettled in Prekmurje. After the completion of the land reform, 14.1 percent of the land in Vojvodina remained in Hungarian hands.[66]

The old Hungarian school system was broken up in the early 1920s. Of the 71 Hungarian-language secondary institutions, only two secondary school departments, an eight-year gymnasium in Subotica, and a four-year gymnasium in Senta were spared. According to official Yugoslav statistics, there were 1,376 lower schools in the Danube Banat in early 1930, with 4,233 departments, of which only 528 taught in Hungarian. The number of Hungarian elementary school teachers fell from 1,832 before the war to 250 in 1941. By then there was not a single Hungarian elementary school class in Baranja. Six Hungarian elementary school departments were permitted in the Banat region after the Croatian Banat was established. A Hungarian department was opened at the teacher training college in Belgrade in 1932.

There were five Hungarian-language dailies in the 1930s: the Subotica *Bácsmegyei Napló* (later the *Napló*), the Novi Sad *Délbácska* (later the *Reggeli Újság*), the *Nép* (initially in Novi Sad, later in Zagreb), and the *Torontál* (later *Híradó*), as well as 11 weeklies and 13 periodicals. The main literary papers were *Kalangya* and the still extant *Híd*.[67]

Austria (*Gerhard Baumgartner*)

Once the Sopron plebiscite had been held in December 1921, the task remained of defining the borders between Austria and Hungary. This was done in 1922–1923 by the Entente's Inter-Allied Border Commission, but attempts were made by small units of Hungarian irregulars in 1922 to prevent certain villages from being annexed to Austria. Such groups occupied, for instance, the German-speaking villages of Luising and Hagensdorf, only to be repelled by regular Austrian and Hungarian forces. When drawing the border, the commission considered the proportions of the national groups among the inhabitants and enquired where they wished to belong. This did not just affect Germans and Hungarians. The Croatian Cultural Association of Burgenland[68] feared that the denominational schools in the Croat-inhabited villages would be taken over by the Austrian authorities, and addressed a memorandum to the Inter-Allied Border Commission calling for these villages to remain in Hungary.[69] So most Croat-inhabited border villages were awarded to Hungary. But in Northern Burgenland the border followed the boundaries of the great estates and the new border placed the Burgenland Hungarians in the position of a minority.

Most of the Hungarian-speakers who remained in Burgenland[70] after 1923 lived in five communities. Three were in the Upper Wart district of Southern Burgenland – Oberwart, Unterwart and Siget in der Wart[71] – and two in Middle Burgenland – Oberpullendorf and Mitterpullendorf. The inhabitants of these villages were descendants of border guards of the late Middle Ages. Since they retained their petty noble status until the nineteenth century, their awareness of being Hungarian equated with their feudal awareness from Early Modern times. They had attained petty nobility as Hungarians and as petty nobility they retained their Hungarian affiliation.[72]

The second group of minority Hungarians consisted of those inhabiting manorial farms in Northern Burgenland. Eight large manorial centers had been established in the second half of the nineteenth century on various large noble estates to the east of Lake Neusiedl, in the western part of the Waasen district. These were settled with tenant-farmer families from Western Hungary, amounting to some 300 people – equivalent to the population of an average Burgenland village. Several manors had their own church, cemetery and Hungarian school. These Hungarians retained a nineteenth-century romantic national awareness based on the Hungarian state ideology conveyed through the school system at the turn of the century. Some manors even had Levente groups in the 1920s.[73] Since the manors in Northern Burgenland formed a Hungarian linguistic island amidst the German-speaking villages, and language use was correlated with social status, the Hungarian language became a negative status attribute for these Hungarian tenant farmers.[74]

The third group consisted of usually bourgeois German-speaking or Croatian speaking families who had turned Hungarian at the turn of the century and were known locally as *magyarón* (pro-Hungarian).[75] They were elderly members of the provincial bourgeois elite, who had received a Hungarian education before the First World War and identified the Hungarian language with bourgeois culture. This symbolic importance had prompted them to teach their children or have them taught Hungarian.

In fact there were five language groups in the area that became Burgenland: Germans, Hungarians, Croats, Slovenes and Gypsies. The Slovenes at that time were living in small numbers in two border villages in the Gyanafalva (Jennersdorf) District. The Gypsies, present since the seventeenth century, were living in 130 localities. They numbered 9,000 in 1920, and 5,000 of them lived in the Felsőőr (Oberwart) District.

Multilingualism had a pace of its own. After the 1880s, a kind of equality of rank developed between the German and Hungarian languages, with the result that many Western Hungarian Germans knew Hungarian as well. Likewise, 57 percent of the Felsőőr Hungarians knew German, as the Felsőőr Hungarians played an intermediary role between Styria and the small towns of Transdanubia, mainly in the wood and timber trade.[76] Exchanging children was very common: Hungarian families would send their children to German villages to study and vice versa. After 1921, the Hungarian and German languages exchanged places, so to speak, as German became the official language in the province, although Hungarian did not lose its prestige in Burgenland automatically. Indeed it kept its cachet, despite the campaign in the 1920s waged against its official use by the new provincial government.

The languages in a district were arranged hierarchically, with German and Hungarian at the top. German-speakers and Hungarian-speakers did not use the other languages, but the Croats would learn the two prestigious languages as well as their own, and Gypsies might speak all three in addition to Roma.[77]

One unusual feature of the Hungarian minority in Burgenland was the fact that they belonged to several denominations. For instance, the three adjacent Hungarian communities of Siget in der Wart, Unterwart and Oberwart belonged to the Evangelical (Lutheran), Catholic and Reformed Churches, respectively. They organized and operated separate associations and were more likely to marry a Croatian-speaking or German-speaking co-religionist than a Hungarian of another denomination. The fourth denomination was religious Jewry (about 4,000 people), most of whom counted as *magyarón* and in some cases had to leave Burgenland in 1921 for that reason.[78]

Some earlier Hungarian legislation remained in force in Burgenland after 1921. The elementary schools were headed, under the Hungarian Education Act, by a board of governors empowered, among other things, to decide the language of instruction. The Burgenland Social Democrats sought after 1921 to extend Austrian school legislation to the province, which would have separated education from religion. The statutes agreed in 1924 were a compromise, whereby the school governors were to be elected democratically instead of being appointed by the Churches. However, the federal Austrian government was led by the Christian Democrats and reversed this ruling in 1927, so that Hungarian education laws applied in Burgenland up to 1937.[79] The teaching of German became compulsory under a 1920 statute. Hungarian could remain the language of elementary education, church services and public administration in minority villages, but further education in Hungarian was no longer available. This affected some 16,000 children. Alfred Wahlheim, Burgenland's first provincial governor, put it like this in 1923: let there be an end to the "Magyar chatter" in classrooms! All Hungarians teaching in secondary education were warned to stop using Hungarian, because "it is a task of the school to raise [pupils] as Germans."[80] The school statistics for Burgenland show that some 2,300 Hungarian-speaking children were enrolled each year between 1921 and 1931, which means that there must have been a cohort of at least 18,400 Hungarian-speaking children aged 6–14 at the beginning of the 1930s. Instead, the 1934 census recorded only 10,442 Hungarian inhabitants in Burgenland, which shows that censuses reflected political inclination, not language use.[81]

The public mood outside the Hungarian-inhabited villages became strongly anti-Hungarian, due partly to the activities of the Hungarian irregulars and partly to the survival of Hungarian education legislation. One mouthpiece for this was the weekly paper of the Burgenland Social Democrats, the *Burgenländische Freiheit*, which called for Hungarian junior school teachers and public employees to be removed from their jobs in schools, local government, the post office and the railways. Some Hungarian local government officers left for Hungary in the 1920s for that reason. The paper even wanted to ban shopping expeditions to

Sopron: "No Burgenlander with any honor in him could go to the stores in Sopron and hand his money to such folk as these!"[82] Ludwig Leser, the deputy provincial governor, set the tone in 1931 at a ceremony to mark Burgenland's tenth anniversary: "Clean out everything that's still Magyar!"[83] Several thousand ministers of religion, teachers and officials accordingly left Burgenland in the 1930s.

An incident in the border village of Hannersdorf in 1927 had national repercussions, when local Christian Democrats fired into a Social Democratic demonstration and one child and one man died. The court in Vienna later acquitted those who had fired the shots, whereupon the Social Democrats set fire to the Supreme Court. Subsequent street fighting left eighty people dead. The political tensions led to civil war in February 1934, causing the collapse of the Austrian Republic and declaration of an authoritarian Christian Socialist state.[84] The new regime was keen to assuage the minorities, who were mainly Christian Socialist supporters. So a new education act for Burgenland was passed, in which the language of instruction in schools depended on the ethnic make-up of the population. Where a minority group accounted for over 70 percent of the local inhabitants, instruction was to be in the native language; where the proportion was over 30 percent, it was to be in two languages.[85]

Outside Burgenland, there were organized Hungarian communities only in Vienna and Graz. The latter had a Hungarian Cultural Alliance established in the nineteenth century and also a Graz Hungarian Society of Academics funded by the Hungarian state. Vienna at the time had a Hungarian community numbering tens of thousands. Before World War I, there were 210,000 people in the city who had originated from Hungary, while 10,922 people declared themselves in the 1923 census to be Hungarian-speaking, although the figure in 1934 was only 4,844. Two focal points were the newspaper *Jövő*, founded by Hungarian communists and social democrats in exile, and the Collegium Hungaricum, an institution established by the Hungarian state in 1924.[86] There were several other Hungarian societies operating in the city.

Notes

1 Irina Livezeanu, *Cultural Politics in Greater Romania: Regionalism, Nation Building, and Ethnic Struggle, 1918–1930* (Ithaca, NY, 2000), pp. 89–188; Nándor Bárdi and Peter Weber, "Kisebbségben és többségben: Iuliu Maniu kisebbségpolitikai nézőpontjai" [In Minority and in Majority. The Views of Iuliu Maniu on Minority Policy], *Limes* (1998) 4: 136–162.

2 *Magyar Népközösség.*

3 On periodization of Romania's policy on the Hungarians, see Nándor Bárdi, "Az ismeretlen vízmosás és a régi országút. Stratégiai útkeresés a romániai Országos Magyar Pártban 1923–1924" [Unknown Gully and Old Highway. Strategic Path-Seeking in Romania's National Hungarian Party 1923–1924], in Nándor Bárdi and Csilla Fedinec, eds., *Etnopolitika. A közösségi, magán- és nemzetközi érdekek viszonyrendszere Közép-Európában* [Ethno-Politics. The System of Relations in Communal, Private and International Interests in Central Europe] (Budapest, 2003), pp. 153–195.

4 The constitutional and minority policy frameworks: Lajos Nagy, *A kisebbségek alkotmányjogi helyzete Nagyromániában* [The Constitutional Position of Minorities in Greater Romania] (Székelyudvarhely, 1994 [1944]), pp. 16–76. A 1937 review of the legal conditions: Sándor Asztalos and Béla Csákány, "A kisebbségi életet legjobban befolyásoló jogszabályok" [The Legal Stipulations Most Affecting Minority Life], in Sándor Kacsó, ed., *Erdélyi Magyar Évkönyv. A kisebbségi magyar polgár kézikönyve, 1938* [Transylvanian Hungarian Yearbook. Handbook for the Minority Hungarian Citizen] (Brașov, 1937), pp. 158–174.

5 On citizenship, see the Romanian act *Lege privitoare la dobândirea și pierderea naționalității române*, to be found in *Monitorul Oficial* (1924) 41 (February 24). For a detailed treatment, see Nagy, *A kisebbségek alkotmányjogi helyzete Nagyromániában*, pp. 76–86. On employment discrimination, see for instance the Romanian act on introducing Romanians into businesses: *Monitorul Oficial* (1934) 161 (July 16). For more detail, see Nagy, *A kisebbségek alkotmányjogi helyzete Nagyromániában*, pp. 163–170, and on language use, see *ibid.*, pp. 109–117 and 148.

6 Sándor Tamás, "A Csíki Magánjavak" [The Csík Private Properties], *Erdélyi Múzeum* (1995) 3–4: 15–55.

7   For a detailed treatment: Nagy, *A kisebbségek alkotmányjogi helyzete Nagyromániában*, pp. 200–207; László Fritz, "România egyenesadó rendszere, mint a kisebbségellenes politika egyik harci eszköze" [Romanian Direct Taxation as a Weapon of Minority Policy], *Magyar Kisebbség* (1928) 12: 437–443.

8   Summaries of the minority policy strategies: Nándor Bárdi, "Die minderheitspolitischen Strategien der ungarischen Bevölkerung in Rumänien zwischen den beiden Weltkriegen," in *Südost-Forschungen 1999* (Munich, 1999), pp. 267–311; Franz S. Horváth, *Zwischen Ablehnung und Anpassung: politische Strategien der ungarischen Minderheitselite in Rumänien 1931–1940* (Munich, 2007).

9   The text of the pact: Imre Mikó, *Huszonkét év. Az erdélyi magyarság politikai története* [Twenty-Two Years. The Political History of Transylvanian Hungarians] (Budapest, 1941), pp. 274–283; reworking: Bárdi, "Az ismeretlen vízmosás," pp. 168–191.

10   Mikó, *Huszonkét év*, pp. 56–65.

11   *Ibid.*, pp. 70–74.

12   The general election results of the National Hungarian Party: Running separately: 3 representatives/3 senators in March 1922, 14/12 in May 1926. On the common governing party list: 10/1 in June 1927. On a joint list with the German Party: 16/6 in December 1928. Running separately again: 10/2 in June 1931, 14/3 in July 1932, 9/3 in December 1933, and 19/3 in December 1937. On the common National Rebirth Front list: 9/6 in June 1939. The National Hungarian Party could poll only about one third of the votes to equal the proportion of the Hungarians in the Romanian electorate – 9.6 percent in 1930. The equivalent proportion for the Germans and their party was about 50 percent. Nándor Bárdi, "Választások a két világháború közti romániai magyar kisebbségpolitikában" [Elections in Interwar Romanian Hungarian Minority Policy], *Magyar Kisebbség* (2000) 4, at http://www.jakabffy.ro/magyarkisebbseg/index.php?action=cimek&lapid=17&cikk=m000405.html. Last accessed April 1, 2009.

13   See Chapter 2 in Part II of this volume, and Ferenc Eiler, *Kisebbségvédelem és revízió. Magyar törekvések az Európai Nemzetiségi Kongresszuson (1925–1939)* [Minority Protection and Revision. Hungarian Efforts at the European Congress of Nationalities (1925–1939)] (Budapest, 2007), pp. 205–211 and 248–251.

14   Imre Mikó, "A romániai magyarság panaszai a Nemzetek Szövetsége előtt" [Complaints of the Romanian Hungarians before the League of Nations], *Magyar Kisebbség* (1938) 24: 581–585.

15   Nándor Bárdi, "Pártpolitika és kisebbségpolitika. A romániai Országos Magyar Párt javaslata és annak visszhangja 1934-35-ben" [Party Politics and Minority Policy. The Proposal of Romania's National Hungary Party and Reaction to It in 1934–1935], *Magyar Kisebbség* (1998) 3–4: 128–185.

16   *Erdélyi Magyar Gazdasági Egyesület.*

17   Horváth, *Zwischen Ablehnung und Anpassung*, pp. 291–323.

18   A broad picture: Sándor Bíró, *The Nationalities Problem in Transylvania 1867–1940* (Boulder, CO/Highland Lakes, NJ, 1992), pp. 507–618. Figures on education: András R. Szeben, "Az erdélyi magyarság népoktatásügyének statisztikai mérlege a másfél évtizedes román uralom alatt" [Statistical Review of Education among Transylvanian Hungarians over a Decade and a Half of Romanian Rule], *Magyar Statisztikai Szemle* (1934) 10: 851–871.

19   *Erdélyi Múzeum Egyesület.*

20   Lajos Kántor, "Az Erdélyi Múzeum-Egyesület problémái" [Problems of the Transylvanian Museum Society], *Magyar Kisebbség* (1930) 9: 309–328.

21   *Erdélyi Közművelődési Egyesület.*

22   Béla Demeter and József Venczel, *Az Erdélyi Magyar Gazdasági Egyesület munkája a román impérium alatt* [The Work of the Transylvanian-Hungarian Economic Association under Romanian Rule] (Budapest, 1940).

23   Bertalan Tárcza, "A Romániai Magyar Dalosszövetség" [The Romanian Hungarian Singers' Association], in Kacsó, ed., *Erdélyi Magyar Évkönyv*, pp. 86–88.

24   *Erdélyi Katolikus Státus.*

25   A broad history of intellectual movements: Ernö Ligeti, *Súly alatt a pálma. Egy nemzedék szellemi élete. 22 esztendő kisebbségi sorsban* [The Palm under a Weight. Intellectual Life of a Generation. 22 Years as a Minority] (Csíkszereda, 2004 [1941]). Individual periodicals and institutions: Edgár Balogh and Gyula Dávid, eds., *Romániai magyar irodalmi lexikon* [Romanian Hungarian Literary Lexicon], I–IV (Bukarest/Kolozsvár, 2002 [1981]). On *Hitel*: Zsuzsanna Török, "Planning the National Minority: Strategies of the Journal *Hitel* in Romania, 1935–44," *Nationalism and Ethnic Politics* (2001) 2: 57–74.

26   *Országos Keresztényszocialista Párt.*

27   *Magyar Nemzeti Párt.*

28 *Egységes Magyar Párt.*
29 Fried, alongside Klement Gottwald, had a key role in the Bolshevization of the Communist Party of Czechoslovakia. Later dropped from the leadership, he was sent as a Comintern advisor to M. Thorez, where he became an architect of the popular front policy of the French Communist Party. See Annie Kriegel and Stephanie Courtois, *Eugen Fried, le grand secret du PCF* (Paris, 1997), p. 447.
30 *Szlovenszkói Magyar Kultúregyesület.*
31 *Csehszlovákiai Magyar Tudományos, Irodalmi és Művészeti Társaság.*
32 *Csehszlovákiai Magyar Akadémikusok Szövetsége.*
33 Named for the theologian Bishop Ottokár Prohászka (1858–1927), who was born in Nyitra.
34 *Csehszlovákiai Magyar Testnevelő Szövetség.*
35 Archiv Ústavu T. G. Masaryka (AUTGM), f. Eduard Beneš, k. 72, Menšiny 1920–1938.
36 The cardinal points of the 12 Hungarian demands put to the Prague Parliament on April 5, 1938, were these: "2. We call for full equal rights, equal rank, and self-government for all nations in the republic… 4. There shall be numbers of Hungarians among officers, employers and workers in offices, state works and public institutions of the Hungarian-inhabited area proportionate to the size of the Hungarian community… 5. We demand that the Hungarian community may conduct and manage for itself the schools and all institutions of public education in a religious spirit. We demand that the deficiency of Hungarian schools be made up urgently. 6. … The land of the Czechoslovak settlements and residual estates shall be shared among the Hungarian farming population… 10. We call for the passage of a law harshly penalizing deprivation of national character or attempts at that. 11. We demand autonomy for Slovakia and Subcarpathia." Digitální knihovna, NS RČS 1918–1920, Poslanecká sněmovna – stenoprotokoly, 3. schuze, 2. června 1920. At http://www.psp.cz/eknih/1935ns/ps/stenprot/145schuz/prilohy/priloh03.htm.
37 On the conduct of Slovakian Hungarians over Munich, see Attila Simon, "A várakozás hetei. A szlovákiai magyarok az első bécsi döntés előtt" [Weeks of Waiting. Slovakian Hungarians before the First Vienna Award], *Limes* (2007) 2: 7–20.
38 *Magyar Nemzeti Tanács.*

39   M. Boldyzhar and P. Mosni, *Derzhavno-pravovyj status Zakarpattia (Pidkarpats'koi' Rusi) v skladi Chehoslovachchyny* [The Constitutional Situation of Transcarpathia (Subcarpathian Rus) within the Czechoslovak Republic] (Uzhhorod, 2001); L. Bianchi, ed., *Dejiny štátu a práva na území Československa v období kapitalizmu* [The History of State and Law in Czechoslovakia in the Period of Capitalism], Vol. II, 1918–1945 (Bratislava, 1973); Petr P. Sova, "Razvytie podkarpattorusskago obshhynnogo y oblastnogo samoupravlenija" [The Development of Public Administration in Transcarpathia], in E. Bachynskyj, ed., *Podkarpats'kaja Rus' 1919–1936* [Subcarpathian Rus 1919–1936] (Uzhhorod, 1936), pp. 68–70.

40   *Kárpátalja településeinek nemzetiségi (anyanyelvi) adatai 1880–1941* [National (Native-Language) Data for the Settlements of Transcarpathia 1880–1941] (Budapest, 1996). On specific ethnic groups: Miklós Rékai, *A munkácsi zsidók "terített asztala"* [The "Laid Table" of the Mukacheve Jews] (Budapest, 1997); Rudolf Jaworski, "Die deutschen Minderheiten in Polen und in der Tschechoslowakei während der Zwischenkriegszeit," *Österreichische Osthefte* (1991) 33: 251–268; Ivan Pop and Paul Robert Magocsi, *Encyclopedia of Rusyn History and Culture* (Toronto, 2002).

41   Act 172 on the powers of the governor of Transcarpathia. A Hungarian text appears in Csilla Fedinec, ed., *Iratok a kárpátaljai magyarság történetéhez 1918–1944. Törvények, rendeletek, kisebbségi programok, nyilatkozatok* [Documents on the History of Subcarpathian Hungarians 1918–1944. Laws, Orders, Minority Programs, Statements] (Somorja/Dunaszerdahely, 2004), pp. 405–407.

42   "328. Ústavní zákon o autonomii Podkarpatské Rusi. 329. Vyhláška o uplnem znenı predpısu o autonomıı Podkarpatské Rusi" [328. Constitutional Law on the Autonomy of Subcarpathian Rus. 329. Decree on the Consolidation of the Rule of Subcarpathian Rus's Autonomy]. In *Sbírka zákonů a nařízení státu cesko-slovenského*, Ročník 1938. Částka 109. Vydána dne 16. prosince 1938 [Official Gazette of the Czecho-Slovak State, Year of 1938. Issue 109. Issued on 16 December, 1938].

43   I. Granchak, ed., *Narysy istorii' Zakarpattia* [Essays on the History of Transcarpathia], Vol. II (Uzhhorod, 1995), pp. 448–454.

44   *Magyar Jogpárt.*

45   *Őslakosok Autonóm Pártja.*

46   *Keresztényszocialista Párt*; *Kisgazda-, Kisiparos és Földműves Párt*.

47   *Magyar Élet Pártja*. M. Tokar, *Politychni partii' Zakarpattia v umovah bagatopartijnosti (1919–1939)* [The Multi-Party System in Transcarpathia (1919–1939)] (Uzhhorod, 2006); Csilla Fedinec, "Magyar pártok Kárpátalján a két világháború között" [Hungarian Parties in Transcarpathia between the Two World Wars], *Fórum Társadalomtudományi Szemle* (2007) 1: 83–110; Aladár R. Vozáry, *A magyar és a magyar nyelvű újságírás a volt Csehszlovákiában. Adatok a magyar újságírás történetéhez* [Hungarian and Hungarian-Language Journalism in Czechoslovakia. Contributions to the History of Hungarian Journalism] (Munkács, 1942).

48   M. Tokar, *Politychni partii' Zakarpattia*, pp. 327–331.

49   *Társadalmi Egyesületek Szövetségének Központja*.

50   *Autonóm Földműves Szövetség*.

51   Béla Angyal, "A csehszlovákiai magyarság anyaországi támogatása a két világháború között" [Subsidies from the Parent Country for Czechoslovakia's Hungarians between the Two World Wars], *Regio* 11 (2000) 3: 133–178; Csilla Fedinec, "Kárpátaljai autonómia-koncepciók 1918–1944 között" [Transcarpathian Concepts of Autonomy 1918–1944], *Kisebbségkutatás* (2001) 3: 450–469.

52   József Kepecs and Zoltán Czibulka, eds., *Kárpátalja településeinek vallási adatai, 1880–1941* [Religious Data of Settlements of Transcarpathia, 1880–1941] (Budapest, 2000); István Bendász, *Részletek a Munkácsi Görög Katolikus Egyházmegye történetéből* [Details from the History of the Mukacheve Greek Catholic Diocese] (Uzhhorod, 1999); Fritz Peyer-Müller, *A Kárpátaljai Református Egyház története a két világháború között – kitekintéssel a jelenre* [The Interwar History of the Reformed Church in Transcarpathia, with a Glance at the Present] (Budapest, 1995); Zsuzsanna Pápai, ed., *Kárpátalja – Római katolikus templomok* [Transcarpathia – Roman Catholic Churches] (Munkács, 2003); István Csernicskó *et al.*, *Útközben. Tanulmányok a kárpátaljai magyarságról* [On the Road. Studies of the Transcarpathian Hungarians] (Ungvár, 1998); M. Palynchak, *Derzhavno-cerkovni vidnosyny na Zakarpatti ta v Shidnij Slovachchyni v 20 seredyni 30-h rokiv XX stolittja* [State–Church Relations in Transcarpathia and Eastern Slovakia in the 1920s and 1930s] (Uzhhorod, 1996); Csilla Fedinec, *A kárpátaljai magyarság*

történeti kronológiája 1918–1944 [The Historical Chronology of the Transcarpathian Hungarians 1918–1944] (Somorja/Dunaszerdahely, 2002).

53   Csilla Fedinec, "Nemzetiségi iskolahálózat és magyaroktatás Kárpátalján" [National School Network and Hungarian Teaching in Transcarpathia], in Lajos Sipos, ed., *Iskolaszerkezet és irodalom-tanítás a Kárpát-medencében. Élményközpontú irodalomtanítás* [School Structure and Literature Teaching in the Carpathian Basin. Experience-Oriented Literature Teaching] (Budapest, 2003), pp. 129–147; Csilla Fedinec, "Kárpátalja közigazgatása és tanügyigazgatása 1938–1944 között" [Public Administration and Educational Management in Transcarpathia in 1938–1944], *Magyar Pedagógia* (1996) 4: 367–375.

54   Balázs Keresztyén, *Irodalmi barangolások a Kárpátok alján* [Literary Rambles under the Carpathians] (Ungvár/Budapest, 1993). Balázs Keresztyén, *Kárpátaljai művelődéstörténeti kislexikon* [Pocket Dictionary of Transcarpathian Educational History] (Budapest, 2001); Gyula Alapy, "Kisebbségi irodalmunk tíz éve (1919–1928) és ennek könyvészete" [Ten Years of Minority Literature (1919–1928) and Its Book Production], in Ferenc Sziklay, ed., *Kazinczy Évkönyv 1898–1928* [Kazinczy Yearbook 1898–1928] (Kassa, 1929).

55   *Ruszinszkói Magyar Színpártoló Egyesület.*

56   Csilla Fedinec, "Magyar könyvkiadás és képzőművészet kapcsolata Kárpátalján (1918-tól napjainkig)" [The Connection of Hungarian Book Publishing and Fine Art in Subcarpathia (from 1918 to the Present Day)], in *Az elsüllyedt jelek. I. A 20. századi magyar könyvillusztráció Magyarország határain kívül 1918-tól napjainkig* [Sunken Signs I. Twentieth-Century Hungarian Book Illustration beyond Hungary's Borders from 1918 to the Present Day] (Budapest, 2003), pp. 138–171; Tamás Gajdó and Éva Balázs, *Magyar színháztörténet 1920–1949* [Hungarian Theater History 1920–1949] (Budapest, 2005); Ödön Faragó, *Írások és emlékek* [Writings and Memoirs] (Ungvár, 1933); Pál Rácz, "Kárpátalja magyar színészete" [Transcarpathian Hungarian Drama Production], *Magyar Írás* (1934) 6: 87–88; Ferenc Sziklay, "A magyar színjátszás Csehszlovákiában" [Hungarian Drama Production in Czechoslovakia], *Erdélyi Helikon* (1930) 670–672.

57   *Mozaik Kultúregyesület; Kárpátaljai Magyar Kultúr Egyesület; Irodalmi és Színpártoló Egyesület.*

58   Béla Popovics, *Munkács kultúrtörténete a korabeli sajtó tükrében* [A Cultural History of Munkács through the Contemporary Press] (Munkács, 2005); Csilla Fedinec, *A kárpátaljai magyarság történeti kronológiája 1918–1944* [The Historical Chronology of the Transcarpathian Hungarians 1918–1944] (Somorja/Dunaszerdahely, 2002).

59   László Balla, "Kárpátalja képzőművészete" [Subcarpathian Fine Art], in Tibor Szöllősy, ed., *Kárpát-medencei magyar paletta* [Hungarian Palette in the Carpathian Basin] (Ungvár/Budapest, 1993); László Balla, *Erdélyi Béla és kortársai* [Béla Erdélyi and His Contemporaries] (Ungvár/Budapest, 1994); Mihály Barát, *Válogatott találkozások. Életpálya- és portrévázlatok, 1970–1996* [Selected Meetings. Career and Portrait Sketches, 1970–1996] (Ungvár/Budapest, 1997); Béla Erdélyi, *Képzőművészet – Ungvár és Ung megye* [Fine Art – Uzhhorod and Ung County] (Ungvár, 1940); József Aba, "Kárpátalja festőművészete" [Subcarpathian Fine Art], in *Új Magyar Művészet* [New Hungarian Art], IV (Budapest, 1944).

60   István Borsody, ed., *Magyarok Csehszlovákiában 1918–1938* [Hungarians in Czechoslovakia 1918–1938] (Budapest, [1938]), pp. 94–95.

61   *Jugoszláviai Magyar Párt.*

62   *Egységes Muravidéki Párt.* László Göncz, *A muravidéki magyarság 1918–1941* [Prekmurje Hungarians 1918–1941] (Lendava, 2001), pp. 118–124.

63   *Szent Gellért Társaság; Társadalmi Egyesületek Szövetségének Központja.*

64   Enikő A. Sajti, *Hungarians in the Voivodina 1918–1947* (Boulder, CO/Highland Lakes, NJ, 2003), pp. 25–89; János Csuka, *A délvidéki magyarság története 1918–1941* [The History of Southern Region Hungarians 1918–1941] (Budapest, 1995), pp. 47–169; Lajos Arday, "A horvátországi magyarok története" [The History of Croatia's Hungarians], in *Fejezetek a horvátországi magyarok történetéből* [Chapters from the History of Hungarians in Croatia] (Budapest, 1994), pp. 9–42.

65   Sajti, *Hungarians in the Voivodina*, pp. 90–125.

66   *Ibid.*, pp. 164–173; Attila Kovács, *Földreform és kolonizáció a Lendva-vidéken a két világháború között* [Land Reform and Colonization in the Lendava District between the Two World Wars] (Lendva, 2004), pp. 169–317.

67   Sajti, *Hungarians in the Voivodina*, pp. 142–163.

68   *Burgenlandi Horvátok Kultúregyesülete/Hrvatsko Kulturno Društvo u Gradišću.*

69   Gerald Schlag, "Die Kroaten im Burgenland 1918 bis 1945," in Stefan Geosits, ed., *Die burgenländischen Kroaten im Wandel der Zeiten* (Vienna, 1986), pp. 171–221.

70   The term Burgenland for the area ceded by Hungary to Austria was coined only in June 1919 but rapidly gained official recognition.

71   Ladislaus Trieber, ed., *Die Obere Wart* (Oberwart, 1977).

72   Ernő Deák, "Wirtschaftshistorische und soziale Aspekte der Neuzeit (1547–1848)," in Trieber, ed., *Die Obere Wart*, pp. 181–249.

73   The paramilitary Levente youth movement was set up in Hungary in 1921.

74   Károly Gaál, *Kire marad a kisködmön? Wer erbt das Jankerl? Über die Kommunikationskultur der Gutshofsknechte im Burgenland* (Szombathely, 1985).

75   Gerhard Baumgartner, "Minderheiten als politische Kraft – das Bauernopfer nationalstaatlicher Politik," in Rainer Bauböck, Gerhard Baumgartner, Bernhard Perchinig and Karin Pinter, eds., *"...und raus bist Du!" Minderheiten in der Politik* (Vienna, 1988), pp. 309–326.

76   Gerhard Baumgartner and Andreas Moritsch, "The Process of National Differentiation within Rural Communities in Southern Carinthia and Southern Burgenland 1850 to 1950," in David Howell, ed., *Roots of Rural Ethnic Mobilization. Comparative Studies on Governments and Non-Dominant Ethnic Groups in Europe 1850–1950*, Vol. VII (New York/Boston, MA, 1992), pp. 99–144.

77   Sándor Győri-Nagy, "Dynamisches Modell zur Minderheitensprachforschung im nordwestpannonischen Raum," in Hans Peter Nelde, ed., *Methoden der Kontaktlinguistik* (Bonn, 1985), pp. 155–167; Gerhard Baumgartner, "Prolegomena zum Sprachverhalten ungarischsprachiger Burgenländer," in Werner Holzer and Rainer Münz, eds., *Trendwende? Sprache und Ethnizität im Burgenland* (Vienna, 1993), pp. 215–235.

78　Ulrike Harmat, "Abschied vom Burgenland. Das Burgenland nach dem Anschluß," in Elisabeth Deinhofer and Traude Horvath, eds., *Grenzfall Burgenland 1921–1991* (Eisenstadt, 1991), pp. 65–104.

79　Österreichische Rektorenkonferenz, ed., *Lage und Perspektive der österreichischen Volksgruppen* (Vienna, 1989); Gerhard Baumgartner, *"6 X Österreich" – Geschichte und aktuelle Situation der Volksgruppen in Österreich* (Klagenfurt/Celovec, 1995).

80　*Aufgabe der Schule ist es, zum Deutschtum zu erziehen.*

81　Gerhard Baumgartner, "Der nationale Differenzierungsprozess in den ländlichen Gemeinden des südlichen Burgenlandes," in Andreas Moritsch, ed., *Vom Ethnos zur Nationalität: Der nationale Differenzierungsprozess am Beispiel ausgewählter Orte in Kärnten und im Burgenland* (Vienna/Munich, 1991), pp. 93–155.

82　*Kein Burgenländer, der Ehre im Leib hat, darf in Ödenburg einkaufen und dieser Sippschaft noch das Geld hintragen.*

83　*Aufräumen mit allem, was noch magyarisch ist!* See Gerhard Baumgartner, "Idevalósi vagyok [I'm Local] – Einer, der hierher gehört. Zur Identität der ungarischsprachigen Bevölkerungsgruppe des Burgenlandes," in Gerhard Baumgartner, Eva Müllner and Rainer Münz, eds., *Lebensraum und Identität* (Eisenstadt, 1989), pp. 69–84.

84　Anton Pelinka, "Der verdrängte Bürgerkrieg," in Anton Pelinka and Erika Weinzierl, eds., *Das große Tabu. Österreichs Umgang mit seiner Vergangenheit* (Vienna, 1987), pp. 143–153.

85　Felix Tobler, Johann Seedoch and Nikola Bencsics, "Die Geschichte des Schulwesens der burgenländischen Kroaten," in Geosits, ed., *Die burgenländischen Kroaten*, pp. 144–170.

86　Gerhard Baumgartner and Stefan Sinkovits, *Kroaten und Ungarn, Vermögensentzug bei burgenländischen Kroaten* (Vienna, 2004).

III. THE WORLD WAR II YEARS
1939–1944

1. RETURNEE HUNGARIANS
Tamás Gusztáv Filep

A significant part of the territory detached from Hungary after World War I was returned between the autumn of 1938 and the summer of 1941. The general basis for redrawing the borders – the Czechoslovak–Hungarian one under the First Vienna Award of November 2, 1938, and the Romanian–Hungarian one under the Second Vienna Award of August 30, 1940 – was ethnic proportions,[1] meaning that the majority of the inhabitants transferred were of Hungarian ethnicity. Hungarian foreign policy was flexible and well informed about local conditions in the period until the attack on the Southern Region in April 1941, and the confidence even of Western powers opposed to the Axis had still not been lost.[2] But the attack, in the wake of a military coup in Yugoslavia, was made as a German ally at Germany's behest, and showed that Hungary's scope for independent policy-making had narrowed, and presaged a future within a Third Reich-commanded alliance system as a belligerent in World War II.[3]

The main feature of Hungary's relations with its neighbors in those years was potential hostility, although the countries concerned belonged to the same alliance system. Slovakia and Romania openly stated their territorial claims against an enlarged Hungary.[4] Influential political figures thought that the factor deciding the fate of the disputed areas would be the claimants' relative zeal in the Nazi interest. Just before the attack on the Soviet Union, the German chancellor promised both Slovakia and Romania that their territorial claims would be met so long as they joined the new war. There was also an area disputed between Hungary and Croatia: the largely Hungarian-inhabited Prekmurje.[5]

None of the hitherto minority Hungarians (except a few communist cells with a couple of hundred members) were able or willing to escape the general feelings of euphoria. The democratic opposition in the Hungarian Parliament and its supporters were as sure as the right-wing opposition and the government and its voters that the territorial gains were just,[6] but the inconsistencies in the new situation that soon appeared were interpreted differently by the formerly minority Hungarians and the formerly state-creating Romanian and Slav national minorities. Some problems stemmed from differences of aim between the government and those returning to Hungary's fold, but many were unconnected with central government intentions. There was a discernible desire among returnee Hungarians to defend regional characteristics from excessive centralization. The inhabitants of reannexed territories were faced with an unaccustomed economic structure and set of social circumstances, often divorced from their markets by the new borders.[7] The Hungarian market had a glut of some products hitherto readily salable beyond the Hungarian linguistic zone. Hungarians and Slovaks who had been transferred from Czechoslovakia, with its more orderly and stable social conditions, comparable to those of Western Europe, thought that their rights would be carried over into Hungary,[8] whereas the enlarged state set as its priority the creation of a uniform legal environment, which meant some curtailments of rights. So Hungary was joined by fragments of the nation with different pre-1941 economic and democratic backgrounds, building up their communities in different ways, and at the same time became a decidedly multi-ethnic state again.[9]

Those problems were soon compounded by wartime economic conditions, in which the frames of production and consumption – including food rationing – were imposed by an increasingly pronounced economic dependence on Germany.[10] These applied generally, but caused enhanced antagonism among the national minorities, who naturally saw themselves as the victims of the boundary changes.

Initially, the question of representation of political interests seemed to be important. In the case of the Hungarians, only the representatives and supporters of former minority Hungarian united parties gained seats in the Hungarian legislature. Although former Upper Hungary and Transcarpathia had been returned by then, they were not covered by the 1939 general elections (after the fall of the Imrédy government) and no further general elections were held until after World War II. Instead, the state "invited" representatives for each returned territory: for Slovakian Hungarians, the United Hungarian Party members who had sat in the Czechoslovakian Parliament and provincial assemblies. Again when Northern Transylvania was returned, the choice was of members of the earlier, now resuscitated Hungarian minority party and its organizations. But the national minorities had no united representation – except for the Rusyns (known officially at the time as Carpatho-Russians or Ruthenians),[11] who set up their own parliamentary club – although the government made some attempt to bring single prominent minority figures into Parliament.

The returned territories remained for various times under military administration before changing to civilian rule. These took different approaches, according to the sources. The military authorities introduced a system that classified the new national minorities by "reliability": the Rusyns scored better than the Slovaks or Croats,[12] and the Romanians and Serbs worse. There were armed clashes between the army and the national minorities in almost every territory, especially during the weeks of the takeover. The Hungarian troops moving into Transcarpathia in mid-March 1939 fought with forces of the infant Carpatho Ukrainian state under Avgusthyn Voloshyn. There were insignificant Romanian partisan activities in Northern Transylvania, followed by reprisals,[13] but more serious clashes with irregular Chetnik forces during the occupation of the Southern Region. There was no military resistance by the Slovaks, but Hungarian gendarmes fired on Slovak demonstrators at Christmas 1938 in Šurany, an act also condemned by Hungarians still remaining in Slovakia.[14] The most dramatic episodes were the raids and massacres in Novi Sad and in the Šajkaš district in January 1942. In the former, several thousand mainly Jewish and Serb civilians were executed by the gendarmerie and the army as reprisals for

Serb partisan strikes.[15] (Officers responsible for the executions were later taken before Hungarian military courts, but they all managed to escape to Germany, returning in the spring of 1944 as German officers. However, eleven gendarmes were given prison sentences of 10–15 years and the Hungarian government began to compensate relatives of the victims.)[16] Most Czechoslovak and Romanian state administrative staff left Hungary after the Vienna Awards, and there was also uncertainty among other non-Hungarian settlers, who had received grants of land.[17] About 200,000 people relocated voluntarily or under Hungarian pressure to Southern Transylvania. (This had been preceded by attacks on Hungarians living there, leading to several tens of thousands of Hungarian departures, voluntarily or under pressure from the Romanian state.) The large numbers of Serbs who had settled in the Southern Region between the wars were forced out after the occupation – holdings vacated in that way were reassigned to Hungarians, including some Székelys displaced from Bukovina, who at the end of the war had to flee again to the territory of today's Hungary.[18]

The General Staff during the period of territorial acquisition was commanded by pro-German military officers (such as Henrik Werth), set upon retaining the reannexed lands and on gaining spoils of war.[19] Against them stood the country's prime ministers (beginning with Pál Teleki), who sought initially to keep the country out of the war or at least minimize the forces sent to the front, and later to survive the world conflagration with the least possible losses of life, materials and territory.

The aim of Teleki and his followers was to resurrect the "Realm of St. Stephen," a program that could be seen as a nation-state ideology intended to thwart or sideline demands by national minorities. In fact the type of country envisaged rested on the idea of a medieval, multinational state in which ethnic communities lived and cooperated harmoniously,[20] although the Hungarians would retain their hegemony. Yet one attempt to dismantle the unified nation state came from within the government: Teleki and Horthy openly espoused Rusyn autonomy in Transcarpathia.[21] This was soon dropped from the parliamentary agenda, due to opposition from the military and from county Hungarian interests, and on account of the signs of imminent war. The sincerity of the intentions can hardly be doubted: as the wartime mood gathered, Teleki said more plainly than ever that the building of society called for loyal minorities and loyalty had a price. (Rusyn autonomy was to act as a harbinger, a pattern for future reorganization of the country.)[22]

Classification of national minorities by loyalty, mentioned earlier, probably suited the purposes of Hungarians living in the returned territories as well: they too distinguished their cohabiting nations by their degree of responsibility for earlier anti-Hungarian measures. The Germans enjoyed a specific position and assessment, with special rights as a result of the alliance system, allowing them to organize as a *Volk*, which meant that Hungarian Germans of military age were enlisted into the Reich army. The consequent conflicts – many Hungarian Germans or Hungarians of German extraction objected to enlistment and called in vain for Hungarian aid – were a sign that the communities of German origin dwelling in Hungary were not all influenced to the same degree by the *volksdeutsche* program. Many turned Hungarian, while others attached more value to their loyalty as Hungarian citizens than to their ancestry.[23] On several occasions there were German–Hungarian disagreements during the boundary changes. The Carpathian German Party in Slovakia, for instance, opposed holding a plebiscite on where the city of Pozsony should belong,[24] and plenty of Germans were against Hungary's invasion of Bačka. Incidentally, the idea of recognizing the national groups as political entities (as had happened with the German *Volk*, due to pressure from Berlin) was rejected by the public and political elite. This was connected with the welcome given to the concept of "Realm of St. Stephen," and the general view that a demand for collective minority recognition would play into the hands of the Reich. However, in principle equality before the law was enjoyed by national minorities, except the Jews, who were styled a "race" and hemmed in by legislation and decrees, despite their usual self-identification as Hungarians.

According to many documents and most subsequent assessments, returnee Hungarian communities were notably democratic and socially sensitive, and strongly critical of the "caste spirit" and hierarchical structure of society in Hungary.[25] They also showed greater understanding of and fellow feeling for national minorities. Many fine everyday examples could be given to support this assessment, but on the other hand, these communities were sensitive to the fate of Hungarians who remained within Slovakia and Romania.[26] They were probably among those who called for reprisals when injuries were done to Hungarian minorities in neighboring countries. They showed dual behavior. It had not been possible while they were a minority for them to develop an officer class experienced in public administration. The gap had to be filled from the parent country and from "reliable" minorities, especially in Transylvania.[27] There are many examples of former minority Hungarians condemning the conduct of latecomers from Trianon Hungary, for ignoring regional values, the "minority mentality" and the demands and sensitivities of members of other ethnic groups. On the other hand, these groups were expecting the state to strengthen their position in relation to the Slavs or Romanians. Few of those who gained positions in the returned territories managed to balance the interests of the state, former minority Hungarians and new national interests.[28]

It became clear also that the former minority political elite could not or would not further the community interests that it ostensibly espoused. A clear example of this was seen in the reform of land ownership. Some estates expropriated under the successor states in the 1920s were broken up again, but not to general satisfaction. Many saw cronyism in the way that the land was redistributed, not rewards for services to the community. There were probably divisions also over the infrastructural improvements in the returned territories and other big investments, and over the economic development programs of great importance and the welfare decisions taken.[29] These reinforced the national identity of the fragmentary societies in many places, helping to preserve them in the forthcoming communist period.

Then and later, many thought that the returned territories should gain a degree of autonomy, or at least that their inhabitants should have a say in local matters. There is no knowing what results that would have had, but the various options gave a foothold for resurrecting the old Upland and Transylvanian parties. The United Hungarian Party *(Egyesült Magyar Párt)* espoused social justice and democratic social egalitarianism, but allied itself in 1938 with Prime Minister Béla Imrédy, who was toying with right-wing radicalism,[30] with the result that Teleki and his group were forced later to integrate into the governing party. Teleki in 1940 promoted the idea of Transylvanian legislators forming a party, to maintain a distance from the governing party, which often yielded to extreme right-wing pressure.[31] In the latter stages of the war, the parliamentary opposition was boosted in Transylvania by the foundation of a local branch of the Smallholders' Party, which managed to work with young representatives of the Transylvanian Party. That allowed the Transylvanians in 1944, when Romania turned against the Axis, to propose unanimously to Horthy that Hungary bail out of the war, and to back a putative attempt to do so in October.[32] After the German occupation, Andor Jaross took the interior portfolio in Döme Sztójay's puppet regime, but prominent Uplanders and Transylvanians condemned the occupation,[33] the Jewish deportations to Germany[34] and continuation of the war.[35]

There also appeared among the wartime intelligentsia in Transylvania ideas for a Central European federation. In 1944, the Hungarian Ministry of Foreign Affairs assisted surreptitiously in securing publication in Switzerland of plans for a separate autonomous Transylvania made by Endre Bajcsy-Zsilinszky, an opposition leader who was to be executed by a collaborationist firing squad on December 24 that year.[36]

Notes

1   Gergely Sallai, *Az első bécsi döntés* [The First Vienna Award] (Budapest, 2002); Béni L. Balogh, *A magyar–román kapcsolatok 1939–1940-ben és a második bécsi döntés* [Hungarian–Romanian

Relations in 1939–1940 and the Second Vienna Award] (Miercurea-Ciuc, 2002). On the invasion of the Southern Region: Enikő A. Sajti, *Hungarians in the Voivodina 1918–1947* (Boulder, CO/Highland Lakes, NJ, 2003), pp. 191–223.

2   On the diplomatic climate, see for instance the following: András D. Bán, *Illúziók és csalódások. Nagy-Britannia és Magyarország, 1938–1941* [Illusions and Disillusionments. Great Britain and Hungary, 1938–1941] (Budapest, 1998); Kim Jiyoung, *A nagyhatalmi politika és az erdélyi kérdés a II. világháború alatt és után* [Great-Power Politics and the Transylvanian Question in and after World War II] (Budapest, 2000), pp. 36–100.

3   Broader implications of the Central European changes of 1938–1941 are considered in Stephen Borsody, *The New Central Europe* (New York, 1993), pp. 59–101.

4   *Ibid.*, pp. 100–101. Analysis of the period of territorial expansion by a Hungarian anti-Nazi politician: Antal Ullein-Reviczky, *Guerre allemande, paix russe. Le drame hongrois* (Neuchâtel, 1947), pp. 15–100.

5   On Prekmurje, see László Göncz, "A visszatért Muravidék 1941–1944" [Prekmurje Returned 1941–1944], in Nándor Bárdi and Attila Simon, eds., *Integrációs stratégiák a magyar kisebbségek történetében* [Integration Strategies in the History of the Hungarian Minorities] (Somorja, 2006), pp. 121–138.

6   Imre Csécsy, "Korszerűtlen napló" [Out-of-Date Diary], in Tibor Valuch, ed., *Radikalizmus és demokrácia. Csécsy Imre válogatott írásai* [Radicalism and Democracy. Selected Writings of Imre Csécsy] (Szeged, 1988), p. 153; "A magyar izraelita vallásfelekezet vezetőinek ünnepélyes ülése a magyar Felvidék visszacsatolása alkalmából" [Grand Meeting of the Heads of the Hungarian Israelite Denomination on the Occasion of the Reannexations of the Hungarian Upland], *Pesti Napló,* November 4, 1938, p. 12; "Ünnepli az egész ország a trianoni határ átlépését" [The Whole Country Celebrates the Crossing of the Trianon Frontier], *Esti Kurír,* November 6, 1938, p. 6. Criticism of the right wing for belittling the achievements: György Apponyi, "Áruló, aki ma megbontja az egységet!" [Those Who Break the Unity Are Traitors!], *Szabadság* (1938) 43: 1.

7   An example of this, among other things: András Tóth-Bartos, "Háromszék vármegye gazdaságának fejlesztésére tett próbálkozások 1940–1944 között" [Attempts to Develop the Economy of Trei Scaune County, 1940–1944], *Limes* (2006) 2: 107–116. There

is also discussion of the economic (and social) problems of the reannexed territories (except the Southern Region) – with a 1960s Marxist outlook but taking a wide base of sources – in Lóránt Tilkovszky, *Revízió és nemzetiségpolitika Magyarországon (1938– 1941)* [Revision and Nationality Policy in Hungary (1938–1941)] (Budapest, 1967), pp. 38–63, 238–244 and 290–296.

8   "Még teljesebb egység felé" [Towards Still Fuller Unity], *Felvidéki Magyar Hírlap*, December 11, 1938, p. 5; on defending democracy: István Borsody, "A program" [The Program], *ibid.*, p. 8.

9   For a uniform review (except the Southern Region), see Tilkovszky, *Revízió és nemzetiségpolitika.*

10 Lajos Jócsik, "A Közép-Duna-medence közgazdasága" [The Economy of the Mid-Danube Basin], in Sándor Püski, ed., *Szárszó. Az 1943. évi balatonszárszói Magyar Élet-tábor előadás- és megbeszéléssorozata* [Szárszó. Lectures and Discussions at the 1943 Hungarian Life Camp at Balatonszárszó] (Budapest, 1943), pp. 83–106.

11 *Kárpátorosz* or *rutén.*

12 Examples of a scholarly approach to the past of nations living partly with the Hungarians: Gyula Szekfű, ed., *A magyarság és a szlávok* [The Hungarians and the Slavs] (Budapest, 2000 [1942]); István Borsody, *A magyar–szlovák kérdés alapvonalai* [The Base Lines of the Hungarian–Slovak Question] (Budapest, 1939); Béla Pukánszky, *Német polgárság magyar földön* [German Bourgeois on Hungarian Soil] (Budapest, 1940); Ladislaus Gáldi and Ladislaus Makkai, eds., *Geschichte der Rumänen* (Budapest, 1942).

13 Criticism of the myth that came to surround this: János Varga, "Levente és értelmezője nyomában. Forráskritikai megjegyzések egy esszéíró történelemidéző módszeréhez" [In Search of the Levente and Its Interpreters. Source-Critical Notes on Historical References by an Essayist], in István Rácz, ed., *Tanulmányok Erdély történetéről. Szakmai konferencia Debrecenben 1987. október 9–10.* [Studies on Transylvanian History. Conference, Debrecen, October 9–10, 1987] (Debrecen, 1988), pp. 212–225.

14 Rezső Szalatnai, "Memorandum. A csehszlovákiai magyarok 1918 és 1945 között" [Czechoslovakian Hungarians in 1918–1945], in József Fazekas, ed., *Vagyunk és leszünk. A szlovenszkói magyarság társadalmi rajza 1918–1945* [We Are and Will Remain. The Sociography of the Hungarians of Slovensko] (Pozsony, 1993), pp. 279–280.

15   Tibor Cseres, *Vérbosszú Bácskában* [Revenge in Bačka] (Budapest, 1991), pp. 61–85; János Buzási, *Az újvidéki "razzia"* [Novi Sad *Razzia*] (Budapest, 1963); Sajti, *Hungarians in the Voivodina*, pp. 342–402.

16   Enikő A. Sajti, *Délvidék 1941–1944* [Southern Region 1941–1944] (Budapest, 1987), pp. 184–187.

17   See Part II, Chapter 7.

18   Their story was summarized by their spiritual leader: Dr. Kálmán Németh, *Százezer szív sikolt. Hazatért és hazavágyó magyarok verőfényes golgotája* [100,000 Hearts Screamed. The Sunlit Story of the Golgotha of Hungarians Returning or Longing for Home] (Obiličevo, 1943). On the deportations and resettlements, see Sajti, *Hungarians in the Voivodina*, pp. 234–297.

19   Lóránd Dombrády, "Revízió háború nélkül?" [Revision without War?], in Idem, *Katonapolitika és hadsereg 1920–1944* [Military Policy and the Army 1920–1944] (Budapest, 2000), pp. 65–76. For details of the military approach to territorial reannexations, see Lóránd Dombrády, *Army and Politics in Hungary 1938–1944* (New York, 2005), pp. 24–306.

20   Summary from a former minority spiritual leader: Miklós Pfeiffer, *A katolikus egyház és a hazai nemzetiségek. Elhangzott a debreceni nemzetiségi előadássorozaton 1942. augusztus 12-én* [The Catholic Church and This Country's Minorities. Delivered at the Minority Lecture Series in Debrecen, August 12, 1942] (Budapest, 1942). See also András Rónai, *A nemzetiségi kérdés* [The Nationality Question] (Budapest, 1942).

21   See Part III, Chapter 2.

22   On the three years following the return: Csilla Fedinec, ed., *Kárpátalja 1938–1941. Magyar és ukrán történeti közelítés* [Transcarpathia 1938–1941. Hungarian and Ukrainian Historical Rapprochement] (Budapest, 2004).

23   On this, see István Fehér, *A bonyhádi hűségmozgalom története* [History of the Bonyhád Fidelity Movement] (Budapest, 1983); Norbert Spannenberger, *Der Volksbund der Deutschen in Ungarn 1938–1944* (Munich, 2002).

24   On the debate between Upland Hungarians (returned to Hungary or in Slovakia) and Slovakian Germans, see for instance (sp) [Pál Szvatkó], "Mecenzéf" [Medzev]. *Felvidéki Magyar Hírlap,* December 14, 1939, p. 1; "A szlovákiai németek és magyarok viszonya" [Relations

between the Germans and Hungarians of Slovakia], *ibid.*, December 28, 1938, p. 7; Szalatnai, "Memorandum," pp. 266–270.

25 Expressing the views of one Upland group: *"Nemzetnevelésünk legnagyobb akadálya a neobarokk szellemiség!* András Károly szerkesztő beszélgetése dr. Pfeiffer Miklós kassai kanonokkal" [The Biggest Obstacle to Education of Our Nation Is the Neo-Baroque Outlook! Editor Károly András Talks to Canon Miklós Pfeiffer of Košice], offprint of *Új Élet*, June 1943. The "Transylvanian spirit" appears, for instance, in Irén Gulácsy, *Erdély jogán és más dolgok. Cikkek, karcolatok* [Transylvania by Right and Other Matters. Articles and Sketches] (Budapest, 1940). Transylvanian writers: "Az írói közösség nyilatkozata" [Statement of the Writers' Community], *Erdélyi Helikon* (1942) 9: 596–604. Position of the Upland intelligentsia: "A Felvidék szellemi gárdája a népi gondolat jegyében akar dolgozni. A virágvasárnapi összejövetel határozatai…" [The Intellects of the Upland Wish to Work along *Népi* Lines. Decisions of the Palm Sunday Gathering], *Érsekújvár és Vidéke* (1939) 20: 1.

26 The source gives examples of both outlooks and of social commitment: István Kristó Nagy, ed., *A lillafüredi írói értekezlet (1942. november). Jegyzőköny* [Lillafüred Writers' Meeting, November 1942. Minutes] (Budapest, n. d.), pp. 70–71, 85–89, 95–98 and 109–112.

27 On appointments in general and the Transylvanian situation, including outside recruits, see Edit Csilléry, "Közalkalmazottak és köztisztviselők Észak-Erdélyben a második bécsi döntést követően" [Civil and Public Servants in Northern Transylvania after the Second Vienna Award], *Limes* (2006) 2: 73–90.

28 Béla Bethlen *Észak-Erdély kormánybiztosa voltam* [I Was Government Commissioner for Northern Transylvania] (Budapest, 1989).

29 On modernization programs for welfare, society and development in returned territories, see Péter Hámori, "A magyar kormány szociálpolitikája a visszacsatolt Felvidéken és Észak-Erdélyben" [Hungarian Government Welfare Policy in the Reannexed Upland and Northern Transylvania], in Bárdi and Simon, eds., *Integrációs stratégiák*, pp. 167–185, and Oláh Sándor, "Modernizációs törekvések a Székelyföldön, 1940–1944" [Modernization Efforts in the Székely Land 1940–1944], in Csilla Fedinec, ed., *Nemzet a társadalomban* [Nation in Society] (Budapest, 2004), pp. 133–150.

30   See Tamás Gusztáv Filep, "A 'felvidéki szellem'-ről és utóéletéről (Közelítések)" [The Upland Spirit and Its Afterlife (Approaches)], *Limes* (2007) 2: 116–120 [1938–1944].

31   On returned Transylvanian politicians: Nándor Bárdi, "A múlt, mint tapasztalat. A kisebbségből többségbe került erdélyi magyar politika szemléletváltása 1940–1944 között" [The Past as Experience. Change of Political Outlook by the Transylvanian Hungarians on Turning from Minority to Majority 1940–1944], *Limes* (2006) 2: 43–70. On the Transylvanian Party leader: Zoltán Tibori Szabó, *Teleki Béla erdélyisége. Embernek maradni embertelen időkben* [The Transylvanianism of Béla Teleki. Remaining Human in Inhuman Times] (Kolozsvár, 1993).

32   An example: László Szenczei, *Az erdélyi magyarság harca (1940–1941)* [Struggle of the Transylvanian Hungarians (1940–1941)] (Budapest, 1946), pp. 35–42. Despite the title, the book covers events after its chosen cut-off point.

33   On Upland Hungarians arrested by Nazis and the Arrow-Cross, executed, or herded into camps, see Tamás Gusztáv Filep, "Utak a náci lágerbirodalomba. Megjegyzések a magyar politikai foglyokról" [Roads to Nazi Concentration Camp Land. Notes on Hungarian Political Prisoners], in Idem, *A humanista voksa. Írások a csehszlovákiai magyar kisebbség történetének köréből 1918–1945* [Humanist Voice. Writings on the History of the Czechoslovakian Hungarian Minority 1918–1945] (Bratislava, 2007), pp. 259–271.

34   The story of the Jews in the returned territories and their deportation has appeared mainly for single cities, for instance the following: Teréz Mózes, *Váradi zsidók* [Várad Jews] (Nagyvárad, 1995), pp. 135–244; Dániel Lővy, *A kálváriától a tragédiáig. Kolozsvár zsidó lakosságának története* [From Calvary to Tragedy. Story of Cluj-Napoca's Jewish Population], 2nd ed. (Kolozsvár, 2005); Sándor Strba and Tamás Lang, *Az érsekújvári zsidóság története* [History of Érsekújvár Jewry] (Pozsony, 2004), pp. 129–172. The campaigns against the Jews of Mukacheve and district and their deportation are discussed in detail in Aladár R. Vozáry, *Így történt! 1944. március 19.–1945. január 18.* [How It Happened: March 19, 1944–January 18, 1945] (Budapest, 1945).

35   The clearest instance was a speech in favor of Jews and political prisoners made by Áron Márton, Catholic bishop of Alba Iulia, on a confirmation tour of Northern Transylvania: "1944. május 18-i

beszéd Kolozsvárott a Szent Mihály templomban" [The May 18, 1944, Speech in the St. Michael Church of Cluj-Napoca], in Pál Péter Domokos, *Rendületlenül... Márton Áron, Erdély katolikus püspöke* [Unflinchingly... Áron Márton, Catholic Bishop of Transylvania] ([Budapest, n. d.), pp. 234–236.

36 Andrew [Endre] Bajcsy-Zsilinszky, *Transylvania. Past and Future* (Geneva, 1944).

2. THE AUTONOMY QUESTION IN TRANSCARPATHIA
Csilla Fedinec

This matter may be divided into periods. Transcarpathia (Carpathian Ukraine) was an administrative region under the autonomy legislation of Czechoslovakia (Second Republic) from October 11, 1938, to March 15, 1939, headed by the pro-Hungarian András Bródy (Andrej Brody) and then by the Ukrainian-oriented Avgusthyn Voloshyn, who sympathized with Ukrainian notions and saw the region in terms of the future of its indigenous Slav inhabitants. The areas returned to Hungarian administration under the First Vienna Award of November 2, 1938, including the cities of Ungvár (Užhorod), Munkács (Mukačevo) and Beregszász (Berehovo), were placed under their pre-1919 counties. Military action then brought the rest of Trianon Transcarpathia under Hungarian rule after March 15, 1939, and the earlier, smaller area, not contiguous with Trianon Transcarpathia and mainly inhabited by Rusyns, was declared to be the "Subcarpathian Governorship." The territory of the region was also affected by the Second Vienna Award.[1]

Under Hungarian military rule the governorship was headed by Julius Marina as commissioner, with Béla Novákovits as military commander. Then came as governors Zsigmond Perényi (July 1939–October 1940), Miklós Kozma (November 1940–December 1941) and Vilmos Pál Tomcsányi (from January 1942). In April 1944, after the region again became a theater of war, András Vincze was both governor and military commander until October 15, when Hungarian administration in Transcarpathia ceased.

On October 11, 1938, the Czechoslovak council of ministers agreed to appoint an autonomous government for "Podkarpatská Rus" (Subcarpathian Rus, or Subcarpathian Ruthenia) known as the Council of Ministers of Podkarpatska Rus. Under the First Vienna Award, 1,523 square kilometers of Podkarpatska Rus (21.1 percent of the region) was transferred to Hungary. In the remainder, Voloshyn established a Carpatho-Ukrainian state with its center in Khust, to which Adolf Hitler gave recognition in the form of a consulate. The constitutional law granting autonomy to "Podkarpatská Rus" was passed in the Prague Parliament on November 22, 1938, having been promised for twenty years in the Treaty of Saint-Germain of September 10, 1919, and the 1920 Czechoslovak Constitution.[2]

Hungary did all that it could to recover the whole of Transcarpathia. In the autumn of 1938, an incident was directed by Miklós Kozma, involving an incursion by the so-called Ragged Guard. This was officially halted, but such border incidents continued.[3] Meanwhile the Poles tried similar tactics to Kozma's, under the command of a professional army officer, Feliks Ankerstein, in what was known as Operation Crowbar in late October and November 1938. The Polish Consulate in Užhorod became a domestic information source.[4]

The decisive events took place in mid-March, when regular Hungarian troops, with tacit agreement from Germany, put paid to the Carpatho-Ukrainian state and its resistance forces, the Carpathian Sich Guard. Then Voloshyn's government in Khust declared the independence of Carpathian Ukraine on March 15. This was merely a symbolic act, as the whole of Transcarpathia had been annexed to Hungary by then.[5]

After the reannexations, the local inhabitants were discontented by a relative loss of freedom of speech compared with liberal Czechoslovak democracy, for the Hungarian system kept public opinion under tight control. This was not just the fault of the Horthy regime, for this was a border region of military significance. Institutions won in "twenty years' struggle" were lost or absorbed into similar institutions in Hungary. On March 15, 1940, the United Hungarian Party was disbanded or absorbed into the Hungarian Party of Life. A decision of the Synod of the Reformed Church of Hungary in October 1939 abolished the Reformed Church Diocese of Subcarpathia, placing it in the Hungarian-based Trans-Tisza Diocese. The Roman Catholic Apostolic Governorship of

Subcarpathia was dissolved by papal command in October 1939 and its area returned to the Diocese of Satu Mare. The authority of the Province of Esztergom was restored over the Greek Catholic Diocese of Munkács in the summer of 1939. Rusyn secondary school teaching was curtailed and most officials were recruited from the "parent country."

Administration of Transcarpathia under Hungarian rule took a curious course. The Hungarian-inhabited band of territory restored by the First Vienna Award was absorbed into the county system, but the Rusyn-inhabited lands beyond remained a special administrative area under the Subcarpathian Governorship based in Ungvár, with three districts styled Ung, Bereg and Maramarosh. One feature was the absence in many parts of clear boundaries, meaning that a community might belong to two different administrative units. Thus Ungvár was the seat of the governorship and of Ung administrative district and of Ung County. Munkács was the seat of the Bereg administrative district and part of Bereg County, whose seat was Beregszász. In education, institutions could be divided even within one building, according to the language of instruction, while geographically these might belong to the Košice, Satu Mare or Subcarpathian educational district. When the Ungvár, Munkács and Beregszász gymnasia were taken over in 1938–1939 by the Voloshyn government, non-Hungarian students and staff were moved into the smaller area of Subcarpathia (Carpatho-Ukraine), where several new gymnasia began to teach in Ukrainian (at Perechyn, Svaliava, Bilki, Rakhiv, Rakoshyno and Velykyy Bychkiv). These were either closed in the following school year or demoted to civil schools. Ungvár Gymnasium was broken into three parts: Hungarian-language gymnasia for boys (Drugeth) and girls (Szent Erzsébet) and a Rusyn-language gymnasium. Munkács's was divided into a Rusyn-language and a Hungarian-language gymnasium (Árpád Fejedelem). Beregszász was left only with a Hungarian-language middle school, while the one in Khust became Rusyn- and Hungarian-language. The Jewish Hebrew schools were closed after the passage of the Jewish Acts.[6]

Even Hungarian inhabitants in the area outside the governorship that had belonged to Podkarpatska Rus in the Czechoslovak period, and then been brought into the county system, retained a feeling for Transcarpathia, expressed, for instance, in 1939 by Árpád Siménfalvy, lord lieutenant of Ung County: "Just as Hungarians and Rusyns fought jointly for their rights in the years of oppression and felt that they belonged as one, so we cannot now raise a Great Wall of China between the habitations of the Rusyns, the administrative district of Subcarpathia, and the activity of the county administration. Hungarians and Rusyns have to be brought closer together."[7]

Prime Minister Pál Teleki saw it as a moral question, after the return of all Transcarpathia to Hungary, to give the Rusyns the territorial, linguistic and cultural autonomy long promised to them. He saw Transcarpathia as the site of a national policy experiment in operating the idea of state of St. Stephen, as he considered the Rusyns to be the minority most loyal to the Hungarian state. Several meetings on the subject were held in March 1939, and the bill on the "Subcarpathian Vojvodeship" and its local government underwent several versions before being presented to Parliament in July 1940. But, shortly afterwards, the prime minister had to withdraw the measure, mainly under the security pressure from the military, and the issue died forever. Teleki's idea of a Subcarpathian Vojvodeship had failed.[8]

It was clear during the debate that the draft had more opponents than supporters. The situation is shown clearly in a statement by Béla Imrédy, who had been drawn into the preparations, having negotiated in September 1938, while still prime minister, with András Bródy. He "raised the question of whether we were prepared to grant Subcarpathia a measure of autonomy in the case of accession. The statement that I made to him then was yes, but we did not detail the matter precisely at that time and tried to keep it rather vague, but as I say, the undertaking to give them autonomy was made firmly. However, I must add that this was stated conditionally, in a case of voluntary accession, meaning that an occupation-type accession such as this, in my view, substantively alters the situation and absolves us morally from the earlier undertakings."[9] It was mentioned in Teleki's circle that Bródy should again be given some political role in Transcarpathia, but in the event, the governorship went to Baron Zsigmond Perényi, who had this to say: "It is true that we assured them autonomy and drew up plans for it, but we did that against the Czechs."[10] Perényi had ties to Transcarpathia as an Ugocsa landowner, and took part between the wars in distributing secret, politically motivated, Hungarian state subsidies in Transcarpathia.

The Rusyn András Bródy was one of the tragic political figures of the period. During his brief period as prime minister in the autumn of 1938 he took a policy line sympathetic to Hungary, seeing that as most appropriate from the national and state-related points of view for protecting the interests of the Rusyns. But he realized after 1939 that he had made a bad choice and turned against official Hungarian policy (unsuccessfully in the event, as he was unable to achieve anything), which had failed to grant Transcarpathia autonomy. Then, under the Soviet system, he was executed for having taken a treacherous pro-Hungarian stance. (Avgusthyn Voloshyn, who had followed an expressly pro-Ukrainian line, also died in a Soviet prison.)

The administrative position of the Subcarpathian Governorship was laid down in Prime Ministerial Order No. 6200 of July 7, 1939, which it would be mistaken to view as a grant of autonomy.[11] The title of the order betrays the fact that it was a "provisional" solution to the question, valid until autonomy should be granted. Transcarpathia had become a difficult issue for the Hungarian government. According to the military command, "The favorable mood of the inhabitants towards the idea of the Hungarian state begins to become unsettled."[12] One big burden was the various vetting committees. The fate of the Jews was one great tragedy in Transcarpathia. Some were taken in 1941 to German-occupied areas of inner Ukraine, while others were deported in 1944 to certain death in Germany.[13] This ethnic group, most of whom identified themselves as Hungarians, became victims of war. There were 78,272 Jewish inhabitants of the region registered in 1941, but only 6,998 in 1946.[14]

Transcarpathia again became a theater of war in April–October 1944, before coming under Soviet occupation.

Notes

1 Csilla Fedinec, "Kárpátalja közigazgatása és tanügyigazgatása 1938–1944 között" [The Public Administration and Educational Administration in Transcarpathia between 1938 and 1944], *Magyar Pedagógia* (1996) 4: 367–375; Csilla Fedinec, "Kárpátaljai autonómia, határváltozások 1918–1944" [Transcarpathia's Autonomy and Border Changes 1918–1944], in Cecília Pásztor, ed., *"... ahol a határ elválaszt." Trianon és következményei a Kárpát-medencében* ["Where the Border Divides." Trianon and Its Consequences in the Carpathian Basin] (Salgótarján, 2002), pp. 415–436; R. Oficyns'kyj, *Politychnyj rozvytok Zakarpattia u skladi Ugorshhyny (1939–1944)* [Political History of Transcarpathia under Hungarian Rule (1939–1944)] (Kyiv, 1997); Charles Wojatsek, *From Trianon to the First Vienna Arbitral Award. The Hungarian Minority in the First Czechoslovak Republic 1918–1938* (Montreal, 1981), pp. 206–208.

2 "328. Ústavní zákon o autonomii Podkarpatské Rusi. 329. Vyhláska o uplném zneni predpisu o autonomii Podkarpatské Rusi" [328. Constitutional Law on the Autonomy of Subcarpathian Rus. 329. Decree on the Consolidation of the Rule of Subcarpathian Rus's Autonomy]. In *Sbírka zákonů a nařízení státu cesko-slovenského*, Ročník 1938. Částka 109. Vydána dne 16. prosince 1938 [Official Gazette of the Czecho-Slovak State, Year of 1938. Issue 109. Issued on 16 December, 1938].

3 Mária Ormos, *Egy magyar médiavezér: Kozma Miklós. Pokoljárás a médiában és a politikában (1919–1941)* [A Hungarian Media Magnate Miklós Kozma. Descent into Hell in the Media and Politics (1919–1941)], Vol. II (Budapest, 2000), pp. 549–572.

4 Dariusz Dabrowski, *Rzeczpospolita Polska wobec kwestii Rusi Zakarpackiei (Podkarpackiei) 1938–1939* [The Republic of Poland to Carpathian Rus (Transcarpathia) 1938–1939] (Toruń, 2007).

5 M. Vegesh, *Karpats'ka Ukrai'na. Dokumenty i fakty* [Carpatho-Ukraine. Documents and Facts] (Uzhhorod, 2004); V. Bodnar and M. Vegesh, *Karpats'ka Ukrai'na v mizhnarodnyh vidnosynah (1938–1939)* [The Carpatho-Ukraine Question in International Politics (1938–1939)] (Uzhhorod, 1997); Lóránt Tilkovszky, *Revízió és nemzetiségpolitika Magyarországon (1938–1941)* [Revision and Nationality Policy in Hungary (1938–1941)] (Budapest, 1967); Csilla Fedinec, ed., *Kárpátalja 1938–1941. Magyar és ukrán történeti*

közelítés [Transcarpathia 1938–1941. Hungarian and Ukrainian Historical Rapprochement] (Budapest, 2004).

6 Increasingly discriminatory anti-Jewish laws were passed in Hungary on May 29, 1938, May 5, 1939, August 8, 1941 and September 6, 1942. These emulated the Nuremberg Laws passed in Germany in 1935. Also see Fedinec, "Kárpátalja közigazgatása."

7 Magyar Országos Levéltár [The National Archives of Hungary], K 28, 45. cs., 96. t.

8 Géza Vasas, "Egy félbehagyott alkotmány. Kárpátalja autonómiájának ügye 1939–1940-ben" [Uncompleted Constitution. The Question of Transcarpathian Autonomy in 1939–1940], in Csilla Fedinec, ed., *Kárpátalja 1938–1941. Magyar és ukrán történeti közelítés* [Transcarpathia 1938–1941. Hungarian and Ukrainian Historical Rapprochement] (Budapest,2004), pp. 157–216; Balázs Ablonczy, *Pál Teleki – The Life of a Controversial Hungarian Politician* (Wayne, NJ, 2007).

9 Magyar Tudományos Akadémia Kézirattára [Manuscripts of the Hungarian Academy of Sciences], Egyed Papers, Ms 10-734/25.

10 *Ibid.*

11 "A m. kir. minisztérium 1939. évi 6.200. M. E. számú rendelete a Magyar Szent Koronához visszatért kárpátaljai terület közigazgatásának ideiglenes rendezéséről" [Royal Hungarian Government Order 1939/6.200 M. E. on Provisional Administration of the Transcarpathian Territory Returned to the Holy Crown of Hungary], in Fedinec, ed., *Iratok a kárpátaljai magyarság történetéhez*, pp. 528–534.

12 Magyar Országos Levéltár, K 28, 123. cs., 237. t.

13 Ágnes Ságvári, "Zsidósors Kárpátalján" [Jewish Destiny in Transcarpathia], in Idem, *Tanulmányok a magyarországi holokauszt történetéből* [Studies on the History of the Hungarian Holocaust] (Budapest, 2002), pp. 33–67; Ágnes Ságvári, "Holocaust Kárpátalján 1941-ben," [Holocaust in Transcarpathia in 1941], *Múltunk* 2 (1999): 116–144; György Haraszti, "Kárpáti rapszódia" [Carpathian Rhapsody], *História* (2004) 2–3: 23–28; Tamás Majsai, "A kőrösmezei zsidó deportálás 1941-ben" [Deportation of the Jewish Population of Yasina in 1941], in Kálmán Benda, Angéla Beliczay, György Erdős and Edit Nagy, eds., *Ráday Gyűjtemény Évkönyve IV–V (1984–85)* [Ráday Collection Yearbook IV–V (1984–1985)] (Budapest, 1986), pp. 59–86; Randolph L. Braham, *The Politics of Genocide: the*

The Autonomy Question in Transcarpathia 255

Holocaust in Hungary, 2nd ed. (Wayne, NJ, 2000); Tamás Stark, *Hungary's Human Losses in World War II* (Uppsala, 1995); Gavriel Bar-Shaked, ed., *Names: the Counties of Carpathian Ruthenia. Part I. Names of Jews Deported from Ugocsa County (Sevlus and Vicinity)* (New York/Paris, 2004); Israel Gutman and Bella Gutterman, eds., *The Auschwitz Album* (Yad Vashem, n. d.); Henry Abrahamson, "Collective Memory and Collective Identity: Jews, Rusyns, and the Holocaust," *Carpatho-Rusyn American* 17 (Fall 1994): 3.

14 Kárpátaljai Területi Állami Levéltár [State Archive of the Transcarpathian *Oblast*], Fond 125, opis 2, delo 67, f. 58–59.

3. CASE STUDIES

Romania (*Béni L. Balogh* and *Nándor Bárdi*)

The Second Vienna Award of August 30, 1940, restored to Hungary Northern Transylvania – two fifths of the territory ceded to Romania under the 1920 Treaty of Trianon. The 60,000 square kilometers of Southern Transylvania remained part of Romania. According to 1930 Romanian census figures, 3,155,922 of the 5,549,806 inhabitants of Transylvania lived in the south, of whom 473,551 (15.0 percent) had Hungarian as their native language and 481,128 had German (15.3 percent). Territorially, the greatest number of Hungarians lived in Arad and Timiş Counties (96,756 and 83,423), as well as in Braşov, Hunedoara and Turda-Arieş Counties (40,000 each).[1] So after the Second Vienna Award there remained in Romania (including the Regat) over 500,000 Hungarians.

The Hungarians of Southern Transylvania entered a radically different existence, as a minority. About 200,000 Hungarians left Romania between the Second Vienna Award and February 1944, and fled to or settled within the enlarged territory of Hungary. The figure includes some 13,200 Bukovina Székely resettled in Bačka.[2] About half of those who left did so within six months of the Second Vienna Award,[3] and a similar number of displaced Romanians arrived in Southern Transylvania. With permission from the Budapest government, almost all Hungarians from the Regat moved, and the flight reached alarming proportions in some parts of Southern Transylvania as well. As a consequence, by April 1941, the number of "ethnic" Hungarians had fallen to 363,000, or 11 percent, from the 440,000 (14 percent) of the 1930 Romanian census figures.[4]

With permission from the head of state, Ion Antonescu, the Romanian Hungarian People's Community held an inaugural assembly in Aiud on November 4, 1940. There a Central Executive was formed and leadership positions vacated after the Second Vienna Award were filled.[5] Elemér Gyárfás (former head of the Catholic Status and the Transylvanian Hungarian Banking Association) became president and Pál Szász (president of the Transylvanian Hungarian Farming Association) vice-president, with Count Bálint Bethlen (chief curator of the Reformed Church) and Elemér Jakabffy (prominent among the Banat community) as Presidential Committee members. Gyárfás also had the support of the Hungarian government, but the leadership was riven from the outset. Several colleagues accused Gyárfás of running the organization single-handed and paying little heed to its internal affairs. At a meeting at Galtiu on May 25, 1944, his policies were denounced by Áron Márton, Roman Catholic bishop of Alba Iulia. Two months later, István Haller (a cooperative leader), Pál Szász and Miklós Gál (a Unitarian leader), resigned from the Presidential Committee, after Gyárfás had used travel difficulties to avoid convening it.[6] In the event, the activity of the organization was more or less paralyzed by the ban on public assembly, the travel problems and the strict censorship of mail and the press. It was active mainly in defending rights, through its central and local offices, and sent regular reports on the Southern Transylvanian Hungarians to the Hungarian Consulates in Arad and Braşov. The branches also did welfare work when conditions allowed, for the system of granting official permits for such activity was becoming stricter. Also operating within the ethnic community was the part of the Transylvanian Hungarian Farming Association that remained in Southern Transylvania, based in Aiud. Its membership had grown from 5,800 to 16,000 by the summer of 1942, as it sought to supply cheaper farming implements, wheat, fertilizer and breeding stock for peasant farmers,[7] but its most valuable side, agricultural training, fell victim to regular harassment.

The want of social institutions and strict ban on public assembly enhanced the importance of the Churches to the Hungarians of

Southern Transylvania. The region included about one third of the Roman Catholic Diocese of Alba Iulia, with 86 parishes and 85,000 members.[8] Bishop Áron Márton was also in charge of the territory ceded to Hungary. Some two fifths of the Transylvanian Reformed Church Province remained in Romania, and had 205 congregations with some 177,000 members at the time of the Second Vienna Award, including 51,000 in the Regat. Most of the latter left for Hungary and the exodus also meant that the membership in Southern Transylvania was hardly more than 100,000 in 1943.[9] Two of the six dioceses in the Királyhágómellék Reformed Church District with 55,000 members also remained in Romania.[10] The Hungarian Lutheran Church Province based in Arad lost only four parishes with 5,000 members by the territorial changes. The Southern Transylvanian membership of 40,000 included some scattered communities, but most lived in a single bloc in the Țara Bârsei district near Brașov.[11] The Unitarians were in a predicament. Although half their members – 24,000–25,000 people – remained in Romania, the seat of the bishop in Cluj went to Hungary, along with most of the Church's assets, both middle schools and the theological academy. Unitarian affairs in Southern Transylvania were conducted by a Representative Council based in Turda.[12]

State education in Hungarian almost ceased in Romania. Most school departments teaching in Hungarian were closed or continued in Romanian. The Hungarian-language denominational schools that remained taught only about half of the Hungarian pupils. In December 1942, the Hungarian Churches in Romania were running seven kindergartens, 179 primary schools, 15 middle schools, one theological academy, and two agricultural, three commercial, and four apprentice schools.[13]

Most denominational schools worked under tough conditions, funded only by diminishing revenue from Church taxes. The departures for Hungary left a chronic shortage of teaching staff, and widespread employment of untrained teachers posed a danger that schools would be closed or stripped of their right to conduct public examinations. Middle school premises were sometimes requisitioned as hospitals.

Intellectual life among the Southern Transylvanian Hungarians was hit by the loss of its cultural center at Cluj, then paralyzed by the censorship, travel curbs and ban on public assembly. It became impossible to hold almost any kind of cultural gathering. Most civil associations were dissolved by the authorities and deprived of their assets and premises. Hungarian clubs and arts centers closed, choral societies were suspended, and there could be no place for plays or other performances. Only in the three cities of Arad, Braşov and Timişoara did there remain any chance for cultural activity, mainly through the libraries. Continuity of Hungarian intellectual life depended mainly on the written word: books, almanacs and the press, but all periodicals in Hungarian were banned in the autumn of 1942. Only in April 1943 could the farming paper *Erdélyi Gazda* appear again, followed in June by the Arad literary journal *Havi Szemle*. Book publication was down to a minimum: 41 titles in 1941, mostly pamphlets, scores and booklets.[14]

Daily life in Romania was governed by the fascist, later military, dictatorship of General Ion Antonescu, who took power in September 1940, and from June 1941 by martial law. The Hungarians suffered also from official discrimination at the central and local level and from anti-Hungarian sentiment, particularly in the presence of the more than 200,000 Romanian refugees, from Northern Transylvania.

The idea of clearing Southern Transylvania of Hungarians became Romanian government policy. One way of effecting this was what was known as forced opting. The Second Vienna Award allowed the Romanians of Northern Transylvania and the Hungarians of Southern Transylvania to opt for Romanian or Hungarian citizenship within six months. Official Romanian organizations encouraged or pressured some Hungarians to sign an option statement resigning their Romanian citizenship. The opting procedures had not been agreed between the two governments in detail, and so the Hungarians did not recognize opting as legally binding. At the beginning of June 1941, the Romanian government issued a confidential order banning public use of the Hungarian language, and there were moves to dismiss certain categories of Hungarian employees. The use of Hungarian was also restricted in postal and telegraph services. These measures were later reversed officially, but restrictions were reimposed by military commands in some districts in 1942. Travel restrictions applied throughout the period, except for one or two short breaks. Within a 20-kilometer-wide restricted border zone, people could not even travel from one village to the next without a gendarmerie pass. The Hungarians of Romania had no representatives at central or even local level, and so no say in matters of direct interest to them. Other serious grievances included the inhuman way in which Hungarian men were treated during military and labor service, billeting of Romanian refugees on Hungarian families, and often unfounded prosecutions in the military courts.[15] Until 1941, the land, stock and farming implements of small-scale and medium-scale farmers were untouched. The assets of Hungarian financial institutions surrounding the Auxiliary Savings Bank in Aiud and the former People's Bank in Braşov grew steadily.[16] The Hangya ("Ant") cooperative center operated well.[17] But thereafter the Hungarians of Southern Transylvania came under mounting economic pressure. The government's aim after the opting requirement was to ruin the Hungarians. This meant overtaxing their artisans, traders, lawyers and physicians, establishing summary courts, compulsory purchases of reconstruction or reannexation loan stock, fabricated charges of economic sabotage, discrimination in distributing utility goods, excessive demands for public work, restricted cross-border tourism, or repeated requisitions of produce or livestock. The Hungarian craftsmen and merchants had no representation in the governing bodies of economic life, and most of the Hungarian employees of the industry were laid off.

The permanent body for protecting the rights of the Hungarian minority was a mixed committee of officers nominated by the German and Italian governments, set up in Braşov in February 1941. An equivalent for Romanian petitioners was set up in Cluj. The Braşov committee received 1,518 complaints in two years and found 242 (16 percent) of them to be just. In 70 percent of cases the response was evasive or the matter was never considered.[18] Almost half the complaints were of some kind of assault. Those to do with land, public supplies or cultural matters made up 11 percent each.

In May 1942, the Romanian government cited persecution of Northern Transylvanian Romanians when proposing to starve Hungarian villages in Southern Transylvania and confiscate all Hungarian property. Armed force was to be used in cases of resistance.[19] The Romanians had to back down again after investigations by German and Italian special commissioners. It proved impractical to remove all Hungarians from Southern Transylvania quickly and easily, although the lot of the Hungarians continued to worsen in 1943–1944.[20]

The main aim of the Romanian government was to retrieve Northern Transylvania as well, and this was served by its ethnic objectives too: to back the Romanians of Northern Transylvania and cleanse Southern Transylvania of Hungarians. Meanwhile, the German minority was given special privileges and was able with Third Reich support to act as a "state within a state," while the Jews were put in a worse situation even than the Hungarians. Budapest saw the Second Vienna Award as a partial remedy for the Treaty of Trianon – a change of rule accepted and agreed to by the Romanians. It could not allow the Southern Transylvanian Hungarians to be chased out altogether, because of its further aims of revision. So it sought to pursue in Northern Transylvania a reciprocal ethnic policy of the kind that was working with the Slovaks. But what ultimately decided the system of relations between Hungary and Romania was the compulsion to join the Axis, although both countries toyed with the idea of bailing out from it.

Slovakia (*Árpád Popély*)

The First Vienna Award of November 2, 1938, restored most of the Upland Hungarians and Hungarian-inhabited areas to Hungary, but about one in ten remained under Czechoslovakian and then Slovakian rule. According to the Slovakian census of December

1938, 57,897 indigenous inhabitants (2.2 percent of the total of 2,656,426) of the Slovakia that became independent on March 14, 1939, called themselves Hungarian by national affiliation.

Most Hungarian inhabitants of the new Slovak Republic lived in and around Bratislava or in the Zobor district near Nitra, but appreciable numbers were found in Slovak towns north of the linguistic border, such as Trnava, Zlaté Moravce, Banská Štiavnica, Zvolen, Banská Bystrica, Levoča, Spišská Nová Ves, Prešov and Michalovce. In social structure, the Hungarian community changed greatly after 1938, with fewer agricultural but more industrial and office workers, and a sizeable intelligentsia.[21]

The Slovak Constitution of July 21, 1939, with its Italian corporatist structure, classed Hungarians and Germans (but not Czechs or Jews) as naturalized national groups. In principle Hungarians had a constitutional right to organize politically and culturally, even to share in state power through a political party, but in practice this was allowed only to the ethnic Germans, who received privileged treatment and came to be a state within a state through their *Deutsche Partei* (German Party). The political representative of the Hungarians was the *Magyar Párt* (Hungarian Party). This, in a sense the legal successor of the pre-Award United Hungarian Party, was long only tolerated by the Slovak authorities and official registration was long postponed, on the reciprocity principle laid down in the Slovak Constitution, and because the Slovaks of Hungary had no official party. Being unregistered prevented the party from undertaking the activity required to represent the interests of the Hungarian minority.[22]

The Slovak authorities eventually granted permission for the Hungarian Party to operate in November 1941, but it still could not do any real political work. The various obstructions meant that its work was confined mainly to the cultural and social fields, and to some extent to the economic. Not once was there a chance to hold a party congress or public mass meeting. The political opportunities were limited to occasional meetings of the presiding committee to discuss issues of the moment. Its president, János Esterházy, was the sole Hungarian member of the Slovak legislature, where he managed to raise Hungarian grievances from time to time and ask for them to be remedied. He also sought out the Hungarian government on several occasions to request help in persuading the Slovak authorities to reduce the pressure on the Hungarian minority.

Among the most important achievements of the party was to build up a network of Hungarian Houses and to give welfare assistance to poor Hungarian families. The Hungarian Houses set up in cities with a Slovak majority became centers of minority social life and were central to maintaining the national awareness and preserving the traditions of scattered Hungarian communities.[23]

Despite strong German and Slovak pressures, joined after October 1944 by pressure from Hungary's Arrow-Cross, Esterházy rejected the idea of reorganizing his party on National Socialist lines. So the Hungarian Party managed to retain its conservative, Christian socialist character within the frames of the fascist Slovak state. Esterházy was also active in assisting the persecuted Jews. His was the sole vote in the Slovak legislature on May 15, 1942, against a constitutional act on deportation of the Jewish population.

After the Arrow-Cross seizure of power, Esterházy was arrested in Budapest in December 1944 and forced to resign as party president, although his party re-elected him on February 3, 1945. In the final days of World War II, the Gestapo issued a warrant for his arrest and he went into hiding. However, he was arrested in the spring of 1945 by the returning Czechoslovak authorities and handed over to the Soviet military authorities. He was then taken off to the Soviet Union along with several other leaders of the Hungarian Party and other members of the Bratislava intelligentsia.[24]

In practice, the cultural life of the Hungarian minority in the Slovak Republic also became confined to the Hungarian Party. There was no state-level institution or budgetary support whatsoever. Almost all the associations outside Bratislava were closed. Only the Toldy Circle and Béla Bartók Choral Society,[25] established several decades before, could continue in the capital. The minority's most important cultural organization, the Slovakian Hungarian Cultural

Association,[26] had been founded in 1925. Its activity was banned in the spring of 1939 and it was only permitted to reopen in a highly restricted form in 1942, when the presidency was taken by Count Mihály Csáky, vice-president of the Hungarian Party.[27]

In the spring of 1939, there were two daily papers (the Hungarian Party's *Új Hírek* and the privately owned *Esti Újság*), a cultural journal (*Magyar Minerva*) and a few provincial weeklies to serve the Hungarian minority. *Magyar Minerva* closed in 1939 and the provincial papers not long afterwards, while the two dailies were banned on the grounds of reciprocity in 1941. However, a Slovak daily paper began to appear in Hungary and two Hungarian papers were allowed again in Slovakia in December 1941: the daily *Magyar Hírlap* and the weekly *Magyar Néplap*, both published by the Hungarian Party. These were published until the Arrow-Cross came to power in the autumn of 1944. The Hungarian press otherwise consisted of a few Catholic papers. Finally, the German authorities in Bratislava permitted the appearance of a National Socialist daily, the *Magyar Szó*, in February and March 1945.[28]

The number of schools teaching in Hungarian was not sufficient either. According to the law, the presence of 30 school-age children was enough to get permission for starting a minority school, but the authorities refused on countless occasions to found a Hungarian school even though the legal requirements for doing so were met. Reciprocity was again the excuse in 1939–1941 for closing several Hungarian middle schools, including the Hungarian teachers' training college in Bratislava and the Ursuline Order's civil school for girls. So in the 1941–1942 school year, the Hungarians of Slovakia had 35 elementary schools, one civil school, one gymnasium, one four-year commercial academy, one two-year trade school and one specialist school for women's occupations.[29]

The Banat (*Enikő A. Sajti*)

The Banat (Bánság) is a term for the parts of the old Hungarian counties of Krassó-Szörény, Temes and Torontál lying between the Rivers Mureş (Maros), Tisa (Tisza) and Danube, and the Carpathian Mountains. It was never a separate political unit. Under the Versailles peace treaties, the Banat was divided between Romania and the Serb-Croat-Slovene Kingdom (later Yugoslavia), with a small corner of Torontál (the Tisza-Maros confluence) remaining in Hungary.

Despite earlier German promises, the Banat was not reannexed to Hungary in April 1941, but occupied by German troops. The German government's excuse was the need to avoid a clash between Hungary and Romania, a rival claimant to the region. There were also fears of domestic crisis in Romania, which had just suffered major territorial losses (of Northern Transylvania to Hungary and Bessarabia and Northern Bukovina to the Soviet Union). Then there were military considerations, as the occupation of the Banat gave Berlin control over important routes such as the railway between Smederovo and the Danube, the confluence of the Danube and the Tisa, and the stretch of the Danube along the Romanian border. The German–Italian agreement on the division of Yugoslavia, signed on April 24, 1941, in the Imperial Hotel, Vienna, promised the Banat to Hungary, but kept it under German military occupation. Yugoslavia was divided into German and Italian spheres of influence, with 98,572 of the 247,542 square kilometers forming the Independent Croatian State. Most of Slovenia fell to Germany, while the province of Ljubljana became an Italian zone of occupation. Italy received most of the Adriatic sea coast and an enlarged Montenegro. Italian troops also occupied parts of Yugoslavia adjacent to Albania. Bulgaria was granted part of Macedonia (28,250 square kilometers). Bačka and the Baranja Triangle went to Hungary without conditions. Hungary undertook to hold talks with Croatia and Germany on the future of Međimurje and Prekmurje, but in the event simply occupied them. The Banat was assigned to Hungary in principle, but with a proviso that it would remain under German military occupation for an indefinite period. Additionally, Hungary was promised a free port on the Dalmatian coast. Serbia was largely confined to its 1912 borders, under German occupation.[30]

According to German figures, the ethnic structure of the Banat in 1941 was as follows: 295,000 Serbs, 120,000 Germans, 95,000 Hungarians, 70,000 Romanians, 18,000 Slovaks and 4,000 Jews. Hungarian figures put the number of Banat Hungarians at 108,732.

So the Germans prevented any advance of Hungarian troops into the Banat, and the plans for a Hungarian military administration were shelved. The Banat Germans held a rally at Pančevo on April 20, 1941 (Hitler's birthday) to demand that an autonomous Danubian German state be formed out of Bačka, the Banat and Srem. This would have proclaimed its accession to the Third Reich. But the German government did not support the idea, in the light of the Hungarian and Romanian territorial demands and the region's ethnic composition. The Hungarian government, confident that the Banat would be reannexed later, tried from the outset to stop ethnic Hungarians from being eased out of the administration. An attempt was also made to persuade Berlin to allow trained officials to be sent into the Banat from Hungary, but this was rejected by the German Ministry of Foreign Affairs, saying that the local Hungarians were demanding more official posts than their proportion in the population justified. The collaborationist government of Milan Nedić in Belgrade issued an order on October 23, 1941, curbing the participation of Banat Hungarians in public administration, which elicited a protest from the Hungarian government. For instance, none of the posts of mayor in the five cities went to a Hungarian. As a result of continuing Hungarian protests, the ethnic proportions in official posts were revised at the end of October, with the result that Hungarians were appointed as prefects of two districts and as a mayor of one city. The privileged position of the Germans was unchanged and their role in the economy was enhanced, as the Banat became an important German economic bridgehead to the Balkans. The failure of Budapest's endeavors became apparent with the dismissal of Hungarians who had taken jobs in local authorities after the collapse of Yugoslavia, hoping for an early move in by the Hungarian army. In Veliki Bečkerek, for instance, local Hungarian officials and employees were dismissed in mid-April with Germans appointed in their stead, and the laying off of Hungarian employees and workers from factories in the city also began. The Serbs in the Banat villages with a Serb majority did not lose their lower-ranking jobs there. The German, Hungarian, Romanian and Serbian languages were all given official status.[31]

On June 5, 1941, the German occupation forces decided without consulting the Hungarians to annex the territory to Serbia, with a separate administrative status. An "auxiliary *ban*" was appointed over it, in the person of a Banat German leader, Josef-Sepp Lapp. His responsibilities included the internal affairs of the Banat and directing four new administrative departments, whose heads, all Germans, were appointed formally by the collaborationist Milan Aćimović, prime minister and minister of the interior of Serbia. Under an agreement signed by the German occupation forces and the Serbian government, the ethnicity of the district, city and parish heads was to match the local ethnic proportions, but the key positions in the economy were to be held by Germans, in the light of the importance of the Banat economy to the German war effort. When a new administrative structure was introduced for Serbia on December 18, 1941, the Banat became one of the country's 14 districts (*okrug*), although still separated from the rest by a customs barrier. Thereafter a deputy to the auxiliary *ban* was chosen from the Hungarian minority, first Ferenc Jeszenszky, then Béla Botka from 1943 onwards. However, a report from the Hungarian Consulate-General in Belgrade suggests that there were attempts to isolate the Hungarian deputy auxiliary *bans*, leaving them unable to do their jobs.

After some shilly-shallying, the Banat Hungarian Public Education Association[32] was allowed to operate under Tibor Tallián, and then under Ferenc Jeszenszky, the former assistant to the auxiliary *ban*. The respected community leader and former Yugoslav senator

Imre Várady was also elected onto the board. The association operated at first as part of the Hungarian Public Education Association in the Southern Region. On German initiative, the name was later changed to the Hungarian Public Education Association in the Danube Region, ostensibly to distance it further from Hungary.

The Hungarian Public Education Association was the only cultural and representative organization for the Banat Hungarians. It successfully intervened, for instance, in the interest of the non-Jewish Hungarians and prevented taking them for labor service in Serbian mines, having them serve in the Banat instead. It was also a determining factor in the post-war fate of the Banat Hungarians that the association aborted a plan for the establishment of a 500-man partisan force among the Banat Hungarians that was to have worn German uniforms and have been under German command.[33]

In the 1942–1943 school year, there were state elementary schools teaching in Hungarian in 84 Banat communities, while 32 had a Hungarian-language kindergarten. Hungarian was also the language of instruction in four private gymnasia, two eight-grade higher gymnasia and six four-grade lower gymnasia, with a total of 900 students, as well as a commercial and a higher elementary school, and seven private boarding schools, including the reopened College of Our Lady in Veliki Bečkerek, about which there were several disagreements during the Royal Yugoslav period. The Hungarian schools suffered severe shortages of teaching staff, and a disproportionately high number of instructors were untrained. These shortages were eventually eased by bringing in teachers from Hungary.

The relations of the Banat Hungarians and Germans had their grotesque aspect, illustrated by the case of a consignment of school uniforms sent to the Banat from Budapest. The German military command refused to distribute them until the braid on them was removed, arguing that it would only lead to scuffles between Hungarian and German students. But the customs office did not have enough hands to remove the braid, and the uniforms remained in bond for two years.

Land was not taken from Hungarians when the Yugoslav land reform was reversed in the Banat, but the expropriated South Slav lands were redistributed only to Germans. The Jewish lands were not parceled out, but placed under Reich administration to supply the German army.

The Jews of the Banat suffered immediate severe reprisals when the territory was occupied. They were deprived of all legal rights and dismissed from business jobs, and their property was confiscated. They could not hold any public office or even use the sidewalks of city streets. In August 1941, they were herded into a relocation center and sent out for annihilation. Only a few hundred of them returned after the Holocaust.[34]

Yugoslav partisans and units of the Soviet Army entered the Banat at the beginning of October 1944. By the autumn, the partisan commander-in-chief, Josip Broz Tito, had set up his command in the small Banat city of Vršac, where he ordered Yugoslav military rule to be imposed on the Banat, Bačka and Baranja on October 17.

The German Reich: Burgenland (*Gerhard Baumgartner*)

The National Socialist movement was already a significant political force in Burgenland by the 1930s. Although illegal in Austria since 1934, the National Socialist Party (*Nationalsozialistische Deutsche Arbeiterpartei*, NSDAP), had many sympathizers and members among the Hungarian-speaking and Croatian-speaking inhabitants as well.[35] Two days before the March 12, 1938, *Anschluss*, the National Socialists of Burgenland held rallies in the Croatian and Hungarian languages, emphasizing the point that their ideology was aimed principally against the Jews and the Gypsies. The festivities at Oberwart to welcome the entry of the Germans featured Hungarians on horseback wearing Hungarian costume. When it came to the April plebiscite designed to legitimize the *Anschluss*, the Hungarian-inhabited villages joined the rest of the Ostmark (former Austria) in voting over 99 percent in favor of confirming the annexation to the Reich. The Evangelical pastor at Siget in der Wart, who objected to the open voting system, was branded a communist and dismissed by his congregation. When NSDAP headquarters in Berlin called for the exclusion of non-German members from the party, the party head in Burgenland refused to carry out the instruction, saying that if he did so, the party would cease to exist in Oberwart, as everyone there was Hungarian.[36]

The province of Burgenland was itself disbanded on April 14, 1939. The Northern and Central Burgenland districts joined the new Gau Niederdonau (Lower Danube) and the Southern Burgenland district of Gau Steiermark (Styria).

By then, the National Socialists in 1938 had expelled the Jewish inhabitants, numbering some 4,000, and confiscated all their property. Most of the Jews fled initially to Vienna, from where those who were unable to obtain foreign visas were sent to concentration camps after 1941.[37] The Burgenland Jews never returned, and with their expulsion the Hungarian-speaking community lost most of its middle class and intelligentsia.

In 1939 the Nazi regime established a special concentration camp for the Gypsies, at Lackenbach in Burgenland. Almost half the 9,000 Burgenland Gypsies were sent in 1941 to the Łodz ghetto in Poland, while the rest were deported to the Auschwitz concentration camp in 1943. Only 900 of them survived the war.[38] The Nazi extermination of the Gypsies was a huge loss to the Hungarian-speaking community in Burgenland, of which they accounted for about one sixth.

The Nazis disbanded all the hitherto independent civil associations in the former territory of Austria, thus ending any cultural activity in the Hungarian villages. An exception was Oberwart's Reformed Reading Circle, which was allowed to continue under Church auspices in a restricted form. All the denominational schools were expropriated after the *Anschluss* and continued as state schools, which meant that teaching in Hungarian ceased. As for the staff of the eight Hungarian-language denominational schools, they were transferred to a German-speaking location, prohibited from teaching, or expelled from the country. But when Berlin proposed to deport the non-German-speaking minorities, this was strongly opposed by the authorities in Burgenland. The German and Hungarian governments were actually negotiating on a possible resettlement at the time, but the Hungarian government never addressed the situation of the Burgenland Hungarians, on which it had no specific information.

The papers of the Hungarian Ministry of Foreign Affairs include only two reports on the position of the Burgenland Hungarians: one by a Sopron university student, and one by a gymnasium student from Hungary passing through. In 1942, the Political Department of the Hungarian Prime Minister's Office appointed János Almássy of Bernstein to preside over the Hungarian associations in the Ostmark. He produced a 14-point program demanding the revival of Burgenland's Hungarian elementary schools, bilingual place-name signs, foundation of a Hungarian-language civil school at Oberwart, and conclusion of a cultural treaty between Hungary and the Third Reich. But there was no known practical effect of this, and Almássy's reports betray the fact that he was not conversant with the situation in Burgenland. Another source, a 1944 report from the Hungarian Consulate-General in Vienna, stated that it was hard to judge the Burgenland situation from Vienna, and complained that it did not interest Hungarian diplomacy in any case.[39]

There was no express Hungarian resistance to the regime, but huge numbers of Hungarians fell victim to Nazi persecution. Not long after the *Anschluss*, two prominent Christian Democratic politicians – Ferenc Prónai, deputy mayor of Eisenstadt, and Imre Faludy, prefect of Güssing – were taken off to the concentration camp at Dachau. Anton von Gömörey, from a noble family in Bernstein, was arrested and ordered to leave the country. Ferenc Rohonczy, a Lackenbach landowner who saved many Gypsies from being sent to a concentration camp, had to flee to Hungary. The most prominent victim among the Vienna Hungarians was Zsigmond Varga, minister to the city's Reformed congregation, who was in touch with opposition circles in the German Churches. He was reported by one of his own congregation, sent to the Mauthausen death camp, and never returned.[40]

Day laborers on the estates of Northern Burgenland generally had ties with the social democratic or communist parties. About 700 took part in a 1939 strike for higher pay. They would visit nearby villages at night to cut down the "Hitler oaks" planted to mark the *Anschluss* and distribute the illegal communist paper. Seventeen of those arrested were sentenced to prison, where two committed suicide. The peasants, artisans, workers and public employees in the underground resistance in Oberwart included some former NSDAP sympathizers and members disillusioned with Nazism, including a former head of the local branch. They collected money for acts of resistance, listened to Entente radio stations, and are said to have planned joint sabotage with Soviet parachutists. The group was discovered in 1944. Five of the 21 members taken to Graz for trial were executed.

Hungarian-inhabited villages all became bilingual under the Third Reich. No more registries were kept in Hungarian; Hungarian names were Germanicized in personal documents. An Austrian citizen who received a passport in 1938 as Gyula Imre was later issued with a travel document as Julius Imre.[41]

The Vienna Hungarians were in a different position from that of those in Burgenland, as the Hungarian associations there were not wound up. A Hungarian House was founded at the Consulate-General under an agreement between the German and Hungarian governments. The Nazis treated this as a foreign cultural institution and did not interfere with its operation. The same applied to the student associations in Graz, Innsbruck and Vienna, which were funded by the Hungarian state, although Jewish members were expelled. The Hungarian House produced a paper called *Értesítő* until 1945.

Many of the 110,000 Jews in Vienna were Hungarian-speaking or held Hungarian citizenship. They could turn to the Hungarian Consulate for help during the Nazi persecutions. The most famous of these was the composer Imre Kálmán, who protested as a Hungarian citizen against confiscation of his property.[42]

In the winter of 1944, *Wehrmacht* forces drove Hungarian labor servicemen up to the Hungarian–Burgenland border, where they were to build a defensive line for the Reich. These labor servicemen, some already on death marches from Bor and other labor camps, were starved and worked to death under inhuman conditions. Yet the system of defenses failed to hold back the Soviet troops for even one day, and the fleeing German forces took their labor service prisoners on death marches further into the Reich. Those too exhausted, weakened or sick to stand the pace were simply killed *en masse*, for instance on the edges of Nickelsdorf, Rechnitz and Deutsch Schützen.[43]

The Soviet forces crossed the Hungarian border and occupied Burgenland on March 29, 1945.

Notes

1   Árpád E. Varga, *Népszámlálások a jelenkori Erdély területén. Jegyzetek Erdély és a kapcsolt részek XX. századi nemzetiségi statisztikájának történetéhez* [Censuses in the Present Area of Transylvania. Notes on the History of 20th-Century Ethnic Statistics in Transylvania and Attached Areas] (Budapest, 1992), pp. 9–19. For ethnic statistics for Transylvania, see http://www.kia.hu/konyvtar/erdely/erdmagy2.pdf.

2   On the resettlement process: Enikő A. Sajti, *Hungarians in the Voivodina 1918–1947* (Boulder, CO/Highland Lakes, NJ, 2003), pp. 250–272.

3   For salient figures on refugees from Romania according to a February 1944 survey: "Main Data of the Refugees from Romania According to the 1944 Survey." *Magyar Statisztikai Szemle* 22 (1944) 9–12: 410.

4   Varga, *Népszámlálások a jelenkori Erdély területén,* pp. 147–148.

5   Romániai Magyar Népközösség. MOL K 63. 1940–27/7. II. 2653–2809, 4–9: A dél-erdélyi magyarság vezetőinek 1940. november 4-iki nagyenyedi értekezlete [Aiud Meeting of Southern Transylvanian Hungarian Leaders on November 4, 1940].

6   Sándor Kacsó, *Nehéz szagú iszap felett. Önéletrajzi visszaemlékezések* [Over Strong-Smelling Mud. Autobiographical Reminiscences], III (Bukarest, 1993), p. 483.

7   MOL K 610. XII. 3/1, 3–13: Az EMGE rövid története és jelenlegi munkája [A Short History of the Transylvanian-Hungarian Economic Association]; *ibid.*, 5/4, 17–31: Szász Pál válasza a gazdasági kérdőpontokra [The Response of Pál Szász to the Economic Questionnaire].

8   *Ibid.*, 6/5, 3–5: 1. A gyulafehérvári róm. kat. egyházmegye rövid története a bécsi döntés óta [A Short History of the Roman Catholic Diocese of Gyulafehérvár since the Vienna Award].

9   *Ibid.*, 6/11, 44–45: Helyzetkép a Délerdélyben maradt Református Anyaszentegyház életéről a II. bécsi döntéstől, 1940. VIII. 31. – 1943. V. 5.-ig [Report on the Activity of the Reformed Mother Church in Southern Transylvania since the Second Vienna Award, August 31, 1940–May 5, 1943].

10   *Ibid.*, 6/7, 3–14: 1. A ref. egyház rövid története a bécsi döntés óta [Short History of the Reformed Church since the Vienna Award].

11   *Ibid.*, 6/1, 305–309: 1. Az egyház rövid története a bécsi döntés óta [Short History of the Church since the Vienna Award].

12   *Ibid.*, 6/3, 1–10: A délerdélyi unitárius egyház válasza a kérdőpontokra [The Response of the Southern Transylvanian Unitarian Church to the Questionnaire].

13   *Ibid.*, 6/4, 279: Összesített kimutatás a romániai magyar egyházak tulajdonában lévő összes iskolákról [Combined Account of All Schools in the Possession of Romanian Hungarian Churches].

14   Gábor Tinódi, "A dél-erdélyi magyarság szellemi élete" [The Intellectual Life of Southern Transylvanian Hungarians], in Éva Záhony, ed., *Hitel. Kolozsvár 1935–1944. Tanulmányok.* I. [Credit. Kolozsvár 1935–1944. Studies I] (Budapest, 1991), p. 305.

15   MOL K 610. XII. 7/1, 201–227: A délerdélyi magyarság helyzete az 1942. évben [The Situation of Southern Transylvanian Hungarians in 1942].

16   Kisegítő Takarékpénztár; Népbank.

17   MOL K 610. XII. 4/1, 3–9: A délerdélyi magyar szövetkezetek részére átadott kérdőpontok [The Response of Southern Transylvanian Cooperatives to the Questionnaire].

18   *Ibid.*, 12/8, 61–63: A délerdélyi magyar kisebbségi panaszok alakulása az 1941–1942. évben [Trends in Southern Transylvanian Minority Grievances in 1941–1942].

19   Arhivele Naționale Istorice Centrale, Fond Președinția Consiliului de Miniștri [National Historical Central Archives, Fond of the

Prime Ministerial Office], 139/1942, 1–15: Conferința privitoare la chestiunea refugiaților din Transilvania de Nord, București, 13 Mai 1942. D-l. Prof. M. Antonescu [Conference Regarding the Question of Refugees from Northern Transylvania, Bucharest, May 13, 1942. D-1. Prof. M. Antonescu].

20   MOL K 610. XII. 5/6, 3–8: Gyárfás Elemér kiegészítő válasza a gazdasági kérdőpontokra az 1943. évi helyzet alapján [Supplementary Response by Elemér Gyárfás to the Economic Questionnaire, Based on the Situation in 1943].

21   László G. Kovács, "A szlovákiai magyarság a második világháború éveiben (1939–1945)" [The Slovakian Hungarians during World War II (1939–1945)], in József Fazekas, ed., *Fejezetek a csehszlovákiai magyarság történetéből* [Chapters from the History of the Czechoslovakian Hungarians] (Bratislava, 1993), p. 133.

22   *Ibid.*, pp. 130–131.

23   *Ibid.*, pp. 139–140.

24   On Esterházy's career, see Gábor Szent-Iványi, *Count János Esterházy: the Life and Works of the Great Son of the Hungarian Highlands* (Portola Valley, CA, 1989); Imre Molnár, *Esterházy János élete és mártírhalála* [The Life and Martyr's Death of János Esterházy] (Šamorín, 2010).

25   Toldy Kör; Bartók Béla Dalegyesület.

26   *Szlovenszkói Magyar Kultúregyesület.*

27   László Tóth and Tamás Gusztáv Filep, eds., *A (cseh)szlovákiai magyar művelődés története 1918–1998* [The History of (Czecho)Slovakian Hungarian Education 1918–1998], Vol. 2 (Budapest, 1998), pp. 225–231.

28   *Ibid.*, pp. 369–373.

29   Gyula Popély, *Hazatéréstől a hazavesztésig* [From Returning Home to Losing One's Native Land] (Bratislava, 2006), pp. 195–244.

30   Enikő A. Sajti, *Délvidék 1941–1944* [The Southern Region 1941–1944] (Budapest, 1987), pp. 108–116; Sajti, *Hungarians in the Voivodina*, pp. 325–328.

31   György Ránki, Ervin Pamlényi, Lóránt Tilkovszky and Gyula Juhász, eds., *A Wilhelmstrasse és Magyarország. Német diplomáciai iratok Magyarországról 1933–1944* [The Wilhelmstrasse and Hungary. German Diplomatic Papers on Hungary 1933–1944] (Budapest, 1986), nos. 339 and 406 (584 and 589–591).

32   *Bánáti Magyar Közművelődési Szövetség.*

33　MOL K–63 Papers of the Political Department of the Ministry of Foreign Affairs 1943–16–12, f[olio]. 31, 110 and 130.

34　Sajti, *Hungarians in the Voivodina*, pp. 336–339.

35　Gerhard Baumgartner, "Die ungarische Volksgruppe des Burgenlandes und die Folgen des Jahres 1938," in Avguštin Malle and Valentin Sima, eds., *Anslus in manjsine v Austriji/ Anschluß und Minderheiten in Österreich* (Klagenfurt/Celovec, 1989); Gerald Schlag, *Der 12. März im Burgenland und seine Vorgeschichte.* Burgenländische Forschungen 73 (Eisenstadt, 1989), pp. 96–111.

36　Dokumentationsarchiv des Österreichischen Widerstandes (DÖW), Faszikel 9643, 27–28.

37　Hugo Gold, *Gedenkbuch der untergegangenen Judengemeinden des Burgenlandes* (Tel Aviv, 1970); Gerhard Baumgartner, "'… konnten wir es nicht glauben, dass unsere Existenz von Staats wegen in Frage gestellt werde!'"; "'Arisierung' und rassisch motivierter Vermögensentzug im Burgenland," in Verena Pawlowski and Harald Wendelin, eds., *Ausgeschlossen und Entrechtet. Raub und Rückgabe – Österreich von 1938 bis heute* (Vienna, 2006), pp. 31–53.

38　Erika Thurner, *Kurzgeschichte des nationalsozialistischen Zigeunerlagers in Lackenbach (1940 bis 1945)* (Eisenstadt, 1984); Florian Freund, Gerhard Baumgartner and Harald Greifeneder, *Vermögensentzug, Restitution und Entschädigung der Roma und Sinti* (Veröffentlichungen der Österreichischen Historikerkommission 23/2) (Vienna, 2004).

39　András D. Bán, László Diószegi, Zoltán Fejős, Ignác Romsics and Győző Vinnai, *Magyarok kisebbségben és szórványban* [Hungarians in Minority and Dispersion] (Budapest, 1995), pp. 701–703.

40　István Szépfalusi, *Lássátok, halljátok egymást!* [See and Listen to Each Other] (Bern, 1980), p. 311.

41　Gerhard Baumgartner, "'Ethnische Flurbereinigung' – ein europäisches Lehrstück am Beispiel des südburgenländischen Bezirkes Oberwart," in Arno Truger and Thomas Macho eds., *Mitteleuropäische Perspektiven* (Vienna, 1990), pp. 141–154.

42　Loránt Tilkovszky, "Kálmán Imre: a világhírű bécsi magyar operettszerző és az Anschluß" [Imre Kálmán: the World-Famous Hungarian Composer of Vienna and the *Anschluss*] *Holocaust Füzetek* 13 (1999): 35–41.

43　Szabolcs Szita, *Halálerőd* [Death Fortress] (Budapest, 1986); Leopold Banny, *Krieg im Burgenland* (Eisenstadt, 1983).

IV. FROM THE END OF WORLD WAR II
TO THE COMMUNIST TAKEOVER
1944–1948

1. HUNGARY AND THE SITUATION OF
THE HUNGARIAN MINORITIES IN 1945
László Szarka

Under the post-World War II agreement between Stalin and Churchill on Eastern European spheres of influence, formulated at Yalta in February 1945, influence in Hungary was to be shared equally between the Soviet Union and the West.[1] This became unrealistic, as Hungary's sovereignty was reduced by accelerated Sovietization in the region in 1946. As for Hungarian minorities, the issue of them became marginal in the Soviet sphere of influence.

Preliminary peace plans drafted by American and British experts even went so far as to revise Hungary's Trianon borders,[2] but by the time that the peace conference began, nobody would back the territorial corrections that the Hungarians included in their draft. Representing the provisional Hungarian government was Minister of Foreign Affairs János Gyöngyösi, who signed an armistice agreement with the main victorious powers: the United States, the United Kingdom and the Soviet Union. It meant that Hungary conceded that the war was lost, and undertook to disarm the German forces still on its soil, hand German assets over to the Allies, intern German citizens, and contribute to the war against Germany eight cavalry divisions commanded by the Allied (Soviet) High Command.[3] Furthermore, Hungary "accepted the obligation to evacuate all Hungarian troops and officials from the territory of Czechoslovakia, Yugoslavia, and Rumania occupied by her within the limits of the frontiers of Hungary existing on December 31, 1937," and "repeal all legislative and administrative provisions relating to the annexation or incorporation into Hungary of Czechoslovak, Yugoslav and Rumanian territory." Under Article 19, the Vienna Awards of 1938 and 1940 were "declared to be null and void."[4] Hungary was to pay the Soviet Union $200 million, and Yugoslavia and Czechoslovakia a total of $100 million over six years in war reparations. The Allied Control Commission established was chaired by General Kliment Voroshilov, representing the Allied (Soviet) High Command, who signed the armistice on the Allies' behalf.

As the Eastern Front advanced across Romania, Czechoslovakia, Yugoslavia, Hungary and Austria from August 1944 to May 1945, the positions of the Hungarian minorities changed dramatically, according to the armistice agreement. But the Soviet occupying forces in Transcarpathia declared a state of emergency and would not allow the Czechoslovak civilian regime to return, despite a prior bilateral agreement. The *de facto* government there was the Carpathian Ukrainian People's Council, formed under Soviet control in November 1944 to operate as a puppet government. In the summer of 1945, the Hungarian government made a single timid approach in relation to the parts of Transcarpathia with a Hungarian majority. The Soviet military responded by extending to neighboring areas of Hungary the deportation of Hungarian men already underway in Transcarpathia.[5] In line with earlier undertakings by President Edvard Beneš and in the light of the situation produced by the Soviet army, Czechoslovakia signed a treaty on June 29, 1945, ceding Transcarpathia to the Soviet Union. Soviet rule and law were introduced formally on January 22, 1946, through legislation by the Ukrainian Soviet Socialist Republic, of which Transcarpathia became part. Most of the ethnic Slovaks among the Transcarpathians exercised their right to resettle under a Czechoslovak–Soviet option agreement. Several hundred ethnic Hungarians sought likewise to resettle in Hungary, but the rigid attitude of the Soviet authorities meant that very few succeeded.[6]

There was a similar worsening in the position of the Hungarians of Czechoslovakia. The government program adopted in Košice on April 5, 1945, sought to eliminate both the German and the Hungarian minority, by depriving each of them of its rights and setting about deporting each of them *en masse* to its respective parent country.[7] The intention was to forestall a repetition of the

Czechoslovak carve-up of 1938–1939 by forming a purely Slav nation state. Beneš issued a series of decrees making the position of the Germans and Hungarians increasingly untenable.[8] In Slovakia, these decrees were often overlaid by orders of the Slovak National Council establishing, for instance, people's courts and a national trusteeship. Discriminatory orders were also issued by the caretaker commission acting for the provincial government of Slovakia and by individual Slovak commissioners.

There followed a wave of deportations, forcible resettlement and internment, along with accompanying deprival of political, social and minority rights, which ultimately pushed Hungary into negotiations in December 1945 about an exchange of population promoted by Prague.[9] When negotiating, the government of Ferenc Nagy tried to impede the Czechoslovak policies of depriving ethnic Hungarians of their rights, resettling them, and forcing them to assimilate. The bilateral agreement of February 27, 1946, was seen as a move towards an international solution for the Upland Hungarians.

Soviet military administration of Northern Transylvania was followed on March 8, 1945, by a return to Romanian rule.[10] Once the Soviet-backed Groza government had formed, representation of the Romanian Hungarians was taken over by the left-wing Hungarian People's Union, which committed itself to resolving the Hungarian question within Romania. In Hungarian government circles, the main aim of Groza's policy towards the Hungarian minority was seen as the attainment of Romania's peace objectives, meaning that Bucharest sought at all costs to reach prior agreement with Hungary. For this purpose the Groza government exploited the Hungarian People's Union, whose leaders – Gyárfás Kurkó, Edgár Balogh and László Bányai – were influenced by Soviet undertakings and by the realities of an East-Central Europe undergoing Sovietization to put their trust in an "internationalist" solution within the framework of Romania. Many contemporary observers in Transylvania and Hungary saw such trust as ill-considered and submissive, but Bányai declared the following: "The *Realpolitik* of the People's Union has to be continued and adapted to the current situation, if we wish to protect the interest of the Hungarian community correctly. Of course, the People's Union would react in the same way to a situation produced by a possible change in the border."[11]

The clearest alternative to the People's Union approach was one drawn up by Bishop Áron Márton, who pressed for the borders to be drawn up in line with the demands of the Transylvanian Hungarians. But this too failed, under the circumstances, to promote the Transylvanian aims formulated in Budapest during the peace preparations.[12]

Official bodies in Hungary was at that time aware of the revenge killings and other atrocities against Hungarians and Germans being committed by Tito's partisan army and OZNA (security agency, the People's Defense Department, *Odeljenje za zaštitu naroda*) in Yugoslavia, but not a single official document has survived that expresses any protest by the Hungarian government against the high number of Hungarian victims in Vojvodina in 1944–1945.[13] Mátyás Rákosi, a government member and Communist Party general secretary, had been born in Ada in Vojvodina. He held talks in the summer and autumn of 1945 in Novi Sad, but no minutes of these have survived. The minister of foreign affairs, János Gyöngyösi, called only for an end to the internment of male Hungarians in Vojvodina. The losses to the Hungarian community there were compounded by the flight of over 65,000 of them to Hungary in 1944–1946, under the option arrangements. Of the many refugees, the Hungarian government paid close attention only to the fate of those who had been resettled in Bačka from northern Bukovina two years earlier and were being moved on to Hungary in April 1945.

Border issues and treatment of minority Hungarians were important points as Hungary's peace preparations began under István Kertész in June 1945. The experts involved gained detailed, relatively accurate information on the atrocities against Hungarians in neighboring countries. Also briefed regularly on the situations in Vojvodina, the Upland and Transylvania was the head of the Roman Catholic Church in Hungary, József Mindszenty, archbishop of Esztergom.[14]

There was some possibility of adjusting the interwar borders in Hungary's favor at most with Romania and conceivably with Slovakia (now part of Czechoslovakia again). The principle of exchanging land holdings as well as inhabitants was advanced by Minister of Foreign Affairs Gyöngyösi mainly as a reaction to the unilateral deportation ideas in Prague and Bratislava. The left-wing Hungarians in Transylvania espoused the idea of integration into Romania with minority rights. They countered the idea of a wholesale transfer of Transylvania to Hungary, advanced by Bishop Márton, with the idea of an ethnically based transfer of about 4,000 square kilometers.[15]

The Budapest government had no means whatsoever of countering the authorities in Yugoslavia, but that does not excuse the diplomatic silence over persecution of the Southern Region Hungarians.[16]

The Hungarian government stance towards Yugoslavia and its treatment of its Hungarian minority was influenced by three main factors: (1) the memory of the "cold days" in northern Bačka and the uncertain picture received of the Serbian reprisals, (2) the relatively restrained behavior of Tito towards Hungary, compared with that of Beneš, and (3) the population exchange agreement based on the "land with people" principle, which seemed more acceptable than the unilateral transfer envisaged by Prague and Bratislava, with mass internal exile and other measures to encourage departure.

From the outset, the Hungarian government addressed a succession of submissions to the Great Powers and to the Central Control Commission in Hungary on the grievances of the Hungarian minorities in Czechoslovakia and Romania. An official memorandum addressed to the Soviet government on July 2, 1945, requested that Moscow "intervene strongly in future with the governments of the neighboring states to prevent persecution of the indigenous Hungarian population there."[17] The Hungarian government spoke out most strongly against "the Hungarian persecution in Czechoslovakia applying the most extreme fascist measures," because this was not only unacceptable to Budapest, but a danger to "friendly cooperation among the Danubian peoples." The note pointed out that the anti-Hungarian behavior of neighboring countries was also endangering the position of the new Hungarian democracy. Observing, and expecting the Soviets to play a role in curbing, the anti-Hungarian atrocities that occurred in Northern Transylvania, in the Székely Land, and also in parts of southern Slovakia, the note also cited the principles behind the nationality policies of Lenin and Stalin, socialism and pure democracy

Notes

1 For details of the Stalin–Churchill meeting, see Winston S. Churchill, *The Second World War*, Vol. VI (London, 1953), Ch. 10.
2 Ignác Romsics, ed., *Wartime American Plans for a New Hungary. Documents from the U.S. Department of State, 1942–1944* (Boulder, CO/Highland Lakes, NJ, 1992).
3 On the international scope for Hungary after World War II: Ignác Romsics, *Hungary in the Twentieth Century* (Budapest, 1999), pp. 220–224 and 238–245. On territorial questions: István Vida, "A magyar békeszerződés területi kérdései" [Territorial Issues in the Hungarian Peace Treaty], *História* (1987) 1: 26–29.
4 The armistice: http://avalon.law.yale.edu/wwii/hungary.asp. Accessed May 26, 2010.
5 István Vida, "Szovjetunió és a magyar békeszerződés előkészítése" [The Soviet Union and Preparation of the Hungarian Peace Treaty], *Külpolitika* (1997) 3: 75–100.
6 Béla Zseliczky, *Kárpátalja a cseh és a szovjet politika érdekterében* [Transcarpathia in the Spheres of Czech and Soviet Politics] (Budapest, 1998).
7 László Szarka, "A kollektív bűnösség elve a szlovákiai magyar kisebbséget sújtó jogszabályokban 1944 és 1949 között" [The Principle of Collective Guilt in Legislation on Slovakia's Hungarian Minority in 1944–1949], in Idem, ed., *Jogfosztó jogszabályok Csehszlovákiában, 1944–1949. Elnöki dekrétumok, törvények, rendeletek, szerződések* [Rights-Depriving Legal Instruments in Czechoslovakia, 1944–1949. Presidential Decrees, Acts, Orders, Treaties] (Budapest/Komárom, 2005), pp. 7–32. Government program: http://www.mtaki.hu/docs/jogfoszto_jogszabalyok/jogfoszto_jogszabalyok_kassai_kormanyprogram.pdf. Accessed May 25, 2010.

8   The decrees: *Sbírka zákonu a nařízení státu Československého* [Repository of the Laws and Regulations of the Czechoslovak State] (1945) 4: 7–10; (1945) 7: 17–20; (1945) 9: 25–31; (1945) 13: 45–46; (1945) 17: 47–49; (1945) 17: 57–58.

9   Sources: *Hungary and the Conference of Paris, Vol. II. Hungary's International Relations before the Conference of Paris. Hungaro-Czechoslovak Relations Papers and Documents Relating to the Preparation of the Peace and to the Exchange of Population between Hungary and Czechoslovakia* (Budapest, 1947), and *ibid., Vol. IV. Papers and Documents Relating to the Czechoslovak Draft Amendments Concerning the Transfer of 200,000 Hungarians from Czechoslovakia to Hungary* (Budapest, 1947); László Szarka, "A csehszlovák–magyar lakosságcsere helye a magyar kisebbség tervezett felszámolásában 1945–1948 között" [The Place of the Czechoslovak–Hungarian Population Exchange in the Planned Abolition of the Hungarian Minority], *Kisebbségkutatás* (2007) 3: 415–430; Sándor Balogh, *Magyarország külpolitikája 1945–1950* [Hungary's Foreign Policy 1945–1950] (Budapest, 1988), pp. 132–158. A monograph on the 1945–1948 history of the Czechoslovakian Hungarians: Katalin Vadkerty, *A kitelepítéstől a reszlovakizációig* [From Deportation to Re-Slovakization] (Pozsony, 2006 [2001]).

10 An overview with sources: Mihály Zoltán Nagy and Gábor Vincze, eds., *Autonomisták és centralisták. Észak-Erdély a két bevonulás között (1944. szeptember–1945. március)* [Autonomists and Centralists. Northern Transylvania between the Two Invasions (September 1944–March 1945)] (Kolozsvár/Csíkszereda,· 2004) introductory study, pp. 19–107.

11 István Gyöngyössy's report of February 27, 1946: Gábor Vincze, ed., *Források a romániai magyar kisebbség és a magyar–román államközi kapcsolatok történetének tanulmányozásához 1944–1978* [Historical Sources for the Romanian Hungarian Minority and Hungarian–Romanian State Relations 1944–1978] (n. d.), at http://www.adatbank.ro/cedula.php?kod=272. Accessed May 25, 2010.

12 On the ideas of Áron Márton, Roman Catholic bishop of Alba Iulia, and Hungarian political forces outside the Hungarian People's Association, see Gábor Vincze, "A kisebbségpolitikus Márton Áron" [The Minority Politician Áron Márton], *Magyar Kisebbség* (1995) 1: 93–108. On Association strategy, see Mihály Zoltán Nagy and Ágoston Olti, eds., *Érdekképviselet vagy pártpolitika?*

Iratok a Magyar Népi Szövetség történetéhez, 1944–1953 [Interest Representation or Party Politics? Documents from the History of the Hungarian People's Association, 1944–1953] (Csíkszereda, 2009).

13   Márton Matuska, *Reprisals* (Budapest, 1995); Enikő A. Sajti, *Hungarians in the Voivodina 1918–1947* (Boulder, CO/Highland Lakes, NJ, 2003), pp. 405–432; Aleksandar Kasas, *Madari u Vojvodini 1941–1946* [Hungarians in the Vojvodina 1941–1946] (Novi Sad, 1996). Minister of Foreign Affairs János Gyöngyösi's letter to Cardinal Mindszenty appears with the appended briefing document in Márton Matuska, *A megtorlás napjai. Ahogy az emlékezet megőrizte* [Days of Reprisals. As Kept in Memory] (Novi Sad, 1991), pp. 365–370.

14   Stephan Kertész, *Between Russia and the West: Hungary and the Illusions of Peacemaking, 1945–1947* (South Bend, IN, 1984); Balogh, *Magyarország külpolitikája, pp.* 132–158.

15   Gábor Vincze, "Álmodozások kora. Tervek, javaslatok az 'erdélyi kérdés' megoldására 1945–46-ban" [Dream Days. Plans and Proposals for Solving the "Transylvanian Question" in 1945–1946], *Limes* 16 (1997) 2: 59–82.

16   Sajti, *Hungarians in the Voivodina*, pp. 433–460.

17   István Vida, *Iratok a magyar–szovjet kapcsolatok történetéhez 1944. október – 1948. július* [Documents on the History of Hungarian–Soviet Relations October 1944–July 1948] (Budapest, 2005).

2. THE LOSSES OF HUNGARIAN MINORITIES
Mihály Zoltán Nagy

The final days of World War II and the next couple of years were marked in Central and Eastern Europe by forced migration on a vast scale. This applied particularly to the Hungarian-speaking populations of territories that had been reannexed to Hungary under the First and Second Vienna Awards (parts of Czecho-Slovakia and Northern Transylvania) or thereafter militarily (Transcarpathia, Bačka, the Baranja Triangle, Prekmurje and Pomurje).

The changes in the legal position of these Hungarian communities and the measures taken against them depended on several factors. These were the current military situation, the minority policies of neighboring governments, the international image of the Hungarian minorities, new frameworks of national and international law to protect minorities, post-war relations between the three victorious powers, and not least the abilities and diplomatic scope for Hungarian governments to assert their will.

By the summer of 1944, it was obvious militarily that the Allies would win the war. Mass population flights began, alongside resettlement measures taken by Hungarian military and civilian authorities. The first wave consisted largely of Hungarian public servants, above all those who had moved to annexed territories from Trianon Hungary. Then came a much larger, disorganized flood of refugees fleeing before the Red Army in the east and north and the Yugoslavs in the south. In Northern Transylvania, almost 400,000 Hungarians escaped as the front advanced in the autumn of 1944.[1] In the Southern Region, some 13,000–15,000 Bukovina Székely (relocated by the Hungarian government in 1941 in place of Serb settlers from southern Serbia brought in after World War I) fled before the Yugoslav People's Liberation Army and Tito's partisans.

Violent measures began to be taken in the autumn of 1944 by the governments of Hungary's neighboring countries against citizens of Hungarian origin, prompted in Czechoslovakia, Romania and Yugoslavia mainly by a desire for a homogeneous nation state ("pure Slav" in Czechoslovakia, "pure South Slav" in Yugoslavia, and a "united national state" in Romania). Drastic steps were taken to obtain this as soon as possible. Plans were drawn up by the authorities in those countries to resettle or disperse Hungarians, as a way of settling the minority question once and for all.[2] Another blow to the survival and legal status of minority Hungarian communities was the fact that the principle of collective responsibility for the war crimes of Hitler's Germany and the outbreak of the war was extended from the Germans to the Hungarians – in Czechoslovakia throughout the period and in Yugoslavia from the autumn of 1944 to the spring of 1945.

The newly established civilian and military authorities cited pacification as the reason for the internments, which mainly applied to Hungarian men of military age (in Romania),[3] but affected all Hungarians in some countries (Czechoslovakia and Yugoslavia).[4] With the Soviet authorities, the main motive was to provide free foreign labor for industry and agriculture.[5] This participation by alien citizens, which extended to whole ethnic groups, was seen by Moscow as part of the reparations for war damage. The action that came to be known in the Carpathian Basin as *málenkij robot* (short work – as it is known in Hungarian history) was begun by the Soviet military and security organizations on November 13, 1944. Twenty thousand or more are estimated to have been rounded up in Transcarpathia alone and deported to Soviet labor camps,[6] but several thousand Hungarians were taken from eastern Slovakia as well.[7] The Hungarian community in Transcarpathia underwent a Sovietization that drastically reduced its numbers after the Soviet–Czechoslovak treaty of June 29, 1945, legitimized the Soviet expansion and the Transcarpathian territory of the Ukrainian SSR was officially established in 1946.

The 15,000–20,000 rounded up in the Southern Region[8] and the 160 revenge killings in Transylvania (far smaller in number but of great psychological effect on the Hungarians) clearly had political, power-related and social motives. Parties and governments were seeking greater support among the majority nation at a time when many sought revenge for real and perceived injuries under the wartime Hungarian administration.

The legislative institutions in Czechoslovakia[9] had full support from the bourgeois and left-wing (social democratic and communist) parties in basing on the principle of collective responsibility several measures that effectively outlawed the Hungarian and German inhabitants.[10] Deportations from southern Slovakia to the Czech provinces and the Czechoslovak–Hungarian population exchange greatly changed the territorial distribution of the Hungarians: that is, both their proportion of the population in regions and sub-regions and their social structure. Estimates of the size of the two waves of deportation range from 42,000 to 60,000–100,000 Hungarians, including women, children and old people.[11] The enforced population exchange that ensued between April 1947 and December 1948 moved 90,000 Hungarians into Hungary and 72,000 Slovaks into Czechoslovakia. For the Hungarians of Slovakia this was coupled with measures against property rights, such as expropriation of land and confiscation of so-called alien property and deprival of citizenship. The social declassing of the Hungarians coincided with a "Re-Slovakization" campaign (in June 1946) aimed at changing people's social identity. This ostensibly voluntary campaign was justified officially by the need to "re-Slovakize" Slovaks who had become Hungarianized. Intimidation and hopes of escaping the confiscation of their property caused 410,000 Hungarians to apply, of whom 326,000 were officially reclassified as Slovaks.[12] The Hungarians were excluded from the Czechoslovak elections of 1948 and began only in the following year to regain some of their civil rights.

Meanwhile the Hungarians of the Southern Region and Transylvania were encountering different minority policies and norms of minority rights. The political elite of Tito's Yugoslavia saw the Hungarian question solely in terms of power and political interest. After its power had been consolidated, Belgrade began in the spring of 1945 to seek a *modus vivendi* with the Hungarians: the communist leadership would look after the Hungarian and other minorities in exchange for their loyalty to the regime.[13] The Hungarians now had greater language rights and more schools teaching in Hungarian than in the interwar period, but expropriations on the grounds of wartime collaboration and the bias in the land reform further reduced the economic potential of the Hungarian community. The ethnic structure of the Hungarian-inhabited regions was altered radically by the expulsion of the indigenous Germans and a wave of settlement accompanying the land reform: 252,000 Serbs arrived in Vojvodina. In fact the forced and voluntary movements of population led to a greater decrease in the Hungarian minority of the Southern Region than had occurred after World War I. Some 84,800 Hungarian-speaking inhabitants of Vojvodina were deported or fled to Hungary. The 1946 Yugoslav–Hungarian agreement on population exchange was never implemented, but the Southern Region Hungarians in any case lost their intelligentsia and middle class.[14]

The Hungarian question first appeared in Romania in the autumn of 1944 as one of state security and administration. Then, as the territorial dispute between Romania and Hungary came to a head, the Hungarian question became expressly one of security policy, and the policy line, legal measures and treatment of the minorities developed accordingly. Although the administration declared itself to be friendly toward the minorities, it introduced a number of measures detrimental to the Hungarians. Rather than resting on the principle of national affiliation, these established a special status. For instance, the legislation on the land reform introduced the concept of refugees and "absentees." The enabling order setting up the Financial Office for the Administration and Supervision of Enemy Property (CASBI)[15] established a category of "putative enemy," which meant that property was confiscated mainly from members of the Hungarian minority. But the representatives of the Communist Party were interested also in the idea of resettling 400,000–500,000 Hungarians in Hungary, in line with plans drawn up during World War II, on the grounds that these Hungarians had moved into Northern Transylvania from Trianon Hungary during the 1940–1944 period of Hungarian rule. The Romanian proposal for such resettlement by interstate agreement was rejected by Moscow,[16] but the 1949 census returns for Hungary register more than 134,000 persons of Romanian origin, who had left their homes voluntarily or been forced to do so.[17]

The people's courts in countries in the Soviet zone became a means of legitimizing the new political elite and furthering the day-to-day policies of the new regimes. War-crime charges were used as a pretext for intimidating Hungarians and forcing them to leave the countries neighboring Hungary, where the authorities hastened to investigate crimes committed by the Hungarian military and civilian authorities as evidence that the policy of territorial revision had had (ostensibly) inhuman consequences. The court sentences in such cases included expropriation of the whole property of those convicted.

Nor were the minorities in the region assisted by the new frameworks of international law for minority protection. For the Great Powers agreed after the war to wind up the minority protection system established under the auspices of the League of Nations, taking the view that the commitment to universal respect for human rights would suffice to protect the minorities as well.[18] The result was that the minorities were left defenseless.

The voluntary and constrained migrations after World War II caused substantial changes to the ethnic patterns, distributions and proportions of the Hungarian community in the Carpathian Basin. By the end of 1946, 267,430 persons from neighboring countries had settled in or been deported to Hungary. The 1949 census returns show an even gloomier picture, with 367,000 inhabitants of Hungary declaring themselves as refugees from neighboring countries.[19] The return to Hungary of civilians and military personnel deported to the Soviet Union began in 1946. Another factor reducing the proportion of Hungarians in neighboring countries was the mass deportation of Jews carried out in the final stages of World War II, when almost 320,000 Jews identifying themselves as Hungarian were sent to the death camps from Transcarpathia, Northern Transylvania, Upper Hungary and the Southern Region. The declassing of the Hungarian minority speeded up during the war and its social structure changed radically, as the landowning and high and middle bourgeois strata were lost. The processes were compounded by the introduction of the economic system of state socialism, when nationalization and collectivization dealt a fatal blow to the ownership structure of the Hungarian minorities. Thereafter, the prevention of ties with Hungary, the elimination of minority private and collective property, and policies of assimilation meant that reproduction of minority culture and identity was at the mercy of the Communist Parties and the state-creating nation. The end of private ownership and constitutional government left it impossible to operate a separate system of minority institutions. The minority policies of the four countries concerned were also affected by the disappearance of the German and Jewish communities, leaving the Hungarians as the single substantial target.

Notes

1   Mihály Zoltán Nagy and Gábor Vincze, eds., *Autonomisták és centralisták. Észak-Erdély a két román bevonulás között 1944. szeptember – 1945. március* [Autonomists and Centralists. Northern Transylvania between Two Romanian Invasions, September 1944–March 1945] (Kolozsvár/Csíkszereda, 2004), pp. 256–280.

2   On Romania's plans, see Béni L. Balogh and Ágoston Olti, "A roman–magyar lakosságcsere kérdése 1940–1947 között" [The Romanian–Hungarian Population Exchange Question in 1940–1947], *Kisebbségkutatás* (2006) 4: 603–616, on Yugoslavia's, see Enikő A. Sajti, *Impériumváltások, revízió, kisebbségek. Magyarok a Délvidéken 1918–1947* [Sovereignty Changes, Revision, Minorities. Hungarians in the Southern Region 1918–1947] (Budapest, 2004), pp. 350–351, and on those for the Upland Hungarians, see Ignác Romsics, *Az 1947-es párizsi békeszerződés* [The 1947 Treaty of Paris]

(Budapest, 2007), pp. 38 and 41, and Kálmán Janics, *A hontalanság évei* [Years of Statelessness] (München, 1979), pp. 70 and 77–78.

3 Levente Benkő and Annamária Papp, eds., *Magyar fogolysors a második világháborúban* [The Fate of Hungarian Prisoners in World War II], 2 vols. (Csíkszereda, 2007).

4 Sajti, *Impériumváltások, revízió, kisebbségek*, p. 324.

5 Tamás Stark, *Magyar foglyok a Szovjetunióban* [Hungarian Prisoners in the Soviet Union] (Budapest, 2006), p. 88.

6 *Ibid.*, pp. 51–64.

7 *Ibid.*, pp. 65–71.

8 Béla Csorba, Márton Matuska and Béla Riba, eds., *Rémuralom Délvidéken. Tanulmányok, emlékezések, helyzetértékelések az 1944/45. évi magyarellenes atrocitásokról* [Terror in the Southern Region. Studies, Memoirs and Reports of Anti-Hungarian Atrocities in 1944–1945] (Újvidék, 2004).

9 The measures concerning the Hungarians and Germans were laid down in the Beneš decrees (issued by the president in lieu of Parliament) for the whole of Czechoslovakia, and in the orders of the Executive Body (in lieu of the Slovak National Council and provincial government) for Slovakia.

10 For a summary, see the following: Árpád Popély, Štefan Šutaj and László Szarka, eds., *Beneš-dekrétumok és a magyar kérdés 1945–1948. Történeti háttér, dokumentumok és jogszabályok* [The Beneš Decrees and the Hungarian Question 1945–1948. Historical Background, Documents and Legislation] (Máriabesenyő/Gödöllő, 2007); Štefan Šutaj, Peter Mosný and Milan Olejník, eds., *Prezidentské dekréty E. Beneša a povojnové Slovensko* [President E. Beneš' Decrees and the Post-War Slovakia] (Bratislava, 2002); Katalin Vadkerty, *A kitelepítéstől a reszlovakizációig* [From Deportation to Re-Slovakization] (Pozsony, 2006).

11 Árpád Popély, "A csehszlovákiai magyar kérdés 'belső rendezésének' eszközei" [Methods of "Internal Settlement" of the Hungarian Question in Czechoslovakia], in Popély, Šutaj and Szarka, eds., *Beneš-dekrétumok és a magyar kérdés*, p. 52.

12 *Ibid.*, p. 53.

13 Sajti, *Impériumváltások, revízió, kisebbségek*, p. 363.

14 Gizella Föglein, "Magyar–jugoszláv népességegyezmény tervezet 1946" [Draft Hungarian–Yugoslav Population Agreement 1946], *Századok* (1996) 6: 1553–1570.

15   *Casa de Administrare şi Supraveghere a Bunurilor Inamice.*

16   Balogh and Olti, "A román–magyar lakosságcsere kérdése," pp. 603–616, especially pp. 613–616.

17   Sajti, *Impériumváltások, revízió, kisebbségek*, p. 348.

18   Unlike the World War I peace treaties, those of 1947 only specified in the case of Italy the status of the German minority in South Tyrol.

19   Sajti, *Impériumváltások, revízió, kisebbségek*, pp. 347–348.

3 CASE STUDIES

Romania (*Csaba Zoltán Novák*)

On August 23, 1944, the historical parties in Romania (the National Liberal and National Peasants' Parties) managed to oust the military dictatorship of Ion Antonescu and bail out of the war, through a coup headed by King Michael. This move and the September 12 armistice with the Allied Powers (the United States, the Soviet Union and the United Kingdom) was backed by the National Democratic Bloc initiated by the Social Democrats and Communists, which joined the new government, headed until December 2 by General Constantin Sănătescu, which otherwise consisted mainly of military men.[1] Meanwhile the Transylvanian Hungarians returned to active politics through the Hungarian People's Union formed on October 16, 1944, in Braşov, with the author Gyárfás Kurkó as its first president.[2]

The historical parties and the Romanian administration returning to Northern Transylvania treated the Hungarian and German populations there as war criminals. The legislation that established the Administration and Supervision of Enemy Property (CASBI) meant that very large numbers of Hungarians and Germans lost their wealth. All those who had fled to or resettled in Hungary from Northern Transylvania or Romanian territory before the Hungarian–Romanian armistice agreement of September 12 had their entire property sequestered by CASBI. The law was detrimental to Hungarian citizens and businesses and to assets of the Hungarian state in Northern Transylvania and Romania. A campaign was launched in the autumn of 1944 against cooperatives owned by the Hungarian community, some of which were placed under CASBI supervision on the grounds that they had received funding from the Hungarian state. There were severe consequences from a resolution passed at the Bucharest congress of cooperatives in 1945, forbidding the formation of cooperatives on ethnic grounds. This left the Hungarian cooperatives with no option but to join the state cooperative center in July 1947.[3]

The fears of the Hungarian community were raised by atrocities committed by "volunteers," Iuliu Maniu's paramilitary Guardists, and the gendarmerie. Volunteer units formed originally to ensure law and order behind the front set out for the Székely Land to destroy rumored secret arsenals. Volunteers from Braşov arrived in the Sfântu Gheorghe district in the second half of September to sack and pillage several villages and mistreat their inhabitants. Eleven people in Aita Seacă were slaughtered. The Guardist trail of destruction had reached Gheorgheni before it was ended by the military command of the Red Army, which occupied Northern Transylvania in the autumn of 1944.[4] Even more serious than the volunteers' atrocities was the herding of many Hungarians into internment and labor camps at Târgu Jiu, Focşani and Feldioara, where the inhuman treatment and conditions led to the loss of several thousand lives.[5]

The Romanian–Hungarian incidents prompted the Soviets in November 1944 to expel the Romanian administration from Northern Transylvania on security grounds. News of the atrocities also reached foreign countries. The Romanian government's response was to set up a Ministry of Minority Affairs and devise a minority charter that was an advance on the arrangements before the war, except that its implementation was blocked by Romanian officials.

Pressure from the Soviet-backed Romanian Communist Party made for a political situation in which the Sănătescu and ensuing Rădescu governments soon succumbed to crises that the left wing, led by the communists, employed to gain further key governmental and administrative positions. By March 6, 1945, the political situation was so dire and Soviet pressure was so strong that King Michael – blackmailed over the future of Transylvania – agreed to a government headed by Petru Groza of the communist-influenced Ploughmen's Front. The historical parties went into opposition, but

Romanian administration of Transylvania was restored, although the new regime promised full equality for all national groups in Romania. The first move in this direction was to replace the expression "minority" with "nationality" – in other words national community – in line with the terminology of national delimitation (*размежевание*) introduced in Soviet Russia in 1917. There was a favorable turn in education, with an independent Hungarian education directorate operating until 1948, issuing its own textbooks and a separate syllabus for Hungarians. Almost 100 percent of Hungarian schoolchildren were able to study in their native language, and several Hungarian institutes of higher education received permits to operate, including the Bolyai University in Cluj and the Institut Medicine-Pharmacy in Tărgu Mureş.[6] But this educational autonomy for the Hungarians was provisional. It earned the Groza government support from the Hungarian People's Union. Most Hungarians had hopes up to the time of the peace negotiations that the Great Powers would allow some territorial concessions to Hungary. The Union leaders at a meeting in Tărgu Mureş in November 1945 issued a statement as follows: "The nationality question in Transylvania is not a border question." The statement had no effect on the Great Powers dealing with the final delineation of the border, which in practice restored the Trianon borders, causing outrage among the Hungarian public in Transylvania.[7]

Although the Groza government's policy towards the Hungarians had some positive aspects, it proved to be ambivalent in many respects. The Hungarians were adversely affected by the land reform. It was aimed at "landowners" with over 50 hectares, but the legislation included other categories that were to be deprived of their holdings: those residing beyond the country's borders, as well as "collaborators" (with the Hungarian wartime administration) and "fugitives." These categories were ill-defined and were applied in practice exclusively to Romanian citizens of Hungarian or German "nationality," based on simple declarations. The effect in many mixed communities was the tendency for local land distribution committees, consisting of Romanians, to confiscate the property of Hungarians. It emerges from the 1946 report from the Ministry of Agriculture that 87 percent of all land confiscated in Cluj County had been Hungarian-owned, but only 35 percent of those granted land were Hungarian.[8]

Another Hungarian grievance was legislation that only recognized the Romanian citizenship of Northern Transylvanian residents who had been domiciled in Romania before the Second Vienna Award of 1940 and who were Romanian citizens under the law applicable at that time.

The general elections of November 19, 1946, had great importance for the country: there was obvious ballot-rigging behind the 84.58 percent of the votes that went to a so-called Bloc of Democratic Parties formed by the communists, consisting of the Romanian Communist Party, the Social Democratic Party, Tătărescu's Liberal Party, the Ploughmen's Front, the People's Party and the Alexandru faction of the Peasants' Party. The Hungarian People's Union received 7.22 percent. The communists markedly strengthened their position in the new Groza government and began to strive for exclusive power, increasing their attacks on the opposition and using so-called salami tactics to squeeze out their coalition partners. The communists were able gradually to eliminate, one by one, their political opponents and the organizations ostensibly allied with them.[9]

The Romanian Communist Party set about obtaining a monopoly of state power by methods paralleled in several other Soviet bloc countries at that time. The National Peasants' Party was shaken in July 1947 by the arrest and imprisonment of Iuliu Maniu. The National Liberal Party became moribund during the same summer. Having decapitated and eliminated the historical parties, the communists turned on their coalition partners. By the end of the year, the Hungarian People's Union, as the organization representing the interests of the country's Hungarians, had become little more than a formality. Its county and central leaderships were reorganized and its main institutions moved in June from Cluj to Bucharest, which much reduced their effectiveness. Several intellectuals previously prominent in the Union and on the Hungarian cultural scene in

Transylvania were arrested in the period between 1948 and 1952 and spent years in prison.[10]

The final stage in the communist takeover came with the abdication of King Michael on December 30, 1947. The Romanian People's Republic[11] was proclaimed on the same day. Victory for a National Democratic Front (consisting of the communists and their allies) was engineered in general elections held in March 1948, as was a February merger of the Romanian Communist Party and the Social Democratic Party, to form the Romanian Workers' Party. Parliament and the government issued a string of measures in 1948 that consolidated absolute political and economic power for the communists under the label of proletarian dictatorship. Large-scale industrial, mining, insurance and transport companies underwent nationalization in June. Under a reform of education and schools in August, the Church schools were nationalized to ensure a communist monopoly over the ideological education of young people. The surge of nationalization also swept away the Hungarians' autonomous economic and cultural institutions. These measures seemingly applied to the whole population alike, but the loss of civil institutions was especially grave for the minorities, in the light of their role in preserving their national awareness, whereas the national identity of the majority nation was still furthered by the state. Also founded in 1948 was the Securitate, an enhanced system of secret police modeled under the direction of its Soviet counterpart, the NKVD (People's Commissariat for Internal Affairs, *Narodnyj komissariat vnutrennyh del*) That was followed by replacement of the police force and gendarmerie with a uniform militia. In 1949, full communist control over local administration was gained through a system of people's councils.[12]

Czechoslovakia (*Árpád Popély*)

The World War II émigré community headed by Edvard Beneš laid the blame for Czechoslovakia's break-up in 1938–1939 on the Germans and the Hungarians. The intention of what came to be recognized as a government-in-exile by the Allies was to deport

the German and Hungarian minorities after the war and create a
Slav nation state. But the idea of chasing the Hungarians from their
Upland homes as the front advanced was thwarted by the course
that the war took. The Czechoslovak leadership also failed to obtain
endorsement from the Great Powers for displacing the Hungarians or
to have the January 20, 1945, armistice with Hungary stipulate that
the Hungarian population should be expelled from Czechoslovakia.
All that it stated was that administrative officials sent in during the
period of Hungarian rule were to be withdrawn.

While diplomatic moves to expel the Germans and Hungarians
took place, legislation aimed at the two minorities was also being
prepared. The first measures to deprive them of their rights came
during the Slovak national uprising that broke out at the end of
August 1944, when the Slovak National Council heading it issued an
order dissolving Slovakia's Hungarian Party, led by János Esterházy,
and placing restrictions on education and religious services in
Hungarian and German.

What became the basis and source of reference for measures
against the minorities was the Košice Program, adopted on April
5, 1945, by the new government of the Social Democrat Zdeněk
Fierlinger. Chapter VIII cited the principle of collective guilt in favor
of depriving the Germans and Hungarians of their Czechoslovak
citizenship, while Chapter IX covered their responsibility and
punishment, Chapters X and XI expropriation of their property, and
Chapter XV closure of their schools.

Publication of the program was followed by a stream of
presidential decrees, acts of Parliament, and orders of the Slovak
National Council, placing the Hungarian and German minorities
beyond the protection of the law. The presidential action of most
consequence was Constitutional Decree No. 33 of August 2, 1945,
depriving both targets of their citizenship. Other orders announced
confiscation of the property of the Hungarians and Germans,
dissolution of Hungarian associations, dismissal of Hungarians
from their jobs, withdrawal of their pensions and state benefits,
and expulsion of them from universities and colleges and from

local government national committees and political parties. The Hungarians were deprived of the vote. Hungarian schools were closed. Use of the Hungarian language in public life was forbidden, as were publication and importation of Hungarian books and newspapers. In several places, use of Hungarian in public places was also banned. Hungarians were not allowed to own radios. They could be ejected from their housing or obliged to do public work at any time.[13]

The authorities closed the Hungarian schools in the spring of 1945, and thereafter not a single Hungarian school operated in Czechoslovakia until the autumn of 1948. This left about 100,000 Hungarian children unable to study in their native language. Even in purely Hungarian villages only Slovak schools operated, and many were left with no school at all, with the result that illiteracy became rife among Hungarian children, even at the age of ten or older. The teaching of Hungarian could only be continued illegally by volunteers – dismissed Hungarian teachers and priests prepared to risk official reprisals. Some middle school students would regularly cross the closed border to continue their studies in Hungary.

The gravest action was taken in Bratislava, where several thousand Hungarians were interned on May 3, 1945, at a camp in Petržalka. At the same time, the armistice terms were cited as the reason for arresting, interning and deporting Hungarians who had arrived in other parts of Slovakia since November 1938. According to Czechoslovak figures, this had been inflicted on 31,780 Hungarians by the end of June 1945, each being allowed to take with them only baggage weighing up to 50 kilograms.[14]

The United Kingdom and the United States refused at the Potsdam Conference of July–August 1945 to countenance unilateral deportation of Czechoslovakia's Hungarian minority of more than 600,000, although they agreed to the expulsion of the German minority of 3.5 million. The government then sought to rid Czechoslovakia of its Hungarians by forcing a population exchange on Hungary. The agreement signed in Budapest on February 27, 1946, by the Hungarian minister of foreign affairs, János

Gyöngyösi, and the Czechoslovak state secretary for foreign affairs, Vladimír Clementis, allowed for as many Slovakian Hungarians to be removed to Hungary as Hungarian Slovaks volunteered for settlement in Czechoslovakia. Czechoslovakia was also empowered to unilaterally deport Hungarians who had been declared war criminals by the Slovak people's courts.[15]

That encouraged the Slovak people's courts to fabricate thousands of charges. Of the 8,055 persons condemned by the courts up to the end of 1947, 4,812 (over 60 percent) were Hungarians. By establishing that the Hungarian minority was guilty of war crimes, the authorities hoped to justify the confiscations and deportations. The severest sentence was passed on János Esterházy, who was condemned to death by the Slovak National Court in Bratislava in September 1947. (The sentence was not carried out, as Esterházy had been taken prisoner by the Soviets in 1945. On his extradition in 1950, it was remitted to life imprisonment.) The biggest of what often became mass trials was the Košice trial, in which several hundred Hungarians were sentenced to imprisonment and full confiscation of their property in August 1946.

Under such circumstances, the Hungarian government would not agree to begin the population exchange until forced to do so by Czechoslovakia, which began to impose a policy of internal resettlement on its Hungarian population, this meaning deportation to the Czech provinces, justified by their shortage of labor and by the Beneš decree No. 88. Such "recruitment of labor" began on November 1946 and lasted until February 1947, and according to official Czechoslovak records 41,666 Hungarians, including women, children and the elderly, were deported to Czechoslovakia under inhuman conditions in unheated freight cars. The property that they left behind in Slovakia was expropriated and reassigned to Slovak settlers.

Then came the population exchange, between April 12, 1947, and December 1948. Altogether 71,787 Slovaks resettled in Czechoslovakia and 89,660 Hungarians were moved from Czechoslovakia to Hungary. The Czechoslovak authorities tended to move wealthier Hungarians, and so there was a huge difference in aggregate values of property left behind, the Slovaks from Hungary abandoning 15,000 cadastral *hold* (8,500 hectares) of land and 4,400 dwellings, while the Hungarians from Slovakia left behind 160,000 *hold* (91,200 hectares) and 15,700 dwellings. Some 23,000 Slovaks from other parts of Slovakia were also sent to southern Slovakia. They and 47,000 local Slovaks together received 71,000 hectares of confiscated land and 2,507 dwellings.

The post-war Czechoslovak government went further than demanding the restoration of the Czechoslovak–Hungarian border and resettlement of the Hungarian population. It also made further territorial demands on Hungary at the Paris peace conference that opened in July 1946. It sought to broaden the Bratislava bridgehead on the south side of the Danube by annexing five Transdanubian villages, arguing that this would help to protect the Slovak capital from Hungarian artillery attack. In the event, the peace conference awarded to Czechoslovakia only three of the five – Dunacsún (Čunovo), Horvátjárfalu (Jarovce) and Oroszvár (Rusovce) – leaving Rajka and Bezenye in Hungary.[16]

Another move designed to reduce the size of the Hungarian minority in Slovakia was the "re-Slovakization" campaign announced on June 17, 1946. This officially concerned former ethnic Slovak families that had become Hungarian, but the volunteers running the campaign made no secret of the fact that Hungarians re-Slovakizing" themselves would receive back their citizenship and be immune from property confiscation and resettlement, while those continuing to declare that they were Hungarians would remain without legal rights. The none-too-surprising result of this was that 410,820 persons reclassified themselves as ethnic Slovaks, of which 326,679 were recognized as such.[17]

Czechoslovakia did not manage to disperse the whole Hungarian minority, but the resettlement of some Hungarians and the importation of several hundred domestic and foreign Slovaks into southern Slovakia brought about a big change in the ethnic structure of what had been a homogeneous piece of Hungarian linguistic territory before the war. In addition, it left still visible marks on the social and cultural structure of the Hungarians of Slovakia, for those targeted were the urban bourgeoisie and intelligentsia who traditionally had been the creators and vehicles of Hungarian culture, along with owners of large and medium-sized rural landholdings.

The Soviet Union (*Csilla Fedinec*)

Transcarpathia belonged from 1945 to 1991 to the Soviet Union under the official name of the Transcarpathian Territory (*Zakarpatskaja oblast'*). A territory or *oblast* is a unit resembling a Hungarian county, subdivided into districts or *rayons* (*rajonov*), with these *rayons* further subdivided into communities (cities, towns and villages). The region progressively became part of the Soviet system from the start of military conquest in the autumn of 1944 until conclusion of the international treaties at the end of 1945.

The Soviet-directed partisan activity that began in Transcarpathia in 1943 was followed by military intervention in September and October 1944. Heavier fighting took place before the capture of the town of Chop, as the 18th Army on the Fourth Ukrainian Front advanced northwest.

Three powers competed in the autumn of 1944 for control over the region's inhabitants: the local people's committees, the command of the Red Army and the returning Czechoslovak state administration. The Soviet Union and Czechoslovakia had signed agreements in 1941 and 1943 recognizing pre-war borders. Then on May 8, 1944, it was decided that the Soviet armed forces should hand liberated Czechoslovak territories over to the Czechoslovak civilian authorities, but this was not done in Transcarpathia. There the Soviet military backed preparations for a first congress of the People's Committees of Transcarpathian Ukraine, held in Mukachevo on November 26, 1944. The delegates arriving for the congress had not been elected legally in all cases; most communities were left unrepresented. On the other hand, the congress was attended by numerous invited partisans, representatives of the command of the 18th Army and several dozen representatives of Soviet internal security, the NKVD. Not even these preparations could ensure that delegates' opinions were unanimous: there was a proposal for a referendum to decide the territory's post-war status and Transcarpathia's independent statehood. Finally a motion was passed that the inhabitants would request "reunion" with their brethren across the Carpathians, the Ukrainians. The request, in the form of a manifesto, was signed also by some members of the local authorities, the people's committees. Where such committees would not do so, they were dissolved and replaced.[18]

Measures were taken accordingly, and the region was reorganized on Soviet lines. The kind of transition that occurred in Hungary in 1945–1948, for instance, took place in Transcarpathia at the end of 1944 and in 1945.

There was a big change in the social structure. The intelligentsia and some of the officials departed for Hungary or Czechoslovakia. Even before the Mukachevo congress, Hungarian and German men aged 18–55 were called up by the Soviet military command for three days' labor, but were actually sent to the Svaliava concentration camp and then to labor camps in Siberia that the majority did not survive. Those who did returned home only after several years. The German inhabitants fled or were relocated by the Soviets. The Romanians were classified as Moldavians and had to change from the Roman to the Cyrillic alphabet, a situation that was reversed only in the 1990s. The Rusyns were not recognized as a separate nation and were registered as Ukrainians.[19] The size of the Russian community increased strongly, mainly through migration. Of a population of 775,116 recorded in 1946, 527,032 were Ukrainians, 134,558 Hungarians, 72,176 Russians, 12,420 Romanians, 6,998 Jews, 2,774 Czechs and 2,338 Germans.[20]

In education there was continuity of teaching in Hungarian, but only in lower elementary schools in the 1944–1945 school year, which began late. Hungarian general schools also opened in the autumn of 1945, but middle schools did not follow until 1953. There were also Hungarian groups at the teachers' training college in Mukachevo. The first institute of higher education in the territory was the Uzhgorod State University, which opened in October 1945, but taught in Russian, as the language of inter-communal communication in the Soviet Union.

The school system was reorganized, with elementary (lower primary), general and middle schools instead of people's schools, civil schools and gymnasia (academically oriented secondary schools). All previous textbooks were locked away and the literature syllabus was revised as well. The first Hungarian literature textbook of the Soviet period appeared only in 1950, but the majority nation did no better: Ukrainian literature textbooks were banned for "idealizing the recent past of Ukraine too much." The history taught was Soviet history, not those of the various nations in the territory.[21]

The one Hungarian-language paper was the *Munkás Újság*, which appeared for a few months in 1945 before ceasing publication. Thereafter a territory paper and a district paper were translated into Hungarian from Ukrainian, under the titles *Kárpáti Igaz Szó* and *Vörös Zászló*.

The Churches went through hard times in an officially atheist country. Their property was confiscated. In 1949, the Greek Catholic Church was suppressed and its churches were handed over to the Orthodox Church, the last Greek Catholic bishop in Transcarpathia, Teodor Romzha, having been murdered in 1947.[22] All aspects of religion were curtailed. Teachers, those in the uniformed services and those in leading positions could not attend church, or even have a church wedding or hold a baptism.[23]

The prime task for the new regime was nationalization. This covered all denominational schools and other Church property. All but the most rudimentary forms of private economic activity were collectivized, as was the farmland, where the peasants were forced to join their local *kolkhoz* and hand over their implements and livestock.[24]

Representatives of the Soviet Union and a still semi-democratic Czechoslovak Republic signed a treaty on June 29, 1945. Hungary was said to have yielded its claims to Transcarpathia under the armistice of January 20, 1945, while Czechoslovakia would "out of friendship" bow to the will of the people and allow "reunion" of the territory.[25] The Transcarpathian Territory of the Ukrainian Soviet Socialist Republic was officially constituted on January 22, 1946.

Yugoslavia (*Enikő A. Sajti*)

Evacuation of Hungary's military and civilian administration in the Southern Region began at the end of September 1944. On October 17, Josip Broz Tito, commander-in-chief of the partisan army and leader of the Communist Party of Yugoslavia, ordered military rule of the Bačka, Banat and Baranja territories, which lasted 103 days. Thus Yugoslav public administration and the establishment of anti-fascist people's committees began in the Southern Region, as elsewhere, under strict military and Communist Party control. Initially, the Hungarians were expressly excluded from the people's committees. On October 18, total expulsion and internment of the German minority was ordered. Camp internment of the Hungarians began two days later. There were 40 camps set up in Vojvodina, including two notorious labor camps at Bački Jarak and Bukin. The whole Hungarian population was moved out of some villages, for instance Mošorin and Čurug.[26]

There were indiscriminate revenge murders of Hungarians during the autumn and winter of 1944, committed by the advancing armed forces, notably the security units, with the assistance of local Slavs. Exactly how many innocent Hungarians were executed during these "even colder days" is still strongly debated. Figures from the People's Defense Department (OZNA), which performed internal security functions, record that 2,982 Hungarians were executed in Vojvodina. Other sources put the likely figure between 15,000 and 20,000. The tribunals set up to investigate war crimes condemned 899 Vojvodina Hungarians to death in 1944–1945. Death sentences were meted out by military courts early in 1944 to the Hungarian army officers who had led the deadly raids in Novi Sad and southern Bačka early in 1942: Ferenc Feketehalmy-Czeydner, József Grassy and Márton Zöldy. The circumstances have still not been clarified in which Ferenc Szombathelyi, army chief of staff at the time, was condemned to death and executed, although he had been sentenced to life imprisonment earlier by the Hungarian People's Court. Several leading Hungarian political figures in the Southern Region met the same fate, including Lord Lieutenant Leó Deák, Gyula Kramer, who had chaired the Hungarian Cultural Association of Southern Region, and Mayor of Novi Sad Miklós Nagy.[27]

In line with the armistice terms, the Yugoslav authorities deported on a mass scale the Hungarians who had settled in the Southern Region since April 1941. Tens of thousands of others fled for fear of reprisals, including the Bukovina Székely settlers in Bačka. The number of Hungarians who fled or were expelled in the autumn of 1944 is put at 84,800 – more than twice as many as in 1918.

On the communist side, a Hungarian partisan unit named after Sándor Petőfi had formed in August 1943 at Zvečevo in Croatia. Early in November 1944, the Yugoslav Liberation Army began to organize a Petőfi Brigade of some 15,000 volunteers, mostly enlisted men from the Hungarian ranks. Over a thousand of these were killed before the end of the war.

While the Paris peace talks were going on, the head of the Yugoslav peace delegation, Minister of Foreign Affairs Edvard Kardelj, turned to the Hungarians on August 16, 1946, with an unexpected proposal for a voluntary, mutual population exchange agreement. This envisaged exchanging about 40,000 Hungarians in the Southern Region for members of the South Slav minorities in Hungary, but no agreement was ever ratified or put into practice.[28]

Elections of November 11, 1945, for a National Constituent Assembly were held by secret ballot, with women voting for the first time. However, the vote was denied to "enemies of the people." Obviously the Germans, as an ethnic group considered to be collectively guilty of war crimes, were excluded, but so were large numbers of Serbs, Croats and others, on the grounds that they had collaborated with the occupiers, as were "Hungarian fascists," a category that covered not only the Arrow-Cross but even members of the wartime Hungarian Public Education Association. The elections, under the close control of the new regime, brought five politically reliable Hungarians into the legislature. According to the official returns, 90.8 percent of a poll with an 88.7 percent turn-out voted for the People's Front. In Vojvodina, 14.6 percent voted against the People's Front, but this reached 40 percent in some constituencies inhabited by Hungarians.[29]

The National Constituent Assembly abolished the monarchy on November 29, 1945, and proclaimed the Federal People's Republic of Yugoslavia. The federative Constitution, adopted on January 31, 1946, placed the multi-ethnic region of Vojvodina under Serbia as an internally autonomous province. In the Vojvodina provincial assembly of 1945, 37 of the 150 members were Hungarian, as were 26 of the 110 members of the Serbian Parliament.

The Hungarian Cultural Association of Vojvodina (*Vajdasági Magyar Kultúrszövetség*) was permitted to operate on July 22, 1945, and soon became a national organization. The High Commission of the People's Liberation of Vojvodina stated in 1945 that Hungarians had equal status in administrative and public life. The Serbian, Croatian and Slovenian languages were not declared official state languages as they had been in the Kingdom. The 1946 Constitution ensured cultural development and the right to the free use of language to national minorities as well.

The Yugoslav state socialist system, modeled on the Soviet one, oversaw the opening of schools teaching in Hungarian, although they were hampered by an acute shortage of staff. According to official figures, there were 635 Hungarian elementary school sections in Vojvodina in the 1947–1948 school year, with 30,706 pupils, and only 519 teachers, most of them with only a four-year middle school education, or in some cases a one-year or even just a three-month period of teachers' training behind them.

Also opened were three higher and 20 lower high schools for Hungarians. Junior school teachers were trained in Subotica and in Novi Sad, where the College of Pedagogy also trained Hungarian secondary school teachers.[30]

Eighty percent of private companies and financial institutions were expropriated and nationalized in 1945 on the grounds of collaboration with the occupying forces or as alien property. Owners and managers were dismissed and imprisoned. The collectively guilty ethnic Germans had all their goods and property confiscated, as did the Hungarian settlers in Čurug and Žabalj.

The land reform affected all private holdings of over 45 hectares, rented land in excess of 25–35 hectares, and bank and corporate or Church holdings of over 10 or 30 hectares respectively. Local people's assemblies played a big part in carrying out the reform, alongside the state bodies assigned to the task, which often meant that laws and regulations were interpreted strangely, or that much of the land was confiscated by order of the people's courts. Of the land for redistribution, 40.58 percent lay in Vojvodina, of which more than half (58.2 percent) had been confiscated from Germans, as opposed to 37.78 percent in the country as a whole. Nationally, 44,116 families of so-called external or federal settlers received land, of whom 93 percent of whom settled in Vojvodina. The families of the so-called internal Vojvodina settlers numbered 7,031. The total number to be settled in Vojvodina can be estimated at around 252,000, which immediately increased the proportion of Serbs in the province. Almost 300,000 new holdings had been created under the reform by the end of 1947. The resulting national holding structure was dominated by dwarf holdings – 65.6 percent had areas between 0.5 and 5 hectares.[31]

Relations between Hungary and Yugoslavia went well from the start. A Hungarian–Yugoslav Society was founded in October 1945 on the initiative of the two governments. In January 1947, diplomatic relations were resumed at legation level. A Hungarian–Yugoslav cultural agreement was signed in Belgrade on October 15, 1947, and was soon ratified by the Hungarian Parliament. This bound each to further the culture of the other's minorities in its territory and set up related research institutes and university departments. It allowed for study in each other's countries, and exchanges of experts and of scientific and cultural works. On December 6, 1947, President Josip Broz Tito visited Budapest; a treaty of friendship and mutual assistance was signed two days later.

Austria (*Gerhard Baumgartner*)

There were 679 Burgenland lives lost as Soviet troops occupied the whole of eastern Austria in March 1945. The country was divided into four zones of occupation, with Burgenland in the Soviet zone. Public administration was reorganized by an Allied Commission for Austria, under a four-power agreement signed on July 4,[32] but the Soviet military authorities had already called on President Karl Renner in April to form a government. This new government reestablished the province of Burgenland under a constitutional law, and the provincial administration began to operate on October 1.[33] Legislation on war crimes had already been passed in the summer.[34] Former Nazi functionaries were accordingly excluded from public life and several hundred suspected war criminals were charged.[35] The general and provincial assembly elections in November led to the formation of governments of national unity at both levels, headed by the Social Democrats and the Christian Socialists, with Communist Party cooperation.

In the Soviet zone, the occupiers confiscated so-called German property under Order 17 of High Commissioner Vladimir Kurasov. Several large factories and installations came into Soviet hands, along with tens of thousands of hectares of the Esterházy estate in Burgenland, some of which became a state farm, while the rest was distributed among small-scale farmers and farm laborers in northern Burgenland, so strengthening left-wing support among Hungarian inhabitants of manorial estates there.[36] As the Cold War set in, the Soviet authorities took about 120 Burgenlanders off to the gulags on the grounds that they were spying for the Americans. Meanwhile a start was made to restoring Jewish property confiscated in 1938–1945, but few of the Jews who had now settled in America or Israel returned to the province[37] – only one of ten religious congregations was revived after 1945.

The so-called National Socialist Act of April 1947[38] rehabilitated and restored the franchise to most former Nazis. That autumn, the first prisoners of war returned from the Soviet Union, where almost half a million Austrian citizens had been taken prisoner since 1941. The basis for Austria's post-war economic recovery was the Marshall Plan, under which it received USD 960 million.[39] Neither the Austrian government nor the Western powers wanted to see this invested in the Soviet zone. Furthermore, Burgenland had scarcely any industry. The upshot was that Burgenland, home to 4 percent of the country's population, received only 0.33 percent of the American aid.[40]

As the Iron Curtain came down along the Austro-Hungarian border in 1948, Burgenland was cut off from the east and became for decades Austria's most backward border region. Restoration of sovereignty under the Austrian State Treaty signed on May 15, 1955,[41] was conditional on the country's becoming a neutral state. Soviet occupation forces left Burgenland in the same year. The post-war revival of Burgenland was hindered further by the absence of many adult men, for 17,600 soldiers failed to return after 1945 and another 38,000 remained prisoners of war. This contributed in Hungarian villages to a sudden increase in ethnically mixed marriages.[42]

At the beginning of 1945, whole Hungarian units retreated into Austrian territory with the German army. However, they did not settle in Burgenland or the Vienna district, but in Upper Austria, in the American zone of occupation. This led, for instance, to the growth of a sizeable Hungarian community in Linz. Another wave of migration towards Austria came with the deportation of Hungary's indigenous Germans, many of them families who were bilingual in German and Hungarian. Some chose to settle in the border villages of Burgenland. Yet another wave arrived with the 1948 communist takeover in Hungary, most of them making for Vienna.[43]

The most important post-war change for the ethnic Hungarians of Burgenland was the reinstatement of the 1937 Schools Act. This meant that teaching in Hungarian could resume in six elementary schools (at Oberwart, Unterwart, Siget in der Wart, Mittelpullendorf, Albrechtsfeld and Kleylehof). But these turned out to be a blind alley in the Austrian education system, as there was no secondary or higher education in Hungarian available. Parents intending to send their children to gymnasia had to enroll them in nearby elementary schools that taught in German. Local societies continued to function in Hungarian-inhabited manors and villages, but there were no provincial-level Hungarian bodies even in the 1950s.

There were seven variant languages to be found in post-war Burgenland. Alongside the Roma language, the three main languages of the province were found in standard and dialect forms. The typical mother tongue spoken in Burgenland was a rural dialect, but other languages would be used in the standard form. A typical Croat farmer would use a local Croatian dialect in the home, but read the Croatian newspaper in the standardized regional *gradišćansko-hrvatski* (Burgenland Croatian) language, and speak German or Hungarian in a standardized literary form.[44]

The Burgenlanders who were bilingual in Hungarian and German used five language variants: standard Hungarian, literary Hungarian, local Hungarian dialect, standard literary German, the dialect of local German villages and a kind of pidgin Hungarian that lay between the local dialects of the two languages. The last was found only in the Hungarian villages. As for the local dialects of Hungarian, they were of seventeenth-century origin and preserved the vocabulary and grammar of the early modern Hungarian language, including variant terminations, the diphthongization found in all language dialects spoken in Burgenland, and some altered vowel sounds.[45]

The "pidginization" of Hungarian took place through the presence of abundant German loan words, not only for modern institutions and objects that had arisen since the isolation from mainstream Hungarian,[46] but also for verbs and other parts of speech, more commonly in their dialect forms than in those of literary German. These loan words were used with Hungarian prefixes and suffixes.[47]

Not everyone in the Hungarian villages was fully bilingual. Older people would use standard Hungarian, Hungarian dialect and occasional pidgin forms, and spoke German in the local dialect. Those who attended Hungarian elementary school and then

German secondary school were conversant with the full range. This had become restricted among the younger generation, who spoke excellent literary German and German dialect, but Hungarian only in the pidgin dialect form. Similar linguistic developments occurred among Burgenland's Croats and Gypsies.[48]

Notes

1 Andrea R. Süle, "România politikatörténete 1944–1990" [Romania's Political History 1944–1990], in Gábor Hunya, Tamás Réti, Andrea R. Süle and László Tóth, eds., *România 1944–1990. Gazdaság- és politikatörténet* [Romania 1944–1990. Economic and Political History] (Budapest, 1990), pp. 199–274; Dennis Deletant, *România sub regimul communist* [Romania under the Communist Regime] (Bucharest, 1997).

2 *Magyar Népi Szövetség.* For more on this, see the following: Mihály Zoltán Nagy and Ágoston Olti, *Érdekképviselet vagy pártpolitika? Iratok a Magyar Népi Szövetség történetéhez 1944–1953* [Interest Representation or Party Politics? Documents on the History of the Hungarian People's Union] (Csíkszereda, 2009); Mihály Zoltán Nagy, "Érdekvédelem és pártpolitika" [Protection of Interests and Party Politics], in Nándor Bárdi and Attila Simon, eds., *Integrációs stratégiák a magyar kisebbségek történetében* [Integration Strategies in the History of Hungarian Minorities] (Somorja, 2006), pp. 343–366; Tamás Lönhárt, *Uniunea Populară Maghiară în perioada instaurării regimului comunist în România (1944–1948)* [The Hungarian People's Union in Romania during the Period of Building the Communist Rule (1944–1948)] (Cluj-Napoca, 2008).

3 For more detail, see Gábor Vincze, *Magyar vagyon román kézen (Dokumentumok a romániai magyar vállalatok, pénzintézetek második világháború utáni helyzetéről és a magyar–román vagyonjogi vitáról)* [Hungarian Property in Romanian Hands. (Documents on the Post-War Position of Romanian Hungarian Companies and Financial Institutions and the Hungarian–Romanian Property Rights Dispute)] (Csíkszereda, 2000); also see Vladimir Tismăneanu, Dorin Dobrincu and Cristian Vasile, eds., *Comisia prezidențială pentru Analiza Dictaturii Comuniste din România.*

Raport final [The Final Report of the Presidential Commission Examining the Communist Dictatorship in Romania] (Bucharest, 2007), p. 343.

4   Mihály Zoltán Nagy and Gábor Vincze, eds., *Autonomisták és centralisták. Észak-Erdély a két bevonulás között (1944. szeptember–1945. március)* [Autonomists and Centralists. Northern Transylvania between the Two Invasions (September 1944–March 1945)] (Kolozsvár/Csíkszereda, 2004).

5   Andrea Andreescu, Lucian Nastasă and Andrea Varga, eds., *Minorități etnoculturale. Mărturii doumentare. Maghiarii din România (1945–1955)* [Ethnocultural Minorities. Documents. Hungarians of Romania (1945–1955)] (Cluj, 2002), pp. 129–142.

6   Gábor Vincze, "A magyar oktatásügy helyzete 1944 és 1989 között" [The Position of Hungarian Education 1944–1989], in Idem, *Illúziók és csalódások. Fejezetek a romániai magyarság második világháború utáni történetéből* [Illusions and Disillusionments. Chapters of the Post-War History of the Romanian Hungarians] (Miercurea-Ciuc, 1999), pp. 188–196; János Lázok and Gábor Vincze, eds., *Erdély magyar egyeteme 1944–1949 II* [Transylvania's Hungarian University 1944–1949, Vol. II] (Marosvásárhely, 1998).

7   Gábor Makkfalvi [Gábor Vincze], "A marosvásárhelyi Rubicon" [Târgu Mureş Rubicon], in Sándor Pál-Antal and Miklós Szabó, eds., *A Maros megyei magyarság történetéből* [From the History of the Hungarians of Mureş County] (Marosvásárhely, 1997), pp. 252–255.

8   Gábor Vincze, "Gazdaságpolitika vagy kisebbségpolitika? Az 1945-ös romániai földreform a Groza-kormány kisebbségpolitikájának tükrében" [Economic or Minority Policy? The 1945 Romanian Land Reform in the Light of the Groza Government's Minority Policy], *Magyar Kisebbség* (1996) 4: 182–208; Tismăneanu, Dobrincu and Vasile, eds., *Comisia prezidențială pentru*, pp. 342–343.

9   Csaba Zoltán Novák, "A Román Kommunista Párt hatalmi szerkezetének kiépítése Maros megyében, 1944–1948" [Development of the Power Structure of the Romanian Communist Party in Mureş County, 1944–1948], in Nándor Bárdi, ed., *Autonóm magyarok? Székelyföld változása az ötvenes években* [Autonomous Hungarians? Change in the Székely Land in the 1950s] (Csíkszereda, 2005), pp. 380–398.

10   They included Edgár Balogh, Lajos Csőgör, Lajos Jordáky and János Demeter. See Gábor Vincze, "A Magyar Népi Szövetség

válsága" [Crisis of the Hungarian People's Union], in Idem, *Illúziók és csalódások*, pp. 263–292; Mária Gál, "Az MNSZ lefejezése. A koncepciós perek és előzményeik" [Decapitation of the Hungarian People's Union. Shows Trials and Antecedents], *Múltunk* (1997) 4: 147–163.

11   *Republica Populară Romînă.*

12   Ion Bucur, "Naţionalizările din România 1944–1953," *Arhivele Totalitarismului* (1994) 1–2: 313–320; Dennis Deletant, *Communist Terror in Romania: Gheorghiu-Dej and the Police State, 1948–1965* (New York, 1999).

13   On the anti-Hungarian and anti-German legislation of Czechoslovakia, see Árpád Popély, Štefan Šutaj and László Szarka, eds., *Beneš-dekrétumok és a magyar kérdés 1945–1948. Történeti háttér, dokumentumok és jogszabályok* [Beneš Decrees and the Hungarian Question 1945–1948. Historical Background, Documents and Legislation] (Máriabesnyő/Gödöllő, 2007).

14   Jozef Jablonický, *Slovensko na prelome* [Slovakia at the Time of Change] (Bratislava, 1965), p. 398.

15   Popély, Šutaj and Szarka, eds., *Beneš-dekrétumok*, pp. 162–165 and 232–240.

16   On the Paris peace talks and treaty, see Ignác Romsics, *Az 1947-es párizsi békeszerződés* [The 1947 Treaty of Paris] (Budapest, 2007).

17   On deportations, population exchanges and re-Slovakization in Czechoslovakia, see Kálmán Janics, *Czechoslovak Policy and the Hungarian Minority 1945–1948* (Boulder, CO/Highland Lakes, NJ, 1982); Katalin Vadkerty, *A kitelepítéstől a reszlovakizációig* [From Deportation to Re-Slovakization] (Pozsony, 2006 [2001]); Árpád Popély, *A (cseh)szlovákiai magyarság történeti kronológiája 1944–1992* [Historical Chronology of the (Czecho)Slovakian Hungarian Community 1944–1992] (Somorja, 2006), pp. 39–157.

18   S. Vidnjans'kyj, "Ukrai'na ta «ukrai'ns'ke pytannja» v polityci Chehoslovachchyny" [Ukraine and the "Ukrainian Question" in Czechoslovak Politics], in O. Derghacov *et al.*, *Ukrai'ns'ka derzhavnist' u 20 stolitti (Istoryko-politologichnyj analiz)* [Ukrainian Statehood in the Twentieth Century (Historical and Political Analysis)] (Kyiv, 1996); Béla Zseliczky, *Kárpátalja a cseh és a szovjet politika érdekterében* [Transcarpathia in the Spheres of Czech and Soviet Politics] (Budapest, 1998); *"Vozz'ednannja Zakarpattia z Ukrai'noju" Materiali konferencii prisvjachenoi*

60-richchju Vozz'ednannja Zakarpattia z Ukrai'noju ["Reunification of Transcarpathia with Ukraine" Studies of the Conference on the 60th Anniversary of the Reunification of Transcarpathia with Ukraine] (Uzhhorod, 2006).

19 Barbara Dietz, "Anders als die anderen: Zur Situation der Deutschen in der Sowjetunion und der deutschen Aussiedler in der Bundesrepublik], *Osteuropa* (1992) 42: 147–159; G. Pavlenko, *Nimci na Zakarpatti* [Germans in Transcarpathia] (Uzhhorod, 1995); V. Marina, *Problemi etnopolitichnogo rozvitku rumun Zakarpattia (1945–1995)* [The Ethno-Political Position of the Transcarpathian Romanians (1945–1995)] (Uzhhorod, 1995); V. Marina, "Etnokul'turnij renesans rumun Zakarpattia" [The Ethno-Cultural Renascence of the Transcarpathian Romanians], in *Derzhavne reguljuvannja mizhetnichnih vidnosin v Zakarpatti* [State Regulation of Ethnic Relations in Transcarpathia] (Uzhhorod, 1997), pp. 110–115; Tamás Stark, "'Malenki Robot'. Magyar kényszermunkások a Szovjetunióban (1944–1955)" ["Short work." Hungarian Forced Laborers in the Soviet Union (1944–1955)], *Kisebbségkutatás* (2005) 1.

20 Derzhavnyj arhiv Zakarpats'koi oblasti [State Archives of the Transcarpathian *Oblast*], Fond 125, opis 2, delo 67, f. 58–59.

21 Csilla Fedinec, "A rendszerváltás Kárpátalja oktatásügyében 1944–1945-ben" [The Change of System in the Education Question in Transcarpathia in 1944–1945], *Pánsíp* (1997) 3: 30–38.

22 Spelled Tódor Romzsa in Hungarian and sometimes anglicized as Theodore Romzha. He was beatified as a Martyr for the Faith in 2001.

23 Zoltán Fejős, "A kárpátaljai reformátusok helyzete és kilátásai 1946–47-ben" [The Position and Prospects of the Transcarpathian Reformed Church in 1946–1947], *Pro Minoritate* (1997) 1: 33–37; V. Fenych, "Greko-katolyky, pravoslavni i vlada na Zakarpatti (1944–1946 rr.)" [Greek Catholics, Orthodox and Power in Transcarpathia (1944–1946)], in *Carpatica – Karpatika* 35 (2006); Ju. Danylec', "Obmezhennja dijal'nosti pravoslavnyh monastyriv Zakarpattia v 1945–1961 rr." [Restrictions on the Operation of Orthodox Monasteries in Transcarpathia in 1945–1961], *Naukovyj visnyk UzhNU. Serija: Istorija* (2002) 13: 161–165.

24 V. Mishchanin, "Kolektivizacija na Zakarpatti" [Collectivization in Transcarpathia], *Naukovij visnik UzhNU. Serija: Istorija* (2006) 17.

25 *Sbornik dejstvujushchih dogovorov, soglashenij i konvencij, zakljuchennyh SSSR s inostrannymi gosudarstvami* [Valid Treaties,

Agreements and Conventions between the Soviet Union and Outside Countries], Vol. XI (Moscow, 1955), p. 31.

26   On the reprisals, see the following: Márton Matuska, *A megtorlás napjai* [Days of Reprisals] (Novi Sad, 1991); Sándor Mészáros, *Holttá nyilvánítva. Délvidéki magyar fátum I.* [Declared Dead. Hungarian Southern Region Fate, Vol. I] (Novi Sad, 1991); Tibor Cseres, *Titoist Atrocities in Vojvodina 1944–1945* (Buffalo, NY, 1993); Elemer Homonnay, *Atrocities Committed by Tito's Communist Partisans in Occupied Southern Hungary* (Cleveland, OH, 1957).

27   Enikő A. Sajti, "'Teljes szabadságot a népnek…' Hatalmi represszió és kisebbség Jugoszláviában – 1944/1945" ["Full Freedom to the People…" Authoritarian Repression and Minorities in Yugoslavia, 1944–1945], *Bácsország* (2006) 4: 12–13; Gergely Galántha, "Háborús bűnösök kiadatási eljárásai Magyarország és Jugoszlávia között 1944–1948" [Extradition Proceedings of War Criminals between Hungary and Yugoslavia 1944–1948], *Bácsország* (2006) 4: 14–23; Gergely Galántha, "Ellenkritika avagy a 'Szombathelyi mítosz' I–II" [Counter-Criticism or the "Szombathelyi Myth" I–II], *Bácsország* (2007) 2: 77–83, and (2007) 3: 23–31; Jenő Györkei, *Idegen bírák előtt. Szombathelyi Ferenc újvidéki pere és kivégzése* [Before Foreign Judges. Ferenc Szombathelyi's Trial and Execution in Novi Sad] (Budapest, 2002).

28   Gizella Föglein, "Magyar–jugoszláv népességcsere egyezmény tervezet 1946" [Draft Agreement on the Hungarian–Yugoslav Population Exchange 1946], *Századok* (1996) 6: 1553–1570.

29   Magyar Országos Levéltár (The National Archives of Hungary, MOL): XIX-A-1-n Miniszterelnökség. Kisebbségi és Nemzetiségi Osztály iratai 1945–1948 [Prime Minister's Office. Documents of the Minority and Nationality Department 1945–1948], "Z"-887-1945. 2. doboz; Enikő A. Sajti, *Hungarians in the Voivodina 1918–1947* (Boulder, CO/Highland Lakes, NJ, 2003), pp. 461–464.

30   Sajti, *Hungarians in the Voivodina*, pp. 468–469.

31   *Ibid.*, pp. 472–480.

32   "Agreement on Control Machinery in Austria." At http://avalon.law. yale.edu/wwii/waust01.asp. Retrieved December 19, 2009.

33   See Gerald Stourzh, "Verfassungsgesetz über die Wiedererrichtung des selbständigen Landes Burgenland," *Kleine Geschichte des Staatsvertrages. Mit Dokumentarteil* (Vienna, 1975).

34   *Kriegsverbrechergesetz*, 26. 05. 1945, StGBl. Nr. 32.

35 Gerhard Baumgartner, "Entnazifizierung im Burgenland im Lichte des Aktenbestandes des BLA und der Bezirkshauptmannschaften," in Walter Schuster and Wolfgang Weber, eds., *Entnazifizierung im regionalen Vergleich* (Linz, 2004), pp. 303–320.

36 Otto Gruber, *"Albrechtsfeld für Albrechtsfelder!"* (Frauenkirchen, 1997).

37 Alfred Lang, Barbara Tobler and Gert Tschögl, eds., *Vertrieben. Erinnerungen burgenländischer Juden und Jüdinnen* (Vienna, 2004); Gerhard Baumgartner, Anton Fennes, Harald Greifeneder, Stefan Sinkovits, Gert Tschögl and Harald Wendelin, *"Arisierungen", beschlagnahmte Vermögen, Rückstellungen und Entschädigungen im Burgenland.* Veröffentlichungen der Österreichischen Historikerkommission 17/3. (Vienna, 2004).

38 *Das Nationalsozialistengesetz und seine Durchführung* (Hrsg. von der Redaktion der Wr. Zeitung) (Vienna, 1947); *Ausführungsbestimmungen zum Nationalsozialistengesetz* (Hrsg. von der Redaktion der Wr. Zeitung) (Vienna, 1947); Dieter Stiefel, *Entnazifizierung in Österreich* (Vienna/Munich/Zurich, 1981).

39 Martin Schain, ed., *The Marshall Plan. Fifty Years After* (New York, 2001); Michael J. Hogan, *The Marshall Plan: America, Britain and the Reconstruction of Western Europe, 1947–1952* (Cambridge, 1989).

40 Hans Seidl, *Österreichische Wirtschaft und Wirtschaftspolitik nach dem Zweiten Weltkrieg* (Vienna, 2005).

41 "Österreichischer Staatsvertrag." It was signed in Vienna by the ministers of foreign affairs of the Soviet Union, the United States, the United Kingdom, France and Austria, and came into force on July 27, 1955. At http://untreaty.un.org/unts/1_60000/6/16/00010771.pdf. Retrieved December 21, 2009.

42 Peter Csoknyai, "Die sprachliche Entwicklung der burgenländischen Bevölkerung zwischen 1900 und 1971," *Integratio* (1979) 11–12: 23–44; Lajos Szeberényi and András Szeberényi, *Die burgenländischen Ungarn / Az Őrdivéki Magyarok* [Hungarians of the Wart], (Oberwart, 1988).

43 Arnold Suppan, *Die österreichischen Volksgruppen und Tendenzen ihrer gesellschaftlichen Entwicklung im 20. Jahrhundert* (Vienna, 1983).

44 Szilvia Szoták, "Veszélyeztetett nyelvek. A magyar nyelv Burgenlandban" [Endangered Languages. The Hungarian Language

in Burgenland], *Kisebbségkutatás* (2004) 1: 37–50; Siegfried Tornow, *Die Herkunft der kroatischen Vlahen des südlichen Burgenlandes.* Veröffentlichung der Abteilung für slavische Sprachen und Literaturen des Osteuropa-Instituts Slavisches Seminar an der Freien Universität Berlin 39 (Berlin, 1971).

45   The agglutinative suffix *-val, -vel* (often translatable as "with") becomes *-ve* or *-je*. So *Tamással* [with Thomas, in Thomas's case] becomes *Tamásje*, and *autóval* [by car] *autóve*. The possessive suffixes are often archaic: not *lábaim* [my legs], but *lábomék* – i.e. turning the possessive suffix into an infix before the plural termination instead of placing it after it. Diphthongization: füöd for *fold* [land], erdüő for *erdő* [forest]. The short vowel *a* often becomes *oa* and the long vowel *é* turns into *í*. Samu Imre, *A felsőőri nyelvjárás* [The Dialect of Oberwart] (Budapest, 1971); Idem, *Felsőőri tájszótár* [Dictionary of Oberwart Dialect] (Budapest, 1973).

46   E.g. *Bezirkshauptmannschaft* [district office] or *Führerschein* [driver's license].

47   E.g. *beántrágunyi* [apply for] from the German *beantragen*; *jemiedütem* [I'm worn out] from the German *müde* [tired] in its dialect form *mied*; *rosztunom kell* [I must rest] from the German *rasten* in its dialect form *rostn*. An example from Oberwart: "Mit bincsülsz Weihnachtnira?" [What do you want for Christmas?], incorporating the standard German word for Christmas and an adaptation of *winschn*, the dialect form of *wünschen* [want]. Susan Gál, "Der Gebrauch der deutschen und ungarischen Sprache in Oberwart," in Ladislaus Trieber, ed., *Die Obere Wart* (Oberwart, 1977), pp. 309–320.

48   Werner Holzer and Rainer Münz, eds., *Trendwende? Sprache und Ethnizität im Burgenland* (Vienna, 1993).

V. IN THE EASTERN EUROPEAN
SINGLE-PARTY STATES
1948–1989

1. THE MODELS FOR COMMUNIST MINORITY POLICY

Stefano Bottoni and *Zoltán Novák*

The East-Central European countries were engaged after 1948 in building up a Soviet-type socialist system. The biggest political change was to a single-party system. The opposition parties were banned and their leaders arrested and sentenced to imprisonment, or they were forced into exile. The social democratic parties were submerged into the communist parties. Even in Czechoslovakia and Poland, where smaller left-wing parties still operated formally, real power was held exclusively by the Communist Party.[1]

These political changes affected the way in which these countries were run. The main political decision-making bodies in a communist party state were the Secretariat and Politburo of the Communist Party Central Committee. The Council of Ministers and its portfolio ministries became responsible to the Communist Party, not the legislature, and were confined to administrative tasks or executive assignments specifically delegated to them, not to the Parliament. The result was a highly centralized system of state administrative bodies, duplicated at most levels by Communist Party organizations designed to oversee them. Furthermore, the fear of the party's dictatorial power meant that quite trivial questions would be passed up the hierarchy and decided at the top.[2]

Drastic efforts were made by the party state to gain control over the economy. By 1948, almost all private factories, banks and mines had been nationalized without compensation. This was followed by the forced collectivization of agriculture into producer "cooperatives." Strong peasant resistance to this, notably in Poland and Romania, led to bloody reprisals (fines, imprisonments, deportations to labor camps and even executions).

323

This command economy rested on highly detailed, centrally devised plans "disaggregated" down to the lowest production units.[3] Until Stalin's death in 1953 the driving aim of the economic policy was a forced rate of industrialization, especially heavy industry devoted to arms manufacture and other military equipment. International relations were very tense in that period. It was assumed that a third world war could occur at any moment.

The official, so-called Marxist-Leninist, ideology of the communist system was imposed on scientific, scholarly and cultural life, from the arts to mass public information.[4] Confessional schools were nationalized and a standard curriculum was introduced, making Russian the compulsory foreign language and introducing subjects such as dialectical materialism and political economy. The brief history of the Communist Party of the Soviet Union taught was written by Stalin himself. Children of "class aliens" (not of proletarian or poor peasant origin) were deprived of higher education. The position of the intelligentsia became equivocal. University and medical staff, and state employees suffered continual purges, as did the Communist Party apparatus itself. Meanwhile, many children of poor families were given special chances for rapid educational and career advancement, and came later to form an elite giving stalwart social support to the system. Fear and coercion were essential to the working of the Stalinist system, after other incentives and brakes had been removed.[5]

The press and mass media were subject to strict censorship. Daily papers, arts journals and radio stations became mouthpieces for the policies or opinions of the state leadership. They spread the "cult of personality", under which the near-worship of the party leader was orchestrated from Moscow. This implied not just the cult of Stalin, but also of the leaders of each satellite Communist Party as well. The cult took facile forms: vast statues and other artworks of Stalin and his equivalents in each "fraternal" country, which had cities, factories, streets and squares named after them.

One myth that obscured the communist image of society was that of the imminent development of an internationalist proletariat freed of national fetters. Yet the civil war that followed Russia's

1917 Revolution presented the new Soviet state with a jumble of nationalities. The concomitant ethnic antagonisms persisted as potentials for conflict despite communist denials of their existence or reinterpretation of them as class struggle.

Similarly to the Soviet Union, the satellite states of Eastern and Central Europe faced ethnic problems during and after World War II.[6] Policies towards minorities in 1945–1948 ranged from efforts to integrate them to blatant discrimination, the worst case being the way in which some nine million indigenous Germans in Poland and Czechoslovakia were shorn of their property, left stateless, and expelled, having been condemned collectively for collaborating with the Nazis.[7] It was only on October 25, 1948, that the legislation restored to members of Czechoslovakia's Hungarian minority their citizenship and the restricted range of political and civil rights to which citizens were entitled in a communist-run society.[8] In the 1950s, the authorities put an effort into integrating the Hungarians of southern Slovakia, much of it channeled through a Cultural Association of Hungarian Workers of Czechoslovakia (CSEMADOK)[9] founded in 1949. Hungarians became eligible for Communist Party membership, and teaching in Hungarian was resumed at some elementary and middle schools.[10]

Romania, on the other hand, pursued from the outset a policy of political and social integration of ethnic minorities. In 1945, the pro-communist government headed by Petru Groza declared that the 1.5 million indigenous Hungarians had equal rights with the majority. The Hungarians made some headway in rights of language use – some of the linguistic ground gained under Hungarian rule in Northern Transylvania in 1940–1944 was retained. From 1945, Hungarian became an accepted language of the public administration in areas inhabited by the same minority, while the university teaching in Hungarian language continued in Cluj, in the frame of a Romanian state university. There was state support for the Hungarian language in schools and in cultural life. Political representation of the minority was assumed by the Hungarian People's Union, which supported the leftist government. Tens of thousands of Hungarians joined the Romanian Communist Party and came to form 12 percent of the membership.[11]

As the communists took over power across Eastern Europe in 1948, minority policy became an internal affair. That, along with the end of grievance procedures of the League of Nations, the post-war acceptance of the principle of collective guilt, and a tight day-to-day control from Moscow, left the Hungarian party state powerless to influence the minority policy of its neighbors, although the Soviets expected the latter to cease open discrimination.

In Czechoslovakia, the Hungarians regained their citizenship, and the 44,000 people deported to the Czech lands in 1946–1947 were allowed to return home, where Hungarian schooling was permitted up to secondary level and a Hungarian-language newspaper appeared as well. This was a start to the process of integrating the Hungarian community.[12]

1948 brought radical changes in the education and cultural life of the Hungarian minority in Romania. Hitherto the Churches and voluntary institutions had played a central role in the organization and financing of the education and cultural life. The schools with education in minority languages were run by the so-called "historical" Churches (Catholics, Reformed, Unitarians and Lutheran Evangelicals). However, in 1948, almost 2,000 properties and other Church assets were nationalized, and education came under tight state control. The great voluntary institutions – the Transylvanian Museum Society, the Hungarian Cultural Society of Transylvania and the Transylvanian-Hungarian Economic Association – were closed. Running theaters and museums, and publishing of periodicals and books, became a state prerogative, which left the Hungarian community and its institutions dependent on the whims of state policy.[13]

The Hungarians of Yugoslavia, classed collectively as war criminals, suffered marked demographic losses. Reprisals by the Yugoslav partisan troops in the autumn of 1944 cost some 15,000 lives. Over 80,000 ethnic Hungarians left the country, mainly for Hungary. As tempers cooled, Tito's Yugoslavia announced a new minority policy: the Hungarian Cultural Association of Vojvodina was founded on July 22, 1945, and a daily paper called *Magyar Szó*, was launched. Furthermore, over 18,000 poor Hungarian families were granted land. The post-war Yugoslav leadership and legislature in fact paid little heed to the minority question. Nor did the 1948 breach with the Soviets change much in the minority policy of the Yugoslav Communist Party. The worker self-management system introduced in 1950 was extended by the 1953 Yugoslav Constitution to cultural and social activities as well.[14]

The minority question was declared to be solved, but it came up again in the détente period after Stalin's death. The process began with the Twentieth Congress of the Communist Party of the Soviet Union, held on February 14–25, 1956, in Moscow. The criticisms of Stalinism voiced by General Secretary Nikita Khrushchev in his secret speech had been preceded by the release of several millions of prisoners since Stalin's death in 1953, but the speech instigated further political reforms. The strongest reactions to it came from Poland and Hungary, which had experimented with Moscow-approved reform programs in 1953. The first Imre Nagy government, installed in Hungary on July 4, 1953, at Soviet behest, had reversed the forced industrialization of the Mátyás Rákosi regime, allowed peasants to back out of the collective farms that they had been forced to join, and freed an estimated 15,000 prisoners. The speed of the détente process prompted the Soviet Union to apply the brake. Rákosi returned to power in 1955, but public oppositionism, notably by the intelligentsia, could not be remedied.

The changes brought about an increasing Hungarian interest in the minority problems as well. Visits between Hungary and its neighboring countries had been possible since 1948 only for official delegations, but the Hungarian radio broadcasts could be heard throughout the Carpathian Basin and people could subscribe to papers from Hungary. (The comic *Ludas Matyi* and the popular science magazine *Élet és Tudomány* each had 10,000 subscribers in Romania alone.) Hungary's borders with Romania and Czechoslovakia were opened for private visits in August 1956, giving a chance to visitors to experience the change of mood in Hungary.[15]

However, the reception of the 1956 Hungarian Revolution by Hungarians in neighboring countries was ambivalent. Many hoped that the Revolution's democratic and national demands could be realized, but at the same time it was feared that reprisals for failure might spread to all Hungarians who had shown sympathy. Still, there were some small initiatives, although the rebels in Budapest had not voiced any demands for the minority Hungarians. Students demonstrating in Timişoara, Cluj and Bucharest voiced mainly political and social demands. The Roman Catholic priest Aladár Szoboszlay set about organizing a nation-wide conspiracy to overthrow the communists and achieve a Romanian–Hungarian confederation. This was soon broken up by the Romanian secret police, the Securitate, who arrested the plotters. When they came to trial in 1958, ten members of the group were executed and other 47 received sentences of several years' imprisonment or hard labor. There were protests around Oradea and in the Székely Land, organized by the Transylvanian Hungarian and Székely youth associations, which consisted mainly of secondary school pupils. Starting from November 1956 to the early 1960s, the intervention of the Romanian Communist Party and the Securitate led to severe reprisals for all who had shown sympathy for the Hungarian cause. Young people, among whom some under-age, were also arrested and condemned for trying to cross the Hungarian border to join the struggle. One female student from Cluj received a ten-year prison sentence for sending a letter to a friend into which she had copied the poem "A Word about Tyranny" by the Hungarian writer Gyula Illyés. Initially the reprisals targeted all ethnicities, but from 1958 onwards they were imposed disproportionately on Hungarians, Germans and Jews, and above all on the Hungarian intelligentsia. Recent research points to more than 32,000 people in Romania being sentenced to forced labor or internal exile between 1956 and 1964, of whom at least one tenth were ethnic Hungarians.[16]

In Slovakia newspapers from Hungary were banned right after the Revolution broke out. Although the protests were smaller than in Romania, there were gestures of sympathy in Bratislava, where ethnic Hungarians and Germans tried to collect money for the revolutionaries. As in Romania, students were to the fore. Hungarian students in Bratislava managed to hold meetings through CSEMADOK declaring their refusal to condemn the Revolution.

Sympathizers underwent heavy reprisals in subsequent months, with several hundred arrests and a number of people (including soldiers and officers) receiving custodial sentences of several years.[17]

In Ukraine, the Hungarian Revolution reinforced the criticism of the authorities that had begun with the Twentieth Congress. There were several meetings in Transcarpathia where social and other discontent was expressed. Groups sympathetic to the Hungarian Revolution were formed. Several of those who joined them later received prison sentences.[18]

The reactions among the Vojvodina Hungarians were relatively feeble, due partly to the generally favorable minority policies of the Tito regime, but also to traumatic memories of partisan violence in 1944. Yugoslavia played a positive role in November 1956 by accepting some 20,000 refugees from Hungary, many of whom traveled on to the West, although some settled in Hungarian-inhabited areas of Vojvodina.[19]

The 1956 Revolution brought about a change in minority policy mainly in Romania, where the minority elite had made a far more active contribution to local and national administration than in the other neighboring countries. The moral of 1956 for the Romanian regime was that ethnic Hungarians still saw Hungary as their parent country, despite all the concessions and ostensible privileges given to them, and showed no desire to integrate into the Romanian state. So they had to be classed as an unreliable element even if they posed no direct threat to the country's territorial integrity. In 1959, the Bolyai University in Cluj with education in Hungarian language was merged into the Babeş University with teaching language in Romanian. At the united university, Hungarian language became secondary to Romanian. In 1960, elementary and secondary schools teaching in Hungarian began to be merged with Romanian schools. Meanwhile, Hungarian-language technical training was winding up and measures were being taken to alter the ethnic proportions of the urban population. The hitherto large number of Hungarians working in the party and state apparatus found themselves squeezed out, along with the

Jewish-born officials who were Hungarian in culture. The secret police used blackmail and other methods to recruit several thousand
ethnic Hungarians as informers on other members of the Hungarian
community. This was applied particularly in the sector of arts, university and media, but it extended to factories and public institutions
as well. Romania's minority policy in the 1960s was characterized by
the so-called nation-building stage in the transformation into a communist society. Gheorghiu-Dej and his successor Nicolae Ceauşescu
gained greater freedom as leaders after the withdrawal of Soviet occupation forces in 1958, the economic confrontation with the Soviet
Union over the Valev Plan in 1962, and the "declaration of independence" by the Romanian Workers' Party in April 1964.[20]

Czechoslovakia's 1960 constitution defined the country as a
"socialist republic." It contained the first constitutional guarantee of
equality of rights, and stated that minorities had a right to education
and training in their own language. However, the Hungarian minority
lost ground in the simultaneous reforms of public administration
that merged local administrative units (such as the districts of
Dunajská Streda and Komárno), reducing the number of those where
Hungarians were in a majority. The subsequent process of détente
and reform – Alexander Dubček was elected as Communist Party
general secretary on January 5, 1968 – pushed the loyalist Hungarian
leaders into calling for extended minority rights. A proposal was put
out through CSEMADOK on March 12, 1968, for self-determination,
codification of minority rights, a proportionate Hungarian presence
in organs of power, the amendment of the 1960 local administration
reform that resulted in centralization, and the abrogation of the
discriminatory Beneš decrees introduced in 1945.[21]

The deep concern felt in Moscow and other Eastern European
capitals for Prague's commitment to reforms was expressed
retrospectively, *after* the August 1968 invasion of Czechoslovakia
by the Soviet and other Warsaw Pact forces, in the Brezhnev
Doctrine, expounded fully in a *Pravda* article in September
1968 by S. M. Kovalev, and reiterated in a Brezhnev speech to
the Polish Communist Party Congress on November 13. The

intervention had been "dictated by necessity," but "when internal and external forces hostile to socialism are threatening to turn a socialist country back to capitalism, this becomes a common problem and a concern of all socialist countries." The Soviet Union, as "the strongest and most developed socialist power," had a right to intervene in the internal affairs of a "fraternal country." The efforts to restore Soviet hegemony culminated in the Moscow conference of communist parties on June 5, 1969. The contributions made to the invasion of Czechoslovakia by Hungary and three other satellite countries were largely nominal but had strong political significance. One aspect of the "normalization" process that followed was an attempt to settle the Hungarian and Slovak questions. The constitutional act on the minorities of October 27, 1968, granted broader rights for the use of minority languages. On January 1, 1969, Czechoslovakia became a federal state consisting of Czech and Slovak republics, and in the new Slovak government László Dobos, an ethnic Hungarian, was appointed as minister without portfolio for minority affairs.[22]

The political changes in the Soviet Union, the spreading cult of personality surrounding Brezhnev, and a number of new policies that affected various national minorities had repercussions also in the satellite countries and on the Hungarian communities there. The policy aim of rapprochement and development for minority groups appeared in the mid-1960s and gained momentum in the 1970s. This rapprochement taking place in a new phase in the development of socialism would lead to the appearance of a new nation – the Soviet nation. In the Soviet Union this resulted in an increasing Russification of education and public life. The aim was not to revive the traditional concept of the nation, but by developing it to lend legitimacy to the existing power arrangements.[23] This Soviet influence led to emphasis on the national element and national interests in the policies of Hungary's neighboring countries towards their Hungarian minorities, but neither in Romania nor in Czechoslovakia did this work to their benefit. The nation-building of the former was limited to the Romanians, while in federal Czechoslovakia the Slovaks were better placed than ever to counter efforts by the indigenous Hungarians at nation-building and emancipation, despite some protests from leaders of Hungarian minority institutions and from Hungarian elites integrated into the socialist system.

The period between April 1969 and November 1989, when Gustáv Husák was Communist Party leader (and from 1975 also head of state), was marked by a return to "normal socialism" (in other words Soviet-style communist rule). Dubček's replacement by Husák in April 1969 brought about a great wave of such "normalization," a surreptitious terror that eschewed executions. This had its effects also among the influential Hungarians who had come out in favor of the Dubček reforms and were running CSEMADOK. The Slovak government set up a Council of Nations consisting of working committees on social policy, education and cultural affairs for each minority (Hungarians and Ukrainians).

The 1970s witnessed a departure from the minority policy efforts originally proclaimed. One of the first casualties was Rezső Szabó, relieved of his posts as deputy speaker and member of the Presidency of the Slovak legislature. Then László Dobos's position of minister for minority affairs was abolished in 1970. Meanwhile, CSEMADOK had to desist from its limited, implicit representation of the Hungarians' political interests. It was dropped from the umbrella National Front in 1971 and operated thereafter solely as a cultural body.[24]

The educational and language-use rights of Czechoslovakia's Hungarians were also curtailed in the early 1970s. The Ministry of Education made several efforts to introduce Slovak as a teaching language in the Hungarian schools. This was a time when Hungary and Czechoslovakia disagreed on a number of political issues. Opposition activity began in the later 1970s in the Slovakian Hungarian intelligentsia.[25] By the early 1980s there had emerged a generation that rejected the communist system as a whole. The activity of the Charta '77 opposition movement in Prague led to the formation of a Committee for the Protection of the Rights of the Hungarian Minority in Czechoslovakia[26] under the leadership of Miklós Duray, which contacted opposition figures in Hungary. The authorities responded with arrests and interrogations. An independent group of young Hungarian writers, *Iródia*, was formed in 1983. Meanwhile, the proportion of Hungarians in several Slovakian areas sank, due to settlement connected with industrialization.[27]

The events in Czechoslovakia in 1968 led to some ostensible domestic liberalization in Romania. Party General Secretary Nicolae Ceauşescu was opposed to the Prague reforms but gained capital in the West by condemning the Soviet intervention. Despite the liberalization, the Communist Party's minority policy remained ambivalent. Ceauşescu, addressing the Ninth Congress in July 1965, called the "nationality question" a problem that had finally been resolved. In June 1968, he denied the need for new legislation on the Hungarian minority. The Council of Workers of Hungarian Nationality[28] that he founded soon proved to be a formalized gathering of advisers with no right even to convene a plenary session. It failed to exert any specific influence on Romanian Communist Party minority policy in the period between 1969 and 1980, and was then confined to discussing a few aspects of social, cultural and economic activity. However, 1970 saw several cultural developments of practical importance for the Hungarian minority, for instance the foundation of the publishing house Kriterion and the launch of the weekly magazine *A Hét*.[29]

Visits to China and North Korea inspired Ceauşescu to announce in 1971 the "July theses" that opened an era of radical re-Stalinization and a renewed cult of personality. The outcome for the Hungarian minority was a dramatic, mercilessly imposed program of "national communism" designed to create an ethnically homogeneous state by forced assimilation. The remnants of Hungarian education began to disappear. Hungarians were squeezed out of high-prestige professions. Transylvanian cities with a Hungarian majority underwent homogenization via massive housing construction and industrialization. In 1984 the concept of "coexisting nations" began to give way to "Romanian workers of Hungarian origin." Even the toothless Council of Workers of Hungarian Nationality added the word "Romanian" to its name. Anti-Hungarianism became strident as the economy and living standards fell.[30]

The Hungarian community's response to this accelerating process ranged from intellectual opposition movements to mass illegal or lawful emigration to Hungary or the West. In some cases the activities of the Securitate drove Hungarians to suicide. Other persons were reported to have been killed by "car accidents".[31]

The solution adopted for the minority question in the ethnically more diverse Yugoslavia was focused on federalism and autonomy. This was not a window-dressing type of solution as the Soviet federalism, but a real system of social organization that worked until the 1980s. Recognized "nations" – Serbs, Croats, Slovenes, Montenegrins, Macedonians and later Bosnian Muslims – could form their own republics. Communities classed as "nationalities" under the self-management system – Hungarians, Romanians, Slovaks, Turks, Czechs, Bulgarians and Rusyns – had various language and cultural rights. The Albanians of Kosovo and Hungarians of the Banat and Bačka lived in provinces of Serbia that had territorial autonomy as well. Scattered ethnic groups – Jews, Russians or Vlachs (as Romanian-speakers were officially called) – were or were not granted cultural rights according to their degree of dispersion. There was not a chance for vertical only for horizontal organizations: it was not possible to create self-governing organizations of minorities, only professional ones.[32]

From 1981 to 1991, the official political status of the Roma in Yugoslavia was that of "nationality." Yugoslavia had a three-level system: the "nations" of Yugoslavia were Croats, Serbs, Slovenes, Bosnians and Macedonians; the "nationalities" included Turks, Albanians and Hungarians; the rest were "other nationalities and ethnic groups," such as Vlachs and Jews. In practice, however, most of the republics that had their own constitutions considered Roma to be an "ethnic group." For example, in the 1981 Macedonian census, Roma were still considered an ethnic group, and this designation is precisely one of the factors which mobilized Macedonian Roma to political action in the 1980s.

The Hungarians had broad language and cultural rights in Vojvodina Autonomous Province, where Hungarian was one of the five official languages. They made up 22 percent of the population.

There was a Department of Hungarian Studies at the University of Novi Sad and a College of Pedagogy in Subotica. Street names were written additionally in any local minority language. Vojvodina Hungarians lived in better circumstances compared to Hungarian minorities in other socialist countries, because farmers could work on their own land and there was greater openness to the West. The weakness in the Yugoslav model was the rivalry between the republics and an obvious Serb hegemony in many fields.

The 1974 constitution decentralized power and handed it to the republics, creating a regional/national pluralism instead of a political/ideological one. Tito acted firmly against separatist national aspirations, coming especially from the Croats. But the Yugoslav model entered a crisis after Tito's death in 1980, as real power passed from the federal bodies to the republican elites. This political problem was compounded by a deep economic crisis.

The critical situation affected the Vojvodina Hungarians as well. The Serbian elite succumbed to a revived Serbian nationalism and steadily eroded the language and cultural rights won by the minorities. In 1983 there came the break-up of the board of the periodical *Új Symposion*, headed by János Sziveri, which had played a progressive cultural role among the Hungarians. In October 1988, the "yoghurt revolution" carried out by Slobodan Milošević reinforced the Serbian elite, and led to the end of the autonomy of Kosovo and Vojvodina in 1989. Up to then, no institutions had developed to represent Hungarian minority interests. The political elite headed by Nándor Major, last head of the Vojvodina autonomous region, sought to assert Hungarian interests through that body and through the spirit of Yugoslavism.

The policies of Czechoslovakia and Romania towards their Hungarian minorities became an increasing problem for Hungary's foreign policy, intent on preserving unity in the Soviet camp. This prompted the Hungarian Communist Party to redraft the basic theses of Leninist nationality policy, to stress the bridging role that the minorities might play in relations between Hungary and its neighboring countries.[33]

Notes

1   Communist takeover: Norman Naimark and Leonid Gibianski, eds., *The Establishment of Communist Regimes in Eastern Europe, 1944–1949* (Boulder, CO, 1997); Eduard Mark, "Revolution by Degrees. Stalin's National Front Strategy for Europe," *Working Paper 31, February 2001, Cold War International History Project* (Washington, DC, 2001).

2   A succinct account of the Soviet power system: János Kornai, *The Socialist System. The Political Economy of Communism* (Princeton, NJ, 1992), pp. 33–48.

3   *Ibid.*, pp. 110–130.

4   *Ibid.*, pp. 49–61.

5   *Ibid.*, pp. 360–379.

6   Marxist theory and practice: Walker Connor, *The National Question in Marxist-Leninist Theory and Strategy* (Princeton, NJ, 1984). Pre-1945 Soviet nationality policy: Terry Martin, *The Affirmative Action Empire. Nations and Nationalism in the Soviet Union, 1923–1939* (New York, 2001).

7   Still useful on population exchanges: Joseph B. Schechtman, *Postwar Population Transfers in Europe 1945–1955* (Philadephia, 1962); German communities: Aldred M. De Zayas, *A Terrible Revenge: the Ethnic Cleansing of the East European Germans, 1944–1950* (New York, 2006); Detlef Brandes, *Der Weg zur Vertreibung 1938–1945. Pläne und Entscheidungen zum "Transfer" der Deutschen aus der Tschechoslowakei und aus Polen* (Munich, 2005).

8   Benjamin Frommer, *National Cleansing: Retribution against Nazi Collaborators in Postwar Czechoslovakia* (New York, 2005); Katalin Vadkerty, *Maďarská otázka v Československu 1945–1948* [The Hungarian Question in Czechoslovakia 1945–1948] (Bratislava, 2002). See also Štefan Šutaj, *Magyarok Csehszlovákiában 1945–1948* [Hungarians in Czechoslovakia 1945–1948] (Budapest, 2008).

9   The organization still exists under a different name but the same acronym. On the way in which organs of state power were tricked out as civil associations in the communist period, see Kornai, *The Socialist System*, pp. 39–40.

10 Árpád Popély, *A (cseh)szlovákiai magyarság történeti kronológiája 1944–1992* [Historical Chronology of the (Czecho)Slovak Hungarian Community, 1944–1992] (Somorja, 2006), p. 290.

11   Zoltán Csaba Novák, "A Román Munkáspárt magyar kádereinek 1956-os megéléstörténetei" [1956 Life Stories of Hungarian Cadres in the Romanian Workers' Party], *Múltunk* (2007) 1: 122–132; Zoltán Mihály Nagy, "Érdekképviseleti lehetőség – integrációs alku" [Interest-Representing Opportunity – Integration Bargain], in Mihály Zoltán Nagy and Ágoston Olti, *Érdekképviselet vagy pártpolitika? Iratok a Magyar Népi Szövetség történetéhez 1944–1953* [Interest Representation or Party Politics? Documents on the Hungarian People's Union, 1944–1953] (Csíkszereda, 2009), pp. 17–100.

12   Cultural life: László Szarka, "A (cseh)szlovákiai magyar közösség nyolc évtizede 1918–1998. Történeti vázlat" [Eight Decades of the Czechoslovakian/Slovakian Hungarian Community 1918–1998. Historical Outline], in László Tóth and Tamás Gusztáv Filep, eds., *A (cseh)szlovákiai magyar művelődés története 1918–1998* [History of (Czecho)Slovakian Hungarian Education 1918–1998], 4 vols. (Budapest, 1998–2000), pp. 9–80.

13   Gábor Vincze, "Gazdaságpolitika vagy kisebbségpolitika? Az 1945-ös romániai földreform a Groza-kormány kisebbségpolitikájának tükrében" [Economic Policy or Minority Policy? The 1945 Romanian Land Reform in the Light of the Groza Government's Minority Policy], *Magyar Kisebbség* (1996) 4: 182–208; Gábor Vincze, *Magyar vagyon román kézen (Dokumentumok a romániai magyar vállalatok, pénzintézetek második világháború utáni helyzetéről és a magyar–román vagyonjogi vitáról)* [Hungarian Property in Romanian Hands. Documents on the Post-War Position of Romanian Hungarian Companies and Financial Institutions and the Hungarian–Romanian Property-Rights Dispute] (Csíkszereda, 2000).

14   See Ivo Banac, *The National Question in Yugoslavia: Origins, History, Politics (Ithaca, NY, 1984).* On self-management in theory and practice, see Kornai, *The Socialist System*, p. 462 ff. On the Hungarian minority, see Enikő A. Sajti, "The Change of Rule and Reprisals against the Hungarians in Yugoslavia 1944–1946," *Chronica. Annual of the Institute of History University of Szeged* (2003) 3: 114–131.

15   Péter Bencsik and György Nagy, *A magyar úti okmányok története 1945–1989* [History of Hungarian Travel Documents 1945–1989] (Budapest, 2003). Hungarian–Romanian travel regulations: Stefano

Bottoni, "Románia" [Romania], in Csaba Békés, ed., *Evolúció és revolúció. Magyarország és a nemzetközi politika 1956-ban* [Evolution and Revolution. Hungary and International Politics in 1956] (Budapest, 2007), pp. 161–163.

16   Stefano Bottoni, Márton László, Klára Lázok and Zoltán Novák, eds., *Az 1956-os forradalom és a romániai magyarság (1956–1959)* [The 1956 Hungarian Revolution and Romania's Hungarians] (Csíkszereda, 2006).

17   Juraj Marušiak, "Az 1956-os magyar forradalom és Szlovákia" [The 1956 Revolution and Slovakia], *Múltunk* (2007) 1: 58–103; Edita Ivaničková and Attila Simon, eds., *Maďarská revolúcia 1956 a Slovensko. Az 1956-os magyar forradalom és Szlovákia* [The 1956 Hungarian Revolution and Slovakia] (Šamorín/Bratislava, 2006).

18   Natália Váradi, "Az 1956-os forradalom és szabadságharc visszhangja Kárpátalján" [The Reaction in Transcarpathia to the 1956 Revolution], in Ádám Szesztay, ed., *Együtt: Az 1956-os forradalom és a határon túli magyarok* [Together: the 1956 Revolution and the Hungarians beyond the Borders] (Budapest, 2006), pp. 35–66.

19   Enikő A. Sajti, "Ötvenhatos menekültek Jugoszláviában. A magyar–jugoszláv hazatelepítési bizottságok tevékenysége 1956–1957-ben" [1956 Refugees in Yugoslavia. The Activity of the Hungarian–Yugoslav Repatriation Committees in 1956–1957], in *Évkönyv* [Yearbook] XIV, 2006–2007 (Budapest, 2007), pp. 201–212.

20   Michael Shafir, *Romania. Politics, Economics, Society: Political Stagnation and Simulated Change* (London, 1985).

21   For more, see Árpád Popély, ed., *1968 és a szlovákiai magyarság* [1968 and the Slovakian Hungarians] (Šamorín, 2008), pp. 23–44; Juraj Marušiak, "A magyar kisebbség a normalizációs évek szlovákiai politikájának összefüggéseiben" [The Hungarian Minority in Terms of Slovakia's Policy in the Normalization Years], *Fórum* (2005) 1: 51–75 and (2005) 2: 63–84. Documentation on Rezső Szabó, a prominent Hungarian politician: *A CSEMADOK és a Prágai Tavasz. Beszélgetések, cikkek, előadások, dokumentumok* [CSEMADOK and the Prague Spring. Conversations, Articles, Lectures, Documents] (Pozsony, 2004).

22   Popély, *1968 és a szlovákiai magyarság*, p. 34.

23   The word *narod* [people] is used, not *natsiya* [nation]. It may be wiser to see this as a concept of a single Soviet people rather than nation. On Brezhnevite efforts to unify Soviet peoples, see Barbara

A. Anderson, and Brian D. Silver, "Some Factors in the Linguistic and Ethnic Russification of Soviet Nationalities: Is Everyone Becoming Russian?," in Lubomyr Hajda and Mark Beissinger, eds., *The Nationality Factor in Soviet Politics and Society* (Boulder, CO, 1990), pp. 95–130.

24   Popély, *1968 és a szlovákiai magyarság*, pp. 42–44.

25   Antecedents: Marusiak, "A magyar kisebbség."

26   *Csehszlovákiai Magyar Kisebbség Jogvédő Bizottsága.*

27   Miklós Duray, *Kutyaszorító* [In a Tight Spot], I (New York, 1982); Miklós Duray, *Kettős elnyomásban. Dokumentumok a csehszlovákiai magyarság helyzetéről és jogvédelméről 1978–1989* [Double Pressure. Documents on the Situation and Legal Protection of the Czechoslovakian Hungarians 1978–1989] (Bratislava, 1989).

28   *Magyar Nemzetiségű Dolgozók Tanácsa.*

29   Gábor Vincze, "Egy romániai 'fantomszervezet', a Magyar Nemzetiségű Dolgozók Tanácsa születése" [A Romanian Fantom Organization, the Birth of the Council of Hungarian Nationality Workers], in *Emlékkönyv Kiss András születésének nyolcvanadik évfordulójára* [*Festschrift* for the 80th Anniversary of the Birth of András Kiss] (Kolozsvár, 2003), pp. 623–639.

30   *Ibid.*

31   Jenő Szikszai, a high school teacher of Brașov, committed suicide in 1977; the Reverend Géza Pálfy of Odorheiu Secuiesc was arrested in 1982 for "agitating against the government," taken away and delivered one week later to a hospital, where he died shortly afterwards; Ernő Ujvárossy of Timișoara, a parishioner of the Reverend László Tőkés, was found murdered in the woods outside Timișoara on September 14, 1989.

32   A broad picture: Gábor Vajda, *Az autonómia illúziója. A délvidéki magyarság eszme- és irodalomtörténete (1972–1989)* [The Illusion of Autonomy. Intellectual and Literary History of the Southern Region Hungarians] (Szabadka, 2007). Analysis of a generation and its main periodical: György Szerbhorváth, *Vajdasági lakoma. Az Új Symposion történetéről* [Vojvodina Feast. From the History of the *Új Symposion*] (Pozsony, 2005).

33   György Földes, *Magyarország, Románia és a nemzeti kérdés 1956–1989* [Hungary, Romania and the National Question 1956–1989] (Budapest, 2007).

2. HUNGARY AND THE HUNGARIANS
BEYOND ITS BORDERS
Nándor Bárdi

The Soviet Union was a dominant influence on Hungarian foreign policy for forty years. The October 1956 declaration by the Imre Nagy government of Hungary's neutrality and withdrawal from the Warsaw Pact could not lead to independence in a world divided into two camps. After the Soviet military reoccupation of November 4, 1956, the imposed Kádár government struggled hard to gain any international acceptance until 1963. Then there began a process of divergent development by the Soviet bloc countries, with mounting assertion of national interests and competition for access to Western technology and economic contacts. But there was still no appreciable policy on the Hungarians in the Rákosi period or most of the Kádár period. Only in the 1980s did Hungary gain the required freedom of foreign policy and did it become politically acceptable to view the Hungarian cultural nation as a unit with boundaries different from those of the Hungarian state.[1]

The Treaty of Paris left no means of ensuring the unity of the Hungarian cultural nation. The Left saw the only prospects of doing so in a confederal scheme based on the shared destiny of Central European peoples and in expanding bilateral relations. Yet the underlying reason behind COMINFORM'S 1948 breach with Yugoslavia was precisely the fact that Stalin would stand for no regional offsets or autonomous organizations within the communist movement. That left open only appeals based on Leninist nationality policy (language and individual rights for the minorities engaged in building socialism and accepting democratic centralism and Communist Party leadership). However, other ideological reasons took precedence over nationality policy. One such was the principle of automatism, whereby the class war ends national antagonisms and the minority question becomes an internal one for each country, as the relation to socialism overrides all national differences. The elite owes its allegiance to communism, not national identities. After Stalin's death, and the resumption of peaceable relations with Yugoslavia in 1955, there began efforts aimed at independent action within the socialist world system. That was followed by divergence of state and regional interests between countries with varying socio-economic features. An attempt to integrate these was made through the economic organization COMECON, offering a systematic division of labor. Hungary tried through this in 1962–1968 to strengthen regional cooperation, but found no partners for doing so.

Kádárite foreign policy marked a departure from that of the period up to 1956. It rested on constructive loyalty – Hungary's internal structure had departed furthest of any in the socialist camp from the Soviet model, but in foreign policy it remained loyal to Moscow.[2] So raising the question of Hungarians abroad and of neighborly relations in general came second to defending the unique Kádárite (Hungarian) model. Hungary had no success with the Romanian or the Czechoslovakian Communist Parties in seeking to promote the Leninist norms of nationality policy or to gain acceptance for the purported bridge-building role of minorities. Only bargains struck with various elite groups in Hungary led by the mid-1980s to a policy that incorporated the collective rights of such minorities.

The restricted public discourse of the 1947–1949 period, discussing the Czechoslovak–Hungarian population exchange, presented the problem of Hungarians abroad as a conflict. Then the subject vanished from the press up to the autumn of 1956. Propaganda after the defeat of the Revolution presented it in a context of condemnation of nationalism and attempts at territorial revision. The matter of the minorities became a subject again at the end of the 1960s for Gyula Illyés and some other members of the cultural and scientific elite. Discrimination against them then appeared in the illegal publications of the democratic opposition (*Beszélő, Párizsi Magyar Füzetek*) as a human rights issue. The critical situations, particularly in Romania, began to be publicized in ever more varied ways in 1983.[3]

The government's foreign policy role was assumed in the Rákosi years by the Communist Party leadership. The Communist Party, having failed to influence the treaty terms or forestall the Hungarian–Czechoslovak population exchange, trusted after 1948 that it could defend Hungary's state and cultural interests through talks with other countries' communist leaders (with local Hungarian communists alongside them). There was a measure of success with the Czechoslovaks, due more to international relations than to "comradely" ones. The population exchange was halted at the end of 1948; deportations of Hungarians from southern Slovakia ceased in October 1949. This was helped along by the Soviet policy of promoting stabilization. Claims of financial compensation were abandoned in favor of pressure to restore the Hungarian school system and ensure real choice of identity for the Hungarians who had been forcibly Slovakized, while Slovakian Hungarian communists appealed against the nation-building, expansionist efforts of the Slovak communists to the party leadership in Prague, which was struggling against Slovak particularism in any case.[4]

Relations with Romania were frozen after the king's abdication and the nationalizations, rather than revitalized as they were in Czechoslovakia. The two leaderships vied at the peace talks to promote their countries' claims regarding to Transylvania, hoping to gain domestic prestige thereby. That worked only for Bucharest, as the Soviet Union came down firmly on Romania's side. Attempts were made to assuage Hungarian bitterness at the return to the pre-war borders with propaganda about cooperation, and to dispel unease among Hungarians in both countries by displaying the ostensible successes of the Hungarian People's Union.[5] But the Romanian communists as state leaders saw in their Hungarian colleagues enemies who had pushed territorial claims only three or four years before. After the excommunication of Yugoslavia and the nationalizations, the policy of presenting the position of Transylvania and its Hungarians in a good light gave way to one of isolating them from Hungary. The two sides could not agree on the nationalized assets of the Hungarian state and legal entities. The negotiations ended with mutual abandonment of such claims, causing a loss of over $200 million for the Hungarian state.[6] After 1949, those with property in both countries could no longer cross the border. Personal visits virtually ceased and bilateral trade fell back. Rákosi cited Moscow's directives when complaining in 1949 that the border situation was worse than it had been before the Hungarian annexation of 1940, but the Romanian leadership (including the ethnic Hungarian minister of finance, László Luka) pleaded a need for vigilance,[7] against internal class enemies and up to 1955 for fear of inimical Yugoslav action. Hungary after 1949 was in the forefront of socialist countries for propaganda against Tito. Yugoslavia by that time was building up a new minority Hungarian cultural elite and providing a network of schools and cultural institutions, while Hungary practiced severe discrimination against its much smaller communities of indigenous Serbs, Croats and Slovenes and began running down the already modest system of South Slav minority institutions.

In the personal and power struggles that ensued after Stalin's death, Gheorghe Gheorghiu-Dej, as party chief and prime minister in Romania, presented Rákosi as a Hungarian nationalist as opposed to Imre Nagy. Even after the rapprochement brokered with Khrushchev, Tito refused to meet Rákosi because of the extreme anti-Yugoslav campaign that he had waged earlier.[8]

Never once right up until the 1980s was the issue of the Transcarpathian Hungarians raised in Soviet–Hungarian relations.[9] Nor did the Hungarians abroad feature in the revolutionary demands made during the two weeks of the 1956 Imre Nagy government. Territorial changes were not raised at governmental or local level, despite later propaganda claims to the contrary. The main aim was to consolidate the political leadership and institutionalize the country's independence. Yet the Revolution had a marked effect on policy towards Hungarians abroad, in two ways. First, it emerged that Hungarians in Romania, Yugoslavia, Czechoslovakia and the Soviet

Union, following the news on the radio, identified strongly with events in Budapest and their ideological and political implications. This "lack of integration" of views turned minority Hungarian endeavors in Transcarpathia, Slovakia and Romania into a matter of state security, in the eyes of the communist leaders of the majority nation. This later gave a pretext for institutional, educational and language-use measures aimed at homogenization and discrimination under the guise of integration. Secondly, the consolidation process after the defeat involved political and economic help (trade credits and loans) from neighboring countries to the Kádár regime, including the breach of the asylum granted to Nagy in the Yugoslav Embassy and his handover to Romania, support in the UN and the communist movement, the participation of activists from Transcarpathia and southern Slovakia in party work inside Hungary, and imports of Hungarian-language papers and books from neighboring countries.[10]

Events in the Kádár period to do with Hungarians abroad may be divided into four phases.

The phase of political consolidation lasted from November 1956 until July 1963, when the "Hungarian question" was dropped from the UN agenda and Western recognition ensued. János Kádár, Ferenc Münnich and Gyula Kállai headed a party and government delegation to tour neighboring socialist countries in 1958 to thank them for their assistance since 1956. They stressed the point that Hungary made no territorial claims and saw the position of the Hungarians as an internal matter for each country,[11] thereby conceding that the achievement of socialism transcended national cultural characteristics and the principle of unity. This concession allowed neighboring countries' leaders to narrow the range of Hungarian-language institutions, with their separatist potentials. The new Hungarian regime was striving for outside acceptance and internal consolidation, and lacked the means to prevent such curtailment of the Hungarian minority institutions even had it wanted to. Examples included the March 1959 merger of the Romanian-language Babeş and Hungarian-language Bolyai universities in Cluj, alteration of the borders of the Hungarian Autonomous Province to increase the Romanian proportion of inhabitants, and replacement of

Hungarians with Romanians in leading positions (December 1960). The 1958 education act in the Soviet Union turned schools teaching in minority languages into bilingual schools, as part of a drive for Russification. Such minority schools were also changed in Hungary in the 1960–1961 school year, after which only arts subjects were taught in the minority language, on the grounds that pupils needed to be conversant in the state language in practical daily life.[12]

That change was a tragic one for minorities in Hungary, conforming as it did to tendencies towards uniformity and homogenization throughout the Soviet bloc in the 1960s. Nor was there in Hungary any trade-off like the one in Romania or Czechoslovakia – national traditions of independence were not strengthened by it, and nor did the authorities gain any legitimacy through national symbols or rhetoric. For one thing, a regime that had endorsed the presence of Soviet occupation forces could not talk credibly of Hungarian national independence. For another, the situation in Hungary differed from that of in the other socialist countries, due to its particular form of internal legitimation, resting partly on a freeing of society from ideology and on an expansion of private freedom. This is precisely why the Kádár period may also be called the "Kádár-regime". The emphasis came to be on a higher standard of living, not on national independence, as the prime national value.[13] Thirdly, it should be noted that Kádár as head of the single-party system held such a plebeian conception about the nation, in which national sentiment was identified with the revisionist/nationalist, manipulative rhetoric and legitimation of the Horthy system. He saw the reappearance of the national symbols in the 1950s and 1960s as a return to pre-1945 nationalism. His insensitivity to the fate of the Hungarians in neighboring countries can be put down to the same fear. Finally, questions involving Hungarians in neighboring countries could not be raised in Hungary before the second half of the 1960s, because the party leaders were committed believers in supranational socialist integration, for instance in COMECON division of labor. Thus nationalism took its place alongside ideological revisionism as the main ideological threat.[14]

Tying in with this was the "nation debate" initiated by Erik Molnár in 1966, in which national independence struggles were contrasted with the modernizing, supranational role of integration and economic development found in the Habsburg realms. But paradoxically, it was the public debates on this that restored acceptance of the history-forming role of the "nation."[15] In policy terms, change ensued when Romania countered Soviet integration efforts with its own 1944 policy of a separate road, separate paths of development (heavy industry priorities), and separate foreign policy interests (in relation to China and Western Europe). Furthermore, the Romanian press began to emphasize the Romanian nature of the parts of Moldavia annexed by the Soviet Union in 1964. So moves by the Hungarian party leadership on the Transylvanian Hungarians suited Soviet interests as well. This all became public in 1967–1968, when Romania was the only socialist country that failed to break off diplomatic relations with Israel, when it was the first to recognize the Federal Republic of Germany, and when it condemned the Soviet military intervention in Czechoslovakia in 1968. At that point, the Hungarian Writers' Union held its first debate on the bodies of literature of Hungarian communities abroad and stated the responsibility that Hungary bore towards them.[16] Open discussion of the Hungarians abroad was no longer condemned as nationalism.

The Communist Party took the matter up as well. The Central Committee's Agitprop Committee met in March 1968 to discuss the relations with Hungarian literary life abroad, seen as part of Hungarian culture. It called for responsibility for it and greater support. By August 1969, the committee was discussing not only literature but the whole cultural situation of the Hungarian-speaking communities in neighboring countries. The practical tasks came before the Politburo as well.[17] Officially the ideology of dual affiliation was proclaimed. Minorities in Hungary and Hungarian minorities in neighboring countries had ties to their national culture and to that of their country of citizenship. They formed a bridge between the two nations, a means of overcoming historical prejudices. That did not change the domestic nature of the nationality question, but culture and education for Hungarians abroad became prominent in private inter-party and diplomatic discussions with neighboring countries. Minority-related contacts with Yugoslavia increased so intensively that a brake was put on information about them. Czechoslovakia would not accept the notion of a bridging role, and once local Hungarian prominents in 1968 (such as László Dobos) had been dismissed, minority-related ties fell back. Silence over the Transcarpathian Hungarians continued at Soviet–Hungarian talks, but cultural relations improved.

The greatest degree of conflict was to be found in relations with Romania. Up to 1968, the Romanian Hungarian literary elite had objected to Hungarian Writers' Union interference, but by the mid-1970s protests to the party center in Bucharest were being coupled with appeals to the makers of Hungarian cultural policy, headed by György Aczél. What precipitated this was the burden on the Romanian Hungarian community placed by Ceauşescu's declared policy of homogenization, new obstacles to starting classes in minority schools, and new curbs in 1974 on offering lodging to visitors of non-Romanian origin.

An important stage in this transformation of policy was a 1972 constitutional amendment, which treated the national minorities of Hungary collectively and declared their equality of rights. Still more decisive was an Agitprop committee statement in 1974, which cannot be interpreted outside the context of the problems of Hungary's minorities abroad. It drew a distinction between the political nation and the cultural nation (Hungarian citizens and self-declared Hungarians), recognized a right of dual affiliation, and stated that a prior requirement for the practical implementation of collective minority rights was good cooperation among the socialist countries.[18] The thesis was first aired in Hungarian diplomacy at a UN conference on minority protection held at Ohrid, Yugoslavia, in July 1974.[19] It sought to make bilateral discussions of the issue compulsory. János Kádár first alluded to the 1,100-year presence of the Hungarians in Europe and to the loss of territory after World War I in a widely noticed address to the Helsinki Conference on July 31, 1975. More importantly, the Helsinki Agreement gave neighboring countries a further guarantee of the inviolability of their borders, and the Third Basket provided a basis for Hungary to maintain ties with Hungarians abroad, through its principle of the free flow of ideas. A year later, in December 1976, the problems of Hungarians in neighboring countries came before the highest executive body of the Communist Party, the Politburo. It was still considered to be an internal issue, but at the same time it represented a foreign policy task for Hungary. The most appropriate means of advance were to raise it at bilateral interparty discussions, to ensure that Hungary's minorities were treated in an exemplary way, and to arrange the appropriate state budgetary coordination for the purpose.[20]

This new concept was promoted at a summit meeting of Kádár and Ceaușescu in June 1977. The Romanians had pressed for such a meeting, while Hungary's party leaders insisted that such a summit should follow specialist talks from which concrete agreements could emerge. There was some success in this respect on the question of each country opening consulates, but nothing shifted in Romania's increasingly centralized policy of homogenization and discrimination against the Hungarians.

Four reasons can be posited for the changed treatment of the question of the Hungarians abroad in the period after the Kádárite consolidation and attempt at supranational socialist integration. The most important was the Soviet permission to criticize Romania's separate road. Then came the need to formulate Hungary's own interests as its foreign policy became more professional, in response to its separate development path and need to acquire Western technology. The third reason was the fact that the Kádár regime sensed in society a tension that had to be dispelled, or to put it another way, an increase in the bargaining power of certain elite groups. This meant primarily Gyula Illyés, Sándor Csoóri and the *népi* writers.[21] They acted as intermediaries over the problems of the minority Hungarians, which earned the latter a publication ban in the 1980s. The international reputation and connections of the democratic opposition in the 1980s allowed them also to exert strong pressure at home and abroad, presenting the problem as one of human rights and airing it frequently in samizdat literature. To the same period belong the editors of the Transylvanian Hungarian samizdat publication *Ellenpontok* (Counterpoints) and the members of the Duray Committee. (Miklós Duray founded the Legal Aid Association of Hungarian Minority in Czechoslovakia. As a result he was imprisoned in 1982–1983 and 1984–1985. The group protesting against that in Budapest was the Duray Committee.) One influence on Romania's image in Western eyes was the Hungarian Press of Transylvania, which worked with the Hungarian Human Rights Foundation to keep the international public informed of the situation with regard to human rights.[22] Another factor in the change to more forceful representation of the national interest and the problems of the cultural nation was the publicity and connection-building work done in Hungary by members of Hungarian elites abroad.

Conditions changed in several ways in the 1980s. It was important that the Czechoslovak and Romanian Communist Parties came largely to ignore Leninist norms of nationality policy, making it steadily less effective for Hungarian party leaders to call them to account in those terms. There arose new groups of Hungarian minority elite, which recognized how the minority question could not be handled within the anti-democratic frames of state socialism, an opinion shared increasingly by opposition groups in Hungary.[23] Also important was the fact that the debates on historical, national, and human rights matters were largely taking place in public. This tied in with the way in which the increasingly rigid Romanian and Czechoslovak systems defended themselves ideologically and from the weakening dictatorship of Hungary and built up an enemy image of it.

The period that began in 1975–1977 reached a turning point in 1982, when an extremist anti-Hungarian work appeared in Romania with official backing. Ion Lăncrăjan's *Cuvint despre Transilvania* (Thoughts on Transylvania) dubbed as territorial revisionists not only the Hungarian left-wing of Romania, but also János Kádár. In the autumn came the arrest and exile of the editors of *Ellenpontok*. In the same week Duray was arrested in Bratislava. All three events attracted strong attention abroad and protests in Hungary,[24] but the official Hungarian government response was subdued, showing a desire to avoid conflict and to renew negotiations. The Hungarian party leaders were reluctant to embroil themselves in international debates, and to speak out in favor of Duray or the *Ellenpontok* editor Géza Szőcs would be to defend Eastern European dissidents and declared opponents of state socialism. Furthermore, this became linked in Czechoslovakia's case with the protests over the joint Gabčíkovo–Nagymaros barrage scheme on the Danube, which had become a domestic issue in Hungary as well. In 1985, Kádár received help from Prague against the Bratislava leadership on the issues of bilingual schooling and place-name usage. Rather than engage in historical polemics with Romania, the three-volume Hungarian *History of Transylvania* that appeared in 1986 after five to eight years' work sought to present "scientific truth."[25] The same intention lay behind the foundation in 1985 of the Group (later Institute) for Research into Hungarian Studies. Such measures had a liberating effect on the Hungarian public at home and abroad, and enhanced their sense of nationhood.

That does not mean that the whole party leadership identified with the cultural nation, the concept of human rights claims, or the tasks arising from them. The key figures were Mátyás Szűrös and Csaba Tabajdi, heads of the MSZMP Central Committee Foreign Affairs Department, under pressure from the *népi* writers and the democratic opposition. Hungary made clear at the Helsinki follow-up meetings in 1985–1988 the stress that it placed on the problems of Hungarians abroad, the bridging role that it ascribed to minorities, its rejection of forcible assimilation, the need for positive discrimi-nation in minority policy, minority contacts with their kin-state, the continuing attention that the problems required, and the status of this as a gauge of democracy. As mounting numbers of refugees arrived from Romania, these were the grounds on which Szűrös stated on the radio in January 1988 that the Hungarians beyond Hungary's borders were part of the Hungarian nation and the Hungarian government bore responsibility for them.[26]

Just a few months later, permission was given for a demonstration in Budapest in June 1988 against the Romanian plans to destroy villages. It was the first unofficial mass protest allowed since 1956. Romania responded by closing the Hungarian Consulate-General in Cluj-Napoca. The new party general secretary, Károly Grósz, tried to remedy matters at a summit meeting with Ceauşescu in Arad, but without success. As the grievances in Transylvania and Slovakia built up and Soviet *glasnost* made it possible to undertake more in Transcarpathia, there was a need for a standing body to coordinate government action. An advisory National Minorities College with an invited membership was formed in the autumn of 1989, but was soon replaced by a College of National and Ethnic Minorities under the Council of Ministers, headed by Tabajdi. This brought to fruition the institutionalization of Hungary's policy towards Hungarians abroad.[27]

Notes

1   On Kádárite foreign policy generally: Mihály Fülöp and Péter Sipos, *Magyarország külpolitikája a XX. században* [Hungary's Foreign Policy in the 20th Century] (Budapest, 1998); Csaba Békés, *Európából Európába. Magyarországi konfliktusok kereszttüzében 1945–1990* [From Europe to Europe. Hungary in the Crossfire of Conflicts 1945–1990] (Budapest, 2004), pp. 237–256. On Kádárite policy on Hungarian minorities: Lajos Arday, "Magyarok a szomszédos államokban – külpolitikánk változása" [Hungarians in the Neighboring Countries – Changes in Our Foreign Policy], in Bálint Balla, ed., *Sztálinizmus és desztálinizáció Magyarországon. Felszámoltuk-e a szovjet rendszert?* [Stalinism and De-Stalinization in Hungary. Did We Wind Up the Soviet System?] (Bern, 1990), pp. 177–202; György Földes, *Magyarország, Románia és a nemzeti kérdés 1956–1989* [Hungary, Romania and the National Question 1956–1989] (Budapest, 2007); Pál Pritz, "Magyarország helye a 20. századi Európában" [Hungary's Place in 20th-Century Europe],

in Pál Pritz, Balázs Sipos and Miklós Zeidler, eds., *Magyarország helye a 20. századi Európában* [Hungary's Place in 20th-Century Europe] (Budapest, 2002), pp. 27–56. On inter-Hungarian relations: Ignác Romsics, "Nemzet és állam a modern magyar történelemben" [Nation and State in Modern Hungarian History], in Pritz, Sipos and Zeidler, eds., *Magyarország helye*, pp. 7–26; Nándor Bárdi, *Tény és való. A budapesti kormányzatok és a határon túli magyarok kapcsolattörténete. Problémakatalógus* [True Fact. Budapest Governments and the History of Their Contacts with Hungarians Abroad. Catalogue of Problems] (Pozsony, 2004), pp. 90–100.

2   Békés, *Európából Európába*, p. 238.

3   Béla Pomogáts, "Illyés Gyula 'válasza'. A magyar kisebbség védelmében 1977–1978" [Gyula Illyés's "Reply". In Defense of the Hungarian Minority 1977–1978], *História* (1997) 9–10: 56–60; Lajos Für, *Kisebbség és tudomány* [Minority and Science] (Budapest, 1989); Péter Dippold and Gyula Balla, *A szomszéd országok magyarságának ügye a magyarországi független (szamizdat) kiadványokban* [The Case of Neighboring Hungarian Communities in Samizdats from Hungary], Ms. Országos Széchenyi Könyvtár Kézirattára (former TLA collection: 371/87); "Nemzetiségi irodalom válogatott bibliográfiája" [Selected Bibliography of Minority Literature], *Magyar Kisebbség* (1995) 1: 114–117 [1922–1952]; (1995) 2: 218–222 [1953–1963]; (1996) 1–2: 356–259 [1964–1968]; (1996) 3: 205–208 [1969–1971]; (2002) 1: 339–342 [1990].

4   Árpád Popély, ed., *Iratok a csehszlovákiai magyarság 1948–1956 közötti történetéhez* [Documents on the 1948–1956 History of the Czechoslovakian Hungarians] (Somorja, 2008); József Kiss, "A csehszlovákiai magyar kisebbség helyzete a cseh–szlovák viszony keretei között (1948–1960)" [The Position of the Czechoslovakian Hungarian Minority within the Frames of Czech–Slovak Relations (1948–1960)], *Fórum* (2003) 3: 3–24.

5   *Magyar Népi Szövetség.*

6   Mihály Fülöp and Gábor Vincze, eds., *Vasfüggöny keleten. Iratok a magyar–román kapcsolatokról (1948–1955)* [The Iron Curtain in the East. Documents on Hungarian–Romanian Relations (1948–1955)] (Debrecen, 2007), pp. 22–23.

7   *Ibid.*, pp. 31–37.

8   Fülöp and Sipos, *Magyarország külpolitikája, pp.* 377–379.

9   Arday, "Magyarok a szomszédos államokban," p. 198.

10   Stefano Bottoni, "Románia," in Csaba Békés, ed., *Evolúció és revolúció. Magyarország és a nemzetközi politika 1956-ban* [Evolution and Revolution. Hungary and International Politics in 1956] (Budapest, 2007), pp. 155–177; István Janek, "Csehszlovákia," in Békés, ed., *Evolúció és revolúció*, pp. 178–204; Edita Ivaničková and Attila Simon, eds., *Maďarská revolúcia 1956 a Slovensko. Az 1956-os magyar forradalom és Szlovákia* [The 1956 Hungarian Revolution and Slovakia] (Šamorín/Bratislava, 2006); Stefano Bottoni, Márton László, Klára Lázok and Zoltán Novák, eds., *Az 1956-os forradalom és a romániai magyarság (1956–1959)* [The 1956 Hungarian Revolution and Romania's Hungarians] (Csíkszereda, 2006).

11   "Kádár János pohárköszöntője Marosvásárhelyen a MAT párt és néptanácsi vezetői által adott díszebéden, 1958. február 25." [János Kádár's Toast in Târgu Mureş on a Ceremonial Lunch Given by the Leaders of the Party and People's Councils of MAT, February 25, 1958], *Népszabadság*, February 26, 1958; Andrea Varga and Gábor Vincze, "Kállai Gyula nemhivatalos látogatása Bukarestben 1959 nyarán" [Gyula Kállai's Unofficial Visit to Bucharest in the Summer of 1959], *Magyar Kisebbség* (1999) 1: 89–92.

12   Gábor Vincze, *A romániai magyar kisebbség történeti kronológiája* [Historical Chronology of the Romanian Hungarian Minority], at http://vincze.adatbank.transindex.ro/index. php?action=ev&ev=1960. Entry for December 22, 1960. Accessed June 10, 2010; Árpád Popély, *A (cseh)szlovákiai magyarság történeti kronológiája 1944–1992* [Historical Chronology of the (Czecho)Slovak Hungarian Community 1944–1992] (Somorja, 2006). Entry for April 9 at http://www.forumhist.sk/index. php?p=kronologia&t=a&xp=&w=&Data_Id=&syear=1960 &MId=&Lev=&Ind=8&P=index,hu,#top. Accessed June 10, 2010; Balázs Dobos, "Kisebbség-politika és kisebbségpolitikai intézményrendszer Magyarországon 1948–1993 között" [Minority Policy and Institutional System in Hungary 1948–1993], *Regio* 18 (2007) 3: 147–172.

13   Miklós Szabó, "Magyar nemzettudat problémák a huszadik század második felében" [Problems of Hungarian National Awareness in the Second Half of the Twentieth Century], in Idem, *Politikai kultúra Magyarországon 1896–1986. Válogatott tanulmányok* [Political Culture in Hungary 1896–1986. Selected Studies] (Budapest, 1989), pp. 225–251.

14   Melinda Kalmár, *Ennivaló és hozomány. A kora kádárizmus ideológiája* [Food and Dowry. The Ideology of Early Kádárism] (Budapest, 1998), pp. 244–253.

15   On the main nation debates in the 1960s and 1970s, see Iván Zoltán Dénes, "Önrendelkezés, nemzet, nacionalizmus. Egy értelmezés kontextusai" [Self-Determination, Nation, Nationalism. Contexts of an Interpretation], *Regio* 13 (2002) 4: 58–78.

16   *Élet és Irodalom*, May 18, 1968. This was denied by the Hungarian writers abroad and was discussed at the Debrecen Days of Literature in 1990. A summary: "A romániai magyar irodalom 1970–1990" [Hungarian Literature in Romania 1970–1990], *Látó* (1991) 2–3; notably Vilmos Ágoston, "A levágott kéz felelőssége" [Responsibility of the Severed Hand], *Látó* (1991) 3: 347–356.

17   Meeting of the HSWP CC Agitation and Propaganda Committee, August 5, 1969. Magyar Országos Levéltár 288. f. 41. cs. 121. őe.

18   "A szocialista hazafiság és a proletár internacionalizmus időszerű kérdései" [Current Issues of Socialist Patriotism and Proletarian Internationalism], *Társadalmi Szemle* (1974) 10: 32–47.

19   Rudolf Joó, "Az ENSZ és a nemzeti kisebbségek védelme" [The UN and National Minority Protection], *Külpolitika* (1976) 4: 60–73.

20   "Kádár János beszéde a Helsinki Konferencián, a Záróokmány aláírása alkalmából, 1975. augusztus" [Address to the Closing Session of the Conference on Security and Cooperation in Europe, August 1975], in János Kádár, *A szocializmus megújulása Magyarországon. Válogatott beszédek és cikkek 1957–1986* [Renewal of Socialism in Hungary. Selected Speeches and Interviews 1957–1986] (Budapest, 1985), pp. 379–382. As Kádár put it, "The most ardent desire of all European peoples is peace. If possible, this is even truer of the Hungarian people, whose home was for centuries at the crossroads of campaigning armies and who had to make enormous sacrifices to survive and protect their state against the threat of destruction. In this century, after the useless sacrifices of the First World War, the territory of vanquished Hungary was reduced to one third of what it had been..." (p. 379). The HSWP CC discussed "policy affecting the Hungarian community in the neighboring socialist countries" on December 20, 1976, and then revised the report: Magyar Országos Levéltár 288. fond. 5. csop. 707. őe. 29-48 f.

21   Those whose work focused on the people (*nép*) of the countryside and their perceived Hungarian qualities.

22 *Erdélyi Magyar Hírügynökség; Magyar Emberi Jogok Alapítvány.*
    Gyula Illyés, *Hajszálgyökerek* [Fine Roots] (Budapest, 1971); Gyula
    Illyés, *Szellem és erőszak* [Spirit and Violence] (Budapest, 1978);
    Gyula Illyés, "Előszó" [Foreword], in Kálmán Janics, *A hontalanság
    évei* [Years of Statelessness] (Bern/München, 1979); statements to
    foreign papers: *Die Presse*, January 13, 1978; *The Times*, May 8,
    1978; *International Herald Tribune*, August 27, 1979. A bibliography
    of publications on Hungary's illegal publications: Dippold and Balla,
    A szomszéd országok magyarságának ügye. A new edition of the
    Romanian illegal publications: Károly Antal Tóth, ed., *Ellenpontok*
    [Counterpoints] (Csíkszereda, 2000). On the rights movements
    of the Czechoslovakian Hungarian minority: Miklós Duray, ed.,
    *Kettős elnyomásban. A csehszlovákiai magyar kisebbség társadalmi
    jogvédelmének tíz éve (1978–1988)* [Under Double Oppression.
    Ten Years of Social Protection of Rights of the Czechoslovakian
    Hungarian Minority] (Pozsony, 1994); *A magyar kisebbségek
    nemzetközi érdekvédelmének dokumentumtára 1976-tól* [Documents
    on International Protection of Hungarian Minorities since 1976], at
    http://www.hhrf.org/dokumentumtar/. Accessed May 25, 2009.
23 Generation groups and initiatives seen as dissident: Nándor Bárdi,
    "Generation Groups in the History of Hungarian Minority Elites],
    Regio 16 (2005): 109–124. Open conflict with official Hungary broke
    out over Sándor Csoóri's anti-regime foreword to Miklós Duray,
    Kutyaszorító [In a Tight Spot] (New York, 1982). János Hajdú
    reacted in "Utószó egy előszóhoz" [Afterword to a Foreword], *Élet
    és Irodalom*, September 16, 1983.
24 Gábor Vince, "Lăncrăjantól Lăncrăjanig. Fejezet a magyar–román
    kapcsolatok nyolcvanas évekbeli történetéből" [From Lăncrăjan
    to Lăncrăjan. Chapters from the History of 1980s Hungarian–
    Romanian Relations], *Magyar Kisebbség* (2006) 3–4: 263–352. More
    on harassment of the *Ellenpontok* group: János Molnár, *Az egyetlen.
    Az Ellenpontok és az ellenpontosok története* [One and Only. The
    Story of *Ellenpontok* and Their Supporters] (Szeged, 1993). On July
    23, 1984, a so-called Duray Committee formed in Budapest, which
    called in its first briefing on everyone to press for Duray's release.
    See http://www.duray.sk/index.php?option=com_content&task=view
    &id=235&Itemid=2. Accessed May 20, 2009.
25 The text in English: http://mek.niif.hu/02100/02109/html/308.
    html#309.

26   Documents and reactions at the time: Csaba Tabajdi, ed., *Mérleg es számvetés. A magyarságpolitikai rendszerváltás kezdete* [Balance and Account. The Beginning of the Change of System in Policy towards Hungarian Communities] (Budapest, 2001). Summarizing the foreign policy outlook in the party: Mátyás Szűrös, *Magyarországról – külpolitikáról* [On Hungary – on Foreign Policy] (Budapest, 1989), pp. 70–72. Background for this was obtained from four meetings of the HSWP CC Agitation and Propaganda Committee in 1987 to review the position of the neighboring Hungarian minorities region by region.

27   Róbert Győri-Szabó, *Kisebbségpolitikai rendszerváltás Magyarországon. A Nemzeti és Etnikai Kisebbségi Kollégium és Titkárság történetének tükrében (1989–1990)* [Change of the Minority Policy System in Hungary. History of the College of National and Ethnic Minorities (1989–1990)] (Budapest, 1998).

3. DEMOGRAPHIC FEATURES
Patrik Tátrai

The communist takeovers in East-Central Europe came shortly after the Treaty of Paris had reinstated Hungary's post-Trianon borders (with a small adjustment in favor of Czechoslovakia). For the many Hungarians living as a minority, this marked the end of a post-war campaign of collective vengeance, reprisals and exiles. The first post-war censuses of 1948–1951, taken in an atmosphere antagonistic towards minorities, recorded 2.4 million people outside Hungary whose head of household declared them Hungarian. Wartime fatalities, the extermination of Hungarian-speaking Jews, mass post-war flights of population, and other events such as re-Slovakization, population exchange and deportations had reduced the aggregate number by almost a million people.

The number of Hungarians rose again as times became more peaceful. This was due not only to demographic factors, but also to the return of prisoners of war and deportees. The rise in the absolute number continued until the early 1980s, with strong regional differences of course, amounting to about 450,000 over thirty years, but the proportion of Hungarians in the population had fallen. In the last decade of communist rule, absolute numbers of Hungarians decreased everywhere except in Slovakia and Burgenland, as did the population of Hungary itself. By about 1990, the number of Hungarians in neighboring countries was down to some 2.7 million.

The main factors influencing the demography of these Hungarians were their status as a minority and the area in which they dwelt. Both strongly affected their rates of natural increase and of migration.

The post-war rate of natural increase among Hungarians in all neighboring countries was below the rate of the population as a whole.

Up to 1961, births exceeded deaths among Hungarians in all the four largest communities (of Slovakia, Transcarpathia, Transylvania and Vojvodina), but this was reversed, first in Vojvodina and then in Transylvania, producing a natural decrease. In Croatia, Prekmurje and Burgenland, the number of Hungarians had been stagnating or falling ever since Trianon. This can be explained in terms of their small numbers, and also, especially in Slavonia and Burgenland, by their scattered settlement pattern.

The demographic data in Slovakia show that the rate of natural increase remained positive until the end of the communist period, even among Hungarians, mainly because of high birth rates in Žitný ostrov. The highest figures, recorded in the 1950s, were followed by a steady fall that became drastic in the mid-1980s. Like Žitný ostrov, Medzibodrožie in southeastern Slovakia also had high rates of natural increase, but aging and decline were and are long-established trends in the Levice and Veľký Krtíš districts.[1]

Traditionally the rate of natural increase in Transcarpathia was high, as it was throughout the northeast of the Carpathian Basin. Data by ethnic group are lacking, but the mainly rural Hungarians certainly maintained a positive rate of increase until the change of system, although the 1989 census showed a decrease in absolute numbers, explainable by assimilation and by migration to Hungary in the 1980s.

The Hungarian inhabitants of Transylvania, like the population of Hungary, stopped increasing in the early 1980s, although the rate of natural increase stayed positive in the Székely counties until the turn of the millennium. Natural increase did not turn into decrease in northwestern Romania (Satu Mare and Sălaj Counties) until 10–15 years later than in the rest of Transylvania.[2] So the loss of some 100,000 Hungarians from the province between 1977 and 1992 was probably due mainly to emigration. Only 63,427 Hungarians left the country legally in that period, but it is thought that there were about 30,000 illegal departures.[3]

At the opposite extreme to the high fertility of northwestern and northeastern Transylvania is the low family size in the Banat, where the indigenous Swabian (German) custom of only children was soon adopted by Hungarians and Romanians as well. These demographically unfavorable figures spread across the frontiers to the southeastern corner of Hungary and much of Vojvodina.

It follows from this that the Vojvodina Hungarians have shown some of the worst population data (birth rate, death rate) for decades. Their numbers have been eroded by natural decrease since 1969.[4] This has been exacerbated since the 1960s by migration abroad, mainly of people of productive age, which accelerated the aging further.

Only Yugoslavia became a large exporter of labor in the 1960s. The policy of closed borders in Czechoslovakia, the Soviet Union and Romania up to the 1980s meant that migration was mainly internal and due to "socialist" urbanization offering jobs and better living conditions. The main goal of this urban development was a process of modernization that drew vast numbers of people from the countryside into the cities, through a forced rate of industrialization (especially in heavy industry) that soaked up the spare rural labor. This coincided with agricultural collectivization in the 1950s and early 1960s, as larger-scale farming made smaller labor demands.[5] Spatial mobility was accompanied by social mobility, which in turn increased the number of ethnically mixed marriages and the rate of assimilation, especially in urban areas. Characteristic of the period was monocentric development based on county and district capitals. Romania was unusual in having closed cities (such as Târgu Mureș), where only the favored (usually from the majority nation) could settle. Urbanization in the neighboring countries also served the implicit purpose of altering the prevailing ethnic structure.

Except in Slovakia and Austria, the Hungarians were overrepresented in urban areas at the beginning of the period, compared with the majority nation. This was changed by the processes just described. The Hungarian minorities with the highest level of urbanization in 1990 were in Vojvodina and Transylvania (58.7 and 56.1 percent respectively). In other regions the proportion of Hungarians in urban areas fell far short of that of the total population (Prekmurje 15.9 percent, Croatia 35.8 percent, Transcarpathia 37.7 percent, Slovakia 39.5 percent).

Urban development in Slovakia was focused on the two big centers of Bratislava and Košice, but in general development was almost wholly in Slovak-inhabited areas or along the language border. The cities in the latter (Nové Zámky, Levice, Lučenec, Rimavská Sobota and Rožňava) were targets of Slovak colonization. The Hungarians lost their majority there in the post-war years,[6] and although large numbers of Hungarians also moved there from the 1960s onwards, this did not greatly increase their proportion. Meanwhile, growing numbers of Hungarians also moved to Slovak-inhabited cities, where communities of a few hundred were rapidly assimilated. The same applied to migrants to the more developed Czech regions.

The main targets of migration in Transcarpathia were cities on the language border that had once had Hungarian majorities (Uzhgorod and Mukachevo) and the old county capital (Beregovo) which lay in the Hungarian-speaking area. These urban areas were within commuting distance of Hungarian-speaking villages along the Hungarian border, and the area retained its ethnic homogeneity, but the number and proportion of Hungarians in urban areas stayed low except in Beregovo and Chop. The Hungarian community increased by only 10,000 in 1959–1989, due to simultaneous emigration to Hungary and Soviet destinations outside Transcarpathia (in the case of relatively skilled labor).[7]

Urban development was greater in Romania than it was in other socialist countries. Transylvania's urban inhabitants, a little over 1.1 million in 1948, had increased fourfold by 1992. Their proportion rose from 19 percent to 57 percent. The increase, fastest in the 1950s and 1960s, typically took the form of directed internal migration, whereby an estimated 800,000 ethnic Romanians arrived in Transylvania from beyond the Carpathians, most of them (80 percent) settling in Southern Transylvanian cities. Meanwhile far fewer – an estimated 250,000 – migrated across the Carpathians from Transylvania. One geographical feature of the development is a divide between Northern and Southern Transylvania. The south developed a greater concentration of industry (the Jiu Valley, the Karaş–Severin industrial area, and the Braşov–Sibiu–Deva–Timişoara axis) that attracted settlers to a greater extent, while in Northern Transylvania the fastest population growths were in the county capitals, with the industrial center Baia Mare prominent.[8]

Ethnic politics can be seen behind urban development in Vojvodina as well. Novi Sad, close to Belgrade, was chosen for the provincial capital. Rapid development there has been matched in Zrenjanin and in the Belgrade satellite town of Pančevo, both lying in Serb-inhabited areas. Meanwhile the population of Subotica, where Hungarians are still in a majority, is about the same as it was between the world wars. However, it was not the urbanization in Vojvodina that lay behind the drastic change in ethnic structure. The decisive factor was emigration, in which the Hungarians were overrepresented. The effect of the concurrent immigration from less developed republics (Macedonia and Montenegro) was not primarily on Hungarian-inhabited areas.

The main post-war alterations in spatial ethnic structure occurred in the cities. Meanwhile, the rural Hungarian-speaking territory shrank in size only in certain areas, mostly where attempts were made to intrude settler villages into it during the land reform.

Deportations and population exchange in Slovakia pushed the language border southward from Levice. There were marked advances by the Slovaks around Košice, southward from Trebišov, and in the Nitra district. Efforts were made to break up the bloc of Hungarian habitation by founding settler villages on the Danubian Plain (Podunajská Rovina). Cities such as Senec, Galanta, Šaľa, Nové Zámky, Levice, Lučenec, Rimavská Sobota, Rožňava and Košice still had Hungarian majorities in 1941, but had Slovak majorities by about 1950.[9] These changes tended to blur what had been a sharp Hungarian–Slovak ethnic divide, turning a Hungarian-inhabited bloc into one of mixed population. Around 1990, the Hungarians still formed an absolute majority in twelve cities and a plurality in one, Moldava na Bodvou, where the Slovaks have since become a majority.

In the rural areas of Transcarpathia, there has been substantial change only in the parts that belonged to the Hungarian county of Ugocsa (the Vinogradovo district), where the Greek Catholic community, with its dual identity, tended to declare themselves Ukrainian after the change of system. Of the cities, Uzhgorod and Mukachevo underwent a rapid change in ethnic structure due to the deportations and high immigration by Ukrainians and Russians. The Hungarians also lost their majority in Vinogradovo and Tyachevo, but retained it in Beregovo and Chop. At the time of the collapse of the Soviet Union, the vast majority of Hungarians were still living in a relatively homogeneous bloc along the plains bordering Hungary.[10]

In terms of ethnic topology, Transylvania differs greatly from the regions mentioned so far, as the Hungarian community is less compact. There are two major blocs (the Székely Land and the areas along the borders of north Bihor, Satu Mare and Sălaj with Hungary) separated by a zone of sporadic Hungarian settlement in isolated groups of villages (such as Țara Călatei). Transylvania's larger cities have sizable Hungarian communities, but they make up only 10–25 percent of the inhabitants. In Satu Mare County there is a mounting German identity among Hungarian-speaking Swabians, while throughout the province there has been a tendency for the Hungarian-speaking Gypsies to see themselves as distinct.[11]

Of all Hungarian-speaking regions, the contraction has been greatest in the area between the Székely Land and the Partium, especially the Banat and Câmpia Transilvaniei. The best measure of how scattered the community is can be derived from a comparison of the figures for native language and national affiliation. Unfavorable assimilation processes can be assumed to be at work in areas where the latter exceeds the former. The native-language figures are strongest in the bloc of Hungarian-inhabited territory that consists of Covasna, Harghita, Mureş, Sălaj, Satu Mare and Bihor Counties. (A native-language majority is typical of all the Hungarian communities in neighboring countries except those of Croatia and, since the Yugoslav wars, Vojvodina.)

The forced industrialization and urbanization in Romania began in the 1950s to decrease the Hungarian proportion of the urban population, and the Romanians became the majority in the large cities. (This happened successively in Baia Mare, Cluj-Napoca, Oradea, Satu Mare and Târgu Mureş.) About 1990, 13 cities in the Székely Land still had a Hungarian majority (of which Târgu Mureş has since gained a Romanian majority), but only four with a Hungarian majority and one with a Hungarian plurality elsewhere: Salonta, Valea lui Mihai, Carei and Cehu Silvaniei. The Romanians have since become a majority in Marghita.

During the socialist period in Vojvodina, western Bačka and the middle and south of the Banat were the districts where the rural Hungarian ethnic territory shrank fastest. Novi Sad, as the provincial capital, soon became Serbianized and the proportion of Hungarians sank below 10 percent. Much ground was lost in other cities as well, such as Temerin. Around 1990, the Hungarian ethnic territory extended over northern Bačka and the northern part of the Banat, from the border down to Temerin in the south. Except in the bloc along the River Tisa, the break-up was accelerating. According to the 1990 census, Hungarians still made up a local majority in nine cities of Vojvodina, but only a plurality in Subotica.

The processes of urbanization and migration in Croatia, Slovenia and Austria affected the Hungarian community only to a moderate extent. In Croatia, the only places to retain their Hungarian complexion were the villages of the Drava Triangle (Baranja) by the Danube and a couple of places in Slavonia, but the majority of Hungarians in Croatia live as a local minority. The Hungarian-inhabited villages along the border in Prekmurje have rising numbers of Slovene inhabitants, but the Hungarians are still in a majority in most of them. The only two places in Austria with a Hungarian majority, Unterwart and Siget in der Wart, are both in southern Burgenland, whereas the more recent, post-1956 immigrants have mainly settled in the economically more prosperous northern Burgenland, with the result that the spatial concentration of the Hungarians has continued to decline (see Table 1).

Table 1. Proportion (%) and number of ethnic Hungarians in neighboring regions[12]

	Slovakia	Transcarpathia	Transylvania	Vojvodina	Croatia	Prekmurje	Burgenland
1941	21.5	27.3	29.5	28.5	1.5	20.1	3.5
	761,434	233,840	1,744,179	473,241	71,400	16,852	10,442
1950	10.3	17.4	25.7	25.8	1.4	10.8	1.9
	354,532	139,700	1,481,903	428,932	51,399	10,246	5,251
1960	12.4	15.9	25.1	23.9	1.0	11.0	1.9
	518,782	146,247	1,558,254	442,561	42,347	9,899	5,033
1970	12.2	14.4	23.8	21.7	0.8	10.0	0.5
	552,006	151,949	1,597,438	423,866	35,488	9,082	1,491
1980	11.2	13.7	22.5	18.9	0.6	9.3	1.5
	559,801	158,446	1,691,048	385,356	25,439	8,617	4,147
1990	10.7	12.5	20.8	16.9	0.5	8.5	2.5
	567,296	155,711	1,603,923	339,491	22,355	7,637	6,763

Notes

1 László Gyurgyík, *Magyar mérleg. A szlovákiai magyarság a népszámlálási és a népmozgalmi adatok tükrében* [Hungarian Balance Sheet. Slovakia's Hungarians in the Light of Census and Migration Data] (Pozsony, 1994), pp. 72–78.

2 Valér Veres, "A romániai magyarság természetes népmozgalma európai kontextusban, 1992–2002 között" [National Population Movements of Romania's Hungarians in a European Context, 1992–2002], in Tamás Kiss, ed., *Népesedési folyamatok az ezredfordulón Erdélyben* [Demographic Processes at the Turn of the Millennium in Transylvania] (Kolozsvár, 2004), pp. 41–42.

3 Árpád E. Varga, *Fejezetek a jelenkori Erdély népesedéstörténetéből. Tanulmányok* [Chapters from the Population History of Present-Day Transylvania. Studies] (Budapest, 1998), pp. 242–248.

4 Károly Mirnics, *Kisebbségi sors* [Minority Destiny] (Újvidék, 1993), p. 25.

5 József Benedek, "Urban Policy and Urbanisation in the Transition Romania," *Romanian Review of Regional Studies*, 2 (2006) 1: 51–64.

6 László Szarka, "A városi magyar népesség számának alakulása a Magyarországgal szomszédos országokban (1910–2000)" [The Trend in Urban Hungarian Population in Countries Neighboring Hungary], *Kisebbségkutatás* 10 (2001) 4: 57–67.

7 Károly Kocsis, Zsolt Botlík and Patrik Tátrai: *Etnikai térfolyamatok a Kárpát-medence határainkon túli régióiban (1989–2002)* [Ethnic Spatial Processes in the Regions of the Carpathian Basin outside Hungary (1989–2002)] (Budapest, 2006), pp. 60–61.

8 Károly Kocsis, *Erdély etnikai térképe – Harta etnică a Transilvaniei – Ethnic Map of Transylvania 1992* (Budapest, 1997).

9 Károly Kocsis and Eszter Kocsis-Hodosi, *Ethnic Geography of the Hungarian Minorities in the Carpathian Basin* (Budapest, 1998).

10 *Ibid.*

11 Varga, *Fejezetek a jelenkori Erdély népesedéstörténetéből*, p. 266.

12 Károly Kocsis, "Magyar kisebbségek a Kárpát-medencében" [Hungarian Minorities in the Carpathian Basin], in Zoltán Bihari, ed., *Magyarok a világban. Kárpát-medence* [Hungarians in the World. The Carpathian Basin] (Budapest, 2000), p. 16.

4. COLLECTIVIZATION AND RURAL CHANGE

Nándor Bárdi and *Márton László*

The communist accession to power in all Central European countries except Austria began a process of social and economic transformation according to the Soviet system of central planning and absolute state control. The nationalization of banking, industry and commerce left the peasantry in the rural areas as the largest stratum by far of private owners working independently of the state. Official state socialist ideology ordained that the agrarian revolution should occur in two stages: land reform (redistribution to eliminate feudal inequalities), then collectivization. The Communist Party leaders of all these countries except Yugoslavia hesitated to begin the latter for fear of encountering strong resistance and endangering food supplies. The Soviet Union, however, wanted to speed up the transformation of Central and Eastern Europe, as a response to the Cold War and in the interest of homogenization. So COMINFORM[1] at its meeting in June 1948 bowed to Soviet pressure and issued a resolution calling for collectivization to begin. The process in most countries took over ten years and was spread over three stages, in 1948–1952, 1953–1956, and 1957–1962.[2]

The aim of collectivization was to gain party state control over as much rural private property as possible. It was also designed to break the economic power and social status of the kulaks or rich peasantry, as the land reform had that of the large-scale landowners. For the relative prosperity and better farming methods of the kulaks gave them a social and cultural leadership in rural society that the Communist Party sought for itself. The resistance to collectivization, assumed to be kulak-led, was to be broken and the poor and landless peasantry ostensibly empowered like the urban proletariat.[3] In other words, collectivization was part of a process of institutionalizing the party state and imposing its authority. In some minority areas such as Slovakia and Transylvania, land reform and collectivization further weakened the relative social position of the Hungarian ethnic group, which was more strongly represented in the landowning class and rich peasantry than in society as a whole.

The collectivization process included eliminating the institutions of economic and social autonomy in the village (such as village magistrates), while commandeering others for propaganda purposes (such as peasant circles). Collectivization also covered the assets of earlier forms of communal property (common forest and farmland, vineyard associations), which were abolished. This mimicked the earlier elimination of civil and voluntary society in the cities, to further social homogenization. It included most bodies that served to foster awareness among the minority Hungarians.

Traditional rural society in most Hungarian-inhabited areas in the later 1940s was economically stratified, but diligence and sound farming could earn social respect. Sons of such richer peasants could be sent to urban schools to qualify for rural professional positions: schoolteachers, priests, or village notaries. The elimination of this peasant elite altered the traditional paths of social mobility and leader recruitment in the countryside. Leading positions in villages and collective farms in the 1950s went to landless or poor peasants who were loyal to the new regime but lacked standing in their communities.

The huge numbers of young people whom collectivization left without land or work had to move to urban areas, where forced industrialization had caused a chronic shortage of labor. This reduced the rural population and steadily modified its age structure, while weakening the cohesive traditions and customs of rural society. Also weakened was the principle that "land marries land." The 1960s brought erosion of the three-generation social and economic model, at various speeds in various countries. Public education was mixed with ideological propaganda, not least against the Churches, whose assets had already been confiscated, so that the traditional values of rural life broke down. Church-related customs died down or died out, for instance in Roman Catholic villages the Good

Friday processions, the blessing of the wheat, and beating of the parish bounds. Centrally directed pursuits played an increasingly important role in rural popular culture.

In Romania, the March 1945 land reform act ordered the expropriation of the lands of those who had fled the country or were "absentees." This affected the Hungarian community badly. There was relatively little land in Northern Transylvania to redistribute among some 100,000 applicants, but about 80 percent of it was Hungarian-owned. The ethnic proportions in the Székely Land were little affected, as most of the applicants were Hungarian too, but redistribution weakened the community considerably in areas where the Hungarians were not in a majority. The members of the local land distribution committees had a direct interest in maximizing the redistribution, as they too were applicants.[4]

In April 1946, the two Hungarian cooperative centers[5] complained at a joint congress that the government backing for the cooperative movement had all gone to the Romanian cooperatives, while Hungarian cooperatives were being intimidated in some parts of the country. The government plan was to subordinate the Hungarian movement to the Romanian one by obliging Hungarian cooperatives to join the Romanian county centers to gain access to goods. Then in June 1947, the national cooperative movement ordered that 57 out of the 537 mainly consumer cooperatives were to be wound up. Hungarian members of the national movement were supposed to retain their independence after joining and be able to supply villages with cheap consumer durables and credit, but in addition they had to submit to a purge of officers in the name of "internal democratization."[6]

Similarly important was the restoration of the legal status and assets of the Ciuc Private Properties[7] (over 60,000 *hold* – 34,200 hectares – of forest and significant holdings of real estate and factories), but this was done in a way that prevented them from becoming the independently managed property of the Ciuc County villages. They were renationalized in 1948 and distributed to several state-owned enterprises.[8]

Collectivization in Romania proceeded in four phases. In the first, full-scale collective farms were set up forcibly in 1949–1953, but they met strong nationwide resistance. The process was not forcibly continued in 1954–1955, but attempts were made to form looser associations. In 1956–1957, collectivization reemerged in political rhetoric as an expectation, and forcible methods of organizing the peasants into cooperatives resumed in the summer of 1958.[9] By April 1962, 94 percent of the agricultural land was farmed collectively by cooperatives or state farms (in other words state-owned enterprises). Peasant holdings in Romania averaged less than 10 hectares in area and had very little equipment. Some 76 percent of the population still lived in rural areas in 1948.[10]

One weapon used in 1949 to force peasants to collectivize was a system of fixed depressed prices far lower than market prices. The compulsory deliveries at these prices, coupled with various taxes and levies, expropriation of equipment and land, and discriminatory financial regulations, kept rural society in fear and under great pressure. There was persecution of those on the kulak lists, including deportation and imprisonment, that affected almost 170,000 peasants in 1949–1953. Collective farms paid lower rents to machinery depots, received preferential state loans, sold produce at higher prices, and had access to consumer durables. They also enjoyed two tax-free years with a 20 percent cut in delivery obligations. Yet only 8.2 percent of farmland in 1953 belonged to the "socialist" sector, including the 300 state farms.

The looser associations of the next phase meant that members did not have to make over their land. They just worked it communally and received tax concessions. Often such associations existed only formally as a defense against discrimination. Other concessions were also made. The targets of the five-year economic plan were halved in 1953 and consumer rationing ceased in 1954. At the end of 1956, the system of forced deliveries of crops, fodder and milk was replaced by purchasing. Furthermore, collective farms, associations, and those tilling less than one hectare of land were exempted from meat delivery quotas. However, all Soviet bloc countries except Poland resumed forced collectivization after a meeting of Communist Party delegations in Moscow in November 1957. This coincided in Romania with hardening of the political system in 1958–1959, involving violence labeled as class struggle, backed by security police methods. As a result, 94 percent of Romania's farmland belonged to the "socialist" sector by April 1962.[11]

The process had few features specific to one ethnic nation or another, but the superior local institutionalization of Hungarian villages and the many commonly owned estates in the Székely Land may have been extra sources of conflict. But the Hungarian regions, unlike several Romanian-inhabited counties, saw no open rebellion. Other methods were used. According to historian Sándor Oláh, the method of survival consisted of unofficially retrieving property rights, recording false data, simulating ignorance, postponement and passiveness, shifting the burden onto other institutions and persons, holding back performance, theft, building up networks of cooperation and mutual assistance, and denying obligations. What was needed to prevent collectivization turning into national conflict was that the state and the party at local levels be represented by ethnic Hungarians. So the elimination of private ownership and the political and economic control over the district all took place in Hungarian language.[12]

In Czechoslovakia, there were close links between land reform and denial of rights and deportation of minorities. A presidential decree of June 21, 1945, placed all agricultural holdings over 50 hectares and all forest holdings over 100 hectares in state hands. Most expropriated land belonged to indigenous Germans and Hungarians. It was redistributed solely to Slav applicants. By October 1946, 293,000 hectares had been seized in Slovakia: 108,000 from Hungarians, 56,000 from Germans, 33,000 from Hungarian and German firms, and 95,000 from "traitors and enemies to the Slovak nation."[13]

Expropriation of estates over 50 hectares was also decreed by the land reform act of the spring of 1945. However, most of the estates concerned were not redistributed, but incorporated into the state farms and agricultural cooperatives that were being formed. There were some 900,000 producers in Slovakia in 1946, of which 35,000 had holdings of 20–50 hectares. Tax obligations and delivery quotas that were almost impossible to meet, coupled with the stigma of the kulak lists, meant that these farmers were keen to hand over their estates to a state farm or cooperative as fast as possible. The formation of cooperatives began in Slovakia in September 1948. A few weeks later, redistribution of land seized from Hungarians stopped and organization of cooperatives began in Hungarian-inhabited villages as well, mainly with Slovak leaders. According to Slovak Communist Party ideology at that time, the Slovak peasantry had been squeezed out of the southern lands for centuries and it was time for them to get their own back. The population exchange sent most of Slovakia's Hungarian medium-scale and large-scale peasant farmers to Hungary, or in some cases the Czech lands. They made way for repatriating Slovaks or the landless from the north of the country, but the newcomers lacked the requisite equipment and in some cases basic farming skills. These groups were won over to collectivization more easily than those who were told to hand over to Slovak or Hungarian small-scale peasants the farmland and forest that they had bought or inherited themselves.[14]

Recruiting Hungarians into cooperatives was a prime task for the newly organized CSEMADOK. For this purpose János Kugler, a Hungarian, was appointed as head of the Agriculture Department of the Slovak Communist Party Central Committee and editor of a new Hungarian-language farming daily called *Szabad Földmüves* [Free Cultivator]. In April 1950, CSEMADOK head Gyula Lőrincz took the campaign against bourgeois nationalism so far as to discern Hungarian nationalism in the ethnic basis on which Hungarian cooperatives were run.[15]

From 1951, agricultural cooperative members were granted plots of land of half a hectare each, but organization was still slow. The gradualism (four types of cooperative introduced successively) and the voluntary principle were just a formality. When the pressure was relieved somewhat in 1953–1954, there were withdrawals on a mass scale in eastern Slovakia, and in the southern, Hungarian-inhabited, districts two thirds of the cooperatives collapsed. This can be ascribed not only to social resistance, but also to lack of state support and agricultural expertise. Collectivization picked up again in 1957–1958. By 1960, 88 percent of the agricultural land in Slovakia belonged to the "socialist" sector. Later came mergers (after the Soviet pattern) that produced massive collective farms covering several settlements.[16]

The Slovaks who settled in Hungarian villages after the population exchange and deportations to the Czech lands included the new leaders of the cooperatives. Their ignorance of local conditions, the lack of state funding, and the passive survival tactics of locals meant that production failed to reach even wartime levels. Rural living standards dropped in the early 1950s. The other big change was the ensuing mechanization of farming, which led to a mounting surplus of labor. This affected as much as a third of the Hungarian population, and led to migration to the cities: to the mining and industrial centers of the Czech lands and to Bratislava. Long-distance daily or weekly commuting became common.[17]

The end of the war of liberation in Yugoslavia was followed in July 1945 by a freeze on sales or transfers of land, and a month later by legislation on land reform and resettlement. The maximum award was to be 20 hectares. Land expropriated from indigenous Germans and from "enemies of the people" – a category interpreted to include many Vojvodina Hungarians – went in a Colonization Land Fund. Another 500,000 *hold* (285,000 hectares) were set aside for certain settler categories, notably veterans of the Yugoslav People's Army. A quarter of the confiscated land came from deported Germans and the great landowners. The colonization program brought into Vojvodina 50,000 Serbian families, numbering about 250,000 people. Such settlers from other parts of the country were assigned about 33 percent of the land; 26 percent went to state farms. One difference from the 1921 land reform was that some landless Hungarian peasants also benefited. About 670,000 hectares of land – 45 percent of the farmland in the province – was seized from about 90,000 owners.[18]

The Yugoslav Communist Party was the first in the region to launch a collectivization campaign in 1946. By the end of the year, 20,012 farms had joined 248 cooperatives. The number reached 730 in 1951, then began to decline. The proportion of cultivated land still in private ownership was 41.7 percent in Vojvodina, 91 percent in the rest of Serbia, and 77 percent in Yugoslavia as a whole.[19]

This eventually unsuccessful campaign was backed from 1946 by a system of compulsory deliveries explained on a propaganda level by the need to supply the cities. In practice huge demands were made of a chosen two or three dozen richer peasants in each village, with confiscation and prison awaiting those who failed to meet their quota. Altogether 2,295 persons in Vojvodina received such sentences in 1946–1950, yielding 21,500 hectares of land for transfer to the cooperatives. This bankrupted the homestead economy, as unoccupied buildings were rapidly stripped. The peasants of Hungarian-inhabited areas were overrepresented as victims, compared with the Serbian-inhabited Srem region of Vojvodina. The March 1951 amnesty came as a huge relief: remaining prison sentences were waived and total expropriation of land replaced by a partial one.[20]

The fact that the Yugoslav leadership, at odds with the Soviet Union and its satellites after 1948, was unable to collectivize the country's agriculture was recognized officially in March 1953, and the cooperatives (to a large extent in Vojvodina) were disbanded. Two months later the maximum landholding was reduced from 20 to 10 hectares, and a further 102,000 hectares of confiscated land was transferred to the agricultural combines (state farms). The state promised compensation in 30 installments spread over 30 years, but it was never paid.[21]

The rationalization of land boundaries that ensued in the 1960s and 1970s was intended to group smaller holdings into one or two tracts. In practice the boundary commissions showed a preference for large-scale farms, granting them huge tracts of more fertile land. Peasants with larger holdings were also at an advantage if they were contracted to supply large agricultural concerns. Peasants who farmed smaller holdings were generally given a single tract of poorer land at some distance from the settlement. By 1978, boundary adjustment had affected a quarter of the arable land in Vojvodina. The agricultural combines also gained an advantage from the prior rights of land purchase that they enjoyed until the later 1980s.[22]

About one third of the Hungarian households in Vojvodina were farming individually at the end of the 1980s, but half the farming households combined it with commuting to work. The number of small holdings in northern Bačka, mainly inhabited by Hungarians, rose continually to around 100,000. This was influenced to some extent by a 1988 amendment to the federal constitution raising the maximum holding size from 10 hectares to 30. A change of outlook towards the villages and peasantry appeared in the "green plan" financed from foreign loans, which offered preferential credit for mechanizing private farms and introducing livestock farming.

The Hungarians in Transcarpathia, the Transcarpathian *oblast* of the Ukrainian SSR in the Soviet Union, largely occupied the most valuable land along the River Tisa. At the end of the 1960s, 66 percent of the population was living in villages, but the proportion engaged in agriculture was much lower, as sizeable numbers commuted to the chemical, precision engineering and other works of Uzhgorod, the engineering and timber-processing factories of Mukachevo, the brick, furniture and canning factories of Beregovo, the rail transshipment depots of Chop and Bat'ovo,[23] or seasonal work further north.

It was May 1946 before the return began of the Transcarpathian Hungarians aged 18–50 who had been sent to forced labor after the war. By that time the local Communist Party apparatus was compiling kulak lists, collecting compulsory state loans, and imposing delivery quotas. The least resistance was punished by forced labor in the Donets Basin.[24]

The first *kolkhoz* was set up at Eseny in 1945 with scant equipment. By 1947, 68,500 *hold* (39,000 hectares) had been taken from Church and secular estates and redistributed. As grants were made, "land communities" and "production groups" were set up – 630 of them by 1947. By 1948, the number of *kolkhoz* had risen from 27 to 188. A year later the regular *kolkhoz* numbered 478 and collectivization was over. Subsequent mergers left 168 *kolkhoz* and 16 state farms in the *oblast* in 1968.[25] The most important agricultural concerns were in the Hungarian-inhabited areas in the 1960s. Each *kolkhoz* covered three or four villages. The Beregovo district had 14 *kolkhoz* and three state farms (two for vineyards and one for stockbreeding). About 10 percent of the 90,000 hectares were vineyards or orchards. The two foremost *kolkhoz* were the Lenin in the Beregovo district and the Border Guard in Vinogradovo.[26]

By the 1980s, peasants from Velyka Dobron' were growing early produce under plastic sheeting and selling it in city markets, for, despite the collectivization, crops grown on household land still made a big contribution to family income. Most land was used as orchards, vineyards or vegetable plots. The supply difficulties in the Soviet Union meant that the rural population still met many of its own needs until the end of the 1980s.[27]

Notes

1   COMINFORM (the Information Bureau of Communist and Workers' Parties) was founded in September 1947 to orchestrate opposition to the US Marshall Aid plans. Although mainly a channel for Soviet instructions to other parties, it also let them gingerly coordinate views or even hint at reluctance. It was dissolved in 1956 in a gesture to Yugoslavia.

2   The main treatments: Nikola Gaćeša, *Agrarna reforma i kolonizacija u Jugoslaviji 1945–1948* [Agrarian Reform and Colonization in Yugoslavia 1945–1948] (Novi Sad, 1984); Samuel Cambel, *Päťdesiate roky na slovenskej dedine. Najťažšie roky kolektivizácie* [Fifty Years in the Slovak Village. The Hardest Years of Collectivization] (Prešov, 2005).

3   The Kádár regime imposed by the Soviets in November 1956 was named the Hungarian Revolutionary Worker-Peasant Government (Magyar Forradalmi Munkás-Paraszt Kormány), as a sign of the

importance attached to the peasantry. Point 10 of its program was "To develop agricultural production, abolish compulsory deliveries and grant aid to individual farmers," but collectivization was resumed in 1959.

4   Gábor Vincze, "Az 1945-ös földreform: magyar föld román kézen" [The 1945 Land Reform. Hungarian Land in Romanian Hands], in Idem, *Illúziók és csalódások. Fejezetek a romániai magyarság második világháború utáni történetéből* [Illusions and Disillusionments. Chapters in the Post-War History of Romania's Hungarians] (Miercurea-Ciuc, 1999), pp. 151–170.

5   The cooperative centers *Kaláka* ["Community Work"] and *Szövetség* ["Alliance"] covered 1,200 Hungarian cooperatives in Romania.

6   Gábor Vincze, "A magyar szövetkezetek küzdelme önállóságuk megvédéséért" [The Hungarian Cooperatives' Struggle to Retain Independence], in Idem, *Illúziók és csalódások*, pp. 171–186.

7   *Csíki Magánjavak.* They arose from a grant made by Joseph II in 1783 to fund border regiments. They contributed much to regional economic development in the late nineteenth century but were nationalized by Romania in 1923. See http://hdl.handle.net/2437/88075. Accessed June 28, 2010.

8   Ágoston Olti, "A csíki magánjavak a második világháború után" [Ciuc Private Properties after World War II], in Nándor Bárdi, ed., *Autonóm Magyarok? Székelyföld változása az "ötvenes" években* [Autonomous Hungarians? Change of Székelyföld [Székely Land] in the 1950s] (Csíkszereda, 2005), pp. 84–111.

9   Cooperatives in the Soviet bloc bore a formal resemblance to Western cooperatives, but in effect membership was compulsory and there was no collective control over assets. Members elected officers by endorsing a single candidate picked by the communists. See János Kornai, *The Socialist System. The Political Economy of Communism* (Princeton, NJ, 1992), pp. 76–83.

10 D. Cătănuş and O. Roske, *Colectivizarea agricultirii în România* [Agricultural Collectivization in Romania] (Bucharest, 1990); Dorin Dobrincu and Constantin Iordachi, eds., *Ţărănimea şi puterea. Procesul de colectivizare a agriculturii în România (1949–1962)* [Peasantry and Power. The Process of Collectivization of Agriculture in Romania (1949–1962)] (Iaşi, 2005).

11 Sándor Oláh, *Csendes csatatér. Kollektivizálás és túlélési stratégiák a két Homoród mentén (1949–1962)* [Silent Battlefield.

Collectivization and Survival Strategies by the Two Homorod Rivers (1949–1962)] (Csíkszereda, 2001), pp. 9–28.

12 *Ibid.*, pp. 199–257.

13 Árpád Popély, *A (cseh)szlovákiai magyarság történeti kronológiája 1944–1992* [Historical Chronology of the (Czecho)Slovakian Hungarian Community 1944–1992] (Somorja, 2006), pp. 65 and 111.

14 László Pukkai, *Mátyusföld I. A Galántai járás társadalmi és gazdasági változásai 1945–2000* [Matušova zem I. Social and Economic Change in Okres Galanta 1945–2000] (Komárom/Dunaszerdahely, 2002), pp. 115–117.

15 Popély, *A (cseh)szlovákiai magyarság*, pp. 178–179.

16 Sándor Gál, *Szociográfiák* [Sociographical Accounts] (Pozsony, 2004), pp. 199–200.

17 *Ibid.*, pp. 256–281.

18 István Ternovácz, *Pusztulj, kulák! Parasztsanyargatás a Vajdaságban* [Perish, Kulak! Oppression of the Peasantry in Vojvodina] (Budapest, 1996), pp. 7–8. Somewhat different but more detailed figures on the land transfers appear in Enikő A. Sajti, *Hungarians in the Voivodina 1918–1947* (Boulder, CO/Highland Lakes, NJ, 2003), pp. 473–479.

19 Lajos Arday, "Magyarok a szerb–jugoszláv Vajdaságban, 1944–1989" [Hungarians in Serbo-Yugoslav Vojvodina, 1944–1989], in Lajos Arday, *Magyarok a Délvidéken, Jugoszláviában* [Hungarians in the Southern Region and Yugoslavia] (Budapest, 2002), pp. 225–226.

20 Ternovácz, *Pusztulj, kulák!*, pp. 8–12.

21 *Ibid., p. 12.*

22 Arday, "Magyarok a szerb–jugoszláv Vajdaságban," pp. 226–227; Ternovácz, *Pusztulj, kulák!*, pp. 14–16.

23 Freight was transferred between broad-gauge (1,520 mm) Soviet stock and standard-gauge (1,435 mm) stock from Hungary and elsewhere.

24 Kálmán Móricz, *Nagydobrony* (Beregszász/Budapest, 1995), pp. 68–69.

25 András S. Benedek, *A gens fidelissima: a ruszinok* [The Gens Fidelissima: The Ruthenes] (Budapest, 2003), p. 68; *Istorija gorodov i sel Ukrainskoj SSR* (Kyiv, 1982), p. 69; I. N. Grozdova, "Etnokulturális folyamatok napjainkban a kárpátaljai magyar lakosság körében" [Ethno-Cultural Processes Today among the Hungarian Inhabitants of Transcarpathia], in Gyula Ortutay, ed.,

Népi kultúra – népi társadalom [Folk Culture – Folk Society], V–VI (Budapest, 1971), pp. 457–466.

26   József Botlik and György Dupka, eds., *Ez hát a hon Tények, adatok, dokumentumok a kárpátaljai magyarság életéből 1918–1991* [So This Is Our Land... Facts, Data, Documents on the Life of Hungarians in Transcarpathia 1918–1991] (Budapest/Szeged, 1991), pp. 76–77.

27   Móricz, *Nagydobrony*, pp. 71–72.

5. THE EDUCATION QUESTION
Csilla Fedinec

It became urgent in February 1948 for Czechoslovakia to settle its relations with Hungary, as a new period of Stalinist single-party dictatorship and membership of the socialist camp opened.[1] So the reintroduction of Hungarian-language teaching gained exceptional symbolic significance. In the autumn of 1948, Slovak-taught schools opened parallel Hungarian classes, but two years later, separate Hungarian schools opened as well. Much was done to further them by the Cultural Association of Hungarian Workers of Czechoslovakia (CSEMADOK) and by the Communist Party of Slovakia Central Committee's Hungarian Committee. The result was a broad system of schools that taught in Hungarian in the early 1950s: almost 600 elementary schools, and by the 1960s, also 22 Hungarian gymnasia (high schools).

The position of the minorities was affected by the Prague Spring of 1968, for the Slovak demands for greater autonomy fed Slovak nationalism, but the leadership stood firm on minority rights legislation and called for proposals from the minority organizations. The memorandum that CSEMADOK compiled in March 1968 included a demand for an autonomous Hungarian school system. This process was halted and indeed reversed by the Soviet-led invasion by the Warsaw Pact countries in the autumn.

The period of normalization under Gustav Husák brought several attacks on the educational and language-use rights of the Hungarian minority. Hungarian-language teachers' training was run down, and the number of Hungarian gymnasia was reduced to 18 at the turn of the 1980s, while mergers of Hungarian elementary schools had reduced their numbers by half by 1989. There was an attempt to reduce the use of Hungarian in schools. Several Hungarian middle schools changed to teaching certain subjects in Slovak. In the second half of the 1970s, elements in the Slovak government drew up a plan to allow Hungarian-taught education to wither away, which led to the formation of a Hungarian dissident movement in Slovakia. The Legal Defense Committee of the Czechoslovakian Hungarian Minority[2] was founded to draw public attention to the minority's grievances and to use what means it could to combat them. The leading figure was the young Bratislava intellectual Miklós Duray.

Higher education in Hungarian was provided in the Hungarian language and literature teachers' training faculty at Comenius University in Bratislava and in the teachers' training program at the University of Nitra.

The Hungarian-taught school system in Transcarpathia, ceded to the Soviet Union in 1945, continued uninterrupted.[3] Hungarian-taught lower elementary education in 1944–1945 was extended in the following year to the eight years of elementary school. The Moldavian schools also counted as minority schools, as did one school teaching in Slovak that closed after a year, but for almost twenty years, the Ministry of Education of the Ukrainian Soviet Socialist Republic preferred to refer to such schools obliquely as "non-Ukrainian- and non-Russian-taught schools."

The first minority middle schools, four Hungarian and four Moldavian, opened in 1953–1954. Thereafter the number of Hungarian-taught middle schools continued to rise, but the overall number of Hungarian-taught schools remained between 90 and 100. That year, classes that were taught in Russian or Ukrainian were opened for Hungarian children, in an effort to increase the effectiveness of Russian teaching, already a compulsory subject. In 1966–1967, a quarter of all Hungarian-taught schools included such parallel classes. By 1989 there remained 50 schools teaching solely in Hungarian.

Hungarian teachers' training began in 1947 in Khust and 1950 in Mukachevo, as did a faculty of Hungarian language and literature at Uzhgorod State University in 1963, but all three taught only specialist subjects in Hungarian, and so Hungarian-taught education effectively ended with high school. There were no official

Hungarian kindergartens, but Hungarian would have been used by nursery teachers in Hungarian-inhabited villages.

The Soviet system established over about twenty years the conditions for native-language schooling, but thereafter there was no development, but rather in fact something of a retreat at the end of the 1980s. The textbooks came from an office of the state textbook publishing enterprise in Uzhgorod, as they do today. These, apart from those for Hungarian language and literature, are translations of the officially set Russian or Ukrainian textbooks. The first textbook for Hungarian literature was written by the Hungarian writer Antal Hidas, who lived in Moscow, and appeared in 1950. Later textbooks were penned by teachers, writers and editors in Transcarpathia. These literature books provided the only available information for schools on Hungarian history, as this was not taught at all before 1989. They also included (in Hungarian) information on Ukrainian literature, but Russian literature was taught separately. In Hungarian literature, the emphasis was on the Moscow émigré writers (Máté Zalka, Béla Illés, Sándor Gergely and others), while a quarter concerned the "outstanding figure in the world revolutionary movement" Sándor Petőfi. There was hardly a mention of any Hungarian writing after World War II.

Educational autonomy was won by the Hungarians of Romania under the Groza government of 1945–1948, which was friendly towards them,[4] but this changed with the nationalization of education. The education act of August 3, 1948, applied the Soviet model to Romania's whole education system. Some Hungarian middle schools closed, but for higher education the years 1948–1950 marked a peak, with native-language teaching at Bolyai University, the separate Hungarian Arts Institute, and the agricultural and technical colleges in Cluj-Napoca, as well as a new Hungarian medical university in Târgu Mureş.

The Hungarian-taught system of education began to shrink in the 1950s. First Hungarian-taught engineering courses ceased, and then a party and government resolution in 1956 called for the Romanizing of minority elementary and middle schools.

Finally, in March 1959, Bolyai University was subsumed into Babeş University. The medical school in Tărgu Mureş closed in 1962. By the mid-1960s, the Hungarian-taught options remaining were the Protestant and Roman Catholic theological colleges and the Tărgu Mureş Drama College. Native-language vocational training also ceased and most Hungarian middle schools had a mixture of Hungarian- and Romanian-taught classes. There was still some teaching in Hungarian in the Hungarian, philosophy and history faculties at Babeş University.

Some educational grievances were redressed under the influence of the 1968 events in Czechoslovakia. Some middle schools returned to teaching only in Hungarian in 1968–1971. Hungarian-taught classes or departments were started at a handful of vocational secondary schools.

But Act 273 of May 13, 1973, discriminated directly against minority elementary schools in stipulating that 25 pupils were necessary to start a fifth-grade class and 36 for a secondary school class, whereas in every place where schools working in languages of "cohabiting national communities" existed, Romanian-taught departments or classes had to be provided irrespective of the number of pupils requiring them. So a rising proportion of Hungarian elementary and secondary students had to study in Romanian.

In the 1980s it became the practice to send newly qualified Hungarian teachers to Romanian-speaking districts. The mid-1980s marked a low point in Hungarian education in Romania. Separate Hungarian middle schools closed and Hungarians hardly won any places in higher education. It seemed that a truncated society was developing, with no intelligentsia of its own.

In Yugoslavia[5] minority schools were allowed to open in August 1945, right after the post-war executions and deportations that the Hungarians had suffered. The message was that they could expect to gain their minority rights "despite their crimes," but only from the new communist regime, not via separate minority bodies or support from the parent country. Yet most Hungarian elementary and middle school teachers were deported or fled the country. The acute shortage could be eased only with crash courses for untrained replacements. Attendances at Hungarian-taught primary schools reached a post-war peak in the mid-1950s and then declined steadily – by 35 percent between 1966 and 1986. The contributing factors included the ageing and dwindling of the minority and the opening of bilingual (or more rarely trilingual) schools. The number of teaching staff, on the other hand, rose rapidly until the mid-1970s before beginning to fall slowly, so that pupil/teacher ratios and school standards were high. By the early 1960s there were chances also for those not studying in Hungarian to improve their language abilities. Initially, the backbone of the middle school system consisted of classic gymnasia – six such schools were teaching in Hungarian in the early 1950s. However, mergers between schools teaching in different languages soon followed, concealed behind a "fraternity – unity" slogan. The Serbo-Croat- and Hungarian-taught schools were combined into school centers in 1956. The 1975 education reform replaced the classic gymnasia by "two-plus-two" middle schools – two years of academic education plus two of vocational training. This meant that middle schools could open in larger villages that had never had one, but it led to a decline in quality. By the end of the 1980s, only 63.8 percent of Hungarian-taught middle school graduates continued their studies. The forced spread of vocational training was abandoned in favor of standard four-year (ninth to twelfth grade) middle schools. Despite some advantages, the bilingual system had the drawback of assisting in the assimilation of the minority.

One big advance in higher education was the foundation of Novi Sad University in 1954, followed by a Hungarian faculty in 1959 and an Institute of Hungarian Studies in 1968. Several other colleges and university departments began to teach in Hungarian: the Novi Sad Academy of Drama in 1972, and a Hungarian-taught department at Maribor in 1966, followed by a department of Hungarian language and literature in 1980. Hungarian training of infants' school teachers began in Novi Sad at secondary level in 1952 and rose to college level in 1973. Hungarian teachers were trained from 1945 onwards in Subotica, where the college taught in Hungarian for a decade before turning bilingual. College-level teachers' training commenced in Novi Sad in 1946 and moved to Subotica in 1978, where teachers of mathematics, physics, chemistry, Hungarian and Serbo-Croat were trained. From 1973 there was uniform (elementary and secondary) teachers' training in Hungarian that included education, psychology, sociology, methodology, Marxism-Leninism and civil defense. Wider self-management under the 1974 Constitution gave greater powers to minority provincial and local management of education, for instance through the Vojvodina Education Council.[6] It became possible to give more emphasis to Hungarian language, history, music and art. The progress ended with the wave of Serbian nationalism at the beginning of the 1980s and the fragmentation of the country during the Yugoslav wars.

Notes

1   Béla László, "A (cseh)szlovákiai oktatásügy szerkezete, valamint közigazgatási és jogi keretei 1945 után" [The Structure of the (Czecho)Slovak Educational System, and Its Administrative and Legal Framework after 1945], in László Tóth, ed., *A (cseh)szlovákiai magyar művelődés története 1918–1998* [History of (Czecho)Slovak Hungarian Culture 1918–1998]. Vol. II. (Budapest, 1998)

2   *Csehszlovákiai Magyar Kisebbség Jogvédő Bizottsága.*

3   Csilla Fedinec, *Fejezetek a kárpátaljai magyar közoktatás történetéből (1938–1991)* [Chapters from the History of Transcarpathian Hungarian Education (1938–1991)] (Budapest, 1999); Csilla Fedinec, "Nemzetiségi iskolahálózat és magyaroktatás Kárpátalján" [Minority Schools and Hungarian Education in Transcarpathia], *Fórum Társadalomtudományi Szemle* (2001) 1: 63–82; Károly D. Balla, *A hontalanság metaforái* [Metaphors of Statelessness] (Budapest, 2000), pp. 22 and 59–60; Kálmán Soós, "Magyar tudományos élet Kárpátalján" [Hungarian Scientific Activity in Transcarpathia], *Magyar Tudomány* (1993) 5: 635–638; Lajos Sipos, ed., *Iskolaszerkezet és irodalomtanítás a Kárpát-medencében* [School Structure and Literature Teaching in the Carpathian Basin] (Budapest, 2003).

4   László Murvai, *Fekete Fehér Könyv* [Black White Book] (Kolozsvár,
     1996); Gábor Vincze, "A romániai magyar kisebbség oktatásügye
     1944 és 1989 között" [Romanian Hungarian Minority Education
     between 1944 and 1989], in Idem, *Illúziók és csalódások. Fejezetek
     a romániai magyarság második világháború utáni történetéből*
     [Illusions and Disillusionments. Chapters in the Post-War
     History of the Romanian Hungarians] (Csíkszereda, 1999),
     pp. 187–224; Gábor Vincze, ed., *Történelmi kényszerpályák
     – kisebbségi reálpolitikák. Dokumentumok a romániai magyar
     kisebbség történetének tanulmányozásához* [Forced Paths of History
     – Minority Realpolitik. Documents for the Study of Romanian
     Hungarian Minority History], Vol. 2, 1944–1989 (Csíkszereda,
     2002), pp. 247–248.
5   Lajos Tóth, *Magyar nyelvű oktatás a Vajdaságban 1944-től
     napjainkig* [Hungarian-Language Education in Vojvodina from
     1944 to the Present Day] (Szabadka, 1995); Lajos Bence, "Egy
     elmulasztott lehetőség margójára (A kétnyelvű oktatás harminc éve
     Szlovéniában)" [In the Margin of a Lost Chance (Thirty Years of
     Bilingual Education in Slovenia)], in Sándor Győri-Nagy and Janka
     Kelemen, eds., *Kétnyelvűség a Kárpát-medencében* [Bilingualism
     in the Carpathian Basin], Vol. 2 (Budapest, 1992); Enikő A. Sajti,
     *Impériumváltások, revízió, kisebbségek. Magyarok a Délvidéken
     1918–1947* [Sovereignty Changes, Revision, Minorities. Hungarians
     in the Southern Region 1918–1947] (Budapest, 2004).
6   *Vajdaság Tanügyi Tanácsa.*

6. THE DEVELOPMENT OF CULTURAL, ARTISTIC AND SCIENTIFIC INSTITUTIONS

Tamás Gusztáv Filep

The socialist ideology of the post-war Soviet camp took a strong hold on culture. No end was served by parallel literary languages, or artistic trends or scientific schools that differed from official ones. Not even the term "minority" was acceptable, as all citizens were ostensibly equal in a socialist country. Although several minorities in East-Central European countries belonged to ethnic groups dominant in another country, socialist ideology attached no importance to this: they were severed automatically by the political borders. Defending the interests of Hungarians outside Hungary became the task of the party state under which they lived, to be carried out by ethnic Hungarian members of that party or other activists in Hungarian-inhabited areas. There were functions in political and cultural life only for those who accepted and conformed to the new order. The minorities were denied their historical and cultural traditions until the 1960s, when selected elements and fragments were restored as parts of a distorted "progressive tradition," significant only if seen as antecedents of the new order.[1]

The minority communities were shorn of their leaders. Many of the intelligentsia who had traditionally fulfilled that role had left. Educational and cultural institutions were nationalized and Churches were placed under tight control. Books, newspapers and periodicals conformed to the system and relied on state funds. Large numbers of cadres with a peasant or worker background were shot into professional, cultural and educational posts at the whim of the new elite. The bourgeoisie in an organized form vanished, along with the private sector that supported them. The cultural elite, hitherto open to influences from Western Europe, had to abide by the tenets of socialist realism, or at least its outward forms and expressions.[2] The exception was Yugoslavia, after the 1948 break with Moscow, where parallel cultural idioms and modernist literary trends appeared as early as the 1960s.[3]

Politics assigned to the arts and sciences a propaganda role, and gave a spurt of growth to mass culture for similar reasons. Such aims lay behind the Hungarian radio and television services set up in neighboring countries.[4] The broadcasting hours assigned them were often derisory, but they were part of the window-dressing, and at the same time opportunities for indigenous Hungarian intelligentsia to seize or even exploit.

There was a similar mechanism behind the movement of successive intellectual generations from the state's politicized system of education into the minority cultural institutions. Native-language higher education was confined to Hungarian departments of universities and to teachers' training, except in the first decade in Romania, when there were also Hungarian art and agricultural colleges, for instance. But on the whole the neighboring countries cut back such provisions. The statistics show a smaller proportion of Hungarians with a higher education (and in the professions for which such qualifications were required) than of the population as a whole. Minority education and culture were skewed towards the humanities and literature, which left the minority technical and scientific intelligentsia unable to contribute to their own culture.[5]

Cultural freedom varied among state-socialist countries, yet the most difficult situation was faced by the indigenous Hungarian minority of Burgenland in Austria, the one neighboring country with a democratic system (despite the Soviet military and political presence in the east of the country up to 1955). The Burgenland Hungarians were fragmented.[6] Their cultural activity was confined to the Churches, state Hungarian-taught elementary education, and voluntary local bodies, night schools, and basic literacy. Not until 1968 was there a Burgenland Hungarian Cultural Association, or until 1977 a Hungarian National Council (formed under the Act on Ethnic Groups). In the 1980s, the University of Vienna began some teaching in Hungarian, so that new schoolteachers could be trained.

In 1988, a Hungarian Institute was founded in Unterwart, mainly for research into community documents, as the product of a period during and after the Cold War when Burgenland Hungarians could make contact with Hungary again.[7]

By then there were institutions for minority research in several successor states. Yugoslavia had its Institute of Hungarian Studies, and an Institute for Ethnic Studies in Ljubljana, focusing on Slovenia's Italians and the small Hungarian population. In Romania there was a little group of minority researchers at the Nicolae Iorga Institute of History, Romanian Academy of Sciences in Bucharest, but it was disbanded in the 1980s. Czechoslovakia also had an Academy Institute in Košice.[8] The findings of such groups hardly registered with the Hungarian public, and the attitude of their founding authorities remained passive, as exemplified by dissipation of the initial interest in the Institute of Hungarian Studies. Private scholarly initiatives and efforts led to the formation of unaffiliated, in some cases illegal, groups, concerned more with defending than with researching their communities. Among the best known were the Czechoslovak Committee for Protection of the Rights of the Hungarian Minority,[9] and the *Limes* Circle formed in Bucharest in the later 1980s.[10] Efforts towards Hungarian cultural cohesion in Yugoslavia were made by the Hungarian Language Society of Vojvodina until it was banned in the early 1970s.[11] The most promising group of theorists were those who gathered round the Cluj-Napoca philosopher and essayist György Bretter at the turn of the 1960s and 1970s, but successive members left Romania after Bretter's death.[12] Ernő Gáll and József Aradi, as editors of the periodical *Korunk* in the 1980s, brought forward a number of younger social researchers.[13] The WAC-Center for Regional and Anthropological Research in Miercurea-Ciuc was a semi-legal organization, serving a purpose shared by the scientific theory circle in Sfântu Gheorghe.[14] The greatest number of results in minority research in all the neighboring countries was obtained in the fields of Hungarian literature and language, the history of narrower periods, some areas of cultural anthropology, and the institutional history of culture.[15]

Books in Hungarian reappeared in Czechoslovakia in 1949: the publishers Pravda produced a series in 1949–1952. The role was taken over in 1953 by another state publisher that was subsumed into a third in 1956 and continued as Tatran in 1963.[16] The Hungarian branch of that became the publisher Madách in 1969. Hungarian books appeared in Transcarpathia from Kárpáti and the textbook concern in Uzhgorod. The firm Józsa Béla Athenaeum operated in Romania from 1944 to 1948, when a state publishing enterprise was formed. This had a minority division from the outset and assumed the name Literary Publishing in 1960.[17] Others included Kriterion – expressly for minority publications and the main firm in the field throughout the period – and Hungarian sections at three other firms.[18] Three publishers produced Hungarian books in Vojvodina,[19] followed later by two others.[20] No books in Hungarian appeared in the Prekmurje district of Slovenia until 1961, when the task was taken up by the local Hungarian association.[21]

The range of newspapers and periodicals narrowed, especially the latter, where a single pattern prevailed. In Yugoslavia, the pre-war left-wing paper *Híd* resumed publication in 1945. There also appeared the periodical *Új Symposion*, which represented literary modernism and was of interest over the whole Hungarian-speaking area, although its influence was equivocal, and a couple of other journals with narrower readerships.[22] In Romania there was only a literary weekly initially, followed by two others in Târgu Mureş, and a lively weekly in Bucharest capable of discussing social and cultural issues.[23] Only in 1958 was it possible in Czechoslovakia to start a periodical resembling an almanac that grew into a review appearing ten times a year.[24] There was no Hungarian periodical in Transcarpathia during the Soviet period, although the *Kárpáti Kalendárium*[25] and various almanacs helped to substitute for this. The press palette in each country included an official Hungarian daily and other publications for children, youth, professions (law, natural history, politics), and the arts (Transcarpathia was poorest in this respect), but all were required to reflect official ideology. The language in science magazines was much criticized, often because

Hungarian expressions for concepts to do with subjects not directly linked to minority life were not widely known.[26]

Literature and literacy in a broader sense play a big part in minority life and in preserving identity. The greatest scope for this between the two world wars lay with the *népi* literary movements, which concentrated on the lives of rural people and were blended with the heritage of the labor movement. The *népi* writers of a socialist type gradually drew towards socialist realism, questioning the deeper national commitments of the working class. The other canon opposing this was modernism in literature, outstanding examples of which were able to address the century's overall problems of existence, although the mass of linguistic experimentation leading up to this drew the charge that its failure to consider communal problems counted as desertion in the face of the problems of destiny. The contradictory reception of this can be traced to the post-war elimination of the literary language variants and to the exclusion from culture of many of the layers of tradition. Contributions also came, of course, from the many contradictions to be found in mass culture.

The valuable literary works often described the restrictions on rights and freedoms, regardless of whether they slotted into existentialism, or the absurd, for example, or the trends dominant in Western Europe at the time, or whether they found their means of expression in the local milieu and subject matter. Furthermore, seemingly more abstract language often increased the permitted scope for expressing opinions on social matters.[27] Direct allusions to the minority situation often called for abstraction on grounds of censorship or self-censorship. Nor were they free of ambiguities and euphemisms. It should be noted that the life's work of some authors, built up over decades, can be fitted into one trend or another.[28]

How far acceptance in Hungary affected the creation of a minority canon is something on which research is only beginning. The reception in Hungary for one or two exceptional such writers played an important part in drawing the parent country's attention to minority literature.[29] General agreement developed in the 1970s and

1980s about the most valuable features of minority literature. Pride of place in Yugoslavia went to the works of Nándor Gion, who gave epic form to the history of the Southern Region Hungarians from the turn of the century to the early 1940s. Similar appreciation went to novels by László Dobos, Gyula Duba and others on the period of rights deprivation in Czechoslovakia from the end of the 1960s. More popular in Hungary at the time were the essays and historical plays of András Sütő, who opened a new stage in his career with an essay-novel on his home village and villagers entitled *My Mother Pledges Easy Dreams*.[30]

Hungarian theater abroad ranged from traveling players to bricks-and-mortar theaters with permanent companies. Full theater life was confined to Romania:[31] Timişoara, Oradea, Satu Mare, Cluj-Napoca, Târgu Mureş and Sfântu Gheorghe, as well as a Hungarian opera and puppet theater in Cluj-Napoca. Most of these survived through the communist period, despite some organizational changes – Hungarian and Romanian sections were often merged in the Ceauşescu period. Romania was also the only neighboring country that trained Hungarian actors and directors, at the István Szentgyörgyi Drama Institute,[32] founded in Târgu Mureş in 1948 from the drama section of the Arts Institute in Cluj-Napoca. A Romanian section was added in 1976. Annual colloquia of minority theaters in Romania began in 1978, based at the State Hungarian Theater in Sfântu Gheorghe. The Hungarian People's Theater[33] in Subotica, Yugoslavia, was founded in 1945, sharing its management from 1951 with the Croatian People's Theater. In Novi Sad there were amateur performances, and a number of public performances between 1953 and 1973 by the Hungarian drama department of Novi Sad Radio. This developed into the Novi Sad Theater founded in 1974 and later a separate company.[34] The Slovakian State Village Theater founded in 1950 had a Hungarian section that in 1952 became the Hungarian Regional Theater based in Komárno.[35] One gain from the Prague Spring was the Thália in Košice, which opened in 1969. Transcarpathia had only amateur drama in Hungarian, at Beregovo's People's Theater. Theater companies in all neighboring countries toured. Attempts were made to foster a modern dramatic idiom, notably by the Romanian theaters and those of Novi Sad and Košice. They often premiered local Hungarian drama, which flourished in the 1970s in Transylvania, and to some extent in the Southern Region. One great achievement of the period was the life's work of the Cluj-Napoca director György Harag.[36]

Czechoslovakia was the only neighboring country with a dedicated Hungarian cultural organization.[37] Apart from acting as a channel for ideological control, it organized and promoted commemorations, camps, and other regional and local events. In the other countries, the Hungarian institutions were not separate, but cultural events in majority Hungarian-speaking areas were held in Hungarian, with varying provisos.

Notes

1   See Stefano Bottoni, *Sztálin a székelyeknél. A Magyar Autonóm Tartomány története (1952–1960)* [Stalin among the Székelys. The History of the Hungarian Autonomous Region (1952–1960)] (Csíkszereda, 2008), pp. 128–134.

2   Two monographs on Romanian and Czechoslovakian Hungarian literature published at the time: Lajos Kántor and Gusztáv Láng, eds., *Romániai magyar irodalom 1944–1970 [Romanian Hungarian Literature 1944–1970], 2nd rev. ed.* (Bucharest, 1973); András Görömbei, *A csehszlovákiai magyar irodalom 1945–1980* [Czechoslovakian Hungarian Literature 1945–1980] (Budapest, 1982).

3   Imre Bori, *A jugoszláviai magyar irodalom története* [The History of Yugoslavian Hungarian Literature] (Újvidék/Belgrád, 1998), for instance.

4   Attila Z. Papp, *A romániai magyar sajtónyilvánosság a kilencvenes években. A működtetők világa* [Romanian Hungarian Press Publicity in the 1990s. The Realm of the Operators] (Csíkszereda, 2005), pp. 41–57; Tihamér Lacza, "A magyar sajtó Szlovákiában 1945 után" [The Hungarian Press in Slovakia after 1945], in Tamás Gusztáv Filep and László Tóth, eds., *A (cseh)szlovákiai magyar művelődés története 1918–1998. II. Oktatásügy–közművelődés–sajtó, rádió,*

televízió [The History of (Czecho)Slovakian Hungarian Education 1918–1998, Vol. 2: Education – Public Education – Press, Radio, Television] (Budapest, 1998), pp. 378–426.

5   An attempt to gauge the problem in a Czechoslovakian Hungarian context: Tihamér Lacza, "Műszaki és természettudományi értelmiségünk helyzete és szerepe" [State and Role of Our Technical Scientific Intelligentsia], in Idem, *Ember a szóban* [Man in Words] (Bratislava, 1985), pp. 41–53.

6   Many aspects of the various Hungarian groups in Burgenland are covered in the descriptive social study by István Szépfalusi, *Lássátok, halljátok egymást!* [See and Listen to Each Other] (Bern, 1980, 2nd ed. Budapest, 1992).

7   György Éger, "A burgenlandi magyarság. Vázlatos áttekintés" [The Burgenland Hungarians. An Outline], in Idem, *Regionalizmus, határok és kisebbségek Kelet-Közép-Európában* [Regionalism, Borders and Minorities in East-Central Europe] (Budapest, 2000), pp. 195–237.

8   Lajos Für, *Kisebbség és tudomány* [Minority and Science] (Budapest, 1989).

9   On its activity, see Miklós Duray, *Kettős elnyomásban. Dokumentumok a csehszlovákiai magyarság helyzetéről és jogvédelméről 1978–1989* [Double Pressure. Documents on the Situation and Legal Protection of the Czechoslovakian Hungarians 1978–1989] (Pozsony, 1993 [1989]).

10 See Gusztáv Molnár, ed., *A transzcendens remény. A Limes-kör dokumentumai 1985–1989* [Transcendent Hope. The *Limes* Circle Documents 1985–1989] (Csíkszereda, 2004).

11 *Vajdasági Magyar Nyelvművelő Egyesület.*

12 A recent selection with bibliography: György Bretter, *A felőrlődés logikája (Esszék, értelmezések, jegyzetek)* [The Logic of Pulverization. Essays, Interpretations, Notes], ed. László Tóth, intr. and bibliography Béla Mester (Budapest, 1998).

13 Ernő Gáll, *Napló I. 1977–1990* [Journal I. 1977–1990], ed. Éva Gáll and Dávid Gyula (Cluj-Napoca, 2003); Ernő Gáll, *Számvetés. Huszonhét év a* Korunk *szerkesztőségében* [Account. 27 Years in the *Korunk* Offices] (Kolozsvár, 1995).

14 *Kulturális Antropológiai Műhely.* Zoltán A. Biró, József Gagyi and János Péntek, *Néphagyományok új környezetben. Tanulmányok a folklorizmuskutatás köréből* [Folk Traditions in a New Context.

Studies in Folklore Research] (Bucharest, 1987); Zoltán Rostás, ed., *"Hát ide figyelj édes fiam..."* Esszék az ifjúságkutatás köréből ["Listen, Son." Essays in Youth Research] (Bukarest, 1989). A volume of work by the Sfântu Gheorghe group: Levente Salat, ed., *Tény és való. Tudományelméleti írások* [Fact. Writings of Scientific Theory] (Bukarest, 1989); Károly Veress, "A tudományelmélet sepsiszentgyörgyi műhelyéről" [The Sfântu Gheorghe Workshop of Scientific Theory], *Erdélyi Múzeum* (1999) 1–2: 132–142.

15   A concise account of Hungarian science and scholarship in Czechoslovakia, Romania and Yugoslavia at that time: Für, *Kisebbség és tudomány, pp.* 116–224.

16   *Pravda Kiadóvállalat; Csehszlovákiai Magyar Könyvkiadó; Szépirodalomi Könyvkiadó; Tatran Szlovák Szépirodalmi és Művészeti Könyvkiadó.*

17   *Állami Irodalmi és Művészeti Kiadó; Irodalmi Könyvkiadó.*

18   *A Kriterion műhelyében. Beszélgetések Domokos Gézával a Kriterion Könyvkiadóról* [In the Kriterion Studio. Talks with Géza Domokos on the Kriterion Publishing House], ed. Dénes Dálnoki Szabó [György Beke] (Budapest, 1988). The other firms: *Dacia; Ifjúsági* (from 1970 *Albatrosz*); *Pedagógiai és Didaktikai Kiadó.*

19   *Híd Könyvkiadó Vállalat* (1946–1949); *Testvériség–Egység Könyvkiadó* (1948–1959); *Minerva* (from 1954).

20   *Forum Könyvkiadó* (from 1957); *Tartományi Tankönyvkiadó Intézet* (1965–1994, issuing textbooks in five languages).

21   *Muravidéki Magyar Önigazgatási Érdekközösség* [Prekmurje Hungarian Self-Management Community], 1960–1980; *Magyar Nemzetiségi Művelődési Intézet* [Institution for Hungarian Nationality and Culture].

22   György Szerbhorváth, *Vajdasági lakoma. Az* Új Symposion *történetéről* [Vojvodina Feast. From the History of the *Új Symposion*] (Pozsony, 2005). The other journals: *Létünk; Üzenet.*

23   *Utunk* (1946); *Igaz Szó* (1953); the revived *Korunk* (1957); *A Hét* (1970).

24   *Irodalmi Szemle.*

25   A consideration of its role: Lajos Szakolczay, "A *Kárpáti Kalendárium* irodalmi mellékletei 1970–1973," in Idem, *Dunának, Oltnak* [For the Danube, for the Olt] (Budapest, 1984), pp. 165–172.

26   Examples analyzed in Czechoslovakian Hungarian papers: László Zeman, "Nyelvi tallózás a *Természet és Társadalom* lapjain"

[Language Gleanings from *Természet and Társadalom*], in István Jakab, ed., *Hogy is mondjuk? Nemzetiségi nyelvhasználatunk – nemzetiségi nyelvművelésünk* [How Do We Say It? Minority Idiom – Minority Language Use] (Pozsony, 1976), pp. 113–121.

27   Exemplified in studies of Romanian Hungarian works in Gusztáv Láng, *Látványok és szövegek. Tanulmányok és kritikák* [Sights and Texts. Studies and Reviews] (Miskolc, 2006).

28   Prominent writers of the time included Ádám Bodor, Gizella Hervay, Sándor Kányádi, József Méliusz, István Nagy, Géza Páskándi, András Sütő, János Székely, Domokos Szilágyi and Géza Szőcs in Romania, Károly Ács, Imre Bori, István Domonkos, Nándor Gion, Ferenc Fehér, János Herceg, István Koncz, Ottó Tolnai and László Végel in Yugoslavia, Gyula Duba, Sándor Gál, Lajos Grendel, Árpád Tőzsér and Zsigmond Zalabai in Czechoslovakia, and László Balla, Géza Fodor, Magda Füzesi, Vilmost Kovács, Zoltán Mihály Nagy and László Vári Fábián in the Soviet Union. A uniform summary of the period: András Görömbei, *Kisebbségi magyar irodalmak (1945–1990)* [Minority Hungarian Literatures (1945–1990)] (Debrecen, 1997)

29   An early, consistent exponent of this: Mihály Czine, *Nép és irodalom* [People and Literature], II (Budapest, 1981).

30   *Anyám könnyű álmot ígér.* Compendia of persons and institutions in minority literature: Edgár Balogh and Gyula Dávid, eds., *Romániai magyar irodalmi lexikon. Szépirodalom, közírás, tudományos irodalom, művelődés* [Romanian Hungarian Literary Dictionary. Literature, Journalism, Scientific Writing, Cultivation] I–V (Bukarest/Kolozsvár, 1981–2002); László Gerold, *Jugoszláviai magyar irodalmi lexikon (1918–2000)* [Yugoslavian Hungarian Literary Dictionary, 1918–2000] (Újvidék, 2001); Zoltán Fónod, ed., *A cseh/szlovákiai magyar irodalom lexikona 1918–2004* [Lexicon of Czech/Slovakian Hungarian Literature 1918–2004), 2nd rev. ed. (Pozsony, 2004).

31   An ample pocket dictionary of Romanian Hungarian theater: *Színjátszó személyek.* A Hét *évkönyve 1982* [Theater People. Yearbook of *A Hét*, 1982] (Bukarest 1982). More comprehensive: Sándor Enyedi, *Rivalda nélkül. A határon túli magyar színjátszás lexikona* [No Footlights. Encyclopedia of Hungarian Theater Abroad] (Budapest, 1999).

32   *Szentgyörgyi István Színművészeti Intézet.*

33   *Magyar Népszínház.*

34   See Zsuzsanna Franyó, ed., *Az újvidéki színház harminc éve* [Thirty Years of Novi Sad (Hungarian) Theater] (Újvidék, 2004).

35   *Magyar Területi Színház (MATESZ).*

36   István Náray, ed., *Harag György színháza* [György Harag's Theater] (Budapest, 1992).

37   *Csehszlovákiai Magyar Dolgozók Kultúregyesülete (CSEMADOK).* On this and the general picture, see László Tóth, "Köz–művelődés–történet. Szempontok és adatok a csehszlovákiai magyar (köz) művelődés lehetőségeihez és fejlődési irányaihoz 1945–1998 között" [Public–Culture–History. Scope and Development of Czechoslovakian Hungarian Culture and Public Education], in Idem, *Köz–művelődés–történet. Három tanulmány* [Public–Culture–History. Three Studies] (Budapest, 2000), pp. 220–324.

7. CASE STUDIES

Romania (*Stefano Bottoni* and *Csaba Zoltán Novák*)

The history of the Hungarian minority in 1945–1989 may be divided into five main periods, according to changes in domestic politics affecting them and to developments in the Romanian Communist Party's (PCR) minority policy. The years 1945–1947 can be seen as a transition: the communists needed Hungarian votes in Transylvania to combat the Romanian bourgeois parties, while the Paris peace negotiations called for a wholly different minority policy from the one before 1940. These changes were made through the Hungarian People's Alliance (MNSZ),[1] as a communist partner organization. Then in 1948–1956 came Stalinist-type integration of the Hungarians, followed in 1957–1965 by a period dominated by reprisals for the internal repercussions of the 1956 Hungarian Revolution. The Communist Party's minority policy in 1965–1971 was one of seeming liberalization. Then from 1971 up to 1989, especially in the mid-1970s, came the erection of Ceauşescu's totalitarian dictatorship. This national communism, stained with neo-Stalinism, was accompanied from 1983 by increasingly open conflict between the communist leaders of Romania and Hungary.[2]

Apart from the instauration of the socialist system, the biggest change for Hungarians in the post-war period was in the ethnic structure of the big Transylvanian cities,[3] with the disappearance of the Jews and Germans,[4] and the dismantling of the traditional Hungarian social and economic institutions.[5]

Under the communist regime, political integration of Romania's Hungarian community into the state structure involved various institutions. In the initial stage (1945–1948) it was undertaken by the aforementioned Hungarian People's Alliance, a minority organization that became in 1948, after the communist seizure of

397

power, a mere "conveyor belt" for the single-party state's instructions. In 1953 the organization was even encouraged to "dissolve itself."[6]

The Transylvanian Hungarians, with their own system of minority institutions, were affected more than the rest of the population by the economic, cultural and social changes introduced by the communist authorities. The party denied any need for collective rights and emphasized a policy of individual integration. Denominational schools felt victim to the education reform of 1948, ending a parallel system that had given relative autonomy to schools teaching in Hungarian. A total of 468 Catholic, 531 Reformed, 34 Unitarian and 8 Evangelical schools were nationalized with all their assets.[7]

A turning point for minority policy came in 1952, when Romania, on Soviet insistence, created a Hungarian Autonomous Region (RAM)[8] in the Székely Land, but at the same time, Hungarians in positions of authority outside the Hungarian Autonomous Region began to be systematically removed. The autonomous region reflected the Soviet Leninist principles of territorial federalism; according to the Soviet constitution, national minorities were granted areas in which to enjoy linguistic and cultural rights. The idea was mooted on September 7, 1951, by two Soviet advisers seconded to Romania, P. Arkhipov and P. Tumanov, in a memorandum addressed to General Secretary Gheorghe Gheorghiu-Dej, outlining two possible forms for the new region to take. One was to have covered about one fifth of Transylvania (the Székely Land and the Mezőség: Ținutul Secuiesc and Câmpia Transilvaniei), with about one million inhabitants and the city of Cluj as its seat. The other covered only the smaller, ethnically more homogeneous area of the Székely Land (the former Mureş-Turda, Ciuc, Odorheiu and Trei Scaune Counties). After long discussions the second was chosen, and the region's creation was confirmed by the new Constitution issued on September 21, 1952. According to the 1956 census, its 13,500 square kilometers contained 731,387 inhabitants, of whom 565,510 (77.3 percent) declared themselves to be of Hungarian ethnicity. In the regional capital Târgu Mureş (Marosvásárhely), a similar proportion of Hungarians

(74 percent) could be found. Hungarians also provided some 80 percent of the party leadership and public officials, including the Communist Party first secretary (Lajos Csupor), the president of the People's Council/Consiliul Popular (Pál Bugyi) and the provincial head of the Securitate or secret police (Mihály Kovács). These men, though, owed their first loyalty to the Romanian party state and did not pursue politics on a national basis.[9] "Autonomy" in this case did not mean self-determination: the Hungarian Autonomous Region was under the same tight control as the other Romanian provinces, and had to implement decisions taken by central authorities. The only substantive difference was that Hungarian could be used freely at all levels of administration, and several cultural institutions were founded in the 1950s in Târgu Mureş: the State Sekler Theatre, the István Szentgyörgyi Academy of Dramatic Art, the literary journal *Igaz Szó*, and the bi-weekly cultural paper *Új Élet*, followed in 1958 by a radio station broadcasting mainly in Hungarian.

The new direction that Romanian minority policy took in the aftermath of the 1956 Hungarian Revolution brought with it in 1958–1959 criticism of the region's ethnic Hungarian leaders. The main charge was of turning a blind eye to so-called "Hungarian nationalism." In the end the Parliament, on December 24, 1960, passed a constitutional amendment altering the region's boundaries. To be known henceforth as the Maros–Hungarian Autonomous Region[10] (RMAM), its territory and ethnic composition were substantially altered. Two Sekler districts were transferred to the Braşov region, and the districts of Sărmaş, Târnăveni and Luduş, with a Hungarian proportion of around 20 percent, were annexed to the Maros–Hungarian Autonomous Region, making it a larger region with about 800,000 inhabitants, of whom 61 percent were Hungarian and 35 percent Romanian.[11] A politically driven change of elite during 1961 replaced most of the Hungarian and Jewish functionaries with Romanian cadres.[12]

Although the Romanian authorities were forced by Soviet pressure into agreeing in 1952 to set up the Hungarian Autonomous Region, they made good use of it in subsequent years to justify pursuing homogenization in other parts of Transylvania, mainly in the cities, and refusing to recognize the minority's specific cultural and social heritage and needs. There was a similar intention behind the merger of Hungarian-taught educational institutions after 1956, ostensibly to end segregation, and behind the abolition in 1959 of the National Minority Committee within the Romanian Communist Party Central Committee. Classes taught in Romanian were added to Hungarian educational institutions at lower and higher levels. Mergers of schools in multi-ethnic communities resulted in parallel sections and classes, while Romanian-taught classes were introduced into hitherto Hungarian-taught schools. The direct outcome was a fall in enrolment in Hungarian-taught secondary education.[13]

As ideological pressures mounted after 1956, they were felt most forcefully by the minorities. The nationalist turn of Romanian communism was also reflected in new terminology referring to non-Romanian ethnic groups. In 1959, the term "national minority" and the previously frequent references to the "multinational" character of the Romanian state were ousted by a new definition, "the Romanian people and the cohabiting national groups." According to party ideologists, "national minority" implied forming a separate cultural nation. Nationhood would have given its members equal rank with the state-creating Romanian nation, despite their smaller numbers. The new formulation made it plain that the cohabitants were subordinate to a "master nation." Also designed to stress the primacy of the Romanian nation was the revived national dogma of Daco-Roman continuity: the formation of the Romanian nation was said to have occurred under the Roman Empire, so that the Romanians were also the sole indigenous ethnic group in Transylvania, joined there only in the Middle Ages by the conquering immigrant Hungarians and colonist Germans. This outlook was reflected in the first comprehensive history of Transylvania to appear since the war, under the auspices of the Romanian Academy.[14]

After Gheorghiu-Dej's death, the post of Communist Party general secretary went on March 22, 1965, to Nicolae Ceauşescu, whose foreign policy of moderate independence from the USSR was accompanied up to 1971 by a certain degree of intellectual liberalization. That not only reinforced Romanian nationalism, but also gave greater scope to Hungarian cultural institutions. The separate foreign policy road had started under the Dej leadership, which in 1964 rejected an economic plan for Romania (and Bulgaria) to serve as a granary for the Soviet bloc, and issued on April 27 a *Declaration of the Romanian Workers' Party's Position on Questions of the International Communist and Workers' Movement*, expressing the country's relative independence within the socialist camp.[15] This independent policy emerged strongly in 1968, when Romania refused to join in the Warsaw Pact's military intervention in Czechoslovakia, and denounced it as imperialist aggression. Later in the 1970s Ceauşescu developed this relatively autonomous foreign policy into a framework for the whole political system. While canvassing for public support, the party leaders in June 1968 held a meeting with prominent members of the ethnic Hungarian intelligentsia. Ceauşescu rejected a request for a minority statute, but progress was made on several other matters (new institutions, periodicals, language-use rights).[16] Hungarian-language TV broadcasts began, and in Bucharest a minority publishing house (Kriterion, headed by Géza Domokos) and a modern weekly cultural paper (*A Hét*) were started. On the other hand, the Maros–Hungarian Autonomous Region was abolished, due to a more general change in local government structure driving it back to the earlier county system. Although plans were issued for a "grand Székely county" covering the newly established Harghita, Covasna and Mureş Counties, ructions in the national and regional party leaderships led to a compromise. There would be no "grand Székely county," but the disputed districts of Târgu Secuiesc and Sfântu Gheorghe would not be transferred to Braşov County, leading to the creation of the country's smallest county, Covasna. With slight adjustments, the three counties of Harghita, Covasna and Mureş resulted from the old Hungarian Autonomous Region.[17] There was a strong Hungarian majority in the first two (85 percent in Harghita and 78.4 percent in Covasna, according to the 1977 census), but the proportion in the new Mureş County (the three districts of the Câmpia Transilvaniei – Sărmaş, Târnăveni and Luduş – plus Sighişoara district) was only 44.3 percent. That circumstance allowed central authorities to speed up the homogenization program that had started in the early 1960s in Mureş County, and especially in the city of Târgu Mureş. Cultural and political leadership within the Hungarian community of Transylvania moved from Cluj and Târgu Mureş to smaller Székely cities such as Sfântu Gheorghe and Miercurea-Ciuc.

Another development in 1968 was the formation within the Socialist Unity Front of a Council of Workers of Hungarian Nationality.[18] With no paid staff, offices or decision-making power, this body was granted some advisory capacity until about 1974, when it became merely a piece of window-dressing. Its members initially were prominent members of the Romanian Hungarian intelligentsia, but by the mid-1980s they had been wholly replaced by loyal party functionaries of Hungarian ethnic origin. As a consequence, the Council of Workers of Hungarian Nationality could be used by Ceauşescu as a propaganda instrument, for instance in public quarrels with Hungary.[19] The process of cultural homogenization peaked in the 1980s, when the public thinking and expression of identity of the Hungarian minority were curbed in a number of ways. Any book that promoted Hungarian self-awareness was placed on the forbidden list at the Kriterion publishing house. Internal measures banned publication of apparently innocent works dealing with ethnography, art history, linguistic or literary criticism. Similar moves were made at the Cluj-based Dacia publishing company as well. Hungarian-language TV broadcasting ceased in January 1985, and a single order by telephone was enough to silence the Hungarian regional radio studios in Târgu Mureş and Cluj-Napoca. Central Hungarian-language broadcasts on Bucharest Radio were reduced from 60 to 30 minutes a day.

The performing arts were constrained heavily in the 1980s, as the Communist Party kept a tight hold on repertoire. Most ethnic Hungarian playwrights and even contemporary writers from Hungary were banned. Most new ethnic Hungarian graduates found it hard to get jobs in Transylvania. In 1988, 689

of 951 fresh Hungarian graduates were forced to work outside
Transylvania, while thousands of Romanian colleagues had been
assigned to Hungarian-inhabited counties.[20] Yet Hungarian-taught
higher education (and implicitly secondary education as well) was
threatened by staff cuts. The state in the 1980s ceased to advertise
posts vacated by retirement and the examinations needed for
academic advancement were no longer held, preventing ethnic
Hungarians from gaining access to academic life and the most
prestigious professions.

Czechoslovakia (*Árpád Popély*)

There were radical changes in 1948 for Czechoslovakia and for its
Hungarian minority, deprived of its rights since 1945. As in other
Soviet-bloc countries, the communists under Klement Gottwald
squeezed out the bourgeois parties and set about building a Stalinist
single-party dictatorship.

The communist takeover brought no immediate benefits to
the Hungarian minority, as the communists had been the main
exponents of anti-Hungarian policy. The new Soviet-inspired
constitution of May 1948 did not provide for any minority rights,
and the indigenous Germans and Hungarians were still unable
to vote in the general elections at the end of the month. In 1948,
710 Hungarian-inhabited communities were given newly created
Slovak names. (Tornalja became Šafárikovo, Párkány became
Štúrovo, Bős became Gabčíkovo, Diószeg became Sládkovičovo,
and Nagymegyer became Čalovo, for instance.)

However, the Soviet Union wanted orderly relations among the
countries in its sphere, and Czechoslovakia had to mend its relations
with Hungary, for which the main condition was the restoration of
the rights of Czechoslovakia's Hungarians, which began on October
25, 1948, with the return of their citizenship.[21] Then came an end
to expropriation of their land up to a ceiling of 50 hectares, the
foundation of a weekly (later daily) paper, *Új Szó*, in Bratislava on
December 15, 1948, the establishment of the Cultural Association

of Hungarian Workers of Czechoslovakia – CSEMADOK – headed by the ethnic Hungarian painter Gyula Lőrincz on March 5, 1949, and the opening in the autumn of 1948 of Hungarian-taught classes in Slovak elementary schools, followed in 1950 by the revival of Hungarian-taught education in separate elementary and middle schools. The population exchange and re-Slovakization programs were halted at the end of 1948, and in the early months of 1949 it became possible for those deported to the Czech lands to return to their homes. The preparation of decisions affecting the Hungarian community and implementation of them were entrusted not just to the Slovak Communist Party leaders but to a Hungarian Committee, on which such party workers from the pre-war Czechoslovak communist movement as István Major, Gyula Lőrincz and István Fábry were included.[22]

It was against that background that in Budapest on April 16, 1949, Czechoslovakia and Hungary signed a symbolic treaty of friendship, cooperation and mutual assistance. It was followed in July by the Štrbské pleso Agreement, which settled the financial disputes between the two countries. Hungary, for instance, dropped its claims for compensation for the property left behind by Hungarians arriving from Czechoslovakia. Finally, a Czechoslovakian–Hungarian Cultural Agreement was signed in Prague on November 13, 1951, but the clauses on minority rights and mutual support for minorities fell victim to Czechoslovakia's opposition.

There were attempts in the late 1940s and early 1950s to settle the political, economic and social situation and reintegration of the Hungarian minority, in the form of party resolutions. It again became possible for Hungarians to join the Communist Party – several, including Lőrincz and Fábry, entered the central committees of the Czechoslovak and Slovak parties – and the various mass organizations. Hungarians were added to several national committees. In 1954 it was possible for Hungarians to vote and stand in the general elections, and several Hungarians were elected to the Prague and Bratislava assemblies.[23] In principle it became possible to use Hungarian for official contacts in Hungarian-inhabited districts and institutions, and the names of Hungarian-inhabited communities were to be posted in both languages. But in practice these resolutions were never published and the observance of them was never checked within the restrictions of a party state.[24] There were no organized reactions to the 1956 Hungarian Revolution among the Hungarians of Czechoslovakia. Memories of post-war deportations were fresh and no one dared speak out in favor of revolution. There were only isolated manifestations of sympathy (in hymn-singing in church, wearing mourning ribbons, and laying wreaths on military graves). Even so, the fear of how the Hungarian inhabitants would behave was so strong in the authorities that the Hungarian (and the Polish) reserves were left out of the mobilization order to the Czechoslovakian army early in November 1956.[25]

Importantly, the constitution of 1960, which changed the country's name to the Czechoslovak Socialist Republic,[26] expressed the equality of citizens and declared minorities' right to education and culture, but practical policy towards the Hungarians remained equivocal. The biggest blow was the 1960 reform of public administration, for mergers of small local government districts often involved combining a mainly Hungarian district with a mainly Slovak one to its north, so that the number of districts with a Hungarian minority decreased by two (Dunajská Streda and Komárno).

After CSEMADOK had been set up, the cultural needs of the Hungarian minority were served by the Hungarian Territorial Theater in Komárno founded in 1952, then by the short-lived Czechoslovakian Hungarian Book Publishers and the Czechoslovakian Hungarian Folk Art Ensemble (1953), the Young Hearts Hungarian Folk Art Ensemble (1957) and the literary periodical *Irodalmi Szemle* (1958). *Új Szó* was joined by new weekly papers: *Szabad Földműves* for farming (1950), *Új Ifjúság* for youth (1952), *Dolgozó Nő* for women (1952) and the CSEMADOK cultural paper *A Hét* (1956).[27]

CSEMADOK's activity was ambivalent. It had been founded mainly to popularize communist ideas and enforce party resolutions. Yet its work was vital in the years after the period of the deprival of rights, in reorganizing the minority's cultural activity, collaborating to reopen Hungarian schools, and setting up almost all the Hungarian institutions. From time to time it also attempted to take up the cause of the Hungarians, especially in the freer atmosphere of the 1960s. The reform policy of the Prague Spring, associated mainly with Alexander Dubček, who was elected as head of the Czechoslovak Communist Party in January 1968, covered democratization, economic reform, reorganization of the law of the state, and a promise to settle the national minority question. It had the support of CSEMADOK, which put forward proposals on March 12, 1968, covering, for instance, minority self-government, legislation on minority rights, proportional representation on state bodies, foundation of a Ministry of National Communities, rectification of the 1960 changes in public administration, expansion of the minority school system, and reappraisal of the anti-Hungarian laws passed after 1945. The new, reformist leaders of CSEMADOK (László Dobos as president and Rezső Szabó as general secretary) took part in discussing the proposals for a constitutional act on the minorities, although they were soon deadlocked.

When the Prague Spring was crushed on August 21, 1968, by the military intervention of the Soviet Union and four other Warsaw Pact countries (including Kádár's Hungary), so was any chance of a reassuring settlement to the minority question. The constitutional act passed on October 27, 1968, granted the minorities the right to education in their native language, to association for minority social and cultural purposes, to a native-language press and information, and to use of their language in official contacts, but the clauses on self-determination were removed.[28]

The Hungarian minority, incidentally, was as opposed as the Czechs and Slovaks to the Soviet-led intervention. They were inimical to the arriving Hungarian troops, seeing them as occupiers, not liberators. CSEMADOK and the Czechoslovakian Hungarian writers, communists and young people all issued condemnatory statements. Hungary's troops withdrew on October 20–31, but the Soviets remained until 1990.

On January 1, 1969, Czechoslovakia became a federation of Czech and Slovak socialist republics. Dobos joined the Slovak government as minister of minority affairs and chair of the government's National Minority Council. Rezső Szabó became one of the vice-chairman of the National Minority Committee of the Slovak legislature. In April 1969, Dubček was replaced as head of the federal party by Gustáv Husák. Despite the new constitutional act, the so-called normalization system abolished minority organizations or left them as formalities. Among those replaced by pro-Soviet officials were the reformist heads of CSEMADOK. The political restoration also obstructed the assertion of the minority's constitutional rights. The language rights and the schools of the Hungarian minority were frequently attacked in the 1970s and 1980s. For example, it became illegal for the Hungarian press to refer to Slovak-inhabited settlements by their Hungarian names. The Hungarian teacher training in Nitra was scaled down. The Slovak education portfolio from 1978 onwards advanced several plans for turning Hungarian-taught schools into bilingual ones or steadily introducing Slovak as the language of instruction.

News of the plans to end Hungarian schooling aroused strong opposition from the minority Hungarian intelligentsia and even from CSEMADOK, which directly promoted the formation of a Committee fot the Protection of the Rights of the Hungarian Minority in Czechoslovakia.[29] Formed in 1978 and directed by Miklós Duray, this was the one rights-defense body to continue operating illegally until the fall of the communist system, although its staff were harassed by the secret police (Duray was imprisoned twice). It managed to orchestrate a wave of protest that helped to dissuade the authorities from pursuing their plans for bilingual education.[30]

The other outstanding figure in the Hungarian opposition apart from Duray was Kálmán Janics, who was deported and published important studies in Hungarian émigré journals in the West. These and a monograph entitled *Years of Statelessness* did much to advertise how the Hungarian minority was being deprived of its rights.[31]

Yugoslavia (*Árpád Hornyák*)

Three of the member socialist republics of the post-war federal Yugoslavia had a Hungarian minority: Serbia (in the Autonomous Province of Vojvodina), Croatia and Slovenia. The Hungarian community in Vojvodina shrank considerably after the war in absolute and proportional terms. About 80,000 emigrated, mainly to Hungary, and post-war reprisals took a toll in tens of thousands. The relative significance of the Hungarian community was reduced by the massacre or expulsion of most Jews and many Gypsies during the wartime Hungarian occupation and by almost total removal of the German community, whose members were branded as collective war criminals after the war. The vacancies created were filled by several hundred thousand South Slavs, mainly Serbs from backward regions, under a conscious policy of building up the Serb presence. The first post-war census, taken in 1948, recorded 496,492 Hungarians in Yugoslavia (3.2 percent of the population), of whom 428,750 lived in Vojvodina (26 percent), in contiguous settlements along the right bank of the River Tisa and in large numbers in northern Bačka. The 50,000 Hungarians of Croatia lived mainly in the Drava district and the 10,000 in Slovenia in the Mura district.

But as passions cooled, Tito's Yugoslavia announced a new "national" policy. Over 18,000 landless Hungarian households gained by redistribution under the land reform. Furthermore, the minorities were disproportionately strong in the ruling Communist Party, and sizeable numbers of Hungarians gained political positions. However, there was no scope allowed for collective political organization of the Hungarian minority or representation of its interests, due to the centralist nature of the communist system, and to the implementation of the principle of 'fraternity and unity'.

Another weakening factor was the fact that the whole Hungarian elite vanished after World War II. There were no more minority institutions: the Communist Party of Yugoslavia held a monopoly of political power and activity.[32] The Hungarians and the other minority communities could not put forward plans or aspirations, elect leaders, or control their lives institutionally. They seem to have been affected by the sweeping social and economic changes to a greater extent than the majority. The collectivization also lost the Hungarians their Church property, and paradoxically their communal property as well, making it impossible for them to keep up their social activities.[33] Yugoslav policy on industrial production, especially heavy industrial production, meant initially that many small-town factories in the Southern Region were dismantled and their plants moved to new centers in more backward parts of the country, but new industry began to arrive in the 1950s. The transformation of the country and the economic structure in the Hungarian-inhabited areas brought about a drastic change in the social structure of the Hungarian community. Before the war, two thirds of the Hungarians lived in the countryside, 11 percent worked in industry, and another 11 percent were artisans and traders. The proportion working in agriculture fell rapidly after the war, and so did agriculture's share of production. By the 1970s, the share of agriculture in Vojvodina's social production was down from 59 percent to 31 percent.[34] The change was more conspicuous still in the Drava district, where 39 percent were working in industry, and in the Mura district, where industry was providing three quarters of the jobs in the social (state and cooperative) sector.[35]

Tito's policy on the minorities was for show. Although he broke with the earlier efforts at forcible assimilation, he emphasized tacit assimilation instead. He recognized the rights of minority individuals but obstructed any communal organization by the more substantial minorities. Yugoslav minority policy was tolerant mainly in the fields of political representation, education, culture and language use. In political representation particularly there were great efforts to attain equality or equality of rights.

The Yugoslav leaders allowed the minorities freedom to use their native language and provided them with their own institutions, but from the outset the aim was to make these as characterless as possible in national terms. Political, academic and civil careers were assured to the Yugoslavian Hungarian intelligentsia, but efforts were made to divorce them from their environment and native language.[36] For the most prestigious Hungarian institutions were based in Novi Sad, which isolated Hungarians who worked in them from the main bloc of Hungarian settlement far to the north.

Hungarian-taught education in Yugoslavia was in a better position than in the other successor states. There emerged in the 1950s a network of gymnasia, specialist secondary schools and specialist training schools teaching in Hungarian that covered the province quite well, although not perfectly. The acute shortage of teachers was eased when the new University of Novi Sad included in 1959 a Hungarian faculty offering qualifications for middle schools' Hungarian teachers, and founded an Institute of Hungarian Studies in 1969. But this was the last Hungarian-language higher education institute established, and its intake was cut by the provincial authorities, which contributed to a situation where recruitment to teaching fell below replacement level. (In 1984, Hungarians made up almost 20 percent of Vojvodina's population, but accounted for only 10.3 percent of those in higher education.)[37] The number of elementary and secondary pupils taught in Hungarian fell drastically in the 1960s, due to disguised assimilation, a rise in mixed marriages, and large numbers of Hungarians working abroad.

Several Hungarian-language periodicals were founded in the 1944–1948 period. The daily *Magyar Szó* appeared in the autumn of 1945, and so did papers for children and young people. The aggregate membership of Hungarian cultural associations rose, and was much higher than before the war. There were 62 in operation in 1948, but over 100 took part four years later in the Hungarian Festival Games held at Palić, near Subotica.[38] The umbrella organization for all areas of culture was the Hungarian Cultural Association of Vojvodina[9] formed in Subotica in the summer of 1945. However, this "voluntarily" merged in 1948 with the Vojvodina Public Education Association. This meant that it became only a department, and the change involved a move from Subotica to Novi Sad that divorced it from its mass base. Hungarian drama followed a similar course.

Hungarian-taught schools began to reopen in 1945 for the Hungarian minority in Croatia, who numbered about 50,000, but as in Vojvodina, the biggest problem was a shortage of teaching staff. A Croatian Hungarian Association[40] was set up in Osijek in November 1949, with a weekly paper, *Magyar Néplap*. After a year's gap this was replaced in 1951 by the pictorial *Képes Újság*, with a print run of 2,500–3,800 in that period. The Association played a seminal part in organizing cultural activity through local societies founded in almost every Hungarian-inhabited village. There were 83 in the early 1950s, 62 of them cultural, 12 devoted to game hunting, and 9 devoted to sports and physical education. Croatia's Hungarian community underwent the fastest decline and numbered only 22,355 in the 1991 census.[41]

The Hungarian community in the Mura district was in a similar position to those of Vojvodina and Croatia, undergoing the same processes: inward migration, and the foundation and later dissolution of cultural associations. A weekly paper, *Népújság*, was printed in some 2,000 copies. Changes came with the 1959 party resolution and the 1963 constitution, which gradually expanded the scope for the Mura Hungarians. The constitution assigned the minority question to the constituent republics. Slovenia decided on exemplary treatment, with an eye to easing the position of the Slovene minorities in Italy and Hungary.

After the 1948 split between Tito and Stalin, Yugoslavia gained greater scope for diplomatic, economic and political maneuver than the other state-socialist countries. Its policy on national communities and minorities proved more flexible as well. Yugoslavia had to ward off constant attacks from COMINFORM and the socialist countries in the years after 1948. One defense was to reinterpret Marxist principles and introduce in 1950 what came to be known as worker self-management. This partial devolution of executive power embraced benign gestures and a more tolerant policy towards the minorities. The 1952 Palić Games were held at a time when relations between Yugoslavia and Hungary were at their coldest. However, the threat from the north and east perpetuated the party state's fear of minority self-organization, as shown by the disbanding of the Vojvodina Hungarian Cultural Association. The Yugoslav leadership and its tightly controlled legislature paid little heed to the minority question in the post-war years. Not until March 24, 1959, did the League of Communists of Yugoslavia's Central Committee Executive pass a resolution on the subject. The dual-affiliation formula employed meant that the minorities were part not only of their nation of origin, but also of the country of domicile, and the greater their equality of rights the smoother their development would be. The party resolution declaring them to be integral parts of the socialist Yugoslavian community took care to avoid the injustice of ignoring minority members when filling important party state posts. It called for closer attention to bilingualism, and welcomed the operation of local minority cultural organizations, as binding forces at commune and district level, but did not see a need to combine them in an organizational sense. The 1963 constitution preferred to call the minorities national minorities.[42] That of 1974 allowed vertical republic-wide national minority organizations in Croatia and Slovenia, but not in Serbia, where 90 percent of the Hungarian community lived. (The main reason was fear of giving rights to the large Albanian population in Kosovo, Serbia's other autonomous province.)

The relative benefits of Yugoslavia's economic and political reforms were necessarily extended to the intellectual activity in Vojvodina and among the country's Hungarians. The economic, political and cultural situation of the Hungarians and other minorities became far better than in neighboring countries. They were able to enjoy the relatively positive changes of the period as citizens of equal rank. The literary and cultural journal *Új Symposion* was founded in January 1965, acting as a channel between world literature and that of the Vojvodina Hungarians. Its foundation coincided with initial efforts by the Yugoslav leadership to develop a supranational "Yugoslav nation" that went beyond the traditional notions of a nation. There was willingness among most of the Vojvodina Hungarian intellectual elite to sacrifice the traditional Hungarian concept of nation to such Yugoslavism. Several of its members held high posts in the province's political and institutional leadership.[43] In this way they managed for a time to win the sympathy and support of the Yugoslav reform communists. But when they began, in line with literary tradition, to criticize the negative aspects of society, the authorities clamped down and the initiatives were banned, along with the existing institutions.[44]

The roots of Vojvodina's autonomy reached back to the 1690s, when various privileges were granted to the Serb settlers by Emperor Leopold I, during and after the great northward migration of the Serbs. A territorially separate Crown Land known as the Serbian Vojvodeship and the Banat of Temes[45] was established by the Habsburg government in 1849, but abolished again after ten years, when the territory was subsumed into the Hungarian county system. There was no separate administrative entity under Yugoslavia either, until Vojvodina was organized as an autonomous province of Serbia in 1945. However, that had no practical effect before the 1960s, or real significance until the 1974 constitution granted the province a status equivalent to that of a republic.

The 1953 constitution of Yugoslavia extended the system of self-management to the fields of culture and society, initiating a process of decentralization that peaked with the 1974 constitution, which effectively also broke the Communist Party up into separate territorial parties. Power in Vojvodina was taken by a group that kept an eye on local interests and included some Hungarians who identified wholly with Yugoslavism. This leadership was ousted in the autumn of 1988 by the "yoghurt revolution" of Slobodan Milošević's Federation of Serbian Communists and by the virtual abolition of Vojvodina's autonomy six months later.

The Soviet Union (*Csilla Fedinec*)

The 1945–1991 period in which Transcarpathia (official name in the Soviet era: *Zakarpatskaja oblast'* [Transcarpathian Territory]) belonged to the Soviet Union is divisible from the Hungarian point of view by the following turning points: the 1945 Soviet–Hungarian agreement on sovereignty over Transcarpathia; the Twentieth Congress of the Communist Party of the Soviet Union in 1956, where cautious post-Stalinist reforms were announced, resulting in some concessions also on Hungarian affairs in Transcarpathia; the foundation of the Forrás [Source] Youth Studio in 1967, which formulated some political submissions on behalf of the Hungarian majority; finally, the foundation in 1989 of the Transcarpathian Hungarian Cultural Association as the first local body for the protection of the local Hungarian community's interests.[46]

There was consternation among the inhabitants of Transcarpathia at the changes brought about by Soviet rule, which were radical and violent even by comparison with the sufferings undergone during World War II. They were intimidated by the persecution of kulaks and political show trials. Nationalization affected every branch of the economy. The peasants were herded into collective farms, and shorn of their land, tools and livestock. Each household was left with only a small plot of land for its own use, but some communities had remarkable success with some garden crops. Velyka Dobron', for instance, became famous for its potatoes and peppers.[47] Petrovo became something of a model community as the center of a collective farm (kolkhoz), and its chairman, Andor Bíró, was the one Hungarian representative in the Supreme Soviet.[48] There was substantial inward migration from other parts of the Soviet Union. It was the practice throughout the country for graduates to be posted for two or three years far away from their native area. Those drafted into the army served in units beyond Ukraine. Many Transcarpathians took seasonal work in "Russia" or became security guards accompanying trains carrying produce. This earned several times their normal wages for two or three summer months.

There had never been appreciable industry in the area, and only smaller component factories were relocated there from other republics during the Soviet period. This meant that the break-up of the Soviet Union caused a further economic trauma. One big economic factor was the railway system. Rail links between Czechoslovakia and Romania, and between Hungary and Poland, had been important geopolitical factors since 1919. Chop and Bat'ovo (along with Brest further north, now in Belarus) formed a main western gateway for Soviet goods before the break-up of COMECON, playing a vital part in passenger and freight traffic.

The official atheist ideology of the Soviet Union confined religion in Transcarpathia within the walls of the churches. No Communist Party member, teacher or state office holder could attend church, not even weddings or baptisms. Church property was also nationalized, and many churches were closed or used as atheist museums or stores. In 1949, the Uniate or Greek Catholic Church in communion with Rome was forcibly merged into the Orthodox Church. Priests who refused to make the move were deported to labor camps. Some three quarters of the Transcarpathian Hungarians belonged to the Reformed Church, while the remainder were Greek Catholic or Roman Catholic. There were difficulties with training priests, as the only Catholic seminary was in Riga, Latvia. The clergy of the Reformed Church were trained at courses in Beregovo. After 1989 it became possible for Catholic or Reformed clergy to be brought from Hungary, and somewhat later for Transcarpathians to pursue theological studies abroad.[49]

Hardly any great artists of old (such men as Gyula Virágh, Gyula Ijjász, Andor Novák, Sámuel Beregi or Károly Izai) survived into the Soviet period, but the first generation of the Transcarpathian school remained: Béla Erdélyi, József Boksay and Emil Grabovszky. Erdélyi failed after the war to start an artists' association, although he was made chairman of the local branch of the Ukrainian republican association. From this official position he tried to start an art college in Uzhgorod, but it closed after a few months in favor of a secondary school for industrial design. Among the early pupils of both were István Szőke, László Habda, Gyula Sztaskó, Pál Balla, Erzsébet Kremninczky, Miklós Medveczky, Edit Luták Medveczky, János Sütő, and others including the highly original Anna Horváth and the painter József Garanyi, both from Beregovo. Erdélyi was soon sidelined, although he had registered as a Ukrainian, despite not speaking the language. As he remarked, "I'm a Ukrainian of

French culture and German native language [both parents were Swabians], who speaks Hungarian best."[50]

The local press was communist-run: the daily *Kárpáti Igaz Szó*, *Kárpátontúli Ifjúság* for the young, translated word for word from a Ukrainian original, *Vörös Zászló* in Beregovo, *Kommunizmus Zászlaja* in Vinogradovo, and *Kommunizmus Fényei* in Uzhgorod. The first three especially had literature columns, but the state publisher issued only one or two Hungarian books a year. The other chance of publication was in the literary supplement of the popular annual *Kárpáti Kalendárium*, which appeared for forty years from 1957. Almost the whole of all these papers except *Kárpáti Igaz Szó* was translated, but their literary sections printed original Hungarian work. Chances of publication abroad were very rare.

Books in Hungarian appeared from the Hungarian department at the textbook publisher and from the publishing house Karpaty. Schools in Ukraine followed the pre-war Soviet curriculum until 1947, with slight adjustments to party resolutions that appeared. The ban on "foreign-language" textbooks at the end of 1944 covered not only Hungarian ones, but also those issued earlier for the Slav population by the Prosvita society, the Subcarpathian Scientific Society, and other associations closed after the war. All local history content was withdrawn, with the result that a whole generation grew up unaware of its own history. Another purge came in 1956, when all language and literature textbooks, including the Hungarian ones, had to be cleansed of references to Stalin and praise of him. The textbooks for schools teaching in Moldavian could be imported from the Moldavian SSR, but those used in Hungarian-taught schools had to be translated from Russian, except those for Hungarian language and literature. The very first Hungarian literature textbook for Transcarpathia, which appeared in 1950, was written by Antal Hidas, who lived in Moscow, but the rest were written by locals (Dezső Csengeri, Gizella Drávai, László Balla, Erzsébet Gortvay, and others).[51]

The local state publishing house Karpaty was not specifically for the Hungarian minority, but it had a Hungarian department and it began in 1959 also to publish jointly with firms in Hungary. By

1970 it had issued 1,800 titles in a total of 20 million copies, some of them sold in Hungary. Only one or two single-author works of prose or poetry per year appeared in Transcarpathia, but the almanacs and anthologies provided authors with broader publishing possibilities. From 1945 to 1983, the only scope for Hungarian writers anywhere between Tyachevo (Ukrainian: Tyachiv) and Uzhgorod was the literature studio attached to the Beregovo paper *Vörös Zászló*. In 1971, László Balla, editor-in-chief of the *Kárpáti Igaz Szó*, published an article (anonymously) accusing the Forrás [Source] Literary Studio in Uzhgorod of spreading bourgeois ideas and of being apolitical and anti-Soviet. At that time, the Beregovo studio provided the only refuge. Later the daily *Kárpáti Igaz Szó*, still with Balla at the helm, also gave chances for writers to see their work in print on a page labeled "Momentum." In 1988, this gave way for a year and a half to a separate cultural magazine supplement called "New Shoot."[52] Another substitute for book publication in 1979–1986 took the form of 14 verse booklets published as part of the paper (which had its print run of 40,000), along with an anthology of one verse each from 15 poets. A traditional Transcarpathian almanac or "calendar" was published by Karpaty throughout the period under various titles.[53]

The promise of the Twentieth Congress of the Communist Party of the Soviet Union in 1956 was belied by arrests in response to a wave of sympathy for the Hungarian Revolution, but in 1957 it became possible to buy books and subscribe to periodicals from Hungary. Hungarian radio and television programs could be picked up in most of the Hungarian-inhabited areas of Transcarpathia. The short programs in Hungarian made at the Uzhgorod studios of the Soviet state channel RTV were popular mainly in the Upper Tisa district, where Hungarian stations could not be picked up until the advent of satellite broadcasting in the 1990s. Although the international border sealed Transcarpathia off from Hungary – foreign travel was allowed only after lengthy procedures, once every two years, for the purpose of visiting close relatives – the broadcasts, books and periodicals kept the Hungarians of Transcarpathia relatively well informed.

Foremost among the many folksong and dance ensembles was the Hungarian Melodies Chamber Ensemble, the Tisza Song and Dance Ensemble, and the People's Theater in Beregovo (headed by Ottó Schober), which opened in 1952 and operated for 40 years. Prominent among the musicians were Dezső Zádor, who had been a pupil of Bartók's in the 1930s, István Márton, and the critic Tibor Boniszlavszky.[54]

The Hungarians had no separate political or civil organization at that time, and the vacuum was filled by literary societies. Most of the writers, poets and journalists had graduated in Hungarian from the Uzhgorod State University. There worked Sándor Fodó, seen as the leading intellectual, who would become founding president of the Transcarpathian Hungarian Cultural Association in 1989. But the university department and its role were equivocal, as its teaching and research did not receive sufficient recognition, although it sufficed to provide common ground and encourage common thinking among young Hungarian intellectuals.

The literary society that wrote history, so to speak, in that period was the Forrás Youth Studio, formed in 1967 by Hungarian majors at Uzhgorod State University, having previously issued a typewritten samizdat entitled *Együtt* [Together] in the autumn of 1966. The leading light was the poet Vilmos Kovács. After this was banned, they found a chance to publish in the periodical *Kárpátontúli Ifjúság*, under whose auspices the studio came into being. Its members – József Zselicki, Gyula Balla, András S. Benedek, László Györke, and others, with some help from Kovács and Fodó – went beyond literary activity to draw up two petitions (in the autumn of 1971 and the spring of 1972) for collective rights for the Hungarians, addressed to the district party committee and to the top party and state leadership in Moscow. That precipitated an official campaign against "manifestations of Hungarian bourgeois nationalism" and military conscription of some students from the university, although they were able to complete their studies later. Forrás was replaced in 1971 on ideological grounds by the Attila József Literary Studio, to act as a spokesman for Soviet literary ideas. This group gathered around the newspaper *Kárpáti Igaz Szó*, whose editor-in-chief László Balla cooperated actively in quelling the dissidents, with the result that the former Forrás activists were left with nowhere to publish. Those years gave rise to a dominant sense of grievance in the Transcarpathian Hungarian writers. In 1975 Balla used *Kárpáti Igaz Szó* to publish a series of articles entitled "Soviet Hungarians," the name that he coined for an ostensible "new category of men" on the ethnic map of Europe. It became official policy to treat the Moscow émigré writers – Máté Zalka, Béla Illés, Antal Hidas, Sándor Gergely, and so on – as the literary classics, rather than seeking tradition in Hungarian literature as a whole or in local Hungarian writing.

The Attila József Literary Studio was steadily sidelined. When it was revived in 1988, it was as the Attila József Creative Community, for all creative Transcarpathian Hungarians, not just writers and poets, with Károly D. Balla, György Dupka and Sándor Horváth as its co-chairmen. However, it dwindled in the 1990s without officially dissolving.

As for the one series of literary pamphlets bound up with the *Kárpáti Igaz Szó*, archived in its Uzhgorod offices, it was pulped in the 1990s, ostensibly by accident. This fittingly symbolized the end of the Soviet period.

Austria (*Gerhard Baumgartner*)

The Hungarian Revolution in the autumn of 1956 posed a huge challenge to Austria, as the Soviet military intervention sent a flood of refugees into the country. About 180,000 Hungarian refugees arrived in Burgenland in the next three months, including the whole teaching staff of Sopron's College of Mining and Forestry, which moved on as a group to Canada in 1957, where the government founded for them a new college at Powell River, near Vancouver. Austria set up several large transit camps, from which the Hungarians were sent to Vienna and onward to a number of Western countries. Also set up in 1956 was the great refugee camp at Traiskirchen. On

December 19, the refugee camp at Eisenstadt received a visit from the US vice-president, Richard Nixon. Most of the refugees later left Austria for other countries: only 18,000 remained by the beginning of 1959. In Vienna, the United Nations built new apartment blocks to house them.[55] The 1956 refugees brought a considerable change in the structure of the Hungarian-speaking community in Vienna. For several decades there were two groups divided by their attitude to the Hungarian state. The 1956-ers would have nothing to do with it, but the established Hungarian cultural associations in Vienna kept up relations with the Kádár regime. The Austrian state set up a separate secondary education system for Hungarian refugees, under which 746 Hungarian students studied in five separate, Hungarian-taught gymnasia. The last school-leaving exams for 1956-er Hungarian students was held in 1963, after which the gymnasia were closed.[56]

The economic and social structure of the Burgenland villages changed fundamentally in the 1960s. Land ownership patterns several centuries old had ensured that dwarf holdings and smallholdings existed side by side with the great estates, but these smallholders became obliged in the 1960s to commute as workers to earn their living, to the industrial areas of Vienna, Lower Austria and Styria.[57] A good example was Andau: this was Austria's biggest cattle-breeding community in 1959, with over 2,000 head, but the last cow was sold in 1969. The people of Andau began commuting the 100 kilometers to Vienna in special trains. Meanwhile, mechanization reduced the demand for farm labor on the manorial farm centers. The laborers moved first to nearby villages and then to the cities.[58] The farm centers with purely Hungarian inhabitants became totally depopulated, and the former laborers were rapidly assimilated, as Hungarian had only been a "servants' language" in their eyes. The want of a complete Hungarian education system in Burgenland meant that there had been no Hungarian minority elite. This function was assumed in the 1960s by 1956-ers or other immigrant members of the intelligentsia from Hungary. In the Upper Wart at the end of the 1960s, the Catholic congregation in Unterwart, the Reformed congregation in Oberwart, and the Evangelical congregation in Siget in der Wart all had clergy born in Hungary. The Austrian government of Bruno Kreisky, having signed with Italy an agreement on the status of South Tyrol (Alto Adige/Südtirol), sought also to settle the position of Austria's minorities. The first step was a secret native-language census, in which all inhabitants were invited to state their native language anonymously. More important was the 1976 act on ethnic groups,[59] which granted five indigenous minorities certain language rights, official Chancellery representation, and state financial support. However, the rights of the Carinthian Slovenes, the Burgenland Croats and the Vienna Czechoslovaks had been guaranteed by interstate treaty, and so they refused to recognize the new act or delegate representatives to the new Ethnic Group Councils. The Burgenland Hungarians were the only community to form, in 1959, such an Ethnic Group Council, whose inaugural meeting Kreisky also attended. However, the act recognized as indigenous only the Burgenland Hungarians, not the migrant groups in Vienna and other cities.[60] In 1980, the Burgenland Hungarian Cultural Association submitted a memorandum to the Austrian government calling for the development of Hungarian secondary and higher education institutions, the erection of bilingual place-name signs, and recognition of Hungarian as an official language.[61] It became apparent within a few years that the Ethnic Group Council was not capable of pursuing the Hungarian minority's aspirations, and so the Cultural Association declared in 1983 that it was demanding the same minority rights for Hungarians as the Croats and Slovenes had received under the State Treaty in 1955.[62]

The first boost in cross-border links came in 1974: the Iron Curtain opened at least from one direction and it became possible for Austrians to visit Hungary without a visa. The value of Hungarian for communication in Austria increased only in 1988, when Hungary waived most passport restrictions for its citizens and tens of thousands of shoppers flooded into Burgenland and Vienna. Then Otto von Habsburg, deputy speaker of the European Parliament and son of Hungary's last king, joined Imre Pozsgay, a leading reform communist and state minister, in making a symbolic first cut in the barbed wire across the frontier at Sopron on August 19, 1989, and a mass of waiting East German tourists seized the chance to flee to the West.[63] This Pan-European Picnic marked an important breach in the division of Europe. By Christmas the Eastern European communist dictatorships were falling successively and the change of system had begun. The rest of the barbed wire dividing the Hungarians of Burgenland from Hungary was removed in the summer of 1990, after 45 years.

The villages of southern Burgenland had been closed communities until the mid-1960s. Not until then did people start commuting from them to neighboring towns and to cities such as Vienna and Graz. Hitherto every aspect of daily village had been tied to the home village, in a form of village life that provided a basis and framework for various distinct dialects to flourish as the natural means of communication. Hitherto it had been expected that those marrying into a Hungarian-speaking village would learn the dialect, and most of them did. Every Burgenland village contained some people who had mastered the local language alongside their own, and that new language would be the local dialect, not literary Hungarian.

The survival of the village dialects was assisted by strong ties to local cultural traditions. Each dialect was linked with verses for Luca[64] or for the best man at weddings, with beating out winter, with Carnival, with traditional village frolics, and with traditional songs sung on such occasions, so that the dialects acted as a cultural and social bond, producing in Burgenland a kind of village ethnicity.[65]

By the mid-1970s, social modernization was breaking this traditional world up. The commuting workers left the village each morning and returned at night, or returned only at weekends. Also breaking up was the extended family structure, for several generations were decreasingly likely to live under one roof. While households still included three generations, the commuting did not affect language use greatly, as the grandparents stood in for the parents and taught the children the local speech. But if a young couple lived separately or moved to another village, there was no way to transmit the minority dialect. It may not have been coincidental that this was when the first Burgenland Hungarian cultural association was formed, as if in response to these developments. The trends were noted by the rural clergy, who prompted the formation of institutions whose forms and demands were intended to offset the damage to the old village framework. This was successful to some extent through the financial and political support received after the 1976 minority act came into force and the Burgenland Hungarians received official recognition.

Notes

1 *Magyar Népi Szövetség.*
2 Vladimir Tismăneanu, Dorin Dobrincu and Cristian Vasile, eds. *Comisia prezidenţială pentru Analiza Dictaturii Comuniste din România. Raport final* [The Presidential Commission for the Analysis of the Communist Dictatorship in Romania. Final Report] (Bukarest, 2007), pp. 332–351.
3 Changes in the ethnic structure of Transylvania's urban population, as a percentage:

	Population	Romanian	Hungarian	German	Jewish
1930	936,418	34.9	37.9	13.2	10.4
1948	1,118,904	50.2	39.0	7.2	2.0
1956	1,753,044	56.2	31.6	8.3	0.4
1977	3,558,651	69.3	23.8	4.8	0.2

Detailed analysis: Árpád E. Varga, "Városodás, vándorlás, nemzetiség. Adatok és szempontok az erdélyi városi térségek etnikai arculatváltásának vizsgálatához" [Urbanization, Migration, Affiliation. Data and Criteria for Examining Change in the Ethnic Complexion of Transylvanian Urban Areas], in Árpád E. Varga, *Fejezetek a jelenkori Erdély népesedéstörténetéből. Tanulmányok* [Chapters from the Population History of Present-Day Transylvania. Studies] (Budapest, 1998), pp. 180–217.

Census data on changes in the language and national-group
relations in three major cities:

	All	Romanian	Hungarian
		1948	
1	47,043	11,007	34,943
2	82,282	26,998	52,540
3	117,791	47,321	67,977
		1956	
1	65,194	14,623	48,077
2	99,663	35,644	59,072
3	154,723	74,033	74,155
		1977	
1	127,783	44,491	81,234
2	170,531	91,925	75,125
3	262,858	173,003	86,215

1 = Târgu Mureş, 2 = Oradea, 3 = Cluj-Napoca

4   Emigration of the indigenous German population became
widespread in the late 1960s and early 1970s. The figures were
16,019 in 1950–1966, 440 in 1967, 614 in 1968, 2,675 in 1969,
6,519 in 1970, 2,848 in 1971, 4,374 in 1972, and 7,577 in 1973. For
more detail, see the following: Tismăneanu, Dobrincu and Vasile,
eds., *Comisia prezidenţială*, p. 361; Dennis Deletant, *Ceauşescu
şi Securitatea. Constrângere şi disidenţă în România anilor 1965–
1989* (Bucharest, 1998) = *Ceausescu and the Securitate: Coercion
and Dissent in Romania, 1965–89* (Armonk, NY, 1995), p. 125;
Georg Weber, *Emigration der Siebenbürger Sachsen. Studien zu
Ost-West-Wanderung im 20. Jahrhundert* (Wiesbaden, 2003), p.
444. Emigration of Romanian Jews peaked in the 1950s and 1960s.

Sample figures: 47,071 in 1950, 40,625 in 1951, 21,269 in 1961, and 25,926 in 1964. For more on this, see the following: Carol Bines, *Din istoria imigrărilor în Israel* [The History of Migration to Israel] (Bucharest, 1998), pp. 92–94; Radu Ioanid, *Răscumpărarea evreilor. Istoria aordurilor secrete dintre România şi Israel* [The Ransom of the Jews: The Story of an Extraordinary Secret Bargain between Romania and Israel] (Bucharest, 2005); Liviu Rotman, *Evreii din România în perioada comunistă 1944–1965* [Jews in Romania during the Communist Period 1944–1965] (Iasi, 2004).

5   Tismăneanu, Dobrincu and Vasile, eds., *Comisia prezidenţială*, pp. 332–354.

6   Mihály Zoltán Nagy and Ágoston Olti, eds., *Érdekképviselet vagy pártpolitika? Iratok a Magyar Népi Szövetség történetéhez 1944– 1953* [Representation of Interests or Party Politics? Documents from the History of the Hungarian People's Association 1944–1953] (Csíkszereda, 2009); Tamás Lönhárt, *Uniunea Populară Maghiară în perioada instaurării regimului comunist în România (1944–1948)* [The Hungarian Popular Union during the Communist Takeover in Romania (1944–1948)] (Cluj-Napoca, 2008).

7   Gábor Vincze, *Illúziók és csalódások. Fejezetek a romániai magyarság második világháború utáni történetéből* [Illusions and Disillusionments. Chapters of the Post-War History of the Romanian Hungarians] (Csíkszereda, 1999), p. 196.

8   *Magyar Autonóm Tartomány/Regiunea Autonomă Maghiară.*

9   A full account of the Hungarian Autonomous Region: Stefano Bottoni, *Sztálin a székelyeknél. A Magyar Autonóm Tartomány története, 1952–1960* [Stalin and the Szeklers: A History of the Hungarian Autonomous Region, 1952–1960] (Csíkszereda, 2008).

10 *Maros-Magyar Autonóm Tartomány/ Regiunea Mureş-Autonomă Maghiară.*

11 Bottoni, *Sztálin a székelyeknél*, p. 418.

12 *Ibid.*, pp. 422–424.

13 Andrea Andreescu, Nastasă Lucian and Andrea Varga, eds., *Minorităţi etnoculturale. Mărturii documentare. Maghiarii din România (1945–1955)* [Ethnocultural Minorities. Testimonial Documentation. Hungarians in Romania (1945–1955)] (Cluj, 2002), pp. 460–482.

14   C. Daicoviciu, Şt. Pascu *et al.*, eds., *Din istoria Transilvaniei*. I–II [History of Transylvania I–II] (Bucharest, 1960–1961). On the ideological output of the Ceausescu regime: Katherine Verdery, *National Ideology under Socialism – Identity and Cultural Politics in Ceausescu's Romania* (Berkeley, CA, 1995).

15   *Declaraţie cu privire la poziţia Partidului Muncitoresc Român în problemele mişcării comuniste şi muncitoreşti internaţionale, adoptată de Plenara lărgită a C.C. al P.M.R. din aprilie 1964* [Declaration of the Romanian Workers' Party's Position on Questions of the International Communist and Workers' Movement, Adopted by the Enlarged Plenary CC of P.M.R. April 1964] (Bucharest, 1964), p. 55.

16   Csaba Zoltán Novák, "A 'nyitás éve', 1968. A romániai magyar értelmiségiek találkozója Nicolae Ceauşescuval" [1968, Year of Opening. The Romanian Hungarian Intelligentsia's Encounter with Nicolae Ceauşescu], *Múltunk* (2008) 2: 229–266. On the relations of the intelligentsia and the authorities: Gail Kligman, *The Politics of Duplicity: Controlling Reproduction in Ceausescu's Romania* (Los Angeles, CA, 1998); József D. Lőrincz, *Az átmenet közéleti értékei a mindennapi életben* [Public Values of the Transition in Daily Life] (Csíkszereda, 2004).

17   Csaba Zoltán Novák, "A megyésítés és a nemzetiségi kérdés Romániában 1968" [Division into Counties and the Minority Question in Romania 1968], in Nándor Bárdi and Attila Simon, eds., *Integrációs stratégiák a magyar kisebbségek történetében* [Integration Strategies in the History of the Hungarian Minorities] (Somorja, 2006), pp. 405–421.

18   *Magyar Nemzetiségű Dolgozók Tanácsa.*

19   Gábor Vincze, "Lăncrăjantól Lăncrăjanig. Fejezet a magyar–román kapcsolatok nyolcvanas évekbeli történetéből" [From Lăncrăjan to Lăncrăjan. Chapters from the History of 1980s Hungarian–Romanian History], *Magyar Kisebbség* (2006) 3–4: 263–352.

20   Vincze, *Illúziók és csalódások*, p. 219; Gábor Vincze, ed., *Történeti kényszerpályák kisebbségi reálpolitikák II. Dokumentumok a romániai magyar kisebbség történetének tanulmányozásához 1944–1989* [Historical Paths of Minority *Realpolitik*, II. Documents from the Study of the History of the Romanian Hungarian Minority 1944–1989] (Csíkszereda, 2003), pp. 448–450.

21 József Gyönyör, *Terhes örökség. A magyarság lélekszámának és sorsának alakulása Csehszlovákiában* [Difficult Heritage. Population and Destiny of the Hungarian Community in Czechoslovakia] (Pozsony, 1994), pp. 264–265.

22 Árpád Popély, *A (cseh)szlovákiai magyarság történeti kronológiája 1944–1992* [Historical Chronology of the (Czecho)Slovakian Hungarian Community 1944–1992] (Somorja, 2006).

23 Nominations had to be endorsed by a communist-controlled front, which made a single endorsement in each district. Voting was compulsory but meant ticking "yes" or "no" for the one candidate. Despite secret balloting, it was far from safe to post a "no" vote or spoil a ballot paper.

24 Gyönyör, *Terhes örökség*, pp. 266–268.

25 On Czechoslovak repercussions of the 1956 Revolution, see Edita Ivaničková and Attila Simon, eds., *Maďarská revolúcia 1956 a Slovensko. Az 1956-os magyar forradalom és Szlovákia* [The 1956 Hungarian Revolution and Slovakia] (Šamorín/Bratislava, 2006).

26 *Československá socialistická republika.*

27 László Tóth, ed., *A (cseh)szlovákiai magyar művelődés története 1918–1998* [The History of (Czecho)Slovakian Hungarian Culture, 1918–1998], II (Budapest, 1998), pp. 236–257.

28 Participation by the Hungarian minority in the 1968 reform is covered in Rezső Szabó, *A Csemadok és a Prágai Tavasz* [CSEMADOK and the Prague Spring] (Pozsony, 2004); Árpád Popély, *1968 és a csehszlovákiai magyarság* [1968 and the Czechoslovakian Hungarians] (Somorja, 2008).

29 *Csehszlovákiai Magyar Kisebbség Jogvédő Bizottsága.*

30 On the committee, see Miklós Duray, ed., *Kettős elnyomásban. Dokumentumok a csehszlovákiai magyarság helyzetéről és jogvédelméről 1978–1989* [Double Pressure. Documents on the Situation and Legal Protection of the Czechoslovakian Hungarians 1978–1989] (Pozsony, 1993).

31 Kálmán Janics, *A hontalanság évei. A szlovákiai magyar kisebbség a második világháború után 1945–1948* [The Years of Statelessness. The Slovak Hungarians after the Second World War 1945–1948] (Munich, 1979), (Budapest, 1989); English edition: *Czechoslovak Policy and the Hungarian Minority 1945–1948* (Highland Lakes, NJ/ Boulder, CO, 1982).

32 Nándor Bárdi, *Tény és való. A budapesti kormányzatok és a határon túli magyarok kapcsolattörténete. Problémakatalógus* [True Fact. Budapest Governments and the History of Their Contacts with Hungarians Abroad. Catalogue of Problems] (Pozsony, 2004), p. 39.
33 *Ibid.*
34 László Domonkos, *Magyarok a Délvidéken* [Hungarians in the Southern Region] (Budapest, 1992), p. 115.
35 *Ibid.*, p. 116.
36 József Botlik, Béla Csorba and Károly Dudás, *Eltévedt mezsgyekövek. Adatok a délvidéki magyarság történetéhez* [Lost Boundary Markers. Notes on the History of the Southern Region Hungarians] (Budapest, 1994), p. 290.
37 Károly Mirnics, *Kis-Jugoszlávia hozománya. Írások az asszimilációról és a kisebbségről* [Dowry of Little Yugoslavia. Writings on Assimilation and Minorities] (Budapest, 1996), p. 49.
38 Botlik, Csorba and Dudás, *Eltévedt mezsgyekövek*, p. 199.
39 *Vajdasági Magyar Kultúrszövetség.*
40 *Horvátországi Magyar Szövetség.*
41 Mirnics, *Kis-Jugoszlávia hozománya*, pp. 311 and 316.
42 The distinction between *kisebbség/manjina* and *nemzetiség/ nationalna manjina* is not easy to convey fully in English. The second underlines the idea that a minority is an integral part of the nation, not just an ethnic entity. *Ustav Socijalističke Federativne Republike Jugoslavije*, Član 43. [The Constitution of the Socialist Federal Republic of Yugoslavia, Article 43], at http://sr.wikisource. org/wiki/Устав_Социјалистичке_Федеративне_Републике_ Југославије_(1963). Accessed August 11, 2010. László Rehák, *Kisebbségtől nemzetiségig* [From Minority to National Community] (Újvidék, 1979), p. 171.
43 Béla Csorba and János Vékás, eds., *A kultúrtanti visszavág. A Symposion-mozgalom krónikája 1954–1993* [Auntie Culture Strikes Back. Chronicle of the *Symposion* Movement 1954–1993] (Újvidék, 1994), p. 175.
44 It has to be said that the Hungarian-language institutional system itself took part in punitive action against the offenders, by making it impossible for them to operate and excluding them from membership. *Ibid.*
45 *Woiwodschaft Serbien und Temeser Banat.*
46 *Kárpátaljai Magyar Kulturális Szövetség.*

47	Kálmán Móricz, *Nagydobrony* [Velyka Dobron'] (Beregszász, 1995).
48	"'Járok egyet a természetben.' Interjú Bíró Andorral" ["I Go for a Walk in Nature.' Interview with Andor Bíró], *Kárpáti Igaz Szó,* June 23, 2005.
49	Memoirs: István Bendász, *Öt év a szögesdrót mögött: egy kárpátaljai pap a Gulag munkatáboraiban* [Five Years behind Barbed Wire: a Transcarpathian Priest in the Labor Camps of the Gulag] (Abaliget, 2000); Pál Forgon, *Ott voltam, ahol a legszebb virágok nyílnak: egy kárpátaljai magyar református lelkész a Gulagon* [Where the Fairest Flowers Bloom: a Subcarpathian Hungarian Reformed Pastor in the Gulag] (Budapest, 1992); József Zimányi, *Tűzoszlopoddal jéghegyek között. Egy ref. lelkész életútja* [Pillar of Fire amid Hills of Ice. Life of a Reformed Pastor] (Budapest, 2006); Barna Horkay, *A Keleti Baráti Kör. Egy ref. lelkész életútja* [The Eastern Friendly Circle. Life of a Reformed Pastor] (n.p., 1998).
50	I. Pop, "Zakarpats'ka shkola zhyvopysu jak fenomen nacional'nogo i kul'turnogo vidrodzhennja" [The Transcarpathian School of Painting as a Phenomenon of National and Cultural Revival], in G. Pavlenko, ed., *Carpatica – Karpatyka. Aktual'ni problemy istorii' i kul'tury Zakarpattia* [Carpatica. Current Problems of History and Culture of Transcarpathia] (Uzhhorod, 1992), pp. 181–196; László Balla, *Erdélyi Béla és kortársai. Kárpátalja képzőművészeinek három nemzedéke* [Béla Erdélyi and His Contemporaries. Three Generations of Transcarpathian Artists] (Ungvár/Budapest, 1994).
51	Csilla Fedinec, "A magyar irodalom a kárpátaljai oktatásban 1944-től napjainkig" [Hungarian Literature in Transcarpathian Education from 1944 to the Present Day], *Literatura* (2001) 4: 409–426.
52	*Lendület; Új Hajtás.*
53	I. Holopenkov and P. Rospopin, eds., *Knygy vydavnyctva "Karpaty" (1946–1970)* [The Books of Publishing House Karpaty (1946–1970)] (Uzhhorod, 1970); László Sándor, "Kárpátukrajnai magyar könyv- és lapkiadás, nyomdászat és könyvkereskedelem 1918–1980-ig" [Carpatho-Ukrainian Hungarian Book and Press Publication, Printing and Book Distribution 1918–1980], *Magyar Könyvszemle* (1983) 2: 186–191; László Sándor and Ferenc Botka, "A kárpátukrajnai magyar könyvkiadás irodalmi bibliográfiája 1945–1960" [Literary Bibliography of Carpatho-Ukrainian Hungarian Book Publication 1945–1960], *Irodalomtörténet* (1961) 3: 355–371; Csilla Fedinec, "Magyar könyvkiadás és képzőművészet kapcsolata

Kárpátalján (1918-tól napjainkig)" [Connection of Hungarian Book Publishing and Fine Art in Transcarpathia (from 1918 to the Present Day)], in Idem, ed., *Az elsüllyedt jelek. I. A 20. századi magyar könyvillusztráció Magyarország határain kívül 1918-tól napjainkig* [Sunken Signs I. 20th-Century Hungarian Book Illustration beyond Hungary's Borders from 1918 to the Present Day] (Budapest, 2003), pp. 138–171; Csilla Fedinec, "A Kárpáti Kiadó Kalendáriuma (40 év címszavakban)" [The Almanac of Publishing House Karpaty (Forty Years in Titles)], in *Kalendárium '96–'97* [Almanac 1996–1997] (Uzhhorod, 1996), pp. 153–167.

54   Ljuba Siselina, "A volt Szovjetunió nemzeti politikája és a kárpátaljai magyarság" [The National Policy of the Former Soviet Union and the Hungarians of Transcarpathia], *Regio* 3 (1992) 2: 166–174; János Penckófer, *Tettben a jellem. A magyar irodalom sajátos kezdeményei Kárpátalján a XX. század második felében* [Character in Deed. The Specific Initiatives of Hungarian Literature in Transcarpathia in the Second Half of the 20th Century] (Budapest, 2003); György Csanádi, *Régi beregszásziak* [Old People of Beregovo] (Beregszász, 2001); György Csanádi, *Sorsfordító évek sodrában. Fejezetek Beregvidék történelmi múltjából* [In the Current of Fateful Years. Chapters of Bereg District History] (Ungvár, 2004); Ottó Schober, *Színfalak előtt, mögött, nélkül. Epizódok a Beregszászi Népszínház történetéből* [Before, behind, without the Scenes. Episodes from the History of the People's Theater of Beregovo] (Ungvár/Budapest, 1995); Balázs Keresztyén, *Kárpátaljai művelődéstörténeti kislexikon* [Pocket Dictionary of Transcarpathian Cultural History] (Budapest, 2001); Károly D. Balla, *Kis(ebbségi) magyar skizofrénia* [A Minor/Minority Hungarian Schizophrenia] (Ungvár/Budapest, 1993).

55   Csaba Békés, Malcolm Byrne and János M. Rainer, eds., *The 1956 Hungarian Revolution. A History in Documents* (Budapest, 2003); György Litván, János Bak and Lyman H. Letgres, eds., *The Hungarian Revolution of 1956. Reform, Revolt and Repression 1953–1963* (London, 1996); Tibor Méray, *Thirteen Days that Shook the Kremlin* (New York, 1959); James A. Michener, *The Bridge at Andau. The Story of the Hungarian Revolution* (London, 1957); Ibolya Murber and Zoltán Fónagy, eds., *Die Ungarische Revolution und Österreich 1956* (Vienna, 2006).

56   Ernö Deák, *Ungarische Mittelschulen in Österreich nach 1956* (Vienna, 2006).

57   Heinrich Wedral, "Pendelwanderung, Abwanderung und die Situation auf dem burgenländischen Arbeitsmarkt," in Traude Horvath and Rainer Münz, eds., *Migration und Arbeitsmarkt* (Eisenstadt, 1987), pp. 18–34; Günter Karner, "Pendeln: Schicksal oder Chance," in Horvath and Münz, eds., *Migration und Arbeitsmarkt*, pp. 35–44.

58   Gerhard Baumgartner, Eva Kovács and András Vári, *Entfernte Nachbarn – Jánossmorja und Andau 1990–2000 / Távoli Rokonok– Jánossmorja és Andau 1990–2000* (Budapest, 2002).

59   Imre Gyenge, "Die Wandlungen der burgenländischen Ungarn. Ein Augenzeugenbericht," *Integratio* 11–12 (1979): 23–33.

60   Ernö Deák, "Die Ungarn in Wien: eine unsichtbare Volksgruppe?," *Integratio* 15 (1982): 115–132.

61   Ludwig Szeberényi, *Die ungarische Volksgruppe im Burgenland und ihr Volksgruppenbeirat* (Vienna, 1986), pp. 35–36.

62   *Maideklaration des Burgenländisch-Ungarischen Kulturvereins.* See Szeberényi, *Die ungarische Volksgruppe*, p. 37.

63   Andreas Oplatka, *Der Riss in der Mauer – September 1989. Ungarn öffnet die Grenze* (Vienna, 2009).

64   St. Lucy's Day (December 13).

65   Gerhard Baumgartner, "Der nationale Differenzierungsprozess in den ländlichen Gemeinden des südlichen Burgenlandes," in Andreas Moritsch, ed., *Vom Ethnos zur Nationalität: Der nationale Differenzierungsprozess am Beispiel ausgewählter Orte in Kärnten und im Burgenland* (Vienna/Munich, 1991), pp. 93–155.

VI. FROM THE CHANGE OF REGIME TO THE RECENT PAST 1989–2005

1. MINORITY RIGHTS
IN INTERNATIONAL RELATIONS
Balázs Vizi

The question of minority rights protection was sidelined in international domain after World War II. The horrors of the war had inclined the United Nations, founded in 1945, to concentrate on furthering world peace, stability, and the universal protection of human rights. The accepted wisdom in that period was that minority rights could be ensured by protecting human rights as a whole and prohibiting discrimination, especially on a racial, national or ethnic basis, and thus any reference to minority rights was omitted from the 1948 UN Declaration of Human Rights.[1] It was rare for international human rights instruments to mention minorities at all, the most prominent exception being the 1966 International Covenant on Civil and Political Rights,[2] long the sole international human rights treaty to allude to the right of persons belonging to minorities to their culture and identity.[3]

Not until 1989–1990 did the minority issue come to the forefront of international politics again, as the authoritarian rule of the Communist Parties of Central and Eastern Europe fell apart. Democratic transition was often accompanied by grave ethnic conflicts in the region. This applied especially to the break-up of the Soviet Union and of Yugoslavia, as national and ethnic communities in the former socialist federations started to claim not only political freedom but also the right to self-determination. The secessions of the Soviet republics were replete with such conflicts (one example being that of the Russian minority in the Transnistria region of Moldova), and so was the gaining of independence by the Yugoslav successor states (Bosnia-Herzegovina, Croatia, Macedonia and Slovenia).[4]

The disintegration of the Soviet Union and the wars in the ex-Yugoslav region in 1991–1999 provoked serious international public attention on the situation of national minorities. These concerns were reflected in the European context within the framework of international co-operations both in security and human rights issues. The Copenhagen Document on the Human Dimension, adopted on June 5–29, 1990, by the Conference on Security and Cooperation in Europe (CSCE; from 1994 the Organization for Security and Cooperation in Europe, OSCE), was the first significant step in setting the standards on the human rights of minorities in Europe, listing various cultural, linguistic, educational and political rights belonging to members of national minorities.[5] This was followed by the adoption of the Helsinki Document of the CSCE in 1992, which established the office of the High Commissioner on National Minorities, whose tasks, through the diplomatic channels of the CSCE participants, were to provide "'early warning' and, as appropriate, 'early action' at the earliest possible stage in regard to tensions involving national minority issues that have the potential to develop into a conflict within the CSCE area, affecting peace, stability, or relations between participating States."[6] In the event, the High Commissioner in the last decade has gone beyond diplomatic activity to prepare comprehensive reports and proposals for the states on developing their minority rights legislations (for example, on the situation of Roma in Europe, on minority education, on language rights, and on the political participation of minorities).[7] The fact that minority rights protection is not just a European concern was reflected in the 1992 UN Declaration on the Rights of Persons Belonging to National or Ethnic, Religious and Linguistic Minorities.[8]

However, these were only political statements, not backed by legal commitments from the CSCE participant states – they did not qualify as full recognition of minority rights under international law. Such a move could not be expected from a mainly security-focused international organization, such as the CSCE/OSCE. The Council of Europe seemed to be a much more suitable organization for these endeavors. Several attempts were made in the early 1990s to have the Council of Europe prepare such a treaty. The first outcome was the 1992 European Charter for Regional or Minority Languages, which defines the scopes for minority language use, from education to state administration, allowing any subscribing state to choose the degree to which it accords these legal commitments on providing rights to its minorities. Moreover, even though the Language Charter clearly has effects on the situation of minorities, its declared goal is limited to the protection of regional or minority languages. The first international treaty to deal expressly and comprehensively with the rights of national minorities was the Framework Convention for the Protection of National Minorities, agreed within the Council of Europe in 1995. This enunciated the main principles in treaty obligations under international law, precluding, for instance, for instance, discrimination based on membership of a national minority, and stipulating that state parties should encourage and promote the protection of minority identity, language and culture.[9] The Framework Convention acknowledged that protection of minority rights "is part of the international protection of human rights and as such falls within the scope of international cooperation."

But neither the Framework Convention nor the Language Charter states plainly what states have to do, or what rights states must grant their minorities if their minorities' identities are to be preserved. Furthermore, implementation of these agreements is monitored only by committees of experts and the political body of the Committee of Ministers – there is no recourse to an international court if a signatory state infringes rights agreed under these treaties.

The international documents merely formulate goals that each state may attain by incorporating them into its policies and legislation. For instance, there is no international document to define what size of minority would warrant a separate state university teaching in the minority language. The international standards are confined to stating that minorities have a right to appropriate education in their own language, but largely leave it to each state to decide how to meet this requirement.[10]

Thus the international protection of minority rights raises some complex issues. There is serious debate between states about whether there exist so-called collective rights applicable not to individuals but to minority communities, such as the right to self-government or autonomy. These questions are left open in the international documents that states have endorsed by consensus. The formulation of coherent, detailed international legal obligations proceeds in a cumbersome fashion, not only because states in Europe differ subjectively in their views on the consistency of minority rights, but also because of objective difficulties: the wide variety of demographic and sociological situations and degrees of organization found among the minorities themselves.

However, increasing emphasis has been placed in international politics on how states treat their minorities. It was seen that states and international organizations were encouraged to increase the protection of minorities in the 1990s by the perceived threats of war and violent conflict. It was recognized that the more successful is the accommodation of minority rights according to the needs of minority communities, the smaller the likelihood of majority/minority conflict developing in a state. So minority protection was conceived in the context of the protection of human rights as an important international commitment for states to make.

A new development came when the European Union, the paramount political and economic entity of institutionalized international co-operation in Europe, joined the OSCE and the Council of Europe in paying serious heed to the minorities of Central and Eastern Europe. The 1993 summit of the EU, which set the Copenhagen Criteria for the accession of Central and Eastern European states, placed great stress on political criteria, including the protection of minorities. This was a big change for an organization that historically had seen European integration mainly in terms of economic integration and creating a single market.

The EU accession process for the early Central and Eastern European candidates, including Hungary, began in the spring of 1998. The European Commission issued every year a regular report ("the EU government" so to speak) on how far the Copenhagen Criteria had been met by candidate states, including developments in the position of the minorities. The extreme political importance of EU membership meant that the candidate countries strove to meet the political requirements, even though they were not legally binding.[11]

This could be seen mainly in the strengthening of social integration measures for the Roma. In 2002–2004 a new Treaty Establishing a Constitution for Europe was prepared, in which, on Hungary's proposal, it was stated for the first time that the Union had recognized in Community law the rights of those belonging to minorities. When the ratification process was terminated at the end of 2007 after rejection of the European Constitution by French and Dutch voters in referenda, it gave way to the Reform Treaty, which eventually took the form of the Treaty of Lisbon, which retained the reference to minority rights unchanged.[12]

All in all, the 1990s marked a big advance, as the question of minority protection and the situation of minorities came to the fore in international politics. The international community has now taken responsibility for their situation, the protection of their human rights, and the preservation of their identity – and not simply for fear of ethnic conflict. A further important development in the last 15 years, apart from the international documents adopted, is that any dispute over the minorities is no longer seen simply as an internal affair. The importance of international cooperation is universally recognized. This has been seen in the 2000s in international debates on the relation between kin-state and cross-border kin-minorities,[13] the implementation of specific minority rights, the right of minorities to self-government or autonomy.[14] Although since the late 1990s minority issues seem to be less important for the international community, the international documents adopted in the past decades are determining for handling internal and international debates on minority rights.

Notes

1   Cf. Patrick Thornberry, *The Rights of Minorities and International Law* (Oxford, 1991), pp. 113–123.
2   This was adopted by the UN General Assembly on December 16, 1966, and came into force on March 23, 1976.
3   "Article 27: In those States in which ethnic, religious or linguistic minorities exist, persons belonging to such minorities shall not be

denied the right, in community with the other members of their group, to enjoy their own culture, to profess and practise their own religion, or to use their own language." See http://www2.ohchr.org/english/law/ccpr.htm. Retrieved December 28, 2009.

4   For more detail, see John Ishyama and Marijke Breuning, *Ethnopolitics in the New Europe* (Boulder, CO, 1998).

5   Text: http://www.ena.lu/document_conference_human_dimension_csce_copenhagen_29_june_1990-020004650.html.   Retrieved December 28, 2009.

6   http://www.osce.org/documents/mcs/1992/07/4048_en.pdf. Retrieved December 28, 2009.

7   On the high commissioner's activity, see Walter Kemp, ed., *Quiet Diplomacy in Action – the OSCE High Commissioner on National Minorities* (The Hague, 2001).

8   In addition, the General Assembly adopted a declaration on the rights of indigenous peoples in 2007.

9   Mark Weller, ed., *The Rights of Minorities. A Commentary on the European Framework Convention for the Protection of National Minorities* (Oxford, 2006); text: http://conventions.coe.int/Treaty/EN/Treaties/Html/148.htm. Retrieved January 5, 2010.

10   *Ibid.*, Article 8.

11   Gabriel Toggenburg, ed., *Minority Protection and the Enlarged European Union: the Way Forward* (Budapest, 2004).

12   This was signed by member states on December 17, 2007, and came into force on December 1, 2009. The reference to minorities runs thus: "The Union is founded on the values of respect for human dignity, freedom, democracy, equality, the rule of law and respect for human rights, including the rights of persons belonging to minorities. These values are common to the Member States in a society in which pluralism, non-discrimination, tolerance, justice, solidarity and equality between women and men prevail." See http://www.consilium.europa. eu/uedocs/cmsUpload/cg00014.en07.pdf. Retrieved January 5, 2010.

13   See, for instance, Zoltán Kántor, Osamu Ieda, Iván Halász, Balázs Vízi, Balázs Majtényi and Stephen Deets, eds., *Beyond Sovereignty: from Status Law to Transnational Citizenship?* (Sapporo, 2006).

14   Cf. Kristin Henrard, *Devising an Adequate System of Minority Protection* (The Hague, 2000).

2. HUNGARIAN MINORITIES
AND THE CHANGE OF SYSTEM, 1989–1991
László Szarka

The system changes in East-Central Europe in 1989–1991 brought changes that were revolutionary in many ways. Monopoly communist power, after a brief transition, yielded to a democratic, parliamentary, multi-party system, and a Soviet-style command economy to a market-led one of privatization and free enterprise dominated by multinationals. But the gap left by the previously proclaimed communist notion of equality and the social, political and economic polarization that ensued brought symptoms of crisis to all societies in the region. The gap between the newly rich and the newly unemployed became a gulf, while both changes were often undeserved. Middle-class impoverishment and mounting destitution in the rest of society led to doubts about whether the newly proclaimed equality of opportunity meant anything at all.

On a great-power level, the changes of system came from Gorbachev's reforms and rapprochement with the United States. The transforming force was trade unionist in Poland, constitutional in Hungary, "velvet" in Czechoslovakia, violent in Romania, and generated in East and West Germany by the fall of the Berlin Wall and the rise of reunification. The Soviet Union collapsed in 1991 and Czechoslovakia and Yugoslavia gave way to new states as well. The end of the Soviet bloc meant the end of its military and economic manifestations, the Warsaw Pact and COMECON. One of the early intimations of irreversibility was a spate of admissions to the Council of Europe.[1]

Opposition forums were developed meanwhile by all the main minority ethnic groups in the region. As democratic programs were written, a free press appeared, and parties and movements were founded, minorities naturally joined in the process of creating the institutional system of political pluralism. They were simultaneously quick to institutionalize their relations with parent countries that were likewise reformulating their obligations to their minorities abroad. This renewed "parental" role was codified as follows in Paragraph 6.3 of Hungary's revised constitution, promulgated on October 23, 1989: "The Republic of Hungary shall bear a sense of responsibility for the fate of Hungarians living outside her borders and shall promote the fostering of their links with Hungary."[2]

Minority Hungarian communities in the Carpathian Basin could rely on initiatives from the reformers and dissidents in the state Communist Parties, on student movements, literary and cultural groups and clubs, voluntary and Church organizations, and on democratic initiatives among independent, opposition intellectuals. This steadily gained support meant that legal protection for minorities featured large within the illegal organizations of the 1980s. So the minority Hungarian movements and parties that emerged during the change of system had various antecedents.[3]

The changes that began in the Soviet Union in 1985 were mainly diplomatic. Tensions between the two superpowers began to ease. But Mikhail Gorbachev, unusually young for a Communist Party general secretary, sought domestic political changes as well, labeled *glasnost* (openness) and *perestroika* (transformation). The early period was marred by secretiveness about the disastrous accident at the Chernobyl nuclear power station, which undermined the credibility of glasnost for the world. By 1988, it was clear that the Soviet Union could not be modernized by reforms alone, and a process began that culminated in August 1991, when Gorbachev announced that the Soviet member republics would conclude a new treaty of association. This sparked an attempted coup by the army and secret service, forestalled by Boris Yeltsin, president of the Russian Federation, and forces loyal to him, but Gorbachev returned to power only symbolically. The Creation Agreement of the Commonwealth of Independent States, signed on December 8, 1991, at Belovezhskaya Pushcha, meant in effect that the Soviet republics had won their independence. The superpower had been replaced by new states, one of which was Ukraine, which included Transcarpathia.[4]

Intellectuals, writers and artists were instrumental in Transcarpathia when the Transcarpathian Hungarian Cultural Association was formed at Uzhgorod (soon to become known as Uzhhorod) on February 26, 1989, with Sándor Fodó as its first president.[5] It announced in its program that it would further the cultural and political interests of the community, and was soon expressing a need for provincial and national self-government. In the autumn of 1991, the council of Berehove (the former Beregovo) District proposed that the territory of Transcarpathia be declared an autonomous region and that the territory of Berehove District become a Hungarian Autonomous District. A referendum on the two types of autonomy was held in December 1991: in this, a clear majority of voters expressed support for autonomy for the Transcarpathian *oblast* and the creation of a Hungarian autonomous district of Berehove. However, this had no consequences.[6] One big move in inter-state relations came on March 1, 1989, with the opening of a minor frontier crossing at Astely (Astej)/Beregsurány, which enabled Transcarpathians to visit Hungary with simplified border procedures.

In the final years of the Husák era (1969–1989) in Czechoslovakia, the work of the Czechoslovakian Hungarian Minority Protection Committee[7] founded in 1978 proved decisive, with help from the samizdat and the official press in Hungary. The writer and geologist Miklós Duray was put on trial in January 1983, but the case was dropped. The Slovakian Hungarian public was mobilized by curbs on their language and education rights and by the increasing difficulties being faced by Hungarians in Transylvania. Ever more students and members of the intelligentsia joined in the defense of minority rights. The clergy who had been sidelined for their activity in 1968 became active, and so did activists of the Cultural Association of Hungarian Workers of Czechoslovakia (CSEMADOK´)[8] and several other groups. There were protests over Czechoslovak infringements of civil and human rights and the general lack of legality, from Charta '77, secret Slovakian Catholic organizations, and the rights movements among the Hungarian minority, all of which showed exemplary civil courage.[9]

Resistance to the negative political initiatives of the Husák regime received ever-wider support. The Slovakian Hungarian writers' group became active. CSEMADOK under the chairmanship of Zoltán Sidó was the one legal cultural organization to make its view heard on the party state's system, the state-owned publisher Madách Kiadó played an increasingly frequent opposition role, and rising numbers of Hungarian university students joined in the work of minority legal protection, connection-building and information.

Slovakian Hungarians were among the first to join the "velvet revolution" that broke out with a mass student protest in Prague on November 17, 1989. A group of ethnic Hungarian intelligentsia in Šaľa anticipated all other Czechoslovakian groups by founding the Independent Hungarian Initiative on November 18.[10] Cooperating closely with newly founded national movements, the Czech Civil Forum and the Public against Violence in Slovakia,[11] it appealed on November 20 to Slovakian Hungarians to join a national strike aimed at ousting the communists. Two days later the Initiative, headed by Lajos Grendel, László Szigeti, László A. Nagy and Károly Tóth, joined the Public against Violence Coordinating Committee. Emphasis in its statements was placed on securing collective rights for national minorities through legislation, and on full self-administration in the cultural and educational fields.[12]

An Initiative nominee, Sándor Varga, gained a vice-premiership in the new multi-party government of Milan Čič, formed on December 12, 1989, while László A. Nagy became deputy speaker in the legislature in 1990. The Initiative nominee in the government that formed after the 1990 general elections was Gábor Zászlós, likewise as a deputy prime minister.

Two other Hungarian political movements arose in January 1990. Groups of Hungarian Catholic intelligentsia initiated the Hungarian Christian Democratic Movement,[13] which focused in its program on securing the rights of Slovakia's national minorities. It also espoused the cause of minority autonomy, but it emphasized from the outset the question of representation of the minority cause in the government structure.

Also founded at this time as a classic minority umbrella party was the Coexistence Political Movement (for Democracy and the Rights of National Minorities), by Miklós Duray, who had returned at the end of November 1989 from an 18-month study trip to the United States.[14] It entered into an electoral alliance with the Christian Democrats and proved efficient at mobilizing the Hungarian community. The demand for autonomy featured in its program from the outset, alongside settlement of the legal and political status of the minority and improvement in its cultural economic position.[15]

The minorities in Romania were under mounting pressure over plans by the Ceauşescu regime for village resettlement and homogenization. Romanian–Hungarian relations became highly strained towards the end of the 1980s, due to the mass flight and emigration of Transylvanian Hungarians to Hungary and the public demonstrations in Hungary against the regime and its resettlement plans.[16] A local conflict arose over the removal of the militant Reverend László Tőkés from the Timişoara Reformed Church in September 1989. Official Hungarian protests were joined on December 16 by a demonstration by his parishioners and Romanians in solidarity with them. This precipitated the December 1989 Romanian revolution, for after a couple of days the civil disobedience spread across the city and then the whole country, as a national movement against Ceauşescu. Attempts by the security police and the army to crush the protests caused many casualties, but the demonstrations swelled and much of the army came over to the demonstrators' side. The events on December 21–25, 1989, toppled the regime. The dictator and his wife were sentenced to death by a summary military court and executed immediately. Serious armed clashes continued in Timişoara, Bucharest and other big cities between security forces loyal to the old regime and demonstrators and the military units on their side.[17]

The leading factor behind the December 1989 revolution became the National Salvation Front, as a new organ of state power.[18] Among those who joined its presiding committee were Géza Domokos, who had done much for Hungarian culture as manager of the state-owned

Kriterion publishing company, and László Tőkés, a symbolic hero of the revolution. The Front duly included in its first proclamation on December 22 a pledge of equality before the law for the national minorities. Once the legal frames of political pluralism were in place, a group of Romanian Hungarians, mainly from Bucharest, issued a proclamation on December 25, calling on the Transylvanian Hungarians to form local branches of a new Democratic Alliance of Hungarians in Romania. This was registered on January 26, 1990, as a political body of "national public and interest representation."[19]

The individual and collective rights of the minorities were duly recognized on January 5, 1990, by the National Salvation Front, which committed itself to drawing the minorities into the institutions of state, in line with the Gyulafehérvár (Alba Iulia) resolution of December 1, 1918.[20] The Alliance initially placed great emphasis on cooperation with the Front, in line with the December 25 proclamation, but it soon made clear its demands for communal rights for the Romanian Hungarians, to be codified in new national minority legislation, and minority participation in the legislature, executive and judiciary. The Alliance's interim leaders – Géza Domokos, László Tőkés and Károly Király – called for minority language-use and education rights to be granted immediately. Within the Alliance, the initiators in Bucharest began to be relegated, and its center of gravity moved to the Székely Land, Târgu Mureş and Cluj-Napoca in Transylvania.

The process of building up the Alliance and rapprochement between Hungarians and Romanians was severely affected by the anti-Hungarian riots in Satu Mare and Târgu Mureş in March 1990. The situation in Târgu Mureş became tense after a march of 100,000 Hungarians with books and candles on February 10, calling for language and education rights. The appearance of a sign in Hungarian at one of the city's pharmacies was enough to start local Romanians organizing a counter-demonstration for March 19. Rumors of Hungarianization measures were spread by the local Romanian press. Károly Király, as a vice-premier in the interim government, could not prevent an escalation into open conflict, which suited some national and local Romanian politicians. The Romanian parties and local interests forced Előd Kincses, Mureş County chairman of the Alliance, to resign. Romanian villagers moving on the city on March 19, armed with axes, attacked the city offices of the Alliance. Only the intervention of the army could save the writer András Sütő, who had been seriously beaten, and several local Alliance figures. Six lives were lost in the mass violence in the main square, and the television pictures shocked opinion in Transylvania and around the world. The dramatic nature of the events was emphasized by a wave of Transylvanian Hungarian emigration numbering several thousand. One important side-effect: the violence in Târgu Mureş provided a pretext on March 26 for resurrecting the secret police, which had been disbanded on December 30, 1989.[21]

Faced with indecision by the Bucharest government and nationalist efforts within it, the Alliance broke with the Front. At the same time, there broke out in the Alliance internal disputes among various groupings and political forces, leading to a weakening of the reform communist and moderate wing (with the relegation of Károly Király) and an advance by the young, radical trends (with the appointment of the poet Géza Szőcs, former editor-in-chief of *Ellenpontok*, as general secretary) and to some temporary compromises in the party. Domokos remained as president and Tőkés as honorary president. All trends received seats on its national board.

A total of 18 parties including the Alliance won seats in the general elections, held at the same time as presidential elections. Transylvanian Hungarians won 12 seats in the Senate and 29 in the Chamber of Deputies, making them the second-largest force after the Front, which gained a two-thirds majority. The Alliance was now on the defensive against nationalism fomented by the Front and the chauvinist Vatra Românească ("Romanian Hearth"), formed on February 7, 1990, in Târgu Mureş, in a parliamentary system that left little leeway for opposition. The Alliance, after the Târgu Mureş events, found it hard to light on a political style to match its importance. A solution was found in the Democratic Convention[22] formed on August 6, 1990, with other opposition groups, which became a vehicle for joint action with Romanian parties and renewal of the methods used in minority political activity. A radical, autonomist group within the Alliance, pressing for assistance from Hungary and the international community, managed for a while to increase its support at the expense of the moderates who sought cooperation with Romanian parties and factions of government.[23]

Yugoslavia was unique, as its transformation timetable was dictated by the process of state disintegration. Eight years after Tito's death, the Federation of Yugoslav Communists as state party could not and would not curb the threat of Serbian nationalism any longer, for national conflicts of interest appeared inside the party as well. The first casualty was the status of the autonomous provinces: Vojvodina, and Kosovo and Metohija.[24] Behind the Serbian nationalist notions lay the conviction that only a unified Serbia freed of provincial autonomy could impose Belgrade's centralism on the other republics and hold the Federation together.

The crisis in post-Tito Yugoslavia began with this program of Serbian renewal. The implicit intention of enhancing Serbian domination, the efforts to shift internal ethnic borders, and the reinterpretation of the federal system to suit Serbia pushed the Yugoslav state into open crisis. Effort went at first into curbing the administrative autonomy and sovereignty of the republics of Slovenia, Croatia, Macedonia, Montenegro and Bosnia–Herzegovina. Then in October 1988 came the "anti-bureaucratic revolution" and attendant nationalism that lost Vojvodina its autonomous status.[25]

The Serbian efforts to centralize and restrict minority rights led to serious disturbances among the majority Albanians in Kosovo in January 1989, reinforced in February by a miners' strike. The Albanian demands received support from other republics, heightened by the sharp responses of the Serbian state and party leaders. On June 28, 1989, Serbian President Slobodan Milošević chose the site, Gazimestan, and the 600th anniversary of the baneful Battle of Kosovo on St. Vitus' Day 1389 to announce to a mass rally that he was "restoring Serbian unity," thus provoking the first declaration of independence by the Kosovo Albanians on July 2.[26] The federal legislature, meeting in Belgrade on August 8, 1990, amended the constitution to allow multi-party government throughout Yugoslavia. However, this version of the constitution did not recognize the minorities as communities, which left Vojvodina and Kosovo with only nominal status. Incitement to xenophobic antagonism towards minorities and neighboring countries increased, which enhanced the risk of armed conflict.

Faced with these conditions, a group of Hungarian intellectuals initiated by András Ágoston launched a petition for minority education rights on December 13, 1989. It was signed by almost 18,000 Yugoslavian Hungarians. Five days later, Ágoston called together a committee of intellectuals (István Beszédes, János Boldizsár, Károly Dudás, Sándor Hódi, Tamás Korhecz, Frigyes Kovács, Zoltán Siflis, László Szekeres, János Tóth and János Vékás) to submit the founding document of the Democratic Fellowship of Vojvodina Hungarians.[27] The initiators, acknowledging the consequences of the national and republican lines that had emerged, made their call for the collective rights to Serbia. The Fellowship, officially inaugurated in 1990, laid its main emphasis on "minority self-government on the personal principle" as the most appropriate legal form for asserting the collective interests of the Vojvodina Hungarians.[28]

Slovenia and Croatia seceded from Yugoslavia in June 1991 after a short conflict. Their independence was recognized by the European Community countries on January 15, 1992. On April 27, 1992, the rump of Yugoslavia adopted the fourth constitution in Yugoslavia's history. This rump consisted of a federal community of states between Serbia and Montenegro. That was the situation when the congress of the Fellowship, meeting in Kanjiža on April 25, finalized its "Memorandum on the self-government of Hungarians living in the Serbian Republic." The document, presented as a proposed constitutional amendment, was the most comprehensive expression hitherto of a system of Hungarian self-government on the triple basis of personal rights and regional and local self-government organizations.[29] Hungary, along with Poland, was the regional pioneer in dismantling the party state and eliminating communist dictatorship during the years of transition. Cooperation between the opposition groups and the reformers within the state party (by no means free of conflict) appeared also in handling the issue of the Hungarian minorities. This was a constant topic in the émigré papers and the samizdat publications in Hungary, notably the periodical *Beszélő*. Apart from the numerous documents and news items that appeared, there were reinterpretations of the basic issues of Hungarian national and minority policy from such hands as Gyula Illyés, Sándor Csoóri, Miklós Duray, Gáspár Miklós Tamás, Géza Szőcs and Mihály Hamburger. Important thematic definitions came from writers, artists and scholars who had recently settled in Hungary, such as Attila Ara-Kovács, Iván Bába, András S. Benedek, Géza Páskándi, Pál Bodor, Miklós Hornyik, Károly Lábadi, László Tóth and others.[30]

Important changes were made in the official policy of the Hungarian party and government. Imre Szokai and Csaba Tabajdi, writing in the daily *Magyar Nemzet* on February 13, 1988, called the relation between the government and the Hungarians minorities ripe for rethinking "at this stage in the renewal of Hungarian socialism." They argued plainly in favor of the unity of the cultural nation and called the defense of the minority Hungarians a task of Hungarian foreign policy.[31]

The half-hearted initiatives of 1968 had been blocked, but official foreign policy took wing again in the early 1980s, when the initiative of Imre Pozsgay's reform supporters in the Hungarian Communist Party and of the national line represented by Mátyás Szűrös led in 1985–1986 to a declared intention of changing minority policy. The new emphases under the Németh government derived mainly from Minister of Foreign Affairs Gyula Horn and Minister of Education Ferenc Glatz. Yet the opposition at home and among the Hungarian minorities rightly called one of the big failings of

Kádárite foreign policy the meager activity that Budapest showed as the situation for Hungarians in Transylvania and Slovakia worsened. The consensus for changing domestic and foreign policy during the change of system covered not only multi-party democracy and restoration of the sovereignty of the Hungarian state, but also responsibility for the Hungarian minorities in neighboring countries and institutionalized acceptance of that. The need for such support was writ large in the government and party programs of 1989–1990.[32] It entailed building up responsible relations with the Hungarian communities concerned. The Antall government expressly declared that they formed an integral part of the Hungarian nation, that the Hungarian state bore responsibility for their survival and destiny, and that support would be given for the programs devised by the minorities.[33] What came to be known as the Antall doctrine placed the task of decision-making in the hands of the elected political representatives of each minority community concerned. Antall underlined the point that his government saw the political movements and parties, and the development of forms of personal, local and regional autonomy, as stabilizing factors integral to the processes occurring in Europe and capable of benefiting neighborly relations. In support of the policy of concluding basic treaties with neighboring countries, he stated that Hungary opposed any change in external or internal state boundaries, but it expected minority rights to be observed consistently. It was to the credit of the Antall government that it brought to the notice of neighboring countries and the outside world (although on occasions in an overly spectacular and emotive way) the fact that the cause of the Hungarian minorities abroad was a central and priority task of Hungarian foreign policy.[34]

Notes

1   See Frederic Bozo, Marie-Pierre Rey, N. Piers Ludlow and Leopoldo Nuti, eds., *Europe and the End of the Cold War. A Reappraisal* (London, 2009), Lee Edwards, *The Collapse of Communism* (Stanford, CA, 1999), and Hans Lemberg, "Osteuropa, Mitteleuropa, Europa, Formen und Probleme der 'Rückkehr nach Europa'," in

Jürgen Elvert, ed., *Der Umbruch in Osteuropa* (Stuttgart, 1993), pp. 15–28.

2   Iván Halász and Balázs Majtényi, "Felelősség a határon túli magyarokért" [Responsibility for Hungarians Abroad], in András Jakab, ed., *Az Alkotmány kommentárja* [Commentary on the Constitution], 2 vols. (Budapest, 2009), pp. 344–349. On interpreting the concept of the Hungarian nation, see László Szarka, Balázs Vizi, Balázs Majtényi and Zoltán Kántor, eds., *Nemzetfogalmak és etnopolitikai modellek Kelet-Közép-Európában* [Concepts of Nation and Ethno-Political Models in East-Central Europe] (Budapest, 2007). On the variety of nation concepts in Europe and East-Central Europe, see the recommendation of the Parliamentary Assembly of the Council of Europe adopted on January 26, 2006, on the basis of a report by Romanian Hungarian Senator György Frunda: *Recommendation 1735 (2006). The Concept of "Nation".* At http:// assembly.coe.int/main.asp?Link=/documents/adoptedtext/ta06/ erec1735.htm. Accessed May 2, 2010.

3   On the ethno-political context of the change of system in East-Central Europe, there is a useful volume of studies analyzing the demographic, historical and political development of the Hungarian minorities: László Szarka, ed., *Hungary and the Hungarian Minorities. Trends in the Past and in Our Time* (Boulder, CO/Highland Lakes, NJ, 2004). On the region as a whole, see Jerzy Kranz, ed., *Law and Practice of Central European Countries in the Field of National Minorities Protection after 1989* (Warsaw, 1998).

4   On the national question's role in the break-up of the Soviet Union, see Ronald Grigor Suny, *The Revenge of the Past: Nationalism, Revolution, and the Collapse of the Soviet Union* (Stanford, CA, 1993).

5   *Kárpátaljai Magyar Kulturális Szövetség (KMKSZ).*

6   Basic documents and timeline of minority Hungarian self-organization: Nándor Bárdi and György Éger, eds., *Útkeresés és integráció. Határon túli magyar érdekvédelmi szervezetek dokumentumai* [Search and Integration. Documents of Hungarian Interest-Representing Organizations Abroad] (Budapest, 2000). For a survey of the attempts, see Nándor Bárdi, "Cleavages in Cross-Border Magyar Minority Politics, 1989–1998," *Regio* 11 (2000) 1: 3–36. On the Transcarpathian documents on this period, see pp. 479–500, and for a chronology (1989–1998, András Jánki), see pp. 793–812; for a detailed account of events, see György Dupka, ed.,

A KMKSZ történetéből. Dokumentumok, tények, adatok [From the History of the Transcarpathian Hungarian Cultural Association. Documents, Facts, Data] (Ungvár, 1993), pp. 118–164.

7   *Csehszlovákiai Magyar Kisebbségi Jogvédő Bizottság.*

8   *Csehszlovákiai Magyar Dolgozók Kulturális Szövetsége (CSEMADOK).* The variations of the name are: 1949–1966: Csehszlovákiai Magyar Dolgozók Kultúregyesülete; 1966–1969 and 1971–1990: Csehszlovákiai Magyar Dolgozók Kulturális Szövetsége; 1969–1971: Csehszlovákiai Magyar Társadalmi és Kulturális Szövetség; 1990–1993: Csehszlovákiai Magyarok Demokratikus Szövetsége; since 1993: Szlovákiai Magyar Társadalmi és Közművelődési Szövetség–Csemadok.

9   The documents of these movements appear in Miklós Duray, *Kettős elnyomásban. Dokumentumok a Csehszlovákiai magyarság helyzetéről és jogvédelméről 1978–1989* [Double Pressure. Documents on the Situation and Legal Protection of the Czechoslovakian Hungarians 1978–1989] (Pozsony, 1989); a detailed account of events is to be found in Árpád Popély, *A (cseh)szlovákiai magyarság történeti kronológiája 1944–1992* [Historical Chronology of the (Czecho)Slovakian Hungarian Community 1944–1992] (Somorja, 2006), in the section on 1977–1990, pp. 349–458.

10   *Független Magyar Kezdeményezés (FMK).*

11   *Občanské fórum (OF); Verejnosť proti násiliu (VPN).*

12   Oral history volume of source value: Árpád Popély and Attila Simon, eds., *A rendszerváltás és a csehszlovákiai magyarok (1989–1992)* [The Change of System and Czechoslovakia's Hungarians (1989–1992)] (Somorja, 2009); a treatment of the change of system: Eleonóra Sándor, "A rendszerváltás magyar szemmel" [The Change of System through Hungarian Eyes], in József Fazekas and Péter Hunčik, eds., *Magyarok Szlovákiában. I. Összefoglaló jelentés (1989–2004)* [Hungarians in Slovakia. I. Summary Report (1989–2004)] (Somorja/ Dunaszerdahely, 2004), pp. 23–50.

13   *Magyar Kereszténydemokrata Mozgalom.*

14   *Együttélés Politikai Mozgalom (a Demokráciáért és a Nemzeti Kisebbségek Jogaiért).*

15   On the foundation of Slovakian Hungarian parties, see László Öllős, "A magyar pártok programja" [Program of Hungarian Parties], in Fazekas and Hunčik, eds., *Magyarok Szlovákiában*, pp. 51–77; basic documents: Bárdi and Éger, eds., *Útkeresés és integráció*, pp. 201–264. For a 68-clause draft proposal by the Hungarian

Christian Democratic Movement "on the situation and rights of national minorities and ethnic groups," see *Új Szó*, February 16, 1993. The Coexistence Political Movement documents "Basic principles of territorial self-government and personal autonomy" and "Local government, alliances between settlements, and public administrative reorganization" were policy yardsticks: Bárdi and Éger, eds., *Útkeresés és integráció*, pp. 232–237.

16   On the position of Romanian Hungarians and their role in Romanian–Hungarian relations, see Béla K. Király, ed., *The Hungarian Minority's Situation in Ceausescu's Romania* (Highland Lakes, NJ, 1994), and György Földes, *Magyarország, Románia és a nemzeti kérdés 1956–1989* [Hungary, Romania and the National Question 1956–1989] (Budapest, 2007).

17   The most comprehensive account so far of the 1989 events in Romania is Peter Siani Davies, *The Romanian Revolution of December 1989* (Ithaca, NY/London, 2005).

18   *Frontul Salvării Naționale.*

19   *Romániai Magyar Demokrata Szövetség.* Documents on the Alliance: Bárdi and Éger, eds., *Útkeresés és integráció*, pp. 21–72; timeline (Frigyes Udvardy), pp. 691–695. For a brief history, see Miklós Bakk, *The Democratic Alliance of Hungarians in Romania* (Budapest, 1998).

20   See Section 1.3. *Romániai Magyar Szó*, January 7, 1990.

21   See Marius Oprea, *Moștenitorii Securității* [The Heirs of the Securitate] (Bucharest, 2004), on how this came about.

22   *Demokratikus Konvenció.*

23   Miklós Bakk, "Az RMDSZ első öt éve" [The First Five Years of the Democratic Alliance of Hungarians in Romania], in Miklós Bakk, István Székely and Tibor T. Toró, eds., *Útközben. Pillanatképek az erdélyi magyar politika reformjáról* [On the Way. Snapshots of the Reform of Transylvanian Hungarian Politics] (Miercurea-Ciuc, 1999), pp. 88–113. The main analyses of the Alliance: http://www.adatbank.ro/belso.php?alk=33&k=5. Accessed May 7, 2010.

24   The province became Kosovo (*Socijalistička Autonomna Pokrajina Kosovo*) in 1974, but Serbia reverted to the style Kosovo and Metohija (*Autonomna Pokrajina Kosovo i Metohija*) in 1990. Metohija refers historically to its western districts.

25   For an account of political organization by Hungarians in Yugoslavia, see Bárdi and Éger, eds., *Útkeresés és integráció* (1989–1993, János Vékás), pp. 771–781.

26   The name of the province derives from the "Field of Blackbirds" (*Kosovo polje*) where the battle occurred. See Noel Malcolm, *Kosovo: A Short History* (New York, 1998).

27   *Vajdasági Magyarok Demokratikus Közössége* (*VMDK*).

28   Documents on Vojvodina Hungarian political activity in 1989–1990 appear in Zoltán Kalapis, Péter Sinkovits and János Vékás, eds., *Magyarok Jugoszláviában '90. A Vajdasági Magyarok Demokratikus Közösségének évkönyve 1990* [Hungarians in Yugoslavia '90. Yearbook 1990] (Újvidék, 1991), pp. 57–165.

29   "Memorandum a Szerb Köztársaságban élõ magyarok önkormányzatáról," in Éva Hódi and Sándor Hódi, eds., *Esély a megmaradásra. A VMDK évkönyve 1992* [Chance of Survival. VMDK Yearbook 1994] (Ada, 1992), pp. 87–107.

30   Gyula Balla and Péter Dippold, "A szomszédországok magyarságának ügye a magyarországi független (szamizdat) kiadványokban" [Hungarians in Neighboring Countries in Hungary's Independent (Samizdat) Publications], *Regio* 2 (1991) 1: 162–163. Relations between authority and the opposition on the affairs of Hungarians abroad: Földes, *Magyarország, Románia és a nemzeti kérdés*, pp. 322–330 and 336–352.

31   *"Mai politikánk és a nemzetiségi kérdés"* [Our Policy Today and the Minority Issue]. The article and reactions to it: Csaba Tabajdi, ed., *Mérleg és számvetés. A magyarságpolitikai rendszerváltás kezdete* [Balance and Account. The Beginning of the Change of System in Policy towards Hungarian Communities] (Budapest, 2001).

32   On this, see Róbert Győri Szabó, *Kisebbségpolitikai rendszerváltás Magyarországon a Nemzeti és Etnikai Kisebbségi Kollégium és titkárság történetének tükrében (1989–1990)* [Minority-Policy Change of System in Hungary in the Light of the History of the National and Ethnic Minority Committee and Secretariat (1989–1990)] (Budapest, 1998).

33   "Kormánynyilatkozat a magyar kisebbségekről" [Government Statement on the Hungarian Minorities], *Új Magyarország*, August 19, 1992.

34   Géza Jeszenszky, "Antall József a nemzetpolitikus" [József Antall the National Politician], *Valóság* (1995) 1: 79–94; Wolfgang Zellner and Pál Dunay, *Ungarns Aussenpolitik 1990–1997: zwischen Westintegration, Nachbarschafts- und Minderheitenpolitik* (Baden-Baden, 1998), pp. 211–230.

3. THE POLICY OF BUDAPEST GOVERNMENTS TOWARDS HUNGARIAN COMMUNITIES ABROAD

Nándor Bárdi

What is known colloquially in Hungary as *nation policy* – policy on minority Hungarian communities – is used since the 1990s to cover state policy towards the Hungarians abroad. The stance of the state towards the Hungarian nation, cultural heritage and envisaged future, and towards the basic values of the European Union, has the nature of an identity policy. But the state's position on the ethnic and national minorities of Hungary (sectorial policies on minorities and the Roma) and on European national minority and ethnic issues can be expressed in ethno-political concepts. Beyond these framework concepts there can be distinguished as a sectorial field the policy towards the Hungarian community. This specific field of nation policy covers the relation system pertaining between Hungary and the Hungarians beyond its borders: international and bilateral minority protection, institutional operation of Hungarian–Hungarian relations (that is, relations between the kin-state and the minorities outside), and support for minority Hungarian communities. This sectorial policy can also be divided into integration, language and institutional policies between the government and the Hungarian minority concerned in the other Central European countries[1]

The Antall and Boross governments (May 1990–July 1994) had three concurrent goals in international relations: European integration, good neighborly relations, and addressing the problems of Hungarians abroad. They undertook in foreign policy to protect the Hungarian minorities through international forums, based on norms of human and minority rights, and to secure collective rights for them. At home the intention behind the 1993 Minority Act was to provide, instead of individual and language rights for national

456

and ethnic minorities, a self-government design that could act as a model for Central Europe. The third tenet was to recognize the sovereignty of Hungarian parties outside the country as bodies representing community interests, and to heed their views on issues affecting them.[2]

The practice of the Németh government (November 1988–May 1990) was followed initially in using as the institutional framework for policy on the Hungarian community the College and Secretariat of National and Ethnic Minorities headed by Géza Entz (appointed in May 1990).[3] In June 1992, the handling was placed on a higher administrative level, with a new Government Office for Hungarian Minorities Abroad,[4] a parallel Illyés Public Foundation to channel governmental and budgetary support to the Hungarians abroad, and a special department in the Ministry of Education to deal with professional issues. The biggest new institution to be set up was Duna TV in 1992, as a television channel specifically broadcasting for the Hungarian communities abroad.[5]

The international policy of the Horn government (July 1994–July 1998) was marked by debate on the basic treaties required by the Western powers as a condition for Euro-Atlantic integration. The series began with the Hungarian–Ukrainian basic treaty of December 1991, but this was not ratified by Parliament until May 1993. Similar pacts followed with Croatia and Slovenia in 1992. To all three were attached separate commitments by the parties to ensure minority rights. One requirement was settled relations with the three newly established countries, while international recognition of their state sovereignty was contingent on a declaration in favor of the European norms of human and minority rights.[6] But there was conflict over efforts at autonomy and minority protection by Coexistence, the Hungarian Christian Democratic Movement and the Hungarian Citizens' Party in Slovakia in the former, and with the Democratic Alliance of Hungarians in Romania in the latter,[7] and the debate on these two treaties came to dominate the Horn government's policy towards neighboring countries. For the government after 1994 had to present such a policy, capable of handling conflicts, before the culmination of Euro-Atlantic integration: the 1997 accession to NATO. It was vital for political activity concerning Hungarians abroad not to pose or even seem to pose a threat to the region's stability. The issue became one of foreign policy and was subordinate to the priorities of integration. So the main European norms of minority rights were incorporated into the Hungarian–Slovak basic treaty, despite strong debate on the matter. However, these were just individual human rights, not the collective minority rights that local Hungarian politicians were calling for, and were to be monitored only by a committee with advisory powers set up in March 1995. A year and a half later, a Hungarian–Romanian basic treaty was concluded in September 1996, despite Democratic Alliance of Hungarians in Romania opposition. To this, relevant documents on minority protection were appended too, but, contrarily to the Slovak case, it was laid down in a separate footnote that Recommendation 1201 of the Council of Europe was not taken to refer to territorial autonomy on an ethnic basis. Little was achieved by either of the mixed committees designed to provide minority protection guarantees under the treaties. Nor was more heard of the promised separate agreements with Romania on the return of Church property, restitution for the goods expropriated from the Hungarian community, and settlement of the issues of native-language use and minority education.[8]

Meanwhile, there were big changes in Hungarian–Hungarian relations and subsidization policy. Basically the government regarded the Hungarians abroad as deprived groups, for which it bore a constitutional responsibility. But the rhetoric changed: future autonomy gave way to prosperity in the country of domicile as the envisioned way of handling the problems. The heads of the Government Office for Hungarian Minorities Abroad – Csaba Tabajdi, László Lábody and Erika Törzsök – stressed the need for economic back-up, the importance of political activity in local and regional government, and stronger initiatives towards modernization and social development. Efforts to further these were made by including local representatives into the New Handshake Foundation[9] and the Illyés Public Foundation, specifically concerned with economic development. On the political side of Hungarian–Hungarian relations, the government sought contact with elite groups still in a position to negotiate with the majority political force on a national and local level: the Community of Hungarian Intellectuals in Transcarpathia as against the Transcarpathian Hungarian Cultural Association, the Vojvodina Hungarian Association opposing the Democratic Community of Vojvodina Hungarians, of the Slovakian Hungarian parties, the Hungarian Christian Democratic Movement and the so-called moderate wing of the Democratic Alliance of Hungarians in Romania.[10]

The foreign policy scope for the Orbán government (July 1998–May 2002) increased along with the country's geopolitical weight, after Hungary had gained NATO membership before its neighbors. This, combined with the support that Hungarian minority parties gave to Euro-Atlantic political forces in their own countries and their role as coalition partners, meant that the Hungarian minority question could no longer be represented as an internationally destabilizing element. Moreover, Hungary's economic growth had resumed, which meant that more could be spent on subsidization.[11]

The focus shifted from crisis management and support for developing local institutions onto the financing of programs. The Apáczai Public Foundation was set up in December 1998 expressly for supporting education and training. Separate Hungarian institutions of higher education were established (the Sapientia Hungarian University of Transylvania in Cluj Napoca, Târgu Mureş and Miercurea-Ciuc, and the Selye János University in Komárno, both in 2001) and existing ones were assured of regular budget support (the Berehove teacher training college and the Partium University in Oradea). The allocation to the Illyés Public Foundation was raised significantly and the media for Hungarians abroad (the news service and Duna TV) were further developed.

Institutionally speaking, the Government Office for Hungarian Minorities Abroad passed from the Prime Minister's Office to the Ministry of Foreign Affairs and was overseen by the portfolio's political state secretary, Zsolt Németh.

The Schengen Agreement brought a danger that Hungary's contacts with Hungarians in Transcarpathia, Vojvodina and Croatia, outside the Schengen area, would be impeded. By then it was clear that the efforts of Hungarians abroad towards gaining autonomy had failed and they could not be approached legally as regional communities. Discussion of such problems and formation of a supra-party consensus had lain behind the convening under the Horn government of the first official Hungarian–Hungarian summit in July 1996. Then came a second meeting at Pápa before the signing of the Hungarian–Romanian basic treaty, but without governmental participation. A conference was held in February 1999 in Budapest, with the government and the political parties of Hungary and Hungarians abroad represented, where it was agreed to form a Hungarian Standing Conference as a liaison.[12] This political consultative body met at least annually under the auspices of the Hungarian prime minister of the time and operated by agreement, not according to legal provisions. Its main contribution was to promote expert forums meeting several times a year under state-secretary chairmanship. These became the main channels by which the administration addressed the problems of the Hungarians abroad. At the second meeting of the Hungarian Standing Conference in December 1999, the Hungarian parties outside Hungary called for legislation on the legal standing within Hungary of the Hungarians abroad. The Act on Hungarians Living in Neighboring Countries, enacted in June 2001,[13] covered native Hungarians in all neighboring countries except Austria, granting them rights to stated concessions in culture, science, employment, medical care and travel, through a Hungarian Certificate issued on application by Hungary's authorities, based on recommendations from specific institutions authorized to do so. This was passed with support from all political parties except the liberal Alliance of Free Democrats, and cognizance of it was taken by all neighboring countries except Romania and Slovakia. The former appealed on the grounds of infringement of state sovereignty and ethnic discrimination to the Venice Commission of the Council of Europe, which ruled in October 2001 that a kin-state had a right to dispense cultural support to non-citizen members of its nation, but in doing so it should work to obtain consent from the host state and to avoid discrimination. For national identity, the Commission required not just personal choice but also the formulation of objective criteria. These were provided in a government order: the diplomatic mission would confirm that applicants for a Hungarian Certificate spoke Hungarian, or were somewhere registered officially as Hungarians, or were members of a Hungarian organization, or appeared as Hungarians in a church register. In December 2001, the Romanian side issued a separate statement of agreement with the Hungarian government, the main point in which extended the three-month concessionary work permit to all Romanian citizens. On the act's application to Slovakia, the Orbán government failed to reach agreement with the Commissioner for Enlargement of the EU and the OSCE high commissioner on national minorites.[14]

The Medgyessy government (May 2002–September 2004) placed the question of Hungarians abroad within its declared policy for national consensus. Its main purpose was to gain acceptance of the Status Law from neighboring countries. It accordingly amended the act in June 2003, with Fidesz and the Hungarian Democratic Forum voting against the change. The reference to a single Hungarian nation was removed from the preamble, and concessions on social insurance, medical care and employment were removed. However, the financial support for education in the mother tongue provided by the kin-state became available also for families with a single child, and irrespective of ethnic affiliation, the sole requirement being to attend a school teaching in Hungarian. The Slovak government would consent to the distribution of such support only if it was received by the education institutions (not the parents) through the mediation of a foundation (December 2003).

After the government change, the Government Office for Hungarian Minorities Abroad returned to the Prime Minister's Office, under the secretary responsible for international relations. But the influence of László Kovács, minister of foreign affairs and Socialist Party president, and the diplomatic moves associated with the Status Law meant that the Ministry of Foreign Affairs and the party leaders of the Hungarians abroad had an increasing say. This was due to the stance of the Hungarian government that the decisions concerning support for Hungarians abroad should be left to the representatives of the latter. Thanks to the favorable domestic political position of the Democratic Alliance of Hungarians in Romania, the Statue of Liberty in Arad was re-erected in a public square (in April 2004) and the Romanian government decided to build the Northern Transylvanian motorway in 2003–2004), although the Hungarian government helped indirectly in both cases.

The Hungarian–Hungarian policy of the first Gyurcsány government (September 2004–April 2006) was marked by debate on dual citizenship. The question of citizenship for Hungarians abroad not resettling in Hungary had come up in the summer of 2003. For Hungary as an EU member was expected to require visas for visitors from two countries – Ukraine and Serbia–Montenegro – with large native Hungarian communities. One solution was to award them Hungarian citizenship without the requirement of residence (passports). Dual citizenship was forbidden by Ukrainian law, but the Serbian government stated several times that there was no obstacle. In the autumn of 2003, Hungarian organizations in Vojvodina collected 50,000 signatures in support and submitted them to Budapest. This provided the Budapest-based World Federation of Hungarians[15] with a basis for initiating a referendum in Hungary. Held on December 5, 2004, it called on Parliament to introduce legislation on preferential naturalization procedures, by individual application, for non-Hungarian citizens domiciled outside Hungary who declared themselves members of the Hungarian nation.

All parliamentary parties in Hungary agreed that it was unfortunate to hold a referendum on this, but when it was announced, in September 2004, the two sides gave voters different advice and dual citizenship became a very divisive issue. Prime Minister Gyurcsány rejected it outright on the grounds of its purported social consequences: a potential influx of settlers, international rejection, and disruption to the political balance of the Hungarian electorate. Fidesz had warned before the campaign against increased migration and weakening of efforts to gain autonomy for Hungarians abroad, but in the campaign it endorsed the clear support for dual citizenship given by legitimate organizations of Hungarians abroad. The opposition presented the issue of passports as one of strengthening relations and national reunification, saying that the drawbacks could be guarded against when Parliament legislated. It questioned the credibility of the government's arguments and accused it of betraying the national interest. The prime minister's response was to extend the concept of nation policy from relations between the Hungarian state and Hungarians abroad to social modernization of Hungary and all Hungarians. (This effectively placed the legal emancipation in Hungary of Hungarians abroad in the same policy bracket as pension, welfare and employment problems.) The prime minister intended to advance a sober, long-term, national (democratic, patriotic) vision of the future, as against the right-wing demand for dual citizenship, with ostensibly unforeseeable results.

The referendum was invalid;[16] this strengthened Gyurcsány's political position at home, but in Hungarian–Hungarian relations it alienated the Hungarian parties abroad from the Socialist–Free Democrat coalition government in Hungary. In January 2005, the prime minister announced a Program of National Responsibility, including a Homeland Program package. Meanwhile, the leaders of the Hungarian communities abroad established a Forum of Hungarian Organizations Abroad.[17]

Three policy strategies for the Hungarian community emerged in the decade and a half after the change of system, none of which could be exclusively associated with the right or the left. Apart from citing international norms and patterns, the minority protection approach starts from the premise that good relations with neighboring countries are needed before the problems of Hungarian minorities can be handled. This lay behind the policy of concluding basic treaties, with mixed committees on minority issues to handle the problems. Emphasis was given to each minority community finding ways of handling its problems within its own country, especially where the Hungarian party was a partner in government. Hungary could assist primarily by diplomatic means. The same

approach appears in the rhetoric about strengthening Hungarian
minority societies economically and socially. These considerations
were basic to Hungarian community policy under the left-wing
governments, along with anti-nationalist discourse (condemning
symbolic politicizing and national rhetoric).[18]

The ideology of national unification envisages unity extending
across nation-state borders that could be institutionalized by breaking
such borders down (through EU integration). Viewed in this light,
the minority societies are severed limbs of the Hungarian nation
dwelling in other countries. The political unity of the Hungarian
ethno-cultural community was symbolized by the Hungarian
Standing Conference and by the Hungarian Certificate as the link
with the Hungarian state on an individual level.[19] Beside the pan-
national outlook, the concept of a "contractual nation" was put
forward to institutionalize the development separate from Hungary
of the Hungarian regional communities in the seven other countries,
as well as the assertion of their specific interests. The premise was
that the Hungarian administration had to formulate its relations
with each regional community separately and vice versa.[20] The idea
of unifying the nation without altering frontiers, along with rhetoric
emphasizing symbolic, nation-building gestures, appears mainly
among Hungary's right wing. The third approach – starting from
EU integration – emphasizes regionalization, trusting common
regional interests to prevail over ethnic antagonisms.[21] Sectorial
policy-makers regard developing border areas and regionalizing the
individual countries as means with great potential for the integration
of minority Hungarian communities and the system of Hungarian
cultural institutions, as well as for their own country. They seek to
achieve this by establishing development regions and cross-border
regions to meet local requirements (involving historical and ethnic
characteristics). Some envisage these regions giving rise to regional
autonomous institutions, which might be needed to shield national
identity from nation-state interference.

The political consensus that has emerged among political
parties in Hungary is to treat minority Hungarian communities

as separate entities and assist the reproduction and development of their national identity, both politically and by supporting their institutions. However, achievement of this has been thwarted by party rivalries and Hungary's deteriorating economy. This and the abortive referendum – seen by Hungarians abroad as rejection of their desire for emancipation – have devalued it for Hungarians abroad and caused nation-policy issues to be sidelined in Hungary itself.[22]

Notes

1 Nándor Bárdi, *Tény és való. A budapesti kormányzatok és a határon túli magyarok kapcsolattörténete. Problémakatalógus* [True Fact. Budapest Governments and the History of Their Contacts with Hungarians Abroad. Catalogue of Problems] (Pozsony, 2004), pp. 13–37.

2 Judit Tóth, "Az elmúlt évtized diaszpórapolitikája" [The Diaspora Policy of the Last Decade], in Endre Sik and Judit Tóth, eds., *Diskurzusok a vándorlásról* [Discourses on Migration] (Budapest, 2000), pp. 218–251; a comprehensive analysis of the Antall government's foreign policy: Pál Dunay and Wolfgang Zellner, *Ungarns Aussenpolitik 1990–1997. Zwischen Westintegration, Nachbarschafts- und Minderheitenpolitik* (Baden-Baden, 1998).

3 *Nemzeti és Etnikai Kisebbségi Kollégiuma és Titkársága.*

4 *Határon Túli Magyarok Hivatala.*

5 Ferenc Mák, "Az új nemzeti politika és a Határon Túli Magyarok Hivatala (1989–1999)" [New National Policy and the Government Office for Hungarian Minorities Abroad (1989–1999)], *Magyar Kisebbség* (2000) 3: 237–293.

6 Hungarian basic treaty texts appeared in *Magyar Kisebbség* (1996) 4 (thematic issue). The stance taken by Hungary's parliamentary parties is analyzed by Róbert Győri Szabó, in "A parlamenti pártok és az alapszerződés (1994–1997)" [The Parliamentary Parties and the Basic Treaty (1994–1997)], *Magyar Kisebbség* (2000) 4.

7 *Együttélés, MKDM, MPP* and *RMDSZ.*

8 Árpád Sidó, János Fiala, Dávid Vincze and Balázs Jarábik, "A szlovák–magyar alapszerződés hatásvizsgálata" [A Study of the Effect of the Slovak–Hungarian Basic Treaty], *Regio* 14 (2003) 1: 111–119;

Miklós Bakk, "Az RMDSZ mint a romániai magyarság politikai önmeghatározási kísérlete 1989 után" [The Romanian Hungarian Democratic Alliance as an Experiment in Political Self-Definition by Romania's Hungarians after 1989], *Regio* 10 (1999) 2: 81–116.

9   *Új Kézfogás Alapítvány.*

10   *Kárpátaljai Magyar Értelmiségiek Fóruma, KMKSZ, Vajdasági Magyar Szövetség* and *VMDK*. Bárdi, *Tény és való*, pp. 109–123; Csaba Tabajdi, "Négy év kormányzati munkájának mérlege, és a jövő feladatai" [Account of Four Years' Government Work and Tasks for the Future], in Csaba Tabajdi, *Az önazonosság labirintusa* [The Labyrinth of Self-Identity] (Budapest, 1998), pp. 587–608.

11   Csaba Lőrincz, "Nemzeti érdekek érvényesítése Magyarország csatlakozása során az euroatlanti államok közösségéhez" [Assertion of National Interests during Hungary's Accession to the Community of Euro-Atlantic States], in Zoltán Kántor, ed., *A státustörvény – Előzmények és következmények* [The Status Law – Antecedents and Consequences] (Budapest, 2002), pp. 185–206; Zsolt Németh, *Magyar kibontakozás* [Hungarian Development] (Budapest, 2002).

12   MÁÉRT. The main MÁÉRT documents: Kántor, ed., *A státustörvény*, pp. 158–181; a critique of the work of the MÁÉRT expert committees: Dániel Hegedűs, *A Magyar Állandó Értekezlet (MÁÉRT) szakértői bizottságai munkájának elemzése az 1998 és 2002 közötti kormányzati ciklusban közpolitikai eszközökkel* [Analysis of the Work of the Expert Committees of the Hungarian Standing Committee under the 1998–2002 Government, by A Public Policy Approach] (Budapest, 2008).

13   Act LXII/2001. More detail appears in http://www.magyarorszag.hu/english/abouthungary/data/foreign/minorities/act.html. Retrieved January 11, 2010.

14   Analyses, timeline and documents: Osamu Ieda, Balázs Majtényi, Zoltán Kántor, Balázs Vizi, Iván Halász and Stephen Deets, eds., *Beyond Sovereignty? From Status Law to Transnational Citizenship* (Sapporo, 2006); influence and outcomes: Zoltán Kántor, Balázs Majtényi, Osamu Ieda, Balázs Vízi and Iván Halász, eds., *The Hungarian Status Law: Nation Building and/or Minority Protection* (Sapporo, 2004); studies in Hungarian: Kántor, ed., *A státustörvény.*

15   *Magyarok Világszövetsége.*

16   For a referendum to be valid, over 25 percent of the electorate must vote for the proposal or against it. In this case there was a 37.49

percent turnout, but neither the proportion of the electorate voting in
favor (18.90 percent) nor against (17.75 percent) was high enough for
validation.

17 Nándor Bárdi, "A 'mumusok' és a 'kék madár'" [The "Bogeymen"
and the "Blue Bird"], in T. Csaba Haris, ed., *Magyar külpolitika az
Európai Unióban* [Hungarian Foreign Policy in the European Union]
(Budapest, 2005), pp. 32–58; data, analyses and documents on the
dual citizenship debate: http://www.kettosallampolgarsag.mtaki.hu/.
Retrieved January 9, 2010.

18 Tabajdi, *Az önazonosság labirintusa*; Erika Törzsök, *Kisebbségek
változó világban* [Minorities in a Changing World] (Cluj-Napoca,
2003); János Kis, "Nemzetegyesítés vagy kisebbségvédelem" [Nation
Unification or Minority Protection], *Élet és Irodalom*, December 17,
2004.

19 Zsolt Németh, "Vezérszónoklat a státustörvényről" [Keynote Speech
on the Status Act], in Németh, *Magyar kibontakozás*, pp. 191–197.

20 László Szarka, "Szerződéses Nemzet" [Contractual Nation],
in Kántor, ed., *A státustörvény*, pp. 407–409; Zsolt Németh,
"Mozaiknemzetből szerződéses Nemzet" [From Mosaic Nation to
Contractual Nation], in Németh, *Magyar kibontakozás*, pp. 123–129.

21 The most important attempt was the bilingual publication *Provincia*
in Transylvania, headed by Gusztáv Molnár: http://www.provincia.
ro/cikk_magyar/archivum.html. Retrieved January 9, 2010. From the
minority protection viewpoint, the most important plan for regionalist
autonomy came from Miklós Bakk, *Kerettörvény a régiókról, 2003*
[Framework Law on the Regions, 2003], at http://www.adatbank.ro/
html/cim pdf503.pdf. Retrieved January 9, 2010. For an economic
development program, see Erika Törzsök, ed., *Szülőföld Program.
Stratégiai tanulmány* [Homeland Program. Strategic Study]
(Budapest, 2005).

22 A full account of the preparatory materials for Hungary's 2008
strategy: László Szarka, ed., "Az új magyar külkapcsolati stratégia
előmunkálatai" [Preparations for the New Hungarian Foreign Policy
Strategy], *Magyar Kisebbség* (2006) 3–4: 7–231.

4. DEMOGRAPHIC PROCESSES IN MINORITY HUNGARIAN COMMUNITIES*

László Gyurgyík

The Hungarian communities in neighboring countries generally have a "distorted" social and demographic structure, in the sense that their individual social, settlement and demographic attributes are less favorable, or more backward, than those of the population as a whole. For the main basis for comparison is the population of their political domicile – the country whose majority community has defined for them the political, economic and demographic scope in which the reproduction of their community has occurred, in the decades since the role of a minority was thrust upon them.

The changes are shown here mainly through the last two census returns and the demographic data. (Figures for Hungarians in this section therefore record self-identification, within the constraints of the census forms and other returns.) The censuses at the turn of the 1980s and 1990s, the start of the period, took place at various times. The earliest came in 1989 in the Transcarpathian region of Ukraine, then still part of the Soviet Union. Most neighboring countries held theirs in 1991, but Romania's was a year later. The censuses of a decade later fell in 2001 in Slovakia, Croatia, Ukraine and Austria, and in 2002 elsewhere. Ukraine's was unusual in being completed only at the third attempt.[1]

The figures for Hungarians living in the neighboring countries can be examined in two respects. As a first approach, the tendency can be compared with that of the population as a whole in their political domicile, although the examination in most countries has been confined to a narrower historical or geographical area long inhabited by Hungarians (*Table 1*).

Table 1: The change of number and rate of Hungarians in neighboring countries

The date of the census		Around 1990			Around 2000		
Country	Dates of the censuses	Total	Proportion of Hungarians among them	%	Total	Proportion of Hungarians among them	%
Slovakia	1991, 2001	5,274,335	567,296	10.8	5,379,455	520,528	9.7
Ukraine	1989, 2001	51,452,034	163,111	0.3	48,416,000	156,600	0.3
Romania	1992, 2002	22,810,035	1,624,959	7.1	21,680,974	1,431,807	6.6
Serbia	1991, 2002	9,778,991	343,942	3.5	7,498,001	293,299	3.9
Croatia	1991, 2001	4,784,265	22,355	0.5	4,437,460	16,595	0.4
Slovenia	1991, 2002	1,965,986	8,503	0.4	1,964,036	6,243	0.3
Austria	1991, 2001	7,795,786	33,459	0.4	8,032,926	40,583	0.5
Total	1991, 2001	103,861,432	2,763,625	2.7	97,408,852	2,465,655	2.5

The number of Hungarians living in most neighboring countries hardly differs from the number in the areas of each country historically inhabited by Hungarians. It is noticeable that the number of Hungarians has *fallen* in all neighboring countries except Austria. There the number of Burgenland Hungarians makes up only a fraction of the Hungarian population in Austria as a whole, which has risen greatly through migration.[2]

The demographic processes among Hungarians in most neighboring countries can be seen more clearly if the survey is restricted to the territory of longstanding Hungarian settlement (*Table 2*). This has been done for Ukraine (Transcarpathia), Romania (Transylvania), Serbia (Vojvodina), Slovenia (Prekmurje) and Austria (Burgenland).[3] With Slovakia and Croatia, the demographic processes are examined over the whole country.[4]

Table 2: The change of number and rate of Hungarians
in the cross-border areas

Area	Total	Proportion of Hungarians among them	%	Total	Proportion of Hungarians among them	%
		Around 1990			Around 2000	
Slovakia	5,274,335	567,296	10.8	5,379,455	520,528	9.7
Trans-carpathia	1,252,288	155,711	12.4	1,254,614	151,516	12.1
Transylvania	7,723,313	1,603,923	20.8	7,221,733	1,415,718	19.6
Vojvodina	2,013,889	339,491	16.9	2,031,992	290,207	14.3
Croatia	4,784,265	22,355	0.5	4,437,460	16,595	0.4
Prekmurje	14,291	7,243	50.7	12,698	5,212	41.0
Burgenland	270,880	6,763	2.5	277,569	6,641	2.4
Total	21,333,261	2,702,782	12.7	20,615,521	2,406,417	11.7

The data in the two tables show strong differences of population between the regions examined and the countries as a whole. (The aggregate population of the seven countries in the 2000s was 97 million and that of the regions examined fewer than 21 million.) But the number of Hungarians recorded in each country in 2001–2002 scarcely differs from the number in the regions examined: 2.466 million and 2.406 million respectively. Most of the 60,000 come from the difference between the number of Burgenland Hungarians and the total in Austria. Let us look at the changes in each case.

The number of Hungarians in Slovakia in 1991–2001 fell by 8.2 percent, from 567,296 to 520,528 – from 10.8 to 9.7 percent of the total population, that is, below 10 percent for the first time. The demographic tendency differed in the country as a whole: the population in 1991–2001 rose by 2 percent (105,120), from 5,274,335 to 5,379,455, mostly by natural increase, but with not inconsiderable net migration as well.[5]

The number of Hungarians in Transcarpathia in 1989–2001 fell by 2.7 percent, from 155,711 to 151,516, so that the proportion of Hungarians in the *oblast* decreased from 12.5 to 12.1 percent. Meanwhile, Transcarpathia's population scarcely changed: a rise of 0.2 percent (2,326) from 1,252,288 to 1,254,614. Births exceeded deaths up to the end of the 1990s, but a natural decrease set in around the turn of the millennium. The population has been falling since 1995 due to net emigration being higher than the natural increase.[6]

The number of Hungarians in Transylvania in 1992–2002 fell from 1,603,923 to 1,415,718 – a decline of 188,205 or 11.7 percent, causing the proportion of Hungarians to fall from 20.8 to 19.6 percent. Transylvania's population in the same period fell by 6.5 percent, from 7,723,313 to 7,221,733, mainly due to sizeable net emigration and changes in census counting techniques.[7]

The number of Hungarians in Vojvodina in 1991–2002 fell from 339,491 to 290,207 – a fall of 49,284 or 14.5 percent, bringing the share of Hungarians down from 16.9 to 14.3 percent. The population rose by 0.9 per cent (18,103), from 2,013,889 to 2,031,992, due to Yugoslav war-related immigration. (The indicators of migration in Serbia in the 1990s were very unfavorable. The population growth in Vojvodina has been negative since 1989, and in 2000 the number of births was 10,000 higher than that of deaths.)[8]

The three smaller communities of Hungarians abroad also fell in number and proportion – those of Croatia from 22,355 to 16,595 (down 5,760 or 25.8 percent), those of Slovenia from 7,243 to 5,212 (down 2,031 or 28 percent), and those of Burgenland from 6,763 to 6,641 (down 1.8 percent).

Three main factors lie behind the way in which the Hungarian communities have dwindled: natural increase or decrease, demographic processes, and assimilation processes. The examination here is confined to the four areas with sizeable numbers of Hungarian inhabitants: Slovakia, Transcarpathia, Transylvania and Vojvodina.

The easiest of the three factors to estimate is natural increase or decrease. Breakdowns of migration data by national group are not always available, but the trends in the birth and death figures for the Hungarian community can be estimated quite easily by examining the demographic data by country and administrative unit.

A big loss was caused by acceleration of the natural decrease in the Hungarian population, to which several factors contributed. (The number of births was declining steadily in most neighboring countries and was coupled with a steady rise in the average age of the inhabitants.) The most important was an uncertain social and economic situation, but alternative lifestyle changes were reducing the number of marriages and raising the age of marriage, which meant a decrease in fertility. It can also be seen that the biological reproduction of Hungarian women (number of offspring produced) is higher than their ethnic reproduction (number of offspring registered as ethnic Hungarians). The official migration statistics by ethnic group largely include only the latter and reflect latently an inter-generation plane of assimilation. In general, the bigger the difference between biological and ethnic reproduction, the higher the proportion of mixed marriages in the group concerned. For most children born to mixed marriages are registered as members of the majority nation and only a small proportion as members of the minority. (In Slovakia 20 percent of the offspring of mixed marriages are registered as Hungarian,[9] in Transylvania one third,[10] and in Vojvodina 20–30 percent. There are no such figures available for Transcarpathia.) The Hungarian communities in all neighboring countries have seen their natural increase turn into a decrease. There are annual national demographic statistics available for the natural increase/decrease of the Hungarians in Slovakia and Transylvania, but the figures for the other areas are estimates. The annual number of Hungarian births in Slovakia fell by a third in 1991–2000 (from 6,707 to 4,498) but the death figure fell by 11 percent (from 6,270 to 5,554). This means that the natural increase in the Hungarian population of Slovakia turned into a decrease in 1994. The number of Hungarian births in 1990 was over 800 higher than the number of deaths in 1990, but in 2000 it was over 1,000 lower. Between the last two censuses (1991–2001), the aggregate natural decrease can be put at around 2,000; its rate changed from +1.5 to –1.9 per thousand.[11]

Population trends for the Transcarpathian Hungarians can only be estimated. The natural increase in the *oblast* became a natural decrease around 2000, but the switch was earlier for the Hungarians, probably before 1990. Deaths outnumbered births among the Hungarians throughout the period between the censuses. The estimated annual average natural decrease of around 3 per thousand led to a decrease of about 5,000.[12]

The birth rate for Hungarians in Transylvania declined from 14,616 in 1992 to 10,615 in 2002, a fall of 27 percent, and the death rate from 23,906 to 20,944 (–12.3 percent). This produced to a natural decrease of 8,000–11,500 over the 1992–2002 period, with 107,437 more deaths than births.[13]

The available data for Vojvodina are incomplete, due to warfare. An estimate can be made by comparing annual national demographic data with Hungarian demographic figures available for certain years. The province had the highest rate of natural decrease of all the four Hungarian-inhabited areas examined – around 10–11 percent over the period between the censuses, leading to a probable decrease of around 30,000.[14]

Examining the migration processes is more complicated still. The demographic figures for each country include a component for "registered" international migration, but "hidden," unregistered migration may be a multiple of it. Another factor to consider when estimating the magnitude of the migration processes is the fact that the criteria for counting the Hungarian population may change between censuses. Available data show that the net migration of Hungarians varies widely from territory to territory, as do the factors behind it.

The migration loss among the Hungarians of Slovakia in 1991–2001 may have been around 2,000. This relatively low number is corroborated by the relatively low number of Slovakian citizens recorded in Hungary's migration statistics. The relatively low loss is explained by the fact that Hungarian employees from Slovakia mainly commute daily to work in Hungary or Austria. Relatively few choose to settle in Hungary. The economic incentive to work abroad is the lowest in any of the four areas examined, and the settlement pattern of Hungarians in Slovakia makes daily or weekly commuting to Hungary feasible.[15]

There is a wide band between the upper and lower estimates for Hungarian emigration from Transcarpathia. Some estimates put the number who settled in Hungary in the 1990s at 5,000, while others suggest 25,000–30,000. The latter is more likely to be the combined number of those working with (or without) work permits or studying in Hungary.[16]

The Romanian Statistics Office recorded a population decrease of more than half a million in the 2002 census. This was largely because all those residing abroad were counted in the 1992 census, but only those who had been abroad for less than one year were counted in 2002. The methodological difference also affected the fall in the number of Transylvanian Hungarians counted. About 100,000 Hungarians left Transylvania between 1992 and 2002 to live abroad permanently, of whom 80,000 are now living in Hungary.[17]

Warfare was the main determining factor of migration among the Vojvodina Hungarians. Some 60,000 Vojvodina Hungarians fled abroad in the 1990s, of whom 20,000 settled abroad, although it is not known how many have returned since. The census also recorded no small number of Hungarians who were also living abroad and were unlikely to return.

The third deciding factor behind the fall in the number of Hungarians in some regions is assimilation. This cannot be measured directly from census or demographic data, or only with difficulty. A figure has been put on it by subtracting natural increase and net immigration from change in population.

Two aspects of the processes of change in national affiliation among the Hungarians in Slovakia can be distinguished – not just the move towards identifying with the Slovak nation, but a noticeable shift in the direction of the Roma. With the relative strength of the factors behind the assimilation processes working on the Hungarians of Slovakia, the strongest is origin, and the weakest the national affiliation of the spouse. Between the two lie language of schooling and depth of knowledge of the Hungarian language. All are affected, of course, by the proportion of Hungarians in the place of residence and by sex and age. Here are some data to illustrate the assimilation processes: 95 percent of those of purely Hungarian origin identified themselves as such, but only 20 percent of those of mixed origin did so. Adding in the other factors, it was found that 99 percent of those of purely Hungarian origin who had attended elementary school in Hungarian, spoke Hungarian to a high standard, and were married to a Hungarian identified themselves as Hungarian. Of the pure Hungarians who had attended elementary school that taught in Slovak, 33 percent identified themselves as Slovak.[18]

The census data for Transcarpathia show dissimilation in the direction of the Hungarians, less because of change in the Ukrainian/ Hungarian ratio than because of legislative changes in favor of the minority, prompting some who had recorded themselves as Gypsy, Ukrainian or Slovak to write "Hungarian" in 2001. The question is whether a more or less formal allegiance (a "statistical" switch of nation) will continue to swell the Hungarian community, or whether it was simply prompted by an administrative change. Meanwhile, it can be assumed that the progeny of mixed marriages between Hungarians and Ukrainians/Rusyns will tend to benefit the majority nation.[19]

Assimilation appears to be the weakest factor in the decline in Transylvania's Hungarian community. Only 18–19 percent of

Hungarians marrying in the 1990s contracted a mixed marriage, while the proportion of mixed marriages by the Hungarians of Slovakia was 25–28 percent. Only 2 percent of Transylvanians of purely Hungarian origin recorded themselves as Romanian. The loss due to assimilation and change of national allegiance can be put at about 30,000.[20]

A different kind of dissimilation appears among the Hungarians of Vojvodina, where it was common in multi-ethnic areas for partners in mixed marriages to record themselves as "Yugoslav" in their national allegiance. Some of these have altered or reverted to "Hungarian" since the dissolution of Yugoslavia. But this formal ethnic reversion does not change the inter-ethnic relations between Hungarians and Serbs, and a high proportion of mixed marriages still produces a marked rate of decline in the Hungarian numbers. The fact that some "Yugoslavs" declared themselves to be Hungarians in 2002 and may have belonged to the minority community ten years earlier only means that the number of Hungarians in 1991 was underestimated and the decline in the 1990s was higher than recorded (*Table 3*).[21]

Table 3: Informative data
on the countries of Central and Eastern Europe (2005–2006)

	Hungary	Slovakia	Ukraine	Romania	Serbia	Croatia	Slovenia	Austria
Number of population (thousands)	10,076	5,390	47,425	21,604	9,400	4,448	2,004	8,199
Territory (km²)	93,029	49,035	603,700	238,391	77,444	56,694	20,273	83,870
Population density (per capita/km²)	108	110	80	91	106	83	99	97
GDP (per capita/USD)	10,833	8,638	1,020	4,559	3,200	15,550	17,259	37,220

The decisive factors behind the fall in the minority population differ in their weights in the four regions. Even where their rankings were the same, the events behind them were quite different. If the data for each region are aggregated, the loss displayed proves in some cases greater and in others smaller than the sum for the three groups of factors. This is partly because the groups of factors cannot be distinguished mechanically, and can be identified only with difficulty, if at all, so that the same causal relation may be classed under different factors in different cases. Furthermore, the difference between the sum of the three factor groups and the total recorded may be affected by methodological differences between the two censuses – as a kind of measurement error.

All in all, caution is needed when evaluating the trends and factors behind population estimates for minority Hungarian communities, as their relative weights vary widely between regions. The decline in Slovakia is due mainly to assimilation processes. Transcarpathia is the one area with a direction of change in formal ethnic allegiance that favors the Hungarians. In Transylvania, a high loss due to migration and low fertility goes together at present with a low rate of loss from changes in ethnic affiliation. In Vojvodina, the sharp decline in Hungarian numbers is due to migration, a marked natural decrease, and assimilation.

Table 4: The estimated magnitude of the determining factors of the Hungarian population in four cross-border areas in the 1990s

Territory	Decrease	Natural Increase/ Decrease	Migration Difference	Assimilation
Slovakia	47,000	– 2,000	– 2,000	– 38,000
Transcarpathia	4,000	– 5,000	– 5,000	+ 5,000
Transylvania	193,000	– 100,000	– 100,000	– 30,000
Vojvodina	50,000	– 30,000	– 40,000	– 20,000

Notes

1   József Molnár and D. István Molnár, *Kárpátalja népessége és magyarsága a népszámlálási és népmozgalmi adatok tükrében* [The Population and Hungarian Community of Transcarpathia Seen through Census and Demographic Data] (Beregszász, 2005), p. 6.

2   Gerhard Baumgartner, "Ausztria magyar nyelvű lakossága a 2001-es osztrák népszámlálás tükrében" [Austria's Hungarian-Speakers in the Light of the 2001 Austrian Census], in László Gyurgyík and László Sebők, eds., *Népszámlálási körkép Közép-Európából 1989–2002* [Census Review of Central Europe 1989–2000] (Budapest, 2003), pp. 161–163.

3   Tamás Kiss, "Az erdélyi magyar népességet érintő természetes népmozgalmi folyamatok: 1992-2002" [Natural Demographic Processes among Transylvania's Hungarian Population], in Tamás Kiss, ed., *Népesedési folyamatok az ezredfordulón* [Demographic Processes at the Turn of the Millennium] (Kolozsvár, 2004), pp. 9–10.

4   László Gyurgyík, "A 2001-es szlovákiai népszámlálás első eredményei" [The Initial Findings of Slovakia's 2001 Census], *Regio* 12 (2001) 3: 247–249; László Sebők, "A határon túli magyarság néhány népességszerkezeti jellemzője és perspektívái" [Some Population-Structure Features and Prospects of Hungarians Abroad], *Kisebbségkutatás* (2002) 2: 237–246

5   László Gyurgyík, *A magyarság demográfiai, település- és társadalomszerkezetének változásai.* [Changes in Demography and Settlement and Social Structure of the Hungarian Community], in József Fazekas and Péter Hunčík, eds., *Magyarok Szlovákiában (1989-2004). Összefoglaló jelentés. A rendszerváltástól az Európai Uniós csatlakozásig. I. kötet* [Hungarians in Slovakia (1989–2004). Summary Report. I. From Change of System to European Union Accession] (Somorja/Dunaszerdahely, 2004), pp. 141–182.

6   Molnár and Molnár, *Kárpátalja*, pp. 20–25.

7   István Horváth, "A 2002-es romániai népszámlálás előzetes eredményeinek ismertetése és elemzése" [Initial Findings and Analysis of Romania's 2002 Census], in László Gyurgyík and László Sebők, eds., *Népszámlálási körkép Közép-Európából 1989–2002* [Census Review of Central Europe 1989–2000] (Budapest, 2003), pp. 80–96.

8   Sebők, "A határon túli magyarság."

9   László Gyurgyík, *Asszimilációs folyamatok a szlovákiai magyarság*

körében [Assimilation Processes among Slovakia's Hungarians] (Bratislava, 2004), pp. 51–53.

10 György Csepeli, Antal Örkény and Mária Székelyi, *Grappling with National Identity* (Budapest, 2000), pp. 130–135.

11 László Gyurgyík, *Népszámlálás 2001. A szlovákiai magyarság demográfiai, valamint település- és társadalomszerkezetének változásai az 1990-es években* [Census 2001. Changes in the Demography and Settlement and Social Structure of the Hungarian Community of Slovakia in the 1990s] (Pozsony, 2006), pp. 91–92.

12 Molnár and Molnár, *Kárpátalja*, pp. 64–67.

13 Kiss, *Népesedési folyamatok az ezredfordulón*, pp. 10–18.

14 László Sebők, "A délvidéki demográfiai folyamatok – elsősorban a magyarok vonatkozásában – az erdélyi magyar népességet érintő természetes népmozgalmi folyamatok: 1992–2002" [Southern Region Demographic Processes – Mainly in Relation to Hungarians – and Natural Demographic Processes among Transylvania's Hungarians: 1992–2002], in Kiss, ed., *Népesedési folyamatok az ezredfordulón*, pp. 318–322.

15 Gyurgyík, *Népszámlálás 2001*, pp. 92–97.

16 Molnár and Molnár, *Kárpátalja*, p. 21.

17 István Horváth, "Az erdélyi magyarság vándorlási vesztesége 1987–2001 között" [Migration Loss of the Transylvanian Hungarians 1987–2001], in Kiss, ed., *Népesedési folyamatok az ezredfordulón*, pp. 67–78.

18 László Gyurgyík, "On Assimilation and Change of Nationality Based on Surveys Conducted among Hungarians Living in Slovakia," *Regio* 8 (2005): 128–133.

19 Molnár and Molnár, *Kárpátalja*, pp. 21–22.

20 Sándor N. Szilágyi, "Az asszimiláció és hatása a népesedési folyamatokra" [Assimilation and Its Effects on Demographic Processes], in Kiss, ed., *Népesedési folyamatok az ezredfordulón*, pp. 157–234.

21 László Sebők, "A 2002-es szerbiai népszámlálás kérdőjelei, különösen a Vajdaság vonatkozásában" [Doubts over the 2002 Serbian Census, Especially in Relation to Vojvodina], in Gyurgyík and Sebők, eds., *Népszámlálási körkép*, pp. 127–128.

* Sources of the tables: Molnár and Molnár, *Kárpátalja*, p. 6; Sebők, "A 2002-es szerbiai népszámlálás," pp. 127–128; Kiss, "Az erdélyi magyar," pp. 9–10; Gyurgyík, *A magyarság demográfiai*, pp. 141–182; Gyurgyík and Sebők, eds., *Népszámlálási körkép*, pp. 127–128; Baumgartner, "Ausztria magyar nyelvű," pp. 161–163.

5. THE EDUCATION ISSUE
Attila Papp Z.

Provision of native-language education for Hungarians abroad is a major recurrent issue in minority communities, whose political efforts on its behalf picked up after the changes of system in East-Central Europe. For the development of native-language education there had previously run up against political barriers, erected on internationalist or national grounds. So arguments in favor of teaching in Hungarian contributed to the grievance-driven political activity that imbued the minority elites in the 1990s, in some cases overshadowing discussion of the concepts that underlay the education. The effects of this can be felt to this day. The prime function that minority schools have, according to nation-related concepts, is to protect the minority and nurture its identity, but rival interpretations of education as a service look beyond native-language cultivation and protection towards a main aim of strengthening pupils' eventual labor market position.[1]

In terms of education policy, Hungary's neighbors can be placed in two groups. Croatia, Slovenia and Austria have relatively small numbers of Hungarians, but there is largely adequate provision of Hungarian or bilingual instruction in basic and higher education. Maribor University in Slovenia, for example, offers courses for teachers of Hungarian language and literature at elementary and secondary levels, to supply the bilingual institutions in the Prekmurje district. In Croatia, Osijek's Josip Juraj Strossmayer University has a Hungarian Language Department. Notable among the educational institutes in Hungarian-inhabited communities is the same city's Croatian Education and Cultural Center. The University of Vienna offers Hungarian Studies. Native-language teaching in Hungarian-inhabited communities in Burgenland has ceased, but it has been replaced by teaching of Hungarian as a school subject and by a bilingual gymnasium (academically orientated high school) founded in Oberwart in 1992.

The other group of neighboring countries – Romania, Slovakia, Serbia and Ukraine – inherited a Soviet type of education system marked by strong centralization, a predominance of technical subjects in secondary and higher education, and compulsory secondary education coupled with a shortage of higher education and early, largely irreversible, specialization. Apart from Romania, these were all new countries in a new political situation, where education policy was intended to further the requirements of the nation state, by fostering identification and loyalty among their citizens. Education in the East-Central European countries not only was affected by systemic change but also contributed to it.[2] The changes in higher education were spectacular, but the extent and centralization of the school system slowed its reactions to the new political and economic requirements.

Each of these countries can be said, in the 1990s, to have devised its educational programs to meet nation-state demands, which partly obscured the collapse of the old political and economic system. The construal given to the education system – that it was a basic national institution – made the leaders of Hungarian communities abroad all the more concerned to have secondary and higher educational institutions that taught in Hungarian. Education became a key symbolic element in political activity. The nation-building logic of majority and minority collided over the question of the language of instruction and the national character of educational institutions, leading to some physical clashes – for instance in Târgu Mureş, and over alternative education in Slovakia.

The clashes of elites appear mainly in their ideas for transforming higher education. The symbolic and specialized debates on developing Hungarian-taught higher education took place on two planes: in majority–minority relations (majority opposition to or scrutiny of efforts to found or expand minority institutions), and as an internal matter (concerning the question of which part of the minority elite had the right to carry out the development, and who could best obtain funds for this from the state concerned or from Hungary). These accompanied an intensive process of founding institutions. By the beginning of the twenty-first century, all major regions of Hungarian habitation had separate state or private institutions of native-language higher education.

The new institutions teaching in Hungarian appeared on what was becoming a mass, expanded market for higher education, which meant that the state system had to respond. The opening of the Sapientia Hungarian University of Transylvania – founded in 2001 with campuses in Cluj-Napoca, Miercurea-Ciuc and Târgu Mureş, on the initiative of the Hungarian Churches in Transylvania,[3] but funded almost exclusively by the Hungarian state – prompted Cluj's state-run Babeş–Bolyai University to expand its range of Hungarian-taught courses. Likewise, the opening of the mainly Slovak state-financed Selye János University in Komárno in October 2003, teaching in Hungarian, speeded up the establishment of a Faculty of Central European Studies at the Konstantin University in Nitra, already an important factor in Hungarian-language teachers' training. The internal Hungarian minority conflicts over higher education development normally became politicized. Examples can be found in each region. In Ukraine, the Ferenc Rákóczi II Transcarpathian Hungarian Institute in Berehove was controlled by the Transcarpathian Hungarian Cultural Association, but Uzhhorod National University by the rival Hungarian Democratic Federation in Ukraine. The Sapientia project in Romania led the Cluj academic elite to question repeatedly the Churches' role in founding, although not funding, the university, in a period when the Reformed Church bishop László Tőkés (founder, by the way, of the Partium Christian University in Oradea) was at political loggerheads with the largest minority political force, the Democratic Alliance of Hungarians in Romania.[4] Academics associated with the Bratislava and Nitra institutions in Slovakia saw the foundation of Selye János University as a victory for the Hungarian Coalition Party, not as an educational advance. Such internecine conflicts have been exacerbated by the funding received from Hungary, which thereby becomes a factor in domestic rivalries and affects the course followed by Hungarian educational development abroad.

The participants in minority education have not been active in national education policy-making, despite their parliamentary representation and even role in government. The strong dichotomy seen in the legislative background to education policy in each country produced a curious mixture of structures in minority education, some inherited from the previous period and some adapted to EU expectations. The present legislation in Romania is EU-compatible, but the process of implementing it was repeatedly delayed for want of political backing, with the result that the Romanians had to fall back on temporary government orders. Slovakia had yet to pass a new public education act by the end of 2007 and preparations for doing so had hardly begun. The 1984 act inherited from the socialist period was amended from time to time. The European Structural Funds were available, but the minority teaching community was unable to avail itself of them. In Ukraine, the uncertainty factors were the legacy of the Soviet system, challenges from Ukrainian national renewal, and new conflicts to do with commitments to observe EU norms. The national educational development doctrine adopted in 2002 named education as the key development issue for the Ukrainian state, nation, society and individuals, and for the country's competitiveness. But the declared aims of education policy will call for serious effort from a strongly centralized, underfunded education system. A new act on public education was passed in Serbia in 2004. The country took part, in the early years of the twenty-first century, in several international programs designed to implant the requirements and principles for educational reforms. However, that openness was offset by memories of the Yugoslav wars of the 1990s and occasional nationalist overtones, accompanied by apathy among teachers and emigration by young people.

The conditions and scope for these education systems in the early twenty-first century are affected not only by the political and legal frames, but also by aspects of demography. The number of children in the Hungarian minorities of all these countries was falling. In Transylvania, for instance, the number of Hungarians of elementary school age fell by 42 percent between 1990 and 2008, and that reduction would reach secondary and higher education over the next ten years. The fall in the Hungarian elementary school population in Slovakia was 20 percent between 2001 and 2006. It was being forecast that the number of secondary school students would fall by more than 30 percent by 2011 and of those in higher education (the 20–24 cohort) by half by 2020. Similar reductions are forecast for Vojvodina: the number of ethnic Hungarians in higher grades of elementary school (the 10–14 cohort) would fall by about 25 percent by 2012 and the higher education roll by almost 40 per cent by 2022. There are no detailed figures available for the mainly rural Hungarians of Transcarpathia, but this group too suffered a demographic decline of 20 percent in 1989–2001 as the Hungarian community aged.

The figures for educational attainment were also negative in many respects. The proportion of Hungarians in Romania with a higher education was lower than the national average.[5] The proportion of Slovakian Hungarians with only elementary schooling was far higher than the national average and the proportion with higher education only 5 percent, against a national figure of around 10 percent.[6] The Hungarians of Transcarpathia showed a relatively high number of secondary school graduates but a very low number of graduates of higher education.[7] The Vojvodina Hungarians also showed a relatively high proportion with only elementary schooling and lower than average proportions for secondary school and higher education graduates.[8] Thus in all four countries, the proportion of Hungarians relative to the average falls as educational attainment rises.

In view of those demographic and educational attainment figures, education policy among the minority Hungarians sought to reduce such differences between native Hungarian-speakers and the majority. Professional and political opinion among the minority Hungarians dwelt on the underrepresentation of Hungarians in higher education and the narrow range of available courses taught in Hungarian. This concern led directly to the initiation of higher education development projects in Transcarpathia, Transylvania, Slovakia and Vojvodina, designed to compensate for "ethnic" disadvantage and create educational equality of opportunity.

In Transylvania in the 2007–2008 academic year, 61 courses were taught in Hungarian at the Babeş–Bolyai University in Cluj-Napoca,[9] and 12 at the Partium Christian University in Oradea (which grew out of the earlier István Sulyok College).[10] Sapientia University in Cluj-Napoca, Miercurea-Ciuc and Târgu Mureş offered 19 courses in the fields of economics, social science, arts and engineering.[11] There was other state higher education available in Hungarian in Târgu Mureş (University of Medicine and Pharmacy, Szentgyörgyi István University of Dramatic Art) and Bucharest (Hungarian studies). Denominational higher education in Hungarian occurred at the Protestant Theological Institute in Cluj-Napoca and the Theological Institute of Alba Iulia.

Hungarian-taught higher education was offered in Slovakia in 2006–2007 at the Konstantin University in Nitra – whose long-established Hungarian-taught courses of teachers' training were hived off from the Faculty of Central European studies in 2004 – and at Selye János University in Komárno, which had courses in theology, economics and teachers' training. Hungarian language and literature could be studied at the Comenius University in Bratislava, where the department was set up in 1951, and since 1996 in the Philology Faculty of Dél Mátyás University in Banská Bystrica.[12]

In Transcarpathia, Hungarian minority higher education was set up at the foundation-run Ferenc Rákóczi II Transcarpathian Hungarian Institute in Berehove, with Hungarian funding. This was offering courses in teachers' training, horticultural engineering, economics and IT, and Hungarian, English and Ukrainian language courses, leading to degrees accredited in Ukraine, and recognized also in Hungary as university degrees under a bilateral treaty. Such courses were being taught in five departments and the Adult Education Center in 2007–2008. Other Hungarian-taught courses were available at the state Uzhhorod National University, where a

Hungarian-language section, the Faculty of History of Hungary and European Integration operates at the Historical Department opened in 2008, and by the Hungarian-language section of Teachers' Training College of Mukacheve State University.[13]

In Vojvodina, teaching in Hungarian within the state higher education system was available at the Technical College and Teachers' Training Institute in Subotica, and the Department of Hungarian Studies, University of Novi Sad. Some courses were also taught in Hungarian in the Economics and Civil Engineering faculties in Subotica, University of Novi Sad and at the Academy of Arts in Novi Sad. A Hungarian-taught Teachers' Training Faculty opened at Subotica University in October 2006.[14]

Hungarian-taught higher education in neighboring countries was also being offered by extra-mural branches of Hungary-based institutions: in Transylvania by Szent István University (based in Gödöllő), the University of West Hungary (Sopron), Károli Gáspár University of the Hungarian Reformed Church (Budapest), the College for Modern Business Studies (Tatabánya), Dennis Gabor College (Budapest), the University of Debrecen and Sámuel Tessedik College (Békéscsaba); in Slovakia by Corvinus University (Budapest), Budapest University of Technical and Economic Studies, Komárom City University, the University of West Hungary, the Horticultural Faculty of Kecskemét College, the University of Miskolc, the College of Modern Business Studies and Dennis Gabor College; in Transcarpathia in the 1990s by Nyíregyháza College, the Horticultural Faculty of Szent István University and Dennis Gabor College; Szent István University and Dennis Gabor College offered courses in Vojvodina, too.[15] The motive behind these initiatives was partly to fill gaps in availability, but there were financial spurs as well. The parent institutions could claim capitation grants from the Hungarian Ministry of Education even for students in neighboring countries, or, where the course did not qualify, fees could be charged. Some extra-mural branches remain, but others were superseded by the local higher education initiatives.

It makes educational and economic sense to bring the developments in higher education, with the regional strategies and those of certain institutions, into line with the demographic and labor market trends. The declining numbers of the students will soon place the institutions and their supply in a new situation, especially where there are duplications. These days the Hungarian higher education system abroad cannot be divorced from market forces: market logic applies among the institutions teaching in the minority and in the majority language, and among those teaching in Hungarian as well. Further challenges derive from the change to the Bologna system and the EU accession of Hungary, Slovakia and Romania. In wider terms, higher education institutions abroad that teach in Hungarian (and the research facilities associated with them) face problems of future staffing, the expansion of higher education, the social imbedding of higher education, the recognition of Hungarian-taught courses no longer being an end in themselves, the absence of regional research strategies, the expansion of network cooperation, and the financing of courses and researches. Accreditation of courses may also be hit by local legislative changes and by conflicts between majority and minority political elites.[16]

Transylvania has the biggest system of elementary and high schools teaching in Hungarian, although demographics have reduced the number of schools or sections by a third in recent years. In 2006 there were around 1,400 Hungarian-language kindergartens and schools with 180,000 pupils. Slovakia had almost 49,000 pupils in 377 elementary and high schools conducted in Hungarian. An extra task for minority education in Transcarpathia was to switch from teaching Russian as a subject to teaching Ukrainian, in line with the official language of state. The Hungarian-taught system consisted of 106 schools: 11 primary schools, 52 elementary schools, 34 high schools, 2 gymnasia and 7 lycea, with almost 20,000 pupils. Three quarters were teaching exclusively in Hungarian, while others had sections teaching in Ukrainian or Russian attached. In Vojvodina Hungarian was the language of instruction in 2004–2005 in 78 elementary schools in 26 communities with some 18,000 pupils, and in 12 administrative districts in 34 high schools (10 gymnasia and 23 specialist middle and trade schools) with some 6,700 pupils.

The other main area of change in minority Hungarian education is secondary education. An important part has been played by local associations of Hungarian teachers. Minority secondary education in the countries examined is largely theoretical in nature, with the added impetus going into the humanities, education studies and the social sciences, where an attempt can be discerned to compensate for decades of state neglect. For the Hungarian minority in particular, the artificially inflated scale of teaching of scientific and technical subjects was not complemented after the change of system by sufficient attention to vocational training.

In Romania, specialist, trade-related subjects could only be taken in Romanian in the 1990s, but the possibility of teaching them in the minority language opened up with legislation in 1999, with the requirement that the technical vocabulary be taught in Romanian as well. The restrictive rules governing the minority education system meant that most of Romania's Hungarian-taught high school population went to schools teaching theoretical, not vocational, subjects. In 2002–2003, for instance, these accounted for 63 percent of enrollment, while the remaining 37 percent could choose between arts, sports, education and technical specializations, of which the last accounted for over 30 percentage points. The situation in minority vocational schooling was hampered not only by the low intake proportion, but also by a poor range of trades offered and by regional differences in availability, compounded by inadequate infrastructure, indifference from businesses, a dearth of qualified Hungarian instructors, lack of provision for extension training, and a shortage of manuals and textbooks in Hungarian.[17]

Data for Slovakia show a similar shift from vocational towards gymnasium schooling, with the former stabilizing at 28–30 percent. Another factor contributing to the low prestige of vocational schools was the fact that most of those completing them failed to find jobs in their trade. The schools had become divorced from reality in many respects. Their courses were unrelated to actual labor market demands and imparted practical or theoretical knowledge, not skills. Such schools also had low prestige and low intakes in Transcarpathia.

There were two vocational lycea involved, one teaching entirely in Hungarian in Yanoshi (Makkosjánosi) and one with Ukrainian and Hungarian sections in Berehove, where a Hungarian class is started if more than 25 students apply for it.

Similar compensatory logic accompanied the spread of high schools maintained by Churches and civil organizations (foundations). Erasing the aftermath of centralization is a long task, in which non-state schools teaching in Hungarian make a breach in the state monopoly, but in some regions come to teach the elite or students selected by ability.[18] In Transcarpathia in 2006–2007, for instance, there were seven selective Church-run gymnasia teaching in Hungarian: the Reformed Lyceum in Pyjterfolvo, the Sándor Sztojka Lyceum in Karachin, the St. Stephen Lyceum in Mukacheve, the Reformed Lyceum in Velyki Berehy and the Reformed Lyceum in Velyka Dobron'.[19] Church schooling is far more widespread in Transylvania: there were 20 Church high schools accounting for 12 percent of the places in Hungarian-taught education in 2006–2007. In the same year, 989 pupils in Slovakia were attending Church-maintained elementary schools that teach in Hungarian and almost 700 such gymnasia. Selective high schooling in Hungarian began at two gymnasia in Vojvodina in September 2003: the Philological Grammar School "Dezső Kosztolányi" in Subotica and the Science and Mathematics Secondary Grammar School for Gifted Students in Senta.[20] Also Church-maintained is the Diocese Classic Gymnasium and Diocese Seminary "Paulinum" in Subotica,[21] where teaching is in Croatian and Hungarian and the leaving examination is accepted by all Serbian institutes of higher education.

The difficulties faced in elementary and secondary education taught in Hungarian differ from region to region, but some can be considered general: reorganization of schools in response to demographic changes, teaching the state language, attracting trained teachers to rural areas and retaining them there, the feminization of the teaching profession, the need to develop extension training for those teaching in Hungarian, the justification and efficiency of education programs in areas of scattered Hungarian habitation, and the need to integrate the schools of Hungarian-speaking Gypsies.[22]

In addition, it is important to mention the expansion of adult education.[23] In Romania and Slovakia there seems to be the requisite legislation and market demand for the system to expand on a market basis, but in Transcarpathia and Vojvodina it covers mainly IT and foreign-language learning, through non-profit foundations.

Notes

1   John U. Ogbu, "Variability in Minority School Performance: a Problem in Search of an Explanation," in Evelyn Jacob *et al.*, eds., *Minority Education: Anthropological Perspectives* (Norwood, NJ, 1993) is, among the various interpretations of minority education, worth singling out. Also see Mikael Luciak, "Minority Status and Schooling – John U. Ogbu's Theory and the Schooling of Ethnic Minorities in Europe," *Intercultural Education* (2004) 4: 359–368 on its applicability to Europe, and Adél Pásztor, "National Minorities with Respect to Education. The Case of Hungarians," *Review of Sociology* (2006) 2: 5–35, on an attempt to adapt it to Hungarians abroad. There have yet to be detailed studies of the effectiveness of Hungarian minority education. Applicability to Hungarians abroad of some findings of the PISA and PIRSL international comparative competence tests are discussed in Örs Csete, Attila Papp Z. and János Setényi, *Magyar oktatás az ezredfordulón* [Hungarian Teaching at the Turn of the Millennium] (Budapest, 2010). A typology of minority education can be found in Attila Papp Z., "Hatékonyság vagy méltóság. A kisebbségi oktatás változatai és kihívásai" [Effectiveness or Equity. Forms and Challenges of Minority Educations], in Margit Feischmidt ed., *Etnicitás. Különbségteremtő társadalom.* [Ethnicity. Society that Divides] (Budapest, 2010).

2   Tamás Kozma, *Kisebbségi oktatás Közép-Európában* [Minority Education in Central Europe] (Budapest, 2005).

3   The term "Transylvanian Hungarian historical Churches" is used in accounts of the foundation process, e. g. on the Sapientia University website, at http://www.sapientia.ro/hu/kronologia.html (accessed February 28, 2010), but the names and affiliations "eight founding leaders" are not specified. "Historical" Churches had privileges over other denominations in Hungary until the mid-twentieth century. The term reappeared in 1998 but is harder to interpret for Transylvania.

Romania of☒cially recognizes 18 denominations. The three biggest to worship mainly in Hungarian are the Roman Catholics, Reformed and Unitarians.

4   *Democratic Alliance of Hungarians in Romania/Uniunea Democrată Maghiară din România.*

5   For more detail, see Attila Papp Z., "Átmenetben: a romániai magyarok társadalmi pozícióinak alakulása 1992–2002 között" [In Transition: Trends in the Social Positions of Romanian Hungarians 1992–2002], *Regio* 19 (2008) 4: 155–230.

6   For more detail, see László Gyurgyík, "A szlovákiai magyarok társadalomszerkezete a 90-es években" [The Social Structure of the Slovakian Hungarians in the 1990s], *Regio* 19 (2008) 4: 77–101·

7   See also Ildikó Orosz, István Csernicskó, Pál Ambrus and Olga Kristafori, *A magyar nyelvű/nyelvi oktatás stratégiai kérdései Kárpátalján* [Strategic Issues in Teaching in and of Hungarian in Transcarpathia] (Ms., 2008).

8   For more detail, see Róbert Badis, "A vajdasági magyar népesség társadalmi szerkezete két népszámlálás tükrében, 1991, 2002" [The Social Structure of the Hungarian Population of Vojvodina in the Light of Two Censuses, 1991 and 2002], *Regio* 19 (2008) 4: 102–154·

9   http://www.ubbcluj.ro/. Accessed February 28, 2010.

10   http://www.partium.ro/. Accessed February 28, 2010.

11   http://emte.ro/. Accessed February 28, 2010.

12   Béla László, László Szabó A. and Károly Tóth, eds., *Magyarok Szlovákiában IV. kötet. Oktatásügy (1989–2006)* [Hungarians in Slovakia, Vol. IV. Education (1989–2006)] (Somorja/Dunaszerdahely, 2006)·

13   Orosz, Csernicskó, Ambrus and Kristafori, *A magyar nyelvű/nyelvi oktatás.*

14   For detailed demographic and school statistics, see Irén Gábrityné Molnár and Zsuzsa Mirnics, eds., *Oktatási oknyomozó. Vajdasági kutatások, tanulmányok* [Educational Investigation. Researches, Studies in Vojvodina] (Szabadka, 2006)·

15   *SzentIstvánEgyetem,Nyugat-magyarországiEgyetem,KároliGáspár Református Egyetem, Modern Üzleti Tudományok Főiskola, Gábor Dénes Főiskola, Debreceni Egyetem, Tessedik Sámuel Főiskola, Corvinus Egyetem, a Budapesti Műszaki és Gazdaságtudományi Egyetem, Komáromi Város Egyetem, Kecskeméti Főiskola Kertészeti Főiskolai Kara, Miskolci Egyetem, Nyíregyházi Főiskola, Szent István Egyetem Kertészmérnöki Kara.*

16 For more detail on these challenges, see Attila Papp Z., "A Kárpát-medencei magyar felsőoktatási és kutatási térség lehetősége" [Scope for Hungarian Higher Education and Research in the Carpathian Basin], in András Görömbei and Károly Manherz, eds., *Az együttműködés esélyei* [Chances of Cooperation] (Debrecen, 2007), pp. 43–52.

17 Rita Fóris-Ferenc, "Kisebbségi oktatás Romániában felső középfokon" [Minority Higher Education in Romania], in Kinga Mandel and Attila Papp Z., eds., *Cammogás. Minőségkoncepciók a romániai magyar középfokú oktatásban* [Trudging Along. Quality Concepts in Romania's Hungarian Higher Education] (Csíkszereda, 2007) pp. 45–94.

18 For more on Church schools, see *Educatio* (2005) 3 (on Church and education) and Fóris-Ferenc, "Kisebbségi oktatás Romániában."

19 *Péterfalvi Református Líceum, Kárácsfalvi Sztojka Sándor Líceum, Munkácsi Szent István Líceum, Nagyberegi Református Líceum, Nagydobronyi Református Líceum.*

20 *Kosztolányi Dezső Tehetséggondozó Gimnázium; Bolyai Matematikai Gimnázium.*

21 *Paulinum Püspökségi Klasszikus Gimnázium.*

22 For more on these challenges, with regional summaries, see Örs Csete, ed., *A Magyariskola Program fogadtatása a Kárpát-medencében* [The Reception of the Hungarian School Program in the Carpathian Basin] (Budapest, 2006)

23 An account in English of Romanian Hungarian and minority adult education and vocational training in general: Attila Papp Z., "The Relationship between Adult Education and Professional Training in Schools (in the Minority Context)," in Attila Z. Papp, ed., *Kihasználatlanul. A romániai magyar felnőttképzés rendszere* [Unusable. Romania's System of Hungarian Adult Education] (Miercurea-Ciuc, 2005), pp. 232–239. On minority adult education see Irén Gábrityné Molnár, ed., *Képzetteké a jövő. A felnőttképzés háttere Észak-Bácska iskolahálózatában* [The Future Belongs to the Qualified. The Adult Education Background in the School System of North Bačka] (Szabadka, 2008, Budapest, 2005), Mária Kulcsár and Károly Tóth, "Felnőttképzés Szlovákiában" [Adult Training in Slovakia], *Regio* 16 (2005) 2: 3–26, and Ildikó Orosz, István Csernicskó, Kálmán Soós and László Brenzovics, "A kárpátaljai magyar felnőttképzés és szakképzés esélyei" [Chances for Hungarian Adult Education and Vocational Training in Transcarpathia], *Regio* 16 (2005) 2: 27–56.

6. THE POSITION OF THE HUNGARIAN LANGUAGE
Orsolya Nádor

In language policy terms, Hungarian appears in three main contexts: as a majority language, a minority language, and a foreign language. These contexts may each bridge several categories, some educational (for example, Hungarian as a less widely known, a language of origin, or a secondary language) and others related to situation and political position (as the native language of a scattered group, a lost language, or a regional official language).[1]

The concept of Hungarian as a minority native language arose after the treaties that followed World War I, which left over three million native speakers as "Hungarians abroad." Since then more than eighty years have not passed without leaving their linguistic mark. Territorial variants of the language have arisen, minority Hungarians have gradually become bilingual, and Hungarian has been increasingly affected by the majority language in various registers, notably in the vocabulary of technical terms, but also in grammatical structure, where traces of Slovak, Romanian, Serbian, Croatian, Slovene, German and Ukrainian have appeared.[2]

The concept can be approached from several directions, mainly in the field of applied linguistics, those of sociolinguistics, dialectology, psycholinguistics, neurolinguistics, language policy and language planning. Each field has applied universal scientific findings to Hungarian relations. This has given rise to research into Hungarian-pairing linguistics, the question of multi-centrism, sociolinguistic study of minority territorial variants of Hungarian, study of language switching and the process of language loss, interpretation of endangered status, language inequality and discrimination through political decisions affecting and curtailing minority language use, and examination of linguicism in relation to certain groups of Hungarian-speakers. Linguistics lagged far behind historical and political developments in only beginning to concern itself in the last third of the twentieth century with the social and psychological attributes of linguistic communities. Before that, issues concerning minority languages had appeared in other scholarly contexts, in works of history, law (the legal history of Hungarian as a state language) or ethnography (dialects, phraseologies). The minorities appeared in the linguistics of Hungarian mainly in philological activity to do with research into language history, etymology and historical topics, and with contacts between the majority and minority languages. However, linguistic surveys were affected by the change of system and by the alteration in European attitudes towards minorities. Today, Hungarian scholarship is falling into line with universal linguistics as the political borders are dismantled. Research cooperation in this field was almost impossible before the changes of system. Now the Hungarian Academy of Sciences is cooperating with language institutions in neighboring countries (the Hodinka Antal Institute, the Gramma Language Institute, the Attila T. Szabó Language Institute, the Samu Imre Language Institute, the Scientific Society for Research into the Hungarian Community, and the Hungarian Language Corpus in Vojvodina) to formulate new dictionary entries and in language policy and education policy researches in all fields. Among the fruits has been the TERMINI website, where lists of "cross-border" words and publications on the subject are available.[3]

The main criteria of Hungarian as a minority language are these:

- Use of the language is restricted; it plays a subordinate role to the majority language.

- Defects of linguistic competence appear, especially in official and specialist parlance.

- The intra-communal prestige and extra-communal assessment of the language differ from place to place.

- Members of minority language groups steadily become bilingual, and Hungarian is not the dominant language in all cases.

-   Depending on minority size and political status and on settlement conditions, bilingualism may take the form of substitution or augmentation.

Restriction of language use and competence in using it are closely linked. One cardinal point of majority policy in successor states is their stance towards the minorities in their midst. László Szarka distinguishes four kinds of legal position over language in East-Central Europe: 1. The concept of the official (state) language is laid down in the Constitution and applies solely to the language of the majority nation (in Slovakia and Romania, and in the Yugoslavia of Milošević in the 1980s and 1990s). 2. The concept of the official (state) language is laid down in the Constitution, but along with the country's minority languages, as regional official languages (in Slovenia and Croatia, and in part in Austria, Ukraine and post-2002 Serbia). 3. The state or official language is laid down not in the Constitution but in other legislation (in Poland). 4. The concept of an official (state) language is not stated in the Constitution or in other legislation (in the Czech Republic and Hungary).[4]

With Hungarian in neighboring countries, the typical case has been of attempts to encourage the advance of the majority language at the expense of the minority one through stigmatization or by narrowing the field where it can be used, openly or on the grounds of ostensible practicality. As a first step, the minority language is relegated in settling official matters, orally or in writing. Then the shortcomings of native-language education lead to gaps in specialist vocabulary. These days, minority Hungarian children usually receive the bases of education in their native language, but find that they are hampered in secondary and higher education, the route to full linguistic competence, because they are taught in the state language. It is hard to maintain the prestige of the minority native language if the route to self-improvement lies through the majority language. The minority community has accorded for decades a high intrinsic value to its native language, irrespective of the language-policy environment, resting on appreciation of the local linguistic variation and archaic forms, in relation not only to the local majority language but also to the standard language of Hungary. This appreciation helped to ensure until recently that the type of bilingualism found in the Hungarian community was an augmenting one in which the native language retained dominance. More recently, linguistics scholars have warned of a retreat by the native language from its decisive role, due to various social processes (such as enhanced mobility, break-up of rural communities, and commoner mixed marriages) so that a substitutive type of bilingualism has become more frequent, which may lead to a switch from Hungarian or its loss as a native language.

There have been big changes in language laws over the decades since the Hungarians became a minority. Between the wars, much of the minority saw the situation as temporary, and competence in the language was fully maintained. The second, socialist period brought a gradual decline in competence. After the changes of system, there was a clear deterioration in the face of impatient, restrictive measures by new nation states. The present division of the minority Hungarians between those within the EU and those outside it or aspiring to membership makes it harder to take advantage of the developments in international language-related legislation.

The position of Hungarian as a minority language, in terms of language policy, can be defined historically in the first, interwar period in Romania, Czechoslovakia, the Serb-Croat-Slovene Kingdom, and Austria. The early measures by successor states made quite clear to the Hungarians the difference in rights and extent between a majority and a minority native language. All states concerned signed the minority protection treaty in Saint-Germain-en-Laye in 1919, which included specific clauses on freedom of language use: the minorities, irrespective of race, language or faith, would have equal rights in employment, worship and all areas of public life. But these commitments were not seen as binding by the new states, which cited historical grievances in their constitutions and language laws as grounds for curbing the minorities' natural rights and native-language use.

The process by which national languages formed in the nineteenth century was mainly internal: assembly from a host of variants of a common standard for orthography and usage. This joined with moves to end the use of outside languages, as curbs on the role and prestige of the national language.

The national languages became vehicles of national identity. Their weight increased appreciably when inequalities among languages and ethnic groups became enshrined in legislation. As Szarka states,

> The symbolic, political function of the majority nation's language was laid down in the constitutions of the region's countries, and... in Slovakia, Ukraine, Serbia, Slovenia, Poland, and since 2001 Hungary, in separate language laws. In these the national language is seen as the means of expression of the nation state, the means of clear communication within state activity and public administration, the vehicle of national cultural values, a basic element of national identity, a national cultural treasure, the means of common communication among all citizens, protected and developed by specific institutions.... Majority national languages without exception enjoy official status as a state language, as opposed to minority national languages, which... according to legislation in the region have won official regional status in Slovenia, Croatia, Ukraine... and Serbia in minority-inhabited areas. In the other countries, the language rights of the minorities are not recognized as official languages, but were enhanced in the last decade of the twentieth century by some limited concessions on language use.[5]

The measures of successor states clearly overlap. The constitution or legislation based on it typically includes riders that contradict the country's treaty commitments. For instance, general freedom of use of native language is curbed by a threshold qualification, usually stipulating that the minority comprise 20 percent of a given population. Education laws may specify that non-denominational schools teach in the state language, thus forcing Hungarian middle schools and colleges to close or change their language of instruction. Frequent use is made of name analysis, as notoriously circumstantial evidence of an earlier "Hungarianization," not in any case admissible under the treaty commitments, and so is official registration of Hungarian names in forms found in the majority language. Curbs on minority communities introduced in judicial and administrative practice may contravene not only treaty commitments, but also the constitution or superior legislation. It is interesting that all successor states have resorted to gerrymandering to prevent a minority language from attaining the necessary figures of speakers in the local population to qualify for language-use rights. Official place names are changed to mirror translations in the majority language or altered to existing majority usages.

Taking the new Yugoslav state as an example, such discrimination occurred in Hungarian-inhabited areas with a Serb/Croat/Slovene majority. An extra tax of 10–50 percent was levied on commercial signs in Hungarian, or they had to be vetted by the police. Customers entering catering establishments, workshops or retail outlets had to be greeted in the new state language. The minority language could not be used in post offices or on railways even for information. Hungarian schools were nationalized, had their financing reduced, or were closed. The premises of middle schools were expropriated and their teaching aids were removed. Hungarian schools were confined to taking pupils who had escaped the attentions of official name analysis up to 1927. New place names were devised and introduced in 1922, whereby only 42 of Hungarian-inhabited 335 settlements kept their original name, others being translated or adorned with a Slav prefix or suffix. The scope for Hungarian speakers to use their native language worsened further in 1929, when the language was banned in all public offices and the remaining Hungarian officials were dismissed.

After brief extension of Hungarian rule over much of the Hungarian-inhabited territory in 1938–1944, the assimilation resumed after World War II under a different political cloak. There was still no legal recourse against language discrimination. Up until the Helsinki Final Act of 1975, minority affairs were treated as internal matters or were susceptible only to external influence through Moscow. The second period began almost everywhere with physical and intellectual reprisals. Only gradually did some communist front organizations of the Hungarian community appear, based on a new basis of class discrimination imposed by communist ideology. In still ostensibly democratic Czechoslovakia in 1945–1948, it was forbidden to use Hungarian in public, Hungarian schools were closed, Church services could not be held in Hungarian, and no periodicals or books in Hungarian could appear. The extreme Stalinist totalitarianism that followed the communist takeover of Czechoslovakia in 1948 meant that years passed before a system of state-controlled minority cultural institutions emerged. Conditions were similar elsewhere, although Czechoslovakia's several-year outright language ban was unique. Some positive moves were made in Tito's Yugoslavia in the last third of the twentieth century: Hungarian began to be taught as a "neighboring" language in Vojvodina's Serbian schools, Hungarian press and book publishing revived, and an institute of Hungarian studies was founded at Novi Sad University. But Romania in the last years of the Ceauşescu regime took openly discriminatory measures, declaring a program of "national homogenization." Hungarians were referred to as ethnic Hungarian or Hungarian-speaking Romanians. Unrealistic population proportions were imposed as a requirement for native-language schooling and pressure was put on Churches to introduce Romanian language services.

The territorial reorganizations of 1989–1990 failed to bring peace and quiet to the region's minorities. Nationalism was typically strengthened in the new states, along with mounting grievance-based antagonism to minorities. Emphasis was laid on the primacy of the state and national language and successive new curbs were placed on minority language use: Slovakia's language laws of 1991 and 1995, Romania's 1994 law on public administration, and Serbia's 1991 law on language use and 1992 and 1998 education laws. Each restricted public appearance of minority languages as incompatible with the concept of a nation state, especially in the fields of public administration, exercise of civil rights, schools and public education. Exceptions in relation to Hungarian were Ukraine and Croatia, which respected the linguistic and cultural rights of their proportionally smaller Hungarian communities while engaged in bitter struggles against far larger Russian and Serbian minorities respectively.

The concept of a state language is often confused or identified with that of an official language. Szarka cites Jenő Kiss's definition of a state language as one with a historically privileged position within a nation state, enjoying unlimited usage, as opposed to disadvantaged minority languages without such status. György Szépe in his definition of "the language of citizens" brings to the fore the communal and state administrative functions of national and official languages, along with their historical, political and symbolic function. He is quoted by Szarka as saying that "the national languages symbolizing the state and native land – think of national anthems, the national literary composition known to all, the community-forming force of historical slogans – for a long time represented the state only symbolically, but with the codification of language rights in the twentieth century they have become state languages in a legal and administrative sense, while retaining earlier symbolic, even sacred functions now adjusted to the needs of each state." According to Szépe, "This symbolic function of the official language – especially if it is the language of the native land – lends positive additional meanings and a strong emotional tinge."[6]

Change in the language rights of the Hungarian minorities in the Carpathian Basin and some diminution of the discrimination against them followed at the end of the 1990s, reaching a stage in the 2000s where the right to use the native language was granted *de jure*. Slovenia, Croatia, Serbia and Ukraine accepted Hungarian as a regional minority language. Romania, Slovakia and Austria also introduced measures that allowed minority languages to be used more widely. At present, Slovakia appears to adhere most consistently to a state-language concept emphasizing the primacy of

Slovak, backed by a persistent official perception of the minorities as factors that still threaten the national interest and the country's sovereignty and territorial integrity, as they once did in the 1930s and 1940s, irrespective of subsequent commitments such as the EU membership of Hungary and Slovakia and their ratification of the European Charter for Regional or Minority Languages.[7] The laws on public administration and education in Romania remain inconsistent, failing to rule on the language rights of minorities. The fragile multilingual tradition of Yugoslavia was a casualty of the ethnic Yugoslav wars of the 1990s, before which Vojvodina had been in an enviable position for several decades. Only after the Yugoslav successor states had stabilized politically could ethnic and linguistic order return. The constitution of Slovenia proclaims the concept of regional minority languages to exist and defines their scope for official use. Croatia acknowledges the existence of indigenous minorities. Serbia guaranteed regional use of minority languages in summer 2002. Surprisingly, Austria did not give Hungarian similar treatment in the Burgenland communities of Unterwart, Oberwart, Oberpullendorf and Rotenturm an der Pinka until May 2000.

These changes are positive, but decades of linguistic inequality have left their mark, so that the *de facto* Hungarian-speaking community outside Hungary cannot fully exploit the language rights belatedly gained. Surveys show that the proportion giving the majority language preference is increasing. The minority language has only a limited area of influence, extending over fewer registers than the version spoken in Hungary itself. It shows increasing signs of its contacts with the majority language and its prestige is falling. These are sure indications of a linguistic assimilation that can only be slowed by a considered minority and language policy based on international agreement.

Notes

1　Gábor Tolcsvai Nagy, *Nyelv, érték, közösség* [Language, Value, Community] (Budapest, 2004), pp. 10–147.

2　István Lanstyák, *Nyelvből nyelvbe. Tanulmányok a szókölcsönzésről, kódváltásról és fordításról* [From Language to Language. Studies on Word Loaning, Code Changing and Translation] (Pozsony, 2006), pp. 15–170; János Péntek and Attila Benő, *Nyelvi kapcsolatok, nyelvi dominanciák az erdélyi régióban* [Language Connections, Language Dominance in the Transylvanian Region], Szabó T. Attila Nyelvi Intézet publications 1 (Kolozsvár, 2003), pp. 9–141.

3　See http://ht.nytud.hu/htonline/present.php?action=hatartalanitas. Accessed March 20, 2010.

4　László Szarka, "Államnyelv, hivatalos nyelv – kisebbségi nyelvi jogok Kelet-Közép-Európában" [State Language, Official Language – Minority Language Rights in East-Central Europe], in Orsolya Nádor and László Szarka, eds., *Nyelvi jogok, kisebbségek, nyelvpolitika Kelet-Közép-Európában* [Language Rights, Minorities, Language Policy in East-Central Europe] (Budapest, 2003), p. 20.

5　*Ibid.*, p. 16.

6　*Ibid.*, pp. 17–18.

7　Hungary ratified the Charter in 1995 (in relation to Croatian, German, Romanian, Serbian, Slovak and Slovene) and Slovakia in 2001 (in relation to Bulgarian, Croatian, German, Hungarian, Polish, Romani, Rusyn and Ukrainian).

7. CULTURAL AND SCIENTIFIC ACTIVITY AMONG HUNGARIAN MINORITY COMMUNITIES
Nándor Bárdi, Csilla Fedinec and *Attila Papp Z.*

The institutional position of Hungarian minority culture altered radically with the systemic changes in Central Europe. State cultural policies directed from a Communist Party center gave way mainly to grassroots organization of minority communities. The arrival of the rule of law and private property relations brought great scope for institutionalization. However, state subsidies shrank considerably, except in Austria and Slovenia. An attempt was made to compensate for this with a system of subsidies from Hungary, directed at institutionalizing and developing intensive relations with a Hungarian ethno-cultural community extending beyond Hungary itself. This changed entirely the institutions and the content of minority Hungarian cultural life. Efforts hitherto, literature-centered and concerned chiefly with encouraging language use and conserving cultural heritage, were joined by aims of disseminating knowledge about the minority community in each locality or region and meeting its cultural needs. This meant presenting and developing the Hungarian cultural heritage (intellectual and material), and reinforcing national self-awareness and distinctiveness. The minority communities became a pronounce in public life not just as representatives of a distinct culture, but as institutionalized social groups. Literature lost its central importance to patterns of cultural consumption found in Hungary, fostered by intensive relations and common mass media.[1]

A survey by the Institute for Ethnic and National Minority Studies of the Hungarian Academy of Sciences found almost 3,000 Hungarian minority cultural institutions and organizations at the turn of the millennium. These were most widespread in Romania (1,700), then Slovakia (560), followed by Serbia (400), Ukraine (160) and Slovenia (33). This meant an average of about 900 Hungarians per institution, except in Slovenia, where the number was about a third of that. Most were multi-functional cultural centers and organizations, three quarters of which defined themselves in almost all regions as Hungarian institutions. The exceptions were Croatia and Slovenia, where the proportion was about 60 percent. The most widespread forms were music and dance groups (about 500), followed by knowledge-disseminating youth clubs (250), drama groups (about 100), and various artists' workshops (70). Decisive among collections and in the community cultural sphere were libraries (about 400), followed by museums (80) and other collections. The press was dominant in cultural dissemination (300), followed by book publishing (80), then television, radio and Internet portals (60). Two thirds of these institutions had been founded after 1989, although 60 percent of the public collections dated from before then. An important tendency in the previous decade had been the steady increase in importance of institutions independent of the state, although state and increasingly local government-run cultural institutions (such as cultural centers) were still playing a vital role in areas where Hungarians were in a majority. Book publishing and the media were the most marketized, while two thirds of the public collections were still publicly funded.[2]

After the change of system, there were attempts by existing Hungarian institutions (CSEMADOK in Czechoslovakia, the KMKSZ in the Ukraine, EMKE in Romania, and the Yugoslavian Hungarian Cultural Society)[3] to offer a centralized frame for the new minority institutions. It soon became clear that only institutions capable of responding directly to local cultural demands were viable, and organization from above largely gave way to a type of institution that stressed further education and provision of methodological assistance. Model examples were the Hungarian Cultural Institute in Lendava (*Magyar Nemzetiségi Művelődési Intézet*), the Hungarian Institute of the Burgenland-Hungarian Cultural Club (*Burgenlandi Magyar Kultúregyesület*) and the Central Hungarian Library, both in Unterwart. In 1996, the Forum Minority Research Institute in Šamorin began to act as a library center, documentation center and scientific and public institution for its region, and as an integrator of minority research in Slovakia. Since 2004, the CSEMADOK

Cultural Institute in Dunajská Streda has acted as a methodological center. In Senta, the Institute for Hungarian Culture in Vojvodina founded in 2005 coordinates the scientific and documentation work in the region as the one institute dealing with the methodology of community culture and librarianship.[4]

Literature adjusted itself to a new canon. It is now possible to talk of a universal Hungarian literature, not a division between Hungary's literature and those of neighboring minority communities. Literature can be structured in terms of aesthetic values, not geographical boundaries. The idea behind literature that reflects the communal problems of minority Hungarian society is being relegated to the background by increasingly professional social scientific research. The Bratislava journal *Kalligram* is also influential in universal Hungarian literature. A decisive role among post-1989 Slovakian Hungarian writers and literary historians is played by the oeuvre and intermediary role of Lajos Grendel. The decade after the change of system has brought fulfillment in the work of László Vári Fábián and Károly D. Balla – the latter runs the most intensive Hungarian literary portal.[5] In Romania, major summarizing works by writers who began their careers in the 1950s (András Sütő, Sándor Kányádi, János Székely and István Szilágyi) appeared in the 1990s, while poets Géza Szőcs and András Ferenc Kovács, active since the 1970s and 1980s, reached fulfillment and became known also in Hungary. The best-known Transylvanian writers of the generation who began their careers just before or after the change of system are András Visky, Zsolt Láng, Jánoo Dénes Orbán and László Lövétei Lázár. Vojvodina had the most modern regional Hungarian literature in the 1970s and 1980s: the *Új Symposion* generation. This continued not only with those who settled in Hungary, but also in the work of Ottó Tolnai, the poetry of István Beszédes, and the prose of Ildikó Lovas and György Szerbhorváth.[6]

Marketization of book publishing meant, incidentally, that publishers in Hungary could freely export to neighboring countries after 1989. The biggest change, though, was that the number of books bought fell to a fifth of what it had been in the 1980s. The pre-1989 state-owned, monopoly publishers in Hungarian, who had played a role in minority intellectual and public life (Madách in Bratislava, Kriterion in Bucharest and Cluj-Napoca, and Fórum in Novi Sad) lost their dominance after privatization. What developed was an undercapitalized book publishing sector of several firms that relied mainly on competitive applications for funding, publishing some 400–450 titles a year between them. The better-known publishers that have emerged since the change of system include Mentor, Komp-Press, Polis, Pallas-Akadémia, Pro-Print and Koinonia in Romania, and Kalligram, Mery Ratio and Lilium Aurum in Slovakia. The Hungarian publisher with the most titles in Transcarpathia is Intermix of Uzhhorod.[7]

Theater, like reading and book-buying, lost its importance in post-1989 Hungarian minority culture, but it gained in professionalism and integrated more closely with Hungary. This is represented most clearly at the Festival of Hungarian Theaters beyond the Borders, which began to be held annually in Kisvárda, Hungary, in 1989. The full-time companies have been joined by the Gyula Illyés Hungarian National Theater in Berehove, the Csík Playhouse in Miercurea-Ciuc, Theater Figura Studio in Gheorgheni, and the Sándor Tomcsa Theater in Odorheiu-Secuiesc. The greatest attention has been accorded to the productions of Gábor Tompa in Cluj-Napoca and Attila Vidnyánszky in Berehove.[8]

The fine arts, not being dependent on language, have shown the strongest transnational influences and connections. Overall Hungarian arts associations have formed, but more intensive work is done in the growing number of training establishments, project groups and artists' colonies. As important as the structural changes have been the expansion of the training and scholarship systems and the addition of complex visual culture and art actions to the traditional branches of art. Private Hungarian universities in Cluj-Napoca and Oradea in Romania have multiplied their intakes by offering photography, film, media and visual culture courses. Hungarian cinema in Transylvania has produced almost 300 motion pictures since 1989, most of them documentaries, with the periodical *Filmtett* playing a central role. The action base set up at Sfântu Gheorghe by Imre Baász holds regular festivals of live art, through which the consciously Transylvanian performances of Gusztáv Ütő have become internationally known. One of the most effective performance artists today is Ilona Németh of Dunajská Streda, who raises issues of universal importance reinterpreted in a minority context. The Contemporary Collection at Dunajská Streda makes conscious collection efforts in all Hungarian-inhabited regions. Another decisive influence is the mediation work of Bálint Szombathy of Vojvodina. Gábor Hushegyi of Bratislava stands out among the art critics.[9]

The press was probably the medium that reacted most sensitively to the changes, from the early 1990s onward, and often contributed to them directly. The changes took place on three planes: in the press, on the audiovisual plane, and on the Internet. New papers were founded and existing ones underwent a renewal of content. The launches were often designed to strengthen some locality, while the existing papers served to manifest renewal among old and new elites, introducing the vocabulary by which the changes became comprehensible to readers. To put it another way, the press created anew the day-to-day ideology required for preserving and maintaining the identities related to minority existence. Thus it became a constant field of conflict among minority elites, and the reorganizations of ownership often took on a political tinge.[10]

Yet the structure of the press did not alter radically. There remained in every region central papers (from the Hungarian minority's point of view) that had appeared for decades: the county papers in Transylvania (*Hargita Népe, Háromszék, Szabadság, Népújság, Bihari Napló, Szatmári Friss Újság*), *Új Szó* (established 1949) in Slovakia, *Magyar Szó* (established 1944) in Vojvodina, and the Uzhhorod *Kárpáti Igaz Szó* (established 1920) in Transcarpathia. Not that there were no major new papers, of course – the minority elite made continual efforts to acquire press mouthpieces by direct or indirect influence. That endeavor after 1989 lay behind the Transylvanian *Krónika* and *Romániai Magyar Szó* (the post-1989 successor to *Előre*), and *Kárpátalja*, published in Berehove.

Although the structural renewal of the written press served as the yardstick, there were important changes also in radio and television. In each region, the surviving state-financed, state-controlled Hungarian-language radio and television stations were joined by new local stations, and satellite dishes meant that Hungary's television channels could be picked up as well. The Hungary-based Duna TV could be received in all the minority regions from 1993, and these days the Hungarian commercial stations can be picked up to a large extent as well. Meanwhile, the neighboring countries' commercial TV stations have also developed enormously into strong competition for the Hungarian stations.[11]

The third field of renewal in the media beyond Hungary's borders has been the emergence of Internet news portals. These represent strong competition to the press in all countries, as they often lend a new tone to coverage of public affairs. There is already competition among them, and allegiances have developed to specific political forces. The other media also run websites, to take local, regional, pan-Hungarian and international information to a wider public and circumvent shortcomings of newspaper distribution. Transylvania's best known site is www.transindex. ro, whose operators define it less as a portal than as a "project," with forums, blog facilities and columns accompanied by relatively little news as such. Other portals of note are www.hirek.ro and www.erdely.ma. Notable sites elsewhere are www.karpatinfo. net for Transcarpathia, www.vajdasagma.info for Vojvodina, and Slovakia's www.felvidek.ma, www.bumm.sk, www.parameter. sk. In addition there are institutional sites for scholarship, science and culture, and most numerous of all, local portals with news and forums designed to boost a sense of community. There are major thematic, cultural, literary and other specialized portals, notably www.zetna.org in Vojvodina, www.bdk.blog.hu in Transcarpathia, www.katedra.sk in Slovakia, and www.langos.at in Burgenland. Notable here are databanks (bibliographies, statistics, link collections, digital libraries and document collections, registers and dictionaries) such as www.foruminst.sk, www.adatbank.ro, http://

adattar.vmmi.org and www.mtaki.hu.[12] A new arrival in March 2006 was www.emagyar.net, to connect so-called eMagyar points in various regions with financial support from Hungary. However, a problem for all Hungarian minority portals has been traffic at a low level that precludes self-financing. Many supply their pages from servers in Hungary.[13]

The media changes helped to transform the scholarly activity that furthered Hungarian self-awareness beyond Hungary's borders. The arts and social sciences were tied closely to Hungary by connections, funding and their language orientation, while the pure and applied sciences built up stronger international links and embedded themselves more deeply in the system of scientific institutions of their country. The emphasis on literature in the period before the change of system meant that this was the field in which the first serious research projects and schools emerged, thanks particularly to Mihály Czine, Mihály Ilia and András Görömbei.

There are almost 1,000 postgraduates in neighboring countries who publish in Hungarian, many with doctorates awarded since 1989 (some in Hungary) and positions in higher education. Some are integrated into their own country's academic institutions. Others work at Hungarian research stations funded by foundations,[14] usually attached to universities or independent professional bodies. Such integration and management in Slovakia was performed in the 1990s by the Mercurius Group, and since then by the Forum Institute and Gramma Language Office. The biggest groups of Hungarian researchers are in the Central European Studies Faculty of Konstantin University in Nitra and at János Selye University in Komárno. The role is played in Transcarpathia by the Hungarian Studies Center at the state Uzhhorod State University, and increasingly since the mid-1990s by the Limes (now named after Tivadar Lehoczky) Institute of Social Research, attached to the Ferenc Rákóczi II Transcarpathian Hungarian Institute, and by the Hodinka Antal Institute. The broadest promoter in Romania is the Transylvanian Museum Society with six specialized departments. Several fields are served by separate associations and foundations, mainly based in Cluj-Napoca: the

János Kriza Ethnographical Society, the Attila T. Szabó Linguistics Institute, the Max Weber Society, the István Apáthy Society, the Entz Géza Foundation for Cultural History and the WAC-Center for Regional and Anthropological Research in Miercurea-Ciuc. These are run mainly by university staff, but research and publications are covered by the Sapientia Foundation Institute for Research Programs, funded by the Hungarian state, while the Hungarian departments at Babeş-Bolyai University have a separate research coordinator: the Hungarian University Federation from Cluj-Napoca. Similar processes occurred in Serbia to those in Transcarpathia: alongside the University of Novi Sad, Faculty of Philosophy, Department of Hungarian Studies arose new workshops of social science that have assumed the task of molding self-awareness in centers of Hungarian habitation. The broadest research management and publishing role is played by the Scientific Association for Hungarology Researches in Subotica. In 2006, the Identity Minority Research Institute was founded specifically for sociological research, under the aegis of the Vojvodina Hungarian Cultural Institute. Hungarian scientific activity in Croatia is coordinated by the Society for Hungarian Science and Art in Croatia in Zagreb, with over 60 members, the most important work being associated with Károly Lábodi. There is scientific coordination also done in Lendava (Slovenia) and Unterwart (Austria). The main journals are *Fórum* in Šamorin, *Erdélyi Társadalom*, *Korunk*, *Magyar Kisebbség* and *Web* in Cluj-Napoca, *Híd* and *Létünk* in Novi Sad, *Aracs* and *Bácsország* in Subotica, *Muratáj* in Lendava, and *Kisebbségkutatás*, *Pro Minoritate* and *Regio* in Budapest.[15]

The subject matter of research has changed. The descriptive works presenting the cultural and social heritage (national identity) typical before 1989 have lost ground to examinations of the operation of minority and regional communities, institutional sub-systems, and specific social processes. Simultaneously, specialization is occurring, although this cannot run as deeply in a narrower, numerically smaller minority Hungarian environment as it does in Hungary or among majority researchers in neighboring countries. The most widespread research projects best known internationally have to do with bilingualism, variants of living language, and language policy. Miklós Kontra initiated research that has been going on for decades into the progressive multi-centeredness of Hungarian. Questions of language design have been tackled by István Csernicskó, Lajos Göncz, István Lanstyák, János Péntek, Gizella Szabómihály and Sándor N. Szilágyi.[16] Of most importance to the self-awareness of minority communities have been the census analyses, enquiring into the processes of demography and social structure, notably by László Gyurgyík, István Horváth, Tamás Kiss, Károly Mirnics, József Molnár, Árpád E. Varga and Valér Veres.[17]

The main methodological innovation in the social sciences was the mass survey. Several regions and majority/minority relations have been covered by major surveys. The Ferenc Balázs Institute has repeatedly used questionnaires on the subject of change in values. György Csepeli and Antal Örkény ran an examination of inter-ethnic relations in the Carpathian Basin in 1997. Ferenc Gereben carried out surveys of national awareness through reading habits. Changes in religious observance were mapped sociologically by Miklós Tomka. Kálmán Gábor looked at youth culture in terms of adaptation. The Institute for Ethnic and National Minority Studies of the Hungarian Academy of Sciences cooperated with groups beyond the borders on the Carpathian Panel of 2007, to examine the relationships of social and employment positions with value systems.[18]

Surveys of ethnography and cultural anthropology play an important role in revealing the features of minority everyday life. Important names here are József Liszka of Slovakia, and the Cluj-Napoca and Miercurea-Ciuc schools of ethnographers: Vilmos Keszeg, Ferenc Pozsony and Vilmos Tánczos, and Zoltán A. Biró, József Gagyi and Sándor Oláh.[19] At the opposite pole is political philosophy, where important changes have been made in the interpretation of the concept of a minority and ethno-political and legal relations by adapting modern political multiculturalism and collective rights to situations that vary from country to country. The Hungarian-language literature on this has been dominated by László Öllős of Slovakia, Alpár Losoncz of Vojvodina, and Miklós Bakk and Levente Salat of Transylvania.[20]

Looking at studies of history that go beyond local history and general knowledge, there are well-known cultural and social historians in Transylvania, such as Ákos Egyed, Gusztáv Hermann, Zsigmond Jakó, András Kiss, András Kovács, Sándor Pál-Antal and Judit Pál. Minority and regional history has become increasingly a subject of Hungarian historiography, in Hungary and in neighboring countries alike. These research projects are reflected also in this book.

Notes

1   General works on post-1989 changes, by region and field: Zoltán Bihari, ed., *Magyarok a világban. Kárpát-medence* [Hungarians in the World. The Carpathian Basin] (Budapest, 2000); Slovakia: Tamás Gusztáv Filep and László Tóth, eds., *A (cseh)szlovákiai magyar művelődés története 1918–1998. II. Oktatásügy–közművelődés– sajtó, rádió, televízió* [The History of (Czecho)Slovakian Hungarian Education 1918–1998, Vol. 2: Education – Public Education – Press, Radio, Television] (Budapest, 1998); József Fazekas and Péter Hunčík, eds., *Magyarok Szlovákiában 1989–2004. Összefoglaló jelentés. A rendszerváltástól az Európai Uniós csatlakozásig. I* [Hungarians in Slovakia 1989–2004. Summary Report. From the Change of System to European Union Accession. Vol. 1] (Somorja/Dunaszerdahely, 2004); Gábor Csanda and Károly Tóth, eds., *Magyarok Szlovákiában. Kultúra (1989–2006)* [Hungarians in Slovakia. Culture (1989–2006)] (Somorja, 2007); Romania: *Romániai magyar politikai évkönyv* [Romanian Hungarian Political Yearbook] from 2000, ed. Barna Bodó; Serbian Hungarians: volumes published by Magyarságkutató Tudományos Társaság since 1997: http://www.mtt.org.rs/publikaciok/ mtt_konyvsorozatok/index.php. Accessed March 29, 2010.
2   István Fábri, "Examination of the Hungarian Institutional System beyond Hungary's Borders," in Éva Blénesi, Kinga Mandel and László Szarka, eds., *A kultúra világa. A határon túli magyar kulturális intézményrendszer* [The World of Culture. The System of Cultural Institutions among Hungarians Abroad] (Budapest, 2005), pp. 93–115.
3   *Csehszlovákiai Magyarok Demokratikus Szövetsége* [Democratic Association of Hungarians of Czechoslovakia]; *Kárpátaljai Magyar Kulturális Szövetség* [Transcarpathian Hungarian Cultural

Association (CAOHIS)]; *Erdélyi Magyar Közművelődési Egyesület* [Hungarian Cultural Society of Transylvania]; *Jugoszláviai Magyar Művelődési Társaság* [Hungarian Cultural Society of Yugoslavia].

4 *Vajdasági Magyar Művelődési Intézet.* The websites of the main arts centers: CSEMADOK: http://www.csemadok.sk/; EMKE: http://www.emke.ro/; Hargita County: http://www.ccenter.ro/?action=elso &sid=fokeres&id=0&lng=1; Vojvodina Hungarian Cultural Institute: http://www.vmmi.org/rolunk; Hungarian Minority Cultural Institute, Lendava: http://www.mnmi-zkmn.si/; Forum Institute, Šamorin: http://www.foruminst.sk/. Sites all accessed March 29, 2010.

5 UngParty: http://www.hhrf.org/up/index.htm. Accessed March 29, 2010.

6 A comprehensive collection of studies: András Görömbei, ed., *Nemzetiségi magyar irodalmak az ezredvégen* [Minority Hungarian Literatures at the End of the Millennium] (Debrecen, 2000). Studies: András Görömbei, "A kisebbségi magyarság és irodalma az ezredvégen" [The Minority Hungarian Community and Its Literature at the End of the Millennium], in Görömbei, ed., *Nemzetiségi magyar irodalmak*, pp. 7–28; Péter Szirák, "A regionalitás és a posztmodern kánon a XX. századi magyar irodalomban" [Regionalism and the Postmodern Canon in Twentieth-Century Hungarian Literature], in Görömbei, ed., *Nemzetiségi magyar irodalmak*, pp. 29–60. On the disjunctive nature of Hungarian literature: Károly D. Balla, ed., *Vízumköteles irodalom?* [Visa Required for Literature?], internet conference, 2003, at http://mek.oszk.hu/02200/02288/html. Accessed March 28, 2010.

7 Gyula Dávid, "A romániai magyar könyvkiadás egy új évezred határán" [Hungarian Book Publishing in Romania up to the Turn of the Millennium], in Barna Bodó, ed., *Romániai magyar politikai évkönyv 2000* [Romanian Hungarian Political Yearbook 2000] (Kolozsvár/Temesvár, 2000), pp. 129–141; Gábor Csanda, "Az irodalmi élet átalakulása és intézményei" [Transformation of Literary Activity and Its Institutions], in Csanda and Tóth, eds, *Magyarok Szlovákiában*, pp. 14–16; Géza Juhász, *Könyvkiadás, könyvterjesztés, könyvcsere* [Book Publishing, Distribution, Exchange]. On Serbia: http://www.bibl.u-szeged.hu/mirror/zetna/zetna/zek/folyoiratok/66/ juhasz.html. Accessed March 29, 2010; Attila Simon, ed., *A határon túli magyar tudományos könyvkiadás* [Academic Book Publishing among Hungarians Abroad] (Somorja/Dunaszerdahely, 2005), with bibliographies for each country. Sándor Enyedi, *Színészek, színházak, városok. A határon túli magyar színházművészet lexikona* [Actors,

8   Theaters, Cities. Dictionary of Hungarian Theater beyond Hungary's
     Borders] (Budapest, 2005).
8   Otto A. Bodó, "Több nyelven magyarul" [Hungarian in Several
     Languages], *Criticai Lapok* (2009) 5, at http://www.criticailapok.hu/
     index.php?option=com_content&view=article&id=34295. Accessed
     March 30, 2010.
9   There is a fine arts periodical in Hungarian in Romania: *Erdélyi
     Művészet*. For Serbia there is a special Hungarian reference work:
     Valéria Balázs and Valéria Arth, *Délvidéki magyar képzőművészeti
     lexikon* [Southern Region Hungarian Fine Arts Dictionary]
     (Budapest, 2007); Gábor Húshegyi, "Kortárs és jelenkori magyar
     képzőművészek" [Contemporary and Present-Day Hungarian Arts],
     in Csanda and Tóth, eds., *Magyarok Szlovákiában*, pp. 67–94. Major
     exhibitions in Budapest were held at the Ernst Museum in May 2006
     and the GPS-Ismeretlen Szcéna in 2007 and 2009.
10   Attributes of the minority press in Romania are analyzed in Attila
     Papp Z., *Keretizmus. A romániai magyar sajtó és működtetői 1989
     után* [Framism. The Hungarian Press in Romania and Its Operators
     after 1989] (Csíkszereda, 2005).
11   Critical analyses of the minority self-image projected from Hungary:
     Vilmos Ágoston, *A határon túli magyarság és a magyar közszolgálati
     média* [Hungarians Abroad and the Hungarian Public Media]
     (Budapest, 2005). Media usage: Tivadar Magyari, "Gyorsjelentés a
     romániai magyarok médiahasználatáról" [Interim Report on Media
     Usage by Romanian Hungarians], *Erdélyi Társadalom* (2005) 1: 151–
     168. In relation to Slovakia: Zsuzsa Lampl, "A szlovákiai magyarok
     kulturális fogyasztásának néhány szelete" [Some Slices of Cultural
     Consumption by Slovakian Hungarians], in Csanda and Tóth, eds.,
     Magyarok Szlovákiában, pp. 209–221.
12   Website addresses in the paragraph were accessed on April 2, 2010,
     although www.felvidek.ma was announcing an indefinite suspension
     for financial reasons.
13   The most-visited minority Hungarian-language portals have traffic
     of under 20,000 a day, but would need 300,000 to support themselves
     from advertising. The proportion of hits from servers in Hungary
     in 2008 was about 40 percent for Transindex and 70 percent for
     Kárpátinfo.
14   The Hungarian Academy of Sciences' Hungarian Scholarship Abroad
     program set out to integrate research outside Hungary in Hungarian
     and about things Hungarian. http://www.mta.hu/index.php?id=1384.

Accessed March 30, 2010; research venues: http://www.mta.hu/ index.php?id=1729. Accessed March 30, 2010.

15 *Mercurius Csoport; Fórum Intézet; Gramma Nyelvi Iroda; Selye János Egyetem; II. Rákóczi Ferenc Kárpátaljai Magyar Főiskola; Lehoczky Tivadar Társadalomkutató Műhely; Hodinka Antal Intézet; Kriza János Néprajzi Társaság; Szabó T. Attila Nyelvészeti Intézet; Max Weber Társaság; Apáthy István Egyesület; Entz Géza Művelődéstörténeti Alapítvány; Kulturális Antropológiai Műhely; Kutatási Programok Intézete; Sapientia– Erdélyi Magyar Tudományegyetem; Kolozsvári Magyar Egyetemi Intézet; Magyarságkutató Tudományos Társaság; Vajdasági Magyar Művelődési Intézet; Identitás Kisebbségkutató Műhely; Horvátországi Magyar Tudományos Társaság.*

16 Summary of Hungarian language variants outside Hungary: Anna Fenyvesi, ed., *Hungarian Language Contact outside Hungary. Studies on Hungarian as a Minority Language* (Amsterdam/Philadelphia, PA, 2005). Integration of variants into the language corpus: http:// ht.nytud.hu/htonline/present.php?action=hatartalanitas. Accessed March 30, 2010. Activity centers: János Péntek, "Termini: the Network of Hungarian Linguistic Research Centres in the Carpathian Basin" *Minorities Research* (2009) 11: 97–123.

17 László Gyurgyík and László Sebők, eds., *Népszámlálási körkép Közép-Európából 1989–2002* [Censuses in Central Europe 1989– 2002] (Budapest, 2003). Árpád E. Varga, works: http://www.kia.hu/ konyvtar/erdely/nepes.htm. Accessed March 29, 2010.

18 Ferenc Dobos, ed., *Az autonóm lét kihívásai kisebbségben* [Challenges of Autonomous Existence in a Minority] (Budapest, 2001); György Csepeli, Louk Hagendoorn, Antal Örkény and Mária Székelyi, "Research. Representation of Coexistence in Transylvania; Slovaks and Hungarians in South Slovakia; Majority and Minority in Hungary," in Peter Huncik, ed., *Confidence Building in the Carpathian Basin* (Bratislava, 2000), pp. 24–157; György Csepeli, Antal Örkény and Mária Székelyi, *Nemzetek egymás tükrében. Interetnikus viszonyok a Kárpát-medencében* [Nations Reflected in Each Other. Inter-Ethnic Relations in the Carpathian Basin] (Budapest, 2002); Ferenc Gereben, *Olvasáskultúra és identitás. A Kárpát-medence magyarságának kulturális és nemzeti azonosságtudata* [Reading and Identity. Cultural and National Self-Awareness among Hungarians of the Carpathian Basin] (Budapest, 2005); Ferenc Gereben and Miklós Tomka, *Vallásosság*

és nemzettudat vizsgálódások Erdélyben [Examinations of Religious Feeling and National Awareness in Transylvania] (Budapest, 2001); Ferenc Gereben, ed., *Hungarian Minorities and Central Europe. Regionalism, National and Religious Identity* (Piliscsaba, 2002); Béla Bauer *et al.*, eds., *MOZAIK 2001 Gyorsjelentés. Magyar fiatalok a Kárpát-medencében* [Interim Report. Young Hungarians in the Carpathian Basin] (Budapest, 2002); Attila Papp Z. and Valér Veres, eds., "Kárpát Panel 2007. A Kárpát-medencei magyarok társadalmi helyzete és perspektívái. Gyorsjelentés" [Carpathian Panel 2007. The Social Situation and Prospects of Carpathian Basin Hungarians] (Budapest, 2007). The largest research database on the subject: *Erdélyi vonatkozású társadalomtudományi kutatások adatbankja* [Database of Scientific Research Relating to Transylvania], at http://kutatasok.adatbank.transindex.ro/. Accessed March 30, 2010.

19   József Liszka, *A szlovákiai magyarok néprajza* [The Ethnography of Slovakian Hungarians] (Budapest/Dunaszerdahely, 2002). The Cluj ethnographers and János Kriza Ethnographical Society: Vilmos Keszeg, "A romániai magyar néprajz kutatás egy évtizede" [A Decade of Hungarian Ethnographical Research in Romania], in Vilmos Tánczos and Gyöngyvér Tőkés, eds., *Tizenkét év. Összefoglaló tanulmányok az erdélyi magyar tudományos kutatások 1990–2001 közötti eredményeiről* [Twelve Years. Summary Studies of Transylvanian Hungarian Scientific Research], 3 vols. (Kolozsvár, 2002), pp. 119–170. The WAC-Center for Regional and Anthropological Research, Miercurea-Ciuc: http://www.kam-wac.ro/index.php?option=com_frontpage&Itemid=1. Accessed March 30, 2010.

20   László Öllős, *Emberi jogok – nemzeti jogok. Emberi és polgári jogok-e a nemzeti kisebbségek jogai?* [Human Rights – National Rights. Are Rights of National Minorities Human and Civil Rights?] (Somorja/Dunaszerdahely, 2004); László Öllős, *Az egyetértés konfliktusa. A Magyar Köztársaság alkotmánya és a határon túli magyarok* [Conflict of Agreement. Hungary's Constitution and the Hungarians beyond the Borders] (Somorja, 2008); Alpár Losoncz, *Európa-dimenziók* [European Dimensions] (Újvidék, 2002); Miklós Bakk, *Politikai közösség és identitás* [Political Community and Identity] (Kolozsvár, 2008); Levente Salat, *Etnopolitika – konfliktustól a méltányosságig* [Ethno-Politics – from Conflict to Equity] (Marosvásárhely, 2001).

8. CASE STUDIES

Austria (*Gerhard Baumgartner*)

One feature of today's Austrian minority policy is the absence of considered strategy: its direction is set by factors of foreign or, more rarely, domestic policy.[1] Foreign policy pressure resulted, for instance, in recognition of the Vienna Hungarians in 1992, division of the Czechoslovak national group in the same year, and recognition of the Romanians in 1993. The rights assured to minorities by Austrian law do not seem deficient at first sight, but not all the stipulations apply in practice. For example, several demands and 45 years went by before multilingual place name signs required under the 1955 Act of State were erected in Burgenland, giving German/Hungarian place name signs to the communities of Oberwart/Felsőőr, Unterwart/Alsóőr, Siget in der Wart/Őrisziget, and Oberpullendorf/Felsőpulya.[2]

Domestic political pressure has applied only in education policy.[3] Bilingual education became possible all over Burgenland in the 1990s only because school rolls had fallen by 50 percent in the 1980s while the number of teachers had grown by 150 percent. The teachers were public employees, which put the provincial government in a difficult situation. They could only be found employment by increasing the number of school classes, which was possible if classes became bilingual, for which a relatively low minimum number of pupils was required. The remaining places were taken up by pupils from Hungary and Slovakia who commuted across the borders each day. In 1992–1993 there were 35 children in Burgenland infants' schools receiving instruction in Hungarian, while the two Hungarian-language elementary schools had 50 pupils and the one Hungarian civil school 55. In the same academic year, 220 pupils in 11 Burgenland elementary schools chose Hungarian as an optional subject, as did 229 pupils in civil schools. There were 229 students being taught in Hungarian at the secondary and higher levels. Such teaching in Burgenland is still regulated by legislation on minority schooling from 1937, as amended in 1994. This guarantees minority-language teaching in all communities where the minority accounts for at least 50 percent of the inhabitants. However, the 1994 amendment also allows for optional minority-language teaching in all schools where seven or more pupils opt for it. In 1992, a bilingual federal gymnasium opened in Oberwart, with Croatian/German and Hungarian/German sections and all subjects taught in both minority languages. The school currently has about 200 students. There has also been a People's College of Burgenland Hungarians operating in Oberwart since 1989.[4]

Burgenland has two quarterly publications published in Hungarian: the *Őrvidéki Hírek* and *Őri Füzetek*. The *Bécsi Napló* is a newspaper published in Vienna by the Central Federation of Austrian Hungarian Associations that appears six times a year. The Burgenland provincial studios of ORF, Austrian national broadcasting service, began to air a 25-minute Hungarian television program four times a year in 1990, rising to six times since 2000. There is also a weekly 45-minute radio program and a daily 5-minute news bulletin. From 1998 to 2004, there was a private radio station, Antenna 4, broadcasting in four languages from Pinkafeld, but it ceased when funding from the Federal Chancellery was withdrawn.[5] Vienna's only Hungarian-language radio station – the privately owned Vienna Hungarian Radio – started up in 2006 and is run by various groups of young people of Hungarian origin.

Figures on the size of the Hungarian community in Burgenland vary. In the 1991 census, 6,763 Burgenlanders stated that they used the Hungarian language in everyday life. Interestingly, this figure has been stable for decades, while the other minorities have been steadily decreasing in size. According to a survey by the Roman Catholic Church in Burgenland, taken in 1987, some 7,000 different Burgenlanders went to a Hungarian mass or requested spiritual guidance or other services for churchgoers during the year. According to the results of a mini-census taken in 1994 by the Austrian state and the Burgenland Provincial Statistics Office, there were 14,000 Burgenlanders who could speak Hungarian to various degrees.[6] This put the proportion of those knowing Hungarian fairly high, and also showed people recording themselves as either German-speaking or Hungarian-speaking, depending on the social and political climate at the time of the census.

Table 1. The Hungarian population of Austria
based on language spoken, 1971–2001[7]

	1971	1981	1991	2001	1991–2001	1991–2001, %
Burgenland	5,673	4,147	6,763	6,641	- 122	-1.80
Vienna	8,413	8,073	13,519	15,436	+1,916	14.17
Lower Austria	2,088	1,159	5,440	8,083	+2,643	48.51
Styria	1,028	543	1,863	3,115	+1,252	57.20
Upper Austria	915	953	3,218	3,849	+ 631	19.61
Carinthia	234	197	490	738	+ 248	50.61
Salzburg	215	301	793	1,095	+ 302	38.08
Tirol	223	15	671	956	+ 285	42.47
Total for Austria	*19,117*	*15,875*	*33,459*	*40,583*	*+7124*	*21.29*

A comparison of the 1991 and 2001 census data shows that the Hungarian-speakers became the most numerous group in Austria among the speakers of recognized minority languages, with a sharp rise in numbers in all provinces except Burgenland.[8] This is explained in eastern Austria by migration to seasonal and black economy work, while in western Austria the number working in the travel industry has grown, partly because of a rise in the number of Hungarian tourists.

One milestone in the history of the Hungarian minority in Vienna was recognition as an indigenous ethnic group, awarded in 1992. This gave them a representative on the Council of Ethnic Groups and entitled them to state support – rights that the Hungarian associations in Graz, Linz and Salzburg have yet to receive. Contributions to the increase in the Vienna Hungarian community were made by the Yugoslav wars and by the mounting popularity of the University of Vienna with students from Hungary and Slovakia. The traditional dividing line between the pre-1945 and post-1956 arrivals has faded.[9]

The position of the Hungarian-language group in Burgenland differs strongly from those of the Croats and the Roma. The latter have partly become assimilated and partly become wholly marginalized, while the Croats are politically divided into large Social Democratic and People's Party camps. The Hungarians are divided in quite different ways: on one side there are the old Hungarian villages consisting of communities with distinct historical identities, and on the other there are the post-World War II settlers. The latter arrived either as refugees after 1956 or for economic reasons after 1989,[10] and now hold the leading positions in the language group. This has caused a marked dividing line between the minority elite and the indigenous Hungarians. The group identity lies close to the Hungarian identity of the twentieth century and has little to do with earlier forms of identity.

It can be said of the Hungarian ethnic group of Burgenland that they are divided in a social sense, but the divisions speak different languages hardly intelligible to one another. The recently arrived *magyaró* are at home in local and standard German and in the Hungarian literary language, but unfamiliar with "pidginized" Hungarian or even with local Hungarian dialect. The families who arrived after 1956 or 1989 themselves speak standard Austro-German and standard Hungarian. In addition, the long-established Northern Burgenland Hungarians descended from families of hired agricultural labor speak both standard and dialect German and a quite distinct western dialect of Hungarian, and cannot follow the archaic dialect spoken by the indigenous Hungarians of the Upper Wart region.

The Hungarian villages of Burgenland are in a paradoxical situation. Just as the Hungarian education was being reintroduced at all levels (infants', primary, civil and gymnasium), children whose mother tongue was Hungarian were all but extinct. Their parents are no longer able to pass on their knowledge of the language and must rely on the education system to teach it. The preservation of the village language has become associated since 1986 with a "romantic" desire, while knowledge of Hungarian has had a practical side since the opening of the border. For one thing, knowledge of the language is necessary to tap a mass purchasing power from Hungary. For another, the open border has given Burgenland Hungarians a comparative advantage in tasks relating to the burgeoning Austro-Hungarian relations. Thirdly, social contacts with Hungarians beyond the local community have suddenly become stronger. The children who learn their Hungarian in school speak a quite different Hungarian from that of their parents or grandparents.

The structure of the Burgenland Hungarian minority has altered considerably in the last decade.[11] Earlier it consisted of a network of minority groups speaking different dialects. Now the minority has become scattered across the whole province as individuals,[12] tending to use the standard Hungarian language. It remains to be seen whether this newly implanted standard Hungarian language can gain a real minority social basis in Burgenland. One requirement for that is for the minority to rise above its traditional internal rivalries.

Croatia (*János Vékás*)

The last Yugoslav census in 1991 recorded 22,355 self-described Hungarians in Croatia, whereas 121,000 people of Hungarian ethnicity had dwelt there in 1910[13] – a demographic loss greater than that of any other Hungarian minority beyond Hungary's post-Trianon borders. Their position was worsened by the bloody process whereby an independent Croatia emerged from the fragmentation of Yugoslavia, as bloody as the one in neighboring Bosnia-Herzegovina.

Croatia's declaration of independence on June 25, 1991, was followed by the secession of mainly Serbian-inhabited districts covering a third of the republic's territory, with active assistance from the Serbian-led Yugoslav army. The ambition of the self-styled Republic of Serbian Krajina was to detach these districts from Croatia and attach them to Serbia. They included the Drava district of south Baranja and east Slavonia, where four fifths of the indigenous Hungarians lived, as a majority in several communities.[14]

The Hungarians came out in favor of independent Croatia, many of them taking up arms, but they had to flee before the advancing Yugoslav army, which wrought devastation in their villages. Over 1,000 Hungarians were killed and about 8,000 fled. Churches, public buildings and dwellings were looted and destroyed, and about 50,000 Serb colonists were brought in from other parts of Bosnia and Croatia.[15]

Croatia reoccupied the quasi-state in 1995, but the return of refugees of Hungarian ethnicity commenced only in 1997, in the face of many difficulties. The Hungarian state contributed a 200 million-forint reconstruction fund in 1999, which was used to rebuild the Reformed church of Kopačevo and the arts center of Zmajevac. These ceremonially reopened on November 13, 1999, in the presence of the Croatian and Hungarian prime ministers. The Hungarian prime minister was also present on January 26, 2002, at the rededication of the rebuilt Reformed church of Korog.

But the economy and the job market had collapsed, and hardly three quarters of the refugees returned. The Croatian census of 2001 found 16,595 people of Hungarian ethnicity, 9,784 of them in north Baranja County.[16]

The legal situation of the Hungarians in Croatia can be described as stable. [17] Croatia was keen to meet expectations for minority protection in its quest for international recognition of its independence and eventually for EU membership. The first constitution, of 1990, already stated that indigenous national minorities had a right to free expression of their national identity, free use of their writing system, and cultural autonomy.[18] Dedicated laws were passed in 2000 allowing for native-language education and regulating its use in detail. The 2000 amendment to the constitution introduced the requirement of a qualified two-thirds majority for amendment of legislation to do with minorities and provides for their representation in Parliament.[19] The 1999 electoral act reserved five seats in Parliament for minorities, including one for the Hungarians. The act on parliamentary constituencies has created a separate constituency covering the whole country for this purpose. The act on electoral rolls assigned the task of preparing such rolls for minorities to the state administration. In 2002 came an act on the minorities with constitutional force, one paragraph of which defines their political representation in Parliament and local government, and permits the formation of minority local government bodies in local or county governments where the minority accounts for 1.5 percent of the population, or exceeds 200 (500 for counties).[20] In the event, the 2007 elections led to the formation of Hungarian minority local governments in five counties, seven cities and ten villages.[21]

Vertical organization of minorities had been permitted under the party state in Croatia. The successor to the supreme Hungarian body founded in 1949, the Federation of Croatian Hungarians, remained after the change of system.[22] However, several of its leaders left for Hungary during the war. The Hungarian People's Party of Croatia[23] that they founded at Zmajevac on March 23, 1990, was unsuccessful in the elections. The leaders remaining in Croatia set up a Provisional Presidency of the Federation of Croatian Hungarians in 1990, and on April 6, 1993, in Zagreb a Democratic Union of Hungarians of Croatia, headed by Sándor Jakab.[24] This performs the tasks of representing the Croatian Hungarians in Parliament and scores consistently well in local elections. It also does significant work in publishing and educational organization.

The Democratic Alliance's HUNCRO Newspaper and Book Publishing Co., founded in Osijek in 1996, dominates the dissemination of information, with a weekly *Új Magyar Képes Újság*, a monthly *Horvátországi Magyarság*, and a children's paper *Barkóca*. Programs are broadcast in Hungarian on the Osijek and Croatian Baranja radio stations and on Slavonian Television. The educational associations to split from the Democratic Community are grouped under a Federation of Hungarian Associations.[25] This includes the Croatian Hungarian Teachers' Association, formed in 1996.[26] In the same year a Society for Hungarian Sciences and Arts in Croatia was founded in Zagreb by 65 scientists and scholars with postgraduate degrees.[27]

Education is among the Croatian Hungarians' biggest problems. In the 1989–1990 school year there had been 41 Hungarian educational institutions with over 2,500 students, but by the turn of the millennium both figures had halved. In 2006–2007, only 148 children attended a Hungarian infants' school and 256 attended one of the five elementary schools teaching in Hungarian. (Another 15 schools taught 729 children Hungarian as a native language, and there was a bilingual section in Zagreb with 14 pupils.) The only secondary school teaching in Hungarian was attached to the Educational and Cultural Center of Hungarians in Croatia, with 67 students. Most of the surviving institutions worked under poor conditions, with substantial subsidies and help with teachers' training from Hungary.

The other grave problem is unemployment. Modernization has not begun in Hungarian-inhabited villages to the same extent as it has in equivalent Croat-inhabited ones. Returning Hungarian refugees were not given their jobs back in state-owned firms, and the proportion employed in the state administration is smaller than their proportion of the population.

Hungary and Croatia signed a treaty in Osijek on April 5, 1995, protecting the rights of Hungary's Croatian and Croatia's Hungarian minority and set up a mixed minority committee to implement it.[28] The two governments held a joint meeting in Budapest on January 26, 2006. The problems of the Hungarian community in Croatia mentioned could be solved by cooperation between them.

Romania (*Nándor Bárdi*)

The Hungarian elite in Romania is determined by Romania's Hungarian national minority, by creating and operating a system of institutions that covers the ethno-cultural community as far as possible. This system can be divided into sub-systems: representation of political interests, local government posts, religious affairs, education, publicity, culture and public education, and voluntary institutions.[29] The country's policy towards the Hungarians and the minority community's legal and economic situation are decided by the institutional frameworks within Romania itself.

Of key importance is the protection of interests, undertaken largely by the Democratic Alliance of Hungarians in Romania (DAHR). The history of the system of interest representation since 1989 can be divided into five phases.[30]

1. The first lasted until the Braşov conference of 1993. There had been simultaneous initiatives by the intelligentsia in Timişoara, Cluj-Napoca and Bucharest in December 1989 to assert the separate interests of the Hungarians. The joint DAHR started its life with a statement on December 25 and was headed by Géza Domokos, then manager of the Kriterion publishing company. The interim executive formed at the end of February 1990 stated that the DAHR intended to act as an umbrella organization for all Hungarian interest-protecting, cultural and religious bodies. The development of local and county bodies owed much to Domokos's contacts in literature, journalism and the arts. Even at the first congress in Oradea in April 1990, there was opposition to the strategy of working through the reform communist National Salvation Front[31] and there were calls for a line based on basic democratic principles of human and international rights. This line was represented by Géza Szőcs, a returned political émigré, backed by the Union of Hungarian Youth Organizations.[32] An attempt was made to handle the clash between the two strategies by electing Domokos as president and Szőcs as secretary-general, with offices in Bucharest and Cluj-Napoca respectively.[33] After the parliamentary elections of May 20, 1990, had made the DAHR the

second-largest political party in the country, the anti-Hungarian measures taken by the new government shifted the DAHR towards the right-wing forces of the party system, concerned with basic democratic values. The Democratic Convention was formed with other opposition organizations.[34] After the September 1992 elections, the post-communist Democratic Front for National Salvation[35] was capable of ruling as a minority government only with support from the communist and nationalist parties, and the DAHR sought allies on the center-right. This also applied in the foreign relations of the Alliance, as the DAHR became the country's first party to join the European Democratic Union (of European Christian Democratic parties) in May 1993. The DAHR managed to broaden its scope at the time that Romania was admitted to the Council of Europe, through an American visit by László Tőkés and through efforts by György Frunda in the Council of Europe. The internal strains over strategy became specific and reached a climax at the 2nd Congress in Târgu Mureş in May 1991.[36]

The political means of striking bargains in Bucharest was opposed increasingly by those trusting in pressure from abroad on the grounds of minority and democratic rights. This amounted to a call for partner-nation status: treating Romania's Hungarians not as a set of minority individuals, but as a national community with power-sharing rights, as a distinct political entity. It went on to develop concepts of autonomy and minority law, and successive political declarations, memoranda and petitions expressing a demand for political emancipation. Meanwhile the elite was changing. The local and national elections replaced increasing numbers of DAHR politicians who had belonged to the pre-1989 cultural elite with younger people, many with technical qualifications, and representatives of local and regional interests. The multiplicity of strategic interests and values led in 1992 to various ideological platforms forming within the DAHR. Out of the Union of Hungarian Youth Organizations arose the Reform Bloc headed by Tibor T. Toró, from the Székely Land Political Group arose the Transylvanian Hungarian Initiative headed by Ádám Katona, and from the group of liberal experts arose the Liberal Circle chaired by Péter Eckstein-Kovács, then in 1993 the Social Democratic–New Left Bloc.[37] Internal democracy and pluralism were to be ensured not only by the platforms but also by legally constituted political associations – the Romanian Hungarian Christian Democratic Party and Association of Romanian Hungarian Employees – and by trade, professional and social associations: the Transylvanian Museum Society, Hungarian Cultural Society of Transylvania, Romanian Hungarian Farmers' Association, Hungarian Teacher's Association of Romania, and so on.[38] The third pillar of internal pluralism was the DAHR's 21 county and district organizations. All these changes were instituted at the 3rd Congress, held in Braşov in January 1993, along with a structural reform that followed the principles of the "state model." The chief decision-making body ("legislature") is now the Council of Association Representatives, and the executive ("government") is the Executive Presidency, with divisions for its various programs. The intention was to complete this self-governing model with the election of party office holders through secret and direct general internal elections among the Hungarians of Romania. The two rival leaders resigned at the Congress, after which Béla Markó was elected as president and Csaba Takács as executive president.[39]

2. The second period of DAHR history, in 1993–1996, was one of many conflicts. Some concerned criticism of Romania's Euro-Atlantic integration and the DAHR's minority position on the Hungarian–Romanian basic treaty. Others derived from government policy: operation of prefectures in the Székely counties, the act on the national anthem, debate on the education act, problems of the Romanian community in the Székely Land, and so on. The third group of conflicts arose between László Tőkés and DAHR members of the legislature Attila Verestóy, György Tokay and György Frunda.[40] Beyond the relations with the Romanian administration, this conflict was about the desirable legal status and autonomy of the Hungarian community of Romania, more generally about the tension between adherence to a political vision for the future and the day-to-day assertion of minority political interests through a bargaining process within the system of political institutions.

Béla Markó and the parliamentary leaders gained strength from the increasingly professional process of party politics. The fourth congress, in Cluj-Napoca in May 1995, amended the statutes so as to benefit the territorial branches and party-like activity, not the platforms. The internal elections to clarify power relations within the DAHR were not held. The Operative Council and the president gained a bigger say in decision-making. The "people's party" character (ideological openness, strong party and electoral apparatus) was strengthened at the expense of the autonomy model.[41]

3. The third phase, in 1996–2000, was marked by participation in the country's right-wing government coalition. November 1996 elections gave the Democratic Convention and the Social Democratic Union a 53 percent majority.[42] There were three reasons for DAHR participation in the government: the stabilizing effect of its 7 percent support in Parliament, the fact that Hungarian votes had been decisive in Emil Constantinescu beating Ion Iliescu in the presidential election, and the international credit that the DAHR gave to the government through its known strong commitment to Euro-Atlantic integration. The importance of the latter became clear when the DAHR's ability to further its language use and educational demands lasted only until July 1997, the NATO summit in Madrid, for once Romania was admitted to the second circle of candidates for accession, it became less vulnerable over its minority and human rights record. Apart from some emergency government orders and legislative amendments, the DAHR's chief victory was the foundation of the Minority Protection Bureau with a broad mandate and regional offices. Also important was the addition of state-secretaryships for minority matters to the Ministry of Education and Culture. The debates within the DAHR mainly concerned its coalition role and the institutional prospects for voluntary organization. Here a key element was the question of a separate Hungarian-language state university, which was not included in the government programs of Victor Ciorbea or Radu Vasile. The party program at the 6th Congress of the DAHR put stronger emphasis on regional interests focused on Transylvania.[43]

4. In the fourth phase, the parliamentary elections in the autumn of 2000 were won by the Social Democratic Party (successor to the National Salvation Front and the 1992–1996 Party of Social Democracy).[44] The new government was not joined by the DAHR, but in exchange for annually renewed national and county agreements in 2000–2004, it agreed to support the governing party, which was in a minority in Parliament. This yielded an amendment to the law on public administration in favor of minority-language usage, a significant increase in state-sponsored higher education in Hungarian, an operating permit for the Sapientia Transylvanian Hungarian University of Sciences funded by the Hungarian state, and the foundation of separate Hungarian secondary schools. The land act was also amended in line with the interests of the Hungarian community – communal property was recognized as a form of ownership, meaning that such cooperatives could be refounded and regain their holdings. One step of great regional importance was the start made on building the A3 Expressway through Northern Transylvania. There was great symbolic significance in the re-erection of the Statue of Liberty in Arad in 2004.[45] The local influence of DAHR branches was greatly increased by agreements reached at county level.[46] There were attempts to form an internal opposition to the Operative Council (consisting of Markó, Verestóy, László Borbély, Frunda and Csaba Takács), but these did not succeed. Tőkés's post of honorary president was abolished at the 7th Congress, held in Satu Mare in January and February 2003, and it was agreed that those standing against the DAHR in elections would lose their membership automatically. This substantially weakened the positions of Tőkés and the groups opposed to Markó. Meanwhile Tőkés began to organize an autonomy movement at grassroots level. As a result the Hungarian National Council of Transylvania was formed under Tőkés's leadership, and in October 2003 the Székely National Council was formed with József Csapó as president.[47] The autonomy program of these two unregistered organizations was rejected in the legislature in 2004 by all parties except the DAHR group.[48]

5. The fifth phase began with the parliamentary elections of November 2004. Independent candidates of the still unregistered Hungarian Civic Party headed by Jenő Szász, mayor of Odorheiu-Secuiesc, ran on Romanian party lists gaining 1 percent of the vote, and the DAHR campaigning for autonomy goals obtained 6 percent. The liberal-democratic grouping formed a coalition government with the DAHR and the Humanist Party. It included a DAHR vice-premier, three ministers (territorial planning, information systems and commerce), nine state secretaries, four prefects and eight sub-prefects. The program included a minority act, decentralized administration and finance, foundation of development regions important to the Hungarians, and construction of a Transylvania Expressway. Romania's accession to the European Union on January 1, 2007, attained a major foreign policy objective pursued by the DAHR for 15 years.

Table 2. Election results
of the Democratic Alliance of Hungarians in Romania

Date	Representatives	Senators	Votes (thousands)	Polls (%)
1992	27	12	811/831	7.4/7.5
1996	25	11	813/838	6.6/6.8
2000	27	12	737/751	6.8/6.9
2004	22	10	628/637	6.1/6.2

Romania's post-1989 policy towards the Hungarians, the way in which the government approached the Hungarians was strongly influenced by the party struggles in Romania (post-communists against the right) and by international relations (the demands of Euro-Atlantic integration).[49]

The first National Salvation Front statement, on December 24, 1989, promised Romania's minorities full equality of rights. There followed a special statement on January 5 that held out the prospect of ensuring individual and collective rights. But by the end of January 1990, conflict between national communities had broken out after the Hungarian state secretaries in the Front, along with the DAHR, had declared a short-term goal of founding separate Hungarian middle schools. The Front was attacked as unpatriotic, in the period leading up to the promulgation of the constitution in June 1991, by the anti-communist parties, for making institutional concessions, while fears aroused of the Hungarians and of Hungary were being used to justify a range of anti-democratic measures. The two factors coincided in the events in Târgu Mureş in March 1990: a demonstration by the city's Hungarians for a separate Hungarian Bolyai Gymnasium and native-language education, and mobilization of the Romanian masses, filled with fear of ostensible Hungarian separatist endeavors. The street clashes seemed to justify the leaders of the National Salvation Front in founding successor organizations for the political secret police (*Securitate*), which was supposed to disband at just that time.[50]

The constitution and the basic treaty with Hungary denied the principle of collective rights and institutional protection of minority rights, thus hindering the institutional development of a separate Hungarian cultural and political community. The 1991 constitution offered no legal guarantees of rights for minorities, and discriminated against them by declaring Romanian to be the sole official language (§13). At the Neptun Meeting in June 1993, the government made concessions specifically to some moderate DAHR politicians in separate bargaining. This lent cachet to the politicians concerned and provided useful international publicity.[51]

Negotiation of the basic treaty with Hungary in 1995–1996 was the main test of strength in this period. The Hungarian side strove to include the main international norms of minority rights, but the Romanian side opposed any codification of international agreements. The talks were broken off in 1993, but resumed under international pressure by a new Hungarian government in 1995. The biggest dispute was over Council of Europe Recommendation 1201/1993, defining the concept of a national minority, opposing change in demographic relations in minority-inhabited areas, asserting rights of minority self-organization and official use of the native language, and proclaiming the right to establish autonomous administrative bodies with special status in areas where a minority formed a majority of the inhabitants. In the end the basic treaty cited three international documents, including Recommendation 1201, to which a footnote was attached, stating that it was not being interpreted as ensuring collective rights. The DAHR refused to endorse the treaty.[52]

Policy towards the Hungarian community up to 1996 was personified in President Ion Iliescu. It continued to be an issue at government coalition level in the subsequent period as well. After the Democratic Convention and its ally the DAHR took power in 1996, the government sought to found the Minority Protection Bureau (a constitutional requirement) and ensure language rights and other reform measures through emergency government orders. However, these were not ratified by the legislature, or they were ratified only after compromises had been made. The obstacle in this period was less the government than the resistance of both coalition and opposition (socialist and nationalist) parties, impeding the foundation of the Bolyai University, seen as the key to a separate Hungarian system of institutions in education.[53]

When the Social Democrats came to power in 2000, the DAHR gave extra-governmental support under agreements reached annually between the two parties. The Hungarian Status Law (more precisely the issue of setting up a network of offices in Romania to implement the law, and that of the financial support for education in the mother tongue provided by the kin-state), as well as the legal and political integration of the Transylvanian Hungarian University of Sciences were two issues on which advances were made, thanks to good DAHR bargaining positions. Also important was the 2003 constitutional amendment.[54] Once again part of the government after the 2004 elections, the DAHR sought to advance positive discrimination through the minority act.[55] However, it failed to get the concept of cultural autonomy past its coalition partners (as a non-local government-based institution hitherto alien to

Romanian public administration). Romania's minority policy today rests on ensuring equal individual rights, with separate institutions envisaged through language usage and voluntary social organization. Here the political weight of the DAHR is decisive (by stabilizing the government majority and through high performance by some of its politicians). Its bargaining position becomes effective from a position of integration into government policy. The "Romanian model," also bandied abroad through the government participation of the minority party, has become widespread practice in the region. Integration of the minority political elite has brought with it the official view that the minority elite is competent to judge in the affairs of its own community, although it also means that Hungarian efforts are confined within the prevailing political system. Efforts to alter the political frames (for instance by constitutional amendment, proposing minority legislation, or altering the divisions of public administration) have elicited immediate conflicts and government questioning of the legitimacy of those representing the minority. Also within the province of the minority political elites is the financing of minority institutions out of public funds.[56]

The legal status of Romania's Hungarians – and implementation of policy on the Hungarians – is set by the 1991 constitution as amended in 2003. Romania is a nation state whose official language is Romanian. The constitution defines several minority rights: to ethnic identity, native-language education, parliamentary representation, and use of the native language in court proceedings. But these were phrased generally, in terms of future legislation that has yet to be passed, with the result that the basic principles lack legal guarantees. Moreover, a series of acts passed up to 1996 put constraints on the minorities' equality before the law and equality of opportunity. The state security act (June 1991) declared "separatism of a segregatory nature" inimical to the state. Under the public administration act (November 1991) local government measures could be suspended at any time by the state-appointed prefect, and the language of local government meetings and administration was to be Romanian exclusively. The severest restrictions came in the June 1995 education act: classes taught in Romanian were to be available in every locality; Romanian was to be the language of official school documents; minority groups could not be organized at the expense of Romanian-taught education; Romanian history and geography were to be taught in Romanian; "specialist education" was to be in Romanian too.[57]

Major changes came after the 1996 change of government brought the Hungarians into the coalition. The Ciorbea government amended the language-use terms of the public administration act in an emergency government order (22/1997). For instance, minority members could use their native language for administrative business in communities where the minority made up 20 percent of the inhabitants. There information in public institutions and place name signs had to feature the minority language as well. This was passed also by Parliament in 2001 under a 2002 agreement between the Social Democrats and the DAHR. With the education act, a similar ameliorating government order was followed by legislation in 1999, guaranteeing the right to study in the native language from kindergarten to university. However, this did not allow for the foundation of a separate state-sponsored Hungarian university.

Further advance in minority law came with anti-discriminatory legislation tabled in 2000 by the minister of minority affairs, Péter Eckstein-Kovács, and passed in 2002. This gave general access to an anti-discrimination council.

The 2003 constitutional amendment guaranteed private property, denominational education, and abolition of compulsory military service, and ensured native-language use in public administration, public offices, and the judiciary. The concept of a unified nation state remained in the constitution but no proposal was adopted that was detrimental to the Hungarians. After 80 years, the question of minority-language use had been settled. A similar advance was the primacy given to EU law over national law.

The economic situation of the Romanian Hungarians was affected strongly by restitution legislation. The act on returning farmland and forest holdings was amended in a way favorable to them in 2001. Another 2001 act returned estate illegally confiscated between 1945 and 1989. The terms applied to all confiscated real estate and provided for compensation where it could not be returned. In 2002 came an act on returning Church property. Implementation began the following year. There had been 1,957 applications by the end of 2005 and 387 positive decisions had been reached. A 2004 act on communal real estate allowed associations, foundations and their legal successors to receive compensation too.

The DAHR had pushed for a minority act since 1991 and tabled a bill in 1993, but to no avail. Romania promised such an act when acceding to the Council of Europe and the European Union. It featured in the program of the post-2004 right-wing coalition government, but the draft submitted foundered on disagreements within the coalition.

The economic position of the Romanian Hungarians differed little from the national tendencies. The deciding factor has been the economic and geographical position of Hungarian-inhabited communities. Privatization and reorganization of the financial system was slow until the incoming Ciorbea government's reforms began in 1996. Loss-making firms were wound up; domestic consumption and subsidies fell; privatization accelerated; small and medium-sized firms were supported; forest and farmland was returned to its owners; regional development programs started. Behind a fall in GDP (+4.1 percent in 1996, -7.3 in 1998, and +2.1 in 2000) lay capital shortage, disorderly ownership relations, and a 40 percent black economy, but inflation, budget deficit and unemployment eased steadily.

By 2005 there were 5,600 partly or wholly owned firms from Hungary registered in Romania – 5 percent of all those in which there was foreign investment. Hungary's aggregate stake of €360 million put it 13th as a source (2.7 percent of the total). This went mainly into small firms in Hungarian-inhabited areas.

The economic positions of Romanian Hungarians are affected by business expertise gained from contacts in Hungary, but this advantage goes together with emigration by many in marketable professions. Transylvania and the Partium were at a medium level of development, but Hungarian-inhabited communities have fallen behind in applying for EU development funds. Much unemployment is hidden, with many farming tiny, hardly mechanized holdings by hand or taking temporary jobs abroad. Collective ownership of land and forest is an institution in Transylvania, with each village holding common property restored since the new millennium. This form was confirmed by an DAHR-initiated government order. But peasants are still suspicious of communal cultivation, and the Hungarian rural population is ageing rapidly.[58]

Publicity and education are treated in other chapters, but two more sub-systems remain. The three largest religious denominations (Reformed, Catholic and Unitarian) cover 93 percent of Romanian Hungarians. The Reformed Church has two districts (centered at Oradea and Cluj-Napoca) and the Unitarian Church one (Cluj-Napoca). The Roman Catholics have four dioceses in Transylvania (Satu Mare, Oradea, Timişoara and Alba Iulia) and the dioceses of Moldova (Iaşi) and Bucharest. Over half the Hungarian Catholics in Romania belong to the diocese of Alba Iulia, which Pope John Paul II raised to an archbishopric. The other dioceses come under Bucharest's authority. Hungarians form a diminishing proportion of Romania's Roman Catholics: 60 percent in 2002. One problem is the question of native-language worship for the Csángó Hungarians of Moldova, where there has been slow movement in local congregations under pressure from the Vatican. The main advance in Church policy has been the passage of the Church affairs act in December 2006. This stresses the Romanian Orthodox Church's role in national history, but without declaring it the state religion. The main innovation is a separate budget fund to support the Churches.[59]

By 1996 there was a system of several hundred institutions covering science, scholarship, education, music, and the fine, applied and performing arts, integral to Romanian Hungarian civil society.[60] National bodies were the Hungarian Cultural Society of Transylvania with its Hungarian houses, and in scholarship and science the Institute of Research Programs of the Sapientia

Hungarian University of Transylvania, the Hungarian Technical Scientific Society of Transylvania, and the Hungarian University Federation from Cluj-Napoca.[61] (Affiliates of the last include the János Kriza Ethnographical Society, the Max Weber Society for sociologists, and the Géza Entz Foundation for art historians.)[62] Foremost among the public collections are the city libraries of the Székely Land, especially their museums.[63] Other important repositories of Hungarian cultural heritage in Romania are the Archbishopric of Alba Iulia and the archives of the Transylvanian Reformed Church District, the museums of Sfântu Gheorghe and Miercurea-Ciuc, the Teleki Téka library in Târgu Mureș, the Elemér Jakabffy Foundation's documentary center in Cluj-Napoca, the Internet portal of the Transylvanian Hungarian Databank, and for scheduled historic buildings, the Transylvania Trust. There are Hungarian theaters in nine Transylvanian cities, a separate Hungarian opera house in Cluj-Napoca, and two professional folkdance ensembles in the Székely Land. These are complemented by several hundred amateur clubs and groups concerned with heritage, folk dancing and folk music, and folk arts. The Hungarian book publishers of Transylvania (Mentor, Kriterion, Pallas-Akadémia, Polis, Pro-Print, and others) issued almost 300 titles a year in the early years of the millennium.[64]

This system of institutions had emerged by the turn of the millennium. Thereafter the emphasis was on financing it and operating it as efficiently as possible. But it emerged that the services necessary to preserve Hungarian self-awareness in communities with a non-Hungarian majority (adult education, library, heritage preservation, and so on) could not be provided by voluntary Hungarian associations alone, whereas in Hungarian-majority communities this could be done. So the focus in the former group has shifted to making the state and local government institutions multilingual.

Serbia (*János Vékás*)

Of all the minority Hungarians in neighboring countries, those of Yugoslavia suffered most, although the degree varied from republic to republic. The situations there had differed in earlier decades, but their ways parted irrevocably after the break-up of the federal state. The last Yugoslav census in 1991 recorded 378,000 persons of Hungarian ethnicity, of whom 90 percent (340,000) lived in Vojvodina.[65] By this time the federal state hardly existed in more than name,[66] but the republics had no chance of parting in peace, faced with Serbia's view that the right of self-determination belonged not to them, but to the individual nations of Yugoslavia.[67] Of the 8.5 million Serbs (36 percent of the population), 1.4 million dwelt in Bosnia-Herzegovina and 600,000 in Croatia. The Hungarians were innocent victims of the merciless Yugoslav wars. Those who fared worst were the Hungarians of Baranja and the parts of Slavonia overrun by Serbia. Next came those of Vojvodina, many of whom fled abroad before threats of conscription, economic collapse and psychological warfare. Least affected were those of Slovenia, who soon joined the Hungarians in Hungary and Slovakia (and later Romania) in the European Union.

Slovenia, Croatia and Macedonia voted for independence after the Yugoslav break-up, in referenda in 1991, and recognized Bosnia-Herzegovina as independent in 1992. In that year Serbia and Montenegro federated as the Yugoslav Federal Republic. The name changed to the State Alliance of Serbia and Montenegro in 2003, before they became separate states in 2006.

The Vojvodina Hungarians were in a very unfavorable position during the great socio-political upheavals of the time. Their numbers had halved since the annexation of 1920 and had begun to fall even faster in the 1970s. The census of 1991 found only 340,000 people in Vojvodina who declared themselves Hungarian – hardly more than three quarters of the 1961 figure of 440,000. This was partly due to assimilation, partly due to emigration, and still more due to the low birth rate typical of the region.

Another problem for the Hungarians of Vojvodina was a scattered settlement pattern. Far fewer dwelt in areas with a Hungarian majority than was the case in Romania or Slovakia. There had been large-scale colonization after both world wars,[68] and a steady process of urbanization, favorable socially and economically, but leaving them open to assimilation.

The Hungarians had lower than average schooling and training, and were underrepresented in highly paid fields such as financial services and social and political organizations.[69] But they showed up well in small-scale industry and in farm equipment levels. Even under socialism many were self-employed.

Serbia's two provinces, Kosovo and Vojvodina, had enjoyed a measure of self-determination within Serbia since World War II. The 1974 constitution had given them a status hardly different from that of the six republics. In Kosovo's case, this assisted the Albanians (85 percent of the population) to assert their national interests, but this did not apply in Vojvodina, where the Hungarians made up only 15 percent.[70]

One drawback during the transformation was a ban on nationally based vertical organization and public debate on minority relations. There could be no sociological or demographic research. As the crisis worsened, pressures to depart were put on the opposition intelligentsia, which might have taken the lead during the change of system.[71] Much of the Vojvodina Hungarian community kept aloof from politics. Although forbidden to discuss it during 50 years of socialism, they remembered the fate of many innocent Hungarians at the hands of the partisans in 1944–1945 and the peasants who were chased off their land.[72]

Earlier policy was to promote awareness of a "Yugoslav Hungarian nation,"[73] especially after Tito fell out with Stalin in 1948, while Hungary was under tight Soviet control. The partial success was partly due to higher standards of living in Yugoslavia than in Hungary in the 1960s and 1970s.

As the country broke up, Serbia encouraged Serb communities in Croatia and Bosnia-Herzegovina to declare separate "republics" in areas where they formed a majority, with the intention of annexing them later. This called for homogenization of the Serbs and incitement to nationalism, which created a mood in which system change in Serbia itself could be postponed. Serbia had cited "national unification" when dismissing the dogmatic political leadership of Vojvodina[74] and ending its autonomy. So the first opposition movements there voiced general demands for democratization, not just national ones. When it became clear that the national question had to be at the focus if any advance was to be made, the Hungarian participants in these movements founded the Democratic Fellowship of Vojvodina Hungarians.[75]

During the Cold War Tito developed the Yugoslav People's Army into one of the best equipped in Europe. The 1974 Yugoslav constitution gave the republics a large part in running the armed forces. The chiefs of staff tried to centralize it after Tito's death in 1980, but this was resisted, especially by Slovenia. When the federal organizations became paralyzed, almost all army officers made for their home republic and reported for duty there.

When Slovenia declared its independence, the republic's defense units were swept aside in days by the Yugoslav army there, although that was not its prime intention. It set about furthering Serbia's interests by helping substantially to arm the local Serbs in Croatia. It then retreated into Bosnia, and when Serbia recalled all its citizens, most of the military equipment was handed to the Bosnian Serbs.

It became increasingly hard to fill the army ranks, and mobilization took ever more violent forms. In October 1991, huge numbers of reservists were called in from Hungarian-inhabited parts of Vojvodina, and when word went round that they would be sent to the front, there were mass demonstrations throughout the province. After calls for peace from crowds of several thousand in Senta and Ada, local government assemblies called for a referendum on whether local citizens supported the war. The Presidency of the Democratic Fellowship of Vojvodina Hungarians appealed to the state presidency and chiefs of staff to demobilize Hungarian conscripts until the army "returned to activity defined by constitutional frames."[76] As news of battlefield casualties spread, a flow of refugees began. By May, some 25,000 Hungarian conscripts had left for Hungary, while those who stayed and resisted conscription at home lost their jobs.[77]

The UN Security Council imposed a range of sanctions on Serbia in 1991–1996, deeming that its leaders could be blamed for the worsening ethnic conflicts in former Yugoslavia. This caused a dire economic crisis: production halted, half the workforce was sent on compulsory leave, the army cost vast sums of public money, and the cost of looking after the refugees pouring into Serbia soared. This further fed the emigration by the Hungarians, and by other communities. Meanwhile ground was gained in the economy by mafia activity in connivance with the political leadership.

The Democratic Fellowship played a dual role, encouraging activity within the community, and representing the community politically at home and abroad. In the latter it had success in federal, Serbian and provincial elections, receiving votes proportional to 75–80 percent of the Hungarian inhabitants on the electoral roll and winning eight or nine seats in the province. But it failed to gain a seat in the 250-member Serbian legislature, which in 1991 passed a language law banning official use of Hungarian forms of place names. In 1992, the schools act allowed only state-owned elementary schools. Hungarian-language arts and information facilities could operate only with heavy support from Hungary. Local government had almost no independent powers. The number of Hungarians employed in courts and state administration dwindled. A 1995 inheritance act ruled out inheritance by anyone who had fled abroad from conscription.[78]

From the outset the Democratic Fellowship saw parliamentary representation as inadequate for securing minority rights. The vital element in maintaining proportionality and minority self-identity in important areas of civil equality was separate institutions run by the Hungarians as a form of minority autonomy. The Democratic Fellowship has made three autonomy proposals during its existence:

1. A 1990 move for autonomy on a personal basis would have made Vojvodina Hungarians competent to decide matters affecting them regardless of their place of residence or proportion of the inhabitants.[79]
2. The "triple autonomy" concept of 1992 envisaged territorial autonomy for the majority Hungarian communities of north Bačka, special legal status for Hungarian-majority communities outside that territory, and personal autonomy for all Vojvodina Hungarians.[80] Serbian President Slobodan Milošević received a Democratic Fellowship delegation and promised to set up an expert group to negotiate on how to implement the autonomy. Nothing came of that. Pressure on the Democratic Fellowship was stepped up: its leaders were beaten up, shots were fired at their houses, grenades were thrown into their yards, they lost their jobs, and army call-up papers were sent to them, to encourage them to flee abroad.[81] After the 1993 elections, Milošević offered a coalition to the Democratic Fellowship, which had won five seats in Parliament. This was rejected.
3. The "modernized" autonomy concept of 1995 returned to personal, rather than territorial, autonomy.[82] This did not prove acceptable either. It seemed realistic because the international community, through the heads of the Yugoslavia Conference held at that time, recommended the broadest possible autonomy for the Croatian and Bosnian Serbs, but such proposals were still rejected out of hand by the Serbian government, which sought annexation, not secure minority rights in neighboring republics.

Meanwhile, a militarily strengthened Croatia was obliterating the "Republic of Serbian Krajina" established on its territory, while the war and genocide in Bosnia-Herzegovina had prompted NATO intervention and international control. Serbia seemed to be moving towards peace at last, and neither the international community nor the government of Hungary wanted to push hard for Vojvodina Hungarian autonomy at that time.

Both the Serbian and the Hungarian government saw the autonomy demands of the Democratic Fellowship leaders as disturbing factors.[83] This prompted efforts to fragment it by withholding subsidies and denying the administrative conditions for it to function.[84] Of the six successor parties, the Alliance of Vojvodina Hungarians formed in 1994 had the best electoral success, holding one of the posts of deputy speaker in the Serbian legislature in 1997–1999.[85] The concept of autonomy on a personal basis was taken further by the Democratic Party of Vojvodina Hungarians registered in 1997 by the former Democratic Fellowship president András Ágoston.[86]

But peace was still a long way off. The Kosovo Albanians also thought that the time had come to secede. The Serbian military efforts to break them did not stop short of mass murder, which could only be forestalled by bombing the country's main military and industrial installations. After the defeat of 1999, when Kosovo came under the control of UN peacekeeping forces, a new surge of refugees arrived in Serbia, and a high proportion were settled in Vojvodina, still an economically more developed province.[87] This brought change not only in ethnic proportions, but also in mentality.[88] Only the restraint shown by the Hungarians prevented matters degenerating into nationally based clashes, especially in west Bačka.[89]

Milošević was unable to live down his defeat in Kosovo. His position wavered, as a result of the Dayton Agreement signed in December 1995 and his "betrayal" of the Bosnian Serbs, and he was able to hold on to power only through serious election rigging. In September 2000 he lost the federal presidential election to Vojislav Koštunica, a joint opposition candidate. In December, the opposition won the Serbian parliamentary elections as well, and a government was formed by Zoran Đinđić, president of the Democratic Party. The Alliance of Vojvodina Hungarians took six parliamentary seats and joined the coalition, with its leader, József Kasza, as a deputy prime minister.

On March 12, 2003, soon after Milošević was arrested and extradited to the Hague to face charges of war crimes by the international court, Prime Minister Zoran Đinđić was murdered by former special-unit members of the Serbian police. A state of emergency was declared, and by the time that it ended, the political scene had become so fragmented that general elections had to be held on December 23, 2003. The most votes went to the extreme nationalist Serbian Radical Party, but it was unable to form a government even with its ally the Socialist Party of Serbia.[90] But none of the Hungarian parties gained a seat, as they failed to reach the threshold of 5 percent of the poll. Only in 2007 did the Alliance manage to gain three seats, after a 2004 amendment to electoral law waived the threshold for minority parties.

The international community gave exceptional support to the new Serbian leadership in launching the process of democratization. In exchange Serbia was expected to hand over war criminals and guarantee human and minority rights. The first happened hardly at all and the second very slowly.

The House of Representatives in February 2002 passed an act on the powers of autonomous provinces that restored to the Vojvodina government some of the powers that it had held before 1989, but left the financing of the administration in the hands of the Serbian legislature.

Also in 2002, the House of Representatives of the Yugoslav Federation passed a minorities act that became part of Serbia's legal system after the Serb-Montenegrin community of state was dissolved.[91] This authorized the foundation of national councils of the minorities as expressions of their collective communal interests, but they were elected not by the members of the minorities but by a college of electors operating under strong state influence, and the powers given to the councils were very limited.[92] The Hungarian National Council formed in that year took over the founders' rights of the daily *Magyar Szó* and weekly *Hét Nap* from the Vojvodina House of Representatives.[93] However, its meager resources were inadequate, under market economic conditions, to run the Vojvodina Hungarian institutions hitherto heavily subsidized by the state. Most of the capital of the Forum Publishing Company had been used up, and it had relied on support from the Hungarian state during the war years. The Hungarian sections of Novi Sad Radio and Novi Sad Television were cut back, along with their range of reception and broadcasting time. Hardly any new institutions appeared. Furthermore, there had been a sharp demographic deterioration. Some 340,000 persons in Vojvodina had declared themselves Hungarian in 1991, but only 290,000 did so in the 2002 census.[94] Conscription and penury had sent mainly the younger and better qualified Hungarians abroad.

All the minority Hungarian communities of the Carpathian Basin had looked proudly to Hungary at the beginning of the 1990s, as a leader in the change of system, democratization, and socio-economic catching up of Eastern Europe, while its neighboring countries still struggled with internal crises. That admiration gave great impetus to the idea of national cohesion. It was a huge change especially for the Vojvodina Hungarians, who faced mounting Serb nationalism after the collapse of the Yugoslav ideal and the end of Yugoslavia's economic advantage over Hungary. By mid-decade it was clear that "redemption" would not come from Hungary either, as it had many barriers to dismantle before it could become an equal member of the European Union. On December 5, 2004, Hungary held a referendum on whether to grant citizenship to the Hungarians beyond its borders.[95] The result made it clear to the Vojvodina Hungarians, among others, that the idea of cohesion alone would not ensure prosperity for the supranational Hungarian community.

Slovakia (*Judit Hamberger*)

Czechoslovakia's political, economic and social transformation, which started with the Velvet Revolution of November 17, 1989, produced a multi-party, democratic political and legal system that allowed the half-million-strong Hungarian community to enter the local (self-governmental) and national (parliamentary) politics. They won some 10–12 percent of the seats in the first free and democratic general and local elections. But Czechoslovakia's dissolution on December 31, 1992, put them instead in the nation state of Slovakia.[96]

Liberal, Christian Democratic and national/ethnic political organizations arose among the Hungarians in 1989/1990, along with some other minor ones. The first (on November 18, 1989) was the liberal Independent Hungarian Initiative (FMK) led by Károly Tóth, then László A. Nagy. In the spring of 1990 came the Hungarian Christian Democratic Movement (MKDM) led by Kálmán Janics and later Béla Bugár, and the Coexistence Political Movement initiated by Miklós Duray.[97] The last two ran together in the first free elections in 1990. From the summer of 1990 to the summer of 1992 the FMK joined in the democratization process as part of Slovakia's democratic governing coalition and was a devotee of the joint governance with the majority nation's democratic forces. The other two joined the parliamentary opposition. In the 1992 elections, the FMK gained only 2 percent of the poll and failed to gain representation in Parliament. It became the Hungarian Civic Party (MPP) in January 1992.[98]

Outside political and legal pressures (notably the amendment to the electoral law on February 1998) persuaded the three minority Hungarian parties to form first an electoral alliance (Hungarian Coalition) and then the combined Hungarian Coalition Party (MKP),[99] of which Bugár became president. The Christian Democrats played a conciliatory role, trying to settle debates among the factions over collective and individual minority rights, and rival concepts of cultural, educational and territorial autonomy. Various programs and strategies were prepared, but to no avail. The main aim in 1990–1996 was to win a legal status of territorial local government. The local government rally in Komárno on January 8, 1994, can be seen as an attempt to emphasize this aim.[100]

In 1995, the Hungarian government sought to stabilize the legal and political position of Slovakia's Hungarians by signing and ratifying the Slovak–Hungarian Basic Treaty. The ratification process in Slovakia took a whole year, as the treaty included the Council of Europe Recommendation 1201/1993, which permitted territorial local government alliances that in principle might be taken as territorial autonomy.[101]

The third Mečiar government of 1994–1998 brought for the Slovakian Hungarians severe curbs on their minority-language rights. One coalition member was the extreme right-wing, anti-Hungarian Slovak National Party, which advocated restrictive language and education policies, a resistant stance in relations between Slovakia and Hungary, and attempts to restrict minority Hungarian culture and limit the role of Hungarian functionaries even in areas where the Hungarians formed a majority. These anti-minority measures by ministers belonging to the National Party were supported also by Prime Minister Mečiar. The minister of culture, from the National Party, sought to introduce "alternative education" in schools teaching in Hungarian, whereby it would become compulsory to teach certain subjects in Slovak. Slovakian Hungarian protests against this in 1995–1996 were successful, partly thanks to support from the Organization for Security and Cooperation in Europe (OSCE).[102] (In retaliation, the minister later sacked several Hungarian school principals who had opposed his assimilatory plans, one of which was to make Slovak the language of administration in schools, meaning that even students' educational certificates would have ceased to be bilingual.) The Hungarian parties also called on EU and NATO member countries for help against new discriminatory measures in language use, cultural financing and local government.[103]

The third Mečiar government in 1995 replaced the Nationality Council with a Minority Council alongside the government, in which the minority delegates had only advisory powers. The Council's internal balance of power effectively blocked decision-making on minority matters.

The second act on the state language, which was passed at the end of 1995 and came into force on January 1, 1997, declared Slovak to be the exclusive language in public administration and public life, with penalties for breaching that. This, at EU behest, should have been offset by an act on minority-language use, but this did not materialize until July 1999, when the Hungarian Coalition Party joined a new governing coalition. Before that, the third Mečiar government had forbidden Hungarian members by law from addressing the legislature in Hungarian.

In July 1996, the legislature passed an act gerrymandering local government boundaries to prevent any territory emerging as an ethnic Hungarian unit. The Hungarian Coalition had pressed for three counties where Hungarians would have been in a majority (centered on Komárno, Rimavská Sobota and Kráľovský Chlmec), but the new act precluded any such arrangement. The aim of the agreed law was to deliberately fragment the Hungarian-majority areas, and thus obstruct the Hungarian territorial self-governing ambitions.[104]

The so-called Blue Coalition of Slovak democratic parties reached an electoral agreement on December 3, 1997, with the coalition of the three Hungarian parties, laying down principles for future cooperation in government. The Slovak parties declared Slovakia to be the state of all its citizens, not just of the Slovak nation. After the general elections of September 1998, the Blue Coalition and the Hungarian Coalition Party formed their first coalition government under Mikuláš Dzurinda in November, following a coalition agreement of October 28 obliging the Hungarian Coalition Party to abandon for the duration of the government its demands for ethnically based autonomy, foundation of a separate Hungarian university, and reappraisal of Czechoslovakia's Beneš Decrees of 1945–1946 imposing collective guilt and sanctions on indigenous Hungarians and Germans.[105] It also stated that the government would accept the verdict of the Hague International Court over the Gabčíkovo–Nagymaros dispute with Hungary,[106] and refrain from initiating changes in the language of instruction in schools teaching in Hungarian.[107]

The Hungarian Coalition Party pressed during the first Dzurinda government of 1998–2002 for extended minority rights, an end to the illegalities committed against minorities in 1945–1948, and a regionalized administrative system. It sought to strengthen democratic institutions of minority politics and culture, render the budget support for minority cultures systematic, and relieve the economic, social and environmental problems of Hungarian-inhabited southern Slovakia. As agreed, the Hungarian

Coalition Party took the portfolios of minority affairs and regional development (Pál Csáky as deputy prime minister), environmental affairs (László Miklós) and building construction (István Harna). Bugár, the Hungarian Coalition Party president, was elected as a deputy speaker of the legislature. It was not granted a separate post of state secretary for minority affairs in the Ministry of Education and Culture.[108]

There was only partial success for the Hungarian Coalition Party over land expropriated (mainly from Hungarians) in 1945–1948, ownership of the disputed class of farmland known as the untitled lands, drafting of a bill on minority-language use rights, and expansion of the scope for native-language education. Only under the second Dzurinda government (2002–2006) would Minister of Agriculture Zsolt Simon achieve the transfer of the untitled lands to local government ownership and overhaul the land registry system.

Some coalition parties refused to back a government reform of local government based on twelve *kraj* (regions), preferring a solution less favorable to the Hungarians, which divided the country into eight *kraj* running north and south, in all of which the Hungarians in the southern Slovakian belt would have been in a minority. None of the other coalition parties supported a Hungarian Coalition Party counter-proposal for turning the main bloc of Hungarian settlement into a thirteenth *kraj* based on Komárno. In the event, the Hungarian Coalition Party in the legislature overruled its own branch organizations and remained in the government, despite this serious political defeat.

However, the Hungarian Coalition Party had some successes in government. A prime ministerial bureau for human and minority rights was founded at the end of 1998, as was a division of the government and a parliamentary committee with the same mandate. On April 14, 1999, a Minority Council chaired by Pál Csáky was formed. The minority representatives, the chairman, and the vice-chairman were the only voting members. A government commissioner was appointed to coordinate Roma affairs and several Roma-related government programs began.[109]

The first Dzurinda government used accelerated procedures to amend the state language act provision on bilingual certificates in school. The powers of local and district school councils were increased pending later legislation. The government saved the Hungarian Thália Theater in Košice from financial collapse and gave a grant towards renovation of the building. On June 16, 1999, the government voted to grant 1.9 million koruna from the cultural budget to the Slovakian Hungarian Social and Educational Association (CSEMADOK). Smaller minority cultural institutions that had been merged in the Mečiar period became independent again.

The government introduced a bill on the use of minority languages in communities with at least 20 percent of minority inhabitants. This was passed by the legislature in July 1999 in a truncated form not supported by the Hungarian Coalition Party. Nonetheless, the use of Hungarian for official purposes began to increase again under the two Dzurinda governments. District offices under Hungarian control soon had bilingual forms, signs and leaflets. Both languages appeared on signs in most official buildings. Dzurinda himself ushered through the legislature Slovakia's ratification of the Council of Europe's Charter for Regional or Minority Languages, which was signed in Bratislava in 2002.

The Hungarian Coalition Party was able to halt the decline in the number of schools teaching in Hungarian. Some new Hungarian-taught middle and elementary schools were founded. Hungarians were appointed to head education departments in several districts. Independent school inspection centers were set up. The Ministry of Education recognized the Szkabela–Bóna Slovak language teaching methodology, devised by two Slovakian Hungarian teachers, as an official method, and supported it. In the early spring of 2000, Hungary and Slovakia signed an equivalence agreement recognizing each other's university qualifications, and extension courses began at Konstantin University in Nitra for graduates of teachers' training colleges in Hungary.[110]

Tensions within the coalition eased during the second Dzurinda government of 2002–2006 as the Party of the Democratic Left failed to gain seats in the legislature. The old problem of Hungarian-language university training for teachers was resolved. In 2001, the senate of Nitra University rejected the plan for a separate Hungarian faculty despite the government decision. However, in 2002 the Hungarian Coalition Party pressed for a separate Hungarian university in Slovakia, which was included in the second Dzurinda government's program. The government approved on March 13, 2003, a statement of intent and schedule of foundation for the new Selye János University in Komárno, with faculties of education, economics and Reformed Church theology teaching in Hungarian.[111] This was endorsed by the legislature on October 23, 2003, and inaugurated on January 17, 2004, in the presence of the Slovak and Hungarian ministers of education, Martin Fronc and Bálint Magyar. The first rector was Sándor Albert. Meanwhile the Faculty of Central European Studies opened at Nitra University, with around 800 students being taught in Hungarian by 50 teachers.

The same government also provisionally settled the statutes of the Danube-side Museum[112] in Komárno, a central museum of the Hungarian community, along with the reopened Historical Museum of Hungarian Culture,[113] part of the Slovak National Museum in Bratislava.

Slovak public opinion looked favorably on all the Hungarian contributors to the two governments of 1998–2006: Pál Csáky, deputy prime minister, and the portfolio ministers István Harna (construction), László Miklós (environmental protection), Zsolt Simon (agriculture), László Gyurovszky (regional development) and briefly László Szigeti (education). Despite compromises, semi-successes and failures, the party's government work fostered the growth of a common (con-social) model of Hungarian–Slovak government, but implementation of it suffered from the lack of a strategic inter-party partnership to place the minority question on new foundations. Want of support from partners in government prevented the Hungarian Coalition Party from presenting a minority bill that could provide a lasting solution. After 2006, control of minority policy reverted to the governing parties, without reference to minority aspirations.[114]

In Hungarian–Hungarian relations (that is, relations between the parent country and the minorities outside), preoccupation with government work lost the Hungarian Coalition Party some of its earlier initiating role. This was clear when application of Hungary's status law to Slovakia was blocked for a time by the Slovak government: the Hungarian Coalition Party failed to persuade its own coalition parties of the law's positive sides.

Despite domestic and foreign policy successes, the economic consolidation under the Dzurinda governments had grave social costs. The general election of 2006 replaced the coalition with one consisting of the strongly populist SMER (Direction, the social democratic party of Robert Fico), Vladimír Mečiar's Movement for a Democratic Slovakia, and Ján Slota's nationalist Slovak National Party.[115]

Slovenia (*János Vékás*)

Slovenia's secession was the least troubled aspect of the break-up of Yugoslavia, for three reasons. Firstly, the republic's frontiers largely followed the ethnic boundaries. Secondly, modernization and Europeanization were advanced, which helped to draw international support. Thirdly, Slovenians had long been preparing for self-determination. They did not see Yugoslavia as the frame for their own national development.[116]

Slovenia was the first Yugoslav republic to set about amending its constitution to enable political pluralism and equal treatment for all forms of ownership. This was done in conjunction with the opposition. The federal constitutional court ruled the amendments unconstitutional, but it emerged that the federal authorities no longer had the means of imposing its rulings.

The first free parliamentary and presidential elections were held on April 8, 1990. There was no antagonistic difference between the old regime and the opposition over the need for national independence. Thus DEMOS, the combined opposition party, won 55 percent of the seats in the legislature, but Milan Kučan, former member of the Central Committee of the Federation of Yugoslav Communists, was elected president. On June 2, 1990, the legislature issued a declaration of the sovereignty of the Slovenian state, which was put to a referendum on December 23, in which 88.5 percent of the votes were in favor of sovereignty and independence.[117]

The legislature announced on January 31, 1991, that the process of secession from Yugoslavia would begin. The constitution was amended accordingly on February 20, and Slovenia's independence was announced on June 25 (as was Croatia's).[118]

On the following day the Yugoslav federal government pronounced that the declarations by Slovenia and Croatia were unlawful and empowered the army to regain control of the international frontier posts that Slovenia's border guards had taken over. The subsequent ten-day war between the territorial guards of the federation and those of Slovenia ended when the former retreated.

Slovenia's formal declaration of independence followed on October 8, 1991. A tribunal set up by the International Yugoslavia Conference concluded on January 11, 1992, that Slovenia met all criteria for recognition as an independent state. It was recognized on the following day by Austria, Belgium, the UK and the Vatican, and by the other European Communities members within a few days. On March 22, 1992, Slovenia became a full member of the OSCE, and on May 1, 2004, the first Yugoslav successor state to accede to the European Union.

The Hungarians and Italians of Slovenia enjoy a special position. The constitution declares them indigenous, autochthonous minorities (there were 2,258 Italians at the time of the 2002 census), grants them broad collective rights, and recognizes them as national minorities under international law.[119] The constitution also mentions the Gypsies (numbering 3,246 in 2002) and orders that their position be defined in separate legislation.[120] Much more populous, however, are the "new minorities" (numbering 230,000 or 11.5 percent of the population): mainly Serbs, Croats and Bosnians from other Yugoslav republics. They do not have collective rights in Slovenia, merely protection from discrimination, albeit with exceptions. Legislation that followed the declaration of independence gave those of Slovenian descent automatic citizenship, while those originating from other republics had to apply.[121] More than 18,000 residents who failed to do so by the deadline simply had their domiciles removed from the records in 1992. The constitutional court of Slovenia then declared this to be unconstitutional,[122] but when a referendum was held in 2004, 95 percent voted against restoring those rights of domicile.

It emerged after the change of system and independence that the number of Germans in Slovenia was far greater than earlier censuses had suggested. This became clear when they began to organize. Slovenia still refuses to recognize them as an indigenous minority, not least because the new German associations have lodged claims for compensation for collective injustices suffered after World War II.

In all censuses held in Yugoslavia, over 95 percent of the ethnic Hungarians in Slovenia were found in the Prekmurje district detached from Hungary after World War I, almost all in a largely continuous band along the border. But numbers have steadily declined, between 1953 and 2002, from 11,019 to 6,243 in Slovenia and from 10,581 to 5,429 in Prekmurje.[123] Emigration is a factor, as Prekmurje is the country's least developed region. Furthermore, its total population has declined. The Slovenian government is attempting to right this by offering annual competitive funding for economic development of the Italian and Hungarian indigenous minorities. In 2007, €2.1 million was awarded, of which Hungarian businesses in underdeveloped, ethnically mixed communities received preferential loans totaling €1.26 million and grants totaling €200,000.[124]

Also significant is the assimilation of the Hungarian community. This is clear from the rising proportion since 1981 of native Hungarian-speakers who declare themselves Slovenian by national affiliation. Yet the position of the Hungarian minority is unrivalled in the Carpathian Basin in legal status and *per capita* institutional provision. The 1991 constitution guarantees the right to preservation and development of self-identity, education in the native language, establishment of associations, and ties with Hungary, as well as representation in local government and the national legislature.[125] What is more, Paragraph 64 gives minority representatives a right of veto over legislation that expressly affects the interests of the minority concerned. Parliamentary and local assembly representatives of each indigenous minority are elected from separate electoral rolls.[126] Paragraph 80 states that "the Italian and Hungarian communities will each elect one representative to the National Assembly." (The Hungarian representative was Mária Pozsonec, who was succeeded by László Göncz in 2008.)

The rules define most minority rights territorially and specify "mixed communities": in the Hungarians' case Lendava, Moravske Toplice, Šalovci, Hodoš and Dobronak. These elect Hungarian local government bodies, which in turn elect a National Hungarian Self-Governing Body, which has existed in Slovenia since 1975. The act on self-governing national communities came into force on December 4, 1994, allowing minority self-government at community level. The local elections in Lendava, Hodoš-Šalovci and Moravske Toplice were followed by elections to the Community National Council, which chose from its numbers an 18-member Prekmurje Hungarian National Council. In the 1998 local elections, Hodoš and Dobronak also elected representatives and formed a minority self-governing council. In January 1999, the Prekmurje Hungarian National Self-Governing Community elected a 21-member council, changing its name to the Prekmurje Hungarian Self-Governing National Community on July 12.[127]

There was parallel development in the system of arts institutions. The Institute for the Information Activity of the Hungarian National Community founded on May 21, 1993, took over the weekly paper *Népújság* and the Prekmurje Hungarian Radio, which had been going since 1958. Early in 1994 the Institution for Hungarian Nationality and Culture began with László Göncz as director, and since 1995 Hungary and Slovenia have jointly financed a Lendava arts center. The Association of Hungarian Writers in Slovenia was founded in the spring of 1997 and the Association of Hungarian Scientists of the Prekmurje Region in October 2002. The Reformed Church of Slovenia was constituted on May 23, 1993, with about 500 members.[128]

There has been steady erosion in education. Official figures show that the five bilingual elementary schools in Prekmurje had 844 pupils in 2006–2007, while the one bilingual middle school, in Lendava, had a roll of 340, and 263 children attended bilingual kindergarten.[129] Hungarian has been taught at Maribor University since 1966; there has been a Faculty of Hungarian Language and Literature there since 1980.

The Hungarian–Slovenian Minority Protection Agreement was signed in Ljubljana on November 6, 1992.[130] A Hungarian–Slovenian Minority Mixed Committee was set up on April 4, 1995, in Ljubljana to monitor its implementation. The two countries also signed a basic treaty in 1992.[131]

Major improvements in communications between this small Hungarian community and Hungary have occurred. A railway link opened between Murska Sobota and Zalalövő on May 16, 2001, and a new road frontier crossing opened at Čepinci–Kétvölgy on March 28, 2002. The two governments agreed in 2004 that all Slovenian–Hungarian frontier crossings would open to third-country traffic from the date of the two countries' EU accession (May 1, 2004). Border controls were lifted on December 21, 2007, under the Schengen Agreement.

Ukraine (*Csilla Fedinec*)

Separatist action gained many countries independence in the twentieth century. The "right to secede" was also enshrined in successive Soviet constitutions (1924, 1936 and 1977), but it only became possible in the post-Soviet sphere in the 1990s. Europe, the birthplace of the nation state and nationalism at the end of the eighteenth century, seemed likely to be its graveyard towards the end of the twentieth. The strongest signs of its return were the Soviet, Yugoslav and Czechoslovak break-ups into successor states organized on a nation-state basis,[132] hastened by Gorbachev's calls in the mid-1980s for *glasnost* and *perestroika*. Hungary was among the first countries to recognize Ukraine's independence in 1991.[133]

Three main documents determined the legal status of the minorities in the new country: the statement of minority rights (1991), the act on national minorities (1992) and the constitution (1996). They stated, among other things, that resident minorities form part of the Ukrainian people. Minority affiliation can be chosen freely, and there are possibilities for monolingual and bilingual signs in the minority language. Numerous places in Transcarpathia have regained their original names and many Hungarian-related statues and memorial tablets and signs have been erected. The Hungarians make up 0.3 percent of the population, almost all of them living in Transcarpathia. They had no political organization before 1989. The intellectual and ultimately political sphere made only a cultural appearance, mainly in literature and art. Change could only be sensed in the second half of the 1980s.[134]

The earliest organization to form (and still the largest) was the Transcarpathian Hungarian Cultural Association, in 1989.[135] A rapid change of generation took place in it with the election of Miklós Kovács as president. This brought a sharp change of outlook that permanently polarized the Transcarpathian elite. Earlier Cultural Association supporters and several newer bodies combined in 1994 as the Forum of Transcarpathian Hungarian Organizations.[136] This takes the view that the cause of the Hungarians in Ukraine can be pursued effectively by cooperating with Ukrainian political forces. In doing so it cannot ignore the city of Uzhhorod, the capital of the oblast, with its main institutions and university with Hungarian faculties, from which the Hungarian elite was recruited, although the city's role in the community has declined since 1989. The Cultural Association is based in the Tisa-side districts, where it presses for Hungarian autonomy and a Hungarian educational area.

The position of the Forum was steadily taken over by the Hungarian Democratic Federation in Ukraine, founded with Sándor Fodó as president in October 1991 by the Transcarpathian Hungarian Cultural Association, Cultural Federation of Hungarians in Lviv, and the Association of Hungarians in Kiev.[137] However, at the June 1995 general assembly of the Democratic Federation in Uzhhorod, its general secretary, Tibor Vass, said that there was nothing to report on its activity, as it had not operated. In March 1996 a new president was elected, Mihály Tóth, a member of the Ukrainian legislature. In 1997 the Transcarpathian Hungarian Cultural Association suspended its membership of the Democratic Federation, so making the split into two camps permanent.

In the intervening general elections, each organization has seen a seat in the legislature as reinforcement of its legitimacy, and this has several times resulted in rivalry between Hungarian candidates. In 1990, Fodó, then president of the Cultural Association, stood, but then suddenly stepped down and urged his supporters to vote in the Cultural Association's name for a Ukrainian candidate, Vasyl Shepa, which they did. In 1994, the organizations that had seceded from the Cultural Association chose Mihály Tóth, who managed to beat Fodó, not least because the latter's campaign relied strongly on discrediting his opponent. Four years later Tóth lost to the new Cultural Association president, Miklós Kovács. Fodó, running on the list of the Social Democratic Party of Ukraine (United),[138] was far behind. This move brought him before the ethics committee of the Cultural Association, but with no consequences. The Social Democratic Party of Ukraine (United) did not withdraw from Hungarian public life; in the 2002 elections it launched the party's Berehove chairman, István Gajdos, against Miklós Kovács, supported by the Cultural Association. The Democratic Federation lined up behind Gajdos. Kovács's chances were lessened also by the candidacy of an unknown namesake, who took some of his votes. The seat was won eventually by Gajdos, by order of the Supreme Court, after several recounts, appeals and complaints.

In the wake of the election scandals, the then governor of the *oblast*, Hennadiy Moskal, chided Hungary for giving Kovács open support, saying that it was not the first time that disputes among Ukrainian Hungarian associations had been soured by such direct intervention. The general meeting of the Cultural Association said in a statement that Gajdos's election was due to crude abuses and destruction of voting papers, with the result that the result did not reflect the will of the voters. Kovács had received a clear majority in the communities where Hungarians were a clear majority of the population, meaning that the Cultural Association's legitimacy was unquestionable. Kovács's complaint was taken up by the European Court of Human Rights.

Legitimacy was at the heart of the debate. The Cultural Association's main charge against the Democratic Federation was that it did not take part and its chosen member of the legislature represented a Ukrainian party that was in power. Taking the voting papers at face value, Kovács was "self-nominated" and Gajdos was the candidate of the Ukrainian Social Democratic Party (United), as civil associations could not stand. Gajdos did his political reputation further harm in 2004 by crossing the floor to the Socialist Party of Ukraine faction, after the balance of power was changed by the presidential elections.

The situation changed radically in the 2006 general elections, with the formation of the first Hungarian parties: the Transcarpathian Hungarian Cultural Association–Hungarian Party in Ukraine chaired by Kovács and the Hungarian Democratic Party in Ukraine chaired by Gajdos.[139] Neither had a realistic chance of reaching the 3 percent threshold for seats in the legislature. The real stake was local government representation. During the elections, the Hungarian parties attracted attention from Ukrainian political forces, which meant that they could put up joint lists. The appearance of the Hungarian parties gave a boost to support for other minorities to form parties. In the early 2007 elections, the candidate of each Hungarian party found a place on a large party's list, but neither gained a seat in the legislature.

The autonomy question arose in a context specific to Transcarpathia, for the Rusyns, not recognized by the authorities as a minority, also made autonomy claims in the early 1990s, with some practical steps being taken between the declaration of Ukraine's independence on August 24, 1991, and the formation of the Commonwealth of Independent States on December 8. The autonomy demand by the Society of Subcarpathian Rusyns was supported by the Berehove branch of the Transcarpathian Hungarian Cultural Association, which soon afterward proposed a referendum on setting up a Hungarian autonomous area. This was supported by the local authorities and a referendum announced for December 1. While 90 percent of the country's voters came out in favor of independence for the republic, 78 percent of votes in Transcarpathia were cast in favor of special status for the region, and 81.4 percent in the Berehove *raion* supported founding a Hungarian autonomous area. However, the referendum had no legal consequences. Signs of a split in the Cultural Association were apparent in 1992, with the handling of this being one of the points at issue. The Hungarian–Ukrainian basic treaty of 1992 made no mention of the matter. The council of the Transcarpathian *oblast* almost immediately rejected the local Hungarian draft for establishing the Berehove Hungarian Autonomous Area. Hungarian cultural autonomy remained on the agenda of the Ukrainian–Hungarian Mixed Committee and was raised at the April 1993 meeting in Uzhhorod of President Leonid Kravchuk and Prime Minister József Antall. In May the Mukacheve conference of the Society of Subcarpathian Rusyns formed a shadow government of *Podkarpatska Rus* (the official name of Transcarpathia in the Czechoslovak period), announcing the move in Bratislava and causing tensions between Ukraine and Slovakia. These scandals marked the end of Rusyn organization. Kuchma, seeking re-election in 1999, campaigned in Transcarpathia, assuring the Hungarians that he would support their autonomy if elected. After the presidential election, legislation was passed establishing a free economic zone in Transcarpathia, but there was silence over cultural autonomy, and creation of a separate Hungarian school network came to seem a more realistic goal.

An important role in the civil sphere was played by the 1993 Transcarpathian Community of Hungarian Intellectuals, chaired by György Dupka, one merit of which was to begin a series of events in 1996 called the Transcarpathian Hungarian Local Government Forum. In 2001, the Local Government Association of Border Communities was founded.[140] Various professions now have associations (Hungarian teachers, librarians, artists, physicians, peasants, business people, and so on). There have been essential changes in culture and education.[141] In the early 1990s, Hungarian infants' schools opened and scope for Hungarian-taught education improved. Denominational schools appeared alongside the state institutions, and several secondary schools started Hungarian groups. The state-accredited Ferenc Rákóczi II Transcarpathian Hungarian Institute opened, mainly with funds from Hungary. In 2005, Uzhhorod National University opened a Hungarian History and European Integration Faculty. Scientific workshops appeared: the Tivadar Lehoczky and Antal Hodinka institutes in Berehove, and the Center for Hungarian Studies in Uzhhorod. Since 1994, there has been a Gyula Illyés Hungarian National Theater, and since 1990 the Imre Révész Society of Transcarpathian Hungarian Painters and Applied Artists. The press proliferated (*Kárpáti Igaz Szó, Kárpátaljai Szemle, Ukrajnai Magyar Krónika,* and so on), but it was still not possible to buy or subscribe to papers from Hungary, largely for economic reasons, and state book publishing in Hungarian ceased for want of funds. Instead, private publishers have been winning competitive funding from Hungary to produce Transcarpathian works. The main book publishers include Galéria in Uzhhorod (Károly D. Balla) and Mandátum in Berehove (János Penckófer). Intermix Kiadó of Uzhhorod and Budapest, the largest book publisher by number of titles, was founded in 1992 with György Dupka as manager. Its Transcarpathian Hungarian Books series includes poetry, prose, sociology, local history, ethnography, documentary publications, and so on. Institutions have also taken to publishing books, and local Internet portals have appeared.[142]

The Churches play important charitable, educational and cultural roles. They are present increasingly in welfare services. They were the first to open Sunday schools for those in areas of scattered Hungarian habitation. The biggest problem in Transcarpathia and throughout Ukraine has been the critical economic situation.[143] The large-scale structure of farming practically disappeared in the 1990s and almost all industrial production ceased, with the result that unemployment rose to around 20 percent. Personal savings accumulated in the Soviet period were frozen indefinitely. The region was devastated in 1998 and 2001 by flooding of the River Tisa. Many had little option but to make a living out of illegal cross-border trading or by working temporarily in Hungary or Slovakia. Only a small proportion of the joint ventures started have been in the production sectors. The situation changed at the beginning of the twenty-first century only insofar as local businesses found it harder to recruit labor. Those who have prospered out of illicit trading are unwilling to abandon it, although it has detrimental effects on society. The legislation on the Transcarpathian free trade area of more than 700 hectares and investment concessions covering the whole of Transcarpathia were intended by the government as measures to stimulate the economy.

Economically motivated emigration, a national problem, increased vastly in the 1990s. The country's population fell from 52.1 million to under 49 million between 1989 and 2001, with migration accounting for no small proportion of the decrease. In 1991–1993, the migration balance was still positive and the population rose by almost half a million, but then the decline set in, with a net 620,000 inhabitants lost to emigration in subsequent years, most of them qualified or skilled. The three main target countries are Israel, Germany and the United States. Mass emigration from Transcarpathia began in the 1980s, with the targets being the Czech Republic, Slovakia, Israel, Germany and the United States, but with Hungary taking by far the most. Almost 85 percent of ethnic Hungarians migrating from Transcarpathia – 30,000 people – have chosen Hungary as their destination. They also apply for citizenship, although dual citizenship is not recognized by the Ukrainian constitution. Large numbers study at colleges and universities in Hungary, and many still at school do not return either. All this is changing the social structure of the Hungarian community. According to the 2001 census, 151,500 of Transcarpathia's 1,254,600 inhabitants were ethnic Hungarians (12.1 percent).[144] The proportion of Hungarians classing Hungarian as their native language hardly changed between the 1989 and 2001 censuses, one reason being that a higher proportion of the Hungarian-speaking Gypsy community declared themselves ethnic Hungarians in 2001.

Notes

1   Peter Pelinka, "Minderheiten im politischen System Österreichs," in Rainer Bauböck, Gerhard Baumgartner, Bernhard Perchinig and Karin Pinter, eds., "…und raus bist Du!" *Minderheiten in der Politik* (Vienna, 1988), pp. 23–28; Gerhard Baumgartner, "Volksgruppenpolitik in Österreich 1945–1999" [Minority Policy and Politics in Austria 1945–1999], in Peter H. Nelde and Roswitha Rindler Schjerve, eds., *Minorities and Language Policy / Minderheiten und Sprachpolitik / Minorité et l'aménagement linguistique* (Sankt Augustin, 2001), pp. 183–192.

2   Gerhard Baumgartner, "Minderheitenpolitik im Burgenland. Politik burgenländischer Minderheiten 1945–2000," in Roland Widder, ed., *Geschichte des Burgenlandes in der Zweiten Republik* (Salzburg, 1999), pp. 15–54.

3   *Burgenländisches Minderheitenschulgesetz 1994.* BGBL. 202/1994; HKDC Kroatisches Kultur und Dokumentationszentrum, ed., *Vorteil Vielfalt. 10 Jahre Minderheitenschulgesetz für das Burgenland* (Eisenstadt, 2004).

4   Dieter Kolonovits, *Sprache in Österreich* (Vienna, 2000); Heinz Tichy, "Die rechtlichen Voraussetzungen für die Erteilung des Unterrichts in den Volksgruppensprachen," in Wiener Arbeitsgemeinschaft für Volksgruppenfragen – Volksgruppeninstitut, ed., *Unterricht und Bildung in den Volksgruppensprachen* (Vienna, 1987), pp. 11–57; Burgenländische Forschungsgesellschaft, ed., *Zweisprachigkeit als Chance. Ungarischunterricht im Burgenland* (Eisenstadt, 1995); Andrea Kaiser, *Zweisprachige Volksschulen im Burgenland*, Doctoral dissertation (Klagenfurt, 1995).

5   KUGA – Kulturna Zadruga, ed., *Manjine i medije – med izolaciom, integraciom i šutnjom. Odredjivane položaja / Minderheiten und Medien – zwischen Isolation, Integration und Funkstille. Eine Standortbestimmung* (Großwarasdorf, 1993).

6   Werner Holzer and Ulrike Pröll, eds., *Mit Sprachen leben. Praxis der Mehrsprachigkeit* (Klagenfurt, 1994).

7   Gerhard Baumgartner, "Ausztria magyar nyelvű lakossága a 2001-es osztrák népszámlálás tükrében" [Austria's Hungarian-Speaking Population as Seen in the 2001 Census], in László Gyurgyík and László Sebők, eds., *Népszámlálási körkép Közép-Európából 1989–2002* [Censuses in Central Europe 1989–2002] (Budapest, 2003), pp. 158–170.

8　Statistik Austria, *Volkszählungen im Burgenland 1981-2001.* Umgangssprache Burgenland–Gemeinden und Ortschaften (Vienna, 2002); *Statistisches Handbuch der Stadt Wien 1992* (Vienna, 1992).

9　Pál Deréky, "Magyarok Ausztriában és Nyugat-Németországban" [Hungarians in Austria and West Germany], *Integratio* 16 (1984).

10　Éva Kovács and Attila Melegh, "'Lehetett volna rosszabb is, mehettünk volna Amerikába is'. Vándorlástörténetek Erdély, Magyarország és Ausztria háromszögében" ["It Could Have Been Worse, We Might Have Gone to America." Migration Stories from Transylvania–Hungary–Austria], in Endre Sík and Judit Tóth, eds., *Diskurzusok a vándorlásról* [Discourses on Migration], Yearbook of the Hungarian Academy of Sciences' Institute of Political Sciences (Budapest, 2000), pp. 93–152.

11　Károly Cserján, "Magyar identitás Ausztriában" [Hungarian Identity in Austria], in Nóra Kóvács, ed., *Tanulmányok a diaszpóráról* [Diaspora Studies] (Budapest, 2004), pp. 41–49; Szilvia Szoták, "Az identitás 'morzsái'. Őrvidéki civil szervezetek a magyar nyelv és kultúra fennmaradásáért" [Crumbs of Identity. Civil Associations for Preserving Hungarian Language and Culture in the Wart], in Boglárka Bakó and Szilvia Szoták, eds., *Magyarlakta kistérségek és kisebbségi identitások a Kárpát-medencében* [Hungarian-Inhabited Districts and Minority Identities in the Carpathian Basin] (Budapest, 2006), pp. 209–224.

12　Statistik Austria, *Volkszählungen im Burgenland 1981–2001*; Adelheid Bauer, "Volkszählung 2001. Umgangssprache im Burgenland," *Statistische Nachrichten* (2002) 9: 636–641.

13　Károly Kocsis and András Bognár, *Ethnical Map of Pannonian Territory of Croatia* (Budapest, 2003).

14　Here local Serbs founded a second quasi-state on June 25, 1991, the Serbian Autonomous Territory of Slavonia, Baranja and West Srem (*Srpska autonomna oblast Slavonija, Baranja i Zapadni Srem*). This joined the Republic of Serbian Krajina on December 24, 1991.

15　For more detail, see Ferenc Mák, "Magyarok Horvátországban" [Hungarians in Croatia], *Magyar Kisebbség* (1997) 3–4: 258–278.

16　Mirjana Lipovšćak, ed., *Stanovništvo prema državljanstvu, narodnosti, materinskom jeziku i vjeri. Popis stanovništva, kućanstva i stanova 31. ožujka 2001. Knj. 2* [The Population According to Citizenship, Nationality, Language and Religious Affiliation, March 31, 2001. Vol. 2] (Zagreb, 2002); *Naselja i stanovništvo Republike*

Hrvatske 1857–2001 [The Settlements and Population of the Republic of Croatia 1857–2001] (Zagreb, 2005), CD–ROM.

17 On the Croatian model of minority protection: Siniša Tatalović, "Model of the Realization of Ethnic Rights of National Minorities in the Republic of Croatia," *Politička misao* (1997) 5: 27–41.

18 "Ustav Republike Hrvatske" [The Constitution of the Republic of Croatia], *Narodne novine* (1990) 56.

19 "Zakon o uporabi jezika i pisma nacionalnih manjina u Republici Hrvatskoj" [Law on the Usage of the National Minorities' Language and Writing in the Republic of Croatia], and "Zakon o odgoju i obrazovanju na jeziku i pismu nacionalnih manjina" [Law on the Teaching of and Education in the Mother Tongue of the National Minorities], *Narodne novine* (2000) 51.

20 The constitutional amendment: "Promjena Ustava Republike Hrvatske" [The Change of the Croatian Constitution], *Narodne novine* (2000) 113; the minority electoral act: "Zakon o izborima zastupnika u Hrvatski državni sabor" [Law on Election of Members of the Croatian Parliament], *Narodne novine* (1999) 116; the act on electoral constituencies: "Zakon o izbornim jedinicama za izbor zastupnika u zastupnički dom Hrvatskoga državnog sabora" [Law on the Constituencies for the Election of Representatives in the House of Representatives of the Croatian National Parliament], *ibid.*; the act on electoral rolls: "Zakon o popisima birača" [Law on Voters], *Narodne novine* (2007) 116; the constitutional act on the rights of national minorities: "Ustavni zakon o pravima nacionalnih zajednica" [Constitutional Law on the National Board], *Narodne novine* (2002) 155; the act on the bylaws of local government bodies deciding the ethnic proportions of representative assemblies: "Zakon o izboru članova predstavničkih tijela jedinica lokalne i područne (regionalne) samouprave" [Law on Election of Members of Representative Bodies of Local and Regional Governments], *Narodne novine* (2001) 33.

21 Nemzeti Kisebbségügyi Hivatal [Office for National Minorities], *Izvješće o provođenju Ustavnog zakona o pravima nacionalnih manjina i utrošku sredstava osiguranih u državnom proračunu Republike Hrvatske za 2007. godinu za potrebe nacionalnih manjina* [Report on the Implementation of the Constitutional Law on National Minorities and the Expenditure of Funds Allocated from the State Budget of Croatia in 2007 for the Needs of National Minorities] (Zagreb, 2008), pp. 223–224.

22   The Croatian Hungarian Cultural and Educational Federation
      (*Horvátországi Magyar Kultúr- és Közoktatási Szövetség*) was
      formed in Osijek on November 29, 1949. *Horvátországi Magyarok
      Szövetsége. Évkönyv 1* [Yearbook of the Croatian Hungarian
      Federation 1] (Eszék, 1979), p. 67.
23   *Horvátországi Magyar Néppárt.*
24   *Horvátországi Magyarok Demokratikus Közössége.*
25   *Magyar Egyesületek Szövetsége.*
26   *Horvátországi Magyar Pedagógus Szövetség.*
27   *Horvátországi Magyar Tudományos és Művészeti Társaság.*
28   Implemented by Act XVI/1997. *Magyar Közlöny* (1997) 28.
29   The Democratic Alliance of Hungarians in Romania (*Romániai
      Magyar Demokrata Szövetség*) won 186 of the 3,137 posts of mayor
      in local elections in June 2004, and 111 (5.9 percent) county council
      seats. Of the Hungarian-inhabited counties, it has a majority on the
      councils of Harghita, Covasna and Satu Mare, but no representatives
      on those of Hunedoara, Alba and Timiş, or Timişoara city. Several
      localities with a Romanian majority elected a Democratic Alliance
      mayor: Jimbolia, Satu Mare, Reghin and Marghita.
30   *Romániai Magyar Demokrata Szövetség* – sometimes translated as
      Democratic Union. For a comprehensive analysis, see Miklós Bakk,
      The Democratic Alliance of Hungarians in Romania (Budapest,
      1998). For a chronology, see Frigyes Udvardy, "A romániai magyar
      kisebbség kronológiája 1990–2003" [Chronology of Romania's
      Hungarian Minority 1990–2003], at http://udvardy.adatbank.
      transindex.ro/. Accessed April 13, 2010. The statutes appear in Nándor
      Bárdi and György Éger, eds., *Útkeresés és integráció. Határon
      túli magyar érdekvédelmi szervezetek dokumentumai* [Search
      and Integration. Documents of Hungarian Interest-Representing
      Organizations Abroad] (Budapest, 2000), pp. 45–200. Some of the
      best analyses appear in János Márton and István Gergő Székely, eds.,
      Elemzések az RMDSZ-ről [Analyses of the Democratic Association
      of Hungarians in Romania], at http://www.adatbank.transindex.ro/
      belso.php?alk=33&k=5. Accessed April 13, 2010.
31   *Frontul Salvării Naţionale.*
32   *Magyar Ifjúsági Szervezetek Szövetsége.*
33   Two memoirs: Géza Domokos, *Esély II. Visszaemlékezések 1989–
      1992* [Chance II. Memoirs 1989–1992] (Miercurea-Ciuc, 1997); Géza
      Szőcs and Farkas Wellmann Endre, eds., *Amikor fordul az ezred*
      [When the Millennium Turns] (Budapest, 2009).

34 *Demokratikus Konvenció / Convenţia Democrată.*

35 *Frontul Democrat al Salvării Naţionale.*

36 An account from the "radical" side: Zsolt Borbély and Krisztina Szentimrei, *Erdélyi magyar politikatörténet 1989–2003* [Transylvanian Hungarian Political History 1989–2003] (Budapest, 2003).

37 *Reform Tömörülés; Székelyföldi Politikai Csoport; Szabadelvű Kör; Szociáldemokrata-Újbaloldali Tömörülés.*

38 *Romániai Magyar Kereszténydemokrata Párt; Romániai Magyar Dolgozók Egyesülete; Erdélyi Múzeum Egyesület; Erdélyi Közművelődési Egyesület; Romániai Magyar Gazdák Egyesülete; Romániai Magyar Pedagógusok Szövetsége.*

39 *Szövetségi Képviselők Tanácsa; Ügyvezető Elnökség.* On internal pluralism and the self-governing model: Miklós Bakk, "Az RMDSZ első öt éve" [The First Five Years of the Democratic Alliance of Hungarians in Romania], in Miklós Bakk, István Székely and Tibor T. Toró, eds., *Útközben. Pillanatképek az erdélyi magyar politika reformjáról* [On the Way. Snapshots of the Reform of Transylvanian Hungarian Politics] (Csíkszereda, 1999), pp. 95–103; Tamás Sándor, "Egy nemzetiségi társadalom belső normatív rendszere" [Internal Normative System of a Minority Society], Ms., 1996, OSZK Kézirattára (ex Teleki Alapítvány document 1709/97).

40 Key debate documents: László Tőkés, "A Hatalom uszályában" [In the Barge of Power], *Romániai Magyar Szó*, August 7, 1993; György Frunda and László Borbély, "Lármafák égetése" [Lighting Alarm Signals], *ibid.*, August 25, 1993; Federal Council of Representatives position on the Neptun affair: *Bihari Napló*, September 28, 1993; campaign against Tőkés by Benedek Nagy, Democratic Alliance representative: *Romániai Magyar Szó*, January 17, 1995, and *Erdélyi Napló*, January 18, 1995.

41 On the people's party model: Miklós Bakk, "Modellviták – rejtett stratégiák" [Debates on Models – Concealed Strategies], in Miklós Bakk, *Lassú valóság* [Slow Truth] (Kézdivásárhely, 2002), pp. 199–205. On the operation of the Operative Council: János Márton, "Válságstáb vagy legfőbb döntéshozó testület? A Szövetségi Operatív Tanács működése 1993–2005 között" [Crisis Team or Top Decision-Making Body? The Operation of the Operative Council in 1993–2005], in Barna Bodó, ed., *Romániai magyar politikai évkönyv* [Romanian Hungarian Political Yearbook] (Temesvár/Kolozsvár, 2005), pp. 16–37.

42   *Convenția Democrată; Uniunea Social Democrată.*

43   *Mérlegen: Az RMDSZ a koalícióban, 1996–2000* [In the Balance: the Democratic Alliance in the Coalition, 1996–2000] (Kolozsvár, n.d.); Nándor Bárdi and Zoltán Kántor, "The Democratic Alliance of Hungarians in Romania in the Government of Romania from 1996 to 2000," *Regio* 13 (2002) 5: 188–226.

44   *Partidul Social Democrat; Partidul Democrației Sociale.*

45   Designed by György Zala and completed in 1890, it marks the execution of 13 Hungarian army officers by the Habsburgs after the 1848–1849 Hungarian War of Independence. The work suffered from vandalism after the Romanian accession and was dismantled in 1925 by government order. Despite protests from some Romanian groups, it was restored in its original position on April 25, 2004.

46   Political program compared with practical politics: János Márton, "A romániai magyar társadalom sajátos kérdései az RMDSZ 1996–2002 közötti programjaiban és politikájában" [Specific Issues of Romanian Hungarian Society in the Programs and Policies of the Democratic Association of Hungarians in Romania, 1996–2002], *Magyar Kisebbség* (2003) 4: 295–359 and (2004) 1–2: 529–572.

47   *Erdélyi Magyar Nemzeti Tanács; Székely Nemzeti Tanács.*

48   All Hungarian autonomy plans and the main analyses appear in Zoltán Bognár, ed., *Romániai autonómia-elképzelések 1989 után* [Ideas for Autonomy in Romania since 1989], at http://www.adatbank. transindex.ro/belso.php?alk=48&k=5. Accessed April 13, 2010.

49   A comprehensive picture of the institutional framework of Romania's minority policy: Levente Salat, ed., *Politici de integrare a minorităților naționale din România. Aspecte legale și instituționale întro perspectivă comparată* [Integration Policies Regarding National Minorities in Romania. Legal and Institutional Aspects in a Comparative Perspective] (Cluj-Napoca, 2008).

50   Tom Gallagher, *Romania after Ceaușescu: the Politics of Intolerance* (Edinburgh, 1995); Christoffer Andersen, *Resurgent Romania Nationalism. In the Wake of the Interethnic Clashes in Tirgu Mures March 1990*, at http://www.edrc.ro/docs/docs/Andersen_senior_ thesis.pdf. September 1995. Accessed April 14, 2010. Human Rights Watch report: http://www.hrw.org/legacy/reports/1990/WR90/ HELSINKI.BOU-02.htm. Accessed April 14, 2010.

51   The US Project on Ethnic Relations arranged a meeting at Neptun on the Romanian coast on July 15–17, 1993, between three unmandated Democratic Alliance legislators (László Borbély, György Frunda and György Tokay), and Viorel Hrebenciuc, government secretary-general and head of the National Minority Council. The latter agreed to reserve 300 places at Babes-Bolyai University for those seeking to study in Hungarian, to rescind the order for primary schools to teach history and geography in Romanian, and to extend to minorities the order that a Romanian-taught class had to be opened wherever there were ten Romanian applicants. The purpose was to publicize and legitimize Romanian minority policy in the West in advance of accession to the Council of Europe. For the 1993 contribution by Tőkés and the other key debate documents, see Note 36.

52   For debate documents on the basic treaty, see *Magyar Kisebbség* (1996) 4: 59–108.

53   A summary of Romanian Hungarian ideas on higher education: Nándor Bárdi, Anna Berki and Szilárd Ulicsák, eds., *Az Erdélyi Magyar Tudományegyetem megvalósíthatósági tanulmánya* [Feasibility Study for the Transylvanian Hungarian University of Sciences] (Budapest, 2001), pp. 11–27. Documents of the debate around the Hungarian private university appear in *Magyar Kisebbség* (2000) 2: 161–171; the first few years' experiences: *Magyar Kisebbség* (2006) 1–2: 7–150.

54   Attila Varga, "A román Alkotmány módosításának időszerűsége" [The Urgency of Amending the Romanian Constitution], *Magyar Kisebbség* (2002) 2: 3–16.

55   Balázs Orbán and János Márton, "Elemzés a 2005-ös kisebbségi törvénytervezetről [Analysis of the 2005 Minority Bill], in Bodó, ed., *Romániai magyar politikai évkönyv, 2005,* pp. 155–198.

56   The Minority Council was set up alongside the government in 1993, followed in 1997 by the Council of National Minorities (*Consiliul Minorităţilor Naţionale*) as a consultative body. It included the 19 minority organizations also represented in the legislature. Its main task was to distribute funding from a separate budgetary fund for minorities. The fund was raised when the Alliance joined the government in 1996. Hungarians have been represented on the Council since 2001 by the Communitas Foundation founded in 1998, not the Alliance. The allocation in 2007, made partly by competitive bidding, was 10,770 million lei (ca. HUF 810,000 million).

57   Ildikó Fülöp Fischer and Éva Cs. Gyímesi, "A tanügyi törvény nemzeti kisebbségeket érintő szakaszainak elemzése és következményei" [An Analysis of the Articles of the Education Act Concerning National Minorities and Their Consequences], in Bárdi and Éger, eds., *Útkeresés és integráció*, Document 35.

58   It is questionable to what extent there is a distinct minority economy. Ideas on this are documented in Ákos Birtalan, "Gondolatok az önálló gazdasági életről kisebbségi létfeltételek közepette" [Ideas on Distinct Economic Activity under Conditions for Minority Existence], *Magyar Kisebbség* (1999) 2–3, and the next, themed economic issue (1999) 4. Since 2000, the economic question has arisen in a development policy context: *Magyar Kisebbség* (2003) 1, (2003) 2–3, and (2005) 3–4. Broad accounts: Tamás Réti, *Közeledő régiók a Kárpát-medencében. Dél-Szlovákia, Erdély és a Vajdaság gazdasági átalakulása* [Converging Regions in the Carpathian Basin: the Economic Transformation of Southern Slovakia, Transylvania and Vojvodina] (Budapest, 2004); Gyula Horváth, ed., *Székelyföld* [The Székely Land] (Budapest/Pécs, 2003); Gyula Horváth, ed., *Északnyugat-Erdély* [Northwest Transylvania] (Budapest/Pécs, 2006); Gyula Horváth, ed., *Dél-Erdély és a Bánság* [Southern Transylvania and the Banat] (Budapest/Pécs, 2009).

59   Károly András, "Tények és problémák a magyar kisebbségek egyházi életében" [Facts and Problems in the Religious Life of Hungarian Minorities] *Regio* 2 (1991) 3: 13–37; Zoltán Bihari, ed., *Magyarok a világban. Kárpát-medence* [Hungarians in the World. The Carpathian Basin] (Budapest, 2000), pp. 417–431.

60   According to a survey by the Institute for Ethnic and National Minority Studies of the Hungarian Academy of Sciences, the system's cultural institutions in 2004 consisted of two archives, 47 museums and local displays, 32 other collections, 29 book publishers, 140 periodicals, 28 radio and TV stations, five Internet portals, 51 theater, opera, puppet, mime and other acting companies, 182 musical ensembles, 104 dance groups, 21 literary clubs, 30 fine, applied, photographic and ethnographical studios, three film studios, 82 institutions disseminating knowledge of the country, and 733 education institutions with several functions. The results are analyzed in Zsombor Csata, Dénes Kiss and Tamás Kiss, "Az erdélyi magyar kulturális intézményrendszerről" [The Transylvanian Hungarian System of Cultural Institutions], in Kinga Mandel, Éva Blénesi

Case Studies (1989–2005)   571

and László Szarka, eds., *A kultúra világa. A határon túli magyar kulturális intézményrendszer* [The World of Culture. The System of Hungarian Cultural Institutions beyond the Borders] (Budapest, 2005), pp. 50–75.

61 *Erdélyi Magyar Közművelődési Egyesület; Erdélyi Múzeum Egyesület; Erdélyi Magyar Tudományegyetem Kutatási Programok Intézete; Erdélyi Magyar Műszaki Tudományos Társaság; Kolozsvári Magyar Egyetemi Intézet.* See Dénes Kiss, "A romániai magyar kulturális intézményrendszer adatbázisa" [Database of the Romanian Hungarian Cultural Institution System], at http://kulturalis.adatbank. transindex.ro/; websites of some major institutions: www.eme.ro; www.emke.ro; www.kjnt.ro. All accessed April 14, 2010.

62 *Kriza János Néprajzi Társaság; Max Weber Kollégium; Entz Géza Alapítvány.*

63 Székely Museum, Sfântu Gheorghe: www.szekelynemzetimuzeum. ro; Csík Székely Museum: www.csszm.ro. Both accessed April 14, 2010.

64 General accounts: József Somai, "Romániai magyar civil szféra" [The Romanian Hungarian Civil Sphere], in Bodó, ed., *Romániai magyar politikai évkönyv, 2001*, pp. 81–96; Gyula Dávid, "A romániai magyar könyvkiadás az új évezred határán" [Romanian Hungarian Book Publishing around the New Millennium], in Bodó, ed., *Romániai magyar politikai évkönyv, 2001*; Ottó A. Bodó, "Erdélyi magyar színjátszás" [Transylvanian Hungarian Theater], in Bodó, ed., *Romániai magyar politikai évkönyv, 2003*, pp. 204–208.

65 *Popis '91. Stanovništvo. Knjiga 3. Nacionalna pripadnost – detaljna klasifikacija* [Census '91. Population. Vol. 3. National Identity – A Detailed Classification] (Belgrade, 1993).

66 The 1974 constitution gave republics and provinces powers of veto over political decision-making. "Ustav Socialističke Federativne Republike Jugoslavije" [The Constitution of the Socialist Federal Republic of Yugoslavia], *Službeni list SFRJ* (1974) 9. Right after Tito's death, the members of the collective presidency of state were delegated by the federal units. "Amandman IV. na Ustav Socialističke Federativne Republike Jugoslavije" [Amendment IV of the Constitution of the Socialist Federal Republic of Yugoslavia], *Službeni list SFRJ* (1981) 38.

67 Debate on this punctuated Yugoslavia's history. The strongest statement in the pre-collapse period: Kosta Mihailović and Vasilije

Krestić, *Memorandum of the Serbian Academy of Sciences and Arts. Answers to Criticisms. Published on the Decision of the Presidency...* April 23, 1993 (Belgrade, 1995), pp. 117–119.

68   Some 100,000 people arrived in Vojvodina after World War I, 250,000 after World War II. The details are in three works by Nikola Gaćeša: *Agrarna reforma i kolonizacija u Bačkoj 1918–1941* [Agrarian Reform and Colonization in Bačka 1918–1941] (Novi Sad, 1968); *Agrarna reforma i kolonizacija u Banatu 1919–1941* [Agrarian Reform and Colonization in the Banat 1919–1941] (Novi Sad, 1972); *Agrarna reforma i kolonizacija u Jugoslaviji 1945–1948* [Agrarian Reform and Colonization in Yugoslavia 1945–1948] (Novi Sad, 1984).

69   See *Popis '91.*

70   For documents on the constitutional development of Vojvodina, see *Autonomija Vojvodine. Izabrani spisi* [The Autonomy of Vojvodina. Selected Papers] (Novi Sad, 1976). For pro-autonomy party views on the national minority question after the autonomy of Vojvodina had been ended, see *Autonomija Vojvodine danas. Rasprava na okruglom stolu održanom, 9. I. 1993. u Novom Sadu* [The Autonomy of Vojvodina Today. The Round-Table Discussion Held on January 9, 1993, in Novi Sad] (Novi Sad, 1993).

71   On communist party views on Vojvodina, see *Aktuelna pitanja razvoja međunacionalnih odnosa u SAP Vojvodini* [Current Issues of the Development of Interethnic Relations in the Socialist Autonomous Province of Vojvodina] (Novi Sad, 1970). For example, see the documents of the 1983 political demolition of the *Új Symposion* staff: Béla Csorba and János Vékás, *A kultúrtanti visszavág. A Symposion-mozgalom krónikája 1954–1993* [Auntie Culture Strikes Back. Chronicle of the *Symposion* Movement, 1954–1993] (Újvidék, 1994).

72   On the reprisals: Márton Matuska, *A megtorlás napjai* [Days of Reprisal] (Novi Sad, 1991) = *Retaliation* (Budapest, 1995); Sándor Mészáros, *Holttá nyilvánítva* [Pronounced Dead] (Budapest, 1995 [1991]); István Ternovácz, "Pusztulj, kulák! Parasztsanyargatás a Vajdaságban" [Perish, Kulak! Oppression of the Peasantry in Vojvodina] (Budapest, 1996).

73   The most conspicuous advocate of this was Imre Bori, who began in the early 1960s to argue that the specific socio-economic situation had "led to the development of a separate, autonomous spirit among

the Yugoslavian Hungarians." Imre Bori, "A jugoszláviai magyar kultúra ma" [Yugoslavian Hungarian Culture Today], *Új Symposion* (1969) 50: 17–20. See also Nándor Major, "Elágazó utak" [Diverging Roads], *Híd* (1969) 4: 433–436.

74　The Serbian leadership used Kosovo Serbs to mount mass demonstrations in July 1988 in several Vojvodina communities. Speakers argued that Vojvodina's autonomy prevented Belgrade from defending the rights of Kosovo Serbs there. Pressure from the Novi Sad demonstration led to the resignation on October 6, 1988, of the Vojvodina leaders, who opposed changing the constitutional position. For details: Sava Kerčov, Jovo Radoš and Aleksandar Raič, *Mitinzi u Vojvodini 1988. Godine rađanja političkog pluralizma* [Rallies in Vojvodina 1988. The Years of the Birth of Political Pluralism] (Novi Sad, 1990).

75　*Vajdasági Magyarok Demokratikus Közösségét (VMDK)*. Its four published yearbooks include seminal documents and a detailed chronology: Zoltán Kalapis, Péter Sinkovits and János Vékás, eds., *Magyarok Jugoszláviában '90. A Vajdasági Magyarok Demokratikus Közösségének évkönyve 1990* [Hungarians in Yugoslavia '90. VMDK Yearbook 1990] (Novi Sad, 1991); Éva Hódi, Sándor Hódi and János Vékás, eds., *"Sokáig éltünk némaságban." A Vajdasági Magyarok Demokratikus Közösségének évkönyve 1991* ["We Lived for a Long Time in Silence." VMDK Yearbook 1991] (Ada, 1992); Éva Hódi and Sándor Hódi, eds., *Esély a megmaradásra. A VMDK évkönyve 1992* [Chance of Survival. VMDK Yearbook 1994] (Ada, 1992); Éva Hódi and Sándor Hódi, eds., *A balkáni pokolban. A VMDK évkönyve 1993* [Balkan Inferno. VMDK Yearbook 1993] (Ada, 1992).

76　Presidency of the VMDK: "Kérelem a JNH kötelékeibe besorolt magyarok ideiglenes leszereléséről" [Petition on the Temporary Demobilization of Hungarians Serving in the Yugoslav National Army], in Hódi, Hódi and Vékás, eds., *A balkáni pokolban*, pp. 255–256.

77　On refugee numbers, see the Serbian government memo to the Serbian House of Representatives, No. 05 9–283/92–253, May 21, 1992, citing Federal National Defense Secretariat data. On dismissals, this was stated: "In Temerin, for instance, 58 were dismissed between September and December 1991, all Hungarians." See Magdolna Nagy, "Otthon és munkahely nélkül" [No Home, No Job], *Magyar Szó*, January 12, 1992.

78   Zakon o službenoj upotrebi jezika i pisama. *Službeni glasnik Republike Srbije* br. 45, July 27, 1991; Zakon o osnovnoj školi. *Službeni... br.* 50, July 25, 1992; Zakon o teritorijalnoj organizaciji Republike Srbije i lokalnoj samoupravi. *Službeni... br.* 47, August 3, 1991; Zakon o nasleđivanju. *Službeni... br.* 46, 1995. The passage was set aside by Serbia's Constitutional Court in 2003.

79   Council of the VMDK: "Önkormányzatot! Kezdeményezés a személyi elven alapuló kisebbségi önkormányzat létrehozatalára" [Local Government! Initiative for the Establishment of Minority Local Government on a Personal Basis], *VMDK Hírmondó*, November 23, 1990, p. 8. Reprinted in Bárdi and Éger, eds., *Útkeresés és integráció*, pp. 358–359.

80   General Assembly of the VMDK: *Hungarian Autonomy. The Position of the DCHV on Autonomy* (Budapest, 1992).

81   Árpád Hajnal, "Elnökverés Nemesmiliticsen" [Beating Up a President in Svetozar Miletić], *Magyar Szó*, October 26, 1993, p. 8; "Rálőttek a VMDK vezetőjének a házára" [VMDK Leader Shot at in His House], *Ibid.*, May 31, 1992; "Bombát dobtak az udvarba" [Bomb Thrown into Yard], *Tiszavidék*, February 21, 1992; Béla Csorba, "Nem tettem eleget a behívóparancsnak" [I Ignored My Call-Up Order], *Magyar Szó*, January 12, 1992.

82   General Assembly of the VMDK: *Kezdeményezés a Szerb Köztársaságban élő magyarság önkormányzatának létrehozására* [Proposal to Establish Autonomy for Hungarians in the Republic of Serbia], *VMDK Hírmondó*, special issue, February 17, 1996, pp. 2–9. Reprinted in Bárdi and Éger, eds., *Útkeresés és integráció*, pp. 417–426.

83   Péter Sinkovits, "Horn békés megoldást sürget" [Horn Calls for a Peaceful Solution], *Magyar Szó,* October 20, 1995, pp. 1 and 3.

84   For the documents, see András Ágoston and János Vékás, eds., *A botrány* [The Scandal] (Újvidék, 1994).

85   *Vajdasági Magyar Szövetség (VMSZ).*

86   *Vajdasági Magyar Demokrata Párt (VMDP).*

87   According to the 2002 census, 5 percent of Serbia's population were refugees, but the proportion was three times as high in Vojvodina (9.2 percent) as in Central Serbia. Petar Lađević and Vladimir Stanković, eds., *Izbeglički korpus u Srbiji. Prema podacima popisa stanovništva 2002* [The Refugee Body in Serbia. According to the Data of the 2002 Census] (Belgrade, 2004), p. 39. In 1996 the number approached

600,000, but about 110,000 had obtained Serbian citizenship by 2006. Danijela Korać Mandić *et al.*, *Integracija kao dugoročno rešenje za izbeglice i raseljena lica u Srbiji - analitički izveštaj. Srpski savet za izbeglice* [Integration as a Long-Term Solution for the Refugees and IDPs in Serbia – An Analytical Report. Serbian Refugee Council] (Novi Sad, July–October 2006). Those people who were relocated from Kosovo to the territory of Central Serbia and Vojvodina are called *interno raseljena lica* [internal IDPs].

88 At Hrtkovci in Srem, for example, one person was murdered on June 28, 1992, others badly injured, and several repeatedly harassed. The tensions prompted 253 Croatian and Hungarian families to move away, raising the proportion of Serbs from 20 to 80 percent within weeks. Perica Vučinić, "Mir i nemir Julijane Molnar" [The Peace and Discomfort of Juliana Molnar], *Borba*, July 2, 1992, p. 14.

89 The proliferating anti-Hungarian incidents in Vojvodina in the 2000s occurred mainly in areas frequented by refugees. *Projekat Afirmacija multikulturalizma i tolerancije u Vojvodini 2006–2007* [Project of Affirmation of Multiculturalism and Tolerance in Vojvodina 2006–2007] (Novi Sad, 2006), p. 4.

90 *Srpska radikalna stranka, SRS; Socijalistička partija Srbije, SPS.*

91 Zakon o zaštiti prava i sloboda nacionalnih manjina. *Službeni list SRJ* br. 11, February 27, 2002.

92 The specific ministry order on the electoral college to elect the National Minorities Council: Pravilnik o načinu rada skupština elektora za izbor saveta nacionalnih manjina. *Službeni list SRJ* br. 41, July 26, 2002.

93 "Osnivačka prava nad listovima manjina preneta nacionalnim savetima," *Dnevnik*, June 30, 2004.

94 Socioeconomic attributes of the population and the minorities: *Etnički mozaik Srbije. Prema podacima popisa stanovništva 2002* [Ethnic Mosaic of Serbia. According to the Data of the 2002 Census] (Belgrade, 2004).

95 The initiative came from outside the party system and was opposed initially by both main parties. It failed to attract the necessary support despite a volte-face by Fidesz, Hungary's main opposition party, and neutrality from the governing Socialist Party, as it faced voter concerns about economic results, political manipulation of the issue, and doubts about the legality under EU law of discriminating between ethnic Hungarian and other citizens of neighboring countries.

96   On the break-up of Czechoslovakia and Hungarian attitudes to it, see Judit Hamberger, *Csehszlovákia szétválása. Egy föderációs kísérlet kudarca* [Czechoslovakia's Dissolution. End of a Federative Experiment] (Budapest, 1997).

97   *Független Magyar Kezdeményezés (FMK); Magyar Kereszténydemokrata Mozgalom (MKDM); Együttélés Politikai Mozgalom.*

98   *Magyar Polgári Párt.* Eleonóra Sándor, "A rendszerváltás magyar szemmel" [Change of System through Hungarian Eyes], in József Fazekas and Péter Hunčik, eds., *Magyarok Szlovákiában. I. Összefoglaló jelentés (1989–2004)* [Hungarians in Slovakia. I. Summary Report (1989–2004)] (Somorja/Dunaszerdahely, 2004), pp. 23–50. Separate interviews with the main participants in the change of system: "Elbeszélt történelem. A rendszerváltás évei" [Narrated History. Years of System Change], in the 1999–2000 issues of *Fórum Társadalomtudományi Szemle.* Analysis of beginnings and party programs: Iván Gyurcsík, "A szlovákiai magyar pártok karaktere és genezise" [Character and Origin of the Slovakian Hungarian Parties], *Regio* 7 (1996) 3: 169–191; László Öllős, "A magyar pártok programjai" [Programs of the Hungarian Parties], in Fazekas and Hunčik, eds., *Magyarok Szlovákiában. I,* pp. 51–78. Activity of Hungarian parties: László Szarka, "Kisebbségi többpártrendszer és a közösségépítés" [Minority Multiparty System and Community Building], in Fazekas and Hunčik, eds., *Magyarok Szlovákiában. I,* pp. 79–99; election results: *ibid.,* pp. 100–103.

99   *Magyar Koalíció Pártja, MKP.*

100   The Komárno rally on January 8, 1994, was the most important Hungarian event of the decade. Over 3,000 out of 5,000 invited Hungarian local assembly members and mayors appeared. In their statement they called Slovakia's Hungarians a nation of equal rank with the Slovak nation and called for special legal status, political institutionalization, a self-elected representative body for the Hungarian-inhabited area, minority local government organizations, and local government units with a Hungarian majority. *Önkormányzat az önrendelkezés alapja. A szlovákiai magyar választott képviselők és polgármesterek nagygyűlésének hiteles jegyzőkönyve* [Self-Government on a Self-Determining Basis. Minutes of the Rally of Slovakia's Elected Hungarian Representatives and Mayors] (Komárom, 1995).

101 Árpád Sidó, János Fiala and Balázs Jarábik, "A szlovák–magyar alapszerződés hatásvizsgálata" [The Effectiveness of the Slovak–Hungarian Basic Treaty], *Regio* 14 (2003) 1: 111–119, and at http://epa. oszk.hu/00000/00036/00049/pdf/07.pdf. Accessed April 24, 2010.

102 This 56-nation *ad hoc* UN organization has its roots in the Conference on European Security and Cooperation that led to the East–West Helsinki Final Act in 1975. The OSCE seeks to resolve ethnic tensions as an element of the third (human) dimension of security. See http://www.osce.org/activities/18805.html. Accessed April 26, 2010.

103 Zsigmond Zalabai, *A nyelvi jogokról: Mit ér a nyelvünk, ha magyar? "Táblaháború" és a "névháború" szlovákiai magyar sajtódokumentumaiból 1990–1994* [Language Rights: How Much Is Hungarian Worth? "Sign Wars" and "Language War" in Slovakian Hungarian Press Documents, 1990–1994] (Pozsony, 1995); József Berényi, *Nyelvországlás. A szlovákiai nyelvtörvény történelmi és társadalmi okai* [Language and Country. Historical and Social Reasons behind Slovakia's Language Law] (Pozsony, 1994); Gizella Szabómihály, "A szlovákiai magyarság nyelvi helyzete" [The Language Situation of Slovakia's Hungarians], in Károly Tóth and Gábor Csanda, eds., *Magyarok Szlovákiában, III. (1989–2006) Kultúra* [Hungarians in Slovakia III (1989–2006). Culture] (Somorja, 2007), pp. 261–278.

104 László Szarka, "Közigazgatási reform és kisebbségi kérdés" [Administrative Reform and the Minority Question], *Kisebbségkutatás* (2001) 1: 8–28.

105 See Section 4.4.

106 The communist governments of Czechoslovakia and Hungary concluded a treaty in Budapest on September 18, 1977, on construction of two barrages with hydroelectric power plants and other installations, along their common length of the Danube. The two countries were to share the power generated equally. The scheme involved diverting most of the flow of the Danube along a 16-kilometer navigable headwater canal from Dunakiliti to what would have been a peak-hour hydroelectric plant at Gabčíkovo combined with a shipping lock. The uneven flow of the peak-hour plant was to have been compensated by a tailwater reservoir and a barrage and hydroelectric plant at Nagymaros, 95 kilometers downstream. The scheme was to have side-benefits for shipping safety and flood protection. Hungary withdrew unilaterally from

the treaty in May 1992 on economic, environmental and aesthetic grounds, but Slovakia pressed ahead with a modified scheme and claimed high damages under international law. The modified scheme came into operation in 1996. In a 1998 judgment (http://www.icj-cij.org/docket/index.php?pr=269&p1=3&p2=1&case=92&p3=6. Accessed April 26, 2010), the Hague court concluded that the Treaty of Budapest was still valid but had been breached by both parties, who were to settle the outstanding issues by negotiation. This they still seem unlikely to do.

107   On the coalition agreement: József Reiter, "A szlovákiai Magyar Koalíció Pártja kormányzati tevékenységének első négy hónapja" [The First Four Months of Government Activity by Slovakia's Hungarian Coalition Party], *Magyar Kisebbség* (1999) 1: 182–193. On its implementation: József Reiter and Szilvia Reiter, "A szlovákiai Magyar Koalíció Pártja kormányzati tevékenységének első éve" [The First Year of Government Activity by Slovakia's Hungarian Coalition Party], *Magyar Kisebbség* (1999) 4: 190–202.

108   Judit Hamberger, "A Magyar Koalíció Pártja a szlovák kormányban" [The Hungarian Coalition Party in the Slovak Government], in Fazekas and Hunčik, eds., *Magyarok Szlovákiában. I,* pp. 105–124; Ferenc Boros, "A Dzurinda-kormány nemzetiségi politikájáról" [National Minority Policy of the Dzurinda Government], *Fórum Társadalomtudományi Szemle* (2002) 1: 125–144.

109   Many Roma in Slovakia are native Hungarian-speakers.

110   On educational questions: Erzsébet Dolník, "Iskolarendszerek, törvényalkotás, az iskolaügy területén" [School Systems and Legislation in Educational Affairs], in Béla László, László A. Szabó and Károly Tóth, eds., *Magyarok Szlovákiában. IV. köt. Oktatásügy (1989–2006)* [Hungarians in Slovakia IV. Education (1989–2006)] (Šamorin, 2007), pp. 36–45; Béla László, "Szlovákiai magyar felsőoktatás" [Slovakian Hungarian Higher Education], in *ibid.,* pp. 117–149; Béla László, Nóra Varga and Zoltán Sidó, "A szlovákiai magyar pedagógusképzés és felsőoktatási intézmények" [The Hungarian Teachers' Training and Institutions of Higher Education in Slovakia], in *ibid.,* pp. 157–190.

111   Hans (János) Selye (1907–1982) was a Vienna-born Canadian endocrinologist of Hungarian origin who investigated and coined the terms "biological stress," negative "distress," and positive "eustress." He lived in Komárno in his childhood.

112 *Duna Menti Múzeum.*
113 *Magyar Kultúra Történeti Múzeuma.*
114 On Fico government policy on minority status and the Hungarians:
     Judit Hamberger, *A feszült szlovák–magyar viszony okairól* [Causes
     of Slovak–Hungarian Tension], at http://www.kulugyiintezet.hu/
     szempont/Hamberger_Judit-szlovak-magyar.pdf. Accessed May 28,
     2010.
115 *Smer – sociálna demokracia; Hnutie za demokratické Slovensko;
     Slovenská národná strana.*
116 Edvard Kardelj, Tito's chief ideologist, wrote even in 1939: "There
     was no way that the path to this community could lead via artificial
     weakening of each nation's individuality or forcible mergers of them,
     as many of us in the so-called integral Yugoslav camp imagined.
     On the contrary, it led via reinforcement of the individuality of each
     nation and its culture, which is the irreplaceable source of general
     human culture." Edvard Kardelj, *A szlovén nemzeti kérdés fejlődése*
     [Development of the Slovene National Question] (Novi Sad, 1961).
117 Sovereignty declaration: "Deklaracija o suverenosti države Republike
     Slovenije" [Declaration of State Sovereignty of the Republic of
     Slovenia], *Uradni list RS* (1990) 26. Referendum: "Zakon o plebiscitu
     o samostojnosti in neodvisnosti Republike Slovenije" [Act on the
     Plebiscite on the Independence of the Republic of Slovenia], *Uradni
     list RS* (1990) 44.
118 Constitutional amendment: "Ustavni amandma XCIX k Ustavi
     Republike Slovenije" [XCIXth Constitutional Amendment to the
     Constitution of the Republic of Slovenia], *Uradni list RS* (1991) 7;
     declaration of independence: "Temeljna ustavna listina o samostojnosti
     in neodvisnosti Republike Slovenije" [Basic Constitutional Charter
     on the Independence of the Republic of Slovenia], *Uradni list RS*
     (1991) 1.
119 "Ustava Republike Slovenije" [The Constitution of the Republic of
     Slovenia], *Uradni list RS* (1991) 33.
120 "Zakon o romski skupnosti v Republiki Sloveniji" [The Law on
     the Roma Community in the Republic of Slovenia], *Uradni list RS*
     (2007) 33.
121 "Zakon o državljanstvu Republike Slovenije" [Law on Citizenship of
     the Republic of Slovenia], *Uradni list RS* (1991) 1.
122 "Odločba Ustavnega sodišča. št. U–I–246/02–28" [Decision of the
     Constitutional Court. No. U–I–246/02–28], *Uradni list RS* (2003) 36.

123 *Popisi na Slovenskem 1948–1991 in Popis 2002* [Censuses in Slovenia 1948–1991 and the 2002 Census] (Ljubljana, 2001), p. 19; in more detail: Milivoja Šircelj, *Verska, jezikovna in narodna sestava prebivalstva Slovenije: popisi 1921–2002* [Religious, Linguistic and Ethnic Composition of the Population of Slovenia: Censuses 1921–2002] (Ljubljana, 2003), p. 163.

124 "Javni razpis za dodelitev sredstev za ustvarjanje gospodarske osnove za avtohtoni narodni skupnosti za leto 2007" [Tender of 2007 for the Allocation of Resources to Generate an Economic Base for Indigenous Ethnic Communities], *Uradni list RS* (2007) 100.

125 "Zakon o posebnih pravicah italijanske in madžarske narodne skupnosti na področju vzgoje in izobraževanja" [Law on Special Rights of the Italian and Hungarian National Communities in the Field of Education], *Uradni list RS* (2001) 35.

126 "Zakon o volitvah v državni zbor" [National Assembly Elections Act], *Uradni list RS* (1992) 44.

127 "Zakon o samoupravnih narodnih skupnostih" [Law on Self-Governing Ethnic Minorities], *Uradni list RS* (1994) 65. *Községi Nemzeti Tanács; Muravidéki Magyar Nemzeti Tanács; Muravidéki Magyar Nemzeti Önigazgatási Közösség; Muravidéki Magyar Önkormányzati Nemzeti Közösség.*

128 *Magyar Nemzeti Tájékoztatási Intézet; Magyar Nemzetiségi Művelődési Intézet; Szlovéniai Magyar Írók Társasága; Muravidéki Magyar Tudományos Társaság.*

129 *Slovenski šolski sistem v številkah* [The Slovenian Education System in Numbers] (Ljubljana, 2007), p. 52.

130 "Zakon o ratifikaciji sporazuma o zagotavljanju posebnih pravic slovenske narodne manjšine v Republiki Madžarski in madžarske narodne skupnosti v Republiki Sloveniji" [Act on Ratification of the Agreement on Providing Special Rights of the Slovenian Minority in the Republic of Hungary and Hungarian Communities in Slovenia], *Uradni list RS-MP* (1993) 6; "1996. évi VI. törvény a Magyar Köztársaságban élő szlovén nemzeti kisebbség és a Szlovén Köztársaságban élő magyar nemzeti közösség különjogainak biztosításáról szóló, Ljubljanában, 1992. november 6-án aláírt Egyezmény kihirdetéséről" [Act VI/1996 on the Agreement Signed in Ljubljana on November 6, 1992, on the Special Rights of the Slovene National Minority Dwelling in the Republic of Hungary and the Hungarian National Minority Dwelling in the Republic of Slovenia], *Magyar Közlöny* (1996) 17.

131 "Zakon o ratifikaciji pogodbe o prijateljstvu in sodelovanju med Republiko Slovenijo in Republiko Madžarsko" [Law on Ratification of the Treaty of Friendship and Cooperation between Slovenia and the Republic of Hungary], *Uradni list RS-MP* (1993) 6; "1995. évi XLVI. törvény a Magyar Köztársaság és a Szlovén Köztársaság között Budapesten, 1992. december 1-jén aláírt barátsági és együttműködési Szerződés kihirdetéséről" [Act XLVI/1995 on Proclamation of the Treaty of Friendship and Cooperation Signed in Budapest between the Republic of Hungary and the Republic of Slovenia], *Magyar Közlöny* (1995) 45.

132 Rogers Brubaker, *Nationalism Reframed: Nationhood and the National Question in the New Europe* (Cambridge, 1996).

133 S. Kul'chyc'kyj, "Utverdzhennja nezalezhnoi' Ukrai'ny" [Establishment of an Independent Ukrainian State], *Ukrai'ns'kyj istorychnyj zhurnal* (2001) 3: 49; M. Derzhaljuk, "Ugors'ka polityka shhodo Ukrai'ny na suchacnomu etapi" [Hungarian Policy towards Ukraine Today], in O. Derghacov *et al.*, *Ukrai'ns'ka derzhavnist' u 20 stolitti (Istoryko-politologichnyj analiz)* [Ukrainian Statehood in the Twentieth Century (Historical and Political Analysis)] (Kyiv, 1996); I. Skyba, "Zakarattja u systemi mizhderzhavnyh vidnosyn Ukrai'ny i Ugors'koi' Respubliky (1991–2004)" [The Transcarpathia Question in Ukraine's and Hungary's Relations (1991–2004)], in V. Smolij *et al.*, *Ukrai'na–Ugorshhyna: spil'ne mynule ta s'ogodennja* [Ukraine–Hungary: Common Past and Present] (Kyiv, 2006), pp. 251–270.

134 István Csernicskó and Ildikó Orosz, *The Hungarians in Transcarpathia* (Budapest, 1999); Bárdi and Éger, eds., *Útkeresés és integráció*, pp. 793–811; Nándor Bárdi, *Tény és való. A budapesti kormányzatok és a határon túli magyarok kapcsolattörténete. Problémakatalógus* [True Fact. Budapest Governments and the History of Their Contacts with Hungarians Abroad. Catalogue of Problems] (Pozsony, 2004), pp. 109–112 and 140; Miklós Kovács, *Üzenet a kalapács alól* [News from under the Hammer] (Ungvár, 1998); L. Lojko, *Gromads'ki organizacii' etnichnyh menshyn Ukrai'ny: pryroda, legitymnist', dijal'nist'* [Social Organizations of the Ukrainian Ethnic Group: Ideology, Legitimacy, Operation] (Kyiv, 2005), pp. 267–273; M. Tovt, *Mizhnarodno-pravovyj zahyst nacional'nyh menshyn (tendencii' suchasnogo rozvytku)* [International Legal Protection of National Minorities (The Present Situation)] (Uzhhorod, 2002).

135 *Kárpátaljai Magyar Kulturális Szövetség (KMKSZ)*.

136 *Kárpátaljai Magyar Szervezetek Fóruma (KMSZF)*.

137 *Ukrajnai Magyar Demokrata Szövetség; Kárpátaljai Magyar Kulturális Szövetség; Lvovi Magyarok Kulturális Szövetsége; Magyarok Kijevi Egyesülete.*

138 *Social-demokratychna partija Ukrai'ny (ob' jednana).*

139 *KMKSZ–Ukrajnai Magyar Párt; Ukrajnai Magyar Demokrata Párt.*

140 *Magyar Értelmiségiek Kárpátaljai Közössége; Kárpátaljai Magyar Önkormányzati Fórum; Határ-menti Települések Önkormányzati Szövetsége.*

141 István Csernicskó, *A magyar nyelv Ukrajnában (Kárpátalján)* [Hungarian Language in Ukraine (Transcarpathia)] (Budapest, 1998); Ferenc Gereben, "Nemzeti és kulturális identitás Kárpátalján" [National and Cultural Identity in Transcarpathia], *Pro Minoritate* (2000) 1: 166–170; Ildikó Orosz, *A magyar nyelvű oktatás helyzete Kárpátalján az ukrán államiság kialakulásának első évtizedében 1989–1999* [The Situation with Hungarian Language Teaching in Transcarpathia in the First Decade of Ukrainian Statehood, 1989–1999] (Ungvár, 2005); *Kárpátaljai Magyar Képző- és Iparművészek Révész Imre Társasága 1990–1995* [Transcarpathian Hungarian Imre Révész Society of Fine and Applied Arts, 1990–1995] (Ungvár, 1995).

142 http://bdk.blog.hu; www.karpataljaforum.net; www.karpatinfo.net, and so on.

143 Jevhenij Zhupan, "The Humanitarian and Socio-Economic Situation in Transcarpathian Rus' Today," *Carpatho-Rusyn American* 20 (1997) 1: 7–9; B. Djachenko and Je. Erfan, "Misce migrantiv u strukturi suchasnogo rynku praci" [Migrants on the Labor Market], *Naukovyj visnyk UzhNU. Serija: Ekonomika* (2005) 8; Zsombor Csata, "Vendégmunka-vállalás a határon túli magyarok körében" [Taking Work Abroad among Hungarians beyond Hungary's Borders], in Ferenc Dobos, ed., *Az autonóm lét kihívásai kisebbségben* [Challenges of Autonomous Existence in a Minority] (Budapest, 2001); "Zakon Ukrai'ny Pro special'nu ekonomichnu zonu 'Zakarpattia'" [Law on the Transcarpathian Free Economic Zone], *Oficijnyj visnyk Ukrai'ny* 16 (2001).

144 József Molnár and István D. Molnár, *Kárpátalja népessége és magyarsága a népszámlálási és népmozgalmi adatok tükrében* [Transcarpathia's Population and Hungarian Community in the Light of Census and Demographic Data] (Beregszász, 2005); Károly Kocsis and Eszter Kocsisné Hodosi, *Ethnic Geography of the Hungarian Minorities in the Carpathian Basin* (Washington, DC, 2001).

VII. OTHER HUNGARIAN-SPEAKING COMMUNITIES IN AND BEYOND HUNGARY'S NEIGHBORING COUNTRIES

1. HUNGARIAN-SPEAKING JEWS IN THE CARPATHIAN BASIN

Viktória Bányai

The Jews of Hungary gained individual civil rights in 1867 and religious rights in 1895. This meant that by law they had equality of rights as individuals and state recognition as a historical (longstanding) religious denomination alongside the main Christian denominations. The legislature thereafter treated the Jews collectively as a religious denomination and individually as Hungarian citizens adhering to the "Israelite" religion (Judaism) – until the passage of the racial theory-based second and third acts on the Jews in 1939 and 1941. There were divisions of various kinds among 5 percent of the inhabitants of pre-Trianon Hungary (excluding Croatia) who were Jews by that definition (911,000 people in 1910). They had strong social, economic, cultural and ideological differences, and even the law provided a state-recognized framework for their religious differences. For when the Jews in the late nineteenth century came under pressure from the state to organize themselves into a national religious institution analogous to the main Christian churches, there emerged within Hungarian Judaism not one but three denominations, at ground level and nationally: Neolog, Orthodox and Status Quo Judaism.[1] The last sought to preserve the situation before the Neolog/Orthodox split had occurred and implied that they were not adherents of either faction, but in time their communities became organized into a third denomination. In 1910, 43 percent adhered to Neolog Judaism, 52 percent to Orthodox, and 5 percent to Status Quo.[2] Territorially, the Neolog were dominant in Budapest, most of Transdanubia, the Danube–Tisza region, and the Southern Region, the Orthodox in Upper Hungary and as far south as Győr-Moson and Sopron Counties, and in the northwest: there were very few Neolog communities northeast of a line from Kassa to Nagyvárad. The most populous Status Quo communities were found along the borders between the areas dominated by the other two denominations, in Léva, Vác, Eger, Gyöngyös, Nyíregyháza and Marosvásárhely.[3] The inter-denominational differences appeared in attitudes towards adjustment to the expectations and customs of majority society and modern life, or in their rejection of these. Most Neolog communities adopted the lifestyle and outward appearance of the majority society, while the Orthodox demanded full observance of the traditional religious prescriptions, even at the cost of a measure of isolation. However, there were differences of approach to language, schooling, dress, and so on, within the Orthodox denomination as well. More western Orthodox communities turned to the use of Hungarian, while among the ultra-orthodox and Hasidic communities of the northeast, especially in Transcarpathia and Northern Transylvania, Yiddish remained as the everyday language, although other languages were used to communicate with the outside world. Both in 1910 and in 1941, about 80 percent of Jews in the Carpathian Basin were exclusively or primarily Hungarian-speaking. Up to the end of World War I, assimilation was in the forefront of the aims for the whole Jewish population of the region to such an extent that they themselves became Hungarianizing factors in some minority areas. It is important to add that assimilation of the Jews was not a one-way process. Hungarian Jewry, through their social contacts and mutual influences, contributed to introducing modern cultural traits and became in general the main vehicle of modernization.

Understandably, Trianon was a huge blow to Hungarian Jewry as well. Its numbers fell from 910,000 in 1910 to 473,000 in 1920. 48 percent of Hungarian Jewry found themselves outside the new borders.[4]

Dilemmas

The change of sovereignty prompted the Jewish population in all successor states to decide or at least consider their situation.[5] While in post-Trianon Hungary the main trend remained the continuation of assimilation, in the detached territories paths opened up to a community of interest with the Hungarians, to choosing various types of Jewish national identity, or to assimilating into the new majority nation. It is hard to gain a true picture of the proportions who chose each course and what changes in attitude occurred over time, for one unconcealed purpose behind the censuses taken in the successor states was to prove that the new ruling nations were in a majority, and the ethnic and language data in them tended to be political statements.

Identification with Hungarian national awareness – self-definition as adherents of Judaism belonging to the Hungarian minority – remained throughout as one of the decisive individual and communal strategies adopted. Many Hungarian Jewish journalists, politicians and artists worked for Hungarian interests and cultural endeavors, with loyalty to the Hungarians as their political program. For example, there was Oradea's militantly anti-Zionist Neolog chief rabbi, Dr. Lipót Kecskeméti (1865–1936). He and many of his flock joined the minority Hungarian Party formed in Transylvania.[6] Several memoirs relate how older people brought up under Dualism would don their *kippot* (prayer caps) and stand to attention if the Hungarian National Anthem was played, or greeted with joy the return of Hungarian rule in World War II, although they would be tragically disillusioned and betrayed by it.

However, there were several factors that were to weaken that pursuit of assimilation. One was the surge of anti-Semitism that appeared in post-war Hungary: the brutalities of the White Terror and the passage of the *numerus clausus* act in 1920, limiting Jewish access to university places. Jews initially sympathetic to the Hungarians were alienated to some extent by the news that they heard from the "mother country." This stance was displayed, for instance, in the 1921 book *Jews Facing a Dilemma*, by the well-known literary historian Aladár Komlós (1892–1980), who came from an Upper Hungarian assimilated Jewish family. He pointed to the many Jewish lives lost in the pogrom at Orgovány, which had been carried out by detachments of officers.[7] It has to be emphasized that the distancing from the Hungarians was political, not linguistic or cultural. There remained Hungarian-speaking Jewish communities and centers of culture and journalism in Košice and Bratislava in Slovakia, Užhorod and Mukačevo in Transcarpathia, Arad, Cluj, Sighetu Marmației and Târgu Mureş in Transylvania, and Subotica and Novi Sad in the Southern Region.[8] There and elsewhere in the interwar period a wide range of Hungarian-language Jewish papers appeared, showing that the linguistic situation was unchanged. The best-known Jewish paper in Transylvania was the pro-Zionist *Új Kelet,* founded in Cluj in 1918 under Ernő Marton, which was revived in Tel Aviv in 1948.[9]

The new state authorities in each case sought to dissociate the Jews from the Hungarian minority, to cut the size and proportion of the latter. One important weapon in Czechoslovakia, Romania and the Serb-Croat-Slovene Kingdom was to go against Austro-Hungarian practice and treat the Jews as a separate ethnic group, irrespective of their native language.[10] This also relieved the Jewish communities in detached regions from the pressure to assimilate again, for the policy of the political leaders of each new majority nation was not to assimilate Jews, but simply to have them distance themselves from the Hungarians by expressing their loyalty to the new state. It was enough if members of Hungarian-speaking Jewish communities identified themselves as members of the Jewish national minority. The new regimes therefore supported the new Jewish movements and parties with a national or Zionist basis. Zionism – the movement, spawned intellectually by the Budapest-born Theodor Herzl, that sought a Jewish national state of Israel – was highly popular, especially among the younger generation. However, it was still scorned by groups that supported Hungarian assimilation and by ultra-Orthodox and Hasidic communities, the latter on the religious grounds that it involved unauthorized people assuming the task of the Messiah.

Orthodox and Hasidic rabbis were also concerned that the burgeoning of Zionism coincided with mounting interest among younger Jews in the atheist and left-wing movements (social democratic and communist) that could flourish in the liberal political climate of Czechoslovakia. They saw the conservative Hungary of old as far preferable. But they too had to adapt to the new conditions. They saw ethnically based political activity as the best way forward for committed religious Jews practicing in a traditional way, and offered instead of the secular national movements the Orthodox religious alternative of a movement known as Agudat Yisrael.

Assimilation into the new majority nation was chosen only by a small number, and hardly at all before the 1930s. One reason was the brevity of the period: it took time to adopt the new language (usually through education taught in it) and the associated cultural traditions. This, along with left-wing ideology that supersedes or overrides the nationality question, would become a frequent choice in the period after the Holocaust.

Slovak nationalists were inimical to the Jews from the outset, as a community loyal to the old Hungarian regime. Nor did their leaders change their stance in the interwar period. But Masaryk's Czechoslovakia as a whole was the one successor country to attempt a political system similar to the Western democracies and eschew discriminatory measures up to 1938. The Orthodox communities that predominated in the Upland were coordinated by an Orthodox Bureau in Bratislava. The political forum on a minority basis was the Jewish Party, founded in 1918, which had branches in all Slovakian cities with an appreciable Jewish community.

Transcarpathia, also annexed to Czechoslovakia, holds a specific place in the history of Hungarian Jewry. Many of the Jews there followed Hasidism, the mystical spiritual movement of Judaism. Their religious customs and folklore differed from those of the Jews in other parts of former Hungary. Furthermore, their everyday language was Yiddish. There was also an upsurge of Hasidism in

Transylvania, where whole communities had arrived in Hungary from Galicia during World War I, for instance that of Yisrael Hager, *rebbe* of Vyzhnytsia, in Oradea. Their rapid spread prompted Dezső Schön to write a novel.[11]

The proportion of Jews in Transcarpathia was an exceptionally high 14 percent, which included proportions of 27 percent in Užhorod and 43 percent in Mukačevo, where the Jews formed the largest community,[12] representatives of the Jewish parties had a right to address the city assembly in Yiddish or Hebrew, and the public library had a Hebrew/Yiddish section. There were strong Jewish nationalist, Zionist presences in the Transcarpathian cities, and several (including Užhorod and Khust) started schools teaching in Hebrew, the best-known being the Hebrew Gymnasium of Mukačevo, founded in 1924.[13]

Romania in 1919 was the last country in Europe to legislate for equal rights for Jews. (The act was incorporated into the 1923 constitution.) Religious recognition ensued under a 1928 act on religious affairs. So the Jews of the Regat had been tied up in different campaigns, and different cultural and linguistic traditions also delayed cooperation with the communities of Transylvania. The local associations – the Transylvanian Orthodox Central Bureau (1920) and the Association of Transylvanian–Banat Israelite Communities (1922) – were derived from counterparts in Hungary.[14] Meanwhile a Zionist association organized on an ethnic basis – the Transylvanian Jewish National Federation[15] – was formed in 1918 and proved to be a strong communal force for pursuing Jewish interests. The community began to make an impact in local and national politics with the foundation of the Transylvanian Jewish Party in 1930.[16]

There were communities of over 10,000 Jews in Cluj, Oradea, Timişoara, Satu Mare and Sighetu Marmaţiei, making the Transylvanian Jews the strongest community of any in the detached regions. Hungarian Jewish writers and journalists played a big role in minority Hungarian life.[17] In the Dualist period, the trend especially in Neolog communities had been to send their children to Hungarian state or parish schools (suspending their own), but the 1920s brought an upsurge of denominational schools to provide Hungarian-taught education, including some middle schools (in Oradea, Timişoara and Cluj), although the last could not continue after 1923, when the use of teaching in Romanian became compulsory.[18]

One special feature of Southern Transylvania was the survival of a Jewish community that was Sephardic, as opposed to Ashkenazi, like the vast majority of the Jews in the Carpathian Basin.[19] Sephardic Jewish tradition derived from the Jewish community of Spain, which was expelled under the Alhambra Decree of 1492 and spread as a diaspora through the Maghreb and the Balkans, and in the wake of the Ottoman incursions as far as Hungary and Transylvania.[20] Traditional Sephardic communities survived into the twentieth century in Alba Iulia and Timişoara.

Vojvodina Jewry also faced the dilemma outlined earlier. Responses can be divided into two groups. Some clung to their pre-1918 traditions of close ties with the Hungarians, and others wished to be loyal to the Yugoslav King Alexander II. The latter was typical of Novi Sad and its environs, and of younger Jews, who were responsible for building up active Zionism in the province. The Jews loyal to the new state were grouped in the Novi Sad Jewish Association, and received extra state subsidies in exchange.

The new Austrian province of Burgenland had once contained some significant Jewish communities. Those settled by the Esterházy princes (in Eisenstadt/Kismarton, Mattersdorf/Nagymarton, Kittsee/Köpcsény, and so on) and the Batthyány counts (in Rohonc/Rechnitz) had enjoyed autonomy and exerted a decisive economic and cultural influence on Hungary's Jews up to the early nineteenth century, but by the end of that century these had been lost and most had moved to Vienna. The remaining Orthodox communities of a few hundred people formed a Burgenland Orthodox Bureau in 1920. By 1934 there were only 3,600 Jews in the province, and these would flee or be annihilated, deported, or moved to Vienna after the *Anschluss* of 1938.[21] Their home towns were then declared *Judenrein* (free of Jews) and their synagogues demolished. The communities did not revive after World War II, but they are remembered in the Austrian Jewish Museum in Eisenstadt.

The Holocaust

Once the gains by the Vienna Awards of 1938 and 1940 had been retaken, the restrictions in Hungary's so-called Jewish acts applied to them, and conscription into the labor service began. The first stage in the tragedy came in the summer of 1941, when "stateless" Jews without Hungarian citizenship were rounded up, deported, and massacred near Kamenets-Podolsky.[22] Yet despite the many thousands of lives lost and the deportations to neighboring countries in 1941–1942 – before the German occupation – most Jews in Hungary still felt that they were protected.

After the German occupation on April 16, 1944, the Jews (and those legally classed as such) were confined in ghettoes and deported. The task was carried out according to gendarmerie districts, from east to west, starting in Transcarpathia and Northern Transylvania. The deportee trains that left between May 15 and July 8 were bound for the death camps of Auschwitz. Some 445,000–450,000 people were sent off within weeks, mainly women, children and the elderly, as men of working age were in the labor service by then. Only the Budapest Jews herded into the ghettoes escaped deportation, but they suffered greatly at the hands of the Hungarian Arrow-Cross movement, legalized by the quisling prime minister, Döme Sztójay.

The Holocaust scholar Randolph L. Braham estimated that the war cost 266,000 Jewish lives in the reannexed territories.[23] It is worth recalling that in Northern Transylvania (occupied by Hungary under the Second Vienna Award of August 30, 1940) almost three quarters of the Jews perished, while the number of Holocaust victims in Southern Transylvania was one or two thousand. Although in 1942 Jews were also deported from there (from Timişoara and Arad) to Transdnistria, where tens of thousands of Jews from other parts of Romania were annihilated, Romania then stopped this and allowed them to emigrate to Palestine.[24] So in 1943 and 1944, Jews from Northern Transylvania, Hungary and other countries were trying to escape *into* Romania and thence via Bucharest and Constanţa to Palestine.[25]

Aftermath

After the war some thousands or tens of thousands of Jews returned to some regions to start a new life. The numbers of survivors are put at 35,000–40,000 from Northern Transylvania, 40,000 from Southern Transylvania, 20,000 from Transcarpathia, 10,000 from the southern, mainly Hungarian-speaking, strip of Slovakia (and 27,000 from the whole of Slovakia), and 3,000–5,000 from Vojvodina.[26] However, many survivors did not return to their native regions, or, on discovering that all their kin and community were gone, and encountering a frequently hostile reception from non-Jews, they immediately departed again for Israel or for Western countries. Some 10,000 Transcarpathian survivors settled as Czechoslovak citizens in the Czech lands, especially Sudetenland, and so when the Soviet Union gained sovereignty over the province, in June 1945, there were hardly 4,000 Jews to be found there.[27] All the survivors faced great difficulties, as communities that were devastated and robbed of their wealth, and were without their religious leaders. At least in the larger communities, the communities weathered out the difficulties and social and educational institutions were reorganized. The main aid came from the American Jewish Joint Distribution Committee (Joint).

The acts and decisions of the survivors of the Holocaust were aimed above all at freeing themselves of the burden of the "Jewish Question". Both communism and Zionism appeared to offer rapid, radical solutions, and indeed for a while they worked hand in hand. Large numbers of Jews joined the Communist Party, seeing it as a haven from persecution. Many were then to be disillusioned by the anti-Zionist trials and the anti-Israel policies that the Communist Party came to proclaim. Others sought freedom to pursue their

Jewish identity in Western countries with long liberal traditions, or were simply unable to come to terms with a native land that had rejected them and massacred their families. Some Jews moved from the detached territories into Hungary. Others chose to remain, reacting by hiding their Jewishness, even from their own children, and seeking full integration into the majority society.

Emigration to Israel was most intensive in 1948, the year that it was founded, and in the following few years. The population flow was further increased by the communist takeovers in Romania and Czechoslovakia, for the new authorities seized control of the Jewish organizations and expelled the international Jewish organizations providing relief to the Jews there. Jewish community life was kept within narrow religious, denominational bounds.

The loss of ground by Jewish culture and community life in the communist period hastened emigration, which continued within the limits set by the policy of each state. The Yugoslavs differed from the other communist regimes in not impeding emigration or the activity of international Jewish organizations. Before leaving the country, emigrants had to renounce their citizenship, which meant that their real estate passed to the state.[28] In Romania, after a period of isolationism in 1951–1958, another 106,000 Jews had left the country by 1966. Thereafter the Ceauşescu regime demanded and received from Israel a capitation fee averaging US $3,000 for each emigrant. By the end of the 1980s, only 6,000 out of the post-Holocaust community of 80,000 Jews remained in Transylvania.[29] A new wave of emigration from Slovakia commenced in 1968.

The Jews of Transcarpathia were the community in the toughest position after World War II. The borders were closed in the autumn of 1945, and only from the mid-1970s would the Soviets allow substantial Jewish emigration, under pressure from abroad. Returnees from long periods in labor camps and immigrants from provinces further east actually increased the Jewish population to about 12,000 in 1959.[30] Communities had to register before they could operate, and obtaining a permit proved impossible in many cases. According to a report in 1950, there were only four registered communities: in Uzhgorod (later to become known as Uzhhorod), Mukachevo, Beregovo (later to become known as Berehove) and Khust. Places of worship belonged to the state under Soviet law, and the synagogues were seized even from the registered communities.[31]

In the provincial towns of all countries in the region there remain only cemeteries as a memorial to the old Jewish communities that vanished after the Holocaust and the depopulation of communist times.

The Present Day

Today the Jewish inhabitants of the detached territories live mainly in the big cities, in communities numbering only a couple of hundred, of whom no more than 30–40 attend the synagogue or Jewish institutions. The holding of services is often prevented due to a lack of the prescribed quorum (10 males).

In many places there is a generation gap between the dwindling elderly, drawing their tradition from childhood and home, and younger people, often from mixed marriages, who have discovered their Jewish identity in recent years and are still learning the traditions. The middle generation of those who grew up under communism is absent from the community. In Transylvania, since the last rabbi (Ernő Neumann of Timişoara) died, there has been no one to replace him.[32] There is tension between the communities of the diaspora, intent on maintaining their own traditions, and the policy of assisting emigration to Israel. Particularly in Transcarpathia, even the remnants of the Hungarian Jewish families have moved to Israel since the change of system. Many Vojvodina Jews decided to do the same during the Yugoslav wars.

There is a dwindling community in the neighboring countries that senses a dual, Hungarian and Jewish, affiliation.[33] Relations with communities in Hungary have been enlivened by annual meetings in Debrecen since 1999. These have become an important event in the community life of the Jews of the Carpathian Basin.

Notes

1   On the schism: Jacob Katz, *A House Divided: Orthodoxy and Schism in Nineteenth-Century Central European Jewry* (Hanover, NH, 1998).

2   Kinga Frojimovics, "The Threefold Path: From the Split to the Forced Unification," in Anna Szalai, ed., *In the Land of Hagar. The Jews of Hungary: History, Society and Culture* (Tel Aviv, 2002), p. 109.

3   For a map, see *ibid.*, p. 107.

4   József Kepecs, ed., *A zsidó népesség száma településenként* [Numbers of the Jewish Population by Settlement] (Budapest, 1993), p. 37.

5   Lya Benjamin, "The Determinants of Jewish Identity in Inter-War Transylvania," *Studia Judaica* (1996) 5: 68–77.

6   Moshe Carmilly-Weinberger, *A zsidóság története Erdélyben, 1623–1944* [The History of Jewry in Transylvania, 1623–1944] (Budapest, 1995), pp. 216–218.

7   Álmos Koral [Aladár Komlós], *Zsidók a válaszúton* [Jews Facing a Dilemma] (Prešov, 1921).

8   Anna Szalai, ed., *Previously Unexplored Sources on the Holocaust in Hungary. A Selection from Jewish Periodicals 1930–1944* (Jerusalem, 2007), pp. 7–8.

9   Carmilly-Weinberger, *A zsidóság története Erdélyben*, pp. 272–274.

10 For a general view of the region: Ezra Mendelsohn, *The Jews of East Central Europe between the World Wars* (Bloomington, IN, 1987).

11 Dezső Schön, *Istenkeresők a Kárpátok alatt* [Seekers after God under the Carpathians] (Budapest, 1997 [1935]).

12 Mendelsohn, *The Jews of East Central Europe,* pp. 142–143.

13 Anna Szalai, "The Yearbooks of the Jewish High School in Munkács, 1938–1943," in Szalai, ed., *Previously Unexplored Sources*, p. 138.

14 *Erdélyi Ortodox Központi Iroda; Erdély-Bánsági Izraelita Hitközségek Szövetsége.* György Gaal, "Az erdélyi zsidóság az első világháborút követő időszakban" [Transylvanian Jewry in the Post-World War I Period], *Korunk* (1991) 8: 1029.

15 *Erdélyi Zsidó Nemzeti Szövetség.*

16 Attila Gidó, *On Transylvanian Jews. An Outline of a Common History* (Cluj-Napoca, 2009).

17 Carmilly-Weinberger, *A zsidóság története Erdélyben*, pp. 235–260.

18   Gaal, "Az erdélyi zsidóság," pp. 1030–1031.
19   *Ashkenaz* was a medieval Hebrew term for the German territories, borrowed from Genesis 10.3.
20   *Sephardi* was a medieval Hebrew term for Spain, borrowed from a place in Israel: Obadiah 1.20. Moshe Carmilly-Weinberger, "Spanish (Sepherdi) Communities in Transylvania and Banat in the XVIIth–XIXth Century," *Studia Judaica* (1991) 1: 39–52.
21   Herbert Rosenkranz, "Das Judentum Burgenlands am Vorabend der Schoah," in Shlomo Spitzer, ed., *Beiträge zur Geschichte der Juden im Burgenland* (Ramat Gan, 1994), pp. 143–160.
22   Randolph L. Braham, *The Politics of Genocide, I–II. The Holocaust in Hungary* (New York, 1994), pp. 205–214.
23   Braham, *The Politics of Genocide*, p. 298.
24   Zoltán Tibor Szabó, "Az erdélyi zsidó közösség sorsa a második világháborút követő időszakban (1945–48)" [The Fate of the Transylvanian Jewish Community after World War II (1945–1948)], *Korunk* (2004) 8: 78.
25   Moshe Carmilly-Weinberger, *The Road to Life* (New York, 1994).
26   Tamás Stark, *The Hungarian Jewry during the Holocaust and after the Second World War, 1939–1949. A Statistical Review* (New York, 2000), p. 115.
27   Károly Lusztig, "A gyertyák csonkig égnek. A kárpátaljai zsidóság sorsa a Soá után" [Candles Burn Down. The Fate of Transcarpathian Jewry after the Shoah], *Múlt és Jövő* (1992) 3: 89.
28   Attila Pejin, *A zentai zsidóság története* [The Fate of Senta Jewry] (Senta, 2003).
29   Attila Gidó, "Zsidó jelen-lét Romániában" [Jewish Present and Presence in Romania], *Regio* 15 (2004) 3: 3–21.
30   Lusztig, "A gyertyák csonkig égnek," p. 89.
31   *Ibid.*, pp. 91–92.
32   Gidó, "Zsidó jelen-lét Romániában," p. 9.
33   *Ibid.*, p. 21.

2. HUNGARIAN-SPEAKING
JEWISH COMMUNITIES OVERSEAS
Viktória Bányai

Emigration

Jews from Hungarian-speaking territories settled in numerous countries, but in many they simply integrated with an existing local Jewish community instead of building up their own framework, meaning that their subsequent history cannot be traced even if they appeared in the immigration statistics. This section concerns the development and institutions of Jewish communities that were Hungarian-speaking or tied to Hungarian tradition in some form, based on available data, which are often fragmentary or inaccurate. The main centers are Israel and North America (the United States and Canada), but Western Europe, South America and Australia also became important destinations, particularly after World War II and 1956.

The impetus behind Jewish emigration in the Dualist period, around the turn of the twentieth century, was mainly economic, especially from poorer counties in the northeast, but political motives also became important in the interwar period. Many young people barred from higher education by the 1920 *numerus clausus* legislation in Trianon Hungary set out for Western Europe and North America, some to become world-famous. The Zionist movement and consequent emigration to Palestine were strong in all the successor countries. In Hungary's case this speeded up towards the end of the 1930s with the passage of the Jewish laws, and even then only a few thousand took that route, most preferring to make for the United States. The number who managed to leave during the war was tragically low – between five and ten thousand. The real flood of emigration began only after the Holocaust and peaked in 1947–1949. In the countries in the Soviet sphere of influence, it preceded the communist takeover, when the borders would close, and it coincided with the formation of the state of Israel. This short period was the only one when the majority of the Jews leaving Trianon Hungary went to Israel.

Jewish emigration continued in the communist period as far as political conditions allowed. Some 20,000–25,000 Jews left Hungary after 1956 (a third for Israel, and two thirds for North America, Australia or Western Europe). The emigrants found new homes and a new country, but their departure was an irreparable loss to the inhabitants of the Carpathian Basin.[1]

Israel

It is not widely known that there existed in the second half of the nineteenth century a small Hungarian Jewish community in Palestine, which grew into one of the largest and most prosperous groups in the still-small Jewish community there. This Orthodox community was not Hungarian-speaking, but Hungary as its source country remained an important part of its self-identity. The Hungarian *kollel* (mutual educational and benefit society) founded in Jerusalem in 1858 was headed by Yosef Chaim Sonnenfeld (1849–1932), who was responsible in the 1880s for instituting a quarter of the *Batei Ungarin* (Hungarian houses) in the city. From this community arose also the first Jewish agricultural settlement in Palestine, Petah Tikva.[2] The thinking of the leading intellect among them, Akiva Yosef Schlesinger (1837–1922), resembled in many ways the goals of the later Zionist movement (revival of the Hebrew language, cultivation of the land, self-defense and a new education system), the decisive difference being that Schlesinger and his associates based all this on the strictest observance of Orthodox principles, in farming and community life as well. This was the approach that Szombathely-born Yehoshua Stampfer (1852–1894) took as the first leader of Petah Tikva. His son Shlomo Itzhak became the first mayor of what by then was a city.[3]

Such ultra-Orthodox groups from Hungary and Hasidic Jewish groups came to form the extremist movement that continues to reject on religious grounds the state of Israel, including Israeli citizenship, although they have lived in Israel for several generations. The Neturei Karta (Guardians of the City) movement arose in 1935 and disagreed with the Zionist efforts to found a state and political aims.[4] Its adherents, in the Mea Shearim quarter of Jerusalem and the city of Bnei Brak, receive strong backing from the Satmar Hasidim in the United States.

Quite differently structured and motivated emigrant groups arrived in Palestine from the Carpathian Basin in the interwar period. Most were young and had been prepared for their *aliyah* by a Zionist organization. Many were professionals (engineers and architects) intending to use their expertise to build the country.[5] They were helped in settling and integrating by the Hitachdut Olei Hungaria – Hungarian Immigrants' Association – founded in 1920, which had branches in several cities, and even a Hungarian lending library in Rehovot, and began to produce information materials in the 1940s. The organization still exists as a focal point for the older generation of Holocaust survivors, and it also aims to assist recent arrivals. Hungarian-speaking Jewish immigrants seeking a communal, agricultural life, mainly young Zionists from Transylvania, founded their own kibbutzim, for instance the Dalia kibbutz in 1939.

There are relatively reliable figures for numbers of immigrants into Palestine/Israel. Around 10,000 arrived from Hungary between 1919 and the foundation of the state of Israel in May 1948, another 10,000 in 1948–1949, and some 13,000 in 1950–1957.[6] These relatively small numbers would seem to justify the proposal by Israeli Radio in 1961 to cease broadcasting in Hungarian, but it became clear to the Israeli public in the subsequent bitter debates that many of the Jews arriving from other countries in the Carpathian Basin also had Hungarian as their native language, so that the number of Hungarian-speaking Jews resident in Israel was put between 125,000 and 200,000 or even more. It seems realistic to accept the smaller of those numbers, but it is also worth considering that the biggest Hungarian paper, *Új Kelet*, was selling 20,000 copies a day in 1960, at a time when many other Hungarian publications were appearing: pamphlets from Zionist organizations, publications by the Israeli army and political parties, papers from origin-based communities, Orthodox religious papers, and literary, artistic and social periodicals. These and the books published in Hungarian feature in a bibliography by Zoltán Féder that emphasizes the importance of the Hungarian reading public in Israel.[7] Centers of social life were the Hungarian speakers' clubs that operated in places such as Nahariya, Kfar Saba and Petah Tikva.

After the Holocaust, many societies were started by people who had come from particular cities, such as Oradea, Dej, Sighetu Marmației, Dunajská Streda, Eger, Mád, Baia Mare, Kisvárda and Karcag, to help survivors keep in touch, to immortalize once-flourishing communities in books, and to arrange for cemeteries to be maintained. Another act of commemoration is the Memorial Museum of Hungarian-Speaking Jewry in Safed.[8] It is rare for the children or grandchildren of Hungarian-speaking Israelis to retain the Hungarian language, due to the natural process of assimilation, often speeded up by a decision taken after the Holocaust not to teach their children the language of a society that rejected them.

United States

Historians of American Jewry make mention of immigrants from Hungary from the 1848–1849 War of Independence onwards, and some Jewish veterans of that conflict went on to take part in the American Civil War.[9] Immigration on a large scale (65,000–70,000 people) began in the 1880s and continued until World War I. Most of the immigrants came from impoverished Orthodox families, who earned their living in light industry and retail trading. The focuses were New York and Cleveland, but there were Hungarian Jewish organizations in other cities, such as the Herzl Society and the Máramaros Sickness Benefit Society in Chicago, offering benefits and funeral rites, and organizing social events, rather as the Chevra Kadisha had done for the Diaspora in the Middle Ages. In New York, the immigrants from Hungary occupied a defined block of land in the Jewish quarter of the Lower East Side, and then, as they rose socially, they formed a Hungarian Jewish neighborhood in Yorkville at the turn of the century.[10]

Those arriving in the United States around the turn of the century had a double or triple identity (as American Hungarian Jews) that was altered substantially by events in Hungary in the 1920s. In religion, they integrated into the general Jewish community instead of founding institutions of their own, and socially and politically they distanced themselves increasingly from the general, which is to say predominantly Christian, Hungarian institutions, withdrawing from American Hungarian affairs. So they became Americanized in language and customs more quickly than the other Hungarians.

But this did not mean there was no Hungarian Jewish social life between the wars or after the Holocaust. For instance, there was a Hungarian Jewish weekly newspaper, *Egyleti Élet*. Based on the New York census returns of 1950, it has been estimated there were 31,000 Jews born in Hungary. The city was also where the World Association of Hungarian Jews was formed in 1951,[11] and a Bnai Zion Hungarian Club still operates there.

The paradox of Hungarian Jewish history is that the Satmar Hasidim, one of the Eastern Hungarian Hasidic groups most opposed to linguistic and cultural assimilation, became after World War II the mainstay of Hungarian Jewish tradition in America, and to a lesser extent Israel. Its head, Joel Teitelbaum (1887–1979), settled in New York in 1947, where he reestablished in Brooklyn (Willamsburg and Borough Park) a congregation that has become the world's second-most populous Hasidic group. They stick strictly to their traditions, foods and religious folklore, and to the Hungarian language, although not as their first language, of course.[12]

Canada

There are Hungarian Jewish communities in Montreal and Toronto. Since 1961, the *Menora-Egyenlőség*, describing itself as the newspaper for Hungarian-speaking Jews in North America, has been published in Toronto.

South America

Jews from Hungary arrived in the countries of South American between the world wars and after the Holocaust. Separate organizations were set up in the countries with the largest Hungarian populations – Argentina, Brazil, Venezuela and Uruguay – but these have dwindled or disappeared, due to the lack of further immigration. That has happened, for instance to the Argentinean Association of Hungarian-Speaking Jews in Buenos Aires, once the center for a number of pursuits (sports, drama and charitable events) and publisher of *Hatikva*, a paper that was once distributed throughout the continent, but whose membership is no longer of Hungarian origin.[13] The loss of a Hungarian-language Jewish press leaves only networks of personal contacts. However, the Hungarian News Agency list of Hungarian organizations abroad includes two other organizations, the Community of Hungarian Israelites in Montevideo, and the Hungarian Mother Tongue Israelite Congregation, founded in São Paolo in 1931 [14]

Notes

1   Tamás Stark, *The Hungarian Jewry during the Holocaust and after the Second World War, 1939–1949. A Statistical Review* (New York, 2000), p. 170.
2   "Opening of Hope": Hosea 2.17.
3   David Giladi, "The Jews of Hungary and Eretz Israel," in Anna Szalai, ed., *In the Land of Hagar. The Jews of Hungary: History, Society and Culture* (Tel Aviv, 2002), pp. 128–131.

604 Minority Hungarian Communities in the 20th Century

4 Norman Lamm, "The Ideology of Neturei Karta, according to the Satmarer Version," *Tradition* 12 (1971) 2: 38–53.

5 Alexander Emed, *A magyarországi cionista mozgalom története, 1902–1948* [History of the Hungarian Zionist Movement, 1902–1948] (Budapest, 2002), pp. 115–136.

6 Stark, *The Hungarian Jewry during the Holocaust*, p. 160.

7 Zoltán Féder, *In Israeli Libraries. Two Bibliographies. A: The Bibliography of the Literary Works in the Hungarian Language from Israel, 1928–2002* (Tel Aviv, 2004).

8 *A Magyar Nyelvterületről Származó Zsidóság Emlékmúzeuma.* At http://www.hjm.org.il/. Retrieved August 31, 2010.

9 Robert Perlman, *Bridging Three Worlds. Hungarian-Jewish Americans, 1848–1919* (Amherst, MA, 1991), Chapter 7.

10 *Ibid.*, pp. 135–142. Cf. Gerald Sorin, *A Time for Building. The Jewish People in America* 3 (Baltimore, MA/London, 1992), p. 71.

11 *Magyar Zsidók Világszövetsége.* At www.whjo.org. Retrieved August 31, 2010.

12 Israel Rubin, *Satmar. Two Generations of an Urban Island* (New York, etc., 1997).

13 *Argentínai Magyar-ajkú Zsidók Egyesülete.* Nóra Kovács, "Baráti kapcsolatok hálózatában. Magyar zsidó bevándorlók első és második generációja Buenos Airesben: Integrációs stratégiák és identifikáció" [In a Network of Friendship. The First and Second Generation of Hungarian Jewish Immigrants in Buenos Aires: Integration Strategies and Identification], in Nóra Kovács, ed., *Tanulmányok a diaszpóráról* [Diaspora Studies] (Budapest, 2004), pp. 96–121.

14 Hungarian News Agency MTI press databank, at http://magyarsag. mti.hu/Pages/Organizations.aspx?menu=2. Retrieved August 31, 2010.

3. THE CSÁNGÓS OF MOLDAVIA
Zoltán Ilyés

The ethnic name Csángó, meaning migrant or wandering, is applied to several Hungarian-speaking or originally Hungarian-speaking groups in and outside the Carpathian Basin. The largest are the Roman Catholic Csángós of Moldavia, who dwell beyond the Eastern Carpathians. Along the Upper Trotuş River in the historical county of Ciuc are the Ghimeş Csángós, descendants of eighteenth-century settlers from the Székely Land and Romanians from Moldavia. Furthermore, there are several villages of Hungarians belonging to the Evangelical (Lutheran) faith in the Şapte Sate and Ţara Bârsei districts near Braşov, whom local Székelys call Csángós.

The Moldavian Csángós, "Hungarians beyond the borders" even before Trianon, came to form, together with the Hungarians of Transylvania, the largest Hungarian minority in any country. This might have encouraged them to pursue education in Hungarian language, religious life and culture and strengthened their Hungarian identity – integrating them into the nation, so to speak – but in the event it did not. First, the Romanian nation state pursued a rigid minority policy on the Moldavian Csángós, and such integration was also discouraged by the Moldavian Roman Catholic Church's commitment to the Romanian nation. The Moldavian Csángós do not have a community of experience with the Hungarians of historical Hungary. They do not look back at the period of linguistic renewal and national awakening as being decisive to their national identity.

The Moldavian Csángós themselves are not uniform in their origin, dialect or culture. To this day many are inclined to consider themselves as descendants of the Hungarians of the Etelköz, who absorbed other nomadic groups, notably Cumans. However, the research of Gábor Lükő in 1932–1933 made it clear that some of the ancestors of the Moldavian Hungarians had settled in the

Middle Ages and were heirs to the Hungarian cultures of Szamos and the Tisza Valley, while others had arrived as part of the flight and resettlement of Székelys in the eighteenth century.[1] Based on historical, literary and ethnographic research, Lükő drew the modern distinctions between the archaic culture of the northern Csángós in the Románvásár (Roman) district, that of the southern Csángós around Bacău, and that of the Székely Csángós around Siret, Tazlău and Târgu Trotuş in Neamţ and Bacău Counties.[2]

Pál Péter Domokos from Ciuc, who collected Moldavian folk poetry and folk songs in 1929–1933, helped to reawaken Székely and pan-Hungarian fellowship and to delineate a fifth dialect area of Hungarian folk music.[3] A very thorough critique and account of the source materials was published by László Mikecs in 1941.[4]

The Csángós were subject to strong Romanian nationalist pressure in the interwar period, including the attentions of the Iron Guard, although linguistically they were largely assimilated by then. In 1941 Iosif Petru M. Pal, a Franciscan minister in Moldavia, devised a theory of the Romanian origin of the Moldavian Csángós. This still influences the Romanian concept of the group and contributes to legitimizing the self-image of the Roman Catholic Church elite in Moldavia.[5] The Romanian state commissioned Dr Petre Râmneanţu of the Sibiu Institute of Hygiene (part of the University of Cluj) to investigate the Romanian origin of the Moldavian Csángós using blood tests and measurements of physical and anthropological parameters in the worst tradition of race biology.

During the repatriation of the Bukovina Székelys in 1941–1942, settlers also went to Bačka from some Moldavian Csángó villages, such as Cleja, Vladnic and Găiceana, and were resettled in 1945 in the homes of Swabians deported from villages in Tolna and Baranya Counties. A drought in 1946–1947 brought further moves to Hungary despite an equivocal stance by the Hungarian authorities, fearing a mass migration and the setting of a precedent for migrants from northern Transylvania, and by their Romanian counterparts, from whom came alternate encouragement and discouragement.

Many Csángós acquired emigration permits by bribing officials in Bucharest.[6] After the war, the communist-inspired Hungarian People's Association[7] set up 35 schools teaching in the Csángós' Land. These ran from 1948 to 1959, with intermissions, and are still remembered appreciatively, but they began to shrink and close after 1953 due to opposition from Romanian education officials and the Roman Catholic Church and the dissolution of the Association.[8] Furthermore, the plethora of Romanian loan words in Csángó dialect meant that many pupils struggled with standard literary Hungarian. (One informant who attended junior school in Vladnic said that the pupils could not understand, for instance, the title of a piece in their reader: "Stripping and shelling the sweet corn.")[9] Some of the teachers imported from the Székely Land had no knowledge of Romanian and they were pedagogically unskilled to help them. In the absence of local Hungarian institutions the language was spoken only in the home, and the urge for parents to support the schools was weak. There was little support from cultural events laid on by the Hungarian People's Association, which were replete with communist and atheist propaganda. Romanians in neighboring villages began to see the Csángós as ardent left-wingers, yet in fact they were strongly religious.

Intensive post-war collection of folk songs by János Jagamas, József Faragó and Zoltán Kallós continued for twenty years. Kallós and György Martin also researched the archaic Moldavian/Carpathian dance culture of Romanian origin, while Károly Kós, Judit Szentimrei and Jenő Nagy completed a monograph on Moldavian Csángó folk art. Their work and that of a younger generation of ethnographers – Péter Halász, István Pávai, Ferenc Pozsony and others – turned the Moldavian Csángós into one of the most intensively studied ethnographic groups in Europe. There was interest beyond Hungary particularly in the hitherto unknown old-style folk songs, ballads, laments and archaic prayers, as a valuable heritage of Hungarian culture. The Romanian state has sought to offset this wealth of ethnographic evidence with the publication of works that sought to trace the Csángós back to Transylvanian Romanians and present their ethnographic materials as wholly Romanian. The most notorious of these works was a book on the origins of the Moldavian Csángós by Dumitru Mărtinaş that appeared in 1985, and in English translation in 1999.[10]

The pastoral work of the Transylvanian Franciscans among the Moldavian Csángós had practically ceased by the last third of the sixteenth century. Thereafter the work was done by a separate missionary district staffed mainly by Bulgarian, Polish and Italian priests. When the Roman Catholic Diocese of Iaşi was founded in 1884, Romanian became the general preaching language, and the cantors who had kept alive the prayers and psalms of the Hungarian-speaking congregations in liturgical practice had largely died out. Many stories are told of Roman Catholic priests with Romanian sympathies who knew no Romanian when they were children and still spoke Hungarian to their mothers, yet looked down on the archaic speech mixed with Romanian words of their congregations and forbade the "devil's language" in church. This image of "janissary" priests apparent in Hungarian discussion and even in scholarly works reflects a failure to appreciate the pressure applied to the Moldavian Roman Catholic Church, from the mid-nineteenth century onwards, by the Romanian nation state, and other pressure experienced due to its position as a minority denomination in an overwhelmingly Orthodox society. The Romanian nation state, strengthening its administrative hold, would recognize only the Orthodox Church as the state religion, and used a number of techniques of coercion to persuade the Roman Catholic Church to abandon the using of another language, which was seen as reflecting an ambivalent loyalty to the nation and the Romanian-speaking community. Even in the 1930s and 1940s, its wholly Romanianized priesthood and congregations still suffered threats and discrimination from the state: their loyalty to Romania was questioned and they were threatened with deportation.[11] In many cases it faced simple anti-Catholicism, which impelled it to define itself as Romanian. One response in Moldavia was to adopt a name that was at variance with Catholic universalism, calling itself "Romanian Catholic" (*român catholic*), instead of "Roman Catholic" (*romano-catolic*). These pressures do not excuse the Roman Catholic priests who banned the Hungarian language and harassed its speakers, often against the pleas of their congregations, even calling for assistance from state agencies. In 1938, for instance, the priest of Lespezi had the gendarmerie arrest the cantor of the village, who was rebelling in favor of celebrating mass in Hungarian, and conduct house-to-house searches for prayer books and hymnals in Hungarian.[12]

By 1989 there was no longer widespread support for initiatives to reintroduce the Hungarian-language liturgy into Moldavian Roman Catholic churches: the most committed proponents of this were a group in Pustiana. This may have been due to the categorical dismissal of the idea by the clergy, the way in which generations had grown up with the Romanian liturgy by then, the fact that Romanian was the first language for many of the young, and/or the undeniably active Church life in Moldavia. Nor was there any support from the Vatican, which saw in the proposal only a likelihood of superfluous conflict within the Moldavian clergy that would not make clerical life easier in predominantly Orthodox Romania. All such proposals were simply referred to the Diocese of Iaşi. This left only occasional Hungarian-language masses celebrated in secret by priests from Hungary or Transylvania, and a single, annual Hungarian mass permitted by the diocese, held at Cacica in Bukovina, the most important place of pilgrimage for Moldavian Catholics.

The twentieth-century demography of the Moldavian Csángós, with the degree of language change and assimilation, can be traced in official census returns, but these need to be augmented and contrasted with local linguistic, ethnographic and sociological findings. A historical demographic analysis by Vilmos Tánczos showed that the number of Roman Catholics in Moldavia had risen from 109,953 in 1930 to 240,038 in 1992. These did not include an estimated 50,000 Csángós who had moved to Transylvania or an estimated 15,000 in the rest of Romania. Behind this spectacular increase lie some clear processes of acculturation and assimilation that had begun in the latter half of the nineteenth century. In 1930, 21.7 percent of the Catholics recorded described themselves as Hungarian, but in 1992 this was down to 0.8 percent (1,826 people, of whom some 500 were living in Moldavian Csángó villages and the rest in cities, where they were mainly of Transylvanian origin. In terms of self-identification, therefore, the half-century of political effort by the Romanian nation state and the Diocese of Iaşi was successful. But the often loaded census returns, collected with the priests and local officials prompting the "right" answers, say little about the level of Hungarian-language knowledge or identification with Csángó Hungarian culture. Based on averaging Tánczos's local findings, the number of Csángós who speak Hungarian and live in Moldavia can be put at about 62,000.[13]

Many Csángós who moved to Transylvania communicated in Romanian at work and in daily life, even in the Székely Land. Ferenc Pozsony showed that this was not only because of the material and symbolic advantages of identifying with the Romanians, but also due to threatening attitudes by those in authority: Csángós were forbidden to attend Hungarian-language masses and urged to call for Romanian masses. In daily life, the archaic Hungarian of the Csángós, spiced with loan words from Romanian, may have caused them comprehension problems in their contacts with the Székelys. So the assimilation processes that began in Moldavia were completed in a Hungarian environment.[14]

The figures for self-identification and native language cover identity patterns and degrees of assimilation that vary from village to village. Pozsony, surveying a sample from Ciuc in Bacău County, found that 41.8 percent ticked Hungarian, 23.8 percent Csángó, 5.3 percent Hungarian Csángó, 5.9 percent Romanian Csángó, 13.4 percent Catholic, and 9.8 percent Romanian.[15] Attila Hegyeli in a similar survey in nearby Somuşca found 35.9 percent of respondents describing themselves as Csángó in language, 27.8 percent as Romanian and 22.8 percent as Hungarian, but for national affiliation the responses were 44.3 percent Romanian, 36.1 percent Csángó, 4.6 percent Hungarian, and 3 percent Catholic.[16] Despite the many options offered in the questionnaires, it is clear that Roman Catholicism is the attribute that most respondents wish to emphasize. The findings of identity surveys may also vary according to the ethnic affiliation of the researcher or questioner. This suggests that the Csángós, caught between the opposing efforts of rival nation states and associated readings of history, may behave, understandably, like chameleons, adjusting to the current situation. The rival nation states of Central and Southeastern Europe expect straightforward identities and affiliations, and thus the Csángós, with their "pre-national" form of identity, find themselves unwittingly a subject of contention.

The identities and cultures of the Moldavian Csángós, after centuries of coexistence and Romanian schooling, cannot be judged by the same gauge of national affiliation or the same coordinates of the Carpathian Basin as can be applied in the case of the Transylvanian Hungarians, for example. The archaic culture, old-style Hungarian speech, and wealth of folklore that appeal to outsider Hungarians symbolize to the Moldavian Csángós themselves their backwardness and poverty, which young people especially would like to see the back of as soon as possible. In this situation, and with no system of Hungarian-language institutions, the language of modernization, advancement and self-fulfillment appears to many to be Romanian, or more recently Italian or Spanish.[17]

It would be a mistake to belittle the importance of those who have completed their higher education in Hungarian since 1989, although most never return to their home district, for want of appropriate jobs there. Moldavian Csángós did not take work in Hungary in large numbers, but those who did so likewise contributed to improving the prestige of the Hungarian language, standard of knowledge of it, and strength of identity with the Hungarians. In Vladnic, for instance, the competence of younger people in Hungarian was perceptibly better in 2001 than in 1990, although some were inclined to mix Budapest slang with their Székely-style Hungarian. As for the post-modern development of identity, the Moldavian Roman Catholic Church has to reckon with the secularization of young migrant Csángós. The Church will not regain its earlier reputation or comprehensive role in influence on daily life. This means not only freer morals and a decline in traditional respect for its authority, but greater freedom to change or choose an identity.

The Moldavian Csángós were engaged originally in arable farming and stockbreeding. This occupation pattern began to change only with post-World War II industrialization. Most Csángó women took very low-paid work for the local collective farm, while the men commuted to nearby cities or to construction sites or factories elsewhere in the Regat or in Transylvania, where whole families would sometimes move from the 1970s onwards. The Moldavian Csángó villages were simpler and poorer than those of the Romanians, due to large families, isolation, qualification disadvantages, and low inter-generational employment mobility. After 1989 came the closure of many workplaces that had employed Csángó men. (From Vladnic alone, there were three busloads of commuters to Bacău, but by 2001 only two or three villagers were still doing it.) The urgent need to earn a livelihood led to migration of workers to Hungary, Israel, Italy and Spain on such a scale that the Roman Catholic Diocese of Iaşi sent priests to Italy to cater for the Csángós there.

The Association of Moldavian Csángó-Hungarians,[18] founded in 1990 to protect their interests and promote traditional culture based on their language, cited Romanian school legislation in petitioning for teaching of Hungarian language, literature and culture to children of parents requesting it. Despite repeated threats and verbal or occasional physical aggression, applications for tuition in Hungarian were made by the parents of 7 pupils in Lespezi, 29 in Pustiana, and 25 in Cleja. The education office in Bacău gathered 598 signatures for a petition in Lespezi stating that the teaching of Hungarian was superfluous. The Association then started extra-curricular Hungarian tuition in village halls and private homes – in 2000 in Cleja, and in 2001 in Somuşca, Pustiana, Galbeni, Fundu Răcăciuni and Gioseni. The county education office then tried to obstruct this through litigation against the organizations and foundations providing the instruction, and local teachers of Hungarian were harassed by the local police. The situation normalized after the Council of Ministers of the Council of Europe adopted a resolution affording protection to Csángó culture in 2001, and the Romanian authorities permitted two weekly lessons of optional Hungarian between seven and eight a. m. in the local state schools. In the 2005–2006 school year there were 1,187 pupils taking part in the scheme: 725 in state schools and 369 as an extra-curricular activity.[19]

There are several organizations and cultural associations that have formed since 1989 to assist in sending Moldavian Csángó students to Hungarian-taught schools in Transylvania and Hungary, find hostel accommodation, and award scholarships. Pupils in the first eight grades are sent regularly to camps conducted in Hungarian in Transylvania and Hungary. On the Romanian side, the idea of the Romanian origin and culture of the Csángós is propagated by the Dumitru Martinaş Association, founded in 2001.

The Csángó festival organized annually since 1990 in Jászberény and the Csángó ball held since 1997 in Budapest are the gatherings of Moldavian Csángó folklore, where the people of Hungary can become more familiar with Csángó instrumental folk music and dances, showing a fair amount of Romanian influence as well, and can listen to and learn the Moldavian folk songs.

The questions of language and minority rights for the Csángós have become topics in European discussions on minority rights and the protection of endangered minorities. On May 4, 2001, the Finnish rapporteur Tytti Isohookana Asunmaa presented a report entitled "Csángó Minority Culture in Romania" to the Parliamentary Assembly of the Council of Europe, based on an extensive visit in 1999, which led the Council of Europe to formulate a nine-point recommendation to Romania, calling among other things to native-language teaching, Church masses in the "Csángó language," recognition and support for Csángó organizations, presentation of Csángó culture in Romania, and assistance for regional economic renewal.[20]

* * *

Apart from the Moldavian Csángós, three other groups in Romania have been called Csángós colloquially.

The Ghimeş Csángós live in the villages of Lunca de Sus, Lunca de Jos, Ghimeş-Făget, Cădăresti and Coşnea in the Ghimeş Pass on the borders of Moldavia and Transylvania, where their ancestors migrated in the seventeenth and eighteenth centuries from Ciuc Székely and Moldavian Hungarian and Romanian villages. They are engaged mainly in upland stockbreeding and forestry. Isolation has meant that their folk culture preserves an ancient layer of Székely peasant culture.[21]

The Ţara Bârsei or Seven-Village Csángós call themselves Hungarians but are called Csángós by others. They are the surviving descendants of eleventh-century Pecheneg border guards in villages in the southeast extremity of Ţara Bârsei, near Braşov: the four villages that make up today's Săcele (Baciu, Turcheş, Cernatu and Satulung), as well as Tărlungeni, Zizin and Purcăreni. Several other Ţara Bârsei villages are also grouped with them: Apaţa, Crizbav, Satu Nou, Hălmeag and Jimbor. They adopted the Evangelical (Lutheran) faith of the Brassó Saxons. Many emigrated to Romania before World War I. They were prominent as drivers of hired carriages and taxi cabs in Bucharest in the 1930s.[22]

Also informally referred to in the past as Csángós were the *Bukovina Székelys*. Several thousand Székelys had migrated from Csík (Ciuc) and Háromszék (Trei Scaune) to Moldavia after the *Siculicidium* or Mádéfalva massacre of 1764, in the reign of Maria Theresa, but were resettled in the province of Bukovina (today Suceava County) by the Habsburg court in 1776–1786. The province, which had been ceded to Austria under the first partition of Poland in 1775, was relatively sparsely populated. The habit of referring to them as Csángós spread in the Hungarian press in the 1880s, but was never adopted by the Bukovina Székelys themselves. Two of these settlements, Laudonfalva (Bălcăuţi) and Tomnátik (Tomnatek), were abandoned at the end of the nineteenth century, but Fogadjisten (Iacobeşti), Istensegíts (Ţibeni), Hadikfalva (Dorneşti), Andrásfalva (Măneuţi) and Józseffalva (Vornicenii Mari) became severely overpopulated. A campaign to resettle the inhabitants in Hungary led to the foundation of the Lower Danube villages of Hertelendyfalva (Vojlovica), Sándoregyháza (Ivanovo), and Székelykeve (Skorenovac), but there were also moves to Gyorok (Ghioroc) in Arad County (1888–1892), Déva (Deva, 1910), Vajdahunyad (Hunedoara, 1892), Babsa (Babşa) in Temes County (1900), Vice (Viţa) in Kolozs County, Magyarnemegye (Nimigea de Jos) in Beszterce-Naszód County (1900), Marosludas (Luduş) in Maros County (1905), and Sztrigyszentgyörgy (Streisângeorgiu) and Csernakeresztúr (Cristur) in Hunyad County (1910). This affected 6,000–7,000 people in all. In 1930, under Romanian rule, there were 15,650 people in the Hungarian villages of Bukovina. The remainder were moved by the Hungarian state to the occupied region of Bačka in Serbia in 1941, but in the autumn of 1944 they had to flee into Transdanubia (in Hungary), where about 13,000 of them moved onto smallholdings in Tolna County vacated in 1946 by deported Swabians. The descendants of the Bukovina Székelys today live along the Lower Danube (in the Pančevo district of Vojvodina) and in the villages around Déva and in Transdanubia, mainly in Bonyhád, Kakasd, Tevel and Egyházaskozár.[23]

Notes

1   Gábor Lükő, *A moldvai csángók I. A csángók kapcsolatai az erdélyi magyarsággal* [Moldavian Csángós. I. The Csángós' Ties with the Transylvanian Hungarians] (Budapest, 2001).

2   Ferenc Pozsony, *A moldvai csángó magyarok* [The Moldavian Csángó Hungarians] (Budapest, 2005), pp. 8–23.

3   Pál Péter Domokos, *A moldvai magyarság* [Moldavian Hungarians], 5th ed. (Budapest, 1987).

4   László Mikecs, *Csángók* [Csángós] (Budapest, 1989).

5   M. Iosif Petru Pal, *Originea Catolicilor din Moldova* [Origins of the Moldavian Catholics] (Săbăoani-Roman, 1941).

6   Pozsony, *A moldvai csángó magyarok*, pp. 49–51.

7   *Magyar Népi Szövetség.*

8   Pozsony, *A moldvai csángó magyarok*, pp. 52–55.

9   *"A kukorica hántása és fosztása."*

10   Dumitru Mărtinaş, *The Origins of the Changos* (Iaşi, 1999).

11   Marius Diaconescu, "The Identity Crisis of the Moldavian Catholics – between Politics and Historic Myth. A Case Study: the Myth of Romanian Origin," in Sándor Ilyés, Lehel Peti and Ferenc Pozsony, eds., *Lokális és transznacionális csángó életvilágok* (Cluj-Napoca, 2008) (= Idem: *Local and Transnational Csángó Lifeworlds* (Cluj-Napoca, 2008)), pp. 81–94.

12   Pozsony, *A moldvai csángó magyarok*, pp. 86–87.

13   Vilmos Tánczos, "A moldvai csángók lélekszámáról" [On the Numbers of Moldavian Csángós], in Ferenc Pozsony, ed., *Csángósors* [Csángó Destiny] (Budapest, n.d.), pp. 7–32.

14   Pozsony, *A moldvai csángó magyarok*, pp. 55–56.

15   Ibid., p. 157.

16   Attila Hegyeli, "Hat nemzetiség egyetlen faluban? Egy moldvai csángó falu etnikai identitásáról" [Six National Groups in One Village? Ethnic Identity of a Moldavian Csángó Village], in Pozsony, ed., *Csángósors*, pp. 83–96, 88.

17   See Balázs Boross, "'Majd egyszer lészen, de nem most'" ["One Day, but Not Now"], *Pro Minoritate* (2002) 4: 48–62; Pál Hatos, "Szempontok a csángókutatás kulturális kontextusainak értelmezéséhez" [Criteria for Interpreting the Cultural Contexts of Csángó Research], *Pro Minoritate* (2002) 4: 5–16; Vilmos Tánczos, "Szappan a kredenc sarkán, avagy a csángókérdés tudománya és politikája" [Soap on the Sideboard Corner, or the Science and Politics of the Csángó Question], *Kisebbségkutatás* (2001) 1: 53–62.

18   *Moldvai Csángómagyarok Szövetsége/Asociaţia Maghiarilor Ceangăi din Moldova.*

19   See Pozsony, *A moldvai csángó magyarok*, pp. 195–200.

20   Tytti Isohookana-Asunmaa, "Recommendation 1521 (2001). Csango Minority Culture in Romania," in Klara Papp-Farkas, ed., *Endangered Minority Cultures in Europe* (Budapest, 2002), pp. 131–133; Tytti Isohookana-Asunmaa, "Report – Csango Minority Culture in Romania Doc. 9078," in Klara Papp-Farkas, ed., *Endangered Minority Cultures in Europe* (Budapest, 2002), pp., 109–130.

21   László Kósa, "A gyimesi csángók hagyományos élete" [Traditional Life of the Csángós of Gyimes], in Zoltán Kallós and György

Martin, eds., *Tegnap a Gyimesben jártam...* [Yesterday I Went to Gyimes...] (Budapest, 1988), pp. 5–17; Zoltán Ilyés, "Identity as Resource in a Small Region: the Example of Gyimes], in Győző Cholnoky, ed., *Minorities Research. A Collection of Studies by Hungarian Authors 2006.* No. 8. (Budapest, 2006), pp. 29–38.

22 Lehel István Kovács, *Hétfalusi csángó tájszógyűjtemény* [Dialect Word List of the Seven-Village Csángós] (Cluj-Napoca, 2005); Emese-Gyöngyvér Veres, *Barcasági körkép. Egy kulturális antropológus terepmunka-tanulmánya*i [Review of Ţara Bârsei. A Cultural-Anthropological Fieldwork Study] (Budapest, 1996).

23 Bertalan Andrásfalvy, "A bukovinai székelyek kultúrájáról" [Bukovina Székely Culture], in Gyula Ortutay, ed., *Népi kultúra, népi társadalom* [Folk Culture, Folk Society] (Budapest, 1973), pp. 7–23; Ádám Sebestyén, *A bukovinai székelység tegnap és ma* [Bukovina Székelys Past and Present] (Szekszárd, 1989).

4. HUNGARIAN-SPEAKING GYPSIES IN THE CARPATHIAN BASIN

Péter Szuhay

The number of Gypsies in Hungary and in the neighboring countries is not known precisely. The numbers estimated by the researchers are about three times higher than the numbers of self-identified Roma recorded in the censuses. In 2001 fewer than 200,000 people declared themselves as Gypsy/Roma in Hungary, while the number of the persons considered or regarded as Gypsies by the majority society was about 600,000. The ethnic structure of the Gypsies in Romania (especially in Transylvania), Slovakia, Ukraine's Transcarpathia and Serbia's Vojvodina is more complex and less homogeneous than that of the Gypsies in Hungary.

Gypsies in the neighboring countries do not always speak a common language with Gypsies of Hungary, whether the latter are Vlach Gypsies (Roma), whose mother tongue is Romani, along with Hungarian, or the Boyash Gypsies ("trough-carving" Gypsies), whose mother tongue is a dialect of Romanian in addition to Hungarian. Hungarian in such cases serves as the intermediary language. The same role is not fulfilled by Romanian in Transylvania or by Slovak in Slovakia, because in the neighboring countries there are Gypsy groups who speak the language of the local or regional majority, but do not speak the dominant language of the whole country.

If we consider the Gypsies (Roma) living in the Carpathian Basin who declare themselves as such, two groups can be distinguished among them (in terms of a distinction adopted as a scientific convention): those who speak one of the Gypsy languages or dialects, and those who do not speak a Gypsy language. Most speakers of the Gypsy languages speak Romani, previously known in Hungary as the Vlach Gypsy language. This language has several dialects. Dominant in eastern regions (including Transylvania) is Kalderash (Kelderás), and Lovari (Lovári) in Slovakia and Hungary, but there are groups who speak the Cerhári and Másári dialects of equal importance.

Other languages spoken by the Gypsies are the Carpathian Gypsy language, which is spoken by the earliest Gypsy groups who settled in the former Nógrád, Hont and Gömör Counties, and the language of the Sinti, strongly influenced by German, and spoken in the western part of the Carpathian Basin. Most researchers recognize as a Gypsy language the Boyash tongue, which largely preserves the Romanian language in its state before the language reforms that took place during the nineteenth and the twentieth century. This language developed in isolation from the Romanian-speaking environment on the territories of present-day Hungary, Slovakia and even Croatia, and it is spoken by the groups of the trough-carving Gypsies.

All speakers of a Gypsy language also speak another language as their native tongue. They rarely show uncertainty about their identity, considering and calling themselves Gypsies or Roma, but in mixed ethnic areas they may speak the locally dominant language to the same level as their mother tongue and another widely spoken local language as well.

Apart from the language differences, the main distinctions among Gypsies are those of lifestyle, which can be both chosen and inherited. They can be distinguished by whether they are settled or nomadic, and by the traditional occupations practiced The terminology used in Hungary mostly differs from that which is used in Transylvania, where it is customary to talk of "tent-dwelling" Gypsies and "house-dwelling" Gypsies. The latter are called "house-dwelling" Gypsies – by themselves, and also by the "tent-dwelling" Gypsies, or by the majority population – if they have been settled for a long time, and if they are firmly integrated into the local social division of labor, but have not merged (or been accepted) into the majority society. "Tent-dwelling" Gypsies settled only a few generations ago. Their migrations and migrant trades are remembered at least on a mythical level. They keep track of tribal or clan ancestry, and typically they have a strong sense of Gypsy identity. "House-dwelling" Gypsies tend to be agricultural day-laborers or casual workers, doing tasks for peasants on the farm or around the house; they might also be musicians, adobe-makers, basket-makers or blacksmiths. Most "tent-dwelling" Gypsies used to be coppersmiths or tinkers. Ethnographers label them as Kalderash (Kelderás). Many call themselves "Gábor" Gypsies, even adding that they are "noble Székely Gypsies," descendants of Áron Gábor (as has been described recently).

One third of all the Gypsies of the world live in the Carpathian Basin, as Károly Kocsis noted at the beginning of his account of the demographic situation of the Roma after 1990.[1] The latest censuses counted 579,000 people (2 percent of the population) who identified themselves as members of the Gypsy nationality and whom 291,000 (1 percent) stated that they have Gypsy language as their native language. The first figure includes 246,000 in Transylvania, 90,000 in Slovakia, and 14,000 in Transcarpathia. Expert estimates from 2001, however, put the number of those who are regarded as Gypsies in the Carpathian Basin to 2.6 million, of whom 1.4–1.5 million live in Transylvania, 600,000 live in Hungary, and 380,000 live in Slovakia. This means that some 9 percent of the total population are Gypsies, and they probably outnumber the Hungarians in Transylvania. "They are concentrated mainly in the northeast and east of the Carpathian Basin, not in the mountains, but in the hilly areas on the rim of the Great Plain: the Gömör, Spiš, Šariš, South Zemplén and Košice districts of Slovakia, Nógrád, Borsod-Abaúj-Zemplén and Szabolcs-Szatmár-Bereg Counties and the mid-Tisza district in Hungary, and in Romania in the mainly flat edges of Satu Mare, Bihor, Arad and Timiş Counties, and the Transylvanian Basin. Elsewhere there are appreciable numbers in Hungary's Baranya and Somogy Counties, in the Serbian parts of the Banat and Belgrade, and in Budapest and Bratislava. Despite east-to-west and village-to-city migration, the Gypsies today live mainly in the same places as they did when they were surveyed in 1893. Gypsies live mainly in less urbanized, traditional rural areas with a mixed ethnic and religious structure, where it used to be relatively easy for them to find a place in the local social division of labor. […] The number of those with a declared Gypsy affiliation grew most between 1991 and 2001 in northern Hungary, the Budapest region (50–70 percent), the Partium (34–39 percent), the Hungarian-inhabited districts of southern Slovakia (51 percent), Bačka (57 percent) and Prekmurje (51 percent), due mainly to natural increase, economically motivated immigration and, not least, ethnic dissimilation. The last entails a mounting awareness of being Gypsies among people who had hitherto recorded themselves as Hungarians. More and more Hungarian-speaking Gypsies are declaring themselves Gypsies, especially in southern Slovakia, Eastern Hungary, and the Hungarian-inhabited districts of Satu Mare, Bihor, Sălaj and Arad Counties in Romania."

In the period up to the end of World War II the main socio-political development for the Gypsies, as well as for the Jews, was the Holocaust and its antecedents. We can reconstruct the events for each country using the book by Barna Purcsi.[2]

In Romania notions of "racial biology" began to spread in the 1930s, along with concepts such as "ethnic purity," "ethnic groups of a lower rank" and "ethnic promiscuity." The "minorities of non-European origin," the "burdensome minorities," in other words the "Gypsies, Jews and others" were perceived as "bio-ethnic peril" in Romania at that time. This was the beginning of the modern racial ideology proclaiming the "racial superiority of the Romanians." The annexation of the northern part of Transylvania by Hungary, after the Second Vienna Award, spared the Hungarian-speaking Gypsies from some of the wartime suffering undergone by those in Romania, where first 11,441 nomadic Gypsies and then 13,176 settled Gypsies were deported.

After Germany occupied Serbia, the military government ordered in 1941 the registration of the Gypsies, and they were forced to wear a yellow armband marked Zigeuner (Gypsy). Inscriptions prohibiting Jews and Gypsies sprang up on the streets, in stores, on buses and streetcars. Incidents provoked by the German military and executions of groups taken hostage had caused the deaths of 10,000–15,000 people of Gypsy origin in Serbia by 1942.

Registration of Gypsies in Croatia was ordered in July 1941 by Minister of the Interior Andrija Artuković. Inscriptions appeared in public places forbidding the entry of "Serbs, Jews, nomadic Gypsies, and dogs." The racial policy of the Ustaša regime aimed the creation of a Croatia consisting of Catholic Croats and Muslim Bosnians and the elimination of such "alien elements" as the Orthodox Serbs, the Jews and the Gypsies. They stated the following "The basis of the Ustaša movement is religion. We have three million bullets for the minorities: the Serbs, the Jews and the Gypsies." The Ministry of the Interior ordered in August 1941 that the so-called "white Gypsies" (the Muslims) should not be harmed and they should be treated as Aryan. This decree was widely flouted by the Ustaša authorities and death squads. In September 1941 the Ustaša began to round up the Bosnian Gypsies, the Serbs and the Jews for deportation to Jasenovac, Đjakovo, Stara Gradiška and Loborgrad. In 1942 the kiln of the Jasenovac Pottery was adapted to operate as a crematorium. In May they began cremating the dead bodies there but the weak and the ill were thrown into the brick kilns while they were still alive. Gypsies were also brought to Jasenovac from other camps, such as Stara Gradiška.

In Košice, Czechoslovakia, there was a trial in 1924–1929 in which 19 Gypsies from Moldavia were accused of cannibalism – the accusations proved to be unfounded but this episode helped to whip up anti-Gypsy feeling. In 1927 legislation was introduced against nomadic Gypsies, requiring them to register at the place where they would spend the night and ask for residence permits. The proclaimed purpose was to "civilize" the Gypsies, but the outcome was to deprive them of their civil rights. The authorities issued 39,000 Gypsy identity documents in 1936. Southern Slovakia, with most of Czechoslovakia's Hungarian-speaking Gypsies, was reannexed to Hungary under the First Vienna Award of 1938, and thereafter they shared the fate of the other Gypsies in Hungary. The Gypsies and Jews in Slovakia were conscripted into the labor service by an order issued on January 18, 1940. Gypsies were banned from entering parks, coffee houses or restaurants, and from using public transport.

"Forced-labor establishments" were set up in the vicinity of the factories where there was a labor shortage, and the Gypsies and other "anti-social elements" were interned there. In 1941 municipal authorities were required to expel Gypsies. The Gypsies of Slovakia actively supported the uprising against the Tiso government in the summer of 1944.

The Austrian gendarmerie counted the Gypsies in Burgenland on two occasions, arriving at figures of 5,480 in 1925 and 6,032 in 1927. Other figures from the same period showed 5,188 and 7,164, with another 1,600 living elsewhere in the country. Yet other estimates put the number of Gypsies outside Burgenland at around 3,000. The criminal police ordered the arrest of 3,000 Gypsies from Burgenland – 2,000 men of working age and 1,000 women – and their deportation to concentration camps. In 1939, 440 Burgenland women were interned at a camp in Ravensbrück for trading or working without a license, or as "asocials" engaged in telling fortunes. All those were declared "asocial" who avoided police investigations and interrogations, those who married non-Gypsies and fled to avoid sterilization, and even those who left their homes without a permit. By April 30, 1945, when the camp was liberated, it held an estimated 5,000 Gypsy women. On March 1, 1943, began the deportation of Gypsies from Austria (they were overwhelmingly Hungarian-speaking Gypsies from Burgenland) to the "Gypsy family camp" in Auschwitz–Birkenau. Deportations were completed by the end of the month.

The post-war position of Hungary in the Soviet political sphere brought an end to open persecution of the Gypsies. The monograph by Zoltan Barany has been used as a source for the following country-by-country account of events related to Gypsies.[3]

Romania sought to settle the nomadic groups at first and later started to disperse the larger Gypsy settlements. Masses of unskilled Gypsies, similarly to the case of Hungary, were drawn into the post-war agricultural collectivization and extensive industrialization, which lent their situation the appearance of assimilation. In fact, the question of awarding the Gypsies national minority status never arose, and policy-makers hardly dealt with their situation after the mid-1970s.

The Roma in the countries of the former Yugoslavia were probably in the most favorable position in the region. Nobody sought to settle the nomadic groups. The solution to any potential problems came through economic conditions in which agricultural communities no longer required migrant artisans or traders, meaning that the nomads were "settled" naturally by a drastic fall in demand for their services. Furthermore, the Gypsies were assisted towards equality by the multicultural nature of Yugoslav society, with its range of ethnic, religious and, to a certain extent, linguistic allegiances. In 1981, they were granted the same communal status as the Albanians or the Hungarians. This gave rise to several dozen social and cultural associations and brought the Gypsies into public life. In some areas, the Romani language began to be taught in schools and Romani radio and television programs were broadcast. The name Roma was used for the first time here in order to replace the term Gypsy, which was considered pejorative.

Emphasis in Czechoslovakia was placed on two political goals: providing full employment for Gypsies capable of work, and dissolving Gypsy settlements (there were around 1,300). There were also campaigns against illiteracy and the "parasitic way of life." About 221,000 people were registered as Gypsies at the end of the 1940s, most in the east of the country. The renewed plans for the dispersed resettlement meant regularly and methodically moving Gypsies from settlements in Slovakia to the western (in other words Czech) territories, where there were relatively few of them. By 1968 this program had clearly foundered on inadequate funding, widespread social protests, sabotage at the middle levels of power, and resistance from the Roma themselves. The Gypsies were then given national-minority treatment for a couple of years, and allowed, indeed encouraged, to set up their own agricultural cooperatives and social and cultural associations, but these were all disbanded in 1973 on the grounds that they had not performed their function of integration. The authorities returned to the earlier approach of assimilation, as part of which hundreds of Gypsy women with several children were sterilized after 1980.

In Burgenland the conception of the state about the Roma remained unchanged after World War II. The Ministry of the Interior issued an order for resettling the Gypsies, as asocial elements and potential criminals, as late as 1948. In 1993, the Roma and the Sinti were recognized as ethnic groups; the schools act of 1994 enabled mother-tongue education for Roma, and a People's College of Burgenland Roma was founded. Romani can also be used in writing; the Graz University linguistics faculty has produced a Romani–German dictionary.

Among the citizens of the Soviet Union living in Transcarpathia (which is now part of the post-Soviet Ukraine) there are estimated to live some 20,000–30,000 Roma. They have lived in almost all parts of Transcarpathia for centuries, the largest communities being in Mukacheve, Uzhhorod, Berehove, Khust, Chop and Rativtsy. The majority of them speak Hungarian, but those living closer to the Carpathians have shifted their language to Ukrainian.

Writing about the contemporary economies of the Gypsies, Alain Reyniers noted the following: "Gypsy members of the intelligentsia, community representatives, and a stratum of proletarianized Gypsies working in industry and agriculture emerged over the four decades of communism. However, the Gypsies as an ethnic group have not developed harmoniously. Although their social stratification has become more complex, the marginalization of the majority has become more severe. This was accelerated by the disappearance of their traditional trades – pursued by only a small number of Gypsy craftsmen – coupled with the disintegration of the traditional social structures that had hitherto governed their relations with non-Gypsies, and the growing uncertainty of their position on the job market. The extensive industrialization of the 1950s and 1960s called for large quantities of unskilled labor. Gypsies found work in industry on a mass scale, but they still received the less socially valued, badly paid jobs, for which qualifications were not required and which other members of society were not prepared to do (street sweeping, cleaning, grave-digging). Their mass employment in jobs requiring few qualifications had negative effects. Regular earnings from such jobs did not encourage Gypsy families to direct their children towards the school system, of which they remained suspicious, while leaving them with only a toehold on the labor market."[4]

At the end of the 1980s, large numbers of Gypsies in Romania followed the earlier example of the Saxons in seeking refuge in Germany, while others moved into the Romanian villages that the Saxons had abandoned. According to a report by the German authorities in 1990, almost 18,000 Roma from Romania had requested asylum; two years later the number had reached 34,000. The years that followed the collapse of the Ceauşescu regime increased the potential migration in subsequent years, but it also heightened the ethnic tensions between the Hungarians or Romanians and the Gypsies. Probably the worst incident occurred in 1993 in Hădăreni, where a crowd of 750 Hungarians and Romanians murdered four Roma, chased out 130 others, and set 17 houses on fire.[5]

Following the dissolution of the two Czechoslovak republics, the Roma-related conflict increased between the successor states. The Czech Republic sought simply to repatriate to Slovakia the Roma who had originated from there. The Czech Republic is the country in the region that takes the hardest policy line against the Roma. There and in Slovakia attacks on the Roma occur most frequently. In July 1995, some 30 skinheads attacked local Roma residents in Hronský Beňadik and set one Roma youth on fire: he later died because of his burns. Significant Roma emigration began in the second half of the 1990s, initially to Britain and Ireland, and later to Scandinavia and Canada. This prompted several countries to reintroduce visa requirements for visitors from Slovakia, for longer or shorter periods. A cut in social benefits in the spring of 2004 led to severe riots and looting among the Gypsies of Trebišov and a drastic police response.[6]

The stance of rural Hungarians towards Gypsies is often one of contempt and rejection. Yet Hungarians collectively expect the Gypsies to "rally round" at census time, and by asserting their secondary identity as Hungarian-speakers lend support to Hungarian minority efforts to assert educational, cultural and language rights. And the Roma seem increasingly unwilling to do this.

Notes

1 Károly Kocsis, "A Kárpát-medence változó etnikai arculata (1989–2002)" [The Changing Ethnic Face of the Carpathian Basin (1989–2002)], *Kisebbségkutatás* (2003) 4: 712–713.

2 Barna Gyula Purcsi, *A cigánykérdés „gyökeres és végleges megoldása". Tanulmányok a XX. századi „cigánykérdés" történetéből* [A "Radical and Final Solution" to the Gypsy Question. Studies on the Twentieth-Century History of the Gypsy Question] (Debrecen, 2004).

3 Zoltan Barany, *The East European Gypsies. Regime Change, Marginality, and Ethnopolitics* (Cambridge, 2002), pp. 118–129.

4 Alain Reyniers, "Gondolatok a cigány gazdaságról" [Thoughts on the Gypsy Economy], *Eszmélet* (2002): 54. http://www.freeweb.hu/eszmelet/54/reyniers54.html.

5 István Haller, "Hadrév – hat év után" [Hădăreni – Six Years On], *Korunk* (1999): 9.

6 Csaba Dömötör, "Felszínre törő roma indulatok Szlovákiában" [Roma Passions Emerging in Slovakia], *Européer*, March 8, 2004.

5. THE HUNGARIAN DIASPORA
BEYOND THE CARPATHIAN BASIN UP TO 1989
Ilona Kovács

The Hungarian diaspora in the West began with a surge of economic emigration at the turn of the twentieth century, before the break-up of historical Hungary, and was directed mainly towards America, particularly the United States. Up until the outbreak of World War I, it caused an annual average of 100,000–120,000 people to leave the country. Even if the returnees and the numbers for minorities are deducted, it meant a total loss of some 460,000 native speakers of Hungarian. Those seeking a new home were mainly from the peasantry and the working and artisan classes, who were prompted by the unfavorable pattern of ownership and poor economic conditions. Some 90 percent of the emigrants sought passage to the United States.[1] There was also appreciable pre-1914 emigration to Canada, of an estimated 15,000.[2] Post-war US immigration restrictions meant that only about 40,000 Hungarians arrived there between 1920 and 1940; the remaining emigrants went to European countries, South America or Canada instead. The favored countries were Argentina, Brazil and Venezuela in South America and Germany, France, Belgium and the Netherlands in Europe. But by then the emigration was not confined to manual workers. It was joined after the defeat of the 1919 revolution by a stratum of left-wing intelligentsia, and in the second half of the period by many Jewish artists, writers, journalists, scientists and industrialists fleeing from the discriminatory laws. The centers of the left-wing émigrés were Vienna, Paris, Berlin and London, from where some went to fight in the Spanish Civil War.

After World War II the center of the left-wing and democratic Hungarian intelligentsia abroad became Paris. Only after World War II did large numbers of Hungarian emigrants make for Australia. The post-war Western diaspora was swollen by two main waves of emigration. The '45-ers included the "national emigration" of Tibor Eckhardt and his circle and the '47-ers the "democratic emigration" of Ferenc Nagy, Béla Varga, Imre Kovács and their associates. At the end of the war in 1945, some 120,000 Hungarian refugees remained in Austria and Germany in prisoner-of-war and refugee camps. The smaller, but politically significant, wave after 1947 was made up of people who had acknowledged the 1945 constitution and contributed to the first stage of Hungary's democratic transition, but left as the coalition government collapsed and the Communist Party took over. Most were politicians of the Smallholders', Peasants' or Social Democratic Parties and rightful owners of nationalized assets. The two waves together became known as the DPs (displaced persons): it took a new agency, the IRO, and several years to distribute them among Western countries, many not leaving the camps until 1950 or 1951. The varying estimates allow only broad figures to be given of how many went where: 26,000 to the United States, 10,000 to Canada, 3,000 to Australia (but according to one source 14,000), 8,000 to France, 5,000 to Belgium, 4,000 to Britain, 3,000 to Argentina (but according to another source 14,000), and 2,300 to Sweden. Israel placed no restrictions on immigration of Hungarian Jews, taking in some 100,000 over subsequent decades.[3]

The development and survival of the diaspora communities resulted not only from economic and political conditions at home, but also from labor demand and the attitude taken to aliens and minorities in the recipient countries. The earliest Hungarian communities in the West grew up in the United States and Canada before World War I. Immigrants worked in mines and factories and on railway construction. In Canada they were recruited to found new agricultural communities. The many millions of European immigrants into the United States placed a considerable burden on the original Anglo-Saxon society. In many cities 70 percent of the population changed. The newcomers brought with them foreign languages and customs, which met with resistance and debate among existing Americans, although immigrant labor was needed urgently as industry burgeoned. The newcomers were defenseless against their employers, lived under tough conditions, and formed a despised section in society, but they earned more than they had at home and found democratic rights and freedoms that they had not had before. They were free to build their communities, use their languages, and operate their institutions. Although they were expected to integrate, fit in, and respect the recipient society, and received various forms of assistance and training for doing so, assimilation was not required until the second generation. The public stance changed in World War I, when society felt threatened, and although the feeling died down after the war, economic depression led later to strict rules of entry into Canada and immigration quotas in the United States.

After both world wars, most recipient countries sought manual laborers, most of whom started on the lowest rung of the social ladder, irrespective of their previous position or qualifications. Success for immigrants came in most cases from industry, attitude, talent and good fortune. Europe was able to absorb only a smaller quantity of refugees after World War II, while the United States would accept immigrants from Hungary, an enemy country during the war, only after political checks and guarantees of a livelihood. The South American countries, on the other hand, would take refugee labor and talent without restriction. Migrants and political émigrés after both world wars met with problems of livelihood, language and acceptance of their qualifications, but in no country of Europe or the Americas did they face a crude policy of assimilation, although stronger pressure was applied in Australia. However, a conscious policy of toleration and a multicultural concept of society did not appear in the legal and institutional system until the 1960s and 1970s.[4]

Early immigrants from all countries settled close to each other in blocs, so that veritable Hungarian quarters and settlements arose. Those with a sense of business set up Hungarian workers' hostels (boarding houses), stores, bars, banks, printing presses and other service provisions. Hungarian was spoken within the community, with local schoolchildren often acting as interpreters for adults in the outside world. These Hungarian communities were replenished after World War I with new arrivals, but the post-World War II refugees and the second generation, with their higher qualifications and better language skills, attained higher positions in society and soon moved out to better neighborhoods and became scattered. The old Hungarian streets and quarters emptied and took on a new demographic complexion. The process was hastened by changes of economic structure in mining and industrial areas.

Although there were internationalist socialists, liberals and communists among the emigrants to America and Europe, most had a national commitment, including the Jews. The principles were those of 1848 and Lajos Kossuth, and their big day of celebration was March 15.[5] Among the arrivals after World War II were some extreme right-wingers and anti-Semites, but they met with strong resistance in the forums of the national conservative émigrés. The earlier immigrants had not been devoid of political differences, but the refugees and émigrés after World War II differed widely in their views. This often caused clashes and debates, especially between '45-ers and '47-ers, and in some cases with the liberal democratic refugees of 1919 found in the circles around Oszkár Jászi and Mihály Károlyi, or with the extreme right wing. The frictions became apparent in their organizations and press as well.

The post-World War II Western diaspora members were united in their rejection of the Soviet-installed communist regime of Mátyás Rákosi. Organization of political activity and international protest began in the refugee camps. Of the many political bodies, one that played something of the role of an émigré parliament was the Hungarian National Committee,[6] based in New York and headed by Béla Varga. Consisting of leading Hungarians who had emigrated before the war, having played some part under the Horthy regime, and of members of the post-1945 democratic forces, apart from the extreme left and extreme right, it was well placed to coordinate action among the old and new moderate, conservative forces. The refugees with an army or gendarmerie background were covered by the branches of the World Federation of Hungarian Veterans.[7] The US administration, as part of its Cold War activity, established the Free Europe Committee and Radio Free Europe.[8]

The Western diaspora set up in each country institutions for preserving and asserting their identities and traditions, and ensuring national, religious and political cohesion and communications: churches, societies, newspapers, schools, drama clubs, community houses, radio stations and other services, to match the rate of immigration and features of each recipient country. Such organizations were ubiquitous, but differed in size and consistency. They were well frequented by the still-isolated Hungarian communities of the early period. Their cohesive function remained important in the ensuing age of generation change and geographical dispersion, but typically involved only 5–10 percent of the community.

The pillars of this system of institutions for immigrants and émigrés were the associations. Relief clubs began to form in the United States in the 1880s, and by 1910 there were more than a thousand of them. The first in Canada was founded in 1901, and by the 1930s they covered all the cities where Hungarians lived. In Europe, economic immigration began relatively early in France, where similar bodies were in place by the 1920s. By 1921, the number of Hungarian–American institutions exceeded 2,000. Several hundred formed in other countries of settlement, including Church, lay and political bodies. A number were built up into national networks, such as those involving health plans (sickness benevolent societies, aid societies) and churches in the United States. Several bodies provided cohesion at a national level: the American Hungarian Federation, the Hungarian Reformed Federation of America, or the American Hungarian Catholic Society.[9] Equivalents elsewhere – the Partnership of German Emigration, the South American Hungarians' Federation and the Australian Hungarian Federation[10] – played a part in coordinating and funding Hungarian community life. One worldwide body was the Hungarian Scout Association in Exteris, formed in 1946, which gained importance in the diaspora with new-found methods for stimulating Hungarian awareness in the next generation.[11]

Also important to preserving awareness of Hungarian identity among adults were several local and other cultural associations and scientific societies, such as the Széchenyi Society and the Rákóczi Foundation in Canada, the Hungarian Society and the American Hungarian Foundation in the United States, and the Mindszenty Hungarian Academy of Science and Culture, and the Péter Pázmány Free University in Argentina.[12]

Many political associations were founded before and during World War II, such as the Human Rights League of the Social Democratic Organization and the anti-fascist Hungarian Independence Movement in France, and the British Hungarian Council, formed with a similar purpose in the United Kingdom.

The press was prominent from the outset among the Western diaspora, as a means of communication and communal organization. There were political, Church, denominational, cultural, literary, social scientific, and youth papers, as well as comic papers, sports papers and magazines. They ranged from local newsletters to national dailies, and numbered in all perhaps a thousand titles. Many were short-lived, but others persisted for decades or longer. As time went by, dailies became weeklies, monthlies or quarterlies. Most were produced wholly for a Hungarian-speaking readership, except for a few designed to inform international opinion, but many became bilingual as time went by, to cater for the new generation. The first began to appear regularly at the turn of the twentieth century: the Cleveland *Szabadság* and the *Amerikai Magyar Népszava*, for example. Other papers, such as *Katolikus Magyarok Vasárnapja* and *Kanadai Magyarság*, appeared at the end of the 1920s, as did the South American *Délamerikai Magyarság* and *Délamerikai Magyar Újság*, or after 1945, such as the Vienna *Bécsi Napló* and the periodicals *Hadak Útján*, *Hungária*, *Látóhatár* and *Új Magyar Út*. The émigré Hungarian papers led to several Hungarian journalists' associations, the first being the Association of Hungarian Journalists Abroad,[13] chaired by József Nyírő and later by Albert Wass.

The outlets for Hungarian literary and scholarly self-expression were the printing presses and publishers. The post-1945 emigration brought the Western diaspora a generation of writers of outstanding value: László Cs. Szabó, Sándor Márai, Zoltán Szabó and others.

Larger papers had presses of their own, but neither they nor the independent publishers could develop into substantial, profitable businesses: the number of works published seldom exceeded a dozen. The most prolific after 1945 were Amerikai Magyar Kiadó in Munich, Kárpát Kiadó in Buenos Aires, Kossuth Kiadó in Cleveland, Ohio, and Occidental Press in Washington, DC. The only other intellectual outlets were the press and the Hungarian broadcasts by Radio Free Europe and the BBC.

The Churches soon began to organize and build, for instance in the final years of the nineteenth and early years of the twentieth century in North America, in the 1920s and 1930s in South America, and in the 1940s and 1950s in Australia. Hungarian clergy could work in Australia, but it was the end of the 1950s before they were allowed to form a Church on an ethnic basis. The Roman Catholic and Reformed Churches were prominent, but Greek Catholic, Evangelical (Lutheran), Baptist and Jewish congregations also appeared as specifically Hungarian congregations using the Hungarian language to converse and for services. There are known to be 42 Hungarian Roman Catholic and 102 Hungarian Reformed congregations in the United States, where all the denominations mentioned are represented. Elsewhere, the Roman Catholics were strongest in South America, but other denominations appeared. The Roman Catholic and Reformed Churches dominated in Europe. The Reformed Church, as a national Church, was crucial initially in preserving the Hungarian language and identity abroad. It ran hundreds of summer and weekend schools, obtaining textbooks and libraries from Hungary, and later producing and publishing its own. The close ties to the mother Church broke in World War I, after which efforts were made to train clergy by offering Hungarians born in the United States university-level tuition in the Hungarian language. The Roman Catholics also organized schools, including some full-time ones, but in that case the law prohibited the sole use of Hungarian as the language of instruction. The ties broke finally after World War II, but the Catholics were strengthened in Europe and overseas by the arrival of many monks, nuns and priests as refugees. In 1950, the Pope appointed a Hungarian apostolic visitor to oversee the pastoral care of the Hungarian diaspora in the West. The Hungarian translation of the New Testament by Gellért Békés and Patrik Dalos was published in 300,000 copies by Actio Catholica. Important teaching institutions, movements and centers were set up, such as the Hungarian youth organization Pax Romana, American Hungarian Csíksomlyó (Youngstown, OH) and St. Gerard's Abbey (São Paulo).[14]

The aging Western diaspora, who were gradually being assimilated into their host countries' culture, received a temporary boost with a new wave of refugees in 1956, due to the 1956 Revolution. This injected new life into the scattered Hungarian communities, but also brought about big changes. Various estimates have been made of how many refugees there were, but broadly speaking, some 200,000 people had left Hungary by the end of 1956: 10,000–11,000 of them returned, while the rest settled in the West. Most crossed the border into Austria, where the superhuman task of receiving them was carried out in a praiseworthy way. About 20,000 of them crossed instead into Yugoslavia, where they were also welcomed. Following a UN appeal, Western governments extended assistance to Austria and received sizable numbers of refugees: 12,700 went to France, 15,500 to Germany, 21,000 to Britain, 12,000 to Switzerland, and 10,000 to Belgium, the Netherlands and Sweden between them. The United States took 40,000, Canada 26,500, Australia 11,000, and South Africa 1,300. Most of those in Yugoslavia reached these recipient countries via Italy.[15]

These refugees were received with a sympathy, amazement and respect not accorded to earlier immigrants, and given special treatment and concessions, both officially and from local people and established Hungarian communities. Later the previous Hungarian immigrants noted that the '56-ers were able to integrate more easily because they did not have to climb each rung of the immigrant ladder, but were given immediate access to higher education and support in establishing their livelihood. Still, most Hungarian groups received them with pleasure and expectation.

The '56-ers were far from uniform. Many had fled persecution after taking up arms or otherwise assisting in the Revolution, including communist supporters of the government of Imre Nagy. Others had escaped discrimination on the grounds of class background or political views. Quite a number were looking for higher education and an academic career or success in their profession. Others were attracted by the freedom of thought and personal development. Many sought rapid integration in language and way of life, especially for their children. On the other hand, the stratum brought renewal in terms of identity and political consciousness to Hungarian organizations and social life. But differences of generation and of social and political experience and upbringing sometimes led to conflict, new objectives, and the founding of new associations and institutions. Above all there arose so-called freedom-fighter bodies among those who had served in the National Guard or as military or intellectual leaders: the Hungarian Freedom Fighters' Association headed by Béla Király, the World Federation of Hungarian Freedom Fighters under Lajos Dálnoki Veress, and the World Federation of Hungarian Freedom Fighters (National Guards) under Gergely Pongrátz.[16] One émigré organization of '56-ers from the intelligentsia was the Petőfi Circle, which eventually settled in New York, still headed by Pál Jónás, as it had been in Budapest. The Union of Hungarian Writers Abroad, based in London, had a similar constituency, but included pre-1956 émigrés as well.[17] Chairing it in succession were György Faludy, Pál Ignotus, and then Tibor Méray. The Imre Nagy Institute of Political and Social Studies was set up in Brussels with György Heltai, who had been state secretary at the Ministry of Foreign Affairs under Nagy, as its director, while János Horváth was elected to preside over the Kossuth Foundation in New York.[18] All these bodies had been formed right after the defeat of the Revolution, in Austria or elsewhere in Europe. Most of them received American financial support through the Commission for a Free Europe or other US agencies, under the Cold War program. There were additional institutional supporters of the communities of '56-ers in other European countries too, such as Switzerland and West Germany.

The most important organization was a political one: the Hungarian Committee, registered in March 1958 by post-World War II émigrés and '56-ers, which settled in New York.[19] This replaced a National Committee of the earlier émigrés. One '56-er organization that joined it was the Hungarian Revolutionary Council formed in Vienna in November 1956, mainly by exiled Smallholders' Party and Social Democratic Party revolutionary leaders. Another organization that dissolved itself without joining the National Committee was the Government Representation, which sought to represent the Nagy government under the chairmanship of Anna Kéthly, the only member of that government to have ended up in the West. The Hungarian Committee elected as its president Béla Varga, who had held the same post in the dissolved National Committee. Its members were divided equally between the earlier émigrés and the '56-ers, but it committed itself wholly to the cause of 1956, and like the other 1956 organizations, saw representation of Hungarian interests as its prime task: drawing attention to 1956 and Hungary, and drawing conclusions from 1956. This was especially important between November 4, 1957, and December 20, 1962, while the "Hungarian question" – that of the armed suppression of the Revolution by the Soviets and of the legitimacy of the Kádár government – remained on the agenda of the UN General Assembly. National Committee members sought to influence public opinion by argument, presenting witnesses, and holding debates on the UN report.

Most of the '56-ers were young; some 8,000 of them were students. This posed the problem of student organizations for those studying at the Hungarian schools and the universities of various countries. There was a demand from young families for Hungarian-taught elementary education, reinforced by the weekend or occasionally full-time tuition in Hungarian-taught or partly Hungarian-taught schools run by the Churches or the Scouts (in Cleveland, New York, New Brunswick, Passaic, Toronto, Buenos Aires, São Paulo, and so on). At the secondary level, the *Hungarian Gymnasium* that operated at Burg-Kastl in Germany from 1984 to

2006 was particularly important. Multicultural concepts were put forward in several countries in the 1970s, in relation to schools and to identity-reinforcing cultural activities, and moral and financial support was received from minority programs.

Even in the early period of exile, Hungarian university students established a successor organization to the 1956 Federation of Hungarian University and College Students' Associations.[20] This was joined by large numbers of Hungarian students in European universities, and had active branches, for instance in West Germany. It operated until 1966. A North American association of Hungarian students also sprang up, and in parallel with that, Hungarian branches arose in the social democratic and Catholic youth movements. These organizations provided a good school and intellectual environment for future Hungarian graduates, who went on to establish throughout Europe the most fertile forums of the émigré Hungarian intelligentsia, holding regular conferences and meetings. The most important of these were based in the Netherlands, Vienna, London, Bern, Lugano and Geneva.[21] Similar bodies appeared in the United States.[22]

Around each appeared various press and book publications. Although many were short-lived, they were often replaced quickly, and many of those that survived until the 1990s were repatriated to Hungary, although some outlived their purpose, at home or abroad, and closed.[23]

The events in Hungary and abroad after 1956 had a marked effect on the political and the cultural organizations and the entire Hungarian diaspora in the West. The 1963 amnesty that ended the years of reprisals and the subsequent milder policies in Hungary caused debates and divisions among the Hungarians abroad. There were clashes over the question of continuing the isolation and rejection of the *de facto* regime or opening up official contacts with it. For the Hungarian authorities sought contacts with the diaspora of various kinds, with some modest successes, such as the series of Mother Tongue Conferences that began in 1970. The other major effect of subsequent East–West *détente* was to reduce the financial support that the West gave to the émigré opposition. As the money dwindled, so did the importance of the émigré organizations and press, and the influence of Radio Free Europe. The 1975 Helsinki Conference gave backing to the efforts to improve the legal political position of the Hungarian community in the Carpathian Basin. The Hungarian Human Rights Foundation was established under the chairmanship of László Hámos.[24] The radical turning point for the Hungarians in the West came with the changes in Hungary in 1990.

Notes

1　Julianna Puskás, *Ties that Bind, Ties that Divide: 100 Years of Hungarian Experience in the United States* (New York/London, 2000), p. 25.

2　Susan Aykler-Papp, "Hungarians in Canada," in Ilona Kovács, Lászlóné Faragó and Júlia Gál, eds., *Hungarica to Be Found in Libraries Abroad: a Directory 13* (Budapest, 1997), p. 23.

3　Kázmér Nagy, *Elveszett alkotmány: a magyar politikai emigráció: 1945–1975* [Lost Constitution: Hungarian Political Emigration] (Budapest, 1984), pp. 209–213; Gyula Borbándi, *A magyar emigráció életrajza: 1945–1985* [Biographies of Hungarian Émigrés: 1945–1985.], Vols. I–II (Budapest, 1981), Vol. I, pp. 108–140

4　Albert Tezla, *Hazardous Quest. Hungarian Immigrants in the United States: 1890–1920: a Documentary* (Budapest, 1993), pp. 221–381; Puskás, *Ties that Bind*, pp. 189–190 and 259–269; Tibor Frank, "Patterns of Interwar Hungarian Immigration to the United States," *Hungarian Studies Review* 30 (2003) 1 2. 3 27; Egon Kunon, *Magyarok Ausztráliában* [Hungarians in Australia] (Budapest, 1997), pp. 123–146 and 161–163; Judit Némethy Kesserű, *Szabadságom lett a börtönöm: az argentin magyar emigráció története: 1948–1968* [My Freedom Became My Prison: The History of Hungarian Emigration to Argentina] (Budapest, 2003), pp. 29–34.

5　The anniversary of the outbreak of Hungary's 1848 Revolution.

6　*Magyar Nemzeti Bizottmány.*

7　*Magyar Harcosok Bajtársi Közössége.*

8　Steven Béla Várdy, *The Hungarian Americans: the Hungarian Experience in North America* (New York/Philadelphia, PA, 1990), pp. 47–87; Puskás, *Ties that Bind*, pp. 173–178; Borbándi, *A magyar emigráció életrajza*, pp. 141–173.

9   *Amerikai Magyar Szövetség; Amerikai Magyar Református Egyesület; Amerikai Magyar Katolikus Egylet.*

10 *Németországi Emigráció Munkaközössége; Dél-amerikai Magyarok Szövetsége; Ausztráliai Magyar Szövetség.*

11 *Külföldi Magyar Cserkésszövetség.*

12 *Széchenyi Társaság; Rákóczi Alapítvány; Magyar Társaság; Amerikai Magyar Alapítvány, Mindszenty Magyar Tudományos Akadémia; Pázmány Péter Szabadegyetem.*

13 *Magyar Újságírók Külföldi Egyesülete.*

14 Stephan Thernstrom, ed., *Harvard Encyclopedia of American Ethnic Groups* (Boston, MA/London, 1980), pp. 462–471; Puskás, *Ties that Bind*, pp. 206–241; Borbándi, *A magyar emigráció életrajza*, pp. 224–267; Egon Kuncz, *The Hungarians in Australia* (Melbourne, 1985), pp. 88–102; Némethy Kesserű, *Szabadságom lett a börtönöm.*

15 *KSH jelentés az 1956-os disszidálásról: az illegálisan külföldre távozott személyek főbb adatai: 1956. október 23–1957. április 30.* [Central Statistics Office Report on Defection in 1956: Main Data of Persons Illegally Leaving for Abroad], *Regio* 2 (1991) 4: 175–176.

16 *Magyar Szabadságharcos Szövetség; Magyar Szabadságharcos Világszövetség; Magyar Szabadságharcos (Nemzetőr) Világszövetség.*

17 *Petőfi Kör; Magyar Írók Szövetsége Külföldön.*

18 *Nagy Imre Politikai és Társadalomtudományi Intézet; Kossuth Alapítvány.*

19 *Magyar Bizottság.*

20 *Magyar Egyetemisták és Főiskolai Hallgatók Egyesületeinek Szövetsége (MEFESZ).*

21 *Mikes Kelemen Kör; Bornemissza Péter Társaság; Sepsi Csombor Márton Kör; Katolikus Magyar Egyetemi Mozgalom and Európai Protestáns Magyar Szabadegyetem; Svájci Magyar Irodalom és Könyvbarátok Köre; Dies Academicus Hungaricus Genevensis.*

22 *Magyar Öregdiák Szövetség–Bessenyei György Kör* (New Brunswick, NJ); *Magyar Baráti Közösség–Itt-Ott Találkozó* (Lake Hope, OH); *Amerikai Magyar Tanárok Egyesülete* (American Hungarian Educators' Association (Chevy Chase, MD).

23 *Nemzetőr* (Munich); *Irodalmi Újság* (Paris); *Új Látóhatár* (Zurich, Paris, Munich); *Bécsi Magyar Híradó* and *Bécsi Napló* (Vienna); *Kanadai Magyar Hírlap* (Toronto/Montreal) and *Kanadai Magyarság*

(Toronto); *Független Magyarország* (Australia); *Magyar Műhely* (Paris); *Szivárvány* (Chicago).

24 Puskás, *Ties that Bind*, pp. 270–278; Gyula Borbándi, *Emigráció és Magyarország: nyugati magyarok a változások éveiben: 1985–1995* [Emigration and Hungary: Hungarians in the West in the Years of Change: 1985–1995] (Basel/Budapest, 1996), pp. 137–343.

6. SOME SOCIAL AND DEMOGRAPHIC FEATURES OF THE HUNGARIAN DIASPORA IN THE WEST AND ITS INSTITUTIONS
Attila Papp Z.

Scattered communities of Hungarians have existed in the West since the second half of the nineteenth century. This section looks at the migration processes that helped to establish them, and notes what demographic and social information can be gathered about them. The main source for their origin and maintenance was a surge of mass emigration from Hungary that peaked in the years before World War I. To this can be added the natural increase in the ethnic population and recruitment of later refugees or migrants. The concept of "Hungarian refugee or migrant" is defined broadly as including others besides those leaving from the area that was within the territory of Hungary at the time of departure. Those of Hungarian ethnic affiliation arriving from various other regions tended to join those from Hungary, but there were also efforts to maintain a regional identity discernible in the names and aims of the organizations established.[1]

It is important to explore the demographic features and the institutions of the Hungarian diaspora in the West, as research-based literature on the subject is sparse. It has taken second place to studies of the minority Hungarian communities in the Carpathian Basin, on which detailed social, economic, political and demographic information is available, while the information on the Hungarian diaspora in the West is less reliable and gathered in a less disciplined way. Motives of ethnic mission and activism, current also in the Carpathian Basin before the change of system in 1989, dominate over the dispassionate methods that are designed to dispel these in a scientific way.

Table 1. Numbers of Hungarian citizens
migrating to America, 1871–1913[2]

	USA immigration figures	Seaport figures	Official statistics from Hungary
1871–1879	5,597	7,682	-
1880–1889	115,252	164,119	-
1890–1899	235,895	261,444	-
1900–1909	1,094,116	1,171,758	854,584
1910–1913	410,480	433,230	315,498
Total 1871– 1913	*1,861,340*	*2,038,233*	-
Total 1900–1913	*1,504,596*	*1,604,988*	*1,170,082*

Almost two million Hungarians migrated abroad in 1871–1913, mainly for economic and livelihood-related reasons. The numbers peaked in the first decade of the twentieth century, when almost a million migrations were recorded in various sources. Almost half a million more left Hungary in the years up to 1914. During this period of mass migration, almost three quarters of the emigrants were men, of whom three quarters were in their best working years of 20–49, while only 3 percent were over 50. Hardly more than a quarter of those leaving the country were Hungarians (26.3 percent) and a similar proportion were Slovaks, but there were sizable numbers of Croats (16.6 percent) and Germans (15 percent) as well.

By the end of World War I, the conditions for international migration had altered. The United States, hitherto the top destination, tightened its policies, introducing an origin-based quota system. As a result, interwar migration from Hungary to the United States was under 50,000. However, that temporarily increased the number going to Canada (25,000–30,000 in 1924–1930), most of them from the countryside. To a smaller extent there was also migration by Hungarian citizens to South America, especially Brazil and Argentina, likewise mainly to agricultural jobs. Nor were the changes in the direction of migration confined to overseas. Within Europe, the main destinations in the 1920s were France and Belgium, but in the 1930s it became Germany, although in these cases temporary migration was commoner than it was among immigrants to the United States, from which about a quarter of the arrivals from Hungary in 1899–1913 returned. All in all, the scale of emigration decreased between the wars, but the proliferation of destinations meant that the communities of the Hungarian diaspora were more scattered. That was still more true of the post-World War II and post-1956 migrations.

More than eleven million people in Europe were left in foreign countries at the end of World War II, of whom about eight million had been repatriated by the summer of 1947. However, about a million and a half did not want to return. The International Refugee Organization (IRO), a UN agency, managed between July 1947 and the end of 1951 to coordinate the settlement of a million displaced persons (DPs) in refugee camps in Germany and Austria, and where possible in overseas countries. According to IRO figures, some 17,000 people of Hungarian origin were sent to the United States, and rather more than 3,500 to France. Canada took 16,500 such Hungarian citizens between 1946 and 1955, and Australia had taken 11,500 by 1954. Other estimates suggest that some 10,000 Hungarian DPs went to South America and 5,000 to the Scandinavian countries. Economic and political criteria were applied by the recipient countries. The United States, for instance, set tight political controls designed to exclude immigrants compromised by an Arrow-Cross or fascist past. Other countries were interested primarily in the aspects of appeal to the labor market. Some 20 percent of the DPs were of Jewish origin, most of whom went to Palestine (after 1948, Israel).

There was a more or less complete cessation of migration in 1949–1956, due to the restrictions applied by the communist regime: hardly more than 2,500 people emigrated from Hungary legally.

Then came an exodus of about 200,000 after the defeat of the 1956 Revolution, which caused serious demographic losses at home,[3] although it helped to restock diaspora communities. Earlier waves of migrants had founded the associations, Churches, Scout troops and other organizations of the Hungarians abroad, but their longer-term survival was ensured by subsequent waves. Furthermore, the '56-ers formed organizations of their own.

The emigration did not stop there. Annual numbers of emigrants up to the change of system, legal or illegal, ranged between 3,000 and 6,000: altogether some 130,000 Hungarian citizens left between 1960 and 1989. Official Hungarian data show that legal and illegal emigration were about equal in the 1960s and 1970s, but illegal emigration was much higher in the last decade of state socialism (*Table 2*).

Table 2. Legal, illegal and total emigration between 1947 and 1989[4]

	Legal	Illegal	Total
1947–1955	2,553	n. d.	2,553
1956–1962	20,703	193,835	214,538
1963–1979	36,713	40,725	77,438
1980–1989	14,931	30,266	45,197
Total	74,900	264,026	339 726

There was some reduction in migration to the West after the change of system in 1989, but it resumed, and Hungary also became a transit country, from which many foreign citizens (including those of Hungarian ethnicity) emigrated further. The exodus westward increased after Hungary's accession to the EU in 2004. The real scale of this can only be estimated from records in the recipient countries, not from official Hungarian statistics. In 2008, for instance, the latter record 359 migrations but aggregated European immigration figures show the arrival of 26,661 Hungarian citizens, of whom 70 percent went to Germany. The departures from Hungary are well documented, often from a variety of sources, but estimating the number of Hungarians resident in foreign countries runs up against various obstacles in all but a couple of countries. The first question is who to consider a Hungarian. Most people who emigrated from Hungary after World War II are likely to be Hungarian, unless there has been a personal, voluntary decision to hasten assimilation.[5] But information from recipient countries is inadequate here, as ethnic Hungarians will also have migrated there from countries other than Hungary and that fact may not have been recorded. Native language is an important criterion of national affiliation, but there are several ways to define native language, and some national censuses do not gather data on native language at all.[6]

Table 3. Hungarians and persons of Hungarian ancestry
in the USA, Canada and Australia (census data)[7]

Country	Census date	No. of Hungarian ancestry	No. speaking Hungarian at home
United States[8]	1980	1,776,902	178,995
	1990	1,582,302	147,902
	2000	1,398,724	117,975
	2006	1,563,081	n. d.
Canada	2001	267,255	23,685
	2006	315,510	21,905
Australia	2001	62,507	24,485
	2006	67,625	21,565

Despite these uncertainties, it is possible to obtain some kind of picture of the Western diaspora and its magnitude (*Tables 3–5*). There are some ostensibly expert, although insufficiently documented, estimates, and there are detailed official figures available in some recipient countries. This applies to the three most prominent destinations – the United States, Canada and Australia (*Table 3*) – and to some South American and European countries that record country of ancestry and/or year of immigration, or where the number of Hungarians can be estimated from figures for religious affiliation.

The United States has about a million and a half residents of Hungarian ancestry, which does not imply a native Hungarian-speaking population of this size. Census questionnaires after 1980 asked, alongside "ancestry," not about native language but about language spoken at home. This criterion is matched by only 8–10 percent of those of Hungarian ancestry in 1980–2000. Data on native language were last gathered in 1970, when respondents were asked about the language that they had spoken in childhood, not about their ethnic ancestry. This produced a figure of 447,000 native Hungarian-speakers in 1970. Research using similar methodology done in 1979 gave a figure of 421,000, in other words a reduction of only 6 percent.[9] Thus around 1980 about a quarter (23.6 percent) of those of Hungarian origin were native Hungarian-speakers. Projecting this onto the 2000 census data gives a maximum of 330,000 (not taking assimilation into account) native Hungarian-speakers. Canada enquires after language use as well as ethnic origin, among other things about native language and language spoken at home. Of the 315,510 people of Hungarian origin in 2006, both parents were Hungarian in only 88,685 cases (28 percent). Of these, 75,595 (24 percent) gave Hungarian as their native language and only 21,905 (7 percent) spoke Hungarian in the home. The proportions in 2001 were 28.8 and 8.8 percent respectively. Australia likewise asks about origin, and the respondents may refer to two forebears. Combining these produces a figure of 62,507 people with Hungarian ancestry in 2001 and 67,625 in 2006. The language question, as in the USA, refers to the language spoken in the home, not the native language. It can be deduced from the figures that 39 percent of those of Hungarian ancestry in 2001 (24,485 people) spoke Hungarian at home in 2001 and 32 percent (21,565 people) in 2006.

An important observation about these three countries is that the proportions of those of Hungarian origin who are native speakers and who speak Hungarian in the home are similar. The proportion speaking Hungarian in the home is much higher in Australia, however. This points to a higher proportion of ethnically homogeneous marriages there and a smaller degree of assimilation.

Comparing South American and European data from various sources, they appear to differ by orders of magnitude in some countries (above all where census data do not detail ethnic or national affiliation sufficiently). Argentina and Brazil, the two South American countries with the largest Hungarian colonies, show wide discrepancies (*Table 4*). Germany's, France's, Belgium's and Sweden's estimates appear to be the most reliable in Western Europe (*Table 5*). It is fairly simple to arrive at estimates from census data in the Latin American countries, by assuming that Hungarians living in each are of four kinds: those born in Hungary, those originating from countries neighboring Hungary, and the children of either of these two groups. The responses to questions about country of birth and information about live births make it easy to count those originating from Hungary and their offspring. Those originating from Romania, Yugoslavia/Serbia and the former Soviet Union/Ukraine can be estimated from the responses to the question on religious affiliation: Roman Catholics and Protestants can be assumed to be Hungarian. With those from Slovakia/the former Czechoslovakia there is no such religious divide, but half the immigrants have been counted as Hungarian (a deliberate overestimate) and the same fertility rate is assumed. There was no enquiry into religion in the most recent census in Argentina, and so the proportions found in Brazil have been superimposed on Argentina as well. This method of estimation obviously has its limitations, for it is questionable whether children born to Hungarian mothers will remain Hungarian. Nor do the calculations consider third- and fourth-generation Hungarians, who may have retained their identity in some form.

Table 4. Estimates for Hungarians living in Latin American countries

	1996[10]	2000[11]	2006[12]	IPUMS[13]
Mexico	100	300	n. d.	n. d.
Costa Rica	n. d.	1,100	n. d.	n. d.
Venezuela	5,000	4,500	4,000–5,000	2,600
Brazil	60,000	70,000	5,000–10,000	14,000
Peru	150	2,000	n. d.	n. d.
Chile	2,000–3,000	2,000	n. d.	1,115
Uruguay	5,000	3,500	4,000–5,000	n. d.
Argentina	40,000	40,000	20,000–30,000	12,000
Paraguay	150	n. d.	n. d.	n. d.
Colombia	150	n. d.	n. d.	n. d.
All	*112,450–113,450*	*123,400*	*33,000–50,000*	*29,715*

Using this procedure on the most recent census data in Argentina and Brazil, it was found that some 12,000 first- and second-generation Hungarians may be living in the former and some 14,500 in the latter. Proportionate results were obtained for Chile and Venezuela, although they are lower than previous estimates. It is worth noting that the Argentinean estimate seems realistic, as similar results have been obtained by other methods.[14] With Brazil, our estimate is closest to HTMH.

According to the 1999 census returns in France, the number of citizens or holders of residence permits born in Hungary is about 10,000.[15] To this need to be added the numbers of live births and of Hungarians arriving from other Carpathian Basin countries, along with their descendants, making a total of about 20,000. The figures for Germany suggest a dynamic increase since 1996 that may be plausible: it has been mentioned that according to 2008 data,

Germany was home to 70 percent of the Hungarian citizens registered in Western Europe (about 19,000 people). Adding the 1996 figure, the number of children born to these, and the number of arrivals from other countries in the Carpathian Basin gives a minimum total of 100,000, which is not far from the 120,000 estimate made by the National Association of Hungarians in Germany (BUOD).

For Belgium there are two reliable starting points: the known figure of some 3,500 Hungarians who arrived after 1956, and an official figure of some 2,000 Hungarian citizens living there in 2006. Thus the number of Hungarians can be put at 7,000–8,000. The estimates for Sweden, based on official figures,[16] come to 25,000–35,000. In 2002, for instance, there were 13,935 people who had been born in Hungary, and about the same number born in Sweden but with Hungarian antecedents, giving a total of almost 28,000 people with ties to Hungary. To these can be added ethnic Hungarians from other parts of the Carpathian Basin, notably Transylvanians, recorded as being from Romania. Of the 12,172 Romanian-born immigrants, 6,808 arrived in the 1980s and may well be Transylvanian Hungarians. It is not possible to say accurately what proportion of the 12,000 immigrants from Romania, 2,000 from Ukraine, or 75,000 from the former Yugoslavia are of Hungarian origin, but aggregating the lowest estimates produces a total of 35,000.

It is important to add that Hungarians and people of Hungarian origin dwell in other parts of the world. Sources already quoted suggest that there are 200,000–250,000 Hungarian-speakers in Israel, from Hungary and other parts of the Carpathian Basin. There are also some 10,000 in Africa and 30,000 in Asia. However, in Israel's case even the lower figure is probably an overestimate. The IPUMS database found 51,000 people who had been born in Hungary in the 1972 census returns, and only 23,000 in the 1983 census returns.[17] These two censuses asked those over 15 about the language that they used in daily life,[18] which produced figures of 21,000 in 1972 and 15,000 in 1983. However, Israel is a special case, as many of those arriving there saw it as a homecoming, not emigration, and the younger generations would rather speak Hebrew.

Table 5. Estimates for Hungarians living in European countries
outside the Carpathian Basin

	1996[19]	2000[20]	2006[21]
Austria	60,000	40,000–45,000	40,000
Belgium	10,000–15,000	14,000–15,000	5,000–6,000
Cyprus	n. d.	n. d.	2,000–3,000
Czech Republic	n. d.	20,000	19,000–20,000
Denmark	2,000	4,000	2,000–4,000
Estonia	n. d.	n. d.	150
France	50,000	40,000–45,000	15,000–19,000
Finland	n. d.	n. d.	1,000
Greece	n. d.	n. d.	n. d.
Netherlands	10,000	11,000–12,000	8,000–10,000
Latvia	n. d.	n. d.	300
Lithuania	n. d.	n. d.	120
Poland	n. d.	n. d.	500
Luxembourg	n. d.	n. d.	2,000–3,000
Britain	25,000	25,000–30,000	25,000–30,000
Germany	62,000	120,000	120,000–160,000
Norway	3,000	4,000	3,000
Italy	10,000	9,000–10,000	n. d.
Portugal	n. d.	2,000	n. d.
Spain	200	n. d.	n. d.
Switzerland	20,000	18,000–20,000	20,000–25,000
Sweden	25,000	25,000–27,000	30,000–35,000
All	*277,000–282,000*	*332,000–354,000*	*289,470–354,670*

So far an attempt has been made to measure emigration to
countries and estimate "potentially" the number of Hungarians
dwelling there. Whether those Hungarians or people of Hungarian

origin actually belong to the Hungarian diaspora as a community is a matter for further research. Research in the United States and Argentina suggests that some 5–10 percent of those of Hungarian origin take part in some organized Hungarian-style activity. This kind of activity may involve 10-15 percent elsewhere.[22] The least information is available for the "working-class" diaspora and for less successful migrants, who may end up on the periphery of a Hungarian community or even of society as a whole, and have a lower potential for asserting their interests or organizing themselves institutionally.

The forms of organization are varied and susceptible to categorization in several ways, not least because each larger group formed its own organization. The fraternal organizations in the United States were founded in the 1880s. Those whom they insured were mainly workers (against accident and sickness). There were newspapers associated with them, and they also held balls and other community-building events. However, the Western organizations took a kind of post-emigration turn after the change of system in Hungary in 1989, whereby their functions shifted towards maintaining ethnic Hungarian culture and mediation between cultures.

The decisive role in preserving ethnic identity in the Western diaspora today is played by the Churches and the Scout movement, and the weekend Hungarian schools that they run. That is not to say that other organizations do not contribute[23] or have not importance (in cultural, intellectual, higher educational, political, lobbying, press and internet community fields).[24]

Organization of Hungarian-language religious congregations began towards the end of the nineteenth century. Today the Hungarian Reformed Church has the most congregations in the United States: 64.[25] The Hungarian Reformed Church in America has 32 and the US Calvin Synod Conference of the United Church of Christ 27. Four belong to the American Presbyterian Church, and one is independent (the Akron, Ohio, Free Hungarian Reformed Church). There are Hungarian-language congregations in 12 places in Canada and 8 in Australia. Argentina and Brazil, and such Western European countries as Germany, the Netherlands, Sweden,

Switzerland, the UK and France each have at least one Protestant congregation.

It was harder to build up Roman Catholic institutions using Hungarian as a working language, not least because the Church is universal and more hierarchical. By the beginning of the twentieth century the USA had almost 100 such Catholic congregations, but the number has fallen since to 16 Roman Catholic and six Greek Catholic congregations, not all of which use Hungarian in the liturgy.[26] There were Roman Catholic congregations elsewhere as well: 18 in Canada, six in Australia, and several congregations, missions and monastic communities in South America.

Also important is the progress made among Hungarians by the Baptist Church. These are grouped in North America under the Hungarian Baptist Convention of North America, whose member congregations are summoned at least three times a year. There are ten congregations that officially belong to it. There is also a Hungarian Baptist congregation in Melbourne, Australia.[27]

The Churches play an important role in maintaining ethnic or national awareness in the Hungarian diaspora. So, understandably, the challenges of assimilation are felt most strongly in their community life. There are often problems not only with replacing clergy (especially for the Catholics), but with retaining the congregation when the number of Hungarians is declining. There is sometimes debate within the diaspora Churches about the relative emphasis to be placed on keeping up the faith or on sustaining the Hungarian community.

Organization of the Hungarian Scout movement in the West began in 1945, when the Hungarian Scouts Association formed in 1912 was revived in the refugee camps. Troops were formed in the camps, assisted by the Teleki Pál Scout Association formed in 1946, and spread among those who emigrated to the United States, Canada, South America, Australia and Western Europe. Meanwhile the Scout movement in Hungary was merged in 1948 into the communist Pioneer movement, after which the Association took the name Hungarian Scouts Association, then for a while the Hungarian

Scout Federation in Exile, and after the movement became legal again in Hungary in 1989, the Hungarian Scout Federation in Exteris. The spread of the Scout movement in the United States began with Gábor Bodnár and his troop, and the Federation moved to headquarters in Garfield, NJ. It continued to strengthen over subsequent decades and today involves 4,000 Scouts in 70 troops, having peaked in the 1980s with 6,200 Scouts in 84 troops.[28] One of the big challenges is the rule that only those conversant with the Hungarian language may take part, with the result that the declining numbers of Hungarians and the pressures of assimilation make recruitment increasingly difficult.[29]

The Churches and Scouts support most of the weekend Hungarian schools serving the Hungarian diaspora in the West, although other voluntary bodies are also involved. There are 26 known schools in the United States, 15 in Germany, and 14 in Sweden, but they cover other countries too. A few of them are daily (for instance at the 'Toronto Magyar Gimnázium" or Helicon School in Toronto) and one or two schools or classes are state-run (such as the Hungarian-language high-school class in Bankstown in Australia).[30] Nor it is unusual for weekend schools to include a creche or a kindergarten as well.[31]

One big challenge for most Church or voluntary schools is to recruit suitably qualified teaching staff. Another is to have suitable teaching materials, where Hungary can provide only a measure of support. There is still aversion in some places to textbooks from Hungary or even to adaptation of them to local needs.[32] Since the 1970s, materials for weekly tuition prepared jointly by educationalists in Hungary and from Western communities have been published by the International Society for Hungarian Language and Culture (Mother-Tongue Conference) and used successfully in several places. Another important question is whether weekend courses can contribute in a broader sense to social integration and complement the lives of young people in schools not taught in Hungarian. There have been positive developments in some countries, where Hungarian can gain official recognition. Germany has "accredited Hungarian tuition" and some US states (such as California) award high-school credits for knowledge of the Hungarian language.

One question central for schools and all Hungarian organizations in the West was whether they could cooperate and how far they took note of one another. The operating logic of some includes keeping up a common umbrella organization (the Churches or the Scouts), while others have started to form networks recently, for instance schools – the Association of Hungarian Teachers in North America (MITE) – and bodies representing special interests. The Western European Association of Country Organizations of Hungarians[33] formed in 2001, and a similar body in Latin America in the summer of 2004.[34]

Other political and professional umbrella organizations that formed earlier in the United States include the American Hungarian Educators' Association, the American Hungarian Foundation, the American Hungarian Association, the Hungarian American Coalition, the Hungarian Human Rights Foundation, the Hungarian Studies Association and the Hungarian Communion of Friends. The primary purpose of the umbrella organizations and their members is to preserve and encourage use of the Hungarian language and culture, since the Western diaspora faces its greatest challenge from assimilation. This is clear from the demographic figures given earlier, and it is apparent on an individual level in the daily lives of people of Hungarian origin living in the West, for a great many factors work against their ties to the parent country and retention of the Hungarian language and culture in a linguistic environment far removed from that of their native language. Yet the organized frameworks of Hungarian life have been retained for decades, if in random and equivocal ways, meaning that an intermediary role can still be played. The Hungarian Alumni Association/György Bessenyei Circle in the United States, for instance, has for over fifty years provided lecturing or exhibition opportunities for over 300 prominent Hungarian writers, scientists, experts and artists from Hungary, its neighboring countries and the West, mainly at Rutgers University in New Jersey.

The task of mediating between cultures is inconceivable among the Hungarians in the West without a sense of mission.

The US sociologist Károly Nagy sees this as "implant[ing] a sense of mission in and among ourselves, to convey the realities of the Hungarian community to Western countries. This... also provided a reason why our children, young people, and fellow citizens should retain their Hungarian language and culture in Western countries... to become spokesmen for the interests and problems of the parts of the Hungarian nation."[35]

Finally, there is the question of what supra-ethnic values the institutional framework can project and in what relation they stand to the cultural, political and economic changes in Hungary in recent decades. Lack of scholarly study means that these often stop short of anything more than simplistic activism not backed by actual knowledge of conditions in Hungary and the neighboring countries. On the other hand, the solidarity and voluntary activity of the Western diaspora Hungarians over the decades present an exemplary alternative of civil organization that contrasts sharply with the *étatist* approach among the Hungarians of the Carpathian Basin.

Notes

1   In several countries and communities, those of Transylvanian, Vojvodina/Southern Region or Upland origin formed organizations of their own. Such organizations can still be found in the United States, Sweden, Austria and elsewhere.

2   Julianna Puskás, *Kivándorló magyarok az Egyesült Államokban, 1880–1940* [Hungarians Emigrating to the United States, 1880–1940] (Budapest, 1982), pp. 443–446. Júlia Puskás and Zoltán Fejős, "Migráció Közép-Kelet Európában a 19. és 20. században" [Migration from Central-Eastern Europe in the 19th and 20th Centuries], *Regio* 2 (1991) 4: 22–48, or Miklós Szántó, *Magyarok Amerikában* [Hungarians in America] (Budapest, 1984), pp. 106–108.

3   On the demographic outcomes, see László Hablicsek and Sándor Illés, "Az 1956-os kivándorlás népességi hatásai" [Population Effects of the 1956 Emigration], *Statisztikai Szemle* (2007) 2: 157–172.

4   Pál Péter Tóth, "A nemzetközi vándormozgalom szerepe a népességfejlődésben" [The Role of International Migration in

Population Development], in Tamás Faragó and Péter Őri, eds., *Történeti demográfiai évkönyv, 2001* [Yearbook of Historical Demography, 2001] (Budapest, 2001), p. 336.

5   There are cases where emigrants are reported to have lost their ability to speak Hungarian after only a couple of years.

6   This has been the case with US censuses since 1980, where respondents are asked only about the language spoken at home, which may not be Hungarian in the case of a mixed marriage. Another barrier is that descendants of immigrants whose native language is Hungarian may not speak the language or feel a Hungarian affiliation. Responses may also be influenced by census-taking methodology, as appears in the phrasing of example answers on US and Australian census forms. Then there is of concealment of ethnic origin. Related demographic problems are discussed in more detail in Pál Péter Tóth, "Magyarok a nagyvilágban" [Hungarians in the Wide World], *Kisebbségkutatás* (2001) 4: 40–46.

7   US Census Bureau, Census 200 special tabulation PHC–T43; Idem, 1990, CPH–L–149; Idem, Ancestry of the population by state: 1980 (Suppl. Report PC80–S1–10); Immigration and citizenship highlight tables, 2006 census. Statistics Canada Catalogue Nos 97–557–XWE20006002 and 97–562–XCB20006012; Australian Bureau of Statistics, Tables 20680–u16–Australia and 20680–c37c–Australia.

8   American Community Survey (ACS) 2006 data. On methodology: Levente Pakot, "A 2000. évi amerikai népszámlálás jellegzetességei és kihatása az amerikai magyarok számbavételére" [Features of the 2000 US Census and Its Effect on Counting US Hungarians], in Attila Z. Papp, ed., *Beszédből világ. Elemzések, adatok amerikai magyarokról* [A World from Speech. Analyses and Data on American Hungarians] (Budapest, 2008), pp. 357–396

9   See Zoltán Fejős, "Magyarok az Egyesült Államokban az 1980-as években (Demográfia, társadalmi adatok, fogalmi problémák)" [Hungarians in the US in the 1980s (Demography, Social Data, Concept Problems)], in *Magyarságkutatás 1988. A Magyarságkutató Intézet Évkönyve* [Hungarian Community Research. Yearbook of the Hungarian Community Research Institute] (Budapest, 1988), pp. 177–216.

10 Gyula Borbándi, *Emigráció és Magyarország: nyugati magyarok a változások éveiben: 1985–1995* [Emigration and Hungary: Hungarians in the West in the Years of Change: 1985–1995] (Basel/Budapest, 1996).

11   Data of the Magyarok Világszövetsége (Hungarians' World Association, MVSZ).

12   HTMH (Határon Túli Magyarok Hivatala), *Jelentés a Kárpát-medencén kívül élő magyarság helyzetéről* [Report on the Situation of Hungarians Living outside the Carpathian Basin] (Budapest, 2006). (http://www.hhrf.org/htmh/?menuid=060209)

13   Minnesota Population Center, Integrated Public Use Microdata Series, International: Version 5.0 [Machine-readable database] (Minneapolis, 2009). Thanks to MPC and the statistics offices of the countries for making the databases available.

14   László Kósa estimated the number of native speakers at 10,000 in 1980, and Dénes Balázs arrived at a figure of 15,000 See László Kósa, ed., *A magyarságtudomány kézikönyve* [Manual of Hungarian Community Studies] (Budapest, 1990); Dénes Balázs, *Argentína, Uruguay* (Budapest, 1988), p. 85.

15   The data also appear in the 1996 HTMH report.

16   Statistika Centralbyrån (SCB) Befolkningsstatistik del 3, 2002, 20, 70 and 74.

17   The number born in Hungary cannot be reconstructed from the IPUMS database for the 1995 census, but it must have been under the 1983 figure. The average age in 1983 of those born in Hungary was 57.8 years, and of those using the Hungarian language on a daily basis was 66.5 years.

18   The question in English read, "What language(s) do you speak daily?" It was omitted from the 1995 census.

19   Borbándi, *Emigráció és Magyarország.*

20   Data of the Magyarok Világszövetsége.

21   HTMH, *Jelentés a Kárpát-medencén kívül élő magyarság helyzetéről.*

22   HTMH suggests 10 percent for South America. Elsewhere the proportions are 10–15 percent. Borbándi, *Emigráció és Magyarország* presumes such a level of involvement in Denmark, calling this "a proportion found in other countries as well" (p. 68). But this segment does not necessarily overlap with those who speak Hungarian in the home. It has been found in many countries that non-Hungarian speakers with Hungarian forebears may also take part in Hungarian institutions, sometimes in a leading role.

23   There were some 700 known US organizations in 2008. On their structure, see János Márton, "Az Amerikai Egyesült Államokban

working magyar szervezetek, közösségek adatbázisának fontosabb jellemzői" [The Main Features of the Database of Hungarian Organizations and Communities in the USA], in Papp, ed., *Beszédből világ*, pp. 299–313. Also see http://www.mtaki.hu/uj_intezeti_ kiadvanyok/papp_z_attila_amerikai_magyarok.html. Retrieved November 18, 2010. Hungarian institutions in almost all countries in the world can be sought in the press databank of the Hungarian News Agency MTI, which lists them by activities. http://www.mti. hu/magyarsag/szervezetek/ Retrieved November 18, 2010.

24   Some of these are detailed elsewhere in this volume by Ilona Kovács. Borbándi, *Emigráció és Magyarország*, also summarizes them.

25   The establishment of the Reformed Church bodies and conflicts among them are described in Béla Várdy, *Magyarok az Újvilágban: az észak-amerikai magyarság rendhagyó története* [Hungarians in the New World: the Unusual History of the North American Hungarians] (Budapest, 2000). The latest figures appear in *Bethlen Almanach 2009* (Ligonier, PA, 2009).

26   See István Mustos, "Magyar nyelvű szolgálat és oktatás az amerikai magyar katolikus egyházakban" [Hungarian-Language Service and Teaching in American Hungarian Catholic Churches], in Károly Nagy and László Papp, eds., *A magyar nyelv és kultúra megtartása. USA 1997* [Retaining Hungarian Language and Culture. USA 1997] (Budapest, 1998), pp. 65–67, and Attila Miklósházy, S. J., *A tengeren túli emigráns magyar katolikus egyházi közösségek rövid története Észak- és Dél-Amerikában, valamint Ausztráliában* [A Short History of Overseas Hungarian Catholic Parishes in North/South America and Australia] (Toronto, 2005), pp. 13–67. Bishop Miklósházy also reports on a number of Hungarian religious communities for men and women.

27   See www.evangeliumihirnok.net. Retrieved November 18, 2010.

28   See Gábor Dömötör, *Cserkészet, magyarságszolgálat...* [Scouting, Service to the Hungarians], http://www.kmcssz.org/. Retrieved November 18, 2010; Várdy, *Magyarok az Újvilágban*, pp. 468–470.

29   On the interpretation and challenges of scouting, see Papp, ed., *Beszédből világ*, pp. 107–135.

30   The most famous school in Western Europe was the Hungarian Gymnasium run at Burg Kastl, Germany, from 1957 to 2006.

31   Examples: Béla Bartók Hungarian School and Kindergarten, Boston, MA; Széchenyi Hungarian School and Kindergarten, New

Brunswick; kindergartens or creches in Augsburg, Darmstadt, Frankfurt/Main, Stuttgart etc., Germany.

32   For the USA, see Szilvia Németh, "Hétvégi magyar iskolák az USA-ban – 2008 (Interjú- és dokumentumelemzés)" [Weekend Hungarian Schools in the USA – 2008 (Analysis of Interviews and Documents)], in Papp, ed., *Beszédből világ*, pp. 264–297. Earlier: Zoltán Fejős, "Az anyanyelvi oktatástól az etnikus kultúra átörökítéséig (Magyar iskolaügy Amerikában 1890 és 1940 között)" [From Native-Language Teaching to Handing down Ethnic Culture (Hungarian Schooling in America between 1890 and 1940)], *Magyarságkutatás* (1990–1991); Éva Kovács, "Magyar iskolák az Egyesült Államokban – 1996-ban [Hungarian Schools in the US – 1996], in Nagy and Papp, eds., *A magyar nyelv és kultúra megtartása*, pp. 34–35; Károly Nagy, "Magyar iskolák az Egyesült Államokban" [Hungarian Schools in the United States], *Új Látóhatár* (March/April 1965). On Germany: Márta Illés-Molnár, *Magyar iskolák Németországban 2008. A Németországi Magyar mint Származási Nyelv* [Hungarian Schools in Germany 2008. Hungarian as a Language of Origin in Germany], http://www.buod.de/docs/iskolaugyibizottsag/beszamolo.pdf.

33   http://www.nyeomszsz.org/. Retrieved November 18, 2010; members in the UK, Austria, Czech Republic, Denmark, Estonia, Finland, Germany, Lithuania, Latvia, the Netherlands, Norway, Poland, Sweden and Switzerland.

34   http://www.lamoszsz.org. Mem*bers in Argentina, Brazil, Chile, Costa Rica, Paraguay, Uruguay and Venezuela.*

35   Károly Nagy, "Tavaszi remények, gondok" [Spring Hopes and Troubles], *Bécsi Napló* 31 (2009) 2. Elsewhere "Magyarok Amerikában" [Hungarians in America], *Korunk* (2004) 6: 57–61. Nagy paid tribute to Erika Dedinszky for her work on poetry by János Pilinszky in the Netherlands and Vince Sulyok for his work on Sándor Csoóri and Sándor Kányádi in Norway, Lóránt Czigány for a history of Hungarian literature in English, Ádám Makkai for two volumes of Hungarian verse translated into English in the US, and others for English-language studies of key events and people in Hungarian history. Nagy translated for a US university publisher important studies by István Bibó. He lists a further twenty ethnic Hungarian literary translators in Europe and America and their "outstanding achievements of recent years."

7. THE CONTACT DIALECTS OF HUNGARIAN
Miklós Kontra

Any regular contact with speakers of another language or dialect can have an effect on the way we speak. When about 3 million native speakers of Hungarian became citizens of Czechoslovakia, Romania, Yugoslavia and Austria, they came into increasing contact with speakers of Slovak, Ruthenian, Ukrainian, Romanian, Serbian, Croatian, German and other languages. The new international borders drawn after World War I disregarded the ethno-linguistic boundaries in the Carpathian Basin and turned formerly majority Hungarians into minority Hungarians overnight, in a similar fashion to "members of the Spanish culture" who "woke up one morning to find themselves citizens of the United States"[1] when the USA annexed New Mexico following the Treaty of Guadalupe Hidalgo in 1848. This had two kinds of linguistic effects: 1) Hungarian regional dialects in the circum-Hungary countries began diverging from the regional dialects in post-World War I Hungary,[2] and 2) the increasing contact with speakers of Slovak, Romanian, Serbian, and so on, gave rise to *contact dialects* of Hungarian, that is, varieties of Hungarian that show the effects of language contact and are unknown and unused by Hungarian-speakers in Hungary.

The effects of the post World War I border changes on the indigenous Hungarians in what are today Slovakia, Ukraine, Romania and Serbia are shown in Table 1.

According to Pál Péter Tóth, the number of Hungarians in the neighboring countries decreased from 3 million in 1920 to 2.4 million in 2000.[3] However, the percentage of Hungarians *vis-à-vis* the majority nations' populations decreased even more (Table 1).

Table 1. The effects of post-World War I international border changes on indigenous Hungarians in Hungary's four neighboring countries: total numbers (N) and Hungarians as a percentage of the total population of Slovakia, Transcarpathia (Ukraine), Romania and Vojvodina (Serbia)

	Slovakia		Ukraine		Romania		Serbia	
	N	%	N	%	N	%	N	%
1921	650,597	21.68	111,052	18.1	1,423,459	9.96[4]	371,006	24.2
2001	520,528	9.67[5]	166,700	13.4[6]	1,431,807	6.60	290,207	14.3[7]

At the end of the first decade of the twenty-first century, indigenous Hungarians belong to one cultural nation and eight political nations. According to the theory of political or civic nation, national identity is defined on the basis of citizenship. According to the theory of cultural nation, it is defined on the basis of language and culture. Since the collapse of the Austro-Hungarian Empire, Hungarians have defined themselves as a cultural nation. By contrast, says Gal, "Majority politicians in the circum-Hungary states have most often taken the 'civic' stance. This was the Hungarian position before 1918, and is currently legitimated in the post-socialist region by pointing to its espousal by prestigious Western states."[8]

Throughout the twentieth century, state borders changed frequently, and, as a result, many people have held five different citizenships without ever leaving their hometown. Deportations, population exchanges, ethnic cleansing and other similar acts have been used to create homogeneous nation states. The language rights situation of Hungarian minorities has varied from country to country and from time to time since 1920, but most of Hungary's neighboring states have exercised linguicist policies towards their Hungarian minorities. (*Linguicism* is social discrimination between groups of people defined on the basis of language.[9]) The Hungarians in Slovakia, Ukraine, Romania and Serbia are overrepresented in blue-collar trades and underrepresented in higher education. Gal observes that in those states "where there are large Hungarian minorities (Romania, Slovakia, Ukraine, Serbia), the language issue has remained the focus of political dispute for the twenty years since the end of communism."[10] Control over the reproduction of the national languages influences jurisdiction over schools and can result in bilingual programs that "turn out to be submersion or transition programs that take Hungarian-speaking youngsters into Serbian."[11]

Hungarian linguists did not recognize, let alone contemplate, the linguistic consequences of World War I for many decades. Then, in 1995, Lanstyák proposed that Hungarian be viewed as a *pluricentric language*, that is, a language that has more than one standard variety (similar to, for instance, German, which has a standard variety in Germany, another one in Switzerland and a third one in Austria). Thus the standard variety of Hungarian spoken by Hungarians in Slovakia, or that spoken in Romania, is recognized as somewhat different from the standard Hungarian in Hungary. These standards show the effects of bilingualism and must not be viewed as "impure, corrupt, degenerate" varieties.[12] In a lecture delivered at the Hungarian Academy of Sciences in 2002, Szilágyi made a well-argued proposal to revise the periodization of Hungarian linguistics. He suggested that the *modern Hungarian period* (which is held to begin in 1772 and to continue to the present day) should end in 1918, and that the period following World War I should be regarded as the *latest period* (*legújabb kor* in Hungarian), because it is since the end of World War I that Hungarian has been spoken as a native language not only in Hungary but in several other states as well.[13]

Domains of language use – One important consequence of the language hierarchies in Slovakia, Ukraine, Romania and Serbia is seen in what domains and to what extent Hungarian is used in those countries. Data gathered for the Sociolinguistics of Hungarian outside Hungary project[14] reveal that in 1996 most Hungarians in Slovakia, Ukraine, Romania and Serbia used their mother tongue overwhelmingly with family members and neighbors, and in church, but in more official domains such as a doctor's office, bank, local

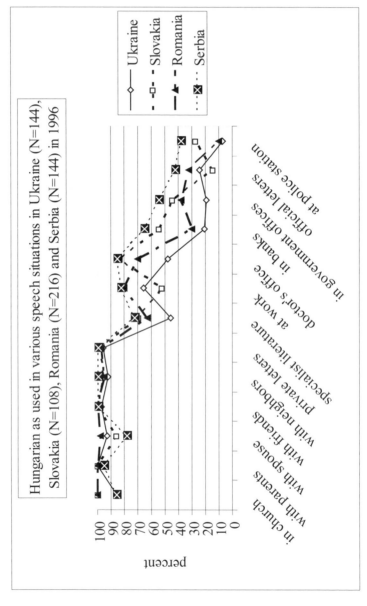

Figure 1.

Hungarian as used in various speech situations in Ukraine (N=144), Slovakia (N=108), Romania (N=216) and Serbia (N=144) in 1996

government office or police station those who used Hungarian alone or Hungarian and the majority language together fell well below 50 percent of our respondents. See Figure 1.[15]

As Figure 1 demonstrates, use of the Hungarian national minorities' mother tongue tends to be restricted to the family; it may be used at work in some cases, but its use in official contacts is very limited.

Attitudes to varieties of Hungarian – Reviewing the studies conducted in the mid-1990s[16] Susan Gal notes that the Hungarian minorities operate with a dual evaluative scheme: "With the economic lens, minority Hungarian speakers see the state languages as 'better' than Hungarian, since their chances of upward social mobility are better with higher education in the state language" but "With the aesthetic and cultural lens, Hungarian is valued very highly by its speakers in all countries."[17]

Minority Hungarians also rank the regionally distinct forms of Hungarian, including their own variety. The Hungarian used in Transylvania is valued most highly in all the countries. Hungarians in Transcarpathia also evaluate their own variety as beautiful, in contrast to Hungarians in Slovakia, who devalue their own distinctive forms of Hungarian, as do those in Serbia and the countries in the southwest (Croatia, Slovenia and Austria). Gal is correct in stating the following: "Hungarian speakers in Hungary make no allowances for the linguistic effects of bilingualism. This, and the somewhat divergent local forms used by minority speakers are heard by metropolitan Hungarians as provincial and chronotopically 'backward' or unsophisticated."[18] In a recent study, Menyhárt shows that over half of the Hungarian primary school children in a village in southern Slovakia report that their speech patterns are identified by Hungarians in Hungary as different from those heard in Hungary (Figure 2), and the most telling feature is their use of borrowed words from Slovak, such as *párki* 'hot dog' (which is *virsli* in Hungary) or *horcsica* 'mustard' (*mustár* in Hungary). See Figure 3.[19]

Hungarians in Hungary are strong supporters of standard language ideology: that is, they believe in the existence of a "correct

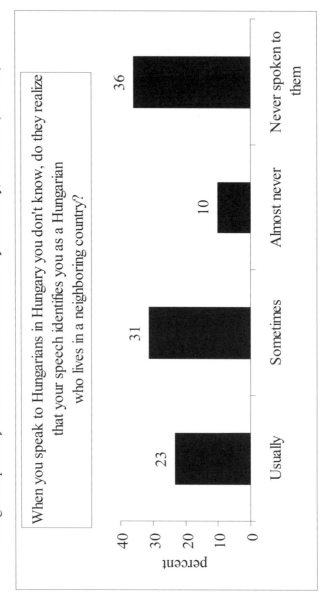

Figure 2. Awareness of the varieties of Hungarian spoken in and outside Hungary as perceived by Hungarian primary school children in Vrakúň/Nyékvárkony, Slovakia (N = 115)[20]

Figure 3. What feature of your Hungarian speech gives you away as a Hungarian from one of Hungary's neighboring countries? Respondents are Hungarian primary school children in Vrakúň/Nyékvárkony, Slovakia (N =115)[21]

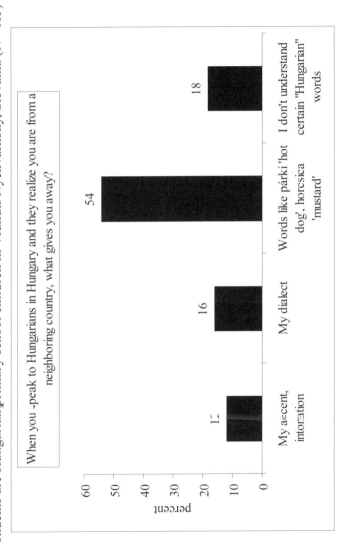

When you speak to Hungarians in Hungary and they realize you are from a neighboring country, what gives you away?

Hungarian" and expect everybody to use it in nearly all speech situations. Linguistic stigmatization of, and social discrimination against, those speakers who use "incorrect" Hungarian are both extremely widespread, and "in the pan-European regime of monolingualism and standard language"[22] borrowing words from the majority language, code-switching (the alternate use of Hungarian and another language) and other language contact phenomena "lead to stigma and to self-deprecation. Judgmental encounters with purist linguists and teachers also create problems of self-confidence."[23]

Vocabulary differences – Some regionalisms date from before 1918: for instance, the present-day Transylvanian word *laska* 'ribbon noodles' is *tészta* in standard Hungarian in Hungary. Use of this regional word can create temporary misunderstanding between a Transylvanian and a metropolitan Hungarian-speaker. International words that were used by Hungarians before 1918, for instance *internátus* 'boarding school', *katedra* '(university) chair' or *penzió* 'pension' have become old-fashioned in metropolitan Hungarian but continue to be used as colloquial words by Hungarians in the neighboring countries.[24]

Lexical changes induced by contact with the majority languages can be of several kinds. First, a Hungarian word can obtain a new meaning due to contact with another language (semantic borrowing), as is the case with *szemafor*, which means '(railway) semaphore' in Hungary but 'traffic light' in Romania, Slovakia, Serbia, Ukraine, Croatia and Slovenia. Second, calques (word-for-word translations into Hungarian) are often used: for example, *feljátszik* 'record something on tape or video' in Slovakia equals *felvesz* in Hungary, *előadótanár* 'associate professor' in Romania equals *egyetemi docens* in Hungary, *elölát* 'plan something' in Serbia is *tervez* in Hungary.[25] Third, the most conspicuous effect is the use of direct borrowings from the majority languages, for example *abonament* 'bus pass' in Romania (which in metropolitan Hungarian is *buszbérlet*), *avansz* 'advance payment' in Ukraine (metropolitan Hungarian *előleg*), *delikvencia* 'delinquency' in Serbia and Slovakia (metropolitan Hungarian *bűnözés*). Under the influence of a contact

language, minority Hungarians may use a different form of the same international word from that used by metropolitan Hungarians: for example, all Hungarians in Hungary use *infarktus* 'heart attack' but the Hungarians in all the seven neighboring countries use *infarkt*.[26]
Our study conducted in 1996 in seven countries[27] has revealed statistically significant differences in the use of universal contact variables, that is, variables that vary both in Hungary and in the neighboring countries, and one of whose variants has an analogous variant in the contact languages. In metropolitan Hungarian, compound profession nouns with the component -*nő* 'woman' are only used when it is important to stress the referent's gender. Such nouns were used by significantly more Hungarians in the neighboring countries than in Hungary. Figure 4 shows the respondents in seven countries on the written sentence completion task *Anyám egy középiskolában tanít, ő tehát...* (*tanár* 'teacher' or *tanárnő* 'teacher + woman') 'My mother teaches in a high school so she is a...'.

Grammatical differences – The use of place name suffixes by Hungarians 75 years after the Treaty of Trianon shows some of the grammatical effects of the borders drawn after World War I. First, a review of the rule for Hungarian place name suffixation is in order. The majority of Hungarian city and village names take the surface cases or *on* cases (for example *Budapest-en* 'in Budapest') whereas some names denoting Hungarian settlements and all names of foreign cities take the interior cases or *in* cases (for example *Tihany-ban* 'in Tihany, Hungary' and *Boston-ban* 'in Boston, USA'). The role of the semantic feature 'foreign' in suffix choice can be illustrated by such a pair as *Velencé-n* 'in Velence, a village in Hungary' and *Velencé-ben* 'in Velence [= Venice], a city in Italy'. The Hungarian vs. foreign distinction is often interpreted as "belonging to historical (pre-1920) Hungary" vs. "outside historical Hungary." In our study we hypothesized that Hungarians in Hungary and those across the borders will differ in their use of place name suffixes: the latter will use the surface (*on*) suffixes for place names outside historical Hungary but within the state in which they live (for example, Hungarians in Yugoslavia will favor *Koszovó-n*),

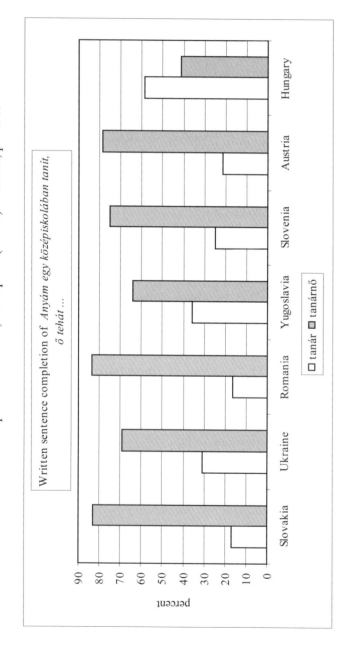

Figure 4. The use of overt gender marking of profession nouns by Hungarians in seven countries. Written sentence completion. N = 807, chi-square (df = 6) = 73.118, p < .001[28]

whereas Hungarians in Hungary will use the interior (*in*) cases for these places (for example *Koszovó-ban*). Two such place names were chosen to gather the data: *Craiova* (a city in Oltenia, Romania) and *Koszovó* (in 1996 an autonomous region in southeast Serbia). Both have always been outside historical Hungary.

In one task, informants were required to choose one of two words (*Craiován* or *Craiovában*) that best fit the sentence *Az egyik ismerősöm fia ... volt katona* 'The son of an acquaintance of mine was a soldier in...'. In the other task, respondents had to choose the more natural sentence of these two: 1) *Koszovóban folytatódnak a tárgyalások az albánok és a szerbek között* and 2) *Koszovón folytatódnak...* 'Negotiations between the Albanians and Serbs in Kosovo continue.' Country-by-country analyses show that significantly more respondents in Romania chose the "home suffix" with *Craiova* than respondents in the other countries (see Figure 5).

Figure 5. Choice of *Craiovában* vs. *Craiován* by Hungarians in seven countries. N = 818, chi-square (df = 6) = 109.501, p < .01

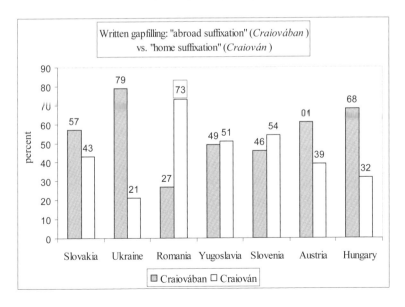

The same "home suffixation" was favored with *Koszovó* by respondents in Yugoslavia and Slovenia: only 20 to 27 percent of the respondents in five countries chose the "home suffixed" form *Koszovón* as more natural, but 61 percent in Yugoslavia and 78 percent in Slovenia judged it more natural than the "abroad suffixed" *Koszovóban*. (The chi-square test shows this difference to be significant: N = 830, chi-square (df = 6) = 130.475, p < .01.)

The explanation for the effect of border changes on the use of place name suffixes comes from Szilágyi: in categorizing a place name, what is important is whether or not the place is in an area where Hungarians or speakers of Hungarian (potentially) live, or are perceived to potentially live. Speakers may vary in their perception of different places, hence the variation in language use. Hungarians in Romania perceive the Romanian regions beyond the Carpathian Mountains (which have never been part of Hungary) as places that they could themselves inhabit, and consequently they say and write forms such as *Craiová-n* 'in Craiova', which are highly unusual for Hungarians in Hungary.[29]

There are several other contact-induced effects on the grammar of minority Hungarian-speakers. When respondents had to choose the more natural sentence of these two for 'I saw you on TV yesterday', a) *Tegnap láttalak a tévében* and b) *Tegnap láttalak téged a tévében* (where use of the overt object pronoun *téged* is induced by the contact with Slavic languages), statistically significant differences were found between metropolitan and minority Hungarians. However, minority Hungarians are not homogeneous in their language use. One factor that plays a role in creating heterogeneity is the number of speakers of Hungarian with whom one is in daily contact. Hungarians who constitute a local majority (over 70 percent of the local population) show fewer contact effects than those who form a local minority (less than 30 percent of the population). For instance, 28 percent of the local-majority Hungarians in Slovakia, Ukraine, Romania and Yugoslavia judged the contact-induced sentence with the overt object pronoun (*Tegnap láttalak téged a tévében*) to be more natural, as opposed to 38 percent of the local-minority Hungarians. This difference is statistically significant (N = 536, chi-square (df = 1) = 6.056, p < .05).[30]

Language maintenance, shift, and the role of education – As was indicated by the previous finding, the high or low concentration of Hungarian-speakers in a locality has a strong impact on the maintenance of Hungarian. Low speaker numbers are one of the factors in language shift: that is, the process whereby a group of Hungarian-speakers stops using Hungarian and starts using another language. This process is all but completed in Oberwart/Felsőőr, Austria,[31] and is undoubtedly taking place in several parts of the Hungarian-speaking regions. In the early 1990s, more than half of the minority Hungarians lived in settlements with a local Hungarian majority: 70 to 77 percent of the Hungarians in Slovakia, Transcarpathia (Ukraine) and Slovenia, and approximately 56 percent each in Vojvodina (Yugoslavia) and in Romania formed a local majority in the villages and towns where they lived. In 1991 there were 1,410 localities with a Hungarian majority population in the neighboring countries. Linguistic assimilation is shown, for instance, by the number of native Hungarian-speakers in Croatian-majority territories being 12 percent lower than those of Hungarian ethnic affiliation.[32]

A very influential factor in minority language maintenance and shift is education, which can contribute to the maintenance (reproduction) of a linguistic minority or its demise. Where the dominant (state) language is taught *additively* (in addition to the pupils' mother tongue), chances for maintenance are much better than in situations of *subtractive* teaching (when the state language is taught at the cost of the mother tongue). The right of Hungarian minorities to education through the medium of their mother tongue was more or less recognized throughout the twentieth century. Typically, there has been an inverse relationship between the number of students studying in mother-tongue-medium schools and the level of their education. For instance, Gal notes that in Slovakia "Roughly 80% of Hungarian-speaking children go to Hungarian primary schools; this figure drops to 50% for secondary education and is even lower for technical education."[33] The subtractive language policy pursued in Slovakia is evident in Gal's diagnosis: "While Slovak is taught in Hungarian schools, Hungarian is not taught in Slovak schools, so that parents who decide to send their children to Slovak schools give up all possibility of Hungarian educational input."[34]

Such education can easily result in what Lanstyák and Szabómihály[35] term *language lapses* and *language gaps*. The former denote cases when a speaker is temporarily unable to recall a word or a grammatical structure with which s/he is otherwise familiar. By the latter the authors mean cases when a required word or structure is not part of the speaker's linguistic system at all. These phenomena contribute a great deal to bilingual Hungarians' linguistic insecurity and may lead to register attrition. For instance, Hungarians in Romania often find it hard to write an official letter in Hungarian, since they have had hardly any opportunity to write them in their mother tongue. Language gaps have also become evident recently among Hungarian school teachers in Slovakia, who find it difficult to write class registers and school reports in Hungarian now that it has become legally possible. It is evident that such language gaps are the result of restrictive language policies or violations of the minority speakers' linguistic human rights.[36]

The choice of the medium of education has been shown to have important effects on the linguistic development of bilingual Hungarians. For instance, Lanstyák and Szabómihály demonstrated that monolingual Hungarian high school children exhibit systematic differences in their use and judgment of different forms of Hungarian from their bilingual peers in southern Slovakia. A further difference has been established between bilingual Hungarian pupils who go to schools with Hungarian as the medium of instruction and those who go to schools with Slovak as the medium. For instance, when the three groups of high school children had to insert one of two forms that best fit the sentence provided, significant differences were shown in their choice: the Slovak-contact-induced form was used to a much greater extent by the Slovak-medium pupils than the monolingual Hungarian form. See Figure 6.

Sentence to complete:
Jó napot kívánok. A ... jöttem, panaszt szeretnék tenni.
'Good afternoon. I have come to see the boss, I would like to lodge a complaint.'
Choice (a)   *főnökhöz* (monolingual Hungarian form)
Choice (b)   *főnök után* (induced by Slovak *ísť za niekým*)

Figure 6. Choice of contact-induced *főnök után* vs. monolingual Hungarian *főnökhöz* by three groups of high school children: Hungarians in Hungary, Hungarians in Slovakia with Hungarian as medium of instruction (Slovakia_H) and Hungarians in Slovakia with Slovak as medium of instruction (Slovakia_S) (N = 806).[37]

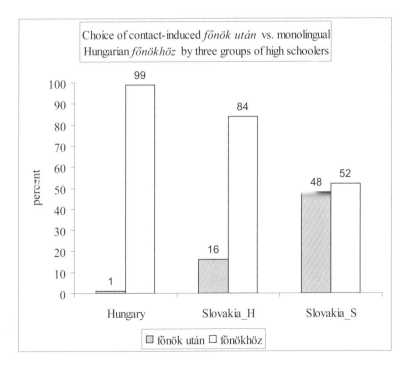

Lanstyák and Szabómihály have found that the linguistic differences between the Slovakia_H and Slovakia_S students are much greater than those between the Hungary students and the Slovakia_H students, despite the fact that the latter groups study in schools 40 to 50 kilometers apart, while the two bilingual groups often study in the same building. Thus the choice of Slovak as the medium of instruction clearly contributes to linguistic divergence (and possibly a shift to Slovak).[38]

Mother-tongue-medium education for the Hungarian minorities in most if not all of the neighboring countries suffers from legislation that makes minority-language-medium education seem a privilege, or something over which the minority pupils only have themselves to blame if they find school too difficult. "Equality" is provided by state-language education for all, without regard to the pupils' mother tongue.[39]

One other problem influencing the linguistic skills of minority Hungarians is how the state languages are taught to them in schools. In most cases they are taught as if they were the mother tongue of Hungarians. What usually happens is that a school subject such as "Romanian language and literature" is identical in the curriculum for Romanian pupils and for minority pupils, although the teaching should serve radically different purposes. For Romanians the goal is to educate mother-tongue (L1) speakers of Romanian in Romanian language and literature, but for Hungarians and other minorities the goal is to enable them to acquire Romanian as a second language (L2). If the same methods and teaching materials are used to teach the state language as an L1 and an L2, the result can only be that Hungarians do not acquire Romanian well enough in school, which later renders them disadvantaged.[40] Such practice, the denial of the right to learn an L2 as an L2, constitutes educational malpractice,[41] is a violation of linguistic human rights in education, and generates social conflicts in Slovakia, Ukraine, Romania and Serbia.

Notes

1 David Marshall, "The Question of an Official Language: Language Rights and the English Language Amendment," *International Journal of the Sociology of Language* (1986) 60: 40.

2 See, for instance, József Menyhárt, Károly Presinszky and Anna Sándor, *Szlovákiai magyar nyelvjárások* [Hungarian Dialects in Slovakia] (Nyitra, 2009).

3 Pál Péter Tóth, *A nemzetközi vándorlás szerepe a kárpát-medencei magyar népességfejlődésben* [The Role of International Migration in the Development of the Hungarian Population in the Carpathian Basin] (Budapest, 2007).

4 These figures are from 1930: see Attila Benő and Sándor N. Szilágyi, "Hungarian in Romania," in Anna Fenyvesi, ed., *Hungarian Language Contact Outside Hungary: Studies on Hungarian as a Minority Language* (Amsterdam, 2005), p. 135.

5 István Lanstyák and Gizella Szabómihály, "Hungarian in Slovakia," in Fenyvesi, ed., *Hungarian Language Contact Outside Hungary*, p. 49.

6 These figures are from 1989: see Károly Kocsis, *Kárpátalja mai területének etnikai térképe/Ethnic Map of Present Territory of Transcarpathia (Subcarpathia)* (Budapest, 2001).

7 These figures are from 2002: see Károly Kocsis and Saša Kicošev, *A Vajdaság mai területének etnikai térképe/Ethnic Map of Present Territory of Vojvodina* (Budapest, 2004).

8 Susan Gal, "Hungarian as a Minority Language," in Guus Extra and Durk Gorter, eds., *Multilingual Europe: Facts and Policies* (Berlin/New York, 2008), p. 221.

9 For similarities between linguicism in the USA and Central Europe, see Miklós Kontra, "Language Rights Arguments in Central Europe and the USA: How Similar Are They?" in Douglas A. Kibbee, ed., *Language Legislation and Linguistic Rights* (Amsterdam/Philadelphia, PA, 1998), pp. 142–178, and its translation into Romanian: "Dreptul la exprimare în limba maternă în Europa Centrală şi în Statele Unite ale Americii. Similitudini şi diferenţe," *Altera* (2000) 15: 43–61.

10 Gal, "Hungarian as a Minority Language," p. 222.

11 *Ibid.*, p. 218.

12 István Lanstyák, "A magyar nyelv központjai" [Hungarian as a Pluricentric Language], *Magyar Tudomány* (1995) 10: 1170–1185.

13   Sándor N. Szilágyi, "A magyar nyelv a Magyarországgal szomszédos országokban" [The Hungarian Language in the Neighboring Countries of Hungary], in Csilla Fedinec, ed., *Értékek, dimenziók a magyarságkutatásban* [Values and Dimensions in the Research of Hungarians] (Budapest, 2008), pp. 105–117.

14   See Miklós Kontra, "Contextualizing the Sociolinguistics of Hungarian Outside Hungary Project," in Fenyvesi, ed., *Hungarian Language Contact Outside Hungary*, pp. 29–45, and several other chapters in the same book.

15   Anikó Beregszászi and István Csernicskó, ... *itt mennyit ér a szó?: Írások a kárpátaljai magyarok nyelvhasználatáról* [...What is the Value of a Word Here?: Studies on the Language Use of Transcarpathian Hungarians] (Ungvár, 2004), p. 62.

16   See Fenyvesi, ed., *Hungarian Language Contact Outside Hungary*.

17   Gal, "Hungarian as a Minority Language," p. 225.

18   *Ibid.*, p. 227.

19   József Menyhárt, "Sóspálcika? Az magyarul ticsinki" [Salt Stick? It Is *ticsinki* in Hungarian], in Erzsébet Zelliger, ed., *Nyelv, területiség, társadalom* [Language, Territoriality, Society] (Budapest, 2007), pp. 333–347.

20   *Ibid.*, p. 343.

21   *Ibid.*

22   Gal, "Hungarian as a Minority Language," p. 228.

23   *Ibid.*

24   István Lanstyák, "A magyar szókészlet szétfejlődése 1918 után" [The Divergent Development of the Hungarian Vocabulary after 1918], in Fedinec, ed., *Értékek, dimenziók a magyarságkutatásban*, p. 127.

25   *Ibid.*, p. 128.

26   *Ibid.*, p. 129.

27   Miklós Kontra, "Hungarian In- and Outside Hungary," in Ulrich Ammon *et al.*, eds., *Sociolinguistics/Soziolinguistik*, 2nd completely revised and extended edition, Volume 3 (Berlin/New York, 2006), pp. 1814–1815.

28   In the captions of Figures 4 and 5, N equals the number of respondents in the study. The result of the chi-square test is presented (with the degree of freedom in parentheses), followed in this case by "p < .001". In plain English this means that there is less than one in a thousand chances that the differences shown in the figure for the seven countries are due to chance. In other words, this is a statistically significant

result, and we can be sure that it is no accident that the majority of respondents in Hungary used *tanár* but the majority of all other respondents in the neighboring countries used *tanárnő*. In Figure 5, $p < .01$ means that there is less than one in a hundred chances that the difference in the data between respondents in Romania vs. the other countries is caused by chance.

29 Sándor N. Szilágyi, *Hogyan teremtsünk világot? Rávezetés a nyelvi világ vizsgálatára* [How Shall We Create a World? Guide to the Study of Linguistic Worlds] (Kolozsvár, 1996), pp. 26–29.

30 Kontra, "Contextualizing the Sociolinguistics," p. 39.

31 See Susan Gal, *Language Shift: Social Determinants of Linguistic Change in Bilingual Austria* (New York, 1979).

32 Károly Kocsis and Eszter Kocsis-Hodosi, *Ethnic Geography of the Hungarian Minorities in the Carpathian Basin* (Budapest, 1998), p. 25.

33 Gal, "Hungarian as a Minority Language," p. 217.

34 *Ibid.*

35 Lanstyák and Szabómihály, "Hungarian in Slovakia," p. 65.

36 See Tove Skutnabb-Kangas, *Linguistic Genocide in Education – or Worldwide Diversity and Human Rights?* (Mahwah, NJ, 2000).

37 Based on István Lanstyák and Gizella Szabómihály, *Magyar nyelvhasználat – iskola – kétnyelvűség* [Hungarian Language Usage – School – Bilingualism] (Pozsony, 1997), p. 109.

38 *Ibid.*, pp. 135–142.

39 See Miklós Kontra and Sándor N. Szilágyi, "A kisebbségeknek van anyanyelvük, de a többségnek nincs?" [The Minorities Have a Mother Tongue but the Majority Do Not?], in Miklós Kontra and Helga Hattyár, eds., *Magyarok és nyelvtörvények* [Hungarians and Language Laws] (Budapest, 2002), pp. 3–10.

40 Sándor N. Szilágyi, "De ce nu-şi pot însuşi copiii maghiari limba română în şcoală?" [Why Can't Hungarian Children Learn Romanian in Schools in Romania?], *Altera* (1998) 7: 131–148; Idem, "Probleme ale predării limbi române în şcolile minorităţilor" [Why Hungarian Children Cannot Master the Romanian Language in School], in Olga Murvai, ed., *Conferinţa naţională de bilingvism 16–17 iunie 1997* [National Conference on Bilingualism, June 16–17, 1997] (Bucharest, 1999), pp. 215–235.

41 For the term *educational malpractice*, see John Baugh, *Out of the Mouths of Slaves: African American Language and Educational Malpractice* (Austin, TX, 1999).

8. POPULATION MOVEMENTS
IN THE CARPATHIAN BASIN
Tamás Stark

The main force behind the social and political changes in the former Austro-Hungarian Monarchy after the Great War came from a vision of the future: of the nation state as a rightful fusion of the constructs of nation and state. The new states that appeared after 1918 rested on conscious, institutionalized nation-building by their majority nations. Yet they contained substantial minorities, and anxiety about the prospect of disintegration led to efforts, within the scope offered by the international situation, to erode the social and economic advantages of any such groups as did not belong to the majority nation, and to assimilate them. The number of Hungarians living in neighboring countries duly declined by one million over the next ninety years. The territories that would be detached from Hungary after the Great War had held 3,175,000 persons of Hungarian national affiliation in 1910, but only 2,174,921 such persons in 2001. The loss was greater still in proportional terms: from 31.1 percent in 1910 to 17.6 percent in 2001.[1] This section examines the contribution to the process made by the migration of Hungarians.

About 10 percent of the Hungarians outside the Trianon borders of Hungary, 350,000 people, moved into Hungary between 1918 and 1924. According to figures from the National Office for Refugees, there were 107,000 arrivals from Czechoslovakia (which then included Transcarpathia), 197,000 from Romania, 45,000 from Yugoslavia, and 1,200 from Austria.[2] Between the mid-1920s (by which time neighboring countries had introduced legislation on citizenship and Hungary had tightened its residence conditions) and 1940, a further 10,000 arrived from Romania and 3,000 from Yugoslavia, disregarding unregistered immigrants.[3]

Romania and Yugoslavia followed strong assimilation policies between the world wars. Even the more democratically organized Czechoslovakia fell far short of the "Switzerland-of-the-East" policy that it proclaimed. In Hungary, its own national minorities were not seen as a big domestic issue between 1919 and 1938, as they made up less than 10 percent of the population, but this issue emerged again after the territorial acquisitions of 1938 and 1941. Hungarian governments sought to conserve or restore the pre-war ethnic structure in the expanded territory and throughout the Carpathian Basin. This meant automatic rejection of any proposals for population exchanges, which would have altered that structure substantially. A proposal for a population exchange with Czechoslovakia was turned down at talks at Komárom in October 1938, and so was one with Romania at talks at Turnu Severin in August 1940, prior to the Second Vienna Award brokered by Germany and Italy. A similar proposal by the Croatian government was rejected in 1942.[4]

Hungary's efforts to restore the pre-1918 situation were focused on reversing the Czechoslovak, Romanian and Serbian settlement programs in the returned southern strip of Slovakia. After the First Vienna Award of November 2, 1938, the agricultural settlers and a total of some 5,000 public employees were removed in November and December.[5]

The Second Vienna Award of August 30, 1940, which returned Northern Transylvania to Hungary, was followed by mass spontaneous movements of people. Romanian settlers who had arrived after 1918 moved to the Regat. Indigenous Hungarians in Southern Transylvania made for Hungary, in a migration accelerated by a rapid deterioration of their prospects of making a living. The Hungarian government was dismayed, for its policy was still to sustain the Hungarians' numerical, cultural and economic weight in Southern Transylvania in the hope of further territorial revision in Hungary's favor. It tightened entry conditions substantially in the spring of 1941, yet foreign police records still showed 190,132 people arriving from Romania between September 1940 and February 1944.[6] Meanwhile 221,000 Romanians were fleeing from Northern

Transylvania,[7] which negated the increase produced by Romanian settlement schemes after 1918.

Hungary's leaders sought to restore 1918 ethnic proportions in occupied parts of the Southern Region after Germany's invasion of Yugoslavia in April 1941. The civilian authorities registered 48,067 persons in 1941 who had moved in after 1918 and stayed after the withdrawal of Yugoslav forces.[8] These were primary targets for the local Hungarian administration and armed forces, but neither the German command in Belgrade nor the puppet Serbian regime would take them, as they were inundated with tens of thousands of Serbs expelled from Croatia. For want of an agreement, the Hungarian authorities in the Southern Region began to expel them unilaterally. According to Hungarian sources, 15,000 "indigenous" Serbs were deported between April 1941 and the end of the year,[9] but German sources put the figure at 35,000 and the Refugee Commission set up by Milan Nedić's puppet government in September 1941 put the number of returnees from the reannexed territories at 80,000.[10]

The Hungarian community in the reannexed territories was boosted further by the arrival of public officials. According to Hungary's Central Statistics Office (CSO) and Ministry of Welfare reports after 1945, the numbers of immigrants and returnees were 26,000 to the regained Upland territory and Transcarpathia, 24,000 to Northern Transylvania, and 14,000 to the Southern Region.[11] Although the purpose was not settlement but to restore the pre-1918 ethnic status quo, two small-scale settlements occurred, both from beyond the 1918 borders into the Southern Region. Some 17,700 Székelys were came from Bukovina under an agreement with Romania from Bukovina,[12] and 1,552 Hungarians from the Bosnian villages of Gunja, Vucijak and Brčko were rescued from partisan warfare. These migrations were relatively small. Nonetheless, there was a dramatic change in Hungary's population structure in the last two years of the war.

The so-called Jewish Question featured high on the government and parliamentary agenda in the period when Hungary was gaining territory on four occasions. The National Assembly passed three acts (usually known as the Jewish laws) between 1938 and 1941 that curtailed the civil and economic rights of the Jews, who thenceforth were not classed as Hungarians. The political leaders rejected successive requests from the German authorities for deportation of the Jews before German military occupation on March 19, 1944, installed a new regime under Döme Sztójay. This was replaced, after an unsuccessful attempt to bail out of the war led by head of state Miklós Horthy, by the quisling government of Ferenc Szálasi, which eagerly met the German demands for full deprivation of Jews' rights and for their deportation. The number of victims of what came to be known as the Holocaust can be estimated from the difference in the size of the community before and after the war, although the historical sources leave broad margins of error. Some 70,000–100,000 people were liberated from the Pest Ghetto,[13] and at least another 20,000 were still in safe houses at the end of the war.[14] Another 20,000–30,000 survived the war with false papers.[15] Thus the number of survivors in Budapest can be put at 110,000–150,000. According to Government Repatriation Commission figures,[16] 68,000 deportees returned to the post-war territory of Hungary.[17] Apart from the Budapest liberated and returnees, there was a third large group of survivors, consisting of Jews from the provinces drafted for labor service. These may have numbered 20,000–40,000.[18]

Based on historical sources, the number of survivors in the present-day territory was certainly more than 190,000 and probably fewer than 260,000.[19] The number of liberated and returnees in territories reannexed in 1938 was about 80,000, giving a total of 270,000–340,000 for the territory that Hungary controlled in the war. The 1941 census recorded 780,000–820,000 citizens covered by the Jewish laws, and given the wide margins for numbers of liberated and returnees, it can be said for sure only that the Jewish community had certainly lost fewer than 550,000 and more than 440,000 members by the end of the war.[20] It must be stressed that handing over the provincial Jews to the Germans for extermination markedly weakened the Hungarian communities in areas of mixed settlement – Transcarpathia and Northern Transylvania – at a time when it was priority government policy to restore and maintain their numbers. The number of Jews in the territory gained from Czechoslovakia sank from 30,000 to 10,000. There had been 115,000 Jews in Transcarpathia, but fewer than 20,000 returned in 1945 to the Soviet-annexed area. Only 44,000 of the 151,000 Jews in Northern Transylvania remained at the time of the liberation, and only 4,000 of the 14,000 Hungarian Jews did in the Southern Region.[21]

The war against the Jews struck a greater blow to the country than the actual warfare, for the number of military deaths, likewise hard to estimate, was a good deal lower than the number of Jews lost. The former were registered by the 22nd Department of the Ministry of Defense. By the end of October 1944, there were 256,431 names on its register of wounded, missing, certified prisoners of war, and those who had died in battle.[22] No account was taken of the number of military deaths between November 1944 and April 1945. The greatest number of the eroding Hungarian military forces was lost in the siege of Budapest, where the number of fallen, missing, and wounded has been put at 50,000 by military historians.[23] Bearing in mind the spring actions, the figure of 256,431 up to October 31, 1944, must be raised to more than 300,000 by the end of the war. Military historians and available Soviet documents suggest that 50–75 percent of the fallen and missing can be counted as having died, as can one third of the wounded, so that the total military loss of life can be estimated at 140,000–180,000. A detailed account of civilian losses was given in June 1945 by the CSO. Combined figures for the country's post-war territory show that 44,490 civilians lost their lives in military action, air raids, and land attacks.[24] The greatest losses by area – 8,568 lives according to the CSO – were in Budapest.[25] Prisoners of war are integral to warfare, but in the campaigns of the Soviet army they were more than a side effect, they were an aim. For the system of labor camps for foreign internees and prisoners of war was set up in September 1939, at the very beginning of the war, as the Soviets drew no distinction between civilians and military, and the war was intended not only to spread the communist system, but to meet immediate labor needs. Beside that economic need lay motives of collective punishment and ethnic cleansing as well.

The CSO, in details prepared in 1946 for the Paris peace talks, put the number of Hungarians taken prisoner by the Soviets at 600,000, based on data from the Ministry of Defense Losses Department, enquiries about prisoners reaching the Ministry of Foreign Affairs, and Soviet war reports.[26] The Division for Prisoners of War and Internees at the Soviet People's Commissariat for Internal Affairs (NKVD) recorded some 530,000 Hungarian prisoners, but the figure is for arrivals in the Soviet Union, excluding transit camp inmates or those who died in transit.[27] The bulk of those taken were civilians. The circumstances in which they were gathered and deported point to the existence of special NKVD units in each territory, engaged in shipping them out. The number of civilians taken from the present-day territory of Hungary (according to individual and group requests for information reaching the Prisoners of War Department at the Ministry of Foreign Affairs, and estimated numbers deported from Budapest) was 120,000–200,000. Local research in Transcarpathia, the reannexed areas of the Upland and Transylvania adds more than 50,000 to this.[28]

The data on returnees are uncertain and to some extent contradictory. There was no central registration of these in Hungary before July 1946, and the estimates vary between 100,000 and 150,000. The 1947, 1948 and 1949 figures of the Prisoner of War Reception Committee in Debrecen add up to another 220,000 returnees. However, there were still prisoners returning in the early 1950s, after the reception camp was closed. According to the most optimistic estimates and calculations, at least 200,000 Hungarians died in Soviet captivity.

When the Red Army and Romanian forces that changed sides arrived at the southeast limits of the Carpathians, some of the inhabitants of Transylvania began to move westward. This favored the Romanian efforts to create a nation state, as the evacuees were Hungarians and Germans from an ethnically mixed area. Just two days after the Romanian change of sides on August 23 there were

Ministry of the Interior orders to intern Germans and Hungarians in Transylvania and the Banat if they were "dangerous to the order of state." A bigger trauma (although one that involved fewer victims) was caused by a campaign of vengeance launched in Transylvania by Romanian paramilitary units raised in Bucharest at the end of August 1944. The events meant that about 400,000 Hungarians left Northern Transylvania in the autumn of 1944. A CSO survey suggests that 102,000 settled in the post-war territory of Hungary instead of returning to their native province after the fighting.[29]

The Front reached the Southern Region at the end of September 1944. Vigorous ethnic cleansing ensued in areas occupied by Tito's partisans, lasting from October 1944 to the spring of 1945 and conducted by the Department of People's Protection (OZNA) and by partisan units. At least 10,000 Germans were killed, and German sources estimate that another 60,000–70,000 died in the internment camps.[30] The Vojvodina OZNA head Svetozar Kostić Čapo stated later that Ministry of the Interior forces killed about 20,000 Hungarians.[31] Serbian Hungarian authors, based on other recollections, eyewitness testimony and local documents, give total figures for Hungarian victims of 15,000–20,000.[32] Some 60,000 Hungarians left the Southern Region before or after the terror,[33] including some 14,000 public employees and another 14,000 Bukovina Székelys who had arrived during 1941.

The Germans and Hungarians were the main obstacle to creating a Slav nation state in Czechoslovakia as well. The three main Allies agreed to deportation of the Germans at the Potsdam Conference, but despite Czechoslovakia's efforts and Soviet support for them, it did not agree to resettlement of the 600,000-strong Hungarian minority. Czechoslovakia then sought a population exchange agreement with Hungary, its experts envisaging that 300,000–500,000 Slovaks from Hungary would move in, yet only 105,000 residents of Hungary had declared Slovak to be their native language in the 1931 census. The Hungarians remaining after the population exchange would then be dispersed by internal resettlement and further unilateral expulsions. Official harassment of the Hungarians of Czechoslovakia eventually persuaded the Hungarian government to conclude a population exchange agreement on February 27, 1946, whereby the numbers resettling in each direction would be the same. In the event, only 73,000 Slovaks left Hungary for Czechoslovakia. About one third of the 600,000 Hungarians of Slovakia were resettled in Hungary, including those deported unilaterally for having settled after 1938, and the ostensible war criminals. The vast majority of the Hungarian community remained where they were.

Implementation of the population exchange agreement had not even begun before the Czechoslovak Ministry of the Interior decided on June 17, 1946, to deport 200,000 Hungarians unilaterally, but this was rejected by the Western allies, despite strong Soviet backing for it, and an obligation to receive the Hungarians of Slovakia was not included in the Treaty of Paris. The thwarted plan gave way to efforts to "resolve" the problem internally. Presidential Order No. 88/1945 on the obligation to work provided grounds for moving Hungarians on a mass scale into areas of Sudetenland evacuated by the Germans. This affected 44,129 Hungarians in 1946–1947,[34] and they were able to return to their home district only after several years. In place of the deported Germans and Hungarians there arrived 130,000 Slovaks from Romania, Poland, Yugoslavia and Bulgaria, along with a further 25,000 from Transcarpathia, under a June 29, 1946, population exchange agreement with the Soviet Union, although Ukrainian sources put the last figure at about 12,000.

The persecution and the organized and voluntary resettlements brought Czechoslovakia close to its goal of becoming a state of Czechs and Slovaks, but such ethnic homogenization was prevented by the fact that most of the Hungarians remained. After the communist takeover in 1948, the Soviet Union switched from supporting the plans for a nation state to demanding of the new Czechoslovak leadership a peaceful conclusion to the ethnic conflict.

There was little feeling in Hungarian society against indigenous Germans (Swabians). Tension had arisen in some provincial communities over *Volksbund* activity and SS recruitment, but there had been no open clashes. Nor was feeling against them roused by the German occupation of March 19, 1944. Once the Soviet army arrived, the members of the local German community were put in the dock, but there were no serious atrocities committed against them. The motives were economic, rather than matters of principle: the provisional post-war government had to cope with some 100,000 refugees from the lost reannexed territories, and used the land reform legislation of March 17, 1945, as a means of confiscating Swabian land, prior to deporting the Swabians to Germany.

The government, with support from the political parties, requested in an oral note to the Soviet Union on May 26, 1945, that it agree to the deportation of 200,000–250,000 "fascist" Germans to the Soviet zone of Germany. Some 490,000 people in the post-war area of Hungary had declared themselves as linguistically or ethnically German in the 1941 census. Thus half the community was condemned for such acts as joining the *Volksbund* or serving in the SS, even as enlisted men. The request was granted on the grounds of the Allied agreement at Potsdam, for Lieutenant-General Vladimir P. Sviridov, head of the Allied Control Commission, had called on the Hungarian government one week after Potsdam to prepare to deport 400,000–450,000 Germans. Despite Potsdam, Sviridov's strong intervention, and the government's own request, the political leadership was unprepared, and the earlier unanimity among the parties broke down in August 1945. Minister of Foreign Affairs János Gyöngyösi argued several times in the Council of Ministers that punishing the Germans on the grounds of their affiliation was to subscribe to Hitler's principles and create a precedent on which neighboring countries could act against their Hungarian minorities.[35] Nonetheless, the government decided in August to deport the whole German community, with full support from the Communist Party and the National Peasants' Party.

The lack of domestic political support and the problems with resettling the deportees in the Western zones of Germany meant that only about 160,000 Hungarian Germans had been deported by the time that the campaign was stopped on June 15, 1948. The deportations and spontaneous departures meant that the 500,000 Hungarian Germans were reduced in number to 200,000–220,000. The political climate meant that in the 1949 census only 22,455 declared German to be their native language and 2,600 claimed German as their national affiliation.[36]

Hungary's total loss between 1941 and 1949 can be put at 800,000–1,000,000. The campaigns of revenge led about 300,000 Hungarians to leave their native areas for the territory of Trianon Hungary. So the loss within the area of present-day Hungary can be put at 300,000–400,000. However, census data show a decline for that period of 111,000, which means that the loss was offset to a large extent by natural increase and immigration. So, in purely demographic terms, the population losses from Nazi genocide, warfare, Soviet imprisonment, and deportation of indigenous Germans were much reduced by the arrival of masses of Hungarians from neighboring countries. The population of the present territory did indeed decline, but it was also replaced to some extent.

Movements of citizens of the socialist countries, even within the Soviet Bloc, were severely curtailed from 1948 to the mid-1950s. Emigration was seen as a malaise that socialist transformation of society would cure. Travelers in or out of the socialist countries were seen as potential enemies; to have relatives or connections abroad was suspect. This mistrust had a strong effect on relations between Hungary and Hungarian communities abroad.[37] International migration affected 523,579 people in Hungary between 1947 and 1989, of whom 370,000 were emigrants.[38] Of these 192,000 had left by April 1957 after the 1956 Revolution. Overrepresented were young people, and people from Budapest and Western Hungary. The main targets were Austria and Yugoslavia as transit countries, with 43,000 and 16,000 respectively, the United States with 30,000, the United

Kingdom with 20,000, Canada with 15,000, West Germany with 12,000, and Switzerland with 10,000.[39] The decisive majority of immigrants into Hungary after 1956 (1,500–2,000 a year) came from minority Hungarian communities, in direct proportion to their size. Altogether 113,372 immigrants arrived between 1948 and 1989, of whom 22,761 were naturalized or had their citizenship restored.[40] The number of arrivals from neighboring countries began to rise in about 1973, but a relatively much bigger increase came in 1988, when Hungary recognized refugee status. In October 1989, Hungary acceded to the Geneva Convention, which granted refugee status to those who could show that they were being persecuted on national, political, religious or racial grounds. This was important particularly to the many illegal arrivals after 1986, who had come as tourists and remained in Hungary.

Year	No. of immigrants	No. of refugees
1987	1,239	-
1988	5,774	12,173
1989	10,180	17,448
1990	17,129	18,283
1991	20,500	54,693

Of the 127,000 refugees who arrived in Hungary in 1988–1994, 42 percent were from Romania and 55 percent from Yugoslavia. Of immigrants, 67 percent were from Romania, 9 percent from Yugoslavia, and 8 percent from successor states of the Soviet Union. Of the refugees, 65 percent were ethnic Hungarians.[41] Of the immigrants in the 1980–1991 period, 20.5 percent had a higher education, as did 6.2 percent of the refugees. The proportions of white-collar workers were 44.1 among the immigrants and 15 percent among the refugees. Of the immigrants 35 percent were dependants, while the proportion of dependants among the refugee population was only 14 percent.[42] Mass flows of refugees began to move to Hungary after 1988 from several directions, as this was the first socialist country to recognize refugee status. Within these, the influx of those of Hungarian national affiliation was decisive. The flows eased markedly in 1994, but the net immigration for the 1990s was 161,000, at a time when Hungary's rate of natural increase was negative, but they were mainly at the expense of minority Hungarian communities.

Notes

1   István Hoóz, "A nemzetiségi struktúra átalakulása a Kárpát-medencében" [Change in the Minority Structure in the Carpathian Basin], *Statisztikai Szemle* (1996) 11: 930–939.

2   *Országos Menekültügyi Hivatal.* Emil Petrichevich Horváth, *Jelentés az Országos Menekültügyi Hivatal négyévi működéséről* [Report on Four Years' Work of the National Bureau of Refugee Affairs] (Budapest, 1924), p. 37. On the social position and integration of the refugees: István Mócsy, *Radicalization and Counterrevolution: Magyar Refugees from the Successor States and Their Role in Hungary, 1918–1921* (Los Angeles, CA, 1973), pp. 303–338.

3   Árpád Hornyák, "A magyar kisebbségi kérdés a magyar kormány délszláv politikájában a harmincas években" [The Hungarian Minority Question in the Hungarian Government's Yugoslav Policy in the 1930s], in Nándor Bárdi and Attila Simon, eds., *Integrációs stratégiák a magyar kisebbségek történetében* [Integration Strategies in the History of the Hungarian Minorities] (Šamorín, 2006), p. 76.

4   Ferenc Sz. Horváth, "Határon innen és határon túl. Népességcsere és áttelepítés mint az erdélyi kérdés megoldása (1937–1942)" [Within and beyond the Border. Population Exchange and Relocation as a Solution to the Transylvanian Question], *Limes* (2006) 2: 7–18; Béni L. Balogh and Ágoston Olti, "A roman–magyar lakosságcsere kérdése 1940–1947 között" [The Romanian–Hungarian Population Exchange Question in 1940–1947], *Kisebbségkutatás* (2006) 4: 603–616.

5   Károly Kocsis, "Telepítések és az etnikai térszerkezet a Kárpát-medence határvidékein, 1944–1950" [Settlements and the Spatial Ethnic Structure in the Border Areas of the Carpathian Basin, 1944–1950], in Sándor Illés and Péter Tóth Pál, eds., *Migráció.*

Tanulmánygyűjtemény, I [Migration. Collection of Studies I] (Budapest, 1998), p. 126; also see Kálmán Janics, *A hontalanság évei* [Years of Statelessness] (Munich, 1979), p. 206.

6   The National Central Authority for Alien Controls (KEOKH) figure appears in Béni L. Balogh, "Az erdélyi magyar menekültkérdés" [The Transylvanian Hungarian Refugee Question], *Regio* (1999) 3: 250.

7   *Ibid.*, p. 251; also see Joseph Schechtman, *European Population Transfers, 1939–1945* (Philadelphia, PA, 1962 [1946]), p. 430.

8   Enikő A. Sajti, *Hungarians in the Voivodina 1918–1947* (Highland Lakes, NJ, 2003), pp. 234–249.

9   Péter Gosztonyi, *A magyar honvédség a második világháborúban* [The Hungarian Defense Force in World War II] (Budapest, 1992), p. 55; also see C. A. Macartney, *October Fifteenth. A History of Modern Hungary II* (Edinburgh, 1961), p. 13; János Csim, *Adalékok a Horthy hadsereg szervezetének és háborús tevékenységének a tanulmányozásához (1938–1945)* [Towards a Study of the Organization and Wartime Activity of Horthy's Army (1938–1945)] (Budapest, 1961), p. 59.

10   Sajti, *Hungarians in the Voivodina*, pp. 234–249. Estimates of the Hungarian victims in Serbian literature vary between 25,000 and 150,000. The lowest appears in Slobodan D. Milošević, *Izbeglice i preseljenici na teritoriji okupirane Jugoslavije, 1941–1945* [Refugees and Immigrants in the Occupied Territories of Yugoslavia, 1941–1945] (Belgrade, 1981), p. 276. For higher estimates, see Aleksandar Kasaš, *Mađari u Vojvodini 1941–1946* [Hungarians in Vojvodina 1941–1946] (Novi Sad, 1996), p. 39. The source for 150,000 was someone from the German military command in Serbia, right after the Hungarian withdrawal from Bačka, who was referring to intentions, not facts. See György Ránki, Ervin Pamlényi, Lóránt Tilkovszky and Gyula Juhász, eds., *A Wilhelmstrasse és Magyarország. Német diplomáciai iratok Magyarországról 1933–1944* [The Wilhelmstrasse and Hungary. German Diplomatic Papers on Hungary, 1933–1944] (Budapest, 1968), p. 581.

11   Central Statistics Office Archives, bequest of Gyula Barsy; Edit Csilléry, "Közalkalmazottak és köztisztviselők Észak-Erdélyben a második bécsi döntést követően" [Civil and Public Servants in Northern Transylvania after the Second Vienna Award], *Limes* (2006) 2: 73–90.

12 Sajti, *Hungarians in the Voivodina*; József Oberding Ősi, "A buko-
    vinai székelyek dunántúli letelepítése" [The Settlement of the
    Bukovina Székelys in Transdanubia], *Agrártörténeti Szemle* (1967)
    1–2: 185; Schechtman, *European Population Transfers*, p. 436.

13 On the survivors, see Elek Karsai and László Karsai, *A Szálasi-per*
    [The Szálasi Trial] (Budapest, 1988), pp. 605–606; Jenő Lévai, ed.,
    Eichmann in Hungary (Budapest, 1961), p. 160; Lani Yahil, "Raoul
    Wallenberg – His Mission," *Yad Vashem Studies* (1983) 43; Arieh
    Ben-Tov, *Facing the Holocaust in Budapest* (Geneva, 1988), p.
    323; Rezső Rudolf Kastner, *Der Kastner-Bericht über Eichmanns
    Menschenhandel in Ungarn* (Munich, 1961), p. 241.

14 Szálasi's ministers, Gábor Vajna and Gábor Kemény, testified in his
    trial that there were some 40,000 deportees in protected houses in
    November 1944, about half being moved to the Pest Ghetto early in
    December. Karsai and Karsai, *A Szálasi-per*, pp. 248 and 421.

15 Jenő Lévai, *Fekete könyv a magyar zsidóság szenvedéséről* [Black
    Book on the Sufferings of Hungarian Jewry] (Budapest, 1946), p.
    315, citing a report of the Hungarian Office of the World Jewish
    Council. See Alexander Grossmann, *Nur das Gewissen* (Waldgut,
    1986), pp. 260–270.

16 *Hazahozatali Kormánybiztosság.*

17 Rita Horváth, "A Deportáltakat Gondozó Országos Bizottság
    története" [History of the National Committee for the Care of
    Deportees], *Magyar Zsidó Levéltári Füzetek* (1997) 1: 25; Hadtörténeti
    Levéltár, Budapest, 1947 eln. 1333.

18 For source details, see Tamás Stark, *Hungarian Jews during the
    Holocaust and after the Second World War, 1939–1949* (Boulder,
    CO, 2000), pp. 61–68.

19 Similar conclusions came from CSO statisticians trying to estimate
    the number of Jewish survivors just after the war. See Árpád Snyder,
    "Becslés Magyarországnak a második világháború következtében
    elszenvedett emberveszteségeiről" [Estimate of Hungary's Losses
    of Life in World War II], *Magyar Statisztikai Szemle* (1946) 1–6:
    3–4, and Lajos Thirring, "Megjegyzések a Zsidó Világkongresszus
    Magyarországi Képviseletének a magyarországi zsidók helyzetére
    vonatkozó adataihoz" [Notes on Data on the Situation of Hungarian
    Jews from the Hungarian Office of the World Jewish Council], MOL
    Jelenkortörténeti Gyűjtemény XIX-J-1-a-II. 21.t. 29/Be/1946.

20   For more detail, see Stark, *Hungarian Jews during the Holocaust*, pp. 121–141.

21   Sources for data on Jewish communities in reannexed territories: *La Population Juive de la Transylvanie de Nord* (Bucharest, 1945); András S. Benedek, *Kárpátalja története és kultúrtörténete* [History and Cultural History of Transcarpathia] (Budapest, 1995), p. 47; Ernő Marton Archives, Yad Vashem Archives, I. M. 2625/4; American Jewish Archives, Cincinnati, WJC, H96, A14/3/93. S.

22   The number of fallen was 37,490, wounded 88,296, and missing 124,890. Hadtörténeti Levéltár, HM Békeelőkészítő anyag 3. doboz A/II. 31. 37.490.

23   On the war history research, see Tamás Stark, *Magyarország második világháborús embervesztesége* [Hungary's Human Losses in World War II] (Budapest, 1989); for a more detailed treatment, see Tamás Stark, *Hungary's Human Losses in World War II* (Uppsala, 1995).

24   "Tájékoztató gyorsfelvétel a községek, városok közérdekű viszonyairól" [Rough Survey of Public Interest Relations in Villages and Cities], *Magyar Statisztikai Szemle* (1946) 1–6: 16.

25   *Városi Szemle* (1945) 1: 54–55.

26   Hadtörténelmi Levéltár, HM Békeelőkészítő anyag, 2. doboz A/1. 94/4766.

27   *Voennoplennye v SSSR, 1939–1956. Dokumenty i materialy* [POWs in the USSR. Documents and Materials] (Moscow, 2000), pp. 295–297.

28   On the sources for statistics of civilian deportees, see Tamás Stark, "Cleansing and Collective Punishment: the Soviet Policy towards Prisoners of War and Civilian Internees in the Carpathian Basin," in Steven Béla Várdy and T. Hunt Tooley, eds., *Ethnic Cleansing in 20th Century Europe* (Boulder, CO, 2003), pp. 489–502.

29   *Az 1949. évi népszámlálás* [1949 Census)], Vol. IX (Budapest, 1950), p. 13.

30   John R. Schindler, "Yugoslavia's First Ethnic Cleansing," in Várdy and Tooley, eds., *Ethnic Cleansing in 20th Century Europe*, pp. 366–368.

31   Kasaš, *Mađari u Vojvodini*, p. 178.

32   Sándor Mészáros, *Holttá nyilvánítva* [Pronounced Dead], Vol. I: *Bácska* [Bačka] (Budapest, 1995 [1991]), pp. 200–203. The findings of Hungarian researchers in Serbia well summarized: Béla Csorba, Márton Matuska and Béla Riba, eds., *Rémuralom Délvidéken. Tanulmányok, emlékezések, helyzetértékelések az 1944/45. évi magyarellenes atrocitásokról* [Terror in the Southern Region. Studies,

Memoirs, and Reports of Anti-Hungarian Atrocities in 1944–1945] (Novi Sad, 2004); Sajti, *Hungarians in the Voivodina*, pp. 405–432.

33   Stark, *Magyarország második világháborús embervesztesége*, p. 72.

34   Štefan Šutaj, "A Déli akció" [The Southern Campaign], *Regio* (1992) 2: 92.

35   László Szűcs, ed., *Dálnoki Miklós Béla kormányának minisztertanácsi jegyzőkönyvei, 1944. december 23.–1945. november 15.* [Council of Ministers Minutes of the Dálnoki Government, December 23, 1944–November 15, 1945], Vol. B (Budapest, 1997), p. 58.

36   Zoltán Czibulka, Ervin Heinz and Miklós Lakatos, eds., *A magyarországi németek kitelepítése és az 1941. évi népszámlálás* [Deportation of Hungary's Germans and the 1941 Census] (Budapest, 2004), p. 35.

37   The ideological attitude of the period is well reflected in Miklós Szántó, *Magyarok a nagyvilágban* [Hungarians in the Wide World] (Budapest, 1970), p. 6. On illegal crossing of borders: György Irsay, *Örökre száműzve... adatok 1500 száműzött magyar történetéhez* [In Exile Forever. Data on the Hungarian History of 1,500 Exiles] (Gyoma, 2003). On scope for foreign travel: Péter Bencsik, "Documents of Passage, Travel Opportunities and Border Traffic in 20th Century Hungary," *Regio* 2 (2002): 51–71.

38   An overview: Pál Péter Tóth, "International Migration and Hungary," in Pál Péter Tóth and Emil Valkovics, eds., *Demography of Contemporary Hungarian Society* (Highland Lakes, NJ, 1996), pp. 139–170. Data on this: Pál Péter Tóth, *Haza csak egy van? Menekülők, bevándorlók, új állampolgárok Magyarországon (1988–1994)* [Only One Home Country? Refugees, Immigrants, New Citizens in Hungary (1988–1994)] (Budapest, 1997), p. 65.

39   Mária L. Rédei, "Nemzetközi népességmozgás Magyarországon" [International Movements of Population in Hungary], in Pál Tamás and András Inotai, eds., *Új exodus. A nemzetközi munkaerőáramlás új irányai* [New Exodus. New Directions in the International Flow of Labor] (Budapest, 1993), pp. 184–200.

40   Pál Péter Tóth, "A vándormozgalom szerepe a magyar népességfejlődésben" [Migration's Role in the Development of the Hungarian Population], in Pál Péter Tóth, ed., *Bevándorlás Magyarországra* [Immigration into Hungary] (Budapest, 2006), p. 105, with an annual breakdown.

41   Tóth, *Haza csak egy van?*, p. 84.

42   Tóth, "A vándormozgalom szerepe," p. 195.

BIOGRAPHIES OF KEY PERSONALITIES

Ágoston, András (born 1944)

Vojvodina lawyer, journalist and politician. A journalist and a manager of the Novi Sad Forum publishing concern before the change of system, he was behind the foundation in December 1989 of the Democratic Community of Vojvodina Hungarians (VMDK). As president of this and the Hungarian Democratic Party of Vojvodina that he founded in February 1997, he has sought personal autonomy and proportionate parliamentary representation for Hungarians in Serbia, and the option of dual nationality.

Balla, László (1927–2010)

Transcarpathian poet, writer, translator and editor. He became editor in 1965 of the daily *Kárpáti Igaz Szó* in Transcarpathia, later converting it from a simple translation of its Ukrainian equivalent into a full Hungarian newspaper. He retired in 1987. He did seminal work in the 1960s–1980s in promoting Hungarian literature in Transcarpathia and in public life in its Hungarian community, but his contribution came in for some criticism after the disintegration of the Soviet Union.

Balogh, Edgár (1906–1996)

Transylvanian political writer, editor and politician. Although of Transylvanian origin, Balogh went to high school in Bratislava and university in Prague, becoming the leading figure in Sarló (Sickle), a Marxist youth group among Czechoslovakian Hungarians. In 1935, he was deported to Romania and worked as a journalist. He joined the board of the communist-affiliated National Federation of Hungarian Workers (1934–1940), and after 1945 became a vice-president of the Hungarian People's Alliance (1945–1946), the editor of the Cluj daily *Világosság* (1944–1948), and rector of the city's Bolyai University (1948–

697

1949), before being jailed on false charges (1949–1955). He was later deputy editor-in-chief of the journal *Korunk* (1957–1971).

Bánffy, Miklós (1873–1950)

Transylvanian politician and writer. A member of Parliament from 1901 to 1918, he became Hungarian minister of foreign affairs in 1921–1922, and then returned to Romania in 1926. There he initiated and financed several cultural movements, including the periodical *Erdélyi Helikon* and the newspaper *Ellenzék*, as well as writing plays and novels under the pseudonym Kisbán. He became a senior lay official of the Reformed Church, then chairman of the Hungarian People's Community in 1939–1940, and a member of the Hungarian legislature again after the reannexation. He was on the staff of the Cluj literary periodical *Utunk* in 1944–1949, before moving back to Hungary.

Bethlen, György (1888–1968)

Transylvanian politician and expert on agriculture. His public activity began with the annexation of Transylvania. He joined the presiding committee of the National Hungarian Party in 1922 and served as its president in 1926–1938. He pursued a conservative policy aimed at defending the rights, estates and social positions of the Hungarian minority. He withdrew from politics in the period of royal dictatorship in 1938–1940, but entered the Hungarian legislature after the Second Vienna Award. He spent several years in Romanian prisons after World War II, and then worked as a manual laborer.

Bori, Imre (1929–2004)

Vojvodina literary historian, editor and university professor. He began teaching Hungarian in elementary and secondary schools in 1951, and then became professor of the Hungarian department at the University of Novi Sad until his retirement in 1995, serving concurrently as director of the Institute of Hungarian Studies (1979–1981) and editor of the periodical *Híd* (1984–2004). As the most influential cultural politician of his time, he stood for the development of a separate Hungarian culture within the specific social and economic conditions of Yugoslavia.

Bródy, András (Andrej Brody) (1895–1946)
Transcarpathian politician. Originally an elementary school teacher, he fought in World War I, and then studied law in Budapest. After the change of sovereignty he became a newspaper editor in Transcarpathia, then a founder and later president of the Autonomous Agricultural Union, and in October 1938 the region's first prime minister. He joined the Lower House of the Hungarian Parliament in 1939. In 1946, he was tried for collaboration in Uzhgorod and executed.

Bugár, Béla (born 1958)
Slovakian Hungarian politician. He entered public life after Czechoslovakia's 1989 revolution. He was a founder of the Hungarian Christian Democratic Movement, its president in 1991–1998, then president of the Hungarian Coalition Party (1998–2007). In 2009 he became founder-president of the Now/Bridge Party. A member of the federal legislature in Prague in 1990–1992, he has been a member of the Bratislava legislature continuously since 1992. In 1998–2006 he was a deputy speaker of Parliament, as he has been again since 2010.

Csoóri, Sándor (born 1930)
Writer and politician. He worked on a literary paper in 1953–1956, and as a journalist in the 1960s and a film scriptwriter in 1968–1988. He joined the periodical *Hitel* as editor in 1988 and became editor-in-chief in 1992. He was a leading light in the people's national opposition in the 1960s and later in the preparations for the change of system. He served as president of the World Federation of Hungarians in 1991–2000. In 1992 he sponsored the idea of Duna Television, a station for Hungarians abroad.

Csuka, Zoltán (1901–1984)
Writer, translator and literary activist. He left for Yugoslavia after the fall of the 1919 Hungarian Soviet Republic. There he became a motivating force within Hungarian literature in Yugoslavia and a translator of South Slav literature. He founded and worked for several Hungarian periodicals in Vojvodina (*Út,*

Képes Vasárnap, Vajdasági Írás, Kalangya). He returned to Hungary in 1933, and in 1944 became editor of *Láthatár,* which he had founded. Having been executive manager of the Hungarian–Yugoslav Society (1947–1948) and editor of its paper *Déli Csillag* (1947–1949), he was arrested for spying in 1950 and sentenced to 15 years' imprisonment, but was released in 1955.

Dobos, László (born 1930)
Slovakian Hungarian writer, publisher and politician. During the Prague Spring of 1968, he was president of the Hungarian cultural organization CSEMADOK, a member of the Prague and Bratislava legislatures, and a minister without portfolio responsible for minority affairs in the Slovak government. He was dismissed as minister in 1970 and from his CSEMADOK post in 1971, when he was also excluded from the Communist Party and the Prague and Bratislava legislatures. After the 1989 change of system he became a vice-president of the World Federation of Hungarians, director of the Madách publishing firm in Bratislava, and for a short while honorary president of CSEMADOK.

Domokos, Géza (1928–2007)
Romanian Hungarian politician, writer and translator. On completing his university studies in Moscow, he returned to Romania to work as a journalist. In 1961 he became editor-in-chief of the minority department at the literary publishers in Bucharest, then becoming manager of the new minority publisher Kriterion from 1970 to 1989. He was an alternate member of the Romanian Communist Party Central Committee from 1969 to 1984. He was a decisive organizing figure in Hungarian cultural life in Romania in the 1970s and 1980s. He chaired the Democratic Union of Hungarians in Romania from 1990 to 1993, when he withdrew from public life.

Domokos, Pál Péter (1901–1992)
Transylvanian ethnographer and schoolteacher. After studies in Miercurea-Ciuc, Debrecen and Budapest, he returned to Transylvania to teach singing and music in teachers' training

colleges. His first folksong collection tour of Catholic villages in Moldavia in 1929 was followed by regular work on folk music and culture among the Csángós. He headed the Cluj teachers' training college from 1940 to 1944, and then moved to Budapest, where he was a ministry employee until he was dismissed in 1949. He then taught at various elementary and secondary schools until his retirement in 1961.

Duray, Miklós (born 1945)
Slovakian Hungarian geologist and politician. On the CSEMADOK and the Hungarian Youth Association boards in Czechoslovakia in 1968–1969, he was a Bratislava geologist in the 1970s and 1980s. He became well known in the Czechoslovakian Hungarian opposition when he set up the Minority Rights Defense Committee, being imprisoned in 1982–1983 and 1984–1985. After the system change he was founder-president of the political group Coexistence (1990–1998), vice-president of the Hungarian Coalition Party (1998–2010), and a member of the Prague and Bratislava Parliaments.

Egry, Ferenc (1864–1945)
Upper Hungarian bell-founder and politician. Bells from his foundry at Kisgejőc (Mali Hejivci) can be found today all over Central Europe. He was an activist in the Independence Party in the final years of the Austro-Hungarian Monarchy, and in Transcarpathia in the Czechoslovak period was a leader of the Smallholders' Party, later the Hungarian National Party, and then of the United Hungarian Party. He was a senator in 1924 1929 and a seconded member of the Hungarian legislature from 1939.

Esterházy, János (1901–1957)
Slovakian Hungarian landowner and politician. President of the National Christian Socialist Party in Czechoslovakia from 1932, he became executive president of the United Hungarian Party in 1936. He was a member of the Prague legislature in 1935–1938 and of the Bratislava legislature in 1938–1944. In the wartime Tiso period, he was in internal opposition, voting

against deportation of the Jews and giving sanctuary to some Jews and others in hiding. Deported to the Soviet Union in early 1945, he was sentenced to death by the Slovak National Court in his absence. This was commuted to life imprisonment. He was behind bars in Czechoslovakia from 1949 until his death.

Fazekas, János (1926–2004)

Romanian Hungarian politician. On joining the Romanian Communist Party in 1945 he worked initially in its youth movement. He was a Central Committee member from 1954 to 1984, as well as minister of the food industry (1961–1965), a deputy prime minister, and a member of the government Executive Committee (1975–1980). After 1956, he was responsible for Hungarian minority affairs, as a confidant of Ceauşescu and the Romanian Hungarian holding the highest public office, but he was edged out in the mid-1980s.

Fodó, Sándor (1940–2005)

Transcarpathian university professor and public figure. He was a professor in Uzhgorod State University's Hungarian Faculty from 1967 to the 1990s, except in 1971–1976, when he had to work as a stoker and proofreader. He was president of the Transcarpathian Hungarian Cultural Association from its foundation in 1989 to 1996, then its honorary president until his death, but no longer had influence over it.

Gajdos, István (born 1971)

Transcarpathian politician. Graduating in mechanical engineering and law, he later moved from commerce into politics, as a member of the Ukrainian legislature in 2002–2006 for the Social Democratic Party of Ukraine (united), then the Ukrainian Socialist Party, and secretary of the legislature's Human Rights and Minorities Committee. Since 2002 he has been president of the Ukrainian Hungarian Democratic Association. He was elected mayor of Berehove for two consecutive terms in 2006 and 2010.

Gyárfás, Elemér (1884–1945)

Transylvanian politician and writer on economics. After law studies in Cluj, Budapest and Paris, he became an official, then a lawyer in Dicsőszentmárton (Târnăveni). He was the state leader of Kis-Küküllő County in 1917–1918. In 1922, he joined the leadership of the Romanian National Hungarian Party. He was a member of Parliament for Csík County in 1926–1938. He headed a lay organization of the Transylvanian Roman Catholic Church (Catholic Status) and the Transylvanian Hungarian Banks' Association. In 1940–1944 he stayed in Romanian-ruled Southern Transylvania as president of the Hungarian People's Community.

Hámos, László (born 1951)
American Hungarian human rights activist. Having studied at the University of Pennsylvania, from 1976 he headed the Committee for Human Rights in Romania and its successor, the Hungarian Human Rights Foundation, as co-founding president. The latter, an NGO, seeks to provide US support to the Hungarians of the Carpathian Basin, and improve and publicize their human rights position.

Hodža, Milan (1878–1944)
Slovak politician and journalist. As the foremost Slovak politician in the First Republic, he sat in the Prague legislature for the Republic Agrarian Party (1918–1938), serving as a minister several times and as prime minister of Czechoslovakia in 1935–1938. He then went into exile. His book on his postwar regional plans, *Federation in Central Europe*, appeared in London in 1942.

Hlinka, Andrej (1864–1938)
Slovak Roman Catholic priest and politician. A leading figure in the Slovak national movement before 1918, he was founder-president of the Slovak National Party, which later called itself the Hlinka Slovak National Party. Once Czechoslovakia was founded, he campaigned against Prague centralism, for Slovakian autonomy. The party that he led became strongly nationalist, anti-Semitic and anti-democratic in its principles.

Hokky, Károly (Charles J. Hokky) (1883–1971)
Transcarpathian politician. He studied arts in Cluj and Budapest, and worked as a secondary school teacher in Budapest and then

Kassa (Košice). He fought on the Eastern Front in World War I. In 1921 he became general secretary and later executive of the Christian Socialist Party of Transcarpathia, based in Sevľuš (Vynohradiv), then a member of the provincial assembly from 1928 and of the National Assembly of Czechoslovakia from 1929, and a senator from 1935. In 1939 he became a member of the Hungarian Parliament. He emigrated overseas before the Soviet occupation.

Jakabffy, Elemér (1881–1963)

Romanian Hungarian lawyer, politician and columnist. He practiced law in Lugos (Lugoj) and was a member of the Hungarian Parliament in 1910–1918. He was a vice-president of the National Hungarian Party in Romania in 1924–1938, a member of Parliament in 1927–1938, a representative of Romanian Hungarians at the Congresses of European Nations in 1925–1936 and a founding editor of the journal *Magyar Kisebbség*. He withdrew from public life after 1945 and was in internal exile in 1949–1954.

Kardelj, Edvard (1910–1979)

Slovenian politician and publicist. An organizer of the Slovenian resistance movement from 1941, he was the author of the 1943 AVNOJ resolution defining the federative structure for Yugoslavia. As Yugoslav minister of foreign affairs he headed the delegation to the Paris peace talks in 1947. In 1963 he became speaker of the federal Parliament. He remained a member of the highest bodies of the Yugoslav League of Communists and a close associate of Tito. He defined the theory of "self-management" socialism.

Kecskeméti, Lipót (1865–1936)

Transylvanian rabbi and politician. A graduate of the rabbinical institute in Budapest, he became rabbi of the Neologist congregation of Nagyvárad (Oradea) from 1890 until his death. He was a celebrated preacher and a devotee of Hungarian-language Jewish culture. He continued to advocate cultural and political assimilation after the Treaty of Trianon, thus remaining an anti-Zionist in the interwar period.

Király, Károly (born 1930)

Romanian Hungarian politician. He began in the youth bodies of the Romanian Communist Party, attended the Komsomol school in Moscow in 1956–1957, and graduated from the Stefan Gheorghiu Party Academy in 1963. He was party first secretary of Covasna County in 1968–1972. He was also vice-president of the Hungarian National Council of Workers, which was set up at that time. He was a member of the party's Central Committee in 1969–1974. He resigned his party position in 1972 and in 1978 wrote a letter of protest criticizing the party leadership. In December 1989 he was elected onto the leadership of the National Salvation Front.

Korláth, Endre (1881–1946)

Transcarpathian politician. Before the change of sovereignty he practiced as a lawyer in Ungvár (Užhorod), before becoming a city official and then attorney-general of Ung County in 1917. He was a founder of the Transcarpathian Hungarian Party of Law and the Transcarpathian Hungarian Party Association in the Czechoslovak period. In 1924 he became a member of the National Assembly and then a senator, as well as Transcarpathian executive secretary of the Hungarian National Party in 1925. Seconded into the Hungarian Parliament in December 1938, he was appointed as lord lieutenant of Ung and Bereg a month later and then elected to Parliament.

Kós, Károly (1883–1977)

Transylvanian architect, writer and designer. He qualified as an architect at Budapest Technical University in 1907, and then worked in various firms and studied the folk architecture of Transylvania. He helped to initiate political activity among Romania's Hungarians in 1921. In 1924, he and some Transylvanian writers founded a publishing firm that began in 1926 to issue an arts journal, *Erdélyi Helikon*. He became the leading figure in "Transylvanianism," a movement among the Romanian Hungarian elite that combined concern for regional interests with affiliations to the Hungarian nation.

Kovács, Miklós (born 1967)

Transcarpathian politician and political scientist. He graduated in history from Uzhhorod State University and in political science from Budapest's Eötvös Loránd University. He was then a local councilor for several terms, was a member of the Ukrainian legislature in 1998–2002, and sat on its Standing Committee on Human Rights, Religion and National Affiliation. He has chaired the Transcarpathian Hungarian Cultural Association since 1996 and teaches at the Ferenc Rákóczi II. Transcarpathian Hungarian Institute.

Kovács, Vilmos (1927–1977)

Transcarpathian writer, poet and literary activist. Having studied finance and economics, he worked as an accountant from 1945 before becoming an editor in the Hungarian department of the Karpaty Publishing House in Uzhgorod in 1958–1971, but then became unemployed. He began to write literature in the 1950s. At the turn of the 1970s he became a decisive literary and political figure at the Forrás Studio in Uzhgorod. He moved to Hungary in 1977 but was already mortally ill.

Kurkó, Gyárfás (1909–1983)

Romanian Hungarian politician and political writer. He began his political career in the Union of Hungarian Romanian Workers, and then in 1944–1947 became president of its successor, the Hungarian People's Union. His calls for the need to retain an autonomous Hungarian system of institutions were at variance with the communists' minority policies. He was arrested in the autumn of 1947, convicted of treason in 1951, released under a general amnesty in 1964 and rehabilitated in 1968. He worked for the rest of his life in a Braşov factory, at his own request.

Major, Nándor (born 1931)

Vojvodina writer, journalist and politician. He graduated from the Teachers' Training College in Novi Sad, then worked from 1950 as a journalist, becoming editor-in-chief in the periodical *Híd* in 1957. He joined the staff of the paper *Magyar Szó* in 1962, and then became an editor and deputy manager at the

Forum publishing enterprise. His political career began in the mid-1970s as Tito began to pick off so-called liberals. He was a provincial secretary of the League of Yugoslav Communists from 1974, then national executive secretary from 1978. In 1982 he joined the Vojvodina Presidium, as its last president. He was expelled from the party in 1989.

Makkai, Sándor (1890–1951)
Transylvanian theologian and writer. After university studies in Kolozsvár (Cluj) and Budapest, he gained a doctorate in philosophy in 1912, and then worked as a divinity teacher and clergyman, and from 1918 as a theology professor. He was elected as bishop of the Transylvanian Reformed Church district in 1926. Until the mid-1930s, he argued that moral renewal was the appropriate response to a minority existence, but in 1937 he wrote an article entitled "It Cannot Be," in which he declared that a minority existence was not worthy of man.

Markó, Béla (born 1951)
Transylvanian poet, politician and editor. Graduating from Cluj-Napoca University in Hungarian and French in 1974, he served in 1974–1989 as editor of the Târgu Mureş periodical *Igaz Szó* and then in 1989–2005 as editor-in-chief of the journal *Látó*. In 1990 he became a Mureş County senator representing the Democratic Union of Hungarians in Romania and in 1993 the organization's president. He was a deputy prime minister in 2004–2007, responsible for cultural, educational and EU affairs. He was again appointed as deputy prime minister in December 2009.

Márton, Áron (1896–1980)
Transylvanian Roman Catholic bishop. He was ordained as priest in 1924 after theological studies at Alba Iulia. He then served as a priest and a divinity teacher in Ditrău, Gheorgheni, Târgu Mureş, Sibiu and Cluj. He was consecrated as bishop of Transylvania in 1938, and stayed in Alba Iulia in 1940. He dissociated himself from the Hungarian People's Association in 1946. He was arrested and given a life sentence in 1949, but

was freed in 1955. He was under house arrest in Alba Iulia from 1957 to 1967.

Németh, Zsolt (born 1963)

Politician. He graduated in economics and sociology from Budapest's Karl Marx University in 1987, and then studied the theory of nationalism as a doctoral student at the Hungarian Research Institute in 1987–1990. He became a Fidesz MP in 1990, a Ministry of Foreign Affairs state secretary in 1998–2002 and again in 2010, and between the two terms leader of the parliamentary Foreign Affairs Committee. As initiator of the Concession Act, he is a major figure in the formulation of Fidesz policy on Hungarians and minorities.

Paál, Árpád (1880–1944)

Transylvanian politician and columnist. After legal studies, he was chief recorder of Udvarhely (Odorhei) County in 1908–1918, then the real head of the county from November 1918 to January 1919, after which he organized resistance against the invading Romanian forces. For this he was arrested by the Romanians, but he was released after 16 months. From 1920 he was on the staff of the newspaper *Keleti Újság* and was politically active. In 1928–1930 he was a member of the legislature for the National Hungarian Party. He became editor-in-chief of the Oradea newspaper *Erdélyi Lapok* in 1932. The bourgeois radicalism that he promoted in the later 1920s turned in the 1930s into sympathy for German Nazism.

Pataky, Tibor (1888–1953)

Hungarian politician. After studying law in Kolozsvár (Cluj) and Vienna, he joined the Central Statistics Office in Budapest in 1912, moving to the Prime Minister's Office to head the Second National Department from 1922 to 1944, dealing with minority problems in Hungary, contacts with and support for Hungarian communities in neighboring countries, and the affairs of Hungarians living abroad. He was pensioned in 1945 and sent into internal exile in 1951–1953.

Sterliczky, Dénes (1888–1953)

Vojvodina lawyer and politician. He was a secretary, and then sat on the Presidential Council of the Yugoslavian Hungarian Party founded in 1922, and was editor-in-chief of its paper, the *Hírlap*. He was a member of the Yugoslav legislature in 1927–1929, a member of the governing board of the Hungarian People's League Association in Yugoslavia, and several times a delegate to the European Minority Congress. In 1933 he became editor of the journal *Magyar Könyvtár*. He withdrew from public life in 1941–1944, but was deputy president of the Subotica district People's Front after 1945.

Szenteleky (Sztankovits), Kornél (1893–1933)

Vojvodina writer, poet and physician. A noted figure in Yugoslavian Hungarian literature, he started the literary papers *Vajdasági Írás* (1928) and *A Mi Irodalmunk* and *Kalangya* (1932) He also set up the Kalangya Library system. He saw local impact as a prime task for Vojvodina Hungarian literature and the intelligentsia.

Szent-Ivány, József (1884–1941)

Upper Hungarian landowner, writer and politician. The founder and president (1919–1925) of the Hungarian National Party, he remained its paramount leader, and represented it in the legislature from 1920 to 1938. He strongly supported the idea of self-organization of the Hungarians of Slovakia within the Czechoslovak state. He became a member of the Budapest Parliament after the First Vienna Award of 1938.

Szépfalusi, István (1932–2000)

Evangelical cleric, "sociographer" and cultural activist. After studying theology in Sopron and Budapest in 1950–1955, he studied history and interpreting at Graz University in 1962–1968, having moved to Austria in 1955. (His mother was an Austrian citizen.) There he began to serve in 1956 as a Hungarian minister within the Austrian Evangelical Church. He taught translation and interpreting at Vienna University.

He was the founder and organizer of the European Protestant Hungarian Free University and the Péter Bornemissza Society, whose publications he edited.

Szüllő, Géza (1872–1957)

Upper Hungarian landowner and politician. He was president of the National Christian Socialist Party in 1925–1932, in the legislature in 1925–1938, and chair of its parliamentary club. After the First Vienna Award of 1938 he was appointed in perpetuity to the Hungarian Upper House, where he joined the opposition in defending parliamentarian principles. He withdrew from public life after 1945.

Tabajdi, Csaba (born 1952)

Politician and diplomat. Graduating in international affairs in Budapest in 1974, he joined the Ministry of Foreign Affairs, working for seven years as cultural attaché in Moscow. He joined the Foreign Affairs Department at the Hungarian Socialist Workers' Party Central Committee in 1983–1989, and then headed the secretariat of the government National and Ethnic Minorities' College. He was a Socialist member of Parliament in 1990–2004, and political state secretary for minorities at the Prime Minister's Office in 1994–1998.

Teitelbaum, Joel (1887–1979)

Transylvanian rabbi. A member of a rabbinical dynasty in Northern Transylvania, he was rabbi of Carei and then Satu Mare before the Holocaust. He escaped on a Kastner train before the deportations. After the war, he resuscitated the so-called Szatmár Hassidic congregation in New York, making it larger than it had been, based on principles of autonomy and separation that excluded all state influence or support, even from Israel, which on religious grounds he did not consider legitimate.

Tomić, Jaša (1856–1929)

Serbian politician, writer and journalist. A founder of the Versec (Vršac) group of socialists, he edited the paper *Zastava* and was a leader of the youth movement in opposition to Hungary's Serbian National Party. He then founded Hungary's Serbian

Radical Party in 1884. In 1918, he took the lead at that party's Grand National Council and Grand National Assembly in Novi Sad in declaring the secession of Bačka, the Banat and Baranya from Hungary and their accession to Serbia.

Tóth, Mihály (born 1954)

Ukrainian politician and lawyer. Originally a construction engineer, he began to deal with minority rights in the 1990s, receiving a candidacy degree in the field. In 1994–1998 he was a member of the Ukrainian legislature and its Human Rights and Minority Committee. After the turn of the millennium he became honorary president of the Ukrainian Hungarian Democratic Association and a senior staff member at the V. M. Koretsky Institute of State and Law of the National Academy of Sciences of Ukraine.

Tőkés, László (born 1952)

Transylvanian Reformed Church cleric and politician. He was an assistant minister in Braşov and Dej, but was dismissed for criticisms in 1984. In 1986 he began to serve in Timişoara, but still criticized Church policy and the government policy of flattening villages. A TV interview on this in 1989 earned him dismissal from his parish, but the people of the city protested and he became a leader of the Romanian revolution. In 1990 he became bishop of Timişoara and honorary president of the Democratic Union of Hungarians in Romania. In 2003 he became president of a new body, the Hungarian National Council of Transylvania. He joined the European Parliament in 2007 and became a vice-president of the Hungarian National Council in 2010.

Várady, Imre (1867–1959)

Lawyer and politician in the Banat. An Independence Party member of the Hungarian legislature in 1905–1910, he conducted the defense of some arrested and interned Serbian politicians in 1914. He joined the Freemasons in 1911 and became a head of the new Vojvodina lodge in 1921. He was co-president of the Hungarian Party of Yugoslavia and a Yugoslav legislature member in 1927–1929. In 1939 he became the one Hungarian to be made a senator. For a time after 1945 he joined the board of the Yugoslavian People's Front.

Voloshyn, Avgusthyn (1874–1945)

Transcarpathian politician and educationalist. Politically active in the 1920s and 1930s, he founded and headed the Transcarpathian National Christian Party in 1923–1939 and was a member of the Czechoslovak legislature in 1925–1929. After Munich he became a state secretary in the first government of Transcarpathia and prime minister in the second. On its collapse he settled in Prague and ran the education faculty at the Free Ukrainian University. In 1945 he was imprisoned in Moscow by the Soviet Secret Service and died soon afterwards.

THE AUTHORS

Béni L. Balogh (born 1961, Timişoara, Romania)

With a degree in philosophy and history from Babeş–Bolyai University in Cluj-Napoca, Romania, he was on the staff of the Romanian-taught lyceum in Orăştie from 1984 to 1989. He then moved to Komárom-Esztergom County Archives in Hungary, and also became editor of the journal *Limes* in 1997. Having taken an archivist's course at the Humanities Faculty of Eötvös Loránd University, Budapest, by correspondence, he gained a university doctorate in 1997 and a PhD in 2010. He carried out frequent research in Romanian archives from 1994 to 2008.

Research field:
Hungarian–Romanian relations in the 1930s and 1940s.

Selected publications:

Az erdélyi magyar menekültkérdés 1939 és 1944 között [The Transylvanian Hungarian Refugee Question in 1939–1944]. *Regio* (1999) 3–4: 243–265.

A magyar–román kapcsolatok 1939–1940-ben és a második bécsi döntés [Hungarian–Romanian Relations in 1939–1940 and the Second Vienna Award]. Csíkszereda. Pro-Print, 2002.

"A dél-erdélyi magyar kisebbség helyzete (1940–1944)" [The Position of the Southern Transylvanian Hungarian Minority, 1940–1944]. In *Korrajz 2003. A XX. Század Intézet Évkönyve* (2003 Yearbook of the Twentieth-Century Institute). Budapest: XX. Század Intézet, 2003, pp. 39–53.

"Az idegháború' kezdete. Magyar–román tárgyalások 1940 őszén" [The Beginning of the War of Nerves. Hungarian–Romanian Negotiations in the Autumn of 1940]. In Nándor Bárdi and Attila Simon, eds., *Integrációs stratégiák a magyar kisebbségek*

történetében [Integration Strategies in the History of Hungarian Minorities]. Somorja/Dunaszerdahely: Fórum Intézet/Lilium Aurum, 2006, pp. 101–117.
"Az Antonescu-rezsim békeelképzelései 1940–1944 között" [The Peace Plans of the Antonescu Regime 1940–1944]. *Századok* (2007) 1: 3–27.

Viktória Bányai (born 1971, Budapest)

Having graduated in history and Hebrew studies from Eötvös Loránd University, Budapest, she obtained a PhD in 2001, for which her dissertation received an Academy Youth Prize in 2002. In 2004–2006 she was on a post-doctoral scholarship from the National Scientific Research Foundation. She joined the staff of the Center of Jewish Studies at the Hungarian Academy of Sciences in 1995. She teaches in the Hebrew Studies department of her old university.

Research fields:
Early modern and modern Hungarian Jewish history and art history.

Selected publications:
"Hebrew Literature in Hungary in the Epoch of Haskala." In *Studia Judaica*, Vol. 6. Cluj-Napoca: Sincron Publish ing House, 1997, pp. 169–176.
With Kinga Frojimovics, Géza Komoróczy and Andrea Strbik: *Jewish Budapest. Monuments, Rites, History.* Budapest: Central European University Press, 1999.
Zsidó oktatásügy Magyarországon, 1780–1850 [Jewish Education in Hungary, 1780–1850]. Hungaria Judaica 17. Budapest: Gondolat, 2005.
Ezekiel Landau prágai rabbi (1713–1793) döntvényéből Magyarországi adatok [Rabbi of Prague: Data on Hungary. Ezekiel Landau (1713–1793)]. Hungaria Judaica 22. Budapest: MTA Judaisztika Kutatóközpont, 2008.

Nándor Bárdi (born 1962, Laskod)

After graduating in history from the Department of Nineteenth-and Twentieth-Century Eastern European History at the University of Szeged, in 1987, he lectured at his old university in 1990–1996 on the minority question and the interwar history of Middle Europe. He was on the staff of the László Teleki Foundation's Central European Institute from 1997 to 2006. Since 2007 he has continued his work at the Institute for Ethnic and National Minority Studies of the Hungarian Academy of Sciences. He edits the journals *Regio* and *Múltunk,* and the book series *Sources for the History of the Romanian Hungarian Minority.* He is academic head of the adatbank.ro Internet portal.

Research fields:
Comparative minority studies; compilation of databases on the minorities of Central Europe; analysis of policy towards Hungarians and minorities; changes in the image and constructions of their own societies held by minority elites, notably the Hungarian minority of Romania between the two world wars.

Selected publications:
With Lajos Pándi, *Köztes-Európa 1763–1993* [Middle Europe 1763–1993]. 2nd rev. ed. Budapest: Osiris, 1997.
Tény és való. A budapesti kormányzatok és a határon túli magyarok kapcsolattörténete. Problémakatalógus [True Fact. Budapest Governments and the History of Their Contacts with Hungarians Abroad. Catalogue of Problems]. Pozsony: Kalligram, 2004.
"The History of Relations between Hungarian Governments and Ethnic Hungarians Living beyond the Borders of Hungary." In Zoltán Kántor *et al.,* eds., *The Hungarian Status Law. Nation-Building and/or Minority Protection.* Slavic Eurasian Studies series. Sapporo: Slavic Research Center, Hokkaido University, 2004, pp. 58–86.
"Generation Groups in the History of Hungarian Minority Elites." *Regio* (English edition) 5 (2005) 109–124.

"The Strategies and Institutional Framework Employed by Hungarian Governments to Promote 'Hungarian Minorities Policy' between 1918 and 1938." In Ferenc Eiler and Dagmar Hájková, eds., *Czech and Hungarian Minority Policy in Central Europe 1918–1938*. Prague/Budapest: Masarykův ústav a Archiv AV ČR/MTA Kisebségkutató Intézet, 2009, pp. 33–53.

Gerhard Baumgartner (born 1957, Oberwart, Austria)

A historian, journalist and professor at the University of Applied Sciences, Graz, he heads research at the international group Kanzlei, and is a founding member of the research firm Burgenländische Forschungsgesellschaft, an editorial board member of the history journal *ÖZG*, and project leader of the Name Database of the Austrian Holocaust Victims among the Roma and Sinti. Since 2007 he has been co-opted as an expert on the Roma Genocide Subgroup of the International Task Force for International Cooperation on Holocaust Education, Remembrance and Research. He has lectured at universities in Vienna, Salzburg, Klagenfurt, Budapest and Tel Aviv.

Research fields:
Ethnic and religious minorities in Europe in the nineteenth and the twentieth century; national problems in the Austro-Hungarian monarchy; Austrian minority politics after 1945; the theory of nationalism; the regional history of Burgenland and western Hungary.

Selected publications:
With Andreas Moritsch, "The Process of National Differentiation within Rural Communities in Southern Carinthia and Southern Burgenland 1850 to 1950." In David Howell, *et al.*, eds., *Roots of Rural Ethnic Mobilization*. Comparative Studies on Governments and Non-Dominant Ethnic Groups in Europe 1850–1950 VII. New York/Sudbury, MA: New York University Press/Dartmouth Publishing, 1992.
„6 X Österreich" – *Geschichte und aktuelle Situation der Volksgruppen in Österreich*. Klagenfurt: Drava, 1995.

With Florian Freund, *Die Burgenland Roma 1945–2000. Eine Darstellung der Volksgruppe anhand qualitativer und quantitativer Daten.* Forschungen aus dem Burgenland 88. Eisenstadt: Burgenländische Forschungsgesellschaft, 2004.

With Bernhard Perchinig, "Minderheitenpolitik in Österreich nach 1945." In Herbert Dachs *et al.*, eds., *Handbuch des politischen Systems Österreichs*, 4th ed. Vienna: MANZ'sche Wien, 2005, pp. 546–560.

With Tayfun Belgin, *Roma & Sinti – „Zigeunerdarstellungen" der Moderne.* Krems: Kunstmeile Krems, 2007.

Stefano Bottoni (born 1977, Bologna, Italy)

Having graduated in history from the University of Bologna in 2001, he obtained a PhD in contemporary European history in 2005, with a thesis on the Hungarian autonomous region of Romania in 1952–1960. He then began teaching the history of contemporary Eastern Europe at Bologna. In 2006, he won a three-year János Bolyai Fellowship from the Hungarian Academy of Sciences, whose Institute of History he joined in 2009 as a research fellow.

Research fields:
Contemporary history of Eastern Europe.

Selected publications:
"The Creation of the Hungarian Autonomous Region in Romania in 1952: Premises and Consequences." *Regio* (English edition) 3 (2003): 15–38.

Transilvania rossa. Il comunismo romeno e la questione nazionale, 1944–1965. Rome: Carocci Editore, 2007.

"Memorie negate, verità di stato. Lustrazione e commissioni storiche nella Romania postcomunista." *Quaderni Storici* (2008) 2: 403–431.

"Reassessing the Communist Takeover: Violence, Institutional Continuity, and Ethnic Conflict Management." *East European Politics and Societies* 59 (2010) 1: 59–89.

Ferenc Eiler (born 1968, Szeged)

A graduate in German and history from the University of Szeged in 1994, he joined the General History of the Modern Period doctoral program at the University of Pécs in 1995–1998. He spent ten months in 1997–1998 as a DAAD research scholar at Johannes Gutenberg University in Mainz, Germany. He joined the staff of the Institute for Ethnic and National Minority Studies of the Hungarian Academy of Sciences in 1998, spending four months in 1999 as a research scholar at the Institute for European History in Mainz, and receiving a Hungarian Academy of Sciences foundation scholarship for 2002–2005. He received a PhD from Pécs in 2005 with a dissertation on "Minority Protection and Revision. Hungarian Efforts at the European Minority Congress 1925–1939." Since 2009 he has held a János Bolyai Research Scholarship.

Research fields:
Minority policy and protection in interwar Central Europe.

Selected publications:
"Németország Duna-völgyi politikája 1920–1938" [Germany's Policy for the Danube Valley 1920–1938]. In Csilla Fedinec, ed., *Társadalmi önismeret és nemzeti önazonosság Közép-Európában* [Social Self-Knowledge and National Identity in Central Europe]. Budapest: Teleki László Alapítvány, 2002, pp. 37–63.
"Német és magyar nemzetpolitikák a két világháború között 1920–1938" [German and Hungarian National Policies between the Two World Wars 1920–1938]. In Nándor Bárdi and Attila Simon, eds., *Integrációs stratégiák a magyar kisebbségek történetében. (Vázlat)* [Integration Strategies in the History of the Hungarian Minorities (Outline)]. Somorja: Fórum Kisebbségkutató Intézet, 2006, pp. 89–99.
"Die Grenzen eines wirksamen Minderheitenschutzes im Rahmen des Völkerbunds." In Ralph Melville, Jiři Pešek and Claus Scharf, eds., *Zwangsmigrationen im mittleren und östlichen Europa. Völkerrecht – Konzeptionen – Praxis (1938–1950)]*. Mainz: Verlag Philipp von Zabern, 2007, pp. 111–127.

Kisebbségvédelem és revízió. Magyar részvétel az Európai Nemzetiségi Kongresszuson 1925–1939 [Minority Protection and Revival. Hungarian Participation in the European Minority Congress 1925–1939]. Budapest: Gondolat, 2007. As editor, with Dagmar Hájková, *Czech and Hungarian Minority Policy in Central Europe 1918–1938.* Prague/Budapest: Prague/Budapest: Masarykův ústav a Archiv AV ČR/MTA Kisebbségkutató Intézet, 2009.

Csilla Fedinec (born 1968, Beregovo, Soviet Union)

She graduated from the Uzhgorod State University, Ukraine, in 1992 and taught there from 1994 to 1999, meanwhile obtaining a PhD in Hungary in 1996. Since then she has been a research fellow, at László Teleki Institute's Center of Central European Studies in 2000–2006 and since 2007 at the Institute for Ethnic and National Minority Studies of the Hungarian Academy of Sciences. She was a Hungarian Academy of Sciences János Bolyai research scholar in 1998–2001, and Sasakawa Young Leaders scholar in 2001–2002. Her research work was recognized with János Váradi-Sternberg Award in 1999 and with For Minorities Award in 2009.

Research fields:
Twentieth-century history of Transcarpathia, the minority question in East Central Europe.

Selected publications:
Fejezetek a kárpátaljai magyar közoktatás történetéből (1938–1991) [Chapters from the History of Hungarian Public Education in Transcarpathia (1938–1991)]. Officina Hungarica VIII. Budapest: Nemzetközi Hungarológiai Központ, 1999.
A kárpátaljai magyarság történeti kronológiája 1918–1944 [Historical Chronology of the Transcarpathian Hungarian Community 1918–1944]. Nostra Tempora 7. Galánta/Dunaszerdahely: Fórum Intézet/Lilium Aurum, 2002.

Iratok a kárpátaljai magyarság történetéhez 1918–1944. Törvények, rendeletek, kisebbségi programok, nyilatkozatok [Documents on the History of the Transcarpathian Hungarian Community 1918–1944. Laws, Orders, Minority Programs, Statements]. Somorja/Dunaszerdahely: Fórum Intézet/Lilium Aurum, 2004.

As editor, with Viktoria Sereda, *Ukrajna színeváltozása 1991–2008: politikai, gazdasági, kulturális és nemzetiségi attitűdök* [Transformation in Ukraine: Political, Economic, Cultural and Minority Attitudes]. Bratislava: Kalligram, 2009.

As editor-in-chief, with Mykola Vegesh, In Hungarian: *Kárpátalja 1919–2009: történelem, politika, kultúra* [Transcarpathia 1919–2009: History, Politics, Culture]. Budapest: Argumentum Kiadó – Magyar Tudományos Akadémia Etnikai-nemzeti Kisebbségkutató Intézete, 2010. In Ukrainian: *Zakarpattja 1919–2009 rokiv: istorija, polityka, kul'tura* [Transcarpathia 1919–2009: History, Politics, Culture]. Uzhgorod: Poligrafcentr "Lira" – Naukovodoslidnyj instytut politychnoi' regionalistyky Uzhgorods'kogo nacional'nogo universytetu, 2010.

Tamás Gusztáv Filep (born 1961, Budapest)

After working in book distribution and marketing in 1984–1989, he became editor of the journals *Unió* and *Regio* in 1990–1992, then organized book aid at the Pro Hungaris Foundation in 1993–1998. He took a librarianship course at Eötvös Loránd University in Budapest. Since 1990, he has been a freelance scholar.

Research fields:
The history of ideas and education in relation to the history of Slovakia's Hungarian minority and twentieth-century Hungarian national awareness.

Selected publications:
As editor with László Tóth, *A (cseh)szlovákiai magyar művelődés története 1918–1998* [The History of (Czecho)Slovakian Hungarian Culture 1918–1998]. 4 vols. Budapest: Ister, 1998–2000.

As editor etc., *Joó Tibor: Történetfilozófia és metafiizika. Válogatott írások* [Tibor Joó: Historical Philosophy and Metaphysics. Selected Writings]. Budapest: Ister, 2001.

A hagyomány felemelt tőre. Válogatott és új esszék, tanulmányok az 1918–1945 közötti (cseh)szlovákiai magyar kultúráról [The Raised Sword of Tradition. Essays and Studies on (Czecho)-Slovakian Hungarian Culture 1918–1945]. Budapest: Ister, 2003.

"A kultúra tehénhimlője. Kemény Zsigmond a nemzetiségi kérdésről 1837 és 1860 között" [The Cowpox of Culture. Zsigmond Kemény on the National Question 1837–1860]. *Pro Minoritate* (2005) 4: 117–152.

A humanista voksa. Írások a csehszlovákiai magyar kisebbség történetének köréből 1918–1945 [The Humanist Vote. Writings on the History of the Czechoslovakian Hungarian Minority 1918–1945]. Pozsony: Kalligram, 2007.

László Gyurgyík (born 1954, Sahy, Czechoslovakia)

He graduated in 1985 in sociology, from Comenius University in Bratislava, and then worked from 1985 to 1990 (with a break of a year and a half) at the same city's Research Institute of Agrarian Economics. He worked as an editor in 1990–1992, then as a freelance researcher, founding the Bratislava Mercurius Social Science Research Group. He moved to Budapest in 1995 to study in the Postgraduate Faculty of Budapest University of Economic Sciences, where he received a PhD in sociology in 2002. He was a senior fellow at the László Teleki Institute from 1999 to 2006. He began teaching at Selye János University in Komárno, Slovakia, in 2005. He has been a researcher at the European Foundation for Comparative Minority Researches since 2007.

Research fields:
The sociology and demography of Hungarian minorities.

Selected publications:
Changes in the Demographic, Settlement, and Social Structure of the Minority in (Czecho)-Slovakia 1918–1998. Budapest: Institute for Central European Studies Budapest, 1999.

Asszimilációs folyamatok a szlovákiai magyarság körében [Assimilation Processes among the Hungarians of Slovakia]. Bratislava: Kalligram, 2004. "On Assimilation and Change of Nationality Based on Surveys Conducted among Hungarians Living in Slovakia." *Regio* (English edition) 8 (2005) 125–140.

Népszámlálás 2001 – A szlovákiai magyarság demográfiai, település és társadalomszerkezetének változásai az 1990-es években [Census 2001. Demographic, Settlement and Social-Structure Changes among Slovakia's Hungarians]. Pozsony: Kalligram, 2006. With Tamás Kiss, *Párhuzamok és különbségek. A második világháború utáni erdélyi és szlovákiai magyar népességfejlődés összehasonlító elemzése* [Parallels and Differences. A Comparative Analysis of Post-World War II Hungarian Population Development in Slovakia and Transylvania]. Budapest: EÖKIK, 2010.

Hornyák Árpád (born 1971, Darmstadt, Germany)

Having graduated from the University of Pécs in 1996, he attended the doctoral school there and obtained a PhD in 2002 with a dissertation on Hungarian–Yugoslav diplomatic relations in 1918–1927. He has continued his research in British, US, Serbian, and Croatian archives with the help of Hungarian and international scholarships.

Research fields:
Hungarian–Yugoslav relations in the twentieth century; the history of Bosnia and Serbia in the nineteenth and the twentieth century.

Selected publications:
Magyar–jugoszláv diplomáciai kapcsolatok 1918–1927 [Hungarian–Yugoslav Diplomatic Relations 1918–1927]. Újvidék: Fórum, 2004.
Pécs szerb megszállása egy szerb újságíró szemével. Milan Glibonjski visszaemlékezései [The Serbian Occupation of Pécs through a Serb Journalist's Eyes. Recollections by Milan Glibonjski]. Pécs: Pécs Története Alapítvány, 2006.

"Die in Jugoslavien lebende ungarisches Minderheit in der ungarische Aussenpolitik zwischen den beiden Weltkriegen (1919–1938)." *Razprave i gradivo. Revija za narodnosna vprašanja* (2007) 53–54: 322–339.

"The Balkan Federation 1866–1948 with Special Regard to Serbian/Yugoslavian Views." *Bulgarian Historical Review* (2007) 1: 217–232.

Találkozások–ütközések. Fejezetek a 20. századi magyar–szerb kapcsolatok történetéből [Meetings and Clashes. Chapters from the History of 20th-Century Hungarian–Serbian Relations]. Pécs: Bocz, 2010.

Zoltán Ilyés (born 1968, Budapest)

He graduated in geography and biology from the University of Debrecen in 1993. He taught in the Geography Department of Károly Eszterházy College in Eger from 1992 to 2008. He has also worked since 1993 in the Cultural and Visual Anthropology Institute of the University of Miskolc, and since 2002 on the staff of the Institute for Ethnic and National Minority Studies of the Hungarian Academy of Sciences. He attended the geology doctoral program of the University of Debrecen in 1994–1997, obtaining his PhD in 1999 with a dissertation on changes of land use and development of the historical cultural landscape of Ghimeş. In the same year he won a DAAD scholarship to Tübingen University, followed by research scholarships to the Herder Institute in Marburg in 2000, and the Leipzig Institut für Länderkunde in 2002. He was a Hungarian Academy of Sciences János Bolyai research scholar in 2001–2004.

Research fields:
Mother tongue and ethnic identity as resources; diasporas; the military and the landscape.

Selected publications:
"Die Wirkung der Exogamie auf den Zustand der Muttersprache und die ethnische Identität." In Elek Bartha *et al.*, eds., *Műveltség és hagyomány* [Cultivation and Tradition]. Yearbook of the Anthropology Department of the Kossuth Lajos University of

Sciences. Ethnographica et Folcloristica Carpathica, Vols. 9–10. Debrecen: KLTE, Néprajzi Tanszék, 1998, pp. 84–98.

"Veränderungen der sakralen Raumstruktur in einer religiösen Kontaktzone der Ostkarpaten. Siedlungsforschung." In *Archäologie – Geschichte – Geographie*, Vol. 20. Bonn, 2002. pp. 187–202.

"Identity as Resource in a Small Region: the Example of Gyimes." *Minorities Research. A Collection of Studies by Hungarian Authors* 8. (2006): 29–38.

"Researching and Interpreting Diaspora. Remarks on Social Science Research into the Diaspora Communities of the Carpathian Basin." In Balázs Balogh and Zoltán Ilyés, eds., *Perspectives of Diaspora Existence. Hungarian Diasporas in the Carpathian Basin – Historical and Current Contexts of a Specific Diaspora Interpretation and Its Aspects of Ethnic Minority Protection.* Budapest: Akadémiai, 2006, pp. 45–63.

"Military Activities. Warfare and Defence." In József Szabó, Lóránt Dávid and Dénes Lóczi, eds., *Anthropogenic Geomorphology. A Guide to Man-Made Land Forms.* New York: Springer: Dordrecht, 2010, pp. 217–232.

Miklós Kontra (born 1950, Budapest)

Currently professor of English applied linguistics at the University of Szeged, from 1985 to 2010 he was head of the Department of Sociolinguistics in the Linguistics Institute of the Hungarian Academy of Sciences, Budapest. He held two Fulbright research scholarships at Indiana University (1992–1993) and Michigan State University (2003) and an ACLS Fellowship at Michigan State (1995–1996).

Research fields:
Primarily: variation in Hungarian; contact varieties of Hungarian in neighboring countries; Hungarian–American bilingualism; educational linguistics; linguistic human rights.

Selected publications:
As editor, with Csaba Pléh, *Hungarian Sociolinguistics* (Special Issue) *International Journal of the Sociology of Language* (1995): 111.

As editor, with Robert Phillipson, Tove Skuttnab-Kangas and Tibor Várady, *Language: A Right and a Resource. Approaching Linguistic Human Rights.* Budapest: Central European University Press, 1999.

As guest editor, *Language Contact in East-Central Europe* (Special Issue) = *Multilingua* 19 (2000) 1–2: 1–195.

As editor, *Nyelv és társadalom a rendszerváltáskori Magyar-országon* [Language and Society in Hungary at the Fall of Communism]. Budapest: Osiris, 2003.

As editor, the book series *A magyar nyelv a Kárpát-medencében a XX. század végén* [The Hungarian Language in the Carpathian Basin at the End of the 20th Century], updated parts of which appear in Anna Fenyvesi, ed., *Hungarian Language Contact outside Hungary: Studies on Hungarian as a Minority Language.* Amsterdam: John Benjamins, 2005.

Hasznos nyelvészet [Socially Useful Linguistics]. Somorja: Fórum Kisebbségkutató Intézet, 2010.

Attila Kovács (born 1973, Murska Sobota, Yugoslavia)

He graduated in history and political science from the University of Pécs in 1997 and then joined the staff of the Ljubljana Institute of Ethnic Studies. He attended the doctoral school of history in Pécs, obtaining his PhD in 2002, when he returned to the Institute of Ethnic Studies, as a full research fellow from 2006. He has taught in the history department of the University of Maribor, Slovenia, since 2008.

Research fields:
Twentieth-century history and position of minorities in present-day Slovenia.

Selected publications:
Földreform és kolonizáció a Lendva-vidéken a két világháború között [Land Reform and Colonization in the Lendva Region between the World Wars]. Lendva: MNMI Lendva, 2004.

"Madžarski eksodus leta 1956–57 s posebnim poudarkom na beguncih, ki so zbežali v Jugoslavijo oziroma v Slovenijo" [Hungarian Exodus in 1956–57 with Special Emphasis on Refugees of 1956 Who had Fled to Yugoslavia and Slovenia] *Prispevki za novejšo zgodovino* 47 (2007) 1: 169–184.

"Die Minderheiten in Slowenien an der Wende vom 20. zum 21. Jahrhundert." In Erika Hammer and László Kupa, eds., *Ethno-Kulturelle Begegnungen in Mittel- und Osteuropa*. Schriftenreihe Socialia No. 94. Hamburg: Verlag Dr. Kovač, 2008, pp. 191–198.

Ilona Kovács (born 1938, Debrecen)

She graduated in Hungarian and librarianship from Eötvös Loránd University, Budapest, in 1961. She obtained a master's degree in library science at Kent State University, Ohio, in 1975, followed by a university doctorate in 1982 and the Hungarian Academy of Sciences' candidacy degree in 1996. She began work in 1961 at the Hungarian Academy of Sciences Library and then held posts at the National Széchényi Library from 1962 until her retirement in 2001. She has spent numerous study and research periods abroad, notably as a Fulbright scholar in the United States in 1995, 2001–2002, and 2003. She is a member of the Association of Hungarian Librarians, the International Association of Hungarian Studies, and the American Hungarian Educators' Association.

Research fields:
Hungarian communities abroad; the question of collecting and preserving Hungarian-related materials; the history of minority cultures, primarily that of the American Hungarians; immigration and emigration history.

Selected publications:
"Problems and Patterns in the Development of Library Services for Ethnic Hungarians in the United States in the First Decades of the 20th Century." *Hungarian Studies: Journal of the International Association of Hungarian Studies* 3 (1987) 1–2: 248–260.

"Ethnic Research and the Hungarica Collection of the National Széchényi Library." *Ethnic Forum. Journal of Ethnic Studies and Ethnic Bibliography* 9 (1989) 1–2: 91–99.

Az amerikai közkönyvtárak magyar gyűjteményeinek szerepe az asszimiláció és az identitás megőrzésének kettős folyamatában: 1890–1940 [The Dual Role of Hungarian Collections in American Public Libraries in Assimilation and Identity Maintenance: 1890–1940]. Budapest: OSZK, 1997.

As editor, with others, *The Hungarian Legacy in America: the History of the American Hungarian Foundation: the First Fifty Years.* New Brunswick, NJ: AHF, 2007.

"Az amerikai magyar könyvtári gyűjtemények, mint az etnikai könyvtári gyűjtemények típusai" [American Hungarian Ethnic Libraries as Types of Ethnic Library Collections]. *Nyelvünk és kultúránk* 38 (2008) 3: 25–36.

Orsolya Nádor (born 1959, Veszprém)

After qualifying as an elementary school teacher in the Hungarian/ Russian department of the Ho Chi Minh Teachers' Training College, Eger, she obtained a degree in Hungarian language and literature and education at Eötvös Loránd University, Budapest, followed by a university doctorate in Hungarian literature outside Hungary in 1988, and a candidate's degree in linguistic studies from the Hungarian Academy of Sciences in 1998. She qualified as a university teacher at the University of Pécs. She has since taught there and at Kecskemét Teachers' Training College. She is currently a senior lecturer in the Linguistic Studies Department of Károli Gáspár Reformed University, Budapest. In 2003–2010 she was on the staff of the Balassi Institute, where she headed the Hungarian language department and developed eLearning materials. Since October 2010 she has been a guest professor in linguistics at the University of Zagreb, Croatia.

Research fields:
History of language policy and language-teaching policy in relation to the Hungarians of the Carpathian Basin; art history, cultural

diplomacy and psycho-linguistic aspects of teaching Hungarian as a foreign language.

Selected publications:
"A magyar nyelv és a nyelvi jogok az anyanyelvi oktatás össze-függésében" [Hungarian Language and Language Rights in Relation to Native-Language Teaching]. *Regio* (1998) 1: 49–81.

Nyelvpolitika. A magyar nyelvpolitika státusváltozásai és oktatása a kezdetektől napjainkig [Language Policy. Changes in the Political Status and Teaching of the Hungarian Language from the Outset to the Present Day]. Budapest: BIP, 2002.

"A kisebbségek anyanyelvi oktatási jogai Kelet-Közép-Európában" [Native-Language Teaching Rights of Minorities in East-Central Europe]. In Orsolya Nádor and László Szarka, eds., *Nyelvi jogok, kisebbségek, nyelvpolitika Kelet-Közép-Európában* [Language Rights, Minorities, Language Policy in East-Central Europe]. Budapest: Akadémiai, 2003, pp. 76–94.

"Teaching of Less Widely Used Languages in Europe and Language Politics." In Johanna Laakso, ed., *Ungarisch unterricht in Österreich: Perspektiven und Vergleichspunkte/Teaching Hungarian in Austria: Perspectives and Points of Comparison.* PUSA 6. Vienna: LIT-Verlag, 2008, pp. 57–65.

"From Monolingualism to Multilingualism in the EU – through Bilingual Minorities (Status Report on Central Eastern Europe)." In Barna Bodó and Márton Tonk, eds., *Nations and National Minorities in the European Union.* Kolozsvár: Scientia, 2009, pp. 65–73.

Mihály Zoltán Nagy (born 1974, Carastelec, Romania)

After obtaining a 1999 degree in history and education from the University of Pécs, he was on the staff of the Transylvanian Museum Association in Cluj-Napoca, Romania, from 2000 to 2010. He is now deputy director-general of the Romanian National Archives.

Research field:
Post-1945 history of the Hungarian minority in Romania.

Selected publications:
"Válságos idők. A dél-erdélyi magyarok internálása és annak hatása a magyarság politikai önszerveződésére (1944. szeptember–1945. szeptember)" [Times of Crisis. The Internment of South Transylvanian Hungarians and its Effect on Political Organization among Hungarians (September 1944–September 1945)]. In Béla Csorba, Márton Matuska, Béla Ribár eds., *Rémuralom a Délvidéken: Tanulmányok, emlékezések, helyzetértékelések az 1944/45. évi magyarellenes atrocitásokról* [Reign of Terror in the Southern Region: Studies, Memoirs, Assessments of 1944–1945 Anti-Hungarian Atrocities]. Újvidék: Vajdasági Magyar Tudományos Társaság/Atlantis, 2004, pp. 51–74.
As editor, with Gábor Vincze, *Autonomisták és centralisták: Észak-Erdély a két román bevonulás között (1944. szeptember – 1945. március)* [Autonomists and Centralists. Northern Transylvania between the Two Invasions (September 1944–March 1945)]. Kolozsvár/Csíkszereda: EME/Pro-Print, 2004.
"A romániai Egyházügyi Hivatal Irattárának hasznosíthatósága az egyháztörténeti kutatásokba" [The Utility of the Archives of Romania's Bureau of Church Affairs for Research into Ecclesiastical History]. In Szabolcs Varga, Lázár Vértesi eds., *Az 1945 utáni magyar katolikus egyháztörténet új megközelítései* [New Approaches to post-1945 Hungarian Catholic History]. Pécs: Pécsi Egyháztörténeti Intézet, 2007, pp. 197–207.
With Ágoston Olti, *Érdekképviselet vagy pártpolitika. Iratok a Magyar Népi Szövetség történetéhez 1944–1953* [Representing Interests or Party Politics. Writings on the History of the Hungarian People's Association 1944–1953]. Csíkszereda: Pro-Print, 2009.
"Protejarea intereselor etnice sau urmărirea liniei PCR. Funcția de reprezentare a intereselor etnice a UPM" [Protecting Ethnic Interests or Following the Path of the Romanian Communist Party. The Hungarian Popular Union's Role in the Safeguarding the Ethnic Interest]. In Agoston Olti and Attila Gido, eds., *Minoritatea maghiară în perioada comunistă* [Hungarian

Minority in the Communist Era]. Cluj-Napoca: Institutul Naţional pentru Problemele Minorităţilor Naţionale/Kriterion, 2009, pp. 115–161.

Csaba Zoltán Novák (born 1975, Miercurea Nirajului, Romania)

Having studied at Elek Benedek Teachers' Training College, Odorheiu-Secuiesc, Romania, in 1991–1996, he also graduated in history in 2002 from Babeş–Bolyai University in Cluj-Napoca, Romania, where he took a master's course in oral history and contemporary history in 2002–2003. In 2004 he joined the staff of Gheorghe Şincai Institute of the Romanian Academy of Sciences, and in 2005 began the doctoral course at its Nicolae Ioraga Institute of History.

Research fields:
Minority history, minority elites, ethnic conflicts, and post-1945 East European history.

Selected publications:
"A Román Kommunista Párt hatalmi szerkezetének kiépítése Maros megyében 1944–1948" [Building Up Romanian Communist Party Power Structure in Mureş County, 1944–1948]. In Nándor Bárdi, ed., *Autonóm Magyarok? Székelyföld változása az „ötvenes" években* [Autonomous Hungarians? Change in the Székely Country in the Fifties]. Csíkszereda: Pro-Print, 2005.
"A megyésítés előkészítése és a nemzetiségi kérdés Romániában 1968" [Preparations for the County Structure and the Minority Question in Romania 1968]. In Nándor Bárdi and Attila Simon, eds., *Integrációs stratégiák a magyar kisebbségek történetében* [Integration Strategies in the History of Hungarian Minorities]. Somorja/Dunaszerdahely: Fórum Intézet/Lilium Aurum, 2006.
"A román külpolitikai gondolkodás magyarságképe 1956 után" [The Post-1956 Image of the Hungarian Community in Romanian Foreign Policy Thinking]. *Limes* (2008) 2: 99–114.
"Anul posibilităţilor? 1968 în România şi problema naţională" [Golden Age? The Minority Question in Romania in 1968]. In Vasile Ciobanu, Sorin Radu eds., *Partide politice şi minorităţile*

naţionale din România în secolul XX. [Political Parties and National Minorities in Romania in the 20th Century]. Sibiu: 4. Techno Media, 2009.

"Politica naţională a PCR la sfârşitul anilor '60 şi începutul deceniulul următor" [The National Policy of the RCP (Romanian Communist Party) at the End of the 60's and at the Beginning of the Next Decade. In Attila Gidó, Gusztáv Olti, *Minoritatea maghiară în perioada comunistă* [Hungarian Minority in Communist Era]. Cluj-Napoca: Institutul pentru Studierea Problemelor Minorităţii Naţionale, 2009.

Attila Papp Z. (born 1969, Gheorgheni, Romania)

He graduated in sociology in 1996 from Western University, Timişoara, and then obtained a PhD in 2006 from Eötvös Loránd University, Budapest. He joined the research staff of the László Teleki Institute in 1999, where he was also head of the Cross-Border Educational Development Program Bureau in 2003–2006. Since 2007, he has been on the staff of the Institute for Ethnic and National Minority Studies of the Hungarian Academy of Sciences, but he also worked from August 2007 to April 2009 as higher education adviser to the Hungarian Prime Minister's Office. Currently he is associated professor of Quantitative Methodology and Sociology of Education at Miskolc University, Institute of Sociology and editor of the journal *Regio*. He has taught at Babeş–Bolyai University in Cluj-Napoca, Romania, and held methodology courses in educational research for young people in neighboring countries [in Miercurea Ciuc, Cluj-Napoca, Berehovo, Subotica, Senta, Komárno, and Budapest]. He has been on a Hungarian Academy of Sciences János Bolyai Research Scholarship since 2009.

Research fields:
Institutional forms among the Hungarians of Romania (publicity, education, adult education, etc.); education systems, methods of organization, demography, and other social aspects of Hungarian communities in the Carpathian Basin and in the West; educational integration of the Roma in Hungary, Romania and Serbia.

Selected publications:
"The Idea of Civil Society in the Romanian Public Sphere." *Regio* 5 (2002) 151–187.
With Szilvia Németh *et al.*, "Guidelines for Abolishing Segregated Education of Roma Pupils. Policy Note." In Szilvia Németh, ed., *Esély az együttnevelésre/Chance for Integration.* Budapest: OKI, 2004, pp. 9–45.
"The Hungarian Press System in Romania during the Nineties: the World of the Operators." *Regio* 8 (2005) 141–153.
"The Institutional Network of the Preservation and Maintenance of National Identity: Press and Media." *Minorities Research* 10 (2008) 35–50.
"Ways of Interpretation of Hungarian-American Ethnic-Based Public Life and Identity." In Attila Papp Z., ed., *Beszédből világ. Elemzések, adatok amerikai magyarokról* [A World from Speech. Analyses and Data on American Hungarians]. Regio Books. Budapest: Magyar Külügyi Intézet, 2008, pp. 426–456.

Árpád Popély (born 1970, Bratislava, Czechoslovakia)

Having graduated in history and Hungarian from Comenius University, Bratislava, in 1993, he studied at the doctoral school of nineteenth- and twentieth-century Hungarian history at Eötvös Loránd University, Budapest in 1996–1999, and obtained a PhD in 2003. He taught at the Hungarian Gymnasium in Bratislava in 1997–2002, before joining the staff of the Forum Minority Research Institute in Šamorín, Slovakia, in 2002. Since 2010 he has also held the post of senior lecturer at Selye János University, Komárno, Slovakia.

Research fields:
Post-World War II history of the Hungarian minority in Slovakia.

Selected publications:
A [cseh)szlovákiai magyarság történeti kronológiája 1944–1992 [Historical Chronology of the (Czecho)Slovakian Hungarian Minority, 1944–1992]. Somorja: Fórum Kisebbségkutató Intézet, 2006.

"A szlovákiai magyarság csehországi deportálása" [Deporting of Slovakian Hungarians to Czech Lands]. In Imre Molnár Imre and László Szarka, eds., *Otthontalan emlékezet. Emlékkönyv a csehszlovák-magyar lakosságcsere 60. évfordulójára* [Homeless Memory. Memorial Book for the 60th Anniversary of the Czechoslovak–Hungarian Population Exchange]. Budapest/ Komárom: MTA Kisebbségkutató Intézet/Kecskés László Társaság, 2007, pp. 48–66.

"A csehszlovák-magyar lakosságcsere és az áttelepítésre kijelölt szlovákiai magyarok névjegyzékei" [The Czechoslovak–Hungarian Population Exchange and Register of Hungarians in Slovakia Assigned for Resettlement]. *Fórum Társadalomtudományi Szemle* 10 (2008) 1: 125–144.

1968 és a csehszlovákiai magyarság. [1968 and the Czechoslovakian Hungarian Minority]. Somorja: Fórum Kisebbségkutató Intézet, 2008.

Iratok a csehszlovákiai magyarság 1948–1956 közötti történetéhez I [Documents on the History of the Czechoslovakian Hungarians 1948–1956. Vol. 1.]. Somorja: Fórum Kisebbségkutató Intézet, 2008.

Enikő A. Sajti (born 1944, Nagyszalonta)

A tenured university professor and holder of a DSc from the Hungarian Academy of Sciences, she graduated in history and Russian from the University of Szeged, where she has taught the nineteenth- and twentieth-century history of East Central Europe and the Balkans since 1975. She is also on the staff of the university's Doctoral School of History, head of its Balkan doctoral sub-program, and a member of its Council.

Research fields
Balkan history of the twentieth century, Hungarian–Yugoslav relations, and the minority question.

Selected publications
Délvidék 1941–1944. A magyar kormányok délszláv politikája [The Southern Region 1941–1944. The Southern Region Policy of Hungarian Governments]. Budapest: Kossuth, 1987.

Hungarians in the Voivodina 1918–1947. Boulder, CO/Highland Lakes, NJ: Social Science Monographs/Atlantic Research and Publications, 2003.
"The Change of Rule and Reprisals against the Hungarians in Yugoslavia 1944–1946." *Chronica. Annual of the Institute of History University of Szeged* 3 (2003): 114–131.
"The Former 'Southlands' in Serbia 1918–1947." *The Hungarian Quarterly* 47 (2006) 1: 111–124.
Bűntudat és győztes fölény. Magyarország, Jugoszlávia és a délvidéki magyarok [Guilt and Victorious Domination. Hungary, Yugoslavia and the Southern Region Hungarians]. Szeged: SZTE BTK Történelem Doktori Iskola, 2010.

Attila Simon (born 1966, Rimavská Sobota, Czechoslovakia)

He graduated as a Hungarian and history teacher in 1989 from Comenius University, Bratislava, and then taught history at Dunajská Streda Gymnasium. He became a fellow of the Fórum Minority Research Institute, Šamorín, Slovakia, in 2001. He obtained a PhD from the multidisciplinary doctoral school at the University of Pécs in 2005, since when he has been a head of department and senior lecturer at Selye János University, Komárno.

Research field:
History of Slovakia and its Hungarian minority, 1918–1945.

Selected publications:
"Az 1956-os forradalom visszhangja a szlovákiai magyarok között" [Reactions of Slovakian Hungarians to the 1956 Revolution]. In János M. Rainer and Katalin Somlai, eds., *Az 1956-os forradalom visszhangja a szovjet tömb országaiban* [Reactions to the 1956 Revolution in Soviet Bloc Countries]. Budapest: 1956-os Intézet, 2007, pp. 229–246.
"A várakozás hetei. A szlovákiai magyarok az első bécsi döntés előtt" [The Weeks of Waiting. Slovakian Hungarians before the First Vienna Award]. *Limes* (2007) 2: 7–20.

Telepesek és telepesfalvak Szlovákiában a két világháború között
[Colonists and Colony Villages in Slovakia between the World
Wars]. Somorja: Fórum Kisebbségkutató Intézet, 2008.
"Zabudnutí aktivisti. Príspevok k dejinám maďarských politických
strán v medzivojnovom období" [The Forgotten Activists.
Contribution to the History of the Political Parties between the
Two World Wars] *Historický Časopis* (2009) 3: 511–530.
*Egy rövid esztendő krónikája. A szlovákiai magyar kisebbség
1938-ban* [Chronicle of a Short Year. The Slovakian Hungarian
Minority in 1938]. Somorja: Fórum Kisebbségkutató Intézet,
2010.

Tamás Stark (born 1959, Budapest)

He graduated in international relations from Karl Marx University of
Economic Sciences, Budapest, in 1983, since when he has worked at
the Hungarian Academy of Sciences' Institute of History, becoming
a senior fellow in 2000. He also holds the Hungarian Academy of
Sciences candidacy degree.

Research field:
Forced movements of population in East-Central Europe, 1938–
1955.

Selected publications:
Hungary's Human Losses in World War II. Uppsala: Centre for
Multiethnic Research, Uppsala University, 1995.
*Hungarian Jews during the Holocaust and after the Second World
War, 1939–1949. A Statistical Review.* Boulder, CO: East
European Monographs, 2000.
Magyar foglyok a Szovjetunióban [Hungarian Prisoners in the
Soviet Union]. Budapest: Lucidus, 2006.
With Pertti Ahonnen *et al., People on the Move. Forced Population
Movements in Europe during the Second World War and in Its
Aftermath.* Occupation in Europe Series Oxford/New York:
European Science Foundation/Berg, 2008.

László Szarka (born 1953, Dolné Saliby, Czechoslovakia)

After graduating in history and Hungarian from Comenius University in Bratislava in 1976, he was a scholarship student at the History Institute of the Slovakian Academy of Sciences until 1977, then on the staff of the Institute's Budapest working group until 1985. He was a fellow and then interim department head at the Hungarian Academy of Sciences' Institute of History in 1985–1995. In 1998–2000 he was program manager of the Institute for Ethnic and National Minority Studies of the Hungarian Academy of Sciences, and then from 2000 to 2009 its director when it became an institute. In that year he became dean of the Teachers' Training Faculty of János Selye University, Komárno, Slovakia, also teaching at Universities of Debrecen and Pécs, Péter Pázmány Catholic University and Századvég Academy of Politics, all in Hungary.

Research fields:
Twentieth-century Czech and Slovak history, the minority question in Hungary and Central Europe (also nineteenth-century), history of the Hungarian national minority, and changes in the ethnic spatial structure and ethno-political strategies of Central Europe.

Selected publications:
Duna-táji dilemmák. Nemzeti kisebbségek – kisebbségi politika a 20. századi Kelet-Közép-Európában [Danube Dilemmas. National Minorities/Minority Policy in 20th-Century East-Central Europe]. Budapest: Ister, 1998.
Szlovák nemzeti fejlődés – magyar nemzetiségi politika 1867–1918 [Slovak National Development/Hungarian Minority Policy 1867–1918]. Pozsony/Budapest: Kalligram/Magyar Kulturális Intézet, 1999.
Kisebbségi léthelyzetek – közösségi alternatívák. Az etnikai csoportok helye a kelet-közép-európai nemzetállamokban [Minority Living Situations – Community Alternatives. The Place of Ethnic Groups in the Nation States of East-Central Europe. Budapest: Lucidus, 2004.

As editor, *Hungary and the Hungarian Minorities. Trends in the Past and in Our Time.* Boulder, CO/Highland Lakes, NJ: Social Science Monographs/Atlantic Research and Publications, 2004.

"Significance of Czechoslovakian–Hungarian Population Exchange in the History of Intended Elimination of Hungarian Minority in Czechoslovakia." *Minorities Research* 10 (2008): 51–65.

Péter Szuhay (born 1954, Miskolc)

He graduated in ethnography and museum studies from Eötvös Loránd University, Budapest, in 1978, and took a second degree in sociology in 1980. Since then he has been on the staff of the Museum of Ethnography in Budapest. He dealt up to the end of the 1980s with the history of peasant farming and celebrations in rural society. He has presented his research in exhibitions, documentaries and studies, and given guest lectures at universities.

Research field:
The society and cultural history of Hungary's Gypsies; ethnic identity and symbolization; social conflicts and ethnic coexistence.

Selected publications:
With Antónia Barati, *Képek a magyarországi cigányság 20. századi történetéből* [Pictures of the 20th-Century History of Gypsies in Hungary]. Budapest: Néprajzi Múzeum, 1993.

"Constructing a Gypsy National Culture" *Budapest Review of Books* 5 (1995) 3: 111–120.

Cigány-kép – Roma-kép. A Néprajzi Múzeum „Romák Közép- és Kelet-Európában" című kiállításának képeskönyve [Gypsy Image – Roma Image. Illustrated Book on International Exhibition "Roma in Central and Eastern Europe"]. Budapest: Néprajzi Múzeum, 1998.

"Eternal Home: A Vlach Roma Funeral in Kétegyháza, Hungary." *Romani Studies (Continuing Journal of the Gypsy Lore Society)* 15 (2005) 2: 91–124.

With Tivadar Fátyol, Gábor Fleck and Edit Kőszegi, *A roma kultúra virtuális háza/Virtual House of Roma Culture, 2006/2008.* Internet presentation.

Patrik Tátrai (born 1979, Szentes)

He graduated in geography in 2002 from Eötvös Loránd University, Budapest, where he obtained a PhD in 2009. He has been on the staff of the Hungarian Academy of Sciences' Geographical Research Institute since 2003.

Research fields:
Fieldwork mainly in mixed areas of neighboring countries: Nitra district in Slovakia, and Satu Mare area and Oradea in Romania.

Selected publications:
"Ethnic Identity along the Hungarian–Slovak Linguistic Border." *Minorities Research* 6 (2004): 64–86
With K. Kocsis and Zs. Bottlik, *Etnikai térfolyamatok a Kárpát-medence határainkon túli régióiban (1989–2002)* [Ethnic Spatial Processes in the Carpathian Regions beyond Hungary's Borders (1989–2002)]. Budapest: MTA Földrajztudományi Kutatóintézet. 2007.
"Ethnic Mapping of Settlements in Historical Szatmár County." In B. Csiki and Zs. Bartos-Elekes, eds., *Descriptio Transylvaniae* [Description of Transylvania]. Cluj-Napoca: Cholnoky Jenő Geographic Society/Babeş–Bolyai University, Faculty of Geography, 2009, pp. 125–132.
Az etnikai térszerkezet változásai a történeti Szatmárban [Changes in Ethnic Spatial Structure in Historical Szatmár]. Budapest: MTA Földrajztudományi Kutatóintézet. 2010.
With Á. Erőss, "Ethnic Features of Symbolic Appropriation of Public Space in Changing Geopolitical Frames – the Case of Oradea/Nagyvárad." *Hungarian Geographical Bulletin* 59 (2010) 1: 51–68.

János Vékás (born 1953, Novi Sad, Yugoslavia)

Having graduated in literature, law and economics, he became managing editor of Radio Ujvidék, Novi Sad, director of Radio Szenttamás, deputy president of the Democratic Community of Vojvodina Hungarians (1990–1996), foreign political adviser to the Hungarian prime minister (1998–2002), and a research fellow of the Institute for Ethnic and National Minority Studies of the Hungarian Academy of Sciences. He has documented the intellectual life of Vojvodina Hungarians in studies, analyses, interviews, bibliographies and chronologies.

Selected publications:
"Spectra: National and Ethnic Minorities of Hungary as Reflected by the Census." In Ágnes Tóth, ed., *National and Ethnic Minorities in Hungary, 1920–2001.* Boulder, CO/Highland Lakes, NJ: Social Science Monographs/Atlantic Research and Publications, 2005, pp. 1–125.
With Ágnes Tóth, "Identität und Migration. Ergebnisse aus der ungarischen Volkszählung 2001." In Werner Mezger *et al.*, eds., *Jahrbuch für deutsche und osteuropäische Volkskunde.* Vol. 47, 2005. Marburg: N. G. Elwert Verlag, 2006, pp. 193–213.
With Ágnes Tóth, "Modernizáció és identitás. A magyarországi kisebbségek társadalmi-gazdasági helyzete" [Modernization and Identity. The Socio-Economic Situation of Hungarian Minorities]. In Imre Kovách *et al.*, eds., *Európai Magyarország 2007* [European Hungary 2007]. Budapest: MTA Etnikai-nemzeti Kisebbségkutató Intézet, etc., 2007, pp. 240–251.
With Ágnes Tóth, "Borders and Identity." *Hungarian Statistical Review* (Special Issue) 87 (2009) 13: 3–30.
Utak. Életinterjúk 1980–1990 [Paths. Life Interviews 1980–1990]. With CD supplement. Zenta: Vajdasági Magyar Művelődési Intézet, 2010.

Balázs Vizi (born 1974, Kaposvár)

After graduating in law from Eötvös Loránd University, Budapest, in 1999, he received a PhD in political science from the Katholieke Universiteit Leuven, Belgium, in 2006. He has worked since 2002 at the Institute for Ethnic and National Minority Studies of the Hungarian Academy of Sciences and since 2004 as a lecturer in the Department of International Law at Budapest Corvinus University of Budapest. He is a senior non-resident research associate of the European Centre for Minority Issues, Flensburg, Germany.

Research field:
International human and minority rights protection.

Selected publications:
"The Unintended Legal Backlash of Enlargement? The Inclusion of the Rights of Minorities in the EU Constitution." *Regio* 8 (2005): 87–108.

"The EU and the Situation of Roma in Hungary in the Accession Process." *Central European Political Science Review* 6 (2005) 2: 66–91.

"Minority Rights in the "New" EU Member States after Enlargement." In H. Swoboda and J. M. Wiersma, eds., *Democracy, Populism and Minority Rights.* Brussels: PSE/Renner Institut, 2008, pp. 77–85.

"Hungary: a Model with Lasting Problems." In Bernd Rechel, ed., *Minority Rights in Central and Eastern Europe.* London: Routledge, 2009, pp. 119–134.

With Zoltán Kántor *et al.*, eds., *The Hungarian Status Law: Nation-Building and/or Minority Protection.* Slavic Eurasian Studies series. Sapporo: Slavic Research Center, Hokkaido University, 2004.

With Zoltán Kántor *et al.*, eds., *Beyond Sovereignty: from Status Law to Transnational Citizenship?* Slavic Eurasian Studies. Sapporo: Slavic Research Center, Hokkaido University, 2006.

BIBLIOGRAPHY*

A. Sajti, Enikő. *Délvidék 1941–1944* [Southern Region 1941–1944]. Budapest: Kossuth Könyvkiadó, 1987.

A. Sajti, Enikő. *Hungarians in the Voivodina 1918–1947.* Highland Lakes, NJ: Atlantic Research and Publications, Inc., 2003.

A. Sajti, Enikő. *Impériumváltások, revízió, kisebbségek. Magyarok a Délvidéken 1918–1947* [Sovereignty Changes, Revision, Minorities. Hungarians in the Southern Region 1918–1947]. Budapest: Napvilág Kiadó, 2004.

A. Sajti, Enikő. *Kényszerpályán. Magyarok Jugoszláviában, 1918–1941* [Forced Path. Hungarians in Yugoslavia 1918–1941]. Szeged: Hispánia Kiadó, 1997.

A. Sajti, Enikő. *Székely telepítés és nemzetiségi politika a Bácskában* [Székely Settlement and Minority Policy in Bačka]. Budapest: Akadémiai, 1987.

Ablonczy, Balázs. *Pál Teleki – The Life of a Controversial Hungarian Politician.* Boulder, CO: Social Science Monographs, 2007.

Ablonczy, Balázs and Csilla Fedinec, eds. *Folyamatok a változásban. A hatalomváltások társadalmi hatásai Közép-Európában a XX. században* [Processes in Change. Social Effects of Sovereignty Changes in Central Europe in the 20th Century]. Budapest: Teleki László Alapítvány, 2005.

Achim, Viorel. *Cigányok a román történelemben* [Gypsies in Romanian History]. Budapest: Osiris, 2001,

Ádám, Magda. *The Little Entente and Europe (1920–1929).* Budapest: Akadémiai, 2003.

Ádám, Magda and Győző Cholnoky, eds. *Trianon. A magyar békeküldöttség tevékenysége 1920-ban. Válogatás* A magyar béketárgyalások. Jelentés a magyar béketárgyalások. Jelentés a magyar béketárgyalások. Jelentés a magyar béketárgyalások működéséről Neuilly-sur-Seine-ben *I–II. kötetéből* [Trianon. The Activity of the Hungarian Peace Delegation in 1920. Selection from Vols I and II of *The Hungarian Peace Negotiations. Report on the Work of the Hungarian Peace Delegation in Neuilly-sur-Seine*]. Budapest: Lucidus Könyvkiadó, 2001.

---

* See full-text-free books on the Internet.

Ágoston, András and János Vékás, eds. *A botrány* [The Skandall]. Újvidék: VMDK, 1994.

* Ágoston Vilmos. *A határon túli magyarság és a magyar közszolgálati média* [Hungarians Abroad and the Hungarian Public Media]. Budapest: EÖKIK, 2005.

Alföldy, Jenő et al., eds. *Haza a magasban. Magyar nemzetismeret II.* [Home Country on High. Hungarian National Knowledge Vol II]. Lakitelek: Antológia, 2002.

Ammende, Ewald, ed. *Die Nationalitäten in den Staaten Europas.* Vienna/ Leipzig: Sammlung von Lageberichten, 1931.

Ammon, Ulrich et al., eds. *Sociolinguistics Vol. III.* Berlin/New York: Walter de Gruyter, 2006.

Andreescu, Andrea, Lucian Nastasă, and Andrea Varga, eds. *Minorităţi etnoculturale. Mărturii documentare. Maghiarii din România (1945–1955)* [Ethnocultural Minorities. Documents. Hungarians of Romania (1945–1955)]. Cluj: Centrul de Resurse Pentru Diversitate Etnoculturală, 2002.

* Angyal, Béla. *Érdekvédelem és önszerveződés. Fejezetek a csehszlová-kiai magyar pártpolitika történetéből 1918–1938* [Interest Protection and Self-Organization. Chapters from the History of Czechoslovakian Hungarian Party Politics 1918–1938]. Galánta/Dunaszerdahely: Fórum Intézet/Lilium Aurum, 2002.

Arday, Lajos. *Magyarok a Délvidéken, Jugoszláviában* [Hungarians in the Southern Region and Yugoslavia]. Budapest: BIP, 2002.

Arday, Lajos. *Reformok és kudarcok. Jugoszlávia utolsó évtizedei és ami utána következett* [Reforms and Defeats. Yugoslavia's Last Decades and What Ensued]. Budapest: BIP, 2002.

Arday, Lajos. *Térkép, csata után. Magyarország a brit külpolitikában (1918–1919)* [Map after Battle. Hungary in British Foreign Policy, 1918–1919]. Budapest: Magvető Kiadó, 1990.

Arday, Lajos, ed. *Fejezetek a horvátországi magyarok történetéből* [Chapters from the History of Croatia's Hungarians]. Budapest: TLA, 1994.

Autonomija Vojvodine. Izabrani spisi [The Autonomy of Vojvodina. Selected Papers]. Novi Sad: Centar PK SKV za političke studije i marksističko obrazovanje, 1976.

Axworthy, Mark W. A. *Axis Slovakia – Hitler'S Slavic Wedge, 1938–1945.* Bayside, NY: Axis Europa Books, 2002.

Babits, Mihály. *Írók két háború közt* [Writers between the Two Wars]. Budapest: Nyugat, 1941.

Bachynskyj E., ed., *Podkarpats'kaja Rus' 1919–1936* [Subcarpathian Rus 1919–2009]. Uzhgorod: Shkol'naja pomoshh', 1936.

Bajcsy-Zsilinszky, Andrew. *Transylvania. Past and Future.* Geneva: Kundig, 1944.

Bakk, Miklós. *The Democratic Alliance of Hungarians in Romania.* Budapest: TLA, 1998.

* Bakk, Miklós. *Lassú valóság* [Slow Truth]. Târgu Secuiesc: Ambrózia, 2002.

Bakk, Miklós. *Politikai közösség és identitás* [Political Community and Identity]. Kolozsvár: Komp-Press, 2008.

Bakk, Miklós, István Székely, and Tibor T. Toró, eds. *Útközben. Pillanatképek az erdélyi magyar politika reformjáról* [On the Way. Snapshots of the Reform of Transylvanian Hungarian Politics]. Csíkszereda: Pro-Print, 1999.

Bakó, Boglárka, ed. *Lokális világok. Együttélés a Kárpát-medencében* [Local Worlds. Coexistence in the Carpathian Basin]. Budapest: MTA Társadalomkutató Központ, 2003.

* Bakó, Boglárka and Szilvia Szoták, eds. *Magyarlakta kistérségek és kisebbségi identitások a Kárpát-medencében* [Hungarian-Inhabited Districts and Minority Identities in the Carpathian Basin]. Budapest: Gondolat/MTA Etnikai-nemzeti Kisebbségkutató Intézet, 2006.

Balassa, Iván. *A határainkon túli magyarok néprajza* [Ethonography of Hungarians beyond the Borders]. Budapest: Gondolat, 1989.

Balázs, Ferenc, ed. *Versek – elbeszélések – tanulmányok tizenegy fiatal erdélyi írótól erdélyi művészek rajzaival* [Verses, Stories, Studies by 11 Young Transylvanian Writers, Drawings by Transylvanian Artists]. Kolozsvár: Minerva, 1923.

Balázs, Imre József. *Az avantgárd az erdélyi magyar irodalomban* [The Avant Garde in Transylvanian Hungarian Literature]. Marosvásárhely. Mentor Kiadó, 2006.

Balázs, Sándor. *Lugosi üzenet* [Message from Lugoj]. Szatmárnémeti: Szatmárnémeti Kölcsey Kör, 1995.

Balázs, Sándor. *Szociológia és nemzeti önismeret (A Gusti-iskola és a romániai magyar szociográfia) Kritikai tanulmány* [Sociology and National Self-Awareness. (The Gusti School and Romanian Hungarian Sociography) A Critical Study]. Bukarest: Politikai Könyvkiadó, 1979.

Balázs-Arth, Valéria. *Délvidéki magyar képzőművészeti lexikon* [Southern Region Hungarian Fine Arts Dictionary]. Budapest: Timp Kiadó, 2007.

Balla, Bálint, ed. *Sztálinizmus és desztálinizáció Magyarországon. Felszámoltuk-e a szovjet rendszert?* [Stalinism and De-Stalinization in Hungary. Did We Wind up the Soviet System?]. Bern: EPMSZ, 1990.

* Balla, Károly D. *A hontalanság metaforái* [Metaphors of Statelessness]. Ungvár/Budapest: Magyar Nyelv és Kultúra Nemzetközi Társasága, 2000.

* Balla, Károly D. *Kis(ebbségi) magyar skizofrénia* [A Little/Minority Hungarian Schizophrenia]. Ungvár/Budapest: Galéria, 1993.

Balla, László. *Erdélyi Béla és kortársai. Kárpátalja képzőművészeinek három nemzedéke* [Béla Erdélyi and His Contemporaries. Three Generations of Transcarpathian Artists]. Budapest: Galéria Kiadó, 1994.

Balogh, Artúr. *Der internationale Shutz der Minderheiten.* Munich: A. Dresler, 1928.

Balogh, Artúr. *Jogállam és kisebbség* [Constitutional State and Minority]. Budapest: Kriterion Könyvkiadó, 1997.

Balogh, Artúr. *A kisebbségek nemzetközi védelme. A kisebbségi szerződések és a békeszerződések alapján* [International Protection of Minorities. Based on the Minority Treaties and Peace Treaties]. Csíkszereda: Kájoni, 1997.

Balogh, Edgár and Gyula Dávid, eds. *Romániai magyar irodalmi lexikon I–IV.* [Romanian Hungarian Literary Lexicon Vol. I–IV]. Bukarest: Kriterion, 2002.

Balogh, Júlia. *Az erdélyi hatalomváltozás és a magyar közoktatás 1918–1928* [Change of Power in Transylvania and Hungarian Public Education 1918–1928]. Budapest: Püski, 1996.

Balogh, Sándor. *Magyarország külpolitikája 1945–1950* [Hungary's Foreign Policy, 1945–1950]. Budapest: Kossuth, 1988.

Bamberger-Stemmann, Sabine. *Der Europäische Nationalitätenkongreß 1925 bis 1938. Nationale Minderheiten zwischen Lobbyistentum und Großmachtinteressen.* Marburg: Verlag Herder-Institut, 2000.

* Bán, András D. *Hungarian–British Diplomacy, 1938–1941. The Attempt to Maintain Relations.* London: Routledge, 2004.

Bán, András D. *Illúziók és csalódások. Nagy-Britannia és Magyarország, 1938–1941* [Illusions and Disillusionments. Great Britain and Hungary 1938–1941]. Budapest: Osiris, 1998.

Bán, András D., ed. *Pax Britannica. Brit külügyi iratok a második világháború utáni Közép-Európáról 1942–1943* [British Foreign Office Documents on Post-World War II Central Europe, 1942–1943]. Budapest: Osiris, 1996.

Bán, András D., László Diószegi, Zoltán Fejős, Ignác Romsics, and Győző Vinnai. *Magyarok kisebbségben és szórványban* [Hungarians in Minority and Dispersion]. Budapest: Teleki László Alapítvány, 1995.

Banac, Ivo. *The National Question in Yugoslavia: Origins, History, Politics*. Ithaca, NY: Cornell University Press, 1984.

Banny, Leopold. *Krieg im Burgenland*. Eisenstadt: Roetzer, 1983.

Barany, Zoltan. *The East European Gypsies. Regime Change, Marginality, and Ethnopolitics*. Cambridge: Cambridge UP, 2002.

Barát, Mihály. *Válogatott találkozások. Életpálya- és portrévázlatok, 1970–1996* [Selected Meetings. Career and Portrait Sketches 1970–1996]. Ungvár/Budapest: Intermix, 1997.

Barcza, György. *Diplomataéveim, 1911–1945* [My Diplomat Years 1911–1945]. Budapest: Európa/História, 1994.

* Bárdi, Nándor. *Tény és való. A budapesti kormányzatok és a határon túli magyarok kapcsolattörténete. Problémakatalógus* [True Fact. Budapest Governments and the History of Its Contacts with Hungarian Abroad. Catalogue of Problems]. Pozsony: Kalligram, 2004.

Bárdi, Nándor, ed. *Autonóm magyarok? Székelyföld változásai az „ötvenes" években* [Autonomous Hungarians? Changes in the Székely Land in the Early 1950s]. Csíkszereda: Pro-Print, 2005.

Bárdi, Nándor, ed. *Globalizáció és nemzetépítés* [Globalization and Nation-Building]. Budapest: Teleki László Alapítvány, 1999.

* Bárdi, Nándor, ed. *Konfliktusok és kezelésük Közép-Európában* [Conflicts and Handling of Them in Central Europe]. Budapest: Teleki László Alapítvány, 2000.

* Bárdi, Nándor and György Éger, eds. *Útkeresés és integráció. Határon túli magyar érdekvédelmi szervezetek dokumentumai* [Search and Integration. Documents of Hungarian Interest Representing Organizations Abroad]. Budapest: Teleki László Alapítvány, 2000.

* Bárdi, Nándor and Csilla Fedinec, eds. *Etnopolitika. A közösségi, magán- és nemzetközi érdekek viszonyrendszere Közép-Európában* [Ethno-Politics. The System of Relations in Communal, Private, and International Interests]. Budapest: Teleki László Alapítvány, 2003.

Bárdi, Nándor, Csilla Fedinec, and László Szarka, eds. *Kisebbségi magyar közösségek a 20. században* [Minority Hungarian Communities in the 20th Century]. Budapest: Gondolat/MTA Kisebbségkutató Intézet, 2008.

* Bárdi, Nándor and Attila Simon, eds. *Integrációs stratégiák a magyar kisebbségek történetében* [Integration Strategies in the History of the Hungarian Minorities]. Somorja: Fórum Kisebbségkutató Intézet, 2006.

Bar-Shaked, Gavriel, ed. *Names: the Counties of Carpathian Ruthenia. Part I. Names of Jews Deported from Ugocsa County (Sevlus and Vicinity).* New York/Paris: Beate Klarsfeld Foundation, 2004.

Bauböck, Rainer, Gerhard Baumgartner, Bernhard Perchinig, and Karin Pinter, eds. *"...und raus bist Du!" Minderheiten in der Politik.* Vienna: Gesellschaftskritik, 1988.

* Baucal, Aleksandar and Dragica Pavlović-Babić. *Quality and Equity of Education in Serbia: Educational Opportunities of the Vulnerable. Pisa Assessment 2003 and 2006 Data.* Belgrade: Government of the Republic of Serbia, 2009.

* Bauer, Béla *et al.*, eds. *Mozaik 2001 Gyorsjelentés. Magyar fiatalok a Kárpát-medencében* [Interim Report. Young Hungarians in the Carpathian Basin]. Budapest: Nemzeti Ifjúságkutató Intézet, 2002.

Baugh, John. *Out of the Mouths of Slaves: African American Language and Educational Malpractice.* Austin, TX: University of Texas Press, 1999.

Baumgartner, Gerhard. *"6 X Österreich" – Geschichte und aktuelle Situation der Volksgruppen in Österreich.* Klagenfurt/Celovec: Drava, 1995.

Baumgartner, Gerhard and Stefan Schinkovits. *Vermögensentzug bei burgenländischen Kroaten und Ungarn.* Vienna: Böhlau, 2004.

* Baumgartner, Gerhard, Eva Kovács, and András Vári. *Távoli Rokonok – Jánossomorja és Andau 1990–2000* [Distant Relatives. Jánossomorja and Andau 1990–2000]. Budapest: Teleki László Alapítvány, 2002.

Baumgartner, Gerhard, Eva Müllner, and Rainer Münz, eds. *Lebensraum und Identität.* Eisenstadt: Prugg, 1989.

* Bécsy, Tamás, Gajdó Tamás, and György Székely, eds. *Magyar színháztörténet III. 1920–1949* [Hungarian Theater History III. 1920–1949]. Budapest: Magyar Könyvklub, 2006.

Békés, Csaba. *Európából Európába. Magyarországi konfliktusok kereszttüzében 1945–1990* [From Europe to Europe. Hungary in the Crossfire of Conflicts, 1945–1990]. Budapest: Gondolat, 2004.

Békés, Csaba, ed. *Evolúció és revolúció. Magyarország és a nemzetközi politika 1956-ban* [Evolution and Revolution. Hungary and International Politics in 1956]. Budapest: Gondolat/1956-os Intézet, 2007.

* Békés, Csaba, Malcolm Byrne, and János M. Rainer, eds. *The 1956 Hungarian Revolution. A History in Documents.* Budapest: Central European University Press, 2003.

Béládi, Miklós. *Válaszutak. Tanulmányok* [Dilemmas. Studies]. Budapest: Szépirodalmi, 1983.

Bence, Lajos. *Hungarians in Slovenia.* Budapest: Teleki László Alapítvány, 1998.

Bence, Lajos. *Írott szóval a megmaradásért. A szlovéniai magyarság 70 éve* [Survival by Written Word. 70 Years of the Slovenian Hungarians]. Lendava: Magyar Nemzetiségi Műv. Intézet, 1994.

* Bencsik, Péter and György Nagy. *A magyar úti okmányok története 1945–1989* [History of Hungarian Travel Documents 1945–2003]. Budapest: Tipico Design, 2003.

Benda, Kálmán, Angéla Beliczay, György Erdős, and Edit Nagy, eds. *Ráday Gyűjtemény Évkönyve IV–V. (1984–1985)* [Ráday Collection Yearbook (1984–1985) Vol. IV–V.]. Budapest: Ráday Gyűjtemény, 1986.

Bendász, István. *Öt év a szögesdrót mögött: egy kárpátaljai pap a Gulag munkatáboraiban* [Five Years behind Barbed Wire: a Subcarpathian Priest in the Labor Camps of the Gulag]. Abaliget: Lámpás, 2000.

Bendász, István. *Részletek a Munkácsi Görög Katolikus Egyházmegye történetéből* [Details from the History of Mukacheve Greek Catholic Diocese]. Ungvár: KMKSZ, 1999.

Benkő, Levente. *Szárazajta* [Aita Seacă]. Sepsiszentgyörgy: H-Press, 1995.

Benkő, Levente and Annamária Papp, eds. *Magyar fogolysors a második világháborúban II.* [The Fate of Hungarian Prisoners in World War II, Vol II]. Csíkszereda: Pallas Akadémia, 2007

Ben-Tov, Arieh. *Facing the Holocaust in Budapest.* Geneva: Henry Dunant Institute, 1988.

Beregszászi, Anikó and István Csernicskó. *... itt mennyit ér a szó?: Írások a kárpátaljai magyarok nyelvhasználatáról* [...What Is the Value of a Word Here?: Studies on the Language Using of Subcarpathian Hungarians]. Ungvár: PoliPrint, 2004.

Berényi, József. *Nyelvországlás. A szlovákiai nyelvtörvény történelmi és társadalmi okai* [Language and Country. Historical and Social Reasons behind Slovakia's Language Law]. Pozsony: Fórum Alapítvány, 1994.

Berey, Géza. *A magyar újságírás Erdélyben 1919–1939* [Hungarian Journalism in Transylvania 1919–39]. Szeged: Ablaka György Könyvnyomdája, 1940.

Bertha, Zoltán and András Görömbei. *A romániai magyar irodalom válogatott bibliográfiája 1971–1980* [Select Bibliography of Romanian Hungarian Literature]. Budapest: Tudományos Ismeretterjesztő Társulat Budapesti Szervezete, n. d.

Bethlen, Béla. *Észak-Erdély kormánybiztosa voltam* [I Was Government Commissioner for Northern Transylvania]. Budapest: Zrínyi Katonai Kiadó, 1989.

Bianchi, Leonard, ed. *Dejiny štátu a práva na území Československa v obdobi kapitalizmu* [History of State and Law in Czechoslovakia in the Period of Capitalism Vol. II]. Bratislava: Vydavateľstvo Slovenskej akadémie vied, 1973.

* Bihari, Zoltán, ed. *Magyarok a nagyvilágban. Kézikönyv a Kárpát-medencében, Magyarország határain kívül élő magyarságról* [Hungarians in the Wide World. Handbook on the Carpathian Basin Hungarians beyond Hungary's Borders]. Budapest: CEBA, 2000.

Bines, Carol. *Din istoria imigrărilor în Israel* [The History of Migration to Israel]. Bucureşti: Hasefer, 1998.

Bíró, Gáspár. *Az identitásválasztás szabadsága* [Freedom of Identity Choice]. Budapest: Századvég, 1995.

Bíró, Sándor. *The Nationalities Problem in Transylvania 1867–1940.* Highland Lakes, NJ: Atlantic Research and Publications, 1992.

* Biró, Zoltán A. *Stratégiák vagy kényszerpályák?* [Strategy or Forced Path?]. Csíkszereda: Pro-Print, 1998.

* Biró, Zoltán A., József Gagyi, and János Péntek. *Néphagyományok új környezetben. Tanulmányok a folklorizmuskutatás köréből* [Folk Traditions in a New Context, Studies in Folklore Research]. Bukarest: Kriterion, 1987.

Bisztray, Gyula and Zoltán Csuka, eds. *Szenteleky Kornél irodalmi levelei 1927–1933* [Literary Correspondence of Kornél Szenteleky 1927–1933]. Zsombor/Budapest: Szenteleky Társaság, 1943.

Bodnar, V. and M. Vegesh. *Karpats'ka Ukrai'na v mizhnarodnyh vidnosynah (1938–1939)* [The Carpatho-Ukraine Question in International Politics (1938–1939)]. Uzhhorod: UzhDU, 1997.

* Bodó, Julianna, ed. *Fényes tegnapunk. Tanulmányok a szocializmus korszakáról* [Our Glowing Past. Studies on the Socialism Period]. Csíkszereda: Pro-Print, 1998.

* Bodó, Julianna, ed. *Helykeresők. Roma lakosság a Székelyföldön* [Seeking their Place? Roma People in the Székely Land]. Csíkszereda: Pro-Print, 2002.

Bodó, Barna, ed. *Romániai magyar politikai évkönyv* [Romanian Hungarian Political Yearbook]. Temesvár/Kolozsvár: Szórvány Alapítvány, 2000–2005.

Boldyzhar, M. *Zakarpattia mizh dvoma svitovymy vijnamy. Materialy do istorii' suspil'no-politychnyh vidnosyn* [Transcarpathia between the World Wars. Materials on the History of Socio-Political Relations]. Uzhhorod, 1993.

Boldyzhar, M. and P. Mosni. *Derzhavno-pravovyj status Zakarpattia (Pidkarpats'koi' Rusi) v skladi Chehoslovachchyny* [The Constitutional Situation of Transcarpathia (Subcarpathian Rus) within the Czechoslovak Republic]. Uzhhorod: UzhDU, 2001.

Borbándi, Gyula. *Emigráció és Magyarország: nyugati magyarok a változások éveiben: 1985–1995* [Emigration and Hungary: Hungarians in the West in the Years of Change: 1985–1995]. Basel/Budapest: Európai Protestáns Magyar Szabadegyetem, 1996.

* Borbándi, Gyula. *A magyar emigráció életrajza: 1945–1985. I–II.* [Biographies of Hungarian Émigrés, Vol. I–II]. Budapest: Európa, 1981.

Borbély, Zsolt and Krisztina Szentimrei. *Erdélyi magyar politikatörténet 1989–2003* [Transylvanian Hungarian Political History 1989–2003]. Budapest: LKD Bt, 2003.

Bori, Imre. *A jugoszláviai magyar irodalom története* [History of Yugoslavian Hungarian Literature]. Újvidék/Belgrád: Forum/Zavod za udzbenike i nastavna sredstva, 1998.

Boros, Ferenc. *Szomszédunk Szlovákia. A diplomata-történész szemével, 1993–1999* [Our Neighbor Slovakia through the Eyes of a Diplomat and Historian, 1993–1999]. Pozsony: Kalligram, 2000.

Borsody, István. *A magyar–szlovák kérdés alapvonalai* [The Base Lines of the Hungarian–Slovak Question]. Budapest: privately published, 1939.

Borsody, István, ed. *Magyarok Csehszlovákiában 1918–1938* [Hungarians in Czechoslovakia 1918–1938]. Budapest: Az Ország Útja, 1938.

* Borsody, Stephen. *The New Central Europe*. New York: Columbia University Press, 1993.

* Borsody, Stephen, ed. *The Hungarians: a Divided Nation*. New Haven, CT: Yale Center for International and Area Studies, 1988.

Botlik, József, Béla Csorba and Károly Dudás. *Eltévedt mezsgyekövek. Adatok a délvidéki magyarság történetéhez* [Lost Boundary Markers. Notes on the History of the South Country Hungarians]. Budapest: Hatodik Síp Alapítvány/Új Mandátum, 1994.

* Bottoni, Stefano. *Sztálin a székelyeknél. A Magyar Autonóm Tartomány története (1952–1960)* [Stalin among the Székelys. History of the Hungarian Autonomous Province, 1952–1960]. Csíkszereda: Pro-Print, 2008.

Bottoni, Stefano. *Transilvania rossa. Il comunismo romeno e la questione nazionale, 1944–1965.* Rome: Carocci, 2007.

* Bottoni, Stefano, Márton László, Klára Lázok, and Zoltán Novák, eds. *Az 1956-os forradalom és a romániai magyarság (1956–1959)* [The '56 Hungarian Revolution and Romania's Hungarians]. Csíkszereda: Pro-Print, 2006.

Bozo, Frederic, Marie-Pierre Rey, N. Piers Ludlow, and Leopoldo Nuti, eds. *Europe and the End of the Cold War. A Reappraisal.* London: Routledge, 2009.

* Bözödi, György. *Székely bánja* [Ban of the Székely]. Cluj: Gloria, 1938.

Braham, Randolph L. *Genocide and Retribution: the Holocaust in Hungarian-Ruled Northern Transylvania.* Boston: Kluwer, 1983.

Braham, Randolph L. *A Magyarországi holokauszt földrajzi enciklopédiája I–III.* [Geographic Encyclopedia of the Holocaust in Hungary, Vol I–III.]. Budapest: Park, 2007.

* Braham, Randolph L. *The Politics of Genocide: the Holocaust in Hungary.* Wayne: Wayne State University Press, 2000.

Brandes, Detlef, Edita Ivaničková, and Jiří Pešek, eds. *Erzwungene Trennung. Vertreibungen und Aussiedlungen in und aus der Tschechoslowakei 1938–1947 im Vergleich mit Polen, Ungarn und Jugoslawien.* Essen: Klartext Verlag, 1999.

Brandes, Detlef, Edita Ivaničková, and Jiří Pešek, eds. *Der Weg zur Vertreibung 1938–1945. Pläne und Entscheidungen zum "Transfer" der Deutschen aus der Tschechoslowakei und aus Polen.* Munich: R. Oldenbourg Verlag, 2005.

Bretter, György. *A felőrlődés logikája. (Esszék, értelmezések, jegyzetek)* [Logic of Pulverization. Essays, Interpretations, Notes]. Budapest: Enciklopédia/Ister, 1998.

Britain, David and Cheshire, Jenny, eds. *Social Dialectology: in Honour of Peter Trudgill.* Amsterdam/Philadelphia: John Benjamins Publishing Company, n. d.

Brubaker, Rogers. *Nationalism Reframed: Nationhood and the National Question in the New Europe*. Cambridge: Cambridge University Press, 1996.

Brubaker, Rogers, Margit Feischmidt, Jon Fox, and Liana Grancea. *Nationalist Politics and Everyday Ethnicity in a Transylvanian Town*. Princeton: Princeton University Press, 2006.

Brunner, Georg. *Nationalitätenprobleme und Minderheitenkonflikte in Osteuropa*. Gütersloh: Bertelsmann Stiftung, 1993.

Buday, László. *A megcsonkított Magyarország* [Severed Hungary]. Budapest: Pantheon, 1921.

Bulla, Béla and Tibor Mendöl. *A Kárpát-medence földrajza* [The Geography of the Carpathian Basin]. Budapest: Lucidus, 1999.

Burgenländische Forschungsgesellschaft, ed. *Zweisprachigkeit als Chance. Ungarischunterricht im Burgenland*. Eisenstadt: Rötzer, 1995.

Buzási, János. *Az újvidéki „razzia"* [Novi Sad Razzia]. Budapest: Kossuth, 1963.

Cadzow, John, F., Andrew Ludanyi, and Louis J. Elteto, eds. *Transylvania. The Roots of Ethnic Conflict*. Kent, OH: Kent State University Press, 1983.

Cambel, Samuel. *Päťdesiate roky na slovenskej dedine. Najťažšie roky kolektivizácie* [Fifty Years in the Slovak Village. The Hardest Years of Collectivization]. Prešov: Universum, 2005.

Carmilly-Weinberger, Moshe. *The Road to Life*. New York: Shengold Publishers, 1994.

Carmilly-Weinberger, Moshe. *A zsidóság története Erdélyben, 1623–1944* [History of Jewry in Transylvania 1623–1944]. Budapest: MTA Judaisztikai Kutatócsoport, 1995.

Case, Holly. *Between States: the Transylvanian Question and the European Idea during World War II*. Stanford: Stanford University Press, 2009.

Cătănuş, D. and O. Roske. *Colectivizarea agricultirii în România* [Agricultural Collectivization in Romania]. Bucureşti: Humanitas, 1990.

Československá statistika. Svazek 9. Sčítaní ludu v republice Československé ze dne 15. února 1921 [Czechoslovak Statistics. Vol. 9. Census in the Republic of Czechoslovakia of 15 February 1921]. Praha: Orbis, 1924.

* Chaszar, Edward. *Decision in Vienna: the Czechoslovak–Hungarian Border Dispute of 1938*. Astor, FL: Danubian Press, 1978.

Chászár, Edward, ed. *Hungarians in Czechoslovakia Yesterday and Today.* Astor, FL: Danubian Press, 1988.

* Cholnoky, Győző, ed. *Minorities Research. A Collection of Studies by Hungarian Authors.* Budapest: Lucidus, 2006.

Churchill, Winston S. *The Second World War.* Vol. VI. London: Cassell, 1953.

Connor, Walker. *The National Question in Marxist-Leninist Theory and Strategy.* Princeton, NJ: Princeton University Press, 1984.

Csáky, Piroska S. *A Frum Könyvkiadó bibliográfiája 1957–2006* [Bibliography of Publishers Forum, 1957–2006]. Újvidék: Forum, 2007.

Csáky, Piroska S. *A jugoszláviai magyar könyv 1945–1970* [Yugoslavian Hungarian Books 1945–1970]. Újvidék: Frum, 1973.

Csanádi, György. *Régi beregszásziak* [Old People of Beregovo]. Beregszász: Bereginfo, 2001.

Csanádi, György. *Sorsfordító évek sodrában. Fejezetek Beregvidék történelmi múltjából* [In the Current of Fateful Years. Chapters of Bereg District History]. Ungvár: PoliPrint, 2004.

* Csanda, Gábor and Károly Tóth, eds. *Magyarok Szlovákiában. Kultúra (1989–2006)* [Hungarians in Slovakia. Culture (1989–2006)]. Šamorin: Fórum Kisebbségkutató Intézet, 2007.

Csatári, Dániel. *Forgószélben (Magyar–román viszony 1940–1945)* [In a Whirlwind. Hungarian–Romanian Relations 1940–1945]. Budapest: Akadémiai Kiadó, 1968.

Cseke, Péter and Gusztáv Molnár, eds. *Nem lehet. A kisebbségi sors vitája* [It Can't Be Done. Debate on Minority Fate]. Budapest: Héttorony, 1989.

Csepeli, György, Antal Örkény, and Mária Székelyi. *Grappling with National Identity.* Budapest: Akadémiai Kiadó, 2000.

Csepeli, György, Antal Örkény, and Mária Székelyi. *Nemzetek egymás tükrében. Interetnikus viszonyok a Kárpát-medencében* [Nations Reflected in Each Other. Inter-Ethnic Relations in the Carpathian Basin]. Budapest: Balassi, 2002.

Cseres, Tibor. *Titoist atrocities in Vojvodina 1944–1945.* Buffalo, NY: Hunyadi, 1993.

Cseres, Tibor. *Vérbosszú Bácskában* [Revenge in Bačka]. Budapest: Magvető, 1991.

Csergő, Zsuzsa. *Talk of the Nation: Language and Conflict in Romania and Slovakia.* NY/London: Cornell University Press, 2007.

Csernicskó, István. *A magyar nyelv Ukrajnában (Kárpátalján)* [The Hungarian Language in Ukraine (Transcarpathia)]. Budapest: Osiris/ MTA Kisebbségkutató Műhely, 1998.

Csernicskó, István and Ildikó Orosz. *The Hungarians in Transcarpathia*. Budapest: Tinta, 1999.

* Csete, Örs, ed. *A Magyariskola Program fogadtatása a Kárpát-medencében* [Reception of the Hungarian School Program in the Carpathian Basin]. Budapest: Apáczai Közalapítvány, 2006.

Csim, János. *Adalékok a Horthy-hadsereg szervezetének és háborús tevékenységének a tanulmányozásához (1938–1945)* [Toward a Study of the Organization and Wartime Activity of Horthy's Army]. Budapest: Honvédelmi Minisztérium Központi Irattár, 1961.

Csoma, Gergely. *Moldvai csángó magyarok* [Moldavian Csángó Hungarians]. Budapest: Corvina, 1988.

Csorba, Béla, Márton Matuska, and Béla Riba, eds. *Rémuralom Délvidéken. Tanulmányok, emlékezések, helyzetértékelések az 1944–1945. évi magyarellenes atrocitásokról* [Terror in the Southern Region. Studies, Memoirs, and Reports of Anti-Hungarian Atrocities in 1944–1945]. Újvidék: Vajdasági Magyar Tudományos Társaság/Atlantis Kiadó, 2004.

Csorba, Béla and János Vékás, eds. *A kultúrtanti visszavág. A Symposion-mozgalom krónikája 1954–1993* [Auntie Culture Strikes Back. Chronicle of the Symposion Movement]. Újvidék: self-published, 1994.

Csuka, János. *A délvidéki magyarság története 1918–1941* [History of Southern Region Hungarians 1918–1941]. Budapest: Püski, 1995.

Csuka, Zoltán, ed. *A visszatért Délvidék* [The Returned Southern Region]. Budapest: Kalász Irodalmi és Könyvkiadóvállalat, 1941.

Csuka, Zoltán and János Ölvedi, eds. *Magyar föld – magyar nép. (A megnagyobbodott Magyarország községeinek adattára)* [Hungarian Land – Hungarian People. Data on the Villages of Enlarged Hungary]. Budapest: Magyar Írás Irodalmi és Könyvkiadóvállalat, 1943.

Czibulka, Zoltán, Ervin Heinz, and Miklós Lakatos, eds. *A magyarországi németek kitelepítése és az 1941. évi népszámlálás* [Deportation of Hungary's Germans and the 1941 Census]. Budapest: KSH, 2004.

Czigány, Magda. *Kényszerű tanulmányúton – 1956-os magyar egyetemi hallgatók Nagy-Britanniában* [Forced Study Trip. 1956 Hungarian University Students in Great Britain]. Budapest: Jószöveg Műhely, 2007.

Czine, Mihály. *Nép és irodalom II.* [People and Literature, Vol. II].
  Budapest: Szépirodalmi Könyvkiadó, 1981.
* D. Lőrincz, József. *Az átmenet közéleti értékei a mindennapi életben*
  [Public Values of the Transition in Daily Life]. Csíkszereda: Pro-Print,
  2004.
D. Lőrincz, József, Zoltán Biró A. eds. *Szeklerland in Transition. Essays
  in Cultural Anthropology.* Csíkszereda: Pro-Print, 1999.
Dabrowski, Dariusz. *Rzeczpospolita Polska wobec kwestii Rusi Zakar-
  packiei (Podkarpackiej) 1938–1939* [The Republic of Poland to the
  Carpathian Ruthenia (Subcarpathia) 1938–1939]. Toruń: Europejskie
  Centrum Edukacyjne, 2007.
Daicoviciu, C. Şt. Pascu *et al.*, eds. *Din istoria Transilvaniei. I–II* [History
  of Transylvania, Vol. I–II]. Bucureşti: Editura Academiei RPR, 1960–
  1961.
Dálnoki Szabó, Dénes and György Beke, eds. *A Kriterion műhelyében.
  Beszélgetések Domokos Gézával a Kriterion Könyvkiadóról* [In the
  Kriterion Studio. Talks with Géza Domokos on Publishers Kriterion].
  Budapest: Kossuth, 1988.
Davies, Peter Siani. *The Romanian Revolution of December 1989.* London:
  Cornell University Press, 2005.
De Zayas, Aldred M. *A Terrible Revenge: the Ethnic Cleansing of the
  East European Germans, 1944–1950.* New York: Palgrave/Macmillan,
  2006.
Deák, Ernö. *Ungarische Mittelschulen in Österreich nach 1956.* Vienna:
  Zentralverb, 2006.
Deák, Francis. *Hungary at the Paris Peace Conference. The Diplomatic
  History of the Treaty of Trianon.* New York: Howard Fertig, 1972.
Deák, Ladislav. *Hungary's Game for Slovakia: Slovakia in Hungarian
  Politics in the Years 1933–1939.* Bratislava: Veda, 1996.
Deák, Ladislav, ed. *Malá vojna* [The Little War]. Bratislava: Slovac
  Academia Press, 1993.
Deák, Ladislav. *Viedenská arbitráž. 2 november 1938 I–III* [The Vienna
  Award. November 2, 1938, Vol. I–III]. Bratislava: Martin, 2002–
  2006.
Deér, József, ed. *Erdély* [Transylvania]. Budapest: Magyar Történelemi
  Társulat, 1940.
Deér, József, ed. *Siebenbürgen.* Budapest: Történettudományi Intézet,
  1941.

* Deér, József and László Gáldi, eds. *Magyarok és románok II.* [Hungarians and Romanians, Vol. II]. Budapest: Magyar Történeti Intézet, 1943.

Deinhofer, Elisabeth and Traude Horvath, eds. *Grenzfall Burgenland 1921–1991.* Eisenstadt: Kanica, 1991.

Deletant, Dennis. *Communist Terror in Romania: Gheorghiu-Dej and the Police State, 1948–1965.* New York: St. Martin's Press, 1999.

Delfiner, Henry. *Vienna Broadcasts to Slovakia, 1938–1939: a Case Study in Subversion.* Boulder, CO: East European Quarterly, 1974.

Demeter, Béla and József Venczel. *Az Erdélyi Magyar Gazdasági Egyesület munkája a román impérium alatt* [Work of Transylvanian Hungarian Commercial Association under Romanian Rule]. Budapest: Pátria Ny., 1940.

Deréky, Pál. *Magyarok Ausztriában és Nyugat-Németországban* [Hungarians in Austria and West Germany]. Vienna: Integratio 16, 1984.

Derghacov, O. *et al. Ukrai'ns'ka derzhavnist' u 20 stolitti (Istoryko-politologichnyj analiz)* [Ukrainian Statehood in the Twentieth Century (Historical and Political Analysis)] (Kyiv: Politychna dumka, 1996)

* Diószegi, László and Andrea R. Süle, eds. *A romániai magyarság története 1919–1989* [History of the Romanian Hungarians 1919–1989]. Budapest: Magyarságkutató Intézet, 1990.

Djokić, Dejan, ed. *Yugoslavism. Histories of a Failed Idea 1918–1992.* London: C. Hurst, 2003.

Dobos, Ferenc, ed. *Az autonóm lét kihívásai kisebbségben* [Challenges of Autonomous Existence in a Minority]. Budapest: Osiris, 2001.

Dobrincu, Dorin and Constantin Iordachi, eds. *Ţărănimea şi puterea. Procesul de colectivizare a agriculturii în România (1949–1962)* [Peasantry and Power. The Process of Collectivization of Agriculture in Romania (1949–1962)]. Iaşi: Polirom, 2005.

Dombrády, Lóránd. *Army and Politics in Hungary 1938–1944.* Highland Lakes, NJ: Atlantic Research and Publications, 2005.

Dombrády, Lóránd. *Katonapolitika és hadsereg 1920–1944* [Military Policy and the Army, 1920–1944]. Budapest: Ister, 2000.

Domokos, Géza. *Esély I–III. Visszaemlékezések 1989–1992* [Chance, Vol I–III. Memoirs 1989–1992]. Csíkszereda: Pallas Akadémia, 1997.

* Domokos, Pál Péter. *A moldvai magyarság* [Moldavian Hungarians]. Budapest: Magvető, 1987.

Domokos, Pál Péter. *Rendületlenül... Márton Áron Erdély katolikus püspöke* [Unflinchingly. Áron Márton, Catholic Bishop of Transylvania]. Budapest: Eötvös Kiadó/Szent Gellért Egyházi Kiadó, n. d.

Domonkos, László. *Magyarok a Délvidéken* [Hungarians in the Southern Region]. Budapest: Zrínyi Kiadó, 1992.

Dreisziger, Nandor F. *Hungary's Way to World War II*. Astor Park, FL: Danubian Press, 1968.

Duba, Gyula. *Vajúdó parasztvilág. Jelentés a Garam mentéről* [Birth Pangs of the Peasantry. Report from the Garam Valley]. Pozsony/Budapest: Madách/Szépirodalmi, 1974.

Dunay, Pál and Wolfgang Zellner. *Ungarns Aussenpolitik 1990–1997. Zwischen Westintegration, Nachbarschafts- und Minderheitenpolitik.* Baden-Baden: Nomos Verlagsgesellschaft, 1998.

Dupka, György. *„Sötét napok jöttek..." Koncepciós perek magyar elítéltjeinek emlékkönyve 1944–1955* ["Dark Days Came..." Memorial Book to the Show Trials of Hungarian Prisoners, 1944–1955]. Budapest/Ungvár: Intermix Kiadó, 1993.

Dupka, György, ed. *A KMKSZ történetéből. Dokumentumok, tények, adatok* [From the History of the Transcarpathian Hungarian Cultural Association. Documents, Facts, Data]. Ungvár: Intermix, 1993.

* Duray, Miklós. *Kettős elnyomásban. Dokumentumok a csehszlovákiai magyarság helyzetéről és jogvédelméről 1978–1989* [Double Pressure. Documents on the Situation and Legal Protection of the Czechoslovakian Hungarians, 1978–1989]. Pozsony: Madách–Posonium, 1993.

* Duray, Miklós. *Kutyaszorító I.* [In a Tight Spot, Vol. I.]. New York: Püski/Corvin, 1982.

Duray, Miklós. *Önrendelkezési kísérleteink* [Attempts at Self-Determination]. Somorja: Méry Ratio, 1999.

Duray, Miklós, ed. *Kettős elnyomásban. A csehszlovákiai magyar kisebbség társadalmi jogvédelmének tíz éve (1978–1988)* [Double Pressure. Documents on the Situation and Legal Protection of the Czechoslovakian Hungarians 1978–1989]. Pozsony: Madách–Posonium, 1994.

* Eberhardt, Piotr. *Ethnic Groups and Population Changes in Twentieth-Century Central-Eastern Europe. History, Data and Analysis.* Armonk, NY/London: M. E. Sharpe, 2002.

Edwards, Lee. *The Collapse of Communism.* Stanford, CA: Hoover Institute Press, 1999.

Edwin, Bakker. *Minority Conflict in Slovakia and Hungary?* Capelle a/d Ijssel: Labyrinth Publication, 1997.

Éger, György. *A burgenlandi magyarság rövid története* [Short History of the Burgenland Hungarians]. Budapest: Anonymus, 1994.

Éger, György. *Regionalizmus, határok és kisebbségek Kelet-Közép-Európában* [Regionalism, Borders and Minorities in East-Central Europe]. Budapest: Osiris, 2000.

Éger, György and Ádám Szesztay. *Alsóőr* [Unterwart]. Budapest/Ungvár: Száz magyar falu könyvesháza Kht, n. d.

Egry, Gábor. *Az erdélyiség "színeváltozása". Kísérlet az Erdélyi Párt ideológiájának és identitáspolitikájának elemzésére 1940–1944* [The "Transfiguration" of Transylvanianism. An Attempt to Analyze the Ideology and Identity Policy of the Transylvanian Party, 1940–1944]. Budapest: Napvilág, 2008.

* Eiler, Ferenc. *Kisebbségvédelem és revízió. Magyar törekvések az Európai Nemzetiségi Kongresszuson (1925–1939)* [Minority Protection and Revision. Hungarian Efforts at the European Congress of Nationalities, 1925–1939]. Budapest: MTA Kisebbségkutató Intézet, 2007.

* Eiler, Ferenc and Dagmar Hájková, eds. *Czech and Hungarian Minority Policy in Central Europe 1918–1938.* Budapest: MTA Kisebbségkutató Intézet, 2009.

"Az elsüllyedt jelek.". I. A 20. századi magyar könyvillusztráció Magyarország határain kívül 1918-tól napjainkig [Sunken Signs I. Twentieth-Century Hungarian Book Illustration beyond Hungary's Borders from 1918 to the Present Day]. Budapest: Magyar Képzőművészek és Iparművészek Társasága, 2003.

Elvert, Jürgen, ed. *Der Umbruch in Osteuropa.* Stuttgart: Steiner, 1993.

Emed, Alexander. *A magyarországi cionista mozgalom története, 1902–1948* [History of the Hungarian Zionist Movement, 1902–1948]. Budapest: Oneg Sábbát Klub, 2002.

Enyedi, Sándor. *Rivalda nélkül. A határon túli magyar színjátszás lexikona* [No Footlights. Encyclopedia of Hungarian Theater Abroad]. Budapest: TLA, 1999.

Enyedi, Sándor. *Színészek, színházak, városok. A határon túli magyar színházművészet lexikona* [Actors, Theaters, Cities. Dictionary of Hungarian Theater beyond Hungary's Borders]. Budapest: Balassi, 2005.

Eppl, Peter, Béla Rásky, and Werner Michael Schwarz, eds. *Ungarn 1956.* Vienna: Wien Museum, 2006.

Erdélyi, Béla. *Képzőművészet – Ungvár és Ung megye* [Fine Art – Uzhhorod and Ung County] Ungvár, 1940.

Esterházy, János. *A kisebbségi kérdés* [The Minority Question]. Budapest: Ister, 2000.

Extra, Guus and Durk Gorter, eds. *Multilingual Europe: Facts and Policies.* New York: Mouton De Gruyter, 2008.

Fábry, Zoltán. *Az éhség legendája* [Legend of Famine]. Pozsony: Az Út, 1932.

Fábry, Zoltán. *A vádlott megszólal* [The Accused Speaks]. Pozsony: Madách Könyv- és Lapkiadó, 1992.

Faragó, Ödön. *Írások és emlékek* [Writings and Memoirs]. Užhorod: Lám Elemér Rt., 1939.

* Faragó, Tamás and Péter Őri, eds. *Történeti demográfiai évkönyv, 2001* [Yearbook of Historical Demography 2001]. Budapest: KSH NKI, 2001.

Fazekas, József, ed. *Fejezetek a csehszlovákiai magyarság történetéből* [Chapters from the History of the Czechoslovakian Hungarians]. Pozsony: Kalligram, 1993.

Fazekas, József, ed. *Vagyunk és leszünk. A szlovenszkói magyarság társadalmi rajza 1918–1945* [We Are and will Remain. The Sociography of the Hungarians of Slovensko]. Pozsony: Kalligram, 1993.

* Fazekas, József and Péter Hunčík, eds. *Magyarok Szlovákiában I. 1989–2004. Összefoglaló jelentés. A rendszerváltástól az Európai Uniós csatlakozásig.* [Hungarians in Slovakia, Vol. I. 1989–2004. Summary Report. From the Change of System to EU Accession]. Dunaszerdahely: Lilium Aurum, 2004.

* Fazekas, József and Péter Hunčík, eds. *Magyarok Szlovákiában. II. Dokumentumok, Kronológia (1989–2004)* [Hungarians in Slovakia, Vol. II. Documents, Chronology (1989–2004)]. Dunaszerdahely: Lilium Aurum, 2005.

Féder, Zoltán. *In Israeli Libraries. Two Bibliographies. A: the Bibliography of the Literary Works in the Hungarian Language from Israel, 1928–2002.* Tel Aviv: Eked, 2004.

* Fedinec, Csilla. *Fejezetek a kárpátaljai magyar közoktatás történetéből (1938–1991)* [Chapters from the History of Transcarpathian Hungarian Education, 1938–1991]. Budapest: Nemzetközi Hungarológiai Központ, 1999.

* Fedinec, Csilla. *A kárpátaljai magyarság történeti kronológiája 1918–1944* [Historical Chronology of Transcarpathian Hungarians 1918–1944]. Dunaszerdahely: Lilium Aurum, 2002.

* Fedinec, Csilla, ed. *Értékek, dimenziók a magyarságkutatásban* [Values and Dimensions in the Research of Hungarians]. Budapest: MTA Magyar Tudományosság Külföldön Elnöki Bizottsága, 2008.

* Fedinec, Csilla, ed. *Iratok a kárpátaljai magyarság történetéhez 1918–1944. Törvények, rendeletek, kisebbségi programok, nyilatkozatok* [Documents on the History of Transcarpathian Hungarians 1918–1944. Laws, Orders, Minority Programs, Statements]. Dunaszerdahely: Lilium Aurum Könyvkiadó, 2004.

* Fedinec, Csilla, ed. *Kárpátalja 1938–1941. – Magyar és ukrán történeti közelítés* [Transcarpathia 1938–1941. Hungarian and Ukrainian Historical Rapprochement]. Budapest: Teleki László Alapítvány, 2004.

Fedinec, Csilla, ed. *Nemzet a társadalomban* [Nation in Society]. Budapest: Teleki László Alapítvány, 2004.

Fedinec, Csilla and Mykola Vegesh, eds. *Kárpátalja 1919–2009: történelem, politika, kultúra* [Transcarpathia 1919–2009: History, Politics, Culture]. Budapest: Argumentum Kiadó – Magyar Tudományos Akadémia Etnikai-nemzeti Kisebbségkutató Intézete, 2010.

Fedinec, Csilla and Mykola Vegesh, eds. *Zakarpattja 1919–2009 rokiv: istorija, polityka, kul'tura* [Transcarpathia 1919–2009: History, Politics, Culture]. Uzhhorod: Poligrafcentr "Lira" – Naukovo-doslidnyj instytut politychnoi' regionalistyky Uzhgorods'kogo nacional'nogo universytetu, 2010.

Feischmidt, Margit, ed. *Etnicitás. Különbségteremtő társadalom* [Ethnicity. Society That Creates Differences]. Budapest: Gondolat – MTA Kisebbségkutató Intézet, 2010.

Felak, James Ramon. *At the Price of the Republic: Hlinka's Slovak People's Party, 1929–1938.* Pittsburgh, PA: University of Pittsburgh Press, 1995.

Felvidéki mártírok és hősök aranykönyve. Felvidéki irodalmi emlékkönyv [Golden Book of Upland Martyrs and Heroes. Upland Literary Memorial Book]. Budapest: MEFHOSZ, 1940.

Fenyvesi, Anna, ed. *Hungarian Language Contact outside Hungary: Studies on Hungarian as a Minority Language.* Amsterdam: John Benjamins, 2005.

Filep, Tamás Gusztáv. *A hagyomány felemelt tőre. Válogatott és új tanulmányok az 1918–1945 közötti (cseh)szlovákiai magyar kultúráról* [Raised Sword of Tradition. Selected and New Studies on (Czecho)Slovakian and Slovakian Hungarian Culture in 1918–1945]. Budapest: Ister, 2003.

Filep, Tamás Gusztáv. *A humanista voksa. Írások a csehszlovákiai magyar kisebbség történetének köréből 1918–1945* [Humanist Voice.

Writings on the History of the Czechoslovakian Hungarian Minority 1918–1945]. Pozsony: Kalligram, 2007.

Fink, Carole. *Defending the Rights of Others: the Great Powers, the Jews, and International Minority Protection, 1878–1938*. Cambridge: Cambridge University Press, 2004.

Flachbarth, Ernő. *System Des internationalen Minderheitenrechtes*. Budapest: Gergely, 1937.

Földes, György. *Magyarország, Románia és a nemzeti kérdés 1956–1989* [Hungary, Romania and the National Question 1956–1989]. Budapest: Napvilág, 2007.

Fónod, Zoltán. *Üzenet. A magyar irodalom története Cseh/Szlovákiában 1918–1945* [Message. History of Hungarian Literature in (Czecho) Slovakia 1918–1945]. Pozsony: Madách–Posonium, 2002.

Fónod, Zoltán, ed. *A cseh/szlovákiai magyar irodalom lexikona 1918–2004* [Lexicon of (Czecho)Slovakian Hungarian Literature]. Pozsony: Madách-Posonium, 2004.

Forgon, Pál. *Ott voltam, ahol a legszebb virágok nyílnak: egy kárpátaljai magyar református lelkész a Gulagon* [Where the Fairest Flowers Bloom: a Subcarpathian Hungarian Reformed Pastor in the Gulag]. Budapest: Kálvin, 1992.

Franyó, Zsuzsanna, ed. *Az újvidéki színház harminc éve* [30 Years of Novi Sad [Hungarian] Theater]. Újvidék: Újvidéki Színház, 2004.

Fraser, Agnus. *The Gypsies*. Oxford: Blackwell, 1995.

Fritz, László and István Sulyok, eds. *Erdélyi Magyar Évkönyv* [Transylvanian Hungarian Yearbook]. Kolozsvár: Juventus, 1930.

* Frommer, Benjamin. *National Cleansing (Retribution against Nazi Collaborators in Postwar Czechoslovakia)*. New York: Cambridge University Press, 2005.

Fülöp, Mihály and Gábor Vincze, eds. *Revízió vagy autonómia? Iratok a magyar–román kapcsolatok történetéről (1945–1947)* [Border Revision or Autonomy? Documents on the History of Hungarian–Romanian Relations, 1945–1947]. Budapest: Teleki László Alapítvány, 1998.

* Fülöp, Mihály and Gábor Vincze, eds. *Vasfüggöny keleten. Iratok a magyar–román kapcsolatokról (1948–1955)* [Iron Curtain in the East. Documents on Hungarian–Romanian Relations 1948–1955]. Debrecen: Kossuth Egyetemi Kiadó, 2007.

Fülöp, Mihály. *La Paix inachevée. Le Conseil des Ministres des Affaires Etrangères et le traité de paix avec la Hongrie (1947)*. Budapest: Association des Sciences Historiques de Hongrie, 1998.

Fülöp, Mihály and Péter Sipos. *Magyarország külpolitikája a XX. században* [Hungary's Foreign Policy in the 20th Century]. Budapest: Aula, 1998.

Für, Lajos. *Kisebbség és tudomány* [Minority and Science]. Budapest: Magvető, 1989.

Gaál, Károly. *Aranymadár. A burgenlandi magyar falvak elbeszélő kultúrája* [Golden Bird. Narrative Culture in Burgenland Hungarian Villages]. Szombathely: Vas Megyei Múzeumok Igazgatósága, 1988.

Gaál, Károly. *Kire marad a kisködmön? (Wer Erbt Das Jankerl? Über Die Kommunikationskultur Der Gutshofsknechte Im Burgenland).* Szombathely: Vas Megyei Múzeumok Igazgatósága, 1985.

* Gábrityné Molnár, Irén and Zsuzsa Mirnics, eds. *Oktatási oknyomozó. Vajdasági kutatások, tanulmányok* [Hungarian Pragmatist. Researches, Studies in Vojvodina]. Szabadka: Magyarságkutató Tudományos Társaság, 2006.

* Gábrityné Molnár, Irén and Zsuzsa Mirnics, eds. *Vajdasági útkereső. Kutatások, tanulmányok, jelentések* [Vojvodina Search for a Path. Researches, Studies, Reports]. Szabadka: Magyarságkutató Tudományos Társaság, 1998.

Gaćeša, Nikola. *Agrarna reforma i kolonizacija u Bačkoj 1918–1941* [Agrarian Reform and Colonization in Bačka 1918–1941]. Novi Sad: Matica srpska, 1968.

Gaćeša, Nikola. *Agrarna reforma i kolonizacija u Banatu 1919–1941* [Agrarian Reform and Colonization in the Banat 1919–1941]. Novi Sad: Matica srpska, 1972.

Gaćeša, Nikola. *Agrarna reforma i kolonizacija u Jugoslaviji 1945–1948* [Agrarian Reform and Colonization in Yugoslavia 1945–1948]. Novi Sad: Matica srpska, 1984.

* Gagyi, József. *A krízis éve a Székelyföldön* [Crisis Year in the Székely Land]. Csíkszereda: Pro-Print, 2004.

* Gagyi, József, ed. *Egymás mellett élés. A magyar–román, magyar–cigány kapcsolatokról* [Coexistence. Hungarian–Romanian, Hungarian–Gypsy Relations]. Csíkszereda: Pro-Print, 1996.

Gajdó, Tamás and Éva Balázs. *Magyar színháztörténet 1920–1949* [Hungarian Theater History 1920–1949]. Budapest, 2005.

Gál, Kinga, ed. *Minority Governance – Concepts at the Threshold of the 21st Century.* Budapest: LGI ECMI, 2002.

Gál, Mária, Attila Balogh, and Ferenc Imre Gajdos, eds. *Fehér könyv az 1944. őszi magyarellenes atrocitásokról* [White Book on the Anti-Hungarian Atrocities of the Fall of 1944]. Kolozsvár: RMDSZ, 1995.

Gál, Sándor. *Szociográfiák* [Sociographic Accounts]. Pozsony: Ab-Art, 2004.

Gal, Susan. *Language Shift: Social Determinants of Linguistic Change in Bilingual Austria.* New York: Academic Press, 1979.

Galántai, József. *Trianon and the Protection of Minorities.* Highland Lakes, NJ: Atlantic Research and Publications Inc, 1991.

Gáldi, Ladislaus and Ladislaus Makkai, eds. *Geschichte der Rumänen.* Budapest: Sárkány Nyomda, 1942.

Gáll, Ernő. *Napló I. 1977–1990* [Journal, Vol I. 1977–1990]. Kolozsvár: Polis, 2003.

Gáll, Ernő. *Számvetés. Huszonhét év a* Korunk *szerkesztőségében* [Account. 27 Years in the *Korunk* Offices]. Kolozsvár: Komp-Press – Korunk Baráti Társaság, 1995.

Gallagher, Tom. *Romania after Ceauşescu: the Politics of Intolerance.* Edinburgh: Edinburgh University Press, 1995.

Ganzer, Christian. *Die Karpato-Ukraine 1938/39: Spielball im internationalen Interessenkonflikt am Vorabend des Zweiten Weltkrieges.* Hamburg: Verlag Deutsche Ges. für Osteuropakunde, 2001.

Geosits, Stefan, ed. *Die burgenländischen Kroaten im Wandel der Zeiten.* Vienna: Tusch, 1986.

Gereben, Ferenc. *Olvasáskultúra és identitás. A Kárpát-medence magyarságának kulturális és nemzeti azonosságtudata* [Reading and Identity. Cultural and National Self-Awareness in Hungarians of the Carpathian Basin]. Budapest: Lucidus, 2005.

Gereben, Ferenc, ed. *Hungarian Minorities and Central Europe. Regionalism, National and Religious Identity.* Piliscsaba: Pázmány Péter Catholic University of Humanities, 2002.

Gereben, Ferenc and Miklós Tomka. *Vallásosság és nemzettudat – Vizsgálódások Erdélyben* [Examinations of Religious Feeling and National Awareness in Transylvania]. Budapest: TLA, 2001.

* Gerold, László. *Jugoszláviai magyar irodalmi lexikon (1918–2000)* [Yugoslavian Hungarian Literary Dictionary]. Újvidék: Forum, 2001.

* Gidó, Attila. *Úton. Erdélyi zsidó társadalom és nemzetépítési kísérletek (1918–1940)* [On the Way. Transylvanian Jewish Society and Nation-Building Attempts]. Csíkszereda: Pro-Print, 2008.

* Gidó, Attila. *On Transylvanian Jews. An Outline of a Common History.* Kolozsvár: ISPMN, 2009.

Glatz, Ferenc, ed. *Etudes Historiques Hongroises 1990. II. Ethnicity and Society in Hungary.* Budapest: MTA TTI, 1990.

Glatz, Ferenc, ed. *Magyarok a Kárpát-medencében* [Hungarians in the Carpathian Basin]. Budapest: Pallas, 1988.

Gold, Hugo. *Gedenkbuch der untergegangenen Judengemeinden des Burgenlandes.* Tel Aviv: Oleahu, 1970.

Göncz, Lajos. *A magyar nyelv Jugoszláviában (Vajdaságban)* [The Hungarian Language in Yugoslavia (Vojvodina)]. Budapest: Osiris, 1999.

Göncz, László. *Felszabadulás vagy megszállás? A Mura mente 1941–1945* [Liberation or Occupation? Along the Mura, 1941–1945]. Lendava: Magyar Nemzetiségi Művelődési Intézet, 2006.

Göncz, László. *A muravidéki magyarság 1918–1941* [Prekmurje Hungarians 1918–1941]. Lendava: Magyar Nemzetiségi Művelődési Intézet, 2001.

Görömbei, András. *A csehszlovákiai magyar irodalom 1945–1980* [Czechoslovak Hungarian Literature 1945–1980]. Budapest: Akadémiai, 1982.

Görömbei, András. *Kisebbségi magyar irodalmak (1945–1990)* [Minority Hungarian Literatures (1945–1990)]. Debrecen: Kossuth Egyetemi Kiadó, 1997.

Görömbei, András, ed. *Nemzetiségi magyar irodalmak az ezredvégen* [Minority Hungarian Literatures at the End of the Millennium]. Debrecen: Kossuth Egyetemi Kiadó, 2000.

Görömbei, András and Károly Manherz, eds. *Az együttműködés esélyei* [Chances of Cooperation]. Debrecen: MTA Magyar Tudományosság Külföldön Elnöki Bizottság, 2007.

Gosztonyi, Péter. *A magyar honvédség a második világháborúban* [The Hungarian Defense Force in World War II]. Budapest: Európa Kiadó, 1992.

Grad, Cornel and Viorel Ciubuta, eds. *1918: Sfarsit si inceput De Epoca* [1918 the End and the Beginning of an Era]. Satu Mare/Zalau: Editura "Lekton", 1998.

Granchak I., ed., *Narysy istorii' Zakarpattja. T. II.* [Essays on the History of Transcarpathia, Vol. II]. Uzhhorod: Zakarpattja, 1995.

Grossmann, Alexander. *Nur das Gewissen..* Waldgut: Carl Lutz, 1986.

Gulácsy, Irén. *Erdély jogán és más dolgok. Cikkek, karcolatok* [Transylvania by Right and Other Matters. Articles and Sketches]. Budapest: Singer és Wolfner Irodalmi Intézet, 1940.

* Gulyás, László. *Két régió – Felvidék és Vajdaság – sorsa. Az Osztrák–Magyar Monarchiától napjainkig* [Fate of Two Regions: Upland and Vojvodina. From the Monarchy to Today]. Pécs: Hazai Térségfejlesztő Rt., 2005.

Gutman, Israel and Bella Gutterman, eds. *The Auschwitz Album.* Yerusalem–Oświęcim: Yad Vashem – Auschwitz–Birkenau State Museum, n. d.

Gyémánt, Ladislau. *The Jews of Transylvania. A Historical Destiny.* Kolozsvár: Romanian Cultural Institute, 2004.

Gyönyör, József. *Államalkotó nemzetiségek* [State-Creator National Communities]. Pozsony: Madách, 1989.

Gyönyör, József. *Közel a jog asztalához. A csehszlovák állam kezdeti nehézségei, területi gyarapodása, ideiglenes alkotmánya, alkotmánylevele és annak sorsa* [Near the Table of the Law. Czechoslovakia's Initial Difficulties, Territorial Expansion, Provisional Constitution, and Constitution and Destiny]. Pozsony: Madách, 1992.

Gyönyör, József. *Terhes örökség. A magyarság lélekszámának és sorsának alakulása Csehszlovákiában* [Difficult Heritage. Population and Destiny of the Hungarian Community in Czechoslovakia]. Pozsony: Madách–Posonium, 1994.

* György, Béla. *Iratok a romániai Országos Magyar Párt történetéhez. A vezető testületek jegyzőkönyvei* [Documents on the History of Romania's National Hungarian Party. Minutes of Leading Bodies]. Csíkszereda: Pro-Print–EME, 2003.

György Lajos, ed. *Az Erdélyi Múzeum-Egyesület háromnegyedszázados tudományos működése 1859–1934* [Three-Quarters of a Century of Scholarly Work by the Transylvanian Museum Society 1859–1934]. Cluj: Erdélyi Múzeum-Egyesület, 1938.

Győri Szabó, Róbert. *Kisebbség, autonómia, regionalizmus* [Minority, Autonomy, Regionalism]. Budapest: Osiris, 2006.

Győri Szabó, Róbert. *Kisebbségpolitikai rendszerváltás Magyarországon. A Nemzeti és Etnikai Kisebbségi Kollégium és Titkárság történetének tükrében (1989–1990)* [Change of Minority-Policy System in Hungary. History of the National and Ethnic Minority College and Secretariat]. Budapest: Osiris, 1998.

Győri, Illés István, ed. *Metamorphosis Transylvaniae. Országrészünk átalakulása 1918–1936* [Transformation of Our Part of the Country 1918–1936]. Kolozsvár: Új Transzilvánia, 1937.

Győri, Róbert and Zoltán Hajdú, eds. *Kárpát-medence: települések, tájak, régiók, térstruktúrák* [Carpathian Basin: Settlements, Districts, Regions, Structures]. Budapest: MTA RKK, 2006.

Győri-Nagy, Sándor and Janka Kelemen, eds. *Kétnyelvűség a Kárpát-medencében II.* [Bilingualism in the Carpathian Basin, Vol. II.]. Budapest: Universitas, 1992.

Györkei, Jenő. *Idegen bírák előtt. Szombathelyi Ferenc újvidéki pere és kivégzése* [Before Alien Judges. Ferenc Szombathelyi's Trial and Execution in Novi Sad]. Budapest: Zrínyi Kiadó, 2002.

Gyüre, Lajos. *Kassai Napló 1918–1929* [Kassa Diary 1918–1929]. Pozsony: Madách, 1986.

Gyurgyík, László. *Asszimilációs folyamatok a szlovákiai magyarság körében* [Assimilation Processes among Slovakia's Hungarians]. Pozsony: Kalligram, 2004.

Gyurgyík, László. *Magyar mérleg. A szlovákiai magyarság a népszámlálási és a népmozgalmi adatok tükrében* [Hungarian Balance Sheet. Slovakia's Hungarians in the Light of Census and Migration Data]. Pozsony: Kalligram, 1994.

Gyurgyík, László. *Népszámlálás 2001. A szlovákiai magyarság demográfiai, valamint település- és társadalomszerkezetének változásai az 1990-es években* [Census 2001. Changes in Demography and Settlement and Social Structure of the Hungarian Community of Slovakia in the 1990s]. Pozsony: Kalligram, 2006.

Gyurgyík, László and László Sebők, eds. *Népszámlálási körkép Közép-Európából 1989–2002* [Censuses in Central Europe 1989–2002]. Budapest: Teleki László Alapítvány, 2003.

Hajda, Lubomyr and Mark Beissinger, eds. *The Nationality Factor in Soviet Politics and Society.* Boulder, CO: Westview, 1990.

Hamberger, Judit. *Csehszlovákia szétválása. Egy föderációs kísérlet kudarca* [Czechoslovakia's Dissolution. End of a Federative Experiment]. Budapest: Teleki László Alapítvány, 1997.

Hamberger, Judit. *Szlovákokról és csehekről magyar szemmel* [Czechs and Slovaks through Hungarian Eyes]. Pozsony: Kalligram, 2000.

Hanák, Tibor. *Az elfelejtett reneszánsz. A magyar filozófiai gondolkodás századunk első felében* [Forgotten Renaissance. Hungarian Philosophical Thinking in the First Half of This Century]. Budapest: Göncöl, 1993.

Haris T., Csaba, ed. *Magyar külpolitika az Európai Unióban* [Hungarian Foreign Policy in the EU]. Budapest: Manfred Wörner Alapítvány, 2005.

Haslinger, Peter. *Hundert Jahre Nachbarschaft. Die Beziehungen zwischen Österreich und Ungarn 1895–1994*. Paris: Peter Lang Verlag, 1996.

Haslinger, Peter. *Der ungarische Revisionismus und das Burgenland 1922–1932*. Paris: Peter Lang Verlag, 1994.

* Hegedűs, Dániel. *A Magyar Állandó Értekezlet (MÁÉRT) szakértői bizottságai munkájának elemzése az 1998 és 2002 közötti kormányzati ciklusban közpolitikai eszközökkel* [Analysis of the Work of the Expert Committees of the Hungarian Standing Committee under the 1998–2002 Government, by Public Political Means]. Budapest: EÖKIK, 2008.

Henrard, Kristin. *Devising an Adequate System of Minority Protection*. The Hague: Martinus Nijhoff Publishers, 2000.

Héraud, Guy. *L'Europe des ethnies*. Paris: Dencel, 1974.

HKDC Kroatisches Kultur and Dokumentationszentrum, ed. *Vorteil Vielfalt. 10 Jahre Minderheitenschulgesetz für das Burgenland*. Eisenstadt: Rötzer, 2004.

Hódi, Éva and Sándor Hódi, eds. *A balkáni pokolban. A VMDK évkönyve 1993* [Balkan Inferno. The VMDK Yearbook 1993]. Ada: VMDK, 1994.

Hódi, Éva and Sándor Hódi, eds. *Esély a megmaradásra. A VMDK évkönyve 1992* [Chance of Survival. The VMDK Yearbook, 1992]. Ada: VMDK, 1992.

Hódi, Éva, Sándor Hódi, and János Vékás, eds. *"Sokáig éltünk némaságban." A Vajdasági Magyarok Demokratikus Közösségének évkönyve 1991* ["We Lived Long in Silence." The VMDK Yearbook 1991]. Ada: VMDK, 1992.

* Hódi, Sándor. *Magyarok a forrongó Szerbiában* [Hungarians in Seething Serbia]. Tóthfalu: Logos, 2002.

Hodza, Milan. *Szövetség Közép-Európában* [Alliance in Central Europe]. Budapest–Pozsony: Kalligram, 2004.

Hoensch, Jörg. *Der ungarische Revisionismus und die Zerschlagung der Tschechoslowakei*. Tübingen: Mohr, 1967.

Hoensch, K. Jörg. *Die Slowakei und Hitlers Ostpolitik. Hlinkas Slowakische Volkspartei zwischen Autonomie und Separation 1938–1939*. Cologne/ Graz, 1965.

Hogan, Michael J. *The Marshall Plan: America, Britain and the Reconstruction of Western Europe, 1947–1952*. Cambridge: Cambridge University Press, 1989.

Holopenkov, I. and P. Rospopin, eds. *Knygy vydavnyctva "Karpaty" (1946–1970)* [The Books of Publishing House Karpaty (1946–1970)]. Uzhhorod: Karpaty, 1970.

Holzer, Werner and Ulrike Pröll, eds. *Mit Sprachen leben. Praxis der Mehrsprachigkeit.* Klagenfurt: Drava, 1994.

Holzer, Werner and Rainer Münz, eds. *Trendwende? Sprache und Ethnizität im Burgenland.* Vienna: Passagen, 1993.

Homonnay, Elemer. *Atrocities Committed by Tito's Communist Partisans in Occupied Southern Hungary.* Cleveland, OH: Council for Liberation of Southern Hungary, 1957.

Horkay, Barna. *A Keleti Baráti Kör. Egy ref. lelkész életútja* [The Eastern Friendly Circle. Life of a Reformed Pastor]. N.p: Author's edition, 1998.

Hornyák, Árpád. *Magyar–jugoszláv diplomáciai kapcsolatok 1918–1927* [Hungarian–Yugoslavian Diplomatic Relations, 1918–1927]. Újvidék: Forum, 2004.

Hornyik, Miklós. *Határsértés. Válogatott és új írások 1965–2001* [Border Encroachment. Selected and New Writings, 1965–2001]. Budapest: Ister, 2002.

Horváth, Franz S. *Zwischen Ablehnung und Anpassung: politische Strategien der ungarischen Minderheitselite in Rumänien 1931–1940.* Munich: Ungarishes Institut, 2007.

Horváth, Gyula, ed. *A Kárpát-medence régiói I–XII.* [Regions of the Carpathian Basin, Vol. I–XII.]. Budapest: MTA Regionális Kutatások Központ, 2003–2010.

Horvath, Traude and Rainer Münz, eds. *Migration und Arbeitsmarkt.* Eisenstadt: Prugg, 1987.

Howell, David, ed. *Roots of Rural Ethnic Mobilization. Comparative Studies on Governments und Non-Dominant Ethnic Groups in Europe 1850–1950,* Vol. VII. New York: New York University Press, 1992.

Hronský, Marián. *The Struggle for Slovakia and the Treaty of Trianon.* Bratislava: Veda, 2001.

Huncik, Peter, ed. *Confidence Building in the Carpathian Basin.* Bratislava: Sandor Marai Foundation, 1999.

Hungarians in Czechoslovakia. New York: Research Institute for Minority Studies on Hungarians Attached to Czechoslovakia and Carpatho-Ruthenia, 1959.

Hunya, Gábor, Tamás Réti, Andrea R. Süle, and László Tóth, eds. *Románia 1944–1990. Gazdaság- és politikatörténet* [Romania 1944–1990.

Economic and Political History]. Budapest: Atlantisz Medvetánc, 1990.

Hupchick, D. P. and R. W. Weisberger, eds. *Hungary's Historical Legacies: Studies in Honor of Steven Béla Várdy.* Boulder CO: East European Monographs, 2000.

* Hurst, Hannum. *Autonomy, Sovereignty, and Self-Determination. The Accommodation of Conflicting Rights.* Philadephia: University of Pennsylvania Press, 1990.

* Ieda, Osamu, Balázs Majtényi, Zoltán Kántor, Balázs Vizi, Iván Halász, and Stephen Deets, eds. *Beyond Sovereignty? From Status Law to Transnational Citizenship.* Sapporo: Slavic Research Center, Hokkaido University, 2006.

Illés, Sándor and Péter Tóth Pál, eds. *Migráció, Tanulmánygyűjtemény, I.* [Migration. Collection of Studies, Vol. I]. Budapest: KSH Népességtudományi Kutató Intézet, 1998.

Illyés, Elemér. *National Minorities in Romania: Change in Transylvania.* Boulder, CO: European Monographs, 1982.

Illyés, Gyula. *Hajszálgyökerek* [Fine Roots]. Budapest: Magvető, 1971.

* Illyés, Gyula. *Szellem és erőszak* [Spirit and Violence]. Budapest: Magvető, 1978.

Ilyés, Sándor, Lehel Peti, and Ferenc Pozsony, eds. *Lokális és transznacionális csángó életvilágok.* Kolozsvár: KJNT, 2008.

Imre, Samu. *A felsőőri nyelvjárás* [Dialect of Oberwart]. Budapest: Akadémiai, 1971.

Irsay, György. *Örökre száműzve... adatok 1500 száműzött magyar történetéhez* [In Exile Forever... Data on the Hungarian History of 1500 Exiles]. Budapest: p. p., 2003.

Ishyama, John and Marijke Breuning. *Ethnopolitics in the New Europe.* Boulder, CO: Lynne Rienner, 1998.

* Ivaničková, Edita and Attila Simon eds. *Maďarská revolúcia 1956 a Slovensko. Az 1956-os magyar forradalom és Szlovákia* [The '56 Hungarian Revolution and Slovakia]. Šamorín/Bratislava: Fórum inštitút pre výskum menšín/Historický ústav SAV, 2006.

* *Izvješće o provođenju Ustavnog zakona o pravima nacionalnih manjina i utrošku sredstava osiguranih u državnom proračunu Republike Hrvatske za 2007. godinu za potrebe nacionalnih manjina* [Report on the Implementation of the Constitutional Law on National Minorities and the Expenditure of Funds Allocated from the State Budget of

Croatian in 2007 for the Needs of National Minorities]. Zagreb: Ured za Nacionalne Manjine 2008.

Jacob, Evelyn *et al.*, eds. *Minority Education: Anthropological Perspectives.* Norwood, NJ: Ablex, 1993.

Jakab, Albert Zsolt and Árpád Töhötöm Szabó, eds. *Lenyomatok 5. Fiatal kutatók a népi kultúráról* [Reprints 5. Young Researches on Folk Culture]. Kolozsvár: KJNT, 2006.

Jakab, András, ed. *Az Alkotmány kommentárja* [Commentary on the Constitution]. Budapest: Századvég, 2009.

Jakab, István, ed. *Hogy is mondjuk? Nemzetiségi nyelvhasználatunk – nemzetiségi nyelvművelésünk* [How Do We Say It? Minority Idiom – Minority Language Use]. Pozsony: Madách, 1976.

Janics, Kálmán. *Czechoslovak Policy and the Hungarian Minority 1945–1948.* Highland Lakes, NJ: Atlantic Research and Publications, Inc., 1994.

Janics, Kálmán. *A hontalanság évei* [Years of Statelessness]. Bern/München: Európai Protestáns Magyar Szabadegyetem, 1979.

Janics, Kálmán. *A hontalanság évei. A szlovákiai magyar kisebbség a második világháború után 1945–1948* [Years of Statelessness. The Slovakian Hungarian Minority after World War II 1945–1948]. Pozsony: Madách Könyvkiadó, 1992.

Jech, Karel, ed. *Němci a Maďaři v dekretech prezidenta republiky. Studie a dokumenty. 1940—1945. Die Deutschen und Magyaren in den Dekreten des Präsidenten der Republik. Studien und Dokumente 1940–1945.* Brno: Ústav pro soudobé dějiny AV ČR-Doplněk, 2003.

Jinga, Victor. *Migrațiunile demografice şi problema colonizărilor în Romania* [The Question of Migration, Demography, and Colonization in Romania]. Brasov, n.p., 1941.

Jiyoung, Kim. *A nagyhatalmi politika és az erdélyi kérdés a II. világháború alatt és után* [Great-Power Politics and the Transylvanian Question in and after World War II]. Budapest: Osiris, 2000.

Jócsik, Lajos. *Hazatérés – Tájékozódás* [Returning Home, Finding Bearings]. Pécs: Janus Pannonius Társaság, 1942.

Joó, Rudolf and Andrew Ludányi, eds. *The Hungarian Minority's Situation in Ceausescu's Romania.* Highland Lakes, NJ: Atlantic Research and Publications Inc., 1994.

Jordáky, Lajos. *Az erdélyi némafilmgyártás története (1903–1930)* [History of Transylvanian Silent Film-Making, 1903–1930]. Bukarest: Kriterion Könyvkiadó, 1980.

Jordáky, Lajos. *A szocialista irodalom útján* [On the Path of Socialist Literature]. Budapest: Magvető Kiadó, 1973.

Juhász, Gyula. *Uralkodó eszmék Magyarországon 1939–1944* [Dominant Ideas in Hungary, 1939–1944]. Budapest: Kossuth Könyvkiadó, 1983.

Juhász, József. *Volt egyszer egy Jugoszlávia. A délszláv állam története* [Once there Was a Yugoslavia. History of the South Slav State]. Budapest: Aula, 1999.

Kacsó, Sándor. *Nehéz szagú iszap felett. Önéletrajzi visszaemlékezések* [Over Strong-Smelling Mud. Autobiographical Reminiscences]. Bukarest: Kriterion, 1993.

* Kacsó, Sándor ed. *Erdélyi Magyar Évkönyv. A kisebbségi magyar polgár kézikönyve, 1938* [Transylvanian Hungarian Yearbook. The Minority Hungarian Citizen's Handbook, 1938]. Braşov: Brassói Lapok–Népújság, 1937.

Kádár, János. *A szocializmus megújulása Magyarországon. Válogatott beszédek és cikkek 1957–1986* [Renewal of Socialism in Hungary. Selected Speeches and Interviews 1957–1986]. Budapest: Akadémiai, 1985.

Kaiser, Andrea. *Zweisprachige Volksschulen im Burgenland*. Doctoral dissertation. Klagenfurt: Universität Klagenfurt, 1995.

Kalapis, Zoltán, Péter Sinkovits, and János Vékás, eds. *Magyarok Jugoszláviában '90. A Vajdasági Magyarok Demokratikus Közösségének évkönyve 1990* [Hungarians in Yugoslavia '90. The VMDK Yearbook 1990]. Újvidék: VMDK, 1991.

Kalmár, Melinda. *Ennivaló és hozomány. A kora kádárizmus ideológiája* [Food and Dowry. Ideology of Early Kádárism]. Budapest: Magvető, 1998.

Kamenec, Ivan. *Trauma: Az első Szlovák Köztársaság 1939–1945* [Trauma. The First Slovak Republic 1939–1945]. Budapest: Aura, 1994.

* Kántor, Lajos and Gusztáv Láng, eds. *Romániai magyar irodalom 1944–1970* [Romanian Hungarian Literature 1944–1970]. Bukarest: Kriterion, 1973.

* Kántor, Zoltán, ed. *A státustörvény – Előzmények és következmények* [The Status Law – Antecedents and Consequences]. Budapest: Teleki László Alapítvány, 2002.

* Kántor, Zoltán, Balázs Majtényi, Osamu Ieda, Balázs Vizi, and Iván Halász, eds. *The Hungarian Status Law: Nation Building and/or Minority Protection*. Sapporo: Hokkaido University, 2004.

Kaplan, Karel. *Csehszlovákia igazi arca 1945–1948* [Czechoslovakia's True Face 1945–1948]. Pozsony: Kalligram, 1993.

Kardos, Gábor. *Kisebbségek: konfliktusok és garanciák* [Minorities: Conflicts and Guarantees]. Budapest: Gondolat, 2007.

Kárpátaljai Magyar Képző- és Iparművészek Révész Imre Társasága 1990–1995 [Transcarpathian Hungarian Imre Révész Society of Fine and Applied Arts, 1990–1995]. Ungvár: Tárogató, 1995.

Karsai, Elek, ed. *„Fegyvertelen álltak az aknamezőkön..."* Dokumentumok a munkaszolgálat történetéhez Magyarországon* ["They Stood Unarmed in the Minefield." Documents from the History of the Labor Service]. Budapest: MIOK, 1962.

Karsai, Elek and László Karsai. *A Szálasi-per* [Szálasi Trial]. Budapest: Reform, 1988.

Kastner, Rezső Rudolf. *Der Kastner-Bericht über Eichmanns Menschenhandel in Ungarn.* Munich: Kindler Verlag, 1961.

Kemény, Gábor. *Így tűnt el egy gondolat. A felvidéki magyar irodalom története 1918–1938* [How an Idea Disappeared. History of Upland Hungarian Literature 1918–1938]. Budapest: MEFHOSZ, 1940.

Kemp, Walter, ed. *Quiet Diplomacy in Action – The OSCE High Commissioner on National Minorities.* The Hague: Kluwer Law International, 2001.

Kende, Ferenc. *Magyarokról magyaroknak* [On Hungarians for Hungarians]. Újvidék: Farkas, 1940.

Kepecs, József and Zoltán Czibulka, eds. *Kárpátalja településeinek vallási adatai, 1880–1941* [Religious Data of Settlements of Transbcarpathia, 1880–1941]. Budapest: KSH, 2000.

Kerčov, Sava, Jovo Radoš, and Aleksandar Raič. *Mitinzi u Vojvodini 1988. Godine rađanja političkog pluralizma* [Rallies in Vojvodina 1988. Years of the Birth of the Political Pluralism] Novi Sad: Dnevnik, 1990.

Keresztyén, Balázs. *Irodalmi barangolások a Kárpátok alján* [Literary Rambles under the Carpathians]. Ungvár: Intermix Kiadó, 1993.

Keresztyén, Balázs. *Kárpátaljai művelődéstörténeti kislexikon* [Pocket Dictionary of Transcarpathian Cultural History]. Budapest: Új Mandátum Kiadó, Hatodik Síp Alapítvány, 2001.

* Kertész, Stephan. *Between Russia and the West: Hungary and the Illusions of Peacemaking, 1945–1947.* South Bend: University of Notre Dame Press, 1984.

Kibbee, Douglas A., ed. *Language Legislation and Linguistic Rights.* Amsterdam/Philadelphia: John Benjamins, n. d.

Kincses, Előd. *Marosvásárhely fekete márciusa* [Black March in Marosvásárhely]. Budapest: Püski, 1990.

Kinda, István and Ferenc Pozsony, eds. *Adaptáció és modernizáció a moldvai csángó falvakban* [Adaptation and Modernization in Moldavian Csángó Villages]. Kolozsvár: KJNT, 2005.

King, Robert R. *Minorities under Communism: Nationalities as a Source of Tension among Balkan Communist States.* Cambridge, MA: Harvard UP, 1973.

Király, Béla K. and László Veszprémy, eds. *Trianon and East Central Europe.* Highland Lakes, NJ: Atlantic Research and Publications Inc., 1995.

Király, Béla K., Peter Pastor, and Ivan Sanders, eds. *Essays on World War I: Total War and Peacemaking. A Case Study on Trianon.* New York: Brooklyn College Press, 1982.

Király, Károly. *Nyílt kártyákkal – Önéletírás és naplójegyzetek* [Cards Open – Autobiography and Diary Notes]. Budapest: Nap Kiadó, 1995.

* Kiss, Tamás. *Adminisztratív tekintet. Az erdélyi magyar demográfiai diskurzus összehasonlító elemzéséhez. Az erdélyi magyar népesség statisztikai konstrukciójáról* [Aministrative Look. To the Comparative Analysis of the Transylvanian Hungarian Demographic Discourse. on the Statistical Construction of the Hungarian Population of Transylvania]. Kolozsvár: Kriterion – Nemzeti Kisebbségkutató Intézet, 2010.

* Kiss, Tamás, ed. *Népesedési folyamatok az ezredfordulón Erdélyben* [Demographic Processes at the Turn of the Millennium in Transylvania]. Kolozsvár: Kriterion, 2004.

Kligman, Gail. *The Politics of Duplicity: Controlling Reproduction in Ceausescu's Romania.* Los Angeles, CA: University of California Press, 1998.

Kloss, Heinz. *Grundfragen der Ethnopolitik im 20. Jahrhundert.* Vienna/ Stuttgart: Wilhelm Braumüller Universitäts-Verlagsbuchhandlung, 1969.

Kocsis, Károly. *Erdély etnikai térképe 1992* [Ethnic Map of Transylvania 1992]. Budapest: MTA Földrajztudományi Kutatóintézet, 1997.

Kocsis, Károly. *Az etnikai konfliktusok történeti-földrajzi háttere a volt Jugoszlávia területén. Egy felrobbant etnikai mozaik esete* [The Historical and Geographical Background to Ethnic Conflicts in Former

Yugoslavia. A Case of a Blown-Up Ethnic Mosaic]. Budapest: Teleki László Alapítvány, 1993.

Kocsis, Károly. *Kárpátalja mai területének etnikai térképe/Ethnic Map of Present Territory of Transcarpathia (Subcarpathia)*. Budapest: Magyar Tudományos Akadémia Földrajztudományi Kutatóintézet, 2001.

Kocsis, Károly, ed. *South Eastern Europe in Maps*. Budapest: Geographical Research Institute, Hungarian Academy of Sciences, 2007.

Kocsis, Károly and András Bognár. *Ethnical Map of Pannonian Territory of Croatia*. Budapest: Geographical Research Institute, Hungarian Academy of Sciences, 2003.

* Kocsis, Károly and Eszter Kocsis-Hodosi. *Hungarian Minorities in the Carpathian Basin. A Study in Ethnic Geography*. Toronto: Mathias Corvinus, 1995.

Kocsis, Károly and Saša Kicošev. *A Vajdaság mai területének etnikai térképe* [Ethnic Map of Present Territory of Vojvodina]. Budapest: Magyar Tudományos Akadémia Földrajztudományi Kutatóintézet, 2004.

Kocsis, Károly, Zsolt Botlík and Patrik Tátrai. *Etnikai térfolyamatok a Kárpát-medence határainkon túli régióiban (1989–2002)* [Ethnic Spatial Processes in the Regions of the Carpathian Basin outside Hungary, 1989–2002]. Budapest: MTA Földrajztudományi Kutatóintézet, 2006.

Kolláth, Anna. *Magyarul Muravidéken* [In Hungarian in Prekmurje]. Maribor: Slavistično društvo, 2005.

Kolonovits, Dieter. *Sprache in Österreich*. Vienna: Manz, 2000.

* Kontra, Miklós, ed. *Sült galamb. Magyar egyetemi tannyelvpolitika* [Roast Pigeon. Hungarian University Policy on Language of Instruction]. Somorja/Dunaszerdahely: Fórum Kisebbségkutató Intézet/ Lilium Aurum, 2005.

Kontra, Miklós, ed. *Tanulmanyok a határainkon túli kétnyelvűségről* [Studies of Bilingualism beyond Our Borders]. Budapest: MTA Földrajztudományi Kutatóintézet, 1991.

Kontra, Miklós and Noémi Saly, eds., *Nyelvmentés vagy nyelvárulás? Vita a határon túli magyar nyelvhasználatról* [Saving or Betrayal of a Language? Debate on the Hungarian Language-Use beyond the Border]. Budapest: Osiris, 1998.

Kontra, Miklós, Robert Phillipson, Tove Skutnabb Kangas, and Tibor Várady, eds. *Language: a Right and Resource. Approaching Linguistic Human Rights*. Budapest: CEU Press, 1999.

Kontra, Miklós and Helga Hattyár, eds. *Magyarok és nyelvtörvények* [Hungarians and Language Laws]. Budapest: Teleki László Alapítvány, 2002.

* Köpeczi, Béla, *et al.*, eds. *Erdély története III.* [History of Transylvania, Vol. III.]. Budapest: Akadémiai, 1986.

Koppándi, Sándor, ed. *A romániai magyar nemzetiség* [The Romanian Hungarian National Group]. Bukarest: Kriterion, 1981.

Kornai, János. *The Socialist System. The Political Economy of Communism.* Princeton, NJ: Princeton University Press, 1992.

Kornis, Gyula. *Az elcsatolt területek magyar egyetemi ifjúsága* [Hungarian University Youth of the Detached Territories]. Budapest: Magyar Pedagógiai Társaság, 1937.

Kós, Károly, Árpád Paál, and István Zágoni. *Kiáltó szó* [Exclamatory Word]. Budapest: Idegennyelvű Folyóirat K. Leányváll., 1988.

* Kós, Károly, Jenő Nagy, and Judit Szentimrei. *Moldvai csángó népművészet* [Moldavian Csángó Folk Art]. Bukarest: Kriterion, 1981.

Kósa, László, ed. *A magyarságtudomány kézikönyve* [Manual of Hungarian Community Studies]. Budapest: Akadémiai, 1990.

Kovács Kiss, Gyöngy, ed. *Történelmünk a Kárpát-medencében 1926–1956–2006* [The History of the Hungarians in the Carpathian Basin, 1926–1956–2006]. Kolozsvár: Komp-Press, 2006.

Kovács, Attila. *Földreform és kolonizáció a Lendva-vidéken a két világháború között* [Land Reform and Colonization in the Lendava District between the World Wars]. Lendva: Magyar Nemzetiségi Művelődési Intézet, 2004.

Kovács, Éva. *Az asszimiláció ellentmondásai. A kassai zsidóság a két világháború között (1918–1938)* [Contradictions of Assimilation. Jews of Košice between the World Wars, 1918–1938]. Budapest: Országos Széchényi Könyvtár, 2004.

Kovács, Ilona, Lászlóné Faragó, and Júlia Gál, eds. *Hungarica to Be Found in Libraries Abroad: a Directory 13.* Budapest: Országos Széchényi Könyvtár, 1997.

Kovács, János, ed. *Híd 1934–1941.* Újvidék: Forum, 1964.

Kovács, Lehel István. *Hétfalusi csángó tájszógyűjtemény* [Dialect Wordlist of the Seven-Village Csángós]. Kolozsvár: KJNT, 2005.

Kovács, Miklós. *Üzenet a kalapács alól* [News from under the Hammer]. Ungvár: KMKSZ, 1998.

* Kovács, Nóra, ed. *Tanulmányok a diaszpóráról* [Diaspora Studies]. Budapest: Gondolat, 2004.

Kovács-Bertrand, Anikó. *Der ungarische Revisionismus nach dem Ersten Weltkrieg. Der publizistische Kampf gegen den Friedensvertrag von Trianon 1918–1931.* Munich: Oldenbourg, 1997.

Kovacsics, József, ed. *Magyarország nemzetiségeinek és a szomszédos államok magyarságának statisztikája (1910–1990)* [Statistics on Hungary's National Minorities and the Hungarians of Neighboring Countries]. Budapest: KSH, 1994.

Kováts, Miklós. *Magyar színjátszás és drámairodalom Csehszlovákiában 1918–1938* [Hungarian Acting and Drama Literature in Czechoslovakia 1918–1938]. Pozsony: Madách, 1974.

* Kozma, Tamás. *Kisebbségi oktatás Közép-Európában* [Minority Education in Central Europe]. Budapest: FKI, 2005.

* Krammer, Jenő. *A szlovenszkói magyar serdülők lelkivilága. Szociálpszichológiai tanulmány* [The Psychological World of Slovensko Hungarian Adolescents. Social Psychological Study]. Budapest: Nagy László Könyvtár 1935.

* Kranz, Jerzy, ed. *Law and Practice of Central European Countries in the Field of National Minorities Protection after 1989.* Warsaw: Center for International Relations, 1998.

Kugler, József. *Lakosságcsere a Délkelet-Alföldön 1944–1948. Population Exchange on the SE Plain.* Budapest: Osiris, 2000.

Kul'tura ukrai'ns'kyh Karpat: tradycii' i suchasnist'. Materialy mizhnarodnoi' naukovoi' konferencii' (Uzhhorod, 1–4 veresnja 1993 roku) [The Culture of Carpatho-Ukraine: Traditions and Modernity. Proceedings of the International Scientific Conference (Uzhhorod, 1–4 September, 1993)] (Uzhhorod: Grazhda, 1994)

Kuncz, Egon. *The Hungarians in Australia.* Melbourne: AE Press, 1985.

Kuncz, Ödön. *A trianoni békeszerzodes revíziójának szükségessége. Emlékirat Sir Robert Gowerhez* [Need to Revise the Treaty of Trianon. Memorandum to Sir Robert Gower]. Budapest: Egyetemi Nyomda, 1934.

* Kuszálik, Péter. *Erdélyi hírlapok és folyóiratok 1940–1989* [Transylvanian Newspapers and Periodicals 1940–1989]. Budapest: TLA, 1996.

* L. Balogh, Béni. *A magyar–román kapcsolatok 1939–1940-ben és a második bécsi döntés* [Hungarian–Romanian Relations in 1939–1940 and the Second Vienna Award]. Csíkszereda: Pro-Print Könyvkiadó, 2002.

La Population Juive de la Transylvanie de Nord. Bucharest: Congrès Juif Mondial Section Roumanie, 1945.

Lábadi, Károly. *Drávaszög ábécé. Néprajzi és folklór tájlexikon* [ABC of the Drava District. Ethnographical Dictionary]. Eszék/Budapest/Pécs: HunCro-Drávaszög Alapítvány/G Nyomdász BT, 1996.

Lábadi, Károly. *Szétszóratásban: a drávaszögi magyarság sorsüldözöttsége a háborúban, 1991–1998* [Scattered: the Fate of the Drava District Hungarians in the War, 1991–1998]. Budapest/Zágráb: TIMP/MESZ, 2004.

Lacza, Tihamér. *Ember a szóban* [Man in Words]. Pozsony: Madách, 1985.

Lađević, Petar and Vladimir Stanković, eds. *Izbeglički korpus u Srbiji. Prema podacima popisa stanovništva 2002* [The Refugee Body in Serbia. According to the Data of the 2002 Census]. Belgrade: Komesarijata za izbeglice Republike Srbije 2004.

Lakatos, István. *Emlékeim I. Szemben az árral* [My Memoirs, Vol. I. Against the Current]. Marosvásárhely: Appendix Kiadó, 2005.

Lang, Alfred, Barbara Tobler, and Gert Tschögl, eds. *Vertrieben. Erinnerungen burgenländischer Juden und Jüdinnen*. Vienna: Mandelbaum, 2004.

Láng, Gusztáv. *Kivándorló irodalom. Kísérletek* [Emigrant Literature. Experiments]. Kolozsvár: Komp-Press, 1998.

Láng, Gusztáv. *Látványok és szövegek. Tanulmányok és kritikák* [Sights and Texts. Studies and Reviews]. Miskolc: Felsőmagyarország, 2006.

Lanstyák, István. *A magyar nyelv Szlovákiában* [The Hungarian Language in Slovakia]. Budapest: Osiris, 2000.

Lanstyák, István. *Nyelvből nyelvbe. Tanulmányok a szókölcsönzésről, kódváltásról és fordításról* [From Language to Language. Studies on Word Loaning, Code Changing and Translation]. Pozsony: Kalligram Könyvkiadó, 2006.

Lanstyák, István and Gizella Szabómihály. *Magyar nyelvtervezés Szlovákiában. Tanulmányok és dokumentumok* [Hungarian Language Planning in Slovakia. Studies and Documents]. Pozsony: Kalligram Könyvkiadó, 2002.

* László, Béla, László A. Szabó, and Károly Tóth eds. *Magyarok Szlovákiában IV. kötet. Oktatásügy (1989–2006)* [Hungarians in Slovakia Vol. IV. Education (1989–2006)]. Somorja/Dunaszerdahely: Fórum Kisebbségkutató Intézet/Lilium Aurum, 2006.

László, Ferenc and Péter Cseke, eds. *Erdélyi fiatalok. Dokumentumok, viták* [Transylvanian Young People. Documents, Debates]. Bukarest: Kriterion Könyvkiadó, 1986.

László, Péter. *Fehérlaposok. Adalékok a magyar–csehszlovák lakosság-csere-egyezményhez* [White Pages. Contributions on the Hungarian–Czechoslovak Population Exchange Agreement]. Szekszárd: Völgységi Tájkutató Alapítvány, 2005.

Lázok, János and Gábor Vincze, eds. *Erdély magyar egyeteme 1944–1949 II.* [Transylvania's Hungarian University 1944–1949, Vol. II.]. Tărgu Mureş: Mentor, 1998.

Lendvai, Paul. *The Hungarians: a Thousand Years of Victory in Defeat.* London: C. Hurst & Co., 2003.

Lengyel, Zsolt K. *Auf der Suche nach dem Kompromiss. Ursprünge und Gestalten des frühen Transsilvanismus 1918–1928.* Munich: Ungarisches Institut, 1991.

Lévai, Jenő. *Fekete könyv a magyar zsidóság szenvedéséről* [Black Book on the Sufferings of Hungarian Jewry]. Budapest: Officína, 1946.

Lévai, Jenő, ed. *Eichmann in Hungary.* Budapest: Pannónia Press, 1961.

Lévay, Endre. *Dél kapujában* [In the Gateway to the South]. Kecskemét: Szenteleky Társaság, 1944.

* Ligeti, Ernő. *Súly alatt a pálma. Egy nemzedék szellemi élete. 22 esztendő kisebbségi sorsban* [Palm under a Weight. A Generation's Intellectual Life over 22 Years of Being a Minority]. Csíkszereda: Pallas-Akadémia Könyvkiadó, 2004.

Lipovšćak, Mirjana, ed. *Stanovništvo prema državljanstvu, narodnosti, materinskom jeziku i vjeri. Popis stanovništva, kućanstva i stanova 31. ožujka 2001. Knj. 2* [The Population According to Citizenship, Nationality, Language and Religious Affiliation, March 31, 2001, Vol. 2]. Zagreb: Državni zavod za statistiku Republike Hrvatske, 2002.

Liszka, József. *Magyar néprajzi kutatás Szlovákiában (1918–1938)* [Hungarian Ethnographic Research in Slovakia, 1918–1938]. Pozsony: Madách, 1990.

Liszka, József. *A szlovákiai magyarok néprajza* [The Ethnography of Slovakian Hungarians]. Budapest/Dunaszerdahely: Osiris/Lilium Aurum, 2002.

Litván, György, János Bakk and Lyman H. Letgres, eds. *The Hungarian Revolution of 1956. Reform, Revolt and Repression 1953–1963.* London: Longman, 1996.

Livezeanu, Irina. *Cultural Politics in Greater Romania: Regionalism, Nation Building, and Ethnic Struggle, 1918–1930.* Ithaca, NY: Cornell University Press, 2000.

Lojko, L. *Gromads'ki organizacii' etnichnyh menshyn Ukrai'ny: pryroda, legitymnist', dijal'nist'* [Social Organizations of the Ukrainian Ethnic Group: Ideology, Legitimacy, Operation]. Kyiv: Foliant, 2005.

Lőrinc, Péter. *Harcban a földért. A magyar fasizmus jugoszláviai földbirtokpolitikája (1941–1944)* [Struggle for the Soil. The Yugoslavian Land Ownership Policy of Hungarian Fascism]. Budapest: Akadémiai Kiadó, 1977.

Lőrincz, Csaba, Zsolt Németh, Viktor Orbán, and Zoltán Rockenbauer. *Nemzetpolitika '88–'98. Tanulmányok, publicisztikák, beszédek, interjúk* [National Policy '88–'98. Studies, Journalism, Speeches, Interviews]. Budapest: Osiris, 1998.

* Losoncz, Alpár. *Európa-dimenziók* [European Dimensions]. Újvidék: Forum, 2002.

Lővy, Dániel. *A kálváriától a tragédiáig. Kolozsvár zsidó lakosságának története* [From Calvary to Tragedy. Story of Cluj-Napoca's Jewish Population]. Kolozsvár: Koinonia, 2005.

Lukes, Igor and Erik Goldstein, eds. *The Munich Crisis 1938, Prelude to World War II*. London: Frank Cass, 1999.

Lükő, Gábor. *A moldvai csángók I. A csángók kapcsolatai az erdélyi magyarsággal* [Moldavian Csángós, Vol. I. The Csángós' Ties with the Transylvanian Hungarians]. Budapest: Táton, 2001.

* Macartney, C. *October Fifteenth. A History of Modern Hungary Vol. II*. Edinburgh: Edinburgh UP, 1961.

Machnyik, Andor. *Gyakorlati agrár- és szociálpolitika (Csallóköz)* [Practical Agricultural and Social Policy (Csallóköz)]. Pozsony: Kalligram, 1993.

Magocsi, Paul Robert. *The Shaping of a National Identity: Subcarpathian Rus', 1848–1948*. Cambridge, MA: Harvard University Press, 1978.

Magocsi, Paul Robert. *The Rusyn-Ukrainians of Czechoslovakia: an Historical Survey*. Vienna: Braumüller, 1983.

Magocsi, Paul Robert. *Historic Atlas of east Central/Central Europe*. Seattle, WA: University of Washington Press, 2003.

Magocsi, Paul Robert and Ivan Pop. *Encyclopedia of Rusyn History and Culture*. Toronto: University of Toronto Press, 2005.

A magyar béketárgyalások. Jelentés a magyar békeküldöttség működéséről Neuilly s/S.-ben 1920 január–március havában. I–III/B kötet [Hungarian Peace Talks. Report on Work of the Hungarian Peace Delegation at Neuilly S/S in January–March 1920. Vols I–III/B]. Budapest: M. kir. Külügyminisztérium, 1920–1921.

Malcolm, Noel. *A Short History*. New York: New York University Press, 1998.

Malle, Avguštin and Valentin Sima, eds. *Anslus in manjsine v Austriji / Anschluß und Minderheiten in Österreich*. Klagenfurt/Celovec: Drava, 1989.

* Mandel, Kinga and Attila Papp Z., eds. *Cammogás. Minőségkoncepciók a romániai magyar középfokú oktatásban* [Trudging Along. Quality Concepts in Romania's Hungarian Higher Education]. Csíkszereda: Soros Oktatási Központ, 2007.

* Mandel, Kinga, Éva Blénesi, and László Szarka, eds. *A kultúra világa. A határon túli magyar kulturális intézményrendszer* [World of Culture. The System of Hungarian Cultural Institutions beyond the Borders]. Budapest: MTA Etnikai-nemzeti Kisebbségkutató Intézet, 2005.

Manjine i medije – med izolaciom, integraciom i šutnjom. Odredjivane položaja (Minderheiten und Medien – zwischen Isolation, Integration und Funkstille. Eine Standortbestimmung). Großwarasdorf: Kulturna Zadruga, 1993.

Mark, Eduard. *Revolution by Degrees. Stalin's National Front Strategy for Europe*. Working Paper 31, February 2001, Cold War International History Project. Washington, DC: Woodrow Wilson International Center for Scholars, 2001.

Marosi, Ildikó, ed. *A Helikon és az Erdélyi Szépmíves Céh levelesládája (1924–1944) II.* [Helikon and the Letterbox of the Transylvanian Arts Guild (1924–1944), Vol. II.]. Bukarest: Kriterion, 1979.

Martin, Terry. *The Affirmative Action Empire. Nations and Nationalism in the Soviet Union, 1923–1939*. New York: Cornell University Press, 2001.

Márton, Gyula. *A moldvai csángó nyelvjárás roman kölcsönszavai* [Romanian Loan Words in Moldavian Csángó Dialect]. Bukarest: Kriterion, 1972.

Mártonffy, Károly, ed. *Közigazgatásunk nemzetközi kapcsolatai* [International Relations of Our Public Administration]. Budapest: Magyar Királyi Állami Nyomda, 1941.

Masaryk, Tomáš Garrigue. *Demokrácia, nemzetiség. Gondolatok a kisebbségi kérdésről és az antiszemitizmusról* [Democracy, Nationality. Thoughts on the Minority Question and Anti-Semitism]. Pozsony: Kalligram, 1991.

Máthé, Gábor, ed. *Theorie und Institutionsystem der Gewaltentrennung in Europa*. Budapest: Akadémiai, 1993.

Matuska, Márton. *A megtorlás napjai. Ahogy az emlékezet megőrizte* [Days of Reprisals. As Kept in Memory]. Újvidék: Fórum, 1991.

Matuska, Márton. *Reprisals*. Budapest: Püski, 1995.

McGarry, John and Brendan O'Leary, eds. *The Politics of Ethnic Conflict Regulation. Case Studies of Protracted Ethnic Conflicts*. London/New York: Routledge, 1993.

Mendelsohn, Ezra. *The Jews of East Central Europe between the World Wars*. Bloomington: Indiana University Press, 1987.

Méray, Tibor. *Thirteen Days That Shook the Kremlin*. New York: Albert Langen Georg Müller, 1959.

Mészáros, Sándor. *Holttá nyilvánítva. Délvidéki magyar fátum I* [Declared Dead. Hungarian Southern Region Fate, Vol. I.]. Újvidék, 1991.

Michela, Miroslav. *Pod heslom integrity. Slovenská otázka v politike Maďarska 1918–1921* [Under the Slogan of Integrity. Slovak Issue in Hungarian Policy, 1918–1921]. Bratislava: Kalligram, 2009.

Michalka, Wolfgang and Marshall M. Lee, eds. *Gustav Stresemann*. Darmstadt: Wissenschaftliche Buchgesellschaft, 1982.

Michener, James A. *The Bridge at Andau. The Story of the Hungarian Revolution*. London: Secker and Warburg, 1957.

Mihailović, Kosta and Vasilije Krestić. *Memorandum of the Serbian Academy of Sciences and Arts. Answers to Criticisms. Published on the Decision of the Presidency... April 23, 1993*. Belgrade: Serbian Academy of Sciences and Arts, 1995.

Mikecs, László. *Csángók* [Csángós]. Budapest: Optimum, 1989.

Miklósházy, Attila, S. J., ed. *A tengeren túli emigráns magyar katolikus egyházi közösségek rövid története Észak- és Dél-Amerikában, valamint Ausztráliában* [A Short History of Overseas Hungarian Catholic Parishes in North/South America and Australia]. Toronto: n.p., 2005.

* Mikó, Imre. *Huszonkét év. Az erdélyi magyarság politikai története* [Twenty-Two Years. Political History of Transylvanian Hungarians]. Budapest: Studium, 1941.

Mikó, Imre. *Nemzetiségi jog és nemzetiségi politika* [National Minority Law and National Minority Policy]. Kolozsvár: Minerva, 1944.

* Mikó, Imre. *Az erdélyi falu és a nemzetiségi kérdés* [The Transylvanian Village and the Minority Question]. Csíkszereda: Pro-Print, 1998.

Milivoj, Erić. *Agrarna reforma u Jugoslaviji 1918–1941* [Agrarian Reform in Yugoslavia 1918–1941]. Sarajevo: Izdavačko preduzeće Veselin Masleša, 1958.

Milkó, Izidor. *Erdélyi Helikon és vajdasági irodalom* [Transylvanian Helikon and Vojvodina Literature]. Újvidék: Forum, 1966.

Milosević, Slobodan D. *Izbeglice i preseljenici na teritoriji okupirane Jugoslavije, 1941–1945* [Refugees and Immigrants in the Occupied Territories of Yugoslavia, 1941–1945]. Belgrade: IRO Naronda Knjiga, 1981.

Die minderheitspolitischen Strategien der ungarischen Bevölkerung in Rumänien zwischen den beiden Weltkriegen. Munich: R. Oldenburg Verlag, 1999.

Mirnics, Károly. *Kisebbségi sors* [Minority Destiny]. Újvidék: Forum, 1993.

Mirnics, Károly. *Kis-Jugoszlávia hozománya. Írások az asszimilációról és a kisebbségről* [Dowry of Little Yugoslavia. Writings on Assimilation and Minorities]. Budapest: Hatodik Síp Alapítvány, 1996.

Mócsy, István. *The Effects of World War I. The Uprooted: Hungarian Refugees and Their Impact on Hungary's Domestic Politics.* Highland Lakes, NJ: Atlantic Research and Publications, Inc., 1983.

Mócsy, István. *Radicalization and Counterrevolution: Magyar Refugees from the Successor States and Their Role in Hungary, 1918–1921.* Los Angeles: University of California, 1973.

Molnár, Gusztáv, ed. *A transzcendens remény, A Limes-kör dokumentumai 1985–1989* [Transcendent Hope. The Limes Circle Documents 1985–1989]. Csíkszereda: Pallas-Akadémia, 2004.

Molnár, Imre. *Esterházy János 1901–1957* [János Esterházy, 1901–1957]. Dunaszerdahely: Nap Kiadó, 1997.

Molnár, Imre and János Esterházy. *Esterházy János élete és mártírhalála* [The Life and Martyr's Death of János Esterházy]. Somorja: Méry–Ratio, 2010.

Molnár, Imre and László Szarka, eds. *Otthontalan emlékezet. Emlékkönyv a csehszlovák–magyar lakosságcsere 60. évfordulójára* [Homeless Memory. Memorial Volume on the 60th Anniversary of the Czechoslovak–Hungarian Population Exchange]. Budapest/Komárom: MTA Kisebbségkutató Intézet/Kecskés László Társaság, 2007.

* Molnár, János. *Az egyetlen. Az Ellenpontok és az ellenpontosok története* [One and Only. The Story of Counter-Arguments and Their Supporters]. Szeged: Agapé, 1993.

* Molnár, József and István D. Molnár. *Kárpátalja népessége és magyarsága a népszámlálási és népmozgalmi adatok tükrében* [The Population and Hungarian Community of Transcarpathia Seen through

Census and Demographic Data]. Beregszász: Kárpátaljai Magyar Pedagógusszövetség, 2005.

* Monoki, István, eds. *Magyar könyvtermelés Romániában (1919–1940). I. Könyvek és egyéb nyomtatványok* [Hungarian Book Production in Romania (1919–1940). Vol. I: Books and Other Printed Matters]. Kolozsvár/Budapest: Erdélyi Múzeum-Egyesület/Országos Széchényi Könyvtár, 1997.

Móricz, Kálmán. *Nagydobrony* [Velyka Dobrony]. Beregszász: Hatodik Síp Alapítvány, 1995.

Móricz, Miklós. *Az erdélyi föld sorsa. Az 1921. évi román földreform* [The Fate of Transylvanian Soil. The 1921 Romanian Land Reform]. Budapest: Erdélyi Férfiak Egyesülete, 1932.

Moritsch, Andreas, ed. *Vom Ethnos zur Nationalität: Der nationale Differenzierungsprozess am Beispiel ausgewählter Orte in Kärnten und im Burgenland.* Vienna/Munich: Verlag für Geschichte und Politik/ Oldenbourg, 1991.

Mózes, Teréz. *Váradi zsidók* [Várad Jews]. Nagyvárad: Literator, 1995.

Murber, Ibolya and Zoltán Fónagy, eds. *Die Ungarische Revolution und Österreich 1956.* Vienna: Czernin Verlag, 2006.

Murvai, László. *Fekete Fehér Könyv* [Black White Book]. Kolozsvár: Stúdium Könyvkiadó, 1996.

Nádor, Orsolya. *A csehszlovákiai magyar nyelvű könyvkiadás bibliográfiája (1967–1988)* [Bibliography of Czechoslovak Hungarian-Language Publishing, 1967–1988]. Pozsony: Madách, 1992.

Nádor, Orsolya. *Nyelvpolitika. A magyar nyelv politikai státusváltozásai és oktatása a kezdetektől napjainkig* [Language Policy. Changes in the Political Status and Teaching of the Hungarian Language from the Beginnings to Today]. Budapest: BIP, 2002.

Nádor, Orsolya and László Szarka, eds. *Nyelvi jogok, kisebbségek, nyelvpolitika Kelet-Közép-Európában* [Language Rights, Minorities, Language Policy in East-Central Europe]. Budapest: Akadémiai Kiadó, 2003.

Nagy, Csaba. *A magyar emigráns irodalom lexikona* [Dictionary of Hungary Émigré Literature]. Budapest: Argumentum/Petőfi Irodalmi Múzum és Kortárs Irodalmi Központ, 2009.

Nagy, Károly. *Amerikai magyar szigetvilágban* [American-Hungarian Diaspora]. Budapest: Nap Kiadó, 2009.

Nagy, Károly. *Emigránsok küldetésben (Émigré on a Mission): Magyar Öregdiák Szövetség–Bessenyei György Kör–Hungarian Alumni Association: 1960–2000.* New Brunswick/Debrecen: Csokonai, 2000.

Nagy, Károly and László Papp, eds. *A magyar nyelv és kultúra megtartása* [Retaining Hungarian Language and Culture]. Budapest: A Magyar Nyelv és Kultúra Nemzetközi Társasága, 1998.

Nagy, Kázmér. *Elveszett alkotmány: a magyar politikai emigráció: 1945–1975* [Lost Constitution: Hungarian Political Emigration: 1945–1975]. Budapest: Gondolat, 1984.

* Nagy, Lajos. *A kisebbségek alkotmányjogi helyzete Nagyromániában* [Constitutional Position of Minorities in Greater Romania]. Székelyudvarhely: HRKE, 1994.

* Nagy, Mihály Zoltán and Ágoston Olti. *Érdekképviselet vagy pártpolitika? Iratok a Magyar Népi Szövetség történetéhez 1944–1953* [Interest Representation or Party Politics? Documents on the History of the Hungarian People's Union, 1944–1953]. Csíkszereda: Pro-Print, 2009.

Nagy, Mihály Zoltán and Vince Gábor, eds. *Autonomisták és centralisták. Észak-Erdély a két bevonulás között (1944. szeptember – 1945. március)* [Autonomists and Centralist. Northern Transylvania between the Two Invasions (September 1944–March 1945)]. Kolozsvár/Csíkszereda: EME/Pro-Print, 2004.

Naimark, Norman and Leonid Gibianski, eds. *The Establishment of Communist Regimes in Eastern Europe, 1944–1949*. Boulder, CO: Westview, 1997.

Náray, István, ed. *Harag György színháza* [György Harag's Theater]. Budapest: Pesti Szalon, 1992.

Nelde, Hans Peter, ed. *Methoden der Kontaktlinguistik*. Bonn: Dümmler, 1985.

Nelde, Peter H. and Roswitha Klädler Dohjorve, eds. *Minorities and Language Policy*. St. Augustin: Asgard, 2001.

Németh, Kálmán. *Százezer szív sikolt. Hazatért és hazavágyó magyarok verőfényes golgotája* [One Hundred Thousand Hearts Screamed. The Sunlit Story of the Golgotha of Hungarians Returning or Longing for Home]. Obiličevo: Zenélő Kút Könyvműhely, 1943.

Németh, Zsolt. *Magyar kibontakozás* [Hungarian Development]. Budapest: Püski, 2002.

Némethy Keserű, Judit. *Szabadságom lett a börtönöm: az argentin magyar emigráció története: 1948–1968* [My Freedom Became My Prison: History of Hungarian Emigration to Argentina]. Budapest: Magyar Nyelv és Kultúra Nemzetközi Társasága, 2003.

O'Grady, Joseph P. *The Immigrants' Influence on Wilson's Peace Policies.* Lexington, KY: University of Kentucky Press, 1967.

Oficyns'kyj, R.. *Politychnyj rozvytok Zakarpattia u skladi Ugorshhyny (1939–1944)* [Political History of Transcarpathia under Hungarian Rule (1939–1944)]. Kyiv: In-t istorii' Ukrai'ny NAN Ukrai'ny, 1997.

*Oláh, Sándor. *Csendes csatatér. Kollektivizálás és túlélési stratégiák a két Homoród mentén (1949–1962)* [Silent Battlefield. Collectivization and Survival Strategies by the Two Homorod Rivers]. Csíkszereda: Pro-Print, 2001.

Olay, Ferenc. *A magyar művelődés kálváriája az elszakított területeken 1918–1928* [Tribulations of Hungarian Education in the Detached Territories 1918–1928]. Budapest: Magyar Nemzeti Szövetség, 1930.

* Öllős, László. *Az egyetértés konfliktusa. A Magyar Köztársaság alkotmánya és a határon túli magyarok* [Conflict of Agreement. Hungary's Constitution and the Hungarians beyond the Borders]. Somorja: Fórum Kisebbségkutató Intézet, 2008.

* Öllős, László. *Emberi jogok – nemzeti jogok. Emberi és polgári jogok-e a nemzeti kisebbségek jogai?* [Human Rights – National Rights. Are Rights of National Minorities Human and Civil Rights?]. Somorja: Fórum Kisebbségkutató Intézet, 2004.

Oplatka, Andreas. *Der Riss in der Mauer – September 1989. Ungarn öffnet die Grenze.* Vienna: Zsolnay, 2009.

Ormos, Mária. *Civitas Fidelissima.* Szekszárd: IPF Monográfia, 1999.

Ormos, Mária. *Egy magyar médiavezér: Kozma Miklós. Pokoljárás a médiában és a politikában (1919–1941) II.* [A Hungarian Media Magnate: Miklós Kozma. Descent into Hell in the Media and Politics (1919–1941), Vol. II]. Budapest: PolgArt Könyvkiadó, 2000.

Ormos, Mária. *Franciaország és a keleti biztonság 1931–1936* [France and Eastern Security, 1931–1936]. Budapest: Akadémiai Kiadó, 1969.

Ormos, Mária. *From Padua to Trianon, 1918–1920.* Highland Lakes, NJ: Atlantic Research and Publications, Inc., 1982.

Orosz, Ildikó. *A magyar nyelvű oktatás helyzete Kárpátalján az ukrán államiság kialakulásának első évtizedében 1989–1999* [Situation of Hungarian Language Teaching in Transcarpathia in the First Decade of Ukrainian Statehood, 1989–1999]. Ungvár: PoliPrint, 2005.

Ortutay, Gyula, ed. *Népi kultúra népi társadalom* [Folk Culture, Folk Society]. Budapest: Akadémiai Kiadó, 1973.

Österreichische Rektorenkonferenz, ed. *Lage und Perspektive der österreichischen Volksgruppen.* Vienna: Böhlau, 1989.

* Osvát, Anna and László Szarka, eds. *Anyanyelv, oktatás – közösségi nyelvhasználat* [Native Language, Education – Communal Language Use]. Budapest: Gondolat Kiadói Kör/MTA KKI, 2003.

Pál-Antal, Sándor and Miklós Szabó, eds. *A Maros megyei magyarság történetéből* [From the History of the Hungarians of Mureş County]. Tărgu Mureş: Mentor, 1997.

Pál-Antal, Sándor, Gábor Sipos, Andrád W. Kovács, and Rudolf Wolf. *Emlékkönyv Kiss András születésének nyolcvanadik évfordulójára* [Festschrift for the 80th Anniversary of the Birth of András Kiss]. Kolozsvár: Erdélyi Múzeum-Egyesület, 2003.

Palotai, Mária. *Pásztortűz (1921–1944). Egy erdélyi irodalmi folyóirat története* [*Pásztortűz* 1921–1944. History of a Transylvanian Literary Periodical]. Budapest: Argumentum, 2008.

Palotás, Emil. *Kelet-Európa története a 20. század első felében* [History of Eastern Europe in the First Half of the 20th Century]. Budapest: Osiris, 2003.

* Pándi, Lajos, ed. *Köztes-Európa 1756–1997. Kronológia* [Intermediate Europe 1763–1993. Chronology]. Budapest: Teleki László Alapítvány, 1999.

* Pándi, Lajos, ed. *Köztes-Európa 1763–1993. Térképgyűjtemény* [Intermediate Europe 1763–1993. Map Collection]. Budapest: Osiris/ Századvég Kiadó, 1995.

* Papp Z., Attila. *Beszédből világ. Elemzések, adatok amerikai magyarokról* [A World from Speech. Analyses, Data on American Hungarians]. Budapest: Regio Books, 2008.

* Papp Z., Attila. *Keretizmus. A romániai magyar sajtó és működtetői 1989 után* [Allocation-ism. The Romanian Hungarian Press and Its Operators after 1989]. Csíkszereda: Soros Oktatási Központ, 2005

* Papp Z., Attila, ed. *Kihasználatlanul. A romániai magyar felnőttképzés rendszere* [Unusable. Romania's System of Hungarian Adult Education]. Csíkszereda: Soros Oktatási Központ, 2005.

* Papp Z., Attila. and Valér Veres, eds. *Kárpát Panel 2007. A Kárpát-medencei magyarok társadalmi helyzete és perspektívái. Gyorsjelentés* [Carpathian Panel 2007. The Social Situation and Prospects of Carpathian Basin Hungarians]. Budapest: MTA Etnikai-nemzeti Kisebbségkutató Intézet, 2007.

Papp-Farkas, Klara, ed. *Endangered Minority Cultures in Europe*. Budapest: Council of Europe Information and Documentation Centre, 2002.

Párkány, Antal. *Sas Andor helye a csehszlovákiai magyar kulturális életben* [Place of Andor Sas in Czechoslovakian Hungarian Cultural Life]. Pozsony: Madách, 1975.

Pastor, Peter, ed. *Revolutions and Interventions in Hungary and Its Neighbor States, 1918–1919.* Highland Lakes, NJ: Atlantic Research and Publications, 1988.

Pásztor, Cecília, ed. *"... ahol a határ elválaszt"* Trianon *és következményei a Kárpát-medencében* ["Where the Border Divides." Trianon and Its Consequences in the Carpathian Basin]. Salgótarján: Nagy I. Történeti Kör, Nógrád Megyei Levéltár, 2002.

Pavlenko, G. ed. *Carpatica – Karpatyka. Aktual'ni problemy istorii' i kul'tury Zakarpattja* [Actual Problems of History and Culture of Transcarpathia]. Uzhhorod: UzhDU, 1992.

Pavlenko, G. *Nimci na Zakarpatti* [Germans in Transcarpathia]. Uzhhorod: n.p., 1995.

Pawlowski, Verena and Harald Wendelin, eds. *Ausgeschlossen und Entrechtet. Raub und Rückgabe – Österreich von 1938 bis heute.* Vienna: Mandelbaum, 2006.

Pearson, Raymond. *National Minorities in Eastern Europe 1848–1945.* London: Macmillan, 1983.

Peéry, Rezső. *Requiem egy országrészért* [Requiem for Part of a Country]. Pozsony: Pannónia Könyvkiadó, 1993.

Pejin, Attila. *A zentai zsidóság története* [History of the Senta Jewry]. Zenta: Thurzó Lajos Közművelődési Központ, 2003.

Pelinka, Anton and Erika Weinzierl, eds. *Das große Tabu. Österreichs Umgang mit seiner Vergangenheit.* Vienna: Picus-Verlag, 1987.

Penckófer, János. *Tettben a jellem. A magyar irodalom sajátos kezdeményei Kárpátalján a XX. század második felében* [Character in Deed. The Specific Initiatives of Hungarian Literature in Transcarpathia in the Second Half of the 20th Century]. Budapest: Magyar Napló, 2003.

* Pentassuglia, Gaetano. *Minorities in International Law.* Strasbourg: Council of Europe Publishing, 2002.

* Péntek, János. *Anyanyelv és oktatás* [Mother Tongue and Teaching]. Csíkszereda: Pallas-Akadémia, 2004.

Péntek, János and Attila Benő. *Nyelvi kapcsolatok, nyelvi dominanciák az erdélyi régióban* [Language Connections, Language Dominance in the Transylvanian Region]. Kolozsvár: Szabó T. Attila Nyelvi Intézet Publications, 2003.

* Perlman, Robert. *Bridging Three Worlds. Hungarian-Jewish Americans, 1848–1919.* Amherst: University of Massachusetts Press, 1991.

Perman, Dagmar. *The Shaping of the Czechoslovak State.* Leyden: E. J. Brill, 1962.

Petkovics, Kálmán. *A mostoha barázda* [Lone Furrow]. Újvidék: Fórum, 1977.

Petrichevich Horváth, Emil. *Jelentés az Országos Menekültügyi Hivatal négy évi működéséről* [Report on the Four Years' Activity of the National Bureau for Refugee Affairs]. Budapest: Pesti Könyvnyomda, 1924.

Peyer-Müller, Fritz. *A Kárpátaljai Református Egyház története a két világháború között – kitekintéssel a jelenre* [Interwar History of the Reformed Church in Subcarpathia, with a Glance at the Present]. Budapest: Református Zsinati Iroda Tanulmányi Osztálya, 1995.

Pogány, Erzsébet, ed. *Az Együttélés öt éve. Eseménynaptár és dokumentumgyűjtemény 1990–1995* [Five Years of *Együttélés.* Diary of Events and Document Collection 1990–1995]. Pozsony: Együttélés Központi Iroda, 1995.

Pomogáts, Béla. *A romániai magyar irodalom* [Romanian Hungarian Literature]. Budapest: Bereményi, 1992.

Pomogáts, Béla. *Tanulmányok, kritikák* [Studies, Reviews]. Bukarest: Kriterion Könyvkiadó, 1973.

* Popély, Árpád. *A (cseh)szlovákiai magyarság történeti kronológiája 1944–1992* [Historical Chronology of the (Czecho)Slovak Hungarian Community]. Somorja: Fórum Kisebbségkutató Intézet, 2006.

* Popély, Árpád, ed. *1968 és a szlovákiai magyarság* [1968 and the Slovakian Hungarians]. Somorja: Fórum Kisebbségkutató Intézet, 2008.

* Popély, Árpád, ed. *Iratok a csehszlovákiai magyarság 1948–1956 közötti történetéhez* [Documents on the 1948–58 History of the Czechoslovak Hungarians]. Somorja: Fórum Kisebbségkutató Intézet, 2008.

* Popély, Árpád and Attila Simon, eds. *A rendszerváltás és a csehszlovákiai magyarok (1989–1992)* [The Change of System and Czechoslovakia's Hungarians]. Šamorin: Fórum Kisebbségkutató Intézet, 2009.

* Popély, Árpád, Štefan Šutaj, and László Szarka, eds. *Beneš-dekrétumok és a magyar kérdés 1945–1948. Történeti háttér, dokumentumok és jogszabályok* [Beneš Decrees and Hungarian Question 1945–1948. Historical Background, Documents, and Legislation]. Gödöllő: Attraktor, 2007.

Popély, Gyula. *Népfogyatkozás. A csehszlovákiai magyarság a népszámlálások tükrében 1918–1945* [Depopulation. Czechoslovakian Hungarians in the Light of the Censuses 1918–1945]. Budapest: Írók Szakszervezete Széphalom Könyvműhely, 1991.

Popély, Gyula. *Hazatéréstől a hazavesztésig* [From Returning Home to Losing One's Native Land]. Pozsony: Madách, 2006.

Popis '91. Stanovništvo. Knjiga 3. Nacionalna pripadnost – detaljna klasifikacija [Census '91. Population. Vol. 3. National Identity – A Detailed Classification]. Belgrade: Savezni zavod za statistiku (Yugoslavia), 1993.

Popisi na Slovenskem 1948–1991 in Popis 2002 [Censuses in Slovenia 1948–1991 and the 2002 Census]. Ljubljana: Statistični Urad Republike Slovenije, 2001.

Popovics, Béla. *Munkács kultúrtörténete a korabeli sajtó tükrében* [Cultural History of Mukacheve through the Contemporary Press]. Munkács: KMCSSZ, 2005.

Pozsony, Ferenc. *A moldvai csángó magyarok* [The Moldavian Csángó Hungarians]. Budapest: Gondolat, 2005.

Pozsony, Ferenc, ed. *Csángósors* [Csángó Destiny]. Budapest: TLA, 1999.

Pritz, Pál, Balázs Sipos, and Miklós Zeidler, eds. *Magyarország helye a 20. századi Európában* [Hungary's Place in 20th-Century Europe]. Budapest: Magyar Történelmi Társulat, 2002.

* *Projekat Afirmacija multikulturalizma i tolerancije u Vojvodini 2006–2007* [Project of Affirmation of Multiculturalism and Tolerance in Vojvodina 2006–2007]. Novi Sad: Republika Srbija, Autonomna Pokrajina Vojvodina, Pokrajinski Sekreterijat za Propise, Uprevu i Nacionalne Manjine, 2006.

* Prónai, Csaba, ed. *Identitásváltozatok marginalitásban* [Identity Changes in Marginality]. Budapest: MTA Etnikai-nemzeti Kisebbségkutató Intézet, 2005.

Puczi, Béla. *Marosvásárhely, 1990: három napig magyar: egy roma a barikád magyar oldaláról* [Târgu Mureş, 1900: Hungarian for Three Days: a Roma on the Hungarian Side of the Barricade]. Budapest: RSK, 2000.

Pukánszky, Béla. *Német polgárság magyar földön* [German Bourgeois on Hungarian Soil]. Budapest: Franklin Társulat, 1940.

* Pukkai, László. *Mátyusföld I. A Galántai járás társadalmi és gazdasági változásai 1945–2000* [Matušova zem I. Social and Economic Change

in Okres Galanta 1945–2000]. Komárno/Dunaszerdahely: Fórum/ Lilium Aurum, 2002.

Purcsi, Barna Gyula. *A cigánykérdés „gyökeres és végleges megoldása".* *Tanulmányok a XX. századi „cigánykérdés" történetéből* [A "Radical and Final Solution" to the Gypsy Question. Studies on the Twentieth-Century History of the "Gypsy Question"]. Debrecen: Csokonai, 2004.

Puskás, Julianna. *Kivándorló magyarok az Egyesült Államokban 1880–1940* [Hungarians Emigrating to the United States 1880–1940]. Budapest: Akadémiai, 1982.

Puskás, Julianna. *Ties That Bind, Ties That Divide: 100 Years of Hungarian Experience in the United States.* New York/London: Holmes & Meier, 2000.

Püski, Sándor, ed. *Szárszó. Az 1943. évi balatonszárszói Magyar Élet-tábor előadás- és megbeszéléssorozata* [Szárszó. Lectures and Discussions at the 1943 Hungarian Life Camp at Balatonszárszó]. Budapest: Magyar Élet Kiadó, 1943.

Raffay, Ernő. *Erdély 1918–1919-ben* [Transylvania in 1918–1919]. Budapest: Magvető, 1987.

Ránki, György, Ervin Pamlényi, Lóránt Tilkovszky, and Gyula Juhász, eds. *A Wilhelmstrasse és Magyarország. Német diplomáciai iratok Magyarországról 1933–1944* [Wilhelmstrasse and Hungary. German Diplomatic Papers on Hungary, 1933–1944]. Budapest: Kossuth Könyvkiadó, 1986.

Rehák, László. *Kisebbségtől nemzetiségig* [From Minority to National Community]. Újvidék: Fórum Könyvkiadó, 1979.

Rékai, Miklós. *A munkácsi zsidók „terített asztala"* [The "Laid Table" of the Mukachevo Jews]. Budapest. Osiris, 1997.

* Réti, Tamás. *Közeledő régiók a Kárpát-medencében. Dél-Szlovákia, Erdély és a Vajdaság gazdasági átalakulása* [Approaching Regions in the Carpathian Basin: the Economic Transformation of Southern Slovakia, Transylvania and Vojvodina]. Budapest: EÖKIK, 2004.

Romsics, Ignác. *Az 1947-es párizsi békeszerződés* [The 1947 Treaty of Paris]. Budapest: Osiris, 2007.

Romsics, Ignác. *The Dismantling of Historic Hungary: the Peace Treaty of Trianon, 1920.* New York: Columbia University Press, 2002.

Romsics, Ignác. *From Dictatorship to Democracy. The Birth of the Third Hungarian Republic 1988–2001.* Highland Lakes, NJ: Atlantic Resrarch and Publications, 2007.

Romsics, Ignác. *Hungary in the Twentieth Century.* Budapest: Corvina, 1999.

Romsics, Ignác. *Nemzet, nemzetiség és állam Kelet-Közép- és Délkelet-Európában a 19. és 20. században* [Nation, Nationality, and State in East-Central and Southeast Europe in the 19th and 20th Centuries]. Budapest: Napvilág Kiadó, 1998.

Romsics, Ignác, ed. *Trianon és a magyar politikai gondolkodás, 1920–1953* [Trianon and Hungarian Political Thinking 1920–1953]. Budapest: Osiris, 1998.

Romsics, Ignác, ed. *Wartime American Plans for a New Hungary. Documents from the U.S. Department of State, 1942–1944.* Highland Lakes, NJ: Atlantic Resrarch and Publications, 1992.

Romsics, Ignác, *et al.,* eds. *Magyarok kisebbségben és szórványban. A Magyar Miniszterelnökség Nemzetiségi és Kisebbségi Osztályának válogatott iratai, 1919–1944* [Hungarians in a Minority and in Isolated Settlements. Selected Documents of the Hungarian Prime Ministry's Department of Nationality and Minority Affairs 1919–1944]. Budapest: Teleki László Alapítvány, 1995.

Rónai, András. *Atlas of Central Europe.* Budapest: Államtudományi Intézet, 1945.

Rónai, András. *A nemzetiségi kérdés* [Nationality Question]. Budapest: Országos Szociálpolitikai Intézet, 1942.

Rónai, András. *Térképezett történelem* [Mapped History]. Budapest: Magvető, 1989.

Rostás, Zoltán, ed. *„Hát ide figyelj édes fiam..." Esszék az ifjúságkutatás köréből* [Listen, Son. Essays in Youth Research]. Bukarest: Albatrosz, 1989.

Rothermere, Harold Harmsworth. *My Campaign for Hungary.* London: Eyre and Spottiswoode, 1939.

Rothschild, Joseph. *East Central Europe between the Two World Wars.* Seattle/London: University of Washington Press, 1974.

Rubin, Israel. *Satmar. Two Generations of an Urban Island.* New York: Peter Lang, 1997.

* S. Benedek, András. *A gens fidelissima: a ruszinok* [The *Gens Fidelissima*: the Rusyns]. Budapest: Belváros – Lipótváros Ruszin Kisebbségi Önkormányzat, 2003.

S. Benedek, András. *Kárpátalja története és kultúrtörténete* [History and Cultural History of Subcarpathia]. Budapest: Bereményi Könyvkiadó, 1995.

Ságvári, Ágnes. *Tanulmányok a magyarországi holokauszt történetéből* [Studies on the History of the Hungarian Holocaust]. Budapest: Napvilág Kiadó, 2002.

Ságvári, Ágnes, ed. *A magyarországi zsidóság holocaustja, 1944* [Holocaust of Hungarian Jewry, 1944]. Budapest: Jewish Agency, 1994.

Sakmyster, Thomas L. *Hungary, the Great Powers and the Danubian Crisis, 1936–1939.* Athens: University of Georgia Press, 1980.

Salamon, Konrád. *Nemzeti önpusztítás 1918–1920. Forradalom–proletárdiktatúra–ellenforradalom* [National Self-Destruction 1918–1920. Revolution–Proletarian Dictatorship–Counterrevolution]. Budapest: Korona Kiadó, 2001.

* Salat, Levente. *Etnopolitika – konfliktustól a méltányosságig* [Ethno-Politics – from Conflict to Equity]. Marosvásárhely: Mentor, 2001.

* Salat, Levente, ed. *Politici de integrare a minorităţilor naţionale din România. Aspecte legale şi instituţionale întro perspectivă comparată* [Integration Policies Regarding National Minorities in Romania. Legal and Institutional Aspects in a Comparative Perspective]. Cluj-Napoca: CRDE, 2008.

Salat, Levente, ed. *Tény és való. Tudományelméleti írások* [Fact. Writings of Scientific Theory]. Bukarest: Kriterion, 1989.

Sallai, Gergely. *Az első bécsi döntés* [First Vienna Award]. Budapest: Osiris, 2002.

* Sallai, Gergely. *„A határ megindul..."* A csehszlovákiai magyar kisebbség és Magyarország kapcsolatai az 1938–1939. évi államhatár-változások tükrében* ["The Frontier Moves off..." Relations between the Czechoslovakian Hungarian Minority and Hungary in the Light of the 1938–1939 Border Changes]. Pozsony: Kalligram, 2009.

Sándor, László, ed. *Ez volt a Sarló. Tanulmányok, emlékezesek, dokumentumok* [That Was Sarló. Studies, Memoirs, Documents]. Budapest: Kossuth Könyvkiadó, 1978.

Sas, Andor. *A szlovákiai zsidók üldözése 1939–1945* [Persecution of Slovakia's Jews 1939–1945]. Pozsony: Kalligram, 1993.

Schain, Martin, ed. *The Marshall Plan. Fifty Years after.* New York: Palgrave, 2001.

Schechtman, Joseph B. *European Population Transfers, 1939–1945.* Philadelphia, PA: University of Pennsylvania Press, 1962.

Schechtman, Joseph B. *Postwar Population Transfers in Europe 1945–1955.* Philadephia: Philadelphia UP, 1962.

Schlag, Gerald. *Der 12. März im Burgenland und seine Vorgeschichte.*

Burgenländische Forschungen 73. Eisenstadt: Burgenländisches Landesarchiv, 1989.

Schmidt-Hartmann, Eva and Stanley B. Winters, eds. *Grossbritannien, die USA und die böhmischen Länder 1848–1938*. Munich: R. Oldenbourg, 1991.

Schober, Ottó. *Színfalak előtt, mögött, nélkül. Epizódok a Beregszászi Népszínház történetéből* [Before, behind, without the Scenes. Episodes from the History of the People's Theater of Beregovo]. Ungvár/Budapest: Intermix, 1995.

Schönwald, Pál. *A magyarországi 1918–1919-es polgári demokratikus forradalom állam- és jogtörténeti kérdései* [Issues of Constitutional and Legal History in Hungary's Bourgeois Democratic Revolution of 1918–1919]. Budapest: Akadémia Kiadó, 1969.

Schulze Wessel, Martin. *Loyalitäten in der Tschechoslowakischen Republik, 1918–1938: politische, nationale und kulturelle Zugehörigkeiten*. Munich: Oldenbourg, 2004.

* Schuster, Walter and Wolfgang Weber, eds. *Entnazifizierung im regionalen Vergleich*. Linz: Archiv der Stadt Linz, 2004.

Sebestyén, Ádám. *A bukovinai székelység tegnap és ma* [Bukovina Székelys Past and Present]. Szekszárd: Tolna Megyei Könyvtár, 1989.

Seidl, Hans. *Österreichische Wirtschaft und Wirtschaftspolitik nach dem Zweiten Weltkrieg*. Vienna: Manz, 2005.

Seper, Károly. *Alsóőr történetéből. Írások, emlékek és szájhagyomány* [From Unterwart's History. Documents, Memories and Oral Tradition]. Unterwart: Alsóőri Otthon/Unterwarter Heimathaus, 1988.

Seton-Watson, Hugh and Christopher Seton-Watson. *The Making of a New Europe: R. W. Seton-Watson and the Last Years of Austria-Hungary*. Seattle: University of Washington Press, 1981.

Shafir, Michael. *Romania. Politics, Economics, Society: Political Stagnation and Simulated Change*. London: Pinter, 1985.

Sík, Endre and Judit Tóth, eds. *Diskurzusok a vándorlásról* [Discourses on Migration]. Budapest: MTA Politikatudományi Intézet, 2000.

* Simon, Attila. *Telepesek és telepes falvak Dél-Szlovákiában a két világháború között* [Colonists and Colony Villages in Southern Slovakia between the Two World Wars]. Somorja: Fórum Kisebbségkutató Intézet, 2008.

* Simon, Attila, ed. *A határon túli magyar tudományos könyvkiadás* [Academic Book Publishing among Hungarians Abroad]. Somorja: Fórum Kisebbségkutató Intézet, 2005.

* Simon, Attila *Egy rövid esztendő krónikája. A magyar kisebbség 1938-ban* [Chronicle of a Short Year. The Slovakian Hungarian Minority in 1938]. Šamorín: Fórum Kisebbségkutató Intézet, 2010.

Sipos, Lajos, ed. *Iskolaszerkezet és irodalomtanítás a Kárpát-medencében. Élményközpontú irodalomtanítás* [School Structure and Literature Teaching in the Carpathian Basin. Experience-Oriented Literature Teaching]. Budapest: Pont Kiadó, 2003.

* Šircelj, Milivoja. *Verska, jezikovna in narodna sestava prebivalstva Slovenije: popisi 1921–2002* [Religious, Linguistic and Ethnic Composition of the Population of Slovenia: Censuses 1921–2002]. Ljubljana: Statistični Urad Republike Slovenije, 2003.

Skalnik Leff, Carol. *National Conflict in Czechoslovakia: The Making and Remaking of a State, 1918–1987.* Princeton, NJ: Princeton UP, 1988.

Skutnabb-Kangas, Tove. *Linguistic Genocide in Education – or Worldwide Diversity and Human Rights?* Mahwah, N.J: Lawrence Erlbaum, 2000.

Skutnabb-Kangas, Tove. *Nyelv, oktatás és a kisebbségek* [Language, Education and Minorities]. Budapest: Teleki László Alapítvány, 1997.

* *Slovenski šolski sistem v številkah* [Slovene Education System in Numbers]. Ljubljana: Republika Slovenija Ministrstvo za Šolstvo in Šport, 2007.

Smolij, V. *et al.*, *Ukrai'na–Ugorshhyna: spil'ne mynule ta s'ogodennja* [Ukraine–Hungary: Common Past and Present]. Kyiv, 2006.

Sokcsevits, Dénes, Imre Szilágyi, and Károly Szilágyi. *Déli szomszédaink története* [History of Hungary's Southern Neighbors]. Budapest: Bereményi, 1994.

Soós, Katalin. *Burgenland az európai politikában 1918–1921* [Burgenland in European Politics, 1918–1921]. Budapest: Akadémiai Kiadó, 1971

Sorin, Gerald. *A Time for Building. The Jewish People in America Vol. III.* Baltimore/London: Johns Hopkins University Press, 1992.

Sozan, Mihály. *A határ két oldalán* [Both Sides of the Border]. Paris: Párizs Irodalmi Újság, 1985.

Spannenberger, Norbert. *Der Volksbund der Deutschen in Ungarn 1938–1944.* Munich: R. Oldenburg Verlag, 2002.

Spitzer, Shlomo, ed. *Beiträge zur Geschichte der Juden im Burgenland.* Ramat Gan: Universität Bar-Ilan, 1994.

Stark, Tamás. *Hungary's Human Losses in World War II.* Uppsala: Uppsala University, 1995.

Stark, Tamás. *Magyar foglyok a Szovjetunióban* [Hungarian Prisoners in the Soviet Union]. Budapest: Lucidus Kiadó, 2006.

Stark, Tamás. *Magyarország második világháborús embervesztesége* [Hungary's Human Losses in World War II]. Budapes: MTA Történettudományi Intézete, 1989.

Stark, Tamás. *The Hungarian Jews during the Holocaust and after the Second World War, 1939–1949. A Statistical Review.* New York: Columbia University Press, 2000.

Statistisches Handbuch der Stadt Wien 1992. Vienna: Gemeinde Wien, 1992.

Stewart, Michael. *The Time of the Gypsies.* Boulder, CO: Westview Press, 1997.

Stiefel, Dieter. *Entnazifizierung in Österreich.* Vienna/Munich/Zurich: Europa Verlag, 1981.

Stourzh, Gerald. *Kleine Geschichte des Staatsvertrages. Mit Dokumentarteil.* Vienna: Verlag Styria, 1975.

Strba, Sándor and Tamás Lang. *Az érsekújvári zsidóság története* [History of Érsekújvár Jewry]. Pozsony: Kalligram, 2004.

Suny, Ronald Grigor. *The Revenge of the Past: Nationalism, Revolution, and the Collapse of the Soviet Union.* Stanford, CA: Stanford University Press, 1993.

Suppan, Arnold. *Die österreichischen Volksgruppen und Tendenzen ihrer gesellschaftlichen Entwicklung im 20. Jahrhundert.* Vienna: Verlag für Geschichte und Politik, 1983.

Šutaj, Štefan. *Magyarok Csehszlovákiában 1945–1948* [Hungarians in Czechoslovakia, 1945–1948]. Budapest: Lucidus Kiadó, 2008.

Šutaj, Štefan, Peter Mosný, and Milan Olejník, eds. *Prezidenstké dekréty E. Beneša a povojnové Slovensko* [President E. Beneš' Decrees and the Post-War Slovakia]. Bratislava: Veda, 2002.

Szabó, Andrea *et al.*, eds. *Mozaik 2001. Magyar fiatalok a Kárpát-medencében* [Mosaic 2001. Hungarian Youth in the Carpathian Basin]. Budapest: Nemzeti Ifjúságkutató Intézet, 2002.

Szabó, János József. *The Árpád-line. The Defence System of the Hungarian Royal Army in the Eastern Carpathians.* Budapest: Timp, 2006

Szabó, Miklós. *Politikai kultúra Magyarországon 1896–1986. Válogatott tanulmányok* [Political Culture in Hungary 1896–1986. Studies]. Budapest: ELTE/MKKE, 1989.

Szabó, Rezső. *A Csemadok és a Prágai Tavasz* [Csemadok and the Prague Spring]. Pozsony: Kalligram, 2004.

Szakolczay, Lajos. *Dunának, Oltnak* [For the Danube, the Olt]. Budapest: Szépirodalmi, 1984.

Szalai, Anna, ed. *In the Land of Hagar. The Jews of Hungary: History, Society and Culture.* Tel-Aviv: Beth Hatefutsoth, 2002.

Szalai, Anna, ed. *Previously Unexplored Sources on the Holocaust in Hungary. A Selection from Jewish Periodicals 1930–1944.* Jerusalem: Yad Vashem, 2007.

Szántó, Miklós. *Magyarok a nagyvilágban* [Hungarians in the Wide World]. Budapest: Gondolat, 1984.

Szarka, László. *Duna-táji dilemmák. Nemzeti kisebbségek – kisebbségi politika a 20. századi Kelet-Közép-Európában* [Danubian Dilemmas. National Minorities and Minority Policy in 20th-Century East-Central Europe]. Budapest: Ister Kiadó, 1998.

* Szarka, László. *Kisebbségi léthelyzetek – közösségi alternatívák. Az etnikai csoportok helye a kelet-közép-európai nemzetállamokban* [Minority Living Situations – Community Alternatives. The Place of Ethnic Groups in the Nation-States of East-Central Europe]. Budapest: Lucidus, 2004.

Szarka, László. *A szlovákok története* [History of the Slovaks]. Budapest/ Komárno: Bereményi, 1993.

Szarka, László, ed. *Hungary and the Hungarian Minorities. Trends in the Past and in Our Time.* Highland Lakes, NJ: Atlantic Research and Publications, 2004.

Szarka, László, ed. *Jogfosztó jogszabályok Csehszlovákiában, 1944– 1949. Elnöki dekrétumok, törvények, rendeletek, szerződések* [Rights-Depriving Legal Instruments in Czechoslovakia, 1944–1949. Presidential Decrees, Acts, Orders Treaties]. Budapest/Komárno: MTA Etnikai-nemzeti Kisebbségkutató Intézet/Kecskes László Társaság, 2005.

* Szarka, László, Balázs Vizi, Balázs Majtényi, and Zoltán Kántor, eds. *Nemzetfogalmak és etnopolitikai modellek Kelet-Közép-Európában* [Concepts of Nation and Ethno-Political Models in East-Central Europe]. Budapest: Gondolat, 2007.

Szász, Zsombor. *The Minorities in Roumanian Transylvania.* London: Richard Press, 1927.

Szeberényi, Lajos and András Szeberényi. *Az őrvidéki magyarok* [Hungarians of the Wart]. Felsőőr: Burgenlandi Magyar Kultúregyesület, 1985.

Szeberényi, Ludwig. *Die ungarische Volksgruppe im Burgenland und ihr Volksgruppenbeirat.* Vienna: Bundeskanzleramt, 1986.

Szekfű, Gyula, ed. *A magyarság és a szlávok* [The Hungarians and the Slavs]. Budapest: Lucidus Kiadó, 2000.

Szeli, István. *Így hozta a történelem... Vékás János interjúja* [What History Brought... Interview with János Vékás]. Újvidék: Forum, 1988.

Szeli, István. *A magyar kultúra útjai Jugoszláviában* [Paths of Hungarian Literature in Yugoslavia]. Budapest: Kossuth Könyvkiadó, 1983.

Szenczei, László. *Az erdélyi magyarság harca (1940–1941)* [Struggle of the Transylvanian Hungarians 1940–1941]. Budapest: Egyetemi Nyomda, 1946.

Szenteleky, Kornél. *Ugartörés* [Ground Breaking]. Újvidék: Forum, 1963.

Szent-Ivany, Gabor. *Graf János Esterházy.* Vienna: Böhlau, 1995.

* Szépe, György. *Nyelvpolitika: múlt és jövő* [Language Policy: Past and Future]. Pécs: Iskolakultúra, 2001.

Szépfalusi, István. *Lássátok, halljátok egymást! Mai magyarok Ausztriában* [See, Hear One Another! Today's Hungarians in Austria]. Budapest: Magvető, 1992.

Szépfalusi, István, ed. *Találkozások Európával. Bornemisza Péter Társaság 1960–1995* [Encounters with Europe. Péter Bornemisza Society, 1960–1995]. Budapest: Magvető, 1995.

Szerbhorváth, György. *Vajdasági lakoma. Az Új Symposion történetéről* [Vojvodina Feast. From the History of the Új Symposion]. Pozsony: Kalligram, 2005.

* Szesztay, Ádám. *Nemzetiségi kérdés a Kárpát-medencében 1956–1962. Az ötvenhatos forradalom hatása a kelet-közép-európai kisebbségpolitikára* [Minority Question in the Carpathian Basin 1956–1962. Effect of the '56 Revolution on Minority Policy in East-Central Europe]. Budapest: MTA Kisebbségkutató Intézet/Gondolat Kiadói Kör, 2003.

Szesztay, Ádám, ed. *Együtt: Az 1956-os forradalom és a határon túli magyarok* [Together: The '56 Revolution and Hungarians beyond the Borders]. Budapest: Lucidus, 2006.

Sziklay, Ferenc, ed. *Kazinczy Évkönyv 1898–1928* [Kazinczy Yearbook 1898–1928]. Kassa: Kazinczy Kiadóvállalat, 1929.

Szita, Szabolcs. *Haláleröd* [Death Fortress]. Budapest: Gondolat, 1986.

Szőcs, Géza and Endre Farkas Wellmann, eds. *Amikor fordul az ezred* [When the Millennium Turns]. Budapest: Ulpius-ház, 2009.

Szőke, József. *A csehszlovákiai magyar irodalom válogatott bibliográfiája 1945–1985 I–IV.* [Select Bibliography of Czechoslovak Hungarian Literature, 1945–1985, Vol. I–IV.]. Pozsony: Madách, 1982.

Szöllősy, Pál and Bálint Balla, eds. *Európa keresztútjain. Az Európai Protestáns Magyar Szabadegyetem 33 éve* [At Europe's Crossroads. 33 Years of the European Protestant Hungarian Free University]. Basel/Budapest: Európai Protestáns Magyar Szabadegyetem, 2003.

Szöllősy, Tibor, ed. *Kárpát-medencei magyar paletta* [Hungarian Palette in the Carpathian Basin]. Ungvár/Budapest: Intermix, 1993.

Szporluk, Roman. *The Political Thought of Thomas G. Masaryk.* Boulder, CO: East European Monographs, 1981.

Szűcs, Jenő. *Nemzet és történelem. Tanulmányok* [Nation and History. Studies]. Budapest: Gondolat, 1984.

Szűcs, László, ed. *Dálnoki Miklós Béla kormányának minisztertanácsi jegyzőkönyvei, 1944. december 23.–1945. november 15.* [Council of Ministers Minutes of the Dálnoki Government, December 23, 1944–November 15, 1945]. Budapest: Magyar Országos Levéltár, 1997.

Szuhay, Péter and Antónia Barati, eds. *Képek a magyarországi cigányság 20. századi történetéből* [Pictures from the Twentieth-Century History of the Gypsies of Hungary]. Budapest: Néprajzi Múzeum, 1993.

Szűrös, Mátyás. *Magyarországról – külpolitikáról* [On Hungary – On Foreign Policy]. Budapest: Kossuth, 1989.

Szvatkó, Pál. *A változás élménye. Válogatott írások* [Experience of Change. Selected Writings]. Pozsony: Kalligram, 1994.

Szvatkó, Pál. *A visszatért magyarok. A felvidéki magyarság húsz éve* [Returned Hungarians. Twenty Years of the Upland Hungarians]. Budapesti Révai. 1938.

* Tabajdi, Csaba. *Az önazonosság labirintusa* [Labyrinth of Self-Identity]. Budapest: CP Stúdió, 1998.

Tabajdi, Csaba, ed. *Mérleg és számvetés. A magyarságpolitikai rendszerváltás kezdete* [Balance and Account. The Beginning of the Change of System in Policy toward Hungarian Communities]. Budapest: Codex, 2001.

Tamás, Pál and András Inotai, eds. *Új exodus. A nemzetközi munkaerőáramlás új irányai* [New Exodus. New Directions in the International Flow of Labor]. Budapest: MTA Konfliktuskutató Intézet, 1993.

* Tánczos, Vilmos. *Keletnek megnyílt kapuja* [Gate to the East]. Kolozsvár: Komp-Press, 1996.

* Tánczos, Vilmos and Gyöngyvér Tőkés, eds. *Tizenkét év. Összefoglaló tanulmányok az erdélyi magyar tudományos kutatások 1990–2001 közötti eredményeiről* [Twelve Years. Summary Studies of Transylvanian Hungarian Scientific Research]. Kolozsvár: Scientia Kiadó, 2002.

Tanka, László. *Magyarok a nagyvilágban: életrajzok, intézmények, szervezetek* [Hungarians in the Wide World: Biographies, Institutions, Organizations]. Budapest: Panoráma, 2009.

Tapodi, Zsuzsa. *A soha el nem vesző könyv nyomában. Irodalmi tanulmányok* [In Search of Books Never Lost. Literary Studies]. Csíkszereda: Pallas-Akadémia Könyvkiadó, 2008.

Tavaszy, Sándor. *A lét és valóság. Az exisztenciálizmus filozófiájának alapproblémái* [Existence and Reality. Basic Problems of the Philosophy of Existentialism]. Kolozsvár: Minerva, 1933.

Tavaszy, Sándor. *Válogatott filozófiai írások* [Selected Philosophical Writings]. Kolozsvár/Szeged: Pro Philosophia Kiadó/JATE BTK Filozófiai Tanszéke/ JATE Társadalomelméleti Gyűjteménye, 1999.

Teleki, Béla. *A magyar evangélikusság története Őriszigeten* [History of the Hungarian Evangelicals in Siget in Der Wart]. Siget in der Wart, 1979.

Temperley, Harold, ed. *A History of the Peace Conference of Paris. Vol. V.* London: Oxford University Press, 1924.

Ternovácz, István. *Pusztulj, kulák! Parasztsanyargatás a Vajdaságban* [Perish, Kulak! Oppression of the Peasantry in Vojvodina]. Budapest: Hatodik Síp Alapítvány, 1996.

Tezla, Albert. *Hazardous Quest. Hungarian Immigrants in the United States: 1890–1920: A Documentary.* Budapest: Corvina, 1993.

Thernstrom, Stephan, ed. *Harvard Encyclopedia of American Ethnic Groups.* Boston, MA/London: Harvard UP, 1980.

Thornberry, Patrick. *International Law and Rights of Minorities.* Oxford: Clarendon Press, 1991.

Thornberry, Patrick. *The Rights of Minorities and International Law.* Oxford: Clarendon Press, 1991.

Thornberry, Patrick and Maria A. Martin Estébanez. *Minority Rights in Europe.* Strasbourg: Council of Europe Publishing, 2004.

Thurner, Erika. *Kurzgeschichte des nationalsozialistischen Zigeunerlagers in Lackenbach (1940 bis 1945).* Eisenstadt: Roetzer, 1984.

Tibori Szabó, Zoltán. *Teleki Béla erdélyisége. Embernek maradni embertelen időkben* [The Transylvanianism of Béla Teleki. Remaining Human in Inhuman Times]. Kolozsvár: Nis, 1993.

Tilkovszky, Loránt. *Nemzetiségi politika Magyarországon a 20. században* [National Minority Policy in 20th-Century Hungary]. Debrecen: Csokonai Kiadó, 1998.

Tilkovszky, Lóránt. *Revízió és nemzetiségpolitika Magyarországon (1938–1941)* [Revision and Nationality Policy in Hungary 1938–1941]. Budapest: Akadémiai, 1967.

Tilkovszky, Lóránt. *Die Weimarer Republik und die deutschen Minderheiten im Donaubecken.* Budapest: Akadémiai, 1980.

Toggenburg, Gabriel, ed. *Minority Protection and the Enlarged European Union: the Way forward.* Budapest: OSI LGI, 2004.

Tokar, M. *Politychni partii' Zakarpattia v umovah bagatopartijnosti (1919–1939)* [The Multi-Party System in Trans(1919–1939)]. Uzhhorod: UzhNU, 2006.

Tolcsvai Nagy, Gábor. *Nyelv, érték, közösség* [Language, Value, Community]. Budapest: Gondolat, 2004.

Tordai, Zádor and Sándor Tóth, eds. *Szerkesztette Gaál Gábor 1929–1940* [Edited by Gábor Gaál 1929–1940]. Budapest: Magvető, 1976.

Tornow, Siegfried. *Die Herkunft der kroatischen Vlahen des südlichen Burgenlandes. Veröffentlichung der Abteilung für slavische Sprachen und Literaturen des Osteuropa-Instituts Slavisches Seminar an der Freien Universität Berlin 39.* Berlin: Osteuropainstitut, 1971.

* Törzsök, Erika. *Kisebbségek változó világban* [Minorities in a Changing World]. Kolozsvár: A Református Egyház Misztófalusi Kis Miklós Sajtóközpontja, 2003.

Törzsök, Erika, ed. *Szülőföld Program. Stratégiai tanulmány* [Homeland Program. Strategic Study]. Budapest: MEH Európai Integrációs Iroda, 2005.

Tóth, Ágnes, ed. *National and Ethnic Minorities in Hungary 1920–2001.* Highland Lakes, NJ: Atlantic Research and Publications, 2005.

Tóth, Imre. *A nyugat-magyarországi kérdés 1922–1939. Diplomácia és helyi politika a két háború között* [West Hungarian Question 1922–1939. Diplomacy and Local Politics between the World Wars]. Sopron: Soproni Levéltár, 2006.

Tóth, Károly. *Leányvári ébredés. Cikkek, esszék, tanulmányok* [Leányvár Awakening. Articles, Essays, Studies]. Dunaszerdahely: Nap, 1994.

Tóth, Károly and Gábor Csanda, eds. *Magyarok Szlovákiában, III. (1989–2006) Kultúra* [Hungarians in Slovakia, Vol. III (1989–2006). Culture]. Somorja: Fórum Kisebbségkutató Intézet, 2007.

* Tóth, Károly Antal. *Hova-tovább? Az Ellenpontok dokumentumai, esszék, tanulmányok* [Whence Now? Documents, Essays, Studies from Ellenpontok]. Stockholm/Szombathely: Magyar Ökomenikus Önképzőkör/Savaria University Press, 1994.

* Tóth, Károly Antal, ed. *Ellenpontok* [Counter-Arguments]. Csíkszereda: Pro-Print, 2000.

Tóth, Lajos. *Magyar nyelvű oktatás a Vajdaságban 1944-től napjainkig* [Hungarian-Language Education in Vojvodina from 1944 to the Present Day]. Szabadka: Életjel, 1995.

Tóth, László. *Köz – Művelődés – Történet. Három tanulmány* [Public – Education – History. Three Studies]. Budapest: Ister Kiadó, 2000.

Tóth, László, ed. *"Hívebb emlékezésül..." Csehszlovákiai magyar emlékiratok és egyéb dokumentumok a jogfosztottság éveiből 1945–1948* ["As a More Faithful Recollection..." Czechoslovak Hungarian Memoirs and Other Documents of the Years of Denial of Rights]. Pozsony: Kalligram, 1995.

Tóth, László and Tamás Gusztáv Filep, eds. *A (cseh)szlovákiai magyar művelődés története 1918—1998 I–IV.* [History of (Czecho)Slovak Hungarian Culture, 1918–1998, Vol. I–IV.]. Budapest: Ister Kiadó, 1998–2000.

Tóth, Pál Péter. *Haza csak egy van? Menekülők, bevándorlók, új állampolgárok Magyarországon (1988–1994)* [Only One Home Country? Refugees, Immigrants, New Citizens in Hungary 1988–1994]. Budapest: Püski, 1997.

Tóth, Pál Péter, ed. *Bevándorlás Magyarországra* [Immigration into Hungary]. Budapest: Lucidus, 2006.

Tóth, Pál Péter and Emil Valkovics, eds. *Demography of Contemporary Hungarian Society.* Highland Lakes, NJ: Atlantic Research and Publications, 1996.

Tovt, M. *Mizhnarodno-pravovyj zahyst nacional'nyh menshyn (tendencii' suchasnogo rozvytku)* [International Legal Protection of National Minorities. (The Present Situation)]. Uzhhorod: Informacijno-vydavnyche agentstvo "IVA", 2002.

Trieber, Ladislaus, ed. *Die Obere Wart.* Oberwart: Stadtgemeinde Oberwart, 1977.

Trifunovska, Sezana, ed. *Minority Rights in Europe: European Minorities and Languages.* The Hague: Asser Press, 2001.

Truger, Arno and Thomas Macho eds. *Mitteleuropäische Perspektiven.* Vienna: Verlag für Gesellschaftskritik, 1990.

Turczel, Lajos. *Arcképek és emlékezések* [Portraits and Memories]. Pozsony: Madách – Posonium, 1997.

Turczel, Lajos. *Két kor mezsgyéjén. A magyar irodalom fejlődési feltételei és problémái Csehszlovákiában 1918 és 1938 között* [Between Two Periods. Development Conditions and Problems of Hungarian Literature in Czechoslovakia 1918–1938]. Pozsony: Madách, 1983.

Turczel, Lajos. *Visszatekintések a szlovákiai magyar kisebbségi lét első szakaszára* [Looking Back on the First Phase of Hungarian Minority Existence in Slovakia]. Dunaszerdahely: Lilium Aurum, 2002.

Ullein-Reviczky, Antal. *Guerre allemande, paix russe. Le drame hongrois.* Neuchâtel: Editions de la Baconnière, 1947.

Unterricht und Bildung in den Volksgruppensprachen. Vienna: Braumüller, 1987.

Utasi, Csaba. *Irodalmunk és a Kalangya* [Our Literature and Kalangya]. Újvidék: Forum, 1984.

Útközben. Tanulmányok a kárpátaljai magyarságról [On the Road. Studies of the Transcarpathian Hungarians]. Ungvár: KMKSZ, 1998.

Vadkerty, Katalin. *A kitelepítéstől a reszlovakizációig* [From Deportation to Re-Slovakization]. Pozsony: Kalligram, 2006.

* Vajda, Gábor. *Az autonómia illúziója. A délvidéki magyarság eszme- és irodalomtörténetet (1972–1989)* [The Autonomy Illusion. Intellectual and Literary History of the Southern Region Hungarians 1972–1989]. Szabadka. Magyarságkutató Tudományos Társaság, 2007.

Vajda, Gábor. *A magyar irodalom a Délvidéken Trianontól napjainkig* [Hungarian Literature in the Southern Region from Trianon to the Present Day]. Budapest: Bereményi, 1995.

Vajda, Gábor. *Remény a megfélemlítettségben. A délvidéki magyarság eszme- és irodalomtörténete (1945–1972)* [Hope in Intimidation. The Ideological and Literary History of the Southern Region Hungarians 1945–1972]. Szabadka: Magyarságkutató Tudományos Társaság, 2006.

Vallasek, Júlia. *Sajtótörténeti esszék. Négy folyóirat szerepe 1940–1944 között az észak-erdélyi kulturális életben* [Essays in Press History. Role of Four Journals in Cultural Life of North Transylvania in 1940–1944]. Kolozsvár: Kriterion, 2003.

Valuch, Tibor, ed. *Hatalom és társadalom a XX. századi magyar történelemben* [Power and Society in 20th-Century Hungarian History]. Budapest: Osiris, 1995.

Valuch, Tibor, ed. *Radikalizmus és demokrácia. Csécsy Imre válogatott írásai* [Radicalism and Democracy. Selected Writings of Imre Csécsy]. Szeged: Aetas, 1988.

Várallyay, Gyula. *Tanulmányúton: Az emigráns magyar diákmozgalom 1956 után* [Study Trip: the Émigré Hungarian Student Movement after 1956]. Budapest: 1956-os Intézet, 1992.

Várdy, Steven Béla. *The Hungarian Americans: the Hungarian Experience in North America.* New York/Philadelphia, PA: Chelsea Publishing, 1990.

Várdy, Steven Béla. *Magyarok az Újvilágban: az észak-amerikai magyarság rendhagyó története* [Hungarians in the New World: the Unusual History of the North American Hungarians]. Budapest: Magyar Nyelv és Kultúra Nemzetközi Társasága, 2000.

Várdy, Béla and Ágnes H. Várdy. *Hungarian Americans in the Current of History.* New York: Columbia UP, 2010.

Várdy, Steven Béla and T. Hunt Tooley, eds. *Ethnic Cleansing in 20th Century Europe.* Boulder, CO: Social Science Monographs, 2003.

Varga, Árpád E. *Fejezetek a jelenkori Erdély népesedéstörténetéből. Tanulmányok* [Chapters from the Population History of Present-Day Transylvania. Studies]. Budapest: Püski, 1998.

* Varga, Árpád E. *Népszámlálások a jelenkori Erdély területén. Jegyzetek Erdély és a kapcsolt részek XX. századi nemzetiségi statisztikájának történetéhez* [Censuses in Present Area of Transylvania. Notes on History of 20th Century Ethnic Statistics in Transylvania and Attached Areas]. Budapest: Egio/MTA Történettudományi Intézet, 1992.

Vegesh, M. *Karpats'ka Ukrai'na. Dokumenty i fakty* [Carpatho-Ukraine. Documents and Facts]. Uzhhorod: Karpaty, 2004.

M. Vegesh, *Gromads'ko-politychni vzajemovidnosyny Shidnoi' Galychyny i Zakarpattia v 1918–1919 rokah* [The Socio-Political Relations of Eastern Galicia and Transcarpathia in 1918–1919]. Uzhhorod: UzhDU, 1996.

Venczel, József. *Az erdélyi román földbirtokreform* [Romanian Land Reform in Transylvania]. Kolozsvár: Erdélyi Tudományos Intézet, 1942.

Venczel, József. *Az önismeret útján. Tanulmányok az erdélyi társadalomkutatás köréből* [On the Road to Self-Awareness. Studies in Transylvanian Social Research]. Bukarest: Kriterion, 1980.

Verdery, Katherine. *National Ideology under Socialism – Identity and Cultural Politics in Ceausescu's Romania.* Berkeley: University of California Press, 1995.

Veres, Emese-Gyöngyvér. *Barcasági körkép. Egy kulturális antropológus terepmunka-tanulmányai* [Review of Tara Barsei. A Cultural, Anthropological Fieldwork Study]. Budapest: MTA PTI, 1996.

Vékás, János. *Utak – Életútinterjúk 1980–1990.* [Pathes – Life Interviews 1980–1990]. Zenta: Vajdasági Magyar Művelődési Intézet, 2010.

Vida, István. *Iratok a magyar–szovjet kapcsolatok történetéhez 1944. október–1948. július* [Documents on the History of Hungarian–Soviet Relations, October 1944 to July 1948]. Budapest: Gondolat, 2005.

Vincze, Gábor. *Illúziók és csalódások. Fejezetek a romániai magyarság második világháború utáni történetéből* [Illusions and Disillusionments. Chapters in the Postwar History of the Romanian Hungarians]. Csíkszereda: Státus, 1999.

* Vincze, Gábor. *Magyar vagyon román kézen (Dokumentumok a romániai magyar vállalatok, pénzintézetek második világháború utáni helyzetéről és a magyar–román vagyonjogi vitáról)* [Hungarian Property in Romanian Hands. Documents on the Postwar Position of Romanian Hungarian Companies and Financial Institutions and the Hungarian–Romanian Property-Rights Dispute]. Csíkszereda: Pro-Print, 2000.

* Vincze, Gábor. *A romániai magyar kisebbség történeti kronológiája 1944–1953.* [Timeline of Romanian Hungarian Minority History]. Szeged/Budapest: TLA/JATE, 1994.

Vincze, Gábor, *A Historical Chronology of the Hungarian Minority in Romania: 1944–1989.* Oradea: Partium, 2009.

* Vincze, Gábor, ed. *Történeti kényszerpályák kisebbségi reálpolitikák II. Dokumentumok a romániai magyar kisebbség történetének tanulmányozásához 1944–1989* [Historical Paths of Minority Realpolitik, II. Documents from Study of the History of the Romanian Hungarian Minority, 1944–1989]. Csíkszereda: Pro-Print, 2003.

Volkszählungen im Burgenland 1981–2001. Umgangssprache Burgenland – Gemeinden und Ortschaften. Vienna: Bundesverlag, 2002.

Vozáry, Aladár R. *Így történt! 1944. március 19.–1945. január 18.* [How It Happened: March 19, 1944–January 18, 1945]. Budapest: Halász, 1945.

Vozáry, Aladár R. *A magyar és a magyar nyelvű újságírás a volt Csehszlovákiában. Adatok a magyar újságírás történetéhez* [Hungarian and Hungarian-Language Journalism in Czechoslovakia. Contributions to the History of Hungarian Journalism]. Mukacheve: Felvidéki Egyesületek Szövetsége, 1942.

Weber, Georg. *Emigration der Siebenbürger Sachsen. Studien zu Ost-West-Wanderung im 20. Jahrhundert.* Wiesbaden: Westdeutscher Verlag, 2003.

Weller, Mark, ed. *The Rights of Minorities. A Commentary on the European Framework Convention for the Protection of National Minorities.* Oxford: Oxford University Press, 2006.

Widder, Roland, ed. *Geschichte des Burgenlandes in der Zweiten Republik.* Salzburg: n. p., 1999.

Wiener Zeitung, ed. *Ausführungsbestimmungen zum Nationalsozialistengesetz.* Vienna: Österreichische Staatsdruckerei, 1947.

Wiener Zeitung, ed. *Das Nationalsozialistengesetz und seine Durchführung.* Vienna: Österreichische Staatsdruckerei, 1947.

Winkler, Wilhelm. *Statistisches Handbuch der europäischen Nationalitäten.* Vienna: Braumüller, 1931.

Wojatsek, Charles. *From Trianon to the First Vienna Arbitral Award. The Hungarian Minority in the First Czechoslovak Republic 1918–1938.* Montreal: Institute of Comparative Civilizations, 1981.

Záhony, Éva, ed. *Hitel. Kolozsvár 1935–1944. Tanulmányok. I* [Credit. Kolozsvár 1935–1944. Studies. Vol. I.]. Budapest: Bethlen Gábor Könyvkiadó, 1991.

Zalabai, Zsigmond. *A nyelvi jogokról: Mit ér a nyelvünk, ha magyar? „Táblaháború" és a „névháború" szlovákiai magyar sajtódokumentumaiból 1990–1994* [Language Rights: How Much Is Hungarian Worth? "Sign Wars" and "Language War" in Slovakian Hungarian Press Documents, 1990–1994]. Pozsony: Kalligram, 1995.

Zeidler, Miklós. *Ideas on Territorial Revision in Hungary 1920–1945.* Boulder, CO: Social Science Monographs, 2007.

Zeidler, Miklós. *A revíziós gondolat* [The Revisionist Idea]. Pozsony: Kalligram, 2009.

Zeidler, Miklós, ed. *Trianon*. Budapest: Osiris, 2008.

Zelliger, Erzsébet, ed. *Nyelv, területiség, társadalom* [Language, Territoriality, Society]. Budapest: Magyar Nyelvtudományi Társaság, 2007.

Zellner, Wolfgang and Pál Dunay. *Ungarns Außenpolitik 1990–1997: zwischen Westintegration, Nachbarschafts- und Minderheitenpolitik.* Baden-Baden: Nomos, 1998.

Zimányi, József. *Tűzoszlopoddal jéghegyek között. Egy ref. lelkész életútja* [Pillar of Fire Amid Hills of Ice. Life of a Reformed Minister]. Budapest: Éjféli Kiáltás Misszió, 2006.

Zseliczky, Béla. *Kárpátalja a cseh és a szovjet politika érdekterében* [Transcarpathia in the Spheres of Czech and Soviet Politics]. Budapest: Napvilág Kiadó, 1998.

Zsiga, Tibor. *Burgenland vagy Nyugat-Magyarország? (Burgenland oder Westungarn?).* Oberwart: BMK, 1991.

Zückert, Martin. *Zwischen Nationsidee und staatlicher Realität: Die tschechoslowakische Armee und ihre Nationalitätenpolitik 1918–1938.* Munich: Oldenbourg, 2006.

Historical Regions of Minority Hungarian

TRANSYLVANIA [Erdély in Hungarian, Ardeal or Transilvania in Romanian, Siebenbürgen in German]			UPPER HUNGARY or UPLAND [Felvidék or Felföld or Felső-Magyarország in Hungarian]			TRANS [Kárpátalja Zakarpattia	
State affiliations	Period	Historical name of the region	State affiliations	Period	Historical name of the region	State affiliations	Period
Romania	1918–1940	Present-day Transylvania [jelenkori Erdély in Hungarian] = Historical Transylvania (Székely Land, Saxon Land and Counties) + Partium + Maramures + Banat	the Czecho-slovak Republic	1919–1938	Upland [Slovensko in Slovakian, Felvidék or Szlovenszkó in Hungarian]	the Czecho-slovak Republic	1919–1938
			the Czecho-Slovak Republic	1938–1939		the Czecho-Slovak Republic	1938–1939
Hungary	1940–1944	Northern Transylvania [Észak-Erdély in Hungarian]	Slovakia	1939–1944		Hungary	1939–1944
Romania		Southern Transylvania [Dél-Erdély in Hungarian]					
Romania	From 1945 to present	(Present-day) Transylvania [(jelenkori) Erdély in Hungarian]	Czechoslovakia	1945–1993	Southern Slovakia [Južné Slovensko in Slovakian, Dél-Szlovákia in Hungarian]	the Soviet Union	1945–1991
			Slovakia	From 1993 to present		Ukraine	From 1991 to present

Communities in the Carpathian Basin

CARPATHIA in Hungarian, in Ukrainian]	SOUTHERN REGION [*Délvidék* in Hungarian]			BURGENLAND		
Historical name of the region	*State affilia-tions*	*Period*	*Historical name of the region*	*State affilia-tions*	*Period*	*Historical name of the region*
Transcarpathia or Subcarpathian Rus [*Podkarpatská Rus* or *Podkarpatsko* or *Rusinsko* in Slovakian, *Ruszinszkó* or *Kárpátalja* in Hungarian]	the Serb-Croat-Slovene Kingdom	1918–1926	Southern Region [*Délvidék* in Hungarian] = Baranja triangle + Bačka + Banat	Austria	From 1921 to present	Burgenland (in German and in English) [*Burgenland* or *Őrvidék*, or occasionally *Felsőőrvidék* or *Várvidék*, in Hungar-ian, *Gradišče* in Croatian, *Gradiščanska* in Slovenian]
Transcarpathia or Carpathian Ukraine [*Karpats'ka Ukrai'na* in Ukrainian, *Kárpáti Ukrajna* in Hungarian]	Yugo-slavia	1926–1940				
Territory of the Subcarpathian Governorship [*Regents'kyj komisariat Pidkarpats'koi' terytorii'* in Ukrainian, *Kárpát-aljai Kormányzóság* in Hungarian]	Hungary	1940–1944	Southern Region [*Délvidék* in Hungarian]			
Transcarpathian Territory [*Transcarpathian Ukraina* or *Zakarpats'kaja oblast'* in Russian, *Kárpátontúli Ukrajna* or *Kárpátontúli terület* in Hungarian]	Yugo-slavia	1945–1991	Vojvodina (in Serbo-Croat and in English) [*Vajdaság* in Hungarian] = Baranja triangle + Bačka + the Banat + Srem			
Transcarpathian Territory [*Zakarpats'ka oblast'* or *Zakarpattia* in Ukrainian, *Kárpátontúli Ukrajna* or *Kárpátontúli terület* in Hungarian]	Slovenia	From 1991 to present	Prekmurje [*Mura-vidék* in Hungarian, *Pomurska* in Slovenian]			
	Croatia		Baranja, Slavonia and Međimurje			
	Serbia	From 1992 to present	Vojvodina [*Vajdaság* in Hungarian]			

LIST OF MAPS

1. The "Switzerland of the East" proposal by Oszkár Jászi, minister without portfolio, made in 1918
2. Territorial demands on Hungary by neighboring countries (1915–1919)
3. Demarcation lines between Hungary and neighboring countries
4. Population and territory of Hungary transferred to neighboring counties under Treaty of Trianon (1920)
5. The Sopron (Ödenburg) plebiscite
6. Lord Rothermere's 1927 proposals for revising the Trianon borders of Hungary
7. Gyula Gömbös's proposal for territorial revision
8. The First Vienna Award (November 2, 1938)
9. The Second Vienna Award (August 30, 1940)
10. Czechoslovakian colonies established in Hungarian-inhabited areas of Czechoslovakia in 1920s
11. Yugoslav colonies established within Vojvodina in 1920s
12. Transcarpathia (1941–1944)
13. The Southern Region (1941–1944)
14. Ethnic reclassification in Hungarian inhabited villages
15. Hungarian autonomous areas in Romania (1952–1968)
16. Employment and wealth in H. and Hungarian-inhabited parts of neighboring countries, regions in 2008
17. Areas in Transylvania with a Hungarian majority
18. Areas in Slovakia and Ukraine with a Hungarian majority
19. Areas in Vojvodina with a Hungarian majority
20. Areas in Croatia with a Hungarian majority
21. Areas in Prekmurje with a Hungarian majority
22. Areas in Burgenland with a Hungarian majority
23. Csángós in Romania

24. Hungarian minorities and diasporas in the World, around 2000
25. Movements of people and war losses in the Carpathian Basin, 1918–1994
26. Geographic and ethnographic regions of the Carpathian Basin
27. Linguistic composition of the Hungarian Kingdom in 1910
28. Ethnic composition of Hungary and the neighboring countries, regions in 2000–2002 (majority territories based on census)
29. Hungarians in neighboring countries around 2000

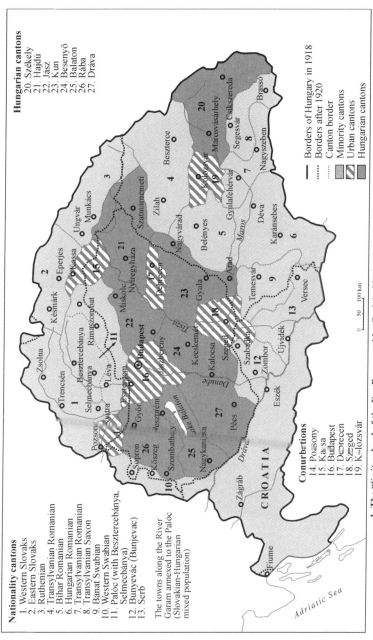

Nationality cantons
1. Western Slovaks
2. Eastern Slovaks
3. Ruthenian
4. Transylvanian Romanian
5. Bihar Romanian
6. Hungarian Romanian
7. Transylvanian Romanian
8. Transylvanian Saxon
9. Banat Swabian
10. Western Swabian
11. Palóc (with Besztercebánya, Selmecbánya)
12. Bunyevác (Bunjevac)
13. Serb

The towns along the River Garam annexed to the Palóc (Slovakian–Hungarian mixed population)

Conurbations
14. Pozsony
15. Kassa
16. Budapest
17. Debrecen
18. Szeged
19. Kolozsvár

Hungarian cantons
20. Székely
21. Hajdú
22. Jász
23. Kun
24. Besenyő
25. Balaton
26. Rába
27. Dráva

—— Borders of Hungary in 1918
······ Borders after 1920
······ Canton border
Minority cantons
Urban cantons
Hungarian cantons

1. The "Switzerland of the East" proposal by Oszkár Jászi, minister without portfolio, made in 1918

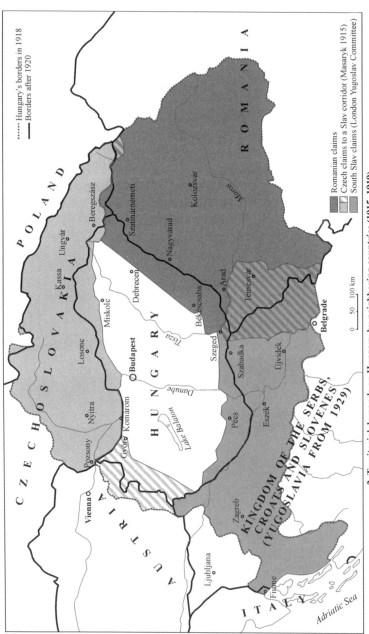

2. Territorial demands on Hungary by neighboring countries (1915–1919)

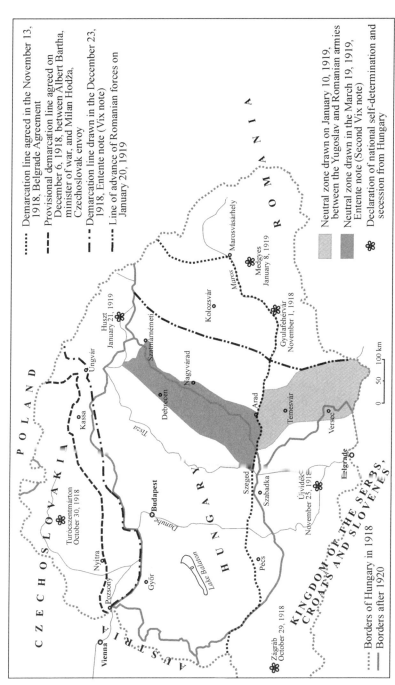

3. Demarcation lines between Hungary and neighboring countries

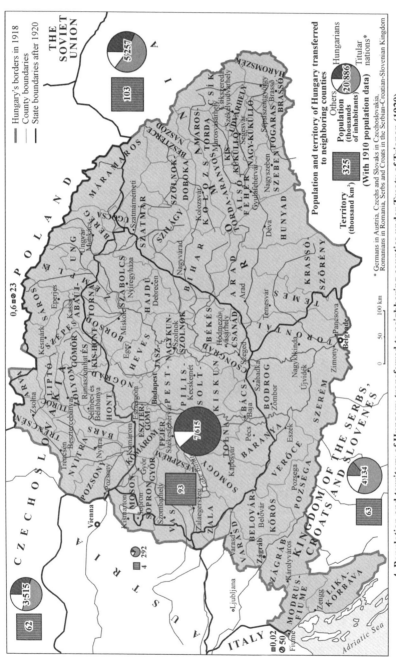

4. Population and territory of Hungary transferred to neighboring counties under Treaty of Trianon (1920)

Maps   815

Votes for remaining within Hungary 65.2%
In Sopron 72.7%
In the eight villages 45.4%

- - - Borders under Trianon (June 1920)
▨ Area covered by plebiscite
(December 1921)
— Final borders after 1923

**5. The Sopron (Ödenburg)
plebiscite**

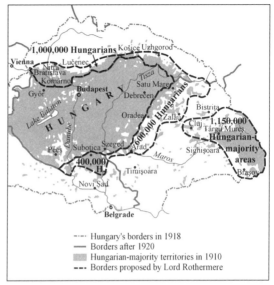

- - - Hungary's borders in 1918
— Borders after 1920
▨ Hungarian-majority territories in 1910
- - - Borders proposed by Lord Rothermere

**6. Lord Rothermere's 1927 proposals for revising
the Trianon borders of Hungary**

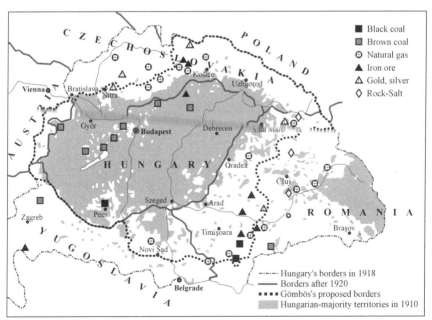

■ Black coal
▨ Brown coal
⊕ Natural gas
▲ Iron ore
△ Gold, silver
◇ Rock-Salt

- · - Hungary's borders in 1918
— Borders after 1920
■■■ Gömbös's proposed borders
▨ Hungarian-majority territories in 1910

7. Gyula Gömbös's proposal for territorial revision

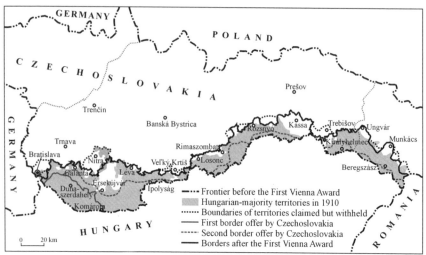

8. The First Vienna Award (November 2, 1938)

9. The Second Vienna Award (August 30, 1940)

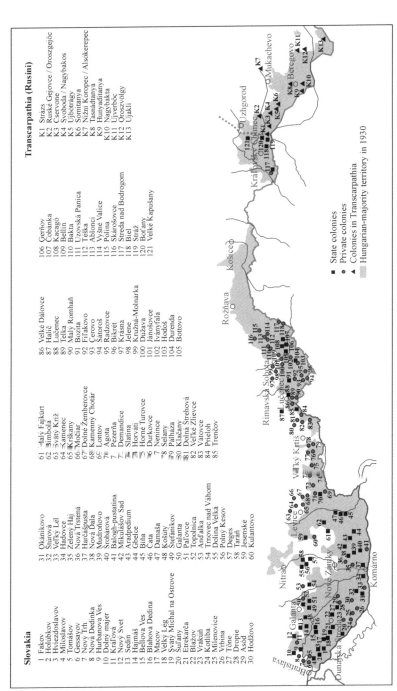

10. Czechoslovakian colonies established in Hungarian-inhabited areas of Czechoslovakia in 1920s

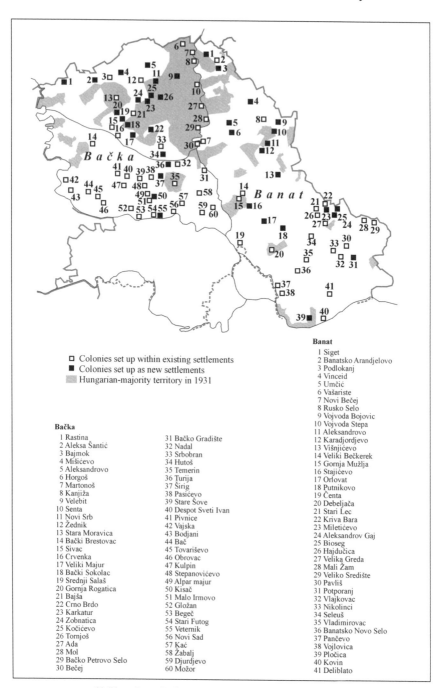

□ Colonies set up within existing settlements
■ Colonies set up as new settlements
▨ Hungarian-majority territory in 1931

Bačka

1 Rastina	31 Bačko Gradište
2 Aleksa Šantić	32 Nadal
3 Bajmok	33 Srbobran
4 Mišićevo	34 Hutoš
5 Aleksandrovo	35 Temerin
6 Horgoš	36 Turija
7 Martonoš	37 Širig
8 Kanjiža	38 Pasićevo
9 Velebit	39 Stare Šove
10 Senta	40 Despot Sveti Ivan
11 Novi Srb	41 Pivnice
12 Žednik	42 Vajska
13 Stara Moravica	43 Bodjani
14 Bački Brestovac	44 Bač
15 Sivac	45 Tovariševo
16 Crvenka	46 Obrovac
17 Veliki Majur	47 Kulpin
18 Bački Sokolac	48 Stepanovićevo
19 Srednji Salaš	49 Alpar majur
20 Gornja Rogatica	50 Kisač
21 Bajša	51 Malo Irmovo
22 Crno Brdo	52 Gložan
23 Karkatur	53 Begeč
24 Zobnatica	54 Stari Futog
25 Kočićevo	55 Veternik
26 Tornjoš	56 Novi Sad
27 Ada	57 Kać
28 Mol	58 Žabalj
29 Bačko Petrovo Selo	59 Djurdjevo
30 Bečej	60 Možor

Banat

1 Siget
2 Banatsko Arandjelovo
3 Podlokanj
4 Vinceid
5 Umčić
6 Vašariste
7 Novi Bečej
8 Rusko Selo
9 Vojvoda Bojovic
10 Vojvoda Stepa
11 Aleksandrovo
12 Karadjordjevo
13 Višnjićevo
14 Veliki Bečkerek
15 Gornja Mužlja
16 Stajićevo
17 Orlovat
18 Putnikovo
19 Čenta
20 Debeljača
21 Stari Lec
22 Kriva Bara
23 Miletićevo
24 Aleksandrov Gaj
25 Bioseg
26 Hajdučica
27 Velika Greda
28 Mali Žam
29 Veliko Središte
30 Pavliš
31 Potporanj
32 Vlajkovac
33 Nikolinci
34 Seleuš
35 Vladimirovac
36 Banatsko Novo Selo
37 Pančevo
38 Vojlovica
39 Pločica
40 Kovin
41 Deliblato

11. Yugoslav colonies established within Vojvodina in 1920s

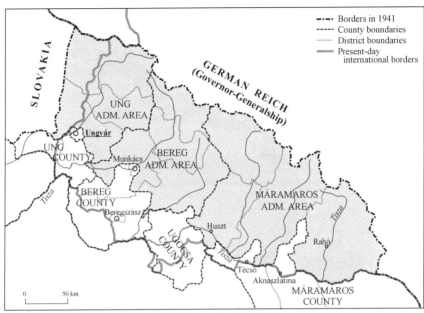

12. Transcarpathia (1941–1944)

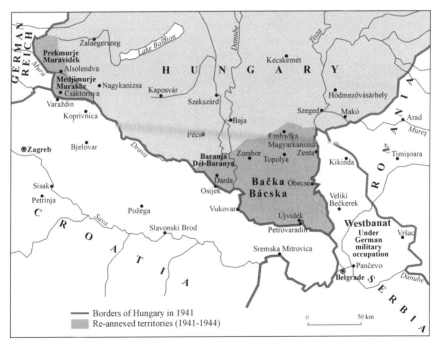

13. The Southern Regio (1941–1944)

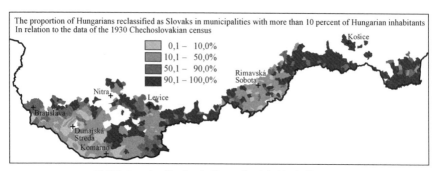

14. Ethnic reclassification in Hungarian-inhabited villages

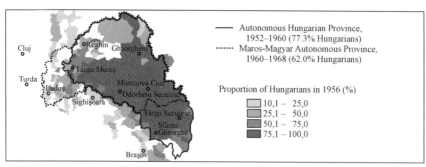

15. Hungarian autonomous areas in Romania (1952–1968)

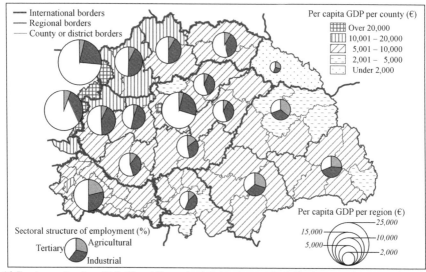

16. Employment and wealth in H. and Hungarian-inhabited parts of neighboring countries, regions in 2008

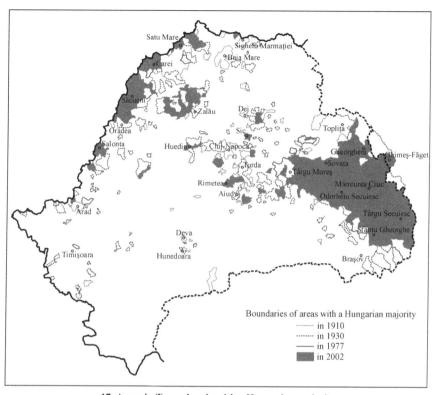

17. Areas in Transylvania with a Hungarian majority

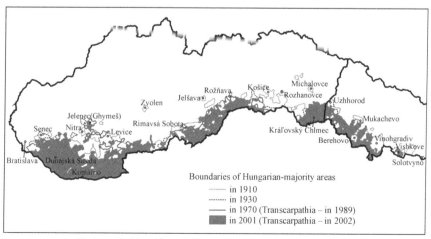

18. Areas in Slovakia and Ukraine with a Hungarian majority

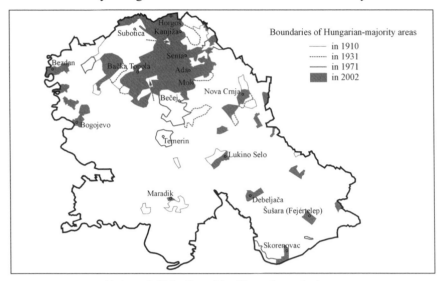

19. Areas in Vojvodina with a Hungarian majority

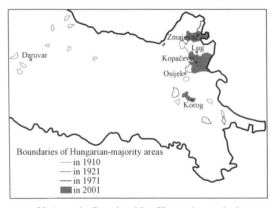

20. Areas in Croatia with a Hungarian majority

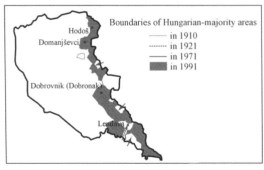

21. Areas in Prekmurje with a Hungarian majority

22. Areas in Burgenland with a Hungarian majority

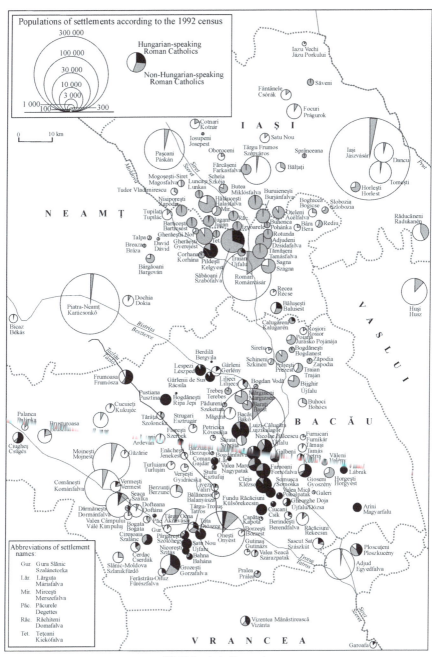

Populations of settlements according to the 1992 census

300 000

100 000

30 000

10 000

3 000

1 000

100   300

Hungarian-speaking
Roman Catholics

Non-Hungarian-speaking
Roman Catholics

0   10 km

Abbreviations of settlement names:

Gur.	Gura Slănic	Szalánctorka
Lăr.	Lărguta	Máriafalva
Mit.	Mirceşti	Merszefalva
Păc.	Păcurele	Degettes
Răc.	Răchiteni	Domafalva
Tet.	Teţcani	Kickófalva

23. Csángós in Romania

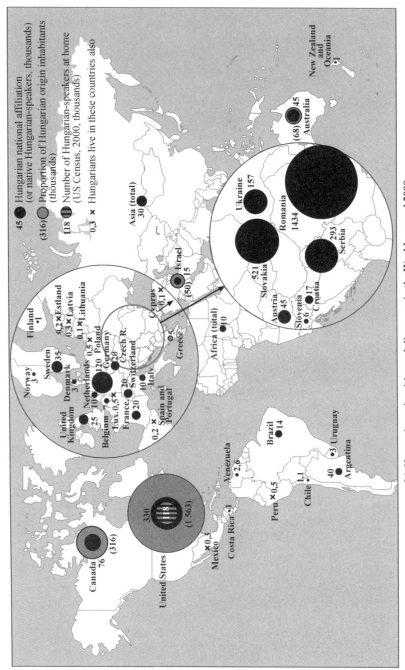

24. Hungarian minorities and diasporas in the World, around 2000

45 ● Hungarian national affiliation (or native Hungarian-speakers, thousands)

(316) ● Proportion of Hungarian origin inhabitants (thousands)

118 ● Number of Hungarian-speakers at home (US Census, 2000, thousands)

0,3 × Hungarians live in these countries also

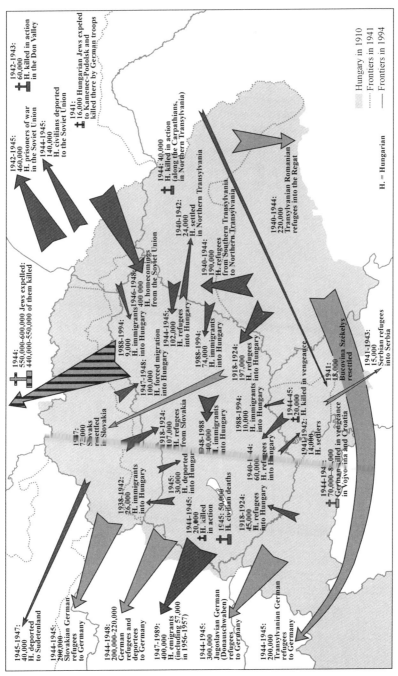

1942–1943:
60,000
H. killed in action
in the Don Valley

1944–1945:
140,000
H. civilians deported
to the Soviet Union

1941:
16,000 Hungarian Jews expeled
to Kamenec-Podolsk and
killed there by German troops

1942–1945:
460,000
H. prisoners of war
in the Soviet Union

1944: 40,000
H. killed in action
(along the Carpathians,
in Northern Transylvania)

1940–1942:
24,000
H. settled
in Northern Transylvania

1940–1944:
190,000
H. refugees
from Southern Transylvania
to Northern Transylvania

1940–1944:
220,000
Transylvanian Romanian
refugees into the Regat

1944:
550,000–600,000 Jews expelled:
440,000–550,000 of them killed

1946–1948:
400,000
H. homecomings
from the Soviet Union

1988–1994:
9,000
H. immigrants
into Hungary

1947–1948:
100,000
H. forced migration
into Hungary

1944–1945:
102,000
H. refugees
into Hungary

1988–1994:
74,000
H. immigrants
into Hungary

1918–1924:
197,000
H. refugees into Hungary

1941:
18,000
Bucovina Székelys
resettled

1941–1943:
15,000
Serbian refugees
into Serbia

1947:
72,000
Slovaks
resettled
in Slovakia

1918–1924:
107,000
H. refugees
from Slovakia

1948–1988:
40,000
H. immigrants
into Hungary

1988–1994:
10,000
H. immigrants into Hungary

1944–45:
20,000: H. killed in vengeance

1941–1942: H. settlers

1941–1942: H. killed in vengeance
14,000:
H. settlers

1938–1942:
26,000
H. immigrants
into Hungary

1945:
30,000
H. deported
into Hungary

1944–1945:
20,000
H. killed
in action

1945: 50,000
H. civilian deaths

1940–1944:
60,000
H. refugees
into Hungary

1918–1924:
45,000
H. refugees
into Hungary

1944–1945: 70,000–8,000
German killed in vengeance
in Vojvodina and Croatia

1945–1947:
40,000
H. deported
to Sudetenland

1944–1945:
200,000
Slovakian German
refugees
to Germany

1944–1948:
200,000–220,000
German
refugees and
deportees
to Germany

1947–1989:
400,000
H. emigrants
(including 57,000
in 1956–1957)

1944–1945:
300,000
Jugoslavian German
(Donauschwaben)
refugees
to Germany

1944–1945:
200,000
Transylvanian German
refugees
to Germany

Hungary in 1910
········· Frontiers in 1941
——— Frontiers in 1994

H. = Hungarian

25. Movements of people and war losses in the Carpathian Basin, 1918–1994

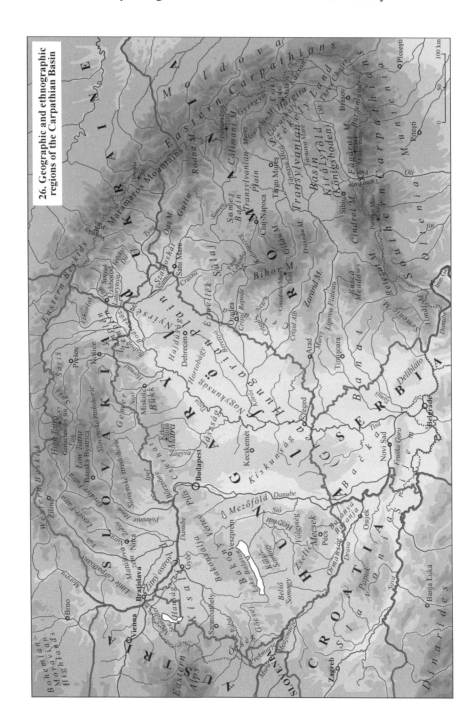

26. Geographic and ethnographic regions of the Carpathian Basin

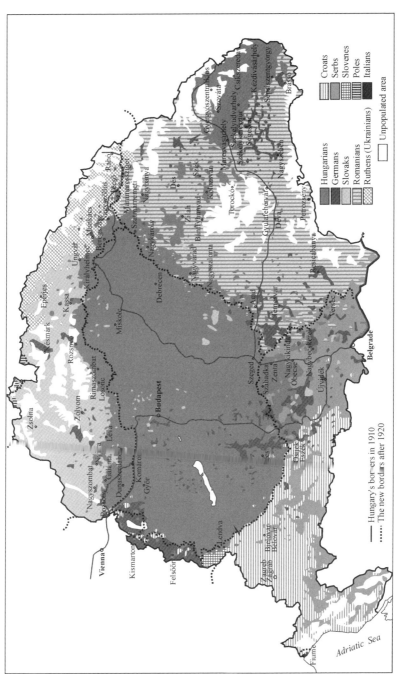

27. Linguistic composition of the Hungarian Kingdom in 1910

Hungarians
Germans
Slovaks
Romanians
Ruthens (Ukrainians)

Croats
Serbs
Slovenes
Poles
Italians

Unpopulated area

—— Hungary's borders in 1910
········ The new borders after 1920

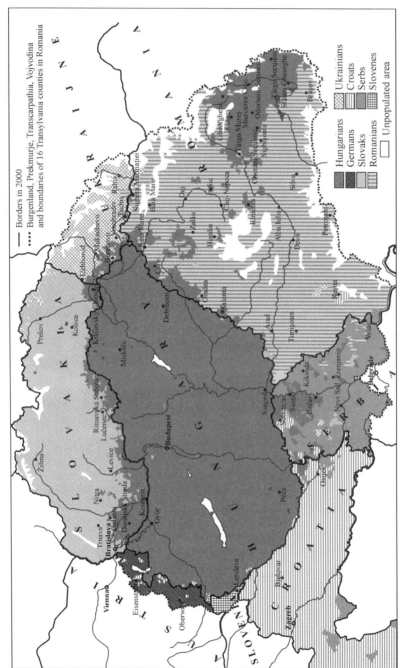

28. Ethnic composition of Hungary and the neighboring countries, regions in 2000–2002 (majority territories based on census)

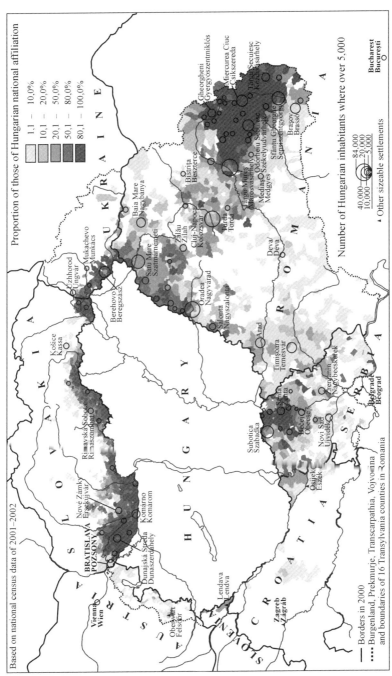

Proportion of those of Hungarian national affiliation

	1,1 – 10,0%
	10,1 – 20,0%
	20,1 – 50,0%
	50,1 – 80,0%
	80,1 – 100,0%

Number of Hungarian inhabitants where over 5,000

84,000
40,000
20,000
10,000 5,000

▲ Other sizeable settlements

Based on national census data of 2001–2002

— Borders in 2000

···· Burgenland, Prekmurje, Transcarpathia, Vojvodina
and boundaries of 16 Transylvania counties in Romania

29. Hungarians in neighboring countries around 2000

Name Index

Aćimović, Milan 267
Aczél, György 347
Ady, Endre 179, 181
Ágoston, András 449, 543, 697
Albert, Sándor 551
Alexander I of Yugoslavia 109, 215
Alexander II of Yugoslav 590
Almássy, János, of Bernstein 271
Ammende, Ewald 21, 99
Angelescu, Constantin 195
Ankerstein, Feliks 249
Antall, József 451, 456, 560
Antonescu, Ion 147, 257, 295, 259
Antonescu, Victor 105
Apáczai Csere, János 459
Apáthy, István 35-37, 53, 56, 510
Apponyi, Albert 47, 81, 142
Áprily, Lajos 182
Aradi, József 388
Ara-Kovács, Attila 450
Arkhipov, P. 398
Árky, Ákos 209
Árpád fejedelem [Prince] 250
Artuković, Andrija 622
Averescu, Alexandru 194, 198
Baász, Imre 507
Bába, Iván 450
Babeş, Victor 329, 382, 482, 485, 510
Bajcsy-Zsilinszky, Endre 241
Bakk, Miklós 511
Balázs, Ferenc 511
Balla D., Károly 419, 505, 561
Balla, Gyula 418

Balla, László 416-417, 419, 697
Balla, Pál 415
Balogh, Artúr 181, 199
Balogh, Edgár 281, 697
Bánffy, Miklós 35, 182, 200, 202, 698
Bányai, László 281, 585, 598
Barany, Zoltan 623
Bárdossy, László 104
Barth, Karl 182
Bartók, Béla 263, 418
Békés, Gellért 635
Bél, Mátyás 485
Benedek, Elek 35
Beneš, Edvard 58, 63, 280-281, 283, 299, 302, 330, 548
Beregi, Sámuel 415
Berinkey, Dénes 34, 37
Bernárd, Ágoston 47
Berthelot, Henri Mathias 36, 54
Bessenyei, György 655
Beszédes, István 449, 505
Beszkid, Anton (Anton Beskyd) 63, 207
Bethlen, Bálint 257
Bethlen, György 198, 698
Bethlen, István 35, 98, 129, 135-137, 142, 161
Bíró, Andor 414
Biró, Zoltán A. 511
Bodnár, Gábor 654
Bodor, Pál 450
Bognár, Cecil 182

Boksay, József 214, 415
Boldizsár, János 449
Bolyai, János 297, 329, 344, 381-382, 482, 485, 510, 531-532, 697
Bóna, Irén 550
Boniszlavszky, Tibor 418
Borbély, László 529
Boross, Péter 456
Botka, Béla 267
Böhm, Károly 181
Braham, Randolph L. 592
Brătianu, Ion C. 31, 102, 194
Brătianu, Vintila 195
Bretter, György 388
Brezhnev, Leonid 330, 331
Bródy, András (Andrej Brody) 144, 210, 248, 251-252, 699
Bugár, Béla 546, 549, 699
Bugyi, Pál 399
Buza, Barna 37
Čapo, Svetozar Kostić 686
Ceauşescu, Nicolae 330, 333, 347-348, 351, 391, 397, 400-402, 445, 499, 594, 626, 702
Charles IV of Hungary (Charles I of Austria) 29, 71
Chopey, Nicholas 62
Churchill, Winston 279
Ciano, Galeazzo 144
Čič, Milan 444
Ciorbea, Victor 528, 534-535
Clemenceau, Georges 36, 39, 45
Clementis, Vladimír 302
Clerk, George, Sir 46-47
Comenius (Jan Amos Komenský) 380, 485
Constantinescu, Emil 528
Czine, Mihály 509
Csáky, Mihály 264

Csáky, Pál 549, 551
Csapó, József 529
Csengeri, Dezső 416
Csepeli, György 511
Csernicskó, István 511
Csomor, István 203
Csoóri, Sándor 348, 450, 699
Csuka, Zoltán 184, 699
Csupor, Lajos 399
Dálnoki Veres, Lajos 636
Dalos, Patrik 631
Darányi, Kálmán 104
Darkó, István 183
Deák, Leó 308
Dérer, Ivan 108
Đinđić, Zoran 543
Dobos, László 331-332, 347, 391, 406-407, 700
Domokos, Géza 401, 445-447, 525, 700
Domokos, Pál Péter 606, 700
Drasche-Lázár, Alfréd 47
Drávai, Gizella 416
Drugeth, György 250
Dsida, Jenő 182
Duba, Gyula 391
Dubček, Alexander 330, 332, 406-407
Dudás, Károly 449
Dupka, György 378, 419, 560-561
Duray, Miklós 333, 349-350, 380, 407, 443, 445, 450, 546, 701
Dzurinda, Mikuláš 548-552
Eckhardt, Tibor 629
Eckstein-Kovács, Péter 527, 534
Egan, Ede 208
Egry, Ferenc 209, 701
Egyed, Ákos 512
Entz, Géza 457, 510, 537

Erdélyi, Béla 214, 416
Esterházy, János 145, 203, 262-263, 300, 302, 311, 591, 701
Fábry, István 404
Faludy, György 636
Faludy, Imre 271
Faragó, József 607
Faragó, Ödön 185
Féder, Zoltán 601
Feketehalmy-Czeydner, Ferenc 150-151, 307
Fenyvesi, Anna 665
Ferdinand I of Romania 53
Fico, Robert 552
Fierlinger, Zdeněk 300
Fodó, Sándor 418, 443, 557-558, 702
Forbáth, Imre 184
Franchet d'Espèrey, Louis 31, 36
Francis Joseph 181
Fried, Jenő (Eugen) 195
Friedrich, István 46, 67
Fronc, Martin 551
Frunda, György 526-527, 529
Fülöp, Árpád 212
Für, Lajos 21
Gábor, Áron 620
Gabor, Dennis (Dénes Gábor) 486
Gábor, Kálmán 511
Gagyi, József 511
Gajdos, István 558-559, 702
Gál, Miklós 257
Gal, Susan 662, 665, 673
Gáll, Ernő 388
Garanyi, József 415
Gellért, St. 46, 136, 215, 635
Gereben, Ferenc 511
Gergely, Sándor 381, 419, 636

Gheorghiu-Dej, Gheorghe 330, 343, 398, 400-401, 705
Gion, Nándor 391
Glatz, Ferenc 450
Gorbachev, Mikhail 441-442, 556
Gortvay, Erzsébet 416
Gottwald, Klement 403
Gömbös, Gyula 129-130, 142
Gömörey, Anton 271
Göncz, Lajos 511
Göncz, László 555
Görömbei, András 509
Grabovszky, Emil 415
Grandpierre, Emil 37, 55-56, 58
Grassy, József 307
Grendel, Lajos 444, 505
Grósz, Károly 351
Groza, Petru 281, 296-298, 325, 381
Gyárfás, Elemér 257, 281, 295, 702, 706
Gyöngyösi, János 279, 282-283, 302, 688
Györffy, Gyula 35
Györke, László 418
Győry, Dezső 184
Gyurcsány, Ferenc 462-463
Gyurgyík, László 468, 511
Gyurovszky, László 551
Haba, Ferenc 214
Habda, László 415
Habsburg, Otto von 421
Hager, Yisrael 590
Halász, Péter 607
Haller, István 257
Hamburger, Mihály 450
Hámos, László 639, 703

Harag, György 392
Harna, István 549, 551
Hegyeli, Attila 610
Heidegger, Martin 182
Heltai, György 636
Herceg, János 185
Herczeg, Ferenc 215
Hermann, Gusztáv 512
Herzl, Theodor 588, 601
Hidas, Antal 381, 416, 419
Hitler, Adolf 98, 103, 143-146, 148-149, 206, 249, 266, 272, 288, 688
Hódi, Sándor 449
Hodinka, Antal 494, 509, 561
Hodža, Milan 34, 206, 703
Hokky, Károly (Charles J. Hokky) 209, 703
Horn, Gyula 450, 457, 460
Hornyik, Miklós 450
Horthy, Miklós 46, 70, 128, 142-143, 148-149, 238, 241, 249, 345, 631, 683
Horváth, Anna 415
Horváth, István 511
Horváth, János 636
Horváth, Sándor 419
Hrabar, Konstantin 207
Husák, Gustáv 332, 379, 407, 443-444
Hushegyi, Gábor 507
Huszár, Károly 46, 67
Ignotus, Pál 636
Ijjász, Gyula 214, 415
Ilia, Mihály 509
Iliescu, Ion 528, 532
Ilku, Pál 212
Illés, Béla 381, 419
Illyés, Gyula 328, 341, 348, 450, 457-459, 506, 561

Imre, Gyula (Julius Imre) 272
Imre, Samu 494
Imrédy, Béla 237, 241, 251
Iorga, Nicolae 388
Isohookana-Asunmaa, Tytti 613
Itzhak, Shlomo 599
Izai, Károly 415
Jagamas, János 607
Jakab, Sándor 523
Jakabffy, Elemér 123, 181, 199, 257, 537, 704
Jakó, Zsigmond 512
Jancsó, Benedek 35, 132
Janics, Kálmán 407, 546
Janovics, Jenő 185
Jaross, Andor 203, 241
Jászi, Oszkár (Oscar Jászi) 34-35, 37, 53, 142, 631
Jeszenszky, Ferenc 267
John Paul II, Pope 536
Jókai, Mór 204
Jónás, Pál 636
Joó, Rudolf 21
Joseph, Archduke 31
Jósika, Sámuel 57
Józsa, Béla 389
József, Attila 418-419
Kádár, Imre 186
Kádár, János 340-341, 344-345, 347-348, 350, 406, 420, 451, 635
Kaigl, Jaroslav 214
Kállai, Gyula 344
Kallós, Zoltán 607
Kálmán, Imre 272
Kánya, Kálmán 104, 143-144
Kányádi, Sándor 505
Karácsony, Benő 182
Kardelj, Edvard 308, 704
Károli, Gáspár 486

Károlyi, Mihály 29, 31-34, 36-38, 52, 54-56, 62, 66, 631
Kasza, József 543
Katona, Ádám 527
Kazinczy, Ferenc 183, 204
Kecskeméti, Lipót 587, 704
Kelemen, Lajos 181
Kemény, János 182, 693
Kerekes, István 209
Kertész, István 282
Keszeg, Vilmos 511
Kéthly, Anna 637
Khrushchev, Nikita 327, 343
Kierkegaard, Søren Aabye 182
Kincses, Előd 447
Király, Béla K. 636
Király, Károly 446-447, 706
Kiss, András 512
Kiss, Csaba 21
Kiss, Jenő 500
Kiss, Tamás 511
Kocsis, Károly 620
Komlós, Aladár 588
Konstantin 478, 485, 509, 550
Kontra, Miklós 511, 661
Korhecz, Tamás 449
Koriáth, Endre 209, 705
Kornis, Gyula 20
Kós, Károly 49, 57, 182, 607, 705
Kossuth, Lajos 60, 631, 634, 636
Koštunica, Vojislav 543
Kosztolányi, Dezső 489
Kovács, András 512
Kovács, András Ferenc 505
Kovács, Frigyes 449
Kovács, Imre 629
Kovács, László 461
Kovács, Mihály 399
Kovács, Miklós 557-559, 709

Kovács, Vilmos 418, 706
Kovalev, S. M. 330
Kozma, Miklós 248-249
Körmendy-Ékes, Lajos 49, 61
Kramař, Karel 63
Kramer, Gyula 216, 308
Krammer, Jenő 181
Kratochwill, Károly 37-38
Kravchuk, Leonid 560
Kreisky, Bruno 421
Kremninczky, Erzsébet 415
Kriza, János 510, 537
Kučan, Milan 552
Kuchma, Leonid Danylovych 560
Kugler, János 371
Kun, Béla 38-39, 45
Kurasov, Vladimir 311
Kurkó, Gyárfás 281, 295, 706
Kurtyák, Iván (Ivan Kurtiak) 210
Lábadi, Károly 450
Lábody, László 458
Lalošević, Joca 66
Lăncrăjan, Ion 349, 426
Láng, Zsolt 505
Lanstyák, István 511, 663, 674-676
Lapp, Josef-Sepp 267
Lehoczky, Tivadar 509, 561
Lelley, Jenő 203
Lenin, Vladimir Ilyich 32, 284, 375
Leopold I of Hungary 7, 413
Leser, Ludwig 222
Ligeti, Ernő 184
Liszka, József 511
Lóczy, Lajos 35
Losoncz, Alpár 511
Lovas, Ildikó 505
Lőrincz, Gyula 371, 404
Lövétei Lázár, László 505

Luka, László 343
Lükő, Gábor 605-606
MacDonald, Ramsay 130
Madách, Imre 389, 444, 506, 700
Magyar, Bálint 551
Major, István 203, 404
Major, Nándor 335
Majtényi, Mihály 185
Makkai, Sándor 181, 707
Maniu, Iuliu 35, 53, 55, 106, 120, 123, 195, 199, 296, 298
Márai, Sándor 633
Maria Theresa 7, 60, 614
Marina, Julius 248
Markó, Béla 527-529, 707
Marshall, George C. 312
Martin, György 182, 551, 607
Mărtinaş, Dumitru 608
Márton, Áron 257-258, 282-283, 704
Marton, Ernő 588
Márton, István 418
Masaryk, Tomáš Garrigue 31, 62, 88, 107, 184, 204, 589
Mečiar, Vladimír 547, 550, 552
Medgyessy, Péter 461
Medveczky, Miklós 415
Medveczky-Luták, Edit 415
Menyhárt, József 665-667
Méray, Tibor 636
Meznik, Jaroslav 207
Michael I of Romania 295-296, 299
Mikecs, László 606
Miklós, László 549, 551
Milošević, Slobodan 335, 413, 448, 495, 542-543
Mindszenty, József 282, 633
Mirnics, Károly 511

Molnár, Erik 346
Molnár, József 511
Molotov, Vyacheslav 145
Moskal, Hennadiy 558
Mussolini, Benito 129-130, 144
Münnich, Ferenc 344
Nagy, Ferenc 281, 629
Nagy, Imre 327, 340, 342-344, 636-637
Nagy, Iván 121
Nagy, Jenő 607
Nagy, Károly 656
Nagy, László A. 444, 546
Nagy, Miklós 308
Nagy, Vilmos 35
Neculcea, Constantin 36
Nedić, Milan 266, 682
Németh, Ilona 507
Németh, László 142
Németh, Miklós 450, 457
Németh, Zsolt 459, 708
Neubauer, Pál 183
Neumann, Ernő 595
Nixon, Richard 420
Novák, Andor 415
Novákovits, Béla 248
Nyírő, József 633
Oláh, Sándor 370, 511
Olay, Ferenc 20
Orbán, János Dénes 505
Orbán, Viktor 459, 461
Oždian, Bedrich 214
Öllős, László 511
Örkény, Antal 511
Paál, Árpád 49, 57, 123, 708
Paderewski, Ignacy 31
Pal, [M.] Iosif Petru 606
Pál, Judit 512
Pál-Antal, Sándor 512

Papp, Antal 136, 480, 503, 642
Pašić, Nikola 31, 102
Páskándi, Géza 450
Pataky, Tibor 135, 708
Paul, Regent 148
Pávai, István 607
Pázmány, Péter 633
Peidl, Gyula 46
Penckófer, János 430, 561
Péntek, János 511
Perényi, Zsigmond 248, 252
Peszkovics, Lukács 121
Peter II of Yugoslavia 148
Petőfi, Sándor 214, 308, 381, 636
Pomogáts, Béla 21
Pongrátz, Gergely 636
Pozsgay, Imre 421, 450
Pozsonec, Mária 555
Pozsony, Ferenc 511, 607, 610
Prerau, Margit 212
Pribičević, Svetozar 68
Prohászka, Ottokár 205
Prónai, Ferenc 271
Purcsi, Barna 621
Rácz, Pál 212
Rădescu, Nicolae 296
Radišić, Elemér 21
Rákóczi, Ferenc II 136, 213, 482, 485, 509, 561, 633, 706
Rákosi, Mátyás 282, 327, 340, 342-343, 631
Râmneanțu, Petre 606
Reményik, Sándor 182
Renner, Karl 311
Révész, Imre 561
Reyniers, Alain 625
Ribbentrop, Joachim von 144-145
Rohonczy, Ferenc 271
Romzha, Teodor 306

Rónai, András 21
Roth, Ottó 35
Rothermere, Harold Harmsworth 129, 132
Rožypal, Antonín 207
Runciman, Walter 144
S. Benedek, András 418, 450
Sáfáry, László 212
Salat, Levente 511
Sănătescu, Constantin 295-296
Sántha, György 214
Sas, Andor 181
Schlesinger, Akiva Yosef 599
Schober, Ottó 418
Schön, Dezső 590
Schulcz, Ignác 203
Selye, János 459, 482, 485, 509, 551
Sidó, Zoltán 444
Siflis, Zoltán 449
Siménfalvy, Árpád 251
Simon, Menyhért 212
Simon, Zsolt 549, 551
Simović, Dušan 148
Slota, Ján 552
Sonnenfeld, Yosef Chaim 599
Šrobár, Vavro 38
Stalin, Joseph 279, 284, 324, 327, 340-341, 343, 411, 416, 539
Stampfer, Yehoshua 599
Stefán, Avgusztin (Avgusthyn Shtefan) 62
Stephen I of Hungary (Saint) 142, 238-239, 251, 489
Stojadinović, Milan 104
Streliczky, Dénes 215
Stresemann, Gustav 129
Strossmayer, Josip Juraj 480
Sulyok, István 485

Supilo, Frano 31
Sütő, András 391, 447, 505
Sütő, János 415
Sviridov, Vladimir P. 688
Szabó T., Attila 181, 494, 510
Szabó, Dezső 142
Szabó, László Cs. 633
Szabó, Oreszt (Orest Sabov) 62
Szabó, Rezső 332, 406-407
Szabó, Zoltán 633
Szabómihály, Gizella 511, 674-675, 677
Szálasi, Ferenc 142, 683
Szarka, László 29, 43, 81, 142, 279, 441, 495, 497, 500
Szász, Jenő 530
Szász, Pál 200-201, 257
Székely, János 505
Szekeres, László 449
Szenes, Piroska 184
Szent István 486; see also Stephen I
Szenteleky, Kornél 184-185, 709
Szentgyörgyi, István 391, 399, 485
Szentimrei, Judit 607
Szent-Ivány, József 108, 183, 203, 709
Szépe, György 500
Szerbhorváth, György 505
Szigeti, László 444, 551
Sziklay, Ferenc 214
Szilágyi N., Sándor 511, 663, 672
Szilágyi, István 505
Szirmai, Károly 185
Sziveri, János 335
Szkabela, Rózsa 550
Szoboszlay, Aladár 328
Szokai, Imre 450
Szombathelyi, Ferenc 150, 308
Szombathy, Bálint 507

Szőcs, Géza 350, 447, 450, 505, 525
Szőke, István 415
Sztaskó, Gyula 415
Sztójay, Döme 241, 592, 683
Sztojka, Sándor (Alexander Stojka) 489
Szüllő, Géza 203, 710
Szűrös, Mátyás 350, 450
Szvatkó, Pál 122, 179, 184, 244
Tabajdi, Csaba 350-351, 450, 458, 710
Takács, Csaba 527, 529
Tallián, Tibor 267
Tamás, Gáspár Miklós 450
Tamás, Mihály 183, 212
Tamási, Áron 182
Tánczos, Vilmos 511, 609-610
Tătărescu, Gheorghe 298
Tavaszy, Sándor 182
Teitelbaum, Joel 602, 710
Teleki, László 22
Teleki, Pál 22, 35, 132, 136, 142, 144, 146, 148-149, 209, 238-239, 241, 251-252, 653
Tessedik, Sámuel 486
Tiso, Jozef 144, 207, 623, 701
Tisza, István 30-31
Tito, Josip Broz 269, 282-283, 287, 289, 307, 310, 326, 329, 335, 343, 408-409, 411, 448, 499, 539-540, 686, 704, 707
Tokay, György 527
Toldy, Ferenc 204, 263
Tolnai, Ottó 505
Tomcsa, Sándor 506
Tomcsányi, Vilmos Pál 248-249
Tomić, Jaša 65, 710
Tomka, Miklós 511

Tompa, Gábor 506
Toró T., Tibor 526
Tóth, János 449
Tóth, Károly 444, 546
Tóth, László 450
Tóth, Mihály 558, 711
Tóth, Pál Péter 661
Tőkés, László 445-447, 482, 526-527, 529, 711
Törzsök, Erika 458
Trumbić, Ante 31
Tumanov, P. 398
Ugron, Gábor 35
Ugron, István 198
Ütő, Gusztáv 507
Vaida-Voevod, Alexandru 102, 194
Valev, Emil 330
Várady, Imre 215, 268, 711
Varga E., Árpád 423, 511
Varga, Béla 181, 629, 631, 637
Varga, Sándor 444
Varga, Zsigmond 271
Vári Fábián, László 505
Vasile, Radu 528
Vass, Tibor 558
Vasyl, Shepa 558
Vékás, János 449, 521, 539, 552

Venczel, József 181
Veres, Valér 511
Verestóy, Attila 527, 529
Vidnyánszky, Attila 506
Vincze, András 248
Virágh, Gyula 214, 415
Visky, András 505
Vitus, St. 66, 68, 85, 215, 448
Vix, Fernand 36, 58
Voloshyn, Avgusthyn 145, 237, 248-250, 252, 712
Voroshilov, Kliment 280
Vozári, Dezső 184
Wahlheim, Alfred 221
Wass, Albert 633
Weber, Max 510, 534
Werth, Henrik 150, 238
Wilson, Woodrow 1, 30, 32, 36, 47-48, 52-53, 63
Yeltsin, Boris 442
Zádor, Dezső 418
Zágoni, István 49
Zalka, Máté 381, 419
Zászlós, Gábor 444
Zhatkovych, Gregory 62-64, 207
Zöldy, Márton 308
Zselicki, József 418

Place Index

All places are located in present-day Hungary unless otherwise stated. The order of the Romanian place names in the bracket is: Hungarian then German. The order of the Ukrainian place names in the bracket is: Hungarian then Russian [and Slovakian].

A – Austria, AA – Argentina, AU – Australia, B – Belgium, BH – Bosnia–Herzegovina, BR – Brazil, BS – Belarus, C – Croatia, CA – Canada, CZ – Czechoslovakia, D – Denmark, F – Finland, FR – France, G – Germany, GB – Great Britain, I – Italy, IS – Israel, L – Latvia, LB – Luxembourg, M – Macedonia, NL– Netherlands, P – Portugal, PL – Poland, R – Romania, RU – Russia, S – Switzerland, SA – Serbia, SK – Slovakia, SL – Slovenia, SP – Spain, U – Ukraine, USA – United States of America, UY – Uruguay

Abara (Oborín; SK) 37

Ada (Ada; SA) 111, 215, 282, 540

Aita Seacă (Szárazajta; R) 296

Aiud (Nagyenyed, Strassburg am Mieresch; R) 257, 260

Akron, OH (USA) 653

Alba Iulia (Gyulafehérvár, Karlsburg; R) 53, 168, 196, 257-258, 446, 485, 536-537, 591, 707-708

Albrechtsfeld (A) 313

Alsóőr (A) 70-71, 517; see also Unterwart

Amsterdam (NL) 132

Andau (A) 420

Andrásfalva (R) 150, 615; see also Măneuți

Apața (Apáca, Geist; R) 614

Arad (Arad, Arad; R) 35, 45-46, 53-55, 172, 257-259, 351, 462, 529, 588, 592

Astely (Asztély, Luzhanka; U) 443

Auschwitz (Oświęcim; PL) 270, 592 623

Babsa (Babşa; R) 615

Bacău (Bákó, Barchau; R) 606, 610 612

Baciu (Kisbács, Botschendorf; R) 614

Bačka Topola (Topolya; SA) 167

Bački Jarak (Tiszaistvánfalva; SA) 307

Baia Mare (Nagybánya, Frauenbach; R) 55, 166, 361, 363, 601

Baja 66

Balassagyarmat 37

Bánffyhunyad (Huedin; R) 55

Bankstown (AU) 654

Banská Bystrica (Besztercebánya; SK) 262, 485

Banská Štiavnica (Selmecbánya; SK) 262

Bártfa (Bardejov; SK) 38

Bat'ovo (Bátyu, [Bat'ovo]; U) 374, 415
Bečej (Óbecse; SA) 151, 184
Beiuş (Belényes, Binsch; R) 168
Békéscsaba 55, 486
Belgrade (SA) 31, 36, 43, 54, 66-67, 104, 111, 114, 121, 133-135, 148, 171, 215-216, 218, 266-267, 290, 310, 361, 448-449, 620, 682
Beregovo (U) 360, 362, 374-375, 391, 415-418, 443, 595; see also Berehove
Beregsurány 443
Beregszász (U) 64, 248, 250; see also Berehove
Berehove (Beregszász, Beregovo, [Berehovo]; U) 17, 64, 207-208, 443, 459, 482, 485, 489, 506-507, 558, 560-561, 595, 625, 702
Berehovo (U) 64, 166, 207-208, 211-214, 248
Berlin (G) 76, 104, 132, 143, 145-146, 239, 265-266, 270-271, 441, 628
Bern (S) 638
Bernstein (Borostyánkő; A) 271
Beszterce (Bistriţa, Bistritz; R) 54
Bezenye 303
Bilki (Bilke; U) 250
Birkenau (Brzezinka; PL) 623
Bled (SL) 105
Bnei Brak (IS) 600
Bologna (I) 487
Bonyhád 615
Bor (SA) 273
Borşa (Borsa, Borscha; R) 147
Boston (USA) 669
Bős (SK) 403; see also Gabčíkovo
Brâncoveneşti (Marosvécs, Wetsch; R) 182

Braşov (Brassó, Kronstadt; R) 54, 111, 172, 256-261, 295-296, 361, 399, 401, 525 527, 605, 614, 706, 711
Brassó (R) 54 614; see also Braşov
Bratislava (Pozsony, SK) 38-39, 59, 85, 109, 144, 159, 166-167, 185, 204, 216, 262-264, 283, 301-303, 328, 350, 360, 372, 377, 380, 403-404, 482, 485, 505-507, 550-551, 560, 588-589, 620, 675, 697, 699-701
Brčko (BH) 682
Brest (BS) 415
Brno (CZ) 204
Brussels (B) 636
Bucharest (R) 29-30, 44, 88, 103-104, 107, 120, 133-135, 194, 196, 202, 281, 296, 299, 328, 342, 347, 388-389, 401-402, 445-447, 485, 506, 525-526, 536, 593, 607, 614, 686, 700
Buda (part of Budapest) 6
Budapest 22, 31, 34-35, 39, 46, 52, 54-56, 67, 88, 103-105, 131-134, 146, 168, 182, 202-204, 213, 256, 261, 263, 267, 269, 282-283, 302, 311, 328, 344, 349, 351, 377-378, 404, 460, 462, 486, 510, 524, 561, 585, 588, 592, 611, 613, 620-621, 636, 643, 645, 666-667, 669, 683-685, 689, 699-710
Buenos Aires (AA) 603, 634, 637
Bukin (Dunabökény, SA) 307
Burg-Kastl (G) 637
Buzitka (Bozita, SK) 159
Cacica (Kacsika, Katschika; R) 609
Cădăresti (Magyarcsügés; R) 614
Čantavir (Csantavér; SA) 111, 215
Carei (Nagykároly, Grosskarol; R) 54, 166, 363, 710
Cehu Silvaniei (Szilágycseh; R) 363

Čepinci (Kerkafő; SL) 556
Cernatu (Csernátfalu, Zernendorf; R) 614
Chernobyl (U) 442
Chicago, IL (USA) 601
Chop (Csap; U) 304, 360, 362, 374, 415, 625
Chust (U) 63, 208; see also Khust
Ciucea (Csucsa, Tschötsch; R) 55, 198
Cleja (Klézse; R) 606, 612
Cleveland, OH (USA) 601, 633-634, 637
Cluj (R) 22, 49, 54, 131, 169, 171, 181-182, 185, 201, 216, 258-259, 261, 297-299, 325, 328-329, 344, 398, 402, 482, 588, 590-591, 606, 697-698, 701-703, 707-708; see also Cluj-Napoca
Cluj-Napoca (Kolozsvár, Klausenburg; R) 351, 363, 381, 388, 391-392, 402, 446, 459, 482, 485, 506, 509-511, 525, 528, 536-537, 707
Constanța (R) 593
Copenhagen (D) 438
Coşnea (Kostelek; R) 614
Craiova (R) 671-672
Crizbav (Krizba, Krebsbach; R) 614
Čurug (Csurog; SA) 150, 307, 310
Csap (U) 38; see also Chop
Csernakeresztúr (Cristur; R) 615
Csíksomlyó (Şumuleu Ciuc; R) 635
Csíkszereda (R) 46; see also Miercurea-Ciuc
Csucsa (R) 36, 55; see also Ciucea
Dachau (G) 271
Dayton OH (USA) 543
Deáki (Deakovce; SK) 59
Debrecen 34, 38, 55, 147, 213, 486, 595, 685, 700

Dej (Dés, Desch; R) 601, 711
Deutsch Schützen (Németlövő; A) 273
Deva (Déva, Diemrich; R) 168, 361, 615
Déva (R) 36, 615; see also Deva
Dévény (SK) 60; see also Devín
Devín (Dévény; SK) 60, 143
Diószeg (SK) 403; see also Sládkovičovo
Đjakovo (Diakovár; C) 622
Dobronak (Dobrovnik; SL) 555
Dorneşti (Hadikfalva; R) 150, 615
Dunacsún (Čunovo; SK) 303
Dunajská Streda (Dunaszerdahely; SK) 330, 377, 405, 504, 507, 601
Eger 586, 601
Egyházaskozár 615
Eisenstadt (Kismarton; A) 70, 271, 420, 563, 591-592
Eperjes (SK) 60, 63; see also Prešov
Érsekújvár (SK) 37, 45, 59-60; see also Nové Zámky
Eseny (Eszeny; U) 374
Esztergom 211, 250, 283
Eupen (B) 81-82
Făgăraş (Fogaras, Fogarasch; R) 168
Feldioara (Földvár, Marienburg; R) 296
Felsőőr (A) 69-70, 220, 517, 673; see also Oberwart
Focşani (Foksány, Fokschan; R) 296
Fogadjisten (Iacobeşti; R) 150, 615
Fundu Răcăciuni (Külsőrekecsin; R) 612
Gabčíkovo (Bős; SK) 350, 403, 548

Găiceana (Gajcsána; R) 606
Galanta (Galánta; SK) 159, 361, 377
Galbeni (Trunk; R) 612
Galtiu (Gáldtő; R) 257
Garfield, NJ (USA) 654
Geneva (S) 94, 98-99, 104, 132, 135, 638 690
Gerňov (Gernyőpuszta; SK) 159
Gheorgheni (Gyergyószentmiklós, Niklasmarkt; R) 296, 506, 707
Ghimeş-Făget (Gyimesbükk; R) 614
Gioseni (Diószén; R) 612
Gödöllő 316, 486
Graz (A) 71, 222, 272, 422, 520, 625, 709
Gunja (C) 682
Güssing (Németújvár; A) 271
Gyanafalva (Jennersdorf; A) 220
Gyergyótölgyes (Tulgheş; R) 36
Gyorok (Ghioroc; R) 615
Gyöngyös 586
Gyulafehérvár (R) 36, 53-54, 196, 446; see also Alba Iulia
Hădăreni (Hadrév; R) 626
Hadikfalva (R) 150, 615; see also Dorneşti
Hagensdorf (Karácsfa; A) 218
Hălmeag (Halmágy; R) 614
Hannersdorf (Sámfalva; A) 222
Helsinki (F) 348, 350, 436, 499, 639
Hertelendyfalva (Vojlovica; SA) 615
Hodoš (Hodos; SL) 555
Homestead, FL (USA) 62
Horgos (SA) 111; see also Horgoš
Horgoš (Horgos; SA) 215
Horvátjárfalu (Jarovce; SK) 303
Hronský Beňadik 626

Hunedoara (Vajdahunyad, Eisenmarkt; R) 168, 256, 615
Huszt (U) 63; see also Khust
Iaşi (Jászvásár, Jassy; R) 536, 608-610, 612
Ibaşfalău (Erzsébetváros, Elisabethstadt; R) 168
Innsbruck (A) 272
Ip (Ipp; R) 147
Istensegíts (Ţibeni; R) 150, 615
Jasenovac (C) 622
Jasiňa (U) 62; see also Jasyna
Jasyna (Kőrösmező, [Jasiňa]; U) 62
Jászberény 613
Jimbor (Székelyzsombor; R) 614
Jóka (Jelka; SK) 38
Józseffalva (R) 150, 615; see also Vornicenii Mari
Kakasd 615
Kamenets-Podolsky (U) 592
Kanjiža (Magyarkanizsa; SA) 449
Karachin (U) 489
Karcag 601
Kassa (SK) 34, 37-38, 46, 60, 167, 202, 585, 704; see also Košice
Kecskemét 486
Kétvölgy 556
Kfar Saba (IS) 601
Khust (Huszt, [Chust]; U) 63, 144, 208, 212, 249-250, 380, 590, 595, 625
Kiel (G) 143
Kiev (U) 377, 557
Kismarton (A) 70, 591; see also Eisenstadt
Kisvárda 506, 601
Kittsee (Köpcsény; A) 591
Osijek (Eszék; C) 411, 480, 523-524
Oşorhei (Fugyivásárhely; R) 54
Padua (I) 31, 54

Kleylehof (A) 312
Kolozsvár (R) 35-37, 46, 53-56, 181, 707-708; see also Cluj and Cluj-Napoca
Komárno (Komárom, SK) 144, 166 204, 330, 377, 391, 405, 459, 482, 485, 509, 546, 548-549, 551
Komárom 45, 202, 486, 681
Kopačevo (Kopács; C) 522
Korog (Kórógy; C) 522
Košice (Kassa; SK) 60, 85, 109, 144-145, 166-167, 181, 185, 204, 212, 250, 280, 300, 302, 360-361, 388, 391-392, 550, 588, 620, 622, 704
Kőrösmező (U) 62; see also Jasyna
Kráľovský Chlmec (Királyhelmec; SK) 548
Lackenbach (Lakompak; A) 270-271
Laudonfalva (Bălcăuți; R) 614
Lendava (Lendva; SL) 504, 510, 555-556
Lespezi (Lészped; R) 609, 612
Léva (SK) 38, 586; see also Levice
Levice (Léva; SK) 166, 358, 360-361
Levoča (Lőcse; SK) 262
Linz (A) 312, 520
Liptovský Ján (Liptószentiván; SK) 183
Lisbon (P) 439
Ljubljana (SL) 265, 388, 556
Loborgrad (C) 622
Łodz (PL) 270
London (GB) 29-30, 132, 628, 636, 638, 703
Losonc (SK) 60; see also Lučenec
Lučenec (Losonc; SK) 60, 166, 216, 360-361

Luduş (Marosludas, Ludasch; R) 399, 402, 615
Lugano (S) 638
Lugoj (Lugos, Lugosch; R) 168, 181, 704
Luising (Lovászad; A) 218
Lunca de Jos (Gyimesközéplok, Nieder-Gimesch; R) 614
Lunca de Sus (Gyimesfelsőlok, Gimesch; R) 614
Lviv (U) 557
Mád 601
Mádéfalva (Siculeni; R) 614
Madrid (SP) 528
Magyarnemegye (Nimigea de Jos; R) 615
Malmedy (B) 81
Măneuți (Andrásfalva; R) 150, 615
Máramarossziget (R) 54; see also Sighetu Marmației
Marca (Márkaszék; R) 147
Marghita (Margitta, Margarethen; R) 363
Maribor (SL) 383, 480, 556
Marosludas (R) 615; see also Luduş
Marosvásárhely (R) 35, 46, 54, 398, 586; see also Târgu Mureş
Marseille (FR) 109
Mattersdorf (Nagymarton; today Mattersburg; A) 70, 591
Mauthausen (A) 271
Mea Shearim (IS) 600
Melbourne (AU) 653
Michalovce (Nagymihály, SK) 262
Miercurea-Ciuc (Csíkszereda, Szeklerburg; R) 377, 388, 402, 459, 482, 485, 506, 510-511, 700
Milan (I) 132
Miskolc 45, 486

Mittelpullendorf (Középpulya; A) 312

Mohács 6

Mol (Mohol; SA) 111, 215

Moldava na Bodvou (Szepsi; SK) 361

Montevideo (UY) 603

Montreal (CA) 603

Moravske Toplice (Alsómarác; SL) 555

Moscow (RU) 283, 288, 291, 324, 326-327, 330-331, 341, 343, 370, 381, 387, 416, 418-419, 499, 700, 705, 710, 712

Mošorin (Mozsor; SA) 307

Mukačevo (U) 64, 109, 163, 167, 207-208, 210-214, 248, 588, 590; see also Mukacheve

Mukacheve (Munkács, Mukachevo, [Mukačevo]; U) 64, 207-208, 210, 486, 489, 560, 625

Mukachevo (U) 304-306, 360, 362, 374, 380, 595; see also Mukacheve

Munich (G) 105, 130, 143-144, 206, 634, 712

Munkács (U) 46, 62, 64, 167, 248, 250; see also Mukacheve

Murska Sobota (Muraszombat; SL) 556

Nagybánya (R) 36, 54; see also Baia Mare

Nagykároly (R) 54; see also Carei

Nagymaros 350, 548

Nagymarton (A) 70, 591; see also Mattersdorf

Nagymegyer (Čalovo; today Veľký Meder; SK) 403

Nagyszeben (R) 7, 53, 55; see also Sibiu

Nagyszombat (SK) 60; see also Trnava

Nagyvárad (R) 37, 45-46, 54-55, 179, 585, 704; see also Oradea

Nahariya (IS) 601

Năsăud (Naszód, Nussdorf; R) 197

Neufeld an der Leitha (Lajtaújfalu; A) 70

Neusiedl (Nezsider; A) 69-70, 219

New Brunswick, NJ (USA) 637

New York, NY (USA) 601-602, 631, 636-637, 710

Nickelsdorf (Miklóshalma; A) 273

Nitra (Nyitra; SK) 60, 144, 166, 262, 361, 380, 407, 482, 485, 509, 550-551

Nové Zámky (Érsekújvár; SK) 59, 360-361

Novi Sad (SA) 65, 151, 167, 181, 214, 218, 237, 282, 307-309, 335, 361, 363, 383-384, 391-392, 410, 428, 486, 499, 506, 510, 545, 588, 591, 697-698, 706, 711

Nyíregyháza 486, 586

Nyitra (SK) 13, 60; see also Nitra

Oberpullendorf (Felsőpulya; A) 70, 219, 501, 517

Oberwart (Felsőőr; A) 69-71, 218, 220, 269-272, 312, 420, 481, 501, 517-518, 673

Odorheiu-Secuiesc (Székelyudvarhely, Odorhellen; R) 54, 398, 506, 530

Ohrid (M) 347

Oradea (Nagyvárad, Grosswardein; R) 54, 166, 185, 328, 363, 391, 459, 482, 485, 506, 525, 536, 587, 590-591, 601, 704, 708

Orgovány 588

Oroszvár (Rusovce; SK) 303

Palić (Palics; SA) 410-411
Pančevo (Pancsova; SA) 266, 361, 615
Pápa 460
Paris (FR) 30, 33, 37, 39, 43, 47, 58-59, 63, 92, 132, 214, 303, 308, 340, 357, 397, 628, 685, 687, 702, 704
Párkány (Štúrovo; SK) 403
Passaic, NJ (USA) 637
Pécs 21, 66
Perechyn (Perecseny; U) 250
Pered (Tešedíkovo; SK) 59
Pest (part of Budapest) 683
Petah Tikva (IS) 599, 601
Petrovo (U) 414; see also Pyjterfolvo
Petržalka (Pozsonyligetfalu; SK) 143, 301
Pinkafeld (Pinkafő; A) 71, 518
Potsdam (G) 301, 686, 688
Pozsony (SK) 13, 38, 59-60, 167, 202, 239, 511, 607, 610; see also Bratislava
Prague (CZ) 31, 49, 60-61, 105-106, 119-120, 133-135, 144, 181, 202, 204-207, 249, 281, 283, 330, 333, 342, 350, 379, 391, 404, 406, 444, 697, 699-701, 703, 712
Prešov (Eperjes; SK) 60, 63, 210, 262
Purcăreni (Pürkerec; R) 614
Pustiana (Pusztina; R) 609, 612
Pyjterfolvo (Tiszapéterfalva, Petrovo; U) 489
Rajka 303
Rakhiv (Rahó, Raho, [Rachov]; U) 250
Rakoshyno (Beregrákos; U) 250
Rativtsy (Rát; U) 625

Ravensbrück (part of Fürstenberg/ Havel; G) 623
Rechnitz (Rohonc; A) 273, 591
Rehovot (IS) 600
Riga (L) 415
Rimaszombat (SK) 58; see also Rimavská Sobota
Rimavská Sobota (Rimaszombat; SK) 58, 166, 360-361, 548
Rohonc 591; see also Rechnitz
Románvásár (Roman; R) 606
Rome (I) 144, 415
Rotenturm an der Pinka ([Vas] vörösvár; A) 71, 501
Rožňava (Rozsnyó; SK) 60, 360-361
Rozsnyó (SK) 46, 60; see also Rožňava
Rust (Ruszt; A) 70
Safed (IS) 601
Saint-Germain-en-Laye (FR) 12, 48, 63, 70, 81, 249, 496
Šaľa (Vágsellye; SK) 361
Salgótarján 45, 81
Salonta (Nagyszalonta, Grosssalonta; R) 131, 363
Šalovci (Sall; SL) 555
Salzburg (A) 81, 519-520
Šamorin (Somorja; SK) 377, 504, 510
Sándoregyháza (Ivanovo; SA) 615
Sankt Vith (B) 82
São Paolo (BR) 603
Sărmaş (Salamás; R) 399, 402
Satu Mare (Szatmárnémeti, Sathmar; R) 54, 131, 166, 211, 250, 363, 391, 446, 529, 536, 590, 710
Satu Nou (Göröcsfalva; R) 614

Satulung (Kővárhosszúfalu, Langendorf; R) 614
Schengen (LB) 460, 556
Scranton, PA (USA) 62-63
Selmecbánya (SK) 12, 38; see also Banská Štiavnica
Senec (Szenc; SK) 361
Senta (Zenta; SA) 111, 114, 214-215, 217, 489, 505, 540
Severin; see Turnu Severin
Sevľuš (U) 208, 213, 704; see also Vynohradiv
Sfântu Gheorghe (Sepsiszentgyörgy; R) 296, 388, 391, 401-402, 507, 537
Sibiu (Nagyszeben, Hermannstadt; R) 7, 53, 172, 194, 361, 606, 707
Siget in der Wart (Őrisziget; A) 220, 269, 312, 363, 420, 517
Sighetu Marmaţiei (Máramarossziget; R) 54, 166, 588, 590, 601
Sighişoara (Segesvár, Schässburg; R) 402
Sinaia (R) 104
Siret (Szeretvásár, Sereth; R) 606
Sirig (Szőreg; SA) 150
Sládkovičovo (Diószeg, SK) 103
Slovenský Meder (Tótmegyer; SK) 145
Smederovo (Szendrő; SA) 265
Solomonovo (Tiszasalamon; Solomonove; U) 159
Solotvyno (Aknaszlatina, [Slatinské Doly]; U) 208
Sombor (Zombor; SA) 67, 216
Somuşca (Somoska; R) 610, 612
Sopron 13, 69-71, 81, 218, 222, 271, 419, 422, 486, 585, 709
Speyer (G) 7

Spišská Nová Ves (Igló; SK) 262
Srbobran (Szenttamás; SA) 151
Stara Gradiška (C) 622
Stari Bečej (SA) 151; see also Bečej
Subotica (Szabadka; SA) 67-68, 114, 121, 171, 181, 186, 215-218, 309, 335, 339, 361, 363, 384-385, 391, 410, 486, 489, 491-492, 510, 588, 709
Šurany (Nagysurány; SK) 145, 237
Svalyava (Szolyva; U) 250, 305
Szabadka (SA) 46, 67; see also Subotica
Szatmárnémeti (R) 37, 45-46, 54-55; see also Satu Mare
Szeged 54-56, 66, 378
Székelykeve (Skorenovac; SA) 615
Székelyudvarhely (R) 54-55, 57; see also Odorheiu-Secuiesc
Szombathely 599
Sztrigyszentgyörgy (Streisângeorgiu; R) 615
Târgu Jiu (Zsilvásárhely; R) 296
Târgu Mureş (Marosvásárhely, Neumarkt; R) 359, 363, 389, 398-399, 402, 446-447, 459, 481-482, 485, 526, 531, 537, 588, 707
Târgu Secuiesc (Kézdivásárhely, Szekler Neumarkt; R) 401
Târgu Trotuş (Tatros; R) 606
Tărlungeni (Tatrang, Tatrangen; R) 614
Târnăveni (Dicsőszentmárton, Sankt-Martin; R) 399, 402, 703
Tatabánya 486
Tazlău (Tázló; R) 606
Tel Aviv (IS) 588
Temerin (Temerin; SA) 150, 363
Temesvár (R) 35, 45, 55; see also Timişoara

Teschen (today Cieszyn [PL] and Český Těšín [CZ]) 81
Tevel 615
The Hague (NL) 92, 94, 543, 548
Tihany 669
Timişoara (Temesvár, Temeswar; R) 55, 168, 172, 185, 259, 328, 361, 391, 445, 525, 536, 590-592, 595, 711
Tiszabecs 213
Tomnátik (Tomnatek; R) 614
Tornalja (Tornaľa; SK) 403
Toronto (CA) 603, 637, 654
Torzsa (Savino Selo; SA) 67
Traiskirchen (A) 419
Trebišov (Tőketerebes; SK) 166, 361, 626
Treznea (Ördögkút, Teufelsbrunnen; R) 147
Trnava (Nagyszombat; SK) 60, 262
Turcheş (Türkös, Türkeschdorf; R) 614
Turda (Torda, Thorenburg; R) 111, 197, 256, 258, 398
Turnu Severin (Szörényvár; R) 146, 361, 681
Turócszentmárton (Martin; SK) 31
Tyachevo (U) 362, 417; see also Tyachiv
Tyachiv (Técső, Tyachevo; U) 417
Újvidék (Novi Sad; SA) 65-66
Ungvár (U) 46, 62-64, 167, 209, 248, 250, 705; see also Uzhhorod
Unterwart (Alsóőr; A) 70, 218, 220, 312, 363, 388, 420, 501, 504, 510, 517
Uzhgorod (U) 306, 360, 362, 374, 380-381, 389, 415-419, 443, 595, 699, 702, 706; see also Uzhhorod

Uzhhorod (Ungvár, Uzhgorod, [Užhorod]; U) 62, 207-208, 443, 482, 485, 506-507, 509, 557, 560-561, 595, 625, 702, 706
Užhorod (U) 62-64, 109, 144, 166-167, 207-208, 211-214, 248-249, 588, 590, 705; see also Uzhhorod
Vác 586
Vajdahunyad (R) 615; see also Hunedoara
Valea lui Mihai (Érmihályfalva; R) 363
Vancouver (CA) 419
Varasd (Varaždin; C) 36
Vatican 210, 216, 536, 553, 609
Velence (I) 669; see also Venice
Velence 669
Veliki Bečkerek (SA) 167, 216, 267-268; see also Zrenjanin
Veľký Krtíš (Nagykürtös, SK) 358
Velyka Dobron' (Nagydobrony; U) 375, 414, 489
Velyki Berehy (Nagybereg; U) 489
Velykyy Bychkiv (Nagybocskó; U) 250
Venice (I) 71, 460, 669
Versailles (FR) 1, 20, 47, 83-84, 87, 118, 143, 146, 265
Vice (Vița, Witzen; R) 615
Vienna (A) 8-9, 31, 71, 99, 124, 144-148, 159, 200, 222, 235, 238, 248, 250, 256-259, 261, 265, 270-272, 279, 287, 298, 312, 387, 419-422, 480, 517-520, 591-592, 621-622, 628, 633, 637-638, 681, 698, 708-710
Vinogradovo (U) 362, 375, 416; see also Vynohradiv

Vladnic (Lábnyik; R) 606-607, 611-612
Vornicenii Mari (Józseffalva; R) 615
Vrakúň (Nyékvárkony; SK) 666-667
Vršac (Versec, Werschetz; SA) 269, 710
Vucijak (BH) 682
Vylok (Tiszaújlak, [Ujlak]; U) 213-214
Vynohradiv (Nagyszőlős, Vinogradovo, [Sevľuš]; U) 208, 704
Vyzhnytsia (U) 590
Waasen (A) 219
Warsaw (PL) 132, 143-144, 330, 340, 379, 401, 406, 441
Washington, DC (USA) 31, 132, 634
Yalta (U) 279
Yanoshi (Makkosjánosi, Ivanovka, [Janosovo]; U) 489

Yorkville (CA) 602
Youngstown, OH (USA) 635
Žabalj (Zsablya; SA) 150, 310
Zagreb (C) 65, 134, 171, 215, 218, 510, 523-524
Zalalövő 556
Zenta (SA) 46; see also Senta
Zilah (Zalău; R) 55
Žilina (Zsolna; SK) 144
Zizin (Zajzon; R) 614
Zlaté Moravce (Aranyosmarót; SK) 262
Zmajevac (Vörösmart; C) 522-523
Zobor (Zobor; SK) 262
Zombor (SA) 67; see also Sombor
Zrenjanin (Nagybecskerek; SA) 361
Zvečevo (C) 308
Zvolen (Zólyom; SK) 262
Zsolna (SK) 38; see also Žilina

Volumes Published in
"Atlantic Studies on Society in Change"

No. 1* T 1	*Tolerance and Movements of Religious Dissent in Eastern Europe.* Edited by Béla K. Király. 1977.
No. 2	*The Habsburg Empire in World War I.* Edited by R. A. Kann. 1978.
No. 3 T 2	*The Mutual Effects of the Islamic and Judeo-Christian Worlds: The East European Pattern.* Edited by A. Ascher, T. Halasi-Kun and B. K. Király. 1979.
No. 4	*Before Watergate: Problems of Corruption in American Society.* Edited by A. S. Eisenstadt, A. Hoogenboom, H. L. Trefousse. 1979.
No. 5	*East Central European Perceptions of Early America.* Edited by B. K. Király and G. Bárány. 1977.
No. 6	*The Hungarian Revolution of 1956 in Retrospect.* Edited by B. K. Király and Paul Jonas. 1978.
No. 7	*Brooklyn U.S.A.: Fourth Largest City in America.* Edited by Rita S. Miller. 1979.
No. 8	*Prime Minister Gyula Andrássy's Influence on Habsburg Foreign Policy.* János Decsy. 1979.
No. 9	*The Great Impeacher: A Political Biography of James M. Ashley.* Robert F. Horowitz. 1979.
No. 10 W I**	*Special Topics and Generalizations on the Eighteenth and Nineteenth Century.* Edited by Béla K. Király and Gunther E. Rothenberg. 1979.
No. 11 W II	*East Central European Society and War in the Pre-Revolutionary 18th Century.* Edited by Gunther E. Rothenberg, Béla K. Király and Peter F. Sugar. 1982.
No. 12 W III	*From Hunyadi to Rákóczi: War and Society in Late Medieval and Early Modern Hungary.* Edited by János M. Bak and Béla K. Király. 1982.

* Vols. T 1 through 19 refer to the series *Tolerance and Discrimination in the Danubian Region*
** Vols. W I through XLI refer to the series *War and Society in East Central Europe*

851

No. 44   *East Central European War Leaders: Civilian and Military.*
W XXV   Edited by Béla K. Király and Albert Nofi. 1988.
No. 46   *Germany's International Monetary Policy and the European Monetary System.* Hugo Kaufmann. 1985.
No. 47   *Iran since the Revolution—Internal Dynamics, Regional Conflicts and the Superpowers.* Edited by Barry M. Rosen. 1985.
No. 48   *The Press during the Hungarian Revolution of 1848-1849.*
W XXVII   Domokos Kosáry. 1986.
No. 49   *The Spanish Inquisition and the Inquisitional Mind.* Edited by Angel Alcala. 1987.
No. 50   *Catholics, the State and the European Radical Right, 1919-1945.* Edited by Richard Wolff and Jorg K. Hoensch. 1987.
No. 51   *The Boer War and Military Reforms.* Jay Stone and Erwin
W XXVIII   A. Schmidl. 1987.
No. 52   *Baron Joseph Eötvös, A Literary Biography.* Steven B. Várdy. 1987.
No. 53   *Towards the Renaissance of Puerto Rican Studies: Ethnic and Area Studies in University Education.* Maria Sanchez and Antonio M. Stevens. 1987.
No. 54   *The Brazilian Diamonds in Contracts, Contraband and Capital.* Harry Bernstein. 1987.
No. 55   *Christians, Jews and Other Worlds: Patterns of Conflict*
T 5   *and Accommodation.* Edited by Philip F. Gallagher. 1988.
No. 56   *The Fall of the Medieval Kingdom of Hungary: Mohács*
W XXVI   *1526, Buda 1541.* Géza Perjés. 1989.
No. 57   *The Lord Mayor of Lisbon: The Portuguese Tribune of the People and His 24 Guilds.* Harry Bernstein. 1989.
No. 58   *Hungarian Statesmen of Destiny: 1860-1960.* Edited by Paul Bödy. 1989.
No. 59   *For China: The Memoirs of T. G. Li, Former Major General in the Chinese Nationalist Army.* T. G. Li. Written in collaboration with Roman Rome. 1989.
No. 60   *Politics in Hungary: For A Democratic Alternative.* János Kis, with an Introduction by Timothy Garton Ash. 1989.
No. 61   *Hungarian Worker's Councils in 1956.* Edited by Bill Lomax. 1990.

No. 62	*Essays on the Structure and Reform of Centrally Planned Economic Systems.* Paul Jonas. A joint publication with Corvina Kiadó, Budapest. 1990.
No. 63	*Kossuth as a Journalist in England.* Éva H. Haraszti. A joint publication with Akadémiai Kiadó, Budapest. 1990.
No. 64	*From Padua to the Trianon, 1918-1920.* Mária Ormos. A joint publication with Akadémiai Kiadó, Budapest. 1990.
No. 65	*Towns in Medieval Hungary.* Edited by László Gerevich. A joint publication with Akadémiai Kiadó, Budapest. 1990.
No. 66 T 6	*The Nationalities Problem in Transylvania, 1867-1940.* Sándor Bíró. 1992.
No. 67 T 7	*Hungarian Exiles and the Romanian National Movement, 1849-1867.* Béla Borsi-Kálmán. 1991.
No. 68 T 8	*The Hungarian Minority's Situation in Ceausescu's Romania.* Edited by Rudolf Joó and Andrew Ludanyi. 1994.
No. 69	*Democracy, Revolution, Self-Determination. Selected Writings.* István Bibó. Edited by Károly Nagy. 1991.
No. 70 T 9	*Trianon and the Protection of Minorities.* József Galántai. A joint publication with Corvina Kiadó, Budapest. 1991.
No. 71	*King Saint Stephen of Hungary.* György Györffy. 1994.
No. 72	*Dynasty, Politics and Culture. Selected Essays.* Robert A. Kann. Edited by Stanley B. Winters. 1991.
No. 73	*Jadwiga of Anjou and the Rise of East Central Europe.* Oscar Halecki. Edited by Thaddeus V. Gromada. A joint publication with the Polish Institute of Arts and Sciences of America, New York. 1991
No. 74 W XXIX	*Hungarian Economy and Society during World War Two.* Edited by György Lengyel. 1993.
No. 75	*The Life of a Communist Revolutionary, Béla Kun.* György Borsányi. 1993.
No. 76	*Yugoslavia: The Process of Disintegration.* Laslo Sekelj. 1993.
No. 77 W XXX	*Wartime American Plans for a New Hungary. Documents from the U.S. Department of State, 1942-1944.* Edited by Ignác Romsics. 1992.
No. 78 W XXXI	*Planning for War against Russia and Serbia. Austro-Hungarian and German Military Strategies, 1871-1914.* Graydon A. Tunstall, Jr. 1993.

No. 79   *American Effects on Hungarian Imagination and Political*
                Thought, 1559-1848. Géza Závodszky. 1995.
No. 80   *Trianon and East Central Europe: Antecedents and*
W XXXII   *Repercussions.* Edited by Béla K. Király and László
                Veszprémy. 1995.
No. 81   *Hungarians and Their Neighbors in Modern Times, 1867-*
T 10   *1950.* Edited by Ferenc Glatz. 1995.
No. 82   *István Bethlen: A Great Conservative Statesman of Hungary,*
                1874-1946. Ignác Romsics. 1995.
No. 83   *20ᵗʰ Century Hungary and the Great Powers.* Edited by
W XXXIII   Ignác Romsics. 1995.
No. 84   *Lawful Revolution in Hungary, 1989-1994.* Edited by Béla
                K. Király. András Bozóki Associate Editor. 1995.
No. 85   *The Demography of Contemporary Hungarian Society.*
                Edited by Pál Péter Tóth and Emil Valkovics. 1996.
No. 86   *Budapest, A History from Its Beginnings to 1996.* Edited by
                András Gerő and János Poór. 1996.
No. 87   *The Dominant Ideas of the Nineteenth Century and*
                Their Impact on the State. Volume 1. Diagnosis. József
                Eötvös. Translated, edited, annotated and indexed with an
                introductory essay by D. Mervyn Jones. 1997.
No. 88   *The Dominant Ideas of the Nineteenth Century and*
                Their Impact on the State. Volume 2. Remedy. József
                Eötvös. Translated, edited, annotated and indexed with an
                introductory essay by D. Mervyn Jones. 1997.
No. 89   *The Social History of the Hungarian Intelligentsia in the*
                "Long Nineteenth Century," 1825-1914. János Mazsu. 1997.
No. 90   *Pax Britannica: Wartime Foreign Office Documents*
W XXXIV   *Regarding Plans for a Post Bellum East Central Europe.*
                Edited by András D. Bán. 1997.
No. 91   *National Identity in Contemporary Hungary.* György
                Csepeli. 1997.
No. 92   *The Hungarian Parliament, 1867-1918: A Mirage of Power.*
                András Gerő. 1997.
No. 93   *The Hungarian Revolution and War of Independence, 1848-*
W XXXV   *1849. A Military History.* Edited by Gábor Bona. 1999.
No. 94   *Academia and State Socialism: Essays on the Political*
                History of Academic Life in Post-1945 Hungary and East
                Central Europe. György Péteri. 1998.

No. 95   *Through the Prism of the Habsburg Monarchy: Hungary*
W XXXVI   *in American Diplomacy and Public Opinion during World*
           War I. Tibor Glant. 1998.
No. 96   *Appeal of Sovereignty in Hungary, Austria and Russia.*
           Edited by Csaba Gombár, Elemér Hankiss, László Lengyel
           and Györgyi Várnai. 1997.
No. 97   *Geopolitics in the Danube Region. Hungarian Reconciliation*
T 11   *Efforts, 1848-1998.* Edited by Ignác Romsics and Béla K.
           Király. 1998.
No. 98   *Hungarian Agrarian Society from the Emancipation of*
           Serfs (1848) to Re-privatization of Land (1998). Edited by
           Péter Gunst. 1999.
No. 99   *"The Jewish Question" in Europe. The Case of Hungary.*
T 12   Tamás Ungvári. 2000.
No. 100   *Soviet Military Intervention in Hungary, 1956.* Edited by
           Jenő Györkei and Miklós Horváth. 1999.
No. 101, T 13 *Jewish Budapest.* Edited by Géza Komoróczy. 1999.
No. 102   *Evolution of Hungarian Economy, 1848-1998. Vol. I. One*
           and a Half Centuries of Semi-Successful Modernization,
           1848-1989. Edited by Iván T. Berend and Tamás Csató.
           2001.
No. 103   *Evolution of Hungarian Economy, 1848-1998. Vol. II. Paying*
           the Bill for Goulash-Communism. János Kornai. 2000.
No. 104   *Evolution of Hungarian Economy, 1848-2000. Vol. III.*
           Hungary: from Transition to Integration. Edited by György
           Csáki and Gábor Karsai 2002.
No. 105   *From Habsburg Agent to Victorian Scholar. G. G. Zerffi*
           (1820-1892). Tibor Frank. 2000.
No. 106   *A History of Transylvania from the Beginning to 1919. Vol.*
           I. Edited by Zoltán Szász and Béla Köpeczi. 2000.
No. 107   *A History of Transylvania from the Beginning to 1919. Vol.*
           II. Edited by Zoltán Szász and Béla Köpeczi. 2002.
No. 108   *A History of Transylvania from the Beginning to 1919. Vol.*
           III. Edited by Zoltán Szász and Béla Köpeczi. 2002.
No. 109   *Hungary: Governments and Politics, 1848–2000.* Edited by
           Mária Ormos and Béla K. Király. 2001.
No. 110   *Hungarians in the Voivodina, 1918–1947.* Enikő A. Sajti.
T 14   2003.

No. 111   *Hungarian Arts and Sciences, 1848–2000.* Edited by László
           Somlyódy and Nóra Somlyódy. 2003.
No. 112   *Hungary and International Politics in 1848–1849.* Domokos
           Kosáry. 2003.
No. 113   *Social History of Hungary from the Reform Era to the End
           of the Twentieth Century.* Edited by Gábor Gyáni, György
           Kövér and Tibor Valuch. 2004.
No. 114   *A Millennium of Hungarian Military History.* Edited by
W XXXVII   László Veszprémy and Béla K. Király. 2002.
No. 115   *Hungarian Relics. A History of the War Banners of the
           Hungarian Revolution and War of Independence, 1848-49.*
           Jenő Györkei and Györgyi Cs. Kottra. 2000.
No. 116   *From Totalitarian to Democratic Hungary. Evolution and
           Transformation, 1990-2000.* Edited by Mária Schmidt and
           László Gy. Tóth. 2001.
No. 117   *A History of Eastern Europe since the Middle Ages.* Emil
           Niederhauser. 2003.
No. 118   *The Ideas of the Hungarian Revolution, Suppressed and
           Victorious, 1956–1999.* Edited by Lee W. Congdon and Béla
           K. Király. 2002.
No. 119   *The Emancipation of the Serfs in East and East-Central
           Europe.* Emil Niederhauser. 2004.
No. 120   *Béla K. Király: Art of Survival. Hungarian National Defense
           and Society in Modern Times.* Edited by Piroska Balogh and
           Tamás Vitek. 2003.
No. 121   *Army and Politics in Hungary, 1938–1944.* Lóránd
W XXXVIII Dombrády. Edited by Gyula Rázsó. 2005.
No. 122   *Hungary and the Hungarian Minorities (Trends in the Past
T 15   and in Our Time).* Edited by László Szarka. 2004.
No. 123, T 16 *Roma of Hungary.* Edited by István Kemény. 2005.
No. 124   *National and Ethnic Minorities in Hungary, 1920–2001.*
T 17   Edited by Ágnes Tóth. 2005.
No. 126   *The Occupation of Bosnia and Herzegovina in 1878.* László
W XXXIX   Bencze. 2005.
No. 127   *Wars, Revolutions and Regime Changes in Hungary, 1912–
           2004. Reminiscences of an Eyewitness.* Béla K. Király.
           Edited by Piroska Balogh, Andrea T. Kulcsár and Tamás
           Vitek. 2005.

No. 128 W XL	*1956: The Hungarian Revolution and War for Independence.* Edited by Lee W. Congdon, Béla K. Király and Károly Nagy. 2006.
No. 129 W XLI	*The History of the Hungarian Military Higher Education, 1947–1956.* Miklós M. Szabó. 2006.
No. 130	*Reform and Revolution, 1830–1848.* András Gergely. 2009.
No. 131	*From Habsburg Neo-Absolutism to the Compromise, 1849–1867.* Ágnes Deák. 2008.
No. 132	*Hungary in the Dual Monarchy, 1867–1914.* László Katus. 2008.
No. 133	*Hungary in the Age of the Two World Wars, 1914–1945.* Mária Ormos. 2007.
No. 134	*Hungary under Soviet Domination, 1944–1989.* György Gyarmati and Tibor Valuch. 2009.
No. 135	*From Dictatorship to Democracy. The Birth of the Third Hungarian Republic, 1988–2001.* Ignác Romsics. 2007.
No. 136	*Hungarian–Soviet Relations, 1920–1941.* Attila Kolontári. 2010.
No. 137	*The Memory of the Habsburg Empire in German, Austrian and Hungarian Right-Wing Historiography and Political Thinking, 1918–1941.* Gergely Romsics. 2010.
No. 138 T 18	*Minority Hungarian Communities in the Twentieth Century.* Edited by Nándor Bárdi, Csilla Fedinec and László Szarka. 2011.
No. 139	*The Second Vienna Award and the Hungarian–Romanian Relations, 1940–1944.* Béni L. Balogh. 2011.
No. 140	*Studies in the History of Early Modern Transylvania.* Edited by Gyöngy Kovács Kiss. 2011.
No. 141 T 19	*A Multiethnic Region in East-Central Europe. Studies in the History of Upper Hungary and Slovakia from the 1600s to the Present.* Edited by László Szarka. 2011.